RICHARD
NIXON
AND HIS
AMERICA

RICHARD NIXON

AND HIS AMERICA

Herbert S. Parmet

KONECKY&KONECKY

Konecky & Konecky
156 Fifth Avenue
New York, N.Y. 10010

This edition published by special arrangement
with Little, Brown And Company.

ISBN: 1-56852-082-4

Printed in the Unites States of America

Contents

For

DANIEL PARMET LANOUE

Who Will Know the Future

Preface

BIOGRAPHY is not the primary force behind this book. The chronicling tendencies of a Boswell have been put aside for a broader purpose: to take up the history, both cultural and political, of the era we have passed through. It is an era that has gone from the Great Depression and Franklin D. Roosevelt to the consequences of overcoming economic disaster and the horrors of a world at war. We have picked up the pieces from those two experiences and have moved on to a future hardly imagined in our youth.

Almost from the start of the postwar period, there have been endless exhumations of the Nixon personality, and he has come down to us in various reincarnations. Most of all, he is familiar as an American version of that ancient Roman conspirator Catiline, or a Clyde Griffiths, the unfortunate protagonist of *An American Tragedy,* who was the victim, as Theodore Dreiser described it, not only of his own needs but of the society as well.

The point here is to understand why Richard Nixon has been such a commanding figure. A combination of timing, skill, and the workings of the historical process introduced him to the American political scene in 1946 and, in the 1970s and 1980s — despite Watergate, despite the resignation, despite the pejorative implications of the pardon — sustained his viability long after he had been discredited.

His era, from his California beginnings and the Voorhis campaign of 1946, spanned the postwar world both at home and abroad. Between Roosevelt and the period that has followed his own presidency — during, in other words, the vital years between the Age of Roosevelt and what Kevin Phillips has noted became "postconservative America" — Nixon's political function was to rationalize two ongoing developments, the progressivism of the New Deal welfare state and the continuing cold war. Nixon has always seen himself as something of a broker playing this role during thirty years of conflict. Contrary to the view engraved in our minds through the cartoons of Herblock, and contrary to the view of many of us who have followed the Republican party, at heart he has always been less the political partisan than a centrist. His emphasis did not assume that the various levels of government could or should fail to protect those who were victimized by the system. Even when he was most identified as an orthodox Republican, his role was to try to steer the Republican party along a middle course, somewhere between the competitive impulses of the Rockefellers, the Goldwaters, and the Reagans.

Nixon personified the children of the New Deal generation who re-gained confidence in American capitalism. They rediscovered the values that seemed to have gone askew. Nixon keenly reflected the priorities that were especially important to those we may identify as the working middle class. They saw in Nixon not a figure of glamor at all, but someone closer to the real gut: a guardian of their intent to secure a piece of the American turf, or their idea of the American dream, and to do so without losing out to those who insisted on changing the rules in the middle of the game by grabbing advantages not available to earlier generations. This was not only the coming of age of the great middle-class majority; we must also understand it as a process of acculturation and assimilation by generations of immigrants. They achieved their security, had faith in the American dream, and contributed a conservative, stabilizing force in the context of American traditionalism.

When reviewing postwar America, then, I believe that Richard Nixon was, in the long run, less distinctive for the peculiarities of his psycho-logical makeup than for his attitudes toward both foreign and domes-tic policies. He provided leadership for a wide variety of second- and third-generation ethnic groups and older-line Republican stalwarts in protecting their interests from the excesses and abuses of welfare state liberalism. At the same time, the Democratic party further polarized society by appearing to become the captive of dissidents and outsiders who were looking to the federal government for special privileges. Those who had made it through the postwar period were now concerned with consolidating their arrival and protecting it. Nixon hoped to bring to-gether a bipartisan coalition of entrepreneurialists of various racial, eth-nic, and class stripes, all bound together in a strong adherence to traditionalism and a very strong sense of American nationalism.

This book is concerned with one who came along not as just another ambitious, self-serving politician but as a leader who tapped the under-lying zones of American discontent. Inevitably, the approach subordi-nates conventional biography to what I think is more significant and useful, the story of how, in his own overtly nationalistic appeal, he har-nessed the unease that lay just below the surface of celebratory blessings of the American existence. To understand Richard Nixon is to attain a more useful comprehension of the thrust of our political culture.

He consented to sit for this portrait. He granted four interviews, eased my access to his family and associates, made available documents that have remained within his private control, and responded to questions that came up during the nearly six years devoted to this book. He never expressed the right to review the manuscript, nor was such an offer made. The only understanding was an implicit one: that a historian of the recent American past take advantage of the perspective of time to further understandings that were inhibited by the passions that dominated the dialogue during his years in public life.

Thus, Richard Nixon, reading this book along with the general public, will find that he emerges from its pages as noteworthy in ways that are not always recognizable from the Herblockian images of the man. There have been, first of all, no truly "new" Nixons. There has been one coherent, consistent Nixon, one whose commitment to what he called "practical liberalism" was unwavering throughout the second half of the twentieth century. Just as consistent was his closeness to the culture of conservative populism, one that saw an idealized vision of capitalism and the demands of entrepreneurialism.

From the end of the war until the rise of the New Right and its capture of the White House, the character of American politics and diplomacy was shaped by the essentials that were common to the Age of Nixon. It was an age of contention. It was an age of uncertainty about the role America could and should play in a confusing and dangerous world. The story of this age transcends the man; it in fact takes us back to the America of the great centennial celebration of 1876 and moves forward to the bicentennial year of 1976, when Richard Nixon expected to lead the nation's celebration.

It is my hope that this account will encourage a more mature level of political analysis by moving away from an obsessive infatuation with the individual and toward an attempt to understand the larger forces that have constituted our political culture.

Acknowledgments

GRATITUDE may seem not only self-evident but perhaps somewhat redundant, but I would prefer to be trite than cavalier. Much has gone into this, and many have made it possible.

The Federal Archives continue to be the basic source, especially those branches that house the Nixon Pre-Presidential Papers at Laguna Niguel, California, and, for the White House years, the Nixon Presidential Materials Project at Alexandria, Virginia. Essential help was given at those repositories by Diane Nixon, Fred Klose, and Joan Howard. Loie G. Gaunt put in many additional hours sorting through the non-deeded papers so generously made available by President Nixon. Sue Ellen Stanley was very helpful and gracious in assisting with a number of requests. The staffs of the Eisenhower and Lyndon Johnson libraries were also of great help, especially John Wickman, Karen Rohrer, Linda Hansen, and Nancy Smith.

Any inquiry into the early years of Richard Nixon must invariably lead to the Richard Nixon Project of the California State University at Fullerton, where I was assisted by Shirley E. Stephenson and had the good fortune to benefit from the compilations that had been organized by Harry P. Jeffrey.

Former president Nixon made himself available for several interviews and helped me gain access to some of his present and former associates. Mr. Nixon's assistant, John H. Taylor, was extremely helpful and courteous in providing information and keeping me up to date, and Carlos Narvaez guided me through some of the presidential papers.

John Ehrlichman and Leonard Garment were kind enough to make their documents available for this project, and Julie Nixon Eisenhower went through the trouble of sending me a copy of the biography of her mother in manuscript in advance of publication. Maurice Stans and Harry Dent provided me with their publications, while Russell Kirk graciously forwarded copies of his correspondence with Richard Nixon. Rabbi Baruch Korff gave me access to the correspondence of the Committee for Fairness to the Presidency, now housed at Brown University. The many others who consented to personal or telephone interviews are listed in the bibliography.

Additional material was ferreted out with diligence and generosity by David Oshinsky, Alonzo Hamby, Nancy Bressler, William Mulligan, Ellen Malino James, Michael Sappol, John White, and Gordon Brooks. I was also fortunate to draw from and be guided by the work of several of my graduate students at the City University of New York, notably Lenore Laupheimer, Jeff Schneider, and Mario Margolies. At the library in my community, Hillsdale, New York, where most of this book was written, Carol Briggs was often helpful in locating hard-to-find books. It was also useful to have access to the facilities at Simon's Rock College at Great Barrington, Massachusetts, and Columbia-Greene Community College at Hudson, New York. Most basic and essential, however, was the help given by my colleagues in the History Department and the administration of my undergraduate school, Queensborough Community College, as well as the graduate school library, both of the City University of New York. To my colleagues at both institutions I owe much for the time, support, and research assistance so vital for this work. The National Endowment for the Humanities helped to defray some of the costs with a useful and timely travel grant.

Joan Parmet not only withstood the difficulties and pressures involved in all this work, as she has in the past, but also provided important help at a number of repositories. She, along with Marie B. Hecht, read through every line of the manuscript, and both did so with editorial pencil in hand. They helped ease the way toward a more readable manuscript, as did Wendy Parmet, who gave me time from her own hectic schedule.

My editor at Little, Brown, Ray Roberts, made this book possible by his confidence in my original proposal, as did my agent, Timothy Seldes. I have also been especially well served by the astute and exacting editorial work of Peggy Leith Anderson, who has kept me on the right track and, at a number of points, from wandering into deep holes. There can be no one better than she at this demanding work. Glenn Speer of the graduate school of the City University of New York took time from his own labors on Richard Nixon and foreign policy and gave me some exceptionally knowledgeable and diligent help, especially during the final preparations of the manuscript. I could hardly have been better served.

Herbert S. Parmet
Hillsdale, New York
July 6, 1989

RICHARD
NIXON
AND HIS
AMERICA

1

Sunrise with Lincoln

SEARCHLIGHT" was on the lawn, tracked by the Secret Service monitoring post at the Old Executive Office Building. His location was hardly unusual, but the hour, before five in the morning, was. Nothing had been done to prepare anyone for a special, unorthodox mission. Egil "Bud" Krogh, the White House aide in charge of security for that day, May 9, had assumed all was normal. The word that Searchlight, the code name for the president of the United States, was up and about before sunrise called for an immediate response.

"My role that night," Krogh later explained, "was basically to be sure that all proper preparations had been made for White House security," for which the full range of protective force had been set into place: the Secret Service, the District of Columbia National Guard, the Executive Protective Service, and the General Services Administration.[1] The danger was not expected at dawn but later, at demonstrations on the Ellipse, the large grassy oval between the White House and the Washington Monument.

For the national capital in 1970, confrontation had become routine. Now the White House was at the center. Fifty-nine city buses were lined up bumper to bumper around the Executive Mansion. "It was a lot easier having buses out there than people," explained Krogh, who had helped develop the plan in anticipation of having the biggest rebellion of all take place right on the streets of the capital.[2]

The crisis had been simmering for at least two weeks, but the coming showdown was nearly a decade old. Across the country, campuses were in turmoil. Bands of students trapped faculty and administrative personnel in their offices. In California, a branch of the Bank of America went up in flames.[3] On April 4, 1968, nearly a year before Richard Nixon became president, civil rights leader Dr. Martin Luther King, Jr., was murdered. "Shoot to kill," Chicago's mayor Richard Daley ordered policemen pursuing looters. Also in the wake of the assassination, a black neighborhood was reduced to rubble in the national capital. By the time Democrats met in Chicago that year to choose an opponent to run against Nixon, Robert Kennedy, their leading candidate, had also been gunned down. Outside the convention hall, up and down Michigan Avenue and in front of the Conrad Hilton Hotel, one mindless fury met another as students and hardened activists pushed the city's law enforcement officers into their own riot. "Bring Us Together" was the appropriate theme of that winning 1968 campaign, but since Nixon had taken office, the rebellions had become even more intense; Nixon's America had neither calmed down nor engaged in civil dialogue.

It had not even responded very much to his leadership. His expectation, as he scribbled on a yellow pad only three weeks after being sworn in, was to become a "Strong in charge President." Since then, however, a year had gone by. He had, by his own estimate, accomplished a great deal, certainly as much as Jack Kennedy had done in *his* first year, and without a Bay of Pigs disaster. JFK had the press with him all the way, and public relations milking every bit of glory. How could he compete if the press refused to give *him* any credit? He was, he decided, the only "strong" president "not revered" by most journalists.[4]

The nature of holding public office, of course, requires popular support. In Nixon's case, concern with image, undoubtedly exacerbated by the Kennedy precedent, became obsessive. He added up other things that the press had ignored: his tolerant treatment of the staff; new social events in the White House; consideration shown opponents. But he noted, in taking stock, he had not done enough to promote his own handling of the presidency, including the image of a hardworking chief executive. He had to put in more time at night. Rarely did he work only one or two hours after eight. His "big play" on November 3, 1969, his speech to the "silent majority" on the need for "peace with honor" in Vietnam, could have yielded even better mileage with more thorough background work. Even his press conferences, he realized, were unsatisfactory, possibly further weakened by the absence of planted questions that could be asked by friendly newsmen.[5]

Once he made the decision to go into Cambodia, he confided to himself that "Every day is the *last — make it count.*" Perhaps this might arouse the sense of purpose in his entire staff; it was a big decision, and if he made it right, there should be "no concern over fluctuation in popularity polls." Old friend Bebe Rebozo had been properly encouraging. While waiting at an elevator door, the man whom the press was pegging as the only one who really had the president's full confidence told him, "This is the big play."[6] It would be dramatic, bold, controversial; above all, it was the right thing to do, to capture the North Vietnamese sanctuary in Cambodia, destroy their headquarters, and relieve the pressures along the Mekong River Valley. There would, he assumed, be the usual protests, but no one could then fault the president for any lack of courage. No, as Bebe agreed, it would demonstrate his ability to make the big play, to assume the decisiveness any president worth his salt needs to employ.

But the April 30 announcement of the "Cambodian incursion" kicked up more hell than even he had expected. Protesters again took to the streets and campuses, raising a din that exceeded anything that had gone before. The man who allegedly had a secret plan for ending the war had instead widened it. The radicalization of dissent seemed complete. Just a few days later, after a night of rioting and fires at the campus of Kent State University in Ohio, four young protesters were killed by National Guardsmen, who had been sent by Governor James Rhodes to restore order. Hundreds of miles away, at Jackson State College in Mississippi, police fired indiscriminately into the dormitory of black women students, killing two and wounding nine. "I think we have to recognize that there is a great deal of fear among adults today and that the feeling of opposition to the war and the Cambodian strike runs deeper on the campus than has anything in recent years," advised a memo to the president from his director of communications. "The daily news reports conveyed a sense of turmoil bordering on insurrection," Nixon later wrote in his memoirs.[7]

Violence even reached the heart of conservative stability, New York City's Wall Street financial center. On Friday, May 8, student antiwar demonstrators, attempting to attract lunch-hour street traffic, were suddenly assaulted by a band of construction workers. Wearing hard hats, which had become the badge of their trade and symbol of counterdissent, they chased the youngsters through the mob of amazed spectators, battering heads whenever they could and scattering the victims throughout the downtown canyons, wounding about seventy before it was all over.

The police (who afterward explained that they were no match for the workers' army) stood with mixed feelings of horror and delight as the hard hats then took off toward city hall. Meanwhile, another angry mob, provoked by missile-throwing students, invaded Pace University, smashing windows with crowbars and clubs and lashing out at those who blocked their way. Other workers ripped off a Red Cross banner at the gate of Trinity Church because they mistook it for a Vietcong flag. Dr. John M. Butler, the rector of the Episcopal church, quickly locked the gates to safeguard the building.[8]

Nixon's postmortem account of those agitated days conveyed a detachment that can variously be described as offering brave, strong, determined leadership; or, to critics, a presidential response that was indifferent and insensitive to the rebellions tearing the nation he had vowed to reunite. Apprehensive about the forthcoming protest of May

9, he wrote, "I felt that we should do everything possible to make sure that this event was nonviolent and that we did not appear insensitive to it."[9] Still, the tactic was to avoid the *appearance* that he was too worried. Nixon the man was in conflict with Nixon the resolute leader. For the sake of history, Henry Kissinger, then adviser for national security affairs, would have to be the hard-liner against the demonstrators, counseling inflexibility until after the completion of the Cambodian operation, while the president cautioned that foreign policy must not be dictated by street protests. Nevertheless, his personal agitation was greater than he would dare reveal.

Reluctant and ambivalent, he had agreed to a suggestion from John Ehrlichman. The White House adviser's son, a Stanford student, had persuaded his father that Nixon should agree to meet with six young men from Kent State who had driven all the way from Ohio to see the president. Nixon's first response was no: the potential for precedents was mind-boggling. Nothing good could come from that kind of session, especially with public opinion adamant against campus rebels. Finally, as Ehrlichman recalls, the president gave in. Shortly after ten-thirty on the morning of Wednesday, May 6, the young men entered the Oval Office.[10]

They were mostly tongue-tied before the president. During one full hour, the communication hardly went beyond halting, embarrassing exchanges. The students, despite their obvious agitation, remained frozen in the presence of the chief executive. Nixon himself found the session trying and unproductive, a test of patience rather than a valuable encounter. His initial reluctance had been justified, and any additional meetings would debase the process. "Why did you put me through it?" was the question Ehrlichman sensed from Nixon afterward. "It was very awkward," recalls Ehrlichman.[11]

Still, the encounter received positive exposure. The student delegation, all between the ages of twenty-one and twenty-four, was able to speak more openly later when facing the press. "All six were well-dressed and clean shaven," reported Robert B. Semple, Jr.'s *New York Times* dispatch. In 1970, that description of student dissenters was itself deemed newsworthy. Apparently better composed in front of the press, they revealed that their grievances went beyond unhappiness over Cambodia. Their encounters with the adult world were unsatisfactory, from the faculty and administration on their campus to decisions being made in Washington. The president listened carefully, they said, and outlined how future unhappiness could be minimized. The White House then also ordered Ehrlichman to prepare an analysis of a Justice Department report on the Kent State tragedy.[12]

The president's session with the students was upstaged by dramatic reports of the closing of scores of colleges. At the same time, unhappiness within the cabinet became public in the form of a letter to Mr. Nixon from Interior Secretary Walter J. Hickel. Hickel, a convert to the cause of environmentalism and already increasingly isolated from the administration, charged that there was a lack of "appropriate concern for the attitude of a great mass of Americans — our young people." They, like himself, were being shut off from the government. The vice president had made them an easy target, treated their motives with contempt, a tactic, wrote Hickel, that "can serve little purpose other than to further cement those attitudes to a solidity impossible to penetrate with reason." The president himself was urged to begin a round of dialogues with individual members of his cabinet.[13] Only one thing was becoming clear: the price of the Cambodian invasion was greater than anybody had anticipated. There was little good news from any quarter that Thursday.

Holding a press conference, then, seemed like the best way to break through. How better to dispel the impression of a remote, isolated president taking refuge in a White House bunker? Even if there were those around him who worried that it could backfire, that he might inadvertently feed the media grist for distortion, Nixon felt he had to take the initiative. He might at least diffuse tensions. So, on prime time that Friday night, only hours after the head-bashing in New York and Hickel's well-advertised distress, the president went before the lights and cameras in the East Room.

He had not held a televised news conference for over three months. His discomfort was obvious. As he faced the newsmen, there was little of the administration's by now familiar combative style, no hint of anything resembling Vice President Spiro Agnew's verbal assaults. He was earnest, almost eager to please his critics. He understood their dismay. He shared their objectives. He, too, wanted to shorten the war.

His responses to questions from the newsmen were not adversarial. He supplied just the sort of information they wanted. The Cambodian invasion had gone better than expected, and he promised that 150,000 additional American troops would be withdrawn from South Vietnam by the spring. In response to whether he really intended to move from an era of confrontation with the Soviet Union to an era of negotiation, he predicted a significant agreement. "The Soviet Union," he explained, "has just as great an interest as we have in seeing that there is some limitation on nuclear arms." Then, in an obvious bid to identify with the concerns of youth, he recalled his own early days in Congress when, in opposition to President Truman, he, like the students, had "the luxury of criticism because they can criticize and if it doesn't work out then they can gloat over it, or if it does work out, the criticism will be forgotten." He had been there himself, and he knew how it felt.

Veteran correspondent Philip Potter of the *Baltimore Sun* then asked the president whether he thought that his use of the word "bums" in condemnation of dissenting students had not helped to inflame the rhet-oric. The comment, made a week earlier, had become Nixon's most publicized remark. "I would certainly regret that my use of the word 'bums' was interpreted to apply to those who dissent," he told Potter. "All the members of this press corps know that I have for years defended the right of dissent. I have always opposed the use of violence. On university campuses the rule of reason is supposed to prevail over the rule of force. And when students on university campuses burn buildings, when they engage in violence, when they break up furniture, when they terrorize their fellow students and terrorize the faculty, then I think 'bums' is perhaps too kind a word to apply to that kind of person. Those are the kind I was referring to." Near the end of the interview, he left open the possibility that he might be available to meet with some of the demonstrators in the White House.[14]

Nixon thereby accomplished his immediate objective. A *New York Times* editorial hailed him for tempering the climate. In Boise, Idaho, Vice President Agnew took the cue from the president's approach. At a Republican dinner, he said he wanted "in some small way" to help cool tempers, and he dropped some of the more inflammatory language from his speech.[15]

Satisfied with his performance, the president returned to the Executive Mansion. "I was agitated and uneasy as the events of the last few weeks raced through my mind," he wrote. His thoughts combined relief with anxiety about what was yet to come. As a student of history, and especially the presidency, he naturally identified his problems with those of the president who had suffered through the war between the North and South. His troubled night, then, had the mystique of mission. Nixon has written that he "slept for a few hours," but the telephone log lists fifty separate calls that were made after the press conference. They began at 9:22 P.M. and concluded with a call to his valet, Manolo Sanchez, at 4:22 A.M., leaving hardly enough time for much more than a catnap. William Safire, a Nixon speechwriter, concludes that he must have slept sometime between his 1:55 A.M. and 3:38 A.M. conversations with Henry Kissinger, with whom he had eight separate talks that night.[16]

A little after four o'clock, the president walked into the Lincoln Sitting Room. He put a Philadelphia Orchestra recording of Rachmaninoff's First Piano Concerto on the turntable. Sanchez heard the music and came in to ask if he needed any help. He found the president looking through the window toward the students who were beginning to gather on the Ellipse. Beyond that grassy area was the Washington Monument, at the southern edge of the planned demonstration.

Yet, at that moment, the president's thoughts were elsewhere, not where the visitors were gathering, not at the scene of the coming protests. They went, instead, to a symbol of conflict and compassion, the marvelous landmark well to the southwest of the Ellipse and past the Reflecting Pool. "Have you ever been to the Lincoln Memorial at night?" the president asked Manolo Sanchez. When Manolo said he had never seen it, Nixon said, "Let's go look at it now."[17]

Krogh, at his command post, then heard that Searchlight was on the lawn. The Secret Service, notified about the odd venture, seemed to the president "petrified with apprehension." He also ordered that his plans be revealed to neither his staff nor the press. Krogh had to act immediately. His call woke up Ehrlichman. "Look," he remembers saying, "I don't know why the president is down there on the lawn, but this town is filled up with a lot of young people who are really geared to expressing their First Amendment rights and it's probably not a good thing for him to be out and about at this time in the morning." He had no choice, Ehrlichman agreed, but to pursue the matter. But by the time Krogh had rushed out to the lawn, Searchlight was gone. Again, this time far more worried, he called his superior. "I think he's taken off," he told Ehrlichman, who ordered him to get another car and track the president's path. "I wanted to stay in the background and just sort of observe what was going on. He had not notified any White House staff people himself."[18]

The incident, wrote Semple, "provided a revealing glimpse of the man who has been under exceptional strain for the past few weeks." Safire later noted that it was the "most impulsive, and perhaps most revealing night of Nixon's Presidency. . . . He broke out of the cocoon that separates the President from the rest of humanity for three hours, enjoyed a taste of real life and the bitter aftertaste."[19] His impulse seemed understandable, but Nixon was communing as much with inspiration as with reality.

Bud Krogh found him just inside the Lincoln Memorial, at the foot of the Great Emancipator's statue. The sun was just coming up and, as Krogh remembers, the "early morning pinkish glow was beginning to rise in the east behind the Capitol building." Nixon had already shown Manolo the carved inscriptions, especially his favorite one: "In this temple, as in the hearts of the people for whom he saved the Union, the memory of Abraham Lincoln is enshrined forever."[20] The engraved quotations, the lonely sculpture of the seated figure, seemed a divine presence. Inescapably, almost mystically, the Lincoln of lore was more tangible than the historical Lincoln.

At that moment, the president, under siege from countless incensed critics, drew emotional and even intellectual support from the Great Emancipator, whose policies, like his own, had also outraged the self-interested and timid. All that was being replayed, only this civil war was Nixon's. Every headline, every additional piece of intelligence reaching the White House, emphasized the vehemence of the opposition. He could assure himself that the great majority remained loyal, but Richard Nixon was too familiar with history not to know that minorities can create civil wars and even revolutions. So, as with Lincoln, enemies were after his hide.

As he and Manolo then turned away and moved toward the steps, they spotted a group of about eight young people. Nixon walked over and reached out to shake their hands. "They were not unfriendly," he later recorded. "As a matter of fact, they seemed somewhat overawed, and, of course, quite surprised." Krogh walked up the steps at that moment and saw "a surrealistic kind of scene because a lot of these kids were obviously tired and obviously disheveled; they had been driving a long way. This was when fatigue clothes were in and long hair, and here he was, in earnest conversation talking to some of these young people."[21]

Did Nixon, like Lincoln, seek out such youthful victims of national turmoil? Safire, for example, describes the sunrise visit as "an impetuous act of compassion," one so lacking in planning that it appeared unconvincing. But there remains a greater probability: any consideration must question the president's conscious priorities. He had reached a moment of crisis, one that forced a dialogue between what was right and what was necessary. "Here's a man who had made a very tough military decision," reflected Krogh fifteen years later. "He had gone in front of the American people and explained why it was essential to do it. . . . He wanted to get out and walk around the city and show it to Manolo and communicate with some of those young people that were there."[22]

Had that been precisely so, Nixon would have directed the Secret Service to take him directly to the Washington Monument and the Ellipse. Nothing, however, suggests that was contemplated. His actions were more sentimental, more those of a seeker of inner guidance or reaffirmation. The moment of crisis led him straight to Lincoln, and that that communion inspired in him awe and the desire for similar presidential immortality cannot be discounted. It bolstered his need to reach out to make himself understood, to plead the cause from the perspective of the president, the leader, the man with the responsibility for making decisions that cannot be fully understood by those who may have to pay the price. He told the surprised little group that gathered around him about his own youth. "Do you realize that many of us, when we were your age, were also willing to die for what we believed in, and are willing to do so today?" "I know that probably most of you think I'm an SOB, but I want you to know that I understand just how you feel." He was reminded of his own days as a law student at Duke. He recalled that his own desire for peace had led him to believe in Chamberlain and to oppose Churchill. He had to. He was raised in a Quaker family. "I was as close to being a pacifist as anybody could be in those times," he said. Then he added that the great question of war and peace was really in their hands, as Lincoln had told his countrymen in his first inaugural address. Nixon then urged his listeners to travel, to get to know the complex world. "I told them," he wrote soon afterward, "my great hopes that during my administration, and certainly during their lifetime, that the great mainland of China would be opened up so that we could know the 700 million people who live in China who are one of the most remarkable people on earth." Manolo tried to interrupt to say that there was a telephone call for him in the limousine, but he told the valet he wanted to go on talking. "Try to understand what we are doing," he told the young people. "Sure you came here to demonstrate and shout your slogans on the Ellipse. That is all right. Just keep it peaceful. . . . Remember, I feel just as deeply as you do about this." He started to explain details about the progress of the strategic arms limitations talks until he saw their attention beginning to wander.[23]

Their hatred for war was understandable, he said. Their feelings were commendable. He urged them not to go from that reaction to a condemnation of our whole system and everything it stood for. Constructive achievements were possible. For example, he explained, most of them came from campuses where racial desegregation had been carried out. But that only created a new kind of segregation. While blacks and whites were now attending classes together, they seemed to have even less contact with each other than before. "You must find a way to communicate with the blacks in your universities," Krogh heard him say.[24]

With Manolo, Krogh, and the Secret Service standing by, Nixon walked down to the base of the memorial. At that point, he saw a group of girls in their early twenties. Krogh asked one of them if she had had any sleep. She confirmed that their night had been spent driving to Washington for the demonstration; they had just arrived and had no idea of where they could sleep. Nixon, eager to greet the later arrivals, asked one girl her age. She said she was twenty-four. "That's Tricia's age," he replied, which seemed to be appropriate small talk. Another young woman, also answering a presidential question, said she was from Syracuse University. The association with the school and its athletic program seemed obvious to Nixon. In an effort to continue the conversation, he noted the prominence of her school's football team.[25]

That parting comment, made just before Nixon and his party left the memorial at five minutes to six, somehow reduced the sunrise visit in his critics' eyes to a trivial, bumbling, insensitive effort to "use" the kids. Only a few days after he had called certain students "bums," Safire wrote, he "had compounded his error by talking condescendingly about trivial matters like football or visiting foreign cities with students who had come in seriousness to protest about the war." Indeed, the young woman from Syracuse who had talked to the president told a reporter, "Here we come from a university that's completely uptight, on strike, and when we told him where we were from, he talked about the football team. And when someone said he was from California, he talked about surfing."[26]

The incident, declared the *Washington Post,* was "a dialogue of the deaf." The effort was dismissed as another example of presidential callousness. As White House chief of staff H. R. "Bob" Haldeman then wrote in a memorandum to speechwriter Ray Price, the treatment of the encounter made Nixon realize "that it would have made more news from the standpoint of the students for him to engage in a spiritual dialogue with them about why we were in Cambodia — why we haven't ended the war sooner — the morality of the war, etc. . . . but as he evaluated the situation . . . [he] felt that perhaps the major contribution he could make to them was 'to try to lift them a bit out of the miserable intellectual wasteland in which they now wander aimlessly around.' " Furthermore, Haldeman reported Nixon as having speculated, " 'I really wonder in the long run if this is all the legacy we want to leave. If it is — then perhaps we should do our job as easily as we can — as expeditiously as we can — and get out and leave the responsibilities of the government to the true materialists — the socialists and the totalitarians, who talk idealism but rule relentlessly without any regard to the individual considerations — the quest for personality that I tried to emphasize in my dialogue with the students.' "[27]

Reluctant to return to the White House, the president led Manolo to the Capitol. The little party consisting of Nixon, Krogh, and the Secret Service, was now joined by Dr. Walter Tkach, the president's personal physician. Unable to unlock the Senate Chamber door at that early hour, they walked through the Rotunda under the Capitol dome and toward the House of Representatives side of the building. There, the president was approached by three black cleaning women. One of them, Carrie Moore, held out a Bible for him to sign. "I read this every day,'" she explained. He responded that "the trouble is that most of us these days don't read it enough." The woman assured him that she read it all the time. Nixon took her hand and said, "You know, my mother was a saint. She died two years ago. She was a saint." Then, squeezing her hand, he added, "You be a saint too," and she replied, "I'll try, Mr. President."[28]

Feeling somewhat exuberant, he wanted to move on. As he did, the entourage grew, with Bob Haldeman and appointments secretary Dwight Chapin joining the presidential party. By that point, the president's aides began to urge that he return to the White House, but he was determined to go somewhere else for breakfast. The only place they could think of as open at that hour was the Rib Room of the Mayflower Hotel. "I'd been a little woozy anyway," remembers Krogh, "because I didn't really sleep the night before very much; hadn't slept at all Friday night. Anyway, we got up there around six-thirty, and we were the first ones in the restaurant." Nixon, in a Washington restaurant for the first time since his swearing-in, ordered corned beef hash with an egg. Then, looking at Krogh, he suddenly asked, "Did you call Ehrlichman?" "Yes, sir," said the youthful aide. "I sure did." "That's too early to call anyone," Nixon responded. "Yes, sir," said Krogh, "it was too early to call anyone."[29]

When the president announced that he wanted to walk back to the White House, Krogh was faced with another security problem. Going by foot would have taken him through Lafayette Park and past the Peace Corps Building, which was occupied by some demonstrators. A Vietcong flag hung from a window. At that moment, the park itself was the last place in Washington for the president to be. "Mr. President," cautioned Krogh, "it's not really the right thing to walk back. We have a lot of demonstrators around the White House right now. There's a perimeter there. We can't get through it." But Nixon insisted that he wanted to walk and headed down Connecticut Avenue. Haldeman, meanwhile, stood alongside the presidential limousine signaling frantically to Krogh to get Nixon into the car. "So I finally went up and just took him by the arm real solid and said, 'We can't walk back. We've got to ride back.' " Finally, the president agreed, and the limousine moved down Connecticut at Seventeenth Street and entered the White House through the E Street entrance, the only way to penetrate the line of buses. The gate that led to the guardhouse swung closed and sealed off the one quiet place along Pennsylvania Avenue.[30]

2

The Thirty-seventh President

POWER MAY OR MAY NOT corrupt, but it certainly can intrigue. That sense of destiny, that messianic impulse, moves the restless, generates its own sense of mission. The lives of Alexander the Great, Julius Caesar, Napoleon, Washington, and Lincoln excite us less as historical curiosities than as role models. Goals created carry the promise of fulfillment, what Friedrich Nietzsche called the "will to power." With that comes the promise of the highest award, immortality. If, as William James pointed out, "we believe that the end is in our power, we *will* that the desired feeling, having, or doing shall be real; and real it presently becomes, either immediately upon the willing or after certain preliminaries have been fulfilled." So basic is that instinct that Julie Nixon Eisenhower assumed she had offered a logical response to a question about her father's drive by making the following observation: "I think he's sort of an idealistic type and this whole idea of a person of destiny. I think that's it. You know, it sounds crazy to talk about that, but that's what some people feel and believe."[1]

No such mission troubled Warren Harding. The ways of democratic politics installed him, after a mundane Senate term, as Woodrow Wilson's successor. Out of his depth, not eager to contribute his own chapter to history, and frustrated by the complexities of leadership, he yearned for his lost Ohio newspaper days. "Lord, Lord, man!" one of Harding's aides said to William Allen White of the *Emporia Gazette*. "You can't know what the President is going through. You see he doesn't understand it; he just doesn't know a thousand things that he ought to know. And he realizes his ignorance, and he is afraid. He has no idea where to turn." Caught in a situation he had not designed, and surrounded by those with more knowledge and more craft, he faced a dilemma not of power but of impotence. The White House had become his prison.

In the company of White, a congenial visitor, Harding naturally turned to the problems of running a small-town daily. He wanted to talk about everything but politics. His greatest distress came from having reached that position of power. "My God," said the president to the editor, "this is a hell of a job! I have no trouble with my enemies. I can take care of my enemies all right. But my damn friends, my God-damn friends, White, they're the ones that keep me walking the floor nights!"[2]

Harding, somewhat like the leopard atop Kilimanjaro, was over his head; today he'd be called an overachiever. His only advantage over Ulysses Grant's plight was that the old soldier had a reputation at stake. But, apart from their individual differences, both careers illustrate how some reputations are not made but destroyed by the presidency. Preferring to believe in how such responsibilities can ennoble even simple souls, we perceive some sort of inevitability about the rise to greatness, the democratic spirit inspiring even ordinary men so that they can perform the wonders that have elsewhere been the task of kings and emperors — mediocrities becoming titanic.

Mythology thereby exalts reality. George Washington, hardly a common citizen, nevertheless left no doubt that he would subordinate his military and social standing for the best interests of his fellow countrymen. Although no longer a commoner by the time he made it to the presidency, Andrew Jackson rose from frontier primitivism and thus confirmed that the Founding Fathers had created a special egalitarianism. Once having taken firm root, the "log cabin" myth embroidered the secular faith. Blatantly used to promote the ambitions of William Henry Harrison, folklore was foisted in more subtle ways, gaining credence from such careers as not only Lincoln's but, closer to our times, Harry Truman's, Lyndon Johnson's, and Richard Nixon's. Even as Americans retained their cynicism about lower-order politicians, the presidency retained its pantheon of nobles. At the same time, the power of the office continued to be regarded as a leveler: small men become great and heroes become mortal.

Nixon has a reputation that was confirmed rather than created by Watergate. Even before the scandals became known, political scientist James David Barber substantiated the validity of his own criteria for predicting presidential behavior. In the case of Nixon, Barber wrote, "it was extremely likely that a man who had spent his life in pursuit of power and had won ultimate power in the political order, would then preside over its dispersal."[3]

For Barber and, indeed, for an entire generation of liberal intellectuals, Nixon's rise marked the nadir of modern American politics. "The real legacy of the Nixon administration," one student of the presidency declared, "was the introduction of a paranoid style of politics that viewed the struggle for power as a form of warfare against enemies."[4] For such critics, the Watergate scandals did more to reaffirm the mendacity that had long since been assumed, something more profound than mere sin. Politicians were, as a profession, susceptible to venality. The man whose career was central to most of their own mature lives was something more than that: more, in other words, than the conventional figure of routine disdain.

Nixon loomed to intellectuals as the personification of the dangerous "Americanist." "Wasn't the whole meaning of 'Americanism' that America was a peculiar land of freedom, equality, and opportunity?" asked historian Louis Hartz some three decades ago, long before the Watergate apartment-office complex was even an excavation on the banks of the Potomac. Freedom, of course, was the key word; but that also became something more, not merely a theme but a permissive code sanctioning individual prerogatives and opportunities for unhampered access. So the paradoxes materialized in easy succession: religious persecution by Puritans who had founded John Winthrop's New World haven for freedom of worship; one of history's more oppressive slavocracies flowed like the River Styx through the utopia dedicated to the "unalienable rights" of man; the secular faith in democracy distorted so that it was possible for Hartz, among others, to observe that "the American 'fascists' were all 'Americanists' to the hilt. . . . When [Huey] Long said that fascism would come to America denying that it was fascism, he had, needless to say, a valid insight into the American ethos."[5] Almost two decades after Hartz's forebodings, Philip Roth wrote a wicked satire called *Our Gang*. The acerbic tract carried a subtitle that served as positive identification of its target: *(Starring Tricky and His Friends)*.

Had his presidency passed without sinister revelations, he still would have been condemned as divisive, as a demagogue who exploited fear and resentment to create majorities. Just as his earlier reputation had been built on deceit, his power was assumed to have been preserved by crafty manipulations of baser popular instincts. Richard Nixon has been the most durable villain of them all.

Once the depth of the abuses of power had been revealed, there was an insatiable appetite for psychological explanations, which, of course, was not unique to Nixon. But noteworthy in his case was the shelfful of volumes specifically devoted to psychobiographical dissections. They scrutinized every known aspect of his life, most particularly as gleaned from early accounts and contemporary interviews.[6] They concluded that he was a psychopathic liar, needed maternal love, disdained his father, and was so full of aggression that he loved mashing potatoes, which was read as proof that he needed outlets for his inner hostilities. Whatever he did next, wrote Arthur Woodstone just one month before the "burglars" were found at the Democratic national headquarters, "it would ultimately prove dangerous" because the president "had to find some

group, some nation, someone, in addition to himself, onto whom he
could project his early guilt."[7]

So it was that satisfaction was achieved, the satisfaction that the American condition could be explained by the neurosis that drove one individual. The sweep of history all boiled down to an unfortunate spell of
idiosyncratic leadership. If only there had been a different navigator,
the ship of state would have sailed in another direction, a vigorous
affirmation of Thomas Carlyle's stress on the importance of the "great
man."

Anybody who had been paying attention would have known that, as in
1945, "victory" was not necessarily the solution. Those who hoped that
Nixon's departure would liberate the nation from a spell in the wilderness soon found themselves in deeper, and sometimes darker, woods.

By 1946, the Roosevelt persuasion had become far weaker, the privileged better positioned to reassert their prerogatives. The objectives
justified the means; uneasiness, the weapons. Such was the struggle for
progress, at least the American way. A New Deal would be superseded
by a Fair Deal, a New Frontier, a Great Society, each an attempt to build
on reforms that were illusory to begin with.

Lyndon Johnson's Great Society became a last-gasp effort by a son of
the New Deal to seize that moment by showing how he would complete
the reforms begun in the 1930s. In an America that had been transformed since Franklin D. Roosevelt's day, Johnson's mixture of progressivism and populism was doomed to ultimate failure even before
Vietnam became a trap.

Only a void remained by the 1970s. Recent memory was hard-pressed
to recall similar doubts, fumbling over solutions, and uncertainty about
the American role, either at home or abroad. Explanations were far
cheaper than options. It may have been the Kennedy assassination, the
war in Vietnam, or the Nixon years and the national "nightmare" over
Watergate. Nobody really knew, but investigators were everywhere. Testing the public pulse, already a national obsession, betrayed an anxiety
about direction. If the shooting in Dallas in 1963 began that decline, as
so many thought, each subsequent incident was but another step down,
for some another erosion of American preeminence, American innocence, American confidence; and, what seemed most troubling to a
highly nationalistic people, the decline of just about every other value.
Far more disturbing to the vast majority was the apparent loss of America's traditional ability to command global respect.

Communications were more sophisticated than ever. A world of tran-
sistors and chips transformed electronic marvels so the universe could
be monitored play by play. The globe had indeed become a village. Never

in history had any society been so saturated with information, and never had that intelligence been so analyzed and digested.

The new articulation became a complexity of symbolism; in a sense, an escape from the inundation of print, verbiage, and graphics. Shyness about betraying the national ethos could be overcome by body language and codes that substituted for direct communications. Attention went to terms that became familiar enough even to the most inattentive: military-industrial complex; eastern establishment; law and order; New Frontier; Great Society; counterculture; "me" generation; affirmative action and reverse discrimination; welfare cheats; neighborhood schools; freedom of choice; gradualism; yuppies; baby boomers; freedom fighters; hippies and Yippies; grass and pot; the "liberal" press; globalism; policeman of the world; Camelot; environmentalism; hard hats; silent majority; Middle America; radical right; born again; nuclear proliferation; and on and on. Nor was there a shortage of slogans calling for the implementation of this or that: Make Love Not War; Draft Beer Not Men; When Guns Are Outlawed, Outlaws Will Have Guns; Right to Life; Freedom of Choice; Gay Rights; Black Power; Take Back the Night; Hell No, We Won't Go; Hey, Hey, LBJ, How Many Kids Did You Kill Today?; Impeach Truman; Impeach Earl Warren; Dump LBJ; Impeach Nixon. Impeach somebody, maybe the twentieth century and modern diseases. And all this came not more than two decades after winning the "most just" of all wars, after finally nailing down Woodrow Wilson's goal of "making the world safe for democracy." Discontent, clearly, was not created by the Age of Nixon. Discontent created the Age of Nixon.

Victor Lasky caught some of that meaning in a 1977 book called *It Didn't Start with Watergate.* Nor, it should be added, did it end with that, either. There was, indeed, a flow, a cycle of our times, of postwar forces and their exhaustion. So it was easy to isolate the germs, spotlight the contaminants and contaminators. As Caligula "is surrounded by his horse," wrote Andrew Kopkind before the inauguration in January 1969, so was the Age of Johnson followed by the Age of Nixon.[8] Others also advertised that despair. Their message became most obvious via the revealing titles of a series of prominent books published between the "golden era" of JFK's Camelot and the rebirth of American pride under Ronald Reagan: *The End of Ideology, The Crisis of Confidence, The End of Liberalism, The End of the American Era, Coming Apart, The Hidden Crisis in American Politics, The Party Is Over: The Failure of Politics in America, The Diffusion of Power, The Retreat of American Power, The Twilight of Authority, The Twilight of Capitalism, The Unraveling of America, Troubled Journey: From Pearl Harbor to Ronald Reagan, Gambling with History: Reagan in the White House,* and *The Unfinished Journey.*

So there is only half-truth to the conventional adage that books cannot be judged by their covers. Their titles do tell a story. But all are indicative of a moment in history. Over a decade after the retirement of Richard Nixon to San Clemente, dispassion may contribute to an understanding of how he was both an architect and victim of an America that was more sanctified than understood. Never had a society worked so hard to make sense out of disorder.

Nixon's career spanned the generations. He was a pre-McCarthy anticommunist detective; ultimately elected four times on a national ticket, matching the record of the champ, FDR himself; thirty-seventh president of the United States, and the only one who left by resigning; the liquidator of the long war in Vietnam; a cold warrior and architect of détente.

"Nixon is a postwar man," Garry Wills pointed out midway through Nixon's first term. "Politically, he does not preexist the year 1946." That bright new day that followed Japan's surrender clouded over more rapidly than seemed possible upon the restoration of peace and the renewal of confidence. Nixon was of that generation, and then some. As Anthony Lewis wrote on the day Nixon turned over his presidency to Gerald Ford, "Richard Nixon has been in public life for 25 years, a period that could fairly be called the age of Nixon in our politics."[9]

Whatever the criteria for approving or disapproving of Richard Nixon, he has been a significant presence ever since the end of World War II. Whether rising beyond Whittier, California, by coming out ahead of Jerry Voorhis, Alger Hiss, and Helen Gahagan Douglas, or sustaining bitter defeats at the hands of John F. Kennedy and Pat Brown and, finally, in the court of public opinion in 1974, Nixon alone — not Henry Wallace, Joe McCarthy, Douglas MacArthur, Dean Acheson, George Wallace, or any number of others — has constantly rekindled controversies. They can hardly be described without at least alluding to his role.

Most politicians are more fortunate. They don't get what they want. Check the *Biographical Directory of the Congress of the United States* and scan the thousands of names that are preserved for history only by biographical vignettes. Unfortunately, that league is not represented by bubblegum cards. Then, at least, their visages would be immortalized, together with appropriate statistics showing electoral triumphs and losses and how they stood on the great questions of the day. Collectors might then be inspired to trade Gores for Colmers, or pay premiums for Atchisons, Baldwins, Bayhs, and Youngs. Maybe a set of the four Hamilton Fishes or the five Frelinghuysens would constitute a prized collection.

No need, however, to rake up nobodies or dynasties. Just consider Nixon's colleagues who arrived with him in the House of Representatives for the first time in 1947. Not since the 1920s had an election produced so many first-term Republicans. Nixon found himself among no fewer than sixty-five GOP newcomers to Capitol Hill. Still, numerous as they were, few became memorable. Only Jacob K. Javits and Thruston B.

Morton might reasonably be regarded as having transcended mediocrity. Although Senate Republicans simultaneously managed a majority with the addition of a more memorable group (in what surely was a fine year for the party if not for the nation) that included Joseph R. McCarthy, John Bricker, William E. Jenner, George W. Malone, William F. Knowland, Arthur V. Watkins, and Irving M. Ives, it was Nixon who would emerge as the most powerful and controversial person over the next three decades.

Why he became the center of such storms transcends psychoanalytical dissections. As Oscar Handlin wrote in *The Uprooted,* "Once I thought to write a history of the immigrants in America. Then I discovered that the immigrants *were* American history." So, too, we might say that once I began to write about Richard Nixon, I found that, however necessary it might be to arrive at some understanding of his emotional as well as his intellectual makeup, it is most necessary to remember that he was a man of his nation and culture.

All our ages are full of ironies, and Nixon's was no exception. During the decades of his maturity, he was never very far from view. Nixon, far more than the post-Roosevelt liberals, reflected the visceral instincts of the mass electorate. Stewart Alsop was on target in 1972 when he wrote in *The Atlantic* that "the social mores and political views of the middle-class American majority are certainly much closer to those of Mr. Nixon than to those of readers of the *New York Review of Books* — or, one suspects, of this magazine."[10] Alsop could well have added that his readers were far more enamored of a wide array of Nixon contemporaries — Adlai Stevenson, Hubert Humphrey, the Kennedys, George McGovern, William Fulbright, Eugene McCarthy, and so on. But Nixon, disasters and all, survived, if not to decorate the American political scene, certainly to articulate the national psyche. Nixon as a man of the people contradicted the perception that he was a sinister betrayer of popular confidence.

Nixon may be seen as an ultrasensitive intellectual (a characterization he would loathe) contending with the necessities of a callous, masculine, and hypocritical society. To succeed, to aspire to what came more easily to the more advantaged, he early recognized the need for accommodation. If Nixon was the quintessential self-made man, the real "figure under the carpet" must be revealed as a highly vulnerable, easily wounded soul who hid himself behind a mask of toughness and demonstrated — as he did in college when he allowed himself to be his football team's cannon fodder — that he could take it. From the start of his political career, he proved that he could also dish it out. His values incorporated recognition of the anybody-can-make-it-if-he's-willing-to-be-enough-of-a-bastard system as the inherent rule determining the game and its winners. It was that system that was to become, for Nixon, a surrogate for inherent advantages. The mythical Abe Lincoln somehow had to be grafted onto the gonads of a Cornelius Vanderbilt.

Even his use of language would have been understood by the old Commodore, to whom it came naturally. The president's fellow countrymen, so offended by the profanities that they never actually heard for themselves from the Watergate tapes, had to be spared by the substitution of "expletive deleted" entries. Actually, the voice was essentially bogus. What the little White House circle — the Ehrlichmans, Haldemans, Mitchells, Magruders, and Deans — heard was the old amateur thespian assuming the language of one displaying the balls of command: General George Patton, a Nixon favorite, reminding the boys they were really men.

"I don't know what the swearing by Nixon connotes," volunteered a thoughtful Hugh Scott when interviewed in 1986. The former senator from Pennsylvania, ex-chairman of the Republican National Committee and his party's leader on the Hill, was clearly searching for answers. "There was really less of that in the leadership meetings or in private meetings with him," he recalled. "Except when he was surrounded by staff, he seems to have felt the need to kind of let go, I don't know, as though he were overcompensating or something to show that 'I'm a regular fella.' . . . When you take it out of context, it sounds like he's a very foul-mouthed individual. Actually, the leadership meetings were on a considerably more dignified level than that. There were very few expletives; basically they were very mild. He rarely ever made a really dirty remark."[11] Nixon had long since learned something about felicitous language. He was not only an amateur actor but a trained debater. The refinement of such skills was, of course, useful to a trial lawyer, but essential to a politician.

If he was going to "make it," he had to cling to a system that had to serve his purposes. With him, the payoff would be the kind of satisfaction that certainly would have appealed to his mother, Hannah, and even the kind of reward that his father, Frank, would have liked. And that was the satisfaction of hard labor. Richard Nixon, then, did not have a fixed ideological base. For him it was something else: a secular faith in success by perseverance. His reward would come by outlasting, outpersisting, outenduring those whose motivation and determination lacked his intensity. He would, somehow, prove the durability of the American Dream.

Nixon's published writings often returned to the question of rule by the wise and the authoritative. If it contradicted his denunciations of elitism, the anomaly seemed to escape him. Typically, he has argued: "The successful leader has a strong will of his own, and he knows how to mobilize the will of others." Moreover, "to wish is passive; to will is active.

Followers wish. Leaders will. . . . [A] Professor can go off on flights into
the stratosphere of the absurd. Those with power have to keep an eye
firmly on the results, the impact, the effect. Leaders deal with the con-
crete." As he told Fidel Castro in 1959, the leader should "of course be
out ahead of the people. He should have a clearer perception than they
of where the country should be going and why, and of what it takes to
get there." In language that springs from Machiavelli, he declared that
"people both love the great leader and hate him; they are seldom indifferent toward him." In Indochina, the French had failed "primarily
because they had not sufficiently trained, much less inspired, the Indochinese people to be able to defend themselves. They had failed to
build a cause — or a cadre — that could resist the nationalist and anticolonialist appeals of the Communists."[12] In his first book, *Six Crises,* and
sprinkled through all his other works, are passages about the rigors of
preparation for leadership. One book, specifically devoted to the problem,
lauded the leadership qualities of people as diverse as Winston Churchill,
Charles de Gaulle, Konrad Adenauer, Nikita Khrushchev, and Zhou
Enlai. He recalled the Chinese Communist leader as "one of the most
extraordinarily gifted people I have ever known, with an incandescent
grasp of the realities of power." Yet, he later cautioned that "many of
history's greatest leaders were disasters for their own people and for the
world because they led in the wrong direction."[13]

That was it: the realities of power, something too often lacking in the
elite, established leadership class. In *The Real War,* he complained that
"too many of America's intellectual and cultural elite have shown themselves to be brilliant, creative, trendy, gullible, smug, and blind in one
eye: they tend to see bad only on the Right, not on the Left. Extremely
sophisticated about ideas in the abstract, they can be extremely simplistic
and naive about the realities of the actual global conflict we find ourselves
engaged in." The history of civilization, he argued elsewhere, "showed
that the leader class rather than the common people were those that
first disintegrated. That here in our country the problem was not the
common people who stood by us — they were the silent majority."[14]

As president, he was confident that he understood his constituency
and frequently alluded to their status. From his position as a westerner
from a modest background, Nixon struck out at what he regarded as
the virtually decadent pillars of the establishment: the press, Ivy League
colleges, and aristocratic professionals. When John Ehrlichman reported
that a prospective nominee to the Justice Department, whose name was
about to be sent to the Hill for confirmation, had gone to Harvard for
a year, the president told him to "take it off the résumé when you go
to the Senate." Ehrlichman responded to Nixon's inquiry and made a
check of the status of Foreign Service officers and found that of one
hundred ambassadors, 55 percent were Ivy League men, whereas but

1.5 percent of all of the nation's college graduates were Ivy Leaguers. That led to the comment that they "were on teams together playing those frilly games — squash, crew." We "must build a new establishment," he said at Camp David on March 21, 1972. "We must assume that the working press is the enemy. Fight them." Our friends are local commentators and editors, he said. Time should be spent with such friends, not the likes of newsmen such as Hugh Sidey or John Osborne. Create a new "establishment" in the press. When Pepsi chairman Donald M. Kendall was admitted to the Business Council, the group that served as liaison to the White House, Nixon observed with satisfaction that Kendall had gone that far without having graduated from an Ivy League school. Turning to three of his chief troubleshooters, George Shultz, Ehrlichman, and Harry Dent, the president advised, "Get some of the non-elite businessmen. They produce. They are with us." At one point, during a cabinet discussion on December 11, 1972, he pointed out that "only Brennan & I come from working class," referring, of course, to his secretary of labor, Peter Brennan, who was rewarded with his post after the hard-hat attack on Wall Street. Once, congratulating Vice President Hubert Humphrey, he cited their commonplace origins by saying, "My dad was a grocer. You came up the pharmacy way." He had little patience when, as Bob Haldeman has recalled, "some college kid was embarrassed by his father because his father was a workman."[15]

Nixon's view of the world owed far more to Thomas Hobbes than John Locke. Life without a strong ruler would indeed be "nasty, brutish, and short." But his outlook was tempered by Jeremy Bentham's essays on the well-being of society. The combination tended him more toward a viewpoint that was intimately related to the American ethos of enterprise and nationalism, and closer to Edmund Burke's concerns about social stability achieved by responsible and authoritative guidance. Such intellectual equipment gave him the flexibility to deal with the Soviets and the Chinese on their own terms. Yet, as reasserted by the events of Watergate, he remained an outsider, just as he had been in 1942 at the Office of Price Administration, alienated from a world dominated by social activists, predominantly eastern, urban, academic, often Marxian, and heavily influenced by Jewish intellectuals. Tenacity and skill enabled him to succeed as well as he did. Garry Wills had it about right when he wrote that Nixon "perfectly summarizes one America, an older and in many ways a nobler America, made up of much sacrifice and anger," one driven by "sheer will and spiritual steam, survivors of the *Pequod.*"[16]

Nixon the President, Leader of the Free World, seemed a distant concept by the first week of June in 1984. In the fourth year of Ronald Reagan's presidency, major problems were, at long last, confined to headlines that could be read with less passion than the sports pages. The Indian government had dispatched troops to quell Sikh terrorists in the Punjab, at the cost of some four hundred anonymous lives. Even more irrelevant was the continuing Persian Gulf war between Iran and Iraq. Reagan was on a three-day state visit to Ireland, where he and his wife had to sit through a speech at Dublin Castle by Prime Minister Garret FitzGerald that rebuked U.S. policy in Central America. The president, after also visiting his ancestral home in County Tipperary, went on to London for a meeting with Prime Minister Margaret Thatcher at a summit conference of the seven major industrial democracies. Meanwhile, without terribly much more attention, jockeying for the Democratic presidential nomination continued. In a Sunday evening debate televised from Los Angeles, an increasingly lonely Gary Hart pleaded for Americans to criticize the president for "a runaway nuclear arms race, a $200 billion annual deficit that is a mortgage against my children's future, runaway pollution, selling off our environment to the highest bidder, and turning his back on equal rights and civil rights." Two days later, however, former vice president Walter Mondale just about clinched the nomination with a solid victory in New Jersey. At Wesleyan University's commencement in Middletown, Connecticut, where Senator Edward M. Kennedy received an honorary doctor of laws degree for his "principled activism," author David McCullough urged the graduates to study history "as a guide to navigation in perilous times. History," added McCullough, "is who we are and why we are the way we are."[17]

History and its lessons were alive in the mind of Richard Nixon. I found him in a thirteenth-floor suite at 26 Federal Plaza, in downtown Manhattan, after going through an unmarked door that was distinguished from others along the corridor only by a small electronic monitoring device. Inside, there were two reception desks, one for the former president's secretary, the other for Secret Service agents.[18] Both main rooms, the outer office and Nixon's, were decorated with White House mementos, especially color blowups of presidential visits with foreign leaders, notably Chinese and Russian.

His large desk was placed catercorner in the room, and he came out from behind it to greet me. I immediately found myself surprised that he was taller and sturdier than I had imagined. At the age of seventy-one, having overcome the trauma of both political disgrace and a critical illness, he was still credible as the former collegiate football player and up-and-coming vigorous politician. He was also the more familiar formal figure, dressed in a three-piece suit (as behooved an ex-president) and self-consciously considerate about personal proprieties. When he autographed his books, he wrote with a traditional fountain pen. Even snapshots of Nixon with his family on Christmas Eve showed him not fully relaxed, although they left no doubt that he was enjoying the company of his grandchildren. I immediately understood the comment of photographer Ollie Atkins that "he's the kind of guy who wears shoes on the beach."[19] He smiled only when there was something to smile about, lest the substance of life be reduced to frivolity. As I contemplated how to get the best of what he had to say, his mind was, in turn, obviously anticipating what I might ask and trying to frame how he would respond.

He was ready, as I had assumed, to talk about Kennedy. The "feeling of loss," Nixon suggested, "certainly at the time of the assassination, was an emotional feeling. There's always a higher degree of mythology about presidents." That was especially true since Kennedy was thought of as a liberal, although, Nixon quickly added, he had conservative tendencies. "It does not mean that it lacked substance. You can't have froth without the beer. It was not so much what he did, but the man, the style, in terms of achievement." Then, giving the matter additional thought, he added, "Lyndon Johnson, for example, was more effective. Comparing that with my situation is like apples and oranges. I was not the pinup boy that JFK was. There was a feeling, despite the way [my] administration ended, that at least it was an administration that knew what it was doing — SALT agreement, Berlin agreement. Domestic affairs, despite the fact we did not have the Congress, we got revenue-sharing and environmental programs."[20]

Still, as we talked, it was obvious that he was not far from either the current Reagan administration or the Republican party. Confident of the president's reelection, Mondale or no Mondale, he remained in close but surreptitious touch with the White House. He wished, he added in confidence, that Mr. Reagan would use more discretion by avoiding references to the Soviet Union as an "evil empire." Nixon thought that was a wholly unproductive public utterance.[21]

All the old clichés about work and his profession monopolizing his thoughts and energies seemed borne out. It was obvious that he could hardly enter the huge office complex without at least a nostalgic glance at the federal courthouse across the square. For that was where Alger Hiss had been tried for perjury in 1949. In what became one of the key exposés of Soviet intelligence activities in the United States during the 1930s, Hiss defended himself against allegations of espionage made by Whittaker Chambers. After the first trial ended in a hung jury, Hiss was finally convicted and sent to prison for five years. Congressman Nixon's tenacity in working to expose the former New Dealer had immediately helped to single him out from among the other young Republicans in Washington, guaranteeing him both prominence and controversy. "Hiss," Nixon reflected, "was the darling of the elitists. The worst thing you could do to the intellectuals [was] to prove them wrong."[22]

A few miles uptown, on Manhattan's East Side, Alger Hiss was also protected from intruders. Even in his eightieth year, and with failing eyesight, he was immediately recognizable as the man whose graceful bearing and smile must have served him very well. Despite all that was known, I came away from exposure to Hiss understanding why he had been so convincing when he had first faced the House Committee on Un-American Activities. His was the certitude of one who knew his innocence and expected ultimate vindication. Watching him, it was difficult to believe that he was once the chief cause célèbre of espionage stories that made headlines in the nineteen-forties.

Before and after his prison term at Lewisburg, Pennsylvania, Hiss held fast to his original story. He had only known Whittaker Chambers by the name George Crosley. He had never passed along classified State Department documents, and he still contended that the deed must have been done by a colleague, Julian Wadleigh, and Chambers himself. The Woodstock typewriter that was alleged to have been used by his wife, Priscilla, to make copies for transmission to Chambers was not the same machine that had been found and produced at his trial. He also held fast to his argument that the typewriter produced in court had actually been one that was reconstructed to match the original by experts retained by the FBI. He continued to make no concession to his accusers even thirty years after his release from prison. Only recently, the Supreme Court had rejected his petition for a writ of error, *coram nobis,* to overturn his perjury conviction. "My success or failure in the courts," he told the press, undaunted, "has seemed almost like a barometer of the Cold War. . . . My conviction has been used by the right wing in politics to try to discredit our liberal political tradition. In particular, it has been used to denigrate the values of the New Deal and of the United Nations, in both of which I took part."[23]

Alger Hiss's loss was calamitous — his reputation, his freedom, his law career, and, within a few years after he got out of jail, his marriage. He had not met Richard Nixon since their confrontation in the congressional hearing room back in 1948. Asking Hiss to recall Nixon was potentially an explosive proposition.

It quickly became apparent, however, that Hiss's Nixon bore only a vague resemblance to the more familiar stereotype. He certainly was, said Hiss, "an opportunistic young congressman," but, he quickly added, "this was true of a great many members of Congress before and since then." While there was "crudity and lack of sensitivity on his part," he was not "a Yahoo," although "he was crude." Despite his education at a good law school, Duke, he was "crass." Yes, agreed Hiss, both he and Nixon were conscious of the class difference that divided them. "While I am not from his background, I'll be frank with you," said Hiss. "I did feel that Nixon was a vulgarian and I'm quite sure that . . . from time to time I was guilty of a certain snobbishness toward him. He may have sensed some of that and it may have annoyed him. In other words, I was being snobbish. . . .

"I can't say he consciously misrepresented the facts," he said. "Nixon was able to fool himself. I think he was able to believe what he wanted to believe," he added, while Chambers was "a pathological liar." Nor would Nixon have undertaken a blind fishing expedition, hoping that persistence and badgering would pay off regardless of the merits. However, "Nixon had a great deal riding on my conviction, so that at that time he was far from objective. . . .

"My complaint," he continued, "is against the people who made use of Chambers as a willing tool. He was obviously under their control in two ways: They could prosecute him at any time. Secondly, they could expose his homosexuality. They could send him to jail. He was really their creature. He soon knew what they wanted him to say."[24]

Hiss did suggest that Nixon "was hostile, browbeating, and attempting to make my answers look bad," but offered nothing specific to show that such decorum parted from normal procedure. What the record does show is what Hiss described as "lengthy, repetitious, and unfriendly" questioning on August 25, 1948. On that day, Nixon "was not seeking the relevant facts but only those that fitted a preconceived pattern inimical to me." Nixon, he complained, wanted to trap him "into some statement which he could imply was contradicted by the records he had and I did not have." Others, namely the committee's chief investigator, Robert Stripling, and prosecutor Thomas F. Murphy, displayed even greater hostility. Nor did Hiss view Nixon as crucial to his prosecution. His "bitterness," he explained, "is for J. Edgar Hoover. Nixon started things, but it was Hoover who carried them through."[25]

So it went. The advocacy of his own innocence remained powerful. The uninitiated, who had not examined the evidence published since his conviction, could easily have been convinced that the wrong man was sent to jail. Still, Hiss appeared as a strange anachronism. Repeatedly, albeit inevitably, because of his concentration on his misdeeds that took place in the 1930s, his frame of reference went back to the New Deal. Ah, he seemed to be saying, those were the times; those were the times when great deeds were being done, when the climate was ripe for the spirit of humanity. And now, we are so far away, having receded and been replaced by an indifferent society.

Listening to the familiar stranger begged another question. That was the moment of caring, Hiss seemed to say — a moment when Americans assumed that their government was vital for human assistance, when the fate of the helpless would not continue to be sacrificed to the marketplace. For those who believed, as Hiss claims, that the New Deal was responsive, subversion appears especially contradictory. Why, if this was the faith of the moment, did such humanitarians nevertheless direct their energies and loyalties, and even risk their lives, to assist not only a foreign power but one with an ideology directly opposed to that of the government that, by their own admission, was sensitive to the needs of its population? And why did that role have the participation of an Alger Hiss? Innocence? Ignorance that the "popular front" was a fraud, bankrupt even before it began. Indeed, as William O'Neill has pointed out, it was "not treason but blindness that discredited Hiss's generation."[26] In the same sense, there was something irrational about the general postwar mood that wanted to get on with tomorrow while discrediting the generation that, for all its faults, kept American democracy alive through its greatest domestic crisis.

It was, as Alistair Cooke has contended, a "generation on trial." The Hiss case was a celebrated affair precisely because it was no ordinary case of espionage. Validation of the bright new world somehow seems to require denigration of the past. For conservatives, it was not enough to cite the shortcomings of the FDR era, not enough to contend, as they did, that men and institutions had been imperfect, that planners in Washington were bringing America dangerously close to "statism" and "socialism." Or, as was repeatedly pointed out, that the advent of war and not the New Deal had lifted the Great Depression. It was much more than a case of misadventures by misty-eyed incompetents: the greatest period of reform in American history was rendered suspect. Naive and even pro-Soviet diplomacy invited the subjugation of eastern Europe.[27] Planners still enticed by the Communist "experiment" found Washington a safe haven.

In all of this, Alger Hiss, who was present at Yalta in 1945, when controversial postwar arrangements were made with the Russians, became the quintessential New Deal brain-truster who, unlike an unspecified number of his colleagues, had the misfortune of being discovered. The rhetoric sometimes made it hard to know which was more despicable, subversion or social welfare. That Hiss himself was convicted of perjury, not of espionage, was almost incidental. The symbolic quality of the verdict was plain. Vindicating Alger Hiss and also accepting Richard Nixon seemed irreconcilable. On the choice of one or the other appeared to rest the history of the times.

For Nixon, as a Republican freshman, the potential prey was inherently attractive. Yet, on balance, it was a mixed bag. "My name, my reputation, and my career," he later recognized, "were ever to be linked with the decisions I made and the actions I took in that case, as a thirty-five-year-old freshman Congressman in 1948."[28]

His motivations stood on their own merits, having little connection with any overarching effort to impugn the loyalties of Democrats. Nixon's voice was not among those calling for a counterrevolution. His was not among the more strident anti–New Deal positions. He emphasized a "new kind of liberalism," somewhat tolerant about the reformist objectives but less patient about how they had been administered. When controls are necessary, he explained, "they must be administered in a business like manner by competent personnel. Government agencies should not be made a dumping ground for crack pots & theorists who use their positions to promote their peculiar ideas of economy & government." Earlier, in applying for the nomination that would lead to his election to Congress in 1946, he expressed the desire to wage an "aggressive, vigorous campaign on a platform of *practical* liberalism [which] should be the antidote the people have been looking for to take the place of [Congressman Jerry] Voorhis' particular brand of New Deal liberalism." His handwritten notes for public comments on the occasion of Lincoln's birthday, as he was about to compete in his first campaign, make the point. They show that he attacked the replacement of "individual enterprise" by a "planned economy." The bureaucracy, "which had reached immense proportions before the war, now threatens to choke the life blood from our economic system," and we "have seen the ugly growth of personal government in which the justice of a man's case is not as important as the influence of his Washington representatives." He confided to a law associate, Leonard Garment, that he was driven by his great interest in world affairs, not by international rivalries or by domestic politics, but by his "pacifist mother's idealism and by the abstract attractions of foreign affairs."[29]

One senses an impatience among the ambitious to get on with politics once the war was over. In those years before he had ever heard of Alger Hiss, Nixon shared that desire. This meant contending with normal, peacetime problems. The world that became Richard Nixon's was in some essential ways little changed from what America had been like back when the nation celebrated its centennial.

3

Two Centuries, One Nation

IN THE CENTENNIAL YEAR of 1876, with the great Civil War in the past, the passion for treating the South like a conquered province was being replaced by schemes for overcoming the first great post–Civil War depression. How better to will the inevitability of a brighter future than by celebrating one hundred years of independence? Yale social scientist William Graham Sumner, injecting some characteristic skepticism into the *North American Review*'s special issue on the centennial, argued that government had become corrupted by the notion that "all men are equally competent to give judgment on political questions."

Nevertheless, he noted, the masses were undaunted by the dismal state of affairs. They were quick to forget great scandals and were untouched by unsavory party politics and the deterioration of public service. The citizens of the democratic republic were behaving as though "the political will of the nation never was purer than it is to-day." The best hope, he held out, was for "instruction and guidance," although that could only be achieved "slowly and by great effort." At least there were signs of that "will," and that was "the best encouragement we have today."[1]

Sumner was, in historian Richard Hofstadter's words, "the metaphysician of the homemade intellectual, and the prophet of the cracker-barrel agnostic" to most educated American contemporaries, "a giant figure in the history of thought."[2] But much of his thinking outside the field of anthropology — and even some of that — was largely inspired by the thinking of an English civil engineer named Herbert Spencer. To those ready to hail Spencer as the greatest philosopher since Aristotle, Sumner was another Emerson.

Sumner and Spencer had much in common. Spencer, twenty years older than the American social scientist, was the product of a lower middle-class English family, which was not terribly different from Sum-

ner's background. Sumner's father, a self-educated worker, had ex-
changed life as an artisan in Lancashire for opportunities in America,
finally settling for work in the repair shop of the Hartford and New
Haven Railroad Company. By the time their sons came face to face,
William Graham Sumner had long since digested — and publicized —
Herbert Spencer's teachings. Both Spencer and Sumner had their most
attentive audiences in the English-speaking lands on either side of the
Atlantic.

What Spencer was preaching, and his disciples were hearing, came to
be known as Social Darwinism. In its purest form, the idea suggested
the folly of man's efforts to attempt, as Sumner later wrote, to "make
the world over." If Sumner, as has been written, "only parroted the
language of Spencer and the classical economists" in the United States,
he nevertheless publicized a notion that, as with Spencer, bound laissez-
faire economics to the hand of God. Not even Adam Smith went so far.
He at least combined his Newtonian "hidden hand" concept with the
assumption of public responsibility for the viability of social institutions.[3]

Social Statics, first published in 1850, contained Spencer's welcome
projection. Writing nine years before the appearance of Charles Darwin's
On the Origin of Species, he foresaw a process of natural selection that was
bound to weed out the unfit and replace them with the fit. Sharing the
Newtonian concepts of natural laws, it followed that interference by mere
man risked creating, not relieving, disaster. Nineteenth-century Americans found far more comfort when Spencer wrote that "society is constantly excreting its unhealthy, imbecile, slow, vacillating, faithless
members." For Americans, especially, he offered "a hopeful philosophy
to a hopeful people," believers in the rewards of self-discipline. As Donald Fleming writes, "Where the Protestant ethic taught men to lay up
riches to the greater glory of God, Social Darwinism taught them to
fulfill themselves to the improvement of the species."[4]

The whole idea made much sense. The theory suited the spirit of an
industrializing America, where laissez-faire was defined as the desire to
boost rather than control commerce. If that sentiment was not fully
appreciated or understood by the working classes and a handful of
reformers, that hardly mattered. The essential point was to let nature
take its course; government intervention in the form of social services,
especially for the poor, would upset the universal design. Only if society
as a whole were on the verge of some sort of breakdown would assistance
be warranted. In a world ignorant of other alternatives, it made sense.
It was, moreover, what many wanted to hear, a vindication of success
that echoed the Puritan tradition, minus Calvin's teachings about social
responsibility that Adam Smith, albeit for other reasons, had urged. The
subsequent appearance of Darwin's studies helped Spencer's authority.

Andrew Carnegie, the industrialist, and John Fiske, the popular historian, became best known among American Social Darwinists. But Sumner's pen spread the gospel, and his post at Yale became his pulpit, converting him into, as Hofstadter has written, "some latter-day Calvin, . . . preaching the salvation of the economically elect through the survival of the fittest."[5] When Spencer later visited America, he was a great celebrity, and Sumner joined with influential leaders of a wide variety of fields to honor the philosopher at a special banquet at Delmonico's.

Sumner's Social Darwinism was the prism through which he viewed America's first century. Civilization itself, he wrote on the eve of the centennial, had best been entrusted to those suitably trained for leadership. How else could one deal with the world of the future? The Founding Fathers had designed a republic; democracy was alien to their concept, an aberration created by forces unleashed by independence. But, in Sumner's view, as society grew more complex, the wisdom of the Fathers became clearer. They had never intended to entrust the popular will with the responsibility for solving a multitude of problems. The very idea would have been even more abhorrent in a nation where "trade and industry have undergone such changes in form and method that success in them demands far closer and more exclusive application than formerly. The social organization is becoming more complex, the division of labor is necessarily more refined, and the value of expert ability is rapidly rising. . . . While the public interests are becoming broader and weightier, the ability of the average voter to cope with them is declining."[6]

One therefore understands why Sumner's article, which helped open the centennial year for at least the readers of the *North American Review,* concluded on a note of optimism only with some obvious difficulty.

"All the world seems to be here in Philadelphia lining the streets," reported the *New York Times* on July 4, 1876. Independence Square, festooned with red, white, and blue bunting, and equipped with a grandstand large enough to hold perhaps five thousand people, was ready for the centennial. Gas jets outlined huge arches along many of the main streets. Broad Street's was the grandest of them all. In front of the Continental Hotel, another spelled out the words "Welcome to All Nations." Internationalism was symbolized by dedicating one arch to the most prominent foreign visitor, Emperor Dom Pedro II of Brazil. As the holiday neared, crowds continued to reach the city, and railroad lines reported that business was two or three times above normal. In the great centennial year, Fairmount Park was the site of the exposition that marked the nation's one hundredth birthday.

From May 10 until that November, visitors filled the area of Fairmount Park north of Girard and Elm avenues. Fairgoers were able to reach the grounds by using the specially built streetcar lines and crossing the newly completed Girard Avenue Bridge ("one of the most pleasing of architectural and engineering achievements in the world"). Another route was by way of the rebuilt Wire Bridge across Callowhill Street, a "handsome and unusually substantial structure."[7] At the park itself, on a plateau 125 feet above the west bank of the Schuylkill River, the gates opened for a fair dedicated to America's first century. The first hundred years were thus left behind, together with the awful memory of a great Civil War, which optimists hoped would be vindicated by the emergence of a nation better disciplined, more unified, and stronger than ever before.

The great fair, advertised as the sixth and largest ever (at least because it covered over 230 acres), fulfilled the ambitions of a planning commission that had been established to outdo all predecessors. The *Guide to the Centennial Exposition and Fairmount Park* tried to advance that objective by expressing the grandeur of the achievement with a compilation of statistics designed to impress the most skeptical. Comparisons with foreign exhibitions were obviously self-conscious, encouraging the enumeration of every conceivable weight and dimension, as though numbers alone certified quality. The *Guide* reveled in numbers.

Size and practicality were paramount, and the wonders of the infant age of machinery were the great attractions. Edison's electric light, the phonograph, a microphone, and Alexander Graham Bell's telephone (which had been patented only that March) drew the most curiosity. But the greatest marvel was the mighty Corliss Engine, the seven-hundred-ton steam powerhouse. Located at the center of the Main Hall, it stood, in the words of William Dean Howells, editor of the *Atlantic Monthly,* as "an athlete of steel and iron with not a superfluous ounce of metal on it; the mighty walking-beams plunge their pistons downward, the enormous fly-wheel revolves with a hoarded power that makes all tremble, the hundred life-like details do their office with unerring intelligence."[8] On opening day, the eight thousand machines in Fairmount Park's great fair suddenly came to life when inventor George Corliss's steam engine (delivering far more power than James Watt had ever conceived) was switched on by President Grant and the visiting emperor. And then it ran, with neither noise nor vibration, a fitting introduction to the age of industry.

An essential part of demonstrating such progress was impressing the outside world. Only twenty-two years had passed since America had helped pry Japan from feudal isolation. In celebrating the centennial, the "liberator" herself seemed self-consciously aware of being not only a child of the Enlightenment but of older worlds. Spacious areas within the gallery were reserved for foreign works, and thirteen ornamental structures originated in other countries. Industrialization encouraged internationalism. At Philadelphia, however, a secondary theme was clear, one distinctively American and very simple: What other nations had prospered from the seeds of so many?

The process also involved discovering as well as being discovered. Visitors were alerted to the expected presence of two large Arab tents, which would "probably be occupied by genuine Bedouins of the desert, affording our citizens ample opportunity for inspection and comparison between Occidental and Oriental home life." Of equal curiosity were the unprecedented numbers of other foreigners from places as remote as the Far East. The majority of such strangers were employed by national pavilions. But most excitement was aroused by the sight of native outfits, especially those from China and Japan. How they were received may be gauged by the characterization of such foreigners in one of America's more esteemed publications, *Harper's Weekly,* which reported the presence of "heathen Chinese."[9]

Distressing to the exposition's organizers were the shocked reactions to some of the art. The major controversy inevitably involved works showing nudes, both male and female. "Whole rooms devoted to the French were barred against the public," reported Howells, "but enough was visible to emphasize the national taste for the nude. When one caught sight of this in paintings just unpacked and standing against the wall, it was as if the subjects had been surprised before they had time to dress for the Centennial, so strongly is the habit of being clothed expressed in the modern face." Sunday pulpit oratory denounced immorality in the Art Gallery. Some defenders of purity damaged pieces of sculpture and defaced canvases, forcing the gallery to close for repairs. When it was finally reopened, canes and umbrellas were ordered checked at the door.[10]

The presence of a Women's Building also provoked some sharp attention. Never before had such a special collection been placed on exhibit. Thirty thousand square feet were used "to display only articles which are the result of feminine skill and labor." The hall included the accomplishments of women "in homes, asylums, missionary fields at home and abroad, sisterhoods, industrial schools, and in the cause of temperance and moral reform." The effrontery of women to have a special show, denounced by critics — even ladies — as excessively "aggressive" and an artificial separation from other accomplishments, was not really out of place. Nineteenth-century America was already finding it hard to stifle feminism: pioneering reformers Lucretia Mott and Elizabeth Cady Stanton had founded the women's rights movement at Seneca Falls, New York, in 1848. Emma Willard had already established her seminary for women, and Oberlin College had long since held co-educational classes. At the Philadelphia exposition, Susan B. Anthony herself, the fighter for women's suffrage, was on the podium. Not surprisingly, as one writer noted, the movement for women's suffrage had already become "embarrassingly militant everywhere in its drive to obtain equal rights."[11]

Still, the politics of post–Civil War America were naturally far more preoccupied with the promotion of commerce and the restoration of a unified nation. One recent student of such fairs has explained that the Centennial Exposition advanced the cause of joining "politicians, business leaders, and scientists in the development and presentation of an ideology of progress that linked ideas about race to nationalism and industrial growth."[12] A more charitable explanation would associate such sentiments with an effort to promote unity by dismissing dissension that had led, first, to a great war, and then to Radical Reconstruction and further political turmoil. The new tone was one of optimism and self-satisfaction.

Symbolic of that change was an addition to the fair of a "club-house" called "The South." Backed by "strong recommendations from leading men of the region, the concession for its erection was cheerfully granted," explained the *Guide*. The two-story building was designed to feature "a band of old-time plantation 'darkies,' who will sing their quaint melodies and strum the banjo before the visitors of every clime. Imagine the phlegmatic German exhibitor with his 'frau and kinder,' gazing with astonishment at the pure and unadulterated 'Essence of Ole Virginny' expounded by a hand from the cotton field, or a solemn-visaged Turk viewing with ill-concealed horror a dusky son of Tophet 'rattling of the bones.' To a student of human nature it will be one of the most interesting sights in the Exhibition," visitors were promised. The end of slavery was commemorated by having American sculptor Harriet Hosmer create a "colossal" statue depicting "the elevation of the negro race under the fostering care of a free government. A colossal female figure, representative of freedom, lifts a child from the earth. Gratitude and wonder rest on the features of the child, while with a calm impress the face of the woman looks upward in confidence for the approval of a higher Power."[13]

Acceptance of divine intervention in behalf of America's past was enough to permit comforting assumptions about His present designs. The 8 million paying customers (fifty cents for adults and twenty-five cents for children) who ultimately passed through the gates represented one out of every five people in the United States. Most of them clearly had their patriotism reinforced; no theme was more prominent than the blessings of a century of progress. But even that anniversary had its dissidents, some of their complaints anticipating later critics, whose view of the fair was anything but kind. A modern critic has complained that the "absence of any overall esthetic coordination of the exhibits produced a bewildering impression." Howells himself denigrated most of the art, exempting only the British exhibit (which offered contributions from Gainsborough and Turner) from his harsher comments. A prominent New Yorker, Benjamin Willis, thought that the money would be better spent by bequeathing "to our posterity the privilege of celebrating the continued existence of the Republic in 1976." One lecturer suggested that the Philadelphia exposition could have been made more truly representational had it displayed a New York tenement house, an abandoned farm, and a corrupt politician.[14]

Moreover, the artificiality of the world represented by the exposition could be seen by anyone who bothered to look across Elm Street, which the *New York Times* reporter evidently neglected to do. "As far as the eye could reach there was not a sign of pauperism nor even of poverty," he wrote on Independence Day. "It spoke of the sobriety of the people, for it gave no token of drunkenness. It spoke in eloquent terms of the regard for sacred things, if not for the Christian foundation of the nation, for it listened with reverence to a prayer it could not hear." Had he glanced at the real world, not far from the 872,320-foot parallelogram that constituted the Main Hall, he would have seen what local police described as the congregating point "for many tramps, peddlers, and boot-blacks," whose homes were "in out-houses, in empty cars of the Pennsylvania Railroad Company, and, in one instance, in a cave." The area had to be cleansed of such "pests and nuisances." The beating to death of one of the centennial's exhibitors, which took place amid that squalor, together with a fire that destroyed four acres of adjacent structures, gave Philadelphia's authorities a good reason to tear down what was left of "Centennial City." By the end of September, the mile-long row of "restaurants, small hotels, beer-gardens, ice-cream saloons, and small shows that have sprung up as if by magic" was all demolished.[15] James Russell Lowell's *Ode for the Centennial* expressed the uneasiness that only infrequently appeared in the public prints:

> *Is this the country that we dream in youth,*
> *Where shams could cease to dominate*
> *In household, church, and state?*
> *Is this Atlantis?*[16]

Critics have overlooked an essential point: the commemoration had everything to do with the U.S. vision for its second century. Fairs sell the future, and the technology on display, with its implications of a better life, appealed to more than Americans. For foreign visitors as well, Philadelphia's displays also marked one hundred years of liberty, of the maturation of the "new man" by celebrating the promise of the joys of abundance. Nor did Howells see any contradiction in his view of the American ideal.

Howells, the editor and author, had grown up in Ohio and had married a second cousin of Governor Rutherford B. Hayes. He had experienced his own brief governmental service by spending the Civil War years in Venice as the American consul. Four of his novels had been published since 1871, the year he became editor-in-chief of the *Atlantic Monthly*. His major work, which came later, was most notable for *The Rise of Silas Lapham*, which dealt understandingly with that object of snobbish derision, the self-made man. By the eighties and nineties, Howells was certainly among America's elite, a genteel reformer. With other "good government" men, or "goo-goos," as they came to be known, he was offended by what he and his friends regarded as the debasement that accompanied the growth of industry and urbanization. Nor were they alone in recoiling against what a later polemicist, Madison Grant, would call the "passing of the great race."

Only slowly, as his work brought him into closer touch with what was really happening, did Howells become a "quiet rebel," even turning to a mild flirtation with socialism. Ironically, such influences began to work their way into Howells's system during the months after his return from Philadelphia and the great fair. Confrontations with Gilded Age realities became inescapable, challenging the comfortable optimism. "Since last week," John Hay wrote to him in 1877, "the country has been at the mercy of the mob, and on the whole the mob has behaved rather better than the country." Howells, that year, undertook his own inquiry, trying to learn more about the underlying causes of the growing social disorder, and the pages of his magazine began to reflect the growing doubts that a Christian utopia had indeed been created in America. He was on his way toward becoming, in the words of a biographer, "the leading literary rebel of his time," who, in *The Rise of Silas Lapham,* was "openly out to demolish what he regarded as the false emotions and outworn clichés of the obsolescent and irrelevant romantic past."[17] *A Hazard of New Fortunes,* therefore, came naturally after his creation of the nouveau riche paint merchant Silas Lapham.

The troubles that finally caught Howells's attention were entirely visible even as the make-believe world of the Centennial Exposition was being concocted. In New York City, the minister of the Presbyterian Church at the corner of Second Avenue and Fourteenth Street, the Reverend Frank H. Marling, had migrated to America from Great Britain. At the church's service marking the nation's centennial, he warned, "These are the times of infidelity." The reverend's harsh judgment was included in a righteous sermon about political and social immorality in his adopted country. He noted the "agonizing cry" about corruption among public officials. Apocalyptically, he added, "If crime and robbery are practiced with immunity in high places, the whole country will be demoralized, and if confidence between man and man is destroyed, the land is imperiled." Mob rule was swallowing liberty. "The sanctity of the marriage vow, the purity of both sexes, the loving obedience of children to parents, are all threatened by manifold and insidious changes, poisoning the very air and invading our very houses," he told the congregation. The Reverend Mr. Marling, who had been in the United States less than a year, warned about newcomers. "The vast hordes flocking to this land," he said, "strike at our national life, which we count most precious, while the ballot gives them a power which they know too well how to use."[18]

Violent conflict was a reality even as the national holiday was being celebrated. From the wild West came word that General George Custer and his five cavalry companies, numbering some 270 men, had been wiped out by Sitting Bull and a force of Sioux and Cheyenne Indians. Details from Little Bighorn, the site of "Custer's Last Stand," were still coming in when news arrived of a July 8 "massacre" in Hamburg, South Carolina. Fighting between 200 armed whites and members of the all-black town's militia, which had been established during the early days of Reconstruction and was under irresponsible local leadership, ultimately helped to convince the state's conservatives to recapture control from the Radical Republicans. National celebrations of liberty and independence were a world apart from such unpleasantnesses, from the contradictions that marked not only American life but the story of human existence. As the British jurist and historian Lord Bryce later noted, "The people see little and they believe less."[19]

The distinctive difference was the mythology. Dedication to "unalienable rights" never attempted to reconcile the contradictions created by racial subordination.[20] It was much easier to rationalize desires for natural access to a permanent source of cheap, expendable labor, whether as servants, harvesters of crops, or warriors. Not even the Civil War and Abraham Lincoln's rededication to freedom had advanced matters much since the Revolutionary War. In the case of Native Americans, competition had intensified conflict; rivalry had, in turn, reduced the image of Indians from "children of nature" to "noble savages" to "children" requiring the "protection" of white "fathers"; finally, they were merely "savages." Thus it was during the Gilded Age that warfare between the contending cultures became most intense, a period marked not only by Custer's plight at Little Bighorn but by the earlier and notorious Sand Creek Massacre in Colorado, all culminating in the battle of Wounded Knee.[21] At the Philadelphia exposition itself, a clear line was drawn between those blessed by God to enjoy the fruits of liberty and inferior tribes standing in the way of progress.[22]

Neither was there much more zeal for going beyond the graduation of slaves to "freedmen." The Hamburg incident was but one example of violence and abuse of power by emancipated blacks that turned even reformers against the more idealistic objectives of the Radical Republicans. Only a few years earlier, impeachment proceedings were conducted against President Andrew Johnson. There was little question that it was nothing more than a blatantly political reaction against what critics damned as his appeasement of an unrepentant South. The gains that had become apparent in the 1860s were diluted, if not completely reversed, during the next decade. Court decisions crippled whatever effectiveness might have been achieved by the Fourteenth and Fifteenth amendments. The death of abolitionist senator Charles Sumner had helped to nullify any protection that might have been made possible for the ex-slaves by the Civil Rights Act of 1875.[23] Responsibility for the political and civil rights of individuals was again completely in the hands of each state.

Intellectuals generally accepted the notion that "the negro race was ground in barbarism." A distinguished visitor from England, Lord Bryce, even while commenting on the fact that American Negroes had been "made full citizens and active members of the most popular government the world has ever seen," saw them as nothing more than "children of nature, whose highest form of pleasure had hitherto been to caper to the strains of a banjo."[24] The words were Bryce's, but the point of view was so universal in America as to constitute a national consensus that could actually assist the process of postwar reunification.

For all their indignation about the crimes of the "slavocracy," northerners hardly rushed to rectify their own inequities. Some progress was made, mainly in New England, but even after the Civil War, blacks were not allowed to vote in most states that had remained loyal to the Union. New York, which had extended the franchise long before the war, reserved for that underclass exclusively the requirement of property ownership. In both North and South, the most intense opposition to political equality came from the most destitute elements. As a cultural historian has noted, "Antagonism between the races becomes acute wherever whites who are in an insecure economic situation find themselves in competition on virtually equal terms with their colored neighbors." Before the Civil War, laborers in such cities as New York and Boston had been among the strongest opponents of the abolitionists. So, too, in Gilded Age America, did the fear of economic competition with blacks mold the sentiments of workers. Again, as in the antebellum experience, newly arrived immigrants were often at the heart of that resistance in urban areas. Bryce, in his travels, observed that "white working men and the labour unions generally refuse to work with coloured men." In southern cities, "where the white working men are most rude and suspicious," he went on, "the jealousy of labour competition [is] added to the jealousy of colour." Intimidation, violence, and simple fraud worked wonders, at first negating and then eliminating what might have constituted a black vote. "We stuffed the ballot boxes. We shot them. We are not ashamed of it," boasted "Pitchfork Ben" Tillman of South Carolina. "With that system — force, tissue ballots, etc. — we got tired ourselves. So we had a constitutional convention, and we eliminated . . . all the colored people whom we could under the Fourteenth and Fifteenth Amendments."[25] Indeed, the institutionalism of racial segregation by means of so-called Jim Crow laws became the major reality of American life, entrenching itself during the decade after the centennial. Lord Bryce recorded the following description of the divided society:

> There is practically no social inter-mixture of white and coloured people. Except on the Pacific coast, a negro never sits down to dinner with a white man, in a railway refreshment-room. You never encounter him at a private party. He is not received in a hotel of the better sort, no matter how rich he may be. He will probably be refused a glass of soda water at a drug store. He is not shaved in a place frequented by white men, not even by a barber of his own colour. He worships in a church of his own. No native white woman would dream of receiving his addresses. Kindly condescension is the best he can look for, accompanied by equality of access to a business or profession. Social equality is utterly out of his reach, and in many districts he has not even equality of economic opportunity, for the white labourer may refuse to work with him and his colour may prove a bar to his obtaining employment except of the lowest kind.[26]

The postwar political process had led directly toward that outcome. A long chain of events had helped to create a Southern labor system based on sharecroppers and tenant farmers, bolstered by ever more rigid racial segregation. The Reconstruction amendments were virtually rescinded if not weakened, including the Thirteenth, which had abolished slavery. The pillorying of President Johnson, in which he escaped conviction by just one vote short of the required two-thirds majority, had once more divided the nation. As historian Allan Nevins has commented, "1876 was an infelicitous time for America to place herself on exhibition."[27]

Obviously, then, those who had hoped for tranquillity after Johnson were in for disappointment during the Grant years. If anything, the new administration, which took office in 1869, only increased revulsion over martial rule. While the president hesitated to use force, in state after state "redeemers" undid the limited achievements of the Reconstruction period. Whatever optimism had followed his replacement of the beleaguered and hapless Johnson soon gave way to a search for restoration of order. Western farmers chafed under post–Civil War debt burdens and pressed for relief through currency depreciation, which, in turn, agitated "sound" money interests. Reformers, Liberal Republicans, Half-breeds, mugwumps, crusaded against what they considered rampant

immorality, a society exploited by villainous greed. Such perceptions
were apparently confirmed during Grant's first term by the exposure of
the Tweed Ring's grip on New York's city hall.

In reality, no part of America was spared profound change. "The
association of social unrest with the imagery of technological violence,"
Alan Trachtenberg has written, "of new city crowds with ignorance and
contempt for culture (or regression to 'savagery') fired the imagination
with nightmarish narrative of impending apocalypse."[28] Clearly, the
United States of the nineteenth century was still experimental. Although
the Civil War had reaffirmed the primacy of the central government,
uncertainty still existed about the durability of political institutions. Postwar conflicts, notably evoked by the Johnson impeachment trial and the
bargain that resolved the 1876 election and placed Rutherford B. Hayes
in the White House, aroused fear that the nation had not really confirmed civil procedures. Farmers became more insecure, victimized by
evils they could only dimly understand, and ready to abandon cherished
habits of individualism for collective action. Thus, it was the time of the
Grangers and of the Free Silver movement; ultimately, their grievances
were expressed through the Populist party and championed by William
Jennings Bryan. Mostly, the sentiment was that of a dilution of the rural
past. Increasingly, the culture and economy were falling under the influence of enlarging corporations and their factories and growing towns
and cities. The new industrial labor force comprised not only the more
recently arrived Irish but growing numbers from eastern and southern
Europe. Even more traumatic was the nationalization of economic forces,
displacing the insularity inherent in subsistence labor. Nothing as severe
had yet been seen as the collapse that followed the Panic of 1873, when
the nation's structural financial weaknesses undermined even remote
economic units.

It was, as Vernon Parrington once wrote, the time of the "great barbecue." Lord Bryce observed that Europeans would always ask about
America, "Isn't everybody corrupt there?" In the South, malfeasance
under carpetbag rule was easily matched by venality elsewhere. One
could build national fame, as did Governor Hayes, by a reputation for
honesty. Legislators at all levels of government were little more than
agents of businessmen. At no time was it more true that differences
among Democrats were no greater than between Tweedledum and
Tweedledee. Republicans were more corrupt simply because they had
more power. Where Democrats held the keys, they took the goods. No
European city, noted Bryce in his famous critique about the failure of
local government in the United States, experienced scandals approaching those of New York, where the public was in 1869–1870 robbed on
a vast scale by the Tweed Ring. The infamous Tammany Hall, the city's
Democratic organization, was only the best-known urban fleecing device.

When Lincoln Steffens later wrote that "the machine controls the whole process of voting, and practices fraud at every stage," he meant Philadelphia, but it also described conditions in New York. William Marcy "Boss" Tweed's famous courthouse construction fraud split the take between the politicos and the businessmen. Originally authorized to be built for no more than $250,000, the structure cost a staggering $5,691,144.26. The city paid $179,729.60 for three tables and forty chairs, and another $350,000 for $14,000 worth of carpeting. Equally absurd was the $41,190.95 for brooms and $7,500 for thermometers — and all at 1870 prices![29]

Diligence in convicting the Tammany leader did wonders for Samuel J. Tilden's political standing. Edwin L. Godkin, who had come to America from Ireland and founded *The Nation* in 1865, called for leadership by "the best class of men." And his publication swayed the elite and most trustworthy.

The "responsible classes" — in other words, those with education, breeding, and wealth — had to assume the burden of saving and purifying the masses from an excess of democracy. Corrupt politicians had to be checked by instituting a merit system to reverse the evils of government by payoffs through spoils. As a leading student of the era has written, "It is indeed ironic that the Gilded Age is indebted to the reformers for its tarnished reputation as well as for its improvement in public morals." Even with that perspective, the immorality cannot be denied, but one can also be challenged to name the real utopias. If such reformers overstated their reactions, they were, in effect, recoiling at the replacement of their idea of order. Grant's support for trade protectionism, demanded by a new class of industrial entrepreneurs, offended nineteenth-century liberals, as did the legitimization of paper money. "The Victorian mind," William Gillette has written, "found it hard to cope with emerging problems of urbanization and immigration, industrialization and unionization, as well as of reconciling order with progress."[30]

The revolt against Grant, then, was inspired by forces more profound than merely presidential ineptitude. "Grantism" is clearly synonymous with corruption. Nor was it fully evident during the early part of the administration. The president's personal reputation is not really rehabilitated, however, by pointing to a few truths. Never was it a matter of his personal corruption. Naïveté, yes; inordinate faith in his appointees and such others as a scheming brother-in-law; even a farcical infatuation with acquiring Santo Domingo — all these certainly existed, but it cannot be forgotten that this was a time when skulduggery was commonplace wherever opportunities existed.

At the very moment of the centennial, attention in the nation's capital focused on the continuing congressional investigation of Grant's administration. The inquiry featured a special committee, presidential protection for immediate aides and even family members, executive privilege, and the impeachment trial of a former secretary of war.[31]

All this confirmed the reformist Liberal Republicans in their hereditary wisdom. Henry Adams, recalling being taken to visit the president in the White House, observed, "The progress of evolution from President Washington to President Grant, was alone evidence enough to upset Darwin."[32] Faith in the purity of their own Christian morality left room for few doubts. Their crusade was as much a manifestation of Protestant missionary zeal as the efforts of ministers laboring in strange lands to convert heathens. They were witnessing moral decay that was attributable less to another fall from grace than to a national transformation of power and psychological relationships.

There was an undoubted sense of well-meaning zeal, suffused with a substantial dose of self-delusion, when Republican liberals, actuating their revolt by holding a presidential nominating convention in Cincinnati, adopted an anti-Grant platform that called not only for civil service reform, but also for fair taxation, a one-term presidency, and a reduction of the national debt. Carl Schurz, in his keynote address, expressed the temperament of the occasion by pleading for the "infusion of a loftier moral spirit into our political organizations."[33]

In 1872, exactly one hundred years before "new politics" Democrats chose George McGovern as their party's nominee, the revolt by Liberal Republicans against Johnson's successor, President Grant, led them — as well as the Democrats — to nominate Horace Greeley, an "odd choice," writes Gillette. He was, as Selig Perlman once said, the "only one who drank deep of the idealism of Brook Farm and at the same time stood close to the labor movement." Greeley, the *New York Tribune*'s publisher, was also, in Gillette's words, "the worst possible candidate because political amateurs assembled to run a national convention of a party without organization represented by delegates without constituencies make political decisions ineffectively." Bostonian Charles Francis Adams, a diplomat and historian, would have been a much more credible candidate, but unfortunately he carried too many burdens for popular appeal. The much-needed Irish vote, especially vital to attract urban Democrats, was put off by Adams's Anglophile slant. His stock was further diminished because he epitomized Yankee aristocracy. His intimacy with the reform movement also left much to be desired, and so Greeley, whom Charles A. Dana of the *New York Sun* called "a visionary without faith, a radical without root, an extremist without persistency, a strife-maker without courage," emerged as the candidate. More to the point, however, was that Greeley's eccentricities had endeared him to antiestablishment purists, including several journalists whose maneuvers behind his candidacy had managed to prevail. At various times, the

Tribune's publisher had been a prohibitionist, utopian socialist, abolitionist, opponent of the exploitation of labor, and spiritualist, and had
campaigned against corsets for women. In short, says Gillette, he had
"brilliantly popularized Republicanism."[34]

When word of Greeley's nomination reached Washington, the salons
on Capitol Hill roared with laughter. William Dean Howells, whose magazine had already endorsed the renegades, recanted in disgust and went
back to Grant. Wrote New York State's old GOP veteran Thurlow Weed:
"Six weeks ago I did not suppose that any considerable number of men,
outside of a Lunatic Asylum, would nominate Greeley for President."
Nevertheless, the Democratic party seconded for itself the candidates
offered by the liberals in Cincinnati. "There was no question," historian
Gillette has since concluded, "that the Democracy still suffered from self-
inflicted wounds of the past: fratricide before the war, obstruction during
the war, and resistance to its result. Long out of power, Democrats
appeared to cultivate blunder and repeat mistakes."[35] Their subsequent
campaign, even with the ostensible advantage of a Liberal Republican
coalition with Democrats, was a model of disorganization, internal dissension, poor funding, and general disarray. Gillette's summation is
worth repeating at length:

> Instead of building a party with a broad base, they conceived a
> party of like-minded men who championed their own causes
> and imposed their own preconceived solutions. Demanding vic-
> tory, they were unwilling or unable to politick among the voters
> and bargain for their support. Indeed some were more inter-
> ested in having their own way than in having a party at all. They
> thought they knew what was good for the people yet they did
> not know the people, care about their problems, or trust them.
> They professed democracy, yet they rejected the notion that
> government should give the people what they want and that the
> people know best what to want. As a result of their lack of
> sustained interest and general competence, they were unrealistic,
> unprofessional, and unpopular.[36]

Words such as those were everywhere exactly one hundred years later.
Richard Nixon led the Republican party to a lopsided victory over a
coalition formed under the Democratic label. They, too, to repeat Gillette's words, "thought they knew what was good for the people yet they
did not know the people, care about their problems, or trust them."
Fragmented, divisive, thoroughly alienated from the Age of Nixon, they
presented the American people with an intolerable vision of what their
administration could bring.

Centennial America was, in significant ways, a very different place from
the invented world within Fairmount Park. Amid fear that the United

States had lost the art of political conciliation and would once again slip into civil war, Democrats and Republicans staged their nominating conventions only days before July Fourth. Republicans, divided between supporters of Grant, who, fittingly, went by the name Stalwarts, and the so-called Half-breeds, who were shocked by the series of scandals in Washington, settled for the sober, straitlaced governor of Ohio, Hayes. Democrats chose one of the richest lawyers in the country, Tilden of New York, who thereby became the wealthiest man to run for the presidency since George Washington. Many Republican reformers, chastened by the Greeley experience but wary of Democrats as the party of "Tammany and Treason," voted to place the puritanical Hayes and his teetotaling wife, Lucy, in the White House. Rumors did circulate about Tilden's soft-money, pro-inflationary tendencies, but the choice remained unexciting. For Republicans, "waving the bloody flag" — reminding voters that the Democrats had been the party of rebellion during the late war — joined the cause of sound currency as a perennially potent issue. As he watched the canvassing, Henry Adams decided that the campaign was nothing more than a conventional struggle in which the same old faces "stand without pretence of reform and idiotically pound at each other."[37]

Fears that conflict would continue to prevail over constitutional government came uncomfortably close to realization when the election results were tabulated, giving neither candidate an electoral majority. As it turned out, because three ex-Confederate states remained in the hands of carpetbagger regimes, resolving the election certified the death of Reconstruction. Tilden, it was clear, had received the bulk of the popular vote and lacked only one additional elector to be declared the winner. But with disputed results from the occupied states — and the canvassing there in the hands of Republicans — Congress appointed a special electoral commission to decide the outcome. Only days before Grant's successor was to be sworn in, Democrats accepted pro-Hayes majorities from those three states in exchange for removal of Union control, and the Republican candidate was accepted as the winner. Ironically, the centennial year presidential election was the most tarnished in the nation's history.

For all that had been achieved during the first one hundred years, then, the second century began with serious questions. The presidency itself was in disrepute, not only because of the way the 1876 election had been settled, but certainly after the trial of Andrew Johnson and Grant's disastrous administration. Unfortunately, too, the specter of sectional disputes could still be aroused by "bloody flag" politics. America, industrializing and urbanizing, was concerned about increasing crime and conflict. Farmers, the mainstays of the nation, were in open rebellion and desperate for relief. Labor's adjustment to factory life and city conditions was equally traumatic. Within the next few years, not only Howells and some of his friends, but Henry George, Henry Demarest Lloyd, Edward Bellamy, Samuel Gompers, Eugene V. Debs, Daniel De Leon, and even Theodore Roosevelt raised fundamental questions about the direction of industrial capitalism. To those who gave the matter much thought, confidence was only illusory.

Few were more certain about how to respond than William Graham Sumner. "Every particle of capital which is wasted on the vicious, the idle, and the shiftless is so much taken from the capital available to reward the independent and productive laborer," he warned in 1883. Such designs must be self-defeating, must, in effect, attempt to subvert "the laws of nature" to "a series of haphazard experiments." A vast army of workers struggled to do its best, providing the essential manpower. They gave society both its foundation and, through routine, unheralded efforts, its wealth. They were, in fact, the victims of "the reformer, social speculator and philanthropist."

Caught in the complexities of the new industrial age, they remained dedicated to the ethic of work, the virtues of sobriety, faith, and patriotism. But their efforts and problems went unnoticed. If there were "true liberty," the laws of nature would be permitted to operate, and, added Sumner, "the Forgotten Man would no longer be forgotten."

Who, then, asked Sumner, is the Forgotten Man? "He is the simple, honest laborer, ready to earn his living by productive work. We pass him by because he is independent, self-supporting, and asks no favors. He does not appeal to the emotions or excite the sentiments. He only wants to make a contract and fulfill it, with respect on both sides and favor on neither side. He must get his living out of the capital of the country. The larger the capital is, the better living he can get." In our modern society, wrote Sumner in the face of a changing America, he was overlooked because "he makes no clamor." But he existed, and in large numbers; he was middle-class and owned property. "He is the clean, quiet, virtuous, domestic citizen, who pays his debts, and his taxes and is never heard of out of his little circle." The Forgotten Man worked, voted, and prayed; "but he always pays — yes, above all, he pays. . . . He is a commonplace man. He gives no trouble. He excites no admiration." He was, further, "weighted down with the cost and burden of the schemes for making everybody happy, with the cost of public beneficence, with the support of all the loafers, with the loss of all the economic quackery, with the cost of all the jobs."[38]

"The Forgotten Man" became Sumner's best-known essay. The image, writes Donald Fleming, "took on great pathos for Sumner as corresponding to his own father, valiantly struggling to keep afloat but too proud to look to anybody else for help." But, as Robert Wiebe has argued, the Forgotten Man was not that far removed from the concerns of nineteenth-century reformers. In either formulation, that of the Social Gospeler or the Social Darwinist, he was the tough undergirding of society. Wiebe quotes Lloyd's comment that when utopia arrives, "it will be the new middle class that will survive and will furnish the human material for the new order."[39]

He did survive, but barely. The silent cog of the industrial age later became the pathetic victim of a world neither wholly agricultural nor wholly industrial, of a world where the basic sectors that were supposed to sustain twentieth-century capitalism were, instead, tearing each other down. In the 1930s Raymond Moley, a Columbia University specialist on politics and criminal law newly recruited for Governor Franklin D. Roosevelt's brain trust, found him once again. Assigned to prepare a major radio address for FDR, one that would promote his presidential ambitions by advancing a positive progressive program, he recalled Sumner. By that time, however, the stable, property-owning, hardworking, quiet American was down and out, not so much ignored by reformers and capitalists alike as sacrificed to the force of natural law run amok. The proud and patriotic were suddenly victims of a world where there was "neither joy, nor love nor light, / Nor certitude, nor peace, nor help for pain"; and there they were, as Matthew Arnold wrote, "as on a darkling plain / Swept with confused alarms of struggle and flight, / Where ignorant armies clash by night."[40] Sumner's Forgotten Man, by-passed by the energy of the new industrial society, was reduced to an abject state. But it was more than that. No less than fifty years earlier, he was at the heart of what ought to make things work.

Sumner's words, as passed on by Moley, became even more memorable as spoken by Governor Roosevelt. Addressing the nation from Albany on April 7, 1932, a fresh voice speaking out in the depth of the great economic calamity declared that "the unhappy times call for the building of plans that rest upon the forgotten, the unorganized but the indispensable units of economic power," and asked that, once again, faith be placed "in the forgotten man at the bottom of the economic pyramid." The speech, as a Roosevelt scholar has pointed out, was "most mild and rather vague," but it was "received as a bold challenge to the conservatives, giving heart to those impatient for change, frightening those wedded to the status quo. . . . To the wealthy and conservative, . . . it was nothing sort of demagogic."[41]

Sumner's parable had become Roosevelt's allegory. The forgotten man recovered and resumed his place. Aided by economic affluence in the post-depression age, he occupied a niche that enabled him, as in Sumner's day, to be identified as a property-owning citizen with a landed stake and faith in his country. It became more fashionable to be known as an employee instead of a worker. In reality, of course, he was a man in the middle, "anchored neither in production nor in administration of the essential goods of society."[42] He was variously blue-collar, white-collar, or new-collar. Even if liberated from smokestacks, he still fell behind the better-born, better-educated, more affluent leaders of the emerging post-industrial society. Progress touched him just enough for a taste of middle-class life-styles that challenged his working-class capacities. He was self-proclaimed middle-class without being an entrepreneur or manager. He was all things that most Americans thought they were doing, gorging themselves at the twentieth-century version of the great barbecue.

His essential place in the hierarchical order had not changed very much. When Dwight Eisenhower and Richard Nixon headed the Republican ticket in 1952, Raymond Moley returned to Sumner and to his own twenty-year-old FDR speech. For Americans, Moley wrote in his magazine column, the "forgotten man" phrase was still valid. What the English called the middle class was our middle-interest group. They constituted "not only a numerical majority, but they own most of the property, save most of the savings, pay most of the taxes, and are most concerned in preserving freedom of opportunity. In the past they have set the tone and character of our political life." But the Democratic party, descendants of the New Dealers Moley had long since left behind, had become "more and more . . . an alliance of minorities," giving Eisenhower the opportunity to "go back to the real majority — the present forgotten majority — and make his appeal. He can rise above economic interest groups, sectionalism, and all the rest of the matters that divide us and appeal to the great interests that unite us." When he accepted the presidential nomination at Miami Beach in 1968, Richard Nixon identified himself with those same "forgotten Americans"; they were also his "silent majority," and not very different from the people Richard M. Scammon and Ben J. Wattenberg then described as the "unyoung, unpoor, and unblack; . . . middle-aged, middle-class, middle-minded." When writing his articulate dissent from the Supreme Court's affirmative action decision in the case of *Johnson v. Transit Agency* in 1987, Associate Justice Antonin Scalia called them the "predominantly unknown, unaffluent, unorganized," the very ones who "suffer this injustice at the hands of a Court fond of thinking itself the champion of the politically impotent." In the populist rhetoric of the Democratic keynote address at the Atlanta convention of 1988, the forgotten American was depicted not simply as left out but as being sacrificed by a government feeding the military-industrial complex.[43]

They were, in each case, whether in Sumner's essay of 1883 or in the words of Democratic keynote speaker Ann Richards over a century later, members of the struggling, working middle class. A sophisticated study of the American electorate called them the "Passive Poor" or "God and Country Democrats."[44]

In centennial America they were just emerging as the by-products of industrial expansion; as the nation neared its second hundredth birthday, they were less forgotten than silent and passive. In the postwar, postindustrial nation, they reached a political maturity that would have been unthinkable during the Gilded Age. They comprised the "real America" that was in touch with Richard Nixon. Together, with one of their own in the White House, they hoped to celebrate the bicentennial.

Had they retrieved William Graham Sumner's centennial essay, they would have read the following words from 1876:

> It is probably the recollection and the standard of this state of things which leads men now on the stage to believe that corruption is spreading and that the political system is degenerating. It is one of the peculiarities of the government of the United States, that it has little historical continuity. If it had more, or if people had more knowledge of their own political history, the above-mentioned opinion would find little ground. The student of history who goes back searching for the golden age does not find it.[45]

4

In the Land of the Golden Bear

IN 1876, California was in its twenty-seventh year of statehood and still a remote outpost, although, by the centennial year, development of the Far West had gone well beyond primitive beginnings. Trails, bridges, and railroad tracks — mostly spur lines — had already moved the continental conquest beyond St. Louis and the Mississippi. The most significant fusion, of course, was the meeting of the Union Pacific and the Central Pacific. San Francisco, the only city of consequence on the West Coast, had just been linked to Los Angeles by tunneling the Central Pacific's tracks through the San Fernando Mountains. Los Angeles, a more southerly settlement in the basin between the San Bernardino Mountains and the ocean, was showing steady growth. Gradually, too, it shed its predominantly Spanish character as newcomers from the east helped to make it look more like the rest of Gilded Age America.[1] Families like the Milhouses and the Nixons were among the settlers in the great Southland — their new frontier — as the territory from Los Angeles to the Mexican border ultimately became known.

The migrants continued to come, constantly extending the edge of settlement. The process was hardly completed when in 1893, historian Frederick Jackson Turner attributed to such newly developed areas the origin of traits characteristic of Americans. "Individualism in America," he argued, "has allowed a laxity in regard to governmental affairs which has rendered possible the spoils system and all the manifest evils that follow from the lack of a highly developed civic spirit."[2]

These "evils" were almost precisely what the Old World aristocracy viewed as the "barbaric" influences festering in the Indian wilderness across the Atlantic. That was the darker side of the egalitarian ideal, the price paid by society for the unbelievable achievements that bemused visitors from lands with castles and royalty. The New World hothouse was germinating destabilization along with democracy. Hardly any nineteenth-century European who visited America — and such travelers were virtually aristocrats by definition — failed to comment on how the absence of legal class distinctions deprived men of the certitude of their station. So it was that that much-quoted French observer of Jacksonian America, Alexis de Tocqueville, concluded that equality of social stations left participation in "wretchedness" open to all men. Mrs. Frances Trollope was astonished to find that young American women preferred to live in "abject poverty" rather than do demeaning domestic work. And gentlemen in mansions, she reported, "spit, talk of elections and the price of produce, and spit again."[3]

However harsh the foreign commentaries, some Americans showed their own disdain. Having become secure and comfortable, the descendants of those who had founded the transatlantic culture were, in turn, skeptical about the Far West. The great stretch of land from San Francisco to the Mexican border seemed especially quaint. Amusement merged with fantasy, aided in time by the rise of Hollywood as the motion picture capital. By the middle of the twentieth century, it seemed more eccentric than serious, a catchall for everything frivolous about American life. Some simply wrote it off as little more than a mecca of the dissatisfied. "If you tilt the whole country sideways," Frank Lloyd Wright is said to have suggested, "Los Angeles is the place where everything loose will fall"; to which John Gunther added that California has "drawn the cream of believers in utopia from everywhere in the union," and the land was "stuck with so many crackpots if only because they can't go any farther." A more recent critic, Will Irwin Thompson, called Los Angeles the "violent juxtoposition of areospace [*sic*] technology and neo-tribal politics," and a great stretch of territory that was "the realization of fantasy." "Precisely because there is no real tradition," he added, "the elders create fantasies of mother, country, God (who is really Uncle Sam in more heavenly attire), private property, flag and family, and on and on in the litany of the nativist." "The land promises escape," added Garry Wills; "since it cannot . . . *keep* that promise, men live in fear," and their "resentment is easily triggered." Accordingly, as Neal R. Peirce has aptly written, "what America is, California is more so." "We *are* the national culture," declared Wallace Stegner, "at its most energetic end."[4]

To the more daring, California had long since become an El Dorado, where late nineteenth-century Americans could enjoy their own Mediterranean pleasure world. Transplanted easterners like Grace Ellery Channing, Abbot Kinney, Charles Fletcher Lummis, Joseph Pomeroy Widney, and Gaylord Wilshire led the way. Kinney appropriately developed a residential community that he called Venice, and Channing saw remarkable geographical similarities between Rome and Los Angeles, which, notes Kevin Starr, in reality became "an Aryan city of the sun." To all, the Pacific Slope was the Garden of Eden they had failed to find in midcontinent. "The great cities of the western valleys," wrote one such pioneer, "will not be cities in the old sense, but a long series of beautiful villages, connected by lines of electric motors, such will move their products and people from place to place."[5]

The lure of the Garden differed little from seduction by fantasy. Utopian communities were a natural part of the dream. "Of all the freedoms for which America stood," wrote a historian of heaven on earth, "none was more significant for history than the freedom to experiment with new practices and new institutions." In a place already blessed with richness of soil and climate, the accident of timing made it that much more attractive for experimental societies. As the United States entered its second century, it also moved into the industrial age. For the established regions of the nation, the agrarian hopes of equality and opportunity were being displaced by a new urban class system.[6] The communitarian movement, begun in the older states, was particularly significant in attracting newcomers to the Southland, ultimately becoming the foundation for at least a dozen cities and towns.[7]

The evolution of the new state made prophets of the Founding Fathers, who had decided that such additions would enter the Union on a parity with the original members. All such migrations, whether from the Old World or from the New, seemed to preserve the common trait: each additional territory, every new infusion of people, reaffirmed rather than recast the old. An enormous alchemy was in the making. California became to the Atlantic seaboard what America was to the Old World.[8]

The movements spurred folks onward almost simultaneously, across the ocean and across the continent. Americans have been taught, for example, about the Reverend Josiah Strong, a minister and author whose concept of mission has come to epitomize the rationale for late nineteenth-century imperialism. To the concepts of economic and military theorists, especially those of Captain Alfred Thayer Mahan, Strong contributed an additional spur, the extension of Christian civilization. His was an American version of what in England Rudyard Kipling called the "white man's burden."

Strong was born in Illinois, and by the age of thirty-eight had won the reputation as a cleric who wanted to convert souls to the American way. Most of what he said and wrote consisted of prescriptions for a better life. None became more renowned than his 1885 treatise, *Our Country,* which brought him both fame and a reputation as a man who wanted to disseminate the gospel to those whose natural fortunes had not made them natives of his land.[9]

Among Strong's concerns was another, equally nationalistic attitude, one reflective of most thoughtful Americans at that time, a time when so many feared that the social order was being challenged. The nation had obviously become both more alien and more urban. Little could be more threatening to life as it had been valued. "During the last ten years," he wrote in 1891, "we have suffered a peaceful invasion by an army four times as vast as the estimated numbers of Goths and Vandals that swept over Southern Europe and overwhelmed Rome." Just as ominous to Strong were the great urban forces emerging as cities became larger and their populations more alien. Fueled by the masses from across the Atlantic, social critics were positioning themselves to bring American institutions to a showdown at the moment of economic crisis. Such radical newcomers, he feared, would have "the means, the fit agents, the motive, the temptation to destroy," thus bringing "the real test of our institutions."[10]

One could hardly avoid the question. Change was everywhere. The Anglo-Saxon nation of farmers — or so it was viewed — was breeding clusters of smokestacks amid tenements filled with greenhorns. "What changes in the character and habits of the American people will this influx of new elements make?" wondered Lord Bryce. Meanwhile, insecurities multiplied. Workers feared for their already tentative positions. Leaders of capital were especially troubled by the labor riot in Chicago's Haymarket Square, which was blamed on anarchists, and they also tempered desires for an abundance of labor with calls for safeguarding against alienism. The Statue of Liberty was installed in New York Harbor that same year, 1886, amid growing alarm about permitting the inundation by foreigners. The question was less whether anything should be done than what would be most effective. Turn-of-the-century reformers banked on the wonders of mass education. As one historian has pointed out, they "attributed the arrogance of bankers, businessmen, and landlords to a confidence that the working-class producers of wealth — divided by race, religion, and ethnicity, mesmerized by the ideology of equal opportunity, awed by the 'genius' of the wealthy — could not identify their enemies, let alone unite against them."[11]

But the mix of newcomers was hardly static. Varied groups came in endless succession, forever changing what it took to educate or "Americanize" the mass. A joint congressional commission had little trouble concluding that, yes, the new breed of Americans was decidedly inferior to the old. The southern and eastern Europeans, the Italians, Jews, Greeks, Poles, and Russians, would never fit in. They were hardly like the Germans, "who made good farmers." They were not even the equal of the Irish, who, after half a century, had at last been recognized as Americans.[12]

Such was the mindset: immigration would not merely affect America, it would remake America. The "city upon a hill" would go down the drain, washed away by the evils once left behind. The flow across America's borders, unregulated through the years except by haphazard, unilateral efforts by individual states (until deemed unconstitutional), could not go unchecked.

At the same time, Lord Bryce's prophecy was a minority voice. Nor would it have been much different had the English visitor been able to muster the technological capacity that would have enabled him to argue his point on prime time over all major television networks. Only traditionalists who took seriously the Emma Lazarus inscription on the Statue of Liberty would have thought him sane of mind for predicting that the new Americans would be proud of their new country, "loyal to the flag, quick to discard their European memories and sentiments, eager to identify themselves with everything distinctive of their new country," and, moreover, neither the unity nor the homogeneity of the country would ultimately suffer.[13]

In reality, the great migrations, once begun, kept building, becoming a constant infusion. America had anything but a set labor force, whether in the textile mills, coal mines, or steel plants. The composition of virtually every industry revealed continuous ethnic changes. If there was a melting pot, it was toward the culture of pluralism. As Herbert Gutman has pointed out, "The changing composition of the working population, the continual entry into the United States of nonindustrial people with distinctive cultures, and the changing structure of American society have combined together to produce common modes of thought and patterns of behavior." As long as they kept coming, they assured the upward mobility of those who had been here longer. As an Australian labor historian has put it, "The faster rates of economic growth in the United States provided greater opportunities for social advancement and the *embourgeoisement* of workers there."[14]

Ironically, the American dream was to a large degree self-fulfilling, made possible by the willingness of each group to take its turn at the bottom for an investment that could be cashed in by their children — and, as it turned out, by later arrivals. The continuing addition of newcomers helped to create not a collection of communal or religious utopias but a land that became, if anything, more emphatically American than the older, more insular regions. Bryce understood all this and even had the precocity to anticipate the Age of Nixon. "Before the year 1950 arrives," he predicted, "the children and grandchildren of the immigrants who have entered since 1885 will be distinguished from other Americans only by their surnames, and sometimes by their features and complexions."[15]

An early biographer has pointed out that nothing about Nixon's family background was especially distinctive. "Preachers, ministers, shopkeepers, school principals, yes," Hannah Nixon told him, "but I can't think of a Nixon or a Milhous holding an office higher than that of sheriff."[16]

True, as Bela Kornitzer explained, that sheriff was John Nixon, who in 1776 gave the Declaration of Independence its first public reading, but that is about as high as one can go in attempting to establish prominence in the Nixon or Milhous genealogy. Both families existed as have most such clans throughout history: more concerned with survival than governance. Even Lyndon Johnson had more distinguished forebears. *His* father was at least prominent in the Texas state legislature.

By the usual criteria, Richard Milhous Nixon was also a little man. Born January 9, 1913, he was the child of hardworking small-town parents. They had migrated along the common path, from the Midwest to southern California. Their story is also by now commonplace, mostly about how the diligent but contentious Francis Anthony Nixon sustained a series of difficulties and was then brought together with Hannah Milhous, a pious and strong woman of the type who personified what is so frequently dismissed as mere mythology about the American frontier spirit. The Nixon-Milhous union settled down in Yorba Linda, southeast of Los Angeles, where Hannah, a devout Quaker, gave her husband religion and five sons.

Richard Nixon's everlasting misfortune was to be split almost right down the line between Hannah and Frank, to behave as the one while wishing the world to believe he was the other. From the Nixon side, Richard got his drive, intensity, tempestuousness, and determination to beat the odds. From the Milhouses, and especially in the person of Hannah, Richard learned the gentleness, consideration, and courtesies that so often astonished those who only knew him as the son of Frank Nixon. To call it a schizophrenic existence is not too strong. "The child is father of the man," wrote William Wordsworth; "And I could wish my days to be / bound each to each by natural piety."

Their respective families certainly were divided, the Milhouses forever regarding Hannah's husband as a dark Irish ne'er-do-well type who was, in Richard's words, a "scrappy, belligerent fighter" while his wife, saintly in just about every account, had the strength of "quiet, inner peace." Hannah's name still evokes reverential tones; she became the model for cousin Jessamyn West's heroine in *The Friendly Persuasion*. Hannah was the mistress of the soft answer who admired evangelist Billy Graham and doing good works, while Frank, hardworking — nobody minimized his industriousness and strong-mindedness — was the opinionated, excitable type, albeit a good leader. As one who remembered both from earlier Whittier days recalled, Frank was "a man of decided opinions." Hannah, almost without exception, was the person "that everybody loved, a very sweet, lovely person that we liked very, very much." The Milhouses were not alone in thinking Hannah all the more remarkable for the lot she had to bear, but they, of course, had the comfort of knowing that Hannah had married beneath her station.[17]

All the more reason for Richard to respect his father. "I remember my old man," Nixon said in his farewell in the White House East Room his last day as president. "I think that they would have called him sort of a little man, a common man. He didn't consider himself that way. You know what he was, he was a streetcar motorman first, and then he was a farmer, and then he had a lemon ranch — it was the poorest lemon ranch in California I can assure you. He sold it before they found oil on it. And then he was a grocer, but he was a great man. Because he did his job, and every job counts up to the hilt regardless of what happens." Frank, what the departing president was telling the world, was the driving force of the family. Even Hannah's sister has so testified.[18]

But what so few people seemed to understand was that he was also Hannah's son. He had her strength and compassion. She was also saintly, as he often remarked. He did everything he could to help her, from worrying about her financial security to making her proud that her son had done so well. There was, for example, the time in 1958 on his vice presidential trip to South America when he planned a Mother's Day surprise from the skies. Without tipping his hand to her in advance (which was why there was ultimate disappointment), he arranged for the pilot of his plane to use his radio equipment so that he could contact his mother. He wanted her to hear for herself how her son, the vice president of the United States, was thinking about her on that Mother's Day and sending his love even while on an official flight to Bogotá, Colombia. The pilot, Colonel Thomas E. Collins, Jr., managed to get airwave clearance from the governments of Ecuador and Colombia and directed his radio bands to Hannah Nixon's Pennsylvania home. One can imagine Nixon's disappointment when she was not there to receive the message.[19]

It was Hannah, in that East Room farewell, whom he talked about with most passion. "My mother was a saint," he said to the teary relatives and aides nearby. "And I think of her, two boys dying of tuberculosis, nursing four others in order that she could take care of my older brother for three years in Arizona and seeing each of them die. . . . She will have no books written about her, but she's a saint."[20] His personal agony was that he was more Frank than Hannah.

Richard's emergence as their dominant boy, the one burdened with major responsibilities, was the direct result of those family tragedies. The family's hardscrabble life became even grimmer with the death of Arthur, their fourth son, of tubercular encephalitis at the age of seven.

Then, after a battle with tuberculosis, they lost their firstborn, Harold, whose ten-year fight for life darkened Richard's youth. When Hannah confined the older brother to a nursing home in Arizona, where she hoped the dry heat would restore his health, seventeen-year-old Richard went to work as a carnival barker. Meanwhile, Hannah earned whatever she could and Frank sold half of the land that surrounded his store, another depressing loss. Such traumas of childhood were best relegated to the hard times of the past but, as in his continuous references to Hannah, impossible to forget.

The Nixons responded to hard times around Yorba Linda by moving to the nearby Friends community of Whittier, where Richard first demonstrated the promise of things to come. Harvard offered him a scholarship, but the costs still would have been higher than attending nearby Whittier College. He also wound up practicing small-town law with the Whittier firm of Wingert and Bewley instead of with an imposing Eastern firm. In later years, John Ehrlichman heard him hark back to his poor California days "over and over."[21]

If, with his background, making it took a fluke, good luck could only be achieved through hard work. No man who then rises from that base can be truly incompetent; indeed, Nixon's reputation was never one of ineptitude. He became known, instead, as Tricky Dick, the most deceitful of them all, a man who reached for power any way he could. From up close, however, it was hardly that simple. As one of his White House aides later put it, Nixon "was the little kid in the schoolyard all the boys were torturing. In order to escape, he has put on different faces and masks." He never forgot much of the sheer torture of growing up. His memoirs include memories of whistles and catcalls when he got on the stage to act for the first time and his clumsiness on the dance floor with the first girl he really liked.[22]

All of this hardly sounds like an exceptional adolescence. Nor should the portrayals of hard work, piety, and small-town life exaggerate young Nixon's provincialism. He and his family were exposed and receptive to the reform impulses of early twentieth-century America. The characteristic ideological tenor of his childhood home tended toward progressivism, reflecting national impulses. His father, despite his attraction to several Republican presidential candidates, voted for William Jennings Bryan. Frank backed Teddy Roosevelt's insurgent Progressives in 1912, Robert La Follette in 1924, and FDR in 1936. Even Hannah, far less the angry rebel and much more traditional, had backed Democrat Woodrow Wilson because of the peace issue. But the influences were more significant in the case of Richard Nixon himself. Dr. Paul S. Smith of Whittier College talked to an interviewer in 1977 and reminisced about his former student. "You see, this is an interesting thing about his life," he said. "He is known as a conservative, reactionary Republican by the American people, but he didn't start out that way." Politically, he was really "nondescript," someone who could have tilted either way. One critical investigation of Nixon's congressional career found that his voting record revealed no "broad recognizable pattern," nor was he identified with any policy.[23]

Even by the end of his long political career, after he had served in the House of Representatives, the Senate, the vice presidency, and the presidency — in short, even after Richard Nixon's extensive record in domestic and international affairs and identification with Republican politics — he was suspected of having no faith stronger than that of "centrist." His identification with the perjury conviction of Alger Hiss not only tagged him as vehemently anticommunist but also distorted his ideological reputation. "His heart was on the right," conceded speechwriter William Safire, although "his head was, with FDR, 'slightly left of center.' " Another speechwriter, Patrick J. Buchanan, considered him "the least ideological statesman" he had ever known.[24]

Simple ideological characterizations never were applicable. The operational Nixon leaned toward accommodation with traditionalism and fiscal conservatism. He retained a Horatio Alger Republicanism more reminiscent of some of the family's progressivism, or even populism. As early as the 1950s, columnist Peter Edson pointed out that a possible Nixon succession to the White House would install a liberal Eisenhower Republican, not a conservative follower of someone like the late Senator Robert A. Taft.[25]

It certainly appeared that way to former California governor Edmund "Pat" Brown. Relaxing in his Beverly Hills law office more than twenty-two years after he had defeated Nixon in a gubernatorial election, Democrat Brown pondered the course of his former adversary's career. "I always felt that RN was really at heart a Democrat, although he didn't show it," he said, reflecting more generosity than animosity toward an ex-rival. Indeed, he seemed happy to talk about him, and remembered how kind and generous Nixon could be.

Brown had always been known as a genial politician of the old school, one who affected little ostentation. Undoubtedly, that accounted for much of his success in California. His recollections of Nixon, then, were in character in their lack of bitterness. Thinking of the former president as one whom birth had made a potential Democrat was one thing, but political veteran Brown also seemed eager to account for Nixon's ultimate course. "I always felt," he added, that "because he was poor [he] got in with those rich Republicans, who changed him."[26]

He could have been a Democrat, agreed Herbert Kalmbach, one of Nixon's attorneys, who won notoriety during the Watergate revelations for having raised hush money. A "Henry Jackson Democrat," Kalmbach said, referring to the longtime senator from Washington. "I know he was very taken with [former Texas governor] John Connally," who was attractive for both his competence and his conservative populism. Kevin Phillips, whose projection of an emerging conservative majority gave ideological support to the campaign strategy for 1968, thought that

Nixon lacked a "long overview of American history and culture," in contrast to his interest in world politics; and, in reality, he "fancied himself" a Tory Democrat. Norman Podhoretz, who steered *Commentary* into conservatism during the 1960s, pointed out that Nixon just happened to be president at a time when the Democratic party was being fragmented. But Nixon himself, said Podhoretz, had changed. "I think that the Nixon presidency was crucial to galvanizing a great many forces that were at work in the country." He was on the verge of creating a "new Republican majority." Podhoretz also saw the political reaction against Watergate "as an extra-electoral coup to keep Nixon from creating a whole new generation of Republicans. The fact that a group of intellectuals were moving away from what the Democratic party was becoming and toward what the Republican party was becoming was creating the climate for the future growth of new attitudes." Midway through Nixon's own presidency, conservative writer William F. Buckley, Jr., asked, "In what significant way has Nixon let the liberals down?" Less than one year later, with the president in Peking, Buckley really cut loose. "Nixon," he wrote, "may yet emerge as the most flexible man of the century, perhaps even as the most deracinated American who ever lived and exercised great power."[27]

Buckley, who had begun *The National Review* in response to Eisenhower Republicanism, had no doubt that Nixon had been far more guilty of betraying the conservative cause. Contemplating Nixon's role, ten years after his resignation from the presidency, Buckley said that "we saw him as completely failing to substantially invigorate the reaction to the New Deal. Now, Nixon we thought of as representing that school of thought, but a little bit to the right because of the whole Hiss episode."[28]

To most conservatives, and certainly to Buckley, normalizing relations with Peking was his greatest crime. "I think that Nixon undermined the hegemonic flavor and integrity of the anticommunist spirit in America," he complained. "He did that primarily not by his approach to China but by the way he behaved in China, what Kissinger called 'the atmospherics.' There was a sycophancy there," and that took the form of going to the Great Wall as a Uriah Heep. "I can't imagine Dean Acheson being quite that way."[29]

Publisher William Rusher, Buckley's *National Review* colleague, while happy that Ronald Reagan was in the White House, was especially acerbic about Nixon. The contempt was ideological, moral, and intellectual. "To Nixon," Rusher explained, "it's all a game of grub. A person who does that misconceives what the twentieth century is about, and what life is about. . . . I do not doubt Nixon's anticommunism. I object to its shallowness."[30]

Even when Nixon, long since the bane of liberal Democrats, first ran for the presidency in 1960, people like Buckley and Rusher had to be persuaded about his conservative legitimacy. Rightist reservations had two main roots. One was his general support for racial equality. As vice president, Nixon had cast a tie-breaking vote in the Senate to ease the overriding of filibusters, which were often (although far from exclusively) used to bury civil rights legislation. He had also drawn close to the Reverend Dr. Martin Luther King, Jr., whom he had first met in 1957, during an official trip to Ghana. He was even made an honorary member of the National Association for the Advancement of Colored People.[31]

Rightists in 1960 were also discontented over Nixon's view of the world, and especially the cold war. Believers in the inevitability of a U.S.-Soviet nuclear showdown had deep reservations about the drift of American policy that Nixon represented. His militant anticommunism, including resistance to the recognition of the People's Republic of China, were insufficiently persuasive. As one of his supporters, Ralph de Toledano, explained on his behalf in late 1959, "It is Mr. Nixon's position that is is better to debate than to obliterate. Not Soviet arms, but Soviet propaganda have [*sic*] pushed the Communists ahead. If we have not convinced the world of our moral, political, and social superiority over the Communists, the fault is our own." When Nixon returned from his 1959 trip to Poland and Russia, where he engaged in the celebrated "kitchen debate" with Premier Nikita Khrushchev, he warned in a popular American magazine about the need to "keep open every possible channel of communication" and cited the importance of serious but patient negotiations. Later, as president, far from moving to strike down Lyndon Johnson's Great Society social programs, he pushed funding to record levels. Under the guidance of a Democrat, Daniel Patrick Moynihan, Nixon tried to reform the welfare system through his Family Assistance Plan. More shocking to conservatives, and a great domestic economic turnaround, was the imposition of wage and price controls in a desperate bid to counter inflation. But international diplomacy, his support of the nuclear nonproliferation treaty, normalizing relations with the People's Republic of China, and the opening to the Soviet Union, all of which brought about the atmosphere of détente, betrayed the conservative cause. Not for the first time was Richard Nixon's system of values, let alone ideological convictions, attacked as nonexistent. Or, as Rusher described with contempt, as "centrist."[32]

"I think he's just very middle-of-the-road," maintained Nixon's devoted younger daughter, Julie, in 1986. "He's certainly not a Reagan, no way. . . . But I don't agree that he's an opportunist and that he only bends with what's going to work. I think he definitely has ideas, principles, and all that guiding him throughout his career." Her husband, David Eisenhower, the grandson of another former president, listened to his wife's analysis and added, "Nixon's administration was definitely making the Great Society work, which is the same posture vis-à-vis that administration as . . . Johnson and my grandfather vis-à-vis the New Deal. Even more so. My grandfather was [ideologically] between Nixon and Reagan. So he could have been a Fair Deal–New Deal Democrat." Then, after more thought, David Eisenhower added: "I say, sure [Nixon] could have been a Democrat — he could have been a Johnson-Humphrey Democrat, but I see that Johnson [and] Humphrey could have been Nixon Republicans as well. What they had in common was partisan politics. Nixon, Johnson, Humphrey — the whole group there in the fifties, the non-Kennedy group, the non-Roosevelt group — all had a lot in common. . . . Nixon's program was defined for him, in a way, by the people who didn't want him to go anywhere. He's a pragmatist."[33]

Nevertheless, whatever the fluctuations and paradoxes, Nixon retained the faith of conservative supporters. Few people knew him longer politically than Robert Finch. Throughout his career, Finch argued, Nixon was remarkably consistent. Instead of change, said Finch, Nixon continually expressed philosophical integrity. The many "new" Nixons were a "matter of style." Herbert Klein, too, another man who was with Nixon during most of his career, was surprised that anyone thought he could ever have been a Democrat. He did, at the same time, concede that Nixon was not deeply involved "in a whole set of philosophies" when he first ran for Congress. His stands were pragmatic, the ones with greatest appeal to the upwardly mobile group of youthful supporters. He was hardly that different from most of those just out of law school who were looking for routes upward. To H. R. Haldeman, who was first attracted to Nixon because of the Hiss case, his conservatism was real.[34]

Such views hardly startled liberals. Nixon and Reagan had both moved to the right: the Virginia dynasty of early America would yield to a California dynasty. Unlike Reagan, however, Nixon neither came of age as an unabashedly liberal, New Deal Democrat nor did he swing to the opposite end of mainstream politics. Reagan's conversion was not only relatively late but long after thorough immersion in an environment that was both strongly associated with organized labor and populated by Hollywood liberals and Jews. Such things were understood, and then written about with explanations that attributed the Reagan movement to his second marriage and the influence of the Davis family, his speechmaking for General Electric, and his reaction to stiff income taxes. Nixon's discovery of the light had had a very different history.

Nixon himself, when interviewed in 1984, disassociated himself from Republican rightists. He insisted that he was neither a liberal nor a conservative. "Neither the Republican nor Democratic parties can win with extremists," he said. His memories of how his father struggled went back to when Frank Nixon lost his job while leading a streetcar workers' strike. He was also influenced by the pacifist Quaker atmosphere provided by his mother and Whittier. "I was basically for small business," he said. "I never was for big business. My source of strength was more Main Street than Wall Street. I went much further than most conservative Republicans with regard to health care. I had a strong commitment to public education and civil rights." At Whittier College, he classified himself as a "liberal," he told an early biographer, "but not a flaming liberal."[35]

Nixon's memoirs, written after his resignation from the presidency, contend that he was closely identified with the reformist impulses of his youth. "The populist elements of my father's politics, the Progressive influence of Paul Smith," he pointed out, "the iconoclasm of Albert Upton, and the Christian humanism of Dr. [J. Herschel] Coffin gave my early thinking a very liberal, almost populist, tinge." He sympathized with much of the New Deal, he has recalled; then he carefully notes that he upheld *"practical liberalism"* (emphasis added). One of Nixon's fellow students at Whittier College, Dean Triggs, acknowledged that he had liberal ideas and "tendencies in many respects as some Democrats. You see," Triggs told an interviewer in 1970, "the real thing he's asking us, is whether we think that this nasty world of politics has forced him to make concessions, character concessions, let's say." By liberal, Triggs also made clear, he meant "in opposition to ultra-conservative."[36]

Whittier College was small, private, and founded in 1901 as a Quaker institution, although it had formally severed its relations with the Friends. Throughout the Great Depression years, the campus was a conservative enclave. A Whittier straw poll just before the presidential election of 1932 gave President Herbert Hoover eighty-two votes, while his Democratic opponent, Franklin D. Roosevelt, received just twenty-six and the Socialist party candidate, Norman Thomas, actually came in second with twenty-eight votes. Still, the atmosphere was relatively untouched by the partisan and ideological issues of the period. Nixon's father, in particular, served as a relatively progressive influence, but Frank's guidance was far less important than the campus environment.[37]

Nixon's early Republican partisanship was significant in the relationship between the young Nixon and his Whittier girlfriend, Ola Florence Welch, the vivacious daughter of the town's chief of police. A warm personality and good sense of humor were additional qualities that made her popular on campus. They became "the campus couple," dating during four of the six years of their friendship. She could have had her choice of young men, but Dick was handsome, a good speaker, and popular, although, she remembers, "we never double-dated with people. He was really a loner." Ola Florence was his only girlfriend at Whittier College. They differed mainly over politics.

Some of it was because he liked to tease her. She came from a family of Democrats and "absolutely adored Roosevelt." But she knew that Dick was more than just "pouring it on me because I was a Democrat." She still wonders exactly why they kept getting into such spats, or why they were so political. But "we kind of were and tended to argue over that." Perhaps it was because his Republicanism was so strong. She remains puzzled that anyone can describe him by using such terms as "progressive" or "liberal." "As far as I can remember him," she says, "he was always conservative." Nor did she doubt that the young man shared the "rabid, feisty" opposition to FDR that was displayed by his "short-tempered" father. Frank, the ex-backer of the Progressive Senator from Wisconsin, Robert La Follette, had begun to sound more like a conservative populist.[38]

Later, when he was a law student at Duke, Dick's public heroes were Justices Louis Brandeis, Benjamin Cardozo, and Charles Evans Hughes, the Supreme Court's progressive minority. Nevertheless, the general attractions of the New Deal seem largely to have escaped him. Among the Roosevelts, his sentiments were far closer to Teddy's than to Franklin's. He registered as a Republican in 1938 and voted for Wendell Willkie in 1940. His faith, he would later write, remained with "the superior merits of a free economy."[39]

At least that was more consistent with the way the public saw him. For a generation of Americans, he was the most durable political representative of the brand of conservatism that sought to modify the New Deal. Not only was communism his target, but so was the "big government" establishment that had been bequeathed by the era of the Great Depression and FDR. The collapse of Nixon's presidency, aborted by the unfortunate circumstances associated with the Watergate break-in, was seen by many conservatives as but an interruption of the trend toward doctrinal purity. When rightist students on the Dartmouth campus in the 1980s, emulating the New Left protesters of the 1960s, waged several years of battle against the college's liberal establishment by publishing an independent dissenting newspaper, they named both Ronald Reagan and Richard Nixon as their guiding heroes.[40]

That young conservative Ivy Leaguers lumped both men together as in the same tradition seems to be stretching a point. The students, who had created some consternation on campus for a number of years among liberals in Hanover, New Hampshire, expressed themselves in their own publication, *The Review*, and had their efforts supported in Buckley's column.[41] The contradiction thus seemed joined: to true believers on the right, Nixon was both a pariah and, paradoxically, a Judas who had used their support but given them the back of his hand. Could they have been so ill informed about recent history as to suffer some of the common delusions about Nixon's role? The reality, however, is that his disgrace and subsequent pardon did not leave him without substantial numbers of sympathizers. For conservatives, in particular, there was an ideological dilemma. Not only, as Buckley and Rusher and others have argued, had he betrayed the cause, but he had also been so casual about constitutional principles and yet retained the allegiance of traditional patriots. What was the source of this support? Did Nixon represent the darker side of politics in a democracy, or is the truth somewhere closer to his own claim, that he really was a representative figure?

The contemplation was troubling. Buckley recalled that "it always struck me as extraordinary to see that Nixon never lost a primary. He just knocked them dead every single time, and this is very difficult for anybody, really, let alone somebody who is sort of manifestly ill at ease with himself." Then, warming to his subject, the conservative writer added, "When I reflected on that a few years ago, I consoled myself — if that's the right word — by concluding that the American people felt sorry for Nixon, a lot of them. . . . My thesis is that they were conde- scending to him, in a sense. They were helping him because they felt sorry for him, because everybody kicked him around."[42]

The conception of Richard Nixon as an outsider, an isolated president shutting himself off from both his staff and the general public, became a piece of conventional wisdom during the Nixon years. And it was true. There was a strong sense of solitary contention, of being under siege as the representative of an embattled, lonely minority, a theme that per- sisted throughout his life.[43] Superficially, it mystified those more familiar with the conventional personalities of politicians. It was only one of many contradictions; in some ways, it remains the key paradox.

His memoirs describe strong childhood humiliation. He recalls his Whittier High School introduction to amateur dramatics. In a scene played with Ola Florence Welch, his effort at tenderness brought "such catcalls, whistles, and uproarious laughter that we had to wait until they subsided before we could continue." When he went on to college, he was usually given character parts. They included, in Nixon's language, the "dithering Mr. Ingoldsby" in a Booth Tarkington play, and a "flaky comic character" created by George M. Cohan. Although he campaigned to have the Quaker college accept dancing on campus, his own efforts on the floor were awkward. He was self-consciously embarrassed when trying to lead partners, who became confused about trying to keep in step with him.[44]

He was equally out of place at athletics. He was a loser with the fresh- man basketball team; not a single victory all season. At football, Nixon was the guy who got into games that no longer mattered, that were either decisively won or lost. Try as hard as he did, and the evidence is strong that no one on the squad gave more of himself, either on the field or off, there was nothing he could do about his mere 150 pounds. One ex-classmate remembered how "tense" he seemed even when he walked. "I mean he didn't have a leisurely, graceful walk," she said.[45] When others were asked about his football days, there was trouble associating him with a specific position on the team.

At least three of those who were interviewed in 1970 used the term "cannon fodder" to explain his role as a practice dummy.[46] As one man remarked, "He used to be the dummy for everybody to tackle. He wasn't quite coordinated enough for a football player. He had two left feet, I think." The wonder to all of them was that he persisted, he took the punishment, repeatedly subjected himself to a "terrific beating" trying to make the football team. One of his former classmates, James J. Grieves, recalled that "he was persistent and he tried with every ounce of strength he had, but he just didn't seem to have the feel for it. But it still didn't discourage him. He kept coming out and coming out. . . . He doesn't know the meaning, as I gather it, of giving up or defeat."[47] Even all that failed to achieve a higher position than the third squad.

Unable to succeed on the field, he nevertheless became a valued member of the squad. Coach Wallace Newman, a University of Southern California graduate, who had helped build up Whittier into something of a local football power by bringing along several fine athletes from his previous coaching job, at Covina High School, learned to respect his tenacity. Nixon, it turned out, contributed something more than cannon fodder. He became vital for the squad's morale. As Newman recalled it, "He'd sit there and cheer the rest of the guys, and tell them how well they'd played." In short, he was an asset on the bench, sitting there, waiting for the outcome to be decided one way or another so he could see some action, but mostly serving to bolster the others. During halftime, he was a one-man cheering squad, demonstrating a powerful sense of spirit that proved infectious. "I think foremost," explained one of the students, "among other reasons that you could really search for his staying on and taking a constant licking, would probably be all embodied in these two things: that he really believed in himself, on the one hand, and he couldn't see himself quitting, on the other, and therefore he stayed it through." The tenacity itself inspired awe. "He stuck it out with the football team," remembered another witness, "sitting on the bench for all the years he was in college. He wanted to play football so he just stuck it out . . . and would appear every time they went out for practice in hopes that he would be called on. . . . Anything he set his mind to do, he didn't give up until he worked it out and he still has that characteristic today."[48]

The sight of Nixon on the bench became so familiar that a little ritual developed between him and Coach Newman. Newman, known to the boys as Chief because he had some Indian blood, would walk over and say, "Nixon, what would you have done on that play?" Then came Nixon's pat response: "Sir," he would explain, "I would've pulled the blanket up just a little tighter around my shoulders."[49]

Nixon learned a lot about losing. He was the stereotype of the grind who succeeds by the seat of his pants. It became obvious that Richard could usually be found at the same place in the library. He could have hidden there forever. His mother reminisced that he was more of a bookworm than the other Nixon children, certainly more than his fun-loving younger brother Donald. As recalled by the son of the man who became Nixon's earliest principal backer, "he spent all his time in the library. He spent very little time on campus socializing." One ex-schoolmate told an interviewer that he was a "working fool." Everything else fell into place: few friends, hardly anything to do with girls, not at all "one of the gang." As one childhood acquaintance recalled, he "didn't have time to be popular."[50]

His first-grade teacher remembered him as "a very quiet, studious boy," who "kept mostly to himself." "He has always been exactly the same," Hannah Nixon told Bela Kornitzer. "I never knew a person to change so little. From the time he was first able to understand the world around him until now, he has reacted the same way to the same situations." "Dick's personality," said a Whittier classmate, "isn't the type that attracts people to him." Nor does the evidence show much difference when he went to law school at Duke University. Even at that more mature stage, his shyness and reserve seemed to suggest going on to a more conventional industrious career with a legal firm rather than anything having to do with politics.[51]

Once out of Duke, Nixon reached for success in the big city. With two friends, he made the rounds of New York's leading law firms. Their names virtually comprised a social register of the most prestigious houses. His companions succeeded, but Dick could only get one "iffy" response.[52] If he wanted to remain in his chosen field, he had no choice but to return to California.

Whittier hardly resembled Wall Street. For a novice, however, he didn't do badly. At Duke, he was advised that if a political career was an option, he should join a hometown law firm. He went to work with Whittier's oldest firm, Wingert and Bewley, and later headed their branch office at nearby La Habra. When World War II came, he moved to Washington and became one of the bureaucrats with the legal staff of the rationing division of the Office of Price Administration (OPA). He found himself, as a writer reported after talking to a former Nixon colleague, "uncomfortable among the liberals, the Eastern law-school graduates, the Jews he rubbed shoulders with on the job. *No one thought of him as a right-winger in those days,* . . . but in style if not in politics he was thought of as conservative (emphasis added)." A Republican lawyer who worked in that OPA office with Nixon gave an account with a far more ideological than psychological twist. "Most of the OPA lawyers were left-wingers," he explained, "and it was natural that Dick and I should develop an affinity for each other.... We both believed in the capitalistic system, but the other lawyers were using rationing and price control as a means of controlling profits."[53]

Several writers have concluded that his experiences with the bureaucracy reaffirmed his own dormant conservatism. Nixon's own explanation acknowledges that his time in the national capital changed his view of government. He had gone to Washington convinced that more could be done. Exposure to the federal bureaucracy made him realize the evils of bigness. "OPA," he recalled, "was government at its best, and there was the patriotic motive to do a good job." At the same time, the young man from California found "an obsessive antibusiness attitude. It opened my eyes to government's arrogance. After the OPA experience, I took a very dim view of controls. I was opposed to controls. I knew that many people in government, who were highly intelligent, wanted to build government bigger at the expense of private enterprise." Nixon often repeated what Chief Newman had told him about how the government had destroyed the Indians by making a once proud people wards and dependents of the state.[54]

Neither Nixon nor others have blamed the failure of wartime controls themselves. The OPA certainly deserves credit for achieving the sort of stability unimaginable during World War I. He was, nevertheless, in tune with those who agreed about the consequences of an unrestrained bureaucracy, one that governed from the top by fiat. The OPA not only set prices but specified regulations governing manufacturing and distribution, even stipulating how butchers were to trim their meat. Historian Barry Karl has pointed out that "the growing hostility to the wartime agencies' invasion of private business enterprise at all levels gave small business a clearer sense of the complaints that the large industries had leveled at the NRA [National Recovery Administration]."[55]

Humiliation and embarrassment forever haunted Nixon, inevitably contributing to both anger and determination. In 1952 he was forced almost literally to crawl back to presidential candidate Dwight Eisenhower for reinstatement as Ike's running mate after responding to charges that supporters had kept a secret fund in his behalf. During Eisenhower's presidency itself, Nixon was alternately displayed before the public with confidence and uncertainty. He had to endure Eisenhower's peculiar reluctance to commit himself before he retained his place on the party's ticket in 1956. During his own campaign four years later, he was left trying to explain exactly what was behind Eisenhower's famous news conference statement that any example of how Nixon had been involved in decision-making would require an additional week of thought. The bitterness of his narrow defeat to Kennedy may have caused the most severe pain of all. And, as a true masochist, he ran for governor of California two years later against the entrenched Pat Brown. Again he lost; this time notoriety resulted from his angry denunciation of the press for having "kicked" Nixon around. From that point, however, he went uphill, the only direction left, back to another presidential nomination and, finally, victory in 1968. The preordained scenario nevertheless prevailed when he later became the first president to resign from office, and the first to leave in disgrace, spared from further legal defenses only by President Gerald Ford's pardon.

Consider, as Nixon-haters refused to do, the pain and embarrassment. On a strictly objective basis, the agony should have been easy to imagine. Within the context of American history, a subject familiar to Mr. Nixon, there had never been anything quite like it. Andrew Johnson's trial back in 1867 was altogether another matter; elements of a political cabal were far more evident; doubts about his own morality were nonexistent. Closer to Nixon's time, in fact, within the realm of his own experience, were the Harding scandals ("I will be an old-fashioned kind of lawyer," he declared as a youngster when he heard about Teapot Dome[56]). Death itself, however, helped spare Harding direct confrontation with how his appointees had fleeced the public till. Even had he lived, the president would likely have escaped the more direct finger-pointing of personal culpability. Only Ulysses Grant, who lived through it all, provided a workable precedent. But even his personal reputation remained sufficiently intact to draw serious support for a third-term boomlet, which didn't come to anything, and a significant corporate position, which did. There was, in short, nothing in the American presidency comparable to Nixon's personal humiliation.

Consider, too, what may have been most painful, the incrementalism of it all: revelations followed by denials followed by confirmations; obstruction of justice; violating the rights of citizens; failure to respond to congressional subpoenas; exposures involving demeaning tactics, petty retributions, fraudulent income tax returns, improper expenditures of federal funds; and, possibly most embarrassing — certainly most damaging — the expletive-studded tapes. Excruciatingly, each step played out before a television-viewing, newspaper-reading public, with the drama rising as the months went by. Finally came the implicit acknowledgment of guilt by acceptance of a presidential pardon. A career notably without much joy thus concluded with embarrassment. Still, after all was done, the aura of Nixon competence remained, and retained enough strength for him to become a presidential adviser (albeit covertly) and, to many, a credible elder statesman.

*   *   *

That, of course, was the enigma of Richard Nixon. He *was* an achiever. It was evident from the start, contradicting all the liabilities. His former Whittier classmate Charles Kendle noted that Richard's personality was unattractive. But Kendle went on to say that "they come to him because of the quality of the man."[57] The outsider had the power to awe more conventional fellows. He may not have been like his fellows. He may sometimes have drawn skepticism, even scorn, but one looks in vain through all their recordings for signs of ridicule.

As one former schoolmate told biographer Earl Mazo, "Since high school Nixon has had an uncommon ability to take advantage of a situation before and after it develops." Then he added: "His success is due to knowing what to do and when to do it, perfect timing in everything." How much was due to responsibility forced upon him at an early age is anybody's guess, but the record is nevertheless impressive. The family's move from Yorba Linda to nearby Whittier followed the displacement of citrus orchards by oil derricks. Once in the new location, in the building that had housed the old Quaker meetinghouse, Frank Nixon opened a general store. Soon, he added gas pumps. Even before entering Whittier High School, Richard did various chores. One job that he did not get but which seems venturesome for one his age, was as an office boy at the *Los Angeles Times*. He was only eleven when he applied by mail, giving the name of his principal as his reference. At the time he began college, he assumed greater responsibility for helping in the store, including the twin burdens of managing the vegetable department and looking after the books. He also spent sixteen weeks working as a handyman and sweeper in a packinghouse and one summer as a janitor at a public swimming pool.[58] Simultaneously, in his sophomore year, he represented Whittier in over fifty debates, including a match with national champions.

Nixon also worked at one of the filthiest jobs, helping growers with smudge pots used to protect orange groves from frost. The going rate was twenty-five cents an hour. Nixon and the other boys, all eager for the opportunity to earn two dollars for eight hours of labor, were often in the fields all night. By morning, when it was time to get to their classes, their faces were covered with grime. When the other boys decided that their labor was underpaid, that thirty cents an hour would be a fairer wage, Nixon dissented. He argued that the growers could not afford the higher amount, and his advice was heeded. He was right, recalled one of the boys.[59]

But winning the respect of his fellow students was only one ingredient of young Richard's success in overcoming his liabilities. A dedicated, serious, and bright student such as he was naturally among those most admired by the faculty. With law school as his ultimate objective, history became his undergraduate major. His interest was perked by Dr. Paul S. Smith's expertise in the practicalities of American politics, but Nixon was also fascinated by the French Revolution. His reading included Voltaire and Rousseau, among other political philosophers, as well as Tolstoy.[60]

Dramatics was also one of Nixon's collegiate interests. The reserved, somewhat shy young man ultimately discovered that the stage was useful for gaining self-confidence. "Dick loved the stage," Dr. Albert Upton said later, "and I think of him as one of the little group of enthusiasts who assisted me in establishing dramatics at Whittier as a recognized curricular activity. He was one of our first successful actors."[61] It was in amateur theatrics that he met, in high school, Ola Florence Welch and later, after he graduated from Duke, Thelma Ryan.

The human cannon fodder and mediocre but persistent athlete simply could not have been dismissed as inept. His high academic standing, number two in the 1934 graduating class, was almost incidental. A Nixon biographer has aptly noted that "it was his never-ending drive that amazed all on the Whittier campus."[62] Whittier, a small school of a little more than three hundred students at Nixon's time, tried to be selective and maintain exacting standards. Although it was not oppressively sectarian, much of the faculty was imbued with a sense of mission. Interviews in later years reveal much pride and surprisingly few barbs at individuals. Contemporaries are, instead, eager to cite the accomplishments of Dr. Smith and to note that the faculty included such prominent people as playwright Maxwell Anderson and author M. F. K. Fisher. They, in turn, expected several students to achieve prominence.

Nixon's relations with the faculty were among the most striking aspects of his life at Whittier. This is especially significant because of the limited interaction with his peers except in groups. When asked about his friends by author Fawn Brodie, Ola Florence Welch, in Brodie's words, "realized only in retrospect that he had almost none." Nor do Nixon's memoirs note specific classmates. But they do acknowledge several members of the faculty, including Chief Newman, the football coach. Newman was dedicated to success and had no illusions about the difference between winning and losing, Nixon wrote.[63] Nor was that outlook very different from that of two later Nixon heroes, General George Patton and Coach Vince Lombardi of the Green Bay Packers.

Still, the formation of such attitudes was leavened by the teachings of Dr. Smith. The historian gave Whittier what was most needed, an avenue to the more sophisticated outside world of scholarship. He had taken his doctorate at the University of Wisconsin under the guidance of Professor Frederick Jackson Turner. One can imagine Smith's delight at arriving in Southern California and unsettling the innocents by lecturing on Charles Beard's analysis of the economic origins of the Constitution. Upsetting shibboleths is almost irresistible to young scholars. "Here was a man who utterly and completely polluted me," one student, Merton Wray, remembered with a smile. "He destroyed all my faith engendered by the Constitutional Oratorical Contest. Here was this young man, this perverter of youth — I hope the irony and satire comes through — here was this perverter of youth that taught history." He was, in Wray's recollections, "very liberal as a young professor (before he became Whittier's president, spent his time raising money, and assumed the conservatism of his surroundings)."[64]

Smith remembered Richard as analytical, not philosophical. His best-known student had begun his college career with a better-than-routine knowledge of both Lincoln and the Constitution. In Whittier High School, Nixon had written an essay on the Constitution. He called it "Our Privileges Under the Constitution." The young student wrote that the framers of the Constitution provided that

> we, their descendants, need not fear to express our sentiments as they did. Yet the question arises: How much ground do these privileges cover? There are some who use them as a cloak for covering libelous, indecent and injurious statements against their fellow men. Should the morals of this nation be offended and polluted in the name of freedom of speech or freedom of the press. In the words of Lincoln, the individual can have no rights against the best interests of society. Furthermore, there are those who, under the pretense of freedom of speech and freedom of the press, have incited riots, assailed our patriotism, and denounced the Constitution. . . .[65]

He followed his mother in admiring President Wilson. "It is interesting how the personality of Woodrow Wilson," Smith recalled, "fascinated the mind of young Richard Nixon." Through his whole political life, he quoted from Wilson more than any other man. Within his own household, the student also learned to appreciate such other heroes as William Jennings Bryan and Theodore Roosevelt. Also included in his reading was the autobiography of the famed Progressive leader Robert La Follette.[66] Lincoln, TR, Wilson, La Follette — their common denominator in the young man's mind had less to do with contemporary progressivism or conservatism, even classical liberalism, and more with what can best be called entrepreneurialism — not quite pure capitalism, but access to enterprise as a natural right for the best interest of men and society. Whatever hindrance might confront that ability, whether originating in capital or labor, had to be restricted.

Although a Quaker by birth, Nixon was more perfunctory about religion than politics, which is why his memoirs emphasize the *political* inspiration he received from Dr. J. Herschel Coffin. Dr. Coffin was a philosopher with a teaching commitment to the principles of a small Quaker college. One of his students, who later became a pastor at the East Whittier Friends Church, remembered Coffin as someone who "stood head and shoulders above any professor that I have had in my academic career."[67]

Whittier itself was only nominally a Quaker institution and far from saturated by that faith. More of the students were actually Methodists, with Quakers being as few as 17 percent. The behavioral objectives of the college, as recalled by a Nixon classmate, focused more on character-building than intellectual development. Nixon himself, as a student in Dr. Coffin's class, was doubtless attracted by the professor's intellectual gifts without becoming more than a conventional Quaker. In fact, the young man's religious devotion, along with his character and temperament, seems to have been somewhere between that of his mother and his father. Frank Nixon had converted when marrying Hannah; and while he joined the family with decent regularity at the East Whittier Friends Church, his devotion was far more casual. In contrast to his wife's pacifism, Nixon's father remained, in the words of one of Richard's uncles, "impetuous, forceful, and outgoing." He was suspected of never having abandoned his native Methodism.[68]

Membership in the Society of Friends was not synonymous with pacifism. Whittier Quakers were part of the California Yearly Meeting. Not only did they have pastors but they were also evangelical and, as such, less liberal and not as dedicated to humanitarian projects as eastern Quakers and the American Friends Service Committee. "We are more insistent upon the matter of conversion and accepting Christ as Saviour than they, the liberal Friends, would be," pointed out a Quaker minister, the Reverend Charles Ball. Ball also added that the evangelical Quakers were more strongly anticommunist. So, too, did they offer more latitude on such matters as the taking up of arms. One established member of the East Whittier Friends Church, for example, shouldered a shotgun to protect his orange groves from thieves who had preyed on the neighborhood. Nixon's father responded to fear of crime by keeping a revolver in the cash register of his grocery store.[69] Richard's later enlistment in the navy and subsequent advocacy of military solutions hardly suited the stereotype of the Quaker unwilling to bear arms.

The reality is that Whittier Quakers represented a wide variety of individual beliefs. There was no "long list" of creeds and doctrines, pointed out one pastor, "but we believe in the priesthood of the believer, and each individual has his or her right and responsibility to go into the presence of God, to seek God's help, to fulfill that will."[70] Sheldon G. Jackson, an authority on Quaker history, placed the matter in better perspective at the time of the Vietnam War by pointing out:

> The pacifistic Quaker stand in regard to peace has more or less been publicized. . . . Yet I think in helping to explain Richard Nixon we have to recognize too that the Quakers have, along with this, tried to maintain an intellectual freedom in which, while they generally espouse certain beliefs, they back up their members who disagree with these certain beliefs. . . . Richard Nixon, who has had this pacificist Quaker background and yet certainly does not take that pacificist stand today, can be considered a good Quaker, because we believe in freedom of conscience and freedom of belief along lines like this. I think that during his college years Richard Nixon did not follow the traditional Quaker viewpoint right down the line. . . . Now possibly his religious background can be the explanation for some of his conservatism, and yet you know that he is liberal in some of his thinking; possibly some of that comes from his experiences in Whittier College and his experiences since. So perhaps the influence in these early years helps to explain what seems to be a kind of conservative foundation to Richard Nixon's philosophy.[71]

Nixon's own attitude was assessed by an early California political associate, who said, "I think that Dick Nixon had, wrapped up within him, the background and solid Quaker philosophy that his forebears had, without necessarily being too closely aligned with some of the older traditions of the church."[72] Nor can anyone argue that Nixon's fondness for an aggressive, body-contact sport like football expressed pacifism.

From Whittier days, Nixon's behavior seemed paradoxical. The desire for a favorable image, recalled a classmate, "was the reason that he went out for football." Even at that early date, the incongruities that marked his career became evident. The so-called loner and bookworm was a campus leader, foreshadowing the sort of dichotomies that characterized his entire life. The Quaker son of pious and pacifistic Hannah campaigned to permit dancing at the college, embodied the football squad's esprit de corps, tried to make the track team, took up acting, enlisted in the Navy, and, although "gambling had been anathema to me as a Quaker," did well enough at poker in the South Pacific to make a down payment on the cost of running for Congress. "He was the finest poker player I ever played against," said a fellow officer. He did win often, Nixon later conceded, but he preferred that others believe his skill was inflated in the retelling.[73] Minor as it may have been, it was another hole he felt needed to be plugged: Nixon the card shark versus Nixon the upright. A continuing pattern of the Nixon career became one of assertion and counterassertion, contradictions that complicated explanations and encouraged controversy.

One example may be drawn from his school days. Reference has already been made to his prominence as a debater. Verbal skills are natural political assets, but Nixon's life also implanted in our collective memory a series of kaleidoscopic images notable less for their eloquence and inspiration than for their contentiousness: charging Jerry Voorhis and Helen Gahagan Douglas with leftist sympathies; using his dog Checkers and a "Republican cloth coat" to sanctify his honesty; associating Harry Truman with the word "traitor"; traveling the "low road" on behalf of Republican congressional candidates; perspiring with obvious discomfort, as though in a police lineup, while debating with a clean-cut, confident-appearing John F. Kennedy; intemperately lashing back at news reporters after losing the California gubernatorial campaign; drawing jeers and thrown objects while engaging in the rhetoric of "a guy running for sheriff"; announcing that American troops had already invaded Cambodia; telling his television audience that he was "not a crook"; resigning from the presidency without admitting to any wrongdoing; calling his mother "a saint" in a maudlin East Room farewell. Such are the montages that were associated with Nixon over three decades. Almost all inspired reminders of his schoolboy training as a debater.

His verbal talents were noted as early as the seventh grade, when he won a debate by arguing in the affirmative on the question, "It is more economical to rent a house than to own one." During his senior year, he won a ten-dollar prize from the school and another twenty dollars from the *Los Angeles Times* for public speaking on the topic "America's Progress: Its Dependence upon the Constitution."[74] His subsequent success on the college debating team was a staple of early biographies.

Later writers, especially those who worked in the shadow of scandals and his resignation, were less inclined to accept such accomplishments at face value. Rather, they suspected, examining those lauded skills would uncover early examples of "dirty tricks." Dr. David Abrahamsen, a New York psychoanalyst who was intrigued by the "two competing" sides of the Nixon personality, uncovered one witness who reported having spotted him cheating at the podium by pretending to quote facts and figures from a blank piece of paper. Another psychobiographer, Fawn Brodie, also working at the low point of the Nixon reputation, included Dr. Abrahamsen's witness as part of her denigration of Richard the debating champion. Those who cited his participating in fifty debates his sophomore year, "the bulk" of which were victories, she pointed out, ignored the "disaster" of the following year. Brodie's "disaster" was a tour that resulted in only one victory and three losses — for Nixon and his colleague — and the cancellation of four other debates through circumstances beyond his control. From Stewart Alsop's 1958 *Saturday Evening Post* article "Nixon on Nixon" she quoted exhortations from Richard to his colleagues that, in retrospect, would diminish a Vince Lombardi's reputation for toughness, but were included to help establish a portrait of ruthlessness. At the same time, she *ignored* the fact that Alsop opened his paragraph with the following judgment: "He was more than good at debating — he was brilliant." "Nixon's delight," Brodie wrote, "was not in solutions but in a place on the platform."[75]

Brodie had access to more than 170 transcripts of interviews with those who had known the young Nixon. To further diminish him as a debater, she cites one as having remembered that Nixon "would always come up with something. . . . Always using the ace in the hole." From the conversation with another former student, Kenneth Ball, she reports that Nixon "would come out suddenly, extemporaneously with some ideas I had not heard of before when we were going over the material for the debate." The pejorative inference was, presumably, clear enough: Tricky Dick hid a lot of ploys up his sleeve. Such an interpretation would have been far less likely had Brodie noted that Ball, in that same conversation, went on to explain that "when he was debating sometimes he would get up there and say things that you would not quite have anticipated in your preparation that he was going to bring out, *because I think he would kind of weave them together as he went along speaking*" (emphasis added).[76] Pre-Watergate interviews were thereby used to confirm post-Watergate verities.

The impressions given by just about everybody who remembered the debater in action, most of them speaking while Nixon was still serving his first term in the White House, reveal just how selective Brodie was trying to be. "He was a debater," said Floyd Wildermuth in 1970. "He was one you couldn't very well beat. I don't remember him as just being a shouter. He was more logical in his argument." Olive Marshburn remembered his ability to respond to unanticipated questions. "His debating ability," Hubert Perry pointed out, "resulted from thoroughness of preparation as much as any one thing, as well as his mental ability to relate to any particular situation, and he certainly was able to handle himself on his feet. . . . He can stand up and talk on most any subject and be convincing, because he had the kind of a memory, I guess, as well as the ability to express himself." A fellow debater, Osmyn Stout, credited Nixon with providing the rebuttals for his teammates. During the opening speeches, he would "write notes like mad. In the rebuttal, he would hand me his notes, and I would just read from his notes. These scrawls were just something terrible to read; they were awful. Nobody else could read them. Only people on our team knew them. And Nixon always had the answers for everybody. . . . He would write these notes, and all I did was pick them up and start talking from the notes. Then the other man would give his rebuttal, and then Nixon would finish up, tie everything together, and win — like that!"[77]

The important thing is that, when everything else collapsed, even Nixon's ability as a debater became suspect; something he must have done with mirrors, or, more like Dick, with tricks. Lost from all this was that Whittier was a small school. Although it gave a lot of importance to the debate team, the mere fact that it was competitive with large institutions was an achievement. For Nixon, from a relatively obscure Quaker college, to have won any notice at all was remarkable. Yet he did. In his senior year, he became the Southern California Intercollegiate Extemporaneous Speaking champion. He also won an extemporaneous speaking contest sponsored by *Reader's Digest.*[78]

Far less controversial were the origins of the Orthogonian Society. The future champion of the silent majority became Whittier's leader of the "nonorgs," the student term for the nonorganized groups on the campus. Much of the basis for what became Nixon's collegiate political prowess was banding together dissidents who resented the Franklins. An outgrowth of an early college debating society, the Franklins served men just as the women had their Palmers. Both prospered because Whittier banned Greek letter fraternities. The reality was that such societies, in a world without formal fraternities and restricted by Quaker egalitarianism, were valued additions to campus life.

To such outsiders as Nixon, the Franklins were the enemy, the organized elite, who had long dominated the campus socially and politically. They wore white shirts with long sleeves, and even were photographed wearing tuxedos. "We used to call them a bunch of kite-flyers," said one Nixon classmate, Newt Robinson. "We didn't think much of the Franklins," recalled another, Herman Fink. "We thought they were a group of society boys, boys that played checkers and chess, ping-pong and badminton."[79] The Franklins were recalled as a group bearing a cultural relationship to Ivy Leaguers. "Sure, the Franklins were the haves and we were the have-nots," Nixon told an interviewer in 1958.[80] "They wanted to overthrow them," remembered one alumnus, "and the ferment was ripe and strong."[81] The time was ready for revolt, and every account places young Richard at the center of the action.

Dr. Upton, the young English instructor who coached Nixon's collegiate theatrical work, was "young, enthusiastic, and saw the need for competition." Upton helped to convince his colleagues about the wisdom of sanctioning the new group. They definitely were the "other" people on campus, as the term "nonorgs" implied. Their core came from the students who were either athletes or closely associated with campus sports. Dean Triggs, one of the young men most actively involved with Nixon in leading the movement, later recalled that "that gang of sixteen was composed of some real rugged characters. They were . . . all making their way. They were not about to get involved in . . . anything expensive. Then, too, they wanted to do their own thinking." "This wasn't a group of society boys," added Herman Fink.[82]

Naturally, symbols were especially important. Who thought up the name Orthogonian Society was far less important than what it meant.

In Greek, *orthogonian* means right-angled; the founders interpreted that to mean "being on the square." As one of them has said, "We were supposed to be square-shooters, up-and-above ordinary people." They wore pins with the insignia of a boar's head. In direct contrast to the Franklins, their white shirts had short sleeves or were rolled up from the cuffs. As though to emphasize the point, their collars were left open, which was how they were photographed for the yearbook. That idea was Nixon's.[83]

Nixon, then only a freshman, became the first Orthogonian president. He also wrote the society's song: "Brothers together we'll travel on and on./Worthy of the name of Orthogonian."[84] Before long, they were competitive with the Franklins, together forming the dominant campus divisions. Nixon's identification with the Orthogonians confirmed his standing as an athlete. It also ensured his political base.

The association gave him entrée to campus government. Qualities that won respect and confidence from classmates had already been established. In his first year at Whittier, he won election as freshman president. He then led the Orthogonians. He had become a leader without personal popularity. Nor is there any evidence that he ever secured such appeal. Not even the most admiring biographers dwell on how well he was liked. But, despite that, he did go on to become vice president of the student body in his junior year and rose to the presidency before graduating. He did it, in part, by enduring the football drills, becoming skillful and developing confidence in campus dramatics, topping a traditional undergraduate competition by somehow finding a four-hole privy, and by his campaign to bring dancing to Whittier. His personal affinity for dancing was virtually nonexistent, but reversing the ancient prohibition was popular enough to justify his advancing the cause. He "sought applause as though it were a substitute for love," Brodie has written, "and the student vote fed this special hunger."[85] She could have added that he was a contradiction from the start.

Few people were indifferent about Nixon. His image evoked thoughts of either someone sinister or one who has been unfairly maligned by those who are truly up to no good. Stewart Alsop once suggested that that was because Nixon was "the cat who walks by himself."[86]

Such characterizations create their own distortions. The essential Nixon was at heart a thorough conformist. Even from his early days, there is little to suggest rebelliousness against established procedures. His initiatives on behalf of the Orthogonians and efforts to bring dancing to Whittier College represent his only substantial departures from a pattern of accommodation to tradition and convention. From youth through postpresidential retirement, his life-style was more prosaic than avant-garde, his demeanor more reflective and thoughtful, the manner of an introspective academic rather than an ambitious politician. Pictures of Richard Nixon donning Indian headdress, chopping wood, or dressed in jeans and sport shirt while on horseback, would be portraits of incongruity. In a world of tweeds and blazers, he clung to the three-piece suit. In a world of technology, he remained comfortable with yellow legal pads and old-fashioned fountain pens. His manner was to watch change and wonder why, worried about the consequences of instability. He pondered, and his mind never stood still. In his presence, it was hard to forget Robert Finch's point about the man's lifelong consistency.

So it should come as no surprise to find that a series of pre-Watergate interviews with early California friends and associates, conducted by students at California State University, Fullerton, contained nothing very unsettling. One young man suggested that the project began "with the idea that Nixon was the prototype of the small-town American who picked up certain values from that town [Whittier] and then has carried them into the White House and found a national response to that."[87]

Whittier was an exacting little college that had its academic pride. Still, young Richard was far more cerebral than his classmates. Except on the athletic field, competence was his hallmark; his efforts were marked by persistence, intelligence, ambition, and sharp competitive instincts. Nothing in the thousands of pages of transcripts denigrates his abilities, and that includes the testimonials of those who did not choose to celebrate him as Whittier's gift to American statesmanship. His emergence as class salutatorian seems fitting.

Witness the recollections of C. Richard Harris, who created the well-known ski-slope caricature of Nixon's nose. Harris's drawing first appeared in *The Quaker Campus* on October 21, 1932. A generation of unflattering cartoons followed that inspiration. Just as in the case of so many that plagued his later career, such as the famous drawings from the pen of Herbert Block (Herblock), there can be little doubt that Harris meant to savage his subject. Harris told an interviewer that he remembered Nixon as one who "set certain goals and figured what was the best way to get there. If it meant sitting on the bench for four years, this was worth the effort. Whatever would further his ends, I've felt, has been his guiding principle."[88] Another classmate remembered Nixon setting his goal on becoming a lawyer and making Jerry Voorhis his first political target. "You know," recalled Osmyn Stout, "when he was a candidate, I could see who were the Republicans here locally that backed him, and I knew that he had sold his soul. . . . They were the most conservative, reactionary people. I knew who they were. Everybody with a liberal frame of mind knew who they represented."

"What are you doing? How can you do this?" Stout said he asked Nixon after he had agreed to become their candidate.

"Sometimes you have to do this," he remembered Nixon telling him.

"You have to do this to become a candidate. I'm going to win." Later, Nixon gave a talk at Whittier in which he advised students that they had to become politicians before they could be statesmen.[89]

One faculty member supposedly responded to that comment by saying that he doubted Nixon knew the difference. The reality is that John Kennedy's advice to mothers that their sons must first become politicians before they can ever hope to reach the presidency is recognized as simple good sense. Had Adlai Stevenson been quoted in the same vein, it would have been used to refute the impression that the two-time Democratic presidential candidate was an egghead rather than a sound politician. Both the Harris and the Stout recollections were naturally conditioned by what they understood about Nixon's later career. The Harris ski-slope caricature, for example, appeared above a caption that said in part: "Nixon is a rather quiet chap about the campus, but get him on a platform with a pitcher of water and a table to pound and he will orate for hours. Last year he toured the northwest with the debate team, leaving a trail blazed with victories and fluttering feminine hearts." Stout, for his part, tempered his disapproving comments by saying that Nixon was not only "an outstanding student in many ways," but he was "also an outstanding person."[90]

The interview with L. Wallace Black adds still another dimension. It fuses the pejorative concept of Nixon the opportunist with a view of political ideology sure to bring surprise, and even outrage, to the accepted categorizations of belief throughout his public career. Black, a contemporary lawyer in Whittier, characterized the political position of the Duke law school graduate who returned to California to join the firm of Wingert and Bewley as follows:

> A lot of people think he lacks sincerity. He seems to give some people this impression. I think this is his main political drawback. He has a hard time compromising. He is extremely idealistic. He is much more liberal than the majority of the party. A lot of Mr. Nixon's liberalism shows through in the kind of political advisors and leaders he's picked for certain key positions in the administration. . . . He had to unite the party, both wings of it. So he has to appeal essentially to both the liberal and the more conservative elements of the party.[91]

Black's definitions will doubtless strike many as idiosyncratic. What he has done, of course, is to borrow varying interpretations of liberalism, progressivism, and conservatism from their contemporary contexts and apply them in seemingly contradictory ways. As used by Black, the term "liberal" is given positive connotations: "liberal" is the correct side, the enlightened view, the classical concept of postfeudal egalitarianism. The antistatist emerges as the true liberal, defending individual freedom from the specter of regimentation. That was precisely the warning of ex-president Hoover and other critics of the New Deal: Roosevelt had advanced the use of government to a level abhorrent to the American way. Enlarged national responsibilities for the economic welfare of each of its citizens, usually viewed as the evolution of the old progressivism into the new liberalism, were actually threatening to undo what a democratic society was supposed to be all about.

Such Hooverian warnings were raised long before the coming of World War II. Even before the Nazi collapse, Friedrich A. Hayek's *Road to Serfdom* (1944) fortified a new generation with intellectual rather than vested-interest arguments that the advance of centralized planning would merely replace old oppressions with new sets of tyrannies. Coincident with Hayek's book, a work by another Austrian economic thinker, Ludwig von Mises, *Omnipotent Government and Bureaucracy,* stated the case for capitalism versus government interference with the "hidden hand" in even more pristine form.[92] Reaching a far greater audience, and — immensely more important — much less easily dismissed as a primer for reaction, was George Orwell's futuristic novel *1984,* published in 1949. With the Third Reich dead and buried, the horrifying possibilities inherent in superstates pointed in only one direction.

In the years between Hayek and von Mises and Orwell, the totalitarian consequences of collectivism were far from universally recognized. Once Hiroshima and Nagasaki finished it all, Americans turned toward replenishing the good life, toward restoration of the world as it had been before the Great Depression, FDR, and the New Deal. The twenties, at least in lore, had been a time of hope and prosperity; what was lacking in the latter was balanced by an abundance of the former. All that had to be done was to tidy up the mess of having to restore a world that was finally made safe for democracy. Then, once Detroit converted to civilian four-wheelers and builders supplied homes for the swollen population and beef, gasoline, and palatable cigarettes returned to the marketplace, demons could be confined to history books. Freedom would at last be restored to the land of the free. As one historian has pointed out, the most important reality of the postwar period may have been "the revolt of *every* group in American society against those controls that directly affected its interests."[93]

Duke helped turn Nixon toward politics. Much about his personality made a political career improbable, and there is little evidence that he went off to Durham with that in mind. Nor, while he was there, did it seem plausible that he would end up that way. Richard the grind was a more recognizable character, one who said his primary concern was to become "the best lawyer in the country." His sobriquet, Gloomy Gus, had far less to do with his demeanor than — as in the comic-strip character origins of the name — the forensic ability to demolish fanciful notions. (The nickname inevitably evolved into just plain Gus, which took its place along with Nix or, especially in the Navy, Nick.) As one of Nixon's former classmates later told Stewart Alsop, "My own guess is that if politics had not sought Nixon, Nixon would never have sought out politics." Another emphasized that, of all Duke students, he was the least likely prospect for politics. Legal scholarship was a far more logical direction.[94]

The Duke experience largely confirmed old undergraduate patterns. Once more, he related better to faculty than to classmates. He made few lasting friends with the other students, not even with any of the three young men (including William R. Perdue, the top graduate in that class of twenty-six) who scrimped by sharing a white frame house off campus, in Duke Forest. Several years after Duke, his mates in Whippoorwill Manor, as they named their forest home, had little trouble recalling him for interviewers. Those more distant from the student had no problem remembering the name but were vague about his personality. As one noted, "You get the distinct impression that most of them know the man much better by reputation than by personal acquaintance." Those who did have clear memories usually describe him by using such characteristic words as "drive," "aggressive," "somber," "competitive," "reserved," "quiet," and "thorough." A librarian said, "He had to know people pretty well to let them see" his frivolous side.[95]

Not a single person remembered that he did any dating while at Duke. Nor did even his Whippoorwill mates know about his continuing involvement with Ola Florence Welch. At Durham, as at Whittier (despite the relationship with her), he struck others as having little appetite for a night life. "He certainly gave no indication of being interested in women or in wasting his time socializing," said an ex-schoolmate. An old friend who did know about Ola Florence said that he "just wasn't the particular type. He didn't have the glamor about him that attracts the opposite sex. He wasn't sexy."[96]

For Dick, it seemed to be Ola Florence or nobody at all. He had asked her to marry him, but that suggestion trailed off into limbo — together with their relationship. She had long since begun to date a man from Covina, Gail Jobe. On a trip back to the coast from Durham, Nixon found that she was with Jobe and refused to see him, but his devotion to Ola Florence continued. After he returned to North Carolina, his letters kept coming. In one of them, she recalls, "he said he wanted to become a lawyer so he could help the poor and the hungry," a suggestion that left unchanged her impression about Dick's conservatism, a characterization that applied even more emphatically to his social behavior.[97]

His election as president of the Duke Bar Association came from respect for his scholarship rather than personal popularity. Once again, as at Whittier, it was hardly the "big man on campus" reputation that would elicit expectations of future prominence. "As a politician, he has had to create himself," another ex-student pointed out, "because it has never been apparent what he really was from his actions."[98]

One student group, which prophetically called itself the Veterans of Future Wars, decided to pick the senior most likely to become a "future candidate for President of the United States." Nixon, however, was by-passed, for all his local accomplishments. He won attention for having boldly challenged one especially intimidating law professor, Douglas Maggs, who "would reduce you to a shamble in class. He'd make you look like an idiot. But I remember Nixon standing him off in our fresh-man torts class." He was on close terms with the dean, served as a con-tributor to the *Law Review,* and was accepted as a member of the prestigious Iredell Law Club. With it all, he managed grades that were just barely below A and high enough for a third-place finish in his graduating class.[99]

But when projecting the probability of future worldly success, Duke's law students named a young man from Louisville, Kentucky, who wound up in the sales department of an underwear company. Much more re-vealing, however, is the comment of a biographer who undoubtedly spoke for Nixon when commenting on such judgments. "Drive didn't seem to count in that popularity contest," wrote Edwin Palmer Hoyt. At Duke, explained Hoyt, Nixon "had neither the time nor the inclination to become known as an entertaining fellow."[100]

And that was true. Nixon was already moving in ways that defied popular tastes. For one, the law school was new and Duke was not the usual place for a Californian. He got there with high grades and strong letters of recommendation from two professors, Paul S. Smith and Albert Upton. Whittier's president, Walter F. Dexter, of some national prom-inence as a Quaker leader, embellished his endorsement with the state-ment that "I believe he will become one of America's important if not great leaders."[101]

Duke got Nixon, thereby giving the young man a crack at the rare law school that he could afford. Amply endowed by the tobacco fortunes of James Buchanan Duke, the school gave him a scholarship of $250, enough to cover matriculation and tuition fees for his first year. Ola Florence, who had gotten to know him better than anyone else at Whittier High and then at Whittier College, had assumed that he would go on to law school. "But the night he found out about the scholarship — oh, we had fun that night. He was not only fun, he was joyous, abandoned," she has recalled, " — the only time I remember him that way. We rode around in his car (he had bought a 1930 Ford in his junior year) and just celebrated."[102]

An additional financial bonus, which paid off in other ways as well, was an arrangement made by the dean, H. Claude Horack, for him to work on a special research problem in criminal law under the auspices of the National Youth Administration (NYA), a New Deal agency. Nixon's assignment, which was not completed until after his graduation, paid thirty-five cents an hour. Such extra ways of earning money were not uncommon among his classmates, but the record suggests that even they recognized Dick Nixon as especially hard-pressed. He had every reason to be grateful. "I believe we've got the best darn law school in the country right at Duke," he wrote to Horack after becoming a member of the bar. "The atmosphere between students and faculty, the small size of student body, and the progressive attitude of the faculty convince me of that fact."[103]

That his experience with Duke would meet his standards for success was not always clear. Most of the other young men had received better undergraduate training. Nixon, three thousand miles from home, felt the stress of insecurity. He later worried about the renewal of his scholarship. "He wrote me these sad letters," Ola Florence has revealed. "He sounded like he was close to quitting two or three times." Anxiety about his class rank led to a break-in of the dean's office. Two of his roommates made it possible to enter through a transom and locate the file with his records, which confirmed that his academic standing had dropped below the top three.[104] But fear about being able to remain on a scholarship was unwarranted. Through it all, Dean Horack emerges as a key figure.

The relationship with Horack was especially close. The dean, who simply referred to the law student as "Nixon," fell into the mold of a succession of male authorities who seem to have become surrogate fathers. In Nixon's case, the temptations are too great not to consider in that context such figures as Paul Smith, Albert Upton, influential Whittier banker Herman Perry, lawyer Tom Bewley, and *Los Angeles Times* newspaperman Kyle Palmer. However imprecise the characterization, the fact does remain that there is strong evidence for saying that they, rather than Frank Nixon, were closely involved in the young man's key decisions.

Crediting Horack was understandable. He was involved in several aspects of Nixon's law school career. When the young man failed to land a position with a New York firm during his Christmas vacation search in 1936, it was Horack he turned to for help in getting an appointment with the Federal Bureau of Investigation. Contacting J. Edgar Hoover, the dean reminded the director of having been invited to refer "any exceptional young man" with interest in the agency. Although he personally thought Nixon's abilities warranted something better, he recommended the student as "one of the finest young men, both in character and ability, that I have ever had the opportunity of having in my classes."[105] Only years later did Nixon learn that his application had been accepted but his appointment had been killed by a budget cut. Having delayed filing for the California bar exam, Nixon then had to tap Horack once again, this time to use his influence to permit him to take the one scheduled for September of 1937.

He feared that graduating from Duke created a potentially serious handicap. That eastern school might not have given adequate preparation for the requirements of the California bar exam. He had, in fact, heard that others had failed because they had spent too little time in cram courses. Providing his usual encouragement, Dean Horack advised that "they will have to flunk all of them if they don't let you by."[106]

Typically, Nixon did not rest on that sort of confidence. He was still completing the NYA research, delving into precedent-breaking decisions involving labor cases, attending the cram course from March until September, first going once, then twice, then three times a week, for three hours a night. A four-week battle against the flu additionally complicated his schedule that spring. Finally, he was among the 46 percent of those who passed the exam; he was sworn in by the California bar at the state supreme court in San Francisco on November 9, 1937.[107] That at last freed him to complete and send to Horack his NYA research.

He was also able to notify the dean that he had accepted a position with the respectable Whittier firm of Wingert and Bewley, which had an office above the Bank of America. He had, in fact, already been assigned a couple of motions to be made before the Los Angeles Superior Court. Horack had advised the student to "go back to your home town and establish yourself in a law firm" if he was really interested in politics.[108]

"I would like to spend a couple of years with some government department before settling down," Nixon wrote right after he took the exam, "but I believe it will be best to settle down and get to work and build up a business — if that can be done. As I remember thats what you advised me to do when I mentioned the possibility of going into the F.B.I. for a while." He added that he had no intention of taking that job even if offered unless the Wingert and Bewley offer should collapse. He also solicited Horack's confirmation that it would be "the best thing to do." As late as the summer of 1943, in a letter to Horack from the South Pacific, Nixon was primarily concerned with making a postwar adjustment to resuming his legal practice. The only allusion to political matters was the observation that there was a "hue and cry already being raised for government aid and control in the field of post war job hunting" and that it might be better for professional associations to prepare to take "care of their own."[109]

While no hint that he was considering entering politics appears in any of the extant letters, there can be no doubt that his coming-of-age at Duke helped to confirm his ultimate direction. Given his own interests, and especially the talk he had often heard from Frank Nixon, politics was something of an inevitability. The latent interest may have been further fired by a lecture Richard heard during his last year that was given by a noted anthropologist, Leonard Cromie.[110] Professor Cromie, who emphasized the function of colleges and universities as training grounds for candidates for public office, was sufficiently impressive for Nixon to discuss the matter with his friends at Whippoorwill Manor. For him to have taken it up with Horack was natural, and the dean's advice about getting started in his own hometown was hardly revolutionary. That there is no evidence of subsequent political exchanges between Nixon and Dean Horack may indicate ideological incompatibility. In 1972, in a discussion at Camp David, Nixon reflected on his old days at Duke, commenting that the law school had "many left-wing deans."[111] Was Horack one of those he had in mind?

Other than joining Wingert and Bewley, Nixon launched his early political ambitions in Whittier in several ways, all characteristic of young attorneys attempting to establish themselves. He became president of the Whittier College Alumni Association and, the following year, was made a member of his alma mater's board of trustees. He was also president of the Duke Alumni Association of California. In Nixon's sole business venture, he joined with some other local men who were trying to freeze and market fresh orange juice, but the gamble fizzled out within less than two years.[112]

On June 15, 1938, Nixon registered as a Republican. During the subsequent presidential election, he did some work for Wendell Willkie's presidential candidacy. His effort to cast a wartime absentee ballot for Thomas Dewey in 1944 was an even more emphatic assertion of partisanship. In several other ways, however, he made tentative advances toward politics. He tried to get himself named to fill a vacancy for the state assembly, but party leaders bypassed him for the nomination. He also served as assistant city attorney of Whittier.[113]

It was then that he met Thelma Catherine Ryan, long since known as Pat Ryan, daughter of a man who his son Tom said "was always chasing rainbows." She was, according to one who knew her at an early age, "a cherubic child with dark sparkling eyes and brown hair . . . with red highlights in it," and cheeks that "'were rather round, with just that little bit of freckling on them that looked so fresh and rather orange more than pink." Her lovely, slender form was not unlike Ola Florence's. What stood out most of all was her eyes, which her daughter Julie has described as having a "soft, pure color [that] gave the impression of endless depth." Her facial structure was dominated by high cheekbones, and that combined with natural poise to exude an image of dignity. Still, "she was fun, and that was what attracted me to her," said one of her former dates.[114] Pat entered Nixon's life not unlike the first appearance of Ola Florence eight years earlier.

He had met the Welch girl when they were both in the senior year high school play. She was Dido, the Carthaginian queen, and he was Aeneas, the Trojan hero, in Whittier's Latin class rendition of Virgil's *Aeneid*. She was petite and beautiful with soft brown eyes and even years later remembered for her enthusiasm and warmth. She was the lead opposite Richard, then in his first play. "It was very romantic," Ola Florence later recalled. "We all wore white gowns. After that we started going together." He was her first date. They were in love from the start, without any doubt that they were "made for each other." "You have no idea," she said much later, "how tremendously interesting and engrossing he was to me, the daughter of a small-town police chief. I considered myself provincial and him worldly." He asked her to marry him. Before it all came to an end, when he was at Duke and she married Gail Jobe, she had come to believe that she "wasn't good enough for him." She later told Fawn Brodie that "I'm sure he would not have made it [to be president] if I had married him. I loved fun too much."[115]

She was unlike Pat, whose dedication to duty kept her loyal to the interests of Nixon's career even when she had to grit her teeth. The Ryan girl was remembered as the "ideal little student who conformed in every way," who "never was silly" or ever "had time to fiddle around after class," so different from Ola Florence's ebullience. Pat, serious, reserved, shy, quiet, even "a little distant" and "stand-offish," was always dedicated to doing the right thing.[116]

Pat was already twenty-six and had spent most of her childhood in Artesia (now Cerritos), only eight miles from Whittier. She first came from the hills near Ely, Nevada, where she was born on March 16, 1912, in a miner's shack that had neither electricity nor running water. Her father's luck never panned out. Will Ryan, whose parents were from County Mayo, Ireland, was among those never compensated for ambition or hard work. With little formal education, he moved from Connecticut and tried to strike it rich in Alaska's Klondike. Will Ryan, who never struck gold and had to settle for the life of a hardworking subsistence farmer, married a widow with two children who had come to America from Germany. Kate Halberstadt Bender Ryan, who was fourteen years younger than her second husband, died when Pat was fourteen. Left with one child from his wife's first marriage who still lived at home, he also had to maintain his and Kate's two sons, Bill and Tom, and their daughter Pat, who was the youngest.

Young Pat became their second mother. "I'm sure that she did a lot of the cooking and housework and things as she grew up. Then," one of Tom's close friends explained, "when the father passed away, the three of them continued to live there for several years even after Tom had gone to college and graduated." Pat's burdens were captured by the Excelsior High School yearbook, which captioned the picture of "Buddy" (as she was known) with the notations that her "intention" was "to run a boardinghouse." Her liability: two brothers. Her occupation: watching Tom. Her talent: watching Bill. She found her treehouse, and escaped to it whenever she could, clinging to the branches with a book and an apple.[117]

The world of the stage offered another early escape. Her interest in the theater led to Pat's role as Penelope Lapham, the older daughter of the paint magnate protagonist of William Dean Howells's *Rise of Silas Lapham.* "Penelope Lapham, in all her girlish moods, gay or serious, was charmingly played by Thelma Ryan," reported the Excelsior yearbook.[118]

Long before she met Richard Nixon, however, she had already experienced much of the real world. Life for Pat involved a wide variety of jobs, including driving an automobile for hire to New York, working as an X-ray assistant in a Bronx hospital, and even appearing as an extra in Hollywood films. She was a teller at the Artesia First National Bank, trying to make enough to pay for her father's terminal hospitalization. She did whatever part-time work she could find, including bookkeeping and janitorial services. She spent a year at Fullerton Junior College and worked her way through the University of Southern California on a research fellowship. With it all, Pat managed to graduate cum laude with a degree in merchandising. "If she had been a rich little gal," said one of Nixon's first cousins, "who had been indulged by her parents, why, I don't think Dick would have been attracted to her. He probably knew pretty well the type of gal he was looking for."[119]

Pat, who looked even younger than she was, became a teacher in the business department of Whittier High School, proving to a colleague that the district superintendent "hasn't lost his eye yet. She was young, full of pep, and very attractive and dressed very nicely. The kids were just crazy about her." She taught classes in typing, stenography, and shorthand. As a new teacher, she was also given duties that included serving as an assistant director of student activities, among them dramatic productions.[120]

Nor was she uninvolved in other matters. Just as Ola Florence, she came from a Democratic background. Will Ryan was loyal to the party preferred by Irish-Americans. He strayed only once, in 1924. Will, as did Frank Nixon, backed the Progressive candidate that year, Robert La Follette. Pat is remembered as a "rabid supporter" of Al Smith against Herbert Hoover.[121] As a teacher, she became secretary of the Whittier branch of the American Association of University Women.

She met Nixon in the same kind of make-believe world in which he had first seen Ola Florence. The Whittier Community Players were chronically pressed to find suitable cast members. In early 1938, director

Louise Baldwin faced the familiar problem of locating leads, this time for a production of *The Dark Tower,* a mystery melodrama by Alexander Woollcott and George S. Kaufman. Mrs. Baldwin's need came to the attention of the assistant superintendent of Whittier's schools. He urged Pat to attend the tryouts that were to be held in the Sunday school room of the St. Mathias Church.

Mrs. Baldwin also needed someone who could play the part of a lawyer. She turned to a Whittier attorney, L. Wallace Black, who pleaded that he did not have enough time. "It was just before noon that she called me," he recalled for an interviewer. "On my way to lunch I ran into Dick in the elevator of the Bank of America building. . . . It occurred to me that Dick would make a good prospect for this part." But Nixon was hardly more enthusiastic about giving his time than was Black. So, as Black reported their encounter, he said, "Well, if you get up there and make a good lawyer, it might bring you some business." Nixon remained noncommittal, so Black called Mrs. Baldwin and advised her to persuade him. That did it. "Dick, I think," said Grant Garman of the theater, "just took one look at her [Pat], at the time he came for the reading of the show, and that was it."[122]

Nixon's interest even exceeded his reaction to Ola Florence. He was dazzled by what has often been described as her titian-colored hair and delicate form. They hardly had any personal conversation, but when the two amateur actors left the church together that first night, he predicted that she would be the one he would marry. Startled, she thought he was teasing; by the time she reached her apartment and met a friend, she said, "I met this guy tonight who says he is going to marry me." Not until two years later was there a serious marriage proposal and a suitable response. When Dick announced his engagement to Pat, Whittier gossip felt that he should have gone with a girl from a better family, preferably one from the town, and certainly with a girl who did not work.[123]

They were married on June 21, 1940, in the Mission Inn at Riverside. Nixon arranged to have a Quaker ceremony. Religion had not been an important part of Pat's life. Pat was, however, as Nixon later wrote, "an independent woman," one who was "traditional, but in a warm way that transcended time and place." She also had the strength and control of Hannah, and it should not be surprising that Nixon would later describe both women in similar terms.[124]

5

A New Day for the Twelfth

FRANK MILHOUS, Nixon's maternal grandfather, served on the board of trustees of Whittier College with Herman Perry. Both friendly and critical accounts recall Perry as a "long-time family friend."[1] He was also the best connection in town.

No one turned Perry down, recalled a Whittier old-timer. Certainly not anyone in town with commercial or political interests. "You just didn't turn him down, because of your connections with the bank and your respect for his ability, and he was a leader. He was a *leader*." Perry was the prime force in persuading his associates to construct a new building for the First National Bank of Whittier, which was later taken over by A. P. Giannini's Bank of America. When the new owners then tried to dump Perry, the country's largest bank was forced to retreat. A little delegation took its case to Mr. Giannini himself and let him know that the branch of his bank could not succeed in Whittier without the leadership of Herman Perry. For the rest of his active career, until five years before his death in 1954, Perry held on as manager.[2]

When Nixon's first political campaign is discussed, Perry is always included among the group of so-called political amateurs whose desire to replace Jerry Voorhis as the Twelfth District's congressman gave Nixon his chance.[3] In truth, the line between amateur and professional was extremely fine, especially tenuous in a state with California's loose partisanship. For the most part, such men were really bound by either fraternal, social, commercial, or partisan political relationships. With the sinister connotation of the words "professional politicians," the amateur was invariably the good guy, a "Mr. Smith Goes to Washington" type who cared about the people instead of the backroom crowd. A puff piece carried by the *Saturday Evening Post* in 1949 tried to paint Nixon with the same type of good-guy colors. Essential for that image was the following sentence: "The amateur politicians began their search for an amateur candidate at a meeting called by Roy Day, manager of the commercial-printing department of the Pomona Progress-Bulletin, which had backed the loser at the last election."[4]

The misleading use of "amateur" suggests an innocence, a popular movement of the disinterested or merely civic-minded. *Saturday Evening Post* readers, for example, were not told that Day, a resident of Pomona, was the Republican chairman of the Twelfth District. He was also known as a rough political operator. As he told an interviewer, "I've never gone on a basis of just playing to play. I like to win and I play hard to win. You have to fight all the way; you never get on the defensive. Nice guys and sissies don't win many elections." Day headed the primary campaign. Nor were the readers informed that Day's initiative was in concert with John S. Barcome. Barcome was chairman of the Los Angeles County Republican Central Committee. Frank E. Jorgensen, an insurance executive, was closely associated with every early Nixon campaign, sometimes as finance chairman and usually responding to various immediate needs.[5]

It is true that Nixon's earliest backers represented a coalition of bankers, Realtors, businessmen, and party workers, as has been charged when the campaign has been portrayed as the product of a cabal of influential men of wealth. They certainly were community leaders. Most of them were already comfortably well off; some prospered later. A few later helped to organize the Lincoln Club, a group of sub-rosa Nixon fat cats from the Newport Beach area of Orange County. Their power was nevertheless relatively limited and minor-league, hardly resembling the holdings of even middle-level industrialists and financiers with national influence. "They weren't a group of wealthy, powerful people," Nixon's daughter Julie has pointed out. "They were small-town people. They had some money, but they certainly weren't pulling the strings like the type of people with power or money." The point is reasonable. Perry himself, for all his local influence and standing as a banker, was not exactly a wealthy man. "At that time," one of Nixon's early backers has recalled, "it was the shopkeepers, the guys who went to the Lions Clubs, the twenties-to-thirties [age] group, a few lawyers."[6] There was, after all, a limit to the amount of power that could be attracted by a thirty-two-year-old political newcomer.

Even a cursory review reveals the Rotarian character of Nixon's initial supporters. Gerald Kepple, a Whittier native, was a lawyer, a member of the state legislature, served on several state boards, and later went on to become a judge. Earl Adams was an attorney, Boyd Gibbons an automobile dealer, Rockwood Nelson an insurance man, Willard J. Larsen a dairyman in the Whittier area, Frank Jorgensen (one of Nixon's managers) a Metropolitan Life Insurance Company vice president, and Arthur Kruse was president of the Alhambra Building and Loan Company.[7]

They were also Herman Perry's friends. Known around town as Uncle Herman, he was also remembered as the local "Mr. Republican," one of those small-town activists whose leadership represents the desires of the Chamber of Commerce and political professionals. His brokership of the "public interest" reconciled "sound moral principles" with "sound fiscal policies" and "one hundred percent American principles." Unable to keep the Democrats from coming to power in the first place, Perry was among those for whom the New Deal was an unfortunate experience that merely confirmed the good sense of having been opposed to FDR. He was also, according to Jorgensen, "the political godfather of young Nixon." "Dick grew up under his wing," said Wallace Black. "He'd seen Dick grow up as a small boy in this town, and as a young man."[8]

Like the Nixons and Milhouses, and like almost everyone else in California, Perry came from somewhere else. He followed a familiar pattern and migrated from the Midwest early in the century. He began his banking career as a bookkeeper with the First National Bank. For the rest of his life, he pursued local business and political interests. In the 1920s, his Republican party activism made him vice chairman of the county committee. "In 1932, however, everyone was suspicious of everybody else," he has written; "there was some name calling, etc. In 1934 to 1936 it became worse. I became so disgusted that I dropped out of politics in 1932 and became just a Republican voter." But before the war was over, Perry was back in politics, pressing the Los Angeles County Republicans to take a more effective role in the local organization.[9]

In 1945, looking ahead to the 1946 election, getting rid of Voorhis was clearly his most important immediate goal. In a very real sense, that would also rid the Twelfth District of the New Deal. Replacing Voorhis was merely one small step toward saving the government from what anti–New Dealers routinely called "statism." Or, as a political friend put it to Perry, "I am convinced that some sort of organization of responsible people, *from all parts of the district* is necessary if we are to elect a man to Congress, who will be representative of the real attitude of most of the people in the district. The people are for the most part conversativ [*sic*] and not in accord with vague 'school boy' ideas about public affairs."[10]

The prerequisite for success, however, was a plausible candidate. Briefly, at least, there were two names prominent in the community; both touched Nixon's life. One was Dr. Walter Dexter, the same man who, as president of Whittier College, had recommended Nixon so highly to Duke. He had since gone ahead to become California's superintendent of education. Personally favored by party leaders, Dexter feared the risks of becoming a candidate. He wanted to be assured of being able to get another position before he could be persuaded to give up his position with the state. All that became moot, only days after he rejected the possibility of his candidacy, when he died of a heart attack. That left another, much more intriguing personality, General George Patton.

Like Dexter, the widely publicized World War II maverick died before the campaign, of an accident on December 21, 1945. Patton was a figure Nixon admired long afterward, and the popular film biography with George C. Scott in the title role was a Nixon favorite. William Safire, a presidential speechwriter, thought that the president identified himself with the general. Patton was also "a patriot misunderstood by carping critics." During the aftermath of the brouhaha in 1952 over Nixon's alleged secret fund, Eisenhower himself compared the two men. Each had erred, he said, and been forgiven; nothing could have better solidified the empathy Nixon felt for Patton.[11] Each had experienced Ike's avuncular righteousness.

Nowhere was Patton's career followed with greater care than in the Twelfth District. His birthplace in San Gabriel was roughly ten miles north of Whittier, and he continued to maintain a local residence. In the same tradition as the draft-Ike movement, nobody knew whether he was a Republican, or seemed to care, but a trial balloon was launched in mid-October for this most celebrated native son. The splash, Roy Day assured Perry, "makes good strategic or psychological 'warfare' material," although he doubted that it would "develop into anything."[12] By then, just three months before Patton's accidental death, Perry had joined with Day and Barcome to steer local Republicans toward a "unity" candidate. Failure to come up with an obvious consensus choice, as Patton surely would have been, left matters open to a tough primary that risked splitting the party and losing to Voorhis virtually by default.

These circumstances eventually led to Nixon. Despite Perry's involvement, that ultimate outcome took several months to become clear. The war was still on when Twelfth District Republicans began to organize themselves, and Lieutenant Commmander Nixon was obviously unavailable. The larger forces of history determined the ultimate direction. The final Japanese collapse came that August. World War II was ending and demobilization was about to begin. At about just that time, readers of twenty-six local newspapers were informed that prospective candidates were invited to appear before "100 interested citizens who will guarantee support but will not obligate the candidate in any way."[13]

So-called fact-finding committees were formed in each of the state assembly districts within the Twelfth Congressional District. They were loosely organized and informal. The primary function of their members was to interview prospective candidates. Eight men applied, including Voorhis's predecessor, John Henry Hoeppel, who promised to keep the

"Jews and the niggers" out of the district. It began to look as though Republican impotence would once again send Voorhis to Washington. An increasingly anxious Perry turned to Dexter, whose personal problems then delayed any resolution of the issue. With the end of the war, men like Tom Bewley, Frank Jorgensen, and Perry began to consider Nixon. Meanwhile, Dexter was still wavering. Somewhat impatiently, Perry sent a brief note to Nixon in Baltimore on Bank of America letterhead asking if he would like to run against Voorhis.[14]

The invitation came just as the lieutenant commander was closing out a number of naval contracts. Under the system for separation from military service, Nixon's forty-nine points made him eligible for early discharge. But he had agreed to stay on for a few months "to clean up the Glenn Martin Co. terminated contracts." As he informed Perry, "since I'm a Bu. Aer. [Bureau of Aeronautics] contracting officer I don't feel I should walk out right in the middle of the negotiations," but he believed he could leave at the start of the new year.[15] Those were the only impediments, and they were hardly serious. In no way did he betray any hesitation. Nor should he have bypassed the opportunity.

His response to Perry was thorough and well thought-out, fully consistent with the "wonderful surprise to learn that I was even being considered for the chance to run against Jerry Voorhis." Perry, according to a fellow member of the fact-finding committee, virtually drafted Nixon, telling him in "no uncertain terms that it was his duty" to take the nomination. "Are you serious?" Nixon asked over the transcontinental wires. "Will I become a candidate for Congress?" Perry firmly replied, "We are not only serious, but we are demanding that you become a candidate for Congress and we will back you."[16]

Hardly more was needed. Nixon assured Perry of his ability to mount a campaign and win. Since Pat had also been working, they had put aside enough cash in the last four years to weather the financial needs. He wrote that the battle could be won by waging an "aggressive, vigorous campaign on a platform of *practical* liberalism" that should become the "antidote the people have been looking for to take the place of Voorhis' particular brand of New Deal liberalism."[17]

Even as Nixon was formulating his response to Perry, Dexter made his decision. The ex-Whittier president then named the man that the banker and others wanted to hear: Nixon, his "brilliant" former student.[18]

The thirty-two-year-old officer hitched a ride west aboard a military air transport plane. The Committee of One Hundred had arranged three sessions to introduce their choice candidate. Nixon, who did not own a civilian suit, wore his navy uniform to a Thursday night dinner in Whittier and to a noon conference at Los Angeles the next day, where he could be presented to Republicans at the statewide level. That Friday evening, November 2, he formally went before the committee at the William Penn Hotel in Whittier. "He seemed intelligent, forceful, and with a capacity for growth," remembered Murray Chotiner, who met him in Los Angeles and later became closely associated with Nixon's early political battles. Reminded of the meeting in 1984, Nixon unhesitatingly used the phrase "practical liberal" to describe his position. Those were the same words used that day when he equated the imposition of government controls with limitations of "individual freedom and all that initiative can produce." Republicans, he pointed out, had crippled themselves in the past by countering Voorhis with such primitivists as Hoeppel. His campaign, he promised, would be "aggressive" and waged along the lines of "progressive liberalism designed to return our district to the Republican Party."[19]

He returned east, faced a backlog of contract termination settlements, and, in those pre–air commutation days, shuttled by rail between Baltimore, Washington, and New York. His capacity for diligence came in handy. He spent many evenings studying Voorhis's voting record, including going over the congressman's book about the Federal Reserve System and the monetary structure. "I believe the main emphasis should be on the constructive program we have to offer rather than on his failures," he wrote to Herman Perry.[20]

On the twenty-eighth of November, in Nixon's absence, the Committee of One Hundred gathered at the YMCA in Alhambra. They were called to order by Chairman Day at 7:00 P.M. Nixon's name was placed in nomination by Kepple. The outcome was never in doubt. The Whittier delegates were able to relax as Nixon's candidacy was boosted by supporters from Pasadena and Alhambra. On that first ballot, Nixon got all but fourteen votes; even those joined the front-runner to make it unanimous. As he had promised, Roy Day telephoned Nixon with the results. At two o'clock in the morning, in his Baltimore apartment, Nixon heard the words, "Dick, the nomination's yours!" The *Los Angeles Times* reported that they had found "a natural candidate." But prophecy was left to Herman Perry, who then warned, "Dick, from now on *you are a marked man*."[21]

The June primary was hardly more than pro forma. The organization and various grass-roots interests had finally joined hands behind a single anti-Voorhis candidate. There was absolutely no room for a maverick. But the Richard Nixon who was discharged from the navy that January and returned to Whittier hardly differed from the man who later sat in the White House. He could easily have vacationed and rested for the coming campaign against Voorhis. That kind of respite would also have been natural considering Pat's advanced pregnancy; their first child, Patricia, arrived on February 21.

The record, however, shows energetic devotion to what was clearly to be an uphill battle. Voorhis, as the incumbent, did not feel that he had to cultivate his district before the primary; he did have a challenger, but he remained in Washington. Nixon's devotion to the task was not unlike what John F. Kennedy was then doing in Boston to win the seat that was being relinquished by James Michael Curley. Characteristically, Nixon did his homework, researching the Voorhis record, preparing speeches, and seeking advice from key people. Meanwhile, back in California, Nixon, as did Voorhis, took advantage of the state's cross-filing system, which allowed candidates to file in both the Republican and Democratic primaries. That served to encourage a Nixon strategy of moderation, one that could attract Democrats along with a broad spectrum of Republicans. Some of the Voorhis support, he knew, was tentative, likely to remain loyal only until the appearance of somebody capable of beating him in November. The hard stuff already being developed to use against Voorhis, the close identification with left-wing organized labor and parallels with the voting record of the openly procommunist congressman Vito Marcantonio should, he advised Perry, be saved for the real campaign. He also assured the press that he would not "straddle the issues."[22]

Most of all, Nixon labored on a kickoff address. To be delivered at the Ebell Clubhouse in Pomona as part of the traditional Republican Lincoln's Birthday observance, it had to establish his presence as that serious challenger. So he went to work with pencils and yellow legal pads, those same canary sheets that remained forever close to his desk, and wrote and rewrote. He wanted to get it exactly right. He wanted to assert faith in a system that could work if it offered hope to individuals, if the masses could have confidence that they and the nation could prosper without the bureaucratic structures that had been created by the New Deal, without the specter of a planned economy. He included not a line that disputed FDR's objectives or that doubted what had been necessary in the nineteen-thirties. Instead, he directed attention to the need to move forward. It was Richard Nixon's first significant public clarification of where he stood. Technically, it began his political career. Delivered on February 12, 1946, the words — at least as they appear in his hand — never became dated.

He could hardly, especially on that occasion, avoid noting his view of the mission of the Republican party. He denied that the GOP was the "party of big business and privilege" but urged that the charge must be recognized. He went on: "Reps live on both sides of the tracks. The interests of all of the people are bound up together and a party which fails to recognize that fact and becomes the tool of one pressure group or another does not deserve to govern. What the country needs is not an adm which will represent big business, nor one which will represent big labor but one that will stand for the interests of *all* the people of the country."

Nor, he added, taking note of the postwar conflicts between labor and management, could the party emulate the Democratic administration, which had "treated the matter as an inevitable *conflict* between labor & management *in which the interests of both were diametrically* opposed. . . . For the Rep Party to follow a policy of taking the side of management in the disputes and to attempt to defeat the right of labor would bring tragedy to this nation."[23]

Circulars distributed throughout the district carried that theme. Nixon was a candidate deserving of bipartisan support. He "knows what it means to earn a dollar — the problems of the working man." He wanted to go forward, not backward, from the New Deal, to make government work better than it could "with the governmental procedures and practices of yesterday." His call was for "a sound progressive program in which government will work with and through private enterprise toward our goal of assuring housing, clothing, food, education and opportunity for every American."[24]

When Twelfth District voters cast their primary ballots, there were no surprises, Voorhis and Nixon emerging easily as their respective parties' candidates. Voorhis got seven thousand more votes overall than Nixon managed, but that was less comfort for the Democratic incumbent than it might appear. His actual share of the total primary vote was down by 6.5 percent from the 1944 level. Still, he *was* the congressman; he had the votes; Nixon was the neophyte with the burden of demonstrating that he could win. When those primary votes came in, people like Roy Day and Herman Perry could not be all that sure.[25]

Challenging the incumbent, almost any incumbent, is usually quixotic; against someone like Voorhis the odds were even greater. Nixon's position was that of a political novice who undertakes a lost cause to either boost his legal career or establish himself in preparation for a serious race at some future date. Winning the June primary was largely a matter of the Republican voters endorsing the choice of the Committee of One Hundred, all of which still left him a long way from actually winning the seat. John Kennedy's simultaneous battle in Massachusetts had been contested; but he was then spared Nixon's need to defeat an established incumbent. Kennedy was already celebrated as a heroic son of the millionaire former ambassador to the Court of St. James's. His political debut made the contest on the West Coast appear relatively insignificant.

Nixon's situation was different in almost every way. Kennedy ran in what was tantamount to a one-party district. All he really had to do for November was to get out the normal Democratic vote, which was a pretty

routine matter for that well-entrenched political machinery. But Nixon
had to contend with an environment that was still "amateurized" by the
weakened party structure that dated back to the days of Progressive
reformers under the governorship of Hiram Johnson. For the forty years
after 1911, California's cross-filing system encouraged bipartisan fluidity
in voting, thereby weakening the power of the professionals. That less-
ened the importance of Voorhis's party affiliation. His personal standing
and usefulness to the district counted far more than any partisan label.
Nixon, very much a partisan Republican and plugged in to his party's
line on the viable issues of the day, had to supply reasons for replacing
a man with considerable popularity. Most of those who supported his
challenge were prepared to settle for giving Voorhis a good scare by
confronting him on the issues. But Nixon, who had been gauging his
opponent's soft spots ever since the fall, had no intention of settling for
a moral victory.

   Nor was there much that was moral about what happened. As important as the election was to his later reputation, Nixon's own recitation
of his "six crises" overlooks that campaign. So did most of the country
at the time. In the long run, what happened in 1946 became better
known. It was an event synonymous with sleaze, filled with maneuverings, replete with dirty tricks. As far as Voorhis was concerned, he had
the misfortune of being remembered less for his own career than as the
first "victim," his name almost interchangeable with Helen Gahagan
Douglas's. Except for Nixon's subsequent reputation, what happened in
California's Twelfth would have been indistinguishable from campaigning across the country to elect the Eightieth Congress. A far from inconsequential matter was that 1946 represented the first realistic
Republican opportunity to regain control over Congress, a dominance
that had been lost back in 1930.

   The combination of California, the land of exotica, and Richard
Nixon, the Catiline of American politics, made the later distortion inevitable. In effect, it was a way of maintaining group innocence by singling out the deviant. John Gunther's *Inside U.S.A.* argued that California
held "in microcosm the fundamentals of almost all American problems
from race relationships to reconversion, from the balance between pressure groups and the democratic process to the balance between factory
and farm." Then he added, in a passage that was both reassuring and
ominous, "If either Fascism or Communism should ever smite this country, it is more likely to rise first in California than in any other state."[26]
It is also perhaps notable that Gunther's more than nine hundred pages
of fact-filled text, which came out in the year after the election, made
not a single mention of the Nixon name.

   To use, for a moment, Gunther's concept of California as a microcosm,
how Nixon came to power illustrates less the malevolence of a single

man than the political consequence of the way America greeted the end of the Great Depression and World War II. The combination of the man and the region, the cultural conditioning of that part of the country at that moment in history, must be applied to recognition of how his career was born. Bruce Mazlish has already wisely noted that Nixon can best be understood against the "turbulent currents of California life, values, and politics."[27]

It is true that from the turn of the century the Pacific slope was, if anything, more agitated than anywhere else in the United States. During the two decades before Lenin reached the Finland Station, California was experiencing its own labor upheavals. The "terror" was enough to induce iron-fisted measures to preserve order. No single individual played the Romanov role better than Harrison Gray Otis, publisher of the *Los Angeles Times,* who was called by reformer Upton Sinclair in his book *The Brass Check* "one of the most corrupt and most violent old men that ever appeared in American public life," and by a more recent writer as "the most savage and effective enemy of labor unionism in the country."[28]

The repressions of an Otis have one thing in common with all repressions, whether imposed by governments or institutions: they betray insecurities; they reveal an inadequacy of consensual acquiescence behind those in power. Otis, in line with southern California entrepreneurs, imposed his "brass check" to keep labor in line. He led the creation of the Merchants and Manufacturers Association, which served as a vigorous counterunionization agency, complete with strikebreakers, special police, and scrutiny of the private activities of every worker. Otis, part of a small clique strong enough to manipulate the political climate for its own interests, was a powerful enough force to sell his methods to most other employers in Los Angeles. Central labor bureaus were set up for each industry. As Kevin Starr has written, Otis and his fellow businessmen "believed with passion and ruthlessness that Los Angeles must be kept an open-shop city with a plentiful supply of cheap industrial labor if it were to have any chance whatsoever of competing with San Francisco and the Eastern United States as a manufacturing center."[29] That was one form of response.

Californians reacted to such charges in various ways. To many romantics the state had become receptive to Edward Bellamy's concept of utopian nationalism. California's Populist party, with its ideas about public ownership, also had ideological links to Bellamy. At the same time, Populist candidates were on the ballots in many parts of the state.[30] To those with property and power to protect, the distinctions that separated such ideologies were moot. Either way, they constituted dangerous radicalism, especially when advanced by such labor movements as the Industrial Workers of the World (IWW).

In California, as elsewhere in the nation, there was evidence that the lower orders were becoming rebellious. The dynamiting of Otis's Los Angeles Times Building in 1910 killed twenty-one employees. That the explosion was planned to intimidate antiunion employees soon became clear.[31] The conspirators, two brothers, were given long prison sentences and more than fifty other unionists were subsequently indicted. An era of labor violence that had erupted with the Molly Maguires of the 1870s was continuing unabated. Capitalist rule was being challenged in a series of industrial clashes.

The most dramatic incident, and also the most damaging to labor, happened in San Francisco in 1916, when California had its own version of the Haymarket episode. Two radical labor activists, Tom Mooney and Warren Billings, were found guilty of killing ten and wounding over forty people when a bomb went off at a parade that promoted preparations for going to war. The affair was almost as celebrated as the Sacco-Vanzetti trial of a few years later, with both leftists and rightists exploiting the event for their own purposes. When Woodrow Wilson's America became a belligerent in World War I, the campaign against antiwar dissent provoked an even more intense reaction against radicalism, which, with President Wilson's active assistance, did much to destroy it.[32]

The battles were not only between labor and capital. The real issue was power. Businessmen were divided between "good government" reformers — that is, progressives — and conservatives who were normally supported by the regular Republican organization. The constant nightmare that got them to close ranks was a mutual fear of socialist government. Divisions in California were already startling. In San Francisco, organized labor was well entrenched and closely involved with the corrupt city government.[33] Otis and his allies were determined to give Los Angeles a different foundation.

Earlier, from 1870 until 1910, control in California, especially the southern part of the state, had been exercised, says historian George E. Mowry, by an "absolute dictatorship" under the Southern Pacific Railway Company, which had absorbed the tracks of the old Central Pacific. Frank Norris's famous novel *The Octopus* recalled how the wheat growers struggled against the greed of the railroad trust. Nowhere else, observed that English visitor Lord Bryce, had a single corporation aroused as much hostility. Between 1895 and 1910, fifty-seven of the seventy-nine rate cases that were argued before California's supreme court were decided in favor of the railroad. As late as 1916, the SP (as it was called) owned over half of one of the state's largest counties and major parts of several others. Maintaining power also meant controlling city machines, which was implemented through what one writer has described as a "Kremlin-like" political bureau. If, as has been written, California history was "one of revolt against Southern Pacific domination," that opposition represented the combined forces of a subservient majority, one consisting of labor and small businessmen. The revolt got behind Hiram Johnson and took him to the governorship in 1911. Johnson ran harder against the SP than against his opponent, and his first term has been called a Camelot for California progressives.[34]

By 1923, consistent with the national post–World War I mood, conservatives had just about routed all remaining progressives. Having won control, they were, as Earl Pomeroy has noted, "concerned more with excluding alien landowners, radicals, and imported goods, or simply with staying in office, than with advancing popular government and social welfare."[35] In 1934 they succeeded, even if only narrowly, in stopping Upton Sinclair's EPIC (End Poverty in California) movement. The state's political coloration underwent a more severe transformation than any other. Republicanism veered more toward establishmentarian respectability. Movements such as Sinclair's and Dr. Francis Townsend's California-based old-age pension scheme were ridiculed, together with various forms of populism, vegetarianism, calendar reformers, and esoteric religious zealots. A social democrat, Culbert Olsen, was elected governor in 1938, but it was very clear that the upper-middle-class progressivism of Hiram Johnson's day was past. Jerry Voorhis himself, a veteran of that EPIC campaign, had long since become more moderate. In 1946, the publisher of the *Los Angeles Times*, Harrison Gray Otis's grandson, Norman Chandler, was sold on Richard Nixon.

For Nixon, the backing was a godsend. For one, he was personally awed at being brought into the inner sanctum of the paper that, while not yet the West Coast leader it has since become, was nevertheless sufficiently dominant in the towns that surrounded Los Angeles. The *Times* was *the* paper of his and most other good Republican families of Whittier. Coming face to face with Norman Chandler and his influential wife, Buff, was exciting for a "small-town lawyer just out of the navy." The paper's support, he later acknowledged, was "tremendously important in assuring my nomination for Congress." He could have gone on about its value in promoting him over his rival, or virtually censoring the Voorhis viewpoint from its pages while heralding the younger man as one who was bringing "a brand of Americanism in our national political affairs which is unmixed by any other ideology; which sees clearly, thinks straight and deals squarely."[36] He was, in short, Norman Chandler's kind of candidate. He was ready for the conservative "Counter-Reformation," unafraid to hit hard at the federal bureaucracy, at communism, at the coddling of labor unions, at all the forms of socialism that were leading the Democratic incumbent by the nose.

Chandler's "find" was made by Kyle Palmer. The longtime political editor was known as Chandler's alter ego. A more recent writer has explained that Palmer "*was* the Republican Party" in the state of California. With the Chandlers ever-conscious of the Otis past, Palmer was less inhibited than his boss in using the paper as an instrument of political power.[37] The editor was closely connected to the Committee of One Hundred, which numbered a brother-in-law among its members. His circle included the well-to-do Pasadena set that had much to say about Twelfth District affairs. Moreover, the Chandlers were movers in state as well as national GOP politics.

While not quite the paper of Otis's day, neither was the *Times* as temperate as in later years. Once taken, its positions were hard-hitting. Palmer devoted most of his pieces to statewide politics and, that year, took on Helen Gahagan Douglas's race in the Fourteenth District, noting that she was favored "by the left-wingers and the Communists" and that the more moderate American Federation of Labor had refused to endorse her candidacy. Even in early October, when he put out an alarm about the power and the need to "counter-vote" the CIO-PAC (the Political Action Committee of the Congress of Industrial Organizations) by getting out the vast "independent" majority, his main concern was with the reelection of Senator William Knowland.[38]

Nixon's race was treated largely as local news, not worthy of frequent or prominent notice in the pages of the *Times*. Palmer, at that point, concentrated more on the issues that surrounded Nixon's efforts rather than on the personality himself. Long political preelection columns by that veteran reporter, for example, completely ignored the names of the Twelfth District's candidates.[39] During the nine months before election day, the *Times* mentioned Nixon in twenty-two articles and ran two pictures, an average of only one story about every two weeks, a count that includes "The Watchman" columns by writer Carlton Williams, whose enthusiastic references matched Palmer's.

The most obvious pro-Nixon bias was the virtual blackout of Voorhis's name. The congressman was mentioned in only eight items that were not directly connected with Nixon's campaign, and they were generally designed to remind readers that the incumbent was favored by the CIO and advocated federal control of water and power as well as a minimum wage law. Voorhis's rejection of Henry A. Wallace, vice president during FDR's third term, was ignored, but the paper did report that the New Dealer had included the congressman in his round of endorsements when he visited California.[40]

Adequate funding was a problem. Nixon's own resources totaled ten thousand dollars in savings. Half went for a down payment on a house in Whittier and the rest represented his financial stake in the campaign. It operated from a makeshift office in downtown Whittier with borrowed furniture, including an old leather couch contributed by Hannah Nixon. As Nixon advised Herman Perry, "The extent of our direct mailing, newspaper advertising and outdoor advertising and the effectiveness of our precinct work will depend upon whether we have sufficient funds available." Until he had enough money to buy civilian clothes, he began to campaign in his naval officer's uniform, which was not exactly the most attractive come-on for recent veterans.[41] For her part, in addition to spending her share of their savings, Pat also helped run the office, kept track of contributions, distributed literature, found ways to keep volunteers most useful, and played the candidate's wife's role by attending coffees in private homes. Nixon had to learn that money would be scarce until he became a winner. All this and logic support the contention of early Nixon biographers that, for all the subsequent publicity given to secret funds, the Lincoln Club, and the support given him by such local fat cats as Asa Call and C. Arnholt Smith, one can easily find better financed campaigns in various parts of the country. The Nixon campaign of 1946 *did* look like a shoestring affair.

There has been an exaggeration of his public relations apparatus for that campaign. It is true that Roy Day hired the services of Los Angeles lawyer Murray Chotiner and that his five-hundred-dollar fee was paid by the Committee of One Hundred. It is also true that Chotiner has since been celebrated as a political merchandiser, one of the earlier operatives who specialized in that field during the postwar era. He was the same Chotiner who became the Republican tutor, the man who toured GOP "political schools" in the mid-fifties and whose campaign guidelines became a primer that Democrats described as "probably one of the most cynical political documents . . . since Machiavelli's *The Prince* or Hitler's *Mein Kampf . . .* a textbook on how to hook suckers."[42] Chotiner's later reputation enabled Nixon's critics to further denigrate his 1946 campaign by depicting Chotiner as a sinister presence.

Even those who deny that Chotiner's role in 1946 has been blown out of proportion find it hard to say exactly what he did.[43] Chotiner did offer Roy Day some potentially useful advice about reaching people: When watching Nixon before audiences, keep your eyes on somebody about six or eight rows out and observe that person's reactions. Note what especially arouses interest.

"We wanted the audience to walk out blazing for Dick Nixon," recalled Day. "But Nixon knew what he wanted to say anyway, and he didn't need much help with his speeches. Nixon has a brain and knows what he is doing."[44]

Only later, because it became so closely associated with the start of Nixon's career, did California's Twelfth Congressional District seem so unique. It embraced the area around Whittier and also included such centers as South Pasadena, Pomona, San Marino, and Alhambra. Recent gerrymandering had virtually equalized the strength of the two major political parties. The preoccupations of the Twelfth were, in most ways, typical of what was going on elsewhere.

Most of all, it was a time of postwar change. In Massachusetts, the hero of *PT-109*, Jack Kennedy, mobilized other returning GIs into a new political force. Veterans were similarly active in the rest of the country. While the war they had just fought and won may have been the most justifiable defense of democracy, there was little to suggest that returning veterans were overflowing with idealistic enthusiasms. Their true aspirations were far simpler, much more in tune with people everywhere: they were eager to get on with deferred desires. Nor had the ideological implications of the war drastically upset biases of old. A War Department survey of returning veterans revealed hostilities toward blacks, Jews, and labor unions. Half the group studied predicted racial "trouble" within the next few years.[45] In California, there were additional sources of tension. Conflicts had been created by the continuous wartime migrations from the rest of the country and, with the end of the war overseas, the release of Japanese-Americans from "relocation" centers. The mixture of rivalries, resentment, impatience, and supernationalistic confidence was an easily exploitable force.

It was undoubtedly the best time for his opponents to do something about Jerry Voorhis. Few could argue that Voorhis had not served with distinction. In 1939, Washington newspapermen named him the most honest congressman and the fifth most intelligent among all representatives on Capitol Hill. His colleagues later cited him as the hardest-working member. Nixon himself wrote to a chief architect of the anti-Voorhis movement: "All agree that he is honest, conscientious and able."[46]

All that about Voorhis was known to Nixon. When he returned to Whittier after graduating from the law school at Duke, his own lawyer was Harold F. "Jack" Petee, who had been one of Voorhis's students at a private school founded by Voorhis's father at San Dimas, California. The older Voorhis had retired from active business and found "something far more worthwhile than stocks and bonds." When interviewed by the present author, Nixon recalled Voorhis as "a very fine man" but one who "just didn't represent the district. He was very ineffective — wasn't able to do much in ten years in Congress." The congressman's "one hundred percent labor backing was not an asset," Nixon said. "Labor was so extreme that they made it seem that they were against the interest of the average workingman."[47] Such comments are about as severe as any that Nixon has ever made about Voorhis. More surprising is the absence of personal recrimination by Voorhis, a matter of some wonder to those with knowledge of that 1946 campaign.

Nixon was a willing and eager instrument in the drive to dump Voorhis. That Voorhis was intelligent, honorable, hardworking, or nice had

very little to do with it. Neither was there much relevance to the imputations of ineffectuality, whatever their merit. The real fear of his
enemies was that either he or his ideas might ultimately *become* effective.
Jerry Voorhis's sin was that he was a free spirit, the son of a millionaire,
a genteel reformer, one whose ideological orientation incorporated a
succession of impulses antithetical to key commercial interests, both
within and beyond the Twelfth District. Still, it was true that he more
clearly belonged to mainstream liberalism of the Harry Truman type,
both in his attitudes toward organized labor and the intensifying conflict
with the Soviet Union. He alone among California's incumbent Democratic congressmen was not endorsed by the national political arm of the
left-wing CIO. As Nixon acknowledged to a Voorhis aide not long after
the election, "Of course, I knew that Jerry Voorhis wasn't a Communist."
The fact is that by 1946 the left regarded him as the least acceptable
liberal in the California delegation.[48]

Voorhis was far out in front of his constituents, especially where labor
was concerned. After Nixon had retired him from the House, Voorhis
advised the founders of the Americans for Democratic Action (ADA) to
"say that we are 'liberals' from the point of view of politics and 'progressives' from the point of view of economics." Still, during the campaign itself, as Nixon has pointed out, Voorhis wanted "to get off the
labor hook."[49]

The reason was simple. In the Twelfth, as in most of the country,
workers were not organized. Increasingly, they identified themselves less
as laborers or workers than as members of the middle class, and with
bourgeois life-styles. Such aspirations implied traditional instincts of independence, an inherent conflict with unionism.

Nixon used attractive appeals that tapped long-cherished values: patriotism, individual economic decision-making, and the belief that people
should be free to work as they saw fit to enhance living standards for
themselves and their families. As one member of the committee that
sought to replace Voorhis put it, even before Nixon was selected as their
candidate, "We do not have a large number of labor union voters and
are in a position to make forthright statements in the interest of the
general public and not simply organized labor." Two days before he got
the nomination, Nixon explained that he was being briefed by "friends
in Washington" on "*the red hot* labor question."[50]

He had concluded, he wrote to Herman Perry a short time later, that
so many "fellow travellers" were "wild about" Voorhis that it would be
foolhardy to take his recent "conservative" line very seriously. Nixon
also decided that the Voorhis voting record was in tune "with the most
radical element of the New Deal group. He is definitely lined up with
Congressman Vito Marcantonio of New York, [Frank E.] Hook of Mich-

igan and Helen Douglas of Hollywood whose political views are not open to doubt." However, he cautioned, Voorhis's popularity would make personal attacks on him backfire. Voorhis's difficulty "seems to be that he attempts to speak on every subject which comes up and consequently fails to concentrate on the issues which are important." His vulnerabilities would lead to defeat only if attacked by "a strong organization which embraced all factions of the party," and that, Nixon urged, must be done under "a progressive platform which will appeal to the rank & file as well as the regular party workers." Such a platform would preserve "our integrity as well because we shall only say what we believe and intend to do."[51]

Herbert Klein first met Nixon during that campaign and remained at his side for most of his political career. In 1946, Klein reported as news editor for the *Alhambra Post-Advocate,* one of the Twelfth District's community papers that enabled Nixon to dominate the local press coverage. Four decades later, Klein, speaking with his characteristic gentle tone and self-assurance, repeated what had long since become the Nixon party line: stories about communism in that campaign have been overblown. "Anticommunism was not really a major issue" during the battle. Nixon's stands were mostly "pragmatic." That pragmatism also led Nixon to appreciate "the importance of good relations with the press and [he] did well in cultivating them."[52]

But there was another party line, one spurred by subsequent interest in what Nixon did and did not do that year. By one account, Nixon had the "ill fortune to fall into the hands of the hobgoblin, fear-and-scare school of persuasion." Another has Kyle Palmer taking "Nixon under his wing in that campaign" and urging him "to hit hard on the anti-Communist line."[53] Such scenarios imagine Nixon as a Manchurian candidate selling his soul to multiple devils and smearing everybody left of center. In effect, then, Voorhis was brought down by strategies and issues formulated largely by the Committee of One Hundred, Murray Chotiner, and the top brass of the *Los Angeles Times,* which effectively lifts the matter from its contemporary setting and suggests that Nixon was the pawn of a devious and corrupt cabal of California rightists.

The record shows something more complex. Correspondence made available for exclusive use of the present study relegates the Chotiners and Palmers mostly to promotional work. The reality is that Nixon's own thorough preparation told him how to rally the anti-Voorhis vote, and, young as he was, his own experience as a debater and acquaintance with public affairs (especially after his stint with the OPA) equipped him with what it took to size up the situation. It would be more accurate to say that the historical moment rather than venality showed the way to victory. Or, as journalist David Halberstam has suggested, "It was a very bad time for a liberal congressman. The mood of the country, particularly in the West and the South, was shifting dramatically."[54]

To note that unfair tactics were common elsewhere that year, and along similar lines, does not justify what happened in the Twelfth. It does much for perspective, however, to realize the validity of Stewart Alsop's observation a quarter of a century ago that "Republicans all over the country were running, like Nixon, against the meat shortage and the CIO-PAC."[55] Hardly a competitive campaign in the nation that year failed to pick up the theme, which was further fanned by the press. A variety of domestic relocations, rivalries, and insecurities, underscored by rising international tensions and espionage stories, made it the most exploitable issue of all. Denials by the Nixon people that communism figured as an issue are disingenuous. *Not to have used it would have made their campaign exceptional.*

The combined trauma of strikes, rising prices, and shortages of food and durable goods heightened frustrations and helped to mobilize dormant antiunionism. Fearful of postwar job insecurity, frustrated by the loss of overtime pay in the face of serious inflation, and resentful that their wage increases had been subordinated to patriotism, workers walked off jobs in record numbers. Almost 5 million wage earners, representing nearly 120 million man-days of work, were involved in stoppages during the year following V-J Day. By the end of the year, the cost of living had gone one-third above pre–Pearl Harbor levels. Americans unaccustomed to labor power could easily view the crisis as almost revolutionary. Especially riled was the South, where the press of CIO organizers combined the specter of worker agitation with assaults against the economic and political disfranchisement of black workers.[56]

CIO organizers became equivalent in many minds to the Industrial Workers of the World (Wobblies), portrayed as radical, irresponsible, violent, un-American, unworthy of American democracy. Significantly, that perception was not confined to management or to antilabor sentiment in the general population. It was also the view of sizable numbers of workers themselves, both the organized and the unorganized. Members of the American Federation of Labor (AFL), the older and rival union movement, said they most objected to the CIO because it was run by Communists and radicals.[57]

But Communists had not taken over American workers, not even CIO members. Nationally, the rank-and-file and leadership was noncommunist, even vehemently anticommunist. Still, political realities were another matter, and so it was significant that no sector of American life was as much under Communist influence as organized labor. John L.

Lewis, by inviting their support in the 1930s, helped make the CIO the best — and therefore the most vulnerable — example.

In June 1941, when virtually all of western Europe was under Nazi control and Hitler was about to launch his blitzkrieg against the Soviet Union, 72 percent of Americans in lower income groups (1 percent higher than the overall average) were for banning membership in the Communist party. When, in mid-1946, the Gallup poll asked what they thought should be done with Communists in this country, almost half who expressed an opinion agreed that they should be either killed or imprisoned. Only farmers were more Draconian-minded than manual workers, the American proletariat. Over 58 percent of the latter, the very people CIO organizers wanted to enroll, favored jailing or capital punishment merely for being Red.[58]

When the fall campaigns began, the issue was intense. One man who had received serious thought as a potential Republican presidential contender, John Bricker, opened the senatorial campaign in Ohio by challenging the Democrats to "bring on your New Deal, Communistic and subversive groups. If we can't lick them in Ohio, America is lost anyway." In San Francisco, FBI director J. Edgar Hoover warned American Legionnaires that "at least 100,000 Communists were at large in the country." The Republican national headquarters distributed 683,000 copies of a thirty-eight-page Chamber of Commerce publication that charged that "practically all CIO unions readily support the PAC" and that the Communist party had direct control over the policies. Inevitably, the New Deal was singled out for having permitted a "Communist penetration of government" that helped lead to such examples of "appeasement" as the "cynical betrayal" at Yalta. The first order for an incoming Republican Congress should be to slam the door on further subversive infiltration of government. Charles Lucey, who covered the elections for the Catholic publication *America*, reported that he found "Communism as sharp an issue on the West Coast as on the Eastern Seaboard."[59]

Both publicly and privately, Nixon's position on the issues kept him within the party's center. At South Pasadena on September 13, the man who closed his political career in the process of achieving détente with the Soviet Union said that the United States had "no more business in [the] political affairs of Eastern Europe than Russia has in political affairs of Latin America. . . . We must settle now with Russia," he urged, "— the problem of peace — the bomb . . . the halt to aggression and an opportunity for all people to choose between democracy and Communism."[60]

Nixon's language that Friday bore an intriguing similarity to comments made just one day earlier by Henry A. Wallace in New York. The speech by the secretary of commerce, whose liberalism had long since made him an outcast among conservatives, told the United States, in effect, to cease meddling with the Soviet sphere of influence. He also called for settlement with the USSR. He went beyond Nixon by calling for something that many American businessmen had been urging ever since the end of the war, increased trade between the two countries. But Wallace's sin was in his mutual condemnation of Great Britain and the United States for helping to provoke the cold war.[61] His message also undercut a hard-line speech given by Secretary of State James F. Byrnes in West Germany just a few days earlier.

Those, of course, were not the only differences. The sponsorship for Wallace's speech that day was tied to the Political Action Committee of the CIO and to its nonunion membership arm, the National Citizens Political Action Committee (NC-PAC). His audience in New York's Madison Square Garden was too left-wing to tolerate any criticism of Soviet aggrandizement in eastern Europe, and such passages were greeted with boos and catcalls. Gilbert Harrison of *The New Republic* immediately applauded Wallace for believing, in Harrison's words, "that peace between the United States and Russia is possible and that competition between Russia and America for the loyalty of the peoples of the world can continue without leading inevitably to violent collision." He also interpreted Wallace's speech as a call for strengthening "the forces of freedom everywhere." Woodrow Wilson's one-time secretary of the navy, Josephus Daniels, congratulated Wallace for furnishing "the chart and compass for the ship of state." Nor were they, at that moment, alone in not interpreting Wallace's words as an apologia for the Soviet Union. The secretary was condemned by the Communist *Daily Worker* and by the *New York Daily News,* which said he had espoused the "peace ideals of the late President Roosevelt" while defending "the policies which are undermining those ideals."[62]

Nevertheless, the Wallace speech became a cause célèbre. His naïveté kept him from anticipating that it would both offend Byrnes and be understood as a condemnation of America's behavior. Liberal anticommunists also hit Wallace for equating U.S. reactions with Russian expansionism.[63] Moreover, delivered as it was before that particular audience, and combined with his reputation, newspaper headlines chose to emphasize that part of his message. Only one paper, a radical daily in New York, *PM,* printed the entire text. The greater the distance from his actual words, the more ominous his heresy appeared. Secretary Byrnes made a vigorous protest to the president. Truman, embarrassed because he had been shown the text for advance approval, forced Wallace's resignation.

The Wallace affair was too significant not to affect the ongoing political climate. In California, as elsewhere, much of that impact rested on distortions of what he had said and misrepresentations of reactions. The

Los Angeles Times, for example, confined Voorhis's reaction to his expression of regret that Wallace was "forced to leave the Cabinet." Readers of the *Pomona Progress-Bulletin* and the *Whittier News,* however, were informed that Voorhis was critical of the NC-PAC-sponsored speech and supportive of Secretary Byrnes.[64] In short, there was little rational middle ground, no forum left for weighing the relative merits of each side. The dialogue had become as polarized as the international situation itself.

That condition was quickly reflected by Nixon's campaign. Just four days after his own evenhanded comments in South Pasadena, the Twelfth District's Republican candidate turned up the anticommunist decibels. There "are those walking in high official places in our country," he said, "who would destroy our constitutional principles through socialization of American free institutions. . . . These are the people who would lead us into a disastrous foreign policy whereby we will be guilty of collusion with other nations in depriving the people of smaller nations the very freedoms guaranteed by our Constitution."[65] Nobody then doubted that he was talking about Henry Wallace. But Wallace himself had become a symbol of New Deal malfeasance; or worse, as Joe McCarthy later charged, "twenty years of treason."

Far from having been a nonissue, as Nixon's detractors would later claim, the matter of communism virtually submerged everything else Nixon was saying. Right from the start, he visualized an America that was dedicated to making the world free for entrepreneurs. Nor did he deny, as did the counterreformationists, that social service responsibilities must come with laissez-faire government, a necessity long since explained by Adam Smith himself. Nixon's call was for a federal government that presided as a guardian rather than engineer. He was talking to a nation for whom FDR "was virtually a god," and, as an early acquaintance pointed out, like that god Nixon had the capacity to arouse "very bitter hatred and animosity."[66] In his own way, Nixon's message was no less direct.

He labeled a "controlled economy . . . a failure" and hailed President Truman's "belated lifting of price controls on meat." A Republican Congress would solve the crisis brought about by the shortage of meat and housing. He called for legislation to outlaw jurisdictional strikes and for transferring rent controls to state and local governments, where they should be administered at "equitable" levels. A typical talking point, especially in pursuit of the veterans' vote, was that "America can best fulfill its obligation to the G.I. by maintaining a form of economic government where an opportunity is given him to do his job. The secret of American success and hope for the future is to give the G.I. a government that allows him to perform the kind of job he has determined to do without restricting him by regimentation."[67]

At the East Whittier Friends Church, he also spoke out for racial harmony. "Let us always remember," he said, "that we in America live under a form of government which recognizes that all men are born free and equal." Then, reciting the names of the most celebrated bigots of the day, Nixon added, "We must be vigilant against the doctrines of the [Theodore] Bilbos and the [Eugene] Talmadges and the Gerald L. K. Smiths, who are just as dangerous to the preservation of the American way of life on the one hand as are the Communists on the other."[68]

Such were the messages that have since been forgotten. If, as Nixon later contended, communism was not the main issue of the campaign, there can be little doubt that it was nevertheless highlighted as the major force behind the domestic discontent that led the GOP to choose "Had Enough?" as the party's campaign slogan. The real central issue, Nixon has written, "was the quality of life in postwar America," a point impossible to refute. But it was also a goal that could, at least theoretically, be reached via more than one path: by bringing New Deal reforms to where the general good would best be served by redistributing national wealth, or by unshackling the economy from those restraints already enacted by liberal Democrats. To argue against the insidious influences of communism, however, was an increasingly effective way of achieving the latter, and the two approaches were hardly mutually exclusive. The anti-Voorhis attacks became as explicit as the Nixon ads that said, "A vote for Nixon is a vote against the Communist-dominated PAC with its gigantic slush fund."[69] The battle between the free enterpriser and the gentleman reformer was a significant test of what the new age might bring.

Early in 1946, as early as that spring — even before the primaries — Jerry Voorhis was "assassinated," as one writer puts it, by his political "friends." The situation was full of ironies. Those who felt he had become too conservative, insufficiently tied to left-wing labor interests, had withheld renewing the approval that had been given to Voorhis by the CIO-PAC in 1944, the first year of its existence. Considering the additional circumstances that governed politics that year, as detailed above, one cannot know what might have happened if, at about the same time, Voorhis's backers in the local, southern California chapter of NC-PAC had not pressed their organization to give him its endorsement. What Voorhis's people then did about that virtual kiss of death remains incomprehensible. As late as September, almost a half-year later, in the words of one study of the 1946 campaign, they had "completely forgotten to tell him" about that potential source of embarrassment.[70]

How else to explain what seems inexplicable? The local committee's attempt to secure NC-PAC's endorsement, even though it was not given, was hardly less useful to Nixon than genuine support from the national headquarters of that organization or from the CIO-PAC itself. Technically, both groups were independent. But they did have overlapping directorates. They were both headed by Sidney Hillman, who died that summer. NC-PAC, founded two years earlier as a nonlabor counterpart of the CIO-PAC, was not Communist-dominated. Still, the prevailing political atmosphere made such distinctions moot, as was the line between a recommended endorsement and one actually granted.

No extraordinary political wiles were needed for Nixon's actions. They would be considered perfectly cricket for the Democratic rival of a popular Republican incumbent on Manhattan's Upper West Side. If the latter had been endorsed by a group within any one of a number of organizations — Birchites, LaRouchites, the Conservative party — with or without his knowledge or consent, for the challenger to cite that kind of backing would be considered routine politics. Nixon's conduct should thus not seem shocking, especially since Voorhis was on the CIO-PAC's favored list in 1944.[71] At the very worst, it was an example of partisan tactics by a challenger out to make the most of his opportunities. Had the incumbent been able to demonstrate repudiation of such sectarian sympathy, embarrassment might have been avoided. But that was what Voorhis failed to do. Not until events forced him to act did he take that step.

How Voorhis could have neglected to defend himself is beyond comprehension. As early as April, Nixon's campaign chairman, Roy Crocker, used the endorsement recommendation to question whether Voorhis was the "choice of a pressure group" or the "representative of all the people." One local paper cited the CIO connection by suggesting that it was somewhat ironical that Voorhis, though born "with a silver spoon in his mouth," was proposing "to represent the common man."[72]

The recommended endorsement was mimeographed and circulated internally in the local NC-PAC branch. Yet, only days later, Crocker said, "Now that the Political Action Committee has publicly endorsed the candidacy of Jerry Voorhis for Congress," thereby clearly referring to the new action rather than to what had happened in 1944. There was, in other words, public knowledge about what had happened even before the primary. Once he became Voorhis's head-on opponent, Nixon himself went on the attack. At a kickoff speech in La Puente, he suggested that it was time "to clean house in Washington." The committee that backed Voorhis was the same "left-wing group" that was headed by James Roosevelt and had preempted the state's Democratic party. Nor could Nixon have been much more direct than he was at a late August rally in Whittier when he said he welcomed "the opposition of the PAC, with its Communist principles and huge slush fund." Again in Whittier, on Labor Day, he welcomed the "challenge of the PAC."[73]

Voorhis answered Nixon on September 11, just twenty-four hours before Wallace's Madison Square Garden address. He denied that he had been endorsed by the CIO-PAC and cited an editorial statement by *People's World* that said he was "against unity with Communists on any issue under any circumstances." The papers carrying that refutation also reported a warning by Nixon's campaign manager that their side was "prepared to offer proof of the present congressman's endorsement by the PAC."[74]

Such exchanges, open as they were, make it hard to understand how Voorhis could have been caught off guard. He has since implicitly acknowledged that such use of his name could have been interpreted as an endorsement. When he heard about the Wallace speech, which had had NC-PAC sponsorship, he requested that the NC-PAC drop "whatever qualified endorsement" had been given. He had, in other words, waited from April until September, then acted only after the brouhaha raised by Wallace.[75]

He was still unprepared, however, for what was about to happen. Despite his front-runner advantage, despite Nixon's own reputation as a debater, it was a Voorhis challenge that set the stage for five platform confrontations. As it turned out, only the first really mattered.

They met on September 13, one day after the Wallace speech. The location was South Pasadena High School, in a community characterized by Paul Bullock in his analysis of the Nixon-Voorhis contest as "predominantly middle-class in population and a strong-hold of bitter-end bigots." Voorhis was left utterly on the defensive, holding a position, "whether he liked it or not," recalled Gerald Kepple, where he was "almost forced to defend the New Deal." Not quite Lincoln versus Douglas, but the event excited a small town in that pretelevision era. "There was no mud-slinging," Kepple added; "there was just straight-from-the-shoulder debating."[76]

The decisive challenge on that platform came from Voorhis, who attempted to rebut the statements about a CIO-PAC endorsement. He demanded "proof." Nixon had the goods. He also had the sense of theater. Dramatically, he placed the mimeographed NC-PAC recommendation in front of his opponent's face. "Voorhis was completely taken by surprise," one of his aides has conceded. Nor was he capable of disentangling the differences between the CIO-PAC, the national NC-PAC, and the local chapter. Nixon then made his point by offering enough evidence to show that distinctions were purely technical. Voorhis "fumbled and was flustered."[77]

He did not ever recover. He tried to disassociate himself from labor. He acknowledged that there was "at least a grave question whether the Communist Party does not exercise inordinate if not decisive influence over state and county organizations." When California Democrats invited Wallace to campaign in the state, Voorhis took to the air and said he would have no part of it. Nor would he brook opposition to Truman's foreign policies, pointing out that "so far Russia, and Russia alone, has remained adamantly opposed" to American initiatives. But Nixon had the issues, the press, the political climate, and the momentum. The Voorhis dilemma is best illustrated by the following excerpt from an editorial that appeared in two of the district's papers: "*Jerry is not a Communist* but not many members of the House have voted against more measures the Communists vigorously oppose than he. It takes a smart politician to get the support of the C.I.O. Political Action Committee in Washington and appeal to the voters at home as a conservative."[78]

Nixon also made effective use of ridicule. In mid-October, one of his newspaper ads denigrated Voorhis's work in Washington by claiming that only one of 132 public bills he had introduced in the last four years had actually been adopted. The reference was to something needed by the district's growers of rabbits. They had been under a price squeeze by the rising cost of feed without compensating increases of OPA price ceilings for their sale of the stock. Nevertheless, Nixon was able to lampoon Voorhis's sponsorship of the Rabbit Transfer Bill. "I assume you have to be a rabbit to have representation in the Twelfth Congressional District," he said at one of his face-offs against Voorhis. That brought the house down. "Voorhis slumped in his chair," Roy Day has reported. "From then on, he [Nixon] had him on the run. That was the ball game right there."[79]

Put out by Nixon's headquarters three days before the election was the accusation that Voorhis had been guilty of consistently voting "the Moscow-PAC-Henry Wallace line." Herb Klein's *Alhambra Post-Advocate* came out with a last-minute salvo. Just a week before the election, an editorial called "How Jerry and Vito Voted" linked Voorhis's record to Marcantonio's. Deceptively, readers were also given the matter-of-fact information that Marcantonio was a Communist.[80] Before the primary, Nixon had promised silence about the Voorhis-Marcantonio parallels he had been gathering; that is, until the "real campaign," and now, thanks to Klein, the Twelfth had the matter in its most explicit form.

Voorhis had been licked, anyway. The same tide that gave Republicans their biggest victory in the House since 1894 carried Nixon to Washington with 56.7 percent of the Twelfth District vote, a majority of 64,784 to 49,431. The *Los Angeles Times* hailed his achievement as "one of the outstanding Republican victories" in the state.[81]

Speaker of the House Sam Rayburn of Texas had predicted a "beef-steak election," an outcome decided by the price of beef and shortages of basic commodities. All, of course, were among the throes of reconversion to peacetime, which so bedeviled an often bewildered Harry Truman. Throughout the nation, moreover, organized labor's stalwarts were most vulnerable. People went to the polls to elect one antiunionist after another — John Bricker in Ohio, Zales Ecton in Montana, James

P. Kem in Missouri, Henry C. Dworshak in Idaho, George W. "Molly" Malone in Nevada, William Jenner in Indiana, and Joseph R. McCarthy in Wisconsin. There were also vehement endorsements for such sentiments as the one expressed by Republican National chairman Carroll Reece, who warned that a victory for "a Democrat-P.A.C. Communist ticket in November would restore the leftists" under Wallace "to their positions of influence in Washington."[82] All in all, it had the makings of a counter–New Deal revolution. For the first time since Roosevelt entered the White House, the Grand Old Party took control of both chambers of Congress, by a margin of 51 to 45 in the Senate and 246 to 188 in the House.

California would have done its share even without Nixon on the ballot. William Knowland, a Republican conservative, was returned to the Senate by winning 55 percent of the vote against Will Rogers, Jr., and Earl Warren, favored by Democrats as well as the GOP, won a second term as governor. Statewide, the party gained ten congressional seats.

The 1946 elections heralded more than a simple transition to a peacetime America. A possible political realignment, premature as it seemed at the time, was beginning to fall into place. Fissures were becoming evident in the old New Deal coalition, widening the cracks that had begun to appear before the war. Southerners were still Democrats to a man; more often than not, however, such loyalty owed more to tradition and the realities of power in Washington than love for what the Roosevelt people had wrought. "I believe we should begin down here to make plans," wrote Congressman Frank W. Boykin of Alabama. "Where would our Party be had it not been for the Solid South?"[83] Even some at the core of the party's northern urban and labor wing, especially Irish Catholics, had shown signs of disaffection for a decade. Fear of communism and the postwar map of Europe now brought additional misgivings.

Harold J. Laski, a prominent member of Britain's Labour party, commented on the American political scene by noting that liberalism under Truman had been insufficient to safeguard labor from the business resurgence. Nor had the left done much to influence his foreign policy. "New lines will have to be laid down," wrote Helen Fuller in *The New Republic,* "between the party proper and the special groups which Franklin Roosevelt welded into the New Deal." Truman, with one eye on the growing propaganda war overseas, issued an executive order establishing the President's Committee on Civil Rights, and with the other on defending his party's probity, began the process of rooting out the "disloyal" in government "to take the ball away from Parnell Thomas" and the Red-hunters in Washington.[84]

Such was the coming of the Age of Nixon.

6

The Game of Grub

THERE MUST HAVE BEEN mixed signals about what
Nixon intended to do once he got to Washington. Ola Florence Welch, remembering his anti–New Deal views and
watching him savage Jerry Voorhis, expected a traditional antilabor,
probusiness conservative. Others, who were not as close to him personally, had different expectations. Judith Wingert Loubert, the daughter
of Jeff Wingert, Tom Bewley's law partner, was a liberal and friendly
toward labor. Her political discussions with Nixon did not discourage
Loubert from believing that Nixon "was going to be a champion of the
underdog and the poor man." The reality was something else, she told
an interviewer halfway into his presidency. Her old friend too often
"sided with the companies rather than what would have been for the
general good of the population." There were also those ex-classmates
such as C. Richard Harris who dismissed Nixon as an "opportunist,"
implying not only that he had become something of a political turncoat
but that he had abandoned his natural progressivism. Paul Smith's 1977
interview stressed that "he was a liberal in a conservative sort of way."[1]

As a freshman, Dick Nixon was among those who assumed that governmental custodianship, necessary while licking a depression and absolutely essential in wartime, ought to be temporary. Once such
emergencies were over, the essential national purpose had to be restored.
Government should then quickly reaffirm that extraordinary powers
were valid only for extraordinary circumstances. As Nixon wrote in late
1945, there could then be a return to "the true principles of the American
constitution," which was nothing less than unleashing the nation's "in-
ventive genius and industrial know-how" that had made for greatness.[2]

His views did not change much once he reached Capitol Hill. If anything, they were reinforced by what happened in Washington, the climate of the country, and the sources of his support. He never parted

from regarding the New Deal as crisis legislation, an essential need whose purpose had come and gone.

He had surprisingly little argument with the goals — but many misgivings over programs that had abdicated responsibilities to the federal government. Nixon acknowledged that any sort of rapid pullback could unsettle the economy, which did not mean that postwar America could afford to neglect making modifications. Ralph de Toledano long ago noted that he "never believed in repealing the entire New Deal." Even a highly critical overview of his congressional career has used the word "magnanimous" to describe his attitude toward farmers, workers, pensioners, and the downtrodden. Such was not the outlook of a reactionary or counterrevolutionary.[3] He shared with FDR's critics the belief that the New Deal, however noble in conception, was in the long run a flawed effort to remake American social and political institutions.

Three recurring Nixon themes were evident from the outset of his public career: the encouragement of individual enterprise, protection of those with modest means from economic hazards as the nation bumped along through the uncertainties of reconversion, and a consistent sense of nationalism and realpolitik in dealing with the rest of the world.

As with any other politician, the Nixon record betrays inevitable inconsistencies. Many involved accommodating constituencies and other political pressures. Along the way, however, myths developed about "new" Nixons. Once again, such perceptions conceded that he was a man of ability but had finally seen the light. In fact, it was an absence of dogmatism that enabled him to respond according to the demands of each situation. Assumptions that he was a hard-shell conservative encouraged the belief that his principles were up for grabs. At the outset he favored the extension of government controls on rents and supported the need to back the construction of additional housing units. His "practical liberalism" also embraced such still touchy human rights matters as abolishing poll taxes (which must be acknowledged as having been a safe position for the Twelfth) and admitting displaced persons from Europe (less secure, dependent on which persons and where they might settle).[4]

From the start, he was far too involved with what he was doing and too well along in becoming, in the words of an early biography, that "dynamic young Republican . . . with a penchant for hard work" to believe that he ever lacked a compass or that he arrived in Washington without a "philosophy of politics."[5] He knew his mind at least as well as any freshman who entered Congress with the class of '46, which also marked the first postwar coalition of northern Republicans and southern Democrats. Not only did they constitute a conservative majority, but they provided a congenial political environment for the freshman from California.

He settled in at the capital both eager and secure about his goals. He and Pat took over an unfurnished apartment in nearby Virginia. Their rent came to eighty dollars a month, which was just about what they could afford. Ignoring the temptations of an environment dominated by the power of money and connections required the saintliness of a Hannah. He could hardly help but note the contrast between his own origins and those who, with less talent, drive, or intelligence, enjoyed the advantages of privilege. Writer Jessamyn West has suggested how being placed in that situation fed resentments about his disadvantages. At their first meeting, Clare Boothe Luce recalls how she was "a little startled by the intensity and passion with which he talked." He was an "enormously tense and keyed-up character."[6]

No contrast was more vivid, and potentially galling, than his early view of Jack Kennedy. From that first month in the Congress and for the rest of his career, Kennedy was a figure who was never very far from the Nixon mind.[7] The wealthy, glamorous young war hero from Boston and Harvard was sworn in together with the serious, almost puritanical thirty-four-year-old from southern California. Kennedy's station in life made him successful by definition. He was Nixon's foil, a wealthy young bachelor, son of a former ambassador to Britain, whose wartime adventures in the South Pacific were publicized in ways not possible for other brave servicemen, who often remained uncelebrated. Even the *Los Angeles Times*, which had virtually overlooked Nixon's own victory, had managed to find a front-page spot to report young Kennedy's election. Kennedy, in the words of one writer, "was the Nixon that Nixon longed to be."[8]

Kennedy had hardly arrived in Washington when his father's manipulative powers made him one of the U.S. Junior Chamber of Commerce's "ten most outstanding young men of the year." Unlike the freshman from California, he took his seat almost as a natural right. It was beside the point that he was indifferent and bored, only too happy to turn responsibilities over to his office staff. His physical distresses, including Addison's disease, were not well known, but his lethargy was hardly a secret on Capitol Hill. The gay young bachelor was also a dedicated skirt-chaser. He had a staff to cover up for his absences and assignations. When he was at work, his mind was elsewhere. Once, under criticism for being gone from his office for long stretches, he said to his secretary, "Mary, you'll just have to work a little harder." His friend, newspaperman Charles Bartlett, has recalled that Jack Kennedy "wasn't a member of the House team," a modest acknowledgment from a loyalist.[9]

The differences between Kennedy and Nixon were important. Nixon was healthy, ambitious, and undistracted. Nary an apologetic word can be found attributing incompetence and ignorance to his youth. He won early attention for dedication and absorption in his work, qualities that became more obvious during that freshman term. With one stroke, for example, he leapfrogged over most other novices on Capitol Hill with a move reminiscent of his college days. He became a prime organizer of the Chowder and Marching Society, the Capitol Hill version of the Orthogonians. The greenest of the novices engineered his own inside coterie. As at Whittier, the Nixon initiative created a political base, one that shared support, information, and access to congressional influence. The group of junior Republicans, which held regular meetings to plan strategy and arrive at decisions about pending legislation, included such future players in Nixon's career as Kenneth Keating, Thruston B. Morton, and Gerald R. Ford.

Making the most of his opportunities, he realized that the levers of power, Kennedy's by inheritance, were not attainable unless he showed he could utilize his circumstances to serve his interests. Kennedy came from money. Money would have to go to Nixon. Kennedy's congressional career earned a gentlemanly C; Nixon's was far more distinguished, but he made his mark by risking the perils of notoriety.

One was a Democrat and the other a Republican. Their constituencies were a continent apart and further separated by striking cultural contrasts. Had they swapped congressional districts, their voting records on Capitol Hill would have been interchangeable. Geography, culture, and sociology wrote the script. Had Kennedy represented Nixon's district, there is no doubt, for example, that he would have voted for the controversial Labor Relations Act of 1947, known as the Taft-Hartley Act. Each had to become less of what he was later to be, for reasons that were predetermined.

Both men were representative of those who came to maturity right after the war. Inevitably, many were veterans eager to forget the recent past and to participate in the great new era of high expectations. Whether in Massachusetts or California, their aspirations were similar. The differences lay in the sociological character of their rock-bottom support. A Dave Powers, for example, was an unemployed Irishman from Charlestown who survived as a member of the "52/20 Club," which meant that, as a discharged serviceman, he was entitled to fifty-two weekly separation allowance checks of twenty dollars each. Between the Bunker Hill Monument, which towered above the working-class three-deckers, and the relic of American liberty moored nearby, the U.S.S. *Constitution*, were the docks of Boston Harbor. The odds were overwhelming that Dave and his neighbors would never advance beyond the daily need to find work as longshoremen. "We were 'townies' and we lived in these three deckers — the Sullivans in the first and the Murphys in the second and the Daughertys at the top," he reminisced when asked to explain his life when he became an early campaign worker and then an aide and sidekick of Jack Kennedy. "But what a wonderful life we had: we thought we were rich, and it was only because we were all as poor as each other and shared in that."[10] Dave, connecting as well as he did with young JFK, was far more fortunate than most. There were also the Ed Berubes, Tom Brodericks, "Yammy" DeMarcos, "Patsy" Mulkerns, Billy Suttons, Joe deGuglielmos, and Clem Nortons. Mostly working-class, and often picaresque, they included those who had earlier been represented by James Michael Curley and later became the constituents of Thomas P. "Tip" O'Neill and Joseph P. Kennedy II.

Nixon's veterans were different. They were much more likely to have come from the officer class. In the immediate postwar period, their link to federal support was more often for matriculating at places like the University of Southern California with the aid of the GI Bill. They were far from the 52/20 Club world and were closer to those later to be known as yuppies.

Pat Hillings, for example, was, like Dave Powers, an Irish Catholic. Hillings and Nixon, however, came together not at the door of a three-decker apartment but while Hillings was a law student at the University of Southern California. Young Pat was an active campus Republican, formed a Young Republican Club in his hometown of Arcadia, and then chaired the Los Angeles County chapter. He went to work as a kind of aide-de-camp at Congressman Nixon's Whittier office. At the age of twenty-eight, Hillings was elected to Nixon's vacated seat and became the youngest congressman ever elected from southern California. He went on to serve four terms, all the while keeping his ears available for Nixon on the state of California politics.[11]

William Price was also a lawyer, with an office in Newport Beach. Price, like Hillings, got to know Nixon in 1947 while in law school. "A group of us established the first Young Republican Club on the USC campus," he said. "Bob Finch had set one up at Occidental and showed us how to do it." The Young Republicans were mostly war veterans. They were on the GI Bill. Their basic concern, however, was not with "American Legion type of bread-and-butter issues." Price added, "We felt like we were the younger group with an opportunity to do something." Like the Kennedy people, they were also concerned about unions, but they viewed organized labor as a negative power.[12]

While both Price and Hillings were veterans, they still belonged to the same generation as Harry Robbins "Bob" Haldeman. Precocious, even with a touch of genius, Bob Haldeman as a boy was nevertheless sent to a private military school for "straightening out." He came out of that training with "a zest for regimen and rigid command structure."[13] He also "found himself" in enough time to graduate cum laude and to go on to UCLA with honors.

Unlike Price and Hillings, Haldeman did not reach military age during the war, but he got at least a remote taste of what was going on by serving two active years in the navy's V-12 training program at UCLA, where he majored in marketing. He also led the campus Christian Science organization and was president of Scabbard and Blade, the national military honorary fraternity. Haldeman was still at college and had just turned twenty when Nixon won his first election, and his graduation coincided with the congressman's reelection for a second term.[14] Haldeman's military bearing, severe crewcut, and reputation for austerity later made him the darkest of the dark villains who occupied the Nixon White House. Any talents for humor, charm, and frivolity on the part of Haldeman — and they were considerable — were hidden from the public by a media veil that concentrated on his "Prussian" severity.

As chief aides to President Nixon, Haldeman and John Ehrlichman, a fellow Christian Scientist friend from UCLA days, became associated in the public mind as Nixon's Rosencrantz and Guildenstern, unquestioning apparatchiks, ready to carry out a putsch if the boss desired. Someone once commented that the only difference between the two was that there were times when Ehrlichman was human. If, as has been suggested, Ehrlichman's rise was "evolutionary," Haldeman's was "inevitable."[15]

Haldeman's family was well above conventional middle-class respectability. Third-generation Angelenos, they had long been prominent in the city's civic and business life. Harry Haldeman, Bob's paternal grandfather, helped to organize the Better America Foundation during the post–World War I Red scare, thereby joining patriotic vigilance against Communists "overrunning" the United States. His civic standing was bolstered as a charter member of the Uplifter's Club and founder of the Hollywood Bowl. Bob's father was one of those whose business sense helped him escape the great stock market disaster and even reach greater prosperity during the depression. In the 1950s, his mother, by then a resident of Beverly Hills, was named woman of the year by the *Los Angeles Times* for her work in connection with the Hollywood Bowl, the Southern California Symphony Association, and welfare activities.[16]

To dismiss Haldeman, as some writers have, as just another public relations man "uninterested in ideological persuasions" overlooks Nixon's attractions for ambitious young men. He was bright, efficient, conservative, Republican, and ready for a career in a new age. His graduation from UCLA and association with the J. Walter Thompson advertising agency coincided with the rising reputation of the congressman from the Twelfth District. He remembers how he was attracted by Nixon's "basic free enterprise and limited government philosophy." He also found himself "fascinated" with the Hiss case, which helped establish Nixon's anticommunism more firmly and drew Haldeman's enthusiastic support. Haldeman was assigned to the Thompson office in New York City when Alger Hiss was indicted and went to trial. Nixon thereafter became Haldeman's hero, an astute and responsible sentinel against communism. Haldeman, who attached himself to the politician's 1956 campaign staff, later recalled Nixon's fear that Joe McCarthy was doing the cause more harm than good.[17]

That, of course, was the common cause of Nixon and Kennedy, the tangible threat to the American future. Kennedy himself lost no time exploiting the issue on Capitol Hill. His efforts, as a member of the House Labor Committee, in securing perjury indictments of two Communists who were United Auto Workers Union officials was hailed as "the opening skirmish between Congress and the American Communist Conspiracy." A *Boston Herald* political writer credited him with flushing out a "conspicuous traitor to this country."[18] There was no doubt that the birth of the Eightieth Congress, rather than the zeal of any single individual, inaugurated what became the new Red scare. While often seen as a bipartisan issue, the initiative was primarily with the Republicans. Strong beliefs fused with good politics. The perception of a Communist espionage apparatus, substantially borne out by later courtroom convictions, automatically placed Democrats on the defensive, as tarred with charges of subversion as Hoover had been deemed responsible for the Great Depression. Once his own anticommunism had bolstered his political standing, Nixon began to attract assistance from the rich and powerful. Helpful support came from the *Los Angeles Times* leadership, which sealed his connections with much of California's power structure.

Then there were people like Dana Smith and Asa Call. Smith was a Pasadena tax lawyer who became visible locally as treasurer of Nixon's 1950 campaign and prominent nationally, as it turned out, for his association with a special fund to help alleviate cash burdens. Well connected in southern California corporate circles, he was the namesake of what has been called "the informal Dana Smith clique," which was involved in real estate, oil, public utilities, and banking. Call, an insurance magnate, was probably more important for his connections than his wallet. A dominant power in Los Angeles business circles, he was a confidant of governors, senators, and presidents. Frank Jorgensen guessed that Call must have often said to candidates, "I'll raise you a number of dollars if I can get it." And, added Jorgensen, "He could usually get it, all right." Such men were but a handful among those who later emerged as Nixon's sponsors, alleviating financial woes and promoting conservative political positions. Through Kyle Palmer and Norman Chandler, Nixon also connected with such other figures as Leonard Firestone, Justin Dart, Louis B. Mayer, and Al Glock, then chairman of the Bank of America.[19]

All that was part of the escalation process, part of an experience common to virtually every politician, at whatever level of power. For a young man showing such promise of rising, rich backers were obviously attractive. Nixon's anticommunism and free enterprise politics made the admiration mutual. As he became better known, there was no shortage of "volunteers" to be helpful. "The pace was important," John Ehrlichman has pointed out. "You won't vault from being a congressman in Whittier overnight. From there it goes up. This was a progressive kind of thing, and Nixon got used to their favors incrementally."[20]

No other common ground was as hidden, and productive, as the Bohemian Club, which began in 1872 as a far western cultural oasis, a watering place for San Francisco literati. Such late nineteenth-century writers and thinkers as Ambrose Bierce, Mark Twain, Bret Harte, Charles Warren Stoddard, Jack London, Henry George, John Muir, and Joaquin Miller socialized there with journalists and mingled with distinguished visitors who had found their way across America. Among the latter were Rudyard Kipling, Lord Bryce, Anthony Trollope, Henry James, and Oscar Wilde.[21]

But the literati began to fade away as one century gave way to another. The commerce of the growing nation transformed the California mainstream, with frontier joie de vivre gradually becoming consumed by corporate joie de vivre. The remaining artists and writers were more likely ornamentations for a new class of financiers, lawyers, oil barons, insurance leaders, and industrialists, together with a scattering of like-minded academics and university presidents. Whether at the club or at the wooded Grove, the 2,700 acres of land covered by California redwoods sixty-five miles north of San Francisco, the well connected became better connected. One sociologist found that a single Bohemian Club outing contained representatives from forty of the fifty largest industrial corporations in the country.[22]

They came from all over to participate in the elaborate rituals and amusements of the all-male environment. One of the more than one hundred subdivisions, or camps, at the Grove, called Poison Oak, featured a Bull's Balls Lunch, where members feasted on delicious testicles transported from newly castrated herds in central California. Elaborate one-night productions cost as much as twenty-five thousand dollars back in 1934. Two-week summer encampments under the giant trees, at the center of which was a beautiful natural amphitheater at the edge of a lake, included a "funeral procession" for the Cremation of Care, a mock banishment to the flames, complete with a dirge, torchbearers, and wearers of red hoods and red flowing robes. "It was the Grove," wrote Richard Reinhardt, "that infused the Bohemian Club with that peculiar mixture of playfulness and pomp, intimacy and grandeur, that differentiates it from any other men's club in America."[23]

Intimacies shared apart from the outside world were the oaths of equality and fraternal ties assuring bonding that would inevitably carry over into the real worlds of business, politics, and government. Membership in the Bohemian Club became a social register. Guest invitations were an exclusive honor. So it was, too, with high-priced entertainers, for whom the privilege of performing before so august an audience was assumed to be sufficient payment. One student of ruling-class cohesiveness in America has observed that "the real spirit of this Bohemia is a *quid pro quo* arrangement between the rich and the talented. The rich patrons, through their wealth, provide a setting within which the creative members can exercise their talents and enjoy the amenities of a first-rate men's club." And all was done with great care to keep such activities hidden from the outside world. Nixon's memoirs, for example, note that his favorite speech, and what he later regarded as "the first milestone on my road to the presidency" was delivered at the Grove in July 1967 and so "received no publicity at the time."[24]

But the club was more than that. It was not a place for just any politician. One had to have cachet; the Bohemian Club was reserved for movers and shakers. Leonard Hall, for example, was a close New York political ally of Nelson Rockefeller. He had also served six terms in the House and had been chairman of the Republican National Committee. None of that was enough to win him a trip to the Grove, let alone membership. He failed to make the grade until the summer of 1961, and that was made possible by former vice president Nixon. "I had heard a lot about the Grove," he wrote in appreciation, "and it lived up to all my expectations."[25] Hall's gratitude is especially revealing, as it emphasizes the relative absence of career politicians. One compilation of members included just one active politico, Richard Nixon. That he was then president of the United States was only incidental.

Nixon made Bohemian early. In January of 1950, the Grove was the site of a fund-raiser for his forthcoming Senate campaign against Representative Helen Gahagan Douglas. His next visit was the following July. There he first met General Dwight D. Eisenhower. Both men were the luncheon guests of longtime member Herbert Hoover. Of the others present at the Hoover camp, only Republican National Chairman Guy Gabrielson was still active in politics. They were all guests of Cave Man, one of Bohemian's "heavy" camps.[26] In 1953, shortly after Nixon became vice president of the United States, he won membership and became a Cave Man.

The Grove, Nixon said in 1984, is a place where "East and West mingles," where the establishment of the Atlantic could meet the establishment of the Pacific.[27] During his presidency, key aides were encouraged to go there as guests. It was as important as traveling to the periodic meetings of the Business Council at Hot Springs, West Virginia.[28] Among their ranks, there were few profound differences about the direction desired for American society. If not all were card-carrying Republicans, their collective conservativism had been well established and unquestioned. Nixon's association with the Bohemian Club helped to stake out his position in the coming battles for power.

Before Pearl Harbor, there were but tentative foreshadowings of the great debate: whether to complete the New Deal agenda or to retrench, take stock of the Roosevelt excesses, and, as Hoover had argued and now Nixon, among others, was repeating, remove the threats to the basic principles of American freedom. Almost simultaneously, another decision had to be made: Had the new lesson of war been to avoid overseas intervention? Or had the experience demonstrated the foolhardiness of the ostrich approach? Over forty years later it would become hard to remember that there was no clear consensus when Richard Nixon first went to Washington. Nor, in the matter of foreign policy, did the interventionism–noninterventionism debate clearly distinguish between left and right. As Nixon had already discovered, even while preparing to compete for a congressional seat, both liberal and conservative Americans were becoming more convinced about the Communist threat.

There was, for example, no shyness about anticommunism on the part of the founders of Americans for Democratic Action. They, too, were in Washington in January 1947, the very month Nixon was sworn in as a member of the Eightieth Congress. That band of liberals included one newly unseated congressman, Jerry Voorhis of California. Acting in the wake of Henry Wallace's departure from the Truman cabinet and subsequent formation of the Wallaceite Progressive Citizens of America, they launched their new organization by staunchly excluding Communists. The exclusion was, in part, a conscious sanitization. One of the founders, Reinhold Niebuhr himself, pointed out that "we cannot have a progressive movement tainted by a suspicion of another loyalty."[29] That stand combined with support for President Truman's cold war policies later brought rebuke for having helped to exacerbate international tensions.

Nixon drew committee assignments that quickly helped to establish his political identity. All were concerned with issues of potential headline caliber, labor and internal security. Little else was as volatile in 1947 as the matters that were handled by the Education and Labor Committee and the House Committee on Un-American Activities. By his first summer, he was able to add another plum, membership in the Herter Committee, which was delegated to scout out the feasibility of the plan outlined by Secretary of State George Marshall for financial assistance to western Europe. Not bad for a freshman. He had made his connections.

Not that Nixon's access was extraordinary, but it did predate his arrival. His military contract work at Baltimore had made it easier to visit Capitol Hill and consult with Republican congressional leaders. Ballots from all 533 precincts of the Twelfth had hardly been counted when Herman Perry took advantage of the young man's earlier groundwork and new success by writing to Joseph Martin, the incoming speaker in the Eightieth Congress. "I trust that you will personally take an interest in him," wrote Perry, "as he has a promising future and considerable drive and ability." Martin's response was polite, routinely political, without, as might be expected, any specific commitments. Whether or not any assistance from Perry was needed, Martin was helpful. He may or may not have had that in mind when he later complained about ingratitude, but there is no doubt that he set the freshman on a productive course.[30]

Assignments to key committees were, of course, instrumental for success as a legislator. In Nixon's case, his memberships did all that and more. They helped to establish identifications that remained with him for the rest of his career.

In mid-February, the same day he made his maiden speech on the House floor, he and Pat went to the White House for the first time, to a reception for freshmen being hosted by the president. In July, he and three colleagues were back at the White House for a private meeting with the chief executive. Nixon later recalled Mr. Truman's "hominess, his democratic attitude, and his sincerity," but also his perplexity in trying to figure out Soviet objectives. "The Russians are like us," said the president while turning a globe with his hand. "They look and act like us. . . . As far as I'm concerned, they can have whatever they want just so they don't try to impose their system on others."[31]

Only a few months earlier, on March 12 — three days before Richard Nixon was admitted to practice before the U.S. Supreme Court — the president had delivered a portentous warning about the importance to the western world of providing military equipment to Greece and Turkey, who were fighting Communist rebellions. The speech, enunciating what became known as the Truman Doctrine, at least temporarily outflanked critics of Democratic "softness" toward communism while, at the same time, undercut those who still hoped for a U.S.-Soviet dialogue. Little wonder that events coinciding with Nixon's legislative debut have been described by one historian as "circumstances that made the nation so restless."[32]

Right from the start, Nixon moved into the heart of the major issues of his time. He later recalled that one of his committee choices, Education and Labor (his second pick after Judiciary), was determined by "the knowledge that the problem of labor-management relations would become one of the most important to confront Congress that year — one with which the entire citizenry would be vitally concerned." He was, of course, right. Few problems seemed as central to the process of restoring the nation to peacetime pursuits. But, as Nixon was also learning, while the special problems of American workers had little to do with the Russians, popular thought often linked unionism to communism. By the time he reached Washington to take his seat, the association had become even more potent. Harry Truman, reacting to the disastrous midterm elections of 1946 and under continuing pressure to do something about internal security, had just appointed a commission to look into the loyalty question. Nor did the new Congress ever stray far from that issue. Its landmark labor legislation of 1947 called for each officer of a labor union seeking a hearing before the National Labor Relations Board to file an affidavit saying that "he is not a member of the Communist Party or affiliated with such party, and that he does not believe in, and is not a member of or supports any organization that believes in or teaches, the overthrow of the United States Government by force or by any illegal or unconstitutional methods." After just one full year of peace, euphoria and hope had deteriorated into skittishness, anxiety, and contention. Gallup pollsters who had shown 82 percent approval for Truman in November 1945 reported that the figure was down to 35 percent by early 1947.[33]

But, as usual, the coming of a new year induced wishful thinking. In Times Square, the New Year's Eve crowd, defying frigid winds from across the Hudson River, was the liveliest since the one that had gathered before Pearl Harbor. For the second year in a row, the wartime brownout was gone; bright neon signs delineated the giant triangular plaza. On Broadway, *Life with Father* was in its eighth year and Jerome Kern's *Show Boat* was winding down. Such stars as Ingrid Bergman, Zero Mostel, James Stewart, Katharine Hepburn, Robert Taylor, Cary Grant, and Judy Garland were all appearing in popular films.

As midnight approached, eyes moved upward toward the tall Times Tower. Along its turrets overlooking the mob below, Tom Ward worked at the job he had been doing for thirty-two years. Aided by two assistants, he prepared to lower the giant ball. As his helpers stood by the halyards used to guide the four-and-a-half-foot, quarter-ton ball from the rail of the turret, Ward waited until a few seconds before midnight and finally shouted, "Let 'er go!" The great ball, its incandescent lights flashing six-foot figures that read "1947," moved downward to what observers thought was the greatest roar and din from horn, bells, and whistles since 1940. Brief flurries of confetti followed from nearby hotel and office windows.

Even at that moment of celebration, uneasiness was just beneath the surface. Horns sold for fifty cents, half the previous year's price. Throughout the Times Square area, novelty shops had adjusted prices to more modest levels. Not many New Year's revelers could afford thirty-five dollars per couple to celebrate at El Morocco, or the fifteen dollars a person for Waldorf-Astoria dinner parties, or the five dollars in its Peacock Alley café. Bargain-hunters could take advantage of the situation by finding reduced prices for scotch, bourbon, and rye, which had generally been overstocked, or, if they went to the right place, they could buy martinis for forty cents instead of a dollar and a quarter. At the information booth north of the Times Tower, a police captain told a reporter, "They know they're going into 1947 with most of their major problems unsolved. You can see it in their faces. These are not the goons of the pre-war days. People are getting some sense, even in their celebrations."[34]

Trouble spots were readily apparent. The *Times* was running a series of articles about how Soviet propaganda was spreading throughout Latin America. Palestine was being rent by increasingly serious terrorism. The incoming chairman of the House Committee on Un-American Activities, J. Parnell Thomas, was somewhat up in arms because of a premature (premature, that is, because it was released before he could get the credit) report detailing a "conspiracy" to promote a Communist revolution in America by wrecking the economy.[35] Senate Republicans, joined by northern liberal Democrats, were organizing themselves to challenge the seating of Mississippi's Theodore Bilbo, considered by many of his colleagues a demagogue and racist.

That little bit of drama escaped the immediate notice of Mr. Truman, whose attention was on the latest, and most promising, new advance in communications. From his Oval Office desk, he was able to watch the first video report from Capitol Hill. The pictures on his television screen showing the opening of the Eightieth Congress came from two Image Orthocon electronic cameras, the latest technological marvel. They were sharp enough so that a bandage on a finger of the House tally clerk could be seen clearly as the image went out over coaxial cables to stations as far away as Philadelphia and New York. The show left the air after the new speaker, Joe Martin, had completed his address. But the few who were able to watch with Mr. Truman heard congressional leaders hail the importance of the new medium in bringing to the American people firsthand views of their government in action.[36]

Thus began the duel between the president and the Republican-controlled Eightieth Congress, before long to become, in Walter Karp's phrase, "necessary enemies," each baiting the other, each exploiting mutual political advantages. No single problem, not even communism, the developing cold war, or the cost of living, divided Americans as heatedly as the labor situation. The most serious of the strikes had passed, but the need to redress the "prolabor imbalance" created during the New Deal was encouraged by a public that was convinced — by the press as much as by its own perceptions — that unions had gotten out of hand. The odds mounted against organized labor and its staunchest friends, ideological liberals and the Wallaceites of the far left.

Those who were looking for a mandate to reverse labor's gains had it, as clear a signal as the public usually gives. Unrest by workers was reported by a Gallup survey as the number-one problem, well ahead of the next most troublesome matters, international relations and inflation. Fully half of those surveyed agreed that workers were not entitled to more pay. When respondents were asked to rank what bothered them most, the survey produced the following objects of general dissatisfaction: the high cost of living, housing, shortages of consumer goods, and family troubles, especially health. Two-thirds of employees themselves expressed a preference for the open shop versus either the union shop or the closed shop, which was favored by just 7 percent. Indeed, as historian R. Alton Lee has reported, "Throughout the country the atmosphere was charged with an air of expectancy that at last Congress would 'put labor in its place.' " The field was fertile for public relations campaigns by small and big business alike, but especially by the well-heeled National Association of Manufacturers (NAM), which consciously aimed its educational drive at "the great, unorganized, inarticulate, so-called middle class; the younger generation; and the opinion-makers of the nation." Newspapers were virtually unanimous in their call for action to curb labor strife.[37]

The situation was only slightly less urgent to President Truman. Absent from his desire was the determination of the National Association of Manufacturers and Chamber of Commerce to weaken organized labor. But very prominent was his need to maintain stability and order, let alone to respond to popular outcries. There was the not incidental fact that, in 1947, organized labor contained 15 million members and had the power to sway some 30 million voters, no minor matter in local and national elections. That, of course, was a factor, but not the only one.

His anger at what he regarded as disruption of the national good by irresponsible unions had already been displayed back in May 1946 when he called for emergency legislation to enable him to draft into the armed forces those who closed key industries. That excess struck even conservatives as totalitarian use of presidential power. Truman had to live that one down for a long time to come. Not known to the general public, however, was that the president had become so angered by the current shutdown of the coal mines that he drafted one of his intemperate undelivered statements to warn union leaders that "patience is exhausted." Ranging beyond his union troubles, the president's notes suggested he should "declare an emergency — call out troops. Start industry and put anyone to work who wants to go to work. If any leader interferes court martial him. Lewis ought to have been shot in 1942, but Franklin didn't have the guts to do it. . . . Adjourn congress and run the country. Get plenty of Atomic bombs on hand — drop one on Stalin, put the United Nations to work and eventually set up a free world."[38]

Later, in early 1947, when coal and railway walkouts were no longer the issue, the president's State of the Union address asked for action to prohibit jurisdictional strikes and certain types of secondary boycotts. There was also his perceived need for machinery to avoid strikes and lockouts, and so he also asked Congress for the creation of a temporary joint commission to study the whole question of labor-management relations. When, just a few weeks later, he reacted strongly against John L. Lewis's United Mine Workers strike in defiance of a court injunction, popular approval was reflected in a Gallup poll that showed the level of approval of his leadership had risen to 60 percent.[39]

Nor was the rest of the governmental process simply sitting back and awaiting executive leadership. The movement to do something about the New Deal's National Labor Relations Act (Wagner Act) had, in fact, been under way for a long time. One hundred and sixty-nine efforts to change that prolabor law had been introduced in the Congress. By 1947 the House and Senate committees with the responsibility for drafting changes were inundated with over one hundred versions of what would constitute "reform." Moreover, individual states became more active in dealing with antilabor legislation since the consequences of the Haymarket riot of 1886. As a result, in 1947 alone, some thirty states went ahead on their own with laws to restrict the power of organized labor.[40]

There never was any doubt about where Nixon stood. Very much a junior member of Education and Labor, along with Kennedy, he took his place when hearings opened on February 5. Before they ended a month later, the committee had heard from more than 130 witnesses. Under the chairmanship of Fred Hartley, a New Jersey Republican, the House panel was clearly eager for stringent measures. Ironically, Hartley had been reelected with the enthusiastic support of William Green and his American Federation of Labor. This "outstanding friend of labor," as Green called him in 1940 was, in reality, so hostile that his elevation to the chairmanship prompted Mary Norton, also from New Jersey but a Democrat, to leave the committee. Fifteen Republicans in all sat on Education and Labor, two-thirds of them, like Nixon, were without prior service; and also like Nixon, they shared disdain for leaders of organized labor because they believed radical unionists were ready to sabotage the interests of their own workers for some Marxist dream. Kennedy's exceptions to all this reflected his labor union constituency, an adjustment not required from the man who represented California's Twelfth.[41]

There is not much doubt about Congressman Hartley's power to shape what came out of the House committee. They heard witnesses who disproportionately sided with management. Hartley also eased the way for significant influence from antilabor Republicans and conservative southern Democrats, in addition to lawyers from the NAM and the Chamber of Commerce. Consequently, drafting the House bill began even before the hearings were concluded. Hartley's tactics also involved loading his bill to make it appear tougher than the Senate version, thereby preparing the way for a final, more acceptable compromise with the measure steered through the upper chamber by Robert A. Taft. As an immediate step, House passage was assured; indeed, it followed on April 17 by the nearly three-to-one vote of 308 to 107.[42] Predictably, the Senate was not far behind, and the final conference report went to the president for his signature on June 9. Thus, Truman was handed a "labor bill of rights" designed to benefit the individual worker.

If American workers failed to benefit from the Taft-Hartley Act, neither were they enslaved, as Truman and its opponents warned. It did, in fact, as historian Donald McCoy has recently reminded us, "regulate labor activity without seriously impairing the legitimate power of unions, just as the Wagner Act of 1935 has restrained outrageous acts by management without crippling it."[43]

Twenty-three years later, when President Nixon sent to Congress a special message on labor disputes in the transportation industry, he recalled that he had "helped write" the Taft-Hartley Act of 1947. His involvement with this landmark legislation, as with so many experiences in Nixon's career, made him the target of quick, simple, and mostly pejorative judgments; in this case, the reputation he acquired was that of a right-wing, antilabor Republican.[44] That impression was given by a *New York Times* headline on February 18, 1947, shortly after the hearings began. "Seven Union Curbs Reported as Set for Bill in House," it announced. For many years afterward, how one voted on Taft-Hartley became *the* litmus test of a pro- or antilabor position, a perception that discouraged a more open analysis.

There was, nevertheless, no evidence that Nixon ever came to regret his role in helping to write the most controversial piece of legislation enacted during the Truman era. The man who became president retained the confidence that enabled him to take pride in his association with the Education and Labor Committee. Events in the United States during the Vietnam War era, as in those early post–World War II years, directed Nixon's attention toward the painful influences of class conflicts.

Nixon continued to insist that the working man needed freedom from exploitation by labor bosses. Wage-earners were central to the capitalist system, not merely pawns in the hands of those who, like unions and Communists, would use them to serve their own ends. The principles of laissez-faire should be as open to them as to any other kind of entrepreneurs. Whatever their grievances, labor's long-term interests lay in partnership and cooperation, not in the creation of provocations that could put them at a disadvantage when dealing with repressive management. Nixon thereby reflected a mainstream view that was vulnerable to the label of paternalism, a disingenuous approach toward the continued subordination of workers, one certainly not expressed by those regarded as labor's friends.

He spoke out at a committee session on Friday morning, February 14, and despite the need to do something and Mr. Hartley's haste to draft a bill, warned against "legislation which somebody may hurriedly have written to take care of a particular situation" and called for a bill that attempted to anticipate future contingencies. "I think it would be far worse for us," he added, "to move too fast and adopt legislation which would encourage industrial strife rather than alleviate it."[45] A year later, after it was all done and Republicans especially were rushing to take credit for having tamed labor, Nixon distributed the following comments to local newspapers in Southern California:

> . . . At that time, it was all too apparent that two extreme schools of thought concerning the type of labor legislation which should be enacted were widely represented in Congress. On the one hand, there were those who wanted to pass a punitive bill which would seriously affect the legitimate rights of labor; on the other hand, there were those who sought to continue, and even strengthen, the labor legislation of the 'thirties which was so discriminatory against both management and the general public interest. . . . It was my intention . . . to attempt to strike a balance between these two extremes and seek enactment of legislation which would discriminate against neither labor nor management and, most important of all, assure protection of the general public's best interests.[46]

That remained Nixon's position toward labor. His was the view of opportunity, one to whom a real bill of rights for the workingman corresponded to laissez-faire for the businessman. Anything else fettered initiative, creating a separate and inherently inferior class. That word, "class," arose repeatedly from his concern. A favorite reference was to the Magna Carta, the charter of liberties conceded when the barons surrounded King John in 1215 and extracted a share of power. If, then, the Wagner Act of 1935 had been hailed as the Magna Carta of union labor, he pointed out several times, "I am convinced that the Congress must also bear in mind that we have a fundamental responsibility to enact legislation in behalf of members of unions." Congress, in other words, had to grant workers a "bill of rights," which would "give rank and file members of unions a voice in their organizations." He called for a "labor bill which is not class legislation, but which is in the best interests of all the people of America." "There are ominous signs today," he told the Merchants and Manufacturers Association of Chicago in early 1947, "of development of two opposing classes in the United States. If this trend continues it cannot help but end tragically for all parties concerned. The trend can be halted only by constructive action by both labor and management. Management has a particular responsibility and should not close its eyes to that responsibility." "We must never forget that the man who suffers most from strikes," he advised his committee colleagues, "is not the employer or the consumer but the man who is forced to go out on strike — the member of the union himself, and I am confident that we will find a great deal of support among union members for a sane, fair, workable national labor policy, which will reduce industrial strife to a minimum."[47]

His position was closer to what Dwight Eisenhower would later call "modern Republicanism," critical of those who analyzed American society as divided along the interests of class instead of the more desirable "corporate commonwealth." The Nixon stance was also far more moderate than a strict representation of his district would have permitted. For those who came to view him as a champion of the small, self-made businessman, it was paradoxical. Such attitudes were then far more likely to be expressed by large corporations than modest entrepreneurs. Remarkably, too, for one whose career was so plagued with negative images, especially for reputedly cynical manipulation of biases and anxieties, that remained Nixon's attitude toward workers. They responded, he continued to believe, not only as wage-earners but as individuals who shared the aims of the larger culture. Thus, Raymond Moley, an original New Deal brain-truster, came away from a series of meetings with Nixon in the spring of 1960 and wrote in *Newsweek* that the then front-runner for the Republican presidential nomination intended to "make his appeal not only to the interests of the union members in their right to democratic control of their own unions, but to their overriding interest in every other national issue." The same man who later, as president of the United States, went head to head against welfare state liberals in courting the votes of workers, understood that "their votes are cast not as members of unions but as fellow citizens in every community where they live — as Americans, and not as a 'working class.' "[48]

At the start of March 1947, he said that the Education and Labor Committee "is interested in preserving free trade-unionism in the United States, and we are absolutely opposed to bringing into the United States Russian communism which would have the effect of destroying free trade-unionism as we see it in the United States." Twelve years later he wrote to reporter Carl Greenberg of the *Los Angeles Times* about a planned California referendum that would couple right-to-work laws (which were legalized by Taft-Hartley) on the ballot with a civil rights issue. "It has been my experience," replied Vice President Nixon, "that these issues tend to divide our citizens along lines of class interest in ways which prejudice our two-party system."[49]

Nor, in 1947, did Nixon merely rely on others' surveys to buttress his views. Right after the hearings began, he talked to some seventy coal miners and their families in Scranton, Pennsylvania. This "grass-roots" survey uncovered, he told his colleagues, evidence to support his point that the workingman wanted freedom from union boss domination. His conversations with the rank and file, as distinguished from the labor officers, elicited their belief in union labor and opposition to crippling legislation, but, as he reported, they were "unanimous in their opinion that some legislation was necessary at this time to restrict the power of certain union leaders who had overreached themselves and were harming the union movement." What they wanted was protection for their rights within the organization. Nixon followed that up the next week by reading from letters written by workers. Stressing that the correspondents generally pleaded that they remain anonymous, he quoted from a United Mine Workers member and his wife who wrote that no union "should become as powerful as the coal miners' union" and that "there should be no one man who says millions may live or not live." Nixon was unambiguous; his references consistently targeted *unions* for restricting workers. "I was elected to smash the labor bosses," he told a newspaperman at the outset, "and my one principle is to accept no dictation from the CIO-PAC."[50]

Nixon's position inevitably created an apparent clash with his colleague from the Northeast, Jack Kennedy. Pedigree and genes had, of course, separated the two. Beyond that, partisanship and political constituencies made the greatest difference, especially the latter. Kennedy himself hardly championed the New Deal, even the advances made by organized labor. A private discussion with journalist Blair Clark about the Wagner Act brought out an "impassioned assault that contained all the conventional anti-labor points." Within the committee, however, as a member of the Democratic minority and representative of a large working-class community, he adjusted his public position so that he differed with Nixon politically rather than ideologically. Although Kennedy signed a minority report opposing the Hartley bill, he came closer to his own hesitations by filing a supplemental opinion. "Management has been selfish. Labor has been selfish," Kennedy wrote. "If repressive and vindictive labor legislation is enacted at the behest of management, a tide of left-wing reaction will develop which may well destroy our existing business system. At the same time if labor continues to insist upon special privilege and unfair advantage . . . I have grave doubts as to the future of the trade-union movement." Then, in wording reminiscent of Nixon's, he warned about legislation that would "bring not peace but labor war" by playing "into the hands of the radicals in our unions, who preach the doctrine of the class struggle."[51]

The two legislators traveled to western Pennsylvania that April for their first public debate. At the Penn McKee Hotel in McKeesport, two of the nation's youngest congressmen faced each other in a public relations forum and stated their differences. To Nixon's contention that the bill upheld the fundamental rights of the workingman, Kennedy replied that it would "be the first shot in a war to end labor peace." His greatest fear, said the Democrat, was that striking down the union shop might "eliminate industry-wide bargaining." In their most pointed difference, Kennedy questioned its sincerity about caring for the welfare of workers and added that "it seeks to strangle by restraint the American labor movement."[52]

At the moment, the greatest political stakes were hardly Nixon's. They were President Truman's. After the overwhelming margin by which the Congress passed the Taft-Hartley bill, each house by more than enough to override a veto, whether or not to sign was the key question. His signature would enact into law legislation that had been the object of his excoriation. A veto, however, would surely be overridden and again expose him to charges of futile and inept leadership. His cabinet officers, with the notable exception of Labor Secretary Lewis Schwellenbach, recommended that he sign. According to Leon Keyserling, of his Council of Economic Advisers, he was about to follow that prudent course. But, as Donald McCoy tells it, "Truman decided on the veto so that he might improve his ability to rally labor and liberal support on later issues and for the 1948 elections."[53] For good measure, he added a vigorous veto message, charging Congress with passing a "slave labor bill."

The House promptly voted to override by 331 to 83, and the Senate followed suit, 68 to 25. From that point on, organized labor's fortunes went mostly downhill.

Philip Murray was born into the Scottish coal pits at Lanarkshire. The son of an Irish-born miner and union leader, young Murray went into the mines at the age of ten as a breaker boy. His family migrated to the United States seven years later, and Murray ultimately became one of America's more respected labor leaders. A lawyer who worked at United Mine Workers headquarters remembered that Murray was a man with "an extremely sweet disposition," one whose concern for those around him evoked a reciprocal loyalty. "Murray knew everybody in the building, knew them by their first names, knew their families, spent a lot of time on their purely personal matters. He was a kindly father figure." Among other things, he was a firm civil libertarian, ready to tolerate divergent points of view. Murray's temperament and intellect pointed naturally toward conciliation rather than confrontation. At his death in 1952, the little man with the Scottish burr had become one of America's most powerful labor leaders as head of the 4 million-member CIO.[54]

Murray, a Roman Catholic immigrant, had been a protégé of the far more colorful and legendary John L. Lewis. On arrival in America, he started out as a miner near Pittsburgh. A battle with a weigh-master that led to a fight after Murray had protested cheating in the weighing of coal led to a long strike and his forcible expulsion from the area by two deputy sheriffs — and, in the long run, the start of a career in organized labor. Thereafter, he rose rapidly through the ranks of the United Mine Workers of America, finally, in 1919, becoming its international vice president under Lewis.[55]

When Lewis staged a revolt against the American Federation of Labor in 1935, Murray joined the dissidents and helped organize what became, in 1938, the Congress of Industrial Organizations. At Lewis's direction, he took up a task the AFL had failed to achieve, the organizing of steelworkers. His success as head of the Steel Workers Organizing Committee made him the first president of their new union. He kept that post until his death even as he rose within the CIO as Lewis's chief lieutenant. When the bushy-browed Lewis, that dominant figure of twentieth-century American labor, kept his vow to resign if FDR was reelected in 1940, Phil Murray took over the CIO. Not long afterward, Lewis turned against his former lieutenant as well. At last, Phil Murray, independent and strong-willed, was his own man and consolidated his personal control.

Murray's career had spanned both world wars. In 1917, President Wilson named him to key state and national committees responsible for overseeing labor and coal production. Under FDR after Pearl Harbor, Murray was a key architect of wartime cooperation. At the very time American Communists were seeking to profit from both the growth of organized labor and wartime discontent, he called for "a new departure for American labor to lead . . . a national government devoted to the general warfare just as much as to the particular interests of labor groups." He then fought to uphold labor's no-strike pledge and called for increased production, all the while holding the reins on the CIO's divergent forces. He also represented his government in trying to build support for foreign labor leaders. Just as firm was his dedication to preserving the CIO's influence within the Democratic party. Murray's support for the organization's Political Action Committee had that as an objective. He expressed his fear that any labor flirtation with a third-party movement "would divide the forces of the Progressives throughout the nation."[56]

At a time when some 15 percent of the membership was under Communist leadership, which had been instrumental in helping to found the

CIO, Murray's opposition to President Truman's early antilabor policies reinforced his need to maintain a united front. That was a time when Murray was leading the battle against big steel, which finally resulted in the signing of the steelworkers' first postwar two-year contract.

Murray, devout Catholic and firm anticommunist, was, in effect, the quintessential New Dealer, attempting to hold together disparate elements in the face of mutual enemies. He hoped, too, just as did Henry Wallace later on, that he could work with and control those who seemed more concerned with the interests of Moscow than of Washington. For the most part he succeeded, even getting the Communists to go along with him at key points, while, at the same time, giving them a free hand within their own affiliated unions.[57] Ultimately, however, he succumbed to the stresses that had begun to eat away at the relatively brief alliance that had weathered the Great Depression and World War II.

His dilemma was not unlike that of New Dealers themselves; or, in a broader sense, the coalition brought together by Roosevelt. There was, within Murray, strength in his conviction that individual workers had the right to their political beliefs. Communism, socialism, liberalism, or conservatism were all ideas capable of being handled within the concept of a democratic society. He was a labor leader keeping his focus on the essential goals, and such conflicting philosophies were irrelevant as long as they did not undermine basic labor objectives. Still, those early postwar years put his principles to the test. They challenged the ability of the CIO itself to survive, reaffirmed his conviction of what was best for the nation in the formulation of early cold war policies, and tried his ability to reconcile his position with the increasingly vehement anticommunism of Catholic trade unionists.

On another level, Phil Murray's dilemma was symptomatic of the dilemma of liberal Catholics. Loyalty to the party of FDR had already been strained in a number of ways. Ever since the Spanish Civil War, Catholic Democrats had found themselves almost wholly at odds with those New Dealers who, for all the neutrality of Roosevelt's hands-off policy, were clearly unconcerned about Communist cooption of the anti-Franco cause. Even before that falling-out, they had been in an uneasy relationship with the so-called popular front, the commitment of a broad spectrum on the American left, which certainly included the crusade to organize workers. Just as Murray had reconciled himself to living with the Communists, so had liberal Catholics. Labor's need was not unlike their own desire for economic and political progress.

Cultural strains, subordinated in the face of economic concerns, were inevitably pushed to the surface. The late thirties brought the antiliberal, anti-Semitic, and, finally, anti–New Deal and even pro-German campaign of the "radio priest" from Michigan, Father Charles Coughlin. Liberal Catholics indeed viewed him as a dangerous rabble-rouser, much the way they would view the 1950s' chief demagogue, Joe McCarthy, but he nevertheless delineated the precise areas of potential contention. Coughlin promoted those issues that remained divisive, allegations of indifference by Democratic policymakers toward the plight of the Church in contrast with their concern for Hitler's victims. Roosevelt's third-term victory in 1940 reflected such discontent, as his support from Roman Catholics dropped off by 13 percent. As the depression eased and America entered the postwar era, Irish Catholics in particular found themselves facing new competition within their ancestral party from newly ascendant ethnic groups. At the same time, American Catholicism was increasingly under fire from liberals and traditional antipapists who warned about the power of the Church, and revived the specter of nativism. Catholics themselves, forced to defend their own Americanism, called attention to the wartime strategies that had left eastern Europe under Soviet domination. Such disaffections were also clearly evident among working-class Catholics, bedrock supporters of Democrats in the urban and industrial north.[58]

That Phil Murray's live-and-let-live policy toward CIO leftists was becoming untenable in the postwar era is hardly surprising. Whatever remained of his old principles soon wore down. When, at Murray's behest, the CIO's executive board introduced a resolution at its eighth convention in November 1946 to counter "the efforts of the Communist Party or other political parties . . . to interfere in the affairs of the CIO," Henry Wallace's followers told themselves that Murray had not succumbed to worries about labor's standing, or Moscow's efforts to exploit workers' anxieties, or how current election campaigns, such as Nixon's in California, had threatened the CIO's standing. Instead, they argued, Phil Murray had capitulated to pressure from the Roman Catholic church and the Association of Catholic Trade Unionists.[59] Myopic and self-serving as was their analysis, their delusion nearly matched the intensity of righteousness.

It was, in fact, easy to ignore the fact that American workers, as was true for liberals in general, were being forced to get out from under the Red cloud for ideological as well as tactical reasons. Those Education and Labor Committee hearings of March and April 1947 emphasized how Communist-led locals had disrupted defense production. Harold Christoffel's role in leading a United Auto Workers affiliate against Allis-Chalmers plants was particularly blatant. That situation, in fact, prompted Jack Kennedy's call for Christoffel's indictment for perjury and won Nixon's colleague early prominence for anticommunism. "KENNEDY ACTS ON 'RED' UNIONS," proclaimed the *Boston Post*'s laudatory headline. Christoffel was later convicted of perjury for denying that his activities were geared to the interests of the Communist party rather than the needs of fellow laborers and finally served sixteen months of a four-year prison sentence. If that was not enough to persuade Murray to clean house, another rationale was supplied when the Progressives, to nobody's surprise, backed Wallace's candidacy to oppose Truman in 1948.[60]

So it went, much of it paralleling both the rise of Wallace at the head of a third party and the House hearings. The CIO's executive board gave Murray what he wanted by passing a resolution that forbade all union officers from belonging to either the Progressives or the ADA, the ADA obviously being thrown in to make disaffiliation from the Progressives acceptable to the far left. The act appeared "confusing and contradictory," noted the Catholic periodical *America,* but it nevertheless editorialized that "the CIO cannot afford to compromise . . . if it wishes to be regarded as a liberal, democratic force in American life." "By fostering and supporting Wallace's candidacy," historian David A. Shannon has written, "the Communists had brought the Communist issue to a head in the C.I.O., and they had lost the battle." The CIO's great purge continued at an accelerated pace, especially after Henry Wallace's presidential candidacy ran into a dead end; behind Murray's leadership, it was effectively completed by 1950.[61]

The long-term direction was toward labor's reunification, with the CIO merging with the AFL in 1955. On the surface, American unionism was disciplining its ranks to join the cold war consensus; or, as labor historian Bert Cochran has put it, the Red issue "defined and determined national attitudes and caught up all labor principles in its web."[62]

Such leaders were heirs to old unionists who had once provided the industrial backbone for the New Deal; they had, in fact, been considerably ahead of FDR's leftward trend, in effect forcing Washington's gradual movement in their direction. The 1930s were a time of intensive organizational activity at various local levels, building toward the drive to unionize the steel and auto industries. Progress was encouraged by such national legislation as the Wagner Act and its creation, the National Labor Relations board, which oversaw collective bargaining. Pushed ahead by the great labor-management conflicts of the depression era, the process also followed a decade of massive movement into the cities by some 6.5 million rural Americans. In conjunction with those whose families had migrated to America during the great flow from Europe until stymied by the immigration laws of the twenties, they created what political scientist Samuel Lubell explained was a "human potential for a revolutionary change," the presence of a ready-made constituency for relief to the lower classes.[63]

By the dawn of the postwar world, they and their families had become the legatees of the American system. As social historian Geoffrey Gorer has explained, "It is this break of continuity between the immigrants of the first generation and their children of the second generation which is to my mind of major importance in the development of the modern American character, which gives rise to what might be called, by analogy with genetics, 'the American mutation.' " Even as the process unfolded, Max Lerner, that perceptive student of American civilization, wrote that "it was his son, the second-generation immigrant, who was lampooned by the novelists as one driven either to imitate or to outdo the 'native Americans' at their own game."[64]

Acculturation and assimilation often meant conservatism, but nothing fed that impulse as effectively as the improved standard of living that became notable during the years that followed Phil Murray's sudden death. The melting pot, to the extent that it existed at all, translated to a lack of class consciousness on the part of the American worker, which has been seen by specialists in labor and immigration as, in the words of one of them, "in part a product of ethnic and racial rivalries, and of the divisive effect of different social conditions in different parts of the country." From there, it was but a short step to "social conservatism," an impetus that came to be increasingly attributed to the insecurities of blue-collar workers. They were to thereby continue the adaptability to the new order that had been a hallmark of preindustrial immigrants.[65]

As early as 1928, before the great crash, labor analyst Selig Perlman noted that although "unionism has emerged as a permanent labor force," it was nevertheless "no more than a minority interest in the American community." Even more striking, because it could just as easily have been written a quarter of a century later, was Perlman's observation that the "material rise in real wages and the disappearance of the more glaring abuses has robbed the labor movement of grounds for telling appeal to public sympathy," a loss he also attributed to "the aggressiveness of many union groups."[66]

By the late forties, union radicalism was on the wane. Incipient at the early stages of the cold war, it was bound to become even more pronounced. Labor's ranks would have responded inevitably to the anti-communist impulse, Murray or no Murray. Right-wing unions within the CIO, such as the Amalgamated Clothing Workers and the Greater New York City CIO Council, had long wanted to purge the leftists.[67] The formulation of such attitudes was as much cultural and tactical as coerced. It was, in fact, the continuation of the long process through which the children of immigrants have joined the national mainstream.

By Murray's death, the labor movement had just about overcome its anarchist, Wobbly, socialist, Communist, and, to a considerable extent, even its social democratic background. "The year 1949–50 was a kind of turning point in American life," sociologist Stanley Aronowitz has noted. "It was not only the man in the gray flannel suit who took the 5:30 from the center city train station back to his suburban ranch house," but the "industrial factory worker as well, formerly encapsulated in the ethnic ghettoes of large cities, was finding his new suburban dwelling a necessity."[68]

Surging consumerism boiled over from the new affluence, with material expectations creating new needs, and it was all interlaced with, first, the peacetime demand for new goods and then the increasing financial burden of protecting the nation from foreign infiltration. Any doubts about the Communists' intentions were dispelled in 1950 when North Koreans invaded the south and when, as the *New York Times* put it, "American troops joined the war against Communist imperialism and aggression."[69]

For many Americans, further confirmation of Communism's expansionist goals was hardly needed, for the threat of subversion haunted not only the labor movement. President Truman had acknowledged as much in 1947 when, responding to pressures to root out the disloyal from government, he issued Executive Order 9835, requiring that every federal employee be screened as a potential security risk. Since then, hearings conducted by the House Committee on Un-American Activities had made it clear that subversives could be found not only among blue-collar wage-earners but among educators and those responsible for Hollywood's movies. Eleven top Communist leaders in the United States had been convicted of sedition and then jailed. Igor Gouzenko, Judith Coplon, Klaus Fuchs, Alger Hiss, and Julius and Ethel Rosenberg had all been tied to Moscow-directed espionage. The Soviets had tightened their grip on eastern Europe and had even extended their domination of Czechoslovakia. They had ended the American nuclear monopoly. In China, Communists had driven Chiang Kai-shek to Formosa. Less than three months later had come Joe McCarthy's explanation that Red successes were not only understandable after what FDR had done at Yalta but hardly surprising, since 205 Communists were employed by the State Department. Coming on top of all that, the Korean invasion virtually confirmed Americans' worst fears. Republicans and Democrats united to back Truman's military intervention.

By the first half of the 1950s, the anticommunist impulse in America reached its zenith, and Richard Nixon's presence as a leading player was of incalculable significance.

If, in the case of the House Committee on Un-American Activities (HUAC), Joe Martin had planned to help boost young Nixon, the move was more shrewd than many contemporaries were ready to grant. Martin has written that he was personally responsible for giving Nixon the chance to sit on a "headline committee." "Some people from the Coast came to us," Martin has explained, "with a high recommendation of Nixon's legal talents. In the end we decided he would be a good man for it."[70]

Martin's account can be interpreted as self-serving hindsight, written a dozen years later, while he was still bitter at the Eisenhower administration's role in enabling congressional Republicans to replace him as majority leader. By Martin's own admission, if he did help Nixon in 1947, it was done under pressure. Certainly, it would have required more than a polite note from Herman Perry. For all the controversy that swirled around that committee, HUAC did offer newcomers the chance to debut with panache. Martin acknowledges that "there were more Republican applicants than there were openings," but not surprisingly fails to explain why, then, the pro-Nixon people were able to exert such influence. More inexplicable is the specter of the assignment having been forced upon Nixon by those same California backers who had pressured Martin. According to Nixon's own account, Martin approached him with an offer he could not refuse but one which, given the committee's reputation, he accepted with trepidation. HUAC was notorious, a gaggle of primitives, "habitually unfair," as Nixon himself later acknowledged, "widely condemned as a 'Red-baiting' group" that routinely was guilty of an "abridgment of civil liberties" while posing as a defender of American virtues against communism. Whittaker Chambers found that his colleagues at *Time* magazine, where he was a senior editor, considered HUAC unworthy of having the cooperation of any "decent man" in Congress.[71]

The testimony of Representative Donald Jackson, another freshman Republican from California and fellow member of the Chowder and Marching Society, then becomes plausible. Jackson reported having witnessed a most agitated Nixon, one who feared the political kiss of death if he accepted the assignment and, while pacing up and down his office in indecision, wondered whether the hazards could not be reduced by working to reform the methods that had made the HUAC so unpalatable to many. Six years later, when the Eighty-Third Congress convened, there were fewer hesitations. Of the 221 freshman Republicans, 185 tried to join the committee.[72]

The obvious point is that Nixon came along at the right time. Nixon, however, recalls another reason. "I was the only lawyer on the committee, so that's why I played such a major role." Ironically, membership on HUAC both established his career and thereafter also plagued him in "reputable" political circles.[73] The passage of four decades has, however, defused much of the passion, neutralized partisan bias, and encouraged reconsideration of Nixon's role. Such thinking may come as a shock to anyone with his head stuck in that period, those wedded to the notion that only a "bunch of reactionaries" harped on New Deal blind spots, labor union transgressions, and the intransigence of Soviet totalitarianism. To the contrary, even one who was "pure" could appreciate the potential combustibility of that mixture. Nixon was not pure. He was, as most assumed, conservative. He was also starting a political career, which is synonymous with ambition; and he fully appreciated the competitive need to make the most of his opportunities. Beyond that, where one draws the line becomes subjective. Nonetheless, it was Nixon, more than any other single person, who restrained HUAC from some of its excesses, enhanced its credibility, and helped to establish its validity as a legislative arm.

Before his time, it lacked almost all of that. HUAC's respectability was virtually zero. Born during the 1930s as a special committee with a mission to scrutinize foreign subversion, notably of the totalitarian fascist or Communist variety, it suffered from a severe loss of public esteem when Martin Dies, a Texas Democrat, took over the chairmanship from John McCormack. The so-called Dies Committee soon became an unseemly example of congressional behavior. Sensational headlines reported the almost imminent undermining of the republic by sinister elements. Concerned readers learned how witnesses were bullied with names and associations tossed about recklessly. One particularly conscientious investigator had to satisfy himself that Kreml hair tonic did not get its name because it sounded like "Kremlin."[74] As the circus continued, Dies forgot about fascism and virtually proclaimed Communist-hunting his speciality. He did not hesitate to laud his own competence over the FBI's. Almost forgotten now because of bigger fish to come, Dies's name was the most prominent among those associated with the "little Red scare." By 1947, he was gone from the scene, having declined to run for reelection. The committee, however, had been substantially upgraded. Acting on a motion by a Mississippi Democrat, John Rankin, the House had made HUAC (as it came to be known) a permanent standing committee.

Speaker Martin's assignment placed Nixon with a body that needed either rejuvenation or abandonment. The absence of Dies had not changed the committee very much. One sign of the times was that no amount of persuasion, regardless of how much agreement there may have been in congressional cloakrooms, would have convinced anybody to risk the blame for the committee's death.

Robert E. Stripling, the chief investigator, was a Dies man, having been brought to Washington by way of the University of Texas. Given his present job upon his discharge from the army, he remained a true believer in HUAC's mission to save America. If only the Justice Department had not aborted hearings in 1941 on Japanese spying along the Pacific Coast and Hawaii, he argued, the committee could have created "enough alarm among the people to have caused the Japanese to abandon their planned attack on Pearl Harbor." It was not that the committee was obsessed by communism, Stripling pointed out, but the postwar menace was no longer the Nazis, who "lack a Fuehrer and a purpose," while the "Communists have both, and combine the fanaticism of Hitler's followers with remarkable guile." After all, there was only one Communist for every 2,277 Russians in 1917, but now there was one for every 1,814 people in the United States. In a book that had its entire last section devoted to a primer on "500 Things You Should Know About Communism," Stripling complained that HUAC had been subjected to "the most determined and articulate abuse by Presidents Roosevelt and Truman, many of their Cabinet officers, liberals, leftists and Reds."[75]

So the most significant change since Dies's time was that HUAC had become a standing committee. Nixon, the only lawyer, was about two decades younger than the average age of the other members. Their years had brought neither distinction nor wisdom. All too often, they were responsible for helping to create the image of HUAC as a den of mediocrity, ignorance, provincialism, and bigotry. Two of Nixon's fellow Republicans, Richard B. Vail of Illinois and John McDowell of Pennsylvania, were also newcomers, although McDowell had served one term before the war. J. Hardin Peterson of Florida and Herbert C. Bonner of North Carolina were veteran southern Democrats. John Wood, a Georgia Democrat who was relinquishing his brief chairmanship, was a sixty-two-year-old who has been described by political historian David Caute as "a gentle but conservative anti–New Dealer." Hostility to FDR and all he stood for also marked the career of Karl Mundt, a forty-six-year-old South Dakota Republican, whose animosities also extended to much of the outside world.[76] Probably the most vehement and most difficult was John E. Rankin.

There was little that was conservative, or gentle, about Rankin. A Mississippi colleague of Senator Theodore Bilbo, a primitive who, without much exaggeration, has been called by John Roy Carlson "probably the most reprehensible politician America ever knew," Rankin as a racist ranked with the most blatant. He struck one interviewer as a "sharp-eyed, shrewd, callous little man, with volatile and fanatic energy." A smattering of *antis* — anti-Semitic, antiblack, anti-Catholic — came from his tongue at almost every opportunity. Speaking on the House floor a half-year before Pearl Harbor, he denounced American Jews as "war mongers" and later said the fight could only be won by exposing "the international Jewish bankers." He once objected to a HUAC investigation of the Ku Klux Klan by saying that the Klan was not "un-American" but "American." Rankin's pro-Klan sympathies were repeated with regularity. His Negrophobia became legendary; with Bilbo, Rankin epitomized the basest culture of the unreconstructed South. His devotion to Jim Crow was also on a par with his anticommunism. John Rankin belonged to that generation for which communism accounted for all that was bad in all that he hated. In 1945, he declared that those who were plotting to "overthrow the government" had their "headquarters in Hollywood." There was no greater "hotbed of subversive activities in the United States." The notion of creating a Fair Employment Practices Commission was ipso facto evil, "the beginning of a Communistic dictatorship the like of which America never dreamed." He needed no evidence of a connection to vow that he would deny Vito Marcantonio his House seat when an anti-Marcantonio campaign worker was killed on election day.[77]

Yet, not so strangely — and this is one of the peculiarities of American politics — Rankin and Marcantonio, who sat in the same chamber but represented different planets, felt they needed each other. They did, in fact, strike up a friendship based more on a sense of humor and irony than anything else. George Smathers, who sat in the House from Florida, recalled hearing Rankin say, "Well, better run — I got to get Marcantonio to get up and cuss me out or I'm going to get defeated." Between those opposites, a bizarre kinship actually existed, a tacit working agreement, one of mutual assistance. "Every time Rankin attacked Marcantonio," recalled Smathers, "that strengthened Marcantonio and every time Marcantonio dumped on Rankin that really made Rankin."[78] Without actually stopping to consider what they were doing, they were, in effect, engaging in a most blatant denigration of their constituents, exploiting them by their biases and offering whatever palliatives were possible, whether or not they made much sense. What was most unfortunate about the caliber of such men was their propensity for derogating from whatever legitimate value HUAC had.

The committee's new chairman was a New Jersey Republican named J. Parnell Thomas, who was not much more elegant than Rankin. To a writer for *Life,* he looked like a character out of Dickens — "Pickwickian, and one could imagine under the circumstances, that the bulge in his coat signifies candy for children."[79]

Thomas's first claim to fame arose from his enthusiasm for exposing the Red menace. But his diligence permitted little patience for anything that interfered with his political opportunities, neither civility, common courtesy, nor the constitutional rights of witnesses. Thomas typified the opportunist who smells ideological and political paydirt. "The immunity which this foreign-directed conspiracy has been enjoying for the past fifteen years must cease," he wrote to Truman in April 1947.[80]

Thomas also managed to do some payroll padding. His confidential secretary informed journalist Drew Pearson that Thomas had pocketed about seven thousand dollars in staff kickbacks. He had also received an additional four thousand in phony expense vouchers. Convicted in 1949 after he changed his not guilty plea to nolo contendere, he was sent to the federal prison at Danbury, Connecticut. Seven years later, down and out and needing a job, Thomas begged for help from Vice President Nixon. "This is not just another appeal from a job seeker," he wrote, "it is from a person who has fought the Republican battles when fight was needed and from who as Chairman of the Committee on Un-American Activities kept the 'red herring' pot boiling at a time when Harry Truman was on the ropes."[81]

When Truman himself instituted loyalty screening procedures for federal employees, Nixon immediately said he was "entirely willing to take the word of the Department of Justice and the F.B.I. that . . . the drastic proposal for investigating Federal employees with respect to their loyalty is . . . entirely warranted." But neither Congressman Nixon nor President Truman could control the fact that the government's acceptance of that need, together with the Justice Department's subsequent release of a list of so-called subversive organizations, only deepened the anxiety.[82]

In this context, Joe Martin's naming of Nixon to HUAC was as much an act of patriotism and intelligent partisanship as beneficence toward a freshman. Nixon and the committee were both gainers. The caliber of his colleagues doubtless made it easier for Nixon to shine, but, as with his service on Education and Labor, his efficiency and competence were unquestioned. Even Fawn Brodie concedes that among his colleagues "he seemed a model of sobriety and reasonableness." Walter Goodman's valuable study of HUAC contends that "the qualities he showed on the Committee would have carried him forward in any event. He was smart, energetic, and a very fast learner of what he needed to know."[83] Neither does the record show a single case of Nixon overstepping the boundaries of legal decorum, beyond the requirements of sharp, intensive cross-examination.[84] Nor, in all the transcripts of committee hearings, can one find a single instance of reckless name-calling or abuse.

Most revealing is the evaluation of Nixon's personal contribution that was made by Robert K. Carr. Carr, a professor of law and political science at Dartmouth, wrote his scholarly study of HUAC *before* Nixon became Eisenhower's running mate in 1952, before, in other words, the full effects of controversy began to confuse what he did and did not do. "It is not hard [*sic*] to overpraise Nixon," wrote Carr, "for he brought to the committee enthusiasm, a willingness to work hard, ability as a lawyer, and a reasonable detachment and sense of fairness, qualities that have been rare among the committee's members."[85]

That was the contrast: Nixon was a rarity for HUAC. The committee's history and reputation were then well established. The Dies-Wood background was hardly rehabilitated by Thomas. The freshman from California, taking his place amid such surroundings, did not immediately fall into line, seduced by the established atmosphere. Looking back to 1947 and given his subsequent reputation, it would be easy to assume that Nixon would have relished the opportunity to make a quick name for himself. The reputation that did emerge from his early days with

HUAC, however, was well stated by Representative John W. Heselton of Massachusetts. Heselton dissented from Nixon's interpretation of the implications of what became known as the Mundt-Nixon bill but nevertheless complimented his colleague for his "tremendously effective, conscientious, and able effort . . . to devise the best possible legislation in a most controversial field. As long as I have known you," Heselton continued, "I have admired your completely straightforward, and intelligent approach to any problem presented to this House."[86]

During Nixon's first year, in the fall of 1947, the committee undertook its much-publicized hearings into Communist influences in the motion picture industry. Insinuations and spurious charges were floated before the public with the sort of abandon that had long since characterized HUAC. The hearings were a clear exploitation of the publicity value obtained by testimony from such film celebrities as actors Robert Taylor and Gary Cooper ("From what I hear, I don't like it [communism] because it isn't on the level") to several screenwriters, producers, and the president of the Screen Actors Guild, Ronald Reagan.

For Thomas, subversion within the motion picture community was akin to communism in government. He had already charged that Hollywood had succumbed to Washington pressures to turn out Communist propaganda. Nixon, although he was not a member of the subcommittee that conducted the hearings, sat in on some of the sessions, but remained only a bit player who watched the parade of film stars.[87]

At several points, he showed his misgivings. One case involved producer Jack L. Warner, who had become a handy target because of his wartime film *Mission to Moscow*, especially under questioning by chief investigator Robert Stripling. While Warner protested that however much the film may have shown the Soviet Union in an excessively favorable light, it was the product of a 1943 war effort comparable to the "American Liberty ships which carried food and guns to Russian allies," Stripling insisted that he was on "dangerous ground" by producing "as a factually correct picture one which portrayed" Russia romantically. Nixon came to Warner's rescue by leading him on to explain how many anticommunist films he had produced, albeit the response was negligible. Another time, when Stripling belabored director Sam Wood for making movies that showed "the sordid side of American life," Nixon observed that films revealing the nation's underside were even being made by those whose loyalty was above reproach.[88]

The Hollywood hearings of 1947 were but the start of a long period of infatuation with the concept of ideological seduction via celluloid. Ten writers were ultimately banned from their professions and then jailed for failure to cooperate with the committee. Over the next few years, other actors, writers, directors, and producers went the same way, victimized by a blacklist aimed at those who pleaded before the committee the constitutional protections of the Fifth Amendment. That careers and livelihoods, apart from individual freedoms, were disrupted and even destroyed was subordinated to what became a national obsession. Nor did it seem to matter that nothing of substance was ever demonstrated. Nothing was revealed that showed how the republic was menaced. All that was demonstrated was the existence of individuals in the film industry, people of varying talent, who were still infatuated by the notion that the answer to society's ills lay in the east.

Much more obvious was the zeal of HUAC and, in particular, Chairman Thomas, who often seemed torn between the question of survival of the United States and survival of the committee. His passion inevitably resulted in one striking early example of what later came to be called McCarthyism. That term involved guilt by association and/or innuendo; a concomitant was the neglect, willful or otherwise, of elementary precautions against false incrimination and the rights of self-defense. Thomas, out for headlines, appropriations, and denigration of Democrats, pounced on what he thought was a perfect victim. Edward U. Condon was a nuclear physicist, one of the most respectable members of the scientific establishment. He had also served with distinction since 1945 as director of the National Bureau of Standards. At the moment, he was caught in a conflict between the White House and Capitol Hill. Truman, having initiated his loyalty program, resisted congressional intrusions. Accordingly, he refused demands that he let HUAC have Condon's file. The committee's immediate target, suspected of constituting key evidence, was an FBI report on the scientist in the file of Commerce Secretary W. Averell Harriman. Harriman cited "the public interest" in refusing to turn over data on the distinguished physicist.[89]

Condon's professional credentials were impressive. He had been involved with developing the atomic bomb virtually from its inception. He played key wartime roles as a member of President Roosevelt's National Defense Research Committee, including helping to organize the Radiation Laboratory, and as an associate director of the Westinghouse Research Laboratories. During the months before the Japanese surrender, Condon devoted himself exclusively to the atomic bomb project while in Berkeley. Most recently, he was a Truman appointee to a committee charged with studying the effects of the Bikini Atoll atomic bomb test. He was also closely associated with the effort of Senator Brien McMahon of Connecticut, a Democrat, to place atomic control in civilian rather than military hands.

As a liberal, Condon continued to believe that the fight for economic and social justice had not been won. Even worse, his bearing was rooted in the 1930s, wedded to faith in progressivism via an alliance of those interested in fighting repression at home and right-wing totalitarianism abroad. Unlike openly anticommunist liberals and socialists, he remained undisturbed about participating with a broad popular front. He was not shy about remaining on friendly terms with men who doubted that the crimes of Stalin and the international dangers of the Soviet Union were legitimate concerns and who thought that those who raised them were engaged in Red-baiting. Worse, they automatically betrayed their own hostility toward progressivism. Whether Condon was naive, or to use some of the contemporary perjoratives, an idealist and visionary and maybe even a fellow traveler, was less significant than the fact that he was out of his decade, an anachronism at a time when conditions required modifications, when the concern was less with redressing the inadequacies of American society than with pinpointing the major source of the Communist threat to national security. In Condon, most members of HUAC were convinced they had found a perfect example of how America had been betrayed by the New Deal mentality.

While not exactly a New Dealer, Condon was close enough to make the point. He had been appointed as director of the Bureau of Standards when Henry A. Wallace was secretary of commerce. That Wallace had no personal connection with Condon was hardly relevant. Other things added up: his wife was described in the report of a HUAC subcommittee delegated to study his case as "an American-born woman of Czechoslovakian descent," which, presumably, was damnation by lineage. He belonged to the American-Soviet Science Society and once sponsored a meeting for the Southern Conference for Human Welfare. His associates included Harlow Shapley, the Harvard astronomer who happened to be a leading supporter of Wallace in the academic world.

All this made him ripe for J. Parnell Thomas. Several newspaper and magazine articles that appeared in 1947 suggested very strongly the imminence of action to be taken about him as a security risk. Condon's efforts to come forth with explanatory information, meanwhile, went unheeded. Nor was Thomas to be put off by the fact that the Atomic Energy Commission was responding to the president's loyalty order by subjecting Condon to the obligatory security check; until it was completed, his status was listed as "pending." In the absence of final clearance, Thomas was ready to take the opportunity to suggest guilt.[90]

Accordingly, the HUAC chairman wasted little time, even while confined to a hospital with gastrointestinal hemorrhages. Presented with a report on Condon by a subcommittee, which he chaired, Thomas brushed away suggestions that the material not be released because its findings were only "preliminary." So the findings, complete with errors and distortions, were made public, less than one week before HUAC sent Congress its request for an annual appropriation of $200,000, double its previous allocation. What mattered, however, was that the public learned that Dr. Condon, "from the evidence at hand, . . . is one of the weakest links in our atomic security."[91] The allegations were made before Condon was given the benefit of a hearing to state his own case.

Condon was able to weather the crisis. For one, he had the benefit of high-powered expertise. His defense was in the hands of such Washington lawyers as Abe Fortas, Thurman Arnold, and Paul Porter. He also had the overwhelming support of the scientific community. The committee, according to Robert Carr, found itself opposed by "an organized, responsible, and highly articulate segment of the American people." To Thomas's everlasting embarrassment, the *Washington Post* revealed that the FBI letter sought by HUAC contained one previously omitted sentence from Director Hoover to Harriman: "There is no evidence to show that contacts between this individual [a self-confessed Soviet espionage agent] and Dr. Condon were related to this individual's espionage activities."[92]

That put off formal pursuit of Condon by HUAC, at least during the Eightieth Congress. Later, a reorganized HUAC, after Nixon himself had gone to the Senate, continued to harass Condon until he resigned from government in 1951. If he was guilty of anything, it was of inadequate attention to his political connections. His profession then honored him by making him president of the American Association for the Advancement of Science.

Nixon, whose personal involvement in the Condon matter was nil since it was handled by a subcommittee, did not keep quiet about the implications of the case. In October of 1948, he asked congressional committees to enable those so accused to testify in their own behalf before they were condemned in public. In December, he conceded in a radio interview that the proceedings had been unfair. Karl Mundt, who had since been elected to the Senate, promptly agreed. The two legislators then suggested a nine-point "code of procedures" to provide greater protection for both witnesses and the accused, most of them drawn from suggestions already made by the Bill of Rights Committee of the Association of the Bar of the City of New York.[93]

Nixon did not hesitate to speak out publicly at other times. A news release issued by his office on May 10, 1947, congratulated a New York State Supreme Court judge for using Solomonic wisdom by upholding the right of Paul Robeson, the black baritone and fellow traveler, to sing in an Albany high school as long as he "should only SING in the high school and must not TALK, as he did recently at Philharmonic Auditorium in Los Angeles when he engaged in a diatribe concerning the advantages of the Russian system of government as compared with the American form (all this between his baritone offerings)." Two weeks later, Nixon addressed the Sales Executive Club in Los Angeles and stressed that "it is essential that we protect the rights of minorities and that we do not infringe on the basic American freedoms." Opposing efforts to stamp out communism by passing laws, he pointed to the need to "differentiate between the Communist or fellow-traveler and the man who happens to disagree with us in political thinking." A "great disservice is done to the anti-communist cause," he wrote to Pat Hillings in 1949, by irresponsible labeling of organizations as Communist front groups. Such advice was consistent with his warning to fellow Republicans that "indiscriminate name-calling and professional Red-baiting can hurt our cause more than it can help it." As late as February 1961, defeated for the presidency and contemplating the governorship of California, Nixon drafted a letter to Otis Chandler praising a lead *Los Angeles Times* editorial on restraining subversive activities; his draft included the following words of caution: "But what we must never forget is that one of the most cherished American ideal [*sic*] is that we must fight with proper methods for those things in which we believe."[94] His legislative career had, indeed, shown attention to "proper methods." What emerges from the entire history of Nixon's membership in HUAC is a pattern of diligence and, when he had reason to believe he was on the right track, persistence.

7

The Great Awakening

RICHARD NIXON'S value to HUAC was immediate. He outperformed his senior colleagues in the less visible functions as well as at the committee's executive and public hearings, including presiding over a legislative subcommittee. One important example was his performance during the fact-finding process that took place on two bills, one by Karl Mundt, the other by Gordon L. McDonough of California. Their purpose was to enact legislation to either curb or outlaw the Communist party.

HUAC began its hearings on measures introduced by Republican congressman Harry Sheppard of California and John Rankin. Neither thought twice about complexities, or constitutionality. They wanted a quick and easy result, to do away with the Communist party by edict, dissolving individual membership together with any political apparatus. Even that was not enough for Rankin. The Mississippian, obsessed with the ability of subversives to corrupt young minds, wanted to make teachers liable to a ten-thousand-dollar fine and a ten-year prison term for conveying *"the impression of sympathy with . . . Communist ideology."*[1]

So poorly were the bills drawn that the propriety of holding hearings to consider them has been questioned. But the fact is that they were given a respectable hearing and, for example, the outlandish testimony by one Walter S. Steele received the kind of courteous treatment that was rare for HUAC.

Steele's appearance on July 21, 1947, once again demonstrated the platform available to even the most extreme anticommunist zealots. His organization, Steele told the committee, was the National Security Committee of the American Coalition of Patriotic, Civic, and Fraternal Societies, which included eighty-four fringe organizations with such names as the Southern Vigilant Intelligence Association, Inc.; Tax Evils Committee of Council Bluffs, Iowa; the Order of Three Crusades, 1092–1192, Inc.;

and the Dames of the Loyal Legion of the United States. Steele's personal "contribution" of over 50 percent of his time "serving the government" was in compiling his own files of subversive individuals and organizations, and that information, he boasted, was shared with several federal agencies. Reform causes, however muddleheaded, were all lumped together with various left-wing groups. Most important, and unfortunate, was the accommodation given by HUAC that allowed Steele to make public the names of people he considered subversives. If his testimony was, as Robert Carr states, "the most irresponsible ever presented to the Un-American Activities Committee," it did not discourage Robert Stripling from disregarding some egregious distortions and going out of his way to praise the vigilante's accuracy.[2]

The positions taken by Steele and, at least inferentially, Stripling, were hardly aberrations. Dealing with subversion by outlawing communism had considerable appeal. HUAC heard from such additional supporters as the Daughters of the American Revolution, the Veterans of Foreign Wars, and the American Legion. Once again, those patriotic organizations believed freedom of speech was a luxury that endangered national security.

Those were, after all, the days immediately after Truman's call for military aid to Greece and Turkey. The stakes, as the president presented them in his dramatic speech of March 12, 1947, were nothing less than the freedom of western Europe; by extension that meant western civilization. As though that were not enough to arouse sufficient vigilance (and yield congressional dollars), he quickly followed through by presenting his plan to monitor the loyalties of government workers. In that context, nothing seemed more logical than doing away with the Communist party itself. Americans no longer needed to be convinced that here was a great exception to guarantees of freedom of speech. Communism, the argument went, was unlike any other ideology. In terms reminiscent of the anti-Catholic nativism of the nineteenth century that linked "papists" to a Roman conspiracy, communism was the faith of those with a primary loyalty to a foreign power. By 1947, three-fifths of Americans were ready to have their government outlaw such membership. "There is hysteria, in Washington and in the country," said commentator Elmer Davis over the ABC radio network later that year; "the Thomas Committee has helped whip it up, so has the not very well-informed clamor of some Congressmen outside that committee; and the result is that we are making ourselves ridiculous in the eyes of the world."[3]

Neither Nixon nor the committee's majority was ready to go so far as to outlaw the party. Nixon has since written that he was opposed to such a step because it would be "inefficient and counterproductive." Such doubts were reinforced by testimony from several prominent Americans, including former ambassador to Moscow William C. Bullitt, American Federation of Labor president William Green, and Eric Johnston of the Motion Picture Producers Association. The most influential dissent came from FBI director J. Edgar Hoover, who cautioned about the effect of driving the party underground and making martyrs out of Communists.[4]

Additional support came from John Foster Dulles. Dulles, then with the law firm of Sullivan and Cromwell (which Nixon had once tried to join), was clearly troubled. "I doubt the efficacy of either of the two bills," he wrote to Nixon, "largely because of the fact that the 'Communist Party' is such a nebulous thing." There would be difficulty in distinguishing between those who would accept the "iron discipline of the party" and those who "are finding in the Communist Party an outlet for a sense of grievance."[5]

By the time the legislative subcommittee continued the series of hearings, this time under Nixon's chairmanship, the Sheppard and Rankin bills had been discarded. Even McDonough's bill, which also involved a ban by condemning anyone "practicing communism" as a "treasonable enemy of the United States," had taken a back seat to the shrewder approach contained in Mundt's version.

The essential idea behind the legislation recommended by the congressman from South Dakota was the registration of individual Communists and their organizations. The rationale involved making them more visible for easy identification during some future emergency.

Nixon presided over the hearings that were held in the Old House Office Building. That his performance was something refreshing for HUAC is clear. They were unfailingly conducted by Nixon with dignity and intelligence. He even began with an introductory statement that offered guidance rather than compliance with preconceived notions. As he wrote to Dulles, "We are also deeply concerned that in our efforts to combat and break up subversive movements through legislation, we do not impair or destroy any of the rights and liberties which we hold so fundamental here in America."[6] Respectable leadership for HUAC was a unique sight. One deprived of that opportunity was Adolf A. Berle, Jr., who testified when Nixon was absent on February 11 and encountered the frustration of having the proceedings turned into a shambles by the antics of Congressman Rankin.

More distressing was the fact that it had little to do with Berle, who was not at all antagonistic. The former New Deal brain-truster, a law professor at Columbia University in 1948, was an accommodating, knowledgeable, and stimulating witness who made no attempt to show disdain for the committee and its functions. He won praise from Congressmen McDowell and Rankin for having been "one of the best witnesses."[7] His major problem that day was the need for patience, a problem directly caused by the absence of Congressman Nixon.

While Berle testified, Nixon was in Bethesda Naval Hospital with a fractured elbow, the result of a fall on the icy steps in front of his Alexandria apartment while carrying little Tricia. Driven to the hospital by his administrative assistant, William A. Arnold, he was X-rayed and the bones were reset.[8] Unfortunately for Berle, that was the only session of the hearings that Nixon missed. Fortunately for the committee, he returned when they resumed eight days later.

That one day's evidence made his value very clear. With Nixon gone, Rankin took over the stage, rendering Acting Chairman John McDowell quite impotent. Berle, a former assistant secretary of state and ambassador to Brazil, labored at reading a statement that questioned the wisdom of legislation aimed at outlawing the Communist party and suggested that such a move would constitute both an oversimplification of the problem and an overreaction to the kind of danger that was involved. Rankin, unrestrained, pushed his way into the center. While Berle composed himself with patience and dignity, the veteran legislator from Mississippi managed to get himself on the record in hot opposition to all of the "crises" worming away at the nation from within. Each and every one involved Communists — in government, in labor unions, in education ("the most dangerous Communists in America are those Red professors"), in the Justice Department persecuting the white people of the South — who "jockey their way into positions of power or influence," and on the radio.[9]

"Mr. Berle," he suddenly asked at one point after the witness had suggested improving visa restrictions, "is it not a fact that the percentage of Communists in the United States is greater today than it was in Russia when they took over?"

"I should be inclined to doubt that," replied Berle. "It would, though, turn on your definition of 'Communist.'"

Unable to get the answer he wanted, Rankin said, "I can understand that this is correct, and I think we can show that," and then added, "and the Communist leaders in this country feel confident that they are going to take over, sooner or later."

"As a danger to the United States," replied Berle, "frankly, I don't see it. — Communism makes sense to certain people in the frozen classes of some European countries. Here it is just blithering nonsense."[10]

So it went. Berle remained controlled, laboring to bring information and expertise to guide the pending legislation, and asking at one point only if Rankin minded if he could finish making a suggestion.[11] The matter becomes more ludicrous when one remembers that Berle was a friendly witness, at least in the sense that he did not obstruct, was not placed on the defensive about his own loyalties, and had no need to plead protection with constitutional guarantees against self-incrimination.

Without Nixon, individuals such as Rankin became throwbacks to the Dies Committee.

Why respect came to Nixon early becomes obvious when comparing the Berle-Rankin exchanges with the events of the day before Nixon broke his elbow. That day's witness was Arthur Garfield Hays, some three decades older than Nixon and best known as a distinguished civil liberties lawyer and a member of the most prominent New York firm specializing in that field. As general counsel for the American Civil Liberties Union (ACLU), he practiced largely constitutional commercial law in New York.

Hays testified before the subcommittee with Nixon chairing the panel. The civil libertarian, of course, flatly opposed attempts to outlaw the Communists. Not only would such laws probably be "unconstitutional" but they would "be futile and defeat the very purpose intended," he told the committee. In a free country, it would be best to meet all dangers without passing oppressive laws, he pointed out. "When you impose penalties on free speech you are corrupting free speech," said Hays. "To say we're going to bar you from politics because of what you believe and we are going to call you a foreign agent just because of what you believe, is beyond my comprehension."[12]

Nixon then reminded Hays that his American Civil Liberties Union itself had barred from office all Communists and fascists as early as February 6, 1940, eight years earlier, after the Russians and Germans had sealed their alliance by invading Poland. How, he wanted to know, could Hays reconcile that with his own present position?

"I am glad you asked that question," said Hays.

"If you can," Nixon shot back, "answer it very quickly."

The ACLU, Hays explained, had been contending with such board members as Elizabeth Gurley Flynn. The former IWW "Rebel Girl" was by then a well-known Communist. Fellow travelers also sat on the board. They were obstructionists. "The Communists," he explained, "regarded civil liberties as a means to an end where the rest of us regard civil liberties as an end in itself. In other words, they were influenced whenever it hit a workingman, but they objected very much to, say, that Henry Ford had a right to go into court and defend his particular view on labor unions. We would defend industrialists just as well as labor unions. . . . When Elizabeth Gurley Flynn came out with an article in the Daily Worker that attacked us all as insincere, that we did not believe in what we were doing, that we are defending big interests, and that we are a bunch of hypocrites; then we discharged Miss Flynn from the board and the rest resigned."

Nixon, getting what he was waiting for, followed through. "The only people who resigned from the board of directors were either Communists or fellow travelers, as a result of that action?" he asked.

"Yes," said the ACLU spokesman.

"In other words," said Nixon, "this change in the board that was made was directed against Communists. In other words, you do not feel that the American Civil Liberties Union could do a proper job with the Communists so you passed a rule against them, but you wouldn't want us to do that on a national level?"

Laughter in the hearing room interrupted the parrying.

Hays, recovered, explained that "we did not want directors who were Communists because we adopted the principle we wanted people running the union who believe in free speech as an end in itself, not as a means to an end. These people believe in ideology as in Russia and we thought people who were on the board should have the same ideas we had."

"That is the way *we* feel," replied Representative Nixon.

Hays fought back. "But you have no right to do it," he insisted. "In 1940 we passed a resolution to the effect that only those who could serve as directors who believe in free speech as an end in itself and who did not believe in totalitarian doctrines and every member had to state that he was not a Communist or Fascist and did not believe in those things. . . . Some people feel Communists belong on our board but we don't want on our board people who do not believe in free speech, but it was on the basis of the resolution that they were put off."

"I think that makes the position of the Civil Liberties Union quite clear to the committee," responded Nixon.[13]

A few minutes later, Hays argued that going after the Communists by branding them as part of an international conspiracy, which was the major rationale for denying the party political freedom, recalled popular attitudes that existed toward American socialists during the 1920s.

"Do you feel that the Socialists of the twenties were as dangerous . . . to our form of government as the Communists are today?" asked Nixon.

"I do," agreed Hays, "because I do not think either of them are at all dangerous."

Nixon: "In other words, you say that as far as danger to the United States is concerned, and insofar as changing our form of government to a totalitarian form of government is concerned, the Socialists and the Communists are just as dangerous."

Hays denied he had said anything of the kind.

"Then what did you say?" Nixon asked.

"I said that since I regard neither of them as at all dangerous, I think one is as dangerous as the other. They are two zeros, in my judgment."

"Then," Nixon reaffirmed, "you do say that one is as dangerous as the other."

"Like zero is to zero," said Hays.[14]

The matter of outlawing the Communist party remained the central piece of contention. Opponents generally agreed that it would be unconstitutional or unwise, or both. They cited the precedent involving free speech and association and the further undesirable effect of driving the party underground, where it would become far more dangerous. But that something ought to be done was clear even to prominent attorney Morris Ernst of the ACLU. Instead of merely targeting the Communist party, Ernst kept pressuring for registering all groups that tried to influence public opinion.[15]

James Burnham, a former Trotskyite and professor of philosophy on the faculty of New York University, was less certain. Burnham, who had just published *The Struggle for the World*, which warned against naive American acceptance of Wendell Willkie's "one world" concept in the face of a conspiratorial Communist menace, was confirming his stature as a leading anticommunist theoretician.[16] Notably absent from Burnham's 1947 book was much alarm over the internal Communist threat.

Only forty-three when he appeared before Nixon's panel on February 19, 1948, Burnham had no doubt about what would happen if the party were outlawed. The fact was, he said, that "the most serious part of the Communist movement is already underground. Illegalization would deprive the underground apparatus of the cover and protection and funds that they now enjoy from the legal organizations."

The defeat of fascist totalitarianism had left the Communist version as the major threat in the world. Nor did Burnham now dispute that the danger was internal as well. The American variety was merely part of a "world-wide conspiratorial movement, politically based upon terror and mass deception, which has for its objective the conquest of a monopoly of world power." To simply "lump genuine Communists together with socialists, liberals, honest progressives and others who may in one or another legitimate way be critical of certain abuses" was a "reactionary tendency" that rendered communism its greatest service. Since neither exposure nor education had been effective deterrents, he argued, the ideology should be outlawed. "If we permit a murderer the free run of our house," Burnham warned, "we can expect that in the end someone is going to get killed."[17]

Still, Burnham's testimony reflected the dilemma of those who, unlike the Steeles and Rankins, had no simple solution. So hedged was his position, in fact, that two general histories of the committee portray him as taking the side of those ready to see the Communist party outlawed.[18] Before he completed his testimony, however, he backed away from that view under Nixon's interrogation.

As though Burnham's statement had not really explained his position, Nixon pressed further. "Do you believe that the American Communist

Party and the American Communists constitute a potential danger to the country which would justify the legislative steps which you have suggested in your statement?" he asked.

Burnham repeated his fear of American communism as the extension of an international empire posing "a very serious danger." Upon further reflection under Nixon's prodding, he had another thought. In approaching the problem, he then suggested, "one has to be very experimental. I would not say, for instance, that tomorrow it should be outlawed without further discussion and the exploring of further possibilities." The Mundt bill, he finally concluded, "would be a good experimental approach."

"An interim approach," said Nixon.

"Yes, to see how that works; and then check up in six months or a year and consider whether further legislation is necessary. I have heard very well-argued cases made for that approach," stated Burnham. While he seemed convinced that outlawing the party might become necessary, he, for one, was not ready to move in that direction just yet.[19]

Nixon had heard what he wanted to hear. The hearings over, he wrote a report in behalf of the subcommittee. The object of legislation, he argued, was the need to strike at the "American cadre of the Soviet-directed communist conspiracy" to keep the alien power from having "the unfair advantages in this conflict of the unrestricted use of illegal means, the cloak of secrecy and fraud, and the assistance and direction of a foreign communist dictatorship."[20] Convinced that registration was wiser than trying to outlaw the Communist party, Nixon joined forces with Mundt and shaped what became known as the Mundt-Nixon bill.

The outcome was essentially a compromise between an outright ban and forcing party members to so identify themselves by registering as Communists. But the real significance has been lost, buried in the endless recountings of congressional responses to mounting anxieties over internal security; lost amid eagerness to point out that passage of legislation justified HUAC's existence, or that the Mundt-Nixon bill became the basis for the more significant McCarran Act of 1950; lost, finally, in the observation that the House version, limited as it was, without an immediate future, was the only piece of legislation that bore Nixon's name.

But the Mundt-Nixon bill's importance was more symptomatic. It took the measure of popular confidence as it existed in mid-1948, a time before Whittaker Chambers made his sensational charges against Alger Hiss, months before the Republican party snatched defeat from the jaws of victory in that year's presidential election; before Julius and Ethel Rosenberg and the Soviet atomic bomb; before the overthrow of Chiang Kai-shek; before the prominence of McCarthy; and before the North Korean drive on Seoul. There was still a relative modicum of reason. Loyal men could still be concerned with process. Safeguarding the Union did not have to mean destroying the Constitution. Above all, Mundt-Nixon demonstrated that the House felt it important to protect itself against charges that it had failed to act.

The final product was a compromise that was not a simple brokering of extremes. The fine point involved a split between outlawing an abhorrent political belief or outlawing those organized to express that belief. One could argue, as did Nixon, that civil liberties were unhampered, that the Communist party was not outlawed, that Americans still retained freedom of political association. The great virtue of Mundt-Nixon was that men of goodwill could claim that they had not surrendered basic constitutional principles even when pressed by the enemies of liberty.

But they had constructed serious obstacles to political freedom. Their major stroke required the annual registration of Communist organizations and their members. Whether a unit was Communist would be determined, according to an amendment offered by Nixon, by whether it was "reasonable to conclude that it is under the control" of the directorship of the international Communist movement. At the same time, although the bill merely required registration, it also provided that any efforts in behalf of a foreign government to establish a totalitarian dictatorship in the United States would bring to those who had previously admitted their membership in the group up to ten years in jail, a ten-thousand-dollar fine, and the loss of citizenship. Reminiscent of the World War I espionage acts was a requirement for the labeling of propaganda sent through the mails or broadcasts made by Communist front or Communist political organizations. Their members were also barred from nonelective federal jobs and denied passports.[21]

But what did the bill really mean? Was it disingenuous to pretend that coercing admission that one was part of an illegal conspiracy was much different from being denied political freedom? Arguments by Nixon and others who advanced their approach over outlawing the Communist party sounded false, as though they were championing civil liberties when, in effect, they were handmaidens to a backdoor assault. Not until key aspects of the bill appeared in a different piece of legislation did the courts get a chance to decide the issue.

The Mundt-Nixon bill was reported out of HUAC on April 29 and immediately became the center of controversy. A resolution passed by the Americans for Democratic Action warned that the bill was a "dangerous and futile attempt to repress the Communists" that would only force Communists underground and drive "well-meaning citizens from virtually every kind of progressive public activity." Nixon, invited to state his case on the ABC radio program "America's Town Meeting of the Air," upheld his achievement as the best of the possible approaches. His prepared remarks stated that he realized "that many well intentioned people who call themselves liberal indulge this fantasy. Let them remember, however, that the liberal who wants to tolerate everything will wake up some day to find that he himself is not being tolerated, but liquidated. It has happened elsewhere and it can happen here."[22]

Three days of mid-May debates revealed the difficulty of congressional moderates. Even J. Edgar Hoover, who supported their fight to kill the bill, arguing that Communists would merely be driven underground, never had a chance. Neither did Representative Chet Holifield's attempt to modify the word "danger" by inserting "potential" for "clear and present." Vito Marcantonio of New York, who had little competition for vigorous leadership of the opposition, scored a debating point by challenging majority leader Charles Halleck to submit the bill to the attorney general for an opinion as to its constitutionality. Marcantonio and his allies cried "fascist," while a congressman from South Carolina declared that the "security of this nation demands that all Communists within our borders be rendered politically and economically impotent." Or, as George A. Dondero of Michigan declared, "The world is divided into two camps, freedom versus Communism, Christian civilization versus paganism, righteousness and justice versus force and violence."[23] The arrival of telegrams from the CIO calling for the bill's defeat only stiffened the determination of its supporters. Amendments to strengthen the bill passed without even perfunctory calls for either standing or teller votes.

Still, the fact remains that Mundt-Nixon was something to argue over rather than vote against. In terms of whether to vote for or against, there simply was no real issue — outside, that is, private chambers. Those who tried to attack HUAC by contending that the committee served no legislative function would now have to try other arguments. Those who questioned Mundt-Nixon's constitutionality knew that statesmanship would come more easily to judges who did not have to face elections. The most conscientious civil libertarians, Democrats as well as Republicans, asked themselves whether they preferred to be memorialized as fallen heroes in the battle for free speech or as legislators noted for their durability. Mundt-Nixon cleared the House on May 19 in a breeze, with two-to-one support from Democrats and virtual unanimity among Republicans. One-fourth of the negative votes came from the New York City delegation. The 319–58 roll call vote, however, failed to assure Senate action.[24]

Once in the upper chamber, the bill remained in the Judiciary Committee, the victim, in effect, of a national debate around the issue of the wisdom of making the Communist party illegal. Most dramatic, and probably most inhibitive to Senate action, was the Stassen-Dewey radio debate that May 15. Broadcast from Portland, Oregon, the two candidates for the Republican presidential nomination argued the issue nationally. Thomas Dewey's warning that it constituted "thought-control" and "an attempt to beat down ideas with a club," as well as "a surrender of everything we believe in" clearly bested Harold Stassen's support for outlawing the party.[25]

In 1948, what historian Caute calls the great fear still had a way to go. What happened during the next two years was far less conducive to homilies about civil liberties. Evidence of internal subversion multiplied, and with sufficient drama to engage the most detached. Countermoves at home took the form of state-required loyalty oaths for teachers and other employees, citizen anticommunist vigilante groups, and, in Peekskill, New York, the clubbing by war veterans of a crowd that had just attended a concert by Paul Robeson, whose pro-Soviet sentiments had marked him a fellow traveler.

The Congress gave new life to Mundt-Nixon via the McCarran Act of 1950. Named after a Democrat, Pat McCarran, a zealous Red-hunter from Nevada, the legislation was enacted over a vigorous Truman veto. For the most part built around the Mundt-Nixon concepts, it exceeded that model in key ways. In contrast with the refusal of the Senate to act in 1948, now only a little band of liberals stood in the way. Even such erstwhile champions of civil liberties as Paul Douglas of Illinois and Hubert Humphrey of Minnesota, in what Caute describes as "a liberal maneuver to divert the cannibal's appetite by promising him a feast of blood," inserted a provision to place Communists in detention camps in the event of a national emergency.[26] Only afterward, in a time of less anticommunist hysteria and less worry about retribution, did the Supreme Court rule that compelling registration contravened protection against self-incrimination contained in the Fifth Amendment. Still, at the time, HUAC's rationale for existence was vindicated, and so was Nixon's role as a leading participant in the making of legislation that was representative of an era.

It may readily be argued that the Mundt-Nixon bill was but one link to the McCarran Act. Alger Hiss and Whittaker Chambers managed to place the entire matter beyond debate; after that, only those who still had illusions were true believers in the progressive dream. For Nixon, the irony was that Chambers's charges against Hiss came after the deliberations over control legislation and after the hesitations of 1948 and inaction by the Senate. His leadership in the celebrated espionage case joined with such external events as the Korean War to condition the climate for something more significant.

Nixon did not delay his initiative until the actual fighting began in Asia. The political opportunity was unquestionably present, but to him, along with a new political generation, the intolerable had gone on far too long. It was most natural for Nixon to use his prominence on the security issue to continue the fight against internal subversion. In January of 1950, just after Hiss was convicted but almost eight months before passage of the McCarran Act, Nixon took the House floor to explain the significance of his own findings. Fittingly, he subtitled his talk "A Lesson for the American People." Ralph de Toledano later called it "the opening gun in a long war."[27]

The message was about the past and the future, about a pattern of laxity and cover-ups involving "considerations which affect the very security of this Republic." As the Hiss case unfolded, the implications became more serious. That a Red network existed was dangerous enough; in the annals of international espionage, it was hardly surprising. But, as Nixon summarized his case that day, to have it systematically ignored and even covered up by Washington was quite another matter. As late as December 1948, the Justice Department had been ready to drop the Hiss case for lack of evidence. Nixon enumerated how time after time no action was taken despite evidence showing the magnitude of the crimes. It had required the dramatic uncovering of the so-called pumpkin papers to compel the action that the government had resisted even after Chambers had produced documents that had been hidden in the dumbwaiter shaft of a Brooklyn tenement. For much of the way, the Justice Department was as great an obstacle as any Hiss had been able to devise.

Nixon spoke with the authority of a man for whom nothing was as glorious as vindication. Still, his approach and tone avoided the excesses that were quickly becoming the staples of headlines. Nixon, unlike some others who rushed to take advantage of the situation, argued that the undermining came not from subversion, not part of a "Red network," but from laxity, a tendency to minimize the danger. "The reason for their failure to act," he explained, was "that administration leaders were treating the reports of Communist espionage on a 'politics-as-usual' basis." As he spoke, he underscored his point by displaying eight pages of photostatic copies in the handwriting of Harry Dexter White, a senior Truman appointee. Thereby, he made the first public revelation of laxity charges that would later be lodged against Truman's administration by Eisenhower's first attorney general, Herbert Brownell. "The great lesson which should be learned from the Alger Hiss case," he concluded, "is that . . . traitors in the high councils of our own Government make sure that the deck is stacked on the Soviet side of the diplomatic table." Read even today, the House speech constitutes a severe indictment of those who clung to the delusions of the popular front. As one writer has put it so perceptively: "The Hiss Case was important because it represented the only successful prosecution of a prominent government official for pro-Communist activities. It gave all those elements in the United States who were so anxious to prove heavy Communist infiltration and dominance of the wartime and postwar American Government a specific case to cite."[28]

For Nixon himself, nothing had matched the Hiss case for drama, shock, and as a glimpse of some of the players who were in Washington during New Deal days. Nor did anything else give the young congressman such quick entrée to senior political leaders and the nation's communications establishment. National attention was, of course, priceless for a young politician. His diligence did help secure Hiss's conviction. If that was the ticket to fame for the thirty-seven-year-old congressman, it was also regarded by his defenders as the main reason for his controversial reputation. During a period when much was written to sort out the reasons for Nixon's image, a 1956 article by journalist Ray Henle catalogued eight liabilities. There was a "ninth reason — one never stated," added Henle. "He put Alger Hiss in jail — and in doing so embarrassed many liberal columnists and Fair Dealers who labelled as 'red herring' Republican attempts to expose Communists in Government. Such public humiliation is hard to forgive."[29]

Henle's point was valid. Nixon's reputation had been made at the price of exposing disloyalty to the United States that was lodged within FDR's New Deal and the establishment-dominated State Department. A considerable portion of Hiss's defense was even based on the assumption that one with his impeccable standing and ties to the elite social establishment could not possibly have been guilty of betraying national security.

There could have been no better vindication for HUAC's zeal in tracking down the Red network and bringing names and faces before the American public. Right after the Hiss-Chambers hearings, chief investigator Robert Stripling made the portentous declaration that "Communist forces now maneuvering in our Government, labor, education, research, religion, entertainment, journalism, radio and other spheres of American life represents a cancerous growth."[30] It was against such assumptions, with all the potential for hysteria, that Hiss had tried to rally his upper-class friends. They were waging class warfare in reverse: Nixon the commoner taking on the American aristocracy, and, of all outrageous things, accusing the privileged of indifference and even complicity in the face of the enemies of capitalism.

The "charges" against Nixon — and it is fair to call them precisely that — can be enumerated as follows: He knew all along that Hiss was probably guilty because of inside knowledge that the New Dealer had belonged to a Communist cell. He thereupon exploited the case for his own political profit, staging a dramatic show complete with a grand exhibit of his prized "catch," aided by that new but still limited technological achievement, television. This version renders his conduct fully

consistent with HUAC's sordid tradition. Such dramatics allegedly included staging a return from a vacation to extract maximum publicity
for himself by focusing attention on his triumphant display of the in-
criminating pumpkin papers. Nixon thereby made the most of his opportunities.

He and his supporters usually respond to such charges by contending
that his misdeed was less in bringing the message than in exposing a
person with the standing, respectability, and connections of an Alger
Hiss. But Nixon has since argued that not until the perjury conviction
did the public wake up to the realities of communism in government.
The earlier alerts had merely "meant opposition to the kind of dictatorial
state socialism that existed in Russia and that many Americans saw as a
negation of everything America stood for."[31]

Democrats could not win that argument. If they decided to reform
ways of old, they had to admit to past laxity. In the hands of certain
extremists, such acknowledgment, implied or direct, would be used to
prove complicity by Roosevelt's "socialists" with the international Soviet
conspiracy. Or, as Allen Weinstein has pointed out, the case confirmed
the failure of their own toleration toward Stalinism.[32]

The lack of greater vigilance is not surprising. During FDR's time,
Reds in Washington hardly seemed worthy of much attention. They
surely were there, but even in Whittaker Chambers's estimation, their
presence in government numbered some seventy-five out of a half-
million federal workers. Moreover, they were in small, scattered clusters;
they were known in several agencies and on some congressional committees. Their major commitment was to influence policymaking rather
than espionage. The period of the Soviet-Nazi alliance was brief, starting
with the weeks before their invasion of Poland and ending with the opening of Hitler's eastern front and his drive toward Moscow in the spring
of 1941. In America, the pact between Stalin and Hitler was the most
fruitful spur for the Communist hunt by the Dies Committee and, in
1940, passage of the Smith Act, making it illegal to "teach or advocate"
the overthrow of the government. Three-quarters of Americans favored
outlawing membership in the Communist Party.[33]

The end of the Soviet-Nazi alliance and, especially, America's entry
into the European war after Pearl Harbor, then relaxed the already
feeble safeguards against increased pro-Soviet influence in Washington.
Revulsion toward Hitler induced sympathy for Stalin's Russia, the heroic
victim of the Wehrmacht. The Soviet Union, even the character of Stalin's personal dictatorship, was easily glorified, as was Mother Russia
herself in a number of wartime Hollywood films, when the great bear
of the east became the heroic, indomitable barrier against the German
superrace. The distance between contempt and romanticization can be
very small indeed, and the United States and the USSR, during that

period of the "strange alliance," submerged many of their traditional differences.[34]

In a climate of both fear and opportunism, exaggeration and portentous predictions were encouraged. Earl Latham, a historian of the Red scare, agreed that Communists' influence in the United States was virtually impossible to gauge and concluded that the "public record supports the finding that there was considerable activity, and that it was not negligible, even if exaggerations are discounted." A more recent examination has demonstrated that what liberals chose not to believe was nevertheless true: Communist cadres, whose leadership rendered the party more potent than its limited membership would indicate, reacted in large measure to directions that came from the Comintern in Moscow.[35]

It took very little to inflame an already frightened nation. Given the cultural loathing toward communism and the handiness of such fear to a wide variety of people who were eager to promote their self-interest — politicians, businessmen, organized ethnic groups, and assorted hucksters of sensation via the printed word and over the airwaves — it was easy to so alarm the nation that it shifted from the complacency of the thirties all the way to the hysteria of the forties and fifties. "Anti-Communism . . . was for the most part easily assimilated into the conservative credo of the 1950s," George H. Nash has written. "Both libertarians and traditionalists discerned in the 'god that failed' a case study for their deepest convictions."[36]

The backdrop was perfect for the dramatics of an Elizabeth Bentley. The matronly Vassar graduate, the former lover of a deceased Russian agent and an admitted ex-courier of secret government documents to Soviet spies, provided the melodramatics that "confirmed" why Americans had reasons for becoming so insecure. She had first told her story to the FBI in 1945 but apparently no action was taken; in 1947 she had repeated her tale before a federal grand jury in New York. Not until 1948, in the midst of preelection politicking, were Bentley's accusations made public.

Appearing before HUAC on July 31, 1948, Bentley told all about her Communist cell. Moreover, she named names; her "traitors" were prominent in New Deal agencies. Bentley, quickly dubbed the "Red spy queen" by the press, became an immediate sensation. HUAC staff members went to work searching for a corroborative witness. That person, who first faced the committee in executive session on the morning of August 3, was a writer and senior editor for *Time*, Whittaker Chambers. Getting him before the committee was the inspiration of Karl Mundt, then the acting chairman, who had received a tip from a New York newspaper reporter. Thus, that August, played out behind closed doors and in open sessions, were the countercharges that resulted from Chambers's naming of Alger Hiss as the government insider who had supplied him with classified documents during the 1930s. Little wonder, as Nixon later recalled, that there was "deep concern among many about the effect of Communists and those who were being used by them. My concern was how deep did the Hiss phenomenon run."[37]

Matters that now seem clear then played out before the public as a complex series of hearings conducted by the House Committee on Un-American Activities. Did Hiss, like Chambers, belong to a Communist cell in Washington during the 1930s? Did Hiss pass on to him government documents, perhaps copied by his wife, Priscilla, on an old Woodstock typewriter? Was Hiss lying when he denied all — espionage, communism, even ever having known Chambers? Was Chambers perjuring himself by implicating Hiss?

To the world, including Richard Nixon, Alger Hiss was no ordinary defendant. The contrast between him and Chambers was vivid. As Nixon would later put it, Hiss was charged with leading a secret and traitorous existence as the "striking representative of the fashionable Eastern establishment — a graduate of Harvard Law School, clerk to a Supreme Court Justice, an aide to Franklin D. Roosevelt at the Yalta conference and one of the major organizers of the United Nations conference in San Francisco." Hiss's "impeccable social and intellectual qualifications" enabled him to plead "innocence by association."[38]

Hiss, in short, was the quintessential New Deal reformer. He exuded the aura of a gentleman bred to social responsibility, the finest product of the class that shared his education and social standing. Tall and lean, he was an especially youthful-looking forty-four, an image caught by the first television cameras ever brought into a congressional hearing room.[39] Even his defense was prepared with the assistance of Dean Acheson. If, as one historian has written, "demeanor evidence were crucial, Hiss would have won easily."[40]

According to a number of writers, both friendly and critical, Nixon received some early information about the activities of certain Communists from Father John Cronin, who taught economics and philosophy at St. Mary's Seminary in Baltimore.[41] Cronin began his career as a student of the progressive Father John A. Ryan, and his work led to the labor movement, where he became a CIO organizer. Before long, he became increasingly conscious of communism within the labor federation. He began to gather data, first on his own and then at the request of the FBI. He exchanged information with William C. Sullivan, who later became one of J. Edgar Hoover's top lieutenants. Cronin drew as well from an interview that Whittaker Chambers gave to the Bureau in 1945. The Bureau also had a memo that described revelations made by Chambers in 1939 to Adolf Berle at the State Department. In response to a request from Archbishop Mooney of Detroit, Father Cronin developed a confidential report, which he circulated among the Catholic hierarchy in November of 1945. The completed document, entitled "The Problem of American Communism," mentioned Hiss. But by that point, the priest's interest in communism cannot be said to have remained confined to domestic subversion. He became convinced that "Soviet plans for world domination" were evident through Comintern activity in the colonial world and in Latin America.[42] That was in 1947; and by then Father Cronin was both the assistant director of the Social Action Development of the National Catholic Welfare Conference in Washington and, from his base in Baltimore, a source of information on communism that was tapped by such congressmen as Charles Kersten of Wisconsin and John F. Kennedy.

Kersten introduced Nixon to the priest. Nixon, according to several reports, read the priest's findings and from them got sensitive intelligence about the activities of such people as Hiss, Chambers, Harry Dexter White, and Elizabeth Bentley. "The priest's briefings of Nixon and Kersten," contends historian Allen Weinstein, in the most comprehensive examination of the Hiss case, "included long discussions of Soviet espionage in America and mentioned the presence of 'certain Communists . . . in the State Department.'" According to this account, Nixon also read a copy of Cronin's report to the bishops, in which Hiss's name was prominent. The significant inference is that at that early date, long before the accusations that were traded during the summer of 1948, Nixon was aware of Hiss's role.[43]

Several things then follow: If he had such knowledge, the information was not shared with anyone, neither then nor later. It also means that any hunches to trust Chambers over Hiss, or suspicions that the latter was being deceitful because of the highly circumspect wording of his responses, were due far less to Nixon's superior acuity, less to his ability to suspect Hiss because he "always qualified his answer by saying that he did not know a man 'by the name of Whittaker Chambers,'" than to his private sources.[44] Without any direct evidence, only on the basis of repeated assertions by the priest that he and Nixon met in February 1947, Nixon has been charged with exploiting privileged information, a case of guilt by association, the historical Nixon versus the Nixon of caricature.

So, for some, the case against Nixon and his involvement in the Hiss case rests on nothing stronger than his subsequent reputation. The most obvious weakness in that analysis, however, is self-evident. It is inconceivable that the Nixon who was so zealous about exposing Communists to further his career somehow kept all of Cronin's information to himself until Chambers testified before HUAC on August 3, 1948. In an apparent contradiction, Cronin himself told Kornitzer that Nixon's "key contribution" in the Hiss case was his *"correct hunch* to trust Chambers rather than Hiss" (emphasis added), which also implies Nixon's ignorance of the information.[45]

Nor is there evidence that Nixon was unduly moved by what happened during the closed session of HUAC on a Saturday at the end of July. Elizabeth Bentley, the fortyish spy queen, told about her dozen years in the Communist Party and named subversives who were employed by the government. Most, like Harry Dexter White, Nathan Gregory Silvermaster, Victor Perlo, Charles Kramer, William Taylor, and Harry Magdoff, were key bureaucrats brought to Washington by the New Deal. Significantly, not a single account suggests that Nixon connected Bentley's testimony with what he should have known earlier from Cronin. Nor was it he who suggested that Chambers, who was known to have been a Communist in the 1930s, be subpoenaed to provide corroboration.

After Chambers first testified, Nixon did not merely go on his own "hunch" about the man's accuracy. He wanted to question Chambers further in executive session. He asked for and received HUAC's support as chairman of a special three-member subcommittee and went to New York on August 7. There, in the federal courthouse, the HUAC subcommittee spent three more hours with Chambers. Under intense questioning, the accuser offered personal details about Hiss that could only have come from intimate acquaintance. Chambers also accepted Nixon's suggestion that his testimony be verified by a lie detector, which Hiss later denigrated as "a proposal to rely on gadgets instead of standard procedures to create an aura of credibility for Chambers."[47]

At that point Nixon could have satisfied himself by rechecking with Father Cronin. Instead, he consulted with *New York Herald Tribune* correspondent Bert Andrews, a prize-winning journalist for stories about abuses of the government's loyalty program. Even after Andrews agreed that Chambers sounded as though he knew what he was talking about, Nixon's typical thoroughness sent him further, to William P. Rogers, the chief counsel for the Senate subcommittee that was investigating the Bentley charges, and to John Foster Dulles, who, along with Andrews, had helped Hiss get his job with the Carnegie Foundation. The expertise of Dulles's brother, Allen, the former Office of Strategic Services spymaster and future director of the Central Intelligence Agency, reinforced Nixon's convictions about Chambers's credibility. Nixon's caution about safeguarding the accused impressed Foster Dulles, who later said that "many people in that position, who appeared to have something sensational, would go ahead without waiting," but Nixon "wanted to be careful about hurting reputations." Dulles and the others relieved any doubts about being on the right track.[48]

For Nixon to favor Chambers over Hiss hardly required advance information from Father Cronin. Hiss was, to Nixon, superficial, privileged, one who, unlike his accuser, faced the world with impeccable social credentials. He symbolized, wrote Nixon, "a considerable number of perfectly loyal citizens whose theaters of operation are the nation's mass media and universities, its scholarly foundations, and its government bureaucracies."[49] Such men advance by pedigree and glamour, deceiving the world with cultivated facades, Nixon argued in *Six Crises,* which appeared a dozen years after Hiss's conviction, and shortly after his loss to John F. Kennedy.

Nixon, in sum, found it easy to believe Chambers. Their mutual attachment was immediate. That the *Time* editor was also a Quaker helped to bring them together. Chambers was the antithesis of the "establishment" Hiss, wrote Nixon, nondescript, awkward, rumpled, a "short and pudgy" figure. He faced the committee with unpressed clothes. A shirt collar, Nixon noticed, was curled over his jacket. He talked not with suave assurance but "in a rather bored monotone." In what must remain as a perfect example of self-conscious association, Nixon recalled that his instincts told him that, "in this case, the rather unsavory-looking Chambers was talking the truth, and the honest-looking Hiss was lying." Like "most men of quality," Nixon wrote, Chambers "made a deeper impression personally than he did in public."[50] He was serious, dedicated, informed, and perfectly pedestrian.

Throughout his career, what Hiss represented was never far from Nixon's mind. In a conversation with John Ehrlichman and Ronald Ziegler, his press secretary, the day before his first Christmas in the White House, the president railed against the press, complaining that "seventy-five per cent of those guys hate my guts. They don't like to be beaten." Ticking off a litany of incidents when he saw himself as victimized by media distortions, he inevitably lit on the matter of Alger Hiss. He was "alone" in that situation, he complained. Ninety-five percent of the columns and stories held that Chambers was lying. They believed Hiss, of course. Hiss was the "epitome" of the eastern establishment, while he and Chambers were "outsiders." That Hiss lied really rankled them. Intellectuals couldn't stand to lose a fight.[51]

At the federal trial for perjury that came after completion of HUAC hearings, Hiss's defense attorney called Chambers "a moral leper"; his background combined subversion and communism and lapses of character. He had even neglected to return books to the Columbia University Library.[52] Chambers was a onetime Wobbly, the confessed courier of government documents for delivery to Soviet agents; he had also provided editorial labor for the *Daily Worker,* articles for the leftist *New Masses,* and, for the American public, an English-language translation of Felix Salten's *Bambi.*

The contrast could not have been more remarkable. Hiss's self-assurance was fortified by confidence in his "integrity, loyalty and veracity" that was vouched for by two Supreme Court justices, Stanley Reed and Felix Frankfurter. Frankfurter said that he had never heard Hiss's reputation "called into question."[53]

Chambers, the sloppy Mr. Everyman, accused the Social Register Mr. Hiss of betraying his country, apparently reversing the natural order of things. Alistair Cooke wondered at a situation "in which the word 'spy' would come to lose its alien attributes and be allowed as a possible role even for a Yale or Harvard man in a Brooks Brothers suit." Walter Lippmann told fellow journalist Richard Rovere, "I know Alger Hiss. He couldn't be guilty of treason." That precocious literary critic Leslie Fiedler chimed in with the afterthought that "the history of Hiss is the prototypical history of the New Dealer at its best: the distinguished years at Harvard Law School, the secretaryship to the almost mythical Justice Holmes, the brilliant career that began in the Nye Committee and culminated at Teheran. . . . Lest the New Dealers seem 'Red-baiters,' they preferred to be fools." Later, when Truman's last secretary of state, Dean Acheson, he of the striped pants and Anglo-Saxon airs, continued to stand by Hiss even after his having been found guilty, an incredulous Senator Hugh Butler of Nebraska said, "I look at that fellow. I watch his smart-aleck manner and his British clothes and that New Dealism, that everlasting New Dealism in everything he says and does, and I want to shout, Get out, Get out. You stand for everything that has been wrong with the United States." Nixon, who merely called Acheson's loyalty "disgusting," reviewed Chambers's book, *Witness,* in the *Saturday Review of Literature* and predicted that "epithets will be directed against it in the drawing rooms, around dinner tables, and during the cocktail hours among the 'better' people." In it, Chambers recalled hearing a wealthy European explain the class culture in America as follows: "In the United States, the working class are Democrats. The middle class are Republicans. The upper class are Communists."[54]

The perception about Hiss was all that mattered, because the reality was generally ignored. The Hisses were "old family" and Alger did have the best of social and political connections. In effect, however, he was self-made. He was, as columnist Murray Kempton put it, "the child of shabby gentility."[55] His father was only forty-two when he lost his dry-goods importing business and, at the same time, faced overwhelming financial responsibilities. Alger was only nine when Charles Hiss committed suicide. The children were mainly brought up by their domineering mother, Minnie Hiss, who continued to make the rounds of Baltimore's civic and women's clubs.

Alger felt the least loved of the family's five children. Brother Bosley was a Bohemian who often ran away from home and, in the end, died of a kidney ailment that may have been alcohol-related. Just two years after brother Bosley's death, Hiss's older sister killed herself by swallowing a bottle of Lysol following a midnight quarrel with her husband. Alger, however, went on to Johns Hopkins University, where he made Phi Beta Kappa, and then became a star at Harvard Law School, both socially and academically. He made *Law Review* and was a protégé of Felix Frankfurter, finally matching the highest immediate aspiration of his peers by clerking for Justice Oliver Wendell Holmes.[56]

His eminence assured, his career in government began as counsel to the Nye Committee, which provided the most authoritative justification for America's pre–World War II isolationism, and included service with Roosevelt at Yalta, which affirmed the internationalist role for the postwar years. He was also prominent at the birth of the United Nations. He had, in effect, recovered and gone ahead of his family's lost stature, and made Washington's Social Register. To simply refer to Hiss as someone with a privileged background was indeed an oversimplification.

Although, like Hiss's, Chambers's family had also fallen, the facade was quite different. He was a writer, translator, editor, poet, and something of a religious mystic. In Kempton's words, "Chambers had traveled a wild, swarm-haunted route, an itinerant worker, a self-asserted veteran of the Industrial Workers of the World. He was unproductive as a writer because he had so much else to do. . . . He was a man who would rather do than write." He substituted faith in communism with a messianic zeal for exposing the great conspiracy. He had seen the light, had come clean, and was warning his fellow Americans about blindness toward the looming menace. "Mr. Hiss," he declared at one point, "represents the concealed enemy against which we are all fighting and I am fighting."[57] As an editor at *Time,* Chambers, to the annoyance of subordinates, was vigilant about ideological impurities infecting their copy.

Raised in what was then the open flatlands of Lynbrook, on Long Island's south shore, Chambers married a girl from Brooklyn, the daughter of Russian-Jewish immigrants. His "weekends," actually two midweek days, were spent away from Manhattan. He commuted regularly to his wife at their farm on Maryland's Eastern Shore. Esther Chambers remained supportive throughout the trial and hearings that followed, conspicuous only for her big black hat, but obviously, together with her husband, an inhabitant of the same world as the Nixons.

The two families began to socialize during that period. There were those occasions when Dick and Pat Nixon drove out to Westminster, sometimes even bringing along Nixon's parents. Frank Nixon had retired and moved east with Hannah to a farm in York, Pennsylvania, not much more than an hour's drive from Maryland's Eastern Shore.

The Nixons provided encouragement and comfort to the Chambers family. Dick was known as "Nixie" to the Chambers children. He was, as Chambers later wrote, "the kind and good, about whom they will tolerate no nonsense." Even then, in his descriptions of Nixon at the farm, he noted that he was both gentle and belligerent. "His somewhat martial Quakerism sometimes amused and always heartened me," Chambers wrote, and when the "kindest of men" talked about Hiss he did so "in his quietly savage way." At one point he said, "If the American people understood the real character of Alger Hiss, they would boil him in oil."[58]

Apart from their ideological differences, a similar relationship between the Nixons and the Hisses would be unimaginable. Not only was Alger from an alien, somewhat forbidding world, but so was his wife. Priscilla's family had been in America even longer than the Hisses. Her father was a trustee of Illinois College and a general agent of the Northwestern Life Insurance Company. Raised as a Quaker, she graduated from Bryn Mawr and won a scholarship to study English literature at Yale, where she met and married another graduate student, Thayer Hobson. She divorced Hobson soon after the birth of their child and then married Alger. They had gone together before she had met her first husband.

Priscilla was short and delicate. She was a "lady" of her class and generation, wore white gloves, and spoke in demure, measured words, except when she became impassioned, which, Chambers testified, brought out a fiery red blush. As between her and Alger, Chambers advised Nixon privately, she was the "red hot" one of the two. Still, Nixon later confessed that "it was hard for me to believe in view of her appearance and the way she acted that she could possibly have been aware of, let alone a part, of a communist conspiracy." She, as a woman, was perhaps even more foreign to Nixon's experiences than her husband, throwing him, as he later acknowledged, off stride and leading him to the one mistake he regretted having made during the hearings, not following up as he should have when she was on the witness stand. Unlike men, Nixon explained, women will rarely compromise to achieve their objectives. "They tend to be total idealists, true believers, whether the cause is on the left or the right."[59] He had never known a woman like Priscilla Hiss.

When, at HUAC's final session on August 25, Hiss challenged Chambers to repeat his charges before the public — and without congressional immunity — Chambers appeared on the "Meet the Press" radio interview program and responded to the very first question by saying, "Alger Hiss was a Communist and may still be one."

Through it all, the centrality of Nixon's role in the internal security controversy was beyond question. He alone among those in the hearing room on August 5, 1948, had been unimpressed by Hiss's initial testimony, doubting the credibility of the man's explanation and becoming pivotal to pursuit of the case. From that point on, Nixon, working with a small staff of five, had taken charge. He prepared the interrogation that included having both men square off against each other at a closed session in New York's Hotel Commodore. Nixon's interrogation broke down Hiss's veracity. As he pressed on, he won over the rest of the committee. From Chambers, he extracted details about the relationship between Hiss and Priscilla, about terms of endearment they used for each other, about hobbies, about how Hiss arranged for the curious disposition of an automobile. All this wore down Hiss's denials that he had ever known "a man by the name of Whittaker Chambers" and undercut his claim that there had simply been a benign relationship with a "George Crosley." Had Nixon not been so effective in advancing the committee's cause by getting Hiss to undermine himself during the closed meetings at the Hotel Commodore on August 17, Chambers later wrote, there would have been no challenge by Hiss to have the allegations repeated by his accuser in a public forum. No statement on "Meet the Press" would have led to no countersuit, no turning over of evidence and the subsequent federal trials. Moreover, it was all done within days. "The case was broken on the seventeenth in the Commodore," recalls Nixon; "the twenty-fifth we wrapped it up publicly. We never saw Hiss after that."[60]

Anticipating a suit after his "Meet the Press" appearance, Chambers went to Brooklyn and recovered government documents, some type-written, some handwritten, some on microfilm, that he had safeguarded at the apartment house of his wife's nephew, Nathan Levine, ten years earlier. Chambers, with a sense of theatrics as well as in the interest of security, placed the microfilm briefly in a hollowed-out pumpkin at his Maryland farm to prevent its being uncovered by hostile Justice Department investigators. It was Nixon who interrupted a Caribbean vacation with Pat to secure the additional evidence that the Justice Department had, in effect, challenged him to produce lest they indict Chambers rather than Hiss for perjury. Stripling and Nixon were photographed together triumphantly displaying the evidence, which Chambers had retained for a decade as his "life insurance." An erroneous report from Eastman Kodak that the company had not manufactured the film at the time Chambers claimed the microfilm copies were made provided a brief period of tension.

While the entire post–pumpkin papers litigation was out of HUAC's hands, it remains valid to say that Nixon's persistence and diligence exposed the most significant breaches of security that were the responsibility of long Democratic rule in Washington.

A grand jury was empaneled and Alger Hiss was indicted on December 15, 1948. After the first trial ended in a hung jury, a second brought in a conviction on two counts of perjury. The statute of limitations for espionage had expired. The five-year sentence, to be spent at the federal penitentiary at Lewisburg, Pennsylvania (forty-four months were actually served), was for having lied about his acquaintance with Chambers in the 1930s and about the fact that, like his accuser, he had been a member of the Communist party.

The Hiss case had an enormous impact. Nothing before it had so dramatically impugned the guardians of the national interest or convinced Americans, including Nixon, of the seriousness of Communist infiltration. On February 9, 1950, two weeks after Nixon reviewed the Hiss case before the House of Representatives, Senator Joe McCarthy spoke to a women's club in Wheeling, West Virginia, and made his celebrated charge that 205 Communists worked for the State Department.

Still, the suspicions about Father Cronin continued, helped in part by Nixon's own silence. In his memoirs, he mentions Cronin just once, in connection with the priest's assistance in the preparation of his acceptance speech for his renomination as the vice presidential candidate in 1956.[61] His earlier work, *Six Crises,* the most detailed Nixon treatment of the Hiss case, totally ignores Cronin. Whatever the reason for Nixon's reticence, there is no evidence that, even if he had been exposed to the doings of Hiss as early as the winter of 1947, the information seemed sufficiently compelling for him to have done anything about it.

Finally, in response to the present author, Nixon has acknowledged the relationship. He recalled that Father Cronin "became one of our most intimate friends during the Vice Presidential years," and he was often a guest in the Nixon household. There was nothing secret or particularly strange about the association. Cronin was of some minor political assistance, including helping to determine the drift of the Catholic vote. Earlier, when Nixon was a member of the Education and Labor Committee, along with Kersten and Kennedy, he found Cronin informative about communism in organized labor. While Cronin's memories about their early meetings report conversations about the Hiss-Chambers case, Nixon recalls that "our talks in that year only involved the subject of communist infiltration into labor unions."[62]

Had Nixon said anything more, it could only have been to acknowledge his failure to follow through after having seen Cronin's list of subversives with Hiss's name. If, in that sense, he was sensitive about having blundered by missing the opportunity, his silence protected the FBI man who did help him. That was Ed Hummel, of the Bureau's countersubversion unit.

Hoover's FBI had, of course, been aware of the allegations about Hiss for a long time. Nothing came of the initial session between Chambers and Berle, in 1939, but a second interview with Chambers in 1945 was followed by corroborating information that made the case a lot more solid. Nevertheless, Hoover cautioned against moving in on Hiss prematurely for fear of revealing confidential sources. His reports to the president and to the secretary of state did help to block a promotion for Hiss and probably led to his resignation from the State Department soon afterward. He went to work with the Carnegie Endowment for International Peace less than two months later.[63]

Still, it was not the FBI but Nixon who laid the groundwork for Hiss's indictment. Nixon advised Chambers to turn over the microfilm he had secured in a pumpkin. As Hoover biographer Richard Gid Powers has written, the director "was bothered and often frustrated by being a step or two behind Nixon and his energetic HUAC investigators."[64]

Nixon, who was charitable to the FBI director during his summary of the case on the House floor in early 1950, recalls that "whatever you want to say about Hoover, he was always very loyal to the boss. He was loyal to Truman, to Roosevelt, etc., and under the circumstances he was loyal to Johnson and he was loyal to me. And in this instance, particularly when Truman called it a 'red herring,' there was no way that Hoover was going to have his boys running around helping the Committee."[65]

The FBI did not get into the case, or question Chambers, until two weeks after Chambers had turned over a number of documents, including the Harry Dexter White photostats, to the Justice Department; they only got into it after Nixon and Stripling drove to see Chambers and learned Chambers had still more documentary evidence, some of which he produced a few days later from the hollowed-out pumpkin. "Therefore, the FBI did not touch the case until after that point. There was no way Ed Hummel could know anything. There was no way anybody could pass anything on to me because Hoover, consistent with his view of very loyally serving the boss, had not done anything with regard to the papers." Had he done so, Hoover or Hummel would have violated a presidential directive issued by Truman on August 5, the day of Hiss's first appearance before the committee, barring any government employee from divulging any loyalty information to a Congressional inquiry.[66] The order, of course, isolated the committee from any possible help from the executive branch.

When the Bureau did enter the case, "then Hummel, through Cronin, kept us informed about what was going on." Later, when Nixon published *Six Crises,* he shielded Hummel by simply stating that "lower echelon" Justice Department employees kept the committee informed. Nixon also recalls that "Hoover was always embarrassed about the fact that the FBI did not play a role in breaking the Hiss case." Nor did historian Athan Theoharis, in his book about the case, find evidence of a close FBI-HUAC relationship in the Bureau's files.[67]

*   *   *

Not until the Hiss trial, Nixon later held, was communism "seen as a clear and present danger to our way of life." To Chambers, wrote Nixon in *Six Crises,* went the credit for helping him realize battles were never over for Communists "so long as they are still able to fight." He also convinced Nixon about the "decay of the philosophy called 'liberalism' " and the "emergence of a liberal heresy called Communism" being played out in a confrontation between two superpowers contending to decide "whose hand will write the next several chapters of human history."[68]

With the Hiss experience very much in mind, Nixon later wrote about the differences between valid concern over internal security and making "a racket of anti-Communism. By exaggerating and making charges they can't prove," he wrote, in an allusion to Joe McCarthy, "they raise doubts as to the very real danger that Communist agents in the United States in fact present. On the other hand, it is just as irresponsible for the radicals of the left to pooh-pooh the danger of Communism at home by denying it exists, even in the face of facts like the Hiss case — thereby adding fuel to the fire of the demagogues on the right."[69]

Still, if the experience was an education for Nixon, the long-term view must be that the Hiss case did not alert Americans as much as it exaggerated the internal menace and thereby exacerbated anticommunism, and anticommunist opportunism, to a new and dangerous level. Before the Hiss case and especially after Truman delivered his speech on the necessity for military aid to Greece and Turkey, three-quarters of the American people were convinced that Russia was bent on dominating the world. Nor did they doubt that domestic Communists owed their primary loyalty to the Soviet Union, a view that was shared by three-fifths who responded to a Gallup poll taken that spring.[70] Virtually everybody without a stake in past policies jumped on the bandwagon. Amid that climate came Nixon, whose pursuit of Hiss served the interests of national security but, unfortunately, also helped lead to the excesses of McCarthy. The blame, however, should be less with Nixon for responding to the Hiss case as he did than to a national culture that permitted the "racket" of anticommunism to prosper. In retrospect, the major difference between Nixon and McCarthy was not only one of responsibility versus disregard of the consequences of recklessness but also that Nixon's tone was much more in accord with the mainstream of public opinion.

Nixon won his fame but paid his price, a point he has made many times since. While, ironically, those who continued to stand by Hiss charged, as one writer notes, that "Nixon and his supporters made Hiss a symbol of what the public feared," the case confirmed Nixon's "McCarthyite" reputation among those most loyal to the concept of the New Deal as the finest moment in American government. It left him, as he wrote in *Six Crises,* the target of "a residue of hatred and hostility" that influenced not only the far left "but also among substantial segments of the press and the intellectual community — a hostility which remains even today." Along with national fame, he became the victim of "an utterly unprincipled and vicious smear campaign" that included charges of "bigamy, forgery, drunkenness, insanity, thievery, anti-Semitism, perjury, the whole gamut of misconduct in public office, ranging from unethical to downright criminal activities." Allen Weinstein has written that "Hiss's fate symbolized for young liberals the quintessence of McCarthyism, its paranoid fear of any public figure to the left of Dwight Eisenhower." Two months after McCarthy's national debut as a Communist-fighter, Nixon's senatorial election campaign committee was advised that "it would be a mistake for Dick to key his major Fresno address on the Hiss case or Unamerican Activities."[71]

As late as the 1956 campaign, at a time when such people as Harold Stassen feared that Nixon was too controversial to remain on the party's national ticket, an aide to New York Democratic senator Herbert Lehman, a bitter opponent of both Nixon and McCarthy, tried to expose "the myth" that Nixon "was the man who tracked down Hiss and secured his indictment and conviction as a spy, perjurer, etc." A member of Lehman's staff, aided by the Legislative Research Service of the Congress, scoured the pages of the *New York Times* and the *Washington Post*. As Lehman's administrative assistant explained, "The whole object of this whole exercise is to ascertain exactly the role the press, at the time, reported Nixon to be playing."[72]

Lehman's researcher, Herbert W. Beaser, soon reported his detailed findings, which included the following sentence: "Nixon, all reporters in Washington know, has been more responsible than any other member of the committee for bringing Hiss Chamber [*sic*] facts into the open. It was Nixon, in fact, who ordered a subpoena served on Chambers — and who got a pumpkin and its contents." The administrative assistant had to acknowledge defeat: "I don't think we can do very much on this business," he admitted. "I don't think we can clearly nail Nixon as a liar, although he undoubtedly is one, in this instance, as in others."[73]

Nixon's defenders remained vigilant against all efforts to impugn his accomplishment. In 1962, publisher Walter Annenberg, one of Nixon's wealthy supporters, refused to permit two affiliates of ABC-TV under his control to carry a network program called "The Political Obituary of Richard Nixon." Annenberg's decision, which provoked a local storm, was over the appearance on the telecast of Hiss, "a convicted treasonable spy," as the publisher's flagship paper, the *Philadelphia Inquirer*, explained. In any event, argued Annenberg, the use of Hiss "was in bad taste and not in the public interest" because of the circumstances of his conviction, "and especially when that man was to comment on the career of a distinguished American who had served his country in high office."[74]

If the Hiss case was really about what Alistair Cooke called "a generation on trial," it was at least as much a trial for the post–New Deal generation as for the New Deal itself. Reluctance to confront the reality of Hiss's guilt combined with defensiveness about the record of both the Roosevelt and Truman presidencies. Once the problem was publicized, however much it may or may not have contributed to postwar disillusionment over the long run, Nixon's name, not McCarthy's, became associated in the public mind as the more credible spokesman. When, after McCarthy's Wheeling speech, Nixon said that the Hiss revelations were only "a small part of the whole shocking story of Communist espionage in the United States," he was both confirming and endorsing the senator's words.[75] Lacking McCarthy's flamboyance, to say nothing about his sheer irresponsibility, Nixon at the same time became more difficult to discredit. Unlike McCarthy's, Nixon's "Red-baiting" was mostly confined to attacking indifference toward the problem rather than the patriotism of a wide range of officeholders and other non-elected individuals. The "fighting Quaker" was, in the long run, far more formidable than "Tail Gunner Joe."

Richard Donovan, writing in *The Reporter* in 1952, noted that the details of Nixon's 1946 and 1950 election campaigns had been pretty much "brushed over" in most recent magazine stories. Tales of dirty tricks and Red-baiting against Voorhis and, later, Helen Gahagan Douglas, were not exactly the sort of material likely to make Nixon very distinctive in those days. At a time when television had yet to become a significant factor, politically or commercially, the Nixon story was more likely to reach the public via puff pieces in such popular magazines as *Life, Look,* and *Time.* What passed as flattery during an era when the American people were first adjusting to the reality of the cold war was how he exposed the Reds — not, as his critics later preferred to emphasize, how he exploited the fear. Nixon's self-promotion in preparation for higher office included a "confidential" memo for "the guidance of Mr. Raymond Moley" that contained the following sentence: "He single-handedly broke the Hiss case wide open when he spotted minute contradictions in Hiss' testimony at a time when all other members of the Committee, including John Rankin and the other Republicans, thought Hiss had cleared himself and were willing to publicly exonerate him." His senatorial campaign against Helen Gahagan Douglas in 1950, although presumably limited to California's voters, featured the national broadcast of a radio talk sponsored by the Committee of Ten Thousand, in which Nixon explicitly detailed how he managed to break the Hiss case despite the obstructions of Attorney General J. Howard McGrath and the Justice Department.[76]

Whittaker Chambers, however, having found the Heavenly City, was not interested in self-promotion. His cause was nothing less than the survival of western civilization, a theme James Burnham later developed in a book with the ominous title *The Suicide of the West.* Chambers spelled out his "god that failed" experience in a 1952 book, *Witness,* which was less an account of the Hiss affair, although it certainly was that, too, than a gospel in the cause of freedom. Only one who had seen Hell could warn about the fires. "Those who do not inform," he wrote about himself, "are still conniving at that evil."[77] As he went along, increasingly discouraged, he joined Bill Buckley's *National Review* as a senior editor but without much optimism that he could save Christianity.

Nor did he, unlike Buckley, value McCarthy. Writing to Buckley on the eve of the Army-McCarthy hearings, which contributed so heavily to the senator's downfall, Chambers doubted that McCarthy had "what it takes to win the fight for the Right." McCarthy was too parochial, too much a radical zealot, one who alienated as many as he convinced, even harming the cause by distracting attention from the Hiss case, "which remains the prime danger to the Left in that field."

Nixon, at least, was enough of an elusive strategist with more "of what it takes." Once the left managed to dispose of McCarthy, Chambers predicted, they would turn on Nixon. But Nixon, through his vice presidency under Eisenhower, made centrist politics a greater priority than anticommunism. As Chambers wrote to Buckley, "The masses must be won by the Republican Left while keeping the Republican Right within the family. Once I hoped that Mr. Nixon could perform this healing bond, holding the Right in line, while a Republican Left formed about him a core."[78]

As the 1960 convention neared, and Nixon's preoccupation with the presidency became most central, the Chambers-Nixon relationship dissolved. With his wife, Esther, Chambers accepted an invitation to visit Nixon, but their Sunday afternoon together was difficult. "We have really nothing to say to each other," Chambers reported to Buckley. The vice president seemed "crushed by the sense of the awful burden" of seeking high office. Chambers felt a sense of "dismay and a gnawing pity" at the overreaching of his old friend. "If he were a great, vital man, bursting with energy, ideas . . . I think I should have felt: Yes, he must have it, he must enact his fate, and ours." But that seemed lacking. "So I came away with unhappiness for him, for all." Then, in a particularly revealing passage, Chambers suggested rhetorically: "Of course, no such man as I have suggested now exists? Apparently not." But still he worried what a defeat would do to Nixon. "In short," he concluded, "I believe he is the best there is; I am not sure that is enough, the odds being so great."[79]

One year later, Chambers knew he was dying. His old friend Nixon had just gone through the pain of defeat in that narrowest of presidential elections. Chambers, writing to him for the last time, encouraged him to overcome the "sense and an impression of political come-down" and compete for the California governorship. "Great character," he advised, "always precludes a sense of come-down, greatly yielding to match the altered circumstances."[80]

Chambers had become a man of religious faith, one intolerant of secular ways; in his own way, an American Aleksandr Solzhenitsyn, little patient with the temporal forces of modern society. And, of course, he knew who Satan was. For all their earlier harmony, he and Nixon were talking about different worlds.

In 1954, when McCarthy's influence was cut down by both the Army-McCarthy hearings and condemnation by his Senate colleagues, Nixon's greater staying power became more apparent. Although the Hiss case is of obvious importance for an understanding of Nixon's career, how it shaped popular responses is of far greater significance. In a perceptive article on Chambers published in 1984, John Judis has cited Chambers's "immense" contribution to the postwar conservative movement. He struck a responsive chord with a new generation with his warning that the "Communist Party exists for the specific purpose of overthrowing the Government, at the opportune time, by any and all means; and each of its members, by the fact that he is a member, is dedicated to this purpose." Burnham, hitherto primarily alarmed about communism as an international menace, followed Chambers's lead with his *Web of Subversion* (1954). While detailing the insidious doings of the disloyal within government, Burnham now saw fit to issue his own clarion call: "During the 1930's and '40's," he wrote, "an invisible web was spun over Washington. . . . The existence of the web, and its general significance, are now, I think, beyond the doubt of any reasonable man who becomes acquainted with the evidence that has already been assembled." Washington, he added, was "only one section of a giant web that stretches with one or another degree of tenacity over the entire earth. Its center is Moscow's Kremlin. This world-wide web is, of course, simply one embodiment of the Soviet Communist world conspiracy." Their ultimate plan was to "draw the web tight, and to suffocate the government from within as part of the process of destroying it."[81]

Burnham, no John Rankin, Martin Dies, or even Joe McCarthy, was, like a new generation of post–New Deal nationalists, devoted to the warning sounded by Whittaker Chambers. Chambers won a posthumous Medal of Freedom from Ronald Reagan in 1984 and, at the thirtieth anniversary dinner of the *National Review,* was lauded by President Reagan and William F. Buckley, Jr., as a hero of the great American awakening.[82]

Chambers's role cannot be overestimated. As Buckley has said, "He reified the hard spiritual case against Communism more successfully than anyone in that generation."[83] Chambers's testimony and subsequent book helped to convince much of the postwar generation that Roosevelt

The Great Awakening							*181*

was an American Aleksandr Kerensky, which meant, of course, that the New Deal was but a prelude to a Soviet-style system of government. Richard Nixon, a charter disciple, may well have prevented the Justice Department from continuing to sit on the evidence. Given the climate of the era and the nature of political competition, whether the Red scare could have been avoided seems highly improbable. What is clear is that, as with the atomic secret, there was a genie that could no longer be contained.

8

Breaking Through

A LREADY IN PLACE by the time of the Hiss conviction were the beginnings of the so-called national security state. The Central Intelligence Agency, created in 1947 to gather information beyond U.S. borders, was quickly expanded to include responsibility for covert psychological and paramilitary operations — all under the "lax" Democratic administration of Harry Truman, all long before the fire bells that were sounded by Chambers, Nixon, McCarthy, and the Korean War.[1] The National Security Council formulated a long-term blueprint committing military power to a no-expense-spared global response to Communist expansionism.

Richard Nixon thus came into this age as inseparable from the problem of internal subversion as Roosevelt was from the New Deal. The publicity gained, he later acknowledged, was "on a scale that most congressmen only dream of achieving."[2] To suddenly shrink from his calling would have implied a repudiation of his major contribution. Of Nixon it may also be said, as of McCarthy and the other Red-baiters of the time, that he was not about to withdraw and leave the housecleaning to Truman's loyalty program or even the FBI. Such would have been inconceivable for an ambitious young Republican, one whose message had cultivated a following as well as a potential winning issue.

He had, by then, become one of the most sought-after Republican speakers. "Do not cater to small group [sic] of intellectual liberals who will not vote for you anyway," advised Father Cronin. "On anything connected with Communism and foreign policy against Russia, work with the man in the street, who is far ahead of the Administration, the Press, and the liberals on these matters. Don't be misled by phony public sentiment created by closed circles of longhairs in New York and Washington."[3]

Cronin's advice was rapidly becoming the cliché of the new era: the *real* America was not along the East Coast. The Atlantic shoreline, home to the old aristocracy, whose intellectuals looked toward Europe and tolerated Fabian socialism, clung to delusions about Russian intentions. Middle Americans were less easily beguiled and far more skeptical.

The New Deal had been useful for its time. Some of Truman's Fair Deal agenda had similar relevance. Nixon and his fellow Republicans worked to orchestrate what they clearly perceived as the winning theme, denouncing New and Fair Deal "softness" toward communism. Their alarm became the foundation, the centerpiece that gave postwar conservatism its dynamic thrust.

Already slipping from grace during those years, despite Truman's surprise reelection in 1948, was Great Depression–inspired economic liberalism. To conservative purists, who digested Friedrich Hayek, Whittaker Chambers, and James Burnham, the vacuum created by the bankrupt notions that had consumed American life since the early thirties could best be filled by faith in pristine capitalism and uncompromising anticommunism.

The Age of Nixon involved brokering the differences between the two groups. Left out of the new majority were progressives who saw themselves as the legatees of early America's socially responsible aristocracy. The inevitable succession became a Nixonian coalition, an alliance between traditional economic conservatives and social conservatives.

All this meshed very well indeed with the combined influence of worldwide and domestic shocks. The problems were real, but nobody knew how real. Nor was there much understanding about how to respond. A consensus did gradually develop over Truman's policy of containing Soviet advances. Americans were convinced that their country must never again be lulled or permitted to become isolated while aggressors could roam freely.

Such realities were not clear at first. Many continued to trust that the great wartime alliance would survive. Their main priorities were to bring the soldiers home and get back to peacetime prosperity. Not many were eager to believe that the Soviet Union, which had done so much to help slay the Third Reich, would become the next threat.

Events soon changed all that. Stalin's behavior justified skepticism about Russian intentions. The Sovietization of eastern Europe rallied public opinion behind Truman and containment. Critics argued that belief in the United Nations was hollow if the United States did not give it the responsibility for collective security, while some prominent conservatives still worried about the high financial cost of internationalism. On the left, Henry Wallace and his Progressives thought that Washington's policies left the Soviets with little choice but to be equally belligerent.

The great political debate began to take on what became its familiar character. Republicans, who had been out of power for nearly twenty years, looked ahead to great success, which seemed assured when challenging one so unpopular and inept as Harry Truman. When, instead, Thomas Dewey lost the election in 1948, the effect was devastating. Republican bitterness was incalculable; backbiting and parochialism marred any sense of unity in defeat. Such devoted supporters of Robert A. Taft as Colonel Robert McCormick of the *Chicago Tribune* lashed out at Tom Dewey for his "me too" campaign. Compounding the anger was that Truman lacked Roosevelt's invincibility. Still, the remnants of FDR's New Deal held fast for the Democratic ticket, despite the absence of evidence that the Republican defeat was caused by a great popular outcry for a new wave of social reforms.[4]

How to regain popular confidence? Simply stated, that was the GOP burden. At the "Battle of Omaha," a two-day Republican conference in early 1949, frustrations were plainly visible. Liberals were blamed for the me-too campaign, which, without offering the voters "real Republicanism," had forfeited the trust of the younger generation. The Republican eastern establishment stood indicted before the rebellious West; angry Taft forces held firm despite a defensive Senator Hugh Scott, the party's national chairman. Scott's efforts to mediate, to formulate a prescription for a middle-of-the-road party, was rewarded with demands that he resign either his seat in Congress or the chairmanship. Scott, who stepped aside as chairman but remained on Capitol Hill for a long time, was among those Republicans who were clearly fighting the odds. The party could no longer afford such impotence. Democratic cooption of the political consensus had to be broken. Worried about "statism" and the "socialistic trend," Republicans were getting desperate about winning some key elections.[5]

Only a few months after the Omaha conference, Pat Hillings, president of the Los Angeles County Young Republicans, met with national Young Republicans at Salt Lake City. Hillings was already sounding out Nixon's possible senatorial candidacy. Such contacts, he assured Nixon, "should stand us in good stead sometime in the future." Not that it was all so easy. Shifts within the GOP were already developing. Those to Nixon's right suspected that, on the national level, he was too close to Scott; within California, he was a potential ally of another moderate, Governor Earl Warren. That complicated matters for Harold Stassen's people, who feared that the Nixonians would ultimately have to back Warren instead of their own progressive for the presidential nomination in 1952. "We felt it natural that he [Stassen] should be wary of us because we were from Warren's home state," Hillings reported to Nixon, "but he should not have sent his agents . . . to smear us . . . without making an investigation of the California YR's and their leaders. Such an investigation would have established that we have an independent organization." But,

Hillings assured Nixon, "you are the only 'rumored' candidate about whom nothing but good things are said as to personality and capability."[6]

Fear that the parties offered voters nothing better than a choice between Tweedledee and Tweedledum also revived thoughts of re-alignment. Different Republicans had gone their own way in 1912, Progressives following Teddy Roosevelt, loyalists sticking with William Howard Taft. In the early forties, Franklin Roosevelt and Wendell Willkie sat together upstairs in the White House and contemplated how the two parties could be realigned. Oren Root, Willkie's grass-roots organizer in New York for the 1940 campaign against Roosevelt, now warned that realignment would substitute class divisions — "all the workers in one party, all ownership and management in the other" — that would be far less satisfactory than letting liberals and conservatives compete for control within the existing structures. After all, wrote Root in 1949, the "issue of civil rights . . . *is not an issue between the Democratic and Republican parties,* but is an issue within each of those parties" (emphasis added). Republicans had such liberals as Wayne Morse of Oregon and Irving Ives and Jacob Javits of New York as minority counterparts of such Democratic conservatives as Harry Byrd of Virginia and Walter George of Georgia. American liberals, concluded Root, should work not toward "a realignment of parties but victory of the progressive wing in both parties."[7]

Root represented a fading GOP impulse. The idea of General Eisenhower as a replacement for Truman in 1948 had appealed to both Democrats and Republicans who had visions of the right man rather than the right party. Many years had yet to pass before the dilution of partisan loyalties would receive close attention, but it was already becoming clear that the resolution of major economic grievances was also blurring such conflicts. The great majority of Americans had hopped aboard FDR's Democratic express during the 1930s and, as yet, there was some justification for occasionally going AWOL but none for desertion. No wonder Republicans had second thoughts about being yes-men.

Opponents of me-tooism moved early in 1950 to draw up a "Statement of Republican Principles and Objectives." An updating of a 1945 declaration, it proclaimed that the real battle was the fight for "Liberty Against Socialism." As further spelled out in the party's statement on foreign policy that came out in August, the repudiation of bipartisanship was all but complete.[8]

Within the political culture of California, that implied the need for readjustment. Reforms left behind by Hiram Johnson created an inadequate structure for partisanship. The system was reinforced by cross-filing for elections. Nonpartisanship and representation by vested interests, such as oil, became more characteristic than any textbook rendition of how a two-party structure is supposed to operate. Primaries became, as one writer described them, "a weird partisan Donnybrook" that weakened conventional political machines and leaders.[9] Still, California had its partisan history that predated the Progressive era. The state was not isolated from the national political structure. Partisanship, for Californians, would continue to be diffused by the old Progressive influences.

Earl Warren's governorship was only nominally Republican and appealed, to the end, across party lines, which was business as usual for California. An article in an Alhambra veterans' magazine, for example, caught that spirit about two potential contenders for the California senatorial campaign in 1950, then still a year away. "In answer to the requests as to what is [*sic*] my politics," the author suggested that "new blood" might be needed in order to establish "which is the mask and which are the features." His reasoning was simple and direct: "Helen Gahagan Douglas is a liberal democrat with some conservative ideas, whereas Richard M. Nixon is a conservative with some liberal tendencies." Why not, then, a joint resolution to nominate both for the Senate?[10]

Congresswoman Douglas, from a liberal, heavily Democratic district in Los Angeles, contemplated a Senate seat, but she had yet to announce that she would enter the primaries. Nixon was still five months away from declaring his own candidacy. "Dear Richard," wrote Douglas to her colleague, enclosing a copy of the magazine, "Have you seen this? I thought it would amuse you. Sincerely, Helen."[11]

A major source of Richard's later trouble was his decision to take on Helen. The effort was entirely logical, dictated by every element of political wisdom. That was the time to move, right after the Hiss case. It was unclear, however, that striking so hard with full advantage of his reputation, exploiting Douglas's vulnerabilities, would also extract a high price. Fighting his way into the Senate thereby reaffirmed his reputation as a ruthless, unscrupulous politician — Tricky Dick, in American political rhetoric. Long after Watergate and the evidence of abuse of power, long after the passions over Vietnam subsided, middle-aged liberals invariably explained their hatred toward Nixon by citing "what he did to Helen Gahagan Douglas."

What Nixon did accomplish was the thorough, decisive defeat of Douglas. But, once again, as with Alger Hiss, the cost was high. He became known for suggesting that she, like Hiss, belonged to the generation that had compromised American interests. "If she had her way," he said at the outset of the campaign, "the communist conspiracy would never have been exposed, and Alger Hiss would still be influencing the foreign policy of the United States."[12] Anonymous telephone calls, a practice which had first been associated with Nixon's 1946 campaign, warned voters about Douglas's associations.

That there were tricks is hardly newsworthy to anyone who ever heard about Richard Nixon and Helen Gahagan Douglas. Still, the case ought to be set straight without fear of destroying comforting myths about "what Dick did to Helen."

Douglas was part of the past that Nixon had been talking about all along. A former singer and Broadway actress, she had a political education that included witnessing European fascism in the 1930s. She believed in the noble goals of the most noble war. First elected to the House in 1944, at the age of forty-four, she came out of wartime America with the ideals of the popular front and the vision of continued collaboration to assure world peace. All she could do was emulate the efforts of thousands of idealists, joining a variety of groups and, as an officeholder, addressing organizations that later turned up on the attorney general's list as "Communist and subversive." As one of 250 sponsors of a Win-the-Peace Conference that met in Washington one year after the end of the war in Europe, she was in the company of a crowd of pinks or Reds. At that moment, when the cold war was developing and had already convinced Churchill to denounce the iron curtain, a declaration by the conference warned that American foreign policy was being taken over by "the economic royalists, the old enemies of peace to whom Roosevelt gave battle more than once." The statement, which also called for an end to colonialism, bore the imprimatur of its far left supporters. Douglas also showed up as a speaker at a dinner meeting of the Civil Rights Congress, which also made the list of subversive organizations. When Henry Wallace visited Great Britain, she blessed his mission by signing a "scroll of greeting" to English progressives. She opposed Truman's call for military aid to Greece and Turkey, urging that the job be given to the United Nations. She denounced the loyalty program itself as smacking of totalitarianism. She objected to HUAC as "a court, with the power to smear innocent names across the nation's headlines," and voted to cut its funding.[13]

Finally, as with so many others of her generation, especially those who made a career of politics, she did some mending and moved to the Democratic center. She broke with Wallace, parting with him over his decision to oppose Truman for the presidency in 1948. She redeemed her opposition to the Truman Doctrine by supporting the Marshall Plan and the North Atlantic Treaty Organization. As a member of the House Foreign Relations Committee, she favored military aid to western Europe. All that left her as a woman with a past, one who trucked with New Deal coddlers of communism. Or, as the *Los Angeles Times* put it, she was a "glamorous actress who, though not a Communist, voted the Communist party line in Congress innumerable times," and was "the darling of the Hollywood parlor pinks and Reds."[14]

She also, as everybody knew, was married to a famous movie actor,

Melvyn Douglas. A political activist, he was also a West Coast leader of the liberal anticommunist ADA. The anomaly of the ADA was that even its exclusion of Communists failed to satisfy the suspicions of the far right, which persisted in charging that it was riddled with Reds. Years before Nixon entered politics, Californians were also told that the actor was the son of a Russian-Jewish immigrant named Hesselberg. In reality, Melvyn was about as Jewish as the ADA was Communist. Edouard Hesselberg's marriage to Lena Shackelford, the daughter of an aristocratic Kentuckian, had seen to that. "Mother so effectively discouraged Jewish religious observances in our home," the actor later reported, "that I did not learn about the non-Christian part of my heritage until my early teens."[15]

Nor, in Helen Douglas's case, was opposition to her based solely on communism, gender, and religion. She alone among California's congressional delegation opposed transferring control of the offshore, tidelands oil back to the states from the federal government. Her stand backed the position of the Truman administration and two Supreme Court decisions that reaffirmed federal control from the low tide line seaward to the three-mile limit. Getting such rights out of the clutches of Washington, which Truman himself had twice prevented by vetoes, was one of the three objectives of the post–World War II oil industry. Holding on to favorable tax depletion rates and setting import quotas on foreign oil were the others.

The tidelands question was pivotal; for a Californian, it was almost a litmus test of liberalism, in some ways more relevant than the Red issue. Believers in federal control were New Deal purists by definition. Kept in Washington hands, oil revenue could, presumably, be used for social programs. Senator Lister Hill of Alabama had suggested that that was one way to provide federal dollars for education. Many progressives were ardent about keeping it out of the hands of "oil barons" and winning points over the broader question of states' rights.

In California, as in the southern Gulf states that were also involved, the issue was especially sensitive among conservative Democrats. Oil, it has been said, controlled the California Democratic party. Wresting it from the government in Washington meant placing decisions in the much more favorable, controllable, and accessible statehouse; at home, that meant Sacramento. But whether the local powers were in Austin, Baton Rouge, or Tallahassee, the issue was similar: not surrendering a financial bonanza to Washington. Banker Roy Crocker, asked about the tidelands as an issue in the campaign, limited his response to the observation that it would be a lot more satisfactory to deal with state officials.[16] The issue not only transcended partisan politics, but even factions within the party.

But the oil question was not all, merely another example of where conservatives thought the federal government had no business. On land ownership and water rights the interests were different but the impact was the same, leaving Douglas in the minority, almost alone among those in political office. Her position involved upholding an old law limiting entitlement to water generated by federal reclamation projects to owners of not more than 160 acres of land. Much of the land was devoted to mass-production crops that required large-scale acreage. The owners, individuals and corporations, were solidly against the limitation. Roy Crocker, Nixon's liaison with the landowners, explained that most California ranchers wanted no federal interference with what they could raise and how much. As with oil, Douglas's efforts to hold the line against that change bucked big money.[17]

Opposition to Douglas also came from California's doctors. Nationally, the American Medical Association, under Dr. Morris Fishbein, was getting the better of a head-to-head battle with President Truman over instituting a national health insurance system. Earl Warren, making his usual bipartisan appeal, had pushed for a statewide medical plan. That the state medical association was vehemently against the governor on that issue hardly brought it much sympathy from Douglas, for whom medical insurance was inseparable from her belief in social welfare services.

Nixon's position on national health insurance resembled his attitude toward organized labor and the question of closed shops. He never denied the need for better protection for Americans, even lecturing medical groups about doing something to remedy the inadequacies. But, in contrast to Warren, Douglas, and the Fair Deal Democrats, he backed a voluntary plan, having already introduced legislation for federal assistance to voluntary programs. Americans, he argued, should have some sort of coverage available to "everybody who should have it" but, at the same time, should avoid anything resembling "compulsory regimentation." His message was easily the more attractive to California doctors, who were further wooed by a Doctors for Nixon Committee.[18]

More than conventional Republican conservatives, however, Nixon kept seeing conflict in terms of a class struggle. Far from the view of traditional emphasis on the role of a responsible aristocracy, his turn of mind focused on a populistic denigration of the privileged. His notes for campaign remarks carried the reminder that people like Hiss and Judith Coplon were neither aliens nor hard-pressed for money. Their ilk, far more than those who worked for a living, was more likely to fall for socialism. National security was too important to be left in the hands of a privileged minority. In the spirit of the party's "Liberty Against Socialism" theme, he emphasized the importance of winning in 1950 to halt society's leftward trend. Otherwise, 1952 was sure to bring more "statism," leaving the country on a leftward course parallel with what was brought to Great Britain by the Labourites. For the Republicans to succeed, his notes emphasized, they "must not stop with negative opposition — indefensible position — opposition to security, wages, housing, medical care. We must believe & sell ideas that we can offer a system which meets the need better — by receiving minimum govt aid & maximum ind[ependent] enterprise & voluntary cooperative effort." They must head off socialism by showing that social services could be accomplished more efficiently.[19]

But none of this made for popular debates and torchlight processions, no more than did land, oil, medical care, or any single issue, except one: communism. "There's no use trying to talk about anything else," Nixon said at one point, "because that's all the people want to hear about."[20] He had helped popularize the issue, and he could hardly back off just when it seemed that everybody cared. Communism remained his central theme.

That was on the popular level. Regional concerns, however, were more immediate. One involved oil. There is little question that, as one writer reported, Nixon received a major share of direct and indirect support from "the wealthy owners of California's oil, private utilities and corporation farms," from, in other words, men who were "well aware of the real issues in the Nixon-Douglas campaign," men with enough sophistication to know that no candidate was a "Communist" or even a "Communist-sympathizer," that that issue was "hogwash." Those concerned with commercial matters, then, led the way in fund-raising, with Asa Call of the Pacific Mutual Company out front, tapping large farmers and the independent oil companies.[21]

The press also went with the big money. A Stanford University Institute of Journalistic Studies survey showed that of twelve representative newspapers, two supported Douglas, nine backed Nixon, and one was neutral. In terms of comparative circulation, the pro-Douglas papers had a combined total of 265,397 readers to Nixon's 1,322,895. Moreover, none of the Douglas papers had a Sunday edition, leaving that field entirely to her opponent. The same study showed that the *Los Angeles Times*'s coverage of Douglas was 59 percent unfavorable; only 5 percent of Nixon's treatment was critical. Douglas's frustration at having to face a virtual newspaper blackout undoubtedly helps to explain her need to gain attention by placing hard-hitting, reckless paid ads in the *Los Angeles Times*.[22]

For California politics, Douglas, like Voorhis before her, was the maverick. Nixon was the orthodox conservative. As the daughter of one of his former law partners recalled, "I think that when he decided to go into politics, it was necessary for him to go to wealthy people . . . and the oil interests to try and see if they wouldn't help him." Such access was not very difficult. Nixon's senior partner, Tom Bewley, specialized in doing legal work for oilmen. Coupling the issue with, as one early biographer says, "the principle of placing responsibility upon state and local governments rather than on the Federal Government, wherever possible," Nixon had no reservations about going along, seconding the positions of both California senators, including the Democratic incumbent, Sheridan Downey.[23]

But oil was not why Nixon ran. Downey, although a former populist who, like Voorhis, had come into politics with Upton Sinclair, had moved rightward rapidly and become a good friend of the oil people. After his own political career, he went to work as a lobbyist for the industry. The evidence shows that Nixon gave his usual amount of serious thought to evaluating the possible consequences of challenging the Democratic incumbent. Most obviously, his calculations told him that whatever Downey's attractions, however little his reputation as a conservative was the cause of any voter discontent, now was the moment for his own effort. Simply put, the Hiss case had made him "hot," and it was the time to strike. Downey himself began the assaults by attacking Douglas for being soft on communism, hitting especially hard at her opposition to the Truman Doctrine. Nixon had, as he wrote to Jorgensen on August 11, 1949, "such an unusual opportunity that the risk is worth taking." Remaining in the House as a member of the Republican minority could hardly bring "any great gain."[24]

But neither Jorgensen nor Herman Perry was pleased about his ambition. At stake was his House seat, and the additional loss of any chance to gain seniority and power. While Perry urged him not to "sacrifice" himself, Nixon's opening came in October, when Congresswoman Douglas entered the Democratic primary to take the renomination away from Downey. At least there was the chance that a split in the opposition, or even a Douglas candidacy, would ease the way. Further encouragement came from Kyle Palmer, whose paper was ready to endorse Nixon for statewide office. That was useful for the Southland, but Nixon then got good news from the north when he was also assured of support from the *San Francisco Chronicle* and the *Oakland Tribune*. The latter was owned by California's Republican senator, William Knowland. The way cleared, Nixon went to Pomona, where he had first declared in 1946, and offered his candidacy, one, he said, that would be "simply the choice between freedom and state socialism."[25]

His strategy was then helped when Senator Downey, amid some skepticism, decided to drop out of the Democratic primary by pleading ill health and his place was taken by Manchester Boddy, publisher of the *Los Angeles Daily News*. Nixon set out to engineer a campaign aimed at uniting anticommunist Republicans and Democrats against a candidate who was a carbon copy of what had gone wrong with the government in Washington. To argue, as does investigator William Costello, that

Douglas's anticommunist credentials were "unassailable" misses the point.[26] She was, as Nixon well knew and has since repeated, not a Communist.

The Douglas campaign also sealed Nixon's closeness to Murray Chotiner. A relationship that began in 1946 matured into a serious political partnership. Chotiner's elevation was the result of a string of victories for Republican candidates in California. He was noted for masterminding Earl Warren's gubernatorial campaign, in addition to his work for Senator Knowland. Chotiner quickly established a reputation that held for the rest of his life. He was present in one way or another in every Nixon fight but the last. No one remained as closely identified with his name as Richard Nixon, a "fundamentally decent man," Garry Wills has written, "until he took up politics and learned too well the lessons of a Murray Chotiner." Two other journalists, astute observers of the contemporary political scene, put it this way: "Chotiner was in many ways the most interesting personality in Nixon's political camp: aggressive, egocentric, a professional among amateurs, brilliant, overbearing, ruthless, engaging, habitually guilty of overkill, constantly enlarging his area of operation. Painted in sinister colors by the press, he was both a public relations problem for Nixon and an invaluable campaign strategist." If any lieutenant was able to push Nixon aside and run the show, it was Chotiner, and even he had trouble. "We only stated the facts," he explained. "The interpretation of the facts was the prerogative of the electorate." Much more direct was his explanation of the prime objective of a successful campaign: "Destroy your opponent."[27]

The decision to use Chotiner was made at a luncheon at the Pacific Union Club in San Francisco, an affair attended by a half-dozen bankers and businessmen and put together by Albert Chester "Bert" Mattei, an oil company president who had been active in northern California politics. "I knew that Murray was very impatient with people who didn't have the IQ that he had," recalled Frank Jorgensen, who was present that day. "He had the habit of a man like that of tramping on them. He'd move ahead. He'd just leave the wreckage behind him, but he would get the job done."[28]

Nixon's own attraction to Chotiner is not hard to understand. Chotiner had the winning hand of the professional. With his experience backing Warren and Knowland, he had been through the complexities of California's politics, which were further compounded by the differences that separated the northern and southern regions. Perhaps of greatest significance were his insights into how to make the most of the relative insignificance of parties in the state's political life. Since politics was also a full-time devotion of Nixon's, it is little wonder that they became good personal friends.

Harder to accept, both morally and tactically, is Nixon's endorsement of Chotiner's approach to winning, not once or even twice but on a continuing basis, so that the black-haired lawyer from Los Angeles figured in his campaign politics as late as 1968. The chemistry can only be understood as an example of Nixon's infatuation with success. A serious matter of judgment is also involved, since it may reasonably be asked whether Chotiner's value was worth the price. Clearly, the harm was apparent to friends as well as critics. Herman Perry, for example, expressed his misgivings to Nixon's secretary, Rose Mary Woods, in 1953: "When Murray develops a little more of the techniques of public relations," wrote the Whittier banker, "I will be one of the first to recognize it and one of the first to give him credit. . . . The only thing I do not want him to do is be the quarterback and call the plays on the team on which I play."[29]

Even if Chotiner called the plays, the patterns were clearly Nixon's. His essential thrust involved burying Douglas under a combined Republican and Democratic protest. With or without Chotiner around to act as quarterback, Nixon's Republicanism had been almost invisible. Hardly anything, including his own press releases, reinforced public consciousness of party affiliation. The strategy was to turn his campaign into an extension of what had propelled his political climb in the first place, the cleansing of government. Nixon would continue to do what he had started to do in the Hiss case, alert "patriotic" Democrats to the betrayals within their own party, a technique perfectly suited to California's system: Nixon the Democratic redemptionist, an all-but-forgotten role.

But it was a strategy nicely facilitated by the withdrawal of Downey, who then backed Boddy over Douglas. Manchester Boddy, who was named Chester at birth, was a poseur with Anglican affectations. One would never have known that his father was a homesteader and he was born in a log cabin. Describing himself as a believer in "Fact, the Dictator," he was reported to have been on both sides of almost every issue imaginable. As a disabled war veteran, he was somehow tolerated and got some American Legion support. Los Angeles's Colonel Blimp, as closely tied to oil as many of the state's politicos, took the shrill anticommunist line against Douglas.[30] He keynoted his anti-Douglas campaign by citing her as "evidence of a state-wide conspiracy on the part of this small subversive clique of red-hots to capture, through stealth and cunning, the nerve centers of our Democratic party." "There's no such thing as being a 'little communistic' or a little socialistic," proclaimed a Boddy campaign sheet, the *Democratic News*. "We've got to stand flat-footed and four-square for our constitutional principles if we are going to preserve our free American way of life." In bright red letters, the paper announced "Record Shows Rep. Douglas Voted With Extreme Radicals."

It was also Boddy, not Nixon and Chotiner, who first linked her record with the much overused Vito Marcantonio. She was, according to one of his widely distributed flyers, "neither truly representative of her sex nor of her party." On April 28, 1950, Boddy's newspaper earned the distinction of using the words "pink lady," which became one of the more memorable terms of the campaign, albeit usually attributed to Nixon. Downey supported Boddy with the following tribute: "He is not an extremist — with him there will be no compromise with Communism or other police state governments." Downey had also helped the cause by making the first connection between Douglas and the Communist party. The alleged Marcantonio-Douglas similarities continued with newspaper ads signed by the Women's Committee for Good Government that alerted Californians that she and the congressman had both voted against a $150,000 appropriation for HUAC. Moreover, "on four previous occasions, Mrs. Douglas and Marcantonio voted in the same way against similar bills to support the investigation of Communists, Fascists and the Ku Klux Klan."[31]

As much as those primaries set the tone for what was to follow, they mercifully came to an end. Douglas swamped Boddy by nearly two to one. Nixon, the beneficiary of cross-filing that attracted many Democratic voters, totaled some 1 million to 900,000 for Douglas.

The atmosphere of Watergate was foreshadowed in 1950. The two situations were, of course, not analogous, and the Douglas and George McGovern campaigns were separated by twenty-two years.

In some ways, they showed how little had changed. Democratic leadership was divided in both eras, not only in Washington and on the local level, but also among the rank and file. Traditional followers of FDR's party were, in each case, severing old loyalties. A variety of cultural and social circumstances blended with perceptions more closely related to questions of nationalism than tactics. Nixon's opponents became befuddled and defensive, overreacting and weakening their own credibility. Most significantly, Nixon's overall strategy in the McGovern campaign was a virtual replay of what he used against Douglas: split the Democrats and siphon off the discontented and disillusioned. "Every campaign," Garry Wills has written, "had taught Nixon the same lesson: mobilize resentment against those in power."[32]

Both campaigns were also overwhelmed by preoccupation with America's role in the Far East. The Truman administration, charged with the "loss" of China to the Communists, was trapped by its own policies and politics, unable to get off the Asian mainland without angering the right. And suddenly, after throwing dollars behind Frenchmen trying to hold on in Indochina, it found itself with its own war in Korea. In the first campaign, the invasion of South Korea, coming right after the spring primary and just before the showdown against Douglas, was a shot in the arm to a Republican candidate with good voter recognition as a staunch anticommunist. In the second instance, a generation later, it was Nixon who, as president, held the more credible military and diplomatic method of ending a long war.

The Douglas fight left its own permanent scar. Although it was primarily over California politics, the situation cannot be seen apart from the national condition. The most obvious circumstance was that the Communist issue was dominant. Republicans fell into line faithfully when Truman moved to assist South Korea, but that was about the limit of bipartisanship for the duration. An immediate objective was regaining control over Congress.

So the struggle was not only in California but, as two historians have noted, "this summer and autumn of fear and crisis witnessed one of the bitterest congressional campaigns in American history." The GOP seized the issue of communism and played it hard, led by the Joe McCarthys, Robert Tafts, William Jenners, and Richard Nixons, but also by such moderates as James Duff and Prescott Bush. Bush's workers brought bus caravans of McCarthyites into the Connecticut city of Bridgeport to defeat William Benton.[33]

And Democrats, too. Researchers for the Democratic National Committee prepared a one-hundred-page document that paralleled statements on issues made by ten Republican senators and congressmen with known Communist positions. New York's liberal senator, Herbert Lehman, one of the few to dare take on Joe McCarthy at an early stage, saw fit to send the following message via night wire to a gathering of Manhattan's Tammanyites: "The situation in the United States and the world today calls for the mobilization of all our energies and all our capabilities for struggle to protect our democracy from its enemies internal and external."[34]

The postprimary campaign began when Douglas charged that Nixon had weakened the forces of freedom in Korea by voting with Vito Marcantonio to cut American aid in half. Her message went to the voters on a yellow sheet that highlighted an alleged Nixon-Marcantonio comparison. "LET'S LOOK AT THE RECORD," it demanded in bold relief. "YOU pick the Congressman the Kremlin loves!" and charged that "Mr. Nixon . . . Cries 'Communist' . . . but on the Korean issue voted consistently in agreement with Mr. Marcantonio, the Communist 'line' follower." At a dinner in Los Angeles's Biltmore Hotel on October 4, she placed Nixon "on the wrong side of all three" key foreign policy votes "which had a profound effect on American defense and security and which were aimed at checking the spread of Communism abroad." As proof of his misdeed, she added, "He was in complete accord with the Communist party-liner, Representative Marcantonio." In a radio talk on

October 30, she claimed that Nixon's vote had "led the Communists of North Korea to believe that they could strike at the Republic of South Korea without opposition."[35]

Douglas was clearly stung, badly weakened by the Downey and Boddy attacks. But her own campaign operators operated with the élan of apprentice butchers and the tactics of desperation. As was true for a number of liberals with vulnerable pasts, she had to be twice as pure. Charging Nixon with having cut the Korean appropriation in half was but one example of her panic.

Her facts were not entirely wrong. He had voted to appropriate just one-half the original amount, a point emphasized on her yellow sheet. A closer reading of what he had done also confirms that he finally supported an appropriation for precisely half that amount.

What Douglas did not say in her effort to burden Nixon with the Marcantonio taint was that not only had her colleague voted for Korean military aid in the past but that his actions were part of his efforts for more, not less, support against Communist expansionism in the Far East. Nor did she indicate that he had gone along with the House majority, largely in protest against omitting Formosa from the aid formula. Opposition also focused on the Truman administration's request for funds for a two-year period, which reduced legislative oversight. When a new bill was drawn up that provided aid for Formosa as well as Korea and included a yearly renewal clause, Nixon voted in its favor. Providing for one year of foreign aid rather than two naturally also resulted in one-half the total amount originally proposed. Douglas's tricky yellow sheet thereby told "the truth."[36]

She was also the wrong person to make that argument. California Republicans were hardly receptive to that kind of approach from a left-wing Democrat. Aside from a few progressive circles, including some basic financing available within the motion picture community, her own political underpinnings were uncertain.[37] The party was as divided as Democrats almost everywhere. Three-quarters of them were Catholics. Any semblance of a party that could come together behind one candidate had just about been demolished by the Downey-Boddy anti-Douglas campaigns. Curiously, even the national coalition Truman had managed to bring together in 1948 was ephemeral, joined more through mutual opposition than common goals.

Outside the deep South, no Democrats wavered as much as Roman Catholics. The process predated Pearl Harbor, but the past five years had been especially contentious. Sensitivity about the reemergence of traditional anti-Catholicism had exacerbated bitterness and insecurity; many critics, especially opponents of the role of the Catholic hierarchy in Franco's Spain and the United States, were fellow Democrats, strange bedfellows for a group still damaged by bigotry. The old battles had not died down. While Paul Blanshard's books were warning about what "Catholic power" was about to do to America, the halls of Congress and courts at all levels were contending with church-state questions. Both parties were on record behind federal aid to education. But whether such funds should be denied to states with segregated school systems and private schools — including, of course, those of various religious denominations — was enough to cause a mini–civil war, not only between North and South, but between liberals and conservatives, and, on the church-state level, Roman Catholics and those opposed on traditional First Amendment grounds or fear of the papacy in America.

That the Democratic party was most hurt by the bloodletting was obvious: the battle was dramatized in 1949 by the open, intemperate dispute over North Carolina congressman Graham A. Barden's effort to deny funds to private schools. The most sensational moment came when Francis Cardinal Spellman of New York denounced Eleanor Roosevelt for "discrimination unworthy of an American mother" because she opposed federal aid to parochial schools. Clare Boothe Luce, a Republican congresswoman and convert to Catholicism, accused liberals of suddenly favoring appeasement now that Russia, not Hitler's Germany, was the threat to civilization. Catholic disaffection, evident even before the war in the person of James A. Farley, longtime political adviser to FDR, had helped give Republicans their congressional victory in 1946. More recently, John Foster Dulles's losing campaign against Herbert Lehman for the Senate seat from New York had barraged heavily Polish-American Erie County with charges of the Democratic "sell-out" at Yalta, which left millions of eastern European Catholics under Communist rule. "The basis of American hopes," McGeorge Bundy wrote in *Foreign Affairs* in 1949, "was the double commitment of Yalta: self-government in Eastern Europe, and cooperation in the United Nations." Nixon himself repeatedly stressed that "America faces the greatest danger after she has won a war." In common with Dulles and what became the standard Republican foreign policy issue of the time, Nixon slashed at the wartime agreements and called for the resignation of Secretary of State Acheson.[38]

California Catholics were no less disillusioned. Economic issues had belonged to the 1930s. Such fears had yielded to the revival of American nativism and the global threat of communism. "I have for some time been making capital for you among my Catholic friends by pointing to your stand on the communism issue of the past two years," wrote Hillings to Nixon during the summer of 1949, "and it is well received. I have sent many of your committee pamphlets to local Catholics with that in mind and knowing that they are traditionally Democrats." Especially positive, noted Hillings, was the "big plug" from "the official Catholic paper for your stand on the Barden bill," which barred public funding for parochial schools.[39] Antidiscrimination and antiappeasement had mushroomed.

By the time Nixon became a candidate, there was little doubt about his ability to cut into that traditional Democratic vote. He got additional help from Archbishop J. Francis A. McIntyre of Los Angeles. The archbishop, even more militantly conservative than Cardinal Spellman, ordered parish priests to deliver several sermons on the dangers of Communist infiltration. To a significant degree, the election hinged on Nixon's ability to woo California's Catholics. "We must appeal to Democrats to help win the election," advised a Chotiner campaign manual. "Therefore, do not make a blanket attack on Democrats. Refer to the opposition as a supporter of the socialistic program running on the Democratic right."[40]

The Catholic strategy also explains why Nixon suggested to Pat Brown, the Democrat then trying to win election as California's attorney general, that they find some ways to reconcile their respective campaigns. "I'll help you if you help me," Brown remembered Nixon telling him. "We won't come out for each other but we'll do something together." What they did together was to assail communism. When the state legislature allocated twenty-five thousand dollars for an antisabotage program, Brown applauded; his fellow Democrat, James Roosevelt, the gubernatorial candidate, avoided being outdone by claiming that the amount was too little.[41]

Nixon also appealed to registered Democrats when he entered the primary by distributing a leaflet that said, "As one Democrat to Another" without identifying his own standing as a Republican. The tactic not only drew fire from the Democrats but a germane question from Boddy's newspaper. Since Nixon was giving the impression that he was a Democrat, wrote the political editor, "some of his critics are wondering if his antipathy to perjury would go far enough to prevent him from using this sort of advertising if he were under oath as Alger Hiss was when Nixon nicked him." But the Nixon appeal also enlisted help from a conservative Democrat from San Francisco, George Creel. Creel, the government's chief propaganda man during World War I, headed a California Democrats for Nixon group that listed sixty-three prominent Democrats. It also put Douglas on the defensive about her own party loyalty. Another denunciation came from the vice president of the California Democratic Women's League, who warned fellow members of her party to "wake up and see where she is trying to lead us."[42]

While historian Donald Crosby has shown that, outside Massachusetts, not much evidence exists to indicate Joe McCarthy was especially persuasive among fellow Roman Catholics, that was not necessarily the contemporary perception. McCarthy had become an overnight anticommunist phenomenon, and his coreligionists, already agitated by the postwar Red menace, were assumed to be his natural audience. Another assumption, of course, was that his message transcended party lines, an essential appeal if Nixon was to win in a state with a heavy Democratic registration. And the senator traveled to the Coast for Nixon on at least two occasions, first during the primary and then for the fall election. When McCarthy told a Nixon rally in March that Truman headed the "administration Communist Party of betrayal," Nixon applauded and said, "God give him the courage to carry on." In October, McCarthy pushed for Nixon via a radio address that called for Acheson to resign and denounced the national leadership as being infiltrated with men who were "international atheistic" Communists and "traitors . . . who are hip-deep in their own failures."[43] Nixon's embrace of McCarthy was more or less par for Republicans in 1950; in any case, it was certainly not evidence of any special relationship.

There was no valid connection between Nixon and two other embarrassments. The first was Gerald L. K. Smith. Smith, who headed the Christian Nationalist Crusade, had a name that was virtually synonymous with not merely anti-Semitism but group hatred. "He was nutty as a fruitcake," said Frank Jorgensen about the "lunatic fringe" Smith, who came out strongly for Nixon. At the very time Nixon was trying to sway Democrats to his side, Smith contributed to the dialogue by pleading to "help Richard Nixon get rid of the Jew-Communists." Certainly not lost on Smith and those who received his message was that Douglas was "the wife of a Jew," referring, of course, to the half-Jewish origins of her husband. Nixon, according to Jorgensen, thought that Smith was "doing more harm than good." He sharply disavowed any connection with Smith, with a statement that denounced "anti-Semitism in whatever form it appears." The Anti-Defamation League (ADL) endorsed Nixon's record as "clear on the question of the hate mongers," and praised him for being "quick to repudiate all such bigots." In denying anti-Semitism, Nixon also reminded voters that his aide and "close friend" Murray Chotiner was Jewish. Another noted anti-Semite, in fact, Robert Williams, attacked Nixon for having a Jew as a campaign manager.[44]

There was also the contention of two who were close to Nixon, Pat Hillings and journalist Ralph de Toledano (who was also Jewish), that the Douglas camp had most to gain by spreading such insinuations. De Toledano suggested an effort to discredit Nixon with the large Jewish vote in southern California, especially Hollywood. Hillings felt they were trying to damage Nixon by exploiting contemporary fear that anti-Semitism was behind the effort to capitalize on the Jewish identities of such people as Judith Coplon and Julius and Ethel Rosenberg. "It began to be developed that anybody who attacked the commies was associated with anti-Semitism," explained Hillings, an observation later echoed by Wilfred Sheed's point that "all the anti-Communists found themselves herded into the same tent, like so many liberals."[45] Neither de Toledano nor Hillings offered evidence for his allegations.

There was some basis for such suspicions. At least that possibility was accepted by the national office of the ADL, which suspected that Nixon had rubbed shoulders too closely with the likes of a John Rankin merely through their HUAC affiliation. As their letter to regional ADL directors explained, "Many professional bigots, for one reason or another, have loudly supported the Congressional Committee except where it has fought bigotry. It is important, however," continued the explanation, "to remember . . . that there is no record of any contact between Sen. Nixon and any of these lunatics."[46] But there had been "contact": mere association with HUAC suggested being in the same league, pursuing the same cause.

Papers in the Nixon files for years afterward show that the rumors were durable, as is common with such gossip. The record also shows that, in frustration, Nixon and his supporters were repeatedly forced to call on Jewish organizational and individual leaders to rebut the charges. They surfaced with particular force when he became a national candidate in 1952.

Some associations that became virtually institutionalized by the fight against Douglas, especially the reputation for questionable campaign tactics and allegations about anti-Semitism, persisted throughout Nixon's career. From that period also came his association with the so-called China Lobby, although it should be said that in the 1940s and 1950s he was merely a bit player among many who were far more active. The lobby's objective involved promoting the lost cause of Generalissimo Chiang Kai-shek and his Nationalists. Having been so prominent in exposing internal security lapses when they involved Soviet subversion, Nixon was far less scrupulous about upholding the fading interests of the government that by late 1949 would be forced by its Communist opponents to take sanctuary on Formosa.

The lobby itself became something of a whipping boy for liberal critics of the Chiang regime. They emphasized the associations of a number of Americans with the corrupt and discredited Nationalists. During the course of the next two decades and Nixon's emergence as an international figure, the victory of the Chinese brand of communism continued to serve as a major modifier of America's Far East policy. As late as 1965, fifty senators and over half the House continued to adopt a China Lobby analysis that encouraged committing more Americans to the war in Vietnam.[47]

The lobby had, in effect, several corridors. One emanated directly from the embattled Chinese Nationalists in their struggle to avoid being driven from the mainland by Mao Zedong. In their defense, they promoted an alliance of businessmen, ideologues, writers, and politicians who publicized the virtues of going to the ends of the earth to keep alive the government of Chiang Kai-shek, the Kuomintang successors to Sun Yat-sen and the glorious republican revolution of 1912.

Gradually, Sun's revolution had become the prize of the Soong family. By the 1920s, China was once again a land where popular welfare was subordinated to the accumulation of wealth and power; this time, the largesse belonged to the Soongs. Their dynasty was closely associated with speculation in silver, commissions for buying military hardware, trading in government bonds, and countless other lucrative enterprises. The peasantry became a source for massive collections of taxes. All was done under a government aided substantially by American money. In 1944, Theodore H. White reported to readers of *Life* that the Nationalist government in Chungking, where the capital had been moved under pressure from the Japanese, was controlled by "a corrupt political clique that combines some of the worst features of Tammany Hall and the Spanish Inquisition."[48]

Little wonder that Chiang, who began as a Communist in the 1920s, was more impassioned about fending off the forces of Mao and Zhou Enlai than defeating the Japanese. To the Chinese masses, the warlords of Tokyo epitomized the traditional enemy. Japan's invasion of Manchuria in 1931 began a process of expansion that subjugated China proper during the years before Pearl Harbor. White, deploring the Nationalists for their priorities, estimated that Chiang was using ten of his best divisions against the Communists rather than trying to defeat the invading Japanese.[49]

The peasantry were, at the same time, exposed to thievery by their own government. Clearly, the Soongs kept the loot all in the family. Or, as an adventurous Russian exporter of Bolshevik terror, Mikhail Borodin, put it, the Kuomintang was "a toilet, which, as often as you flush it, still stinks."[50]

In America, such realities fell on deaf ears; that is, aside from a few scholars and China hands within the government and academia. Far more comforting was continuing the popular romance with China that was sold to Americans during the 1930s. The generalissimo, Chiang Kai-shek, and his exotically beautiful wife were media stars of the day, gallant lords of a backward land, holding off both the Japanese and subversive Communists, cushioning over a half-billion people against the immoralities of atheism and foreign domination, not unlike the old calling of nineteenth-century American missionaries. "Chiang's only similarity to George Washington was false teeth," Sterling Seagrave has written in his comprehensive account of the Soongs. "But in his pious campaign he was portrayed as a heroic Christian soldier, holding the Bible in one hand while fighting off reds and Japs with the other."[51] Madame Chiang,

meanwhile, traveled through the United States selling fantasies and helping to orchestrate support for the regime from a mansion in the New
York City enclave of Riverdale.

The west's mission was to contribute its religion, culture, and certainly
commerce. China's friends were convinced that the key showdowns between the democratic west and the red east would take place in that most
populous of lands. China, with its rapidly swelling numbers, pushing
toward a billion within a few years, was the obvious key to Asia and the
crucial determinant of the balance of power.

Even those who knew better found ready explanations. "Corruption
is *not* the policy of the Kuomintang," declared Clare Boothe Luce. She
added that "free Chinese deplore it as much as you or I do. But murder — mass murder — *genocide is* an official principle of Communists."[52]

"Unfortunately," Mrs. Luce's biographer has written, "most Americans
can see only two of everything, us and them, Left and Right." She and
her associates differed little in spirit from those naive Americans who
rushed to see how Czarist Russia was being replaced by new utopias in
Leningrad and Moscow. The first illusion involved the incipient Soviet
"worker's paradise"; the second, the struggle by "democratic" forces
under Chiang Kai-shek and his Soong allies to save the nation from
extinction by Mao Zedong and his band of revolutionaries. In the second
instance, as in the first, American allies of the cause were found at every
level of government; but their presence among elected officials was far
more prominent on Capitol Hill. The former group had its clear ties,
and directions, to Moscow. The second had a clear connection to the
Kuomintang. In each case, money flowed to agents in the United States.
But Soong dollars were also American in origin, military and economic
assistance recycled to win friends and influence. Much of the flow, including profits from narcotics, was traced by the CIA. President Truman,
when telling his own associates about "grafters and crooks" in Chiang's
government, underestimated by one-half when he suspected they had
roughly a billion dollars in H. H. Kung's Bank of China located in New
York City. Kung, who was the center of Soong money power, was
Chiang's brother-in-law and minister of finance. Moreover, his influence
was uncomfortably closer to friends of the administration than Truman
let on. Walter Lippmann suspected that the government's hands were
tied from exposing the lobby's secret operations because "too many people involved in the scandal were rather important Democrats."[53]

Thus, the combined operations that constituted the China Lobby wove
their own web of subversion. Subversion in this case had nothing to do
with overturning American capitalism. But it had everything to do with
undermining enemies in the State Department. Money and military
equipment were free to flow to the Soongs. The ineptitude and corruption of the Nationalists mattered little, whether attested to by General

George Marshall's 1945 mission to China or even by the far more favorable report by another American envoy, General Albert Wedemeyer.
When General Claire Lee Chennault, of wartime Flying Tiger fame,
testified in Washington on behalf of the China aid bill in 1948, he did
so at a time when his application to keep operating his airline was still
pending before the Chinese government and controlling interest had
actually been taken over by the CIA. Nor was it of much consequence
that Chiang's institutionalized disaster had long since made it obvious
that his complete collapse was only a matter of time. The Soong subversion was less espionage than the corruption of popular perceptions
and the diversion of dollars into a China hole. That the China Lobby's
ranks included such people as editor and writer Max Eastman, Ralph
de Toledano, and James Burnham was ironic. Many were converts from
the left, including, in addition to Eastman, such writers as John T. Flynn,
a former New Deal liberal, and ex-Communist Freda Utley. Joining their
company was the strident anti-Semitic propagandist Joseph P. Kamp.
Even the foremost congressional champion of the Kuomintang, Walter
Judd of Minnesota, was an apostate, but of a different sort. Judd had
first gone to China in the 1920s as a medical missionary, sympathetic to
the Communists, and most concerned about the exploitation of its people. By 1944, he was charging that American Communists had major
responsibility for "China's great present peril."[54] William Loeb, publisher
of the *Manchester* (New Hampshire) *Union-Leader,* was more consistent,
his devotion to Chiang ultimately outlasting Nixon's.

Equally fascinating was the attraction to Republicans of Chiang's fighters for democracy. For some time, the Far East was of greater interest
to members of the GOP, especially those beyond the Atlantic seaboard.
It was Kenneth Wherry, the Nebraska Republican, who allowed his enthusiasm to vow that, "with God's help, we will lift Shanghai up and up,
ever up, until it is just like Kansas City." Additional friends of the lobby
in the House were such Republicans as minority leader Joe Martin. All
joined in drawing blood from Truman and the Democrats, a process of
political temptation made much easier, as John Foster Dulles later explained to Richard Nixon, by the lack of "bipartisan cooperation" in
China policy.[55] But it was not all that simple. Asia-firsters were not all
Republicans; everybody who spoke up for Nationalist China was not a
lobbyist; progressives and fellow travelers were not synonymous.

As in the Communist cases, lines are difficult to draw between leaders,
followers, sympathizers, and friends. While Chiang's brothers-in-law
T. V. Soong and Wellington Koo and such others as H. H. Kung and
his son David Kung actively spread around money and influence, most
"members" of the lobby were merely Kuomintang partisans, in a manner
reminiscent of Communists and fellow travelers of another decade. As
historian Foster Rhea Dulles has shown, documents have revealed "the

willingness on the part of a foreign embassy" — in this case, the Nationalists in Washington — "to interfere in the domestic affairs of the host country."[56] Contacts brought influence, including secret information, with vague references to Nationalist air force officers in Washington prepared to spy on atomic secrets. The major difference between Communist sympathizers and the China Lobby, of course, was that the Soviets were up and the Chinese Nationalists were down. Apart from that, what mattered was the ability of certain groups of Americans to manipulate official policy in behalf of the foreign powers of their choice.

Yet, as with the uncovering of Reds in the New Deal, the significance of the China Lobby has been overblown, offering, in its way, an equally handy explanation for policy failures.[57] For all the diatribes against Truman and Acheson for the famous White Paper of August 1949, which spelled out the futility of the Nationalist cause, the possibilities of continued American assistance had become exhausted with or without the lobby's displeasure. A variety of other reasons compelled U.S. policy to stand firm on the question of the French in Indochina and Chiang on Formosa. However much the generalissimo's publicists wanted the United States to preserve its policy of withholding diplomatic recognition of Communist China, their success was due equally to the Communists' insistence on America's total abandonment of its longstanding support for the Kuomintang. If the lobby had never existed, Truman and most Americans would have connected responding to aggression in Korea with avoiding the mistakes of the 1930s. The willingness to press militarily toward the Yalu River and provoke Peking's intervention in Korea can also hardly be pawned off as a lobby-induced disaster, and the extended and prolonged war that followed was far more instrumental than any effort by publicists, working openly or surreptitiously, in delaying normal relations between the two countries.[58]

What did result was of great political consequence, however: selling the American people the perception of their government's weakness and responsibility for mishandling matters in Asia, for "permitting" communism to flourish, almost as if it were a disease that was allowed to spread while we refused to employ the vaccine. The unfortunate outcome was that politicians, especially Democrats, then reacted as though that indeed had been the case.

Nowhere was the impact of the Nationalist loss as direct and devastating as within the Foreign Service, where specialists found themselves subject to the scrutiny of propagandists fed via a pipeline from Chiang and his crew, especially when a Republican administration replaced Truman. The price there included the naming by Eisenhower's secretary of state, John Foster Dulles, of a courtly, aristocratic Virginian, Walter Robertson, as an assistant secretary of state for Far Eastern affairs. Too inflexible even for Dulles, Robertson confirmed his ignorance of the region by his devotion to the "return to the mainland" fantasy of the Nationalists. His presence in the State Department was also calculated to give pleasure to an old friend of his, publisher Henry Luce, and to the man who probably did more than any other to push his appointment, Walter Judd. Such "expertise" in handling American Far Eastern diplomacy, together with the imputations popularized by the China Lobby, had its natural consequence in the Vietnam imbroglio. The same conditions enabled the China matter to become tied to both the Nixon who defeated Helen Gahagan Douglas in 1950 and the Nixon whose diplomatic breakthrough with China in 1972 was hailed by Senator Edward M. Kennedy as a "lasting monument" to his presidency.[59]

A much more important China lobbyist than Nixon was Whittaker Chambers's boss and Clare Boothe Luce's husband, Henry Luce. His magazine *Time* called the lobby a "mythical dragon." In reality, according to his biographer, Luce was the "pioneer of the China Lobby," a term that best applies to the intellectual and ideological conviction behind Luce's view of the importance to America of that part of the world. At his command, ready to fulfill his desire to "educate" the public, were his other major publications, *Life* and *Fortune*. Luce's full significance may be understood by appreciating the accuracy of Max Lerner's insight that such magazines became "an intermediary between the classes."[60]

At *Time,* journalist Theodore H. White, who spent World War II in China, found that editor Chambers was the man who made the decision between what he saw in China and what Americans could read about it. To Luce, especially, White's dispatches became increasingly irritating. Although Luce had earlier published critical pieces by such people as novelist Pearl Buck, as well as by White, he became more defensive about the need to support Chiang. The fine reporter and writer he had admired had become, Luce wrote, "an ardent sympathizer with the Chinese Communists." White concluded that his boss was "above all, a Christian, and Christianity was the cement by which he meant to bind China and America together."[61]

Luce was too sophisticated, too conscious of his power as a press baron, and, one should add, too complex to approximate some of the caricatures that have represented his outlook. His ideas were anything but primitive. "They were," Wilfred Sheed has written, those of the "Yankee adventurer back in an American setting, with British imperialism shading into American . . . leadership." One novelist who knew him has been quoted as saying that he was "torn between wanting to be a Chinese missionary like his parents and a Chinese warlord like Chiang Kai-shek."[62] If he was, with his power to reach the American public, the best representative of the Chungking government in the United States, he was also a visionary with convictions about the importance of the two countries in the international order.

Under critical questioning by one of his editors about the validity of saying that the United States "lost" China, Luce fired back. To say "lost," Luce agreed, was an oversimplification, but not too farfetched if one could understand "the sense in which we 'had' it. We had it," responded Luce in a memorandum, "in the sense that never in human history did one great (and racially different) country have such a good name in another country as the U.S.A. had in China. In a sense the 'good will' toward the U.S. in China was 'too good' to be true — but there it was."[63]

Keeping China would also have conformed to Luce's vision of what he designated "The American Century." Ten months before Pearl Harbor, Luce's signed editorial in *Life* postulated a global manifest destiny. He considered free enterprise inseparable from American power, which rested on military strength. A Pax Americana required world dominance. Failure to take advantage of the "complete opportunity of leadership" meant sacrificing commercial expansion. America's role left no choice but global leadership. Yes, it was true, wrote Luce to editor Thomas S. Matthews, "a government 'friendly' to the U.S." ruling China "would completely alter the 'balance of power' situation in the world." It would even provide some effective meaning to the cold war containment policy. "The measure of degradation of American policy in the Pacific," he explained to Senator Arthur Vandenberg in 1947, "is the fact that a few guys like Judd and me have to go about peddling a vital interest of the United States and a historic article of U.S. foreign policy as if it were some sort of bottled chop-suey that we were trying to sneak through the Pure Food laws." To complain that China was unworthy of support because it suffered from "corruption and disunity, incompetence and indecision," vices common to other friendly governments, was to forfeit America's need "to work with the world it found and know what world it wanted."[64]

While Luce hoped to proselytize and outargue, others were less suave and cerebral. Among them was one who had been awarded the Order of the Auspicious Star by Chiang Kai-shek after the war, Alfred Kohlberg. Called by one writer "the cement that principally held all the diverse elements of the emphatically non–Red China lobby together," Kohlberg had no misgivings about self-interest and ideology.[65] Although far less known than Luce, he had developed an annual $1.5 million business by moving textiles along a triangular route. Handkerchiefs made from Irish linen were shipped via Belfast to be embroidered by Chinese women, and the finished product was then forwarded to the American market, where they were sold with expensive European labels. Such entrepreneurialism was first-rate, and highly dependent on a cozy relationship with the Kuomintang regime. In China, Kohlberg enjoyed the luxury of being able to work with a government that valued peasants for their cheap labor. In the United States, he needed an administration that overlooked systematic fraud.

Kohlberg's beginnings were almost a cliché among the self-made of the era. Born in San Francisco into a family of German Jews who had left as a result of the revolution of 1848, Alfred began as a campus journalist whose collegiate training came to an end because of the great earthquake of 1906. Instead of going beyond his sophomore year at the University of California, he went into his father's printing plant and remained in business thereafter.[66]

Kohlberg first visited China in 1916. The Chinese Revolution was then only five years old. Sun Yat-sen, replacing the Manchu dynasty, watched with dismay the rise of the Kuomintang, or Nationalists, and the foundation of a parliamentary government. Kohlberg developed his textile business in the early 1920s. His connections with the Kuomintang successors included Chiang Kai-shek and the various Soong in-laws, especially H. H. and David Kung. But Kohlberg's first loyalty was to the generalissimo himself — inseparable, in his self-serving view, from loyalty to America. More than Luce, more than Judd and any other single man, he became an almost direct agent of the Soongs. The handkerchief king became the China Lobby man. The irony of it all, liberal publisher Max Ascoli later observed, was that Kohlberg and his operatives gained almost as much standing among Americans after Chiang's defeat as when they were fighting to keep the regime afloat.[67]

A stocky little man who looked somewhat odd in his long overcoats, Kohlberg became an expert amateur pilot and logged tens of thousands of miles between 1930 and 1941. His business, and much of his lobbying activity, was run from an office at 1 West Thirty-seventh Street, New York City, until it closed down in 1957.

Kohlberg thought he found evidence of skulduggery and an anti-Chiang conspiracy when the Federal Trade Commission banned his misrepresented embroidered imports. He didn't stop his trade, but his activism was spurred. Inspired by additional "evidence," in the form of classified documents somehow obtained and published by the left-wing periodical *Amerasia,* Kohlberg went to work. He helped bankroll the periodical *Plain Talk,* which was edited by Isaac Don Levine, Whittaker Chambers's significant confidant. The lead article of *Plain Talk*'s first issue, in 1946, implicated such government officials and consultants as John Stewart Service, John Davies, John Carter Vincent, General George Marshall, Owen Lattimore, General Joseph W. Stilwell, and Henry Wallace as being part of the "pro-Soviet" group in the State Department.[68] Kohlberg money went on.

He published *The Freeman,* which for a time became an influential conservative periodical (later it merged with *Plain Talk*). To better organize lobbying functions, he helped Clare Boothe Luce establish the American China Policy Association, a group with a board of directors that also included William Loeb, Max Eastman, and Freda Utley. He was also president of the American Jewish League Against Communism, which distributed reams of pro-Nationalist propaganda.

Kohlberg made a greater impact on the Institute of Pacific Relations (IPR), of which he was a member. Since 1925, the IPR had served scholars, businessmen, and many others in and out of government by sifting and coordinating information about the region. Functioning as a private international organization that adopted no partisan or particular nationalistic stance, the IPR keyed its publications to serious informational interest. It was, as political scientist H. Bradford Westerfield has written, "commonly regarded in those years as the authoritative organization for research and publication on the Far East."[69]

Kohlberg, whose own formal education was limited and whose knowledge about communism was admittedly sparse before 1944, went into action because of his realization that the IPR was "the main source for spreading" lies and Communist propaganda about the Chinese government. In 1947, he presented the IPR with charges that its publications failed to criticize the Soviet Union but paralleled "the alterations of the Soviet Union's foreign policy and of the Communist press." His charges were rejected by the organization and probably would have died there, but the thrust of events, especially the "loss" of China, kept them alive — and potent. The Kohlberg analyses were then closely followed by Senator McCarthy, with whom he put in long hours in 1950 preparing allegations against the role of Owen Lattimore, a widely recognized authority on the Far East and onetime editor of the IPR's *Pacific Affairs,* in helping to "sell out" China.[70]

The institute then fell prey to a HUAC subcommittee under the chairmanship of Senator McCarran. The IPR was accused of being in business primarily to promote the interests of the Soviet Union, a charge buttressed with a list of "54 persons connected in various ways with IPR [who] were identified by witnesses as participants in the Communist world conspiracy against democracy." The organization slowly disintegrated during the 1950s. The process begun by Kohlberg, stirred further by McCarthy, and given closer scrutiny by McCarran, left both the institute and its members in a position that was indefensible for that era. Once out of commission, the IPR was succeeded by the Asia Society. The new organization, unlike the old, stated that its concentration would be "mainly on social and cultural activities."[71]

The China Lobby, always amorphous, continued into the Eisenhower fifties, which were, of course, also the years of Nixon's vice presidency As it had in the past, through the Luce and Kohlberg periods, always with Chiang's agents in America not far behind, it took on a new form.

The goal shifted from plotting a counterrevolution on the Asian mainland to simply maintaining the status quo, which, at that point, meant keeping the People's Republic of China in isolation, supporting the Nationalists in their Formosan refuge, and safeguarding the fantasy of someday returning to the mainland.

In those years during and after the Korean War, such goals were among the least controversial in America. Former president Hoover headed a group determined to oppose the admission to the United Nations of the new government in Peking.[72] It launched its drive on October 22, 1953, calling itself the Committee of One Million Against the Admission of Communist China into the United Nations. If nothing else, this updated version of the lobby gave politicians and other prominent Americans a group that could be joined during those years without worrying about some future consequences. It also offered respectable sanitizing for those eager to expunge past leftist affiliations. Prime examples were Senator Paul Douglas and novelist John Dos Passos. A further glance at the names reveals the breadth of the cold war consensus toward American Far East policy: Walter H. Judd, John W. McCormack, John Sparkman, H. Alexander Smith, Charles Edison, Ralph Flanders, Jacob Javits, Whittaker Chambers, Eugene McCarthy, John Bricker, Bennett Cerf, Lucius Clay, Frank Clement, George S. Counts, Ralph de Toledano, James O. Eastland, Frank E. Gannett, William Randolph Hearst, Jr., Herbert Hoover, Hubert H. Humphrey, William F. Knowland, J. Bracken Lee, Emil Lengyel, George Meany, Adolphe Menjou, Margaret Chase Smith, Robert F. Wagner, Jr., William Henry Chamberlin, Warren Austin, Gene Tunney, and General Albert C. Wedemeyer.[73] At last, there was little debate, much harmony, but, ironically, much potential for maligning those who had sailed into even that safe harbor.

The perceptive might note the absence of Joe McCarthy's name, which of course has little to do with how the senator stood on that issue. It had everything to do, however, with the coincidental timing of the Committee of One Million's birth and McCarthy's political demise. Moreover, even though organizational efforts were under way months before the Army-McCarthy hearings and his subsequent condemnation by the Senate in 1954, listing his name would undoubtedly have discouraged many others from signing up. Just as Luce had forged a media bridge between American social and economic classes, this product of latter-day China Lobby influence demonstrated how mainstream political sentiments had been permeated.

But neither was Richard Nixon's name included, and he, of all people, was the chief centrist of America's postwar years. The most obvious reason was that holding the elective position of vice president of the United States inhibited any desire to lend his name to the group, a

consideration that applied to all those within the Eisenhower administration. As Sherman Adams, chief of staff to the president, explained
to the group that solicited his membership: "I have felt that so long as
I occupy my present position, I cannot appropriately lend my name in
this manner."[74]

Upon closer inspection, Nixon's role as an ally of the lobby was, as
many of the controversies that ultimately marred his name, something
less than advertised by such critics as Max Ascoli. In a study of the China
Lobby, Ross Y. Koen lists fifteen of "the most ardent congressional supporters of aid to Generalissimo Chiang Kai-shek and his Nationalist
forces"; Nixon is not among them. But Richard Nixon was a rising star,
and a West Coast Republican. Given the circumstances, total detachment
would have been astonishing. He was an appropriately good friend and
was, in fact, so regarded. H. H. Kung's son Louis donated both money
and encouragement to his campaign against Douglas. "He was, no question, a supporter of ours," Nixon remembers, "contributed I'm sure to
campaigns through the years, and he's a personal friend. As far as his
affecting me, I didn't need to be lobbied on China. It would be like
carrying coals to Newcastle."[75]

That Nixon took the pro-Chiang line is hardly newsworthy. He was
in tune with virtually his entire party on the administration's Far Eastern
troubles. His calls for Acheson's head were exactly what the China Lobby
wanted to hear. He not only condemned the secretary of state but also
diplomat Philip Jessup, who helped write the White Paper on China and
had served as a character witness for Hiss. Just before the returns confirmed his victory over Douglas, Nixon wrote to the editors of the *Sacramento Bee,* "Because of the appeasement attitude of the State
Department toward Communism in China, which has been and apparently still is supported by Mrs. Douglas, China has fallen into the Communist orb," and reiterated his opposition to a UN seat and recognition
for the Mao regime.[76]

Such sentiments naturally attracted Kohlberg to Nixon. He and the
textile importer first met in 1949, one year before his senatorial campaign. But there was no mystery about what was going on. "Because of
the McCarthy exposures and the Korean War raging at that time," Kohlberg later wrote, "and, above all, because of his part in the exposure of
Alger Hiss, and the magnificent speech making record he made, the
campaign was never in doubt."[77]

In fact, it was pro forma. Nixon followed what had become the conventional, and handiest, Republican line against the Democrats; later,
while vice president, he continued to hit hard at the theme. But Nixon
was never as tied to China as was his California colleague Knowland,
the so-called Senator from Formosa. Nixon, too, it should be remem-

bered, unlike Knowland, had his political base in southern California, where pro-Chiang sentiment was, if anything, even stronger.

There is no reason to suppose that Kohlberg found him discouraging in any way. A comparison of Nixon's own handwritten notes of topics for speaking appearances with Kohlberg's recollections of the Nixon he met in 1949 suggests that there was little need to "sell" him on the China problem. The question of not subscribing to the conventional wisdom about Democratic lapses in that part of the world probably never occurred to the congressman. The talking points virtually ignored foreign policy. His preoccupations were primarily with internal security and the growth of liberal paternalism.

Nixon's pitch hardly dismayed an enterprising businessman like Kohlberg, who determined to keep his lines with the rising politician. By the time Nixon became vice president, their correspondence carried "Dear Dick" and "Dear Alfred" salutations, which is not surprising given Kohlberg's energetic lobbying.

Nixon, who had visited Europe as a member of the Herter Committee three years before the Douglas campaign, was nevertheless far better known for his interest in domestic political events than in foreign policy. Still, neither Kohlberg nor the Kungs had any reason to doubt that they had a friend capable of beating Douglas. A New York public relations firm, Allied Syndicates, Inc., which had been doing work for the China Lobby, sent a public relations man named Leo Casey to California. Casey's mission was to help Nixon get a larger portion of the Democratic vote, especially among pro-Douglas blacks. Through the Bank of China, Casey got the funds to organize an Independent Voters Committee for Nixon.

Casey himself found out only later that he had been assigned to the campaign as an agent of the bank. Not only was the bank a repository for the China Lobby, but Casey's instructions from Allied Syndicates called for him to "deliver Nixon" to Major Louis Kung, H.H.'s son. As de Toledano tells it, "Casey was firmly pushed aside by Chotiner when he tried to inject himself into the private councils of the Nixon campaign, and he spent much of his time doing nothing in his suite at the Beverly Hills Hotel." When the election was over, Casey told Nixon all that he himself had learned about his mission. He could not, he explained, go along with any plan that called for him to "deliver" an American senator to a foreign agent. Nixon thanked him for the information.[78]

The lobby's operations had been described earlier, notably by the *New York Times* and *U.S. News & World Report* in 1949. When Owen Lattimore testified before the Tydings Committee (which investigated Joe McCarthy's allegations against the State Department) the next spring, he explained that he was a "victim." But nothing blew its cover and weakened its freedom to operate as much as two articles that ran in Max Ascoli's magazine, *The Reporter,* in April of 1952.[79]

Ascoli, Theodore White has written, "was a strange man," one not easy to like but easy to respect. An Italian antifascist, he fled penniless to New York and married an heiress to the Sears, Roebuck fortune, who set him up with his own liberal magazine. But it was, adds White, "a 'liberal' magazine with vigor, coldness and cut that stemmed directly from its editor-publisher-proprietor." When Ascoli made up his mind, with his unmatched brilliance, he was "excessive" even in the tradition of liberal publishers.[80]

Later in 1952, during the fall presidential campaign, Ascoli ran a series of articles by Ernest Brashear that gave a national readership its first critical impression of Nixon vis-à-vis Voorhis and Douglas. But it was that April, while revealing the operations of the China Lobby and telling about the assignment of Leo Casey, that the magazine tied Nixon to still another questionable step on the young man's route to success. Readers were left with the indelible impression of Nixon as a key player. To reaffirm the point, the magazine carried a caricature of Nixon on the top of a page flanked by the likenesses of David Kung and General P. T. Mow, the deputy chief of staff of the Chinese air force office in Washington. Helen Gahagan Douglas's arch-enemy was evidently "well-connected," in the words of reporter Philip Horton.

But so unconnected were the elements that comprised the pro-Chiang forces in America that the relationship between Nixon and Luce developed far more slowly. There were, of course, several reasons for the publisher's early attractions to the young man. The Hiss case, involving Luce editor Chambers, was the most obvious. Nor did his overall skill as a member of HUAC go unappreciated. Certainly, too, Luce considered Nixon a far more plausible exposer of subversion than McCarthy. Nixon was also, as Luce biographer W. A. Swanberg says, "with the China Lobby all the way,"[81] a statement with the ambiguity to match the definitions of "membership."

Not until he was Eisenhower's man was he really Luce's. The publisher was among those who stood by the vice presidential candidate during the darkest days of the secret fund crisis that marred the 1952 campaign. Luce, who had devoted seven cover stories to Chiang and one to T. V. Soong, the Nationalist minister of foreign affairs, then gave one to the vindicated Ike running mate, and still another when he remained on the ticket in 1956. The second admittedly sounded as though it could have been written by Hannah Nixon. Perhaps that tone was necessary, as an internal memo to Luce explained, "as a defense of Nixon against vilification from other quarters" by redressing "the balance of bias in the public press." Luce stood by Nixon when he became the party's 1960 presidential candidate as "a progressive Republican well qualified to carry on the Eisenhower tradition." But, as a wistful *Life* editorial then put it, "The Kennedy-or-Nixon era will be different. It may be grim or it may be great. It can scarcely be more sunny or fruitful than these Eisenhower years, in which so many age-old visions of the good life first became real."[82]

Luce's wife, Clare, recalled a dinner with Nixon. Then vice president, he had only recently returned from a visit to the Far East; and, as she pointed out, her husband was the only eastern seaboard publisher with "a lively interest in Asia." What remained in her mind was that, unlike Tom Dewey, Nixon "didn't pop his eyeballs," but the meetings she and Harry (everybody's name for Luce) had with him "were always over tense situations."[83]

Their encounters were brief, and without much personal rapport. As on China, they generally saw eye to eye. But for all the boosts given to Nixon by the "Lucepress" (Swanberg's term), the mutuality never approximated what Nixon was able to enjoy with other publishers. Much is already available to show the importance to Nixon of the Chandlers, the Hearst press (especially through its executive Richard Berlin), and Walter Annenberg's communications empire. Luce, for all his essential help, which was never as great as during that 1952 fund crisis, was in another class. China, the Far East, and the ability of a responsible Republican party to hold the line on the Red advance and fulfill the destiny of the American Century were far more important than the ambitions of a young man on the make from California. His publications also failed to note that there was anything unusual about the way Nixon had defeated either Voorhis or Douglas.[84]

Kyle Palmer later acknowledged that they all "took some wild swings, and as California election campaigns go, this was one of the most caustic in the state's history." "It's kind of hard for me to associate the Dick that we knew with what I think a politician has to do to get elected," remembered a Whittier College administrator. Most lamentable about 1950 was that the political atmosphere had become so poisoned and irrational. Outrageous and irresponsible allegations were hardly novel to politics. But none became so impassioned as accusations that the national interest had been subverted on behalf of some foreign agent. In the nation's early days, demagoguery inflamed the public prints about the English and the French. Much nineteenth-century hysteria targeted the papacy, complete with fantasies of a "Romanist" takeover of America. By 1950, the Red scare, taking advantage of peculiar cultural vulnerabilities and electronics, had surpassed all such predecessors. "The real problem is in our society," Anthony Lewis could still write four decades later. "Why do we have this hysterical strain in us about Communism?"[85]

Vito Marcantonio was 1950's most convenient pawn. His own tenden-

cies were clear. No one on Capitol Hill was more faithful to Moscow's
party line. But whether he was right or wrong on any particular issue
became entirely irrelevant. Associating with his views meant ipso facto
damnation. Marcantonio was described by knowledgeable political reporter Warren Moscow as the New York "equivalent of the old Southern
Populist, a man of the people, a fighter against the 'interests,' a hardworking and tireless champion of the social underdog; he was also the
hard-bitten dispenser of political protection to the worst elements in the
community, regardless of party." First elected to the House in the mid-
thirties as a Republican, the handpicked successor of Fiorello La Guardia
was an urban politician from the most heavily Italian-American district
in the United States. They were "loyal to a local boy who had made
good, regardless of his politics," explains Harvey Klehr.[86]

The fact remains that, in 1950, for all that has been said about Douglas's responsibility for having exploited the Marcantonio issue, Chotiner
put it to the most effective use. A special researcher was hired to look
into the Marcantonio-Douglas similarities. Ben Mandel of the HUAC
staff helpfully contributed documentation showing Douglas's various
"front" affiliations as well as a booklet from Congressman George Smathers's primary campaign to unseat Senator Claude Pepper. Smathers, a
Nixon friend, had assailed "Red" Pepper with various tactics that exploited the fear and ignorance of Floridians. Such productive tactics
were carefully studied by Nixon and Chotiner. Manchester Boddy's
"pink lady" label was then used as effectively as "Red" Pepper, with one
additional Chotiner contribution. Douglas's yellow sheet was countered
by the circulation of a "pink sheet" ("All we added," Nixon has since
written, "was the mordant comment of the color of the paper") with the
message that "Mrs. Douglas voted the same as Marcantonio 354 times"
since they both became members of Congress. One measure of the perceived success of the pink sheet was the desire of Democrat for Nixon
George Creel to renew the tactic in 1952. Months before Nixon became
Eisenhower's running mate that year, he tactfully discouraged the old
propaganda master by explaining that the party, neither through its
senatorial nor congressional committees, had adequate personnel to handle the job.[87]

Nixon was smart enough to know that even the Marcantonio strategy
had its limitations. Such voting comparisons are inevitably deceptive,
often even when intentions are honorable. The inherent, and somewhat
fallacious, assumption is that House tallies are reliable gauges of how
individual members have lined up on a given issue. Hidden from the
public are the various procedural ballots and actions on amendments
that often reveal a fuller view of what really took place. Just as far from
view is the mass of minor bills; often noncontroversial, they bring together the votes of representatives of varying ideologies. Any such figure

as "354 times" must necessarily be tailored to misrepresent.[88] The fact is, as William Costello has long since pointed out, that on the eight key roll call votes where Douglas and Marcantonio did not agree, hers were to strengthen, not weaken, the U.S. anticommunist position.[89]

Other tactics followed suit. Postcards reached voters with the following message: "Vote for Our Helen for Senator. We are with you 100%. The Communist League of Negro Women Voters." As in 1946, allegations arose about anonymous telephone calls. Asked whether that tactic was directed at Douglas, Roy Crocker replied, "I think it hurt, yes. It hurt Helen Gahagan Douglas, yes."[90]

Nixon's 2,183,454 votes were 59.2 percent of the total, high in a state with a Democratic majority. In California, as in many places throughout the country, the Roman Catholic vote resumed its 1946 defections from the Democrats, the politics of anticommunism an obvious spur.[91]

Still, as with his encounters with Voorhis and Hiss, the triumph was as costly as it was decisive. His critics, conceded a friendly early biographer, "never fail to observe that in 1950 he conducted a 'vicious smear campaign' against Helen Gahagan Douglas." His reputation was established: a reactionary anticommunist zealot, in bed with both the Chotiners and Gerald L. K. Smiths, willing to throw any falsehood and innuendo against an idealistic lady, the quintessence of political immorality. Richard Nixon, who turned thirty-eight the month he entered the Senate, was thereafter burdened with the sin of ruthless politicking. Democrats, meanwhile, who sought comfort because the Republicans failed to win control of either house or to approximate the customary gains by the "out" party, minimized the significance of losing key New and Fair Deal stalwarts.[92] It was quite enough for Republican conservatives to take full advantage of all the cumulative vulnerabilities of a party long in power.

9

The Ideal Running Mate

NOT EVEN THE SOUTH could be taken for granted by Democrats, a realization that was all the more remarkable given the strong conviction that the States' Rights (Dixiecrat) movement of 1948 had been wrongheaded and self-destructive. As *The Reporter* editorialized, Dixiecrats "succeeded only in bringing down political sanctions against the South." Instead of looking to repeat their split of 1948, even former followers of the Strom Thurmond–Fielding Wright ticket were "looking sideways at the Republicans." "The emotional attachment will diminish," predicted Mississippi newspaper editor Hodding Carter. "Economic progress, population and occupational shifts, the dispersal of concentrated Negro populations — all of these will contribute heavily to the eventual acceptance of two-party politics."[1]

Senator Harry Byrd's machine, the benevolent despotism of Virginia politics, had rebelled early in FDR's day; dissent became sufficiently general by the late thirties for other southern leaders to toy with party realignment. Less than a year after the war, responding to a memorandum that anticipated how the South might react to left-wing domination over the Democratic party, Byrd urged that the only answer was "to organize the South, make its voice heard throughout the West, so as to have an organization ready to meet them when the time comes for the [1948] convention." "The vehemence of the antagonism of the dominant southerners" to the "left-wingism of the Roosevelt and Truman years," recalled correspondent William S. White, "has perhaps never been generally understood."[2]

White had a point: feelings were intense and bitter. Loyalty to the Democracy was, to be sure, not without considerable benefit, even when the party sent a succession of northern leaders to the White House. For the most part, they enjoyed the advantages of one-party states and districts. Unchallenged tenure made for security, obviating fears of not being reelected; in Washington, where seniority was king, they naturally fell into positions of great influence on the most vital committees. Democratic presidents, too, although traditionally from outside Dixie, were forced to adjust their sights to the demands of the party's southern wing. When FDR, Truman, and Kennedy talked about the restraints that inhibited civil rights legislation, they were thinking about the South. Less obvious, but almost as compelling, was their need to trim labor and social welfare concepts for similar reasons. Both sides played the game; the benefits were mutual. As long as there were no egregious aberrations, like the one in 1928 when the national ticket was headed by Al Smith, a "wet" Catholic whose accents were right out of the sidewalks of New York City, frictions were minimized. But there was a breaking point.

As T. Coleman Andrews, a fellow conservative Virginian, pleaded with Byrd in 1950, "I know how strong your ties to the Democratic Party are, and I can understand your reluctance to break with the Democratic Party; but I tell you, Harry, somebody has got to do it." Even if the move failed, Andrews argued, "you could at least have the satisfaction of having tried to save the country from certain tragedy." One year later a member of the party's national committee from Virginia declared, "The time has now arrived . . . when the South will positively refuse not only to make further concessions but demand and insist upon the other segments of the Democratic Party making certain definite and important concessions to us." In March 1952, with the Truman administration ravaged by war in Korea and continued Dixiecrat dissatisfaction, Virginia senator A. Willis Robertson warned Chief Justice Frederick M. Vinson that "another breach in the Democratic Party is threatened which could affect the entire South just as the Readjuster Democratic Party affected Virginia for many years following the War between the States."[3]

In Virginia, perhaps more clearly than elsewhere, Byrd's loyalists oversaw the interests of the established classes. "His state is a government of the gentry — with the gentry's dutiful awareness that it has an obligation to keep the common people happy too," reported Richard Cope. "It is honest, and it is dull; and its opposition to any social change beyond that which its creator initiated twenty years ago is sufficient to keep the state moving at an unimaginative, undramatic, dead-level pace that apparently suits all but a few of its citizens." Only now and then did a maverick appear in opposition. But the normal course of things rested on an easily controllable electorate that excluded the poor and propertyless of both races. "You and I, and many of our friends, do not believe in an unrestricted electorate," wrote Robertson to Congressman Howard W. Smith.[4]

Elsewhere in Dixie, the sixty-year-old vision of a new South had lost none of its appeal to those who believed even more in the words of the journalist who wrote in 1885 about "the importance of giving every possible encouragement to the northern and foreign capitalists to invest their money in the South." Along with such others as Henry W. Grady, the journalistic leader from Georgia, they rallied the forces of capital against "the agrarian spirit." The new South would be an industrial South, salvaged by the spirit of business and enterprise. As historian Paul M. Gaston has written, "Designed to lead the region out of poverty, it made converts by the thousands in all parts of the country of men who looked forward confidently to a South of abundance. Instead, the expectations were unrealized and the South remained the poorest and economically least progressive section of the nation." During the Great Depression of the thirties, President Roosevelt called the South "the Nation's Number 1 economic problem." Still, the idea of a new South lived on, along with the mythology that the South was "undefeated." Not surprisingly, that vision remained so long as the poverty persisted; through the years, the lot of the farmers, and especially those who worked the land with them, sharecroppers and tenant farmers, continued to sink. Little wonder, then, seven out of ten southerners told Gallup interviewers in 1943 that they favored the shift away from agriculture.[5]

The movement was indistinguishable from the insistence on states' rights. The national government that had not hesitated to actively promote and even underwrite the development of the nation's industry was standing in the way of a new South. The aspiration that became so closely identified with Dixieland circles of power meant more than control over offshore tidelands oil deposits and race relations. It meant freedom of enterprise, the unshackling of capital, whether from the North or South, to fulfill the potential of an economy that had been hobbled for too long. The six-thousand-member Southern States Industrial Council urged the elimination of all "non-essential Federal activities" to facilitate "future tax reductions."[6] If they could not benefit from mercantilism, they could at least have the advantages of laissez-faire.

A ruling class is not supposed to feel suppressed. Yet, that was exactly the mood, and the end of World War II exacerbated frustrations. Northern politicians were all too often helping to promote organized labor. The New Deal had done its best to spur unionization and implement wage and hours laws. The Truman succession, instead of understanding the needs of businessmen, continued to play up to that same New Deal constituency. However such politics antagonized conservative businessmen elsewhere in the United States, those from the South felt even more cheated. Worse, the foul deeds were being done by a national government that was in the hands of fellow Democrats.

There was little question about the discontent of the region's aristocracy, the old Jeffersonians who romanticized the glory of the plantation system. They had developed the land, fought for the lost cause, and had worked to put together what had been made chaotic during the days of

Reconstruction. Who better to develop a new South? In 1930, twelve celebrants of the South and its agrarian tradition published a book of essays, *I'll Take My Stand,* that became more noted as a protest against a changing way of life than for having turned heads.

One of the contributors was Herman Clarence Nixon, a historian from Alabama, who was identified as a "pleader of causes for the 'little people.' " Nixon feared that "the human civilization now based on southern agriculture is in no little peril, and industrial civilization under the capitalistic system does not offer a satisfying substitute in human values."[7]

Professor Nixon and his colleagues, who included such literary figures as Robert Penn Warren, Allen Tate, Stark Young, John Crowe Ransom, and Frank L. Owsley, were convinced of the virtues of a community that, if left alone, would reach its own higher potential through intrinsic virtues, mostly the values of a pastoral society. Thus, such southerners taught that they were the ones best suited to prescribe their own reforms. In perpetuating both the myth of the Old South as well as the vision of the new, however, they sold themselves and the rest of the country on the vision that emphasized preserving what were, in effect, feudal advantages. Nowhere else in America did a culture work so hard at celebrating itself, nor so skillfully create a myth. The ordeal of Scarlett O'Hara and the city of Atlanta ablaze retold the wounds that film pioneer D. W. Griffith had preserved for an earlier generation. So it was not hard to understand the bitterness that kept a distinctive sense of solidarity well into the twentieth century.

Equally unsettling was the rising momentum for changing racial relationships. Once the war against the "master race" Third Reich had been won, society itself was about to become transformed. Promoting the ideology of democracy as an international moral crusade raised new expectations about its fulfillment at home. Far more people had jobs than during even the best years of the twenties, and many found their livelihoods by relocating. Nobody resettled as much as southerners, whether by leaving farms to labor in cities or by going to other parts of the country. Blacks followed poor whites in a massive flow toward the factories of the North and West. Outside Dixie, at least, the seeds were being planted for the politics of equality.

Everywhere one looked, established institutions were under siege. In the summer of 1942, southerners passed rumors about black soldiers, armed with even such weapons as icepicks, getting ready to take over power and white women. Meanwhile, reformers in all regions of the country, both sensing the tension and reacting against the anachronistic ways, called for an end to the poll tax system, the mechanism for excluding poor whites as well as poor blacks. In Louisiana, voter registration figures showed that a grand total of 886 blacks were able to cast a ballot during the last prewar election. While the battle for democracy was being fought overseas, not one Negro was eligible to vote in forty-five of that state's sixty-four parishes.[8] After the 1944 Supreme Court decision that outlawed "white primaries," ending that most effective barrier to minority participation, the figures began to move upward.

When black war veterans did get home, having served in a segregated military but with new experiences in the outside world, they neither carried icepicks nor savaged the land of the lost cause. Yet, their demands, including the right to vote, seemed revolutionary to some. Senator Byrd confided to a political lieutenant that "there has been quite a large registration of Negro veterans in Richmond and Norfolk and other large centers. As many as 100 a day have registered in Richmond. I have an idea practically all of them will vote against me." Virginius Dabney, the influential editor of the *Richmond Times Dispatch,* who had been trying to desegregate Virginia's streetcars and buses, expressed his own apprehensions at "the prospect of having hundreds of thousands [of] colored soldiers and sailors returning to the South in the next year or two," after having "received much better treatment in the service than they had before they went in, and they will be bitter and surly, if they feel that no improvement at all has taken place since they left in the South's attitude toward Negroes."[9] Hints of coming changes, of weakening systems of social control, approximated the insecurity that would have accompanied an actual uprising.

One North Carolina woman, a member of the interracial Southern Regional Council (SRC), noted "panic" among her fellow moderates in that organization. "The war is ending too soon," she wrote to a fellow SRC member, Mr. Dabney, "so some of them say; the South has not been taught its lesson. Returning Negroes will not stand for conditions as they are now. This threat of the returning Negro soldier appears repeatedly. I wonder if this panic is present in the Northern white people."[10]

The thing to do, Byrd suggested, was to make sure that "our friends be qualified, as no one can tell what the situation may develop into." Exclusion by class, the senator was in effect saying, must be replaced by racial exclusion, which not only reinforced those coming under siege but was also less vulnerable to populist agitation and far more effectively segmented the opposition. Nothing drove poor whites to voting places as rapidly as the threat of a growing black vote. The potential statewide white turnout was more than enough to compensate, especially when registrars administered literacy tests with a double standard. Thanks to their color and the specter of more blacks at the polls, they found themselves qualified. Still, political scientist V. O. Key, Jr., reported, "the Negro has made the most headway in voting where he is the least political threat to the established order." Then he pondered the failure of "even the warmest advocates of Negro rights" to face the "consequences of suddenly introducing universal suffrage into rural communities where the Negro is poorest, least educated, and least equipped to assume political responsibilities."[11]

Poor whites, tenant farmers — rednecks, dirt-eaters, peckerwoods, whatever they were called — were finding a place in the political and social structure. The agrarian class order was usually more sharply delineated than in urban centers. The vital difference was the absence of any significant middle class, not even, as Key found, an agrarian middle class. The poor of both races were at the bottom, but history and circumstance gave whites their one source of social and economic status — color. An American of European stock could look at his hand and know it would never have the skin of an African. They would never yield that advantage. In Mississippi, for example, Key noted that such "bitterness is compounded by the fact that often Negroes have the best tenant shacks. Class envy is intensified by the difficulty of crossing the line."[12] About all the poor whites had was the pride of racial superiority.

Back in 1897, fourteen years after William Graham Sumner wrote about "the Forgotten Man," a North Carolinian, Walter Hines Page, addressed a group of women students about "the development of forgotten and neglected men." Page, best known for his diplomatic career as Woodrow Wilson's ambassador to the Court of St. James's, was a Jeffersonian Democrat. Born to a slaveholding family that disapproved of the "peculiar institution" and the secession movement, he became closely associated with post–Civil War redeemers who have been described by historian C. Vann Woodward as "middle-class, professional people — schoolmen, churchmen, editors — inspired with humanitarian zeal and a passion for uplift."[13] Their concern with bettering the lot of the region's plain folk was more closely in harmony with the vision of what might become possible in a new South without overhauling the traditional structure of the society. They preferred to remain conscience redemptionists rather than revolutionaries, writing, preaching, and assuming the missionary responsibilities of the privileged classes. They were of landed comfort, not the millionaires of the new age of business and industry.

Page himself chose a career in journalism, which included editorial positions with the *New York World* and the *Atlantic Monthly*. His name lived on through his partnership in the book publishing firm of Doubleday, Page and Company. But his efforts as a reformer for the uplifting of the common man, to which he devoted himself when he took over the *Raleigh State Chronicle*, best expressed what he concluded had to be done in the process of creating a new South.

Page's forgotten men were not the blacks of the South but the region's white tenant farmers. They worked the lands that were owned by the gentry of his own background. "One in every four was wholly forgotten,"

said the forty-two-year-old Page. "The forgotten man remained forgotten. The aristocratic scheme of education had passed him by"; he was
the victim of a concept under which "teaching was controlled by those
who held political power; it was the old system of class education. It did
not touch the masses. They had no part in it." Moreover, they bought
the indoctrination, growing up believing that learning was a special privilege; for them, it was neither desirable nor necessary. "They remained
illiterate, neglected, forgotten." More tragic was that the

> forgotten man was content to be forgotten. He became not only
> a dead weight, but a definite opponent of social progress. He
> faithfully heard the politicians on the stump praise him for vir-
> tues that he did not have. The politician told him that he lived
> in the best State in the Union, told him that the other politicians
> had some hare-brained plan to increase his taxes, told him as a
> consolation for his ignorance how many of his kinsmen had been
> killed in the war, told him to distrust anybody who wished to
> change anything. What was good enough for his fathers was
> good enough for him.

Page then took note of his audience and explained that except for "the
fortunately born and the religious well-to-do . . . all the other women
were forgotten." With an aspiration instead of a plan, he advised, "You
in turn will remember the forgotten child; and in this remembrance is
laid the foundation of a new social order. The neglected people will rise
and with them will rise all the people."[14] But, even as Page spoke, they
were less forgotten than used, and used against themselves.

Some recent post–Civil War assumptions were being abandoned.
Southern aristocrats not uncommonly had faith in the social and political
malleability of the freedmen. The paternalism of the antebellum planter
was clear in the expectation expressed by Governor Wade Hampton of
South Carolina, a Confederate war hero and member of one of his state's
leading families. "As the negro becomes more intelligent," he wrote, "he
naturally allies himself with the more conservative whites, for his observation and experience both show him that his interests are identified
with those of the white race here." Hampton had, in fact, proposed at
least partial suffrage for blacks. Defeat of Radical Republicans, he urged
them, would bring a new era of racial accommodation and harmony.
Even a northern abolitionist and leader of a black Union regiment,
Thomas Wentworth Higginson, came away from a visit to South Carolina
praising the progress he saw toward racial harmony. There was, he wrote
in the *Atlantic Monthly,* no evidence of a plot or "covert plan for crushing
or reenslaving the colored race," and he saw no need for any further
federal interference.[15]

It didn't take long, however, for the Hamptons and other redeemers
of the new South to change tactics. They, along with Yankees who had

hoped to enlist both the conservative white leadership and newly freed blacks in the Republican Party, responded to a new threat. Agrarian discontent, which bred farm alliances and the Populist uprising of both blacks and whites, panicked the old power structure.

For the dozen years before Page's remarks to the North Carolina women, the full force of Jim Crow politics was unleashed. The relative harmony of the few post-Reconstruction years yielded to a new phase, one that was to last until the middle of the next century. Threats to rule by the "Bourbon" gentry were beaten back by appeals to the racial insecurities and fears of southern whites. Just before the Civil War, Hinton Helper, author of the influential book *The Impending Crisis,* had written that "the stupid and sequacious masses, the white victims of slavery . . . believe whatever the slaveholders tell them; and thus are cajoled into the notion that they are the freest, happiest, and most intelligent people in the world." When the war began, as W. J. Cash has commented, "yeoman and cracker turned to the planter, waited eagerly upon his signal as to what to think and do."[16]

During the years of post–Civil War reconstruction, educated southerners, men of property, warned about "Negro domination" and appealed for white supremacy. "In their frantic efforts to stop the revolt and save themselves the conservatives lost their heads," as C. Vann Woodward has written, "and sought to reenact the triumph of earlier years by which they overthrew the carpetbaggers, redeemed the South, and won their laurels." White southern leadership always stood ready to use the votes of poor whites against blacks to maintain social and political control. State after state, during the 1890s especially, enacted new, more stringent regulations segregating the races and eradicating even the limited commingling of the 1870s and early 1880s. During the fifteen years between 1882 and 1897, when Page talked about the forgotten man, lynchings became more routine, with 2,517 officially reported. More revealing was the pattern for each decade. Figures available for the 1880s show that 49 percent of those lynched were black. By the next decade, blacks constituted 72 percent of the victims and rose to 89 percent from 1900 through 1909. The Supreme Court "followed the election returns" in 1883, throwing out five challenges against segregated accommodations enacted by states and then, in the landmark *Plessy v. Ferguson* decision of 1896, upholding the concept of separate but equal. Political leaders such as Georgia's Tom Watson stopped playing David to battle the Goliath of the poor and helped to divide the impoverished, pitting race against race. The South, however changed, wrote Cash, was "still a world in which the first social principle of the old was preserved virtually intact: a world . . . in which a white man, any white man, was in some sense a master."[17]

Whiteness alone secured an acceptable place. "Indeed," George M.

Frederickson has written, "one of the things that made 'the New South' new was the direct exploitation and dependent status of the kind of whites who had been poor but independent landowning farmers under the old regime." By the end of the century, the resurgence of the redeemers had become the policy of the national government as well, even by the same party, as a Boston newspaper put it, that had "carried the country into and through a civil war to free the slave." "It will not be news to any northerners that southern white people show aggression against Negroes," wrote Yale psychologist John Dollard in 1937; "it is almost as well advertised as the plantation stereotype of the goateed planter with his mint julep, the pillared big house, and the happy Negroes singing in their quarters. . . . By adopting the current legend of 'The Old South' we northerners agree not to notice the hostility toward Negroes which southern people tend to understress and which the older abolitionist's ideology in the North overestimated."[18]

Periods of insecurities after each of the two great twentieth-century wars encouraged similar responses. Fear of returning soldiers was not unique to 1945 and 1946. The end of World War I brought a renewal of the old southern apprehension about newly conscious blacks, armed and angry, and together with a new wave of repression, surprising, as Professor Dollard later wrote, "Negro soldiers who came back expecting appreciation for their services."[19] The Ku Klux Klan, reformed just before the war, became newly emboldened and spread its power to the North and Midwest, contributing significantly to the repressive nativism of the early 1920s. Social readjustment was somewhat less traumatic after World War II, but the strains began to show before very long. Moderates like Dabney began to back away from their earlier attempts at desegregating facilities. Ku Klux Klan cross-burning resumed, and violence against blacks compelled President Truman to appoint a special commission on civil rights.

However alarming, the early postwar period failed to equal the violence of earlier days, tempered to a considerable degree by the greater realization of the national shame. "There were fewer lynchings in the South last year," noted Max Ascoli's *Reporter* in 1949, "than there were plays on Broadway about lynchings in the South." There was, instead, the renewed mobilization of resistance against those whose efforts to alter the cozy relationships of the past were viewed as inimicable to the region's economic development. At a meeting of the Kiwanis Club in Jacksonville, the speaker made what one of those present called "a regular Chamber of Commerce talk" about Florida's industries, citing the canning of fruit and citrus concentrates. When he finished, a member of the audience got up and shouted out that he had overlooked Florida's main industry. What was that? he was asked. "The canning of Pepper." The audience erupted into a loud and sustained applause, enjoying the denunciation of Senator Claude Pepper, who, like a handful of other progressives, was more sympathetic to the region's lingering populist sentiments.[20] Whether such people would stage a 1948-style walkout from the Democrats in 1952 was unlikely, but that was of little comfort.

Southern New Dealers like Pepper were on the defensive. A populist with the values of Huey Long was rare. He was unique for his ability to direct a Share-the-Wealth program at the region's impoverished blacks without losing reverence from poor whites. James "Kissin' Jim" Folsom took over the governorship of Alabama determined to rout the Black Belt power that suppressed the poor of both races. "As long as the Negroes are held down by deprivation and lack of opportunity, all the other people will be held down alongside them," he said in his 1949 Christmas message to the legislature. "Let's start talking fellowship and brotherly love, and doing unto others. And let's do more than talk about it; let's start living it." Folsom, whose political career was later killed as much by the bottle as the Bourbons, fully intended to mend Alabama's oligarchic rule, including killing the poll tax, but the Black Belt powers, centering along the region where rich soil combined with vestiges of old slaveholding concentrations, were simply too well entrenched.[21] Pepper had similar opponents, but what did him in was the 1950 campaign of George Smathers, who used some shrewd demagoguery to woo the forgotten man into an alliance with the state's most conservative Democrats.

Gone, too, was the Mississippian remembered as the champion demagogue of them all, Theodore Bilbo. It was Bilbo who, in the words of one of the South's most perceptive students, built "a political career on the old plea of persecution." Much as had Long, Bilbo, from an incredibly poor state, became the messiah of the impoverished. In a public career that lasted from 1916 to 1947, he gave them, writes his biographer, "a taste of rural culture . . . their only source of drama and comedy, of heroes and villains. . . . He knew these people because he was one of them. He knew how to make them laugh and weep, how to soothe them and to arouse their fury. Most of all, he knew how to win their trust — and votes." The son of the aristocratic planter Bilbo defeated wrote that he "was a pert little monster, glib and shameless, with that sort of cunning common to criminals which passes for intelligence." Even the great lords of the delta had little choice but to go along with the "prince of the peckerwoods" because he was the senator and could do a lot more for them in Washington than for their tenants; holding their noses, they voted for him. It may have been, as Key writes, "unsporting and vulgar of him to demagogue about the poor devils" with black skins, but such differences were not all that great. Three decades of Bilbo's power were far more than enough to make his name synonymous with Negrophobia. He was not posturing. His private correspondence is filled with much the same caliber of primitive racism that he expressed in public.[22] Those who failed to see past his extreme "nigger-baiting" forgot that Bilbo's mission was to keep his faith with the rednecks in the hills and on the fields.

But, regardless of how offensive he may have been to civilized Washington, he was also a solid supporter of New Deal welfare and labor legislation. He was there for Mississippi's one-horse farmers on the cotton fields. When he opposed the New Deal, he did so on their behalf. He really did believe, as biographer Chester M. Morgan argues, "that the government ought to insure that somehow men and women who worked so long and hard on American farms would receive an honest livelihood from that labor." Frank Tannenbaum, who had surveyed rural southern poverty, was one of the New Deal intellectuals whose repulsion toward the man did not keep him from admitting that the senator was "a real friend of the people," one who was "consistently always for the under-dog and every vote that he cast was on that side."[23] Bilbo was among a culture of rednecks, shrewder, more articulate, and a champion of the plain folks. His vulgarity was more excessive than unique. In the new America, the America of the second half of the century, his rhetoric was going out of style along with his passions.

Bilbo himself was gone by the fifties, having died before he could win his battle to regain the Senate seat denied him by his colleagues in 1948. There were others, however, both newly elected and holdovers, very different from the Mississippian but all qualified to be considered progressives, New Dealers, or neopopulists. Four, including Huey Long's brother Earl, occupied statehouses. Four others, Estes Kefauver and Albert Gore of Tennessee, and Lister Hill and John Sparkman of Alabama, represented their states in the U.S. Senate. All were as vulnerable to the changing complexion of southern politics, especially the politics of race, as was the national party itself. Still another black-white split seemed certain.[24]

That was what Democrats were determined to avoid as they arrived at Chicago for their national convention in late July 1952. Organized drives behind the recently nominated Eisenhower-Nixon ticket were already disturbingly visible in the South. Most were of the "Democrats for Eisenhower" variety, frequently consisting of the same people who had worked for Strom Thurmond four years earlier. None of this was surprising, because from Virginia to Texas, traditional conservatives were already looking for an alternate ticket. "There is a great deal of talk about Eisenhower being put on the Democratic ticket," wrote Senator John Stennis of Mississippi to Texas colleague Lyndon Johnson, "but I am confident that this will not pan out because we will whip them at their own game on this point. Eisenhower will, however, get a considerable vote in Mississippi and you cannot tell what turn things will take by November." Offshore oil, race, federal controls, domestic spending, unionism, were all helping to drive a new generation toward the despised GOP. Several governors led the way, including James F. Byrnes of South Carolina, followed by "oil governors" like Allan Shivers of Texas and Robert Kennon of Louisiana. In 1952 they were not Dixiecrats; they were "Eisencrats."[25]

The party could hardly afford a fight. With a ticket composed of Adlai Stevenson of Illinois, who had no particular reputation as a civil rights enthusiast, and Alabama's Sparkman, they put forward their best face possible. An effort by northern liberals to head off another bolt by amending the rules to include a "loyalty oath" that would bind all delegates to the national ticket sparked a little rebellion. Virginians protested. They already had their own rule. Any such effort was superfluous; moreover, it was a violation of their state's rights. After a quick caucus, the Virginians countered with a statement that would exempt any state that already had a law that prevented an individual delegate from acting on his own. Once that was put before the convention, a Maryland delegate quickly moved that Virginia be seated. "This victory," stated a memorandum by Lewis Preston Collins, Virginia's delegate-at-large, "was due to an expediency occasioned by fear to crucify the principles" rather than "to any sudden political conversion or renaissance on the part of those in command." That outcome and a milder platform statement on civil rights were sufficiently acceptable to the party's southern wing so that their favorite candidate, Senator Richard Russell of Georgia, felt free to permit his nomination as a candidate under the Democratic banner. At best, some time was bought, but nobody had a clear idea of how the long-term problem could be resolved. Meanwhile, Harry Byrd maintained his "golden silence." He never did come out with a direct endorsement for the Republicans, but on October 17 he told fellow Virginians that he "will not, and cannot, in good conscience, endorse the national Democratic platform or the Stevenson-Sparkman ticket. Endorsement means to recommend and this I cannot do." "Of course I have great respect for Senator Byrd and share his dislike of everything that Trumanism stands for," A. Willis Robertson assured a lady from Chattanooga, "but I listened very attentively to his speech when it was delivered over the radio and I also read it in the press and no where did he say that he is going to vote for General Eisenhower or ask any one else to do so." While Robertson nevertheless remained discreet and took Byrd's cue, his Virginia colleague, Howard W. Smith, kept his old attachment to "the house of our fathers." "I am inclined to believe," Robertson informed Byrd, "that both John Battle [governor of Virginia] and Howard Smith are a little sick."[26]

Such divisions were understandable. The question of race was played down during that national campaign. When Roy Wilkins, director of the National Association for the Advancement of Colored People (NAACP), went to see Stevenson, he found the Democratic candidate barely warmer than his opponent toward a stronger stand on civil rights. Only after much hesitation did the ex-governor of Illinois embrace the idea of a national Fair Employment Practices Commission (FEPC) to outlaw discrimination in employment. The Republicans rested their case on the proposition that it was a matter for the states. In New Jersey, then led by Governor Alfred Driscoll, General Eisenhower declared that such Republican-led states were, in fact, where blacks had been making their greatest gains.[27] The point had considerable merit when also considering such neighboring states as New York, under Governor Tom Dewey, and Connecticut, which, after the generally progressive postwar administration of Raymond Baldwin, was led by John Davis Lodge. That was as far as Eisenhower would venture.

Vice presidential candidate Nixon, in an interview published in *U.S. News & World Report,* repeated the official line. His House record, he said, included two votes for anti–poll tax bills and he was on record for antilynching legislation. Insofar as an FEPC was concerned, his legislative record had already shown that he favored voluntary action by the states. He explained that he opposed segregation in the armed forces (which had formally been abolished by President Truman's executive order in 1948) and was for desegregating the District of Columbia, which was, he added, entitled to home rule. Basically, Nixon explained, "I believe that if we resort to coercion before the people are educated to the point where the coercion would be effective . . . we would have the same situation we had with prohibition. . . . When public opinion is not behind a law, the law will not work."[28]

But Nixon's role on the Republican ticket was not specifically directed at the South. His task was to bring in conservatives on those issues where he was regarded as an asset, so he remained the man who had "convicted" Hiss. The fact that Stevenson had given a deposition in behalf of the accused man made him a natural campaign target. Nixon told a nationwide television audience that he did not question his opponent's loyalty, just his judgment. Even given the knowledge of the quality of Hiss's defense, he said, Stevenson still "testified that the reputation of Alger Hiss for veracity, for integrity, and for loyalty was good." Stevenson, placed on the defensive, explained his endorsement of Hiss as simply having vouched for the man's good character, just as John Foster Dulles had done. In Texarkana on October 27, Nixon returned to his old betrayal-of-the-Democratic-party theme. All of them, Stevenson, Truman, and Dean Acheson, were "traitors to the high principles in which many of the nation's Democrats believe." Hitting still harder in Los Angeles three days later, he said that Stevenson "holds a Ph.D. degree from Acheson's College of Cowardly Communist Containment."[29] Neither the Democratic candidate nor his colleagues would easily forget the excesses of Nixon's rhetoric.

As it turned out, the Eisenhower-Nixon penetration failed to take any Deep South states in 1952, but that is about all that can be said for the ability of the Democrats to hold on to traditional strength. One political scientist took stock of what southern voters had done and exclaimed, "They're acting like Yankees!" Many of them, in fact, were precisely that, drawn to the region by expanding economic opportunities. That kind of Republican constituency was predictable, aided by the organizational efforts of the neo-Bourbons. No one had ever seen so much GOP activity in Texas. The Eisenhower forces in that traditionally Democratic state constituted a coalition of many groups: as enumerated by one scholar, they included newly arrived white-collar workers, discontented conservative Democrats, "nominal Republicans who had become active, presidential Republicans, and real Republicans previously voting in Democratic primaries who thought that at last they saw a chance for the Republican party to be effective."[30]

What was, for the long run, of greatest significance was how closely the shift paralleled the Dixiecrat vote of 1948. The best GOP turnout was in the cities, but even that was greatest where the urban area was closest to the Black Belt. The most surprising gains were in places where Democratic traditional loyalties were most solid. The larger the black population, the stronger the Eisenhower-Nixon vote, which ran ahead of the average statewide totals in two-thirds of such counties. Black Belt counties voted eight times more heavily for the Republicans than in 1948. The old Negrophobia remained a powerful impulse, combining with the economic and cultural appeals of Eisenhower's candidacy, which, wrote Samuel Lubbell, "like the blasting of a dike, served to release forces which had been building up behind the dam of one-party rule." The new redemptionists had spoken, and their signal once more was heeded. As Key observed, rural southern politics "was more cultural than rational. . . . What one did to gain office was distinct, if not unrelated, to what one did in public office."[31]

There was no real controversy about Richard Nixon's first shot at the ticket. In 1952, he was Ike's ideal running mate; one can hardly imagine anyone more suitable, at least by the criteria that determine the succession to power. Of course, the problem then seemed remote: notwithstanding Truman's very recent example, few thought the second spot on the ticket had much value or significance for governing the country. Unifying the party and presenting an attractive ticket for November were all that mattered. Nixon possessed such assets in spades. He was a Republican comer, a California youth sharing the billing with an avun-

cular general who would reach the age of sixty-two by election day; the
new star of the West, where the party's heart was heading; the bane of
subversives, who despite a tendency toward occasional excess in commie-
bashing was a moderate as well as a convinced internationalist.

The senator from California survived an ever-shortening list of potential running mates. Long before any delegates reached Chicago, insider gossip was rife in Washington. Nixon himself had had reasons for
taking such talk seriously since early May. "You are the best man to do
it," Alice Roosevelt Longworth told him at a dinner party. By the time
the Republican gathering in Chicago entered its second day, it was clear
that he was a genuine contender. In midweek, July 10, the *Chicago Daily
News* headlined the rumor of his probable selection. The Eisenhower
camp, daily more confident of beating out Taft, had all but decided.
Even Ike himself was sold on the wisdom of going before the party with
the man who seemed eager, competent, intelligent, and, as he told Nixon,
had not only gotten Hiss but gotten him fairly.[32]

Nixon was, as it turned out, both a pawn and a knight at that convention. The real significance, as the *New York Times* reported, was that
there was "a fundamental change in the direction and control of the
party — a change that has been in the making since 1940."[33] So con-
vulsive was that departure, in fact, that Nixon's place on the ticket was
ultimately jeopardized by the wiles of those who needed him to appeal
to some very strange bedfellows.

It was left to Everett McKinley Dirksen, a freshman senator from
Illinois, to provide the theatrics that did more than anything else to
illustrate Republican fractiousness. In later years especially, his rhetoric
made him something of a celebrity, a showman of the Senate who even
found a mass audience through commercial recordings. But, in 1952,
the "wizard of ooze," the master of purple oratory, the spokesman of
the Taftites on the delegate-seating issue, had his unforgettable moment.

His verbal salvo, rendered from the podium, ended whatever pretense
there was to decorum. His words sparked a fistfight in the Michigan
delegation, a round of applause and countervailing boos, and guests in
the galleries shook their fists, some while standing on chairs. Excited
Republicans and newsmen jammed the aisles. The commotion overwhelmed one New Yorker, who passed out. The GOP was having its
own little civil war, egged on by the man at the podium. At San Francisco's
Cow Palace a dozen years later, the attack came from the delegates
themselves. In each case, the issue was essentially the same. The party
was suffering the throes of its internal conflict, with its agricultural, small-
town, entrepreneurial heartland rebelling against the eastern establishment — and, of course, its patron saint, Tom Dewey.

The pandemonium was beyond anything Dirksen expected, a furor
rooted in Republican geopolitics, more a manifestation of historical bit-

terness than the actual intensity of Dirksen's words. Had he thought about them more carefully beforehand, he would not have been as surprised as he later professed. Facing the delegates, with Dewey seated up front with his New York delegation totally unprepared for what was about to come, Dirksen, a finger aimed at the governor, set off the fireworks: "Reexamine your hearts before you take this action in support of the Minority Report, because we followed you before and you took us down the path to defeat." When all hell let loose, the New York governor confidently assumed that Dirksen's real damage was to himself.[34]

Tom Dewey had become anathema to the party's heartland army of conservatives and rightists, most regarding him as the epitome of everything obnoxious about the eastern establishment. Although a son of the Midwest (Owosso, Michigan) and a graduate of the University of Michigan, Dewey got his law degree from Columbia and had been New York's district attorney par excellence, establishing himself as a gangbuster and public servant who was eloquent and efficient. He liked to think that Republicans were sufficiently fond of the capitalist system to patch its soft spots. But the man who loved to retreat from the big city and play the squire of Quaker Hill at his farm near Pawling was, nevertheless, Manhattan. His backers, his political sources, were centered in GOP strongholds ruled by New York moneymen. Essential parts of his world, they surrounded him in the country no less than in the city.[35]

Ever since his gangbuster days, Tom Dewey had been a distinctive, almost antiseptic, character, somewhat like a well-manicured martinet, short but imposing. He dressed immaculately, had a well-groomed moustache and heavy eyebrows. Phobic about catching germs, he disliked shaking hands, thereby further exuding patrician aloofness. He was, according to philanthropist Sterling Morton, a self-made man who worshipped his creator. Even friends considered him priggish. The image that stuck while he lost to Truman in 1948 was that of a Kewpie doll, much like a groom atop a wedding cake.[36]

His greatest crime, of course, was in being a two-time loser in presidential politics. But the charge that he had run a me-too campaign in 1948 and carried the banner of the eastern establishment, internationalist wing of the party was one that he could never overcome. Robert A. Taft's manager, David Ingalls, issued a formal statement saying that "it is obvious that the convention realizes the fight is between Dewey and the anti-Dewey forces. The Republican party for the third time faces the issue of Deweyism and whether we are going to permit him to lead us down the road to certain defeat in November."[37]

Nothing was more symptomatic of what was happening to the GOP than the letter Dirksen received from former president Herbert Hoover a few days later. "You were the one who emerged from the convention as the leader of our kind of Republicans," assured the comforting voice from the past.[38]

At least for the moment, Nixon was a concession to his kind of Republicans. Still, there was some irony. Nixon in 1952 was not selected for being a rightist. Red-baiting had helped to assure purity, and he had nailed Hiss, but in some quarters that had its minuses as well as pluses. His youth was a contrast with the sixtyish general, and California offered correct geographic balance. Other than that, especially in his international views, he had a record that hardly differed from the outlook of Dewey and the eastern establishment. His own state's conservatives were piqued because they suspected that he had maneuvered the Earl Warren strategy that undermined Taft's bid for the nomination.[39]

For Robert Taft, back at his hotel room after losing his final chance for the presidential nomination, digesting Eisenhower's choice of Nixon exacerbated the pain of defeat. One visitor heard him denounce Nixon as "a little man in a big hurry." Taft conceded that Nixon was clever, but added that "he had a mean and vindictive streak in him which came close to the surface when he couldn't get his way." He hoped that the situation would never permit Nixon to reach the presidency.[40]

Indirectly, at least, Taft tried to keep Nixon off the ticket. In a futile, wholly unrealistic last-minute move that was primarily an effort to salvage some semblance of leverage, Taft let Ike know that he wanted Ev Dirksen. The call, passed on by Senator Frank Carlson of Kansas, was the act of a masochist exploring the intensity of his own pain.

"After what he said," an adviser noted about Dirksen, "I wouldn't wipe my feet on that fellow."[41]

Sinclair Weeks of Massachusetts, chairman of the GOP's finance committee and Eisenhower's future secretary of commerce, noted in his diary that Taft's belated effort to obtain consolation ran afoul of other interests as well. As Weeks recorded the event at the time, "When his name was up, it was promptly killed, not by the 'Eastern Internationalists' (see the Chicago Tribune) but by the great farm state of Iowa and the great ranching and mining state of Colorado."[42]

If Taft had ever counted on Nixon's support, he should have known better. Everything points to Nixon's inclination toward the Eisenhower side long before the Chicago convention and, in fact, before the general became a candidate.

All that can be said is that the California lineup left him with few opportunities for profit by signing on with "Mr. Republican," as Taft had come to be known. The state's senior senator, Bill Knowland, was an ardent Taft man. The only soft spot on the California political hierarchy, Governor Warren, was a favorite son candidate and eager to hold his delegation for an opportunity to capitalize on an Eisenhower-Taft deadlock. For Nixon to side with Eisenhower as early as he did was a long shot. Cynics will, of course, say that it was the only game in town, which ignores some basic realities: Nixon owed Warren nothing and his tepid past support gave him ample reason for resentment. Insofar as Taft was concerned, there was a basic incompatibility, especially over foreign policy.

Moreover, Nixon was simply one of those Americans who admired General Eisenhower. As early as 1947, while the congressman was in Europe, he made the following notation: "Eisenhower of all the generals had the abilities of a military man with none of their stupidities." Nor was he disenchanted when he later visited the general at NATO headquarters in May 1951.[43]

Three months after his trip to Paris, Nixon was explicit about his choice. Writing to George Creel, whose rightward movement had brought him to the conclusion that Eisenhower was "as much of a Welfare Stater as Truman himself," Nixon differed with his old supporter from San Francisco. Eisenhower, he was confident, "will receive the nomination if he consents to run. I share some of the concerns you express but on the other hand . . . I believe it is essential that we put somebody at the top of the ticket who is more sure than Taft appears to be at the present time." A survey of twenty-three thousand California constituents also confirmed for him that they considered Eisenhower by far the strongest candidate. Early in 1952, Nixon turned back Taft's personal appeal for support. He explained that his decision had already been revealed to Knowland and Warren and said that he made the choice because of Eisenhower's qualifications for dealing with foreign affairs. Later, Nixon acknowledged what some eastern establishment people already knew. Eisenhower, in some ways, was even more deeply conservative than Taft, which was less readily apparent because the Ohio senator was so, as Nixon put it, "establishment Republican."[44]

Staking out a pro-Eisenhower position so early in the competition may in retrospect appear to have been shrewd, even a matter of artful deception, making him the only member of his delegation willing to play ball with the other side. One does not, however, have to look closely to realize that Nixon's role was not well hidden. In the crucial battles over credentials involving seating of Taft or Eisenhower people, Nixon took unequivocal positions that favored the "high ground" and "moral principle." The decisive test of strength was embodied in the controversial prenomination Fair Play Amendment, which determined jurisdiction over disputed delegations, all of them from southern states. The tactic was essential to the Eisenhower cause in every way, for it provided the chance to slow down the Taft steamroller powered by the GOP heartland. Nixon became part of that counterattack. He joined with Henry Cabot Lodge and the Dewey strategists behind the general and denounced what he called "the Texas grab" and then, with the bloc of California votes behind him, helped ward off Taft's claims for a share of the Georgia delegation.[45] Nevertheless, his efforts, particularly because of maneuvering within his own delegation, reinforced the view of a Nixon who was little more than a crafty, unprincipled tactician whose services were forever on the open market.

Such hindsight inevitably simplifies his options. Showing his anti-Taft hand so early, as in his letter to Creel, and then holding to that position risked falling into the losing side and bearing political consequences. He chose sides when it was Taft and not Eisenhower who was the party's favorite. Even when the general declared his candidacy and returned from Europe in the spring of 1952, he was still the underdog. Nor, for that matter, did the eventual nominee take the prize before delegations began to shift over after the roll call on the first ballot. Nixon, however, was among those (and they soon became a majority) who feared that Taft would only bring another defeat.[46] Had Taft gone on to win, Nixon would have had to settle for a continued, and possibly permanent, career in the Senate.

Whatever the consequences, there could have been no Nixon-Taft compatibility. Taft himself was, in some ways, more moderate than Eisenhower, whose deep conservatism over fiscal matters was well hidden, but he represented a force that was being generated from the angry right. That position, especially with its implications for foreign policy, was inimical to Nixon's view of the world. In 1952, his notion of where the Republican party had to point was clearly in tune with the general's key backers.

Those eastern establishment people had sized up Nixon early and confirmed his acceptability. He made his first strong entry into their ranks when Governor Dewey invited him as the main speaker at a New York State Republican fund-raiser at the Waldorf-Astoria on May 8. The forum also gave Nixon the opportunity to introduce himself to that wing of the party via a major speech that was broadcast over radio. He fulfilled Dewey's expectations. It would later become commonplace, but at the time it was something of a novelty to see him deliver an important address, before a key audience, without the aid of anything but a brief outline. Later that evening, Dewey introduced him to such other New York Republican bigwigs as J. Russel Sprague, a key leader on Long Island, and Herbert Brownell. Would he object to becoming the vice presidential candidate? Dewey asked. Dewey later remembered that Nixon said he would be "greatly honored." A few weeks later, in a Mayflower Hotel suite in Washington, Dewey introduced him to Eisenhower's inner circle. There he was under some obvious scrutiny, especially about his views on foreign and domestic policy; but, not surprisingly, no commitments were made about the vice presidency. Dewey later recorded his impressions of the Californian: "I thought he was a fine speaker. He had a very fine voting record in both the House and the Senate, good, intelligent, middle of the road, and at this time it was important to get a Senator who knew the world was round. . . . His age was a useful factor. He had a fine record in the war. Most of all, however, he was an extraordinarily intelligent man, fine balance and character." Dewey's biographer, Richard Norton Smith, was later told by the governor's state party chairman that Nixon was "a fifth column" assigned to undermine Warren's California position. He "couldn't think of anybody else who would keep the California delegation in line." Nixon himself later thought that "Dewey saw me as one who could hold the right wing and still be in the center as far as foreign policy, but I had the right-wing support because of the Hiss case."[47]

Eighteen years after that convention, Henry Cabot Lodge clarified the circumstances that established Nixon as a national political leader. Taft's preconvention lead and party standing were so substantial that he could not have been headed off without the full force of the Dewey organization. Eleven men composed the group. Four were holdovers from the governor's 1948 presidential organization, Dewey himself, Brownell, Sprague, and Barak Mattingly. Brownell was made the chief planner, and others, such as Mattingly, were given specific assignments. Also brought in were Paul Hoffman (the Marshall Plan administrator) and Senator Frank Carlson, who was useful for, as Lodge put it, giving "the Kansas flavor."[48]

Another key member of the Eisenhower inner circle was General Lucius Clay. Clay, a fifty-five-year-old, tight-lipped Georgian, was a West Pointer who had served with Ike in the Philippines before the war. After the war, his old friend and commander made him his deputy for the military government of Germany. Eisenhower, in his *Crusade in Europe*, praises Clay for his "brilliant" performance in the initial establishment of the American Military Government in Germany. A crackerjack administrator, perhaps the best in the army, Clay is remembered for his ability to break the Soviet blockade of West Berlin.

Far less well known was Clay the politico. Cited by David Eisenhower as "one of the few figures to bridge Eisenhower's military and political careers," Clay was more than just a link between decades.[49] He knew his way around Washington, first as the son of a man who served fourteen years in the Senate from Georgia, and then as deputy to Office of War Information director James Byrnes and during a War Department assignment under General Brehon Somervell.

Nor were Clay's talents unappreciated by young Richard Nixon. Returning home after meeting Clay during a fact-finding trip to Europe in 1947, Nixon wrote that "I do not believe I have ever seen a military man who had a keener appreciation of economic and political affairs than has General Clay."[50]

The soldier's prestige and connections then served him well in civilian life. By 1951, he had retired from the army and had become chairman of the board of the Continental Can Company and was, moreover, close to such Wall Streeters as financier Sidney Weinberg, which placed him near Tom Dewey. His background and connections made him the ideal man to serve as an intermediary between General Eisenhower and the professional politicians during the effort to get Ike to leave his NATO post in order to campaign for the presidency. Clay, who went on to serve as a key Eisenhower political adviser in both 1952 and 1956, was the man who first informed another early Eisenhower booster, Henry Cabot Lodge, that World War II's most popular general was a Republican.[51]

Lodge himself was up for reelection to another term as senator from Massachusetts in 1952. With young Jack Kennedy about to become his opponent, he expected that it might be disastrous to share the Republican ticket in that eastern state with Taft. Taft, hardly more attractive than a cold water pipe, had a reputation as too much of a hard-shell conservative for easterners and, besides, thought Lodge, did not really understand the world. His was the voice of discredited isolationism, more in tune with the 1930s and Herbert Hoover's continuing fantasies than with the imperatives of collective security and close cooperation with America's European allies.

In a meeting that took place in Dewey's Roosevelt Hotel apartment, Lodge was selected as Ike's campaign manager. Taft's rapid progress seemed difficult to overcome even from the vantage point of November 1951. Given the difficulty of overtaking the senator, Lodge expressed reservations about being asked to play the role. He protested to the group that he was from "the effete East" and had gone to Harvard; his background was "all wrong for that purpose."[52] But there were few other high-ranking Republicans willing to gamble on Eisenhower. Lodge, even if from the wrong part of the country, at least had the advantage of not being known as a Dewey man. At the 1948 convention, he had worked to deadlock the Dewey and Taft forces so the nomination could go to Arthur Vandenberg. If, then, Lodge became the Eisenhower campaign manager and used Deweyites, Dewey himself had to be kept in the background.

A key problem was the California delegation. Ostensibly, at least, Nixon and Knowland were behind their favorite son, Warren. Both had also committed themselves to support the Fair Play Amendment, whose passage was crucial to Eisenhower's success. It was Knowland, however, who worried Lodge. On the Monday before the convention opened, he attended a caucus of the delegation and heard Knowland propose to forgo a vote on the Fair Play Amendment. That, together with his prior knowledge of Knowland, deepened his suspicions. He turned to the most logical ally on the West Coast.

Nixon was known to be "strong" for Ike. He also had major influence with the state's delegation. Nixon also, explained Lodge, was useful because of his appeal to right-wing "Red-baiters such as Bridges." If, Lodge pointed out, there "had been a vote on Eisenhower vs. Taft vs. Stassen vs. Warren, they would not have done nearly as well. If the potential vice presidential candidate was a member of the California delegation, that would be the best insurance of not getting cheated in that delegation. This arrangement was made with Nixon days before the nomination." None of this meant that Nixon was a sure bet for second place, but when on July 11, with Eisenhower's nomination secured, the group of insiders gathered with their short list of running mates there was hardly any discussion about anyone else. Nixon, telephoned by Brownell, made the right noises about surprise and gratitude. His daughter has even written that he was "speechless in disbelief."[53] Back in Whittier, Frank and Hannah watched Nixon's nomination on a television set in Donald's home.

An Eisenhower-Nixon ticket confirmed that Republicans had passed a watershed. The GOP's majority had been forced to swallow realities. Winning was more important than living with Taft on love alone. Even many of those who wore "I Like Ike" buttons, noted Richard Rovere, backed him because he was their only hope. Still, on the eve of the Eisenhower-Nixon nomination, rumors went around the convention hall about a stop-Ike movement sparked by the GOP old guard going down fighting for a Douglas MacArthur–John Bricker ticket. They were more easily roused by General MacArthur, whose keynote address excited the delegates when he accused the Democrats of paving the way for a socialistic or even a communistic state and of refusing to take those military steps that, in the long run, "might have saved continental Asia from Red domination." The next day, only a minority remained impassive when Joe McCarthy promised not to soften his blows on the Communist issue because "a rough fight is the only fight Communists can understand." "I say, one Communist in a defense plant is one Communist too many," he shouted. "One Communist on the faculty of one university is one Communist too many. One Communist among the American advisers at Yalta was one Communist too many. And even if there were only one Communist in the State Department," he concluded, "there would be one Communist too many."[54]

The convention, wrote observer Lester Markel, was a fight between the "Old Guard" and the "New Order." The hold of the former had been broken. "The problem that now confronts the New Order," he wrote, "is whether it can also break the *tradition* of the Old Guard and, more, convince the electorate that it is broken. In brief, it must close the gap between nominee and convention."[55]

That gap was indeed great. The GOP right, in effect blocked from power, returned to their homes as though some infidel had settled in.

The hand of Dewey had not been so well hidden. Neither had the power of New York financial interests and the whole commercial influence of the East Coast. That included Wall Street and the "kingmakers" of the establishment media, which, in their minds, buried Taft and kept the party in the hands of interlopers. One of their enemies, Hugh Scott of Pennsylvania, understood their frustration that if Taft couldn't hold the line "against the pressures of what they regarded as socialism, nobody could."[56] While Ike would rule from his exalted position, the burden for keeping it all together was obviously on Nixon, rather a neophyte for that job.

Two months later, the unexpected brouhaha over the so-called secret fund almost undermined all that. Eisenhower got his chance to pull back from the young man who had aroused so much controversy so quickly, and his advisers had an opportunity to reevaluate the wisdom of their choice. That Nixon clung to the ticket, albeit just barely, was not without a costly trade-off.

Even after being ridiculed for the lachrymose television performance remembered as the "Checkers speech," and never ridding himself of the aura of corruption, he nevertheless emerged as a stronger figure on his own. His talk to the American people, which did much to contribute to the mixed reactions, was watched by the largest television audience as of that time, and it was entirely fitting that the number, nearly 60 million, was not exceeded until his first debate with John F. Kennedy eight years later. What critics have generally failed to see is that the speech, which turned the tide of the crisis, was the first major stroke in his career of the sort of leadership only hinted at earlier, the wooing of the postwar forgotten man. Derision came from a different culture, those who were later described as the "new class": well-educated, affluent, urban, and prominent in the professions as well as the media, which, through that episode, first came to realize Nixon's formidable powers of survival.[57]

On balance, the episode was worth celebrating. Regrettable as the theatrics had been to some around him, forcing both him and Pat to face the humiliation of public laundering of private financial matters, there might have been no career without it. According to the notes of Robert Humphreys, who was then chief assistant to Republican National Chairman Arthur Summerfield, "the whole future of American politics would have been different. . . . Ike would have lost the election. Ike, himself, thought so; . . . Nixon never would have been Vice President. He never would have been able to run for President in 1960. He never would have been able to run again in 1968. In those four hours . . . Humphreys actually made it possible for Nixon to become President of the U.S. 16 years later."[58]

Just about everybody else panicked. Only four years earlier, Dewey had blown his sure thing. As vulnerable as the Truman record was, and as ready as the nation seemed for change, even having a popular general head the ticket did not make the Republicans that secure.

Eisenhower's campaign had been hitting out at the cumulative disenchantment of the postwar years. Republicans promised an "honest deal" for the American people, making the most of influence-peddling scandals that involved close Truman associates. Nixon himself had been condemning the opposition for its "scandal-a-day" administration of national affairs.[59]

On a Thursday, September 18, the liberal *New York Post* carried a different sort of headline: "Secret Rich Men's Trust Fund Keeps Nixon in Style Far Beyond His Salary." Eisenhower, confronted by reporters, agreed that his own "crusade" would be of no avail "if we, ourselves, aren't as clean as a hound's tooth." That comment, Nixon later wrote, made him "feel like the little boy caught with jam on his face." If, as has been written, Eisenhower's desire to win would have led him to retain Nixon as his running mate in any event, that did not seem so clear at the time.[60]

The "secret" fund was not so secret; nor was it anything illegal or unusual. The story about Nixon's office having accumulated a reserve fund was known to papers across the country. When the *Post* broke its account, only seven others followed suit, two of them leading off with a Scripps-Howard piece that columnist Peter Edson wrote in an attempt to explain what was really involved.[61]

When the story broke, the Eisenhower campaign train was headed toward Des Moines for another scheduled speech on the Truman scandals. Eisenhower turned to his younger brother Milton and, noting that whistle-stops would slow their progress, asked him to get off the train and speed ahead by car to get Nixon on the telephone for his side of the story. At least he would know what he was talking about before facing a rally in Kansas City. Milton, unable to make rapid connections, lost out to campaign aide Fred Seaton, who got the vice presidential candidate's explanation in about a five-minute telephone conversation.[62]

The explanation was simple. Whatever secrecy was involved pertained more to Nixon himself, who was less well acquainted with the details than Dana Smith, the trustee of the fund. Smith had taken over as treasurer and chief fund-raiser of contributions by Nixon's supporters. Compensation from the government, which amounted to a $12,500 annual salary plus the cost of one annual round-trip flight between California and Washington and an office with a staff of thirteen, was as inadequate for Nixon as for most of his colleagues. The two-year cost of Christmas cards alone totaled $4,237.54. Once Nixon rose to the Senate, Chotiner suggested that the campaign fund be made permanent, and Smith took over its day-to-day operations. A $25,000 goal was set,

together with a $500 limit on individual contributors. Its long-term ob-
jective was to raise money to cover ongoing activities to assure Nixon's
reelection to the Senate in 1956, and the amount actually raised was
$18,235, not the $16,000 reported by the New York paper. That it was
a "rich man's fund" was only partly offset by the ceiling on contributions.

In every other sense, as with all such political donations, it was hardly
a matter of nickel-and-dime contributions from wage-earners. Its contributors, some seventy-five in all, were drawn from the same group of
upper-middle-class supporters who had sent him to Washington in the
first place: independent oilmen, Realtors, lawyers, stockbrokers, ranchers, and a variety of businessmen and merchants. All that was disclosed
to the press by Smith, including the information that the largest contribution was $1,000. An audit made soon afterward by Price, Water-
house and Company, prominent accountants, and an analysis by the law
firm of Gibson, Dunn, and Crutcher also confirmed that what they had
done was neither secret nor illegal.[63]

Unfortunately, it was not that simple. By using some indignant rhetoric
about the scandals around Truman, Nixon had weakened his own position. He had demanded the resignations of key Democrats for having
intervened with federal agencies to help their friends. The problem was
obviously pervasive, but the legal report by Gibson, Dunn, and Crutcher
showed that Nixon played the same game. In at least two cases, one
involving Dana Smith's problems with the Justice Department, the senator's office interceded on behalf of his contributor.[64]

Yes, there was a fund, Nixon admitted to Fred Seaton, but no personal
benefit was involved. Neither was the money used for any illegitimate
purposes. "So my brother did not modify his speech at all before the
Kansas City people," Milton Eisenhower explained. But "he obviously
was worried. He felt so deeply about the need for absolute integrity in
government . . . that he did not finally clear the matter in his mind until
all the facts were in his possession, until Nixon had made his speech. In
the meantime, he was getting every kind of advice. Many were telling
him to throw Nixon off the ticket." Milton was with that majority. In
hardly any time at all, the matter circulated throughout the Eisenhower
train, immediately splitting the candidate's advisers. One group wanted
Nixon off, while "one wanted to ignore the whole thing." The most
"influential group was insisting that this be turned over to the Senate
committee on ethics." General Clay, who had considered Nixon an ideal
running mate, telephoned the train to keep Eisenhower from making
any statement until he could be met by Herbert Brownell. Both Clay
and Brownell realized that Eisenhower was under great pressure to
disavow the young senator. Not that they thought that "wasn't the right
thing to do," explained Clay. They just wanted Eisenhower to have the
benefit of Brownell's expertise.[65]

Eisenhower was in no mood to make premature decisions. He certainly did not want to kick away any chance for victory. "There is one thing I believe," he said, according to Adams, "if Nixon has to go, we cannot win." But failure to do anything, especially indecisiveness, jeopardized the credibility of his own leadership, his own desires to clean out the "mess in Washington." The onsurging Republicans, other than clobbering the Democrats over communism and Korea, were hitting away at the kind of insidious official immorality that led to the firing or imprisonment of nine important tax collectors and the proliferation of influence-peddling, so-called five-percenters, and such largesse as the giveaway of deep-freeze units and fur coats. Little wonder that Eisenhower was hearing more and more from Republicans who feared they would all go down on election day if Nixon were not dumped. One Citizens for Eisenhower leader from Alabama, Winton Blount, who was made postmaster general by President Nixon in 1969, said that Nixon must be made to "walk the plank. There is too fine a line between the $18,000 of Nixon and the mink coats and deep-freezers of the Administration." He agreed with Eisenhower that "the cause we are working for is bigger than any man." As the phone calls came in from the Citizens people, they struck a similar theme: "Ike could make political capital if he acts strongly and without vacillation. Corruption could be made a live issue by cleaning our own house."[66]

Even as he guarded his own options, Eisenhower was hearing similar warnings from all over. Milton thought Nixon had to go. So did Clay and Paul Hoffman. Newspapers were also quickly falling into line, but especially disturbing was the *New York Herald Tribune*'s agreement, which appeared in an editorial on September 20. Published by Eisenhower's good friend William Robinson, the *Herald Tribune* also had Nixon loyalist Bert Andrews as its chief Washington correspondent. For the *Trib* to join that kind of outcry was tantamount to an official eastern establishment edict from Mount Sinai. Less surprising, but adding to the cumulative pain, was the *Washington Post,* which called for the Republican ticket to provide "an unparalleled opportunity to demonstrate the sincerity of its campaign against loose conduct and corruption in Government."[67]

Senator Knowland was brought to the train as a possible standby substitute. In the middle of it all, a Western Union messenger dropped off a telegram at the Benson Hotel in Portland for Nixon. The wire, from his old acquaintance and political supporter Harold Stassen, advised that unless he yield to a replacement and free Eisenhower to possibly choose Warren, there would be no way to dispel the "cloud."[68]

But, as Humphreys wrote seven years later, "The real furor was confined to the Washington and New York press corps, the Eisenhower train, the Nixon train, a few top-level party leaders and friends of Ike's, and a few editorial writers who called for Nixon's resignation. But what one hell of a furor it was in those circles!"⁶⁹

Nixon, dispirited by his sense of what was coming out of the Republican camp, was sure that Eisenhower wanted him dropped. Unknown to the vice presidential candidate were the comments of financier Bernard Baruch to Eisenhower activist John Reagan "Tex" McCrary. The elder statesman of Wall Street suggested that Nixon should "make a statement to the effect he does not wish to deprive this nation of a great leader and that, therefore, he will retire to the ranks of the private citizen, where he can continue his life dedication, the fighting of communism." He assumed that the *Herald Tribune* editorial had at least had the general's tacit approval. He was also convinced that newsmen with the presidential candidate shared Eisenhower's anti-Nixon sentiments. A study of almost one hundred newspapers nationally indicated that, although most backed the Republican ticket, they were critical of Nixon's action by nearly two to one, with some demanding immediate withdrawal.⁷⁰

Sherman Adams, meanwhile, was his mummylike self. One did not have to know the governor (he had left the New Hampshire statehouse to manage Eisenhower's campaign) very well to notice his doubts about Nixon. Finally, Humphreys and his boss, party chairman Arthur Summerfield, cornered Adams and his wife, Rachel, in the train's drawing room. Summerfield, not feeling well, let Humphreys do most of the talking. As it became heated, Mrs. Adams left the room. Humphreys argued that Nixon must stay on the ticket, citing every reason he could think of. "What do you plan to do?" he asked at one point, "change every piece of literature, every billboard, every campaign poster, every sticker in the land with Nixon's name or picture, and how the hell do you think we are going to do that?" Adams's reply, Humphreys later reminded him, "was icy almost to the point of absolute zero centigrade." He was pulling out all the stops, using every argument, explaining how the whole matter could be handled, but getting nothing but terse, caustic reactions. There was clearly no way that the man who became assistant to the president could conceive of keeping Nixon.

Desperate by that point, Humphreys then said, "All right, answer this one: on Friday morning in Nebraska the General said, 'I intend to talk with him at the earliest time we can reach each other by telephone.' Do you mean to tell me we can convince the American people that for the last sixty hours Dick and Ike have not been able to get together on the telephone when anyone knows that all the General has to do is pick up the phone and call him. No wonder everybody thinks there is a plot to throw Nixon off the ticket."

Finally, Adams came alive. "Instead of jumping across the table and throttling me," as Humphreys recalled, he made no comment and reached for the nearby bank of telephones. The ex-New Hampshire governor directed that a two-way phone hookup between Eisenhower and Nixon be prepared for when the general returned from dinner. Humphreys never learned the identity of Ike's companions at that meal, but it was safe to assume that he was hearing all the reasons for throwing Nixon off the ticket. James C. Hagerty, the general's press secretary, had already issued a statement in Eisenhower's behalf, which applauded Nixon's "determination to drive Communist sympathizers from offices of public trust" and expressed confidence that his running mate would respond to the allegations before the American people "fairly and squarely."[71] A direct talk was something else. Eisenhower hardly knew his partner.

Nixon, meanwhile, had been on his own campaign train. With advance knowledge of the unfolding accusations, he met with his entourage. As to a story that the Nixons had redecorated their Georgetown house for ten thousand dollars in cash, that was gossip. Their new place was set up with furniture shipped from the old home at Whittier, and Pat herself had made the drapes from material bought at a local store. Later, he was even the victim of unfounded charges that he and Pat had pocketed money for their own life-styles and that the funds were also used to cover Dana Smith's gambling losses in Havana.[72] Such rumors, though without any basis in fact, seemed to reflect what some people wanted to believe.

Democratic National Chairman Stephen A. Mitchell quickly called for his resignation and later followed that up with the disingenuous statement that those who could not afford it should not go into politics. With more wisdom than they realized, Murray Chotiner and Bill Rogers, who had agreed to serve as a campaign assistant, thought the entire matter highly overblown. Still, the media reports had their effect. As it proceeded northward, Nixon's campaign ran into crowds carrying hostile signs. Humphreys, who had anticipated such reactions, orchestrated the response. He urged Karl Mundt to denounce the "filthy left-wing smear," then suggested to Nixon, by phone, that he follow the same tactic. At Marysville, California, Nixon was taunted by demands that he tell about the sixteen thousand dollars (the figure in early press reports). He delayed the train and told the crowd that all this had been expected. After his nomination, in fact, he had been warned that "if I continue to attack the Communists and the crooks in this government they would continue to smear me. And," warming up as he sensed the crowd's responsiveness, "believe me, you can expect that they will continue to do so." He reminded them of his role in the Hiss case and added, "Ever since . . . the Communists, the left-wingers, have been fighting me with every smear that they have been able to do." Fred Seaton, calling from the Eisenhower train soon afterward, was pleased to hear from Chotiner how well the crowd had received the explanation. Taunted in Oregon by signs that ridiculed Republicans for having criticized Democratic corruption, Nixon told them that "there are no mink coats for the Nixons. I am proud to say my wife, Pat, wears a good Republican cloth coat."[73]

Outside the immediate Eisenhower camp, there was more support, much of it from traditional conservatives. They saw Nixon as a victim and had little trouble defending him from predictable enemies. One, Robert Taft, was unequivocal, scoffing at a switch. Former president Hoover went further. "If everyone in the city of Washington," he said, "possessed the high level of courage, probity and patriotism of Senator Nixon, this would be a far better nation." Edgar Eisenhower, one of Ike's two younger brothers, disagreed with Milton. He thought the general should stand firm. More anonymous was an indefinable, amorphous mass around the country, neither articulate nor individually influential, unmotivated to carry signs and turn out for campaign trains, but nevertheless with the power to sway the verdict. A private poll conducted by the Gerard Lambert organization reported that fewer than one-fifth of those interviewed saw anything wrong with the fund. Only 10 percent said the revelations would make them less likely to vote for the ticket.[74]

Yet the situation was far from resolved. Humphreys then thought of a way out, following, as he later explained, "a pet theory of mine that when adversity hits, try to convert it into something you can capitalize on." Nixon should go before the American people with his personal plight. The key word was "dramatic": the facts were palatable, nothing was hidden; he had only to appeal to the popular sense of fairness. Summerfield, reached by phone with the idea, gulped at the price tag for a nationwide radio-television broadcast. "Where do we get the money?" he asked. "We simply haven't got it." Asking for free time would have its own complications. The seventy-five-thousand-dollar cost of the broadcast, over four times the amount of the secret fund, was eventually paid by the party's national committee and senatorial and congressional campaign committees.[75]

On the evening of the twenty-first, at about the same time Nixon received his telegram from Stassen, Dewey called to suggest the televised appeal. Dewey, the Republican pariah who tried to keep his hand hidden by using the pseudonym "Mr. Chapman," added an unsettling condition. "I don't think Eisenhower *should* make this decision. Make the American people do it," he said, then added: "If it is 90 to 10, stay on. If you stay on, it isn't blamed on Ike, and if you get off, it isn't blamed on Ike. All the fellows here in New York agree with me."[76]

Just before midnight, Eisenhower himself called to endorse the idea. When Nixon asked whether he could then make a decision, the general remained evasive. He had accepted Herbert Brownell's caution about taking a stand before Nixon's public statement. "I have come to the conclusion," he said, after trying to bolster Nixon's spirits, "that you are the one who has to decide what to do." If, Eisenhower explained, he issued a statement backing him up, he would be accused of "condoning wrongdoing." When Nixon pressed on for some kind of commitment, Eisenhower suggested the possibility that an announcement might not even be necessary. Nixon, clearly left dangling, replied, "General, a time comes in politics when you have to shit or get off the pot!" "Keep your chin up," were Eisenhower's final words.[77]

His future on the line, Nixon broke off his campaign trip, flying from Portland to Los Angeles and proceeding directly from the airport to the Ambassador Hotel. Carefully, he avoided telling reporters about what he planned to say on the broadcast, thereby helping to build both suspense and the size of his audience. The press was also told that he would remain "in seclusion" and work on his talk until airtime.[78]

With just about one hour left before he and Pat had to leave the hotel to go to the El Capitan Theater in Hollywood for the telecast, the telephone rang: "Mr. Chapman" calling. When Nixon heard Dewey's words, presented as an unfortunate message that he had unfortunately been asked to deliver, he knew what course had been sold to Eisenhower: a new running mate. That was the judgment of the general's "top advisers," Nixon was told, but Dewey carefully avoided saying that it was Eisenhower's decision, or even that the candidate had given his personal approval. It was immaterial. The general was running for the presidency. His "top advisers" were directing strategy for a political novice. Nixon needed no other authorization. His talk must go on accordingly, said Dewey, with a careful explanation that he had done nothing wrong but would sacrifice himself lest he risk weighing down the ticket. Not enough time was left for an entirely new script; Nixon had, in fact, only thirty minutes to get to the theater.

"What should I tell them you are going to do?" Dewey asked.

Nixon, who had earlier countered Eisenhower sharply, now, as he recalled it, "exploded." "Just tell them that I haven't the slightest idea as to what I am going to do and if they want to find out they'd better listen to the broadcast. And tell them I know something about politics too!"[79]

The speech on that evening of September 23 was a calculated production, not memorized in the more familiar Nixon fashion, but carefully written and artfully staged. He even called his former Whittier professor Dr. Albert Upton in the wee hours of the morning hoping to locate an appropriate quote from Lincoln that he could couple with a reference to the Hiss case. Three years later, Nixon acknowledged to the Radio and Television Executives Society that he had "staged" the entire show. Pat had been as much of a prop as the American flag. The leading roles were, after all, being played by Richard Nixon, a veteran of amateur theatrics, and Pat Ryan Nixon, a fellow thespian from Whittier days. She sat next to him as he spoke, the camera recording her tense but confident and admiring expression. Earlier, she had warned him that resignation and failure to fight back would be self-destructive. "Your life will be marred forever and the same will be true of your family, and particularly, your daughters."[80]

Had he gone along with Dewey's request, that would have been the end. As costly as changing vice presidential candidates may have been to Eisenhower, he was not convinced that the loss would cost him the election. Eisenhower could not have ignored a public resignation, especially since it would have implied that Nixon was guilty. The general knew that, and so did his advisers. It was typical of him, both in the military and later in the presidency, to let others serve as his mouthpiece in controversial matters and to reserve his options.

But the Nixon affair arose while the general was making the transition from his more familiar military role, where he was secure and shrewd, to his career as president, in which he had yet to become secure and shrewd. The Eisenhower of 1952 had not ever voted, was sufficiently vague about domestic politics to entertain the idea that both parties might make him their candidate by acclamation. He was still at the stage where, as his brother Milton explained, he was "pretty much guided by the advice of the people who had been in politics for a great many years," the same people who advised him to defer to Joe McCarthy by dropping a tribute to General George Marshall from a speech prepared for delivery in Wisconsin.[81]

Many did find Nixon's speech atrocious or, as Stephen Ambrose has written, "thought it was one of the most sickening, disgusting, maudlin performances ever experienced." Walter Lippmann told his dinner guest, "That must be the most demeaning experience my country has ever had to bear." Lucius Clay thought it was the "corniest" speech he ever heard. In *The Nation,* one writer lampooned the performance by writing: "Pretend to be a poor ordinary man fighting the possessors of inherited wealth. Refer to the fact that the standard-bearer of the opposing party inherited money. Mention your own humble origin and your wife's 'cloth coat.' Tell the people that poor men like yourself should represent them in Congress."[82]

A contemptuous minority derided the speech as the unctuous performance of a Uriah Heep. To most, however, he was a figure from a Frank Capra movie, a "Mr. Smith" who had gone to Washington and found himself contending with all the problems that the Mr. Smiths of America could recognize.

What he was charged with doing, Nixon began by acknowledging, would have been morally wrong if the $18,000 had gone for his personal use. But that was not the case: "Not one cent . . . ever went to my personal use. Every penny of it was used to pay for political expenses that I did not think should be charged to the taxpayers of the United States." He cited the reports from his lawyers and accountants, quoting their exonerating words.

That left him with Mr. Smith's problems: owning merely a 1950 Oldsmobile, $3,000 in equity in a California house being occupied by his parents, $20,000 in his Washington property, and just $4,000 in life insurance, plus a GI term policy due to expire in two years. Other than that, "no stocks or bonds; no interest in any other property or business." Placing such assets against $38,500 in debts, mostly represented by mortgages on his two houses, left him with very little. "That's what we have," he told his vast radio and television audience. "And that's what we owe. It isn't very much. But Pat and I have the satisfaction that every dime that we have got is honestly ours." Almost as an afterthought, he said what he had told crowds in the West, "I should say this, that Pat doesn't have a mink coat. But she does have a respectable Republican cloth coat, and I always tell her that she would look good in anything."

Then he told the story about Checkers. Checkers was a little cocker spaniel, "black and white, spotted," sent by a man down in Texas who had heard Pat say the children would like to have a dog. "And you know, the kids, like all kids, loved the dog, and I just want to say this, right now, that regardless of what they say about it, we are going to keep it."

Mr. Smith was going to "continue this fight. I am going to campaign up and down America until we drive the crooks and the Communists and those that defend them out of Washington." Nodding to Pat, he said she was "not a quitter. After all, her name was Patricia Ryan and she was born on Saint Patrick's Day, and you know the Irish never quit." Nor did most Americans share what seemed to be the view of Democratic National Chairman Stephen Mitchell who "says that only a rich man should serve in the Government." It was fine for someone like Governor Stevenson, with his inherited fortune, but remember what Abe Lincoln said? "God must have loved the common people, he made so many of them."

Eisenhower, watching and listening intently from an upstairs room in the Cleveland Municipal Auditorium, where he himself was scheduled to speak, understood all the messages, both direct and indirect. Nixon's challenge hit home. Both Democratic opponents, he had said, Governor Stevenson and Senator John Sparkman, should also bare their financial records. How could Eisenhower now do less? How could Eisenhower be sanctimonious about honesty and refuse to let the public know that he personally had been saved thousands in taxes from *Crusade in Europe,* his World War II book, thanks to a special, generous, and most selective act of Congress? And, as much as he wanted to stand aside from the question of whether Nixon should stay on the ticket, for the younger man to have told the millions out there to relay their desires to the

Republican National Committee was a not-too-subtle denigration of Eisenhower's authority. At the same time, the general, newcomer as he was to partisan politics, unknowing in so many ways of the civilian world, knew the ways of his fellow men. That, more than parliamentary or governmental mechanics, was the secret of his success, in whatever role he served. It did not take him long to understand what had happened. Nor could one so accustomed to positions of command fail to recognize Nixon's precocity and potential for establishing his own ground. He had only to see the emotions of the others in his room. Even Bill Robinson had done a complete about-face. From the auditorium below, where the crowd waiting to hear Eisenhower had listened to the speech on radio, they heard the chants of "We want Nixon. We want Nixon." Lucius Clay walked into an elevator right after that "corniest" speech and saw that the operator was crying. Both men, having spent careers as generals, understood what Nixon had done. Upstairs, Eisenhower went into a huddle with his advisers. There was not much left to decide. His prepared talk on the national economy would have to go. How could he not express admiration for Nixon?[83]

The senator had identified himself with the innocence of Frank Capra's idealistic hero. Years later, when a Whittier College student examined forty-one boxes of the telegrams listeners had sent in response to Nixon's speech, he found clear confirmation of what Nixon had evoked. "It was," reported Donald C. Brandenburgh, " 'the pride of we the American people in Richard Nixon' because he represented the common man, and the homely virtues. Americans reacted positively to the presence of Pat in the TV studio when Nixon was speaking, to the feeling he generated that 'he is like me,' and this cut across monetary and class lines. Nixon brought millions of Americans back to a dream with which they had grown up." "It was corny," agreed a former Nixon classmate from Whittier, "and so many people put it down because 'Oh gosh, he's just putting on an act.' Yet I felt, having known him, that it was really not an act. You perceive these things based on your preconceptions, so many times. Who goes to hear Republicans? Republicans. The Democratic speaker comes to town. Who goes to hear him? The Democrats. There aren't very many of us who try to hear both sides." Another, who knew Nixon from his earliest political days, Gerald Kepple, explained that the American people "are either a thousand percent for you or they will kick you down. . . . The only time an American is in the middle of the road is when he is crossing to get from one side to another." It was true, as two students of the speech later noted, that "as he attempted to build an image of 'honest Dick,' he created the image of 'poor Richard' — poor Richard who had to struggle financially, who was always being attacked through a vicious smear, and who was always the innocent victim."[84]

The Republican National Committee had never experienced anything like it. That the broadcast went off the air before Nixon could give the mailing address of the national committee only strengthened the impact. Not knowing where to turn, listeners reached out to whatever seemed plausible. Calls and telegrams inundated Republican offices everywhere; in desperation, respondents also turned to local television and radio stations. The overloaded San Francisco telephone system became almost inoperative. In Whittier, Kepple recalled, the telephone lines "were so blocked that there was more use of Western Union . . . than for anything that happened in the United States in a hundred years." Nixon, returning to his Ambassador Hotel room, heard that "the telephones are going crazy; everybody's in your corner!"[85]

Within the next few days, the national committee received over 200,000 letters, a load that kept nearly one hundred volunteers working for a month, even overflowing across half the lobby of the Washington Hotel. Out of those envelopes came some $62,000 in contributions. While there was a check for $1,000 and another for $100, most ranged from a quarter to $10. Western Union, meanwhile, lacked the staff to handle the volume of telegrams and had to rush additional personnel to its Washington stations, where the bulk was so great that they were thrown on scales instead of counted. Over 160,000 telegrams were delivered to the main headquarters of the Republican National Committee alone. For every anti-Nixon response, there were 350 in his favor. The Luce publications, which had been sympathetic throughout the crisis, followed through with a seven-page spread in *Life* that was headlined, "Nixon Fights, Wins and Weeps."[86]

But the intracamp tensions were not over. This time the burden was as much Eisenhower's as Nixon's. The American people were with him. Having impressed as a Horatio Alger figure, the senator was determined to continue as Mr. Smith and not play Uriah Heep. Eisenhower told the Cleveland audience that he "would rather have a courageous and honest man by my side than a whole boxcar full of pussyfooters," yet held to his lofty stance by vowing not to be swayed in his decision by "any idea of what will get the most votes. . . . I am going to say: Do I myself believe this man is the kind of man America would like to have for its Vice President?" He then sent Nixon a telegram in which praise for the "magnificent" performance was coupled with words signifying that the ultimate decision would be his rather than the numbers reported by the national committee. He also asked Nixon to join him at Wheeling, West Virginia, his next campaign stop.[87]

Because of the flood of telegrams, Nixon did not receive Eisenhower's and was unaware of even its qualified commendation. His only word came from a news report that stressed the general's continued determination to delay making a decision. Nixon was furious. Little had changed, it seemed, since "Mr. Chapman's" call. Turning to his secretary, Rose Mary Woods, Nixon dictated his own telegram. This one, addressed to Arthur Summerfield, announced that he was taking himself out of the race. Murray Chotiner grabbed it from her hands and ripped it up.[88] Chotiner then put through a call to Summerfield. In no way was Nixon prepared to go crawling to the general, he warned, to beg forgiveness and meekly await his judgment. He was, in fact, ready to resign; meanwhile, he would resume his own campaign schedule, moving on to Missoula and ignoring Eisenhower's request to meet him in Wheeling. That was it; there was no further time for discussion; it was time to go to the airport.

Nixon had the high ground. His own political toughness and sagacity came through. The Eisenhower crowd knew it. Some twenty or thirty minutes later, after they decided they had no other choice, Summerfield called back to get the younger man to reconsider. He reached Chotiner at the airport, only to be told that Nixon was already on the plane and would not get off.

Again, the party's national chairman, acting for the presidential candidate, had to do the pursuing. He told Chotiner he would call Nixon in Missoula. "Clutching this secret to our breasts," Robert Humphreys later revealed, "Arthur and I went back to the hotel suite sometime in the middle of the night . . . and tried to get an hour of sleep before we talked to Nixon. We decided that we would try to promote a Wheeling, W. Va., meeting that night if we could get Nixon back in the frame of mind to stay on the ticket."[89]

The brouhaha was, in effect, all over. Summerfield found after talking to Eisenhower in Portsmouth, Ohio, that the general wanted to know where the national committee stood. Taking a quick telephone poll from Wheeling, he found that all 107 who were reached favored keeping Nixon. The information was immediately wired to Eisenhower on his campaign train, and the decision was made. Summerfield and Humphreys got on the phone to Nixon with assurances that Eisenhower was ready to greet him with his full support. Summerfield then relayed the good news to Sherman Adams at the "next Ike Special stop," Ironton, Ohio.[90]

When Dick and Pat Nixon walked down the steps of the plane at the airport in West Virginia, they were astonished to find Eisenhower running up to them ready to shake hands. "What are you doing here, General? You didn't have to come out to the airport to meet us," said Nixon. "Why not?" said Ike with a big grin and an arm around his running mate. "You're my boy!"[91]

The Checkers speech, as much as the Hiss affair, established Nixon as a political figure. The secret fund affair did something else. Revelations from Adlai Stevenson's office, which began to trickle out even during Nixon's embattlement, that the Democratic presidential candidate had a similar supplementary account, one that was worth far more, helped to confirm that the practice was hardly unique. But the speech itself found its way into the sympathies of the millions who could understand and wanted confirmation that Richard Nixon, although a Republican — the party of big business and Wall Street — shared their everyday anxieties, an altogether different audience from those who thought that the Checkers and Republican cloth coat stuff was "nauseating." Pat had found it hard to swallow. Nixon knew better.[92]

10

Dick and Ike

EISENHOWER'S heart attack in September 1955 was one of Nixon's "six crises." "What I thought of, and what concerned me," he explained, "was not the awesome problems I would have if I should become President, but how I could best handle my immediate responsibility as a Vice President who was now, more than any of his thirty-five predecessors, 'one heartbeat from the presidency.' " Then he added, "How I reacted to this crisis was infinitely more important to the nation and the world than the way I handled the Hiss case or my fight to stay on the ticket in 1952."[1]

Those weeks in the fall of 1955 were anxious ones for the vice president. Reports from Fitzsimons Army Hospital in Colorado kept updating the president's progress and held the key to the vice president's own political future. Temporarily, at least, leadership seemed to be up to Nixon. But the lack of any constitutional definitions about presidential incapacity made the situation vastly more complex. In circumstances with deep political implications, Nixon had to avoid appearing overeager, with the sort of premature "I am in charge" posture that would raise misgivings about Alexander Haig during the Reagan presidency.

Nixon in 1955 was much younger than Haig was in 1981 and less schooled in the ways of White House bureaucracy. Given the delicacy of his situation, he had to have the savvy to understand the difference between discretion and weakness. In mid-October, with many of the immediate difficulties having been resolved, he wrote to Elliott V. Bell that his "primary concern has been to avoid allowing any doubt to be raised."[2] Fortunately, for the nation and the Republican party, good news kept coming from the hospital. The president had intended to serve only one term; now, he might not only be able to complete his four years but also allow himself to be renominated in 1956. As the public was constantly reassured, the "team" had carried on in his absence, the nation had not suffered, and all would soon return to normal.

What really happened was far more significant, for both Nixon and his party. The administration had taken pride in teamwork, thereby minimizing impressions of Eisenhower's importance in decision-making. But, at the same time, the American people still needed to know that he *was* the president, which left Nixon as little more than a symbolic surrogate. As columnist James Reston put it, Nixon could exercise the powers of his office "but cannot exercise the personal power of the President."[3]

Six Crises later hinted at other complications. "There is an old political axiom," Nixon wrote, "that where a vacuum exists, it will be filled by the nearest or strongest power. That had to be avoided at all costs." There could be no "semblance of a struggle for dominance." Scrambles for power, he acknowledged, had taken place in earlier administrations and, despite the "staff system" that operated Eisenhower's "team," such conflicts appeared "to be taking hold in the present one." "You are the constitutional second-in-command and you ought to assume the leadership," Nixon was reminded by Senator Styles Bridges. Bridges, a New Hampshire rival of Sherman Adams, was, of course, eager to keep the assistant to the president from power. "Don't let the White House clique take command," he urged. But Bridges was not alone; his attitude was typical of those who thought Nixon was not doing enough. He and other Nixon supporters had certainly seen the dispatch sent to the *New York Times* only one day after Eisenhower's heart attack that suggested that the president's men would be doing everything possible to make sure that interim power went not to the constitutional second in command but to the assistant to the president, Sherman Adams.[4]

Behind Adams, who, as Washington correspondent Richard Rovere noted, "regards himself as the President's appointed caretaker and is doing everything he can to cut Mr. Nixon down to size," was the commanding figure of Foster Dulles. The secretary of state carried the additional personal authority that owed much to the impression that he was the administration's strongman, a perception that served Eisenhower well politically. But it was never more useful than during that behind-the-scenes power play. That was the moment when Dulles's political maneuvering was far more significant than anything he had ever done about foreign policy. He was, as Nixon later told an interviewer, the general above everybody else. No moves were made during that period without checking in with Dulles.[5]

Dulles was the one man of whom it may be said that he would have been chosen to head the State Department whether the party had won with Dewey or Taft or, for that matter, any other credible Republican.

He was shrewd in a political sense that was seldom apparent to outsiders. His main determination was to escape the trap that swallowed Dean Acheson, to avoid letting himself become victimized by extreme cranks who might even find a Puritan from Sullivan and Cromwell poisoned by the Communist virus. Anticipating such lunacy, Dulles had done his best, tirelessly sanitizing both himself (for, after all, he had vouched for Alger Hiss's integrity) and the State Department. He did his job so well that the Foreign Service was less touched by Joe McCarthy than by McCarthyism. As much as Dulles did thereby demoralize many career officers, he managed to protect himself from the party's old guard, thereby becoming a most useful partner for Eisenhower's efforts to keep Republicans from destroying themselves.

Such self-protection was especially remarkable because of his association with Dewey. The relationship, already of considerable duration, was underscored when Governor Dewey in 1949 appointed Dulles to an interim Senate seat. Before Eisenhower became president, however, Dulles lost it to a Democrat, Herbert Lehman, but he had stayed on as an adviser in Truman's State Department. Negotiating the formal peace treaty with Japan confirmed his contribution to bipartisanship.

In the face of the dilemma created by the president's illness, Dulles was not about to permit a possible vacancy in the executive office to be filled by a vice president whose selection had been prompted by the need to appeal to the Republican right. It was Dulles, then, acting as Eisenhower's quarterback, who determined that it should be Adams, not Nixon, who would be at the president's side in Colorado. Dulles, clearly backed by Eisenhower, was also firm about keeping Nixon as a figurehead.[6]

Nixon acted accordingly. Right after press secretary Jim Hagerty reached him that Saturday night with the news about the heart attack, he avoided the press. He spent that first night hidden in the Bethesda home of Bill Rogers, acting attorney general and a Nixon friend since the Hiss hearings. For the sake of appearances, not least of which was the orchestration of the business-as-usual posture, Nixon presided over both the National Security Council (NSC) and the cabinet. Meanwhile, Dulles used the emergency to enhance the policymaking functions of the NSC.[7]

By the time the crisis ended, Nixon had the first inkling that he was the one whose ambitions were going to have to be placed under tighter control. The sacrificial lamb was being readied for slaughter. Where the administration had succeeded in its first three years — ending the Korean War, pulling the economy out of a brief recession, establishing an opening with the Soviets via "the spirit of Geneva" not very long after Stalin's death — Nixon's name was absent from the credits.

But the negatives fell disproportionately on his side of the table. Even before the swearing-in on January 20, 1953, there had been a considerable pileup. Eisenhower's "high road" approach was balanced by the vice president's mission to arouse the party's more passionate supporters, especially on the right. When Joe McCarthy had to be told off before the American people, the assignment went to Nixon, and it was he who did the work of going public with the first open estrangement between the administration and the buccaneering senator. When, only a few days later, a plan for rescuing the French from pending disaster in Southeast Asia circulated within the administration's high command, it fell to Nixon to float a controversial trial balloon suggesting that American ground forces might be needed in Indochina. More than anybody else in the administration, it was Nixon who campaigned for congressional Republicans in 1954 by carrying out his function as the man who could rally the anticommunist rightists. When the Republicans lost their brief Senate majority as a result of that midterm election, the onus was also Nixon's. The party's right wing, already dismayed by the formal condemnation of Joe McCarthy in late 1954, lost further confidence in the administration when Eisenhower parlayed with Georgi Malenkov and Nikita Khrushchev at the Geneva summit meeting in July 1955.

One thing had become clear by the time Eisenhower had his heart attack: the effort to reinforce the appeal to Republican conservatives confirmed the Nixon stereotype as a hard-line, right-wing demagogue. Simultaneously, moves toward healing cold war tensions provoked distrust among those who feared betrayal of the party's anticommunist principles. Moderate Republicans who had worried about appeasing Colonel Robert R. McCormick, Taft, and McCarthy were beginning to discover that the new dissenters carried such names as William F. Buckley, Jr., Robert Welch, Dean Clarence Manion, and Barry Goldwater. Recalling that rightists had supported him only because of the Hiss case, Nixon said in 1984, "What concerns me about the far right is their tendency to see everything in terms of black and white." Paradoxically, so cantankerous a commentator on the left as journalist I. F. Stone, noting how far to the right some elements were bulging, wrote that Nixon had "become a middle-of-the-road spokesman and conservative papers like the *Washington Star* and *New York Times* find themselves classified more and more as part of the 'left-wing press.' "[8]

Somewhere in the middle of all that was Nixon, and he played his role well. Delicate as the situation was, vulnerable as was his reputation, one can hardly find anything negative about his conduct during those weeks of Eisenhower's recuperation. They needed a good soldier, and he was the man. Before speaking out on foreign policy that October at a gathering sponsored by the *New York Herald Tribune*, he checked in with Dulles. The secretary cited what had been accomplished at the Geneva summit, together with the ongoing talks at the foreign minister level, and urged that "a pretty high and non-controversial note should be struck." At Geneva, Dulles added, the American side was advancing the thesis of renunciation of force as a way of obtaining constructive results in such tension spots as the Middle East and Far East. Nixon thought giving emphasis to such points in his speech would be "going a bit far," and Dulles backed off, but they both agreed that the recent renunciation of force by the Communist regime in Peking should be acknowledged. Nixon also expressed relief at being able to back away from his hatchet man role.[9]

Two days after their conversation, Nixon gave the closing speech of the annual *Herald Tribune* forum on world affairs. He praised the Democratic leaders for supporting the administration, was upbeat about the United Nations, and dropped the charged cold war language that had characterized both his own style and the party's 1952 platform. His language was moderate, carefully balanced, without strident partisanship, and even lacked his usual nationalistic fervor. He failed to accuse the Democrats of having lost China. The speech, described by the *Times* as "more Eisenhower than Nixon" and as the product of advice from friends urging that he become more unifying than divisive, was not even suspected as having been influenced by Dulles.[10]

Nixon was being whipsawed between the inevitability of his succession if Eisenhower should be unable to complete his term — or, at the very least, the possibility of retaining his spot on the ticket in 1956 — and the considerable pressures that were being applied to get him to step aside and take a Cabinet post (this was not to imply he should abandon hopes of getting to the top, as the president said, merely that he would go about it in some other way). He was too controversial, had too many enemies, was a liability to the ticket in the eyes of some influential Republicans. And Eisenhower, being Eisenhower, was not about to be pressured into any decisions before they were absolutely necessary. Nixon's dilemma would have been hard for any man. For someone with his pride and sensitivity, the experience was especially galling. Not until Harold Stassen finally called for unity at the San Francisco convention was he assured of a second term.

The immediate motivations of men and organizations are all too often a mass of ambiguity. Had their ambitions been limited to personal career and power-building, Republican leaders would not have hesitated to join the interests of the northern upper middle classes with disaffected southern Democrats, an alliance that would at least have defined the new political power center. The party would, at the same time, have met such obvious needs as getting out in front on issues like civil rights, deescalation of the arms race, and liberal interpretations of the Constitution's "general welfare" clause. But Republican moderates were not yet ready to concede that their hold over the party was in serious jeopardy.

For many traditional, old-line northern Republicans, cultivating those in rebellion against the Democracy connoted a traumatic reversal of roles, the party of Union and emancipation sponsoring a new generation of redeemers. Lest they be dismissed as romantics, their pragmatic arguments were well prepared. They were not alone, they explained, in not wanting to alienate believers in traditional Republicanism. Consciously or not, they remained attuned to the values that were represented by the *New York Herald Tribune,* the influential voice of the party's internationalist, corporate interests.

The national appeal of Republicanism was rooted as much in small towns and on farms as on Wall Street. A contrary impulse was highly critical of the elite eastern establishment, reflecting values that were more provincial, spiritual, and keyed to handed-down notions of individualism. Robert Taft was dead, but his spirit lived on. As Karl Mundt put it to George Creel during the summer of 1951, "If we permit a problem in semantics and ancient traditions to so badly divide us that city machines in the North who play politics for profit, and left wing fringe groups of the New-Deal Fair-Deal, who play politics for power can win again, those of us supporting such a concept do not deserve victory."[11] To those of the Eisenhower-Dewey persuasion, Mundt and his fellows were the "hard-shells," the "faint hopes," or, more simply, the "troublemakers," who were resistant to what it took to bring the party into the modern age.

The desire to "modernize," a favorite word of Eisenhowerites, rationalized certain contradictions. Spurred by the "team" theoretician, Arthur Larson, Eisenhower eventually talked about "modern Republicanism," a curiously utopian concept that combined liberalism in human relations and conservatism in fiscal management. That notion, together with its lovely ambiguities, was preordained to die an early death, given the shifting foundations of the GOP.

Arthur Larson, a Rhodes scholar who had studied at Oxford and won distinction as a law student, gave up the deanship of the University of Pittsburgh's law school to join the Eisenhower administration as under secretary of labor. He was a thinker in a crowd of businessmen, corporate lawyers, politicians, and one retired five-star general. Conservative intellectuals were only beginning to sprout during the early fifties. Much of that new breed was to his right, leaving him suspect as one who was, in reality, nostalgic for the good old days of the New Deal.

That charge was unfair to Larson, who thought there had to be something between the myth of the free market economy and the advanced welfare state. Larson's efforts to maintain a centrist equilibrium were consistent with the ongoing efforts to keep the party from becoming dominated by its highly nationalistic and isolationist provincial base. The "genius" of the Eisenhower government, he wrote in a 1956 book, *A Republican Looks at His Party,* was the replacement of old interest conflicts with a new consensus. "Now we have as much government activity as is necessary, but not enough to stifle the normal motivations of private enterprise." Moreover, "by bringing about this consolidation of the best forces in American life, President Eisenhower and his associates have, for the first time in our history, discovered and established the Authentic American Center in politics. . . . It is a Center in the American sense of a common meeting-ground of the great majority of our people on our own issues, against a backdrop of our own history, our own current setting and our own responsibilities for the future." The party that held the center, he wrote, "holds a position of almost unbeatable strength." If, Larson noted, "as seems unlikely, the Republicans were some day to nominate a candidate for the presidency who was identified with an extreme conservative position, and if, as seems equally unlikely, the Democrats were to seize that moment to choose a nominee who took over the formula of the great middle way, the Democratic candidate would almost certainly win, and thereafter it would be difficult indeed for the Republicans to get back in."[12]

Larson entered the administration in 1954, his book unfinished and not in print until the summer of 1956. Right after its appearance in those months before his reelection, Eisenhower agreed that "it represented my philosophy of government as well as I have seen it in a book of that size." On election night, at Washington's Sheraton-Park Hotel, he used the term "modern Republicanism" for the first time. The phrase was, in effect, sufficiently ambiguous to be interchangeable with the "New Republicanism" of Larson's "Authentic American Center." Interestingly, however, when Nixon suggested that the party could be "made over to a reasonably conservative progressive Party — and an internationalist Party," Eisenhower was skeptical.[13]

Still, for all his conventional conservatism, Eisenhower was an effective moderating force during his early years. More often than not, his solutions settled on the "broad, humanitarian side of a given issue," recalled Harold Stassen. Stassen, whom Eisenhower had appointed to a cabinet-level post as adviser on disarmament, also remembered how the heart attack changed all that.[14]

Stassen, an old Nixon associate and early supporter, had permitted his own presidential ambitions to disrupt old alliances at the party's Chicago convention. What grew into an obsession about becoming president gradually undermined the effectiveness of the one-time "boy governor." As a young attorney in Minnesota, he had joined the party with the hope of helping to salvage whatever progressive legacy remained from the days of Teddy Roosevelt's Bull Moose revolt. He wanted Republicans to both learn to live with New Deal reforms and adjust to internationalism. At the tumultuous 1940 convention, he urged a liberal candidate and platform, delivered the keynote address, and led the floor fight for Wendell Willkie. He later served as a delegate at the UN's charter session in San Francisco and continued to devote himself to the cause of internationalism and world peace. Within the Eisenhower administration, in fact, he was happy to have his work on disarmament lead to the unofficial designation as "secretary of peace." Such zeal often brought him into conflict with Dulles's closely guarded domain. The idealist and the political infighter were thus joined. Mostly, his reputation suffered the scorn usually directed toward a colleague who cannot be depended upon to observe the rules of political professionalism. The following ridicule became commonplace: "There's one thing about Harold E. Stassen — he likes to go down with his ship, and he doesn't care how many times it's sunk." Or, as historian Stephen Ambrose has added: "One reason Stassen went down with so many ships was that he could never tell when they were sinking under him, indeed couldn't even tell when the ship had hit the bottom."[15]

To Harold Stassen and others around Eisenhower, Nixon represented a contradiction. For any restructuring to be possible, the president kept reminding party leaders, they couldn't begin by "antagonizing Democrats as Democrats." The opposition to Nixon, as *U.S. News & World Report* noted, "was little more than a whisper during the Administration's first two years," but it gained momentum following the president's heart attack.[16]

For those who believed with Stassen in a new Republican party, the time for a Nixon was over. In 1952, he had gone over their heads and appealed to the public. Contrary to their hopes, which carried Eisenhower's approval, it became easier at that moment to leave the ticket intact than to undertake the risks of a midcampaign switch. Since then, however, a number of things had changed. The state of Eisenhower's health — which of course made the vice presidency that much more crucial — was only the most immediate. Nixon's criticism of Truman's handling of the Korean War, and subsequent support for General MacArthur, was in league with the more extreme military solutions. But that had been resolved, with a settlement more in accord with the position of the departed Democratic administration than the rhetoric of Nixon and fellow nationalists. Once he became vice president, Nixon's most prominent association with the Far East was to get himself on record as favoring the use of American ground troops to rescue the French forces from their entrapment at Dienbienphu. Nixon, who has since reaffirmed his regret that nothing was done, has insisted that it was "a case of my sitting in the meetings with Eisenhower and having his views expressed." Nevertheless, at the same time he also acknowledged that the administration was not prepared to accede to Admiral Arthur Radford's designs for a nuclear strike.[17] The affair was but one among many instances when Nixon served the function of reconciling hard-liners to the Eisenhower administration.

The most notable instance, of course, remained the delicate maneuvering with Senator Joe McCarthy. Even when, in March 1954, on the eve of the Army-McCarthy hearings, he was assigned the job of going on the networks in response to the senator, he did it only after some presidential arm-twisting. Within the administration, who but Nixon was in the best position of countering the professional Red-baiter from Wisconsin without tarnishing himself with the pink brush? Agreeing that Communists were "a bunch of rats," he asked his audience — and McCarthy — to remember that "when you go out to shoot rats, you have to shoot straight, because when you shoot wildly it not only means that the rat may get away more easily, you make it easier on the rat, but you might hit someone else who's trying to shoot rats, too." Eisenhower speechwriter William Bragg Ewald, Jr., remembering that performance, later wrote that "the Vice President had appealed to the centrist citizen, the anti-Communist man or woman whom he could persuade to desert the McCarthy formula (chemically, pure anticommunism diluted by disreputable methods) for the Eisenhower formula (chemically, pure anticommunism compounded by fair play and decency)."[18] Played out during the coming months were the three dozen days of televised hearings, which exposed McCarthy's tactics before the American people. Subsequent condemnation by his colleagues drove him off the front pages and destroyed him as a political force.

Nixon, having risen in the cause of anticommunism, suddenly became almost as expendable as McCarthy. Indeed, the months between Eisenhower's heart attack and his decision to run for a second term were a time when the vice president was caught up in the revulsion against shooting rats wildly in the name of internal security. In interviews given seventeen years apart, Sherman Adams and David Eisenhower both raised the same point: the Communist conspiracy issue, which had given Nixon his early glory, had waned by 1956. That was also a period, added Ike's grandson, when the president "underestimated the Republicans." Democrats, regaining the offensive, were turning the tables, profiting to the hilt from Nixon's own questionable tactics. In late November of 1955, Harry Truman recalled that "during the 1952 campaign Nixon called every member of the Democratic party a traitor and at that time I was head of the party."[19]

"Too many Democrats and others," responded Republican columnist

Gould Lincoln, "have mistakenly sought to attribute to Mr. Nixon the charge by Senator McCarthy of Wisconsin that there had been 'twenty years of treason' under the Roosevelt and Truman administrations. The record discloses that this is a complete error." A new "Red issue," noted Lincoln, was being developed by the opposition as an issue for the 1956 campaign, this time fanned by Nixon-haters. The Republican National Committee, finding it increasingly difficult to pretend that Nixon, and by extension the administration and the party, were not on the defensive, was forced to issue a compilation of the record to show that there was nothing at all to substantiate the claims of Truman and his fellow Democrats about any "treason" charges. A news release, issued on February 5, 1956, claimed that "a complete check of all the newspaper accounts of speeches, press conferences, and other public statements made by the Vice President in the campaigns of 1952 and 1954 fail to disclose any instance whatever in which the Vice President referred to the Democratic Party as the party of treason or in which he questioned the loyalty of Mr. Truman, Mr. Stevenson, or other leaders of the Democratic Party."[20]

The fact was that, with the demise of McCarthy, 1952 and 1954 belonged to the past. Nixon, spurred on by Eisenhower himself, had done his job, but had performed only too well. There were too many instances of when it became necessary to deny that Nixon had *actually* impugned in so many words. Inferences, even when not supported by blunt statements, were damaging by their frequency. In compiling its "complete check" of public reports of Nixon's public comments, the national committee had managed to overlook the vice president's Texarkana speech of October 27, 1952. That was where he called Stevenson, Acheson, and Truman "traitors to the high principles in which many of the nation's Democrats believe." True, he never said they betrayed the *nation*.[21] Only a few days earlier, in other comments omitted by the "complete check," Nixon had told the *Kansas City Star* that not only was Truman responsible for the loss of "600 million people to the Communists," but that "there's one difference between the Reds and Pinks. The Pinks want to socialize America. The Reds want to socialize the world and make Moscow the world capital. Their paths are similar; they have the same bible — the teachings of Karl Marx." He need not have been more explicit. The identification of Truman with the Pinks was inescapable. Adlai Stevenson, he said at one point, "gives the American people no hope for safety at home from the sinister threat of communism." More recently, on March 13, 1954, Nixon spoke on television hailing the expected benefits from an end to the war in Korea. This time, with Dean Acheson as his target, there was even less doubt about his meaning. "And incidentally," he added, looking up at the camera almost as an afterthought, "isn't it wonderful that finally we have a Secretary of State who isn't taken in by the Communists, who stands up to them? We can be sure now that the victories that our men win on the battlefields will not be lost in the future by our diplomats at the council table." More language that Democrats never forgot.[22] To hit them the way politicians attack each other was one thing, but insinuations about patriotism and loyalty were another matter.

Nixon's performance on the stump for Republican candidates in 1954 was, in many ways, far more of a bravura feat than two years before. In the face of a national trend back toward the Democrats, toward regaining control of the Congress by the majority party, Nixon was the spark plug, energizing fellow Republicans, fighting to patch up intraparty divisions, and hailing the administration for having saved America from "Trumanism" — all in a forty-eight-day, twenty-eight-thousand-mile whirlwind that foreshadowed his efforts for other GOP candidates in 1964 and 1966. There was little question that, despite the party's predictable losses, he was riding high. "Maybe there wouldn't have been a landslide even if he'd never campaigned," commented *Newsweek,* "but no one will ever convince the Republican rank and file of that."[23] But all that Democrats could remember was his heavy emphasis on communism, which had become more intense as the campaign went along.

Nixon, wrote Stewart Alsop, best approximated Walter Lippmann's description of a "ruthless partisan." Wherever he went, through thirty-one states and ninety-five cities, Democrats were labeled as left-wingers, fully consistent with his belief that communism was the best issue to attract the urban ethnic vote. Stevenson was not allowed to forget his character testimony for Alger Hiss. In Beverly Hills, Nixon suggested that the titular leader of the Democratic party "has been guilty, probably without his being aware that he was doing so, of spreading pro-Communist propaganda as he has attacked with violent fury the economic system of the United States and praised the Soviet economy." On Capitol Hill, Nixon kept arguing, the Democrats were dominated by their "Truman-Stevenson-ADA left wing." When he reached San Francisco, he charged that their party was under the control of men "dedicated to the socialization of basic institutions in this country." When Stevenson later visited and appeared at a Democratic rally in San Francisco's Civic Auditorium, he retorted, "The President smiles while the Vice President smears."[24]

"I think one of the reasons why they are screaming," Nixon wrote to Victor Lasky when it was all over, "is that we were pretty effective in the western states. Did you realize, for example, that west of the Mississippi we gained one Senate seat and broke even on House seats?" He explained his Red-baiting by writing, "My attack was on the ADA left-wingers in the Democratic Party, and as usual, they are trying to throw the cloak of injured innocence around a larger number than themselves."[25]

When Nixon met with the cabinet three days after the voting, however, the Communist issue was notably absent from his analysis. Rejecting any notions that the Democrats had won a mandate, he offered a district-by-district survey of how voters had been influenced by local economic conditions, organizational weaknesses, and personalities. Above all, he emphasized the need for adhering to Eisenhower's "middle of the road." As though to dramatize the need for a sense of energy, he marched a spring-driven mechanical toy across the cabinet table while he stressed that the administration must continue to "beat the drum of achievement."[26]

None of this suggests that Nixon's high-road, low-road campaigning represented some dichotomy in his personality. Rather, it was a conscious, calculated tactic that employed the verbal ability learned from youth. Most important to an understanding of his career is the realization that his appeals were attuned to the national mood. William Costello, for example, in his unsparingly critical compilation of Nixoniana, has shown that, harsh as Nixon's campaign was, "he may have been somewhat more moderate than the party high command." Nothing said or implied by the vice president matched the stridency on the anticommunist issue that was reached by many Republicans on the local level. The campaign behind Senator William Jenner in Indiana, for example, circulated a flier containing drawings of Lenin, Stalin, and Malenkov, with the following message: "We shall force the United States to spend itself to destruction," and warned of "12 billion dollars of *Your* Taxes Given to Russia by Democrats." Yet, in all hypocrisy, Eisenhower virtually took Nixon to the woodshed after the campaign, explaining his displeasure at tactics so offensive to Democrats that working with them would become more difficult. Later, the president, who had wanted Nixon to take the low road, told a close friend that he got "peeved about too much talk in calling the other party 'soft on Communism.' "[27]

The first hint of how the vice president stood came during that period between Eisenhower's recuperation and the public announcement that he would run for a second term. During all the discussions about a possible successor on the ticket, talks that began during his convalescence at Denver, names other than Nixon's headed his list. They ranged from Treasury Secretary George Humphrey, Tom Dewey, Deputy Secretary of Defense Robert B. Anderson, Sherman Adams, Henry Cabot Lodge, Herbert Brownell, Charles Halleck, and William Rogers, to economist Gabriel Hauge, and even such figures from outside politics as NATO commander Alfred Gruenther or his own brother Milton. Nixon usually managed to appear on such lists, but the fact that he was the vice president and that his name often ranked at the middle or the bottom was in itself significant. He was almost regarded as on a par with someone like the party's leader in the Senate, Bill Knowland of California. Eisenhower considered Knowland "a political man" who would "be impossible" and not up to the important job of keeping the likes of a Stevenson, Estes Kefauver, or Averell Harriman from capturing the White House.[28]

From Nixon's standpoint, matters hardly improved once Eisenhower agreed, as Ike wrote to his old friend Swede Hazlitt, that he was forced to "bow my neck to what seemed to be the inevitable." For a four-month period after that Christmas, 1955, the president kept the younger man in limbo, dropping broad and often embarrassing hints in the privacy of the Oval Office — where he suggested on five or six occasions that he would be better off taking a cabinet seat, probably defense — and in press conferences remarks that pointedly evaded any direct commitment. Most painful to Nixon, the offer of a place in the cabinet found its way into the pages of *Newsweek,* obviously, as he later wrote, something that "had come from a White House insider. . . . If Eisenhower had approved the leak, perhaps I had been misreading him all along — perhaps he *was* determined to get me off the ticket and could not understand why I had not taken the hint." More pain came from Eisenhower's press conference of March 7. Asked by Marvin Arrowsmith of the Associated Press about the cabinet offer, the president explained that "the only thing I have asked him to do is to chart out his own course, and tell me what he would like to do. I have never gone beyond that."[29] Behind the scenes, however, Eisenhower was much firmer.

With his mind made up, and having gotten a clean bill of health, Ike followed a business discussion with his secretary of state on the afternoon of February 27 by saying that he wanted to discuss "personal and political" matters. He talked about running again with some regret; he wished campaigning could be made less arduous; the strains of motorcades were particularly trying. But he had been giving more thought to the other name on the ticket. Nixon, he told Dulles, had not gained the popular support he deserved; polls showed the vice president's weakness, he added. He was not at all sure that remaining on the ticket would be in Nixon's best interest. He might have a better future if he followed through by serving on the cabinet, as, say, secretary of commerce.

"You might want to make him Secretary of State," offered Dulles, somewhat whimsically. If Dulles was, after all, truly prepared to step down at that point, there were far more seasoned potential candidates. Nixon had yet to gain the diplomatic experiences of his final years as vice president.[30] Dulles's remark was more likely prompted by the younger man's deepening absorption in foreign affairs, an interest that sometimes came uncomfortably close to impinging on the secretary's field.

Eisenhower, of course, saw the point and laughed. Besides, he told Dulles, he could not escape from his job that easily — unless, however, and this is what he wanted to talk about in the first place, Dulles might become his running mate. He had given primary thought to either the secretary of state or to the man who was perhaps his closest personal confidant on the cabinet, Secretary of Treasury George Humphrey, a self-described "hard-shell" conservative.[31]

Nixon's name then came up again. Dulles pleaded that, at his age, he did not want to look forward to that responsibility and that his personal choice would be Nixon.[32] That option, the obvious one, was not chosen by Eisenhower easily.

He also toyed with running with Frank Lausche, the conservative Democratic governor of Ohio. Ike liked Lausche, was especially delighted at the thought of a Catholic on the Republican ticket, and contemplated that having the governor change his party affiliation would help spark a political realignment. "I'd love to run with a Catholic," the president told party chairman Len Hall, "if only to test it out," and sent Hall and Bob Humphreys to see whether Nixon would step aside for Lausche. Out of deference to his vice president, he cautioned Hall to "be very, very gentle." The GOP chairman was fully aware of the differences between president and vice president, and what they represented. Between the two men, he later recalled, there was a great deal of mutual respect, "but not much dialogue."[33]

Hall found Nixon edgy about not being wanted and yet determined to stay on. "I never saw a scowl come so fast over a man's face," he reported. "But beyond that, we got no response at all. He was so uptight when he heard the suggestion, he just stared at the ceiling." Finally, Hall told the vice president that he should simply tell Ike that he wanted to remain on the ticket. But the idea of reaching out for bipartisan support was never far from Eisenhower's mind. Bob Anderson and Earl Warren were also attractive for that reason.[34]

Newsweek didn't help matters very much by later reporting about a White House stag dinner a day after that March 7 news conference. In Nixon's presence, Eisenhower told the gathering that he couldn't understand why everybody didn't take him at his word. Somewhat disingenuously, he wondered why they failed to comprehend that it would be "improper" for him to reveal his choice before the convention. Nixon, just as he had done four years earlier and as he had vowed to do only a week before following another embarrassing Eisenhower news conference, drafted a statement of withdrawal from the ticket. And, once more, someone intervened, this time Vic Johnston, chief of staff of the senatorial campaign committee, who tipped off the White House. In a matter of hours, Nixon was visited by Hall and Eisenhower aide Jerry Persons. Both urged him to destroy the paper. Hall reassured the vice president that it would, after all, be an Ike-and-Dick ticket. After again trying to convince Nixon to take some cabinet post, this time mentioning either commerce or health, education, and welfare, Eisenhower reassured him that he would "be happy" to have him on the ticket if that was his desire. Privately, however, he explained to Hall right afterward that there were areas of "great opposition to Dick," and then added, "I personally like and admire Dick, and he could not have done better, [but] I think he is making a mistake by wanting the [VP] job." By that point, Nixon was fighting back — in his own way. Quietly, he had secured pledges from some eight hundred convention delegates, more than enough.[35] But no number was sufficient without a word from the president. On April 26, one day after Eisenhower told the press that Nixon had yet to report back his decision, Nixon went to the White House to assert his desire for renomination.

Apart from the excesses of rhetoric that helped to make him so controversial, Nixon was a victim of party changes and a lightning rod for the untouchable Eisenhower. The South, in particular, that area of tentative Republican inroads, was in an uproar, with the Supreme Court's 1954 desegregation decision in *Brown v. Board of Education* placing the region on the defensive. Through 1956, the old "separate but equal" pattern came to an end in hundreds of school districts, especially in Texas and the border states. Massive resistance, defiant through such pseudo-constitutional artifices as interposition, was but among the milder forms of protest. A black leader of a voter registration drive in Lincoln County, Mississippi, was shot to death on the lawn of the courthouse. In Selma, Alabama, also in 1955, over half of those who signed a desegregation petition lost their jobs. A fourteen-year-old black boy, Emmett Till, on a visit from Chicago, was found floating face down in the Tallahatchie River after being accused of whistling at a white woman. The creation of White Citizens Councils and the reemergence of the Klan were among the inevitable additional manifestations, touching off predictable instances of violence. In 1955, the Court, stepping back somewhat, prescribed "with all deliberate speed" as the timetable for racial equality in education. That December, blacks in Montgomery began a boycott of the city bus system that lasted into 1956 and enlisted the leadership of a young minister from Atlanta, Dr. Martin Luther King, Jr.

While the Court and Chief Justice Earl Warren were the principal targets in Washington, the crisis created a dilemma for the president, who thought the *Brown* decision was ill-advised in the first place and then carefully avoided any endorsement along moral lines. All he would say publicly concerned his obvious constitutional responsibility to uphold the laws of the land. Roy Wilkins of the NAACP met with the general before his election and found little reason to expect progress. He thought Eisenhower had a typical "West Point, Old Guard view of racial relations." Nor was there much mystery about Eisenhower's personal attitude. At a White House dinner before the *Brown* decision, the president took Warren's arm and told him that southerners "are not bad people.

All they are concerned about is to see that their sweet little girls are not required to sit in school alongside some big black bucks." Arthur Larson thought he heard a "bombshell" when Eisenhower told him that "I personally think the decision was wrong." "At heart he was a states' righter," acknowledged Jim Hagerty in a 1969 interview with the author, "but not in the evil connotation that it was beginning to develop in those days." Eisenhower, pointed out White House aide Steve Benedict, was totally ignorant of the racial question in the country, an ironic statement when read alongside the president's own comment to General Clay that right-wingers were "the most ignorant people now living in the United States."[36]

Still, whatever the fine distinctions, it is probably fair to say, as did historian William H. Chafe, that "Eisenhower, through his reticence and ambiguity, encouraged segregationists to believe that they had free rein to resist the Supreme Court." A Gallup poll taken during the spring of 1955 showed that, in the midst of the growing massive resistance movement, Eisenhower was extraordinarily strong in the historically Democratic South. While his popularity was high among non-Republicans throughout the country, he was favored by 58 percent of southerners.[37] In August, Gallup's people asked, "What one thing do you like least about the way Dwight Eisenhower is handling his job as President?" Fourth in the list among the five most frequently measured complaints was "He encourages segregation." In late November 1955, the only black man on the White House staff, E. Frederick Morrow, warned that his "mail has been heavy and angry, and wherever I go, people have expressed disappointment that no word has come from the White House deploring this situation [the Till murder]. I always point out, of course, that our Attorney General has followed this situation with interest and skill and that he will act when and if Federal Laws are violated. But this does not still the protestations. There is a clamor for some kind of statement from the White House that will indicate the Administration is aware of, and condemns with vigor, any kind of racist activity in the United States." The president, Benedict later said, would "be wide-eyed at finding out when Morrow would tell him what sort of things were going on. There seemed to have been a certain amount of resistance to believing that things were as bad as they were, just because it almost challenged his whole vision of America."[38]

Given the president's own signals, it should also not be surprising that, within the administration, the politically astute attorney general, Herbert Brownell, took most of the heat. Brownell, charged with enforcing the laws, was attempting to do just that. At the Eisenhower Library, in fact, there is evidence that the attorney general bore the brunt of blame from irate letter-writers, mostly from the South, over the desegregation movement. Moreover, even while maneuvering to avoid upsetting the party's southern support, he was formulating civil rights legislation to be sent to the Congress. His proposals arrived on April 9, 1956, right in the heart of Eisenhower's apparent indecisiveness about retaining Nixon.

Next to Brownell, it was Nixon who had the most opposition in Dixie. "Not one person was for Nixon for Vice President for a second term," reported Hagerty to Eisenhower after a scouting trip through the South that March. As the press secretary explained the situation, "Nixon is in some way connected in Southerner's minds with the Negro difficulty."[39]

Segregationists were on the mark in suspecting that Nixon was not a true friend. His Quaker background was notably free of such bias, and nothing in the record contradicts that history for either the man's public or personal life. In Washington, he and Pat sent their daughters to grade school at Horace Mann, which was both public and integrated, although residential factors limited the number of black students.[40] When Tricia, the older girl, later entered junior high while Julie was still in grammar school, they were both placed in the Sidwell Friends School, an enlightened institution that had no racial or religious barriers. The Nixons had some qualms about giving them a private rather than a public school education. Political life had its responsibilities; in this case, it was setting the proper example. Still, Sidwell was by all odds the better school, and their parents wanted them to go on together and to experience a Friends education.[41]

Wilkins, who was considerably skeptical about Nixon's commitment to civil rights, acknowledged that the vice president was never regarded by blacks as an enemy or hostile to their aspirations. One who was more enthusiastic about Nixon's understanding of the plight of American blacks was Dr. King. King considered him the one leading member of the administration who understood the problems. "I do not need to tell you that he is singing your praises," wrote attorney and civil rights activist Harris Wofford to Nixon after visiting with King in Montgomery. King, who later shocked black friends by saying that Nixon was alone among the potential candidates for the presidency in 1960 who cared about the issue, informed Earl Mazo that "Nixon would have done much more to meet the present crisis in race relations than President Eisenhower has done." From Nixon would have come those much-needed "positive stand[s] on the question of civil rights and the Supreme Court's decision as soon as it was rendered."[42]

In retrospect, the extent of Nixon's assistance seems mild. There should, moreover, be no surprise that it was tempered by his political analysis of both the voters and the party, as, indeed, was the case with virtually everyone else in public life. As the 1950s progressed, and massive resistance heated up, the potential political mileage of having Democrats split along North-South lines, even the specter of Dixiecrats again storming out of one of their conventions, was lost to few Republicans.

The point was strengthened when the party's share of black votes increased in 1956. As Nixon aide Charles McWhorter reminded him, that kind of rebellion would do much to rejuvenate Republican attractions for "independent moderates and conservatives throughout the nation in 1960." But it would do a gross injustice to deny Nixon's intellectual and spiritual commitment to racial equality. Earlier recognition of his attitude had, in fact, brought him honorary membership in a California NAACP chapter (which, during the height of the 1960 election campaign, Eisenhower assured a correspondent, did not mean that Nixon "has any affiliation with the NAACP").[43]

Nixon himself tended to view the problem of equality within the context of the American idea of individual economic progress. In his role as chairman of the Committee on Government Contract Compliance, his stress resembled his attitude toward workers and labor unions. He noted at one cabinet meeting that whenever a group of Negroes got into a desegregated school, the matter became "big news." But it was, he thought, more significant when they actually broke through segregated industries and made it to white-collar jobs. "If the latter is impossible," he said, "then the former is only running them into a dead end."[44]

More publicly, his "trimming" en route to the Republican nomination consisted of emphasizing, as he would later do during his presidency, that "this problem is not limited to the South." While insisting that federal law was not the answer and that public support was a prerequisite for any change, and even arguing that there "has not been, is not now, and should not be immediate and total integration," he still believed there was "no legal, moral, or other justification for denying any American the right to vote." If for no other reason, he pointed out (as had Truman before him and practically every other prominent white civil rights spokesman), progress was necessary because of cold war considerations. "In the world-wide struggle in which we are engaged, racial and religious prejudice is a gun we point at ourselves." In the fall of 1954, when massive resistance was first gaining momentum and the administration was two years away from facing the next election, he made an extemporaneous appeal for desegregating the schools of New Milford, Delaware, where a parental boycott was resisting eleven black students. He pointed out that his own two daughters attended a racially integrated public school system, and predicted that "men and women of good will and good intentions, working patiently together, will find a way to carry out the letter and the spirit of the Supreme Court decision. . . . There is no reason why Americans, regardless of race, creed or color, cannot be educated together." The local school officials who had, meanwhile, capitulated to the parental protests and avoided public statements, privately said that his evident sincerity was deeply moving. He also wrote to a law professor at his old alma mater, Duke, that "there has been far too much discussion of the legal problems involved in this crisis and not enough on the human factors."[45]

Thus he separated himself from his statutory role as Eisenhower's vice president. Returning to that position before the Anti-Defamation League of the American Jewish Committee on September 14, 1955, he laid out the administration's accomplishments — desegregation of the armed forces and the District of Columbia (actually begun under Truman), immigration reform, but, mostly, "equality of opportunity for employment." A change was noticeable, however, when he spoke at a Republican Lincoln Day dinner in New York City. That was February 1956 and in the middle of the contretemps over whether he would succeed himself in the vice presidency. The strictly partisan speech omitted prepared remarks that recited Republican accomplishments in civil rights and dropped a complimentary reference to Earl Warren.[46]

Politics also undoubtedly contributed to Nixon's decision on Rule XXII at the opening of the new session of Congress in January 1957. The rule required a two-thirds vote by the Senate to break filibusters; historically, a filibuster was the final device to abort any civil rights legislation that might somehow be reported out of a committee. Liberals wanting to get around such filibusters clamored for a less stringent voting requirement, such as three-fifths. Even before a vote on such a change, however, there was the question of whether the Senate's rules were in force on a continuing basis or whether each session could make modifications. Because Nixon was presiding officer of the Senate, the decision was his to make. When he ruled with the liberals and permitted the body to vote on the issue, his move was hailed as an important gain for the cause even though the motion failed to pass. It helped clear the way for passage of the Civil Rights Act of 1957. Two years later, Nixon resisted opposition within the GOP and repeated his ruling.[47]

Nixon was not, Jim Hagerty reported to the president, the South's favorite politician. The problem was one he had to manage when he later ran against Kennedy and as he prepared for his revival during the 1960s. It encouraged him to hold off endorsing the omnibus Civil Rights Act of 1964 until it became law, but not even that stopped some southern Democrats attracted to Barry Goldwater's presidential candidacy from being upset that the senator from Arizona had indicated that he intended to give Nixon a top place in his cabinet. Nixon's reputation as a friend of racial equality was that much stronger in 1956, when Eisenhower regarded attracting southern Democrats a vital part of his political restructuring.[48]

Nixon was, at the same time, further embarrassed by his association with Murray Chotiner. Once again, in early 1956, rumors reappeared that

Nixon was anti-Semitic. Robert Williams, a professional anti-Semite, un-wittingly simplified matters by attacking Nixon openly for having a Jew as campaign manager. Chotiner, always expeditious, promptly arranged for a denunciation of Williams in the B'nai B'rith paper, which then carried a lead editorial that declared, " 'Secondary Anti-Semitism' will not work with Richard Nixon."[49]

Other Chotiner problems were not handled so easily. At that particular time, a moment so crucial to Nixon, Chotiner was being investigated in connection with a Senate subcommittee probing influence-peddling in army procurement and racketeer links involving some of his clients with federal clothing supplies. For someone with Chotiner's reputation as a gutter fighter and tutor who specialized in dirty tactics behind Nixon's campaigns, the potential side effects were most disturbing. Much of the press had depicted him as the evil influence behind the vice president's rise to power, as the man who had masterminded the harsh campaigns against Voorhis and Douglas.

Merely asking Chotiner to testify was suspect. Patrick Murphy Malin, the executive director of the American Civil Liberties Union, wired Sen-ator John L. McClellan, the committee's chairman, that the actions of his subcommittee had "overtones of political harassment." The chief attorney on the case was Robert F. Kennedy, the younger brother of a rising Democratic star, Senator John F. Kennedy. Chotiner fired back that spring, charging that chief attorney Kennedy had subpoenaed him as much for his political prominence as for his having received a five-thousand-dollar fee. He also wanted to know whether attorney Kennedy could "explain whether any influence was used in connection with his own appointment as attorney for a subcommittee of a committee of which his brother . . . is a member. And he might also answer how much his family contributed to Democratic party campaign funds, and what mem-ber of his family was appointed to a very high diplomatic post during a Democratic administration."[50] Chotiner always knew how to take care of himself, but not in time to help Nixon.

Whatever the merit of Chotiner's position, and despite his eventual exoneration, the episode confirmed to Eisenhower Nixon's potential li-abilities. There were just too many areas, political and moral, and too many enemies. He had already seen polls that showed an Eisenhower-Warren ticket running some five points stronger than an Eisenhower-Nixon combination.[51]

In this light, complaints about Nixon's not having "grown" or that he was "immature" or not "presidential timber" become code words for Eisenhower's view that the younger man, admirable in so many other ways, had not mastered the political arts. He was a confrontationist, albeit a highly gifted one, and he attracted too many negative connotations.

Eisenhower, in effect, responded with his own tactic, and that was to step back from making a controversial decision openly and incontrovertibly. When, during a press conference briefing, he appeared to verge uncomfortably close to an endorsement of Nixon, he hedged by adding that "he has serious problems. He has his own way to make."[52]

It was, in fact, the president who was uncertain about where the GOP was headed. With committeemen loyal to him firmly established in forty-one of the forty-eight states, he relished the opportunity to mold a new alignment. Some of the more enthusiastic of his friends, like Lucius Clay, even thought the new group might be called Eisenhower Republicans, something Eisenhower himself dismissed as placing too much of the focus on one man. However it would eventually be known, it would follow Arthur Larson's outline by bringing together "conservative" Democrats, especially from the South, and "enlightened" Republicans. Parochial, "self-interest" politicians, especially extremists, would be downgraded. The new consensus would preempt the middle of the road. If he couldn't have Bob Anderson somewhere on the ticket, as the kind of responsible Democrat who could get people to cross party lines, he would fight for it himself. He might even, he thought briefly, run as a Democrat.[53]

Nixon, as Eisenhower saw it, simply failed to fit into that kind of scheme. His loyalty to the party and the administration had been so vehement that he had made enemies galore. Nor was he truly, as some called him, the darling of the old guard. His support of the Eisenhower program of moderation, especially during the months after the heart attack, according to historian David W. Reinhard, "rattled Right Wing Republicans and undercut his conservative support." Nixon opponents were out plugging for Styles Bridges or Bill Knowland. Goodwin Knight, California's new governor and Nixon's intramural rival, wanted it for himself. "There was no love lost at all between Nixon and Knight," explained Caspar Weinberger, then a member of California's state legislature. "In the state committee meetings, there were Nixon people and Knight people and Knowland people." Yet, ironically, because he drew such heat from the opposition, he continued to be seen as a target of the left. "I hope those 'pseudo-liberals' are not going to crowd you out of line for the V.P. nomination," wrote Hearst executive Richard Berlin to Nixon in February. "I have heard considerable rumbling that they have been putting a great deal of pressure on the President to do so." There was also gossip that others who had been wary about keeping Nixon on the ticket in 1952 were saying that he had to go. *Life* magazine highlighted Nixon's problem in an article that said Nixon's partisanship would only qualify him to "be a good Republican President."[54]

But Nixon got some important help from the New Hampshire primary that March. There, a Nixon ally, one who had urged him to assert his power at the time of the Eisenhower heart attack, rightist senator Styles Bridges, rallied fellow conservatives to accomplish an impressive write-in vote. Bridges himself made eighty-seven telephone calls. The result was a triumph of organization, one that carried no imprimatur whatsoever from any source that could be termed New Republican. The tally, which Nixon later described as "surprising" and "unsolicited," showed that 56,464 voters placed their marks alongside Eisenhower's name on the ballot, but 22,202, forty percent of the president's total, took the trouble to enter Nixon's name. Even that failed to budge the president very far when he faced newsmen the next day. Veteran correspondent Merriman Smith asked for his reaction to the New Hampshire vote. Eisenhower made a comment that was little noted at the time: "As far as I am concerned, I will never answer another question on this subject until after August."[55]

August was the month for the Republican nominating convention at San Francisco. That Eisenhower somehow hoped to duck a commitment until then seems clear. He revealed as much at the end of February at a pre–press conference briefing with Jim Hagerty. Hagerty, preparing the president for potential questions, mentioned that he might be asked about the vice presidency. In the file of Ann Whitman at the Eisenhower Library, in Abilene, Kansas, is the following memo describing Eisenhower's response: "The President said he couldn't be sure that the Republican party wanted him. (i.e., Eisenhower), and that he would not say a word about the Vice President until after the President had been nominated. Mr. Hagerty said there might be a question as to whether the President had talked to Vice President Nixon. The President said of course he had talked to Mr. Nixon."[56]

Still, Eisenhower's strategy failed, at least for the moment. Nixon, having agreed to Len Hall's suggestion that he not force the president's hand prematurely, took his stand. When he did, it was after the New Hampshire primary and the day that followed Eisenhower's explanation to reporters that Nixon had yet to get back to him about how he would "chart his own course." "When I heard about this exchange," Nixon has explained, "I knew the time had come to act. The more I thought about it, the more I was convinced that I could not get off the ticket without hurting Eisenhower more than helping him." The next afternoon, April 26, 1956, he effectively called the president's bluff. He could not have been any more direct: he had hesitated to force the issue, he said, but he expected to be on the ticket a second time.[57] Of course, that was precisely what he was doing, forcing his way onto the ticket, knowing that he had the support of Hall and a majority of the national committeemen.

He explained his thinking further: any man would obviously welcome the opportunity to be a vice presidential candidate, especially on an Eisenhower ticket. He would tell the press that he would be prepared to do anything else if conditions should change before the convention.

Then he felt he had to tell the president about Chotiner. The fee was five thousand dollars and was paid to Murray in 1953, not for any connection with the fraud but for professional services. The Senate committee was only going after Chotiner because "he is involved with people who are bad people," something, however, consistent with a lawyer having to represent those with large and varied businesses who also had tax problems. Most of all, he assured the president that he and his staff were clear of any involvement in the matter. His relationship with Chotiner, who was a very good professional politician, "has always been that of an employer with an employee." He added a warning about such investigating committees "going after the friends and relatives of everybody in the Administration from now until election time," and said he wouldn't be "surprised that [my] own people will be the main targets." There was also, for example, the case of his brother Donald, who owned two or three little restaurants in California. He was being picketed by the unions because his workers belonged to an independent union, but Drew Pearson was maintaining that it was the vice president's fault because they would not join the CIO.[58]

Eisenhower's game was, in effect, foiled. He could, at that point, hardly do anything less than what he did: call in his press secretary and say, "Dick has just told me that he'll stay on the ticket. Why don't you take him out right now and let him tell the reporters himself," then adding, in typical Eisenhower fashion, "And you can tell them that I'm delighted by the news." He thought it would be simplest for Dick to "be tackled" by the press.[59]

At three forty-five that afternoon, Nixon faced the White House press corps. "The President has asked me to tell you gentlemen that he was delighted to hear of the Vice President's decision," said Hagerty. Nixon, then asked why he had taken so long to "chart his course," explained that he "had to weigh all the factors involved and to reach a decision" which put the interests of the country first as well as "the best interests of the success of the President in his campaign for re-election and for the continued success of the President's Administration in Washington."[60]

Barely six weeks later, Nixon's future became uncertain once again. To the world at large, the events of June 8 seemed like a footnote to the Eisenhower presidency. "The President has an attack of ileitis (inflammation of the lower portion of the small intestine)," explained Jim Hagerty's press release. "As a precautionary measure he is being taken to Walter Reed Hospital this afternoon. His blood pressure and pulse are good. He has no fever. There is no indication of any heart trouble."

Within twenty-four hours, an anxious public was reassured. The latest illness was not as critical as the heart attack; moreover, his cardiovascular system had withstood the shock. For a man of his age, his recovery was remarkable. Although the attack came late on Friday, by Sunday he was able to walk to a chair, albeit with some assistance. There was no reason, said the doctors, why he would not be able to resume full duties in four to six weeks. Meanwhile, as he had done in the wake of the heart attack, Sherman Adams presided as captain of the Eisenhower team.[61]

Yet, what had happened was hardly that simple; nor was it so trivial that it merely meant that an interim team would carry on in the president's absence, with more important decisions simply deferred for a few days. At Walter Reed, surgeons performed a critical bypass during those early morning hours on Saturday, relieving the obstruction to his ileum and discarding a section of the small intestine. Given his past medical history and his age, sixty-five, the procedure was dangerous, with stress to the heart the greatest threat. The obstruction, which had come on with great pain, left no choice but to operate despite the obvious risk. Unlike what followed the heart attack of the previous fall, there never was any serious question about whether he would change his mind about running again.

In view of his recent history, there was surprisingly little public comment about whether his reelection plans would be changed. So upbeat were the reports from Walter Reed, and so solid had been the prognosis about his heart condition and general health given by doctors in February, that most earlier uncertainties were muted. If Eisenhower himself had any doubts about the wisdom of his decision, they were the inevitable fleeting thoughts between the onset of his pain and recovery from surgery. More important was the renewal of interest about Nixon. The issue had not really died, not even after the president's April statement about welcoming Nixon back on the ticket.

After Nixon told Eisenhower he was ready to chart his own course, the Gallup organization ran a trial heat with the vice president head to head against Governor Christian Herter of Massachusetts. Herter, a quintessential eastern establishment Republican, was well regarded in the Northeast. However, as a potential candidate, he had several serious liabilities, including the fact that he was a severe arthritic who needed a cane. He was also a lackluster campaigner. But he was highly thought of by those who feared that the party was being absorbed by its nationalists. And so Herter was the subject of a direct question posed by Gallup's pollsters to Republican voters: "Suppose the choice for Vice President were narrowed down to Vice-President Richard Nixon and Governor Christian Herter of Massachusetts. Which one would you prefer to have the Republican convention select?" The results were predictable: among those expressing an opinion, Nixon by 83 percent to 10 for Herter.[62]

    The wonder of it all was not that Herter received even 10 percent but that the Gallup organization continued to survey prospects for a Nixon replacement even after April 26 and before the second Eisenhower illness. Between May 10 and May 15, potential Republican voters were handed a card with a list of supposedly eligible replacements. Nixon had no trouble leading the pack, polling 66 percent. Seven others drew a total vote of just 28 percent. The spread between the second name, Stassen, and the last, Herter, was just 5 percent. In between were Dewey, Lodge, Dulles, Knowland, and Milton Eisenhower. Assuming that the survey had any value, Stassen and Dewey were the most credible alternatives.[63]

Harold Stassen's palace revolt was expressed to the president in the Oval Office at nine-thirty on the morning of July 20, 1956, just a month before the party's national conference. Private polls, he told Eisenhower (which had been financed by a group in New York, according to columnist David Lawrence), had shown that he might run as much as six points higher with another running mate. To mend the situation, Stassen was prepared to head a drive in behalf of Governor Herter.

    Few people were as devoted as Herter to the administration's policy of internationalism. Nixon himself always regarded his own early association with Herter as a vital introduction to his understanding of foreign affairs. Moreover, Herter rather than the more partisan Nixon would be in the best position to attract Democrats and independents. The president, according to Stassen's report of their meeting, neither encouraged nor discouraged his proposed coup. About all he emphasized was that Stassen must be seen as acting as an individual and not in any official capacity. Three days later, with the president out of the country, Stassen called a press conference to announce his support for an open convention. Moreover, he added, "I am confident that if the Republican national convention nominated Governor Christian Herter for Vice President, President Eisenhower will be pleased to have him on the ticket." When Eisenhower then returned after a quick official trip to Panama, the White House separated itself from Stassen's move by announcing that he was being given a four-week leave of absence to pursue "certain political activities." In all ways that were public, in other words, Stassen was depicted as a lone wolf in the affair.[64]

    Stassen clearly did not act on his own. Later, when the perennial candidate moved to Pennsylvania and tried to round up support for the gubernatorial nomination, he was quoted as having explained his effort to block Nixon by saying, "I may have done the hatchet job, but it wasn't my brain child." Many years later, Stassen disavowed the quote, denying that it described "my view of my actions in 1956."[65] Nevertheless, Stassen

virtually acknowledged as much in an interview given just before the
Republicans met in San Francisco that year.

> *Question:* If Governor Herter declines to run as Vice President,
> do you have anyone else in mind who would have less detraction?
> *Stassen:* We do not.
> *Question:* You use the expression "we" which conveys the
> impression that you are not alone in this stand, that you are
> associated with others in the Republican Party —
> *Stassen:* That is right.[66]

Stassen's move can best be understood with the realization that Nixon's
status was long in doubt. His future was intertwined with the evolving
decision of whether Eisenhower's heart attack in 1955 would permit him
to run for a second term. The president's physical condition made it
important that the party's future be safeguarded from a vice president
who was regarded as a front man for the right wing. Conservative columnist Frank Kent, for example, pointed out "Mr. Nixon has been
subjected to as vicious, violent and continuous propaganda attacks as
any man in American politics since the days of the Raskob-Michelson
'smear' of Herbert Hoover." He was, in short, the "handiest goat." Even
Eisenhower agreed.[67]

None of this can be ignored when trying to understand Stassen. On July
19, the day before his Oval Office appointment, he wrote to the president
that Nixon "would be an increasing liability" to the ticket because he
had the "strong support of Senator McCarthy and his associates" and
would hinder the "prospects of a lasting peace and success for U.S.
leadership versus communism." Later, in substantiating Nixon's "weaknesses" on the issues, Stassen compiled other liabilities offered "by people
polled who recorded themselves as in favor of the President but against
Mr. Nixon": lack of maturity; indiscreet statements about Asian countries; his association with Chotiner; and unfavorable attitude toward
minorities. Unspecified in all this, except inferentially, were the views
Stassen shared with other liberal Republicans about prospects for world
peace through arms limitations. He had, in fact, unleashed the anti-
Nixon drive immediately after returning from an arms conference in
London. In his letter of July 19, the "secretary of peace" reminded the
president that Governor Herter "has a lifetime record of effective action
reflecting the same philosophy as you have on both domestic and foreign
policy . . . plus an integrity and strength of character of the finest
quality." In an interview the following week with *U.S. News & World
Report,* Stassen reiterated the same theme: Herter would be more compatible with the administration "in both foreign and domestic policy —

labor issues, financial matters — and foreign policy, European and Asiatic."[68]

As Stassen put it to Nixon in writing, an Eisenhower-Herter ticket "is certain to reflect decisively in a number of Senatorial and House seats, and may well be the margin of majority or minority in the Congress."[69]

To those with some access into what was going on, Stassen was hardly on his own. "That such ferment existed within the Republican Party, in high places and in low, has been no secret," revealed *The Reporter,* adding that "the kind of uneasiness that Nixon generates cannot be disposed of so easily. When his enemies aren't attacking him, his friends are gratuitously acquitting him." Such "friends" included some of the most significant and financially powerful segments of the party, hardly people who could be ignored by the president, just as he could not shut his eyes to the *New York Herald Tribune.* Rumors "persisted," according to the newspaper, about backing for Stassen coming from "liberal Republicans, Democrats and independents associated with the National Citizens for Eisenhower movement." To conservative journalist David Lawrence, the anti-Nixon cabal was, at the same time, a "left-wing group" and "New York business and financial men who have been trying all through the present session of Congress to get vast appropriations for foreign aid 'without any strings.' " The involvement of such "leftists" was discounted by Sidney Weinberg, a New York financier and one of the group's founders, but it was clear that Stassen's friends, few as they were, were centered in the nation's largest city. They were, it should be added, swayed by the continuing gossip about Nixon's anti-Semitism. Weinberg even sought reassurances from the Anti-Defamation League.[70]

Tom Dewey himself, a key Nixon backer in 1952, had grown closer to the vice president and remained loyal, so there was a split between the man who had been a three-term governor and the active dissidents. One New York businessman, Arthur J. Goldsmith, used a conference at Harvard to push Stassen. Others were brought together by another early Herter booster, Jacob Javits. Javits, then an attorney general, hosted such people as John Loeb, Jock Whitney, and Nelson Rockefeller at a dinner for Herter in his New York City apartment. "The talk," Javits wrote in his autobiography, "concerned the dangers of war and Soviet expansion, the structural problems of the U.S. economy, and the need to accelerate economic and social development in the less-developed countries." Additional components of the National Citizens for Eisenhower were Ike's bridge companion Sigurd S. Larmon, who was president of the Young and Rubicam advertising agency, and businessman Cliff Roberts, another Ike favorite. At about the time of the Stassen ploy, Larmon informed his political associates, who included Oveta Culp Hobby, Thomas E. Stephens, and Weinberg, that "at the last meeting of our group it was suggested that a 'plan for action' for Citizens for

Eisenhower be prepared." Larmon also explained that he was "delegated to undertake the job." On the eighth of August, three weeks after Stassen acted, the *Herald Tribune* ran a front-page editorial seconding the Citizens' internationalist sentiments, the outlook that brought them together behind Ike in the first place: security from Soviet aggression must be given more importance than "budget-balancing for its own sake"; the U.S. must pursue a coherent continuing foreign economic policy to keep free nations independent; and Washington must aim for "multilateral disarmament" based on effective control and inspection.[71]

One could hardly have missed knowing where eastern establishment Republicanism stood. An editorial in the *Baltimore Evening Sun* said that Stassen's public words were what many "Eisenhower supporters in the East have been saying privately." While most individual Republicans scoffed at the notion, early comments were notably lacking from that coterie. The *Herald Tribune* itself was guarded, not offering a word in support of Nixon and criticizing Stassen only for not having chosen "an appropriate occasion to make public the fact that he preferred Governor Herter — who is one of the country's ablest Governors and public servants — for the post."[72]

A confident James Reston reported in the *New York Times* that "it was generally believed by well-informed Republican politicians in the capital that while Mr. Stassen was not acting at the instigation of the President, he at least had the President's acquiescence in the move for Mr. Herter." Moreover, revealed Reston, he had "personal knowledge that if the President had told Mr. Stassen that he was determined to have Mr. Nixon on the ticket, or even that a public move on behalf of Governor Herter would embarrass the President, today's announcement would not have been made." There were also suspicions within Republican circles, passed on with the aid of a former national chairman, that Eisenhower was trying to gauge the strength of Nixon's opposition. Stassen was introduced at the National Press Club as "the only man in history who ever got a license from the President of the United States to go hunt for 30 days for the Vice President." Eisenhower's handling of the matter did nothing to discourage such gibes. As he reports in his memoirs, when Stassen confronted him in the Oval Office that Friday morning, July 20, he merely said, "You are an American citizen, Harold, and free to follow your own judgment in such matters." But why didn't the president, the former supreme commander and general of the army, who found the Stassen ploy "astonishing," simply tell his subordinate that he would tolerate no such nonsense, that he had already welcomed Nixon to the ticket once more, and that he must stop futile moves that would only divide the party? He couldn't, he reported, because "I was at that moment hurrying to leave Washington for Panama." On July 25, with the president back in the country but while attention was being diverted by the sinking of an Italian liner, the *Andrea Doria,* Stassen offered to drop his drive to replace Nixon if only Eisenhower would come out with an "unmistakeable" statement in support of his vice president. Nixon could hardly be blamed for worrying that Republicans would somehow get the feeling that Stassen was speaking for the president.[73]

Quite legitimately, he feared that such distinctions might be easily lost. Whatever the source of Stassen's inspiration, it caused some overt irritation, but the Eisenhower White House was hardly outraged. "The apparent calm with which the Stassen situation has been handled by the White House does not give any outward indication of the President's personal attitude," wrote one aide, E. Frederick Morrow. "Whether he is angry or not I do not know, but there are strong political possibilities."[74] Whatever annoyance showed, it was suspected, was at least partly because of Stassen's timing. His announcement effectively overshadowed the news of the president's return from a successful conference in Panama.

Stassen may have been impolitic to suggest Herter, but the Massachusetts governor did have friends not far from the Oval Office. If they were not Herter sympathizers, they were Nixon enemies; or they were, as was the case with Sherman Adams, key players, people who, as Nixon recalls, "wanted to do what the Boss wanted." Lucius Clay was more adamant about Nixon. There was no "question Lucius Clay wanted the change," however, and "no question that Stassen continued to press it."[75]

In 1955, when Eisenhower's appointments secretary, Tom Stephens, left the administration to practice law in New York City, it was with the secondary objective of preparing the way for the 1956 convention, a mission that included weighing reactions about retaining Nixon on the ticket. Stephens's function was secret except to the president and an inner circle that included Adams and Clay. Mainly, they were part of a network that gravitated around Ike and accompanied him on recreational trips, especially during his periodic visits to the Augusta National Golf Club in Georgia.[76] "This circle of friends purposely stayed out of the political spotlight," Adams later wrote, "and seldom appeared with Eisenhower at conventions and on campaign trips." As far as Stephens was concerned, he was working for the "Augusta group" and continued his operations throughout 1955 and did not end until the convention. David Eisenhower, recalling Georgia outings with his grandfather, remembered the anti-Nixon influences of the "Augusta crowd."[77] If Stassen's choice was too way out, Nixon's opponents might settle for someone properly available and properly bland (so the bland really could lead the bland), someone with just enough credibility and few enemies, hopefully from the West or South. If he couldn't get Herter, the anti-Nixon sentiment might at least coalesce around a man who did not have the governor's liabilities, someone, in fact, not from the Northeast, not un-

acceptable to the Taftites, not under fire from significant segments of
the party and the electorate.

Eisenhower continued to insist that he wanted an open convention
and held out for one as long as he could. His strongest public praise for
Nixon remained the word "acceptable," even up to the eve of the nominating session at San Francisco. Sherman Adams insisted long afterward
that those who thought Eisenhower had "cooled off" on Nixon "did not
understand" him. He was holding out for an open convention with the
full knowledge that "it would have to be just between Nixon and anyone
Stassen put up." Despite his statement in April, which had virtually been
forced by Nixon, Eisenhower seemed no more decisive about his running
mate than during the secret fund affair — and just about as irritated.
His grandson remembers that "one of his favorite pastimes was sitting
around and saying, 'Now what do we do with Nixon?' " At an August 1
news conference, the president was asked, "Is it not inevitable that we
should conclude that Mr. Nixon is your preference?" Rather than grab
that opportunity to settle matters, he stepped back by saying that "you
have a right to conclude what you please. But I have said that I would
not express a preference. I have said he is perfectly acceptable to me,
as he was in 1952. But I am not going beyond that because in 1952 I
also put down a few others that were equally acceptable to me. So I see
no reason why you should draw the conclusion, but you may if you so
choose." In a sense, it was 1952 all over again, but this time far more
prolonged and anguishing. Nor did Nixon know how he could do anything more. He began to retreat to the isolation of rooms P-53 and
P-55 of the Capitol Building, pacing the floor, his anxiety growing more
intense.[78]

Ike's attitude was remarkable. What made it especially galling was that
Nixon appeared to have won the battle months earlier. His renomination
had been on the line since the start of the year, so his supporters had
taken nothing for granted. "We put Eisenhower on the spot," Pat Hillings
recalls, just as during the Checkers incident after the fund disclosure.
"We had a feeling that Ike was not being properly informed." There
were IOUs to cash in from Republican delegates, committeemen, and
local powers from all over the country, the perks that were made possible
by the vice presidency. Every effort was made to get the most mileage
out of two campaign biographies, both written by Nixon admirers and
with his cooperation, James Keogh's *This Is Nixon,* and Ralph de Toledano's *Nixon.* Multiple copies were circulated to Republicans everywhere.
On the very day Stassen publicized his Herter move, twenty House Republicans expressed themselves "amazed and shocked" and suggested
that he resign. "Harold," said Governor Robert E. Smylie of Iowa, "this
is a pipe dream." Nixon's friend Charles Jones, of the Atlantic Richfield

Oil Company, his tongue loosened by a few drinks at a dinner with Eisenhower, finally blew up and said to the president, "What the hell does a man have to do to get your support?" David Lawrence, applying his "Lawrence School of Prophetic Analysis," calculated via his own poll that the 6 percent Eisenhower might gain by discarding Nixon would actually cost him 20 percent of the "faithful" Republicans. The research division of the party's national committee was collecting additional survey results, all of which, whether from Trendex, the Associated Press, or Elmo Roper, showed Nixon the hands-down Republican favorite.[79]

By the time Eisenhower returned from Panama, after an absence of only three days, he found that a petition supporting Nixon that had been circulated by Hillings had the signatures of 180 of the 203 Republicans in the House.[80]

If that failed to end Eisenhower's latest Nixon-dangling, it at least aborted Herter's career as a vice presidential candidate. Leonard Hall, chairman of the Republican National Committee, was a New Yorker, a Long Island law partner of William J. Casey. Hall was also close to local party leader J. Russel Sprague and Governor Dewey. As Hall's successor as national party chairman put it, he "was not a Nixon admirer." "Len was a very dear friend of mine," said Meade Alcorn. "Len would just shake his head and say, 'Dick is not the man. Dick is not the man.' " Hall would, according to Alcorn, "have welcomed a burst of support for someone else with an acceptable character, but it didn't develop. The Herter thing never caught hold." Hall was finding out how well Nixon had built his support within the national committee. It was becoming clear that an open convention was precisely what would ease the way to a Nixon renomination, but it was better to go to San Francisco under a single banner. Better than anyone else, Nixon would keep the party together.[81]

Hall did not lose much time. He had a plan to scotch the Stassen maneuver. He suggested that Sherman Adams get Herter to nominate Nixon at the convention. "Knowing Herter as I did," Adams later wrote, "I knew that the work that interested him most was in foreign affairs."[82] Would he like "a position of responsibility" in the State Department? the assistant to the president asked Herter. And would he make the Nixon nomination speech? That took care of that. Herter, who replaced Dulles as secretary of state three years later, was no longer Stassen's pawn. As far as Stassen was concerned, however, nothing much had changed. He still plugged for his Eisenhower-Herter "dream" ticket.

Given the president's failure to commit himself, Nixon could only stew while his would-be replacements jockeyed for position. It was hardly remarkable, under such circumstances, that the door was considered wide open for the equally ambitious. Most prominent among them were Governor Theodore McKeldin of Maryland and Goodwin Knight, Warren's successor in the statehouse in Sacramento. Knight, the only prominent Republican to openly support Stassen, feverishly began to tap businessmen for contributions to the host committee in San Francisco. Rumors set their projected goal as $250,000.[83]

Meade Alcorn, then in charge of the committee on arrangements, also received a visit in his Fairmont Hotel headquarters from a fellow Connecticut politico, former congresswoman Clare Boothe Luce. Thanks to Eisenhower, she was currently the American ambassador to Italy.

"I have come to you because I think you're the one who can help me achieve what I have in mind," said Ambassador Luce, as Alcorn remembers the conversation. "I want the nomination for vice president of the United States."

Alcorn advised that she had come to the wrong man. She needed to see the president.

She answered, "I know that you're very close to the president, and I know that you're setting up this convention. I would like to have you lay this before the president. Tell him I would like that nomination. I believe I can be helpful to the ticket. I believe that I can relieve him of some of the difficulties that he is confronted with now by virtue of the situation that developed over Nixon's renomination. I would like to be the first woman nominee on a national ticket."

He hesitated, Alcorn explained; the circumstances of his own relationship with Eisenhower and Nixon and his party position ruled out any idea that he could intervene. He had also distanced himself from the Stassen move behind Herter. It was up to her to take it up with the president himself. "I wouldn't say that she was visibly angry, but she was disappointed. She finally left. The ambassador wanted that nomination so bad she could taste it."[84]

Told in 1985 that corroborating information had been supplied by several sources, Luce flatly denied that she had any such ambitions, saying that she had "more sense than to expect that" and added her denial that she had participated in any "dump Nixon" movement. Others, like Nixon himself, recall that there were "rumors" about her effort at the time. A Luce biographer, Alden Hatch, is more emphatic, citing a "considerable move" to have her replace Nixon. One of her friends, Randolph Churchill, wrote that "if it had been decided to dump Mr. Nixon from the ticket she would have been very glad to have stepped into the breach. The vice presidency has often been the stepping stone to the White House. And short of being Pope of Rome there is probably no other job which Mrs. Luce would more willingly discharge than that of President of the United States."[85]

Eisenhower, of course, pretended that the situation was beyond his control. In trying to reshape the party, he was, ironically, flirting with disunity. But it was more than mere dissension. He was trying to keep the party from bending toward its natural direction, fighting to shape a moderate, internationalist base, one that was basically a bourgeois, upper-class alliance. In essence, his was the pipe dream. Republicanism was reaching not only into the hinterlands of the South and West but downward toward the masses as well. Neither Eisenhower nor Stassen had an adequate base for what they wanted to do.

Stassen seemed to be the only man who didn't know that. Each delegate received one of his open letters that pleaded the case for Herter. Far more discreetly, two of Ike's lieutenants, General Clay and Adams, made desperate efforts to prevent what had been allowed to happen in 1952. Adams pushed for an updated list of potential running mates, and Clay continued a behind-the-scenes dump-Nixon effort while he operated in liaison with Harold Stassen — all with the knowledge of the president. Dewey's continuing loyalty to Nixon was not enough to keep Clay's activities from encouraging rumors that he was in league with the ex–New York governor.[86]

The retired general who had been so instrumental in getting Ike to run in the first place was active at the convention itself. Herbert Brownell recalls that at breakfast with the president at San Francisco he was asked for his opinion about what ought to be done about the vice presidency, a certain indication that at that late date, just hours before the renomination, Eisenhower still had an open mind. Brownell, surprised that the question even came up, responded matter-of-factly that, of course, Nixon was the man. "What am I going to do about Stassen?" was Eisenhower's reply. That was easy, said the attorney general: he should be told in no uncertain terms to get with the team and second Nixon's nomination. "But what went on between them after my breakfast I don't know," says Brownell. "Eisenhower didn't want to make a decision until he had to; that's why he called me in. Indeed, Clay never disclosed to me that he was talking to Stassen."[87]

At about the same time, within forty-eight hours of the renominations, Stassen sent Eisenhower a "personal and confidential" memorandum with the explicit statement that he was in close touch with Clay. Despite their efforts, he reported "no important change in the delegations toward a new Vice Presidential nominee." As unhappy as were such people as Javits and others from New York, they were reluctant to break with Dewey. Californians, despite Goodie Knight's efforts, were being held behind Nixon by both Bill Knowland and the operation of the unit rule. Several others, Stassen made clear, were reluctant to make a break without the right word from the president. Delegations were also receiving telegrams from the public that, to "the best of our information," were

clearly in favor of a change. If, Stassen concluded, Nixon must be retained, it was important that "the responsibility be borne by the Republican organization leaders and delegates and not shifted to the President
individually."[88]

Thus did a putsch seem possible to some bitter-enders even without
any plausible arithmetic when considering the delegate count. As illogical
as it was, Nixon was kept in limbo. Just nine hours before his renomination, Senator Edward Thye of Minnesota called at Eisenhower's
sixteenth-floor St. Francis Hotel suite and was told by an assistant that the
president wanted Nixon. But even at that moment, according to reporter
Fletcher Knebel, he made no effort to give him an unqualified endorsement.[89] What sealed matters was a later visit to the suite by Stassen.

Stassen's surrender was inevitable. However belatedly, even he knew
he was finished, but not until he scrutinized each delegation and came
up with brave, optimistic reports about each Nixon weak spot. We now
know that his performance was pathetic but not quite as Hugh Scott
described it, "an act of political loneliness." Kept waiting for one hour
and forty minutes, he was finally granted an eleven-minute interview,
and that was made contingent by Len Hall and Sherman Adams on his
agreement to follow Herter to the podium to deliver a seconding speech
for Nixon. As Hall told him, "Harold, for weeks you've been forecasting
legions on white horses. They never materialize. You haven't got any
delegates." Forty-one minutes after Stassen left, Eisenhower called a
press conference to announce that Herter's chief promoter would second
Nixon's nomination. He told newsmen that Stassen had been convinced
that "the majority of the delegates want Mr. Nixon." Once more, and
once more with difficulty, the Ike and Dick ticket persevered. "That's
what it all got down to," Nixon later explained. "Brownell and Alcorn
opposed the dump-Nixon move. They feared that it would blow hell
out of the Republican party."[90] Later that day, Eisenhower was renominated unanimously, but Nixon's was just short of perfection as he won
with a vote of 1,323 to 1.

Eisenhower had written the scenario. Only Nixon had to pay the price,
because vice presidents are at the mercy of the White House. Eisenhower
had nothing at all to lose. If he failed to strengthen his ticket, or was
unable to reshape it along "modern Republican" lines, he would at least
keep the Republican gathering at San Francisco from being so predictable. As early as July 27, he told Cliff Roberts that, at the very least,
Stassen's announcement "did stir up some interest. Our program has
been so cut and dried, a little interest won't hurt." Ike had made the
most of what he had. As Harold Boeschenstein of the Owens-Corning
Fiberglas Corporation and chairman of the Business Advisory Council
(later called Business Council) cabled Eisenhower on August 24, "What

a wonderful life you have given to millions of Americans during this past week!"[91]

Her husband's personal ordeal came as no surprise to Pat Nixon. The secret fund episode had taught her to hate politics, to detest the way the game was played, and to be far less forbearing of personal attacks.[92] She had also had to endure the efforts to keep Nixon away from presidential power during Eisenhower's heart attack. If he put up with the political give-and-take, and certainly gave back at least as much as he received, that was his professional world. Her role was to tolerate everything and always look loyal and pleased; and she did, winning the public's admiration for perfection, from her lithe form to bright disposition. She did all the right things, standing by his side as the admiring wife, fulfilling the ceremonial functions, making the right comments to the right interviewers, a superwoman — or whatever Middle America thought was right.

That she bore through the role so well was especially remarkable when the job became harder to take. There was always something very private about Patricia Ryan; one sensed a longing to return to where life was very different from Washington. Watching what Dick had to go through convinced her even more that they should leave at the end of the first term. He would only be forty-four and they could go back to California, where there were many attractions for living the life of an affluent lawyer with a lovely wife and two growing daughters. Each time he had to put up with another political frustration, that solution seemed especially wise. They had one such talk in February of 1954, a time when the heat being created by Joe McCarthy was vexing Nixon and the administration. He even agreed, at that point, that he would do it, give up after 1956 and return to Whittier. She challenged him to put it in writing; he did, then stuck the piece of paper into his own wallet. There was at least one not-so-private suggestion about that plan, although Pat quickly said she meant it "half in jest." While they were driving with good friend Charles G. "Bebe" Rebozo from Fort Lauderdale to Key Biscayne, Pat expressed her hope that one term would be enough, adding that she was not going to campaign again.[93]

Pat's strength had attracted Nixon to her from the outset, tempting speculative psychobiographers to see her as another Hannah. Whatever the similarities may have been, and however enticing the comparisons, Pat demonstrated considerable stoicism and determination. At heart, she knew Dick's life was buried in politics. He was a prisoner and nagging would do no good. When Eisenhower applied the heat directly in 1955 and 1956, wavering between suggestions that Nixon might become a member of the cabinet and doubts that he wanted him at his side at all, even Pat, for all her desire that they flee, told her close friends Jack and Helene Drown that "no one is going to push us off the ticket."[94]

No one knew more intimately than Pat how his activism as vice president, however much a landmark in the evolution of the office, also carried with it the penality of subservience that galled and humiliated Nixon and others who held the position. The Founding Fathers had only provided that he preside over the Senate; not until the Twelfth Amendment (1804) were electors required to cast specific ballots for the vice presidency. During Eisenhower's physical disabilities, the lack of any written provision about his precise role left him with no choice but to obey the White House power structure and give his enemies no ammunition for gossip about hunger for power. So he remained the executive gofer, only adding to previous functions of the office the more active political role as hatchet man, which gave him plenty of headlines and countless liabilities.

So it was, one way or another, throughout his vice presidency, always putting on the correct face about being "Ike's boy" while dying a thousand deaths inside, from the 1952 campaign until the embarrassments when he ran against Kennedy, circumstances so peculiar that explanations were needed for years to come. It was, as he further explained, "awfully hard to get out when you are in the middle of the stream — if it is intended that you stay there."[95] LBJ learned that lesson under Kennedy and Humphrey under LBJ, and each vice president has had to make his accommodation with the same reality, accepting the liabilities along with the advantages.

Asking his wife to tolerate the situation was another matter. This time around, the pain came under less dramatic circumstances and not quite as public, but certainly much more extended; moreover, unlike in 1952, there was no applause for how the young man handled his discomfort. If he put up with it, it was for his political future; if she did, it was because she loved him.

He had just about told the president as much when he went in to see him in March 1956. Nixon was no novice at being blunt with Eisenhower. He was startlingly audacious during the heat of the secret fund affair, letting the Old Man know at that early date that he was not going to be a lackey. Once more, mindful of his ongoing discussions with Pat, to quit or not to quit, he was direct in making his case. "I have one serious problem," he said; "my family. Pat is not at all happy about the prospect of staying in Washington," and, with his eye on the possibility of having the uncertainty dragged out until the late-summer convention, told Eisenhower that "if she feels in August as she does now, I will have difficulty in doing *anything*," and that, he made clear, included settling for a cabinet seat.[96] The fact was, of course, that however the president finally felt, the decision about Nixon's political future was theirs.

Moreover, Pat was only an amateur as an actress, and the real woman began to show through. Barbs about "plastic Pat" implied as much; she was not happy. Even before the latest charade about what Eisenhower really had in mind, Pat was surprisingly candid about the growing discontent, not only for herself but, Hannah-like, for her husband and daughters. She felt his pains over what was supposed to be normal about life at the nation's power center. She tried hard to paint his home life as one of perfection, even telling an interviewer that they never fought. What others said about him was bad enough, but having her daughters exposed to the viciousness was another matter. She banished the *Washington Post* from their home to spare Julie and Tricia the sight of Herblock's latest cartoon attacks. In the summer of 1954, Pat broke down and told a reporter that she hated politics.[97]

There was a limit to her role. The public had long admired how well she played the role of loyal wife, the suffering mate who sat at his side while he told the nation about their personal finances and the family dog; later, even more courageously, she was a heroic figure while fanatic South American leftists spat on her in Caracas. A *New York Times Magazine* article called her "the ultimate good sport," who, from the moment her husband had entered politics, had "gone the whole route, smiling her way through the inedible banquets and endless receiving lines and arrivals and departures at bleak airports all over America. She has listened again and again to a single Nixon speech, somehow managing to muster, for each occasion, the adoring look of total rapt attention," complaining to no one, self-sacrificing.[98]

The public began to sense that she was withdrawn; her discomfort at helplessness showed through, thus the image of artificiality. She was supportive, Nixon has written, but at the same time "an independent woman," one who was "traditional, but in a warm way that transcended time and place." Bill Safire even observed that she "shares his prejudices and scar tissue."[99] By the time she became first lady, the marriage had clearly been subordinated to his career. She went on being the ultimate good sport.

So it went all the time he remained in Washington. Never given to public holding of hands or embraces, they fed gossips who tried to make much of their lack of open affection. It was simply not their style; both had traditional ideas about private and public behavior. However much that was explained, the public thought otherwise. When his presidential career collapsed under the weight of the Watergate revelations, she lost her temper and said, "You have ruined my life."[100]

With Bebe Rebozo, Nixon could get away from all that. There was no question about mutual captivity. Bebe could listen to him by the hour, or they could commune together in perfect silence. That kind of relationship, which deepened as Nixon went on to yet another term under Eisenhower, was in its own way more reciprocal. Bebe was clearly happy to be at the edge of power, and Nixon, for his own part, could unburden himself without guilt. His friend was a refuge, a source of complete trust.

When Adlai Stevenson formally opened the nomination of his running mate to the delegates at the Democratic convention in Chicago, he staged a show that was hard to top, one of the most exciting horse races of any convention. After two ballots, Senator Estes Kefauver of Tennessee was chosen as the Democratic vice presidential candidate, and only after television viewers saw challenger John F. Kennedy come within thirty-three and one-half ballots of the needed majority.[101]

That was not the only explosive moment for the Democrats. Many thought the keynote address by Governor Frank Clements of Tennessee was excessive, that he overstepped political propriety by hitting the popular president as hard as he did, something usually shunned by Ike's more prudent opponents. The attack was the talk of the town. His oratory blamed Ike directly for the vehemence of Nixon's political attacks. The wildest moment of the forty-four separate bursts of applause came when he said that the opposition had waged a "double-faced campaign" with the "Vice-Hatchet Man slinging slander and spreading half-truths while the top man peers down the green fairways of indifference." "In any event," wrote Connecticut's liberal Democrat Chester Bowles to Hubert Humphrey, "it was a very serious mistake."[102]

That was precisely what perplexed the Democrats. Nixon was their only real issue. When one of Ike's speechwriters later told Clay that Eisenhower would not have been sorry to see Nixon replaced with someone else, Clay agreed and also added, "But he wanted somebody else to do it."[103]

Some right-wingers who watched Eisenhower, however, feared that he had another candidate in mind. And Nixon, in their view, was far better than any potential replacement. Bill Buckley remembered that his friends clung to Nixon in 1956 because "they thought of him as the conservative alternative to a Rockefeller, who would have been the obvious compromise. Eisenhower's hesitations," Buckley pointed out, "helped to mobilize conservative support for Nixon."[104] An understandable reaction, here, would be to minimize Rockefeller's importance as a factor so early in the game.

The 1956 campaign, after all, took place more than two years before he was elected as New York's governor and predated by several more years his divorce and remarriage, which complicated his political ambitions. But Buckley was not alone in recalling the Rockefeller factor. Meade Alcorn, who was closer to the man whose name was synonymous with great wealth, did not discount his significance. Substituting him for a deposed Nixon, he knew, would have "rocked the boat."[105]

Even thinking that Rockefeller had any chance to replace Nixon in 1956, or that he wanted to, emphasizes the insecurity of the right wing under Eisenhower's conservative leadership. Rockefeller's name never came from the president's lips as an alternative. Yet, his inclusion by Ike's most informed biographer as "Nixon's chief rival for the position of chosen successor to Eisenhower" must suggest that they were not merely being paranoid.[106]

Rockefeller was a figure whose money and power were never far from view. By the end of that year, he had completed three tours of duty with the Eisenhower administration. If his lineage and background made him at least a symbolic foe of heartland Republicans, his Washington role was even less assuring. A key member of the New York pro-Eisenhower crew, he had joined the new team even before the inauguration. For a year and a half, he served the administration as under secretary of health, education, and welfare, hardly the most popular agency among Taftites. Later, before and after the Geneva summit conference of 1955, he headed the so-called Quantico group and worked with Harold Stassen on disarmament. He lobbied for acceptance of the "Open Skies" proposal that Eisenhower announced at Geneva. Still, his resignation at the end of 1955 as the president's special assistant for cold war strategy, after his strategies had antagonized both John Foster Dulles and George Humphrey, undoubtedly helps account for his absence from Eisenhower's various lists of potential running mates and should have relaxed conservatives. And perhaps it did. For whatever it was worth, Rocky was safely out of the way in 1956, a bit of relief that made the return of Nixon all the more welcome.[107]

Herbert Hoover, a good Nixon friend since Bohemian Grove days, felt especially festive about the inevitable outcome of the Republican convention. After visiting the Stassen headquarters on Market Street, about a dozen of the former president's friends accompanied him to his hotel suite where, with a cake and candles, they celebrated his eighty-second birthday. After he blew at the candles, one refused to die. With an eye on the persistent flame, Hoover said, "That's for Stassen," and then blew it out.[108]

If Stassen was finished, so, in a sense, was Eisenhower, his triumphs all in the past. It was not generally realized, but it was nevertheless true. The decision made that August marked a watershed. Writing less than a week after the nominations, one British correspondent proclaimed the "end of the Eisenhower era" and reported that the political machinery now belonged to Nixon. Joseph L. Rauh, Jr., the activist liberal attorney, seconded the thought that, whether or not Eisenhower was elected, Nixon was the new party leader. Rethinking the decade just a few years later, it occurred to Murray Kempton that the fifties "were not the Eisenhower years but the Nixon years. That was the decade when the American lower class in the person of this man moved to engrave into the history of the United States, as the voice of America, its own faltering spirit, its self-pity and its envy, its continual anxiety about what the wrong people might think, its whole peevish, resentful whine."[109]

So much of Eisenhower's career had been built on accommodation that he was an expert at accepting the inevitable. If he feared that continuing with Nixon might contravene his own vision of the future, such thoughts were irrelevant. At San Francisco, the lingering currents of discontent revolving around the usual array of competing ambitions seemed to dissipate, the age of Ike camouflaged disharmonies that had been building for the past decade. The symbolic moment itself came when Harold Stassen seconded Nixon by tardily discovering that the man he had been scheming to dethrone only a few hours earlier suddenly had the "experience" and "ability" to add luster to a ticket that offered "the best prospect to reach a sound system of world disarmament in hydrogen and other weapons."[110]

For the delegates, who had been given a chance to go wild over the appearance of Hoover on the day before the nomination, there was only one memorable moment, and that was supplied by a lone voice that found a way to dissent from the pro forma ratification of the vice president.[111] A short, gray-haired Nebraskan named Terry Carpenter caused the chairwoman of his delegation to answer the roll call by reporting that "one of our delegates demands the right to place a name in nomination."

At the podium, convention chairman Joe Martin made his confusion plain. "Who does the delegate want to nominate?" came his incredulous question.

"His name hasn't been disclosed to me," replied the lady from Nebraska.

"I must have the name," insisted Martin.

She turned to Carpenter, then talked into the floor microphone: "Joe Smith."

"Who?" demanded Martin.

"Joe Smith."

Not even a political professional like Martin had heard anything like it. Recovering his command, he banged the gavel and announced, "Nebraska reserves the right to nominate Joe Smith, whoever he is."

What happened right afterward was mostly confusion, a moment that stole the convention highlight from the renomination of Ike and Dick, one that could not even have been staged so well by the great general himself. Carpenter, the new center of interest, was overwhelmed by other delegates, reporters, photographers, and a movie actor from California.

George Murphy, of song and dance fame, rushed from the platform, grabbed Carpenter's arm, and demanded to know whether he had the pedigree and fingerprints of his candidate. No, said the Nebraskan; he didn't even have his own. He later told the press that since it was such a dull affair he at least wanted to impress the rest of the country with the openness of the convention.[112]

For the moment, Stassen was back in grace, the virtues of unity and appetite for victory overshadowing intramural bitterness. Nixon, having flown to Whittier to be at the bedside of his critically ill seventy-seven-year-old father, stood in front of the Spanish-style home that evening before well-wishing neighbors and news photographers and explained that Frank Nixon's condition would permit him to return to San Francisco in the morning for his formal acceptance speech. At the Cow Palace, he expressed his "appreciation" for Stassen's statesmanship. His formal remarks before the convention, however, said nothing new. One week later, he rushed back to California and was there when Frank Nixon died on September 4.

Whatever "Joe Smith" meant to Terry Carpenter, the invention became symbolic of the futility that confronted Stevenson. Running against Ike for a second time, he could do little more than turn the stunt into a handy metaphor. In early October, with his campaign showing even less sign of viability than four years earlier, he began to invoke Smith as Everyman, hapless before a government run by General Motors. "It is time," he urged in New York City, "to take government away from GM and return it to Joe Smith."[113]

Farmers, intellectuals, and hard-core Democrats were about all who listened to Adlai. Just about everybody else warmed to Ike more than ever, and, as the campaign progressed, Stevenson's hardships became plain. America's Joe Smiths were becoming indifferent to the bread-and-butter politics of FDR Democrats. Much more appealing was the sense of well-being under Ike, the apparent restoration of his health a clear signal that all was well with America and their world.

It showed in all sorts of ways. Stevenson's early call for suspension of nuclear testing, unilaterally if the Russians refused to go along, was easily dismissed as a naive letting down of the guard, more evidence that Democrats could not be trusted with the essence of security in a dangerous world. Nor did he gain any more credibility by suggesting that the draft be ended. When Poles staged their October uprising against Soviet rule, followed quickly by the short-lived rebellion by Hungarian freedom fighters and its violent suppression, the emergence of new, election-eve international crises only reaffirmed the need for Ike at the helm. Nixon, out campaigning, called Khrushchev the "Butcher of Budapest" and let it go at that, no more inclined than the rest of the administration to do something about liberating the captive peoples.[114]

Not even the Anglo-French and Israeli invasion of Egypt at the end of October, and the coordinated drive to wrest the Suez Canal from the control of President Gamal Abdel Nasser, alerted voters at home to the weaknesses of American Middle East policy. Stevenson, outmaneuvered by Eisenhower on Korea in 1952, was handcuffed once again. He could hardly differ with the administration's actions in ending the assault; besides, the best evidence was that calling off the fighting had the clear support of American public opinion, which registered strong disapproval of the British and French and somewhat milder dissent toward Israel's role.[115] The trio of crises, Poland, Hungary, and the Middle East, fortified the president's political position.

Stevenson's desperation showed in every way. Four years earlier, he had lost the election while establishing his stature and dignity. Now, attacking Nixon, he sacrificed much of that reputation. As the election drew closer, his rhetoric became purple. In mid-September, he charged that "the Vice-President seems to sail downwind no matter which way the wind blows." Nixon, argued the Democratic presidential candidate, was "beloved by the most reactionary wing of Old Guard Republicanism." He warned that the American people "can't imagine putting Richard Nixon's hand on the trigger of the H-bomb. They just don't trust him." By election eve, the specter of Nixon was made even more ominous, his succession more assured. The vice president was but "a heartbeat away" from the top.[116]

In a final campaign speech televised from Boston, Stevenson concluded that an Eisenhower victory would mean that "Nixon would probably be president of this country within the next four years." Then he added, "I recoil at the prospect of Mr. Nixon as custodian of this nation's future, as guardian of the hydrogen bomb, as representative of America in the world, as commander in chief of the United States armed forces."[117]

For Nixon, drawing more direct fire from the opposition than any vice presidential candidate in history was the price of having been, with the possible exception of Aaron Burr, the most controversial man to have held that office. He did, at the same time, offer traces of the style that had attracted such bitterness. With a clear echo of the past, for example, he denounced Stevenson's suggestions about a unilateral nuclear test ban as "treasonable nonsense," thereby again waving the old Red flag in the face of his opponents. His whistle-stopping, especially in the Midwest, included familiar warnings about the "threat of communism." But they were relative aberrations in a campaign that became known for the unveiling of a "new" Nixon. He was more likely to agree that Democrats were "loyal Americans"; or, as left-wing critic I. F. Stone noted right after the convention, to acknowledge "that the Democratic party is legal again." His good behavior was variously explained as getting ready to head the ticket in 1960 and further immunizing Eisenhower from personal attacks. An increasingly perplexed Stevenson then called Nixon a "man of many masks" and an unbelievable "Little Lord Fauntleroy of the Republican party."[118]

The only thing surprising, to some, about the Eisenhower-Nixon re-election was the failure of the crises in Poland, Hungary, and the Middle East to hurt the administration politically. Victory came with better than 57 percent of the vote, and the plurality over Stevenson was twice as high as in 1952. About the only Republican setback was the party's inability to have its winning ticket carry with it a majority in either house of Congress, the first time that had happened in 108 years.

More emphatic was the black shift toward Ike, a reversal of a twenty-year drift away from the party, and accomplished with a minimum of political capital on the part of the president. If anything, his position about desegregation was unchanged. When asked at a mid-September press conference about the town of Texarkana using rangers to keep two students out of a school at which they were registered, he explained that the issue was up to the states, as though the nation's highest court had never spoken. It was largely for other reasons, then, that his share of the black vote nationally went up by five points, to 47 percent. Leading the swing were southern blacks, their voter participation further encouraged by the elimination of the so-called white primaries.[119]

Democrats simply offered less. Stevenson was no civil rights firebrand; nor did his own sense of dignity make him comfortable about groveling after minority group votes. That left a party with its FDR legacy, some northern pro–civil rights liberals and intellectuals, and that was about all. Far from proposing legislation implementing at least the spirit of the *Brown* decision, or enacting one iota of what Truman's Committee on Civil Rights had recommended back in 1947, Democrats remained the party of unreconstructed segregationists. Republican candidates had little trouble directing their appeals to blacks with reminders that the James O. Eastlands and the Talmadges of Georgia were all Democrats. They were also bolstered by Attorney General Brownell's effective challenge to congressional Democrats to produce legislation. Harlem's powerful congressman, Adam Clayton Powell, Jr., made his financial and political pact with the White House and reciprocated with his support, which produced a 16.5 percent increase in the black vote on election day in his district.[120]

Black leadership elsewhere fell into line. Before long, the country's Afro-American newspapers, led by the *Amsterdam News* (New York City) and the *Pittsburgh Courier,* were for Ike and Dick. By election day, the candidates were backed by most of the black press, becoming part of the over three-fifths majority of papers nationally that declared for the ticket. According to an *Editor & Publisher* survey, only 15 percent came

out for Stevenson.[121] One measure of how well the Republicans succeeded was that they not only received the backing of most newspapers,
black and white, but increased their winning margin substantially in
twelve of the fourteen border and southern states.

Nor did Stevenson make much headway with another stalwart of the
New Deal vote, organized labor. "I look for a repetition of '52 in one
important respect," wrote Palmer Hoyt of the *Denver Post* to Nixon in
late September; "namely the pledge by labor leaders of the labor vote
to Stevenson and the fact of the individual members unions voting substantially for Ike." His prophecy was borne out by the final tabulation,
which, according to Michigan's Survey Research Center, showed that
Eisenhower and Nixon got 56 percent of the skilled workers and 53
percent among the unskilled. Others put the figure as high as 58 percent,
with the middle-class percentage calculated as 66.[122]

Mostly, there was no evidence that Nixon was a drag on the ticket.[123]
For the long run, something more significant was happening. A new
generation, one that came of age in postwar America, was shedding
traditional and Great Depression–born Democratic loyalties. The South
was only the most dramatic region of change. In another sense, what
was happening there was similar to movements elsewhere. Whites were
moving upward and taking aim at middle-class life-styles. Whether or
not they had yet arrived was less important to their political ideology
than the fact that there was sufficient expansion in the economy for such
aspirations to be within sight. Along with ethnic and regional shifts, they
were the other potential new Republicans, not merely attracted by Eisenhower but precursors of a more far-reaching trend. The traditional
forgotten men of American culture had become the new aspiring middle
class. In the long run, they were far more congenial to Nixon's antielitist,
antiestablishment, and proentrepreneurial views, together with his appeal to conservative populism, than to what has been described as the
Eisenhower ideal of a "corporate commonwealth."

Before the 1956 election, Claude Robinson, the Republican political
pollster and analyst, identified Nixon's sources of strength. Regionally,
he had the least support along the eastern seaboard and in the West but
was strongest in the Middle West and South. Nixon's primary identification remained as the "man who put Alger Hiss in jail" and with
"McCarthyism." That made him weakest with liberals and Jews, for
whom, explained the report, the "worst symbol" was "persecution."

What sets the Robinson report apart, however, is its clear analysis of
his support from those who longed to establish their identity as members
of the white middle class, or what may be called the aspiring middle
class. Nixon, an economic conservative, was surprisingly strong with
lower-income and nonunion workers as well as with farmers. As Robinson then summarized the essence of the vice president's appeal: "Plain

folks with grade and high school education who hew wood and draw water like Nixon. The anti-Nixon sentiment is particularly evident among the sophisticates . . . Independents, college people, professional men. Also among people of Jewish faith. It is in the reasoning of these people that the keys to voter feeling about Nixon are likely to be most clearly revealed." At about the same time, the American Institute of Public Opinion — commonly identified as the Gallup poll — found the Eisenhower-Nixon combination making gains since 1952 among manual workers, increasing their share from that group by 4 percent to a total of 49 percent. A similar increase was found among families of unionized workers.[124]

What Robinson and Gallup might have pointed out was that Nixon's forgotten Americans constituted the potential swing vote among Democrats rather than the bedrock of loyalist Republicans. He had not only the party loyalists, but also a lower white middle class of skilled and unskilled workers, especially the unorganized, and there were enough of them willing to cross party lines for Nixon to make a difference.[125]

11

The Global Vice President

HOW THE TWO-TERM limitation influenced Eisenhower's last four years in office will always remain something of a mystery. Several circumstances inhibit the ability to make a simple analysis, not the least of which were his age and physical condition. Another possibility is that, despite his continuing popularity, his final term produced a deterioration of the consensus that had kept him in power.

By the time Ike gave way to the much younger John F. Kennedy, the respite from war that followed the Korean armistice had been replaced by American assumption of the French role in Vietnam. The "spirit of Geneva" in the wake of Eisenhower's attendance at the first summit conference in 1955 had been replaced by new sources of deterioration in east-west relations: tension over the continued viability of West Berlin as a free city, the inauguration of space flights and competition for ballistic supremacy that escalated the arms race, the collapse of a projected meeting in Paris following the shooting down of an American spy plane over the Russian heartland, and the dawning of what was bound to be the most competitive arena of all, jockeying among the superpowers for influence among the developing nations, most of them recently decolonialized, soon to be known as the Third World.

Similarly, at home, the early post-McCarthy period was marked by both prosperity and, as Adlai Stevenson learned, a reduction of partisan polarization. Eisenhower's second term was also the period when conservatives in power experienced their greatest frustration over the economy. The standard of living was little aided even when the administration turned in three balanced budgets, not, at least, when the combined strains of inflation, high interest rates, and unemployment brought renewed doubts about Republican ability to manage the economy. There was also a vigorous counterrevolution among white southerners, who were more militant than at any time since Reconstruction. The resurgence of the Ku Klux Klan, the rise of White Citizens Councils, and the arguments of constitutional lawyers seeking to use the Tenth Amendment (states' rights) as a barricade against the intrusions of the Fourteenth (citizens' rights to equal protection under the law), all resisted Martin Luther King, Jr., and the efforts of his Southern Christian Leadership Conference. Suddenly, the notion of "placid fifties" evaporated. If, as one journalist then wrote, the Eisenhower decade was a time of postponement, the coming time of troubles was already visible. Relief from the cold war seemed as remote as ever and the short-lived consensus diminished before fresh perceptions of Soviet supremacy and social and political conflict at home.

Richard Nixon never forgot Earl Warren's advice to seize upon two or three issues at the most and become known for them.[1] During his race for the Senate, his identification with one major theme was complete, and that issue was communism, not only his issue but the bête noire that energized the mainstream of American society, its politics, its economy, its scientific and intellectual debates and advances. So it was that his career moved naturally from the web-of-subversion syndrome to the more advanced demands of cold war diplomacy.

More consistently than any other leader of his generation, Nixon reflected that dominant strain. By 1960, a significant number of Republicans would have preferred to have Senator Barry Goldwater of Arizona take the lead in sanitizing the world for the United States. To a considerable extent, they also drifted toward leaders and organizations that warned that the fight against communism was a new holy war.

Few matters of importance during those years can be understood without recalling what Archibald MacLeish wrote in 1949. "Never in the history of the world," explained MacLeish, one of America's most honored writers, "was one people as completely dominated, intellectually and morally, by another as the people of the United States by the people of Russia. . . . American political controversy was controversy sung to the Russian tune. . . . All this took place not in a time of national weakness or decay but precisely at the moment when the United States, having engineered a tremendous triumph and fought its way to a brilliant victory in the greatest of all wars, had reached the highest point of world power ever achieved by a single state."[2]

At home and abroad, the Communist menace explained the world, not as the "misbegotten child of the Enlightenment," but as the major countervailing force challenging the survival of a spiritually free, economically vibrant, and politically independent American democracy. "Our alternative," Nixon believed, "is progress *with* freedom — and, in fact, progress *because* of freedom."[3] His ups and downs revolved around the same essential battle. So little had changed in the intervening years that the editors of *The Atlantic* saw fit to reprint MacLeish's commentary during Jimmy Carter's final year as president and just before the coming of Ronald Reagan. Through all this, Nixon seemed able to keep abreast of political trends, never championing lost causes while, at the same time, remaining true to his special mission.

Nothing remarkable about his world view came out of those early campaigns. When he was a congressional candidate, domestic matters, especially those of immediate interest to his district, naturally got prime attention. Thus, he was able to argue that, "with the notable exception of dissent toward Democratic policy toward China," his record was "virtually 100%" in support of bipartisanship. His "entire stress" while battling for a second House term, Herb Klein later reminded him, "was on what you had [d]one for the district and on the Herter Committee and how you were needed to carry on this work."[4]

He was, it was true, the only westerner appointed to the nineteen-member Herter Committee; nor can one deny that his youth did not supply some balance. Still, when Speaker Martin assigned him to that "headline committee," it was after having been lobbied by such Nixon friends as Herman Perry and being assured that Herter himself endorsed the choice. Herter, then a congressman, chaired the select committee, which went to Europe in late August of 1947 in an effort to prepare for possible legislation to implement the Marshall Plan. When Nixon returned in mid-October, he became an active fighter for the Truman administration's program, combating a three-to-one sentiment against "give-away" programs through newspaper columns, radio talks, newsletters, and speeches in his district. "These speeches were received very favorably both by the audiences and the newspapers in the District," he later wrote to Rose Mary Woods. When recounting the effort in his memoirs, they were recalled as Nixon's response to the "classic dilemma" of how much a legislator should permit the wrongheadedness of his constituents to influence his vote.[5]

Americans generally shared the misperceptions of California's Twelfth District; or, in less politic terms, provincialism, naïveté, simple ignorance. Nixon, evidently amused, passed on a story he heard in London from General Jimmy Doolittle. The man who had become famous for his wartime air raids on Tokyo told of flying over Athens and looking down at the Acropolis and its ruins when a member of the crew came up to him and said, "Boy, General, our bombers certainly did a job on that place."[6]

Even if we had not done a job on Greece, the effects of war were still very visible to Nixon. He found much of the continent incapacitated and impoverished, vestiges of the recent brutalization. The German cities of Hamburg and Berlin looked like "great gaunt skeletons." He stood in the great hall of Hitler's former chancellery "and as we looked at the ruins and realized what destruction a dictator had brought upon himself and his people by reason of his totalitarian aggression, small thin-faced German boys attempted to sell us the medals which their fathers had won during the war as souvenirs." Not only in Germany, but wherever he went, he found "marked hunger and malnutrition on a universal scale among the people." In Verona, he asked a woman who had a child suffering from a severe case of rickets how they managed to cope in winter. "We go to bed," she replied. When he went to Trieste, he was told by an industrialist that "a good standard of living is the most dangerous enemy of communism," something Nixon hardly doubted. "We further must face the fact that if the people of Europe are faced on the one hand with starvation and no hope of improvement insofar as U.S. aid is concerned," he reported, "and they are confronted on the other hand with the promises of the Communists, that Europe will without question go Communist this winter." Such conditions were ready-made for exploitation.[7]

A shortage of effective leadership worsened the situation. Count Sforza, the Italian foreign minister, typified what his country had to offer as an alternative to those who looked to Moscow for guidance. "Sforza is a very able man," Nixon thought, "but he is suffering from a disease which too many of Europe's politicians are suffering from — old age, not only from the standpoint of years, but from the standpoint of his ability to recognize and cope with new political developments." The aristocrats merely tended to dismiss the Communists as "stupid"; they ignored the need to develop attractive alternatives for Italian youth.[8]

Frenchmen, on both the left and right, were puzzled by de Gaulle, not knowing whether he "will furnish the type of leadership" that was needed. "The difficulty with DeGaulle at the present time," said Nixon as he recorded his notes, "is that he has no program for France and too often acts upon impulse rather [than] upon a pre-determined plan which is needed by the country if it is going to recover." He quoted a French critic who told him that "DeGaulle in political matters thinks that he has a direct telephone line with God and that in making decisions all that he has to do is to get on the wire and get the word straight from God." What made France especially vulnerable to communism was the control Communists held over labor unions. "One of the members of our committee declared that the Communists could probably take over France by telephone at any time that Stalin wanted to order a general strike," he noted. In Italy, Nixon asked a businessman why the church could not be more effective in its fight against the Communists. "I consider myself to be a good Catholic," was the reply, "but on the other hand I do not want the priests in my house every day of the week. I want him there when I am born, when I marry and when I die, and maybe some other day, but no more than that."[9]

Such ineffectual individual and institutional responses were in contrast to Communist capabilities. Meeting with Giuseppe Di Vittorio, the Communist secretary general of the Italian Labor Confederation, Nixon found a talent superior to most of the American trade unionists with whom he had recently met during his work on the Education and Labor Committee. Di Vittorio argued that the right to strike was unnecessary in the USSR, a country not dominated by "capitalist reactionaries and employers." Their absence also made it "impossible for the foreign policy of Russia to be imperialist. Therefore it is not subject to criticism." As with the head of the Italian Communist party, Palmiro Togliatti, Di Vittorio "tied the Communist cause to the cause of Nationalism." Party posters pictured the nineteenth-century patriot Garibaldi and not the Soviet hammer and sickle.[10]

If nationalism was being turned by the Communists to their own advantage, so could the existence of rightist, antidemocratic regimes, something Nixon had expressed himself about long before going to Europe and confirmed by his own observations. It was obvious, as he later pointed out, that authoritarianism was also hindering what could be done to save the continent from "the twin specters of starvation and communism." In notes made as he went, he wrote that "we fought war against Total[itarianism]. We don't intend to subsidize another one. Govt. must not be the status quo — here are the seeds of another war. Must be a new society — with better break for common man — more goods." In Greece, he found popular resistance to any Communist attempt to take over by force, but matters were not helped by a government that in "some instances . . . follows policies which we would term reactionary in the United States." In England, he was warned by Minister of Food John Strachey that "if the people of Europe are faced on the one hand with stark reaction and on the other hand with Communism, they will definitely turn toward the Communists."[11]

Only their own capacity for force seemed to be much of a deterrent. He found the Greeks "individualistic" and opposed to guerrillas waging war against their government from such bordering Communist-dominated states as Albania and Yugoslavia. He asked some Greeks whether they thought that the German occupation was worse than they would find under Communist control and reported that a typical answer was that "the German is a man, the Communist a beast." Near the Yugoslavian border, in Trieste, he found similar revulsion about what had been heard about Communist rule in neighboring territory.[12]

Nixon's original report did not dwell on Red brutality. He emphasized almost entirely the Communist's ability to take advantage of political and economic instability to gradually win control. They had no hesitation about using any means to consolidate power. A typical judgment was the following about the Greek guerrilla situation: "It can definitely be said first that they are Communist led, that second they are Communist financed and supplied, and third that they are working to set up a Communist government which will owe its loyalty to Russia." His conclusion also included, in addition to what was then the standard comment about "lessons" that should have been learned about pre–World War II appeasement, a restatement of Truman's argument for sending military aid to Greece and Turkey: "If we abandon the Greek people to the Communists and allow them to accomplish their purposes, the other countries of Europe will then be easy prey for the threats and aggressive illegal tactics of the Communists in attempting to impose Communism upon other peoples of Europe against their will."[13]

In his published memoirs, however, the five-page description of his Herter Committee experience emphasizes "the violence that sometimes accompanied the communist threat." Nor do the memoirs repeat Nixon's on-the-scene concern about how authoritarianism hurt the cause of anticommunism. They recount the use of nationalism while expanding on his observation that "most of democratic Europe was either leaderless or, worse still, that many in the leadership class had simply capitulated to communism."[14] The consequences of right-wing rule, moreover, which concerned him at the time, were entirely omitted.

When Ralph de Toledano published his book in connection with Nixon's 1956 campaign, he reported that he was told by Nixon four years after the Herter mission that while "there was no more corrupt and unstable government in the world than the government of Greece . . . we recognized that it was not a question of the Greek government or something better, but a question of the Greek government or something worse, and we gave the Greek government the assistance which enabled it to defeat the Communists." That was a lesson Nixon learned, de Toledano added, that the State Department should have learned about China, instead of "splitting hairs over the 'corruption' of the Chinese Nationalists, ignored until it was too late and the seeds for the Korean war had flowered bloodily."[15] Thus was history rewritten just before Nixon became vice president — and later updated. Each version suited some contemporary need.

Essentially his 1947 impressions reinforced his judgment. He also assumed and argued, along with many legislators throughout the country, that economic assistance was a matter of enlightened self-interest. The American economy simply could not be detached from the success of postwar recovery overseas. Domestic manufacturers needed European markets, and farmers were even more desperate. While still in Trieste, Nixon issued a statement that emphasized the importance of foreign aid to "the economic and political future of our own people."[16] The House vote on the Marshall Plan, in which the congressman was part of a comfortable 313-to-82-vote majority, came at a time that coincided with the formal creation of the Progressive Citizens of America behind Henry Wallace and further polarization in the form of an incipient Dixiecrat rebellion against the Democratic party. The moment was the pinnacle of bipartisanship, and there was never any question that Nixon stood with the center. Virtually the entire political mainstream coalesced against opposition coming from the far left and fiscally conservative nationalists on the right.

The trip was educational, modifying some of Nixon's own inexperience and naïveté. His understanding of Communists, their ideology, and their mentality was unformed. He was still learning, "curious to see how their minds worked." Almost with the sense of experiencing a revelation, he reported that, despite their often crude manners, he would never again make the mistake of thinking that "Communist leaders are not very intelligent and very tough men." He found, he recalled thirty years later, that "without our food and aid, Europe would be plunged into anarchy, revolution, and, ultimately, communism." But, while still there, he wrote down the following prophetic notation: "A gov't rises or falls depending on how much it can get from the United States." In Milan, he also learned something about religion and communism. "Power of church; very rich, gives great deal of dough in fight on commies. Priests tell women how to vote at confession."[17]

Most noteworthy about his analysis, especially considering the near panic of some others at the time, was the absence of fear about a coming Red sweep across Europe. To have made such a prediction at the time would have been conventional; it was almost fashionable for western leaders, especially in the United States, to suggest a new barbarian invasion. Nixon's observations were anything but hysterical. No Soviet triumph was imminent. But money, leadership, and dedication were all essential to keep war-scarred nations from reaching out in desperation.

What that experience really did was to introduce Nixon to the living world of European-based imperatives. Largely confined to the eastern wing of the Republican party and to Democrats, they were actually as old as the republic itself. In the more recently updated tradition of Woodrow Wilson, they contrasted with the world of the China Lobby. Whereas the latter confirmed Nixon's heartland GOP orthodoxy, the former helped broaden his global view beyond the bounds of partisan loyalties.

Nixon's exposure to early postwar Europe helped him to understand the relationship between economic hardship and Communist expansionism. In the days before the cold war seemed irreversible, before the Czech coup and the Berlin blockade, his public statements lacked the military bite of later years. Only days after Truman's March 12, 1947, speech requesting a military aid program for Turkey and Greece, he expressed misgivings about the oligarchical government of King George. Before asking Americans for such a commitment, said Nixon, Truman had the duty to explain what kind of government we were proposing to support. "There should be no moral justification for upholding any government which is totalitarian, whether it be on the Right or the Left."[18]

Politically, of course, bipartisanship had its limits. The administration's troubles in the Far East were an Achilles heel too tempting for Republicans to resist, and Nixon stood with his party. Over two years before the collapse of the Kuomintang in Peking, he asked, "What is the difference between the spread of Communism in China and Red influence in the eastern Mediterranean?" The solutions were being proposed by the same people who were trying to save Chiang Kai-shek "by sending pinkos and fellow-travelers to fight Communism." And they were the same people who were backing off after pouring $400 million into the Chinese sinkhole.[19] Such criticism of Truman's handling of developments in Asia were surprisingly in tune with what many Democrats were saying.

That was Nixon before his Herter Committee experience. He recognized how discredited isolationism had become as a way of facing the world, how that innocence had been lost in the fight against Japan and Germany and was being left further behind by mounting tensions with the Soviet Union. That, as the cold war developed, became the collective wisdom, the consensus that brought together a broad spectrum of American opinion. Nixon parted with the center, however, in focusing on the problem of having our fight sabotaged by domestic "pinkos and fellow-travelers," who, he repeatedly stressed, were entrenched in government and labor unions. Even more revealing, especially in the matter of Greece, was a statement made with the passion of old-fashioned Anglophobia that there could be no "justification for intervening anywhere if the primary purpose is to save the British Empire." Then, in words that would be made ironic by future events, he declared that "Congress and the people are entitled to more facts than they have yet been given by the president before we embark upon this drastic venture."[20]

Nixon's position reflected the paradoxical nature of the type of nationalism that was especially common along the West Coast. The vast Pacific was at once a protective buffer and an avenue to the Orient, an object of interest dating back to the early days of the nation and the clipper ships of the China trade. Although at that time the potentials of the American continent were yet to be fully explored, a window on the Pacific also had its attractions. To those with an eye westward, Europe was remote, written off as Iberian fortune-hunters had forfeited the Mediterranean to the Venetians. If form follows function, desire follows the attainable. Europe was, moreover, the past, the motherland, the region of ancient encounters and traditions alien to the spirit and independence of the New World.

What happened to China plainly influenced American thinking about the Korean invasion. On June 25, 1950, little more than a half year after the forces of Mao Zedong secured their hold over the mainland, well over 100,000 North Korean Communist troops, bolstered by 150 tanks and 110 combat planes — hardly a mere border incursion — rushed across the thirty-eighth parallel into South Korea.

Almost immediately, before convening either the Congress or the United Nations, which had overseen the organization of the South Korean government, President Truman sent American air and naval forces to help the South Koreans. The Seventh Fleet was ordered to neutralize Formosa by patrolling the waters between the island and the Chinese mainland. The United Nations Security Council, then called into session (although without the presence of the Soviet Union, which was boycotting the organization for refusing to seat the new regime in Peking), asked member nations to send military aid to repel the aggression and urged a North Korean withdrawal. He was not going to war, said Truman, but when a reporter asked whether it was "a police action under the United Nations," the president agreed that was a fair description.[21] By the end of the month, only five days after the onset of the invasion, the president committed U.S. land forces to keep the peninsula from being overwhelmed. The objective was clear: to free South Korea and to make a point about the importance of deterring aggression. By late summer, while General MacArthur, as commander of the UN forces, was building up his naval and air support, the South Koreans were reduced to an enclave around the southeastern port of Pusan. Aggression had reached its high-water mark. In mid-September, the tide turned, with major assistance from MacArthur's landing on the west coast at Inchon, which outflanked enemy soldiers and hurled them northward. With the south apparently secure, its capital city of Seoul retaken, the general met with President Truman in a much-publicized conference at Wake Island. Together, they sealed an agreement to disregard warnings and push the enemy back, beyond the thirty-eighth parallel. Thus began the fateful drive toward the Yalu River, which ended in disaster with a late November counterattack by over a quarter-million Chinese Communist "volunteers." Once more, the UN forces, led by the United States and the Republic of Korea, dropped back below the line and Seoul fell for a second time. Once more, there was recovery, but no victory; just stalemate.

Few hesitated to assume that the United States had acted to counter the master plan for Russian domination. America, as the *Economist* of London put it, went through "months of degradation."²² Conditioned by tales of spies, real and imagined, and by inexplicable developments abroad, the public braced for assaults that seemed inevitable.

Only a few months earlier, Joe McCarthy had made his bold bid for national headlines. The sudden start of fighting was unexpected only because it began in Korea. Warnings about Red expansionism seemed to have been borne out. There were even expressions of relief that Moscow was showing its true colors. With the exception of a few voices of "dubious loyalty" on the far left, a consensus formed that was as solid as anything experienced during the entire cold war. It seemed as clear to everyone else as it did to Truman that, in his words, "Communism was acting in Korea just as Hitler, Mussolini, and the Japanese had acted ten, fifteen, and twenty years earlier. . . . If this was allowed to go unchallenged it would mean a third world war." Republicans and Democrats, isolationists and interventionists, fell over one another in condemning the latest example of Soviet expansionism and backed the president. Robert Taft, despite misgivings about being "stampeded into war," blamed the "outrageous, aggressive attitude of Soviet Russia." The *New York Times* called the attack "obviously Soviet-authorized." A State Department intelligence report assumed that it must "be considered a Soviet move" and saw the situation as one that tested the will of the United States to face the challenge. The almost immediate denial of responsibility issued by Moscow or the lack of evidence that the conflict went beyond Korean political rivalries became totally irrelevant. Nor did Truman's avoidance of direct accusations make any difference.²³ His military response and the drumbeat of politicians and the press left few Americans doubting what had happened.

To this day, the evidence is somewhat murky, but what is available points to a clash of nationalistic ambitions by the Communist, Soviet-oriented regime under Kim Il-sung in the north and President Syngman Rhee in the south. Each wanted to lead a unified Korea, with Rhee putting as much pressure on the United States for assistance as Kim Il-sung placed on the Russians. The north, with weapons supplied by the Soviets, struck at a moment of Rhee's political vulnerability, the interests of Korean nationalism clearly subordinating Moscow's role. Furthermore, the Russians were led to believe there would be no invasion before August. Caught off guard by their temporary abandonment of the United Nations, they were unable to use their Security Council veto to thwart a countermove. Nevertheless, as two historians have put it, the start of the war brought unquestioned assumptions about the Soviet role and the "chief issue was not *whether*, but *how*, the United States should prepare." That reaction was confirmed by the Gallup organization in midsummer. Sixty-eight percent of the respondents to their survey thought that it was more important that "Russian expansion in Asia and Europe be stopped" than to keep the country "out of a major war."[24]

A true civil war, which is what the conflict in Korea was, came to be regarded as part of the east-west confrontation. The international climate, and political dialogue at home, overlooked the actual three-way tensions created between North Korea, the Soviet Union, and the People's Republic of China. First, in what galled the Pyongyang regime of Kim Il-sung, the Russians, who had equipped its forces, withheld their heaviest military matériel once the war started, limiting their client state to conventional weapons that were no match for what the United States supplied to the south. Support was also limited in other ways, all indicative of less than enthusiastic backing from Moscow, which proposed truce talks in 1951 without much consultation with the Chinese or North Koreans. Nor did the Soviets remain steadfast with the Chinese allies, stepping back from seeing the conflict as a prelude to an American invasion of the Asian mainland and attributing the war to U.S. economic imperialism with Korea as the goal. Finally, while no side wanted to continue the war as much as did Syngman Rhee, with his cherished hope of unification fully dependent upon an all-out American commitment, the withdrawal of support from Moscow gave neither Pyongyang nor Peking much choice but to accept the truce in July 1953.[25] The experience taught the Chinese much about Russian reliability.

Nevertheless, even a president less positive that international communism was the villain would have done the same as Truman. The loss of China was too fresh in that summer of 1950. Another major Communist victory was intolerable. The diplomatic price of inaction would also have been high, given the inevitable perceptions around the world of an America once again immobilized while communism expanded. In all this, there was no way that Korea could not have been made to appear as an example of western resolve. Historian Burton I. Kaufman has put it quite simply: "In fact, after the Communist victory in China, Korea became the only symbol left of America's willingness to contain Communist expansion in Asia. Washing its hands of Korea would be a signal to other Asians that the United States had abandoned them as well." [26] Or as Kaufman then adds, in a passage that, with the alteration of a few words, can be used to describe much of America's cold war experience:

> In other words, the credibility of the administration's foreign policy was at issue in the Korean War, both abroad and at home, both among America's allies and its adversaries. In such a situation of crisis as seemed to face the United States in the summer of 1950, furthermore, the President had to act forthrightly and unequivocally. Anything less would be an indication of weakness on his part, which the enemies of the United States and foes of the administration could use to their benefits. Once Truman and

his closest advisers accepted these basic assumptions — as they did almost immediately after receiving news of the fighting in Korea — there really seemed no course open to them other than the one they followed.[27]

The experience proved unfortunate for Truman's presidency. He relieved MacArthur from his command in April 1951 — a move that brought predictable outcries, including resolutions of impeachment — after the general repeatedly complained that Washington failed to understand that there was "no substitute for victory." MacArthur, even in the face of a Sino-Soviet mutual assistance pact, wanted to take America's first limited war to the Chinese mainland to destroy military bases and industrial capacity. His plans included nuclear weapons and using Chiang Kai-shek's troops from Formosa as a southern diversion. Truman, wanting to keep the war limited, warned that expansion could lead to a major conflagration, and bore the full weight of outrage when he replaced General MacArthur with Matthew Ridgway. The president's popular standing reached a new low. A long military standoff, with sporadically intense battles, paralleled the simultaneous efforts to reach a truce at the tent in Panmunjom.

Meanwhile, Nixon's range broadened. He moved from being one whose political roots had been identified with internal security to someone who, as the frustrations over Korea became more intense, became a prominent participant in the debates over what to do about the war. He, as did most Republicans, applauded Truman's intervention. When Truman fired MacArthur, however, Nixon, then a freshman senator, parted with the president and the concept of fighting a limited war.

Once bipartisanship collapsed, Nixon went with his party. On the day the general was ordered relieved, the senator held the floor of the upper chamber and repeated the common charge that Secretary of State Dean Acheson, in a speech made in January 1950, had just about invited the attack by not including South Korea within the U.S. Far Eastern defense perimeter. But few Americans regarded the territory as vital, especially when the Communists had the entire Chinese mainland, and this was evident by the fact that MacArthur himself had outlined a defensive perimeter similar to Acheson's months earlier when he told a British journalist that "our line of defense runs through the chain of islands fringing the coast of Asia."[28]

Another characteristic of the cold war thereby became evident: various locations, however innocuous by themselves, suddenly acquired symbolic value because they became momentary areas of east-west competition, whether military or psychological.[29] Korea was simply not anticipated as an especially likely arena. But it had happened, and had drawn bipartisan support. With the firing of MacArthur, which symbolized the frustration of a limited war, Truman's opponents could attack him by hailing their maligned military hero.

Nixon, helping to lead the way, wasted no time in sponsoring Senate Resolution 126, which called on the president to reverse himself, to recognize that he had not "acted in the best interests of the American people . . . and should restore General MacArthur to the commands from which he was removed." Americans were "shocked, disheartened, endangered," he declared, and "the happiest group in the country will be the Communists and their stooges." His mail was encouraging, one hundred to one in support. Over a period of months, even while the general's "There is no substitute for victory" was seeping into the consciousness of the American people, Nixon carried on the fight. On an "America's Town Meeting of the Air" radio broadcast, he declared that "we cannot get out of Korea because this would be the greatest possible encouragement we could give to the communist aggressors in Asia and would probably result eventually in the fall of all of Asia to the Communists and then a Third World War. A political settlement with the Chinese Communists is not possible because they insist that such a settlement must give them a seat in the United Nations and control over the Island of Formosa. . . . Therefore, I believe that we have no other choice than to take the necessary steps which will end the war in Korea with victory, and not appeasement." Later, when it came down to accepting an armistice along a cease-fire line that roughly approximated the thirty-eighth parallel — a division, in other words, not very different from where the war would have ended had Truman and MacArthur not decided to push beyond their original objectives — Nixon stood with those on the right, including Dulles, who were steadfastly behind Rhee as the Korean unifier. He saw the Chinese as the chief scourge of the region. If the war accomplished anything, it placed Peking on notice. As he told a national audience after the fighting came to an end, "When the Communists failed to extend their empire by overt aggression in Korea, they lost their chance to extend their control over the other nations in Asia. If they had not been stopped in Korea, the risk of their moving somewhere else in Asia or in Europe would have been increased immeasurably."[30]

He considered Korea a case of outright aggression, pure and simple, never questioning that raw military expansionism, whether Russian or Chinese, was at the heart of the matter. When, as president, he traveled to Peking in 1972 in the much-celebrated opening to China, Nixon and Zhou Enlai recalled the Korean affair in convenient diplomatic terms. Both agreed that "Korea had all been a ghastly miscalculation, fomented by irresponsible men in the Kremlin." But ten years after that, out of the White House and when writing a book called *Leaders,* he returned to the view, as expressed by MacArthur, that the Chinese intervention demonstrated "the same lust for the expansion of power which has animated every would-be conqueror since the beginning of time."[31]

This became evident by the time American diplomacy in the Far East encountered trouble. A good many of the frustrations of trying to resolve postwar problems in the more familiar area of anxiety, Europe, were also present in Asia. The containment of Soviet expansionism that bound the western alliance had little applicability to China. Neither Chiang Kai-shek's regime nor the French colonial holdings in the Associated States of Indochina (Vietnam, Laos, and Cambodia) could be upheld with much credibility as serving either democratic idealism or concepts of self-determination. Too many Frenchmen, especially those tied to commercial ventures in Southeast Asia, wanted to hold on at all costs. The United States, long since recognizing the arguments for independence, was caught in a dilemma, for abandoning France's colonial interests might ease the way for Communist domination over the area. Moreover, placating the French was important in the interest of preserving the western alliance for European defenses. To further complicate matters, it soon became abundantly obvious that while Republicans largely backed President Truman's responses against potential or real Soviet ambitions, the administration's record in Asia was far more vulnerable.

The French predicament became an American dilemma, a determining force that ultimately caused Washington to supercede Paris on the Vietnam escalator. The interests of the Elysée Palace simply could not be ignored. In addition, once Soviet expansionism was assumed as the culprit in Korea, it was easier to blame the problem in Indochina on a civil war that pitted Marxists against prowestern democrats. Casually dismissing those who, like FDR, had recognized the destructive potential of continued colonialism, Truman saw America's role as an effort to prop up both Asia and Europe by accepting France's self-serving interpretation of the problem. The Korean War became the obvious, handy confirmation. Wooing France and containing a Red threat meant underwriting the resistance against the Vietminh, a coalition of nationalists and Communists led by Ho Chi Minh. "Look, you people are making one very bad error," Eisenhower later recalled that he told the French. "You're letting the world, and particularly the people in Indo China believe that you're still fighting a colonial war. You've got to make this thing a matter between freedom and communism."[32]

So the tragedy began to take shape. Even before Eisenhower became president, the State Department concluded that, aside from supporting France, there was no alternative to Communist rule in Vietnam. From there it was pure logic to give an open endorsement to a unified state of Vietnam under the playboy, puppet emperor, Bao Dai. The irony was that the dissolute ruler became, for naive Americans, the potential bearer of Vietnamese freedom. The syllogism was simple: If stopping communism was essential in Korea, why not in Southeast Asia? American financial aid moved continuously upward, totaling $2.5 billion from fiscal 1950 through fiscal 1954, the first Eisenhower budgetary year. Also included, during the final half of Truman's second term, were 539,847 tons of American military equipment.[33]

Inheriting the involvement from the Democrats, just as with the military situation in Korea, left no room for options other than traveling even further along the same disastrous route. As historian George McT. Kahin has put it, "If millions of Americans had been persuaded that their government actually could have prevented the communists from coming to power in China, then it was plausible to assume they might also believe it had the capacity to deny Vietnam to communist control."[34]

What is less likely are suggestions that economic issues were peripheral to American policy in the Far East, either for U.S. interests or for Japan. If that argument has any merit, U.S. policy was again misled. More to the point, it was peripheral, it certainly did not appear that way to the planners.[35]

Washington did act through concern that Japan could succumb to a Marxist-controlled Far East. In the final months of the Truman administration, with American soldiers still bogged down in the Korean hills after two years of frustration, the National Security Council adopted a position paper, NSC 124/2, that cited Japan for its critical need for rice from Burma and Thailand. It was very obvious to the NSC that losing any part of Southeast Asia "to communist control as a consequence of overt or covert Chinese Communist aggression would have critical psychological, political and economic consequences"; all of the region's vital resources, not only rice, but rubber, tin, and petroleum would also be jeopardized. That assumption having been established, nothing changed with the coming of the Eisenhower presidency. Early in the administration, Secretary of State John Foster Dulles said that "if Southeast Asia were lost, this would lead to the loss of Japan. The situation of the Japanese is hard enough with China being commie. You would not lose Japan immediately, but from there on out the Japs would be thinking of how to get on the other side."[36]

At this time, Nixon learned more about Japan and Southeast Asia at first hand. In October 1953, only a few months after the Korean armistice, acting at Eisenhower's suggestion, he and Pat undertook a long goodwill trip to the Asian continent. Before leaving, he underwent three days of briefing; no factor was as prominent as Japan. Tokyo's need for imports, especially foodstuffs, said his briefing book, was as great as ever.

The dependence on foreign commerce for economic welfare was greater than that of any other country. "Only through expansion of its exports of manufactured goods will Japan be able to earn sufficient exchange to pay for its essential imports." The crux of the matter was that there might be no choice. Self-support was inseparable from the prosperity of noncommunist Asia. Expanding economies there "will result indirectly in an increased demand for imports from Japan and elsewhere." That meant maintaining "free" Asian economies open to Japan. Left with no alternatives for their economic viability, the Japanese could well turn away from the west and secure trade ties with a Marxist Southeast Asia, and, warned the briefing book, "it would be a tragedy to world security if Japan were to fall under Communist domination." Vietnam itself was not so much a source for Japan's needs, but its rice, rubber, and coal were attractive to China. Should Peking take that over, the "domino effect" could lead to the subversion of Thailand, Burma, and Malaya and eventual depletion of Japan's trading zone.[37]

The president later made much the same point when he said at a news conference that without that region as a trading area, "Japan, in turn, will have only one place in the world to go — that is, toward the Communist areas in order to live." In meetings with editors and legislative leaders, he was very explicit: "If we don't assist Japan, gentlemen, Japan is going Communist," he warned. "Then instead of the Pacific being an American lake, believe me it is going to be a Communist lake. If we do not let them trade with Red China, with Southeast Asia, then we are going to be in for trouble. Of course, we do not want to ruin our own industries to keep Japan on our side, but we must give them assistance." The point was not one to be treated frivolously, and administration policymakers were persistent, Dulles telling the Los Angeles World Affairs Council that it would require "little imagination to visualize what would happen if Russia, China and Japan become a united hostile group in the Pacific." In his usual plain manner, the president told the cabinet that Japanese industrial power was bound to the resources and manpower of the east. "The Reds are playing their own cards in Japan very well," he said. "They are capitalizing on the pacifist tendencies of the people and on the fact that, after all, the only two A-bombs used in World War II were dropped on Japan."[38]

Japan, along with Indochina, became an essential part of Nixon's itinerary. The United States, Nixon was advised before he and his wife flew across the Pacific, must realize that trade policies in such commodities as rubber, tin, wool, cotton, jute, wheat, meat, and dairy products "will have profound effect on [the] economic and political future of countries concerned, and considerable strategic impact so far as the whole anti-Communist struggle is concerned." While still in Tokyo, he lectured Japanese reporters on the need for that nation's rearmament. The

United States had made a mistake by mandating disarmament as part of Japan's rehabilitation, but the time had come to acknowledge and undo that error, which was made when Soviet intentions had yet to become clear. After his return, he warned that the fall of Indochina would place Thailand in an "almost impossible position. The same is true of Malaya with its rubber and tin. The same is true of Indonesia. If Indonesia goes under Communist domination the whole of South East Asia will be threatened, and that means that the economic and military security of Japan will inevitably be endangered also. That indicates . . . why it is vitally important that Indochina not go behind the Iron Curtain." Nixon kept in mind a point once made by Whittaker Chambers: "What people do not understand is that for the communists, the war in Korea is not a war about Korea, it is a war about Japan." In the same way, Nixon recalled in 1985, "the war in Vietnam was not just about Vietnam but about Cambodia, Laos, Indonesia, Angola, Ethiopia, and Nicaragua."[39] Publicly and privately, it was clear that the administration regarded Japan as the key to the Pacific.

The Far East trip took him to nineteen countries over a ten-week period, giving him his first intimate view of a region that eventually preoccupied much of his thinking. In Malaya, he saw firsthand the "new kind of Communist warfare that was already threatening the stability of the entire region," guerrilla warfare. From Syngman Rhee, he was encouraged about the wisdom of being unpredictable about readiness to use force. In Vietnam, he wore battle fatigues and talked to both French and Vietnamese soldiers.[40]

It was all very discouraging. Once Vietnam was lost, he feared, all of Southeast Asia would inevitably follow, and then Japan or even Australia. Yet, in his last night in Hanoi, he managed an upbeat talk about "the fight of the forces of freedom against the force of totalitarianism which is centered in Vietnam," even adding that "the tide of aggression has reached its peak and has finally begun to recede." To the American counselor of the embassy in Saigon, who shared his outlook, he later explained that "I still believe we must play it publicly on an optimistic note." "Both my parents left Hanoi depressed," Julie Nixon Eisenhower has written, "convinced that the French, if not losing the war, did not know how to win it."[41]

When he delivered his report to the American public just before Christmas, his words were somewhat less than glowing; if not exactly grave, they were at least somber, combining alarm and faith. He stressed accomplishments, dangers, and ideals. "If China had not gone Communist," he explained, "we would not have had a war in Korea." If not for that setback, "there would now be no war in Indochina, and there would be no war in Malaya." Eight hundred million Asians on the Chinese side were sponsoring war in Indochina and Malaya. "They have stirred up revolutions in Burma and Indonesia and the Philippines, and they have supported subversion everywhere in this area." While not actually under the gun, Thailand, too, was being threatened by "subversion within, and by possible Communist aggression at any time from without." Hardly anyplace was safe from the "danger of subversive tactics" attempting to deny popular desires for independence, economic progress, and peace. He made a strong point about Chinese responsibility for disturbances throughout Southeast Asia. Then, the man who had been a chief critic of Truman's policy and key supporter of MacArthur in Korea, added some advice: "We should recognize that the time is past when we should try to reach agreement with the Communists at the conference table by surrendering to them. We are paying the price in Asia for that kind of diplomacy right now." Negotiations, he was advising, entailed risks that were unacceptable.

We were, he made clear, facing an insidious enemy, one quick to foment trouble at every opportunity. Part of their design, he warned, was to create "the impression in the minds of the people that we are arrogant, that we are mean, that we are prejudiced, that we are superior, that we are bent on war rather than on a program that will lead to peace." The most lethal force was subversion and revolution, which were far more potent among those deprived of basic cultural, religious, and economic freedoms. "They want fundamental recognition of their equal dignity as human beings." We, as a nation, could not appeal to their needs, he warned, when we practiced racial discrimination or prejudice. Every violation of such basic rights was "blown up by the Communists abroad, and [hurts] America as much as an espionage agent who turns over a weapon to a foreign country."[42]

Nixon's public report was but one of several indications of his findings — and, to a considerable degree, of the trip's educational value. One outlet came during a two-hour speech to the National Security Council. His performance before that secret body, we have been told, afforded his first recognition as "a respected participant in the nation's foreign policy councils." Information about what he said, which is also available from Nixon's own notes, emphasizes his warning that a collapsing Indochina would carry with it Malaya, Thailand, and then Japan, "since a bulk of her trading was with that area." Then, with NATO as a model, he stressed the need for military encirclement of the "Sino-Soviet empire" by building a mutual defense crescent that would include Turkey, Iran, Pakistan, Indochina, Formosa, and Japan. After a talk with Prime Minister Jawaharlal Nehru of India, he was convinced that an impotent noncommunist Asia was an important promoter of the "neutralism" that attempted to avoid a stake in the cause of prowestern democracy.[43]

His own notes are revealing in other ways. They reaffirm the belief expressed in his public speeches that the Communists were "losing support among peoples everywhere throughout Asia." Read, for example, the following notations from his general impressions: "Communist tide throughout Far East and S. E. Asia beginning to recede. Free world strength on upgrade, probably due to more aggressive policy of United States and the accesses [*sic*] of Communists."[44]

But his tone was far from complacent. Troop morale in Vietnam was poor and not helped by continued talk about a negotiated end to the war. Ho Chi Minh was "far more appealing as a popular leader" than Bao Dai, who was neither in touch with the people nor eager to do anything about it. Nor had the colonial forces done much to develop an adequate native civil service. In a footnote, he added: "In considering Indochina, vital to realize complete control that Chinese have over future status of this war."

His own report failed to substantiate that last point. When he explained the appeal of communism, he pinpointed vital domestic elements. Reds were strong within labor unions and educational institutions and among intellectuals. Popular responses were sympathetic because white Europeans were associated with economic distress and poverty, and there was additional support because they were able to take advantage of local nationalist movements. Independence, it was hoped, would lead to peace, prosperity, and civil freedom, including respect and tolerance for their various religious faiths. "For example," Nixon added, "the sending of missionaries to many of these countries is considered insulting. Missionaries should be reserved for savages." Moreover, he noted, the "American attitude toward S. E. Asia should not be conditioned by the views of the English, French and Dutch who have failed." At the moment, however, "people in Asia do not care for U.S. type propaganda and immediately discount it."

Interestingly, Nixon showed his first awareness of how the United States was being hurt by the publicity about "rooting out" the "disloyal" for security reasons. He offered the following advice:

> The political attacks on the State Department and the foreign service during the last two years in particular [a clear reference to Dulles's efforts to protect his position from attacks by McCarthy], although completely justified in many instances, have cast a public odium on the foreign service. No one wants to make a career in a discredited service and no important Administration officials . . . have defended the service publicly. . . . Neither the Secretary of State nor any other key Department officials has [*sic*] as yet proclaimed publicly that the Department has cleaned house and that there will be an end to firings for political reasons. This has created an atmosphere of considerable insecurity as to the future. . . . There is almost a pathological hatred of [Scott]

McLeod everywhere. [McLeod was administrator of the State
Department's Bureau of Security and Consular Affairs, charged
with identifying "security risks."] He controls the lives and careers of all these people; he is a stooge of McCarthy working in
the State Department; he knows *nothing* about the foreign service
and he has never visited a single diplomatic post outside the
United States. . . . I can guarantee that nothing would improve
morale faster than to have McLeod fired. He is a symbol of
arbitrary, political interference of the worst sort.[45]

As the report illustrates, Nixon was blunt. He was also on his way
toward becoming perhaps the best-informed man in the administration.
"He sure does his homework," remarked an intelligence official, "and if
you don't know the real answer when he asks a question, it's a lot better
to say so." Not hesitating about making his preparation obvious, he made
others uneasy, at times even the secretary of state.[46]

Only months later, when most Americans were relieved that, for the
first time in five years, no young men were in combat anywhere, Nixon
made some off-the-record comments about the situation in Southeast
Asia that, suddenly, raised the crisis at Dienbienphu, where a large
French force had been under siege since November, to front-page prominence. His remarks stirred anxieties within both the administration and
the Congress, distressed the American people, and, on the eve of a
foreign ministers conference on Korea and Indochina scheduled for
Geneva, created new questions about exactly what Eisenhower and Dulles
were planning to do about France's deteriorating colonial position.

The forum was at a Washington luncheon of the American Society of
Newspaper Editors on April 16, 1954, and the remark that made front-
page headlines came during the question-and-answer session that followed his talk. The editor and publisher of the *Evening Herald* of Rock
Hill, South Carolina, Talbot Patrick, asked whether the vice president
thought the United States might consider sending troops to Indochina
in the event of a French withdrawal.

Like the rest of the administration, Nixon had been living with the
crisis for months. He had only recently returned from the area. His
close-up view of the situation, which included meeting with General
Henri Navarre about what further assistance could be offered for the
beleaguered French, gave him insights that left him impatient with the
general indecisiveness that characterized official Washington. Eisenhower, he saw, had gone from seemingly total rejection of any commitment, even telling the American public in a February news conference
that he could not conceive of anything more tragic than for Americans
to get involved in an all-out war in the Far East, to calling Indochina's

defense "of transcendent importance." By late March and early April, it seemed, the president was willing to draw the line; there was no chance that the United States would do much beyond sending a token detachment of two hundred technicians. Any significant intervention could only result from "united action," which meant acting in concert with France, Great Britain, New Zealand, Australia, Thailand, and the Philippines, thereby putting in place the conditions for possible intervention in case of disaster in Indochina. A coalition would, in addition, be a helpful backup for action should the Geneva conference fizzle. United action was also a prelude to some formal mutual security mechanism, especially in Dulles's mind, but to the president it was indispensable before any intervention could gain the approval of Congress and the public. For a president who approved his National Security Council's objective of preventing "Southeast Asia from passing into the Communist plot" but who, at the same time, "could not imagine the United States putting ground forces anywhere" on that mainland, "united action" was the only answer. Most recently, in Nixon's presence, Eisenhower had told the NSC that "we are not prepared now to take action with respect to Dien Bien Phu in and by itself, but the coalition program for Southeast Asia must go forward as a matter of greatest urgency." Having gone a long way toward considering American involvement in the French predicament, even verging for a while on decisive intervention, the president, along with his secretary of state, fell back on the premise that only direct Chinese intervention could justify that kind of response. To Nixon, that meant doing very little.[47]

As he pointed out at the NSC meeting of April 6, united action was completely untested as a way of answering subversive aggression. It evaded the issue in favor of an ambiguous and possibly ineffectual long-range regional organization. Turning to Dulles, Nixon said, "At some point or other, the United States must decide whether it is prepared to take action which will be effective in saving free governments from internal Communist subversion," thereby stating what he, unlike the secretary, regarded as the crux of the matter: the imminence of Marxist penetration by guerrillas rather than through direct intervention. Nixon clearly cited the former as the greater danger.[48]

It also placed him in league with Admiral Arthur Radford, then chairman of the Joint Chiefs of Staff. Both the vice president and the admiral shared abhorrence at permitting the fall of the French base, however others regarded Dienbienphu as merely symbolic. Radford, while agreeing with the rest of the NSC about the inadvisability of committing U.S. ground forces, continued to hold out for what was known as Operation VULTURE, a massive air strike that contemplated the use of tactical atomic weapons.[49] Nixon, wanting to accomplish the same objective while never clearly signing on to the Radford plan, feared that merely falling back on a regional defense agreement missed the point. The United States had to be willing to assert itself right then and there in some significant way to prevent the French collapse.

When, at the editor's luncheon, Mr. Patrick's question came, Nixon didn't hesitate, but he was careful to label the point about the use of troops an assumption and said he doubted it would happen. Then, instead of evading the hypothetical question, he replied that "the United States is the leader of the free world, and the free world cannot afford in Asia a further retreat to the Communists. . . . But under the circumstances, if in order to avoid further Communist expansion in Asia and particularly in Indochina, if in order to avoid it, we must take the risk now by putting American boys in, I believe that the executive branch of the government has to take the politically unpopular position of facing up to it and doing it, and I personally would support such a decision."[50]

Despite having been given off the record, his remarks were revealed in the next day's papers. It was a time of public ignorance of Operation VULTURE. The public was aware that American financial aid was being given to the French and that some personnel were stationed there, but unaware of what else was being contemplated; Nixon's suggestion suddenly raised the possibility that American boys could be thrown into a new conflict. Hardly a word of support came from anywhere. Jim Hagerty, who privately called the statement "foolish," immediately said he could not confirm that Nixon had reflected the president's view. He simply had no knowledge of the story. In Georgia, where Eisenhower was in the temporary White House on the grounds of the Augusta National Golf Club, Dulles hurriedly conferred with the president about how to handle the ensuing protests without weakening his bargaining position with the Communists at Geneva. His solution was to tell reporters that the use of U.S. troops was "unlikely" but not impossible. Defense Secretary Charles Wilson added that his department did not intend to send men to Indochina. Senator Hubert Humphrey, the Minnesota Democrat, complained that congressional committees had not been alerted to the possibility and wanted to know how the administration could reconcile Nixon's remarks with statements that we would not become involved in conflicts on "the periphery of the world — the Korea kind of struggles." Key legislative leaders of both parties — Leverett Saltonstall, chairman of the Senate Armed Services Committee, Alexander Wiley, chairman of the Senate Foreign Relations Committee, Senators Ralph Flanders of Vermont and John F. Kennedy of Massachusetts — all joined in denying that the United States was about to have "another Korea." The publication of Gallup's first postcomment survey merely confirmed what the reactions had already made obvious.

Fully 68 percent of those who responded opposed sending U.S. soldiers; only a little over one-fifth thought the idea had merit.[51]

But Nixon was not discouraged from pressing his alert. The reality, he said in Cincinnati only three days later, was that the Indochinese war was not just a civil war but a matter of aggression, controlled, supported, and directed by Communist China. While the administration had no real desire to send troops, he added, the loss of the area could jeopardize all of Southeast Asia and Japan. The Kremlin could even be sufficiently emboldened to start a world war. Journalist John Chamberlain caught Nixon exactly right when he commented that the vice president "saw from close up that the Indo-Chinese 'civil' war was not a war about Indo-China, but a war about everything from Tokyo to Melbourne, and from Melbourne to the ultimate fate of Communist influence in Italy and France."[52]

Nothing had so stirred American apprehension over the question of peace or war since the negotiations at Panmunjom. The world wanted to know whether the vice president's remarks were an authorized ploy by an administration trying to gauge how the public might accept the possible use of troops.

In truth, although it made little difference, the whole thing was unplanned. One might argue that Nixon was dissembling if he really thought such remarks made before a roomful of newspaper executives could truly be kept off the record; his remarks promptly constituted the lead story, where he was identified only as "a high Administration source" and as a "highly placed official" who was not a foreign policy spokesman. The anonymity was short-lived when the *Times* of London ran an account that fingered Nixon as the unmistakable source and *France-Soir* of Paris left even less to the imagination, while a Republican congressman from Michigan pinpointed him directly in an interview with a local paper. Nevertheless, the evidence offers little beyond the reasonable conclusion that Nixon, consistent with a tendency to overstep, was on his own, giving a reporter a spontaneous answer to a speculative question. He spoke to Dulles a few days later and expressed some pique that the press had not chosen to report the part of his remarks that endorsed everything the secretary was doing. He wanted to endorse the administration's approach in Asia, which, unlike the Korean experience, was not one of "weakness and vacillation." He had not, in any event, intended to make news and hoped that he had done nothing to upset policy. Years later, when he was interviewed for the Dulles Oral History Project at Princeton University, Nixon recalled that in making his highly publicized remarks he was merely reflecting the feelings of the secretary of state.[53]

If he served as a sounding board for anyone, it was more likely the president than Mr. Dulles. In a telephone conversation with Republican senator H. Alexander Smith of New Jersey, only three days after Nixon's remark, Dulles called the matter "unfortunate" and assumed it would soon blow over. That same day, Dulles met with Eisenhower in Augusta and the total absence of any reference to Nixon in the memorandum of that conversation encourages the view that his warning about the use of troops was not out of line one way or the other. When the secretary's sister, Eleanor, was reminded of the matter in 1970, she called the statement "somewhat rash" and added that her other brother, Allen, who was then director of the Central Intelligence Agency, agreed that Foster was not ready to go that far. Later, while recovering from his heart attack, Eisenhower showed his awareness of Nixon's tendency to overstep his authority by sending him a polite but firm note before the secretary left for a foreign ministers conference. Dulles was about to attend the meeting, said the president, with his "complete confidence" and must not be circumscribed in any way.[54]

Ironically, however, in an administration where most bellicose statements were assumed to have come from the State Department, Nixon's controversial remarks fulfilled a presidential function. Eisenhower had already arranged a legislative leaders meeting to demonstrate how cool the Hill was to unilateral intervention. If Nixon's comments served any purpose, they confirmed that the public was not any more receptive. They were also in tune with the Eisenhower-Dulles management of foreign policy, contributing to the cultivation of deliberate ambiguity, a tactic that worked particularly well in the Far East. As the president once indicated in an oft-quoted comment to Jim Hagerty, it was best to "keep them guessing." Kept before the public, at the moment, was the matter of Indochina, and allowed to float was the option of military intervention. Political writer Roscoe Drummond, who was close to the vice president, noted that the remarks about sending troops reflected "Mr. Nixon's awareness of all the information which comes before the National Security Council" and doubted "if Mr. Eisenhower is at all upset." Yet, so inscrutable was Ike, revealed Nixon by implication, that it was not until after Dulles had died that he said that both president and secretary of state were with him "all the way" on the troop issue. Even then, the revelation contains no attribution; nor does the wording indicate that it was said directly by Eisenhower to Nixon. But we do know that the president called him from Augusta shortly after he made the comment about troops and advised him not to worry, suggesting that his words might prove useful in alerting the country to the seriousness of the crisis. When Nixon later published a little book on his own presidential experience with Indochina, he recalled that not intervening in the battle of Dienbienphu was America's "first critical mistake. . . . By standing aside as our ally went down to defeat, the United States lost its last chance to stop the expansion of communism in Southeast Asia at little cost to itself."[55]

What followed is well known and will remain as the textbook example of the incremental and insidious consequences of a diplomatic and military enterprise characterized by uncertainty about the nature of the enemy and the objectives of the mission. Dienbienphu fell in early May. Gradually thereafter, the United States began to supplant the French role in Indochina. At the foreign ministers conference at Geneva, Vietnam was divided into zones separated by the seventeenth parallel. Indochina was no Korea, either historically or culturally, and the line of latitude was different, but the attempted solution was the same, a convenient division of the land into Communist and noncommunist governments. In the north, Ho Chi Minh ruled from Hanoi; in the south, an ascetic Roman Catholic, who had been at the Maryknoll Seminary in the United States and who was known for the intensity of his honesty and fervor of his nationalism, was virtually handpicked by the Americans and installed in Saigon as premier. Subsequent elections legitimized his rule, so Ngo Dinh Diem became president. At least as agreed to at Geneva, the Ho Chi Minh and Diem states were to last until 1956, when the Vietnamese people were to participate in a unifying referendum to end the partition. The arrangement worked out at Geneva had only implicit American support. Dulles judiciously let his presence be replaced by Under Secretary of State Walter Bedell Smith, and, with visions of the Roosevelt-Stalin-Churchill photograph taken at Yalta, avoided being pictured shaking hands with Chinese Communist leaders. By not signing the Geneva accords, the United States also sidestepped official responsibility for permitting North Vietnam to fall under what, at best, was tentative Communist rule.

By the end of 1954, continued American involvement in Southeast Asia was confirmed. Eisenhower committed himself to Diem's support. Dulles, pursuing mutual security, orchestrated a pact at Manila to assure collective defense of the area against an aggressor. The Military Assistance Advisory Group (MAAG) under Colonel Edwin Lansdale, whose fame had come from thwarting Communist guerrillas in the Philippines, worked covertly, along with the CIA, to protect Diem from his enemies, of which there were many: religious sects, the country's Buddhist majority, anticolonialist Communists and nationalists of the Vietcong, and cabals more devoted to largesse and corruption than to any ideology. Through it all, Washington watched the ups and downs, in 1955 almost deciding that Diem could no longer be supported, but, even at that dark moment, managing to prop him up. The Vietnamese mandarin remained as much an indispensable surrogate as a liability. As an NSC

report stated bluntly in late 1955, "U.S. support made it possible for
Prime Minister Diem to continue in office, to consolidate his position,
and to stimulate international sympathy and support for Free Vietnam."
But, too shrewd to be a puppet, he kept his lines open to a variety of
groups that had no desire to see egalitarian democratic reforms replace
the old colonial oligarchy. Diem, the imperial aristocrat, kept his power
base among the military, the country's Catholic minority, the growing
urban middle class in Saigon, and, most traditional in that agrarian
country, the landlords, who regained properties that the Vietminh had
redistributed among the peasants.[56] His insistence upon retaining the
prerogatives of an autocratic nationalist leader, his indifference to the
American desire to create an alternative to anticolonialism, never
stopped being a source of consternation in Washington; in the end, with
John Kennedy in the White House, it cost Diem his life.

Under Eisenhower, meanwhile, he in effect held the Americans hostage by their anticommunist petard. When he knew he could not win
the kind of election provided for at Geneva, he scuttled the plan, which
ended that means of unifying the country, and the United States went
along. However, the Americans warned him, the referendum to sanctify
him as president should show a sufficiently authoritative majority to
confirm his legitimacy. Not leaving anything to chance, the Diem forces
worked to manufacture the vote, in some districts giving him totals that
exceeded the size of the electorate; he got his way with a not-too-modest
98.2 percent.[57]

But Diem was easier to explain to the American people, and safer for
strategic interests, than any alternative, and he remained a client who
made supplicants out of the leaders of the free world. Several years later,
when the NSC and the CIA paved the way for his downfall, controversies
over responsibility for Diem's death (which included manufactured evidence in a fraudulent telegram plotted by Nixon aide Charles Colson)
conveniently overlooked that, far from promoting the free world cause
in Saigon, his was the government that a *Foreign Affairs* writer described
in 1957 as "a quasi–police state characterized by arbitrary arrests and
imprisonment, strict censorship of the press and the absence of an effective political opposition." Even while William Henderson was writing
this article, disparate opponents, Communists and noncommunists, were
building on Diem's internal enemies to bolster the Vietcong by creating
the National Liberation Front. But when that Hanoi-directed force
emerged in 1960, Americans were distracted by Berlin, Cuba, Khrushchev, the Congo, and Francis Gary Powers and his ill-fated U-2 spy
plane. By the time Eisenhower turned the White House over to Kennedy,
he warned that the designs of Hanoi and Peking were posing an even
greater danger to the landlocked kingdom of Laos. Such was the denouement of U.S. assumption of French rule. Whether all that could

have been avoided had Radford and Nixon had their way in 1954 can never be known. The only certainty is that the scenario would have been different, which is not the same as better. But, as Nixon later reflected, it might have been worth keeping the French in power and moving the Indochinese along toward gradual independence rather than forcing the United States to assume responsibility.[58] They could hardly have done worse.

12

Heir Apparent

FEW CAME because they loved him," wrote Nixon after Dulles's funeral; "most had often disagreed with him." Yet, although he "was made to seem and sound like a throwback to cold war rigidity," he was "the most conscientious public man" Nixon had ever known. Those who did not know the man "thought him severe, dour, almost ascetic"; he was, according to the press, "a cold fish, devoid of human emotions" and poised at "the brink" for nuclear war. The real Dulles, however, was "brilliant, disciplined, and deeply religious . . . a man who thought that the life of each individual on earth was important and precious because it was the gift of God."[1] Eisenhower called him an Old Testament prophet; his secretary of state, for all his political and diplomatic strengths, was a misplaced Puritan.

The respective circumstances of the two men, Nixon and Dulles, were superficially very different. They were raised at opposite sides of the continent and separated by age and class, one a birthright Quaker and the other a Presbyterian; one had already risen far above his hard-working grocer father and saintly mother, and the other had merely ascended to his own birthright, heading the State Department.

Still, both looked at the world in much the same way. Nixon felt comfortable with the administration's foreign policy. Dulles became associated with such militant cold war phraseology as "massive retaliation" and "brinksmanship," epitomizing the hard-line deterrents of his day. Emmet J. Hughes, a leading administration speechwriter, recalled Dulles as "a prosecuting attorney who was going to rid the world of communist criminality and he wanted no compromise in the judgment that was to be visited upon him." When, in marked contrast to the stridency of the rhetoric, Dulles spoke in that slow, measured way that Eisenhower found tedious, Nixon claimed not to be put off; he was a learner and listened carefully to the master "because he knew a lot more about diplomacy and human nature, and he knew a lot more about the working of the Communist mind."[2]

Both saw Marxism as an insidious new kind of threat, destructive in a way the world had never before seen. The Marxists' successful weapon, Dulles warned before he became secretary of state, "has been political warfare, with the main reliance placed on revolutionary slogans which arouse the masses to Soviet-dictated violence," exactly what Nixon had seen for himself in both Europe and Asia. They agreed, in a Saturday morning discussion at Dulles's home in 1958, that the prospect ahead with the Russians was for economic warfare. Within the "next two to five years," as Dulles then wrote in a memorandum of their conversation, "the Soviet Union might develop a capability and purpose to wage economic warfare against our free enterprise system by getting control of raw materials and by disrupting the free world markets through dumping of raw materials and/or manufactured goods. There might be a real question as to whether our classical free trade methods based upon profits by private enterprise could survive that kind of a struggle."[3]

It seemed that, along with Eisenhower, Dulles was the newest in a succession of influential elders. Nixon and Pat often dined with Foster and Allen and their wives. It was not unusual for the secretary to telephone Pat to tell her about something particularly good that her husband had done. He also took care to see that the vice president was fully briefed about what was happening at State.[4] While their mutual interest in foreign affairs was strong, they shared more pragmatic concerns.

Foster Dulles, who took over his job after opposing politicians had made mincemeat of Dean Acheson, had the kind of political sophistication that was invaluable for the head of the State Department, and never more helpful than during those trying years. An interim term as a Dewey appointee in the U.S. Senate had helped hone the essentials. In his campaign to win the seat on his own against a liberal challenger, Dulles kept in mind some sage advice about how to woo angry ethnics by stepping up accusations that Roosevelt and the Democrats had connived with Stalin at Yalta to subvert eastern Europe to communism. Although he lost statewide, the theme paid off in Erie County, where he cut deeply into the traditional Democratic vote and showed how middle- and working-class Democrats could be attracted to the Republican ticket. With that lesson in mind, Dulles penned the party's foreign-policy platform for 1952. At once blunt, utopian, and misleading, his plank actually suggested that voting for the GOP would not only "liberate" the "captive peoples" but would also free the United States from "all commitments contained in secret understandings such as those of Yalta which aid Communist enslavement."[5]

Once installed as secretary of state, he betrayed his sensitivity to attacks from the right. On one particular occasion, which drew strong disapproval from careerists, he told subordinates assembled in the courtyard that he expected "positive loyalty" and, further sublimating his pride and good sense, permitted the anti-Red terror to wreak hell in Foggy Bottom and demoralize the Foreign Service. Clearly, it would be Dulles who would appease anticommunists. He succeeded so well that he became the lightning rod, along with Nixon, for attacks on the administration from the left. Eisenhower, typically, remained detached, issued platitudes, played golf, waved and smiled, all the good things Americans had come to expect from their presidents.

Nixon and Dulles, both protectors of the administration, often worried more about their own party's right wing than about Democrats. They harmonized on such matters as maintaining partisan equilibrium, dovetailing allies with balance-of-power considerations, and were always sensitive to perceptions of Soviet-bloc gains, real or imagined.

Their compatibility went beyond professional requirements. Foreign affairs and politics accounted for much of their conversation. Neither was much for small talk, but their nonshop interests also converged. When, for example, someone asked the secretary at a Dulles-Nixon dinner party, "What on earth do you talk about when you don't talk about politics?" the answer was easy: "Sport," he replied. Nixon, who appreciated both, could also understand a man who could feel, as did Dulles, that the "United States is almost the only country strong enough and powerful enough to be moral."[6]

Nixon's introduction to the Dulles family was via Allen, Foster's debonair younger brother, for whom the Herter Committee's European tour had served as a cover for early work with the CIA. But it was the Hiss trial that first brought Nixon into contact with Foster. As chairman of the Carnegie Foundation, Dulles had been instrumental in securing Hiss's appointment as endowment president. Nixon's efforts to alert Dulles about the nature of testimony given by the accused man kept him from making any further endorsements of Hiss, which could have caused political damage, and led to a key role as a rebuttal character witness after Hiss had been indicted by the grand jury.[7]

Their differences were, in part, generational. Dulles was conditioned by the world as it broke down after World War I, Nixon by the loss of the grand illusion after World War II. Operationally and collegially, conflicts of authority produced irritations; the younger man, a relative novice, had the constitutional authority but needed to build up his credentials. So their relationship approximated that of a student and a teacher, but the vice president was not always fully deferential and was, not infrequently, independent.

More than most secretaries of state, Dulles colored the administration's diplomatic character. If its actions were no bolder than under Truman and Acheson, at least the tone suggested otherwise. Having denounced containment as essentially immoral, he joined Eisenhower in steering America's responses along lines that accepted the same limitation of options, despite all that talk about massive retaliation and brinksmanship. He also feigned the unleashing of Chiang Kai-shek for his cherished return to the mainland, but accommodated to the real world by accepting the Korean armistice, Zhou Enlai's authority over China and, throughout the 1950s, the requirement that the United States had to coexist with the Soviet Union. When food riots broke out in East Germany, when the Poles and the Hungarians staged their rebellions, and when Khrushchev made his threats against the continued existence of a partitioned Berlin, Dulles never considered war as an option. The institutionalization of covert operations was the main military escalation from Truman days, but even that was made possible by an expansion of the CIA's authority, which predated the Eisenhower-Dulles years.

All the while, Nixon worked to emerge with his own special identity. For him to become the most involved vice president the country had ever had required the conjunction of several factors. The FDR-Truman succession, in which the vice president had inherited the job with only the most rudimentary knowledge of what was going on, signaled the dangers of that casual approach, especially with America at the heart of a global community. Truman himself, once having undergone his on-the-job training, went without an understudy until his own elective term, and then all he had was Alben Barkley, a fine, gregarious, colorful Kentuckian, a good, loyal politician, and, as he demonstrated at the convention that won him his job, a fiery orator. But the good old likable veep was even older than the president and little better suited to take over in an emergency than Truman had been under Roosevelt. In Eisenhower's White House, the problems of age and health, combined with his faith in a staff system of operation, worked naturally to the benefit of an enhanced vice presidency.

Then there was Nixon himself. Since he had progressed so far, he was less content with a seat in the balcony. Cheerleading from the sidelines was a thing of the past. With greater confidence in his own abilities, an improved sense of being able to command his own professional and popular constituency, he was not about to remain on the bench. Had that been his status, there is not much doubt that he might well have kept his promise to Pat about giving up politics and enjoying a life of affluence with his wife and daughters. But fate and his drive to achieve interfered. Eisenhower's heart attack and additional illnesses guaranteed that Nixon would not be a ceremonial vice president. In the absence of a constitutional amendment (which did not come until 1967), Eisenhower and Nixon took the initiative by drafting a letter of understanding for an emergency transfer of power during a prolonged period of presidential disability.

For Nixon to make foreign policy his primary field of interest could hardly have been more logical. In one sense, he merely changed angles, going from scrutinizing communism at home to monitoring global events. In any case, as his own confidence and sense of mission began to mature, international matters were clearly the most presidential areas of expertise. Americans already had a strong consensus about the character of the affluent society and the relationship of its various components; only questions of tactics marked the debates over how to respond to the cold war. In that climate, achieving a convincing expertise was more important than staking out any advanced or dissenting positions.

Nixon's path toward that goal presented constant dangers. Ike was superbly devious, and Dulles, with his lawyerlike shrewdness, was precise about what he said and how it should be heard; as with any strong department head, he was always vigilant about his prerogatives. Yet, in his own way, Nixon was his match, pushing his views, and even infringing on Dulles's territory (as during the Dienbienphu crisis), always, however, remaining a loyal member of the team. In a sense, the vice president became a third wheel in the formulation of how the administration presented itself to the rest of the world.

In a major issue that came up during the heart of the 1956 election, a crisis in the Middle East, Nixon, whose closeness to Dulles made for natural support of the secretary, went along with a policy that he later came to regret. The conflict that centered on Egypt and Israel and, eventually, the Suez Canal, became serious while Eisenhower was still recuperating from his heart attack; when it reached its climax, and before it was resolved, Dulles was sidelined with his first cancer operation. Nixon, an understudy for much of that part of the drama, was, as it turned out, involved in the preliminaries for several crucial decisions that were in his future.

As the tension increased over the Suez Canal, efforts at achieving what was at best a precarious balance were undertaken against long odds. The government at Tel Aviv had its security to worry about. Survival for a people who had experienced the Nazi holocaust was fated through history and circumstance to depend on achieving stability at the expense of dispossessed Palestinians. Israel's dangers were compounded in a land where Arab fedayeen raiders could strike at will from the sands of the Gaza Strip in Egypt, the Golan Heights to the north, and across the Jordan River from the east. Survival also depended on chronic disunity among their enemies and support from the western democracies. And it sometimes meant acting like the tough kid on the block, one who could

easily hit back and could take care of himself even without bigger brothers. However much it was irrelevant to U.S. interests in the area, the
Israelis assumed that they had little choice but to show their independent
strength by violently retaliating every time fedayeen raiders or others
carried out acts of terrorism within their borders. Nor was there much
doubt that such necessity, in turn, escalated the Middle East arms race
and paved the way for Moscow's influence not only as suppliers for the
Arabs but as the anti-imperialist, anticolonialist good guys.[8]

But the Israelis, having lost the support of the Russians that they had
had at their nation's birth, had also to live with the reality that it was
often only by chance that their needs coincided with the interests of their
western friends. The Suez Canal, neutralized and open to international
shipping since 1888, was one specific case. That waterway, the vital passage through to the Mediterranean from Middle East oil fields, had since
1948 been denied to their maritime traffic by the Egyptian government.
Among European powers with material interests in the area were the
British and French, who feared that they, too, might lose such rights.
Along with most of the west, they particularly dreaded the loss of Arab
oil. The Eisenhower administration also cared about that oil. As the
president noted in his diary, "The oil of the Arab world has grown
increasingly important to all of Europe. The economy of European countries would collapse if those oil supplies were cut off," and, if that happened, "the United States would be in a situation of which the difficulty
could scarcely be exaggerated." But it was far from simple anxiety about
that black gold. He worried about the liabilities of identifying with colonialism, which would be intensified through one-sided support of Israel, and how that could so easily lead to Soviet penetration of the Middle
East. As the president told congressional leaders, the conflict was a "family fight" and although he understood Israeli grievances, prudence was
necessary in order to stabilize the area and safeguard long-run interests
for the entire west. From early on, the administration was convinced
that the west's mutual welfare would be better served by having the
British, who by agreement with Egypt maintained troops along the canal,
remove their forces from Egyptian soil.[9]

British concern over stabilizing the region led the Americans to support the creation of a mutual security agreement, known as the Baghdad
Pact (the United States did not join the pact; Britain, Pakistan, Turkey,
Iraq, and Iran did). The Egyptians, finding themselves surrounded by
western-dominated countries, sought to ease their encirclement through
a military agreement with Syria. Via Czechoslovakia, meanwhile, the
Egyptians were being well supplied with Soviet arms. Most significantly,
and attractively for Egyptian desires to develop the resources of the Nile,
the Russians also offered to help finance construction of the High Dam
at Aswan, which would irrigate useless desert lands and boost the coun-

try's ability to export fine, long-staple cotton. Within days of that offer, and coinciding with the Egyptian-Syrian pact, the State Department moved to blunt Soviet influence by saying that it, too, was ready to help. While Dulles prepared a statement to be sent to Eisenhower at Denver saying that the United States would not contribute to an arms race in the region, the State Department released a warning that Washington would be "strongly opposed to the side which starts a war in the Middle East" and would aid the victim.[10]

Just one month later, on December 11, 1955, David Ben-Gurion, newly reinstalled as Israel's premier, launched a devastating overnight retaliatory raid that struck Syrian military outposts and civilian homes on the slopes of Mount Hermon, north of the Sea of Galilee. Only days later, while the British and Americans were trying to reach an agreement with the Egyptians over Aswan, rioting broke out in Jordanian cities in protest against the Baghdad Pact. Hoping to disentangle it all, Eisenhower was led by his great personal faith in Robert B. Anderson to send that Texan to attempt to work out a settlement between Tel Aviv and Cairo. Anderson told the Egyptian president that Washington was ready to finance the dam and guarantee the inviolability of boundaries. But neither side was buying, the Israelis resisting territorial adjustments and the Egyptians unable to even consider accepting the existence of the Jewish state. Anderson, who began with high hopes, returned a disappointed man.[11]

Matters went downhill from there. The prospect of large crops of fine-grade Egyptian cotton aroused the fears of those in the United States who represented states that feared the potential competition. President Nasser of Egypt, finding out the value of playing off Moscow against Washington, antagonized the latter by stepping up his purchase of military matériel from the Soviet bloc. Nasser's "growing ambition" was a "fundamental factor in the problem," believed Eisenhower, who thought that the State Department might strike a counterbalance by helping to promote the authority of the king of Saudi Arabia. From Congress came demands that the United States match that kind of assistance by sending arms to Israel.[12]

That was no climate for going ahead with money for Nasser to build his dam, and, very firmly — some thought brutally — Dulles said no deal when the ambassador from Cairo came for the money in July.[13] With no funding for Aswan from Washington and the British troops gone, only one week after that rejection Nasser seized control of Suez, immediately contravening the principle of the canal as an international waterway and raising the specter of its closure at his pleasure.

The move astonished Eisenhower along with almost everyone else.[14] It also confirmed the failure of the administration's policy, not only with the Egyptians but also with the British, who had once had thousands of troops helping to protect the waterway. But the immediate effect was the determination by both the British and the French to react with force.

However, Washington, more than Paris or London, was convinced that, as Dulles explained to Nixon and others, the current jam was taking place "because the past Administration had always dealt with the area from a political standpoint and had tried to meet the wishes of the Zionists in this country and that had created a basic antagonism with the Arabs. That was what the Russians were now capitalizing on." People like George Marshall and James V. Forrestal learned that under Truman, when, as secretary of state and defense secretary, respectively, they tried to keep their administration from capitulating to the Jewish vote by eagerly embracing the creation of Israel. In short, the United States could not afford to have that vital zone turn toward the east because of irresponsible acts by traditional allies. Yet, as Dulles told Henry Luce, according to notes taken by his secretary Phyllis Bernau, he was "well aware how almost impossible it is in this country to carry out foreign policy not approved by the Jews. . . . That does not mean I am anti-Jewish, but I believe in what GWashington [*sic*] said in his Farewell Address that an emotional attachment to another country should not interfere." Furthermore, as Dulles later put it to Republican congressman John M. Vorys of Ohio at the height of the effort to force the Israelis to yield their military gains, "We face a critical situation as far as the Arab world is concerned because they are watching closely to decide . . . even if a *Republican* Administration finds it impossible to have a foreign policy the Jews don't approve of and if that is their conclusion they will line up with the Soviets" (emphasis added). During the earlier stages of the crisis, back in 1955, Vorys had attempted to build a "backfire" against the Jewish vote by enlisting the bishop of the Methodist Church of Ohio; now he suggested that alerting Protestant and Catholic churches to get behind the administration's efforts "would straighten things out in a big hurry." The problem with that, Dulles pointed out, was that the only ones out there "ready to be altered" were "extreme anti-Semites" eager for the chance. Moreover, Dulles reminded the congressman, he had to be careful to avoid being anti-Semitic and thus becoming anti-American.[15] The dilemma was real, exacerbated by Nasser's takeover of Suez in July 1956 and, after Dulles's diplomacy attempted to delay any Anglo-French military response, the onset of an Israeli drive in late October across the Sinai Peninsula and straight for the canal.

Would American policy be once again held hostage to the Israeli vote? That was Dulles's dilemma. Not if he could help it. As one of his executive assistants, John W. Hanes, Jr., pointed out long before the seizure of the canal, there was little confidence that Republicans could make much headway with the Jewish vote in any event. Nixon, consulted by Dulles at every step of the way as the Middle Eastern situation unfolded, agreed that politics might create an anti-Arab policy once again. However much it might alienate the Jewish vote, said Nixon, the matter should be dealt with on a nonpartisan basis. David Ben-Gurion's government in Tel Aviv, after some hesitation about going ahead with its attack before the American election, evidently hoped that such political considerations would inhibit official interference before Israel and its western allies could accomplish their mission. He failed to take seriously Eisenhower's warning that "we would handle our affairs as though we didn't have a Jew in America."[16]

Nor, as it turned out — and as Washington was finding out — did England and France truly understand the strength of the American objections. For some months, Dulles's diplomacy with those western allies had been to forestall military action, to keep the Middle East from becoming consumed by a war that might have unlimited consequences and, at the very least, would only reaffirm that traditional colonialist lines had not changed very much. Dulles's message and delaying tactics did, however, encourage the three governments to, in effect, go underground by plotting to wrest control of the canal from Nasser without consulting Washington. Nevertheless, during those late October days, the air between Paris and Tel Aviv was filled with enough electronic messages to indicate that something serious was about to happen. American U-2 spy planes, which had just gone into action that year, were able to keep Israeli mobilization under surveillance.[17]

Nixon himself was away from Washington, making his final week of campaign speeches, when the Israelis began the Suez War by pushing rapidly across the Sinai, rolling back Egyptian forces in disarray, with the canal as their target. In New York City the next afternoon, Tuesday, October 30, the reconvened UN Security Council was informed that British and French troops were headed toward Port Said for "temporary occupation." Britain and France had also sent joint ultimatums to Egypt and Israel demanding the withdrawal of forces to ten miles on either side of the canal. But there were vetoes all around. Using its Security Council vote, the United Kingdom killed an American resolution that called for an immediate cease-fire. Nasser, as was expected, also rejected the Anglo-French ultimatum. He did so even before Prime Minister Anthony Eden and French premier Guy Mollet received Eisenhower's personal message calling for the affair to be settled by the United Nations. The president followed through with several telephone calls to 10 Downing Street asking for a withdrawal. With the approval of his cabinet, Eden wired back that they would go before the Security Council but that they could not afford to see the canal closed or to lose the shipping which passed daily through it. "We have a responsibility for the people in these ships. We feel that decisive action should be taken at once to stop hostilities," he wrote.[18]

On the thirty-first, Nixon called Dulles from Detroit to say that it was more important to reassert firmness and to dispel any notion that America had a "pipsqueak" as president than to worry about how Jews would react. The Republicans didn't have enough of that vote to make a difference, anyway.[19] Small countries had to be kept independent while keeping American boys from becoming involved. That was the point to make, he urged the secretary: reports that tied military action in the area to the failure of our policy must be countered by our assertion of noninterventionism.

On November 5, with the Israeli conquest of the Sinai Peninsula and Gaza Strip complete except for minor mopping-up operations, an Anglo-French airdrop began at Port Said, followed by amphibious landings the next day. Four armies fought on Egyptian soil. The Russians, even while crushing the Hungarian rebellion in Budapest, also pressed demands for withdrawal, pointing out that London and Paris were within range of their nuclear missiles. Even more ominous, and sternly rebuffed by Eisenhower, was Premier Nikolay Bulganin's proposal for a joint U.S.-Soviet military operation to crush the "aggression against Egypt." By the next day, Moscow was announcing that Russian "volunteers" were applying to serve with Nasser's soldiers. On the seventh, the day after American voters reelected the Eisenhower-Nixon ticket, the three invaders accepted the cease-fire calls. Their forces halted in the canal zone, but the waterway itself was still in Egyptian hands and shut down by the wreckage of ships. American opposition, UN resolutions, and, finally, the threats of Russian intervention, were too much. Nixon, prevented by the political campaign from having much of a say in what was going on, was most visible as a spokesman, a role he served in direct connection with Dulles.[20]

The secretary wired ahead to Nixon at Hershey, Pennsylvania, where he was due to deliver a televised campaign speech before three thousand people at the local arena. Adlai Stevenson had just called the administration's Middle East policy a failure and charged that the president should have been able to avert the crisis. As a result, claimed the Democratic presidential candidate, the United States stood alone "in an unfriendly world." Dulles forwarded harder-hitting language to counter such criticism, words that were bound to make headlines. Just before election day, the secretary obviously felt the need to defend the administration's Middle East position in the strongest possible way. For the first time since the start of the cold war, the United States had parted openly from its principal western allies and even found itself on the same side as the Soviet Union. Nixon, loyally attempting to turn a diplomatic setback to the administration's advantage, used Dulles's words and explained that "for the first time in history we have shown independence of Anglo-French policies which seemed to us to reflect the colonial tradition. That declaration of independence has had an electrifying effect throughout the world." It was, in short, as Nixon reminded his audience, a sign of our strength. "The moment we are weak we invite war."[21]

In Washington, Dulles, back from a long round of debates at the United Nations in New York, had severe stomach pains late that night. Rushed to Walter Reed Hospital the next morning, he was in surgery for two and a half hours. Instead of finding what they hoped were kidney stones, they had to cut away a malignant growth that was piercing his abdomen. After his surgery, Dulles recuperated at Key West for two weeks and returned to Washington in early December. Facing a meeting with foreign ministers from America's NATO allies, he drafted an explanation in the form of a speech to be delivered by the vice president. In Philadelphia during the early stages of the Anglo-French-Israeli assault, Eisenhower had declared that "we cannot — in the world, any more than in our own nation — subscribe to one law for the weak, another law for the strong; one law for those opposing us, another for those allied with us. There can be only one law — or there will be no peace." Nixon's message, described by historian Herman Finer as "an elaborate, full-scale state paper," amplified that theme. Recent events were brought on by mishandling on all sides, he conceded; taking the high ground on the "one law" pronouncement, he paid tribute to an alliance that could show enough strength to survive "a period of adversity."[22]

Nixon's private views were often complex; for anyone close to him, it was natural to suspect that, at heart, he had considerable admiration for the Israeli and Anglo-French initiative. It was the kind of potential disagreement that, as Julie Eisenhower points out, has "to be held close to the vest. You can't have a whole lot of Cabinet, even the Vice President — If you have a crisis situation like Suez, how can you have everybody gathering around?"[23] Even given the importance of unifying behind the team, Nixon was then simply too far from the scene where policy was being decided, and he had little choice, especially when campaigning, except to support the White House and the State Department. Moreover, he simply went along with the decision.

Two decades later, he came to believe that "our actions were a serious mistake. Nasser became even more rash and aggressive than before, and the seeds of another Mideast war were planted." Eisenhower, too, he later reported, had come to regret his actions.[24]

In short, Eisenhower's policies had some serious shortcomings. At a time when journalists and other specialists gave so much attention to what they perceived as the truculence of the influence of John Foster Dulles upon American foreign policy, and, in doing so, fell into the public relations trap of underestimating the president's own role, there was inadequate awareness of Nixon's emergence as a distinct force. The irony was that, while still very far from those on the extreme right who actually saw Dulles and Eisenhower as betrayers of U.S. interests, Nixon doubted that responses were firm enough to meet long-term dangers. He could and did welcome the end of fighting in Korea and the avoidance of American bloodshed at Dienbienphu, just as he was also relieved that east and west stopped short of a violent showdown over Suez. Each case, however, left him with the uncomfortable feeling that, as FDR had found convenient to do when dealing with the Russians at Yalta, areas of serious conflict were merely being postponed. His anxieties would doubtlessly have been greater had he been prescient enough to know that each issue would someday stop at his own desk.

The Jewish vote went just about as expected, with those in big cities responding once again to Stevenson's style and imbuing him with New and Fair Deal genes; here and there, there was even some slippage from Eisenhower's 1952 totals. Nationally, however, both Gallup and the Survey Research Center of the University of Michigan showed that American Jews, while still strongly pro-Stevenson, actually increased their support for Eisenhower and Nixon by 2 to 6 percent.[25]

One major consequence of the U.S.-UN-Soviet reaction to Suez was the forced withdrawal of Israeli armies to the original boundaries that had been established by the United Nations in 1948. The retreat was piecemeal, but ultimately pushed by threats of sanctions from Washington. Once Tel Aviv removed troops from their defensive outposts on the Gaza Strip and the entranceway to the Gulf of Aqaba at the southern tip of the Sinai Peninsula, they were replaced by a UN emergency force. Compensation then also flowed through American backing of a series of loans from the World Bank and the reaffirmation of the principle of free navigation.[26] With the immediate crisis over, the administration initiated a Middle Eastern replica of the Formosa Resolution, this one bearing the name of the president.

As had the Formosa Resolution in early 1955, the Eisenhower Resolution gave the administration the congressional blessing it sought to intervene in the region to thwart an "outside" power. Later, in the summer of 1958, Eisenhower used that authority, which was politically desirable if not constitutionally necessary, to send American marines into Lebanon in response to what appeared to be the perilous position of the country's pro-Western president, Camille Chamoun.

Nixon, for his part, increased his own efforts to play a more conspicuous role. The time had come to do more than, as he put it, serve as Dulles's "political eyes and ears." If he could be something like an executive assistant, that would be fine. But that, of course, risked stepping on toes, most notably those of the assistant to the president, Sherman Adams. Responsibility for lobbying on Capitol Hill for legislation of interest to the administration was the prerogative of the White House's own congressional liaison people. Whatever his enlarged role might be, suggested Eisenhower, it must be done "without compromising your necessary attitude of objectivity and non-partisanship," a weird point given how the vice president was actually used. What might be best, Eisenhower ventured, would be helping to prepare legislation dealing with national security matters. Nixon agreed, pointing to his congressional experience, foreign travels, and service as a member of the National Security Council as qualifications. In any event, the president wanted any enhancement to take place without formal publicity.[27]

The real change had little to do with constitutional functions of the vice presidency or impingement of powers over any particular department or agency. Nixon took his "political eyes and ears" overseas. Travel, all coordinated with Secretary Dulles, became a more prominent function of his office than for any previous vice president, reflecting, no doubt, how both the world and his office had changed. There was also Nixon's insatiable curiosity and zest for involvement. He was, for example, present at the unveiling of the new African state of Ghana.

Much better publicized, and of infinitely greater political value, was his trip to South America the following year, 1958. A key figure in an administration that supported rightist Latin dictatorships, Nixon became a natural target for anger at Yankee imperialism. Protests, no doubt fanned by local Communist activists but fed as much by history, placed Nixon and his wife under siege and, at times, perilously close to physical harm. The violence was especially fierce in Caracas, where enraged students rocked their automobile and threatened to maul the occupants. The Nixons were also spat upon — undignified, insulting, but not life-threatening; still, a nightmare for all concerned, not least for those who were assigned to protect the visitors.

The vice president and Mrs. Nixon endured the ordeal with remarkable poise and courage, winning major headlines back home. They were applauded for personal bravery and for having risked their own lives against passionate anti-Americanism. In his ceremonial duties as vice president, Nixon had become the man on the firing line. He was also, at the same time, an adjunct to the secretary of state, doing those things that Dulles thought he should not do for himself.

Occasionally such activities led to a response that embarrassed Nixon and created an impression of confusion at the upper echelons. On September 27, 1958, for example, the vice president came to Dulles's defense somewhat too vehemently. He assumed, incorrectly as it turned out, that someone in the State Department had leaked to the press information that White House mail was strongly against the administration's efforts to back Chiang Kai-shek in his determination to defend the offshore islands of Quemoy and Matsu, which were being shelled by Communist China. Nixon denounced the attempt of a "subordinate to undercut the Secretary of State and sabotage his policy." He later explained that career people were typically "cutting [Dulles's] throat," in league with such elements of the press as the *New York Times*. But in this case Nixon jumped the gun. Had he first checked into the matter, he would have found that the information was released through routine State Department channels. In what had long since become characteristic of responses to such lapses, Nixon was depicted as an overly aggressive vice president displaying his customary lack of restraint, his action quickly labeled a "conditioned reflex" that confirmed old "fascist tendencies."[28]

In all probability, responses would not have been as heated had the situation not taken place in the middle of the midterm congressional election campaign. As he had done in 1954 and 1956, Nixon was out campaigning. All indications projected an uphill fight. Even Eisenhower's emphatic reelection two years earlier had failed to give the GOP enough seats to control either house. In the battle for congressional seats, the combination of higher unemployment and inflation, along with farm belt discontent with the administration's agricultural policies, pointed to the virtual certainty of a weakened minority position. A *New York Times* survey of Wisconsin voters uncovered no evidence of any Democratic shifts to the Republicans, but substantial numbers were going the other way, even in some traditionally conservative areas. It was World Series time, and a discouraged party leader in Milwaukee told a reporter that "I suppose the next thing we'll be blamed for is the Braves defeat by the Yankees."[29]

Nixon used his position to wage what was, in effect, a national campaign, thereby identifying himself even more with the party's fortunes. The process seemed more frustrating than rewarding. Exasperated, Nixon noted to Murray Chotiner, "It is difficult for me to understand how some of these people whose interests and philosophies are so closely tied to the Republican Party think they can sit on their hands financially and otherwise this year, but there are signs that this is the case in several states." It wasn't so much that 1958 could be redeemed, but, as he added, "I think you will agree with me that they should be out working night and day to at least minimize the losses if they hope to salvage anything in 1960."[30]

If such troubles were not bad enough, he was especially disheartened by the personal rivalry in his home state between William Knowland and Goodwin Knight, who was stepping down from the governorship to run against Claire Engle for the Senate. The situation compelled Nixon to make two California campaign swings. "It is awfully rough, people are disheartened," reported Rose Mary Woods to national chairman Alcorn. "The Vice President is 'kicking them in the teeth' to try to arouse them."

Nixon, she told him, said that Knowland and Knight were "behaving like little boys — very bad boys," and he was "trying to shame them out of it." Both Republicans were ultimately beaten on election day, Knowland's defeat at least cutting down one whom Nixon had watched closely as a potential competitor in 1960.[31]

Certainly, no other Republican worked as hard during that campaign. Nor did anybody else chart the party's fortunes so carefully in an effort to keep Republicans afloat despite what promised to be a disastrous political year. Keeping dispirited Republicans from falling apart and establishing a base for campaigning for the presidency two years later were logical expressions of his own self-interest. His efforts had three immediate objectives: strengthening the party's ideological base, placing the opposition on the defensive, and wooing back those Democrats who were obviously uncomfortable about continuing in the same camp with "radicals." "If the radical Democrat candidates are elected the real Democrats will no longer be able to control the party," explained Nixon, pointing out that his own speeches had been sensitive to the "clear-cut difference between the two wings of the party." He told Rose Mary Woods that he thought that George Smathers would "pass along to [Stuart] Symington, [Mike] Mansfield and [John] Kennedy that under no circumstances is RN [Nixon] coming into those states, even tho he has been asked to many times. It's just like Smathers privately says — he doesn't want too many of those states to win because of the radicals. Naturally, Smathers can't say that publicly." [32] Nixon thereby delineated a fourth, more personal goal, one that later emerged with great force during his presidency: attempting to forge an alignment of conservative Democrats with the Republican heartland. In effect, then, he was also discarding the relevance of his own party's more extreme right wing.

He made his major campaign point very forcefully at a party strategy meeting in the White House on October 6. Tarnishing Democrats with the word "socialism" was the best way to please the crowds and place their opponents on the defensive, he advised. His guidance resulted in a manifesto declaring that "we are certain to go down the left lane which leads inseparably to socialism" if Democrats again controlled Congress. On the nineteenth, after completing his campaign swing through the West, Nixon sent a telegram to all Republican congressional candidates which urged taking "the offensive on the issue of the firmness of our foreign policy against Communist aggression. . . . In appealing to Democrats we should point out that Democrats who support our Republican candidates are not deserting their party but that their party is deserting them because of its domination in the Northern and Western states by the radical wing."[33] The word "radical" then became the key, used as a wedge to separate the opposition's divergent groups. Eisenhower himself, in Los Angeles, charged that Democrats were dominated by "political radicals" and, in his own harshest partisan language, held that northern liberals were a challenge to "sane government"; speaking over television from Chicago two days later, the president depicted the Democrats as dominated by radicals and "those of little faith."[34]

Nixon's own speeches reached out to disgruntled Democrats. He even modified his references to Harry Truman. Truman was now a legitimate Democrat, no longer "a traitor to his party," and the Communists were the only "party of treason." Good, patriotic Democrats, he suggested in his set speeches, would not permit themselves to be dominated by the radical, wild-spending Americans for Democratic Action, who were "drunk with visions of votes and not pink but dead elephants." Nor would they permit themselves to be beholden to labor racketeers. Remember, he advised, "labor politicians don't give support unless they get 100% domination of the man they help to elect." Radical Democrats would nationalize such "American institutions" as health, housing, power, and farming. To union supporters in large areas of the country, especially the West, he advised that whatever gains were made by the opposition were bound to come from the "radical" wing of the Democratic party.[35]

The pattern would be repeated later, most notably in 1964 and 1966: Nixon gained while the party lost. Henry Luce's *Life* magazine hailed the vice president as its "most effective campaigner" and praised him for "doing all one man can to update and repoliticize his party."[36]

One thing did seem certain. James Reston reported from Salt Lake City that "one hears very little criticism or even discussions . . . in the areas between the Appalachians and the Rockies" of the foreign policy differences being debated elsewhere. Nor, at least in that part of the country, did he uncover much annoyance with Eisenhower for giving Dulles too much leeway in handling the offshore islands controversy. His image as a great soldier and a good and genial man of peace who was fully in charge was undimmed. About the only criticism Reston heard was that he was somewhat too "wobbly" on the Chinese Communists. "He was tough on them at the beginning and then seemed to pull back," said a retired worker in Parkersburg, West Virginia, and the point was repeated by many others. "The President said these islands were important and he should stick to it," complained a railroad switchman. Most Americans, however, thought that only the defense of Formosa warranted going to war.[37]

Anecdotal samplings, however, showed that Eisenhower's personal popularity was still high but without the magic that seemed to charm his presidency. The public still approved of the man, but verdicts were already coming in from professional president-watchers. Political journalist William V. Shannon adjudged Eisenhower a "transitional figure" who was passing through the American scene without repealing the past or shaping the future. His era was nothing more than "the time of the great postponement"; the general in the White House was not the first great figure of a new Republican age but the "last of an old Democratic generation." Another prominent Washington reporter, Marquis Childs, wrote that it was not too early to decide that Eisenhower "must be put down as a weak president who, ill-prepared for the job, settled in as a 'captive hero.' "[38]

The fact is that, as Eric Goldman has written, the middle of the road was getting bumpy. Ike's famous luck seemed to be giving out. A scandal ultimately forced Sherman Adams to resign just before the election. The Russians, with no advance fanfare, successfully launched *Sputnik* into outer space. Far more damaging, however, was the wobbly economy. Surveys generally showed that voters were either preoccupied with pocketbook issues or were not listening at all. When Gallup asked how much attention they were giving to the elections, 59 percent responded by saying "little" or "none."[39] As 1958 progressed, improvement was noted, but most people agreed it was too little and too late.

Mostly, Americans were preoccupied with themselves. Campaign rhetoric seemed to count for very little. Whatever Eisenhower meant by "modern Republicans" wasn't very clear, anyway. Democrats were good for bad times; Republicans best for, to use Warren Harding's word, "normalcy." Democrats were best for winning wars, Republicans for heading them off while keeping strong. If voters were working and felt secure, even able to afford some luxuries, Eisenhower and the Republicans were fine; if not, they were ready to turn elsewhere.

For political leaders, getting the attention of the voters was the big problem. One reflexive response came from appeals to nationalism; nobody needed to know anything about geography or military logistics, let alone economics and politics, to know that giving in to the Communists was wrong, dead wrong. The lesson was learned at Munich, or should have been, and Roosevelt had done the same thing at Yalta, trying to satisfy Uncle Joe, dealing with the old dictator as if he were a regular guy and ready to play ball. If nothing else was learned, that much was: you can't do business with dictators, and the Communists, Chinese or Russian, embodied every evil plus Marxism. So while few wanted war, fewer still wanted to lose. The offshore islands were remote, barely dots on a map of the China coast; most Americans were vague about where they were. China, however, was another matter, and so was communism. About half of those who had an opinion, 42 percent, thought that the use of atomic weapons was warranted against the Peking government's military installations in case of war over Quemoy and Matsu.[40]

In a way, the offshore islands problem was like Korea all over again. Dulles compared it to Berlin. Either way, the United States was hostage to a client state. "We can break them [the Nationalists] if we cut off aid," he explained to Nixon, "but if you break them, you lose Formosa." If the United States didn't back West Berlin, it would lose Germany; if it displeased Syngman Rhee, it had to be ready to fight in Korea. "So the solution," said the secretary to the vice president, "cannot be found in terms of giving up Quemoy and Matsu. . . . The broad challenge is are we going to keep the Western shores of the Pacific in friendly hands or not?" Nobody seemed to have a solution for the problem. How could he get the "ChiNats" (Chinese Nationalists) to withdraw without pressure that would break them and almost guarantee a Communist takeover of Formosa? If the United States lost Formosa, he told Nixon, "Japan will make terms with Communist China and we will have suffered an overall setback even worse than when we lost the Mainland."[41]

Some years later, when Nixon talked about Dulles and the offshore islands crisis, he emphasized how the secretary was wont to steer carefully between the art of the possible and diplomatic necessities. Dulles thought that the worst thing that he could do would be to ignore congressional and popular sentiments. If, despite resistance, action was needed, he felt that it was his job to create a more favorable climate.[42] Resolving the problem through other means was, however, a first step.

Admiral Radford and Walter Robertson had already been sent to persuade Chiang Kai-shek to evacuate the garrisons on Quemoy and Matsu while the islands were not under fire. One overture, kept classified until recently, involved giving Chiang a protective nuclear curtain to protect the islands if he agreed to withdraw his provocative garrisons. In late September 1958, when Dulles tried to enlist John McCloy for a similar effort, the former American high commissioner begged off. Chiang's resistance would only stiffen, he argued, and the trip would be "something akin public relations–wise to the ill fated mission of General Marshall to Chiang. Again a friend of the President's is called upon to induce Chiang to moderate his attitude toward the Communists."[43]

Skirmishing over the chain of islands in the Formosa Strait, all the way from the Tachens to the north to Quemoy and Little Quemoy near the People's Republic of China port of Amoy, had begun three years earlier. The Quemoys themselves were close enough, as accessible to the Chinese mainland as Staten Island to the rest of New York City. As small and remote as they were, and despite U.S. displeasure, Chiang built up his garrisons to the 100,000 level, one-third of his total ground forces. Continuing to defy advice, he further provoked the Communists by carrying out commando raids. American supervision over such activities was so loose that, at one point, the two Dulles brothers, the secretary of state and the head of the CIA, each confessed to the other over the telephone his uncertainty about whether Chiang's latest raid had been undertaken with American assistance.[44]

For Chiang, holding on to the islands was essential to his fantasy of returning to the mainland. The Communists, however, hoped to cut their supply lines and starve out the garrisons, or to at least make replenishment too costly. The upshot would be, as a Peking radio broadcast put it, to "smash the American paper tiger and liberate" Formosa. Washington was not at all sure they would not succeed. Moreover, given the importance of defending Formosa itself and the nearby Pescadores Islands, which were regarded as vital for defense of Chiang Kai-shek's home base, the offshore islands were regarded as more of a distraction — and possibly symbolic — than strategic. But Chiang considered them essential for the survival of Formosa itself and was uninterested in making fine distinctions between them and the Pescadores. Circumstances, therefore, made the United States a reluctant guardian, hoping somehow to convince an obstreperous junior to act responsibly. Adding to the discomfort, and making an issue out of what should have been discarded quietly, were the eight thousand rounds a day that were being fired onto the islands from Communist coastal batteries. After a long period of shelling in 1954, the guns fell silent, and activity in the area was highlighted mainly by Chiang's buildup and occasional coastal raids; then, on August 23, 1958, the firing resumed.

Former secretary of state Dean Acheson spoke for a great majority when he said that the islands' defense was "not worth a single American life." Walter Lippmann warned that we "would be acting on Chinese territory in a Chinese civil war." The Eisenhower administration had, at least, convinced Chiang to slip his soldiers quietly off the Tachen Islands, the northernmost offshore group, when nobody was watching, at the cost of promising to help defend Quemoy and Matsu. The trouble, Dulles explained to the cabinet in February of 1955, was that the Communists cared not at all to settle for the islands even if they got them free. They really wanted to get rid of the Nationalists altogether and remove that barrier to Communist expansion.[45]

The new round of shelling led to the administration's attempt to bolster the political legitimacy of its military involvement in the area. Eisenhower requested specific authority from Congress to use U.S. forces to protect "Formosa and the Pescadores and related positions, if necessary, in defense of the principal islands," which was given by an 83 to 3 vote in the Senate and 410 to 3 in the House. Thus, by approving the Formosa Resolution, did the Congress acknowledge that the administration might somehow be able to decide whether some particular action against the offshore islands was a prelude to an assault upon Formosa itself. When the shelling resumed in August 1958, it was more intense than ever. After a brief respite, the Chinese Communists announced they would resume by firing only on alternate days. Before it was over, Eisenhower decided that "we were in a Gilbert and Sullivan war."[46]

Nor did the administration's conduct of the situation appear much better in what was, paradoxically, probably its most deft handling of any international crisis. If, in fact, it was the ineptitude that many thought at the time, it was at least rational ineptitude. The Joint Chiefs of Staff urged a policy of "keeping them guessing" about the circumstances that would warrant U.S. military intervention. As far as the public could see, however, the two men, Eisenhower and Dulles, blew hot and cold, the secretary stressing the importance of keeping the islands from falling even at the risk of intervention, and the president alternating between firmness and pieties about peace. They carried on that way throughout September. Dulles, especially, sounded as if there were no alternative to war. "The consequences in the Far East would be more far-reaching and catastrophic than those which followed when the United States allowed [sic] the Chinese mainland to be taken over by the Chinese Communists," he said on September 5 from the presidential vacation base at Newport, Rhode Island. On the eleventh, Eisenhower delivered a television address in which he said he was ready to negotiate and added, "I believe that there is not going to be any war." Sixteen days later the president told viewers that he was taking "the only position . . . consistent with the vital interests of the United States and, indeed, with the peace of the world." Nixon, too, was caught in the confusion, saying on television that the islands must be preserved, only to have Dulles explain the very next morning that the issue could be negotiated.[47]

Behind the scenes, unofficial talks between the Americans and the People's Republic of China were resuming at Warsaw. If they failed, suggested Dulles to UN ambassador Henry Cabot Lodge, the secretary-general might seek a cease-fire and neutralization of the islands. In early October, Dulles told Nixon that "we had always hoped that there would come about not through our talks in Warsaw but through the force of events a de facto cease-fire."[48]

Meanwhile, the president circulated an editorial from the *Kansas City Star* suggesting that the time was ripe for reappraising U.S. Far East policy; nonrecognition and barring Communist China from the United Nations were not going to disappear as issues "when the present crisis is disposed of." Was our position, asked the editorial, really in our own best interest? In case he didn't get the point, the president reminded his secretary of state that the paper "probably more closely reflects Mid Western sentiment than any other paper west of the Mississippi." Over three years earlier, in the aftermath of the Korean War, the State Department had discovered that the Chinese were finding the Soviets becoming less dependable as a source of raw material and military supplies. It all came together, the more evident Sino-Soviet strains and the uncomfortable prospect of being led by Chiang Kai-shek's fantasies and need to serve up jingoism to the American public, to alert Dulles and Eisenhower to the hazards of continuing a potentially self-destructive

policy toward the Chinese Communists. Thus, the offshore islands dilemma would ultimately prove sobering.[49]

Finally, efforts to restrain Chiang paid off. The Communists declared
a two-week cease-fire and resumed with alternate-day shelling. Quemoy
and Matsu continued to be supplied, and it became obvious that the
bombardment was costing more than it was worth. The policy of getting
the Nationalists to reduce the size of their military forces and keeping
the enemy guessing paid off; the shelling soon ceased and the crisis
faded away. It had, in that instance, been profitable not to let either side,
neither America's clients nor the enemy, know precisely when and under
what circumstances the United States might come in.[50]

Nixon concluded his campaign swing with a flying, last-minute visit to
Juneau, Anchorage, and Fairbanks, landing in the Alaska interior on
election eve and receiving what the *Fairbanks Daily News–Miner* called "a
tumultuous welcome unrivaled in the history of the city"; altogether, an
excellent start in the territory that was then on the verge of statehood.
At Anchorage, which "has become sophisticated and un-Alaskan," he
was greeted by a crowd that numbered "at least" two thousand people.[51]

But 1958 was a disaster for the Republican party. Not since 1936 had
Democrats shown such strength, gaining forty-eight seats in the House
and fifteen in the Senate. Almost everywhere, but especially in urban
working-class districts and in the farm belt, Republicans were thrown
for sharp losses.

The reasons were obvious. Economic distress, though less severe than
earlier that year, discouraged workers and farmers. Republicans in several states nonetheless chose that moment to campaign for right-to-work
laws as a way to free workers from unscrupulous labor bosses by outlawing union shops. Nixon knew better. So did Eisenhower. Such candidates as Bill Knowland, who campaigned against Pat Brown for
California's governorship, did not. In a year of dissatisfaction with economic policy, right-to-work provided a handy target.

Some antilabor candidates, such as Knowland, were enthralled with
right-to-work as a winning issue. In part, they were deceived by the
results of a special election held in the San Fernando Valley in 1957,
when the victory of a congressional candidate was hailed as a repudiation
of unionism. The principle of right-to-work seemed to have been vindicated only because some six hundred recruits were brought into the
district to literally haul "enough Republicans to the polls to win," aide
Charles McWhorter told Nixon. Anybody who thought that the outcome
demonstrated antilabor strength was wrong. What it did demonstrate
was the need for some sort of "ideological stimulus such as right to
work in order to make them mad or excited enough to vote."[52]

The election left Nixon discouraged. His staff and Meade Alcorn agreed that the results also revealed the GOP's organizational inadequacies. They had, Alcorn advised Eisenhower, failed to touch "the hopes and the aspirations of the average American." For Nixon, the only positive note was that many of the newly elected Democrats were "spenders" who would be independent of whatever suasion might be exerted by their party's congressional leaders and might thereby enable Eisenhower to score political points by making an issue out of vetoing some of their bills. By the end of the year, even after the first shock of defeat, Nixon lamented to Senator Barry Goldwater that the 1960 nomination looked as though it was going to be worthless, "and I think you agree there is considerable chance that nothing we can do will save the situation." Goldwater, for his part, had suggested that the party should "resume its rightful place as a conservative party," a point that Nixon chose to ignore in his reply.[53]

Yet, only two weeks earlier, the vice president confided to a Harvard law professor that "we need a greater understanding of conservative principles than now exists if we are to offset the plethora of liberal propaganda in the bookstores and on the newsstands." Nixon believed then, and never stopped believing, that individual drive for success was society's most effective economic dynamo. Thirty years later, he appeared on a "Meet the Press" television interview with the same theme. In that era, speaking so soon after the imprisonment of Wall Street arbitrageur Ivan Boesky, he virtually endorsed the ethos of the inside trader. "There is nothing wrong at all with greed," said Nixon, almost quoting from Boesky, but adding, "provided that greed is one that contributes to the wealth of the country, so that the wealth of the country can then handle some of the problems that people have." Then, elaborating on what may be called the value of productive greed, he went on. "Let me tell you, if some people weren't greedy, we wouldn't have the tax money [so] that we could even be talking about more for education, more for health, and the rest."[54] That simple truth, he believed, harsh and cruel as it may have sounded at first glance, and certainly true to the teachings of Hayek and von Mises, was almost impossible to convey in terms of mass value to a society that failed to realize how even well-intentioned "humanitarian" actions by government actually stifled investment and reduced the supply of capital for the public welfare.

Adding to his personal sense of despondence at this time was the lack of much recognition of his own evident leadership. Television and the press seemed far more preoccupied with the rise of two new stars, Democrat Jack Kennedy, who won a massive reelection against just token opposition, and, more important for Nixon, Nelson A. Rockefeller. Making his first run in electoral politics, the attractive multimillionaire submerged New York's incumbent governor under a 573,034-vote plurality and immediately stirred speculation about his future.[55] Almost from the outset, Rockefeller became the media's hope for whatever remained of Republican liberalism. At the same time, understated by the press, was what happened in Arizona, where Senator Barry Goldwater won re-election with over 56 percent of the vote. If they accomplished nothing else, those midterm elections effectively created three potential contenders for the GOP's 1960 presidential nomination, Nixon and, to either side of him ideologically, Rockefeller and Goldwater.

The hazard of being caught in a left-right crossfire was, for Nixon, a far greater problem than the party's organizational inadequacies, although the latter could conceivably negate any success against his leading Republican rivals. John Bricker, defeated for reelection to the Senate from Ohio after his strong support for right-to-work laws, told him that he wished "for once that we could get an issue clear cut between the radicals and the conservatives, who are the true liberals, so this country could know once and for all whether it is going to go completely socialistic or continue as a representative, free government." Clarence Kelland, a popular magazine writer and conservative national committeeman from Arizona, also called for a conservative realignment of the parties. "The Republican Party is on its deathbed as was the Whig party a hundred and thirty years ago," he wrote to Alcorn. "Its only hope of survival is the elimination by operation of Eisenhowerism and of those who have fostered that infection. The miserable invalid gasping under its oxygen tent does not deserve to survive. . . . This is basically a conservative country, but conservatism has had no voice to speak for it and no leadership."[56]

Kelland was close to Goldwater. His candidate for assumption of that leadership was quite obvious. Nixon, watching the restlessness on the right — much of it working up enthusiasm for the senator from Arizona — took his own precautions. "I think that in the next few months, we are going to have to engage in a lot of soul-searching with regard to the future of the Republican Party," he wrote to Fred Clark of the free-market American Economic Foundation. Alluding to what brought down Bricker and other opponents of unions, he hoped Republicans would be "smart enough to present our case in such a way that we do not lead the rank and file of labor to believe that in opposing the extreme views of some of their leaders, we are also opposing the best interests of working men generally."[57]

No one else's career — neither that of "Mr. Republican," Robert A. Taft, nor Tom Dewey, nor Dwight Eisenhower, nor even Ronald Reagan — was as instructive about the fortunes of the modern GOP as Nixon's. Far more than anyone else, he provided that continuity from the generation of Hoover Republicans to a new crop of free-market libertarians who rebounded from New Deal restraints. He, more than any other figure of his generation, bridged cultural and geographic differences to keep in touch with mainstream Republicanism.

How much of all this was understood by Eisenhower is uncertain. The general-turned-politician was too enigmatic — some would call him, paradoxically, shrewd or naive, others too wily — to trust as a witness. He had, after all, moved from the military to the presidency under the banner of traditional conservatism; from there, without breaking stride, to "modern Republicanism"; then as the unlikely sage of a new progressive GOP spirit who, in the face of the Goldwater absorption of the party in 1964, suddenly stranded his moderate dependents. His behavior followed a familiar pattern: embarrassing indecisiveness about how to handle Nixon's secret fund crisis in 1952; shilly-shallying about Joe McCarthy until, providentially, the senator looped a rope around his own neck; vacillating about having Nixon on the ticket again in 1956; and, during his vice president's effort to succeed him in 1960, seeming to remain aloof to the younger man's everlasting dismay even when, at that particular time, there could have been no reason to believe that he had any doubts.

Ike was best at understanding what was possible. He never lost that famed wartime ability to maneuver among differing forces and personalities. As presidents are wont to do, however, he neglected the reshaping of his party or the projection of any coherent vision for the national future. He lacked the abundant missionary appetite of a Ronald Reagan; in the long run, he was salutary but inconsequential. Nixon, however, had neither Eisenhower's phlegmatic complacency nor Reagan's single-minded certitude. His way was not to avoid issues but neither, as was the case with Reagan, was it to let them become traps.

From the moment the Republicans lost in 1958, their future was his future, the prospect of winning the party's nomination the next step in a march to power that was barely a dozen years old. His anticommunism was pugnacious; oratory that befitted a Hiss-pursuer long remained his trademark. Cosmetic changes were made, including weight loss that deemphasized those familiar square jowls. Through the next decade, transformations of the "old" Nixon were less significant, the press notwithstanding, than a shifting GOP and, finally, a shifting nation. Inevitably, both later turned to him.

Rarely has any nation undergone such obsessive self-examination as did the United States during Eisenhower's later years. So introspective was the mood, so compulsive the undertaking, that finally the president himself appointed a special commission to look into the matter. Thus, during those four years before the celebrated Kennedy-Nixon campaign of 1960, prominent Americans signed on to a curious self-examination of a society uncertain about what kind of lumps it was trying to find.

   The most visible contributions came from three sources. The Rockefeller Brothers Fund, headed first by Nelson and later by Laurance,
organized America at Mid-Century, a special studies project, in 1956.
As with any Rockefeller project, the luminaries were not hard to convene.
The Rockefellers spent several hundred thousand dollars and signaled
its importance for all those subsequently enlisted: Chester Bowles, John
W. Gardner, Henry R. Luce, Dean Rusk, Robert B. Anderson, and, from
the Center for International Affairs at Harvard, Henry A. Kissinger.
The second study, organized by Luce for *Life,* ran as a series in the
magazine and later appeared in book form under the title *The National
Purpose.*[58] The Luce crew brought together Gardner plus John K. Jessup,
Adlai Stevenson, Archibald MacLeish, David Sarnoff, Billy Graham,
Clinton Rossiter, Albert Wohlstetter, James Reston, and Walter Lipp-
man. Also appearing in the *Life* series, soon after the nominating conventions, were statements by presidential candidates Nixon and
Kennedy. In February of 1960, Eisenhower fell into line by appointing
the President's Commission on National Goals. The report that came
out of that effort, *Goals for Americans,* was issued just nine months later.
   The Republican party itself enlisted in the search. In early 1959,
Meade Alcorn appointed a forty-four-member Committee on Programs
and Progress. Placed under the chairmanship of a youthful business
executive, Charles Percy, president of Bell and Howell, they were commissioned to stake out a GOP rendition of the national purpose to accept
on behalf of the party the responsibility for making "clear to the individual American his stake and his role in meeting the common challenge." In their case, however, the goal was defined as trying to provide
the party "with a concise understandable statement of our Party's long-
range objectives in all areas of political responsibility." Most notably, in
the effort to take the distant view, they chose the forthcoming bicentennial year, 1976, as the focal point of their studies. "We proceeded from
the premise that we are entering an era which will open new universes
to man — a new world with unique opportunities for human advancement, and tremendous challenges," explained Percy in his report.[59]
   The search for a national purpose assumed, first of all, that a society
dedicated to individual pursuits needed a common justification for carrying on as a nation state. For the most part, all other assumptions fell
into place just as easily: America's responsibility for carrying the free
world burden against the evils of Sino-Soviet communism; the potential
perfectibility of American democracy for justice at home and economic
and moral leadership abroad; the need to mobilize society to meet, not
only the global tests of democracy, but challenges to peacekeeping. All
in all, as the head of the presidential commission noted, the various
studies' conclusions added up to "platitudinous duds," all put forth with
confidence that, somehow, they would enable the United States to exert

itself as a force for good in an evil world. Virtually "everyone who discussed America's mission at the end of the Eisenhower era," historian John W. Jeffries has noted, "insisted that the United States must seize the initiative and advance liberty rather than merely respond to and contain Communism."[60]

Just about every national purpose statement, whether gathered by Luce, Rockefeller, or Eisenhower's national commission, even those most critical of where America had gone wrong, contained some tribute to the American spirit. Their common bond stressed the special qualities of this particular democracy; although it was imperfect, as several acknowledged, there was little doubt that sufficient will could attain the ideal. A commitment to democracy, suggested the Rockefeller panel, could unleash the "goodness and rationality of men." Democratic man was by definition civilized man, respecting others' rights and stature regardless of racial or religious background. "Ideas that have kindled the struggle for democracy in the modern world — the rights of man, the dignity of the individual — have expressed this attitude," they concluded. If men only had the will, they seemed to be saying, and were backed by the moral ideals of a "moral community," society could "join together in a common cause." With words that strikingly foreshadowed what the country soon heard, in loftier form, during the subsequent campaign, the Rockefeller people declared that "the great question is whether a comfortable people can respond to an emergency that is chronic and to problems that require a long effort and a sustained exercise of will and imagination." Nor did the president's own commission offer any doubt about what could be done. "We have never more closely approached a classless society," it announced; "there has been a revolution in the status of women; education is more nearly available to all; most citizens have opportunities which a century ago were dreamed of by only a handful."[61]

Such team efforts showed that it took celebrated minds to sanctify commonplaces and confirm them as gospel for the age. If, in all their work, there were any profound differences among the panelists, they were well hidden; sentiments often resembled old-fashioned Fourth of July exhortations, approximating an updated version of the old Manifest Destiny theme. In the nineteenth century, that theme had produced a momentum for subduing the continent all the way to the Pacific shores. In the twentieth century, the most compelling national purpose was to better prepare the nation, physically, morally, and economically, to resist the "grave" threat posed by Moscow and Peking.

There were only mild doubts, which questioned the temper, not the cause. Archibald MacLeish repeated his misgivings that the nation was succumbing to fear of the Russians. "It isn't just the Russians now: it's ourselves," he wrote. "It's the way we feel about ourselves as Americans.

We feel that we've lost our way in the woods, that we don't know where we are going — if anywhere." Columnist Walter Lippmann declared that "the Roosevelt-Wilson-Roosevelt formulae and policies and programs no longer fit the character of the world Americans are now concerned with, the world as it has developed since the second World War. We are now waiting to be shown the way into the future. We are waiting for another innovator in the line of the two Roosevelts and Wilson."[62]

Luce himself, the sponsor of *Life*'s national purpose project, had effectively pushed the dialogue almost twenty years earlier. When the magazine carried his "American Century" essay on February 17, 1941, it seemed to some that he was going well beyond criticizing 1930s isolationism. Luce saw the future in missionary terms, as the responsibility of a privileged nation. To Luce, the son of a man whose calling had pulled him to China, America was special, the evangelist of the free world.

In those pre–Pearl Harbor days, Luce urged recognition of the reality that we already *were* at war; as a world power, it was our destiny to reject isolationism, to "accept wholeheartedly our duty and our opportunity as the most powerful and vital nation in the world and in consequence to exert upon the world the full impact of our influence for such progress as we see fit and by such means as we see fit." American democracy could not work successfully, he argued, unless it could be made to work in "terms of a vital international economy and in terms of an international moral order." The twentieth century "is our century. It is ours not only in the sense that we happen to live in it but ours because it is America's first century as a dominant power in the world. . . . And finally there is the belief shared, let us remember, by most men living — that the 20th century must be to a significant degree an American Century. This knowledge calls us to action now." At a time when involvement in Europe's war seemed more and more like an unhappy inevitability rather than an opportunity, Luce wrote, "As America enters dynamically upon the world scene, we need most of all to seek and to bring forth a vision of America as a world power which is authentically American and which can inspire us to live and work and fight with vigor and enthusiasm. . . . And now, in this moment of testing, there may come clear at last the vision which will guide us to the authentic creation of the 20th century — our century." Far more in anticipation of the postwar than the prewar world, he called for his country to "be the Good Samaritan of the entire world" because it was "the manifest duty of this country to undertake to feed all the people of the world" who were victims of a collapsing civilization. In the following paragraph, he sounded remarkably like the Girondists of the French Revolution or Trotsky of the Russian: "We know perfectly well that there is not the slightest chance of anything faintly resembling a free economic system prevailing in this country if it prevails nowhere else."[63]

In a real sense, then, Luce never doubted the national purpose. Of Luce, too, it may be said, that, in the dying days of print as the prime means of communication, his was perhaps the clearest voice. The sense of urgency that tied the course of civilization itself to American willingness to influence was never as strong as when the world once again seemed too bleak for neutrality. Hitler's subjugation of much of Europe and tensions with imperial Japan were enough reason to shatter American detachment.

The next war would clearly afford no second chance. Just standing by, as the United States did before Pearl Harbor, was out of the question. Wicked communism attached itself with alarming ease to much of the world, especially nations just gaining independence after long colonial rule. Even if it spread no further, the alliance of the Peking Chinese — or, in general current usage, Red China — with the Moscow Communists was bad enough. Korea was proof of the dangers, and the current struggle to hold on to Southeast Asia demonstrated the continuing nature of the conflict. Who could doubt that the west was under siege?

That was where the focus was restored with the passing of Joe McCarthy and his crusade. Once the domestic squabbling over the internal threat had lifted, the external dangers became the focal point for a new consensus on internationalism. The solidity of such assumptions and scarcity of dissent were remarkable. For a time in the mid-fifties, hopes were stirred when Khrushchev and Eisenhower went to Geneva and clinked vodka-filled glasses to toast coexistence. Eisenhower clearly enjoyed playing Prince of Peace. Dulles, meanwhile, grumbled about appearances and worried that Ike and Nikita were looking as chummy as did FDR and Uncle Joe at Yalta.

So did dissenters from the right. William F. Buckley, Jr., fresh from fighting a holy war against heretics at Yale, dedicated his new *National Review* to the unremitting struggle against Red contamination. A candy manufacturer from Massachusetts, Robert Welch, dramatized the gravity of the crusade when he named his organization after an obscure soldier, John Birch, the "first American to lose his life in China in the cause of freedom." General Robert Wood and Dean Clarence Manion convened America First veterans to pursue anticommunism under the banner "For America." The politics of paranoia, supposedly discredited with McCarthy, were alive and getting stronger, even under the more respectable hunt for the national purpose. So it was with the cold war, which never seemed as cold or apocalyptic as at that late Eisenhower period.

A chilling sequence of events ostensibly confirmed the death of the "spirit of Geneva." Soviet ability to orbit an outer space satellite in October 1957 led to much agonizing that Americans had deceived themselves about the true state of Russian technology, *their* superior scientific education, *their* superior rate of growth, *their* superior single-minded dedication to a cause, "the great advantage of totalitarian nations." Barely a year later, Khrushchev renewed the pressure on West Berlin, calling for the creation of a "free city," while in the United States 81 percent of Gallup's respondents thought that American forces should be kept in the city even at the risk of war.[64] Khrushchev toured the United States in the fall of 1959 and much of the chill seemed gone from the cold war. Suddenly, in May of 1960, all else then seemed to drop from the heavens: a U-2 spy plane was shot down over the Soviet heartland, embarrassing Washington's cover-up and killing a planned summit conference in Paris that spring; rioting anti-American students prompted the Japanese government to cancel Eisenhower's visit; Fidel Castro, hailed by some as a Cuban George Washington after his overthrow of the bloody Batista government, seemed well on his way to letting the Russians sponsor his new order; turmoil in the Congo after independence from Belgium spurred apprehension that Patrice Lumumba was turning to the east for guidance and intervention; in Southeast Asia, Diem's government in Saigon and the Royal Laotians in Luang Prabang forced Washington to contemplate fuller intervention.

Gloom began to strain traditional self-confidence and reaffirmed the introspective obsession with defining the national purpose. When two young men, Nixon and Kennedy, became presidential candidates that summer, they did so against this background of multiplying troubles. If the search for what American society was all about was never meant to be equated with the implementation of specific policy in response to specific developments, it nevertheless gave the enterprise a somewhat Churchillian flavor.

To Kennedy, whose essay in *Life* appeared the week before Nixon's, what the nation faced was a test of collective will. He had begun the year by addressing the Massachusetts legislature and evoking John Winthrop's "as a city upon a hill" simile; now, drawing from David Lloyd George's recollection of how the inspirations of certain young Welshmen had been energized, it became a matter of climbing "to the hilltop." His key phrase was "the combined purposefulness of each of us"; he quickly added that that was *"when we were at our moral best."* That height, that purposefulness, consisted of a common effort, the pulling together of a society dedicated to doing what could not be done by individuals, all directed toward the attainment of the national ideal: the elimination of particular injustices. At a time when arguments for reform were often rationalized by citing how important to America's ability to compete with other nations were the humane qualities of its democracy, Kennedy argued that society had to work toward such objectives even without the motivation of a continuing cold war.[65] His view of the national purpose involved a Churchillian call for sacrifice and dedication that became the dominant theme of Kennedy's appeal.

How Nixon's essay parted from Kennedy's is instructive and, in a broad thematic sense, illustrative of the distinctions that separated the positions of the two men throughout the campaign, which suggests more consensus than conflict. Where Kennedy conceived of the perfection of the democratic process in terms of improved social and economic conditions for each individual, Nixon relied on the potential of men living freely and interacting without, as communism would have it, "a social discipline enforced by tyrannical state power." His analysis allowed no room for gradations of that power; it was either Communist or capitalist, with the latter freeing men to go about their business and reserving to them the options of how to exist and how to compete. "We are a society of individuals," he stated at one point, and that, he left no doubt, was the essential, liberating value. "Our capitalists are not the few but the many." Out of these individual wills came the dynamics inherent in freedom. Rather than enumerate, as did Kennedy, specific objectives that would consist in bettering the human condition — objectives, he noted, that were attractive to backward, newly liberated nations that were most receptive to the palliatives of communism — he proposed that the "goals of man" had to be achieved without sacrificing the essentials of justice and liberty. Here, sounding much more like the Herbert Hoover of the 1930s than like Adam Smith, he argued that the test of what we were ready to do about preserving that state of freedom was what we were ready to do about the "challenge to free society" posed by communism and, by extension, dependence upon government.[66]

People like Kennedy, however, discussed the national purpose in terms of having a "will" or a "desire" to do the right thing. Once granted that assumption, they could declare, as did Kennedy in Washington on the day before announcing his candidacy, that America had gone wrong because "the sense of the promise of America and the will to fulfill it" had been "lost." Implicit in all this was that the "will" could be generated by a "call to greatness," a theme not unlike that used by the Democratic titular leader, Adlai Stevenson.[67]

For Nixon, it was not a calling but an educational process, not merely to stimulate latent humanity, but rather to reach the people so they could be informed that there were certain natural truths, realities that defied mere inspiration. The world could not be remade, he held, in a sense that recalled Spencer, Sumner, and other nineteenth-century Social Darwinists. The system, in other words, would have to operate through its own self-enforcing mechanism, kept in line by the Constitution and by the conflicting multitude of interests anticipated by the Founding Fathers.

Nixon, and conservatives generally, saw that as the best hope for stability and preservation of a climate for entrepreneurialism and, more broadly, freedom. Certain fundamental principles had seemingly been buried under the rubble of the economic crash of the 1930s, but these conservatives were not convinced that it had all come falling down because of a failed structure. Theirs was sophisticated doctrine, one that had little in common with popular notions about the inherent evils of capitalism.

When Nixon complained to Henry Luce that his publications had shortchanged coverage of a speech he had given to the Harvard Business Association, he emphasized that it was the responsibility of Luce and other friendly publishers to help get across "a subject as vital to the people's welfare as this whole matter of taxation, of business to people relationships, and our economic growth requirements."[68]

What actually followed during Nixon's campaign against Kennedy was in large part conditioned by the atmosphere that Luce had helped to create. Nixon, "Ike's boy," had to remain loyal to the record of the past eight years, differing only cautiously, as when he sided with the Democrats about the need for stronger defenses. Such gestures of independence, however, were easily overshadowed by his continued ties to the president. Eisenhower's delayed entry as an active campaigner, moreover, was handled entirely offstage, the warning by the president's physician against arduous speechmaking unknown to the press and public, raising more doubts about the older man's enthusiasm for Tricky Dick. Even more difficult for Nixon was being caught in a squeeze between the GOP's Rockefeller moderates and Goldwater conservatives. The Democratic candidate, of course, had to deal with the matter of his religion, which he did brilliantly, but aside from that he was first to adopt as virtually his own the themes of the national purpose debate. As television broadcaster Howard K. Smith remarked about Kennedy and the report of the president's commission, "One would swear he wrote the document."[69] Just recognizing the legitimacy of a need to define national goals placed Nixon in the position of implying that America had somehow lost its way under Eisenhower.

To Nixon's distress, then, the high ground for that campaign was, in effect, the ability to promote national purpose rhetoric. The theme became indistinguishable from what Kennedy called the "need to get America moving again" and his insistence on the need to regain America's "fallen" prestige.

The outcome of the 1960 election proved very little, which is often true in American presidential politics, where battles are less often resolved along significant ideological — or even leadership — lines than by conditions external to the campaign and the candidates. Nixon, who held out all night before conceding, later emphasized the closeness of the tabulation: only some 113,000 popular votes out of over 68 million cast, a difference of just 2 per precinct. Fraudulent counting in a number of places, especially in Texas and Illinois, where Chicago mayor Richard Daley had reportedly reassured Kennedy that "with a little bit of luck and the help of a few close friends, you're going to carry Illinois," could easily have deprived Nixon of an actual popular plurality. Even a more judicious distribution of the two-candidate vote that went to unpledged electors in Alabama, can be used to demonstrate that more voters actually cast their ballots for a Nixon victory. One method developed by *Congressional Quarterly,* one at least as valid as any other, actually gives Nixon a national popular vote margin of 58,181.[70] Any judicious consideration of that possibility should at least facilitate an understanding of why he believed that he was not rejected by the American people.

The debate over Illinois can probably never be laid to rest. Nixon, in his postelection account, enumerates the precincts where votes outnumbered voters. Mayor Daley, despite policing by the Republican Eagle Eye Program, surely managed to withhold returns until he knew just how many votes would be needed for a statewide plurality. The overall Kennedy margin in Chicago was a healthy 450,000; statewide, fewer than 9,000. His Texas edge was much more substantial, 46,233.[71] Altogether, a total of fifty-one electoral votes were at stake in the two states, twenty-four in Texas alone.

For Nixon to have been declared the winner would have required reversing the entire two-state total, which, in any event, would have been a dubious action. The fact that he needed both states made any change impossible. Texas, where Mexican children were paid to stand by the polls to beg people not to vote Republican because they would "never see their fathers again," had absolutely no provisions for a recount. In any case, there was no chance that the state's Kennedy margin could have been overturned. Moreover, in Chicago, twenty-two precincts were recounted during the first week in December, but the total recovered was too low even allowing what gains Kennedy could have made in a nonpartisan tabulation of downstate Illinois. When considering that the great majority of the counties were in Republican hands, any possibility that a legitimate canvass would have enabled Nixon to pick up more votes there disappears altogether. Moreover, as corrupt as the voting in Illinois and Cook County may have been, "fraud in vote-counting was nationwide — both in their own fraud and Democratic fraud," Theodore H. White, the foremost authority on what happened in 1960, has written. To compound matters even more, Edmund F. Kallina's recent analysis of the controversy has shown that the Cook County recount indicated that more votes were recovered for the three other Republican candidates than for Nixon.[72]

Several of those close to Nixon, including Eisenhower, urged a recount. Nixon disagreed. His judgment was sound, both at the time and with the advantage of greater perspective. The complications and dangers were too great, all arising out of the inevitably lengthy and contentious process. He told Earl Mazo that the "country couldn't afford the agony of a Constitutional crisis — and I damn well will not be a party to creating one just to become President or anything else." Such dangers were sure to be compounded by prolonged court fights that would have gone well beyond the moderating influence of any one man, including Nixon. Victory under such circumstances would hardly have been worthwhile, especially if the Texas vote stood unchanged. There was also the prospect, Nixon later explained, that challenging the results would inevitably give him a "sore loser" reputation that would tarnish his political future.[73]

For those wishing to understand Nixon and the America of his time, there is something more important than attempting to disentangle the matter of who really won. The fact was that Nixon and his associates remained convinced that the election had been stolen from under him. Considering every questionable aspect, including the method used to translate totals for unpledged electors into popular votes, one does not have to fantasize to suspect that more people actually went to the polls wanting Nixon than Kennedy. Virtually every sympathetic account has taken up the theme. Mazo, in an updated version of his Nixon biography that he wrote with Stephen Hess, has repeated much of the investigative work on the situation that he did for the *New York Herald Tribune,* and continues to lean toward the stolen election interpretation. Nixon "was deprived of victory" was the flat-out conclusion of the *Chicago Tribune* and his advocate Victor Lasky. That he had merely turned the other cheek rather than been defeated became a significant theme for supporters of his renomination in 1968 who denied that he really was a two-time loser.[74]

One thing was certain: he could not let it happen again. His second time around in Chicago, when he ran for the presidency against Hubert Humphrey, included a far more elaborate system of monitoring than the Eagle Eye Program. This time, ironically, the Nixon people were also armed with the legal paraphernalia provided by the Kennedy and Johnson–sponsored Voting Rights Act of 1965, which provided for court challenges against voting fraud. The new machinery to safeguard the returns was supervised by an experienced FBI investigator, Louis Nichols. Of more than passing interest, however, was that the machinery was created at Nixon's specific request by Robert R. Mullen.

Mullen was a journalist by trade. During the GOP's 1952 campaign, he served as public relations director of Citizens for Eisenhower. From there, his career moved into ever-closer ties with the CIA. By 1968, CIA agents were on the payroll of Mullen & Company, and it was well established as a CIA front. One CIA director, Richard Helms, explained that "Mr. Mullen did us the patriotic favor of allowing us to put some of our agents abroad under his company." One of those agents was E. Howard Hunt, who later became deeply involved in the Watergate scandal. Shortly afterward, Mullen & Company was purchased by Robert Foster Bennett, the son of a Republican senator from Utah and a friend of Charles Colson. Bennett was also sufficiently close to people in the organization of millionaire recluse Howard Hughes for him to become a suspect as the celebrated "Deep Throat" of the Watergate affair.[75] Most important is that Mullen's front group was already thoroughly associated with intelligence operations in 1968 and, contrary to the CIA's legal mandate, involved in such activities within the United States.

Called Operation Integrity, Mullen's project enlisted more than 100,000 poll-watchers nationally. Texas, of course, was a key point, but so, too, were such areas as the Carolinas, where voters were customarily shuttled back and forth between two states to bolster key precincts.

But the main target was Chicago. Nichols, at the command post, brought in a contingent of additional FBI agents and lawyers, working under the jurisdiction of the statewide office of the United Committee for Nixon and Agnew. A "bucket shop" operation of twenty-five telephones and a task force of lawyers scrutinized the legitimacy of "voters" registered by the Democratic machine. One lawyer signed himself into a Skid Row flophouse and was recruited as a voter, along with the resident derelicts, with the payment of a dollar a head. Although a formal complaint filed under the Voting Rights Act lost in court, the task force salvaged the situation by publicizing substantive findings that were made of violations. When the judge also warned that he might urge the impaneling of a special grand jury and a special prosecutor, copies of his remarks were circulated throughout area pool halls, flophouses along West Madison Street, and the Skid Row area to intimidate precinct workers. According to a subsequent report, the threat worked. Local Democratic leaders suddenly faced a minor rebellion among their usually docile charges. All in all, Operation Integrity was credited in 1968 with slicing in half Humphrey's downtown vote and helped the GOP ticket carry the state with a 135,000-vote margin. Similar claims were made for such other states as Florida, Virginia, North Carolina, and New Jersey. The lesson emphasized by the national Nixon-Agnew campaign was to retain such security operations on a permanent basis. In 1972, Jack Caulfield, a former Bronx policeman who went from undercover work in New York City to a security job with Nixon's 1968 campaign, suggested that something he called Operation Sandwedge should, as a successor of Operation Integrity, be formed to carry out political intelligence for the reelection of the president.[76]

However exaggerated the credit given such intelligence work for the success of the 1968 campaign (which, of course, totally ignored the question of Republican tampering with the electoral process), the experience reinforced Nixon's belief in Roscoe Conkling's well-known dictum that "parties are not built up by deportment, or by ladies' magazines, or gush!" As Nixon surely also knew, his loss to Kennedy in 1960 was influenced by far more significant factors. The Survey Research Center of Michigan calculated that his opponent's religion cost him some 1.5 million ballots.[77] Tennessee, for example, which had twice gone for Stevenson over Eisenhower, carried much of the anti-Catholic Bible Belt vote into the Republican column. Other aspects of the campaign, such as the effect of the four radio and television debates, are hard to calculate. They must have given the younger, less well known Kennedy valuable prominence; his skill, especially as demonstrated during his first head-on session with Nixon before a national audience, made him an equal rival. But what ducking out of debates altogether would have cost Nixon can never be known. The black vote, on the other hand, is clearer. Kennedy's involvement, just days before the election, in getting the Reverend Dr. King out of a Georgia prison (he had been arrested at a sit-in) helped move that already heavily Democratic vote more fully into the Democratic column. Such states as Illinois, Michigan, and South Carolina went for Kennedy by far smaller margins than expected, considering their numbers of black voters.

Still, all that could have been overcome but for the conditions that had plagued Republicans two years earlier. Too few Americans identified themselves as party loyalists, and far too many continued to accept the notion that there was a necessary relationship between Republicanism, big business, and hard times. When Nixon used his Ambassador Hotel telephone to call the president from across the continent the morning after the election, his explanation for what had gone wrong was simple. The GOP was too weak; organization was inadequate; his own vote was some 7 percent ahead of the Republican party, while Kennedy trailed his fellow Democrats. He also could have added that he ran ahead of 235 of the Republican congressional candidates out of the 359 competitive districts, and outpolled GOP gubernatorial candidates in 19 of the 27 gubernatorial contests. As a result of "the disastrous 1958 elections . . . the Republican Party was at its lowest ebb since 1936," he later wrote. And in 1960 the Democrats claimed a 17 million advantage in the two-party division.[78]

As he himself pointed out, everybody seemed to have postmortem advice. "If only" he had refused to debate, or hadn't waged a me-too campaign, or had been more liberal, or more conservative, or had used Eisenhower more, or attacked Kennedy for exploiting the religious issues, or been kinder to the press . . . Somehow, if only he had done this or done that, the 100,000 popular vote plurality would have been overturned, the needed switch of a half vote in each precinct, and, if he had stood his ground about fraudulent canvassing, the 303 to 219 electoral votes could, presumably, have gone the other way.[79]

But what Nixon well knew, and suggested as much by citing "the disastrous 1958 elections," the weak economy had hit Republicans, already a minority party, where they were most vulnerable. That, more than anything else, accounted for the pattern of how people voted. While Roman Catholics backed Kennedy, they did not necessarily do so *because* they were Roman Catholics. Middle- and upper-class Catholics, many of whom had voted for Ike in the last two elections, largely managed to resist the lure of their coreligionist. Blacks were even more wholeheartedly for Kennedy. Even the Jewish vote was more solid. In general, the more affluent vote fell behind Nixon. Of businessmen surveyed by the Research Institute of America, Kennedy's share was only about 20 percent.[80]

Where conditions were depressed, especially in urban regions of the Northeast, Kennedy's vote was one-sided. His early-evening swamp of Nixon in the working-class city of Bridgeport, Connecticut, failed to foreshadow how the race would tighten with the accumulation of additional returns. As the count piled up, it became obvious that pocketbook worries were more likely than religion to drive voters toward Kennedy. In city after city, Nixon's vote depended more on high unemployment than anti-Catholicism.[81]

The problem, reported Nixon's pollster, Claude Robinson, two weeks after the election, was that "too few people . . . think as Republicans, and have confidence in the G.O.P." The party could not hope to regain public confidence without rebuilding, not only through organization and finance but with younger leadership, and behind an ideology compatible with the mass of voters. Only Nixon, Robinson stressed, was closest to the mainstream. Only he could pursue "an acceptable ideology," which should ensure an appeal that would broaden the base of financial contributions. Only Nixon, he warned, could "prevent a suicidal split between the Goldwaters and Rockefeller[s]" and push the GOP rank and file "toward the mean than to the extreme, thus neutralizing the power of extremist leaders."[82]

13

Does It Make a Difference?

UNLIKE CLAUDE ROBINSON, Eric Sevareid was not boosting a particular candidate in 1960; but, as a nationally known journalist, he was reviewing the prospects, and they were not very pleasant. Whereas Robinson was trying to pinpoint mainstream Republicanism, Sevareid wondered whether the term had any functional value or simply connoted what to him seemed a continuation of 1950s Eisenhower-inspired drift. To Sevareid, as to most of his colleagues, it had also become evident that what the voters were being asked to buy had little to do with any of the substantive qualifications. "Wisdom is essential in a President," he wrote, but "the appearance of wisdom will do for a candidate."[1]

Furthermore, not a Lincoln was in sight. Even if one were, he wouldn't be recognized, a fact of life long since obvious to the veteran commentator. "Rarely," in fact, he wrote in a preface to a guide to the candidates that appeared in 1959, "has the private quality of a man been the deciding factor in his election to the White House." If such was true in the past, it was even more so now. In an age of appearances, "the wrapping seems more important than the contents." Given such realities, it was only natural that if a candidate "is of poor and humble origin, he must appear at ease with the rich and powerful; if he is of rich and powerful origin he must make it clear that his heart has always been with the humble and the poor. He must appear, in other words, to be the universal man. We are a complex federation."[2]

By the time the conventions were over, Sevareid's "rule" was again confirmed, embodied by the choices of Kennedy and Nixon. Alas, wrote Sevareid in one of his columns, that campaign summer marked the arrival of the "Organization Man," packaged candidates who stood for nothing but their own ambitions. How they felt about any of the real issues that moved men and women who "dreamt beautiful and foolish dreams about the perfectibility of man, cheered Roosevelt and adored the poor" was virtually unknown. "I can't find in the record," Sevareid went on, "that Kennedy or Nixon ever did, thought or felt these things. They must have been across the campus on Fraternity Row, with the law and business school boys, wearing the proper clothes, thinking the proper thoughts, cultivating the proper people." He would be damned, he added, if he "ever thought one of them would end up running the country."[3]

Kennedy and Nixon did have their similarities, conceded Arthur Schlesinger, Jr., his pen summoned for the counterattack. They both came of age in the 1930s and did represent "the bid of the postwar generation to take over the American government." But, argued the Harvard historian in *Kennedy or Nixon: Does It Make Any Difference?*, it was Nixon, more than Kennedy, who was the midcentury man, "obsessed with appearances rather than with the reality of things, obsessed above all with his own image, seeking reassurance through winning, but never knowing why he is so mad to win or what he will do with his victory." Nixon was neither reactionary, radical, nor conservative, but a condition out of David Riesman's *Lonely Crowd,* the perfect example of an "other-directed" man: driven by externals and reflecting nothing more than the vicissitudes of his environment. Let such a man shift ground on the spot, he would pay no price. He could be for anything, or against anything: "Nixon could be for or against the Taft-Hartley Act, for or against Chiang Kai-shek, and no one would be surprised." Richard Nixon "stands for almost nothing."[4]

Did it *really* make any difference? as Schlesinger's subtitle asked. What could have been more disturbing that August than for liberals who did not share Schlesinger's faith in Kennedy to conclude that their party had merely ratified the political disaster of the Eisenhower-McCarthy fifties? What else would one call pitting their own Nixon against Nixon? "Today unless you are as scurrilous as Nixon," wrote Agnes Meyer, wife of the *Washington Post* publisher, to her friend Adlai Stevenson, "you can succeed only by being as shrewd and organization conscious as Kennedy. . . . A man who believes in character, who loves ideas, high standards, above all loves his country and wishes to serve it for those reasons, has no place in a world in which even the people who play games are professionals. You are the last of the great artist-men such as Churchill, Roosevelt, Wilson. The era of the engineer-statesmen has begun." At lunch later that month, Henry Kissinger argued that the real issue was not who could best manage the status quo; that line would doom Kennedy in a debate with Nixon. "The issue is a new epoch," said the Harvard professor and consultant to Governor Rockefeller. "If we get a new speech and a new spirit, the technical programs will take care of themselves." Among his own circle of liberals, Kissinger's luncheon companion, Schlesinger, had already circulated a privately printed pamphlet that envisioned "a *'qualitative liberalism'* dedicated to bettering the quality of people's lives and opportunities" as a successor to the "quantititave liberalism of the thirties."[5]

Genteel men of breeding, good men all, secure behind families, trust funds, and properties passed down from generation to generation, were talking to each other and hearing very much the same things. Some held public office; others performed their service by accepting appointments from established politicians. There were those who, like Dr. Kissinger, historian and author, had fled Nazi rule and found that, in America, he could break out of his Cambridge office and touch those who had not had the inconveniences of his past. In 1960 it was his privilege to play with the Kennedyites while advising Rockefeller; later, better known for his writings on nuclear strategy, he played with the Johnsons while advising Nixon. With everything else that has been observed about Henry Kissinger, there is a tendency to forget that his two most significant clients, Rockefeller and Nixon, were the men who, in the long run, played for stakes that were as decisive as anything implied by the campaign against Kennedy. Ironically, too, it was within the Republican party itself, the so-called party of the fat cats, that Sevareid's man of "poor and humble origin" clashed with someone who epitomized "the rich and powerful."

Nelson Rockefeller was, in fact, so rich and so powerful that one can understand how hard it would be for him to comprehend that the world was not his. Among the many contemporary estimates of Rockefeller wealth was *Fortune*'s, which suggested $100 million to $200 million as his personal worth, all part of some $2 billion to $3 billion in family assets. He was, suggested Stewart Alsop, "the only potential presidential candidate in our history whose family's personal economic decisions might conceivably have an important national impact."[6]

Rockefeller's grandfather, the original John D., was a parvenu not much different from William Dean Howells's paint magnate, only he was far more successful, far more powerful, far more significant than the fictitious Lapham. He was the quintessential robber baron who savaged competitors, created the Standard Oil monopoly and joined the world of Vanderbilts, Carnegies, Morgans, Goulds, and Harrimans in overwhelming the proper, pious, ministerial architects — the Roosevelts, Fishes, Adamses, Beechers — the "builders" of America. With the surrender at Appomatox, the newly industrializing society unleashed ambitious captains of industry: their capital, replenished by boundless European investments, fueled growth that created a transatlantic industrial revolution. The depastoralization of America had begun. Smokestacks surrounded the flats of worker shanties, denoted mills that went up along streams and rivers that had heretofore flowed through the woods without any particular function.

In America, as in Europe, cities experienced spectacular growth. By fin de siècle, midcentury outposts were transformed into crowded cities. Rural America had not yet vanished, but its steady decline was unsettling enough for those with ties to the past. To worsen matters, the new cities received the human rejects from all over, immigrant laborers becoming as familiar as Currier and Ives families. How much can America take? asked Reverend Josiah Strong in 1885.

> When our urban population has been multiplied several fold, and our Cincinnatis have become Chicagos, and our Chicagos New Yorks, and our New Yorks Londons; when class antipathies are deepened; when socialistic organizations, armed and drilled, are in every city, and the ignorant and vicious power of crowded populations has full found itself; when the corruption of city government has grown apace; when crops fail, or some gigantic "corner" doubles the price of bread; . . . then, with *the opportunity, the means, the fit agents, the motive, the temptation to destroy, all brought into even conjunction, THEN will come the real test of our institutions.*[7]

That, together with lamentations of the "passing of the great race," was the world in which Rockefellers became Rockefellers. Theirs was wealth on a scale unimagined by the American aristocracy that grew from the colonial plantings. But freedom from feudal heritages also brought freedom for new industrial powers, who tried to settle for modern replicas of medieval lordships; only as the Rockefellers, and also the Morgans, Carnegies, and Kennedys soon learned, things cannot be quite the same in a multitiered society, where even state police powers are rarely satisfactory.

Discovering such truths was always painful. It was not that great wealth and authority were exactly commonplace. What mattered was how much they owned of the treasures that could be found. Nelson Rockefeller would ultimately, like Ted Kennedy, rise to his preordained station, enchant the political world with the presence of one not only financially well-endowed but also well-gened and, frustrated that he could not conquer, inexplicably, find emotional satisfactions elsewhere, settling for warm and tender arms instead of the obeisance of a fickle public.

When he first crossed Nixon's path, he had no need for his ultimate refuge. That escape was still years away. The essential difference between the two men, however, as much as all the other obvious differences, was that, to Nixon, Rockefeller's realities were not so much fantasies as indulgences.

He took over the government at Albany and immediately converted the state and the inherited Republican party into a Rockefeller manor. His swearing-in was hardly off the front pages when New York Republicans found themselves among the unwanted, swept out by a determined architect of a new order. Vacancies in the state's supreme court and downstate were filled while ignoring, according to Meade Alcorn's complaint to Nixon, "two excellent, experienced trial lawyers in their middle fifties, both of whom had been approved by the Bar Association."[8] The party's national chairman, also about to become a victim of change, heard the outcry of New York Republicans who, in effect, had been thrown off their ramparts. The new governor didn't give a damn about channels, i.e., working through party leaders, and overturned the orderly patterns maintained by Tom Dewey. Revitalizing the party after four years of Harriman was one thing; so was rewarding the efforts of those who, like L. Judson Morhouse, had plotted the Rockefeller coup and trampled upon the political backs of those who had stood in the way. Both Len Hall and Erie County leader Walter J. Mahoney, the big power around the city of Buffalo, had supported their own gubernatorial ambitions in 1958, which hardly made them natural allies of Rockefeller. But this was unconscionable. Not only were loyal and competent Republicans being sacrificed, but Rockefeller's desire to establish what he called a close-knit organization (an upbeat euphemism for imperial rule) gave key state posts even to Democrats.

"No Republican regulars will want to see Rockefeller or even hear his name," wrote a dismayed Alcorn in February 1959. The new governor was "absolutely murdering the Republican organization in New York City." Upstate, even stalwarts not in Mahoney's tent smelled Eisenhower-type disdain for political perquisites. It followed almost naturally that the president's talented speechwriter, Emmet Hughes, was imported from Washington to continue his work in Albany. Hughes himself had come to personify the nonpartisan intellectual in politics, which seemed to bed him down with Rockefeller very appropriately. The "above politics" charge, in fact, jabbed at the new governor almost immediately, together with conservative Republican and populistic worries that he was too liberal and was trying to use the power of inherited wealth to smother their trusty machine with his personal empire. They were "demoralized and disintegrating rapidly," Alcorn warned Nixon.[9] Even to the more dispassionate, Rockefeller could be seen as on his way to devouring the state's Republican party and taking over the soul of its last GOP governor, Tom Dewey.

That was even apart from the Rockefeller program which, to all intents and purposes, made him anathema to the very party he hoped to lead. His inaugural address, written by Hughes, the maverick Democrat turned Eisenhower speechwriter and author of the "I will go to Korea" campaign vow of 1952, established at the outset what became a trademark Rockefeller characteristic, piety and power. "Our neighborhood is the world," he said in Albany that January. "It is divided, essentially,

between those who believe in the brotherhood of man and the father-
hood of God — and those who scorn this as a pious myth."[10] The sermon
became so familiar that journalistic derision dubbed it BOMFOG.

BOMFOG was, in a sense, Nelson's spiritual link to grandfather Rockefeller, who had apparently written the soon-to-be-overworked phrase in
an old Bible. Its use gradually helped ridicule John D.'s grandson as a
visionary not of this earth, as a preacher trying to atone for the sins of
his privileged heritage. The thought of Rockefeller as president "gives
me shivers, to say the least," wrote the chief curmudgeon of the right,
William Loeb. "The Republic may be in bad shape now, but it certainly
would be pretty nearly done for after HE got it."[11] Publisher of the often
sensational, sometimes lurid, and always outspoken *Union-Leader* of Manchester, New Hampshire, Loeb exerted an influence that exceeded both
his circulation and his good sense. Other Republicans also shuddered
at the thought of Rockefeller.

Rockefeller's reputation as a liberal always did border on the irrational.
Compared with Loeb's, however, his views would seem liberal. Loeb
represented a primitive, populistic, anticommunist nihilism that, in the
American context, often passed for conservatism. When even those more
grounded in reality dismissed the New York governor as a man of the
left, it was appropriate to ask why, and many have. Agreement seems
fairly general that the bloated notion of his liberalism had more to do
with publicity about Rockefeller family charities to humanitarian causes
than to starry-eyed notions of economics, international communism,
peace and war, racism — in short, than to anything of substance that
separated him from Richard Nixon. Hugh Scott, who worked with both
men, simply concluded that they "fitted easily under Ike's 'Modern Republican umbrella.' " Certainly, Stewart Alsop pointed out, there simply
did not exist between Nixon and Rockefeller the areas of disagreement
that separated Dewey and Taft and Eisenhower and Taft. One of Rockefeller's friends predicted that "he'll be the first man to ride to high office
on a tide of philanthropy."[12]

There was little incompatibility about creed, but much to be said about
the state of the political process, in which dialogue bounced back and
forth within a small circle, an area of exchange that did not tolerate the
iconoclastic. Both Nixon and Kennedy had, after all, been drawn into
the national purpose dialogue. Still, the quest remained a Rockefeller
mission that, in essence, involved consolidating for the postwar world
the means of rationalizing for American society the humanitarian principles of the Enlightenment.

Maybe because of that, Rockefeller became the "liberal" and Nixon
the "conservative." As often as writers and biographers may try to explain
that impression, pointing out, for example, as does Garry Wills, that old
John D.'s value system "left a deeper mark on his whole brood than

Whittier did on Nixon," Americans will remain as convinced as were his
Republican contemporaries. One point of difference between the two
men, as Wills has explained, also helped to account for their individual
styles. Nixon, he argued, "has spent his life on the way up — up a particularly jagged cliff. Nelson was *born* on top, king of the mountain, with
only one moral duty, endlessly inculcated — to throw lifelines down to
those stuck on the cliff."[13]

Peter Collier and David Horowitz, in their book tracing the Rockefeller
family story, also made the observation that "people had willingly sus-
pended their disbelief and made the sort of allowances for him they
would not have made for any other politician in America." Almost na-
ively, too, there was remarkably little appreciation for Rockefeller's inherent political base, which, with its array of minority groups and greater
acceptance of welfare liberalism, virtually cajoled progressive juices out
of any politician with statewide ambitions in New York. Journalist Stewart Alsop, who interviewed both Nixon and Rockefeller for a dual study
published in 1960, noted the latter's unquestioning assumption of basic
values, which made for an essential conservatism that was unlike Nixon's.
To Alsop, it seemed "a fair guess" that Nixon "would be a less conservative President than Rockefeller — for he is at heart a less cautious
man." "I'm always willing to take a chance," Nixon told him. "I think
that has been the mark of my political career." In a remarkably prescient
observation, Alsop added: "One can imagine Nixon, far more easily than
Rockefeller, deliberately deciding 'to take a chance' at a time of great
international crisis in order to turn the crisis to the West's advantage, as
he turned the fund crisis . . . to his own advantage."[14]

Only on foreign and defense policies was there any real debate, and
there, more than on domestic affairs, Nixon was circumscribed by his
need to support the administration's record. Had that not been the case,
he, like Rockefeller, would have been on the side of bolstering military
strength. As it was, Rockefeller emphasized the eventual goal of arms
control and disarmament and called for countering what he and the
Democratic candidates claimed was a "missile gap," while Nixon was in
the position of having to defend Eisenhower claims. In an address before
the Academy of Political Science in New York City, however, Nixon
acknowledged that "some more positive courses of action than massive
military deterrence must somehow be found."[15]

Shorn clean of their direct competitive and electoral needs, notions
of Rockefeller liberalism become more farfetched. It was the New York
governor, for example, whose infatuation with a nuclear fallout shelter
program helped set off some of the more extravagant cold war hysteria.
President Kennedy adopted that approach through a conscious desire
to undercut Rockefeller politically when he mobilized the nation to
counter Khrushchev about the continuation of American rights in West

Berlin. Later, he acknowledged that stimulating popular anxieties in quite that way was overdoing the point. Moreover, Rockefeller, elected to Albany four times and presiding over a state with a strongly dovish electorate, nevertheless remained a strong supporter of the American war in Vietnam, a conflict that he neither inherited nor had the direct responsibility to "end with honor." It was Rockefeller as New York's governor who promoted both no-knock and drug enforcement laws before they were adopted by the Nixon presidency, and yet it was the president's record that was remembered and the governor's, with its preventive detention and mandatory life sentences, that was forgotten.[16]

Submerged under the subsequent history of Richard Nixon was how Nelson Rockefeller, the New York "liberal," rode roughshod over advisers with qualms about civil liberties and shaped a drug bill that Joseph Persico, his chief speechwriter, describes as one that "left no hope for rehabilitating an offender guilty perhaps of a single mistake in life." He did so, too, while zealously guarding the "secrets" of his scheme from such interested colleagues as Governor Ronald Reagan of California. Outraged editorial writers helped make the final bill somewhat less Draconian, but, as Rockefeller's successor, Governor Hugh Carey, later pointed out, the law "resulted in injustices in numerous cases and has made courts, prosecutors and jurors reluctant to enforce its provisions," an especially melancholy finding considering that it was not even "effective in reducing drug traffic in New York."[17] Rockefeller, in memory and in GOP folklore, remained the liberal who could have saved the Republican party's progressive soul.

Most of all, Rockefeller was a promoter. His dyslexia relegated him to Dartmouth, then known as a school built around a gym, instead of to Princeton, his first choice. Only days after his graduation, he followed the proper scenario by marrying Mary Todhunter Clark, intelligent, civilized, level-headed, and with the sort of liberal outlook permissible for a straying daughter of Philadelphia's Main Line and the Foxcroft School (Pennsylvania's progressive Democratic politician Joseph Clark was a relative). A Rockefeller-Clark union made no headlines except on the society page. Nor was there anything newsworthy about a Rockefeller devoting himself to various enterprises that balanced government service with overseeing, together with his brothers, the family's vast financial network. Franklin Roosevelt, who was as enchanted by the Rockefeller association as anyone else, sent him to South America, which was laced with the family's money. As assistant secretary of state for Latin America, he played a significant wartime role in securing U.S. acceptance of Juan Perón's Argentina by making possible that government's admission to the United Nations when, after a too-cozy wartime friendship with Nazi Germany, it became a "belligerent" on the Allied side only weeks before Hitler's collapse. He designed an economic and social assistance aid plan for Latin America, the American International Association (AIA), and oversaw its counterpart, the International Basic Economy Corporation, which, as Persico states, was Nelson's "chosen instrument to deliver to Latin America the blessings of Yankee enterprise, the supermarket, mass distribution and low retail prices, all at a fair profit." Rockefeller's hemispheric designs, especially his AIA, became a model for Harry Truman's Point Four Program to aid underdeveloped nations; the entire pattern of enlightened economic assistance, in fact, was a precursor of the Marshall Plan for western Europe.[18]

From the outset of Eisenhower's administration, Nelson Rockefeller played a supporting role, helping to create the new cabinet-level department of Health, Education, and Welfare and becoming its first under secretary. Schemes for federally assisted medical insurance and school construction were also hatched in his office but hardly got past the door, the former shot down by the American Medical Association, which was vigilant about protecting the public from being demeaned if government came to their rescue in times of physical distress. Nelson's vision was, however, much broader, and inevitably returned him to the outer world and grand designs involving war and peace. Eisenhower's dramatic Open Skies proposal, which called for the United States and the Soviet Union to open their territories to aerial surveillance, and which highlighted the Geneva summit meeting in 1955, had Rockefeller's byline.

That Rockefeller formed a working relationship with Emmet Hughes seems natural. Both were essentially irreverent, the writer brilliant, independent, ultimately sufficiently disrespectful of team loyalty for his later book on the administration, *Ordeal of Power,* to be seen as a betrayal of trust. Rockefeller was a Hughes without eloquence. What he lacked in intellectual strength, somewhat traceable to the handicapping effects of dyslexia, was compensated for by the ebullience of his personality and the ability to put his weight behind his desires. Nixon's objectives could only be realized by planning, designing, and plotting, always plotting, figuring the angles, calculating the potentials. Rockefeller assumed he had only to command. He once startled New York mayor John Lindsay and others in his Fifth Avenue apartment when they realized that he was perfectly serious about wanting the removal of two buildings, the YMCA and the Ethical Culture Society headquarters, because they kept him from seeing the Metropolitan Opera House at Lincoln Center from his window.[19]

That was the Rockefeller whose principal home at Pocantico Hills resembled, said Persico, "the official residence of a Middle European chief of state." The main house was decorated with a gallery replete with Picassos, Pollocks, and de Koonings. The vast Rockefeller family acreage in New York's prime Westchester County was not merely a refuge from that twenty-three-room triplex apartment at 810 Fifth Avenue but an estate and art museum that would have been appropriate at the Tuileries. Startling those skeptical about his entry into electoral politics, he overcame the kind of gaffes that were routine for one so far removed from the world where people lived and worked. At an early stage, he tried to clarify how his tax plan would affect individuals by explaining to some reporters how it would apply to an "average" guy who made fifty thousand dollars a year. The newsmen, who surely would have welcomed that salary, were visibly amused, but accounts of the incident do not record that they offered any enlightenment. The cram course on state government he had received as chairman of Governor Harriman's special commission to determine the feasibility of summoning a new constitutional convention had evidently not fully connected his feet to the soil.[20]

Money, his tax plan in particular, became the audacious move that brought Nelson's new administration its wider notoriety. The simple fact was that Governor Rockefeller undertook the conversion of his state into a model for bigger things; it was important to show that he *could* make the trains run on time, literally. He immediately went after the troubled commuter system of the state's great metropolitan region. By "successfully tackling this problem," Bob Finch, who returned from California in 1958 to become Nixon's administrative assistant, advised, Rockefeller would show that "he can master the same growing problem the nation over." Preliminary to that, and all the other designs he had in mind (he had run for the governorship on a "can-do" progressive theme that covered everything from rent controls to health insurance), was fiscal solvency, pulling income into line with expenditures. As Republicans not only in New York but across the nation watched with what can most delicately be called rapt attention, he proposed raising $277 million in new taxes rather than cutting services, thereupon converting the GOP's sensational new vote-getter into the boldest player of them all. Local Republicans were up in arms. Democrats, hurt in the recent election by Rockefeller's successful appeal to independents and their own irregulars, accused him of "soaking the poor." "So this rich character gets elected," Stewart Alsop quoted a New York City taxi driver, "and right away he's got his hand in my pocket."[21]

Rockefeller was en route to creating monuments and deficits. His multistructure Empire State Plaza in Albany would have impressed Napoleon III, and it later challenged the skills of the budget managers. His infatuation with building monuments to mark his reign brought gibes about an "edifice complex." As a first step at the outset of his long years in Albany, however, he won the essentials of his tax program, modifed only slightly by a legislature that followed its leader.

He seemed to have certain "natural qualities," political analyst Samuel Lubell told some friends at a small dinner party, that translated into a

compelling public personality. Rockefeller's personal flair, which made
him a glamorous, likeable figure at Dartmouth in contrast to the Gloomy
Gus of Whittier and Duke, rendered him a strong, attractive campaigner
from the outset: the prince as commoner so much more enticing than
an ambitious plebeian. Hardened upstate New York pols would swoon
and report ecstatically that Rocky — if one could forget who he *really*
was — behaved like one of the boys. "God must have meant Nelson to
be a politician," said an admiring old pro. Even before the governor's
fiscal program became a factor, the Gallup poll showed an interesting
distinction in the respective strengths of Nixon and Rockefeller. Among
Republicans only, the vice president was preferred by two to one. Independents, however, were another matter. Nonpartisans separated the
two men by a statistically meaningless 1 percent. Nevertheless, by the
second month of Rockefeller's administration the central conflict was
already shaping up. His personal appeal, private willingness to use his
great leverage, and demonstrated ability to capture the middle ground,
so needed by the party, were all running athwart the cultural discomfits
of traditional heartland Republicans about considering Rockefeller as a
member of their world. The board chairman of the Upstate New York
Farmers and Traders Life Insurance Company already proclaimed the
governor's "rush to impose taxes" a crippling setback for his presidential
ambitions. Even by mid-February 1959, surveys showed Republicans
rejecting the notion that winning was everything. "Rocky," reported
columnist Gould Lincoln, was "too far left of center" and had already
alienated many conservatives. Additional surveys, bolstering the Gallup
findings, showed Nixon preferred by a wide margin. For all Rockefeller's
mass appeal, argued Lincoln, it was Nixon who was best able to unite
the party.[22] He was certainly to be preferred over a Rockefeller who was
turning his state's existing political structure into a blatant instrument
of his personal power.

Rockefeller, Nixon well knew, could hardly be ignored. Even if the
biggest capitalist of them all could not buy out Republicans everywhere,
his creation of a New York State fiefdom had the potential for serious
obstructionism. New York was still the largest state in the union and its
number of delegates led naturally to preoccupation with the Rockefeller
"problem."

Simple logic could have told Rockefeller that, victory or no victory,
everything was against him. The Republican objectives were to counter
the trend shown in the 1958 election and restore the momentum that
had led them to power under Ike; but, of course, the question was how
to do it without the general. Every bit of evidence — national registration
figures, the party's failure to carry Congress even with Eisenhower's big
win in 1956, and the most recent setback — all indicated trouble ahead.
Republican stalwarts were harmoniously behind a salable program and

credible candidate. Nelson, for all his attractive personal qualities and command of a financial network, posed the least desirable factor: divisiveness. The scenario dictated a centrist healer, one who could reconcile divisions, not dig chasms.

Oddly, in view of Nixon's reputation as a contentious, Red-baiting hardliner whose natural home was with the Republican right, he was associated with some of the same anxieties felt about Rockefeller. That suspicions toward even a centrist agitated heartland Republicans was no surprise to anyone who experienced the national committee's gathering in Des Moines in early 1959, just two months after the disastrous congressional elections. When, for example, Eisenhower kicked off the meeting with a message about the need for an "unremitting effort" to be made for 1960 by a party that had been playing at hibernating, Senator Barry Goldwater shot back with a telegram suggesting that the elephant would come out of hibernation when it knew what direction it should point its trunk. Goldwater, there was no doubt — not Nixon, and certainly not Rockefeller — represented the spirit of those congressional Republicans who dominated the two days in Des Moines. "Let's quit copying the New Deal," urged the Arizona Republican, "seeking only for votes and remember that a two-party system needs two philosophies and not just one." Ideas like "modern Republicanism" were clearly indulgences that had to go, foisted by a president whose indifference to partisan and ideological needs had brought disaster.[23]

Moreover, insofar as Nixon was concerned, he was neither entirely credible as a winner nor satisfactory to conservatives as a departure from the Eisenhower brand of moderation. Party chairman Meade Alcorn, who worked to put things together at Des Moines that January before relinquishing his job because he "simply had to go home and get to work," recalls the regard for Nixon in an "available man" context rather than as a natural heir to Republican principles. There were, Alcorn explained, "a great many who went along with the Nixon move because they felt that it was a greater hope, if not assurance, of peace than getting into a fight over the nomination. There were many — not one or two, but many — quiet exploratory moves made by members of the party in the hope that they could unearth a candidate who would sort of storm the convention, but nobody succeeded in that. I think that Nixon was the beneficiary of a condition in the party that a great many party workers hoped wouldn't explode into a worse situation or a worse fight than we were already in." Such principles applied even to Barry Goldwater, who damned modern Republicanism, damned flirtations with liberalism, thought the party had to move to the right because there was no room on the left, but, above all, wanted to win. If Nixon could keep Republicans in the White House, fine. Meanwhile, as though to ensure that principles would not be sacrificed along the way, Charles Percy's Committee on Programs and Progress was supplied with a set of "tried and true principles" that would retain the spirit of Taft Republicanism.[24]

The specter of Nelson Rockefeller would not disappear. A Gallup poll issued while the Des Moines meeting was still under way showed that he was Nixon's only real rival among the Republican rank and file. Nobody else was really in contention, but Nixon's lead was commanding, 56 to 27 percent.[25]

Nixon's close monitoring of Rockefeller was excessive. The governor's prospects for getting enough delegates never were bright. Still, Nixon took no chances, regarding a Rockefeller challenge as formidable almost by definition. He looked into the millionaire's business involvements, hoping less to confirm the breadth of his fortunes than to expose weaknesses by citing instances of failure. He had Herb Klein check out the ownership of Rockefeller's airplane; if the title belonged to one of the governor's brothers, Nixon reasoned, it could well constitute a violation of the five-thousand-dollar limitation on campaign contributions. Rocky's jugular, if it could be exposed and constricted, was the vulnerability of a blatant capitalist in a capitalist's party that asked for the vote of Everyman. If he could not be sidetracked that way, there was the momentary hope that Senator Kenneth Keating, who represented Rockefeller's own state, could be enticed to shoot for the party's vice presidential nomination. That would really torpedo the governor. All Nels's money could not buy a rewriting of the federal Constitution to permit all electors to vote for two candidates from the same state.[26]

Throughout 1959, especially, the vice president's office was a virtual clearinghouse for intelligence on Rockefeller. Bryce Harlow of the White House staff reported that conversations with key southern Republicans brought the uniformly disturbing opinion that Rockefeller would "sweep" the region and "that Nixon would lose every Southern state," largely because of his pro–civil rights position on the filibuster issue. At the April meeting of the Republican National Committee, when Alcorn was replaced by Thruston Morton, the party's top brass urged unity, and Rockefeller backers were sufficiently in evidence with offers of their own formula. From the West Coast there were warnings of Rockefeller strength as shown by the respected Field poll and urgings that a more aggressive campaign be launched by the early establishment of Nixon clubs. Bill Loeb, in New Hampshire, sounded a similar theme. If Nixon failed to launch an early drive for that state's March primary, warned its strongest molder of public opinion, "we will find that a combination of Dartmouth Alumni plus Rockefeller money will sweep the New Hampshire primary for Rockefeller."[27]

In Rockefeller's own state, much depended on Tom Dewey. Herb

Brownell dined with the governor and told Len Hall, it was later related, that Rockefeller "is one of the most ruthless men he has ever seen in politics. He told him in so many words that he was going to punish anyone in New York who was against him." Dewey, out of politics and into lucrative law, was, in effect, on a tether to the new power in Albany. Of equal importance was his prominence among New York City's Republican business establishment, thereby placing him at the core of any Rockefeller-Nixon competition for support from that valued group. Hall, who was well acquainted with all the principals, advised Nixon that Dewey and Rockefeller lunched at a club at least once a month "and you have to figure out that Dewey will finally land publicly in the Rockefeller camp." Then referring to the man who was so instrumental in making Nixon vice president in the first place, Hall added, "He thinks it is the toughest spot he has been in. In his heart he thinks he is for RN but you know him — with his clients — and his concern with money — when Rockefeller pushes the button some of these fellows who are for RN now will go for NR." Rockefeller, Hall then advised, "would not stop at anything"; nothing should be taken for granted. As one of Rockefeller's associates said, "Nelson doesn't expect you to be a yes-man. But he does expect you to be a Rockefeller man, first, last, and all the time."[28]

Moreover, Nixon had also heard, Dewey was doing some business with the White House. Brownell was trying to push Eisenhower to get him on the Supreme Court, but the president was not convinced about his "judicial judgment." Dewey did, according to gossip in New York, succeed in arranging an Eisenhower-Rockefeller get-together. Elmer Bobst of the Warner-Lambert pharmaceutical company and a Nixon fat cat, also snickered at Dewey's love for money: his arrogance had increased with his income and he was "playing loose with his patriotism" by representing the Japanese government as a lobbyist for $200,000. Another wealthy backer, communications czar Walter Annenberg, later heard that Dewey was angling for a dinner appointment with Nixon, a sure sign of a weakening Rockefeller political outlook. Despite all this, there remained the issue of Nixon's electability. When Nixon's assistant Charlie McWhorter dined at Dartmouth with James Reston, he heard the *Times*'s chief Washington correspondent praise Nixon, along with Lyndon Johnson, as "the two ablest politicians of this century," but Reston doubted that Nixon could be elected. In that state, Bill Loeb was continuing to burn with fear of Rockefeller. By mid-October, he thought it was time to either fight for New Hampshire or concede it to Rocky. "If I didn't think Rockefeller was so bad for the United States," wrote Loeb to Herb Klein, "I wouldn't give a darn because I hate to get mixed up with bunglers like you fellows are in New Hampshire. . . . We often say in New Hampshire the only folks who like us are the plain people — thank God. But it is their votes that you and Nixon need."[29]

Conservatives who watched Nixon and the maneuvering within the party were also confronting the reality that while Rockefeller was merely a red herring in all this, nothing could prevent the vice president's nomination. In December, Ralph de Toledano faced a gathering of the restless on the right. He told a forum sponsored by the *National Review* that the possibility of a Nixon victory "seems to have struck terror in the hearts of certain Republican conservatives" who were elevating "masochism to a political principle"; put off largely by Nixon's civil rights position, they doubted his conservative credentials. "Perhaps it is too liberal, for some conservatives, to grant the privileges of education, voting, housing, economic opportunity, and decent treatment to men because of their religion or the color of their skins," said de Toledano. "If this is so, then Mr. Nixon will have to do without this kind of conservative support."[30]

The discontent may have been at a tolerable level; it certainly was not isolated. Too many who called themselves conservatives feared that signing on for Nixon was like buying a pig in a poke. They questioned his reliability on such issues as medical care for the elderly. They feared imminent surrender on even such sacred prerogatives of states over the federal government as teacher salaries or race relations. Curiously, although these principles were hardly violated by the current Republican administration, author Clarence Budington Kelland wondered whether Nixon would become president "in name only while actually remaining General Eisenhower's Vice-President."[31]

A *Wall Street Journal* lead editorial pointed out that Nixon was no "darling of the conservatives" and was, in fact, "far too liberal on such matters as foreign aid, international development and welfare legislation." In mid-January, shortly after the *Journal*'s editorial, Senator George Aiken of Vermont, a moderate Republican, came out of a meeting with the vice president and told the press that yes, in effect, Nixon was more liberal than the Eisenhower administration, and that included more sympathy for farmers, who had long rebelled against the economics of Agriculture Secretary Ezra Taft Benson. He was even, explained Aiken, "well to the left of much of his vocal support." Aiken, one of those eastern Republicans who had drawn close to Nixon, was also careful to say that the vice president was "not so far to the left as some would want him to go." Nixon even gave a private interview that spring to Arthur Krock, a conservative pillar of the *Times,* and warned that he rejected the "feet-in-concrete" stance of Republican rightists while also opposing liberal concepts of how to use the federal government. "I will be political at times, of course," he told Krock. "But I am damned if I will be demagogic, and make promises the Democrats will make that would bankrupt the country if executed."[32]

*   *   *

The balancing act was deft, but the price was high. Nixon, it seemed, was acting true to form, subordinating principles to tactics. The old Nixon, the anticommunist gut fighter and villain of the Voorhis-Hiss-Douglas wars, had acquired a new mask. He appeared on the David Susskind "Open End" television talk show, and, reminded by the host that Joe McCarthy had produced "a legacy of hate, suspicion and rancor and deflation of our national image" while ineffectually "rooting out subversion," Nixon explained that he had warned the filibustering late senator "on several occasions that it is vitally important to shoot with a rifle in this area and not with a shotgun." That tendency, he explained, had gotten McCarthy into trouble. Investigations into subversion "must be directed at only actions and not to beliefs." Each conservative gesture was balanced by a nod to the center and left; he was neither one way nor the other. He mixed deploring racial injustice with calling attention to its national rather than merely southern dimensions. He denounced the power of organized labor but stood firm against right-to-work laws. At a time when the Soviet launching of *Sputnik* simultaneously set off thousands of anguished missives about how American educators, especially progressives concerned with teaching the "whole child," were overlooking the importance of the mind to the body, he agreed that education deserved priority treatment; still, controls should be kept at state or local levels. He wanted the federal government to balance the budget but joined in the chorus for economic growth. He addressed the American Society of Newspaper Editors in April and told them that he believed in "economic conservatism" and quickly added that "conservatism at its best must be progressive." He was "an economic conservative," he said, "because I believe that conservative economic policies provide the surest and best road to progress for the great majority of the American people." In opening the first of three *Newsweek* columns based on conversations with Nixon, Raymond Moley repeated an observation that others close to the vice president had noted: in the dozen years since he had known Nixon, his philosophy was characterized by "remarkable consistency."[33]

He was also the statesman par excellence. Most dramatically, he was developing to the fullest the process begun with his Far East trip of 1953, of vice presidential involvement with diplomacy. In 1959, little more than three months after Fidel Castro's revolutionaries swept in triumph through Havana, Nixon met with the new Cuban leader informally and on a Sunday in April, in the vice president's private office in the Capitol Building.

Nixon, according to his notes of their conversation, listened to Castro tell about his desire to carry out the will of the Cuban people. It was, Nixon dictated immediately afterward, "almost slavish subservience to prevailing majority opinion — the voice of the mob." In sizing up Castro, nothing impressed the vice president more, not even "his naive attitude toward Communism and his obvious lack of understanding of even the most elementary economic principles . . . in evaluating what kind of a leader he might eventually turn out to be." There was some irony, which was not reflected in his notes, that here was the vice president of a freely elected government, of the world's proudest democracy, seated in the United States Capitol, advising a revolutionary dictator about "slavish subservience to prevailing majority opinion — the voice of the mob." He should know, Nixon told Castro, that "it was the responsibility of a leader not always to follow public opinion but to help to direct it in the proper channels." Nothing very positive was likely to result from departing from "democratic principles on the ground that he was following the will of the people." At a time of "emotional stress," it was important "not to give the people what they think they want . . . but to make them want what they ought to have." He also found Castro as hopelessly naive about economics and capital. "I told him quite bluntly that his best hope as far as the United States was concerned was not in getting more government capital but in attracting private capital," but the hero of the July 26 Movement insisted that plants licensed by the government would serve the interests of Cuba better than privately owned enterprises.[34]

The off-the-record meeting, taking place at a time when Castro was spurned by the White House but was a revolutionary hero elsewhere, is fascinating in retrospect. Each was then doing his own maneuvering at home, Castro in an attempt to consolidate his revolution by satisfying the appetite for revenge against the notorious Batistanos and jockeying, at the moment, between getting support from the United States or the Soviet Union, and Nixon laboring to develop a consensual position among warring Republican factions, getting them to subordinate whatever reservations they had about him for the greater cause of resisting being swallowed up by Nelson Rockefeller. Their meeting also took place close to the preliminary stage of White House hatching of a counter-revolutionary plot against Cuba itself. The plan, in which the vice president played a central part, first involved internal harassment via dropping counterrevolutionaries behind the lines, hiring mob elements to assassinate Castro, and, finally, landing a brigade at the Bay of Pigs. All that was not far off when Nixon concluded his session with the Cuban by deciding that he was "either incredibly naive about Communism or under Communist discipline — my guess is the former," and noted that "his ideas as to how to run a government or an economy are less developed then those of almost any world figure I have met in fifty countries." Nonetheless, he was a power who would have to be dealt with, and, Nixon concluded, "we have no choice but at least to try to orient him in the right direction."[35]

Several months after meeting with Castro, Nixon received a graphic demonstration of the dilemma of leadership, of the difference between responding to mass psychology and, as he himself tried to explain to Castro, of making the people want "what they ought to have." The case involved Caryl Chessman. The most publicized man on California's death row, and probably in the nation, Chessman was condemned to go to the gas chamber. Nixon was not yet his party's candidate for the presidency. As a Californian and the party's front-runner, he could not dodge the issue, not merely questions about Chessman's possible innocence but the broader matter of the death penalty. There were, nationally, fifty-six legal executions that year, but the moral and legal questions were yet to be as easily dismissed as they would be in the 1980s, when another Californian became president.

The Chessman case was, for its day, the equivalent of such passionate death-penalty predecessors as Sacco and Vanzetti and Julius and Ethel Rosenberg. There was even a reaction from the official Vatican newspaper, *Osservatore Romano,* which condemned Chessman's execution as barbaric. Chessman, dubbed the Red Light Bandit, had waged a twelve-year battle for life. Rather than guilt or innocence, the question involved whether he had committed a capital crime. One thing was clear: Chessman had killed nobody; he had been sentenced in 1948 for forcing two women into his car, at gunpoint, to perform fellatio. The issue bounced back and forth within the legal system and the press. Meanwhile, his cause was further publicized through a series of books that Chessman wrote in his San Quentin cell which helped promote the popular belief that a man who had taken no lives should be punished by something less severe than death. As his legal appeals made headlines, San Quentin became the focal point of demonstrations. The Berkeley students who protested and stood vigil outside the prison in 1960 were the vanguard of the Bay Area radicals of just a few years later. Abbie Hoffman, who was among them, recalled that a fellow demonstrator had wondered about it all after both the warden and Governor Pat Brown had expressed misgivings about the May 2 execution: "How does that work?" said the student. "In a democracy, I mean, no one wants to see him die and the state kills him?"[36]

Nixon had, in February of that year, been confronted with the issue of capital punishment. Governor Brown's call for a special session of the legislature to consider abolishing the death penalty led to the inevitable question as Nixon faced a panel of newsmen before the microphones of station KQED in San Francisco. As to killing people for committing crimes, he explained, that was a California issue, one that he ought not to get into. Still, he could not say he was against the death penalty itself; decisions should be made on specific cases. But there was no question that, as a resident of California, he felt that "we should retain" the penalty for "capital crimes" as "a deterrent to crime" as the so-called Little Lindbergh Laws had done. The Quaker, who had long since disassociated himself from any notions of pacifism still identified with that faith, then explained that "while we naturally must be concerned about the lives of criminals that we take, we have a greater concern for the lives of innocent people that might otherwise be taken by criminals if they did not face this deterrent." Fawn Brodie's conclusion that "Nixon was strong for capital punishment" was an overstatement and not precisely the way he had put it.[37]

When the baseball season opened that spring, so did the gates of San Francisco's new stadium, Candlestick Park. Governor Brown was there for the opening and there was a full house. To the fans that day, the name Chessman was about as familiar as Willie Mays. Governor Brown's call for a sixty-day reprieve for the condemned man made him the most despised person in the new ballpark. Twenty-five years later, Brown, an attorney in Beverly Hills, recalled how the fans booed when his name was introduced. Nixon sat alongside him, he also remembered, and, when the noise had subsided, the vice president said to him, "That was a pretty good booing, but it doesn't compare to some I've gotten." Brown thought about that moment fondly and about how gracious it was of Nixon to make that comment at a moment that was personally mortifying. Standing there as governor, with some fifty thousand Californians expressing contempt, was in itself a sort of execution. He never forgot Nixon's effort to assuage the pain. When the vice president himself was then introduced, the crowd gave him a standing ovation.[38]

During the summer of 1959, in a political coup, he went to eastern Europe, debated with Khrushchev in the kitchen of a model home display at Skolniki Park in Moscow, and won major political credit at home — meaning, of course, media prominence — for "standing up to Khrushchev" while selling democracy and the joys of a society that wanted to live in peace. The trip was worth a five-to-six-point boost in Nixon's popular standing, and, as he has reported, it helped to narrow his difference with Kennedy. *Commonweal,* the liberal Roman Catholic periodical, applauded the fact that the vice president "has helped reduce, to some indeterminate degree, the chasm which has divided the Russian and the American peoples."[39] The illusion of détente brightened that fall. Despite some shenanigans, Khrushchev's tour of the United States, which squared him off against American capitalists, labor leaders, opportunistic politicians, Disneyland, and shockingly revealing female backsides on the Hollywood set of *Can-Can,* spurred dreams of a bright new world. A summit meeting in Paris would be followed by an Eisenhower trip to Moscow. After a near blowup over Berlin, the great powers had backed off.

Nixon enjoyed the political breakthrough but was more philosophical about the diplomatic significance. "It is absolutely essential that we keep the 'spirit of Camp David' in its proper context," he wrote to Henry Cabot Lodge. "There is nothing Mr. Khrushchev would like better than to frighten all of his potential critics into silence regardless of what he may have done in the past or does in the future." In short, he had no doubt, he wrote to another correspondent, that Khrushchev "is and will remain a dedicated Communist and will continue to pursue Communism's long term objective of world domination."[40]

Even at that moment of his popular political gain, Nixon's dilemma was clear. The passionate right was blowing its whistles ever more desperately. In New York, Bill Buckley organized an anti-Khrushchev rally at Carnegie Hall. Pointedly, the organist played a Bach fugue, and the mourners included such militant anticommunists as Rabbi Benjamin Schultz, Eugene Lyons, Brent Bozell, Joe McCarthy's widow, Jean, and Dean Clarence Manion. The latter's Manion Forum, a right-wing group, had already called Khrushchev's planned September visit a "national disgrace and worse appeasement than Munich." The alternative, Nixon explained to Dick Berlin, was to convince Khrushchev "that the Marxist view of a divided, exploitive and decadent Free World is hopelessly outmoded and that the only national course of action in a world of nuclear weapons is peaceful competition rather than his present tactic of unilateral aggression."[41]

By late fall, for all the fulminating by people like Bill Loeb, it was also clear that Rockefeller was not strong with those whom he needed to give him the nomination. When paired in trial heats against Kennedy, he did well; against Nixon, there was no contest. In mid-December, only Rockefeller and Nixon did credibly in a purely Republican field, but even then it was no contest: Nixon led by 66 percent to the governor's 19. Entering the New Hampshire primary could only confirm the Rockefeller disaster. Senator Margaret Chase Smith of Maine, whose "Declaration of Conscience" had appealed to Republican civility in the face of Joe McCarthy a decade earlier, then took it upon herself to forestall bloodletting by urging both Nixon and Rockefeller to pledge that, if nominated, each would invite the other to become his running mate in order to have "a team [that] would give the United States its greatest combination of executive leadership in the years ahead."[42]

According to Teamster's Union boss Jimmy Hoffa, however, Senator Smith was not being addle-brained about Rockefeller's strength. Hoffa had his staff prepare a report that showed how Rockefeller could marshal what a Nixon friend described as an enormous "business network, including banks, oil companies, etc., through making available or withholding money, credit, business opportunities, etc.," and thereby "produce a campaign of very considerable magnitude." There were, in effect, many Tom Deweys out there and, Nixon was told, "Rockefeller is going to make a big try for the Republican nomination."[43]

Coinciding with the arrival of that bit of intelligence, on the day after Christmas, Rockefeller, "running into a blank wall," as Theodore White put it, issued a statement that he was not inclined to expend the "time and energy" that would obviously be required to buck "the great majority of those who will control the Republican convention," and made a "definite and final" withdrawal of his candidacy, a gesture he repeated eight years later. The move was made with remarkable political ineptitude. Only a few months earlier, he acknowledged that his decision would be dictated by how Gallup gauged his relative standing with Nixon late that fall. All the energy and investment of time, money, and carrying the torch for the national purpose hinged, so he acknowledged, on how the pollsters calculated the numbers at that particular moment.[44]

But he was Rockefeller, and because he was Rockefeller, few people were convinced that he had really decided the wall was unbreachable. At year's end, Gallup found that 59 percent of those polled were favorable toward Nixon. The same survey, however, reported Jack Kennedy's favorable rating at 62 percent. The significant difference, which most assuredly was not lost on either Rockefeller or Nixon, was that more than twice as many said they were "extremely unfavorable" toward Nixon than toward Kennedy. As Claude Robinson then warned Nixon, "You will be the top target of all the dead cats, rotten eggs, innuendo and snide remarks that the opposition can throw. Without any doubt there is a hard core of 'hate Nixon' voters. We have talked about this . . . but possibly only a psychiatrist could figure it out and even then there would be some question as to the accuracy of the diagnosis. The best theory . . . is that the liberal fringe has a guilt feeling attached to the Alger Hiss case and wishes to blame you for it." Nixon absorbed all this and wrote to Walter Annenberg at year's end that more weeks would have to pass before the full effect of Rockefeller's announcement could be appraised.[45] It was obvious that Nixon had a Dr. Moriarty watching him from Albany.

What made Dr. Moriarty especially dangerous was growing affection for an Arizona senator rapidly winning attention as a conservative stalwart, Barry Goldwater. With Rockefeller apparently out of the way, Republican rightists were far more likely to draw a bead on Nixon's head. The vice president could hardly advertise his moderation and preserve his standing with those of his party who viewed Eisenhower as a betrayer of sound principles. The surging Goldwater activity, as Charles McWhorter reminded him, was a manifestation of "the 'uneasiness and restlessness' of the 'hard core' Republicans over your alleged flirtations with the 'liberals.' " Rather than settle for a middle-of-the-road position, the senator's backers felt they were "entitled to a clear cut choice between a pure liberal and a pure conservative."[46]

No longer a foil for Rockefeller among the rightists, Nixon found his position more precarious. Never a favorite of the eastern establishment but tolerated as long as he could be sold as "Ike's boy," he was vulnerable to attacks from the other side by those who, having gotten rid of one "liberal," were little less inclined to settle for a centrist.

Nixon the accommodator was clearly on Goldwater's mind when he attributed 1960's defeat to failure "to present to this nation a bold political organization unequivocally committed to an easily definable political philosophy." Indeed, as a critic of the Kennedy administration, he was unsurpassed and unrestrained, freshening political dialogue with the sort of astringent dissent that gained him a loyal following on campuses and in young Republican clubs. His private fondness for the president became, in public, a voice that expressed the idea that those dedicated to organized labor and the restoration of the New Deal were attempting to resurrect "statism" in the postwar era. "The brave, bold rhetoric of the New Frontier — the magnificent phrases — stand naked and shivering. . . . The Young men who promised to lead us forward on a dead run have been running in circles. The transfusion just didn't take," he charged after two years of the Kennedy presidency. "The tired old panaceas of the depression '30s, despite their chrome ornaments, aren't working any better today than when they were first tried." Then, with the type of flourish of which more were due to be heard, Goldwater added, "If we, as a people, have lost sight of our national goal, if we are confused, if we are floundering and groping, might we not find an explanation for this confusion in the two-faced images both national parties have presented at the polls in recent years."[47]

That was, in fact, the authentic appeal of the Goldwater drive, a movement that had its immediate origin in Colonel Robert McCormick's charge about me-tooism in 1948. With Goldwater, there were no such compromises. He outdid Nixon as a cold warrior, identifying himself even more closely with everything military and tough. By the time 1960 rolled around he was already on record with a call for the GOP to move to the right because they had gone about as far to the left as they could go. He championed the South, states' rights, and opposition to federal intervention in race relations. In Barry Goldwater, labor leaders, especially United Auto Workers chief Walter Reuther, had their most tenacious opponent. He had stood fast with the twenty-one other Republicans who resisted the Senate's condemnation of Senator Joe McCarthy. A wealthy member of a merchant family, Goldwater also had the rugged good looks associated with a westerner, and, adding to this appeal, spoke as plainly about his convictions as any politician since Harry Truman while avoiding the excesses common to many on the far right. He was, for example, not as wild as Dean Clarence Manion and his Manion Forum or battling congressman Bruce Alger of Dallas, the lord of a fanatic "Mink Coat Mob" of right-wing women, making him and themselves a local legend. In 1960, Alger smelled a Nixon bid for the liberal vote. Goldwater, in contrast, kept his head, recognized that Nixon would be better than any Democrat, and puffed new hope into the hearts of those who, like John Bricker of Ohio, thought that "the American people are ready for a revival of some real old fashioned patriotism." "Thirty years ago the innovators called themselves radicals," wrote the author of *U.S.A.,* John Dos Passos. "Now mostly they call themselves conservatives."[48]

Goldwater's 1 percent among Republicans that January meant that the true believers still needed the numbers to equal their passion; their man had already become the favorite speaker of the grass-roots fund-raising dinner circuit. The Young Americans for Freedom, then some twenty thousand strong and with chapters on a hundred college campuses, were with him to a man. When it hit the stalls that year, Goldwater's *Conscience of a Conservative* did for political action what Hayek had done for economics. Within four years, the best-seller, which was especially popular among college students, went through more than twenty printings. His presence, at the very time when Richard Nixon, the old hero of the anticommunist right, was trying to go all the way, marked what a historian of the conservative movement has noted as "the first thrust of the postwar New Right into presidental politics. Indeed," added George H. Nash, "it is likely that without the patient spadework of the intellectual Right, the conservative *political* movement of the 1960s would have remained disorganized and defeated."[49]

In all this, Goldwater was aided, ironically, by the process that had recently enhanced Nixon's credibility as a statesman, the exchange of visits with Khrushchev. As an official with Manion's group wrote to the president of the Southern California Edison Company, "You can't shake hands with dedicated Communists and break even, Mr. Quinton. If relations should worsen after the trip — and this is quite likely — Mr. Nixon will get the 'rap' for it. He will be dubbed in the public mind as the man who glad-handed Khrushchev and brought it all about. It is not entirely incredible that Mr. Nixon's trip to Moscow was engineered by those who would even risk *war* rather than have him get the nomination." Only months before the convention, the prophecy of Mr. L. F. Reardon, the Manion Forum man, was confirmed when the U-2 plane episode shattered the projected Eisenhower-Khrushchev rapprochement. After the incident, twisting matters the other way with Goldwaterite heat on his back, Nixon could reemerge by exploiting his reputation for being tough on Communists. He had talked tough to Khrushchev in Moscow and stood up to the Russians. That was it; he had made the point; hardly anyone could quarrel with Nixon's spunk. If, at that moment in American politics, public opinion indicated anything other than a consensus about the cold war, it was well hidden, confined to the left bank of the Hudson and the shores of the Charles.[50]

The turn of events also gave credibility to claims that the administration's defense preparations were lagging. Several military analysts and congressional specialists charged the inevitability of a so-called missile gap, by which they meant an approaching period of a few years when Soviet ballistic capability would approximate or even exceed U.S. ability. A logical interpretation was that America would then be far more vulnerable to a first strike. A number of Democrats, notably the ambitious Senator Kennedy, took up the cry. Eisenhower sat firm on his own private, classified information and scorned such critics. Nixon was less sure, tending to agree that more was needed. Rockefeller, who was not restrained by his ties with the administration, was clearly less inhibited. In February, he directed his State Defense Council to follow through by getting legislation for the mandatory construction of air raid shelters.[51]

Thus, more illusions were encouraged. Everybody reached for self-serving "evidence." The Goldwaterites had no reason to permit their minuscule standing in the polls to keep them from pushing for their man. Hadn't Wendell Willkie come from nowhere in 1940? Look how Harry Truman upset all predictions! Rockefeller was out, had not a chance, and was forced to step aside through ideological, cultural, and social incompatibility. Nixon was more concerned with juggling, trying to please the Kellands and the Loebs along with the entire New York crew. Most emphatically, his stands on race doomed him with the right. If Goldwaterites, then, had illusions of at least diverting the party, they were not alone in believing in the potential power of their sectarian thrust. Two GOP moderates, Senators Aiken of Vermont and Javits of New York, drew up a nine-point "Declaration of Purpose." Aiken's explanation was blunt: "We had to do something to counteract pressure from the far right in our party on the convention and on the Vice President himself."[52]

That Nixon approximated their position was clear, especially with his rulings on cloture to weaken filibusters. By 1960, the Reverend Dr. King said that Nixon was the only potential presidential candidate who cared about civil rights. Jackie Robinson, who was a Republican and shared the vice president's view on economics, also gave his support to Nixon.[53] Both men, the human rights leader and the ballplayer — two of the most prominent blacks of their day — saw in Nixon someone whose views on racial matters could be reconciled with their own broader attitudes toward society.

Then, too, southerners were reacting accordingly. Traditional repugnance against Republicanism was gradually being buried in history; upholding the "lost cause" always came first. Of the major political figures,

only Goldwater understood the South. He alone stood uncompromis-
ingly between them and the continuing oppressive Yankee mentality.
Southerners had, in fact, felt betrayed by Nixon. Bryce Harlow's sound-
ings left him convinced that, before Rockefeller's withdrawal, state after
state might actually have preferred the New Yorker, if only to punish
the vice president. Goldwater appeared on a "Face the Nation" television
interview and reaffirmed his understanding of the people of the South
who, on their own, were moving away from violence. Unlike the more
zealous of his supporters, he acknowledged that Nixon would be better
than any Democrat. He, at least, would give Dixieland a fair shake.[54]

Rockefeller, meanwhile, proceeded to demonstrate that the doubters
had been right all along about his noncandidacy. He continued to carry
the anti-Nixon message, becoming something of a latter-day Stassen.
Eisenhower, speaking of both Nixon and Rockefeller, said at one point
that his concern was "that two people — even if they should both become
candidates for the same nomination — who have supported me so long
and faithfully through the years . . . should find themselves publicly at
odds. . . . My opinion is that people can be politically ambitious if they
so desire without necessarily becoming personal antagonists." In a July
news conference, he called Rockefeller "dedicated, hard-working" and,
as he did later when addressing the convention, remained thoroughly
neutral. Once again appeared the pious, holier than thou, disingenuous
general, standing above the battle, safeguarding his chastity and 68 percent Gallup poll approval, while the boys muddied their hands. So circumspect was his position that when South Carolina Republicans
hesitated about Nixon because they doubted his sympathy on racial matters, Goldwater thought that their action secretly "pleased" the president.
Still, in a "personal and confidential" note to Tex McCrary, an original
Eisenhower backer, the president's sympathy for Nixon was plain. He
even empathized with Nixon's difficult position, being "the single accepted 'candidate' of a political party and, at the same time, having to
abstain from acting like one who is already the '*nominee*.' "[55]

These were far from Nixon's only burdens. Kennedy's round of primary campaigns, first in Wisconsin and then in West Virginia, made him
a much more visible potential opponent. By March, the Gallup poll
showed him running even against Nixon in a trial heat. That threat
simultaneously raised new questions about Nixon's electability, whether
he could match a glamorous, popular young Democrat. Moley, loyally
standing by Nixon, compared the "Nixon can't win talk" to the FDR
"can't win" gossip in 1932. Rockefeller had no chance of stealing the
nomination from him, but there was every possibility that the New York
powerhouse could muster sufficient resources to force Nixon to commit
himself in a way that could damage his position with either wing of the
party. As the vice president wrote to Moley in April, he intended "to do

several things in the next few weeks to counter-act the impression first, that I am taking the conservatives for granted, second, that I have shifted my basic philosophical position on major issues, and third, that this will be a repetition of the 1948 campaign." That was as far as he wanted to go publicly, at least until after the nomination, believing it would be best to approach the November election by delaying until then his program of "positive, progressive conservatism."[56]

Such reticence was not easy for one with Nixon's strong convictions; self-imposed restraints required much discipline. Watching the developing situation in the Congo, for example, where the Belgian government was about to grant independence to the new nation that summer, he wrote to Maurice Stans, quite prophetically, about his "concern . . . that we in this country will not recognize the explosive potential in Africa and will fail to fill the vacuum which will be left as the colonial governments move out and as the newly independent states take over."[57]

Noncandidate Rockefeller, meanwhile, had his forums and was sounding like a Republican Kennedy, full of national purpose platitudes and exhortations to the "unprecedented challenge ahead of us." Eisenhower had rescued the party, he said in Washington, from "20 years of wandering in wilderness" and the party must act to keep from losing its way when he left office.[58]

One way to stir up some interest, Eisenhower suggested from behind the scenes, was to leak stories about possible Nixon running mates; such names as Cabot Lodge, Nelson Rockefeller, Bob Anderson, Thruston Morton, Jim Mitchell, Chuck Percy, Fred Seaton, Bill Rogers, Arthur Flemming, Jerry Ford, Charlie Halleck, Prescott Bush, General Gruenther, Hugh Scott, Neil McElroy, and others should provoke speculation. Len Hall and Spyros Skouras, the motion picture magnate and bankroller of Republican causes, both agreed that toying with names other than Rockefeller was silly. They had no doubt that he should be asked.[59]

Assuming that the right wing neither would nor could bolt, nor, for that matter, sit on its hands at election time, the New Yorker would bring most credibility to the ticket, to say nothing about his other natural assets. Eisenhower even thought Nixon could break down any reluctance to accept by offering to, in effect, turn over the White House to Rockefeller after serving one term. Dr. Arthur Burns, former chairman of Eisenhower's Council of Economic Advisers and frequent unofficial political adviser to Nixon, also pushed Rockefeller's name as someone who "would add more strength to the Republican ticket than anyone else." Then, stepping back somewhat, Burns admitted that "I do not quite trust him and therefore great skill will be needed in approaching him. What I fear is that if you offered him the second spot he might turn it down, then tell the entire world about it, and in the process cheapen the Vice Presidency for the man who is finally selected." At the start of May, not five weeks after Eisenhower made his suggestion, Nixon tipped off the press about his "desire" to have Rockefeller. The governor told the world that there was no chance.[60]

The climate was ripe for BOMFOG, and Rockefeller came through. This time, after developing his approach at a Pocantico Hills session with Emmet Hughes, the Brotherhood was the Party. His pronouncement, released one month before the convention, called upon Republicans to reject being led by someone who asks "to meet the future with a banner aloft whose only emblem is a question mark." He was indignant that Nixon insisted on spelling out his program only after he had been nominated, and called for the party's new spokesmen to "declare now, and not at some later date, precisely what they believe and what they propose, to meet the great matters before the nation." His statement, which was received as a dramatic stroke, was widely regarded as not just an attack upon Nixon but also an act of war against his own party, one that did permanent damage to his standing.[61]

The stroke was transparent. Any information Rockefeller wanted about the vice president's positions could be found in all the public outlets on a daily basis. Moreover, and ironically, that very week the McGraw-Hill Book Company published a compilation of major Nixon speeches and papers that covered every conceivable topic. Carefully edited as it was to serve his best interests, and, in a sense, constituting a campaign biography, it nevertheless left little doubt about his ideological location within the Republican party. Nixon had a point, then, when he followed Rockefeller's statement with a challenge of his own, to question him in public about any issue or position about which they were in disagreement. Rockefeller declined the invitation, citing his unwillingness to help Nixon clarify his views.[62]

Nixon sensed that the situation could not be ignored. Too much was at stake, especially when the Rockefeller people ran into a roadblock in the platform committee over the governor's civil rights plank. Charles Percy had already encountered the governor's dissatisfaction with the draft turned out by the committee, which had begun its work in Chicago on July 18, a week before the convention was to open. Rockefeller, unhappy with the work by the more conservative body, insisted on more emphatic language about civil rights and, subscribing as he did to the missile gap theory, wanted to endorse a stronger national defense policy.[63]

Nixon was determined to head off a floor fight, so he called Herb Brownell in New York and asked him to set up a conference. Thus began the much-debated, much-deplored "Compact of Fifth Avenue," which left not only Goldwater sputtering about "the Munich of the Republican Party" but produced such headlines as "Grant Surrenders to

Lee." "A damn sellout," said the head of the Texas delegation, the work
of a "supplicant" at the feet of America's biggest power broker. Nothing
he could have done was as effective in moving Goldwaterites to urge a
declared candidacy. Looking back upon it, however, the most incisive
analyst of Rockefeller's career has noted that while the "meeting seemed
to demean Nixon, it actually revealed his adroit timing in shifting from
the Party Track to the Popular Track, and Nelson's obliviousness to
both."[64] In making his necessary twists and turns, as he did throughout
his career, Nixon was remarkably consistent, doing no less than quar-
terbacking the next play.

What, in this particular case, really sparked the furies was anger that
the platform was being "dictated" from a thousand miles away, and,
from all places, the apartment at 810 Fifth Avenue! "Many of the committee members would have been less than happy with a *Nixon* platform;
when told that what they were being asked to approve was a *Rockefeller*
platform, it was like waving a red cape in front of a bull," Earl Mazo
and Stephen Hess later pointed out.[65] Even more galling was the realization that Nixon had acceded to Rockefeller's ground rules that it
would have to be *he* who acquiesced to the vice president's request for
a meeting and that the vice president would travel to New York at
Rockefeller's request. So it was that Henry IV went to Canossa.

Actually, Rockefeller's version was drafted in Chicago by Hughes and
teletyped to him in New York, where Nixon arrived on the evening of
July 22. After dinner, according to Nixon, "we got right down to brass
tacks." The first hurdle was the vice presidency, which, according to
Nixon's 1962 account, was not offered but discussed; his postpolitical
career 1978 version, however, explains that he "made the gesture of
offering him the position." In either event, the reception was the same:
Rockefeller was no more interested than he had been a few months
earlier which, as Nixon later concluded, was just as well. Rockefeller
would have been a difficult running mate.[66]

Their actual work, which ultimately was seen as Nixon's "surrender"
by the time he reached the convention city, was far from the product
of a closed summit conference between two powerful men. For three
hours, excluding a twenty-minute break at one in the morning, they
participated in a four-way telephone conference. Nixon held the line in
Rockefeller's study while the governor used his bedroom extension.
Their New York end was linked to Chicago via Percy at the Blackstone
Hotel and Hughes in the Sheraton Towers. Then, after much switching
of shifts by operators and one break in their connection, they completed
the so-called Compact ("Treaty" was the preferred noun among those
favoring a sellout analogy). Not until almost dawn did the two men
complete their statement of principles, each accommodating the other's
needs. Nixon's trip was risky, the price potentially high, but, as he has

explained, "by going to see him in New York and working out differences that were more illusory than real, I was able to insure his support for the Republican ticket."[67]

The downside appeared immediately; press reports denounced the treaty as simple surrender. More important than its contents was that, in Mazo and Hess's words, "It *looked* like a surrender." The reality, if anyone cared, was that Nixon and Rockefeller had capitulated to each other's unacceptable items, with the governor yielding to objections about financing for health insurance and federal intervention in labor disputes. As Theodore White wrote soon afterward, "The principles Rockefeller chanted were neither entirely strange nor distasteful to Nixon; indeed, with many of the Rockefeller positions he privately and wholeheartedly agreed." Over defense, however, an issue that separated Nixon more from the president than from the New Yorker, the wording almost sounded as though it came from Kennedy ("There must be no price ceiling on America's security") in its clear suggestion that there were too many restraints to assure adequate strength. When Eisenhower objected to the wording, Nixon went to work with his people to fashion more tactful language for the platform.[68]

What has been lost in all this is that defense was far less touchy than civil rights. For one, Eisenhower's personal pride was not involved; besides, one could always come up with a selective list of the administration's accomplishments. Nixon himself committed the indiscretion of crediting the Republicans for the Supreme Court's *Brown* decision. Nixon and Attorney General Rogers, assisted by a deputy attorney general, Lawrence E. Walsh, had already coordinated their efforts, with Rockefeller via telephone, to turn out a draft that got to Percy and the committee even before the rendevous at 810 Fifth Avenue. Walsh personally took it to Chicago, where those black leaders who had been urging efforts to match the Democratic plank written in Los Angeles were impressed.[69]

The *New York Times* reported that the draft was "strong and temperate." Subsequently, it replaced the committee's original tepid statement. Most impressive, and never precisely reiterated by the final version, was a pledge to use "the full power of government to eliminate discrimination based on race, color, religion or national origin." The acceptance of the need for "direct government" action was unequivocal, and that included the withholding of federal funding for segregated facilities.[70]

By the time Nixon himself got to Chicago, having returned to Washington after meeting with Rockefeller, the rebellion involved civil rights, not defense. Perhaps it was easier to vent anger at the "surrender" by targeting the Nixon-Rockefeller civil rights submission. For a while, a floor fight seemed possible over the issue as Republican delagates from both North and South objected. When Rockefeller told an NAACP rally that he was, indeed, prepared to do battle on the convention floor, he was seconded by one of Nixon's strategists, Hugh Scott.[71]

Nixon, once on the scene, faced reporters and insisted on his right to have the platform reflect his views. "I believe," he told them, "it is essential that the Republican convention adopt a strong civil rights platform, an honest one, which just deals specifically and not in generalities with the problems and with the goals that we desire to reach in these fields."[72] The civil rights plank that finally got through the 103-member platform committee was only mildly more subdued than the Nixon-Rockefeller draft and, in one particular area, gave even greater support to the sit-in desegregation movement.

Arthur Krock concluded that a Nixon victory was bound to elect a president "who will give leadership to enforce sweeping antisegregation laws and court decisions." Unlike the Democrats, the Republicans were not burdened by a bloc of southern dissenters.[73] What might have happened had Nixon won in 1960 will never be known.

The record of that fall's campaign, however, showed that Nixon was in a quandary between such aims and his perception of what it would take to defeat Kennedy. He was haunted by his inherent weakness in the South, a situation further compounded by Kennedy's choice of Lyndon Johnson of Texas as his running mate. When Nixon acceded to Eisenhower's wisdom and shared his ticket with Henry Cabot Lodge, he came to rue his choice when the man from Massachusetts pledged that their new administration would select the first black cabinet appointee. Nixon, not daring to do anything about the situation, remained silent when the Kennedys acted to win Dr. King's release from prison. Having secured a strong civil rights plank, he clearly, as White has written, "befuzzed his original position in Chicago and succeeded, in the end, in alienating Northern Negro *and* Southern white, losing both along with the election."[74] Jackie Robinson and Dr. King broke with him after that. For the Republican party, however, the long-term dividends were obvious. The southern bastion of presidential Democrats was rapidly becoming a shambles.

With the election of Kennedy, everything began to change. The oldest president gave way to the youngest. An era of materialism, avarice, self-indulgence, the hoi polloi's rise to comfort and unbridled ambitions, became distracted by the New Frontier's enigmatic tribute to patriotism, as embodied in the new president's inaugural address: "And so, my fellow Americans, ask not what your country can do for you; ask what you can do for your country." A new Pied Piper was showing the way, and the followers were plentiful. Whatever they may have actually done on election day, to an astonishing degree they claimed that their votes had been for the dashing athletic figure who was further enhanced by having an elegant wife in the later stage of pregnancy, and a toddler.

He did tell them that "America must get moving again," and, whatever that meant, it sounded right. If they really understood every implication — if Kennedy himself knew — there would have been less ambiguity. The outcome would have been less vulnerable to those little "what-ifs" that Nixon later listed in *Six Crises:* the disputed tabulations; Eisenhower's taking up Nixon's cause at the last minute after having done his damage by remarking at a press conference that he needed "a week" to recall how Vice President Nixon had been instrumental in determining policy; Nixon's making good on his promise to campaign in all fifty states, which virtually forfeited to Kennedy the crowded Northeast with its crucial cache of electors; Henry Cabot Lodge's lethargic run for the vice presidency, and unilateral promise to create a black cabinet seat, striking political ineptitude in contrast with the effectiveness with which Lyndon Johnson read the riot act to wary southern Democrats. And the press, always the press: whatever went wrong, especially after the 1960s, was blamed on the ambitious, self-seeking, biased men and women who disdained the jowly Red-baiter who, more and more, had begun to deliver nationalistic homilies about morality. Even in his debates with Kennedy, Nixon deplored Harry Truman's language. A bemused JFK finessed the occasion by saying that the old man's vulgarities were Bess's problem.

It was a time of change. The pendulum of history had, seemingly, swung to the left, but not quite as far as it appeared. Kennedy learned just how limited was that change when he counted the votes and analyzed the Congress and its committees. As he and his fellow New Frontiersmen analyzed the situation, they saw continuity, not revolution.

Yet events followed each other in such rapid succession that the short, romantic presidency that his widow later promoted as a Camelot became, instead, one thousand days of such turbulence that the Eisenhower years looked more and more like a time of placidity. Overwhelmed from the start about how to respond to a Khrushchev speech about "wars of national liberation," the new administration soon toyed with counterinsurgency in a wide array of fields. What to do about Communist absorption of landlocked Laos, let alone South Vietnam, was quickly pushed off the front page by the sending of a tiny brigade onto Cuban shores, only to have them outfoxed almost from the start. Eisenhower, now the squire of Gettysburg, privately sneered at the "Profile in Timidity and Indecision" in the White House, but, forever the patriot, came through in public. Nixon, similarly called upon, could do no less. Nelson Rockefeller, also enlisted under the banner of bipartisanship, emerged from the Oval Office with the president and joined in a plea for the freedom of Cubans trapped under Castro.[75]

Before that year was over, the new president had to negotiate the

Laotian situation without risking the country's total collapse to the Communists, bolster the already imperiled South Vietnamese regime of Ngo Dinh Diem, work behind the scenes to stabilize the tumultuous results of independence for the Congo, and, after meeting with Khrushchev in Vienna, face him down over West Berlin by mobilizing American resources. He also had to meet the reality of the Soviet wall that split Berlin by deploying American tanks that went nose to nose against their Russian counterparts in what was perhaps the most chilling single encounter of the entire cold war. By late 1962, the administration, in direct response to the European situation, adopted a new strategy, the Single Integrated Operational Plan for Fiscal Year 1962, or SIOP-2, which prepared for the possible maximization of American superiority "through a massive, simultaneous nuclear offensive — in preemption if possible, but in retaliation if necessary — against the full set of military and urban-industrial targets in the Sino-Soviet bloc." A preemptive strike, the Joint Chiefs believed, could give the United States victory in a general nuclear war.[76] Also unknown to the public, Castro, never far from Kennedy's mind, became the target of assassination plots. Inherited, as was the Bay of Pigs invasion plan, from the Eisenhower administration, institutionalization of sabotage began with the top-secret Operation MONGOOSE, which was not revealed until 1975. At home, preoccupation with racial disorders in the quest for equality coincided with the search for what to do about the rest of the world, especially the Soviet Union, Communist China, and the growing commitment in Vietnam. By that point, too, the Kennedy Justice Department under his brother Bobby, having had to respond to violence in Alabama and bloodshed over the admission of a black student to the University of Mississippi, was confronted with the Reverend Dr. King's crusade to desegregate Birmingham. Television scenes showed men, women, and children in Alabama being attacked by club-wielding police, dogs, and powerful water hoses. A quarter of a million demonstrators gathered in Washington late that August demanding equal protection legislation. Hardly much time seemed to pass by after that before Kennedy was killed in Dallas and Lyndon Johnson took over.

Part of the Kennedy flair was zest for dramatics, but even he was not that gifted a stage manager. Through that age of trauma and change, Richard Nixon remained the stable force, sustaining themes that seemed compromised and truncated. As *Newsweek*'s Election Blue Extra proclaimed right after he lost to Kennedy, "Richard Nixon is far from dead politically. For the next four years, despite his defeat, he will be the leader of the Republican party in fact, as well as name. And, come 1964, Nixon — if he wants to be — will almost certainly be the man to reckon with in the battle for the GOP nomination for President." Only by rallying around him, Republicans were saying, could they "avoid a war of an-

nihilation between the liberal Eastern wing of the party headed by Gov.
Nelson Rockefeller of New York, and the ultraconservatives, who follow
the rich, personable Sen. Barry Goldwater of Arizona."[77]

He was offstage, but never very far. As a former vice president, as "Ike's
boy," despite the general's enigmatic behavior toward the younger man,
his prestige was high — and even higher because his loss had been so
narrow and his position as the party unifier and titular leader appeared
preeminent. "I really feel," Julie Eisenhower recalls, "that because the
election was so close and because of the cheating and him being the
combative type, the feisty type, that he wanted to redeem '60; he wanted
to go for it in '64."[78] Nixon's determination to vindicate himself is also
better understood when one realizes that the emphasis on Kennedy's
youth has obscured the fact that the former vice president was hardly
that much older, only forty-eight when he left office in January of 1961.

That brought him up against the conflicting needs of keeping open
his political options for the future while, at the same time, providing for
his family. As the daughter of his first law partner back in Whittier has
recalled, his choice of a political career brought the immediate necessity
of tapping funds from the well-to-do, and he subsequently was rarely
at a loss for such assistance. Lesser-known lights leave Washington positioned for cashing in on their contacts and reputations. For most who
serve in even mildly prominent positions, public service is, in reality, a
good long-term investment rather than a financial hardship.[79] If that
was Nixon's desire, he was in an especially strong position, and he could
have accepted any one of an array of corporate directorships and law
partnerships.

"I didn't understand him at first," Bebe Rebozo said of Nixon many
years later. The youngest child of an immigrant Cuban cigarmaker,
Rebozo did almost everything to escape a life of poverty, entrepreneur-
ing his way by pumping gas, recapping tires, chauffeuring tourist limousines, lending money, going into business with boyhood friend George
Smathers, and, finally, by the time he reflected on his long friendship
with Richard Nixon, serving as the respectable president of the Key
Biscayne Bank and Trust Company. By 1974, the cigarmaker's ninth
child was reportedly worth $4.5 million, reaffirming the American
dream.[80]

Sitting in the bank's office in 1985, Rebozo recalled that "I've been
around so long that I'm so close to the wife and the husband and the
two children." Divorced in 1950 — and not remarrying until thirty-four
years later — Rebozo lived in a sprawling white Spanish-style home on
fashionable Bay Lane, right by the Key Biscayne house that Nixon
bought in 1968. "I've never been so close to an entire family," Rebozo
continued. "Tricia's boy is my godson." As Dr. David Abrahamsen has

put it, Bebe "remained the man in the shadows waiting for him," and Smathers's comment that Rebozo and Nixon could "sit in a room for three hours and neither ever say a word" has become part of the lore that has made their friendship legendary.[81]

Still, the oddities have been exaggerated. Rebozo was often there for fun; he brought beautiful women and mixed perfect dry martinis. One night, he and Nixon were seen roughhousing with a rubber raft, each trying to dunk the other and become "King of the Pool."[82]

"Men like Bebe have an old-shoe quality that helps Nixon relax," Steve Hess has explained. If Nixon was not money-hungry, their relationship becomes even more fascinating. Murray Chotiner coached him in the art of politics, but Rebozo's primary function was to help bring financial security without sacrificing his public career.[83]

Still, in Nixon's case, it went beyond that; an almost mystical aura seemed to come out of their relationship, the portrait of two men, so very different in background and culture, establishing telepathic communications. Fascination with their personalities often submerged the reality that money was at the bottom of it all. J. Anthony Lukas, author of the most comprehensive account of the Watergate scandals, has concluded that there was "substantial evidence that Rebozo controlled a fund of cash available for Nixon's private purposes." That they also became best of friends was, of course, helpful, but it was almost incidental. Having gone through all the Watergate investigations, and especially what happened to a $100,000 loan from Howard Hughes, Bebe was obviously more eager to talk about how he and Nixon had gotten on together than about how he had helped his friend make money, although he readily admitted to helping Nixon make money through real estate. After all, Rebozo pointed out, Nixon was worth only $47,000 when he left Washington for California in 1961.[84]

In Nixon's life, Rebozo became both a shadow and a contradiction. Nixon himself has put it aptly: "Bebe Rebozo is one of the kindest and most generous men I have ever known. He is a man of great character and integrity. Yet anyone who read only the press stories about him, his business dealings, or his friendship with me would have had to conclude that he combined the worst traits of Rasputin and Al Capone." They first got together through Smathers, who had been a friend of Rebozo's since they were fourth-grade classmates. Their actual meeting came in 1951 at Smathers's suggestion via a former FBI agent and Miami city manager who had led the Florida Democrat's 1946 campaign, Richard Danner. Danner's involvement only deepens the intrigue because of his later association with Howard Hughes.[85] That all three, Rebozo, Danner, and Hughes, would ultimately become significant players in Nixon's world was virtually guaranteed by the unfolding of a process that was part of an American success story.

Consider, for example, Walter Annenberg, less publicized than Rebozo but, as one of America's wealthiest men, perhaps the fattest cat of them all. By background Annenberg, the lord of Palm Desert, California, would have seemed an improbable master of a Philadelphia Main Line mansion and host to several presidents — Eisenhower, Kennedy, Johnson, Nixon, Reagan.

The incongruity was also akin, as John Ehrlichman has pointed out, to Joseph P. Kennedy's designation as the ambassador to the Court of St. James's by FDR. Whereas Roosevelt sent an Irish Catholic of questionable entrepreneurial repute, President Nixon had *his* laugh by dispatching, as Ehrlichman has put it, the son of a racketeer and a Jew, "a signal to the Eastern, Ivy League blue-bloods who thought they owned that embassy!" Roosevelt had, in fact, done to Annenberg's father, Moses, what he would have loved to have done to Kennedy — sent him to prison instead of London. In 1940, Moses Annenberg, a poor immigrant who had pioneered such gambling sheets as the *Daily Racing Form* and the *Morning Telegraph,* had also become the publisher of the *Philadelphia Inquirer* and mass-circulation detective and movie magazines. His $6 million income was appraised by federal officials as the highest in the United States at the time. His imprisonment for tax evasion, which was a "special project" of FDR's, was called the most sensational tax-evasion conviction in U.S. history.[86]

Moses's son, Walter, vain, powerful, and talented, took over the Annenberg holdings and expanded them into a communications empire. His Triangle Publications hit additional lodes of gold by publishing such popular magazines as *Seventeen* and *TV Guide.* Together with radio and television stations, they enabled the son to far outstrip the father. Annenberg's control over information was, of course, invaluable for Nixon, as for any other politician. In his own way, the publisher was circumspect, giving his support without having to be asked. Annenberg was also discreet about financial contributions. Moneys for the Nixon cause could not be traced to him but came from other members of the Annenberg family.[87]

His closeness to Nixon did not develop until the vice president's second term. By 1958, they were sufficiently chummy for Nixon to relax from an overseas trip by stopping in at Inwood, the Annenberg Main Line mansion. "It was not easy to get close to him no matter how seemingly cordial a relationship you may have had," Annenberg said in 1986. "His being such a very private person, it was not easy to envision him as a gregarious human being. He was not a conventional politician in the sense that conventional politicians are prepared to embrace a snake at any given opportunity." John Cooney, Annenberg's biographer, has offered the most sensible explanation of why two such men were able to relate. "Neither man," Cooney has written, "for all he has gained in life, feels himself firmly rooted as part of the American Establishment, yet each believes himself to be among the staunchest of American patriots." Annenberg, the outsider who built his own golf course at Palm Desert because Jews were excluded from the local country club, termed any talk about Nixon as anti-Semitic as "utter rubbish."[88]

Nixon had also drawn close to the vitamin king, Elmer Bobst, a relationship that began in the earliest days of his vice presidency. One of Nixon's friends remembered that Bobst "looked somewhat like Mr. Magoo." When he said "Good morning," it sounded like a speech to shareholders. A gregarious, conservative businessman, whose father had been a missionary to China, Bobst enjoyed telling stories about how he had built his pharmaceuticals empire. The Nixon family had the run of Bobst's five-bedroom country house at Spring Lake, New Jersey. Bobst also had an attractive Lebanese wife, a home in Palm Springs, Florida, down the street from Joe Kennedy's, and traveled to play golf at Burning Tree in his private railroad car. Nixon found it hard to resist the voluble multimillionaire, and Bobst liked to think of himself as the younger man's father. Later, during Nixon's presidency, Bobst emerged with an $18 million profit after Attorney General John Mitchell intervened to overrule the Federal Trade Commission's objection to a merger between Warner-Lambert and Parke-Davis, which created the country's second largest drug company.[89]

Still, it was not mere money, power, and open pocketbooks that brought men like Rebozo, Annenberg, and Bobst into Nixon's life. His circle of approval included such relatively unknown lights as John A. Mulcahy, who rose from a poor Irish immigrant family to become president of a large supplier of steel equipment and then a major stockholder in the Pfizer pharmaceuticals company.[90] Later, Nixon and his family were closely associated with J. Willard Marriott, who developed an extensive network of hotels and motels. Not surprisingly, they made large financial contributions to his political campaigns. With the addition of a conservative Chicago millionaire, W. Clement Stone, their checks were invaluable, affording a supply of cash that was not always forthcoming from many traditional Republican sources.

For Nixon, as for them, the dynamo was success. He admired the self-driven achievers whether or not they, like him, were propelled by needing to compensate for inherent deficiencies or the limitations unknown to the Rockefellers, Kennedys, and lesser lights. The success drive, while hardly unique to America, was easily converted by mythology via the Horatio Alger myth into a national creed. For Nixon, it was all-encompassing; it provided the rationale, as well, for each of his foreign policy initiatives, ranging from his earlier support of the Truman containment program, which was bolstered by his experiences as a member of the Herter Commission, to the opening of China and the Soviet Union.

Certainly more than Annenberg, but even more than Bobst and Rebozo, Donald M. Kendall personified success. Kendall, white-haired and still handsome by the time he retired in 1986, was a college dropout who sat at the head of PepsiCo, formerly known as Pepsi-Cola, Incorporated. The palace of the soft-drink emperor was a 140-acre estate in New York's Westchester County that constituted a corporate Versailles. Outside Kendall's window, the landscape was decorated with an impressive collection of modern sculpture, works of art but, equally important, testimonials to his rise from a four-hundred-dollar-a-month bottling line worker at New Rochelle, to the chief of Pepsi-Cola's overseas operations. Then, in 1963, at the age of forty-two, Don Kendall became Pepsi's president and chief executive officer, which fulfilled the mission of the boy who began life milking cows on a dairy farm in the Dungeness Valley of Washington State.[91]

Nixon took naturally to a Don Kendall. To Nixon, Kendall was a legitimate entrepreneur, one who had risen through his own drive, intelligence, and initiative. That made him the kind of businessman who would naturally become part of his "new" establishment. "I told Don that we have to realize that the old establishment just like the old establishment in the university community and in the media simply weren't going to be with us and that we had to build a new establishment," said a 1972 presidential memo to Bob Haldeman. He needed people like Kendall, who was among those who ruled America. "The business elite," wrote President Nixon, "if anything, has less guts than the labor elite or the farm elite. What we have to do is to find those few people in the business community who have some reputation as being successful in business but who haven't been taken in by the idea that they must only attach themselves to 'fashionable' causes." Almost ten years earlier, after Nixon had been defeated for the governorship of California and with his political career ostensibly over, Kendall teamed up with Elmer Bobst to make a deal with the New York City law firm of Mudge, Stern, Baldwin, and Todd to give them Warner-Lambert and Pepsi's multimillion-dollar legal business in exchange for taking on Nixon as a senior partner. Bobst was the spark behind that, Kendall remembered, "but it was the two of us who took the company's business into the firm, and, as matter of fact, they did a hell of a good job for us."[92]

After Goldwater's defeat in 1964, Kendall joined Maurice Stans and others in pushing what they called the Issues Research Council. The council was supposedly nonpartisan; in reality, with a targeted budget of $100,000, its function was to give Richard Nixon the staff and apparatus to promote his position as a prominent Republican spokesman during the Johnson years. Stans, himself an Eisenhower veteran, then chaired the blatantly political Congress '66 committee. That, in turn, spawned two other groups, together presumably devoted to Republican fortunes. Their real objective, however, was always kept aloft: providing the means and cadre for a Nixon run for the presidency in 1968. The group, according to Stans, never numbered more than twenty-five, fund-raisers and fat cats, and Don Kendall was among them almost from the start.[93]

Above all, Don Kendall was a businessman, and so making money was his raison d'être. Politics, such as it existed in Kendall's makeup, consisted of the inherited conservatism of the American heartland, and even that escaped being leavened by the Great Depression. His most repeated memory of those days was a vivid recollection of how he managed to put together ten dollars for spending money by skinning calves. He saved his earnings, but then FDR closed the banks. Why what followed should necessarily have happened as it did is not as important as the lesson that remained. "I lost my $10, and my opinion about liberals hasn't changed since," he pointed out. To another Democratic president, Lyndon Johnson, Kendall expressed his outrage at hearing fellow businessmen ask "What difference does it make to us if Vietnam does go communist?" He, for one, had no doubt; the Reds had to be stopped. "I have also been appalled," he wrote to Johnson, "at the position taken by some of the so-called intellectual set who appear to have absolutely no understanding as to what we are fighting for in Southeast Asia."[94] But consistency, like ideology, was less important to the soft-drink czar than the welfare of his enterprises.

"We are always going to have a competitive relationship with the Soviet Union," Kendall explained in 1985, and he saw no reason why he and his company could not engage in some profitable business. He had, he explained, more faith than his friend Dick in the efficacy of world trade as a modifier of international tensions. He was still angry that the U.S. Senate had permitted Henry Jackson, who represented Kendall's home state, to exploit the Jewish vote in furtherance of his national political ambitions by passing the Jackson-Vanik Amendment, which removed most-favored-nation trading status from any nation that restricted its citizens from leaving. Not only did it lower rather than raise the number of Soviet Jews who were able to leave, Kendall argued, but the provision, combined with the premature end of Nixon's presidency, torpedoed détente. The United States and USSR may always be rivals, he added, "but for crissakes we can learn to live with each other and not create the kind of problems that we've got today."[95]

But it was a Pepsi-Cola booth at the American National Exhibition at Skolniki Park, just before Nixon and Khrushchev debated before the cameras and microphones at the model kitchen, that Kendall recalled most fondly. The setting became a turning point in the careers of both Kendall and Nixon, establishing the former as seller of Pepsi and the latter as a salesman of his presidential stature.

The State Department had suggested that the two giant American soft-drink companies, Coca-Cola and Pepsi-Cola, should be on hand to dispense their beverages at kiosks at various locations in the exhibition. Coca-Cola, the larger of the two, turned down the offer. Some of their hesitation doubtless rubbed off on Kendall's superiors, who feared that such public association with the Soviet Union was not worth the potential value of the Russian market. But, as Kendall pointed out, Coke was dominant in western Europe and he thought it was time for Pepsi to penetrate the east. Despite what he recalled was some "abusive" reaction, he went ahead, his public relations gears in full operation. Since his company's current advertising slogan was "Be Sociable, Have a Pepsi," what could be better than having Chairman Khrushchev himself pictured looking pleased with a bottle of Pepsi in his hand? Kendall passed the idea on to the American ambassador in Moscow, Llewellyn Thompson, who then got the assurance of Nixon's cooperation.[96]

Setting up Khrushchev with Pepsi was one thing, but getting him to like it and having the whole thing go off smoothly was another matter. Kendall had the company check out the quality of Moscow's water to make certain that it would mix right with the syrup to be provided by Pepsi. He wanted Khrushchev to compare a Pepsi made with New York water with one made in Moscow. "I knew which one he would like best," he recalled proudly in 1985. As an additional part of the preparations, Kendall arranged for his wares to be accompanied by seven pretty Russian-speaking American girls. They were to supervise the locals responsible for operating the dispensing equipment; they could also be useful, Kendall explained in a 1959 letter outlining his plans, "in case anyone should come up to our booths and start asking questions about the United States and Democracy." To prepare the American girls for that part of the task, Kendall's letter went on, "we are arranging to send the girls to special courses conducted by the State Department to give them a refresher course on our country and what it stands for, as it is expected they will be quizzed constantly."[97]

At the exhibit that July, Nixon followed through. "Don't worry, I'll bring him by," he promised Kendall.[98] With Khrushchev in tow, they stopped at the RCA booth and engaged in what became a preliminary to the kitchen debate, a genuine dialogue in which each man defended his own nation's way of life. When Nixon steered the Soviet ruler to the Pepsi booth, Kendall suggested that he sample the two versions of Pepsi-Cola. Khrushchev sipped both. Predictably, he immediately acclaimed the one made with Moscow water and boasted about the superiority of the

"Russian" product while a photographer caught Khrushchev with Soviet president K. Y. Voroshilov and Kendall, all endowed with Pepsis.

For Kendall, the event was a triumph. American newspapers adopted a variation of the soft drink's ads with such headlines as "Khrushchev Learns to be Sociable." When the Nixon administration later established its détente with Moscow, doors to the east were open to Kendall, and a Pepsi-Cola plant opened in the Soviet Union in 1974. At the suggestion of Ambassador Thompson, Kendall's company reciprocated by selling Stolichnaya vodka in the United States. The chairman and president of the Economic Development Council of New York City, Inc., George Champion, had already recognized Kendall's flair for international commerce by suggesting that he be named to replace William Rogers as secretary of state.[99] Champion, who was one of Pepsi-Cola's directors, must have heard about Henry Kissinger, so one suspects that he was really trying to drive home another point, the importance of international trade.

Less than two years after the Moscow encounter, right after Nixon was getting himself relocated in southern California and first beginning to weigh the idea of trying for the governorship, Kendall was among those who made him an offer to enter the private sector. He called Nixon to tell him he had in mind having him become chairman of the board of Pepsi-Cola International. Nixon clearly did not jump at the idea, so Kendall became more specific. In a long letter late that April, he acknowledged that the company "would gain a great deal of prestige and publicity" by having Nixon oversee its overseas operations and take care of legal matters. Not for a moment, Kendall indicated, did he assume that Nixon's political career had come to an impasse. On the contrary. Pepsi would pay for him and Pat to take "frequent trips abroad where you would have an opportunity to see first hand the problems we are faced with abroad and then come back to this country and be able to make speeches that would help solve these problems which result in your being constantly in the public eye." He would also "never be in a position where anyone could criticize you for mistakes that may occur from time to time." As Kendall learned, that was not how he and his friend could get together. Nor was Nixon much more receptive to similar offers from Annenberg, Robert Abplanalp, and other corporate leaders, all hoping to gain by retaining the services of a recent vice president.[100]

Still, when one considers the Kendalls, Rebozos, and Annenbergs, who had such close access to Nixon, their relationship assumes a more intricate symbiosis than mere fat cat and political puppet. Note, for example, Kendall's admiration of the way Nixon had performed before a dinner held in his honor in October 1985 by a group of black entrepreneurs who were indebted to his administration: "Nixon has a brilliant mind. I went to a dinner last Thursday night, and here he is in his seventies and stood up to a single microphone to a group of black people and gave one of the best talks I have ever heard. How he wove things with his unbelievable memory of his by going through baseball scores and relating things that happened with football players and baseball players and citing the game, and what happened. He's somebody with that great intellect, but he has the ability to get down and communicate with the average guy in the street and make him realize that he cares and that he understands. He's a very shrewd politician. Probably today he can make book on elections better than anybody in this country, and he's just uncanny at that."[101]

"This is a man of great intellectual ability," said Annenberg. But it was in a discussion with another Nixon friend, Robert Abplanalp, the aerosol spray valve magnate, that a different persona was stressed. John Connally recalls that Nixon's two closest friends "in the world, on a personal basis, were Bob Abplanalp and Bebe Rebozo. They were self-made men. So he had an affinity for the average guy that worked and made what he had. This was deeply ingrained in him. That's why I say he's a populist." (One should remember, Nixon pointed out in 1988, the good qualities of nineteenth-century populism.)[102]

One brought up with memories of populists leading a great reform movement found Abplanalp an unlikely crusader. On a morning in 1985, the beefy self-made fat cat sat in the office visibly tense. He had only recently given up a four-pack-a-day cigarette habit. He seemed better suited to his self-professed reputation as a "hard-hat without venom," although, lest one get the wrong idea, he quickly explained that his position "to the right of Attila the Hun" made Nixon seem like "a left-winger."[103]

Abplanalp built his fortune on the new kind of spray can and operated the Precision Valve Corporation from his Yonkers, New York, headquarters. He proudly escorts visitors to the automated assembly line that affixes caps to the cans, and explains that some of the valves are being manufactured for shipment to Japan, where he has a wholly owned company. Although the American aerosol patent has expired, he can go on functioning overseas without local competition because he has the corner on the manufacturing apparatus.[104]

He first met Nixon after the 1960 election, when Abplanalp was in Washington and the former vice president was packing. That was in the spring of 1961, a reference point made easy for Abplanalp because Nixon had just seen President Kennedy after the Bay of Pigs failure. At their introduction, which was arranged by banker and Nixon fund-raiser Cliff Folger, Abplanalp was told that they had been "robbed" in the 1960 election. The aerosol manufacturer then got down to his immediate interest: he needed Nixon for legal work in California. Later, after Nixon failed to win the governorship and moved back to New York, Abplanalp joined Bobst and Kendall in taking his law business to what had become Nixon, Mudge, Rose, Guthrie, and Alexander, "chiefly to keep the government out of [our] hair. We didn't want them to know what we were doing. We were afraid they'd steal our ideas."[105]

Once in New York, Abplanalp was also introduced to Rebozo. The two men became business associates and close friends. Abplanalp is on the directorship of Rebozo's bank and has holdings in the Bahamas, where he owns Grand Cay. He also shares Walker Cay with his friend, and they have developed the island into a resort with a fish hatchery that mass-produces marine specimens.[106]

Abplanalp, doing his best without nicotine, wanted to talk about Nixon. He called himself a Taft Republican to reaffirm his own conservative credentials (during the sixties, he was a supporter of the Tell It to Hanoi Committee), but was hard-pressed to isolate specific examples of where Nixon's views differed from his. Equally obvious was that Nixon had modified his own position to avoid marring their relationship. Politics, as such, was not central. More important by far was having Abplanalp as a personal sounding board, and as someone who could feed Nixon's interest and absorption in being befriended and favored in every way by a man of great wealth, especially one who came up the hard way. "I spent Friday afternoon and all day Saturday on Grand Cay," writes Nixon in his memoirs about his vacation just before the Watergate story hit the papers, "a small island in the Bahamas owned by my old friend Bob Abplanalp. The weather was spotty, but I went for a swim and took a walk around the island."[107] He enjoyed all that, along with Pat, but most satisfying was his own congeniality with the entrepreneurial ethos that struck such a responsive chord with the industrialist. So there was nothing inconsistent about Abplanalp observing that the two of them had little in common politically.

There were, he recalled, occasional flashes of Nixon humor. Later, when Abplanalp bought up some of the San Clemente property held by the former president, the press asked him what he intended to do with it. Abplanalp characteristically undiplomatic, shot back with the comment that he intended to build a "ten-story whorehouse." When the remark, with its potential for being taken literally, hit the newspapers, Nixon sent him a telegram that, as Abplanalp recalled, said, "Bob, save the piano-player's job for me."

Asked what he considered Nixon's greatest strength, Abplanalp began by saying, "This will come as some surprise. I think he's painfully honest. Everybody in the world said to him, 'Burn the tapes.' I offered to do it myself. My suggestion was to call in all the media. You get a can of gasoline, I'll throw in the match. Part of it was he was an attorney, and that would have been a criminal act. How much crap he would have to take was not the consideration. It was illegal and he wouldn't do it. He pictured the worst. Nixon has tremendous strength of character, unbelievable resiliency."[108]

14

A Two-Time Loser

HOWARD HUGHES was the most powerful and dangerous fat cat of them all. One can accurately say that Hughes insinuated himself into Nixon's public life from the outset, established a relationship of convenience, haunted him, and finally became destructive. As Hughes biographer John Phelan has noted, Hughes's interests "were intricately entwined with those of government on federal, state and local levels," which had to be the routine course of business for a man whose contracts from the public purse came to an average siphoning of $1.7 million every day.[1] Such meshing guaranteed that Nixon was hardly alone among Hughes's political connections. But he was among the most durable, and the connection assumed the character of mutal intrigue.

The two men never met. Had they, each would have been wary of the other. They shared a desire for privacy and power, but that was about all. Frank Nixon was worth less then $100,000 at his death, but Hughes's father left his son an oil-well exploration enterprise and the profitable tool company that bore the family name.[2] Howard Robards Hughes built his empire from substantial beginnings. Nixon's admiration for the self-made did not preclude being dazzled by those who, like Rockefeller, Kennedy, and Hughes, had the wealth that gave them institutional clout equal to giant corporations or even nation states. Hughes only had to buy leverage, and the most accommodating thing public servants could do was to provide special services.

Hughes, it was said, was just about the richest man in America; and even if that was not literally true, it hardly mattered. Who could gauge his actual worth? Something over $1.5 billion seemed reasonable, but even that figure did not include the amply endowed Howard R. Hughes Medical Foundation. Clearly, a few million more or less seemed inconsequential; if he was not Croesus, he was a splendid stand-in. Naturally, with that much money and power, officeholders were potential clients. Unlike the more conventional power brokers around Nixon, Hughes could destroy as easily as build.

For much of his later life, it was hard to know whether he was dead or alive. Operationally, whether the voice from within Oz was truly Hughes's was relatively moot. At the time Nixon became president, the Hughes headquarters had already moved from 7000 Romaine Street in Los Angeles to a $9,933-per-week suite atop Las Vegas's Desert Inn Hotel.

So thoroughly did the mad billionaire cloak himself in mystery that his whereabouts, operations, and even the actual moment and circumstances of his death were weird. His uncle, the prominent novelist Rupert Hughes, once said that "I can get through to the Almighty by dropping to my knees, but I don't know how to get in touch with Howard." That Hughes actually existed was confirmed only by the few privileged witnesses of the naked, bedridden recluse, whose sore-infested, drugged body was attended to by five Mormon nursemaids and a staff of six senior male aides, all administered by an ex-FBI agent, Robert Maheu.[3]

First reports that he had died were equally mysterious. A stroke reportedly killed him while airborne on April 5, 1976, from Acapulco, Mexico, to a Houston hospital. The cause was later given as kidney failure. Nevertheless, claims that Howard Hughes had passed away prompted Treasury Secretary William Simon to order the Internal Revenue Service to authenticate the body before starting taxation proceedings against the estate.[4]

In his last years, Hughes's obsession with germs became the chief explanation for the hypochondria that led to his self-imposed insulation in a controlled environment, which meant, in effect, that he had changed his life-style most remarkably. In a day when airplanes were still the playthings of the bold, aviator Hughes had set speed records and won a congressional medal for flying around the world in ninety-one hours. A direct encounter with death came in 1946 when his custom-designed air force reconnaissance plane crashed into Beverly Hills. He created and flew — for a full mile across Long Beach harbor — a plywood seaplane, the *Spruce Goose*. The wooden behemoth, "Hughes's Folly," the result of an $18 million Defense Department contract, led to his final public appearance, three decades before his actual death. In 1947, Hughes, called before a Senate investigating committee looking into war profiteering and political payoffs, gave one of the more petulant, defiant, and rambunctious performances of that era.

The airplane innovator and manufacturer was also a movie magnate who made such films as *Hell's Angels, Scarface, The Front Page,* and *The Outlaw,* for which he marketed the Buxom Bombshell, Jane Russell, personally attending to such details as designing a special cantilevered brassiere for correct positioning of her nipples.[5] His marriage to actress Jean Peters had a history as peculiar as his other eccentricities. His real Hollywood coup, however, was in capturing control of RKO, one of the largest studios.

But the most impressive flow of cash came after he had been forced out of the movie business, in the form of a check for $546 million that closed his sale of Trans World Airlines. As a biographer has noted, his hobbies turned into big corporations. By the time Nixon became president, Howard Hughes had taken over a large chunk of Las Vegas and had clearly established economic dominance over Nevada. In 1974, the government reinstated an indictment that accused him of conspiring with three associates to manipulate stock in Hughes Air West, Inc.[6]

His lucrative defense trade made Hughes the single largest private contractor for the CIA. A mysterious vessel, the *Glomar Explorer,* built at a cost of $350 million ostensibly to gather mineral wealth from the bottom of the seas, was actually trying to retrieve a sunken Russian nuclear submarine. Only later did its real objective become known, together with the fact that it was but one of many projects undertaken by Hughes for the CIA.[7]

Hughes's insinuation into the political power of Nixon's world was one of the things he did best. Senator Lowell Weicker, a Connecticut Republican and member of the Senate Watergate Committee, put it simply: "Everybody was feeding at the same trough." Hughes's connections involved such well-known names as Hubert Humphrey, Bobby Kennedy, Lyndon Johnson, and Democratic senator Joseph Montoya of New Mexico. One can state with confidence that hardly any important politico of Hughes's day escaped. "He manipulated politicians, but he never voted," explained his former financial manager, Noah Dietrich.[8]

Nevertheless, a review of his connections questions the considerable degree of involvement with Nixon; and if not with him personally, with enough associates to establish a strong pattern: Donald and Hannah Nixon, Pat Hillings, Richard Danner, Robert Mullen, Robert Foster Bennett, and most prominently, Bebe Rebozo. In March of 1964, long before Nixon's presidency, a former Republican presidential candidate, Alf Landon, suggested that the time had come for a "frank and complete statement covering the Hughes Tool Company loan of $200,000.00 to your brother in California during the time that you were Vice President of the United States." To Landon, and whenever else the subject — which had first come up in the fall of 1960 — could not be avoided, Nixon replied that he "had no part or interest in my brother's business. I had no part whatever in the negotiation of this loan. I was never asked to do anything by the Hughes Tool Company and never did anything for them."[9] But the haunting continued; the Landons never were satisfied, and Nixon ultimately left public life still under the Hughes curse.

The initial connection came from the 1956 loan to brother Donald, a sum that was actually $205,000, and, legally, from Frank J. Waters to Hannah Nixon. The arrangement involved the then vacant corner at the former Nixon homesite on East Whittier Boulevard and the corner of St. Gertrude's, land that became collateral for money designed to salvage the business enterprises of Hannah's younger son Donald. The Richard–Donald affair was the Nixon counterpart of the LBJ–Sam Houston Johnson tension; later, similar embarrassment was endured by President Carter from the ventures of his enterprising brother, Billy. In each case, sibling jealousy was at work, the more obscure family member hoping to cash in on the other's fame and fortune. In each case, too, the gains were not worth the risks and complications.

Donald, who was some two years younger than Richard, was from early on viewed as the more aggressive go-getter. Of the Nixon children, they were the most competitive. Sheldon Beeson, a first cousin, told an interviewer in 1970 that "Don was never one to make concessions to anyone. He had a pretty determined way about him. . . . He'd always get particularly frustrated at Dick because he couldn't win an argument with Dick, either. Dick would always seem to come out on top, making Don madder than ever, and he just couldn't argue him down." While the older brother was "quiet and studious and very conscientious about everything that he did," Don was "a dynamo," recalled cousin William A. Milhous. "Nobody could keep up with him." When compared with his older brother, he was "boisterous." Another cousin, Dr. Theodore F. Marshburn, recalled Don as apolitical but "already in the market business before Dick ever went into politics." Even more pointed was the observation that "I think that maybe as long as Dick Nixon is Vice-President or in high office, this guy might get by." Far more than Richard, Don was the adventurous entrepreneur. Another cousin thought he was "a charming promoter-type of an entertainer. I mean he can meet anybody so easily and he is so friendly. He's just like a big friendly dog with his tail a-wagging. He comes up, and everybody loves him." Still, the fact was, as John Ehrlichman has recalled, that when Nixon won the presidential election in 1968, Donald boasted that he "intended to make a million in the next four years." His brother Richard maintains that Don "was a totally honest man. He took wonderful care of my mother and so forth. The problem was that he was naive and he was a sucker for con-men." Donald seemed to follow his predestined script; eventually, the road led to the District of Columbia's Virginia Avenue and the building complex known as Watergate. He had placed himself, and his family, in the hands of America's foremost shark, one whose range of operations was as vast as the oceans themselves.[10]

The essential difference between Donald and other small businessmen was that his brother was vice president of the United States. Nothing could have made his plight more attractive to those who, like Hughes, were also in the business of buying politicians. Donald created the predicament by overexpanding and placing himself in a financial crunch.

He got to that pit because of an early illusion of success. He saturated Whittier with a Nixon's Drive-In, a Nixon's Family Restaurant, and a Nixon's Super Market and Coffee Shop, featuring, in the process, a Nixonburger sandwich. He hoped for continued growth by expanding into Anaheim via another fast-food drive-in restaurant. The bottom line, of course, was that the Nixon name was distinctive. When overextension got him into trouble, that was an irresistible asset. As Donald later explained, he "had hoped that the stock offered to the public would be sold by June 1956 and that this financing would enable me to clean up our obligations and arrears and to carry on and expand the business."[11]

But since he was not an anonymous entrepreneur, there were ways out, and such means were usually through people who knew other people. One such acquaintance was Frank Waters. Waters, an attorney who had served in the California legislature, was simply explained as an old family friend. Ingratiating himself with such people as Donald Nixon was also part of his business. The official explanation that Waters was a "friend and supporter" of the vice president was true, but he was also a political attorney for Howard Hughes. He handled disbursements and served as a registered lobbyist for the Hughes Tool Company. Through Harold Stassen, Richard Nixon's long-term acquaintance, Waters knew Vic Johnston. Johnston, like Stassen, was from Minnesota; during the 1950s, he also headed the senatorial campaign committee. It was a fine, fairly well defined — but hardly unique — circle that was always ready for mutual assistance.

Donald was not too naive to take his troubles to Johnston, who suggested that he see Waters. "Don went to talk to Frank," Richard Nixon has explained, "to see if he knew people who might buy stock in the company. I was aware of that."[12]

Therein came the $205,000, technically borrowed by Hannah Nixon from Waters; in reality, it was turned over to Waters by Dietrich from the Canadian subsidiary of the Hughes Tool Company.[13] Later, the deed to the land was held by someone even more obscure than Waters, a Philip Reiner, an accountant who was also asked to become lienholder. Reiner was connected to Hughes through his association with another one of the billionaire's retainees, James J. Arditto, a Waters law partner.

"That was all I knew at the time," said Nixon. He was in Key Biscayne just before Christmas in 1955 when he got a call from either Waters or Johnston telling him that Hughes had made the loan to Donald. "I was shocked. 'My God,' I said. 'Why did they do it?' I was no fool, and I remember so well." He called Donald from Florida and said that his brother must give security for the loan, and it was at his insistence "that he put up my mother's property — you know, the service station, the store, and all the rest — as security."[14]

Also questionable was the adequacy of Hannah Nixon's property as collateral. Donald's claim that it was worth over $200,000 contradicted his mother's official Los Angeles County affidavit that Frank Nixon was worth no more than $100,000 at the time of his death, including that lot. The original purchase price was $5,000, and although the assessed value had gone to $13,000, that meant it could actually fetch no more than $52,000, on the scale of the going price in that neighborhood at the time. But the long-term value was tremendous. The corner plot on the main business thoroughfare through Whittier is now valued in the millions. Of greater significance, and what really raised the question of violations of law, was that the IRS lost little time after the money exchange to rule that the Howard Hughes Medical Institute was tax exempt, a decision that was worth many times the size of the loan. Hughes's other companies also got their own advantages.[15]

The actual loan was executed on December 10, 1956, just one month after the Eisenhower-Nixon reelection, but there is absolutely no evidence that, however unwise the Hughes association, Nixon's immediate interest went beyond helping Donald. If anything, an earlier unfavorable IRS ruling spurred the Hughes Tool Company to come to the rescue of the vice president's brother, whose plight could not have escaped the attention of Waters in any event. The complexity of Hughes's relationships with government agencies certainly compounds the magnitude of Nixon's indiscretion. The affair also subjected him to continuing scrutiny from journalists and political rivals. The Hughes connection was often uncomfortable and awkward for Nixon, which makes his later acceptance of additional Hughes money through Bebe Rebozo even more inexplicable.

Another dilemma caused by Hughes during Nixon's presidency involved plans for an underground atomic test in Nevada. Hughes, by then in his cocoon and obsessed by fears of contamination, was terrified by the continuing series of nuclear explosions. Some could even be felt in Las Vegas. The whole state was his fiefdom by then, or so he thought. He was sure another powerful atomic blast would touch off earthquakes. He sent his then trusted aide, Robert Maheu, to get Bebe Rebozo to have the president call them off. "Please pull out every last stop to delay or cancel this test," Hughes pleaded. He was willing to pay a million dollars. Rebozo, refusing to act on his own, urged Hughes to meet with Nixon himself. But Hughes would not descend from his penthouse even to meet with the president of the United States. "Forget it, Bebe," Nixon remembers telling his friend, and on Thursday, March 26, 1970, the six hundredth nuclear explosion since the opening of the atomic age, and one of the biggest, shook up the recluse in his Las Vegas bed. "Once again," Michael Drosnin has written, "Hughes grabbed a yellow legal pad and, in one last futile gesture, scrawled a threat to leave the country, taking all his assets with him."[16]

Hughes undoubtedly was capitalism run amok. Of him it may properly be said that he was everywhere and nowhere. He and Nixon had communicated only twice by telephone, one call involving having his own commercial jet go to Moscow along with a government jet. Nixon recalls: "He wanted to demonstrate one of our planes before the Russians" in the days when jets were first coming into common usage. Otherwise, he was just a hidden force, creating an ever greater mystique. Before the hysteria over the atomic testing, says Nixon, "he never asked for anything."[17] Perhaps he was sure he didn't have to.

At the time of the loan to Donald, the embarrassment was minor. Robert Kennedy's comment that it was an important reason for Nixon's loss in 1960 was a gross exaggeration.[18] The story broke late in that campaign and interest was mainly confined to California, which Nixon won. Moreover, eastern papers hardly bothered with it, and Theodore White's comprehensive account of the 1960 race ignores the matter altogether.

Only a miscalculation by the Nixon camp gave it any airing before that year's election. Details were made available to several media outlets, including columnist Drew Pearson, but fearing accusations of last-minute mud-slinging without much time left for rebuttals, they all thought it unwise to release what could be interpreted as a bombshell. Without realizing that Pearson and the others intended to hold it until *after* the voting, Nixon's campaign put out a story to offset expected revelations by the opposition. Scripps-Howard columnist Peter Edson got an exclusive that portrayed the loan in terms of pure innocence. There was no mention of Hughes, only that "Mrs. Waters and Donald Nixon's wife had been in high school together and the two families were and still are good friends," which made it "natural" to help Don. Besides, went the Edson account, the money was secured by the value of Hannah Nixon's property deeded to Waters, who then turned it over to Reiner, "one of the creditors who had threatened foreclosure."[19]

Once that version appeared, Pearson released his. Four years after the secret fund incident, in December of 1956, he explained, Nixon's family "received a much bigger financial benefit from the Hughes Tool Co., wholly owned by Howard Hughes." Bob Finch called the Pearson story an "obvious political smear," and Donald Nixon, while acknowledging that the money came from Hughes, explained that it was Waters who was the lender and his mother who had borrowed on her property. "There were no ulterior motives here so far as I know," said Donald's statement. "I have never asked my brother to do anything for me or anyone else in the government; and if I did I know he would refuse."[20]

When the Kennedys came into power, they considered bringing charges against both parties, the Nixons and Hughes, for violations of criminal law. But the paper wall that had been created, including sub-leasing of Hannah Nixon's property to the Union Oil Company, complicated it to the point that the Justice Department decided that the loan had violated no statutes.[21]

The 1962 California race was another matter. Bebe Rebozo, who was most closely involved in the Hughes transactions that figured in the Watergate scandals, recalls that the Hughes issue was "just spillover dirt" that was "foreign" to him at the time. All he knew about the matter was that it was caused by Don Nixon's naïveté and that it had little to do with the outcome. Nixon himself, however, has admitted to the importance of the loan in his fight for the governorship.[22] Any apparent contradiction between their respective memories may be explained when one realizes the incredible lack of discretion that was involved. If Rebozo prefers to forget, it is for a good reason. Instead of regarding the $205,000 affair as a warning of what could happen, Bebe's after-the-fact justification for going ahead with Hughes required dismissing the importance of the earlier embarrassment.

Once the elements of the episode came to light, the loan was impossible to explain without encouraging continued skepticism. The fact that the papers were signed right after the 1956 election aroused suspicions that the parties to the deal had chosen a "safe" moment. The inadequacy of Hannah Nixon's collateral and Waters's closeness to Hughes, followed by the use of two dummy mortgage holders, were additional signs that the whole thing was meant to be hidden. After the 1960 defeat, Donald worried that his business problems had caused the loss. His brother reassured him that it was a minor matter.[23] More accurately, the responsibility was shared.

The affair was grist for Nixon's opponents in California in 1962, especially Republicans who opposed him in the primary, and it remained alive until election day. Nixon, already facing a difficult situation in running against Governor Pat Brown, didn't help his cause by ducking the issue. During his only direct campaign confrontation with Brown, he challenged his opponent to produce direct evidence; but, as Nixon then explained during an eleventh-hour telethon, the governor "stood up . . . cringed and went away like a whipped boy."[24] For all Brown's failure to pin his opponent down on the issue, Nixon could not bury the suspicions.

After his first presidential campaign, despite the loss to Kennedy, Nixon's standing remained high; yet, even then, reporter Neil Morgan observed that his "nature is less clearly understood by the public than that of any other major political figure of his time." Then came his decision to compete with Governor Brown in California, which brought much agreement with President Kennedy's view that it did not make "much sense to run [for the governorship] when he came so close to being President." Speaking to Arthur Krock on the last day of 1962, Kennedy pointed out that the former vice president had forfeited his dominant position. "If he hadn't run, I think you would have to say that Nixon would be up in front. The polls would have put him up in front, and I think he would have been the candidate if he wanted to be. That is why I thought it wasn't necessary for him to run."[25]

There *was* something incongruous about so perceptive a politician risking his future against an incumbent governor. Caspar Weinberger, who became chairman of California's Republican party that summer of 1962, remembered that the California defeat left Nixon "bitter and unhappy and thoroughly finished, as far as he was concerned. The only thing he ever cared about was politics, and he saw this whole thing just closed off. I think that night, he clearly had given up." Repudiation by his home state further signaled the end of his political career. For Nixon and his family there seemed no choice but to go east. "Nobody wanted to stay," remembered Julie.[26] They went to New York, the land of Rockefeller Republicanism.

There he was, in other words, in precisely the place he had shunned when leaving the White House. New York, especially with its Rockefeller-controlled party, never was his political base. Even before the Republicans managed to wrest the statehouse away from Harriman, its anti-Nixon bias was abundantly clear. The men behind Stassen's maneuverings confirmed that. To sidestep a California challenge, however, would appear to signal that, like Tom Dewey, he would retire to a private law practice and concentrate on making money. But, as people like Bryce Harlow recognized, that was not Nixon's bent. Harlow, the presidential adviser, had gotten to know Nixon well during the Eisenhower years and it was with some confidence that, in the wake of the California disaster, he explained to Rose Mary Woods that her boss would not "find lasting satisfaction in [a] strictly mercenary life."[27]

Having rejected commercial opportunities, he of course had options other than risking an encounter against Pat Brown. Early on, Ray Moley tried to convince him of the advantages of becoming the party's national chairman. Moley reasoned that Nixon could follow in the hallowed traditions of Thomas Jefferson, who worked to build a party structure during his vice presidency. He could also make it clear by taking on that job that it would not be used to promote another race against Kennedy in 1964. Besides, argued the ex–New Deal brain-truster, "nothing could so inspire the millions who have been either reluctant Republicans or those who kept clear of the Republican Party. It would also be a rallying point for millions of conservative Democrats who are presently home-less."[28]

They talked about it within days after Nixon's loss to Kennedy, but he never warmed to the idea. Taking over the national committee, he told Moley, might be "committing political hari kari as far as running for any future political office is concerned" and he much preferred to keep his options open.[29] Another choice was to emulate John Quincy Adams and serve a distinguished career in the U.S. Congress, but that, too, might place him on the wrong political track. He would, instead, return to California, practice law, and put together his memoirs. As a private citizen, he could speak freely on the issues, and provide for the financial needs of Pat and their two daughters.

None of this meant that he was turning his back on Washington. The special network of friendly journalists, contributors, and Republicans would not vanish overnight, wherever he was located. Though he was out of power, his prestige remained high. Still, many had no doubt that he had blown an advantage. He should have won; he lost a golden opportunity over a vulnerable opponent. Somewhat the way it had happened after Dewey lost to Truman in 1948, there were those in the party, especially to his right, who complained about the old specter of me-tooism: He had been too gentle with Kennedy, had run a poorly conceived and executed campaign. The youthful comer of the past decade was suddenly a flawed veteran, a reality that was especially striking when he gave a party for Republicans just before stepping down from the vice presidency; they acted as though he was a has-been, and that had to hurt.[30] At this time, power was more likely to be found with Goldwater or Rockefeller. Only time would tell whether he would even want to challenge Kennedy in 1964.

Mindful that Eisenhower remained their strongest attraction, that they had done poorly without him, party leaders recognized that self-interest involved keeping him "alive" even after he retired to Gettysburg. That meant informing the general about what was going on, beyond the political headlines available to the public: marriages, anniversaries, birthdays, all the occasions for maintaining contact with "the right people at the right time" through a confidential newsletter that could serve as a "political survival kit."[31]

To take care of that function, the party got financing from moneymen like banker Cliff Folger and industrialist Harold Boeschenstein and hired twenty-eight-year-old Stephen Hess. A researcher and speechwriter, Hess came from a liberal New York background and then turned elsewhere, both geographically and politically. He studied at the University of Chicago for two years before going on to Johns Hopkins, where he took his degree in political science and also taught courses in American government. His working experience in Washington came as a staff assistant in the Eisenhower administration, and he also served briefly on the public relations staff of the Republican National Committee, all of which made him ideal to handle the assignment for Eisenhower. Once given his special duty by Bryce Harlow, Hess went to work in his Washington office under the name of Stephen Hess Associates.

Hess's newsletter also went to Nixon, which gave him an audience of two, or, as Hess later put it, the most "elite readership in America." Hess recalled that Eisenhower "loved the opportunity to take advantage" of such social amenities. Nixon's reaction was very different: he considered the whole thing distasteful, burdensome; it reminded him of when he had to mimeograph manuscripts back at Duke so professors could hand out to students copies of their unpublishable books. "You don't have to send me those letters anymore," he instructed Hess after he had his fill. "I don't want to be a person who remembers somebody's birthday." The contrast between the two men was inescapable, the general who scoffed at politics and politicians enjoyed maintaining his social connections, while the career pro moved into his own world. Chitchat never was his way.[32]

Much more characteristic was how he dealt with the decision to oppose Brown, a possibility that was under active consideration within weeks of his loss to Kennedy and while his daughters were still completing their school year in Washington.[33] He could, of course, have settled down with the Los Angeles law firm of Adams, Duque, and Hazeltine and kept his future plans an open matter. But that choice never seemed right. There were things he *had* to do and, because they were compatible with his own inclinations about what kind of future was possible, they became what he *wanted* to do. The process consumed several months of indecision, less because of Nixon's reluctance than the wariness of others, especially his family.

California Republicans generally had little trouble with the question. Retaining control over the state capital at Sacramento was their first priority. Brown, they assumed, was vulnerable. He had tripped over Chessman and the death penalty, all of which was confirmed by public opinion polls. In the eyes of people like Weinberger, Nixon's candidacy was far more sensible than risking a loss by going with some relative lightweight. "We wanted to have a well-known candidate at the head of the ticket, and Nixon was clearly that," Weinberger has said.[34] Victory would not only keep him in the news and provide a forum, but decisions about what to do about national ambitions in 1964 or 1968 would still remain in his hands.

Such reasoning had the endorsement of a notable array of Republicans in the rest of the country. Eisenhower, Len Hall, and Cliff Folger argued that he could not expect to raise much money without a political base,

an undoubtedly persuasive argument. How could they continue to tap
their financial sources just for Nixon's convenience if he did not run for
office and disappeared from the headlines? As Nixon continued his
consultations, he found hardly anyone without an opinion, whether or
not it was based on any knowledge of California politics. Herbert Hoover
and General Douglas MacArthur cautioned him to stay out, but Nixon
later cited a letter from Whittaker Chambers that "probably tilted the
scales on the side of running."[35]

One noteworthy aspect of the Chambers letter is that it was dated
February 2, 1961, only two weeks after Nixon turned over the vice
presidency to Lyndon Johnson. Another is that Nixon and Chambers
had for some time had only limited contacts. Chambers knew he was
dying, and it was his last letter to Nixon. "Some tell me that there are
reasons why you should not presently run for Governor of California,"
wrote the man whose revelations launched Nixon's career. "But if it is
at all feasible, I, for what it is worth, strongly urge you to consider this.
There would be a sense and an impression of political come-down? Great
character always precludes a sense of come-down, greatly yielding to
match the altered circumstances. The public impression will then take
care of itself, may, indeed, become an asset. I believe you to be, rather
uniquely, a man who can do this."[36]

Nixon and his friends continued to search for the appropriate decision. Ray Moley remained in close touch on the matter and his own
wavering illustrates the larger problem. In early August 1961, Moley
had visions of Nixon buried under statewide minutiae that would paralyze him as a national spokesman. He would be frustrated by a hostile,
corrupt legislature and be trapped into situations that were "likely to be
dismaying." Any ability to express himself via the printed word in a
manner that might offer "authority and influence" would also be subjected to frustrating interruptions. Mostly, he would be best off preserving himself as "the natural occupant of the vast middle ground
where, I believe, most people stand."[37]

Within two weeks, however, after meeting with Hall and journalist
Victor Lasky, Moley sounded like a different man. The others, he reported, were worried that the party could well nominate Rockefeller in
1964, which "would result in one of the greatest stay-at-home votes in
history" because conservatives would simply write it off. Nixon, of course,
would retain the party faithful, a victory would give him the best of both
worlds, a strong base for running again or, should that not seem wise,
the advantage of falling back on the promise that he would not use the
governorship as a stepping-stone to the presidency; but, as Moley
pointed out, neither would such a pledge necessarily be binding. "Dewey
and Rockefeller made similar promises," he wrote. "I would rather see
you take a chance on losing a few votes by frankly saying that while you

will not actively seek the Presidential nomination, you will be at the service of the party nationally in '64." He should argue for the importance of rescuing California from Brown and the Democrats, even at the price of disclaiming the White House as his ultimate objective. What he might do when 1964 came was not relevant, although being otherwise preoccupied in Sacramento could serve as a "convenient bombshelter that would give him an excuse not to run against Kennedy," a popular incumbent. Besides, as Moley reminded him, "nobody will believe anything you say about serving out the term."[38]

Assumed but somehow brushed aside was his lack of enthusiasm for the governorship itself. Instead, he convinced himself of his own organizational and intellectual strengths, which would enable him to become a credible fighter for California, to deal on a knowledgeable level with the growth problems of the most rapidly expanding state. A contest against Brown was viewed as a fitting warm-up for another national campaign. Political scientists saw California's voting behavior as a reflection of what was happening nationally. Even the fact that the state had about a million more registered Democrats than Republicans was a positive factor in making a chance to win there more attractive. "California will be, more than ever, a national background," wrote Neil Morgan, and the *New York Times* saw the battle over its governorship as the "most important election ever held in a single state."[39] The temptations were too great.

All the positive reasons were marshaled. The state's well-regarded Field poll showed him a potential winner against Brown.[40] Goodwin Knight, the major challenger, faced primary competition from two contenders, most notably Joseph Shell. A former University of Southern California football star and a forty-three-year-old oil executive, Shell attracted strong support from the right. While Knight remained the greatest obstacle, California's central Republican committee was maneuvering him out of the way. The state's leaders could hardly have done more to prepare for Nixon's nomination.

Getting into the fight was intriguing. He was clearly not receptive to the kind of advice Bob Haldeman offered: stay out. Some of those in California whom he canvassed found out, said Weinberger, that he "barely spoke" to them again. Even his political analyst, Claude Robinson, cautioned that Brown's prospects could well improve by election day. Herb Klein was aware that even as "we debated the merits of a Nixon campaign in California . . . it did not really matter whether I and others came down on one side of the issue or the other. Nixon had already made up his mind." He dined at the Chandler mansion with Buff and Norman of the *Los Angeles Times,* and as Mrs Chandler later revealed, "he simply refused to listen. Pat was very uncomfortable and wanted to go home but he ignored her. He drank too much and he kept talking, delivering a monologue. He went on much too long, insisting Pat Brown was just a clown who was headed for certain defeat." So intense was his pitch that they found it too awkward "to inject one other important reality," that he could no longer take the *Times* for granted since Otis Chandler had become publisher. Still, Nixon was too intoxicated by the idea to heed the sense of his good friend George A. Fuller of the Fuller Construction Company, who was the only dissenter when Nixon gathered some twenty-two people together in Washington for advice.[41]

The announcement of his candidacy, made from the Statler-Hilton Hotel in Los Angeles on September 27, brought obvious skepticism from newsmen about whether, if elected, he really intended to serve out his term. When Nixon's statement declared that he would not "seek" the presidency in 1964, they maneuvered him into the clarification that he would neither be the candidate nor the nominee. Another major issue concerned where he stood on the John Birch Society, the group dedicated by candy manufacturer Robert Welch to saving the world from Moscow's Marxist conspiracy; the Birchites' appeal to the far right was causing serious rifts among the state's Republicans. When asked about them, Nixon sharply rejected their support and cited his own anticommunist credentials.[42]

Even with Knight in the race, victory in the primary seemed assured. Knight, bitter since having been brushed aside by Knowland in 1958, withdrew in mid-January. His departure boosted Shell by nine points in the Field poll, which still left him at just the 16 percent level, and gave Nixon far more maneuverability among the Republican electorate.[43] Beating Shell was easy.

But victory itself signaled more trouble. Shell's highest public office was as minority leader of the state legislature. For Nixon to run no better than two to one, with 65 percent of the vote in California's first primary without crossover balloting, was not all that impressive. Nixon's pulling power was also considerably lower than what incumbent Republican senator Tom Kuchel and Governor Brown had managed in their primaries. To win in November, Nixon needed 90 percent of the Republican vote plus 20 percent of the Democrats.[44]

Nixon then made his opposition to the Birchites more emphatic by refusing to endorse two of the state's congressmen, John H. Rousselot and Edgar Hiestand, who were members of the society. Nixon's spurning of Rousselot was especially galling. The congressman represented Nixon's old district and was regarded as a protégé of the former vice president. Compounding the Nixon-Rousselot connection was the fact that his campaign was being run by one of Nixon's charter sponsors from 1946, Roy O. Day. As though that were not enough, their differences were widened when Nixon tried to get the state party to demand that all Republicans quit the Birch Society on the grounds that membership was inconsistent with Republican principles. The resolution that was finally adopted was watered down, partly because of opposition by such other California Republicans as Ronald Reagan, and partly because Nixon's own tactician, Murray Chotiner, hesitated to alienate hard-core Republican conservatives.[45]

Reagan, increasing his political identification with the party's right wing, backed Rousselot and then went over to Nixon, but more ultra-conservative strength was needed if the Republican nominee had any chance to defeat Brown. As Governor Arthur Langlie reminded Nixon about his own experience in the state of Washington, "The burdens of carrying the right wing is [*sic*] always tougher than carrying the extreme left." After his California campaign, Nixon pointed out in a letter to the *New York Herald Tribune* that "many observers believe that Birch opposition was one of the major factors causing my defeat." The assumption was, at best, partly true. Twenty-three years later, Nixon reportedly advised presidential candidate George Bush that "a Republican could afford neither to alienate his conservative base nor to waste time in the fall campaign courting their support." Mindful of his California experience, he was quoted as saying, "You can't win the election just with these people. But you can't win the election without these people, as I learned."[46]

When, at the Los Angeles announcement of his candidacy, he reminded his audience that he had fought Communists all his political life and that "they fought me," he was also placed on the defensive about another matter. In a manner reminiscent of the secret fund and the Hughes loan embarrassment, he had to submit to suspicions of an involvement with Jimmy Hoffa, who had been chosen in 1957 to succeed Dave Beck as president of the International Brotherhood of Teamsters.[47] The Hoffa situation never matched Hughes as an issue, but the experience warrants some detailed explanation as a case study of how questions about Nixon's veracity, even when seemingly unfair, bore substantive relationships to his involvements.

Hoffa continued the union's sordid association with crime and mobsters. His rise to Teamster dominance testified to his ability to survive internal power struggles. As biographer Walter Sheridan has explained, "Hoffa decided early in the game that he would always have more muscle than the other guy. He obtained his own racketeers."[48]

The Teamster leader was genuinely self-made. His father, an unsuccessful coal prospector in Indiana, died when Jimmy was just four, and the youngster took up the chores for the family, dropping out of school at age fourteen. He was only seventeen when he led fellow workers to demand better pay and working conditions, ultimately delivering their new labor organization into the hands of the Teamsters.

The coming of union health and welfare funds placed sustantial resources at their command. Money in trust for Teamster members enabled the organization's officers to profit by setting up companies and making a number of phony investments. Beck himself embezzled more than $350,000 from such funds and was the subject of congressional probes. Under Hoffa, pension money helped to fund a variety of real estate properties, including an apartment house project in conjunction with Clint Murchison, Jr. There was also a half-million-dollar diversion for a potential retirement "paradise" at Titusville, Florida, that was sponsored by the mob-ridden Sun Valley Corporation. The Sun Valley operation brought Hoffa under fire when Senator John McClellan of Arkansas, a conservative southern Democrat, chaired a Select Committee on Improper Activities that had Robert Kennedy as its chief counsel and Jack Kennedy as a member. Only some shrewd maneuvering by Edward Bennett Williams, Hoffa's defense lawyer, spared him from conviction for bribing a juror when he was tried for attempting to plant a spy on the committee.[49] Bobby Kennedy's zeal for catching up with the Teamster boss and putting him in jail became somewhat of a crusade and obsession. Politically, both Beck and Hoffa were inviting targets for those who were eager to use revelations about the Teamsters as a way of besmirching union leaders generally.

It almost seemed paradoxical that the Teamsters, who in so many ways epitomized what antiunion people were railing against, became most closely allied with two Republican presidents, Eisenhower and Nixon. Hoffa, who, as Steven Brill has written, built "a cynical money-hungry, crime-allied, apolitical dictatorship" that created "the widest possible gap between the wealth of the union leaders and that of the rank and file," emulated Beck's 1956 endorsement of Eisenhower by backing Nixon in 1960.[50]

That the vice president was receptive to that kind of help when he ran against Kennedy is hardly newsworthy. The arrangements required no personal meeting; negotiations were left to intermediaries. A key man was I. Irving Davidson, the son of a Pittsburgh rabbi, whose reputation for honesty made him an effective Washington wheeler-dealer, lobbyist, and international operator. Long before the Iranian arms-sale adventures of Albert Hakim and Richard Secord, Davidson exploited the international arms trade. He became a registered agent for the government of Luis Somoza in Nicaragua and was close to the president and his brother Anastasio, who ran the army. Davidson also represented Israel in selling military equipment, such as armored trucks for Fulgencio Batista's forces in Cuba, and to the Haitian government under François "Papa Doc" Duvalier. In 1960, he attended both parties' nominating conventions. He introduced Hoffa to John Connally at the Democratic event in Los Angeles and, at the Republican gathering in Chicago, continued to act as an emissary between Allan Oakley Hunter, a California lawyer who had served in Congress until 1955, and Hunter's friend Vice President Nixon. Hunter informed Nixon that Davidson's interest in Hoffa was based on his "affinity for interesting and controversial personalities, and he wants to continue to negotiate loans; therefore, if ever he has an opportunity to help Hoffa, he will do so."[51]

The Hoffa-Nixon understanding was sealed long before that campaign or even the conventions. What Hoffa wanted was relief from federal prosecution, or, in his terms, he wanted to get the government "off my back." Nixon's need was political help from the Teamsters, and it was in Ohio where they could be most effective.

No state was more under Teamster control, which was particularly powerful in the city of Cleveland. Ohio also had a Democratic governor, Mike DiSalle, who was plainly inclined toward Kennedy. And, since the state had strong rural-urban components, neither party could take its twenty-five electoral votes for granted. Eisenhower won it twice, but Ike was Ike; Truman took it over Dewey in 1948 by a scant margin. Either way one looked at it, Ohio was crucial for Nixon, especially if he ran against Kennedy. It was also important for the Teamsters to dump a long-term Ohio congressman, Bill Ayres. The Akron Republican represented a marginal district and was on Hoffa's "hit" list for voting for the recently passed Landrum-Griffin labor law with its restrictions against boycotts and picketing.[52]

Hunter sounded out the vice president and told Davidson that while it would not be wise for him to accept an official position as an adviser to Hoffa, he was interested in political help from the Teamsters. Hunter agreed to a Sunday meeting with Davidson and Hoffa in Miami's Americana Hotel two weeks before Christmas of 1959. Hoffa was clearly delighted at the chance to meet Nixon's emissary, but, taking no chances, immediately removed his jacket. Hunter assumed that Hoffa was showing that he carried no hidden microphones and did the same.

They managed to clear the air about their respective needs. Hunter, as he afterward described the encounter to Nixon, disclaimed any Nixon initiative or function as his spokesman, except to reaffirm his concern about the vice president's political future. He also made plain that he thought Hoffa and Nixon had much in common: "You were hated by experts, you were both self-made men, you were both dedicated to your respective fields of endeavor, and you both had a lot of guts," was how he reported his words. For Nixon's benefit, Hunter pointed out that Hoffa "leads a clean life, pays his taxes, and obeys the law. . . . [He] does not smoke or drink or chase women. He is very devoted to his wife, and she is very often with him when he travels. He eats regularly, he has dinner at 6:30, and is in bed by 10:30." In turn, Hunter also assured Hoffa that although Nixon disapproved of many Teamster activities, he "did not have the knife out for him personally, and bore no preconceived prejudices against him," which drew an obvious contrast with the Kennedy brothers. Moreover, "having worked your way up in the world, you certainly appreciated the problems of working people and believed in the right of labor to organize and bargain collectively."

Hoffa, whom Hunter found highly articulate and well informed as well as dogmatic about labor-management relations, seemed exuberant at the opportunity for even indirect communication with Nixon. He emphasized the need to get rid of Congressman Ayres, fulminated against Nelson Rockefeller and against Standard Oil, which was fighting his union with tactics that were "as rough, tough, mean and dirty as they have ever been in the history of the Teamsters' relations with the several Standard Oil companies." Hunter thought that, coming from Hoffa, the description was of a "pretty rough league." Most of all, the Teamster leader wanted the federal government off his back. He was confident of winning the Sun Valley case, but it would be costly both in time and money.

In contrast to United Auto Workers president Walter Reuther — who, he contended, was being treated with kid gloves despite what Hoffa alleged was his control of gambling in the automobile plants to provide unaccountable slush funds — he was being harassed by Attorney General William Rogers. The Justice Department was out to "get him" with a series of "nuisance suits." All Hoffa wanted was to "be treated like anyone else." If not, he warned, he had the power to strike back. As Hunter relayed Hoffa's position to Nixon: "He feels that the open endorsement of local officials of his union in certain cities would definitely benefit a candidate, and that the work of individual members of his union, wherever they are, almost without exception, would be an asset to any candidate."

Hunter left with no direct promises, but did say that his own disinclination to serve in any official advisory position to Hoffa did not mean that he would not volunteer "ideas on how his union might undertake political action in the best interests of the country." A few weeks later, Hoffa tried to find out, as Hunter relayed the question to Nixon, "if there were any particular candidates for Congress or the Senate in the western states and Hawaii which we might have special reason for not wanting the Longshoremen to clobber."[53]

Not so quietly, Hoffa and his Teamsters, while avoiding outright support for Nixon, attacked Kennedy's presidential candidacy, most prominently through an editorial in the September 1960 issue of the *International Teamster* magazine and in a vote by the international brotherhood's executive board. Hoffa also denounced the Democrat that summer as the son of a millionaire "who never knew what it was to work." While Hoffa was careful to avoid the kiss of death by openly endorsing

Nixon, Kennedy's loss of Ohio was a major surprise of the campaign, especially since, as DiSalle pointed out four years later, the Democrats worked harder there "than in any of the large states." Drew Pearson, who followed the Nixon-Hoffa exchanges, thought that Teamster support "probably tipped the scales in the state."[54]

That such help had much to do with the outcome there is not supported by the evidence, however. Kennedy carried just ten of Ohio's eighty-eight counties, and those were the areas of prime Teamster strength, including Cuyahoga County, the location of the city of Cleveland. While the Kennedy vote there was less than optimistic expectations, his split with Nixon showed a distinct Catholic-Protestant division. In most places, Nixon's margins coincided with Eisenhower's sources of strength.[55]

The Justice Department, meanwhile, pursued a criminal indictment of Hoffa in the Sun Valley case, charging "flagrant misuse of union funds." Just as that legal step was about to be taken, in what has been described as "an open-and-shut case," a telephone call from Malcolm Wilkie, who headed the department's criminal division, directed the postponement of the indictment and a return of the files for further study. Hoffa got a breather; whether he would be in the clear depended on what the voters did in November. When they chose Kennedy, Attorney General Rogers went ahead with the indictment. Hoffa was sure he had been double-crossed; with the election over, Nixon had reneged about holding off Justice any further. But that was not the case, Hunter then assured the union leader. "I know for a fact that your side of the case was put before the Vice President and that he discussed the case with the Attorney General, Bill Rogers," he wrote to Hoffa. He then explained that losing the election also left Nixon in no "position to exercise any decisive degree of influence. As Vice President he had no authority to order the Attorney General to do anything."[56]

The irony was that Hoffa owed nothing to Nixon; the vice president had fulfilled his part of the bargain and then could do no more as a lame duck. But he could never escape the consequences of having dealt with Hoffa, and the association followed Nixon to the West Coast.

Whether the Nixons would readjust to California was always questionable; circumstances never permitted much of a test, but, for a time, they made a concerted effort. Financially, they were finally in the clear. Becoming a consultant for the law firm of Adams, Duque, and Hazeltine enabled him to estimate that his 1961 income would be around $350,000, higher than the total of his fourteen years in Washington.[57]

After fumbling around with temporary residences, they settled down in their "pseudo-Grecian home," as John Ehrlichman put it, at 410 Martin Lane, in the western part of Los Angeles not far from both Bel-Air and Beverly Hills. Building the ranch house, its sixty-five hundred square feet with seven baths, four bedrooms, three fireplaces, a swimming pool, a spacious library, and a thirty-foot-long living room, stretched the family's assets. Trousdale Estates, where their home was located, was the creation of developer Paul Trousdale, who later had the idea of getting together with some fellow Republicans to buy the *New York Times* so they could "slant its news toward the conservative view for a change."[58]

Nixon's purchase of land in Trousdale's development, however, produced the unexpected — new allegations about improprieties. The *Los Angeles Times* reported that he had received a "celebrity discount" through none other than Jimmy Hoffa. Los Angeles County records showed Teamster Trust Fund involvement in the form of a $42,000 mortgage on the lot, which the Nixons bought for $35,000 as a site for their home.

Part of the financing came from selling their old Wesley Heights home for a $25,000 profit. The rest, it was soon alleged, came with the help of a $42,000 first trust deed that had been placed on Trousdale's property by Jimmy Hoffa's Teamsters' fund. Questions were raised when Nixon's actual cost was shown as $35,000. "Would you explain how you managed to buy a piece of property for $35,000 which had a $42,000 mortgage on it?" he was asked by reporters when he announced his candidacy, implicitly linking the Hoffa matter with the allegations about Howard Hughes. "Was this a gift?" was the reporter's charged question.[59]

"First of all," Nixon explained, "with regard to the price for the lot, I think all the questions on that should be directed to the man from whom it was purchased. I desired to buy a lot in that particular tract. He wished to sell a lot, and I paid the price that he asked. I think it was a reasonable price. As a matter of fact, I might say, incidentally, that builders all over this state and county offered me lots free, which I did not take because I did not think that was appropriate. I would suggest that $35,000 is a great deal of money to pay for a lot, too. Now, with regard to Jimmy Hoffa's $42,000, I can really give you something a lot better than that. That loan, I understand, was made five years ago when I was thinking of living someplace other than in Trousdale Estates. As a matter of fact, five years ago I didn't even know where Trousdale Estates were." The essential matter, of course, was not only that the Teamster expenditure was made so much earlier but that it represented just part of their investment in the developer's enterprise, another deployment of union pension funds. There was absolutely no connection with Nixon's finances. In acknowledging that point, Nixon said with exasperation, "There's nothing left to throw at me."[60]

It was Nixon who, as in his postcampaign letter to the *Herald Tribune* about the price paid for disavowing the John Birch Society, eagerly advanced the notion that he was hurt because he had rebelled against extremism. The press picked up the theme, even while noting, as did the *New York Times,* that there was a mixed pattern in the success of California's conservative candidates.[61]

Nixon was evidently dissembling. He was realistic enough to know that he had much more to gain than to lose by denouncing the group. As a report on the organization by Benjamin R. Epstein and Arnold Forster later explained, "In the Birch Society's penetration of American society, the single most important step has been the infiltration of the Republican Party by Welch's dedicated and indoctrinated cadres." Democrats had their own problems with extremism, but the Birchite factor was far more troublesome to Republicans generally — especially during the three years that followed that 1962 campaign — and nowhere was it as severe as in southern California. Nevertheless, Tom Kuchel ran for reelection on the same ticket as did Nixon, bluntly wrote off the rightists, and still came away with 56.5 percent against his Democratic opponent.[62]

Since Robert Welch's followers considered themselves members of a secret organization, no accurate calculation of their membership was known; at best, because Republicans were outnumbered in California, the Birchites were a minority within a minority. The secrecy of their membership naturally made it hard to gauge their actual strength, but the assumption within the Nixon camp, which was the most generous estimate, was that they at least had the following of one-third of the state's Republicans. By every gauge possible, their membership increased greatly *after* 1962, some 30 percent during the first three months of the next year alone, according to Rousselot. Not until Barry Goldwater's rise in 1964 were the Birchites potent, and then mainly in California's Southland.[63]

Nevertheless, Nixon was careful to distinguish between members of the society and the national organization headed by Welch. He emphasized that he had not taken a stand against them as *individuals* but did not believe Republican candidates "should seek, or accept, the support of an organization whose acknowledged leader has said on several occasions that Dwight Eisenhower and Foster Dulles were conscious agents of the Communist conspiracy."[64]

While nobody questions that Shell was the Birchite favorite, it is equally true that Nixon did not enter the gubernatorial race expecting embarrassment. Defeating Shell, as Pat Brown has pointed out, was more important than the Birchites at that time. When Henry Salvatori, an oil magnate and benefactor of Republican conservatives, brought Nixon together with Shell after the primary, the loser acknowledged the weakness of his position by agreeing to back Nixon — however tepid that support actually turned out to be.[65]

By emphasizing their power, Nixon was overblowing the Birch threat, much as he rose to political prominence in the first place by exaggerating the dangers of internal communism. Taking that stand during the gubernatorial race, moreover, was prudent for California as well as for another potential race for the White House by confirming his image as a moderate, which, in fact, he was. Right after shaking off the Birchite support, he made a point of writing to other prominent Republicans that "it was time to take on the lunatic fringe once and for all"; the party should not have to "carry the anchor of the reactionary right into our campaigns this Fall."[66]

Disavowing the Birch Society was Nixon's play for the bipartisan political center — in other words, the state's Democratic voters — much as Kuchel had achieved. The big difference, of course, was that the senator was a popular incumbent. Nixon was the one running against the man who held the office in Sacramento and, although Brown had image problems and had been weakened by the death penalty fiasco, things had settled down considerably. Recalling that the appeal of his son, Jerry, then only one year out of his Jesuit school training, had influenced his temporary reprieve for Chessman, Brown pointed out that the forty executions actually accomplished during his administration undercut arguments that he was "soft" on crime. In fact, he added, "law and order" was a big issue in the campaign.[67]

Nixon's speechwriters were hard-pressed to focus on an area of Brown's vulnerability. Nixon's teenage daughter Julie was perceptive enough to note at the time that the bumbling, rather plain candidate that Brown appeared to be on television was exactly the sort of man who would attract a popular following. What it all came down to, Weinberger later explained, was that "Nixon was viewed as trying to push out an incumbent governor who hadn't done anything very wrong. And that's a very hard role to play."[68]

There were, in fact, few issues that Nixon, now virtually considered an outsider to the state — and one who repeatedly betrayed his lack of intimacy with all things Californian — could use with good effect to unseat the governor. Before the start of that fall's campaign, he admitted during remarks at Eisenhower's farm at Gettysburg that he was "in a sort of internship." A number of stumbles confirmed that very quickly. On election eve, for example, he referred to himself as a prospective "Governor of the United States." His desire to retain the right-wing Republican vote prompted him to virtually abdicate to Brown some of the state's vital labor and ethnic blocs. About all the governor really had to do was to keep hammering away at the idea that Nixon was using California as a stepping-stone. Nor was his opponent helped when the Hughes loan "corroborated some of the 'Tricky Dick' feeling," recalled Brown, who then added that "Nixon tried to paint me as a stupid Red."

Bumper stickers asked the question "Is Brown Pink?" with the final word printed in the appropriate color. Ironically, given Nixon's repudiation of the organization, they were sold at the American Opinion bookstores operated by the John Birch Society. Eugene Wyman, the Democratic state chairman, charged that the governor was the victim of a smear campaign, but the bumper stickers, at least, were not traceable to Nixon.[69]

Being identified with strong anticommunism, something hardly new to Nixon's career, was better than losing. Disavowing the Birchites decontaminated him from extremism while allowing him to pursue the cause for which he was best known, anticommunism. Pat Hillings, who had contacts among the Democrats, reported in March 1962 that his friends within the other camp feared that Nixon's rejection of the right-wing extremists would free him to open his "big gun" on the leftist reformers of the California Democratic Council. "They are particularly fearful of your attacking the position of the CDC leadership in favoring the admission of Red China [to the United Nations]," he advised.[70]

In taking on communism during that California campaign, Nixon did not suddenly reinvent the issue, as others have suggested. Reaching that conclusion ignores that his campaign embraced a matter that had been pursued by a long-standing state fact-finding subcommittee on un-American activities. For the past two decades, reaching back into the heart of World War II days, the legislators found the hunt for subversives a worthwhile preoccupation. Finally, in late 1961, even as Nixon was preparing to compete for the governorship, the committee, by then under the chairmanship of State Senator Hugh M. Burns, issued its eleventh report. It elucidated in over two hundred pages the "revival" of "un-American activities in California," especially among college students. "Scattered through the universities and colleges of the state are a group of student political organizations," warned the Burns Committee, "ranging all the way from extreme political radicalism to those that advocate a relatively mild brand of socialism." The report, which was issued just a few years before the free-speech movement at Berkeley and the rise of campus antiwar agitation, warned that "the gates have been thrown open to Communists, faculty members, students, and anyone else who cares to utilize the university property as a brawling ground for political controversy." When Nixon was asked at a press conference in mid-September to support his contention that Communist subversion had increased in California, he rested his case by citing the Burns Committee's latest report.[71]

He opened the fall campaign by questioning Brown's ability to deal "with the Communist threat within our borders" and charging that the governor's record "shows not a single item of anti-subversive legislation

in four years." Nixon promised that he would make the state "a model
for effectively dealing with an alien system — communism." He charged
that California's Democratic organization contained "thirty-five Communists." The number was small, he acknowledged, but he stressed that
it was nevertheless important because of their links to the "international
Communist conspiracy" and proposed a three-pronged program of investigation, legislation, and education.[72]

Nixon's desperation encouraged the continued use of Murray Chotiner, despite Chotiner's questionable reputation, which was exacerbated
when he was called to testify before a Senate investigation of influence-
peddling in Washington. The Beverly Hills lawyer, whose work for
Nixon went back to 1946, was not actually charged with any wrongdoing,
but he was viewed as a political liability. Democrats also thought his
arrival as an adviser to Nixon's campaign indicated a shift to the right.
Eugene Wyman called him a "drumbeater for the John Birch Society."
Nixon also directed his campaign manager, Bob Haldeman, to work with
Leone Baxter of the political public relations firm of Whitaker and
Baxter.[73]

Whitaker and Baxter had already become well established, most notably
for their handling of the American Medical Association's $3.5 million
fight to defeat President Truman's proposal for a system of national
health insurance. Clem Whitaker and his associate, Leone Baxter, whom
he then married, were pioneers in a field that later became far more
familiar. Another California political management firm, Spencer-
Roberts, which directed Rockefeller's primary in 1964, began its operations in 1961.[74]

Whitaker started out as a newspaperman, and his wife's background
included working as an organizer and tactician for the Chamber of
Commerce. They collaborated to manage a campaign in 1933, making
them the first professional political publicists. Their mission was pragmatic, not ideological.

Their basic theory was that pressure for a given outcome could be
best achieved by selling the merits of the case to the voters, who were
in the best position to apply pressure. As Richard Harris has written,
they "held that old-fashioned lobbying — persuading, intimidating, and
buying legislators — was costly and, in the long run, uncertain, since a
client could not be sure that legislators would stay persuaded, intimi-
dated, or bought beyond a single legislative session, and the whole un-
pleasant business might have to be repeated every couple of years." Over
a dozen years before they were used by the Nixon campaign, Senator
James E. Murray of Montana called Whitaker and Baxter "a chromium-
plated publicity firm."[75]

The fact was that Whitaker and Baxter knew how to win elections; or at least such fellow Californians as Knight, Knowland, Warren, and Kuchel thought so. All retained them at one time or another. The husband-and-wife team was successful precisely because it brought professionalism to the often chaotic innards of the political game. The extraparty money-gathering was in the hands of what was called the Nixon for Governor Finance Committee. In their fight to unseat Brown, their use of Whitaker and Baxter included the creation of a phony Committee to Preserve the Democratic Party. The appeal was one that Nixon had used before: *real* Democrats, that is, conservative Democrats, must be outraged by what the band of New Dealers and Kremlin-sympathizers had been doing to traditional principles associated with the Jeffersonian-Jacksonian heritage. Using a mailing list of some half-million Democrats regarded as potentially sensitive to that type of sellout, and identifying themselves as fellow Democrats, the committee sent out postcards with questions that were contrived to lead respondents to agree with certain assumptions: Governor Brown was a captive of the "ultra liberal" CDC and had become a tool of their softness toward communism by favoring Communist China's admission to the United Nations, suspension of nuclear testing, approval of "subversive" speeches on the state's college campuses, and giving foreign aid to Communist countries, such as Yugoslavia. Recipients were urged to express their feelings and send in checks to help the cause. The operation, which cost $70,000, brought in $368.50. Another document, in the form of a flier, carried the heading of "Democrats for California" and urged "fellow Democrats" to vote Republican because of the CDC "take-over." Nixon's own headquarters made available such pamphlets as "California, Dynasty of Communism" and "Pat Brown and the CDC."[76]

Democrats took their case to court. On October 22, Judge Byron Arnold of the California Superior Court granted a temporary restraining order against continued use of the postcards; twelve days later, he followed with a temporary injunction. Meanwhile, Nixon accused his opponents of eleven violations of fair campaign ethics and the Republicans filed their own "smear" suits. As if by mutual agreement, most legal action was dropped right after the campaign. In 1964, however, the San Francisco judge made his injunction permanent. Realistically, of course, by then it had no more force than a reprimand, but his decision, ignored at the time, stated that "Mr. Nixon and Mr. Haldeman approved the plan and project as described above and agreed that the Nixon committee would finance the project."[77]

Nixon came out of that campaign as Tricky Dick once more, and, even more damaging with the party pros, as a confirmed loser, now twice over. At a time when Americans were beginning to wander away from the Eisenhower equilibrium, he was finding himself shunned not only by liberals but by the far right as well.

Julie, reflecting back to what her father had let himself in for that year, explained that "he was just so tired that I don't think he was thinking as straight as he would have been. He had undertaken too much. He was doing the *Six Crises*. He had raised over half a million dollars for Republicans by speeches over the country by '61." The pressure from Eisenhower and other Republicans was just too great to resist.[78] Mercifully, almost, the ordeal came to an end even before the voters actually had their say. President Kennedy's successful face-down of Khrushchev over the placement of missiles on Cuban soil helped to spur a Democratic tide.

Nixon was desperate. He could, of course, do nothing less than support the president's dramatic quarantine of Cuba. Along with a number of other prominent Republicans, he had long been urging Kennedy to "take the necessary steps to avoid the building up of a Communist beachhead in Cuba ninety miles from our shore." In mid-September, a month before the missile launchers were detected on the island, he was asked whether he was prepared to "risk nuclear war over Cuba" and replied that he was ready to support the president in taking "any action" that might be needed. On Monday, October 22, appearing on his own paid telethon five and a half hours after Kennedy's announcement of the quarantine, he warned that the Cuban crisis might be a prelude to increased Communist activity in California and reminded his listeners about his own experience as an anticommunist. That Saturday, before conclusion of a withdrawal agreement with the Soviets, he denounced any deal that might remove American missiles from Turkey, because that country would then "inevitably go down the drain because it is right on the border with the Russian aggressions threatening them at every moment." On Sunday, Ronald Reagan went on the air and told listeners that he sort of liked the idea of taking the country back to the days of McKinley. "Under McKinley we freed Cuba." Speaking on election eve, Nixon made a dramatic last-minute plea. He denounced Governor Brown's "smear tactics" in reviving the allegations about the Hughes loan and protested circulars that accused him of being anti-Semitic, anti-Negro, and anti-Catholic.[79]

The next day, 6 million Californians went to the polls and Pat Brown got nearly 300,000 more votes than Richard Nixon. The Cuban missile crisis completely "sealed" the outcome of that election, Nixon later wrote in his diary. He really meant "confirmed," which was what was also immediately accepted as the prognosis for his future beyond California. An ABC-TV news special, which provoked the anger of such Nixon loyalists as Annenberg, was called "The Political Obituary of Richard M.

Nixon" and included an on-air interview with Alger Hiss. Even the *Los Angeles Times* used the following headline above a column on what it all meant: "Nixon's Rise, Fall, Warning for Americans."[80] Had he taken California that year, the party's presidential nomination in 1964 would have been his, unless he preferred to keep his pledge to serve a full term.

The best-remembered incidents from that campaign were not the dirty tricks, the associations with Hoffa and Hughes, or Nixon's disavowal of Birchite support. Much more memorable was what happened the morning after the election at his Beverly Hilton Hotel headquarters.

Nixon's crew was up late the night before. Voting was close and returns were slow, the outcome possibly not certain until absentee ballots could be tabulated. At the moment, they hardly seemed crucial, however; discouraging as the figures were, Nixon predicted a 50.5 to 49.5 percent outcome. When the later numbers came in and defeat seemed probable, Nixon wrote "never" on a yellow pad, defiance that recalled his delayed concession after losing to Kennedy. At about midnight, he reacted to the inevitable and scribbled out a statement. Herb Klein quietly pocketed his boss's concession.

Thoroughly discouraged, Nixon, said Klein, had "a couple of drinks" and fell into a restless sleep. He awoke eager for some coffee. The emotional fatigue was obvious. Please, he asked Klein, keep me from facing the newsmen downstairs. Klein went to the next floor to put them off.

That provoked objections from two Nixon friends, Jack Drown and Ray Arbuthnot. He should tell off the press. Klein, the news professional, had already told them that Nixon had gone home; but Drown and Arbuthnot persisted. It would be a mistake to duck the waiting press. The difference between the friends and the professionals around Nixon, Klein later explained, was that Nixon "expected us to use some judgment. We learned that he didn't mean it."[81] Nixon went downstairs.

Klein later recalled that he listened to Nixon's opening remarks and "knew we were in trouble. I wanted somehow to hide, but there was no place to go." Nixon, "exhausted mentally and physically" from the night before, and not drunk although he had had several glasses of scotch and water, was not fully revived. The reporters, who were eager to ask their questions, "couldn't help seeing his condition," Ehrlichman has written. When Nixon singled out Carl Greenberg as an example of a newsman who *had* given him fair coverage, the *Los Angeles Times* writer was clearly embarrassed. Then, "hung over, trembling and red-eyed," and too "emotionally fatigued," as both Herb Klein and Pat Hillings recall, to enable him to cope with his emotions and the circumstances, Nixon concluded his rambling remarks by adding that they would not have "Nixon to kick around anymore, because, gentlemen, this is my last press conference and it will be one in which I have welcomed the opportunity to test wits with you."[82]

That pathetic performance, even more than the inept campaign itself, showed the world another side of the Nixon who, only a few days before, had gone out of his way to laud the press. That earlier statement, made during a telethon, upheld the need of journalists to have "as much access to information as possible." Then he added, "The very fact a newspaperman is watching keeps a public official on his toes. This is one of the greatest strengths we have over the Communists. We've got to have criticism and surveillance wherever possible." Fine words; still, when he faced newsmen at a moment when California's governorship was lost, along with what seemed left of his own political career, the bitterness poured out. He denounced them, told them off in a way totally unacceptable for any public figure dependent upon popular support. The outburst showed a side of Nixon that was associated with the rest of his career. The press had actually covered the California campaign with remarkable balance.[83]

One matter that did bring protests from the Nixon camp was *Life* magazine's use of writer Mark Harris. Bob Haldeman pointed out that "Harris' questionable Communist-front affiliations and activities, and his complete lack of experience or ability as a political writer or analyst hardly qualify him as the man to report to the nation on Nixon's campaign." CBS's use of political analyst Lou Harris as a consultant was also attacked. The pollster was suspect because he had been used by Democrats President Kennedy and Pat Brown.[84] But such questions were almost routine complaints that are associated with many campaigns, and one has to go very far to say that Nixon lost in California that year because of the press.

Several attempts have been made to quantify the balance of newspaper and electronic coverage of campaigns, but the results have hardly persuaded the convinced.[85] In Nixon's case, and the same could be said of the coverage given most public figures as well as major events, judiciousness of reportage by the media in general is too ambiguous a concept for satisfactory evaluation. Bias and intent clash with conditions determined by technological and commercial considerations. Few issues bring as much heat.

Such were the controversies during Nixon's entire career. When he lost to Kennedy in 1960, there was no argument about where the press stood. Nixon clearly had the backing of an overwhelming majority of the country's newspapers. An organization that monitored coverage for the Republican National Committee acknowledged during the heat of that campaign that the Democratic ticket was ahead "even when the entire media strength of the President is added to the totals of the Republican ticket."[86]

   That same year, after his fourth television debate with Kennedy, Nixon told reporters Robert S. Allen and Paul J. Scott that "the coverage of the campaign by newspapers has been very fair. I have no complaint on that score. In all fairness, I think that should be said." And his point was well taken. Henry Luce's publications gave him their blessing if not their love. Even if he sometimes found Luce's ambivalence and even-handedness disturbing, Nixon could, at least, count more consistently on such other giants as Walter Annenberg, William Randolph Hearst, Frank Gannett, Roy Howard, and Otis Chandler. Of local importance but vital for his crucial New Hampshire primary fight in 1968 was William Loeb and the *Manchester Union-Leader.* Such individual journalists as Earl Mazo, Dick Wilson, Lyle Wilson, Merriman Smith, Walter Trohan, Stewart Alsop, Joseph Alsop, Bert Andrews, Raymond Moley, Ralph de Toledano, Hedley Donovan, James Sheply, and widely circulated conservative writer George Sokolsky, whose column was carried in about 350 papers, were with him all the way. Where any of them parted with the Eisenhower administration, it was because of qualms about its flirtations with liberalism. But they had more confidence in Nixon. In addition, the vice president had kept his close ties to his old friends at the *Los Angeles Times,* where Kyle Palmer was still political editor. By 1968, Nixon had, in addition, also drawn close to another reporter on the staff, Carl Greenberg. Despite all of this, the perception was that 1968 was won *despite* rather than because of the support of the media.[87]

As a Republican, Richard Nixon had the almost automatic support of the businessmen who run America's newspapers. Such traditional partisanship is too well known to need documentation; even FDR's second-term sweep in 1936 was opposed by most of the press, a bias manifested in the unfortunate survey published that year by the *Literary Digest,* which made perhaps the most misguided political prognostication of all time by predicting a Landon victory. Newspaper support continued heavily Republican throughout the Truman and Eisenhower eras. Only Barry Goldwater's extremism in 1964 helped shift to Lyndon Johnson a disproportionate share of the normally Republican press; with Nixon the party's candidate once again four years later, normality returned. A survey compiled by *Editor & Publisher* showed that newspapers with a total circulation of 27 million, numbering 483 in all, endorsed Nixon, while Hubert Humphrey was the favorite of just 93 papers that reached fewer than 4 million.[88]

   Nixon also had many close ties with important communications executives. His files show a personal relationship with Hearst president and chief executive officer Richard E. Berlin. Berlin, who headed one of the country's largest diversified media companies, was a dedicated believer in Nixon as one who understood the menace of Soviet internationalist ambitions. Friends like Berlin were fine, Nixon told Berlin, but press backing too often stopped at the editorial page. "If all the editors and publishers who supported us had done as well as the Hearst papers," he wrote in January 1961, ". . . there is no doubt in my mind but that we would have won the election."[89] More accurately, he could have added that how he was portrayed in the press vis-à-vis Kennedy was the intensification of a long-existing favoritism.

The journalists assigned to do the coverage simply did not like Nixon. That they were mostly Democrats was part of the problem. Nixon was not only a Republican, but the wrong kind of Republican. Hiss, Voorhis, Douglas, HUAC, and Checkers were part of the past but not gone from memory, all associated with the Nixon who belonged with Joe McCarthy, Karl Mundt, Pat McCarran, and William Jenner, the most despised examples of political reaction. To Nixon, as Theodore White wrote of the campaign, such newsmen were "not a brotherhood, but a conspiracy, and a hostile conspiracy at that," and he was skeptical about being able to reach the public over their heads.[90]

Yet, even the *New York Times* — the *Pravda* of the bunch — noted right after his presidential nomination that he "never failed to control completely interviews and press conferences." If, as during school days, he was not exactly their cup of tea, neither was he a buffoon. It was more simply that, as de Toledano has pointed out, Nixon "was kept perpetually on the firing line" and was "bird-dogged by eager reporters whose 'interpretive' stories were often not much more than a polemic." The cumulative effect was so bad, in fact, that his reputation suffered even among those of his colleagues who knew better.[91]

More than ever before, there was open warfare between Nixon and the press. They clashed and embittered and exhausted each other, and were more estranged by the time it was all over. When Nixon first became the party's leader, White has reported, the journalists were somewhat split down the middle. By the time their war of distrust had played itself out, the press had become a Kennedy cheering section.[92]

Peter Lisagor of the *Chicago Daily News,* a longtime political reporter, recalled that there were strange moments during that 1960 campaign. "He wouldn't see us. He began to isolate himself away from the press. There was an episode in New York where he went into hiding in the Waldorf-Astoria Hotel for a couple of days and didn't even do any campaigning. There were some mystifying aspects to it. He brooded a great deal. He felt like he had been made the underdog and that the press was opposed to him, and he was fighting all kinds of hobgoblins." One conservative journalist, Robert D. Novak, has written that "it was easier to gain an audience with the Pope than to see Nixon privately during the 1960 campaign." John Ehrlichman pinpointed the damage. "Somewhere and somehow the working press was lost," he wrote to Nixon after it was all over, "and with them much of the advantage of good local crowds, color events, effective non-televised rallies and the attractive, different human interest items which newspaper readers consume and are moved by because they are different, catchy, easy to remember." What Ehrlichman could have added but did not was that in Kennedy, Nixon had an opponent who exacerbated the situation. The Democrat and the journalists enjoyed each other. Reporters sometimes seemed more a part of his entourage than working professionals.[93]

Nixon simply could not compete, nor did he really try. He did carry out routine, obligatory press briefings and informal discussions. There were even times when he seemed to loosen up and, as the race later tightened, he encouraged his staff to sway reporters' perceptions by what he called "operation confidence." But he had no illusions about becoming their favorite, a predisposition that confirmed the inevitability of a clash. In common with many public figures, he took their criticism as personal and malicious.[94]

Most certainly, the problem went beyond the personalities of Nixon and Kennedy. The Republican candidate was up against what historian Allen J. Matusow has called "an intense subculture at the center of the nation's communication network"; almost all "shared a world view that profoundly influenced the political climate in this election year." Nixon speechwriter Pat Buchanan, noting the role of the men and women of the working press, called them "the first line of defense for American liberals."[95]

How to get around their effect on public information was of no small concern to those who agreed with Nixon about the power of such intellectual elitists. In their view, the situation was made especially critical after the Russians orbited the first space satellite. The American public, young and old alike, were simply not being educated to prepare them for the coming showdown with international communism. Three weeks after the launching of *Sputnik*, Nixon commented privately that "Rome . . . fell because of inner decay, not because of any innate superiority of the invaders from the North. Yet the handful of believers, who but a few centuries before emerged from their refuge in the catacombs, not only brought religious faith to their new masters, but also preserved much of Greek and Roman culture in the process." There was no doubt, he added, that "the real struggle today is a struggle for men's minds," with Americans needing to understand that the Third World's rising expectations were not only economic but "mainly a struggle for equality and against injustice and discrimination." At least, Nixon wrote to Fred Clark, the Russian breakthrough had provoked second thoughts about the pedagogical ideas that have "brought our public schools to such a low state"; despite the inevitable resistance to change, there might at last be "a renaissance of learning" such as the nation had not had since the nineteenth century. Nixon's despair over education was reinforced by publisher John Cowles, who responded to a survey of Minnesota high school students by telling him that "a substantial proportion of our teenagers are either completely unaware of, or out of sympathy with, the basic concepts on which our government was established." At about the same time, a teacher at Bob Finch's old high school in Inglewood, California, wrote of her concern that whereas when she was a student most teachers "were Republican in outlook, if not in party affiliation," her colleagues were beginning to change in ways that were bound to have negative classroom influences. William F. Buckley, Jr.'s *National Review* ran an article by conservative writer Frank Chodorov arguing that "individualism must be offered as first-class radicalism" to college students to wipe away notions of socialism. "We need to produce people who are grounded in the humanities," Nixon told an economic conference in Washington, "people who have an understanding of the world problems with which this country must deal, and of our domestic problems as well." Elmer Bobst feared that Americans tended to ignore problems mostly because they lacked "knowledge coupled with too often a false sense of security. Both lead to smugness and complacency."[96]

The dilemma was especially severe, Nixon explained to Henry Luce, for conservatives wishing to influence public information. "We Republicans," he stressed, would, without the ability to reach out to the masses, be limited to the "serious" audience, which made it all the more vital for such magazines as Luce's to educate the public on subjects "vital to the people's welfare." The crux of the problem, Nixon reminded the man whose publications were in virtually every American home, was that there was a higher calling: conservative voices needed more help from friendly publishers. Little wonder that battle lines had been drawn long before 1960 and certainly, as has been pointed out, long before he entered the White House later in the decade.[97]

Unlike Kennedy, Nixon was of a different culture from the working press. He had to face a new breed of newshounds. No longer could one start as a high school graduate and advance from copyboy to cub and even full reporter. The new men and women were often the products of a liberal education, and with the growing importance of television, were part of the process of remaking how Americans got their information. The new technology was a far cry from the old. A vast network reached out from key media centers, principally New York and Washington. Moreover, the new age of television gave even more power to those two key papers that became the bane of political conservatives, the

New York Times and the *Washington Post.* Both papers set the agenda for much of what was selected for television news coverage; the stories given prominence by their writers and editors became the lead items on screens throughout the country. In that way, more than ever before, those two papers, especially via the tube, determined what news was rated as important for consumption by Americans; they were joined, to various degrees, by the *Wall Street Journal, Time, Newsweek,* and, especially in official Washington circles during Republican administrations, by *U.S. News & World Report.*[98]

They attracted to their staffs a postwar generation of men and women who were the children of business and professional people, including would-be novelists and print reporters. Collectively, the media, as C. Wright Mills wrote, helped push the transformation of American society: "They are also among the most important of those increased means of power now at the disposal of elites of wealth and power; moreover, some of the higher agents of these media are themselves either among the elites or very important among their servants."[99]

These members of the media were at once indigenous to American culture and, at the same time, far removed. They were the quintessential new aristocrats, constituting, in a sense, a modern leisure class. Professional absorptions took them away from labor, their creativity more rewarding than pay, their egos bolstered by what John Kenneth Galbraith had already called "a vicarious feeling of superiority — another manifestation of class atittudes." So readily did they assume that, at least for them, work was not labor, that it was no longer considered remarkable, as Galbraith put it, "that the advertising man, tycoon, poet, or professor who suddenly finds his work unrewarding should seek the counsel of a psychiatrist." By the mid-sixties, when Nixon was presumed to have reached his political dead end because he had preempted the center of the Republican party rather than the nation, U.S. Court of Appeals Judge David Bazelon defined the "new class" as a "growing group of similarly situated people, with distinctly similar purposes, who entrepreneured their way through society by means of an educational qualification rather than by property ownership." *"The New Class,"* Bazelon went on, *"has not invented culture, nor has it devised an initial application of culture to power: it has simply established both of these on a mass basis, and with an income-gathering emphasis. . . .* The New Class is the non-owning class: and they non-own everything important, eventually."[100] They were the new leaders of the postindustrial revolution.

Their distance from the working-class view of the world was increasing. More than when Nixon first began his political career, journalism was shaped by their outlook and values. Unlike Horatio Alger folklore, those in key positions of their professions were highly educated and well paid. As Washington correspondent David Broder wrote, "The fact is that reporters are by no means any kind of cross-section. We are over-educated, we are overpaid in terms of the median, and we have a higher socio-economic stratification than the people for whom we are writing. . . . There is clearly a danger of elitism creeping in."[101]

Broder and his colleagues were overwhelmingly white, male, urban, and politically liberal, and remained consistent with their cultural backgrounds. During the sixteen-year period from 1964 to 1980, less than 20 percent of the media elite backed any Republican presidential candidate. Neither was there much difference between reporters and their editors. A 1971 study showed that most of the media executives, in fact, placed themselves on the left and just 10 percent on the right.

Possibly the biggest shift, however, one Walter Annenberg and his colleagues complained about, was the loss of editorial control by the executive offices. A significant change had taken place since the 1930s in the freedom of the working press to operate outside the confines of such biases. In 1961, a study by journalism professor William Rivers reported that only 7 percent of working newspeople reported such tampering, a far cry from the day when Henry Luce saw nothing wrong with seeing to it that his subordinates dedicated his magazines to the goal of placing Eisenhower in the White House. Little wonder, considering where he stood, Nixon complained in 1984 that "the press couldn't tolerate an intelligent conservative; they thought that anyone with a good education should be one of them." They seemed to him far removed from the concept that the American dream was alive and percolating in the heartland. For Nixon and those on the right generally, the older, happier alliances with the press were breaking down. Even as Americans were becoming more conservative, the men and women responsible for explaining the news were finding themselves freer to probe and critique the way the country was being run. The difference, Irving Kristol has written, was that "the older populist journalism was always ready, when things went wrong, to shout: 'Shoot the piano-player!' The new demagogic journalism is constantly and no less shrilly suggesting 'Shoot the piano.' "[102]

Updated versions of late nineteenth-century populist rhetoric pinpointed the new class as modern reincarnations of Wall Street capitalists, railroad barons, hard-money gold interests, and devilish foreigners. Texas journalist Lawrence Wright remembers that when he grew up in Dallas "the idea of protest seemed foreign and rather crackpot," and he took it for granted that "the country was being controlled by academics in Cambridge and New Haven, and by New York newspaper barons and network executives." He was thrilled along with everyone else he knew when Barry Goldwater suggested that "the country would be better off if we could just saw off the Eastern Seaboard and float it out to sea." The most charitable thing critics said about that modern band of intellectual elitists was that if they were not actually Communists, they didn't give much of a damn about the menace. Bazelon has suggested that opposing the fluoridation of drinking water, which grew as a rightist cause in the early sixties, was one manifestation of the rebellion against the new class.[103]

For Nixon, there was little difference between hostility toward the press and alienation from the new class. In his mind, at least — as to a significant extent in reality — they were part of that same group of intellectual elitists who, while professing empathy for humanity, operated with undisguised disdain for mass values. For the most part, he managed to keep his dislike for them under control. He did have his fourth-estate friends, for one, and political necessities also kept him doing the "right things." So it was not surprising that his enemies were especially delighted when, after losing to Brown, he also lost his composure.

That so-called last press conference was especially enjoyable to the passengers on *Air Force One*. The news was fresh that November day when the presidential plane was on its way to Hyde Park, New York, for the funeral of Eleanor Roosevelt. President Kennedy was accompanied by Chief Justice Earl Warren and at least one member of his cabinet, Arthur Goldberg. "I must remember to smile when I get defeated," said the president, as his group chuckled over accounts of Nixon's obvious self-destruction. One journalist, Mary McGrory, could not decide by looking at their faces who was enjoying the downfall more, the chief justice or the president of the United States. "They had their heads together over the clippings and were laughing like schoolboys," she remembered.[104]

If nothing else, such evidence of Nixon's indiscretion seemed bound to furnish ample ammunition for his Democratic opponents if, after losing to Brown in California, he should actually decide to attempt a comeback. Somehow, however, it never worked that way. The incident showed venom, weariness, unrestrained bitterness, and, most of all, poor sportsmanship, but it never did become a handy weapon. By the time he ran for the presidency in 1968, it became apparent that those who tried to use it against him might end up by shooting themselves. Pat Hillings recalls that when they heard that the Democrats were going to play back that tape, they went through it once more and determined — correctly, as it turned out — that Nixon's outburst was more likely to find sympathy from the larger numbers out there who also viewed the press as the enemy. When television crews played into the hands of wild radicals outside the Democratic convention in Chicago that summer, all doubts were wiped away. The antifluoridationists were not the only ones who had begun to see things Nixon's way.[105]

15

Revolt of the
Red-Diaper Babies

DWIGHT EISENHOWER'S famed good luck eluded Richard Nixon. He just managed to survive the secret fund epi-
sode in 1952, then Eisenhower's heart attack put him through
a long period of anxiety about a second vice presidential term. He and
Pat went through a horrendous experience during their 1958 trip to
South America. Even at the start of his presidential campaign against
Kennedy, when prospects favored the better-known and experienced
Mr. Nixon, a knee injury sidelined him just long enough for Kennedy
to take the initiative. Then, at the critical moment in his campaign against
Brown, the Cuban missile crisis took over the momentum of the final
days, strengthening Democrats, while incumbents seized the opportunity
to respond with patriotic élan. To seal it all, Nixon went before the press
on that unfortunate, ever-to-be-famous morning after and demolished
what was left of his reputation.

Nevertheless, inconceivable as it seemed at the moment, rejection in
California turned out to be fortunate. The governorship could well have
been a trap, his public career brought to a dead end under the gold-
domed state capitol. He had run under the assumption that the big
challenge would be defeating Kennedy in 1964. He further thought that
he could then size up the situation and, if it was one for a sacrificial
lamb, he could sidestep any obligation by citing his pledge to remain as
governor, thereby leaving himself available to compete against some
future nonincumbent.

But, as others have learned, the future was imponderable. The Kennedy assassination did more than remove the incumbent. It installed a
willful politician who skillfully exploited the young president's martyrdom, engineered an impressive series of accomplishments before the
next election, and became a formidable opponent, about as close as we
ever get to a consensus candidate.

Logically, of course, Nixon could have tried to dodge that kind of risk. In the changed atmosphere, however, and with an enhanced track record, it would have been virtually impossible to resist pleas to save the party from either Rockefeller or the Goldwaterites. He would have been the Republican Sir Galahad instead of a has-been, which, as it turned out, was a more advantageous position. Put another way, it is inconceivable that the man who could not resist pressures and temptations to run in the first place would have refused to go to war against Lyndon Johnson, especially once he had taken over in California.

But rejection was an extraordinary experience for the man who had run so well against Kennedy, and California was best forgotten. They were eager to escape to New York, Rockefeller territory, of course, but that hardly seemed to matter, recalled Julie, "so when he went back there he knew that he would be frozen out of all state events."[1] With old friends Elmer Bobst and Don Kendall eager to have him in New York and available to represent their companies' legal needs, Nixon became a senior partner in a prestigious firm there. When merged with John Mitchell's municipal and state bond specialists, the firm — located at 20 Broad Street, just south of Wall and almost within the shadow of the Subtreasury Building — became Nixon, Mudge, Rose, Guthrie, Alexander, and Mitchell. Even if Nixon's rival hovered nearby, Broad and Wall were far less remote than Sacramento. California, as it turned out, was not Nixon's Waterloo, and Broad Street was more like Elba than St. Helena.

One can also argue that the same cold war insecurity about communism that helped to launch Nixon's career so dominated events at home that it made his political survival almost inevitable. He could merely wait for events to fall his way, which, of course, implies that his own outlook remained relatively constant.

Nixon's generation feared Soviet-inspired communism to the virtual exclusion of all other forms of totalitarianism. Meanwhile, the post–New Deal breed of reformers were aided in their activism by the cold war. They, as he, had their solutions to the challenges faced by western democracies. At their simplest, the alternatives represented two differing views of what sort of response would be most appropriate for American leadership. Some argued that it should demonstrate the superiority of middle-class government as, paradoxically, the most effective expression of "people's" democracy, which could be best advanced by emphasizing civil libertarianism and social justice. The more traditional approach aimed at geopolitical supremacy through military counterforce combined with national economic strength. So went the dialogue that, with only minor variations, dominated the age.

Through it all, Nixon remained committed to the latter camp. As the rightists became louder and more numerous, he looked better, waiting, so it seemed, for the world to turn to him. Despite his own mistakes — as differentiated from bad luck — Nixon managed to preserve his eminence (without shedding the "loser" image) and watched things finally go his way. The national consensus that seemed so strong began to unravel. Social upheavals at home merged with the internal paroxysms over the increasingly troublesome war in Southeast Asia to create a tide of reaction and nationalism. By the time he was ready to return, the country was ready for him. Those who had written him off failed to understand the strength of his natural constituency.

By 1968, as Nixon stood on the verge of a resurrection, political scientist Theodore Lowi lamented that the liberal state was "coming to be appreciated as an anachronism." The differences had long been there, but recent experience questioned whether the system was capable "of maintaining the ideal of one nation indivisible."[2]

Such matters existed far from the consciousness of most Americans. Hardly five months after the atomic bombing of Hiroshima and Nagasaki, the high cost of living was the predominant concern of those surveyed by the Gallup organization.[3] The restoration of the level of purchasing power that had been absent since the 1920s, the return of soldiers from long overseas duty, and the settling down with families into homes, cushioned with economic security, was all that they really wanted from the new world order.

Not much more can be said about what Paul Johnson has called the nation's lack of "global coherence." A generation of young historians, taking their cue from historian William Appleman Williams, tried to explain foreign policy in terms of rational behavior. The chic view among New Left historians stressed the clash of market forces among capitalist nations, a continuation of imperialism under new concepts of colonialism. One was as complex as the other, each consisting of ethnocentric bonds, economic security, and cultural instincts that joined mysticism with spirituality. The problems that would later emerge, that exploded during the Nixon years in the streets of America and the halls of Congress, were from the start of the postwar years simmering toward the boiling point. By 1968, Professor Lowi observed that "the crisis of the 1960's is at bottom a political crisis, a crisis of public authority. . . . The crisis deepens because its nature has not even been discovered as yet."[4]

Conservatives and liberals both had illusions. Each defined mass needs within the context of its own ideology. Each drew from a leadership that was well educated, at least upper middle class, and secure economically and psychologically. It took a waterfront philosopher, Eric Hoffer, to define the climate. "The true believer is everywhere on the march," he wrote in a little book first published in 1961, "and both by converting and antagonizing, he is shaping the world in his own image."[5]

When the Nixons moved into their twelve-room apartment at 810 Fifth Avenue, in the wake of the resolution of the Cuban missile crisis, the signals were mixed. Throughout 1963, there were both encouragement and deterioration. The Kennedy administration followed through from the brink of nuclear confrontation to achieve a limited test ban agreement with the Russians. That, plus easing of tensions over the security of West Berlin, indicated the onset of the first substantial détente, a vast step forward since Eisenhower met Khrushchev at Geneva in 1955. In the Far East, however, the Democratic administration in Washington was watching its intransigent client state in Saigon, headed by President Diem, repress dissenting South Vietnamese Buddhists. Soldiers smashed pagodas and protesting monks set themselves afire. Pacification and security were more elusive than ever.

At home, violence brought results when resistance helped dramatize the unobtained goals of racial equality. Starting in Greensboro, North Carolina, students filled local jails by protesting segregation ordinances at lunch counters. Their civil disobedience proved infectious as similar demonstrations spread throughout the South. By 1961, at the start of the Kennedy administration, efforts to overturn traditional segregation were most dramatized when activists, largely northern and often interracial, invaded Dixie. At Anniston, Alabama, a 1960s version of KKK night riders burned a bus carrying freedom riders. The Kennedy administration, reacting through executive action, contributed Justice Department marshals. Guarded — and sometimes halfhearted — encouragement was also given to a voter registration campaign led by a wide array of youthful reformers and interfaith clergymen. Their provocative actions, however, had limitations insofar as the Kennedy administration was concerned. Attorney General Robert Kennedy's request to "cool it" lest the president be embarrassed at his forthcoming meeting with Khrushchev in Vienna only provoked indignation from those activists who could tolerate no compromise. Expert political analyses were not needed to recognize how the conflict was escalating.

At Port Huron, Michigan, a group of activist college students expressed their faith in participatory democracy by drafting a statement that called for a drastic overhaul of national priorities. Thus was born the Students for a Democratic Society, bringing to prominence a young leader named Tom Hayden and a force that, in its movement from reformist liberalism and toward democratization, gradually symbolized the radicalization of a vigorous counterculture.[6]

Still, in the days before the president was assassinated, the national

focus was diffused. Martin Luther King, Jr., with the aid of brutal resistance that shocked the national conscience and shook the economic
consciousness of Birmingham's business leaders, forced a settlement by
making them eager to restore stability. Helped by extremism, he got
Kennedy to abandon the administration's fairly cautious approach to
racial dissension. The president finally requested broad legislative protections for human rights. On August 28, 1963, a quarter-million Americans marched on Washington and crowded before the steps of the
Lincoln Memorial in a massive outpouring that demanded passage of
civil rights legislation. Dr. King's "I have a dream" speech and the peace-
fulness of the gathering made the occasion a memorable success. John
F. Kennedy, relieved that the day had gone so smoothly, afterward
greeted the leaders at the White House and posed for group pictures.
In the weeks that followed, political correspondents concentrated on the
deepening deadlock between the executive and the legislature, and, in-
ternationally, on the process of the landmark nuclear agreement with
the Russians. In early November, impatience with Diem having run its
course, the planners in Washington stepped aside to ease his overthrow.

Henry Luce's American Century was rekindled by the coming of Kennedy. Luce did not say so directly, but there was something romantic
about the new, youthful president, setting the tone and pace for the era.
All that "national purpose" language seemed to come together, crafted
into soaring and inspiring prose. The nation, Tom Hayden has written,
"and my generation, needed Kennedy as president."[7]

Unfortunately, the rhetoric, however inspiring, was overblown. Getting America moving again implied new beginnings, the retrieval of lost
prestige and rejection of the sluggishness under the Eisenhower era,
that time of great postponement. With the guidance of a more activist
federal government, under Kennedy there would be justice at home and
respect abroad for the nation's efforts to extend democracy throughout
the world and arrest the spread of totalitarianism. Led by a glamorous
new first family, the restoration of pride would underlay the new nationalism.

The implicit message naturally encouraged excessive expectations.
Simple arithmetic showed not only the narrowness of his victory over
Nixon — hardly a mandate — but also the power of the political opposition on Capitol Hill. Kennedy talked about "sailing against the wind,"
but, from the outset, those who expected an activist government that
would take command of the lagging struggle for racial equality and
correct the increasing maldistribution of wealth had to brace themselves
for more delays. The president was worried about moving too quickly;
support was still limited. Kennedy needed a second term. Even in his
highly inspirational inaugural address, he had admitted that "all this will

not be finished in the first one hundred days. Nor will it be finished in the first one thousand days, nor in the life of this administration, nor even perhaps in our lifetime on this planet."

The spirit was at least reasonable, the direction a far cry from the mundane Eisenhower approach. Still, under the gloss and rhetoric, little of substance seemed to have changed. Kennedy's first State of the Union address struck a tough cold war note. It also became clear that on the vital issues, especially civil rights, the new executive was also wary about activism. On several issues of interest to liberals, he followed the rituals expected from the first Democratic president since Truman. Mostly, however, as in acting on a report about giving more federal jobs to blacks, he was content to "indicate my interest and put the matter on ice for a while."[8]

The contradiction with the image was plain. Many intellectuals were skeptical about Kennedy all along, and they found their proof through his inaction. A number of prominent critics from the left — Lewis Mumford, Erich Fromm, A. J. Muste, Roger Hagan, Robert W. Gilmore, Staughton Lynd, Robert Paul Wolff, and Nathan Glazer — had little trouble deciding that Kennedy's New Frontier was a fraud. "The rhetoric of the inaugural address," wrote Mumford, "is now too deeply soiled to wash clean. The President, for all the brains he has assembled and picked, is still living in a pre-nuclear world, guided by the stale shibboleths of nineteenth century politics. Instead of correcting the long series of technological miscalculations and human blunders made under Truman and Eisenhower, President Kennedy has committed himself to perpetuating and recklessly pyramiding those errors." James Warburg, the financier, bankrolled the left-liberal Institute for Policy Studies in Washington. Kennedy's critics had little tolerance for explanations that the new president was "shrewdly calculating his legislative demands to just about what the traffic will bear." As late as May 1963, in the wake of Dr. King's crusade to desegregate the city of Birmingham and filmed reports of fire hoses and police dogs forcing back women and children in the streets, Attorney General Robert F. Kennedy met in his Central Park South apartment with writer James Baldwin and other black notables and found that they were impatient with the administration's explanations of why things were not possible.[9]

The right was also let down. Disenchantment began with the disastrous Bay of Pigs operation in April 1961. The Congolese crisis that followed the new nation's independence from Belgium placed a substantial body of American conservatives on the side of the Katanganese rebels. In Vietnam, Kennedy's incremental buildup contributed to the much-criticized policy of "gradualism" that was later held liable for America's military failure there. More unforgivable, in the eyes of his critics, was the undercutting of Diem, which only led to more instability and a deeper

American commitment. When the Soviets placed missiles in Cuba in 1962, there was a faceoff with Khrushchev and a settlement; but that included Kennedy's promise of no further intervention, instead of doing the job that should have been done at the Bay of Pigs. In his final days, Kennedy's embrace of civil rights activism and his moves to secure a treaty with the Russians to limit nuclear testing further repelled the far right. Such critics were barely stilled by the gunshots in Dallas.

If in the end Camelot inspired, it also rode on the reformist mood. Not by coincidence did several best-selling books come out in rapid succession during the next few years to tackle issues that, for the most part, were ignored by contributors to the national purpose debate. In 1958, John Kenneth Galbraith published *The Affluent Society,* with its critique of spending priorities. A young socialist, Michael Harrington, made news in 1962 with what his publishers advertised as "a stark, authoritative portrait of the seamy side of the Affluent Society," *The Other America.* As though to dramatize Harrington's point, James Baldwin's *Fire Next Time* warned that blacks were impatient. Inspired by the French feminist writer Simone de Beauvoir, Betty Friedan's *Feminine Mystique* tried to awaken American women to the fact that they had been educated for servility.

Such works of reform, or, in Theodore Roosevelt's characterization, muckraking, were thoroughly in the American grain. What was remarkable, however, was that from the mid-fifties to the publication of Ralph Nader's crusading *Unsafe at Any Speed* in 1965, there were so many significant books that sounded alarms and found large audiences. One of the classic works, which alerted the world to man's ability to create imbalances of nature, Rachel Carson's *Silent Spring,* appeared in the midst of the Kennedy years.

The ultimate denouement of Camelot, then, was less the creation of a progressive mood, one that embodied racial justice and humanitarian concerns over the quality of survival, than the ability of Kennedy and his brothers to digest and finally articulate preexisting impulses. If there was anything unique about the New Frontier, that was it: the ability to convert the New Deal legacy of governmental activism that targeted consumers rather than producers as the crux of economic well-being into an ideology of social reform suitable to the needs of the postwar generation of liberal baby boomers. It was, in a sense, a throwback to the progressive roots of Herbert Croly's "new nationalism." In a far more complex international economy, it could easily be seen as a new quest for utopia.

Increasingly, there were two nations, one eager for social justice as the most effective safeguard of democracy and the other bent on stability, tradition, and strength to resist a Sovet Union that was viewed as inherently evil and expansionist. That dichotomy carried the substance of political polarization, much of it later attributed to orchestration by the Nixon White House. Consequently, there was a split within the various constituent groups that had been joined by the common causes of the thirties and forties. The strange bedfellows of the post-Reconstruction South — workers engaged in productivity, service and clerical occupations, and the vast range of what became known as minority groups — found themselves participants in a reordering of society that challenged each component group to find its place in the new scheme.

That change, as Nixon found out during his campaign against Kennedy, was full of hazards for the incumbent Democrats. The national party's commitment to civil rights legislation, already a clearly defined two-edged sword, always had potential for partisan bloodshed. Certainly, as conservatives viewed the prospect, the political cost to the sponsors would not be warranted by the gains to society, even to those theoretically first in line for benefits, American blacks trying to emerge as a political force.

If, for example, one were to accept the premise of the opening line of a report by a special assistant to the secretary of labor, Daniel Patrick Moynihan, that "the Negro American revolution is rightly regarded as the most important domestic event of the postwar period in the United States," it is difficult to understand how Nixon could have succeeded by ignoring such implications.[10] Essentially, his adjustment was slight, the modification from enlightened compassion with the needs of an abused minority group to politic accommodation with majority attitudes.

On October 10, 1963, Annenberg's flagship paper, the *Philadelphia Inquirer,* praised him for not diluting his understanding of the civil rights movement by catering to the South. Just a few months later, he addressed fellow Republicans at a Lincoln Day dinner in Cincinnati and called upon "responsible civil rights leaders to take over from the extremists" whose actions could destroy what legislation might achieve. Ray Moley responded in complimentary terms and observed that the "white population in the northern states is becoming increasingly resentful about these demonstrations and boycotts."[11]

Later, it would be tempting to trace Nixon's apostasy away from sympathy toward the movement to both his own political needs and his subsequent work for the Goldwater presidential candidacy. Yet, during that eight-year absence from office, however pragmatic he became, his adjustments were, in effect, a sensitive reflection of mass opinion.

Throughout the period from the Kennedy assassination until his own election, Nixon watched three fairly distinct phases of Democratic administrations contend with the mixed blessing JFK had tried to balance.

The first came in the wake of martyrdom. Lyndon Johnson picked up on that theme, made the cause of comprehensive civil rights legislation his own, and emerged with a more sweeping bill than Kennedy had ever imagined. Overriding the usual filibuster and actually achieving a strong majority for the omnibus legislation was made possible with the help of Senate Republican leader Everett Dirksen. That moment in history included a bipartisan surge behind the notion that government was responsible for ensuring political liberties for all people. Nevertheless, Barry Goldwater's presidential campaign emphasized that he would give the American people a "choice not an echo," and questioned the constitutionality of the pending legislation. Goldwater, having made it his mission to reaffirm conservative principles, and without positive expectations of winning, was rejected precisely because he countered mainstream thinking at that moment of reform.[12]

Achieving economic parity was another matter and was made complicated as machinery gradually replaced manpower on southern farms. In common with economic migrants throughout history, the displaced workers accelerated their exodus. First begun at the time of World War I and undertaken en masse during the second war, it continued during the fifties, which led to the anomaly that became the bane of the great metropolitan centers during the postwar era. Earlier migrants had fallen upon an abundance of jobs for the unskilled, but modernization was also changing all that. Black families just off southern farms were hit from both sides, economic dislocation and the culture shock of contending with big-city life. At the very point when legal equality was being achieved, their income relative to that of whites actually dropped.[13]

The struggle moved to a different arena, the pages of scholarly journals, high-brow magazines, academic forums, and conferences of sociologists and political scientists. Some even met in the Johnson White House. "Great portions of the American middle class simply do not understand the nature of the demand for equality," wrote Moynihan. The dialogue was largely academic, then finally submerged under the backlash that was fanned by the wave of ghetto disorders. "How is it possible," Lyndon Johnson often asked, "that all these people could be so ungrateful to me after I had given them so much?"[14]

He was shocked, even hurt, personally rejected. The revolt of the masses had been in the making for some time, the term "backlash" becoming familiar after the Indiana primary in the spring of 1964, the realization of James Baldwin's prophecy about "the fire next time." A spontaneous street outburst in New York City's Harlem over a minor traffic incident during the summer encouraged economist Eliot Janeway to predict that poor whites, feeling a squeeze on the job market, were on the verge of a racial rebellion against black competition. But disbelief persisted. And there was reinforcement. Johnson, appreciative of polls, months before the election read the results of an Oliver Quayle survey that concluded that political backlash was a potential but not a real threat.

Whatever the number of disaffected Democratic voters, they were more than matched by Republicans backing Johnson.[15] The urban disorders, or "Goldwater rallies" in the view of those most apprehensive about the growing backlash, were yet to peak and have their most devastating political effect.

Sociologist David Riesman declared that the women's movement was "possibly the most lasting legacy of the . . . period of protests."[16] He could also have added that, with the possible exception of the drive for racial equality, it was the most reflective of what was happening to society generally. It was also the most contradictory, creating shifting alliances that redrew well-established patterns.

The reform surge that was so identified with Kennedy and Johnson became both Nixon's burden and opportunity. Everything, in fact, seemed paradoxical. An extraordinary number of women, reported the editors of *Harper's* in 1962, were "ardently determined to extend their vocation beyond the bedroom, kitchen and nursery," but feminism as an ideology was quite another matter.[17] Only through domesticity, Freudians had been arguing, could women maintain stability.

Even a cursory examination of demographics and economics, however, showed the power of social change. By the time Nixon became president late in the decade, the feminist movement had influenced all parts of the country.[18]

Those who knew their history should have been prepared for change. Americans, and American women especially, had long since been subjected to liberalizing ideas that were in contrast with Old World notions. Any social history covering the nineteenth century will invariably recount the number of feminist movements. In some of the western states, in particular, women were able to vote well before there was a Nineteenth Amendment. Some even went to college. Oberlin had opened classes to both men and women as early as 1833. When Lord Bryce toured America, he found that the country's women had the world "at their feet. Society seems organized for the purpose of providing enjoyment for them," he wrote, adding that "she holds in her own house a more prominent, if not a more substantially powerful, position than in England or even in France."[19]

They were, of course, the fortunate few whose accident of birth permitted career goals that set them apart from their contemporaries. For the poor, labor was anything but liberating. In Europe, they worked alongside men in the mines; in America, factory girls were common in the textile mills of New England. Historian Jacqueline Jones has described the burdens of female slaves and their eventual movement from cotton fields to wage labor in southern cities and towns. Immigrant women in late nineteenth-century America did whatever they could to help sustain their families, usually as workers in sweatshops. The more elite among them became office workers, mastering the new turn-of-the-century technology, while schoolteaching became the most logical and respectable career. With the upturn of prosperity after World War I, women became far more prominent outside the home, and the era began to hint at what was still forty years in the future. One avant-garde female, Alice Paul, organized a small National Women's Party that advocated an equal rights amendment. Harvard Law School professor Felix Frankfurter was right when he observed that her group represented professionals rather than "millions of wage-earning women."[20] Even their call for an equal rights amendment betrayed their advantages. Most women were more worried about holding on to what they had than in competing in a man's world. The futility of such competition was especially dramatized during the Great Depression, when married women were commonly told by employers that one breadwinner was all any family should expect. The coming of World War II, however, provided jobs for all who would toil.

The change was more lasting than anyone foresaw. Far more women than ever, even more than during the 1920s, found jobs outside the home. More were also going to college, joining the war veterans. Long since divided by class and caste, women were further separated by new assumptions and opportunities about education, family planning, and the income needs that were regarded as essential for middle-class life. They began to do it all, going to college, holding down jobs, and having babies. Society hardly grasped the implications. Nothing useful came from a 1957 Ford Foundation report that called attention to the problems of working mothers despite its warning that they were sufficiently severe for the federal government to consider helping to fund day-care centers.[21]

The national mood seemed to reject realities. "Feminism" remained a somewhat opprobrious term, too often evoking associations with man-hating and lesbianism. Agnes Meyer, whose husband published the *Washington Post* and whose close friend Adlai Stevenson was the two-time Democratic presidential candidate, anticipated a later antifeminist crusader, Phyllis Schlafly. "Women must boldly announce that no job is more exacting, more necessary, or more rewarding than that of housewife and mother," wrote Meyer in 1950, which was also the year the president of a women's college fortified his case for a feminine curriculum by claiming that home economics majors were less likely to end up in divorce courts. Later, in 1968, erroneous reports about burning of brassieres at the Miss America pageant reinforced popular stereotypes of feminists. The flags and draft cards that went up in flames at about the same time were associated with a demonstration at the pageant that included the tossing of feminine underwear, false eyelashes, and wigs into a "Freedom Trash Can."[22] Women were forgetting how girls were expected to behave.

Such were the liabilities that activists worked to counter. At the start of the 1960s, their organizations continued to oppose the concept of an equal rights amendment. President Kennedy tried to satisfy mounting demands for such an amendment by the tactic of creating a Commission on the Status of Women and naming Eleanor Roosevelt as its first head. The antiamendment objective was more or less confirmed when Mrs. Roosevelt's successor, Esther Peterson, complained that a constitutional amendment was a "headache." The continued opposition, aided by organized labor, also managed to keep calls for an amendment out of both parties' platforms during the 1960s. For the average woman, protection was still more precious than equality. That the latter was so elusive was demonstrated once more when wage disparities persisted despite the enactment of the Equal Pay Act in 1963.[23]

The forces that were at work in all western industrial countries, principally the expansion of the labor market, continued to operate in America. More jobs meant more women in the workplace. The need for work was further fueled by inflation and expectations of the good life, and married middle-class women were discovering the "liberating" influences of labor.[24] For the better-educated, work could actually not be work at all, but a career that brought fulfillment. In *The Second Sex*, which came to the United States in early 1953, Simone de Beauvoir showed that women were breaking away from their historic roles.

When, in the next decade, Betty Friedan's book was published, the country was ready for her analysis. Over a third of married women were at work. Moreover, the drive for racial justice was making a more general point about equality. The coincidental arrival of oral contraceptives for women — the Pill — gave both partners a happier way to cope with family planning and offered women more freedom. Friedan's message found a receptive audience, one that welcomed a rationale for their departure from tradition. It also found affirmation in law, a statute that, in the long run, worked to undercut the ground of those who looked for assistance from an equal rights amendment. Hoping to make the Civil Rights Act of 1964 sufficiently unpalatable so that it would be killed in the process, southern opponents tacked on a provision that also banned discrimination based on sex. Undeterred, President Johnson pushed the entire package and, as historian Carl Degler has noted, it became "the most significant single force behind the new feminist movement."[25] It also remained the last contribution by the federal government, even when feminist groups did an about-face in the 1970s and pushed for an amendment.

Clearly, the problem was beyond the mere passage of new laws. Failure to overcome the cultural lag became evident even from the attitudes of the politically "correct." Stokely Carmichael, the youthful civil rights leader who helped to convert the movement into a revolution with his call for "black power," said at a National Conference for a New Politics that "the position of women in our movement should be prone." Radical feminists also found that male co-workers, for all their lip service to the cause of equality, continued with their chauvinistic ways. "Men sought them out, recruited them, took them seriously, honored their intelligence," Todd Gitlin has written about the Students for a Democratic Society, "— then subtly demoted them to girlfriends, wives, note-takers, coffeemakers."[26] Such experiences helped to convince Friedan to use her royalties to start the National Organization for Women. The birth of NOW in 1966 marked the beginning of a newly energized feminist movement.

Those who reacted most sharply to male dominance and joined NOW were, for the most part, young and well-educated women — and overwhelmingly middle-class. Discouraged by repeated instances of what came to be called sexism, they demanded more than protection. Convinced of the feebleness of existing legislation, they embraced the issue of the right of women to a free choice over their reproductive systems and also placed themselves on record in support of an equal rights amendment.[27]

NOW quickly became synonymous with the mainstream of the 1960s social revolution. Joined by even more vocal feminists during the next few years, they assailed virtually every traditional assumption about family life and the role of women in American society. Some women led the way by establishing day-care centers, publishing feminist magazines, and engaging in scholarly and often vitriolic debates in which they portrayed themselves as members of an abused minority. Tracts that appeared in the late 1960s and well into the next decade left untouched no area of suspected male domination, including the marriage bed. The resemblances to the civil rights movement left little doubt that one was a prerequisite for the success of the other.

There was, of course, an additional similarity. While it became common to attack civil rights activists as radical agitators and even Communists, women on the march were easily denigrated as libbers and lesbians. Much harder for some traditionalists to accept was their anger and ability to articulate grievances. They raised the decibels of the feminist cause far above what the country had ever heard. The political ramifications were striking.

That was hardly less true of the antiwar movement. One sympathetic description of the new radicals explained that "they felt American society supported racism, oppressive institutions, capital punishment, and wars against popular movements in underdeveloped countries."[28] When Dr.

King separated himself from the administration's war policy, he cited the inevitable sacrifice of domestic priorities. Radical women, together with dissenting students, interpreted the escalating commitment to Vietnam as the ultimate immorality of a society that had used bourgeois ideas of sex as a tool for subjugation. Even Lyndon Johnson, for all his fulminating about the "nervous Nellies" who opposed his military policies, was most of all concerned about the creation of a Great Society that would, in effect, complete the unfinished goals of the New Deal. All that, however, was quickly receding, buried under the new reality that began to consume America by the middle and later sixties. Whatever positions may have been taken in the past, nothing defined the political alignments as sharply as the war.

Nixon's position on Vietnam was never very mysterious. He avoided the extremes of total victory or precipitous abandonment. He aimed at a level of military security that could provide for a credible settlement, a position that was totally consistent with his established views of United States global responsibility. Inevitably, that placed him among those with faith in military solutions.

He had done so in the case of Korea, emphatically siding with the MacArthur view over Truman's "police action" concept. He was the boldest of the Eisenhower crew in going public with the possibility of troop support for the French before the fall of Dienbienphu. He came to regret the one instance when he went along with halting the military, Suez, and then left no doubt that he thought the canal should have been taken. During the offshore islands crisis, the administration kept under wraps its offer to take over for Chiang Kai-shek and defend Quemoy and Matsu even at the risk of nuclear attack. When he served as an unofficial spokesman for Dulles, there was nothing surprising about hearing that Nixon was ready for a military solution. His 1960 debate with Kennedy over Cuba trapped him in a contradiction precisely because he was a leading proponent of the Eisenhower administration's plans for toppling Fidel Castro. Right after the Bay of Pigs blew up in the face of President Kennedy, Nixon kept pressing for a military solution. The administration, advised the former vice president, should "find a proper legal cover" for going into Cuba and getting the job done. Openly, however, he kept his adversarial role by disputing Kennedy's criticism of the press for failing to provide better cover for the preinvasion operations in the Caribbean area. On the contrary, Nixon said, "the whole concept of a return to security in peacetime demonstrates a profound misunderstanding of the role of a free press. . . . The plea for security," he added with an observation made ironic by his own subsequent actions, "could well become a cloak for errors, misjudgments and other failings of government."[29]

In many ways, the Vietnamese problem was made to order. His analysis of what was needed differed little from what he had been saying and thinking all along. It also resembled his postpresidential talk about managing conflict to maintain "real peace."

Neither Nixon nor his two Democratic predecessors disagreed about the importance of quarantining South Vietnam from the military incursions of its Communist neighbors. If that flirted with expanding the war, it was, as he argued in a 1965 article, a choice between a "policy involving some risk and another policy involving an even greater risk." He had seen firsthand the importance of containment in Europe. The experiences of the 1950s, including his own up-front view during his trip to the Far East, confirmed that what was vital to stop the Soviet Union also applied to the People's Republic of China in Asia. In the early spring of 1964, Nixon toured the region, stopping in for a visit with Ambassador Henry Cabot Lodge in Saigon. That trip, in which Nixon, according to Ralph Blumenthal of the *New York Times*, "met secretly with the Vietcong and ransomed five American prisoners of war for bars of gold" (all of which Nixon flatly denies as "apocryphal"), enabled him to update his knowledge about the situation. As he further stated in his 1965 article, "The battle for Vietnam is the battle for Asia. If the United States gives up on Vietnam, Asia will give up on the United States and the Pacific will become a Red Sea."[30]

Nixon continued searching for firsthand information. He went overseas and met with foreign leaders, journeys undertaken despite repeated CIA rejections of his requests for pretrip briefings.[31] He traveled to Japan, Taiwan, Vietnam, and Australia on a comprehensive three-week tour in 1965 that further enhanced his authority as the chief Republican spokesman on Asian matters.

When he returned, he lost no time reminding the Johnson administration that he was ready to denounce any wavering in the American commitment. With clear implications for the upcoming congressional elections and the presidential voting to follow, he warned that he and his party would pounce on any effort by the administration to leave Vietnam with a coalition or "neutralist" government. He avoided calling for a showdown with Communist China, but said, in effect, that the military restraints of the Korean War must not be repeated. This time there must be no "Yalu River complex" to keep the United States from being able to pursue the source of aggression. Nor should even friendly nations be permitted to carry supplies to North Vietnam, something that could be enforced by using American sea power to lay down a total embargo of the enemy coast.[32]

The major assumption that reinforced all this, of course, was that, as in Europe, Vietnam was not the scene of a civil war but a power test between Communist and noncommunist rivals. Those who considered that the lack of social reforms was the source of the trouble were fooling themselves. "I recall the conversations I had with several Vietnamese village officials when I was there this Spring," Nixon wrote Joseph Alsop in 1964. "I would ask each one of them individually what his village needed most. None of them came back with the expected answers, e.g., — a new school, more rice, more political freedom, less persecution of the Buddhists, a new well. In every instance, the answer was — military security. And it is small wonder that this was the case in view of the daily reports of murder, rape, maiming and terror which sweep the country-side."[33] Strikingly absent were considerations of Indochinese culture and politics, or, for that matter, just how much of an American military commitment would be needed — or would be possible to wage a "preventive war" twelve thousand miles away.

All of this was very familiar to those who heard the arguments of Secretary of State Dean Rusk. After Nixon presented his views at a luncheon attended by seventy-five leading businessmen in the New York area in 1965, Don Kendall wrote to President Johnson that "they had never heard a Republican support so strongly the policies of a Democratic Administration."[34] Kendall was accurate, but suggestions of "loyal opposition" stretched the point beyond any understanding of what was happening.

The luncheon Kendall had arranged came shortly after the start of Operation ROLLING THUNDER, the sustained bombing of North Vietnam that followed the attack on a military base at Pleiku. In the days before that significant escalation, Nixon could hardly have been called Johnson's advocate. He was, if anything, considerably more of a "hawk," as the term was coming to be used. He warned about losing the war, about forfeiting military initiatives by neglecting the interdiction of Communist supply lines or by even contemplating premature negotiations to stop the fighting. Any attempt to bargain or settle for a neutral South Vietnam, he warned, would be "surrendering on the installment plan."[35]

Only after the bombing was announced did he become Johnson's enthusiastic supporter. Even then he remained skeptical. The bombings themselves, he pointed out to Barry Goldwater, were consistent with the positions both had taken. "My concern now," Nixon added, "is that there may not be an adequate follow-through. I think we must continue to urge that the United States make a command decision to use whatever air and sea power is necessary to cut off the flow of all arms and men from North Vietnam into South Vietnam." A day later, he met the president and Lady Bird in their White House bedroom and pressed for further action. Nor could he have been any plainer than he was with former army secretary Robert T. Stevens later that summer of 1965, just after the administration had boosted U.S. fighting strength by 50,000 troops, which, in addition to being what historian George Herring has called "the closest thing to a formal declaration of war in Vietnam," brought American forces over the 100,000 level. "For the United States to negotiate a peace agreement now which would in any way reward the Communists for their aggression would not only lead to the loss of Asia but would greatly increase the risk of World War III," he wrote to Stevens. The war had to be fought to discourage Soviet expansionist designs, sustain prowestern regimes throughout the region, and contain the Chinese Communists. Richard Nixon, in other words, whether out campaigning in behalf of Goldwater or expressing himself as a private citizen, remained the party's most consistent spokesman about how to handle Southeast Asia — and that left little doubt about the importance of the Chinese danger. China, Nixon declared, was "an unrepentant aggressor nation."[36]

Few Americans doubted the potential expansionism of the Communist regime in Peking. There was considerable conviction that once industrialized and with nuclear capability, the People's Republic posed a greater threat than the Soviet Union itself. Neither the Kennedy nor Johnson administration, bolstered by Secretary of State Rusk, was prepared to make any accommodation with Peking, whether normalization of relations, acceptance of a Taipei-Peking "two-China" policy, or admission to the United Nations. According to foreign policy adviser Walt Rostow, Kennedy believed that Chinese explosion of a nuclear weapon would be "the biggest event of the 1960s." Even the house dove, Chester Bowles, warned that the Peking regime was "far more dangerous" than the alarmist China Lobbyists had contended. With an eye on the treaty to control atomic tests, Kennedy and his closest advisers advanced the notion of inviting the Soviet Union to join with the United States in delivering a preemptive strike against Chinese nuclear installations. Nothing came of that idea, however, even after it was kept alive during the Johnson administration. In October 1964, the Chinese detonated their first atomic device.[37]

Once such power had become a reality, Nixon worried about letting the war go on indefinitely. The South Vietnamese, already war-weary, might well abandon the field, while the Chinese remained unchallenged and increased their nuclear strength. Sharing the anxieties about that threat to the Far East which were held by even such new critics of American actions in Vietnam as Senator J. William Fulbright, Nixon wrote publicly that the situation risked provoking World War III.[38] How to respond was another matter.

His thinking clearly foreshadowed what became known during his own presidency as "Vietnamization." Only days before Goldwater's defeat, Nixon deplored sending American boys to "fight and die in the jungles of Vietnam or anyplace else, unless there is a policy to win — win for America and win for the Southeast Asians." Any blueprint for victory, of course, had to be military. In March of 1966, he informed General Albert Wedemeyer that he agreed with his "recommendation that we should generate military forces from the area of Southeast Asia to fight in South Vietnam and other trouble spots where the communists embark on aggression." Then Nixon added: "It seems that every time the United States becomes involved in this kind of situation we tend to 'Americanize' the whole operation. I shall attempt to develop these proposals in some of my future speeches and articles." A Gallup survey taken eighteen months after Nixon's letter to Wedemeyer showed that three-quarters of those canvassed favored giving the South Vietnamese more responsibility for fighting the war.[39]

Such close correlation between Nixon's views and public opinion was fairly routine. An obvious point is that his nonincumbency gave him an important advantage over the Democratic administrations that had been upgrading the war. Unlike either Kennedy or Johnson, he was free to state the objectives and describe the process without having to account to either the Congress or the electorate. While each of the two Democrats finessed his military response, Kennedy using the subterfuges of a paramilitary war supported by American "advisers" and Johnson the political expediency of measured gradualism, Nixon had the luxury of being forthright. Recent analysts have denied the political necessity for the incremental approach. The American people, they have argued, were prepared to follow the White House lead. There was little appetite for a major war in Asia but, at the same time, the public rejected the thought that the United States would end up no better than had the French.[40] From the vantage point of those in actual power, however, there was little desire to test that proposition.

Moreover, both Kennedy and Johnson faced significant internal opposition. Kennedy's advisers wanted to press Diem to achieve stability through reforms. Johnson, who took over shortly after the chaos that followed Diem's assassination, viewed the war as a threat to his domestic ambitions. When ROLLING THUNDER seemed unlikely to force the Vietcong and the National Liberation Front to beg for peace, Johnson began to encounter the highly publicized opposition from Senator Fulbright and, gradually, the bulk of his own party's majority on the Senate Foreign Relations Committee. As victory began to seem more elusive and some Republicans joined the dissenters, Nixon began to despair over the break in ranks that could only undermine the cause in Southeast Asia.[41]

Those who insist that the war could have been "won" uphold the Nixon view. They blamed the incremental escalation for restricting the full use of American military power. A dedicated desire to see it through to victory would have achieved total mobilization by asking for a declaration of war, which would have defused much of the undermining that took

place on Capitol Hill and brought full support from the American people.[42] The rest of the story might then have been very different, especially
the character of the antiwar movement.

Nixon's zest for a fight — evident since the start of his career — was
reasserted when he joined the attack on Eugene Genovese. Genovese, a
historian at Rutgers University, had announced that "I do not fear or
reject the impending Vietcong victory in Vietnam. I welcome it." As part
of the faculty of a state institution, Genovese had made himself especially
vulnerable. The chance to denounce him in the name of patriotism and
to demand his removal was then exploited by State Senator Wayne Dumont, who was a heavy underdog against a popular governor, Richard
Hughes.

The professor's controversial statement came at a campus demonstration on April 23, 1965, the spring of the teach-ins, local antiwar
forums that became popular after the bombing began. At college
after college, from the University of Michigan to a giant outpouring at
Berkeley, Johnson's policies were denounced by young people and
their instructors who engaged in mutual reinforcements of their own
righteousness in condemning the "immoral" war. Twenty thousand
protesters, most of them led by the Students for a Democratic Society
(SDS), marched on the Washington Monument in the first mass antiwar
outpouring.[43] College and university students, many veterans of the civil
rights wars and, as at Berkeley, battles over campus reforms, began years
of protest over Vietnam.

Relatively speaking, few were aroused, on or off the campuses. Most
Americans were still uninterested or, perhaps more accurately, detached.
Even among the better-informed, whatever the United States was doing
in Southeast Asia was routinely accepted as part of the effort to contain
communism, especially the Red Chinese variety. Bombing North Vietnam was a logical measure to force the enemy's realization that he had
no choice but to abandon his ambitions. Departures from that conventional wisdom were not very easily tolerated. So that when, during that
fall's gubernatorial campaign, the desperate Dumont looked for political
paydirt by capitalizing on the several-months-old remarks, Genovese
achieved sudden notoriety.

Also significant was the reluctance of other prominent Republicans to
include references to the Genovese incident when they spoke in behalf
of Dumont's election, and there was no shortage of party celebrities who
came into the state. Governors John Chafee of Rhode Island, William
Scranton of Pennsylvania, and George Romney of Michigan all visited
to tell New Jersey voters that they should be governed by a Republican.
General Eisenhower also took up the Dumont cause. But on Genovese,
they remained silent.[44]

It must have been the sensitivity of the issue, not the climate of opinion, that persuaded them to avoid joining Dumont's call. By October 1965, the antiwar movement had advanced to a higher plateau. The earlier teach-ins and campus demonstrations seemed relatively benign compared with flag desecrations and draft card burnings. The rebels of the New Left were becoming more brazen, now commanding the media as never before. What had been considered disruptions by the undisciplined and "pampered" was now feared as a threat to national security. Warning that resistance to conscription constituted an act of "unlawful conspiracy," Senator John Stennis of Mississippi urged that the movement be pulled up "by the roots" and ground "to bits." Others saw the hand of Moscow taking over the crowd from more moderate elements. The battle of the campuses, which ultimately undid numerous academic administrators and boosted the careers of others (such as Ronald Reagan, who, early in his California governorship, suggested that it might take a "bloodbath" to stop the more violent disorders), did much to polarize American attitudes.[45]

Unlike the other luminaries who went to bat for Dumont, Nixon was serious about becoming the party's dominant voice on Vietnam. In mid-October, he had called for the use of American sea power to impose a total embargo of North Vietnamese ports. Nevertheless, at the moment, he was eager to subdue antielitist passions by reaching out to intellectuals and the political center. But when he faced an audience of legionnaires at Morristown on October 25 at a preelection appearance, the temptation was just too great. He followed his instincts and pepped up the veterans with a flag-waving support of Dumont's demand. He delighted the local guardians of American liberties by saying that he did not care how Genovese felt about segregation or integration, or whether he was "for free love or celibacy, for Communism or anarchy, or anything else — in peacetime." But this was different, claimed Nixon, "The United States is at war. Genovese is employed by a state university, and he used the state college as a forum to, in effect, give aid and comfort to the enemy. World War II was a big war, and this is a little war. If anyone had welcomed a Nazi victory during World War II there would have been no question about what to do."[46]

Suddenly, it seemed, there were evocations of early California days. "Here is the old Nixon in action," said the disapproving *New York Times*, "posing the spurious choice between freedom of speech for Genovese and 'American boys defending freedom of speech' in Vietnam." Governor Hughes stood behind the professor, as did Rutgers's president, Mason Gross, on the grounds of academic freedom and derided Nixon as having been "recruited from the bottom of the list" to back Dumont's call. Civil libertarians and academics naturally had a nice target. The "real" Nixon was back in form, engaging in the rhetorical hyperbole that had helped to make him a caricature among liberals, ignoring the First Amendment and, in the process, Genovese's rights as a citizen. Three days after his Morristown appearance, Nixon's letter to the *New York Times* reasserted his position by adding that "unfortunately, there are occasions — particularly wartime — when the individual's rights and the nation's security come in conflict." That the country was not legally at war seemed beside the point.[47]

Nixon understood all that. He felt the need to follow through with a statement to clarify his position. Copies went to various friends and supporters, including General Eisenhower. When he spoke at the University of Rochester's commencement in 1966 (ironically, where Genovese later chaired the history department), he chose his language more carefully. His central rationale, as he has explained many times since then, was that Genovese's responsibility was greater because he was employed by a state school. He was using that forum, Nixon told his Rochester audience, "to welcome victory for the enemy in a war in which the United States is engaged." That remark "crosses the line between liberty and license. If we are to defend academic freedom from encroachment we must also defend it from its own excesses." In a similar way, he had argued in 1962 against hiring teachers who resisted California's loyalty oath. As he explained to Julie several years later, he thought that the "fundamental issue" in the Genovese case was that he did not think "that any individual who received his compensation from the state should advocate victory over the United States in a war in which our men are fighting."[48]

Nixon ultimately rested on that contention. The proposition that employment by a public university necessitated one's conformity to any prescribed conclusion, in whatever discipline, is of course dubious. That the United States had not declared war further undermined his case in the eyes of many, although there were those who regarded that point as moot in view of the 1964 Gulf of Tonkin Resolution, which gave the president authority to order military action in Vietnam, and the actual involvement of American soldiers in battle. Nevertheless, the suppression of a point of view in a democracy even in cases of declared war is questionable, and the continuation of freedom of speech under such conditions would hardly be unprecedented. Whatever the arguments among lawyers and civil libertarians, Genovese himself had recognized that there was a distinction between advocating a military or a political victory by later adding the clarification that he meant the latter.[49]

Nixon sought the high ground by alluding to the actions of two Democratic presidents, Woodrow Wilson and Franklin D. Roosevelt. In each case, he claimed, those two wartime leaders had not hesitated to subordinate the "preservation of freedom for all people" to the greater cause of defeating the enemy. He equated the U.S. involvement in Vietnam as it existed in 1965 with the two major declared wars of the twentieth century. He thereby implicitly accepted the assaults on civil liberties that were unleashed by congressional passage of the Espionage Act of 1917 and the Sedition Act of 1918 and post–World War I Supreme Court decisions, which included the jailing of Eugene V. Debs for speaking out against the war.[50]

Supported by Oliver Wendell Holmes's famous "clear and present danger" dictum, the Court in 1919 unanimously upheld the jailing of two antidraft propagandists. Congress had obligingly given Wilson an Espionage Act that, among other specified crimes against national security, outlawed interference with conscription. In the instance of an opponent of dispatching American troops to postrevolutionary Russia, however, Holmes joined Justice Louis Brandeis in dissent with the argument that

> to allow opposition by speech seems to indicate that you think the speech impotent. . . . But when men have realized that time has upset many fighting faiths, they may come to believe even more than they believe the very foundations of their own conduct that the ultimate good desired is better reached by free trade in ideas — that the best test of truth is the power of the thought to get itself accepted in the competition of the market, and that truth is the only ground upon which their wishes can be safely carried out. That at any rate is the theory of our Constitution. It is an experiment, as all life is an experiment.[51]

What Nixon's rationale overlooked was that Wilson's own national security measures, which included the suppression and decimation of the IWW, got out of hand as the stricken president lay impotent in the White House while "patriotic" zealots went on a rampage. Holmes's "clear and present danger" criterion was loosely interpreted by officials at various levels of government to provide license for the repression of unpopular ideas. Nor did the first Red scare that was thereby unleashed, with its reckless record of hysteria and truncation of personal freedoms cherished by traditional conservatives, offer encouragement to cite that period.[52]

Reliance on FDR and World War II was also poor justification for having to make such a "cruel choice." If Nixon was referring to the Smith Act of 1940, he was citing the abridgment of the right to "teach" about the need to overthrow the U.S. government, an excess that had already been effectively dismissed by Supreme Court decisions.[53] Neither the Alien Enemies Act nor the lamentable incarceration of 120,000 Japanese Americans, mostly American citizens, furnishes additional comfort for believing that Nixon later became a civil libertarian. He had not gone very far from his Whittier High School essay on "Our Privileges Under the Constitution" and its concern with the primacy of the state and security over the interests of the individual.[54]

Whatever Genovese's point, Nixon's argument was shaky. One might question the professor's fitness to announce his judgment at a forum attended by students about a matter far removed from his area of academic competence. Given the circumstances, however, it was still very different from subjecting student captives in his classroom to propaganda instead of a professional opinion. The real question was whether, as Nixon contended, Genovese and others surrendered their rights as citizens by participating in such teach-ins and making remarks that were extravagant, or, as in his case, considered by many as heretical or even treasonous because they happened to be on the state payroll. Government employees on every level could conceivably be lumped into that category. In 1965, an estimated one out of every seven Americans was in that group, so that would have constituted a considerable underclass of the disenfranchised.

At the very least, the matter was impolitic for Nixon. It neither helped Dumont's cause nor Nixon's effort to be accepted by the moderate center. New Jersey's voters gave no evidence that it made much difference in the election, which was won by Governor Hughes by a record plurality of 354,000. Nor did Nixon need to add to his anticommunist credentials. The general wisdom was that his entry into the dispute was unfortunate.

The best explanation is that he had no ulterior motive. He spoke his mind and probably got into more trouble than it was worth. Other than emphasize how he felt about the war, the Genovese incident once again revealed his fixation with the entire issue of communism.

It also underscored the character of Nixon's lifelong involvement with that threat to the American way of life. In attacking Genovese, he was not confronting the prototypical young sixties radical whose activism stemmed from a liberal heritage and associations with the civil rights movement. Genovese was more of a link between the radicalism of the thirties and the emerging New Left.

He was a product of the old rather than the new, closer to the bright intellectuals who were tolerated by the New Deal. He came out of radical, first-generation, mostly Italian and Jewish working-class leftists in Brooklyn. It was, in fact, as a student at Brooklyn College that Genovese helped to recruit for a front group, American Youth for Democracy. He then broke with the party because of a falling-out over their tactics, and, in line with the best Communist tradition, was denounced as a reactionary bigot.[55] As a historian, he remained committed to Marxian analyses and became known as a hardheaded, independent thinker. No more than Nixon could he have remained aloof from Vietnam.

He was, however, anathema to Nixon because his leftist orientation seemed endemic to such eastern intellectuals. Rutgers was not Harvard, but it was still a significant university and its affiliation with the state made such heresies that much more unforgivable. If Genovese was no Alger Hiss, he was, in Nixon's view, uncomfortably close to the same alien culture that bore from within and corrupted American principles.

There was but a short distance from Genovese to the Hill case. If, by taking on the professor, Nixon's arguments offended civil libertarians, the matter involving the family of James Hill and *Life* magazine revealed him in another dimension, one that enhanced his standing as a lawyer in at least three ways. It demonstrated once and for all that he was more than just window dressing for his firm, someone whose value merely depended on his ability to attract valuable corporate clients to Mudge, Rose. He showed that with the right opportunity, he could go into court and dispel any doubts about his legal brilliance, enabling him to shine just as he had done nearly twenty years earlier as a member of HUAC. He could also balance the freedoms specified in the First Amendment with state-protected interests in privacy.

For Nixon, however, the opportunity went beyond that. He could, at last, also take on the press in a direct, legal way, not merely as the cantankerous, frustrated politician of the "last press conference."

His concern about the need for protection from an irresponsible press was hardly isolated. Nor was it confined to ideological kinship. Indeed, the Supreme Court's newest member, a liberal, Associate Justice Abe Fortas, who had been nominated by President Johnson in 1965, shared Nixon's apprehensions. As Fortas's biographer has made explicit, the justice was contemptuous of the presence among the working press of so many whom he considered "mongers," "dirty," and "crooked." "It's no different from the McCarthy thing," he once said. "You destroy people by making these accusations. You destroy their self-esteem. The fracas can be brutal."[56]

Fortas, the liberal, who was later forced off the Court, became Nixon's ally in the legal battle that was first fought by Len Garment. Garment, through his senior partner, Randolph H. Guthrie, Jr., received the case in behalf of Hill, a former Harvard classmate of Guthrie's. Hill, along with his wife and three children, had been held hostage by escaped convicts in their home outside Philadelphia. The nineteen-hour nightmare was one of several such incidents that writer Joseph Hayes turned into a composite suspense story for his novel *The Desperate Hours,* which later became a motion picture as well as a play. The Hills, with considerable supporting evidence, argued that Hayes's work was fiction and that its description of the sordidness and brutality endured by the hostage family bore no relationship to their own experience. Nevertheless, *Life* helped to promote the stage version by running a review complete with photographs that rather explicitly established the Hills as the actual victims. The author himself had made no such claim. Encouraged by Guthrie, the Hills brought a "right of privacy" suit against Time Inc. in the state of New York. Garment tried the case and won a settlement that was first set aside as excessive, and Time Inc., the parent company of *Life,* took the case to the U.S. Supreme Court.

Coming so soon after the Genovese affair made it an even more attractive undertaking for Nixon. Garment watched his colleague's "almost obsessive" preparations with awe. Yellow pads piled up with every conceivable argument and possible line of strategy. Nothing was left to chance. "His behavior was not only a matter of professional pride," Garment has written, "but a sign of his determination not to let his recent defeats drive him from the political arena."[57]

That was in early 1966; Garment had known Nixon for less than three years; a far longer relationship still lay ahead. That episode was perhaps among Garment's more remarkable glimpses of Nixon. When he went before the Supreme Court on April 27, with Chief Justice Warren presiding, Nixon's presentation was masterful. He demonstrated the magazine's inattention to the accuracy of its story, or to the implications for the Hill family and their lives. As Nixon wrote shortly afterward in a memorandum, "LIFE just didn't care enough about the Hills. In other words, LIFE was not trying to hurt the Hills; it was trying to use the Hills to help itself." *Life* was trying to justify an invasion of the right of privacy by citing First Amendment protections, which, Nixon then added, "should be treated like the right to reputation in libel cases as being one of those areas where the state has the power, under the Ninth and Tenth Amendments, to give redress to private citizens where they are injured by other private citizens." As Garment watched his colleague before the court, he concluded that "he sounded like a polished professional of the bar — his footing confident, his language lawyer-like, his organization of material sure and clear," a view that was widely shared. John MacKenzie of the *Washington Post* called Nixon's effort "one of the better oral arguments of the year."[58]

What happened the next morning astonished Garment even more. Both men, tired after a momentous day in Washington, returned to LaGuardia Airport later that night. As Garment recalls, "I went home, drank a couple of vodkas, and fell into an exhausted sleep." When he reached his office at ten the next morning, he found on his desk a 2,500-word memorandum that had been dictated by Nixon overnight. It was, as Garment writes, "an act of intellectual self-criticism that beggars description," a legal analysis of the arguments before the court and the constitutional implications that Garment himself "could not have produced that weary night with a gun at my head."[59]

It was not, however, enough to win the case. The immediate vote was 6–3 to uphold the Hills. But Fortas, who had been assigned to the case by Warren, turned out a sixteen-page memorandum that was so vehemently opposed to the minority that it helped inflame an already personally hostile Associate Justice Hugo Black, who forced a delay until the fall in order to reargue the case. That also gave him the summer to turn out a sharp rebuttal. That blockbuster thoroughly undercut Fortas. Black's internal memorandum and behind-the-scenes lobbying won out. In the end, only Warren and Justices John Marshall Harlan and Tom Clark stood with Fortas, making for a 5–4 vote favoring Time Inc. As Garment points out, Nixon's position was backed until the end by two political enemies, Warren and Fortas. The final decision, written by Associate Justice William Brennan, held that for the family to collect they would have to prove that the article was published with "knowledge that it was false, or with reckless disregard for whether it was true or false." With that, it went back to the New York courts. The Hills were able to get a generous out-of-court settlement from *Life*, which was apparently small compensation. Two psychiatrists had testified that the publicity had damaged Mrs. Hill emotionally. She committed suicide in August 1971.[60]

Nixon's loss, however, was short-term. He ultimately had the satisfaction of seeing the court later acknowledge, in the case of *Gertz v. Robert Welch, Inc.* (1974), the extension of a special latitude of protection for private persons from intrusion by the press. The opinion in *Gertz* was written by Associate Justice Lewis F. Powell. The overriding issue, of course, was the perceived overstepping by the press of the rights to privacy by expansive interpretations of the First Amendment, which had helped to create a climate that many believed contributed significantly to the nation's trend toward greater conservatism.

Whether the Hill case did much to counter the bad taste left among many people by Nixon's attack on Genovese is doubtful. More important, Genovese was inspiring a new generation of anti-Americanists. From comfortable middle-class backgrounds, they were far removed from the sons and daughters of workers and farmers who did not go to college, who tried to survive for themselves and their families by taking whatever work was available, and who existed within the society without trying to tear it down. Such ordinary Americans, children of the forgotten man, had little affluence to scorn. But the "new radicals," as two authors of a sympathetic book wrote, were likely to reject the values of their middle-class parents, who, once poor, now desired "to own, to accumulate, to achieve the status and prestige which go with material wealth. . . . They felt American society supported racism, oppressive institutions, capital punishment, and wars against popular movements in underdeveloped countries." Middle-class radicals, unlike blue-collar workers, "demanded purity at home first, and when it was not forthcoming, quickly became convinced that it was impossible, that there was something rotten at the core of American society."[61]

As a group they have been contemptuously called the "Red-diaper babies." Overwhelmingly from left-leaning families, many with radical backgrounds, they were eager to carry out the progressive ideals of their fathers. Their movement was, as Norman Podhoretz later wrote, "turning out to be a movement by the children of McCarthy's victims to avenge their parents in the flesh of the country which had produced him." They were the children of a "new class" of intellectuals, sons and daughters of the postwar bourgeoisie engaging in what Daniel Patrick Moynihan called "a form of upper class aggression." One study by SDS leader Richard Flacks noted that they tended to come from the "educated humanist" type of families. Their humanism was also of the secular type, unless they were Quakers or Unitarians or other denominations that stressed social concerns, and the heavy Jewish representation of student radicals also reflected cultural commitments to civil liberties. The movement seemed to have hit American society almost overnight. In 1959, university administrator Clark Kerr wrote that "employers will love this generation, they are not going to press many grievances. . . . They are going to be easy to handle." Four years later, Kerr lectured at Harvard about the restlessness of undergraduates.[62]

What Kerr also said was at the nub of criticism by Nixon and others. Many college faculty members, wrote editor Max Ways in a special issue of *Fortune,* had "drawn up an indictment of U.S. society out of random observations organized around attitudes of social criteria picked up in the flea market of ideas — mostly odds and ends of Savonarola, Voltaire, Thoreau, Marx, Zola, William Jennings Bryan, and C. Wright Mills." The creation of powerful, independent faculty bodies during the postwar years, especially at the most prestigious research-oriented institutions, was indicted not only by the students at schools like Berkeley, Wisconsin, and Columbia, but also by conservatives who smelled corruption of the young by leftist theorists.[63]

A culture apart from his, the new radicals were long familiar to Nixon. He had come of age on the outside looking in. They, like Hiss and Dean Acheson, were part of the same breed that bloated the Washington bureaucracy. The young Nixon's connections were not even adequate to place him with J. Edgar Hoover's FBI. When he did work for government, with the OPA during the war, the experience confirmed his perceptions that the federal government was riddled with paper-pushers who were full of theories but had little idea of the real world. They, and those like them, were the soft underbelly of American society, the ones most capable of selling out the religious, hardworking masses. The world that he saw, and the world that he thought he saw, was all too ready to rationalize Marxist goals.

Nixon's confrontation with the new rebellion was the inevitable clash of old foes. He saw communism as both an alien thrust and an ideological horror. It belonged to — and was tolerated by — a culture that he detested. To suggest that crude demagoguery motivated his pursuit of the issue misrepresents his conviction that such dangers were manipulating the naive components of the New Left as they had the innocent planners of the New Deal. The same elements that tried to hide the truth in the forties, he felt, were still at work in the sixties. After a spree of antidraft demonstrations in Oakland, California, for example, he turned to Bill Knowland because he could not get an "objective . . . picture of the situation from the columns of the New York Times" to find out "what elements" were responsible. He had little doubt that while "criticism of the war is completely justified and proper," such divisions played into the hands of the enemy and rewarded aggression. When the so-called battle of Morningside Heights disrupted the Columbia campus, he called upon university officials to "rid the campus now of revolutionaries."[64]

What made his outlook especially trenchant was its compatibility with public opinion. Every available survey shows the unpopularity of the demonstrators, even among those who were themselves opposed to the war. By the end of 1967, Lou Harris found that by a ratio of 68 percent to 22 percent, the public considered their activities "acts of disloyalty against the boys fighting in Vietnam." There was even less disagreement that the protesters were encouraging the Communists to fight harder. Harris and others found, then and later, that Americans who had serious misgivings about the war were also upset about the character of the dissent. That sentiment later showed up in the New Hampshire primary of 1968, where much of Eugene McCarthy's support came from that state's hawkish population. Those unhappy with Johnson for not using the military more effectively outnumbered the doves by nearly three to two, something that the administration realized before the voting. After three days in Manchester, journalist Robert G. Spivack reported back that there was "virtually no sentiment for easing up" in Vietnam but plenty for "increasing pressure on Communists." Acting on such information, a Johnson aide suggested to White House political adviser Marvin Watson that "our organization in New Hampshire could ask the Democratic voters in this state to choose sides — the President or the peaceniks." It is, in fact, ironic that Robert Kennedy's victory in that year's Indiana primary was achieved with the help of those who were confident he would be tougher against the Vietnamese Communists and American blacks. Most fascinating, as reported by a team of political scientists, was that only 3 percent of Americans were both against the war *and* sympathetic with the protesters. Nor was there evidence that the electorate had become more dovish by 1968; the decline, rather, was in confidence in the administration's performance. Not surprisingly, then, there was overwhelming popular support for the police against the demonstrators during the riots outside the Democratic convention at Chicago in 1968, and strong sympathy when construction workers attacked young protesters in Wall Street two years later. Even those sympathetic with the goals of the demonstrators, concluded the political scientists, were more fearful of the breakdown of authority and discipline.[65]

It was also a rebellion that spurred a counterreaction from another quarter, elements of the old left, former socialists and Communists of various varieties, veterans of depression-era radicalism who came to find the Democratic party imperfect but congenial. Now, after the Berlin-Moscow pact of 1939, the path that had already been taken by Burnham and Chambers, then by Sidney Hook, Irving Kristol, and Lionel Trilling, was being followed by a later generation of intellectuals who were emerging as neoconservatives. Podhoretz, the ex-socialist and editor of the American Jewish Committee's influential journal of opinion, *Commentary*, thought back to the new direction his magazine began to take. "The neoconservative movement was born in reaction to the New Left," he explained about a movement that all too often included tones of anti-Semitism and "knee-jerk opposition to defense spending that was inconsistent with the need to aid Israel."[66]

As with the earlier apostates, that brought them into league with Richard Nixon, an anticommunist whose passion had little to do with any commitment to the ideals of Locke, Milton, Mill, or similar figures of the Enlightenment. His hatred for Marxism was only weakly related to doubts about the ability of the masses to rule themselves. He did not share Robert La Follette's faith that the best cure for the ills of democracy is more democracy. Neither did he see communism as, in William Rusher's words, "that misbegotten child of the Enlightenment."[67]

The basis for his objections was less the economic implications than the notion of communism as inherently wedded to bureaucracy, a bureaucracy that would inevitably — especially because of Marxist dogma — be controlled by a ruling elite. That elite was the establishment, whether in the Soviet Union or elsewhere. Thus it was, in Nixon's makeup, a conservative populism that reinforced his anticommunism. Implicit in his thinking was a Wilsonian notion of self-determination, but with an important proviso: that governance had to be controlled by strong, enlightened leadership.

16

Men on Horseback

NIXON WAS barely more comfortable with the New Right than the New Left. Among Republicans, he was a man in the middle, hearing from Tom Kuchel about the dangers of extremism and the need for preserving the party's progressivism, and from oil tycoon H. L. Hunt about the virtues of being a loyal rightist. Having been crippled by his California loss and further damaged among ultraconservatives by his repudiation of the Birchites, he could only share with relative passivity the shock of other traditionalists as they watched the takeover by the Goldwater legions. There was a difference between being a responsible, dedicated anticommunist like himself and an extremist. That had been Joe McCarthy's pitfall. It was now the weakness of the Goldwater crowd. At the convention in San Francisco, Nixon cringed when the senator's acceptance speech praised "extremism in the defense of liberty" and knew that the Goldwater New Right crusade had destroyed itself on the spot. After Johnson's easy victory that fall, a wistful Nixon wrote that he wished "more of our conservative friends could recognize the terrible liability of the extremist tag." Later, reflecting on the making of that disaster, he recalled that "we had to keep the Goldwater debacle from destroying the party."[1]

In the process, Nixon was a key player from start to finish, hoping, at first, to head off the enthusiasm for the Arizonan by either becoming a consensus candidate himself by bridging the party's disparate wings, or by working to preserve its structure so that it could function in the future. Of his efforts behind Goldwater after the San Francisco convention, that famous occasion when Nelson Rockefeller was figuratively blown off the platform, Julie Eisenhower has recalled that he was campaigning less for the ticket — which he knew to be doomed, anyway — than "trying to build the party, too. Definitely, he was doing both, as much as he was trying to help Goldwater."[2]

Indeed, nobody who watched Nixon thought he had suddenly "retired" after losing to Governor Brown. Or that the move to New York had anything to do with forsaking politics. One can, in fact, locate many signs that demonstrate that, despite it all, he was remaining open to whatever opportunity might arise, even to opposing Kennedy again. In his mind, the Brown race did not make that impossible. As Eisenhower and Nixon speechwriter Kevin McCann put it to a Republican fundraiser, the perception of him as a two-time loser was "poor arithmetic because as far as I am concerned he was *not* defeated for the Presidency."[3]

If others failed to see it that way, Nixon would simply take advantage of his resources to make it inevitable. After all, his professional backers were limited in number but influential, starting with Len Hall; Fred Seaton, the former Nebraska governor and Eisenhower cabinet member who was a righthand adviser in Nixon's fight against Kennedy; GOP executive committee member and future party chairman, Ray Bliss of Ohio; and Hall's law partner, William Casey of New York. Financing came from friends who were indebted to Nixon, continued to believe in him and his ideas, and were ready to stake much on his future power. They, along with old loyalists such as Bob Finch and Herb Klein, relative newcomers such as Bob Haldeman and John Ehrlichman, and writer Victor Lasky, never abandoned the idea of challenging Kennedy in 1964. Just a week before Kennedy left on that fateful trip to Texas, the former vice president's aides were piqued that another writer, Ralph de Toledano, was doing some work for Goldwater. "Some of our so-called 'friends' really amaze me," noted Rose Mary Woods, while Len Hall agreed that de Toledano always went "where the 'sugar' is."[4]

If people like de Toledano thought there was more gravy elsewhere, they forgot that Nixon's decision to run in California never ruled out trying to beat out Rockefeller or Goldwater in 1964, win or lose. Every analysis of what might happen in California was with the next presidential election in mind. "There are many sizable problems that a candidate must face, many little ones," Hall advised right after Nixon announced his decision to run, "— sometimes irritating — that come up. You take care of the big ones but try to have someone else take care of the small ones."[5]

He was less than certain about risking all by making another try against Kennedy. Still, displaced in New York after a second defeat and confronting a "sizable" problem, Nixon never indicated that he was ready to withdraw to the obscurity of an affluent corporate law firm. "I have been particularly grateful for the fine opportunities that have been offered to me if I should decide to devote my efforts exclusively to legal practice, or to private business," he wrote to a friend. "But, after careful consideration of all the factors involved, I have decided that to the extent my obligation to provide for my family will permit, I should continue to devote as much of my time as possible to participation in public affairs." He later recalled in a memorandum to Bob Haldeman "that from the period after the California election in 1962 until I became a candidate in January of 1968, I was running the whole operation literally on a shoe string — travelling around the world, sometimes on coach flights with only one person with me and sometimes none at all."[6]

The few remaining doubts about his political ambitions were virtually removed when Nixon spoke before the American Society of Newspaper Editors in April 1963, a moment when civil rights demonstrations in Birmingham were overshadowing international concerns. It was a period of relative calm overseas. The Cuban missile crisis had passed and so had the crisis over Berlin. Southeast Asia, of course, continued to ferment, but the assaults by Diem on the Buddhists were yet to come and the administration's great test in Vietnam lay ahead. Nixon, invited to address the editors in Washington, went all out before the important forum (which he had attended as vice president) to deliver a sizing-up of the U.S. international role that was partisan in tone but also impressive for its comprehensive overview of where he thought diplomacy ought to lead. His preparation was characteristically thorough. Steve Hess helped to blend into the speech points made by Dr. Henry Kissinger of Harvard about the weakness of the administration's NATO policy. "Kissinger, as I recall," Nixon explained to Bryce Harlow during the preparation process, "was at one time one of Rockefeller's chief advisers in the foreign policy field. If this is still the case, Rockefeller may be contemplating a similar approach in his speech to the Publishers in New York a few days after the Editors meeting in Washington. This should cause us no concern, however, because if the position is a sound one it will bear repetition."[7]

If, when he spoke in Washington that day, he considered himself a fallen politico, a two-time loser, that was not apparent to anyone who watched. Many immediately remarked that he had not given up on the presidency. He was Richard Nixon carrying the message and cause in a manner that had long since become familiar, and the editors responded with warmth. He even told them that he had reconsidered his "last press conference" remarks after the California defeat and said that, if he were proposing a toast, it would be "to the working press of America, the most underpaid and skilled craftsmen in America." This time, he said, he had the advantage of a being private citizen "speaking without regard to any effect my words may have on my own, my party's or my Administration's political popularity." In response to a question, he said he had no intention of running for office again and suggested that a Rockefeller-Goldwater ticket could beat Kennedy. "If Jack and Lyndon could get together," he said, "Barry and Nelson can."[8]

The speech made the front pages. It had the desired effect of reaffirming his primacy as a Republican spokesman, one whose outlook was increasingly taking a comprehensive view of America's position in the world. With the need to deter Soviet expansionism everywhere as his central theme, he cited every point of the administration's vulnerability. In Cuba, the missiles may have been removed, but it was still a "Soviet beachhead," and a forceful statement of what Washington was willing to do might avoid the need for later military action. Kennedy had rushed troops into Oxford, Mississippi, to safeguard the integration of the University of Mississippi but refused to invade Castro's stronghold. "Red China and Russia are having their differences," he noted, "but we cannot take too much comfort in the fact that what they are arguing about is not how to beat each other but how to beat us. They are simply arguing about what kind of a shovel they should use to dig the grave of the United States." Picking up on Kissinger's theme, he called for a "political confederation" of America and her European allies to share nuclear weapons and develop a common defense strategy. Foreign aid must be targeted to support the "forces of freedom," but, as he explained when questioned later, he would not withhold such assistance from right-wing regimes unless they were clearly part of an international movement aimed at the United States. Underdeveloped countries, however, should get assistance to encourage efforts at population control.[9]

Most striking about Nixon's central message is its familiarity when reread from the perspective of the eighties. To be sure, it had some contemporary rhetoric, as when he said that "to the Communists who say that their goal is a Communist America, we must answer — our goal is nothing less than a free Russia, a free China, a free Eastern Europe and a free Cuba." But his central theme emerged when he charged that Kennedy's policy of containment was essentially defensive in character and was therefore "doomed to failure." "I refuse to accept the contention that our only choice is between coexistence, which is another word for creeping surrender, on the one hand, and no existence on the other hand. I believe there is a responsible strategy which will avoid both war and surrender," he said, and added that "Mr. Khrushchev will not treat us gently because we treat him gently but only when and because he respects our power to deal firmly with him."[10]

In reasserting the prominence of his leadership, Nixon was also keeping alive his perennial theme that there could be no peaceful coexistence, only the managed conflict of perpetual rivalry between the capitalist and Marxist worlds. Of those who thought otherwise, he was contemptuous. As he wrote to William R. Kintner of the Foreign Policy Research Institute a few weeks after his speech, "It is disheartening and sometimes almost frightening to see how much influence Walter Lippmann, with his almost unbelievably muddy thinking, has on so-called intellectuals in this country." Completion of the limited nuclear test ban agreement with the Soviet Union in August left Nixon believing that it "marked the beginning of the most dangerous period of the cold war since it began eighteen years ago." Nixon went to Syracuse, New York, that fall and again tried to bolster the Republican critique of Kennedy through a series of foreign policy speeches. When news about tragedy came from Saigon early in November, he wrote to Karl Mundt that "the Diem murder was the most disgraceful deed to date in our mixed up foreign policy record. It is dangerous to be a foe of Communism and a friend of the U.S." He could not understand, he wrote to Robert Humphreys, "why the Republicans are so reluctant to say a good word for Diem. He was, after all, a foe of communism and a friend of the United States." As an afterthought, he noted, "It is indeed ironical that at a time we condone the murder of Diem we are fawning over Tito, normalizing relations with [János] Kadar, and doing our very best to 'accommodate' Khrushchev. Give 'em hell!!"[11]

Officially, Nixon still held firm against becoming a candidate, preferring to rest on his earlier disavowals. Still, pollsters will be pollsters, and they were probably less inclined to write him off than were party leaders. A Gallup survey taken during the weeks just before the Diem murder showed Nixon ahead of Barry Goldwater among Republicans by four points and trailing by two in a canvass limited to independents. Another test of opinion, taken during that same week, showed that 46 percent, by far the largest number, were critical of the Kennedy administration for pushing integration too rapidly. With such indicators, as the president well knew, politicians begin to revise their strategies. Kennedy left for Dallas on the twenty-first fearing the worst from "free world" voters who had been asked to extend equal rights to their fellow citizens but hoping to squeeze needed campaign money from fat-cat Texas Democrats.[12]

Then, within two weeks after Lee Harvey Oswald became a household name, the papers began to report presidential activity behind Nixon. In early December of 1963, Leonard Hall and Nixon visited Ike for a reassessment of the political climate. Those difficult postassassination days, a time of vast national support for LBJ's accidental presidency, were not very well suited to much overt politicking. Nevertheless, with Kennedy gone, not only was Nixon more receptive, he was also the logical big name to step into the situation. A February Gallup poll placed him eleven points ahead of Goldwater among Republicans, a preference that was also borne out by regional surveys. Further encouragement came from a survey of the personal preferences of 1,606 Republican county chairmen. They liked Goldwater by better than two to one; but when asked for the probable nominee, it was Nixon by 526 to 427 over the senator. He joined Jackie Gleason and Arthur Godfrey on a radio show and when Gleason asked, "Are you going to run?" replied, "I never wear a hat, so it must always be in the ring." Positioning for 1964, however, had long since taken place. Before his assassination, Kennedy had feared that he might have to face the homespun apple-pie righteousness of George Romney, the Michigan governor and father of American Motors's little Rambler. He hoped he would have the good fortune to run against Barry Goldwater, and that the far-right extremist would only go on shooting himself in the foot with comments too outrageous even for the citizens of the United States. That, of course, was the strongest kind of "confidence" skeptics had about Goldwater. As Fred Seaton wrote to Nixon, "The more Barry Goldwater talks, the more he loses support."[13]

At least it seemed that way to self-proclaimed rationalists, most of whom had a remarkable tendency to underestimate what was happening. They knew all about how Nixon had gotten started. Scratch a liberal Democrat and he would immediately recite the list of "victims," all with full consciousness that the process had enabled Nixon to become vice president and a serious presidential contender. They also knew everything they thought needed to be known about Joe McCarthy, the House Committee on Un-American Activities, and, more recently, Robert Welch and the John Birch Society. They knew how well anticommunism played in America, how the Red menace was held responsible for all evils, racial integration, higher minimum wages, labor unions, feminism, and Washington bureaucrats. However well they understood those things, they underestimated the power of the right.

It was easy to dismiss malcontents, crackpots like "little old ladies in tennis shoes" whose natural habitat was in California's Southland, as little more respectable than KKKers; they were thought to be resentful that newcomers were bypassing them in the economic pecking order or eager to protect their newly earned fortunes from a government that seemingly only wanted to tax and tax and spend and spend. For the most part, especially in the days before Dallas, Americans were still secure about the rationality of the political order and the inevitability of progress. That the Eisenhower presidency kept the lid on a right-wing powder keg was only dimly perceived.[14]

There was not much popular awareness of the influence of postwar conservative theorists. They were far less known than a Chambers or even a Burnham, but the writings of Friedrich Hayek, Ludwig von Mises, and Russell Kirk were to the New Right what Herbert Marcuse and Norman O. Brown became to the New Left. Kirk's *Conservative Mind,* for example, appeared just as Eisenhower stepped into political power and went far beyond conventional critiques of New Deal liberalism. It upheld the social order, which, in Kirk's view, had been chipped away by society in defense of humanism, "dramatically catalyzed," in the words of George H. Nash, "the emergence of the conservative intellectual movement."[15] The pages of the *National Review,* which William F. Buckley, Jr., first put out in late 1955, began to bring to the new generation of antistatists the writings of thinkers who, whether or not they supported Joe McCarthy, as did Buckley, were contemptuous of even the way the current Republican administration accepted the magnitude of federal intervention into American economic and social life.

Even before the end of that regime of "modern Republicanism," between the months after Nixon's nomination and Kennedy's electoral victory, eager seekers of a new libertarian utopia gathered at Buckley's estate in Connecticut. Youthful, devoted to seeking the eternal truths of limited government, the destruction of international communism, and the restoration of a market economy, they incorporated such dreams into the so-called Sharon Statement. Thus was born the Young Americans for Freedom, some two years before Tom Hayden's Port Huron Statement produced the Students for a Democratic Society. Like their left-wing counterparts, their movement was born from affluence, not poverty. They were the other side of the coin of the postwar American success story, from families as economically blessed as the New Left but, just having made their money, far more insecure about holding on to it. By the time Kennedy was settling into the White House, their movement had spawned chapters at some one hundred colleges. Numbering about twenty-seven thousand in all within six months after their start in Sharon, Connecticut, they, along with the bulk of the New Right, became familiar to suburban communities, especially in the South and West.[16]

Kennedy's swearing-in only sped up the process. During his first year in office, New York rightists founded a Conservative party, "an instinctive move," Rusher called it, to translate "their principles into effective action in the political sphere." Under the leadership of such Republicans as F. Clifton White and newly elected congressman John Ashbrook of Ohio, who entered politics by way of the Young Republicans, they were as committed to Goldwater as the Progressive Citizens of America had been to Henry Wallace in 1948. "The disarray in the GOP, the slow but steady disintegration of the old Roosevelt coalition in the Democratic party, the growing strength and significance of the South and West on the national scene," Rusher has explained, "— all of these suggested that the time was ripe for the Republican party, under new auspices, to make a major bid for blue-collar support." Richard G. Kleindienst, an Arizona lawyer close to Goldwater and a Republican national committeeman, commented on the plight of his party. "We will never be successful in out-promising the opposition; we will never be willing to appeal to the prejudices and selfish interests of various groupings of Americans based upon differences in race, color, creed and economic status. Nevertheless," he added, "I firmly believe that there is a growing uneasiness in the hearts of a majority of our citizens that they are being neglected and forgotten as individuals." Conservatives had "an astonishingly good chance of up-ending Kennedy nationally," Rusher wrote in his *National Review,* "by taking most of the 165 electoral votes of the southern and border states away from him."[17]

Goldwaterites constituted a moral crusade that rebelled against Republicans who, to their way of thinking, were every bit as utopian as the New Left. They also, however, represented the moral integrity of an earlier era, where patriotism and individualism were taken for granted and the state functioned — if it did at all — as a protector of national security and traditional values. They had few reservations about drawing enemies in bold relief: the eastern Republican "liberal" establishment; the "liberal" media; the wishy-washy, compromising conservatism of the national Republican party, which had performed so ineptly under Eisenhower in defense of American freedoms and in opposition to international communism. More recently, the cause of true conservatism was "sold out" by Nixon in his race against Kennedy and subsequent rejection of California's anticommunist Birchites. Supplied by cadres from among the Young Republicans, organizational work proceeded throughout the country. By 1964, their cause attracted financial contributions from an impressive number of individual donors, a grass-roots movement that was over a dozen times greater than the number who sent dollars for Nixon's 1960 campaign. One especially astute enterpriser, Richard Viguerie, began with that base and employed new computer technology to raise funds through direct mail operations, which enabled him to reach what Barry Goldwater had referred to as the "silent Americans."

The New Right thereby began an end run to reach ordinary Americans by outflanking the media. By the time of Ronald Reagan's elevation to the presidency, Viguerie had collected the largest political mailing list in the country and, with fellow rightist Paul Weyrich, had put together a new coalition. Largely Protestant, and with some militant Catholics and Jews, they became the vanguard for a new moral crusade. One, a St. Louis newspaperman, Pat Buchanan, went to work for Richard Nixon after the Goldwater campaign and then became a link to the more pristine conservatism of Ronald Reagan. Buchanan, never one to qualify his political convictions, later wrote that Nixon was "less a conservative than a fellow-traveler of the right."[18]

Bill Rusher was another New Right pioneer. A midwesterner and descendant of a socialist grandfather, Rusher grew up hearing from his father about how the captains of industry brutalized their workers. As a Princeton undergraduate, he was a Willkie Republican and then backed Tom Dewey, who lost to Truman the year Rusher graduated from Harvard Law School. Rusher's conversion to right-wing conservatism came after his enlightenment about the Communist menace when Whittaker Chambers unmasked Alger Hiss. Liberal ganging up against Joe Mc-Carthy angered him. Convinced about the leftist threat to America, Rusher left private practice in New York to become an associate counsel to the Senate Internal Security Subcommittee, then under the chairmanship of James Eastland.[19]

He had already helped start the *National Review,* which quickly became the most effective outlet for the New Right. Then, as its publisher, he wrote with wit and acerbity in the pages of the outspoken, sometimes unpredictable publication.[20] The Democratic party, Rusher once wrote, "is the primary cancer on the American body politic" and an "ancient conspiracy against good government." He was hardly more charitable about Richard Nixon, whose presidency he regarded as a betrayal of conservative principles. "In a time of troubles when America was looking for definition," he said, "Nixon represented the trouble." Reagan should have been nominated in 1968, not Nixon, and it could have happened if conservatives had not broken ranks to support the likely winner. "Think of what it meant," he pondered. "We would have been spared Watergate and we would not have had that inflation." Hearing Rusher was a reminder that without Whittaker Chambers there would have been no Nixon; without Goldwater, there would have been no Reagan. The Goldwaterite takeover of the party, Rusher has written, led "by demonstrable steps" to Reagan's presidency.[21]

Although the power of such enthusiasts was underestimated before 1964, their capacity for mischief was not. "While Goldwater undoubtedly has a commanding lead at this time among Republicans," Nixon wrote to Walter Annenberg less than a year before the convention, "I don't believe that any of the other candidates can be written off at such an early date."[22]

Nixon then tried something else. Eisenhower had passed on to him a letter from a Temple City, California, man with an allegation about Goldwater's behavior on the Italian front as an Air Force executive officer with the 485th Bombardment Group. The correspondent claimed that the story was known to most of the five thousand men who were in that combat group. He reported that Goldwater was so preoccupied with becoming a military hero to promote his postwar political career that he disobeyed orders and led his squadron over an area where the concentration of antiaircraft flak was so great that some ten bombers were shot down, with the loss of one hundred men. Only the subsequent death in combat of a key witness saved him from a court-martial.

Nixon turned to a friendly journalist, Victor Lasky, the author of a then-current exposé, *JFK, the Man and the Myth.* Lasky's reputation as a conservative muckraker was quite secure, so, for Nixon at least, it was a case of directing the right leak to the right conduit. He suggested that

Lasky might want to check out the story because it was "bound to come
out if Goldwater becomes a candidate for the presidency." He had, of
course, lofty reasons for sending it to Lasky. "It occurred to me that this
kind of libelous material should not be allowed to get wide circulation
before being nailed," he wrote. "Perhaps you might want to dig into it.
Exposing its falsity could make quite a column for you!"[23] In other words,
instead of burying the letter in the "crackpot" files, which he implied
should be done, he preferred to have Lasky air the entire thing and
thereby give credence to something that would otherwise be ignored.

Eisenhower's role in the affair is also noteworthy. He could have discarded that particular piece of mail along with the thousands of other
routine crank letters, but he chose to send it on to Nixon, which at least
implied that it warranted attention. Even a man with Lasky's talent was
not able to do anything with it. Goldwater, alas, never served on the
Italian front.

All that was just before the Kennedy assassination, which also made
moderates more fearful about Goldwater winning the nomination. Kevin
McCann, the Eisenhower speechwriter, thought all could be saved by
going with a Nixon–Milton Eisenhower ticket. But, as he conceded,
the perception of Nixon as a two-time loser and his loss of a politico-
geographical base by moving to New York made that impossible. Another Eisenhower veteran, Jim Hagerty, pressed for action to prevent a
Republican split and to keep the Goldwaterites from turning "this party
into what would be a white man's party. Think what this would do to
us all over the world."[24]

The immediate impact, however, was on the Republican party. Most
of the established leadership agreed with Hagerty. Goldwater was undesirable, but if they had no choice but to live with him, every effort
should be made to limit the divisiveness of his candidacy; certainly, the
drive of the New Right must not undermine the chances of moderates
to run under the party's label. Inevitably, there was hope that Eisenhower, as their most revered living figure, could keep it all in balance,
either by using his prestige to stop Goldwater or by acting in some other
way to preserve unity. Meanwhile, after Kennedy's death, it became
clearer that Nixon had his own ideas about how to resolve matters.

By holding all possible other contenders in check and by keeping a
balance between supporting the senator from Arizona and worrying
about his takeover of the party, Nixon might yet keep the way open for
himself. But an impasse could only be achieved if other potential candidates, those more acceptable to moderates and liberals, could stem the
Goldwater momentum. And it all had to be done without Nixon's active
campaigning. He was in a catch-22 situation: his cause would go begging
if the Goldwater enthusiasts were needed for his nomination. When he

therefore worked to keep them friendly, which included taking a more hostile line toward civil rights, he offended the liberals and moderates.[25]

His only alternative was to engage in a covert campaign, and the Nixon role became perhaps the touchiest of all before the Republicans met at San Francisco to choose the nominees. At least one rival, Rockefeller, had just about knocked himself out of the running by marrying Margaretta "Happy" Murphy less than two years after divorcing his wife of thirty years, the mother of his five children. His opponents were thereby handed what seemed a perfect excuse, and the polls, watched with interest by Nixon's side, confirmed the political damage.[26] That left several others to block Goldwater's way without winning for themselves: Henry Cabot Lodge, George Romney, and William Scranton.

Nixon, then, engaged in his delicate maneuver, which played itself out during the 1964 primaries. In New Hampshire, he maintained a hands-off policy as former governor Wesley Powell, whose blessing was less than helpful, organized a write-in vote. The March 10 count gave him 17 percent, or about half of Lodge's total and 5 percent behind Goldwater's. Nixon's analysis left him upbeat. He and Seaton agreed that Lodge, who was serving the Democrats as ambassador in Saigon and was involved in the overthrow of Diem, was not a serious threat. Besides, said Nixon, he knew for a fact that $100,000 had been spent on the Lodge entry. Lodge himself followed his victory with a telegram stating that he was not a candidate and was precluded from political activity because of his foreign service. The outcome was sufficiently encouraging for Nixon to enlarge his campaign staff. With that confidence, plus a lot of additional chipping-in by Cliff Folger, Len Hall, and State Senator Marvin Stromer to raise the needed $50,000, they organized a Nebraskans for a Free Choice write-in campaign for the May 12 primary. The result was a significant improvement over New Hampshire. Nixon, five days after delivering a "nonpolitical" speech in Omaha, came up with 42,811 write-in votes, or 35 percent of the total, which was not bad considering the fact that Goldwater drew 67,369 as the only candidate on the ballot. The Nebraska outcome was also welcome because it was regarded as a boost for Oregon, where a vital decision had had to be made. Oregon law enabled the state to decide for itself whether to include on the ballot the names of individuals prominently considered as potential candidates. To withdraw, Seaton advised, would necessitate an unequivocal statement that he was not and did "not intend becoming a candidate at the November election."[27]

But the result in Oregon was disheartening, leaving Nixon in fourth place with 17 percent while Rockefeller came in first. It was also enough to compel Nixon to declare his neutrality in the winner-take-all California primary and call on all sides to unite behind the nominee to be selected in San Francisco. For Goldwater, the victory was a big one. He beat

Rockefeller, who was portrayed as a stand-in for Romney and Scranton, by 51.4 percent to 48.6 percent of the popular vote, which gave him the entire eighty-six-member delegation.[28]

Whatever complacency had existed about the reality of Goldwater actually heading the ticket succumbed to panic. Hugh Scott was described by Hagerty as being "scared to death." Goldwater, warned Hagerty, would be a disaster in the large cities, except for some sections of a place like Queens. "It is frightening," he telephoned Nixon by way of Rose Mary Woods, "the more you hear of it. Someone has to do something or you could end up with a 1912. A real, tough, serious split with someone taking a walk." Still, he agreed with Nixon that it was not wise to gang up on the senator.[29]

That was also the weekend of the governors conference at Cleveland. On Saturday, June 6, Governor Scranton met with Eisenhower at Gettysburg. Was it just a coincidence, or were they plotting a last-ditch stop-Goldwater move? The latter seemed much more probable as Scranton left the former president believing that he had been asked to make himself more available for the nomination, as indeed he had. The backing was also timely for another reason: Scranton had a date for that Sunday's "Face the Nation" television interview program.

It didn't take long for word of the Eisenhower-Scranton meeting to make its mark. Clifton White knew the best way to reach the general, through George Humphrey, his good friend and former treasury secretary. Humphrey, who had been Eisenhower's closest soul mate within the cabinet, had no trouble talking bluntly to the general. When he called that Saturday night, his anger plain, he held nothing back. If Eisenhower didn't call off the governor, if he participated in any stop-Goldwater movement, he'd better "stay at a hotel" when he tried to visit the Humphrey estate. That Sunday morning, just two hours before Scranton was to go on the air, and when the rest of the country was prepared to hear a dramatic anti-Goldwater stroke, Eisenhower called the Pennsylvania governor. He hoped, he told him, that he had not given the wrong impression at their Gettysburg meeting and certainly did not want him to engage in any "cabal" against a Republican candidate.[30]

Scranton went on the air and fended off the interviewers with innocuous, evasive statements that offered absolutely no hint of a challenge to Goldwater either through his own candidacy or via any other means. Nor were there any warnings about potential damage to the party. Viewers who expected an historic statement were let down, puzzled. That he had been undercut and left stranded on the air before millions who watched was obvious. The discomfort and embarrassment was as intense as that ever experienced by a major political figure.

That Eisenhower was somehow to blame loomed as an immediate piece of conventional wisdom; but why, why the last-minute retreat? Why did he set up Scranton only to let him hang? All people could do was to speculate, but they could hardly have guessed how Humphrey had gotten to the general; the industrialist's influence over the former president was not as well recognized by the public as by those who had been closely associated with Eisenhower. Nixon could well commiserate with Scranton. He understood the feeling. Ike, by caving in to Humphrey, had let down the party's moderates and set off some panic. "I can't understand things," said Hagerty to Miss Woods. "I don't understand my former boss."[31]

At breakfast in Cleveland that Sunday morning Romney failed to be dissuaded by the other governors when he announced that he intended to make a strong anti-Goldwater statement. He then went public with a press conference and returned to Michigan. In his absence that Sunday evening, hours after the Scranton television fiasco, Rockefeller and James Rhodes of Ohio met privately at Scranton's suggestion. According to an Associated Press wire story, Scranton explained that he still hoped "that we could build someone else, and it may be interesting for everybody to know that it was I who got Governor Rockefeller and Governor Rhodes together that night and suggested to them that we get a hold of Governor Romney who had gone back to Michigan." They did, in fact, call Romney during the meeting to ask him to become the candidate and promised the necessary support.[32]

The next morning, at breakfast with Nixon at the Sheraton-Cadillac Hotel in Detroit, Romney went on about the need to safeguard Republican moderation. He said nothing about becoming a candidate and went no further than to say he was prepared to fight for that position. That evening, he rejoined the governors in Cleveland.

That group, meanwhile, insisted that Nixon join them by Tuesday morning. Nixon, completing his speaking engagements, agreed to fly in on their chartered plane. He arrived after dinner on Monday night, after a flight from Muskegon. When he reached his Cleveland hotel room, he found a note from Romney requesting that they meet before the scheduled governors breakfast the next morning.

Romney arrived at Nixon's suite by 7:00 A.M. He was ready, he told the former vice president, to take on Goldwater. He told Nixon about Scranton's promise to organize their forces behind him and said he would consider it a draft if a majority of his fellow governors asked him to run. That meeting was relatively brief, about fifteen minutes, and Romney then pursued the matter further at the breakfast table with Scranton. As they went on after the meal, two things became clear. Romney was determined to go ahead with his plan and eager to claim Nixon's support. Nixon, still hesitant about offending the Goldwaterites but eager for a deadlock, raised questions about the wisdom of Romney's actions. Was the timing right for such a statement? How would it affect the party?

Didn't Romney have a commitment to the people of Michigan not to become a presidential candidate? If Romney insisted on going ahead, Nixon suggested, the format must be positive and not seen as an anti-Goldwater act. If, under such circumstances, he wanted to do it, that was his right; as for himself, he would remain neutral. Romney then left Nixon and promptly told the press that "several Republican governors" had urged his candidacy.[33]

Nixon's role seemed clear. "After a moment or two," one of the governors later said, "I realized what was happening. Nixon was waiting for us to ask him to run for President. It was unbelievable, just unbelievable." But the governors were not buying, and he was unable to get anything more positive after making several telephone calls to different parts of the country. When Goldwater heard about Nixon's activities, he remarked, "He's sounding more like Harold Stassen every day."[34]

The sad fact was that the centrists were badly disunited. Rockefeller didn't trust Nixon and pointedly excluded him when he got together for a strategy session with Scranton and Rhodes after that Tuesday breakfast. Scranton had appeared little more than an Eisenhower puppet after his "Face the Nation" performance, and none of them had much confidence in Romney as a credible stopper. Against a determined force of Goldwaterites, by that late date they were quite impotent. Not even the senator's continuing weakness in the national polls, which the Gallup organization confirmed in a series of preconvention surveys, mattered very much. Only in the South — that area of increasing Republican strength — was he in front, and there by almost two to one. "The greatest Republican gains in the last fifteen years have been in the South," Goldwater said after the 1962 midterm election, which meant that he would not only vote against the omnibus Civil Rights Act of 1964, which he would have done anyway, but do so loudly and proudly. It was in the South, too, where there were threats of a bolt from the party if it tried to select that "wife-swapper" Nelson Rockefeller.[35] There were lessons to be learned.

Meanwhile, Nixon had allowed himself to be mousetrapped. He couldn't have it both ways: derail the Goldwater express and yet steer clear of a cabal while avoiding the impression that he was engineering a self-serving deadlock. So anxious was he to dispel that impression that he had an aide (probably Sherman Unger, the only man who was privy to the various phone calls and meetings) prepare a detailed chronology to demonstrate that his trip to Cleveland had been at the urgent request of the governors and that he had resisted Romney's efforts to win his support.[36] Still, acceptance of Romney's version encouraged the idea that Nixon was merely using him as a stalking horse for himself.

"When I see the way Scranton/Lodge and Romney have handled themselves," agonized Jim Hagerty, "all I do is sit down and cry. It is just sheer stupidity. It is stupid people who are doing this."[37]

Nixon, meanwhile, couldn't get out of Cleveland soon enough. He did, though, fend off a suggestion from the Goldwater camp that he take second place on the ticket. He could do more for it on his own, he replied.[38]

And, sure enough, Romney's "candidacy" was virtually stillborn. The key people he turned to for assistance, Herb Brownell and Len Hall, were, for one reason or another (mainly because they were against the whole idea), unavailable. Romney, the midwestern Boy Scout, had no choice but to honor his commitment to his constituents and return to his governorship.[39] Scranton, perhaps to compensate for his televised embarrassment, perhaps through a sense of moral responsibility, then declared his candidacy for the presidency. It lasted less than five weeks.

Then came the reality of just how effectively Clif White and his colleagues had engineered the Goldwater takeover. What mattered in the long run was, in Rusher's words, that Republican domination had passed from the eastern wing "into the hands of a new management. And that management wasn't just the Arizona Mafia." Yes, said Goldwater many years later, "and, to be honest, that's the major reason I ran. It was my Convention from the day the doors opened."[40]

In another sense, it really was his, but the process of finding a running mate must have shaken that sense of control. One of the several potential candidates he approached, the Reverend Billy Graham, turned him down. He was "flattered and impressed" but declined with some tactful reasons. "Graham is interested in entering politics," said a report to President Johnson, "and has been for several years. He has the 'bug' — the charm — the personality — the image — he is a ready-made candidate — all he needs is a 'stalking horse.' " What seemed more acceptable, Johnson was told, was that he would only run on a ticket headed by Nixon. The nation's most respected evangelist had been close to every president since Eisenhower. Later, during the 1968 campaign, he did serve as a conduit between Johnson and Nixon. It was Graham, in fact, who helped to persuade Nixon to cancel a campaign motorcade through Chicago by agreeing with seeress Jeane Dixon about a possible assassination attempt.[41]

In the long run, it hardly mattered that Goldwater had to settle for Congressman William Miller of upstate New York. Miller's credentials were limited: he was properly conservative, highly partisan, and a Catholic. Once chosen he seemed to fade away, one of the forgotten also-rans of history.[42]

If Goldwater had no illusions about winning, knowing "damn well that nobody could beat Johnson — and the ghost of Jack Kennedy, too," neither did Nixon — nor, for that matter, anybody else not deluded about a "hidden vote" that supposedly lay in wait for the chance to participate in a race that offered a "choice not an echo." That myth, which had been intriguing some frustrated Republicans ever since Dewey's loss in 1948, never did materialize. Soon after the 1964 election, the Republican National Committee reported that "the percentage of Americans of voting age who actually voted dropped slightly compared to 1960 and was smaller than the percentage voting in 1952."[43] The GOP's 1964 convention was nevertheless significant because it reaffirmed the power of ideology, symbolized the shift of the Republican base, and, in retrospect, became an overture for the configuration of forces that inevitably brought Nixon to the presidency.

In a White House memorandum written in 1970, Nixon recalled that "there is a very good story in how we operated from 1963 to 1968." The most essential single step was his decision not to join the stop-Goldwater crowd and to work hard for the candidate even when it was obvious that the campaign was doomed. Fat cats were betting their money on Johnson, while Goldwater seemed idiosyncratic about making points that upheld New Right purity but frightened voters. Nixon, who later explained the importance of not letting Goldwater's strong conservative supporters "feel that they were completely abandoned by all of those who happened to disagree with some of his views," covered a vast amount of ground. His thirty-six-state swing involved 150 stops in what was less an effort to secure the impossible, which would have been victory for Goldwater and his running mate, than to prevent a disaster for Republicans all along the line. In the process, "I had no idea at all in 1964 that I might be a candidate in 1968."[44]

That comment, made to Haldeman after nearly two years in the White House, could not have been taken too seriously by the young Californian who had become a key member of his staff. Haldeman had been moving closer to the boss. The two met again at the Goldwater convention, an affair that was so thoroughly dominated by the senator and his legions that it was truly his. Nixon, who had been close to the octogenarian ex-president Herbert Hoover since their Bohemian Grove encampments, remembered that during that last summer of his life, the party's eldest statesman thought that the "Goldwaterites should have their day and get it out of their system." Haldeman, who was primarily interested in Nixon's future, hardly thought his boss was ready to let the Goldwater aberration end his political career.[45]

But those who failed to understand what was happening were also deceiving themselves. Easily the most memorable boost for the campaign, aside from Goldwater's own fiery declaration of the virtues of "extremism in defense of liberty," was a nationally broadcast preelection speech by Ronald Reagan, which went far to launch the Republican party's future hero. Political writer David Broder, known for his sobriety, called it "the most successful political debut since William Jennings Bryan electrified the 1896 Democratic convention with his 'Cross of Gold' speech," and enough Americans agreed for $1 million in contributions to flow in as a direct result of that speech. *Time* magazine called it "the one bright spot in a dismal campaign." If, after that delivery of what Reagan called "A Time for Choosing," he became the chief conservative torchbearer, it was by building on Goldwater's then politically suicidal flourishes, which outraged those who thought he was really campaigning to win but delighted those who praised the purity of the new conservative creed.[46] Johnson, for example, did not believe Vietnam was worth an expanded war; Goldwater did. Johnson favored more domestic spending programs, especially for the poor and racially disadvantaged; Goldwater did not. Johnson wanted to fulfill the promise of FDR's New Deal; Goldwater railed against "big government," taxes, and interference with private enterprise.

He lost the election, but the future was with him. That year, for example, was the first time that a greater number of voters turned out from America's suburbs than from the central cities. Ever since the war, metropolitan areas were growing larger and the outlying centers of population were becoming more dominant. Suburbia was the new middle-class capital, and it was a place where everything was disproportionate, from the number of shopping centers, growing children, and automobiles to its share of political power. And that was more conservative and more Republican. About the only increases attributable to the inner cities were the rates of crime, poverty, and the percentage of nonwhites. One did not have to be clairvoyant to see that such continued growth meant more social and political polarization, isolating the middle class even further from what Michael Harrington had called the other America.

But that was hardly the end of it. Republicanism was also becoming southern as well as northern, not merely in the Eisenhower sense of picking up a relatively modern, urban constituency. Goldwater, however, without race-baiting, also managed to reach out to backwater poor whites, to the grandchildren of those who had been led by Tom Watson, Ben Tillman, and Theodore Bilbo. He broadened the southern base, confirming the transformation of the party, and five of the six states he carried were from Dixie. His majorities came from a Republican party that was pushed far more rightward than in the North as it inherited conservative Democrats and lost blacks who were giving up on the party of Lincoln for the party of FDR.[47]

Goldwater, as Tom Wicker later wrote, became the "first Republican Presidential candidate of the twentieth century who was not politically respectable, and Lyndon Johnson embraced the opportunity in a Texas bear hug." Nixon, meanwhile, appreciated the certainty that while his party might not have an incumbent in 1968 it would have a long memory. Then, too, what would the party be worth? The poor showing of Republican congressional candidates in 1958 had hurt in 1960 and, whatever his own ambitions, there was the threat of GOP extinction, or, as a number of political journalists were then speculating, permanence as a minority coterie instead of as a major political force. Nixon felt he had no choice but to campaign as hard as he could.[48]

After Johnson won his 61 percent of the popular vote and forty-four states, the Democratic National Committee proclaimed the failure of Republican efforts to exploit racial and ethnic prejudices. A wide variety of groups had gone more solidly for the president than they had for Kennedy in 1960. An ebullient John Bailey, the party's chairman, found vindication of Johnson's prediction that the "frontlash" reaction against Goldwater would far outweigh the "backlash" of racial prejudice. When trouble followed, Johnson could not believe that things had gone so wrong.[49]

Little wonder. He was updating and expanding earlier remedies for the poor, especially blacks. His Great Society had already picked up from Kennedy and begun its War on Poverty. The Office of Economic Opportunity (OEO) was designing community action programs, which aimed at funneling monies to enable the impoverished to design their own grass-roots solutions. An imposing array of additional programs fell under the aegis of the OEO: the Job Corps, VISTA, a Neighborhood Youth Corps, the Head Start program. Congress, almost as agreeable as under FDR, also provided for financial aid for mass transportation. From that, too, the poor would benefit most. All that was in addition to the omnibus Civil Rights Act. After the defeat of Goldwater, and thereby also the decimation of whatever opposition remained on Capitol Hill, came even more imposing Great Society programs: the Voting Rights Act, which many thought would prove the most significant of all; Medicare; a Model Cities program and Omnibus Housing Act; the establishment of the Department of Housing and Urban Development; higher minimum wages; aid for veterans; more for transportation; and so on. He had the magic touch until it became obvious that he was more enthralled with scoring than administering. In the late summer of 1965, a violent outbreak in the black ghetto of Watts in Los Angeles caught more national attention than any previous disorder. By the following year, the president's clout with Congress disappeared. Both wars, the one in Southeast Asia and the one against poverty, had placed him on the defensive. The consensus for reform became bogged down in bureaucratic conflicts, domestic disorders, and inflation. Racial hostilities that had been relatively muted in large areas of the country became far more blatant, even if usually masked by code language.

As Pat Brown put it, "Whether we like it or not, the people want separation of the races."[50] A new phase had begun. The operative words were "backlash," "law and order," and "crime in the streets," often expressed in tandem with complaints about "welfare cheats," blacks on the dole, and too many children. Why work when the checks keep coming? The Aid to Families with Dependent Children program, a spin-off from the Social Security Act of 1935, became as synonymous with indulgent behavior by lazy blacks as the old horror stories of how freed slaves had corrupted Radical Reconstruction after the Civil War.

Nixon cannot be faulted for advocating compliance with the Civil Rights Act of 1964, but he remained the rationalist who could reason from both points of view. For example, even before the spate of legislation and the start of ghetto burnings, even before "law and order" became a code, he warned about attempting to force racial equality "in an artificial and unworkable manner," which would cause whatever progress had been achieved to backfire. In terms that appealed to forgotten Americans, he deplored the tendency of the Washington bureaucracy, which so often was more representative of the establishment elite, to ignore the problems of middle-class white families who had to labor long hours just to hold on to what they had. They, not the upper-class reformers, would ultimately have to pay the price of social experiments. When, in 1968, the president's National Advisory Commission on Civil Disorders, under Governor Otto Kerner of Illinois, made its report (which included the much-advertised portentous line, "Our nation is moving toward two societies, one black, one white — separate and unequal"), Johnson did an about-face by almost ignoring the study he himself had commissioned. Nixon, far from ducking the issue, spoke out nationally with the argument that its conclusions were too limited. As he wrote to Eisenhower, there was "a need for order as the first requisite if we are to have peace and progress either at home or abroad," and he advised the ex-president that the point drew receptive audiences wherever he went.[51]

That the country had turned was made plain at the polls in 1966. Though still a minority, the Republicans picked up forty-seven seats in the House. Almost all the losers had solidly supported Johnson on the Great Society. Moreover, when Gallup's pollsters took a survey one month before the election, they found voters listing the war in Vietnam, civil rights, racial strife, and increasing inflation as the nation's outstanding problems.[52]

For most Americans, reform movements — especially civil rights — were suspect to begin with. As political writer Meg Greenfield noted in the spring of 1966, "the affluence of labor, Negroes, middle-class white liberals, and machine politicians upon which that strength was based is coming apart."[53] Such antagonisms and suspicions, which had weakened an alliance that was always tenuous at best, were bringing down the coalition that had carried both Kennedy and Johnson. Middle-income whites, especially, were exhausting their patience. Racial turbulence and the virtually traitorous, authority-defiant acts of the most fortunate of America's young people were confirming the sinister suspicions of the vast majority. Even before the urban riots, nearly two-thirds of those surveyed by Gallup were unhappy about the plans for the massive civil rights rally in Washington in August 1963. Nor was there much popular support for the voter registration and freedom rider campaigns that northern whites undertook in the South.

Suspicions that organized conspirators were responsible increased with the disorders that spread across the country from 1964 through 1966. Communists or radicals of one stripe or another were suspected of being everywhere, mischievously upsetting civil order and social patterns. Three-quarters of those surveyed by Gallup were convinced that they had a hand in both the civil rights and antiwar demonstrations. One especially revealing finding by the Harris poll in the spring of 1966 showed that, by more than two to one, poor whites were the most worried about the likelihood of violence by blacks. The reaction reached even into those areas safely distant from the urban chaos, with respondents everywhere agreeing the disorders had eroded whatever was left of their fragile sympathy for the plight of America's minorities. The vestigial cohesion of the post-Roosevelt Democracy was being torn by divisions based on education, race, class, culture, and income. An internal Democratic party memorandum, prepared after the elections and given to President Johnson, included the following statement: *"The single issue which appeared to be critical, and which was calculated to appeal beyond the general target audience of small-town Republicans, was that of race rioting and the pace of Negro advances in our society."* Reformers of the 1960s had pushed matters too far to be further tolerated by the great majority.[54]

That note ended the fears of Nixon and other nonideologues that Goldwater's candidacy foreshadowed the destruction of the Republican party. The most serious watershed in American politics since the New Deal was being crossed. In California, Democratic opponents of a third term for Brown restrained their criticism because of realization that victory for the Republican contender, Ronald Reagan, would make him a national figure. Their restraint collapsed, however, with the outbreak of rioting in San Francisco, and Brown's position was more untenable than ever. Reagan rode on the fear of what was happening to social stability both on campuses and in the streets and went on to defeat Brown by nearly 1 million votes. If Reagan attracted economic conservatives as well, such local candidates as Rosemary Gunning in New York City and

Louise Day Hicks in Boston were the obvious beneficiaries of white middle-income worries about social disorder.

Throughout much of American history, a politician had only to be known for his honesty to win respect; when the backlash came, upholding racial purity of all-white schools was the new way to stardom. Hicks, a member of Boston's school committee, became symptomatic of the resistance movement's shift to the North. A determined opponent of desegregated education, she survived a ten-way nonpartisan primary election to face off against Kevin White for the mayoralty. She made a serious, loud, but failed effort to defeat White. Like Barry Goldwater in 1964, she lost the vote but sanctified the cause, which was confirmed by an analysis of her following that was commissioned for the Johnson administration. The study noted that "when voters were asked to tell us what they consider the major problems of Boston today, racial unrest clearly tops the list, followed by taxes, schools, and education, crime, juvenile delinquency, vandalism, housing, and urban renewal." Moreover, fully three-fourths of the voters thought there were illegitimate recipients of welfare funds. The same number agreed that Boston's blacks were receiving fair and equal treatment. The impulse crossed party and even regional lines. Hicks's ideological kinship was with such other Democratic candidates as Lester Maddox in Georgia, Jim Johnson in Arkansas, and Lurleen Wallace of Alabama, the last a stand-in for a governor not eligible to succeed himself. In Maryland, a Republican, Baltimore County Executive Spiro Agnew, provoked by a rightist challenge that also attracted white supremacists, turned on a passionate defense against extremism that won over liberals and moderates, blacks and Jews behind his "fearless" candidacy to turn back a George Wallace prototype.[55]

The turn in American society was a curiosity to two British members of Parliament, who toured the country and observed the character of the 1966 elections. As a key aide to Vice President Humphrey reported their findings, "They believe that backlash was far more important than it might appear to be. In district after district, and city after city, they found an undercurrent of resentment concerning civil order and gains made by the Negro population. They felt backlash was highly important in the [Charles] Percy and Reagan victories, even though both men were attractive campaigners in their own right." Nixon, then also engaged as a syndicated columnist, warned that Democrats were risking "the next generation" by evoking "racism, demagogy and the backlash" just to win in 1966.[56]

Everywhere one looked, there was evidence of conservative strength, not necessarily enough to overwhelm organizational support for an electoral majority, but surely enough to make the point. The Maryland gubernatorial candidate, for example, was a Democrat named George P. Mahoney, who had come through a three-way primary, perked up his campaign with the rather fetching slogan "Your Home Is Your Castle — Protect It," which was not enough to defeat his opponent, Spiro Agnew, but certainly left the impression that the winner was the more moderate of the two men. For its governor, Georgia chose a blatant primitive on the race question, restaurateur Lester Maddox, who made ax handles the symbol of forcible resistance to desegregation.

Possibly more significant than any partisan clash was the vote in New York City on the creation of a civilian review board. Charges of police brutality had become associated almost exclusively with minority protests about abuse. The combination of street crime, urban disorders, and repeated complaints about unwarranted treatment by white officers gave the vote a polarization and significance that were generally lacking in the city's Democratic-dominated political character. The vote, really a referendum on law and order, with opponents of a civilian review board arguing that it would only further weaken the fight against crime, was also viewed as a verdict on the civil rights movement.

The review board proposal failed by almost three to one, but the vote revealed what was happening generally. Italian and Irish neighborhoods that were adjacent to black districts voted negatively by as much as 90 percent. Jews, traditionally more supportive of racial justice, had also begun to react, led by those who felt most vulnerable to incursions by blacks. One Jewish intellectual, Milton Himmelfarb, asked, "In 1966, was it chiefly education that prompted Jews to vote for the civilian review board, and lack of education to vote against it?" He had no trouble answering his own question: "Perhaps it was prosperity and lack of prosperity. The prosperous could afford their votes. The unprosperous (and elderly), living in apartment houses without doormen and riding subways rather than taxis, may have voted as they did, not because of ignorance but because of concerns explicable by the reality of their lives — a reality against which prosperity shields the prosperous." Not until three years later (an indication that the sentiment was far from fleeting) did Mario Procaccino, a conservative mayoral candidate, say on a New York City radio station that John Lindsay was the voice of "limousine liberals." As Procaccino, an emotional man who contributed other rhetorical flourishes, explained, "I've got the help of the little people on my side. That's the important issue. I don't have the select few. I don't have those people that live in penthouses and who send their children to private schools, and have doormen, and who don't ride the subways. I have the people that sweat as they go into the subway." New Yorkers, especially those in transitional neighborhoods, were demonstrating further movement away from the Democratic party. The white ethnic erosion of old loyalties was unmistakable. Ohio's Polish-American vote was a full 45 percent less Democratic in 1966 than it had been for Kennedy, a state that he lost in 1960. The party was in danger of "losing its base in suburban-urban centers," worried an aide to President Johnson.[57]

The splurge of Democratic social reform was, in short, bumping into the twin obstacles of ethnic rivalry underscored by growing working-class resentment of what was all too often seen as displacement. A new conservative populism was beginning to reshape social and political patterns.

Andy Valuchek, who worked with a black ex-newspaperman, Louis Martin, to oversee ethnic problems for President Johnson, reported on his round of Pulaski Day celebrations in three cities. He found fear about civil rights. "Many of the people who came to me," he wrote to Martin, "claim that they are not anti-Negro, that they would like them to make more progress and not be discriminated against. But they fear that some of the progress the Negro will make will be at their express expense. They fear that since they are on the lowest rung of the totem-pole in the factory, it will not be the Smith that will go but the Nowicki when room will have to be found for the Negro." Valuchek was surprised to find that the most fearful were the oldest, those who had migrated to the United States in their youth. "They wonder whether this is not the beginning of the end of our way of life. The ones who are concerned are those who fled because of the pogroms in their own homelands."[58]

Nixon followed through after the Goldwater campaign by denouncing criticism of the senator for leading the party to defeat, thereby making himself the beneficiary of the hard-pressed right. Under California Congressman Robert Wilson, New York investment banker Peter Flanigan, and Maurice Stans, Eisenhower's old budget director, three fund-raising committees were set up, fed by old reliable fat cats. They financed Nixon's own extensive activities and enabled him to expand his staff beyond Buchanan, who had remained the only full-timer on the payroll. Buchanan already had the assistance of New York public relations man William L. Safire.

Nixon's major achievement, however, was in mobilizing the party's wounded right and clearly establishing his differences with the old stop-Goldwater crowd. Moreover, their cause was consistent with the party's changing political base and the growing reaction against the New Deal welfare state.

Soon after the Goldwater defeat, for example, Senator Everett Dirksen, who understood the drift of things as well as any man, wrote to Nixon about the dominant concern with self-preservation. Americans felt their security threatened by inflation, unemployment, and fears about the soundness of Social Security. As Dirksen then added, "Disregard for law and order and for the property rights of others is a threat. An over burden of taxes is a threat, whether they are direct or indirect, whether they come in the form of a hike in Social Security taxes or in some other form."[59] The disruptions of social change and war, with the simultaneous threats to order and values, simplified Nixon's reconciliation with more conservative elements.

Further encouragement came from the continuation of an intellectual relationship with Russell Kirk, one of the key figures in the rebirth of American conservatism and Edmund Burke's foremost right-wing partisan. Five years younger than Nixon and the son of a railroad engineer in Michigan, Kirk had a basis for dialogue with Nixon. Less a free enterpriser than the politician, Kirk was essentially a moralist, holding that the safety of enduring societal values rested not with those who pursued mammon but with the preservation of structural relationships that were found in lower-middle-class families. His own home was far removed from large urban intellectual centers and in relative isolation at Mount Pleasant, Michigan, near his birthplace. His disdain for eastern intellectuals was based on disapproval of their role as shapers of contemporary American greed.[60]

The Nixon-Kirk contacts, which dated back to the vice presidential years, were revived through their shared views of student disorders and the administration's conduct of the war. They drew closer at the time Nixon became more active in that 1966 congressional campaign, and their relationship lasted through the years of Nixon's presidency. The two men exchanged writings and speeches on the drift of American society and the failure of liberal solutions. "No one knows what the future holds," wrote Nixon to Kirk in December of 1966, "but at least it is most gratifying to realize that whoever is the Republican nominee in 1968 will now have an even chance to win due to our increased strength across the country."[61]

Nixon's efforts included campaigning for Republicans in eighty-six congressional districts in thirty-five states, just as he went to bat for Wayne Dumont. Lyndon Johnson, recognizing the implications for Nixon's potential political resurrection, sneered that he was a "chronic campaigner."[62]

In a sense, Johnson was right. The Stassen of 1964 was still fighting for another life, but 1966 was different, his efforts more credible. There was no question about beating out any obvious front-runners for any nomination. Whatever others might suspect about his motives, they could not fault what he was doing for the party. Whether his work would turn out to be a case of enlightened self-interest was still uncertain. Moreover, he was still weighed down by the past, and his waltz around the stop-Goldwater fiasco had given him little reason for personal encouragement. Still, he remained the grind of old, succeeding in one way or another; if not by making the starting lineup, by rallying the team from the sidelines. The party was leaderless, and Richard Nixon emerged from 1966 far more acceptable than the group that he called the eastern Republican dividers.

His contributions included significant attention to the South. There, more than in any other part of the country, he became a true centrist. He delicately balanced sensitivity to traditional attitudes about black-white relationships with the interests of desegregation and compliance with federal law. He called for Republicans and Democrats to campaign on "issues of the future" instead of race. He advised against insisting on segregation while carefully signaling, as he had done before, not only his understanding of the South but his belief that civil rights was not confined to a single region. As he warned in a newspaper column, "Southern Republicans must not climb aboard the sinking ship of racial injustice."[63]

Still, in another sense, the "chronic campaigner" jab was a foolish overreaction by Johnson. Coming as it did during the weeks before the election, it helped elevate Nixon to greater prominence as chief critic of the administration's handling of the war. In line with Nixon's previous opposition to gradualism, his comments that fall expressed concern lest there be any reduction of military pressure to compel a favorable solution. His position was complex and understandably made him vulnerable to snide comments that old Tricky Dick was simultaneously courting hawks and doves. Why else call for an Asian conference to "solve this Asian war," as he did at the end of September, and couple that with some strong language about UN Ambassador Arthur Goldberg's offer to cease all bombing of North Vietnam in exchange for "assurances" of deescalation by the National Liberation Front?[64]

Nevertheless, there was nothing unique about Nixon's position. It was hardly novel for him to argue that withholding firepower based on mere promises "returns American diplomacy to the naive days of Yalta, Teheran and Potsdam, the days of the secret agreement based solely on the communist promise." Nor was it strange for Nixon to warn, as he had early in September, about an overcommitment of American forces. There had to be a way out, he was saying, either by force to exhaust the enemy or by a regional arrangement for peace, not by creating a situation that would place on "our hands a dependency for a generation to come." As the president prepared to go to Manila that October for a meeting with General Nguyen Van Thieu and Prime Minister Nguyen Cao Ky of South Vietnam, Nixon issued a statement urging Johnson to use the occasion as an opportunity to issue a Pacific charter to set forth a long-range program for peace and freedom in Asia.[65]

When Nixon and Bill Safire read the Johnson-Ky communiqué, they spotted a windfall. American and other allied troops would be withdrawn, it said, "as the military and subversive forces of North Vietnam are withdrawn, infiltration ceases and the level of violence thus subsides," and added that continued military action "must depend for its size and duration on the intensity and duration of the Communist aggression."[66]

Quickly, helped by Safire, Nixon seized on what he clearly understood as a soft-headed position. Without saying so precisely, the formula called for "mutual withdrawal." But mutual withdrawal for whom? By the United States and the National Liberation Front (based, of course, on good faith), not by the Vietcong, who would then be free to resume devastating South Vietnam, almost as though they had not been opposed from the start. Did it also signal an abandonment of a regional solution? Or would we simply have to respond all over again to an inevitable escalation of guerrilla warfare with an even greater commitment of manpower, matériel, and tax dollars?

That rebuke caught Johnson where it hurt and made him hopping mad, not only at Nixon but at the *New York Times* for running his critique. Johnson, according to Bill Moyers, "thought that Nixon was the most vulnerable man in American politics" and fired back with his "chronic campaigner" charge. If the point had not already been made, the president helped make it: the Republican former vice president was in charge of the opposition's fall election campaign. Nixon, placed by Johnson where he wanted to be, was delighted to respond that the "presidential temper" would certainly not keep him from speaking out on Vietnam.[67]

Most of all, what characterized Nixon's work was a vigorous denunciation of the Johnson brand of leadership, holding him responsible for botching the war effort, engineering a Great Society that created a bureaucratic nightmare with mounting inflation, and for what was quickly emerging as the administration's "credibility gap." Nixon was the powerful, effective spokesman, the voice of the party's future rather than its Landon-Willkie-Dewey-Eisenhower past. Statistical analyses of how well "his" congressional candidates succeeded showed that they were the ones who were the most likely to win, which helped to create the impression that their gains were also his. As he followed the election returns from the Drake Hotel on New York's Park Avenue, a friend who watched him reported that he was "like a kid who had won his first race for the state legislature," but, veteran that he was, he took the time to telephone his personal congratulations to each victorious Republican. Not unappreciated was the fact that he had helped to raise between $4 million and $5 million for the congressional elections.[68]

The next year's events only improved Republican prospects. Nineteen sixty-seven was perhaps the longest of the so-called long hot summers. Headlines told of repeated ghetto rioting, with the most violent outburst taking place in Detroit. Other smaller cities and towns were also affected:

Toledo, Grand Rapids, Nashville. The final death toll amounted to 225. Another 4,000 were wounded, and property damage totaled some $112 million. The research division of the Republican National Committee concluded that the summer riots had "starkly dramatized the fact that there is a major crisis in the cities of America," one that defied the billions spent by the ever-enlarging Washington bureaucracy on the problems confronting urban America.[69]

No single "devil" was responsible, as the Kerner Commission confirmed. Americans were, as usual, quick to spot the hand of the Kremlin in it all and far too preoccupied with the threat to order to absorb the sense of outrage in black communities, the frustration of helplessness and abandonment that contrasted so sharply with the extravagant expectations raised by Johnson and other reformers. Unrealistic hopes were also created by such militant competitors of Dr. King as H. Rap Brown, Malcolm X, and Stokely Carmichael, who called for black power while the urban underclass, lacking any hope, sank ever more deeply into social infirmity. In Boston, Kevin White barely warded off Mrs. Hicks by refusing to oppose her antibusing campaign. Political analyst Richard Scammon tracked the continuing demise of liberalism and added up Democratic voters for local Republican candidates in working-class districts. In a Gary, Indiana, white ethnic precinct that had a Croation Hall, the vote was over 90 percent Republican; the district had gone Democratic by two to one in 1964. Publisher Max Ascoli considered Johnson's plight and asked, "What has he done to make himself the object of such revulsion?" "The work of some of the extreme civil rights leadership has hurt us," wrote Louis Martin in an internal memorandum, "although I am certain that we still enjoy the majority support of the rank and file."[70]

The transition from civil disobedience to black power, the transition from movement to revolution, was plainly shredding established alliances. "The old Democratic coalition was being taken over by ideas that were not part of the coalition in the first place," explained Norman Podhoretz in accounting for the rightward shift of his *Commentary*. The "other" Norman, writer Mailer, noted a contrast between the 1963 march on Washington and the procession of antiwar protesters that crossed the Arlington Memorial Bridge in October of 1967. There, in the most dramatic protest assault, they sang and shouted, "Hey, hey, LBJ, how many kids did you kill today?" as they moved toward their objective, a massive sit-in at the Pentagon itself — described by Mailer as that "giant mudpie on the banks of America's Nile, our Potomac!" — to shut down the heart of the "war machine." This time, Mailer noticed, the studied politeness between the races that had belonged to the earlier solidarity was replaced by black militants acting defiantly and even contemptuously toward New Left whites.[71]

The antiwar movement was even harder to take on top of the black revolt. A mass demonstration had taken place in New York's Central Park that spring, with sixty young men burning draft cards and, only five days before the column of protesters moved across the Potomac, Stop the Draft Week was celebrated in Oakland, California, where radicals tried to shut down an army induction center. "A Call to Resist Illegitimate Authority" appeared in the form of a paid advertisement signed by 121 intellectuals who denounced the war on moral and legal grounds and pledged to oppose the fighting "in whatever ways may seem appropriate." As the administration clocked public opinion, it found little evidence that winning the war was thought less important, but there were increasing doubts about why Americans had to carry so much of the load. Within a year, President Johnson was told, the number of Americans who thought that the South Vietnamese should be given greater responsibility for fighting the war had risen by 15 percent.[72]

Nixon, maintaining his eminence in the mounting debate, deplored the trend toward isolationism. No nation had ever "sought to use its power to nobler purposes," he said in September 1967 at New York's Waldorf-Astoria, "but seldom has a nation been so mistrusted in its purposes or so frustrated in its efforts. . . . Increasingly, we are seen as an old nation in a new world." Moreover, it was clear that he was leading a party of opposition that was opposing the conduct of the war and not its purpose. As General Eisenhower had written to George Humphrey that spring, "An abject surrender might be welcomed by a few of the [William] Fulbrights, [Wayne] Morses, and members of the leftish sectors, but I believe it would outrage the vast majority of our citizens." It was not the war that was weakening us, Eisenhower added, as much as "the many unwise domestic programs" that were taking their "toll in money and individual self-reliance." House minority leader Gerald Ford asked in a major address that August, "Why are we pulling our best punches in Vietnam?"[73]

By that point, Nixon's concept of America's place in the global village was well advanced. "The Asian area is going to present some of our major foreign policy problems in the months and years immediately ahead," he had advised in 1965, "and any potential national candidate would strengthen his cause by getting some first hand knowledge of the area." And that was precisely what he continued to do by including Southeast Asia on his itinerary once more, this time as one of his four foreign study trips during the spring of 1967. Ray Price, a former editorial writer for the defunct *New York Herald Tribune* who joined the enlarged staff earlier that year, accompanied him to the Far East, and found that his boss had little need for the prepared briefings about various leaders he was about to meet in Japan, Formosa, South Vietnam, and India. "He knew the countries, knew the problems, and in most cases he already knew the leaders he was going to meet," but he kept pressing for more information. Unfailingly, whether with Prime Minister Eisaku Sato of Japan, Indira Gandhi in India, or Chiang Kai-shek, he found reaffirmation that the administration was merely fighting what he described as a "defensive war of attrition," when getting the upper hand was the real need. While American critics scoffed at the idea of "falling dominoes," Price later reported, "the dominoes themselves did not." Security for the region, that is, preserving the status quo for the noncommunist powers, was clearly up to the United States, the obvious bulwark against Chinese and Soviet ambitions.[74]

With tape recorder in hand, Nixon detailed both the minutiae and more substantial impressions of wherever he went and, traveling with Buchanan, he also reached Europe, Africa, and the Middle East. David Ben-Gurion touched a sympathetic nerve when he added the advice that it was time for the Americans to understand their self-interest by coming to terms with the People's Republic of China. Nixon had, by then, under-taken many such trips, since going overseas with the Herter Committee twenty years earlier. They naturally helped his credentials as a foreign policy spokesman; more important, however, he gained a firsthand un-derstanding of other leaders and an education that separated him from his relatively provincial beginnings. From one of his closer hangers-on, for example, Elmer Bobst, the vitamin king but also a missionary's son, Nixon heard much about the Asian continent. Len Garment, while work-ing with Nixon on the Hill case, was told by Bobst that "he and Nixon agreed that 'the most important thing' to be done in world affairs was to 'bring China into the world.' " Ray Price captured some of that sen-timent when he noted that "more than his critics, he did take those 'little brown people' seriously, as human begins, with the same feelings, the same worth, as the taller white people most Americans were comfortable with."[75]

Nixon was thus well prepared to be serious about making a genuine and well-thought-out run for the presidency. An opening shot came that summer when he faced the moneymen at the Bohemian Grove. He made the most of the opportunity created when he was asked to deliver the Lakeside Speech in honor of Herbert Hoover, who had died in 1964. Once again striking the note of peace within the context of international competition, he stressed the need for diplomacy and trade, but all with insistence on reciprocity.[76]

In October, *Foreign Affairs* published a major analysis by Nixon under the heading "Asia After Viet Nam." Nixon's theme was twofold, both prescient. The Vietnam experience, he warned, would encourage Amer-icans to pull inward, to reject future unilateral intervention to counter Communist insurrections elsewhere. A long-term consequence for Asia, however, related to the position of the People's Republic of China. Temporarily diverted from expansionist goals, the Peking government could no longer be ignored. The reality of its existence necessitated helping "to induce change" to encourage "a turning away from foreign adventuring and a turning inward toward the solution of its own domestic problems." In short, the sort of priority assigned to western Europe after World War II should be given to shoring up Asia. "Only as the nations of non-communist Asia become so strong — economically, politically and militarily — that they no longer furnish tempting targets for Chinese aggression, will the leaders in Peking be persuaded to turn their energies inward rather than outward. And that will be the time when the dialogue with mainland China can begin." There was also Nixon's admonition that "during this final third of the twentieth century, the great race will be between man and change: the race to control change, rather than be controlled by it. In this race we cannot afford to wait for others to act, and then merely react. And the race in Asia is already under way."[77]

But the climate demanded action rather than reflection. The Nixon statement contrasted with the rhetoric of political opportunism, which was attracted as much by the war at home as the battles in Asia and was most marked by a turnabout against the Johnson leadership. "We are directing our concern primarily to the middle-class suburbanites whose reactions could contribute a dangerously strong backlash sentiment," advised one White House memorandum, while even such Johnson stalwarts as Senator Robert Byrd of West Virginia were beginning to speak out openly against the president on civil rights. An immediate casualty was the War on Poverty, which, reported economist Robert Lekachman, "looks suspiciously like a Negro-aid program, and is therefore ripe for destruction." The whole question of race, centering on riots and equal rights, ranked far above any other among the popular concerns, according to data received by the administration. A prominent Virginia attorney and future associate justice of the Supreme Court, Lewis F. Powell, advised a newspaperman that "if civil disobedience is pressed, the ultimate results will either be anarchy or a form of repressive reaction which may be totalitarian in its consequences. In either event, minority groups and races will be those who suffer the most."[78]

A natural product of that climate was the transformation of Governor George Wallace of Alabama from a regional capitalizer of racial tensions into a symbol of resistance. Wallace, who had taken over the statehouse in Montgomery in 1963, was a sturdily built, pugnacious lawyer. He made his start as a loyal Democrat, even something of a liberal in Alabama; he held fast in 1948 when, at the party's national convention, Handy Ellis led the state's walkout against Harry Truman and the pro–civil rights platform. Peter Schrag, writing about the "new" Wallace, noted that a "man who can change from a progressive democrat into a bigot overnight deserves attention." The updated Wallace used the words "out-niggered" to explain why he lost his first gubernatorial race. He later denied ever using that expression, but whether or not he said it at the time, the point was made. No more softness on racial mixing. After he was elected in 1962, his acceptance speech was spiced with the vow of "Segregation now! Segregation tomorrow! Segregation forever!" The racial purity of the state's all-white educational system would be upheld even if he had to personally block "the schoolhouse door." The Wallace who really became a household name, however, was the Wallace who went through the motions of fulfilling that vow before television cameras in front of the University of Alabama. At the end, of course, as according to a script, he stepped aside and yielded to federal court orders and the Kennedy Justice Department. But that final act was off camera, and the governor scored his point as the tenacious battler for the little man.[79]

As the racial conflicts of the mid-sixties spread to the North, so did Wallace's message, touching a nerve that resonated with nonsouthern, working-class whites. "The great pointed heads who know best about how to run everybody's life have had their day," he told an interviewer, "and as a consequence the country's in a mess. My vote was only the tip of the iceberg." Or take, for example, the words that practically became Wallace's trademark: "I would have the Justice Department grab them by the hair — these intellectual morons, these professors, these students tearing up their draft cards, raising money and blood for the Viet Cong — and have them charged with treason, have them tried and put away. . . . We're at war. It doesn't matter whether Johnson has the legal right to send the troops over there." As to his strength, he had an easy explanation. "We got our biggest vote in sixty-four from organized labor," he said. "They're all concerned about crime and property rights. You take a working man, if he lives in a section where law and order break down, he can't just up and move like rich folks can."[80]

Writer Marshall Frady, trying to understand what was becoming the Wallace phenomenon, discovered during his travels through the country "the uneasy feeling that alienations, not only racial but also intellectual, have reached the point in our society where the potential for revolution is more palpable than ever before." And Wallace, Frady observed, was "the ultimate product of the democratic system," and one who represented "the dark side of the moon."[81]

He could no longer be written off as just another segregationist Dixiecrat. "The fact that in 1964 Wallace could come out of the South and find even 10 per cent support for his view, let alone 30 and 40 per cent, is in itself astonishing," said a White House memorandum to Johnson's trusted adviser Marvin Watson. Wallace had, in fact, done surprisingly well after entering three Democratic primaries outside the South; only

Goldwater's subsequent nomination by the Republicans has been credited with defusing his early northern spark. Even at that relatively early
stage in his national reputation, a Gallup survey showed that Wallace
had enough pulling power for a potential 3.5 million presidential votes.
The power of his southern base was confirmed soon afterward when he
was favored by four out of every five people in that region.[82]

It was also too simple to write off all his supporters as bigots. While
racism lingered on, the Jim Crow era was largely dead, killed by the
force of social change, proclaimed unlawful by a plethora of court decisions, and found appalling to the consciences of younger, better-
educated, and more global-minded Americans. For the first time in U.S.
history, it was possible to argue that a majority understood how blacks
were dehumanized, that — as President Kennedy reminded them when
he spoke to the nation on civil rights in June of 1963 — Negroes were
robbed of housing, life supports, political freedom, and longevity itself.
The great second world war had done much to increase such awareness.
Competition with the Soviet Union for propaganda influence with the
rest of the world had done much to disseminate the idea of racial equality
even among less well educated Americans. Critics of a two-tier citizenship
were given more ample reasons for revulsion when television showed
the brutality of southern diehards with their blatant disregard for human
rights. A poll commissioned by *Newsweek* confirmed that most Americans,
perhaps two-thirds, understood that blacks were the victims of the subjugation that contradicted the concept of democratic society. Seven out
of ten questioned even recognized some justification for black demands.[83]
Kennedy, for all his skepticism about being able to overcome the numerical power of the status quo, finally could not resist the demands for
justice.

Dismissing the reaction merely as racism was an oversimplification. If
anything, concluded a group of political scientists, "the drift of white
opinion had been . . . toward a more liberal stance, and hence can hardly
explain a vote which seemed to vibrate with 'backlash.' "[84] Americans
had come a long way since KKK night riders struck at will and everybody
laughed when the little golden girl, Shirley Temple, scolded coal-black
Stepin Fetchit.

When considered alongside such awareness, the rise of George Wallace
seems paradoxical. "*It is quite easy for millions of Americans to agree with him
without feeling particularly guilty about it,*" continued the message to Watson.
"Provided one doesn't delve too deep, *his is a very pragmatic philosophy.* . . . The publicity generated by Wallace, the reaction of extremists,
and the resulting distortion of important issues such as civil rights, Vietnam, and the War on Poverty, will place heavy pressure on the Democratic organizations at the state and national levels." In New Jersey,
Congressman Peter Frelinghuysen's press secretary, Carl Golden, took

an informal survey among the six hundred Republicans who attended a county committee finance dinner and was shocked to find the pro-Wallace support among young and ardent conservatives. Golden reported their view that "Nixon is not really a conservative" and that "Wallace's ideas are more to my liking." Gerald Ford, who was the main speaker at that dinner, later joked at the Gridiron Club that the 1964 Goldwater slogan "In Your Heart, You Know He's Right," was being updated by Wallace to read, "In Your Heart, You Know He's White." Most of all, such Republicans understood that Wallace was serious and so was his potential appeal. He might even force the presidential election into the House, where the existing numbers favored the Democrats. Calculating that thirty-one more GOP seats were needed to gain a majority in the lower chamber if that body were to select the next president, such key congressional Republicans as Melvin Laird of Wisconsin signaled the need to soften the anti-Rockefeller sentiment. All began to batten down the hatches against the backlash, that surge of anger against blacks for wantonly wasting all that "preferential treatment" from the government, while ordinary, hardworking white Americans, who had agreed that justice was long overdue, had borne the costs and were the victims of blatant disregard for law and order. By early 1968, Wallace showed up on Gallup's list of the most admired men in America, placing eighth, just behind Nixon and one ahead of Ronald Reagan.[85]

The situation was tantalizing as well as instructive. Wallace, it seemed, was both a populist and a right-wing extremist. The idea of Wallaceite populism had key support. He had, after all, blessed Alabama with extensive public works projects. Only Louisiana had more people involved in public welfare programs. Ex-governor Jim Folsom, Kissin' Jim, the legendary hero of the poor folks and an uncle of Wallace's second wife, pointed out that he related to Alabama's ordinary people in a way that "surpassed the fondest dreams of every liberal in the state."[86]

The populism part of Wallace suggests advocacy of the little man against society's leviathans. Populism and reformism, well established in the American experience, recall late nineteenth-century efforts to cut down the advantages of power, whether exercised by railroads, bankers, or other interests seeking to profit by exploiting the weak. The Populist party of 1892 championed the cause of debtors against the creditor classes. Their platform contained such declarations as "the power of government — in other words, of the people — should be expanded . . . as rapidly and as far as the good sense of an intelligent people and the teachings of experience shall justify, to the end that oppression, injustice, and poverty shall eventually cease in the land."[87] The formulations were clearly economic.

By that standard, Wallace was an improbable populist, but that definition had its ideological limitations. If one grants the non-Marxian

impulses of the American people, populism becomes no longer synonymous with economic justice but with demagoguery and primitivism,
simplistic and exploitative of resentments, expressing the anti-minority-
group rhetoric attractive to the perceived impotence of the little man,
once again that forgotten American.

So alarmed was T. Harry Williams, the Pulitzer Prize–winning biographer of the South's most famous populist, Huey Long, that he protested the invidiousness of such comparisons. "Wallace is a racist while
Huey Long rarely rode the racial issue," declared Williams; "he has no
vision of the economic order. The absorbing issue with him has been
race, and it was his exploiting of the race issue that elected him Governor
and made him overnight a Southern hero and a national figure. . . .
Huey Long offered a very different kind of politics."[88]

In his use of power, however, Wallace did resemble the Kingfish, as
well as an entire genre of picaresque southern politicians, from Pitchfork
Ben to Kissin' Jim. When confronted with the statutory prohibition
against running to succeed himself in 1966, he solved the problem by
installing his wife Lurleen as a blatant but loyal surrogate; he called the
shots and she signed the bills. Her death in May 1968 inconveniently
placed Lieutenant Governor Albert Brewer in Lurleen's chair, forcing
Wallace to fight to regain power in Montgomery while trying to establish
credibility as a figure who really belonged in Washington. "If I don't
win," he explained to friends, "them niggers are going to control this
state."[89]

His use of race, of course, made him most distinctive from Long. The
goal of Wallace populism fell far short of Long's proclaimed aim of
making "every man a king." He pursued regressive fiscal and labor
policies that left the poor of both races prey to Alabama's business elite.
Wallace's state, for example, was consistently among those that did the
least for the most helpless. A Midwest Research Institute quality-of-life
study showed Alabama near or at the bottom in the key indices of governmental service. Later, in 1975, the Southern Regional Council confirmed that Alabama's poor were taxed more heavily than any other
group. Sales taxes, inherently regressive at best, even extended to such
essentials as medicine and food. Governor Wallace refused to enact a
minimum wage law and blocked efforts to repeal a right-to-work statute
despite Alabama's continued slide beneath the national average in per
capita income. The people were further shortchanged by an educational
system that ranked forty-eighth in per pupil expenditures, and the percentage of those from the state drafted into the armed forces who failed
to pass the military mental tests continued to range in the upper forties.
The "center of gravity of Wallace popularity," as stated by the Survey
Research Center of the University of Michigan, "was clearly among white
skilled workers." Congressman Howard "Bo" Callaway, the Georgia con-

servative, was explicit: Wallace, said the party's future chairman, really belonged with the Republicans.[90]

That the segregationist White Citizens Councils and the Klan supported Wallace was not surprising. KKK leader Robert Shelton took full credit by saying, "We made him governor and we must make him President." The *Los Angeles Times* found Wallace's 1968 campaign permeated by the paramilitary Minutemen and the John Birch Society. Two years later, Wallace was the chief speaker at the society's New York Hilton banquet and wrote the lead article in the December 1970 issue of *American Opinion*, the official Birchite publication. Later, one writer for the *National Review* showed the ideological kinship between the governor and Mario Procaccino by writing that the "Wallace people know that the folks who, for the sake of 'business' stability, have slowly sold them out on social questions are the very ones who cry out over taxes, move to 'safe' school districts or send their children to private schools, and then vote Republican."[91]

"Most middle Americans think the Negro could have helped himself and didn't," wrote the authors of a book based on an issue devoted by *Newsweek* to "The Troubled American." *Newsweek* noted that "there is a pervasive feeling of being cheated by the affluent society." The plainest warning came from Eric Hoffer: "The common man is standing up and someday he's going to elect a policeman President of the United States."[92]

17

Resurrection

AT CHRISTMASTIME 1967, Richard Nixon, already a veteran of two forced retirements, announced to his family that he was serious about running. Pat, the "good sport" who gave her husband all he needed, went along as usual. Tricia and Julie agreed that the situation was very unlike 1964. Instead, as he had predicted after Goldwater's defeat, "the election will be like '60 — one of the closest in history."[1]

The Democratic opposition had torn itself apart. Senator Eugene McCarthy of Minnesota, convinced by dissidents to become the point man for the dump-Johnson movement, began innocuously enough; neither the press nor the country paid much attention. Suddenly, the band of rebels that composed his cadre found their campaign energized by a new turn in the war: what was actually a successful counterattack against the Vietcong translated, ironically, into political defeat for the administration. The combined force of the Tet offensive and McCarthy's upstaging of the president in the New Hampshire primary clinched Robert Kennedy's decision to declare his own candidacy. Nixon predicted that Bobby's entry would further charge up the political atmosphere and might even spur the growing volume of violence at home. By the end of March, a sense of futility about what he could do in Vietnam led to LBJ's dramatic decision not to run for another term. Nineteen sixty-eight, in the words of more than one commentator, marked "the end of innocence — the death of hope." Reporting from his vantage point on Long Island as publisher of *Newsday,* Bill Moyers wrote to Johnson's press secretary, "It is intriguing that when we lose votes, we lose them to Republicans, not to Kennedy."[2]

The events of that spring were but a prelude for what was yet to come; still, at the time, they were so tumultuous as to overwhelm the implications of the president's surprise decision. In April, Martin Luther King,

Jr., was murdered in Memphis, where he had gone to support a strike by that city's black sanitation workers. Violence led to more violence and more ghettos aflame. Frustrated and angry blacks lashed back by torching their own neighborhoods and looting white-owned stores. In Chicago, Mayor Richard Daley gave his famous "shoot to kill" order.

Then, in early June came more shock, more confusion and agony. Robert Kennedy thanked his campaign workers for helping him win the California primary and walked directly into the path of Sirhan Sirhan's bullet. Eugene McCarthy was so shaken that he told Hubert Humphrey he had no appetite to go on with his role; from that point on, his candidacy was perfunctory, a desultory sleepwalk that frustrated his followers.[3]

McCarthy's pro forma status was in direct contrast to the vice president's problems. After expressing his misgivings about the war to Lyndon Johnson at the start of Operation ROLLING THUNDER, Humphrey found his own efforts carefully monitored by the president. That period was, in fact, but a continuation of a most painful vice presidency. Johnson was none to subtle about the possibility of getting back into the race, or, at the very least, holding back from Humphrey the $600,000 available in his special fund if his heir apparent waffled on supporting the administration's prowar policy.[4]

What happened on the streets of Chicago during the Democratic convention in August, however, hurt Humphrey much more. Antiwar demonstrators, bent on making a mockery of the system, created their own battleground outside the convention hall. Mayor Daley's police, all too eager to express their own hatred of privileged antiwar, antiflag, antisociety college students, turned the challenge into their own version of class warfare.

In a time of rising crime and political dissension, no group carried as much pent-up anger as did the police. In trying to fulfill society's demand to emphasize law and order, they too often found themselves among the victims. They faced constant danger with few rewards, and their resentment had been building for some time. They heard themselves called pigs and even worse by upper-middle-class men and women with lifestyles the police saw as an affront to God and country. Baited in the streets of Chicago by the very symbols they found most infuriating — desecration of the flag, blatant and sometimes provocative sexuality by college-age women, feces and urine thrown at them from windows — they disregarded professional restraints and struck back with frightening, indiscriminate violence. A special commission later termed their behavior a "police riot." "Damned if you do, damned if you don't," was the comment of a veteran cop. The attorney general of the United States, Ramsey Clark, acknowledged the unfairness of placing those men where they alone had to cope with everybody else's conflicting furies. "What was worse, in the eyes of many police," historian David Farber has written, "was that it seemed almost like there was a conspiracy between the mass media and the rioters, protesters, and other agitators." Too many liberals had misplaced compassion. The *Chicago Tribune* undoubtedly spoke for most Americans by editorializing that "the blame must be placed on those who have been preaching anarchy, letting people think they can violate laws which they think are wrong. . . . It is impossible to believe that wholesale arson, gunfire, and looting are spontaneous, unorganized, undirected or unprepared."[5]

The antiwar Democrats within the convention hall, noting the street fighting, interrupted their attack against the pro-Humphrey, prowar forces. Senator Abraham Ribicoff of Connecticut stepped to the podium and denounced what was happening to "our children" on the streets. Mayor Daley, in full view of the television audience, spoke his piece from a balcony, shouting obscenities that could easily be lip-read across America. Liberals were, at that moment, so out of touch with their own country that they were ill prepared to understand that the overwhelming majority of Americans were cheering for the Chicago police. What hurt most was the revulsion against the demonstrators among traditional Democrats, workers and ethnic Catholics, who closed ranks behind Daley. The networks and the protesters were the villains, a development that made a significant contribution to popular perceptions of just how "liberal" the media had become.[6]

Yet, in the fight for the nomination, starting with the New Hampshire primary in March, George Romney and not Nixon was the man who suffered most from the press, a victim of his own careless language. Nixon labored under the charge that a two-time loser could not possibly win, but he managed to avoid being placed on the defensive. He kept his footing with the press even as their questions became cagier. As the nation sank that much more deeply into Vietnam and the war dominated the campaign, contending with the media, as Romney learned, became even trickier. As journalist Jules Witcover has written, "If there was press irresponsibility in 1967 and 1968, it existed just as much in giving Nixon a free ride on Vietnam as it did in hounding Romney to political defeat on the same issue."[7]

Public opinion succumbed to two inaccuracies. The first was that Eugene McCarthy's strong showing was a referendum on the peace issue. The second was that Nixon, in direct response to the antiwar sentiment, claimed to have a "secret plan" to end the fighting. Both needed to be clarified.

Misleading campaign rhetoric is hardly unusual. Moreover, Vietnam was, in early 1968, a highly charged subject. Reports solicited by the White House from Democratic state chairmen were almost uniformly gloomy. Many voters who had gone for JFK and then backed LBJ threatened to defect. At the same time, in apparent contradiction to the mood, reports that reached Washington showed only a minority were dovish. John Bailey of Connecticut, for example, as savvy a politician as the Democrats had, advised that all New England states seemed to be in good shape. Oliver Quayle, Johnson's pollster, gauged the frustration that was aroused not only by the enemy's New Year's (Tet) offensive but, in addition, the recent seizure by the North Korean Communists of the U.S.S. *Pueblo*. Quayle urged the administration to make the New Hampshire election a referendum over "whether or not Americans want a policy of appeasement and backing down in Vietnam." The White House advisory to the state's Democrats accordingly highlighted the warning that "Hanoi is listening" to gauge their lack of resolve.[8] The McCarthy vote, as noted before, resulted more from frustration over not winning and despair that the administration did not seem to know how to bring the war to a satisfactory conclusion.

Few presidents have felt as embattled as did LBJ that spring. He turned to Chalmers Roberts of the *Washington Post* and said, "The only difference between the Kennedy assassination and mine is that I am alive and it has been more torturous. . . . The press can bring a man to his knees in a moment but you can't bring me to my knees because I don't depend on you anymore." Just before Johnson's group of wise men convened to ponder what should be done about the war and General William C. Westmoreland's request for additional troops, one of the capital's most seasoned and sophisticated advisers to presidents, James Rowe, warned the president that he needed to do something about Vietnam before the next primary, the big one in Wisconsin. "McCarthy and Kennedy are the candidates of peace and the President is the war candidate," Rowe emphasized. He explained that he was "shocked" by how the White House switchboard was being swamped by the large number of callers protesting the administration's continued justification of pursuing the war. "I have said to you before," Rowe went on, "that the Tet offensive by the Viet Cong is the cause of all this, including the popularity of McCarthy and the entry of Kennedy. . . . There are more hawks and many more doves. . . . McCarthy and Kennedy are the creatures, the symptom and not the cause of the Tet offensive."[9]

Rowe was, of course, right about one essential point: the country was becoming more polarized; but the bitterness of the antiwar reaction had been a long time in coming, and it was easy to misread the mood. The more articulate, the well-connected, the ones with easier access to the nation's communications system, had the best means of getting the message out, and they wanted to believe that the good Democrats of New Hampshire had also come to their senses. The oversimplification of the McCarthy vote became the wrong message. One might argue that much of the national media fell into the trap and turned the "message" into an extravagant example of raised expectations.

It was certainly true about the reports that Nixon had tried to sway the primary by saying he had a "secret plan" to end the war. Clearly, that was another pitfall, and he fell into it much as Harry Truman had taken a reporter's bait by agreeing that, yes, the intervention in Korea might be termed a "police action." Amid the political competition and continuing war-weariness, there was an understandable push among the rival candidates to convince the public that they had some specific solutions. In mid-January, Romney told an audience at Keene State College that he had a plan for a "guaranteed neutralization" of the entire region. The audience gave him a rousing reception, providing a much-needed boost to his confidence, after he explained that the plan involved an "internal settlement" between the National Liberation Front and Saigon.[10]

The potential political mileage of proposed solutions was questionable. In a letter to General Eisenhower in mid-March, Nixon emphasized the importance of avoiding statements that "would in any way restrict the negotiating flexibility" if "we should have the responsibility of leadership in January."[11] By the time these words were written, however, the candidate had already created a new controversy.

Nixon can be blamed for being suggestive. A young lady who heard him while she was a college student bitterly recalled his evasiveness. She sat in the Memorial Building of the University of New Hampshire and listened to him respond to a question about how he would end the war by simply saying, "I'm not telling yet." A memorandum in the files of the Republican National Committee acknowledges that "he did indicate that he had definite ideas on what was needed to end the war, and that the actual Nixon plan was Vietnamization." This version attributes the "secret plan" claim to an unguarded comment made informally before a small group of reporters. Someone put words in his mouth, and he may have swallowed them. The document in the RNC files, which was designed as a guide for handling the controversy, suggests that one reporter "allegedly" asked, "Mr. Nixon, do you have a secret plan to end the war?" Impulsively, the candidate responded, "Yes, I have *a plan* to end the war," without bothering to make a distinction between "a plan" and "a secret plan."[12] What all the stories have in common is evidence of Nixon's desire to demonstrate that he *did* know what to do about Southeast Asia.

That was true. He had been dropping hints all along. "There was a plan," Nixon has recalled; "it was not secret. Instead of reading my lips, you read my record. I had strongly supported stronger military action, including the mining of the harbor at Haiphong. I had made militant speeches on that. I was doing that in part because Eisenhower, while publicly supporting the president, once told me, 'If I have an enemy on the hill with one battalion, you give me two battalions and I can take that hill but I'll take a lot of casualties. You give me a division, I'll take it without a fight.' " Nixon shared Eisenhower's disdain for Johnson's "gradualism" and had made that position plain. He was on record for stronger military action in order to have a better bargaining position, which was part of a "troika" that also included diplomacy and "Vietnamization." That meant, as Nixon described it in many speeches, "unlike the U.S. role in Korea and then in Vietnam, we furnished the arms, we furnished the aid and most of the men; in the future, we should furnish the arms, we should furnish the aid, but they must furnish most of the men. That was Vietnamization."[13]

All this and more was on his mind during a long day devoted to campaigning on the fifth of March, a day that included a swing through several New Hampshire towns and did not end until he flew to Washington for a fund-raising dinner. He told the well-heeled Republicans about the need to keep up military pressure.[14]

When he began that day at a campaign stop in Hampton, Nixon was especially precise. "I say that the American people will be justified in electing new leadership, and I pledge to you that new leadership will end the war and *win the peace in the Pacific*," he told the crowd.[15]

One hardly needed to read between the lines to note the stress on a regional solution, or to have been especially insightful to realize his concern about Communist China. Nixon, even then, as he explained twenty years later, was convinced that "you couldn't have peace in the Pacific without China participating. I was thinking of China not just with regard to Vietnam, but China with regard to Indonesia. At that time, China was in its aggressive state; we thought so, although it had changed substantially. So I felt it very important to develop a relationship with China. The Chinese were still playing the senior partnership role."[16]

Saying that he claimed to have a secret plan to end the war was stretching a point. He also denied that he had in mind a "pushbutton technique" or that his words implied "withdrawal from Vietnam." He even made the none-too-mysterious suggestion that an end could be achieved by mobilizing "our economic, political and diplomatic leadership." In Washington that evening in March of 1968, he repeated the need to keep up military pressure but again emphasized his belief that Johnson had neglected diplomatic and political means.[17]

That he never *said* he had a secret plan, as was thereafter widely repeated, is absolutely clear. That allegation was first put on the wires by an overeager UPI staffer from the agency's Boston office. Although the words were reported without quotes, the distinction was quickly lost. Romney supporters pounced on Nixon to "come clean" with just what he had in mind, thereby helping to establish as a fact that Nixon had used the controversial phrase. Nelson Rockefeller said that Nixon had blundered by not disclosing exactly what he had in mind. It must have been with considerable relish that the governor "wondered" how Nixon could keep his "peace plan" to himself "while hundreds of Americans die each week in Vietnam." A hunt for the alleged phrase was then made by reporters and television researchers who later confirmed the report was false.[18]

The episode was exasperating. Especially hurtful was the presumption of irresponsibility. He decided that he would no longer make any specific or individual criticisms of the president. If he had a "magic formula" or "a gimmick," he told the Associated Press, "I would tell Lyndon Johnson." Nixon's friend George Smathers advised the White House that "he will be talking against the Democratic Party and against certain programs and what he considers to be failings of the Party and its programs."[19] Nixon retreated to more cautious ground.

While critics kept carping, Nixon and his writers scheduled a radio network speech for March 31. Finally, they would have their answer. A three-pronged strategy was about to be spelled out. "We had the speech all ready, but Johnson pulled the plug on us," Nixon later explained. As Safire puts it, Johnson "dropped his bomb" by announcing a bombing halt and startling the public with the statement that he would not be a candidate to succeed himself. "And then," as Nixon recalls, "my hands were tied. It wasn't that I was being such a great statesman. That was part of it. But another reason was that I thought it would be politically bad to do so, politically bad to be trying to talk about a different plan when Johnson's people were negotiating in Paris." Nixon maintained that position through the remaining primaries and until the election in November, disposing of Vietnam as a partisan political issue.[20]

Eisenhower followed every move from his bed at Walter Reed Army Hospital and applauded. One week before Americans voted, he sent Nixon the following list of what needed to be done: "unite the country and bring the social betterments that are so badly needed; deal with dissension and lawlessness at home, while effectively getting at their root causes; cope with the problems abroad, including Vietnam; and change the ingrained power structure of the Federal Government (the heritage of years of Democratic rule), placing more responsibility at State and local levels."[21]

The Republican convention in Miami Beach was marked by political infighting. The tension came from maneuvering by Ronald Reagan's forces, hoping to convert the California governor's last-minute declared candidacy into victory if, with the assistance of Nelson Rockefeller's own ambitions, Nixon could be kept from winning on the first ballot. The two great extremes of the Republican party, apart as much politically as geographically, were devising an ideological standoff that could deny Nixon his majority. Rockefeller had withdrawn from contention in March but little over a month later changed his mind; he arrived in Florida hoping to sway delegates who had denounced him in San Francisco four years earlier. Nixon, needing the Republican center, had counted on George Romney to help keep the others at bay. Ironically, Rockefeller also banked on Romney, considering him the best bet to block Nixon. But Reagan had suddenly become the real threat, mustering heavy support from southern delegates and a wide range of old Goldwater fans, including Phyllis Schlafly, William Rusher, and Jeane Dixon, whose ESP told her that Strom Thurmond was destined to be the one to install the former actor in the White House.[22] She pegged Thurmond right but tied him to the wrong man. Nixon, who had swamped the opposition in the New Hampshire and Wisconsin primaries, blocked the developing pro-Reagan tide and made it on the first ballot. Not by much, however — a plurality of 51 out of the 1,333 votes recorded.

Nixon's acceptance speech, although pitched heavily at the law-and-order issue, also provided a blueprint for the coming administration that was far more prophetic than anyone realized. He declared that he represented the "forgotten Americans — the non-shouters, the non-demonstrators," the dynamos of the "American dream," working together to carry forth the "greatest engine of progress ever developed in the history of man — American private enterprise." He also declared that his goal was "justice for every American" while denying that "law and order is the code word for racism."[23]

By naming Governor Spiro Agnew of Maryland to round out the ticket, Nixon signaled his determination to redirect the course of the Republican party. Agnew, who was instrumental in making Nixon's own nomination possible, was a fortunate choice in some surprising ways. For one, he suited the Nixon instinct for grabbing attention by making the "big play." He also met Nixon's multiple requirements. Steve Hess has noted that "if you put all the conflicting Republican elements into a computer, and programmed it to produce a Vice-President who would do least harm to party unity, the tape would be punched SPIRO T. AGNEW." Only with Agnew's help could Nixon reshape the GOP by bringing together northern moderates with rightward-leaning southerners, many themselves refugees from the Democratic party. Only Agnew, it was assumed, could mollify traditionalists from the urban areas of the North along with such people as Harry Dent, South Carolina's Republican chairman, who acknowledged that "we were concerned about the consequences to Thurmond if Nixon won and proved to be anti-South and liberal like LBJ." The fears of the South Carolinian were not eased by the many warnings he heard at Miami about "Tricky Dick."[24]

Agnew's background belonged to a conventional New Deal Democrat. Born in 1918, he came of age during the Great Depression. His father, a poor immigrant, made his way through the American world by becoming a restaurateur. The son pushed on, studied law, and abandoned Greek Orthodoxy for Episcopalianism. Young Spiro — known to his friends as Ted (his middle name was Theodore) — took the next step toward assimilation by changing his political affiliation. Getting elected as chief executive of Baltimore County was a perfect springboard toward the governorship of Maryland, an office he won during that backlash year of 1966, when race was at least an implied factor in just about every political dialogue.

In contrast with what went on elsewhere, he came out of that campaign perceived as a moderate, even a progressive who advocated open housing and equalized welfare payments. When he took over Maryland's statehouse, the American Conservative Union called Agnew a "liberal," a view that was not confined to the far right.[25] As far as most Republicans were concerned, Agnew reaffirmed that judgment when he then latched on to Nelson Rockefeller — of all people — and, both publicly and privately, urged him to fight for the party's nomination.

The other "finalists" included Governor John Volpe of Massachusetts and Howard Baker of Tennessee. "For the North," as one southerner then said, "it was Volpe. For the South, it was Baker. Nobody looked hard at Agnew. We were all looking higher and lower." People saw what they wanted. Baker served in the Senate from Tennessee and was the son-in-law of the powerful Everett Dirksen. His political identification was acceptably southern and his philosophical bent conservative, not an attractive package for northern Republicans who were still skeptical about dealing with Nixon. Geographically and ideologically, Volpe had little on his side save his Italian heritage. White House counselor Leonard Garment has remarked that Nixon was attracted to such "foreign ethnic types." Three years earlier, Nixon had seemed to advise Volpe to prepare for bigger things to come when he suggested that he broaden his background by finding out more at first hand about Asia rather than taking still another trip to Europe.[26] Italians, who were at this time rushing toward Republicanism, were especially valuable because of their concentration in states with significant numbers of electoral votes.

The way in which Agnew came to be chosen demonstrates Nixon's careful winnowing process. Advisers were brought together in a series of meetings designed to generate and review lists of candidates who were then discarded as politically undesirable, enabling Nixon's predetermined choice to rise to the top. The methodology was as complex as it was cunning, leaving Nixon with the rationale to do exactly what he wanted. It also served several other purposes. It shielded the presidential candidate from what was essentially *his* personal decision for *his* running mate and established the aura of a party consensus. And by considering many candidates, it flattered their egos, making them more willing to coalesce behind the final choice. The also-rans included Representative George Bush, a Texas Republican, and senators Robert Griffin and John Tower. Within the councils of the advisers, only Oregon senator Mark Hatfield, New York mayor John Lindsay, and Nelson Rockefeller were anathema.[27] All in all, some fifty potential running mates were used in that connection.

The name of William Scranton, the retired governor of Pennsylvania and the veteran of the stop-Goldwater movement, was included to keep him out of Rockefeller's arms. Nixon asked Walter Annenberg to broach the idea to Scranton, who now recalls that the overture was haphazard. Restless and eager to circulate throughout the convention hall, he left his seat and got some exercise by "walking around in everybody's parade. Walter had a box which was for people who were not delegates. He stopped me and we began chatting. He made the proposition to me," one that left no doubt that he was talking for Nixon. But Scranton was firm, and predictable; he repeated his vow not to return to politics after leaving the governorship in 1966.[28]

Not even Hugh Scott, the most powerful Pennsylvanian on Capitol Hill and a Republican from Philadelphia, knew about the Scranton "offer." But Scott did remember that Nixon pursued the ex-governor in other ways. He recalled that Nixon told him he had "offered him anything he wanted — secretary of state, Court of St. James's; anything he wanted, I told him he could have. He didn't want anything."[29] He did, after the election, accept an assignment from Nixon as his special emissary to the Middle East and later chaired the President's Commission on Campus Unrest.

A name that emerged from a deliberative group was Nixon's old side-kick Bob Finch, then California's lieutenant governor. From second in command in Sacramento to understudy in Washington would be quite a jump, a stretch of credibility that Finch himself acknowledged. Not only that but, as he has also pointed out, pairing him with Nixon, despite his friend's move to New York, would have created a constitutional anomaly at least in spirit by asking the electors to select two Californians. Finch, always the loyal helpmate, then deferred to Rogers C. B. Morton. A Kentuckian by birth who had become a Maryland congressman, Morton at least came from an appropriate state, Agnew's, which was one step closer to reality. Morton then displayed modesty by saying that his credibility would not be as great as Finch's.[30]

Nixon kept to himself while most of the early maneuvering was going on. He hid away on Montauk Point, on Long Island's eastern end, to rest and work on his acceptance speech. Meanwhile, he and all who spoke for him stuck to the vow that his running mate would be acceptable to all regions of the country, a statement that, by its very nature, gave the rebellious, pro-Reagan South the greatest veto power.

Nevertheless, all his preparations and rounds of meetings with advisers and politicos, especially from the South, still left the matter of choosing a vice president agonizing, and there is no doubt that he struggled over the question before making his decision. Nor should one assume that it was made while ignoring the power of George Wallace.[31]

Paradoxically, the argument has also been made that Nixon expected that he was getting a moderate by going for Agnew. Nixon himself has advanced that idea, stating that Agnew was placed on the ticket because he was acceptable to that wing of the party. He has also minimized the selection's connection as part of a border states strategy, although he notes with satisfaction that he "won the right part of the South." Others have suggested that Nixon was actually misled by Agnew's reputation.[32] However, even if one were to grant that he was deceived, the analysis would have to assume the unlikely scenario that that was one time Nixon's advance work was sloppy.

In fact, Agnew's reputation for moderation had vanished long before. Right after Martin Luther King's assassination that spring, the governor, a big man who read little and set his political compass by his instincts, faced down some one hundred middle-class black leaders from Baltimore by suggesting that they shared responsibility for the city's riots. Agnew assumed that the uprising was an organized revolt and that they, the minority leaders, should have foreseen the situation. The black power militant Stokely Carmichael had visited Baltimore only a few days earlier, so the notion of a conspiracy did not seem completely farfetched. But lack of evidence did not stop Agnew. He dressed them down, a white man lecturing to black elites about how *they* had failed. They were appalled; about eighty walked out. One of them even decided that Agnew was "as sick as any bigot in America."[33]

Agnew's apparent conversion did not stop there. He denounced the Kerner Commission report's concern about continuing black-white tensions as the voice of "white racism" and, in other ways, displayed the kind of hostility toward minorities that was common among members of the white working class who, like the Chicago police, felt their interests were being sacrificed for the sake of social change.

Clearly, none of this shook Nixon's faith in Agnew as a moderate. His responses as Maryland's governor were not those of an extremist or a hard-liner but justifiable instances of leadership in the face of violence and the breakdown of law and order. "I was impressed by the fact that he was named as a progressive governor," Nixon has recalled. "Frankly,

I would have agreed with him on throwing some of these people out of his office [*sic*]. I think it was the only thing he could do. I didn't pick him because he was a nut on the right."[34]

Thus when Nixon designated "Spiro Who?" that August, it was because Agnew was a border state governor whose presence would help sway those vital electoral votes; and he was acceptable to South Carolina senator J. Strom Thurmond, who extracted a high price for helping deliver Dixie to Nixon rather than Reagan. In addition, Agnew had stood up for law and order, which, as Nixon guessed, would play as well in the North as in the South.

Nixon had first connected with Agnew some four months before the convention, at a moment when he was most available. He had just been effectively snubbed by Rockefeller, a public relations disaster made possible by his own bravado. Agnew's arrogance and insensitivity encouraged him to have far more faith than was actually warranted about the New Yorker's wanting to become a candidate. Acting with little more than wishful thinking, Agnew, who expected to play a major role in Rockefeller's campaign, invited a dozen reporters into his office to watch a press conference at which the governor would presumably tell the world about his desire to become president.

What happened next was mortifying, certainly an oversight by the Lord of BOMFOG, and demolished Agnew's immediate standing. When the New Yorker appeared on the screen that March 21, his words contained an unequivocal declaration of his noncandidacy. Party leaders, he explained, were turning to Nixon.[35] Made aware that Agnew had been humiliated, Rockefeller tried to patch it up. But it was left to Nixon to mollify the wounded governor.

Two of Nixon's people grabbed the chance to bring them together. For some two hours, only days after the Agnew embarrassment, Agnew and Nixon had a get-acquainted session at his office at 20 Broad Street. Nixon liked what he saw. He was usually taken by self-confidence, and he decided that the governor was a man of strength. Agnew was also impressive for the way he had worked his way up from his immigrant background. That he happened also to come from Maryland made him even more attractive. Nixon recalls that Agnew expressed a vague interest in a future nomination to the Supreme Court.[36]

Pat Buchanan, no lover of liberals or moderates, kept his boss up to date about the governor's activities, and Nixon followed through in a number of ways: phone calls, consultations for advice, contacts utilizing a variety of handy excuses. In early May, newspaper reports included Agnew on Nixon's list of potential running mates. According to a Nixon aide, his mind was pretty much made up by June. It was not like Nixon, he added, "to go down to the convention and wait until the night before to have in mind who he wanted as Vice President." He arrived at Miami

Beach, in other words, with ace-in-hand when he reassured anxious southerners that they would not be upset.[37]

The consultants, who met in various rooms of the Hilton Hotel, were part of an elaborate camouflage. "Frankly," said one, "I knew he didn't want any of us. Why not call Agnew? But we went on with the charade." Nixon had not only decided on Agnew, but the governor's shadow hovered over a more extensive deal. At a meeting with southern leaders, Nixon settled what was, in effect, their separation from the man who was his most dangerous obstacle to the party's nomination, Ronald Reagan. To this day, William Rusher insists that Reagan could have been a winner. "Many were sincerely convinced that Nixon, though not as conservative as Reagan, was conservative 'enough' — whatever that might mean," the *National Review* publisher has written. "The nomination of Richard Nixon that year was the work of conservatives who — let me say it, sadly and perhaps a little bitterly — ought to have known better." If only they had held out, a number of conservatives continue to insist, the country would have had Reagan in 1969 rather than being forced to wait until 1981.[38]

Grass-roots enthusiasm, real and potential delegate strength, and the enticements of his closest backers brought Reagan into the picture. The California governor announced his availability after the Republicans had gathered in Miami Beach. As the imminence of Nixon's nomination closed in, and the talk that he was a loser, an untrustworthy Tricky Dick, hovered, the desperate right turned toward the man whose election as California's governor produced a new hope. Just as Nixon seemed to have clinched the prize, a rush to Reagan among southerners had ominous possibilities for Nixon's hoped-for first-ballot victory. Potentially, the delegates were far more Reagan's than Nixon's or Rockefeller's. Only Nixon's stronger national standing prevented a massive defection, and that support was constantly on the verge of cracking.[39] Failure to wrap it up on the first ballot could well be fatal, sending off signals of weakness that would drive delegates toward someone more attractive.

Nixon later found it hard to forgive Reagan for that move at Miami. He had long had reason to believe in the governor's noncandidacy. Various accounts have Reagan assuring both Nixon and Goldwater during the summer of 1967 that he intended to stay out of the race unless Nixon "stumbled." Yet, throughout the country, not only in the South, Reagan's strength was becoming more compelling. An associate of Leonard Garment, a man who managed Congressman Peter Frelinghuysen's campaigns and served as the New Jerseyite's eyes and ears, returned from a New England vacation and reported that "the biggest interest . . . growing almost like a prarie [*sic*] fire, is in Ronald Reagan. Not one thing about him being an actor, or being a Right-Winger. . . . Just that he seems to have done a fine job as Governor of California, that he is not a 'nut,' and most of all, that he is tremendously appealing. I was amazed at the depth and breadth of deep, serious interest in Reagan."[40]

One incident that particularly upset southerners was a leak by Herb Klein designed to keep liberals in line, suggesting that Mayor Lindsay and Mark Hatfield were being considered for the number-two spot. Nevertheless, most delegates held fast, especially after a group of Republicans from Louisiana and Georgia were assured that the *Miami Herald* story about Hatfield was a plant. Its author, confronted with his published claim, refused Dent's challenge of a three-hundred-dollar bet that he was wrong. Nixon has since recalled that "it was close" on naming Lindsay, but "we found that that wouldn't fly."[41]

Before even contending with competition from George Wallace, Nixon had to stem the rush toward Reagan. In the face of that surge, Nixon had no choice except to assure southern committeemen that he understood their view on civil rights. He did not intend to retreat from his support of the Supreme Court's 1954 desegregation decision, but southerners' aversion to busing for desegregating schools was another matter. They were assured about his conviction that forced busing had serious implications for the entire country. Pragmatically, he also met Thurmond's concerns about South Carolina's cotton industry, accepting the need for protection against textiles from Japan and other countries. Southerners, as they reiterated during a meeting in an Atlanta motel on the last day of May, were also concerned about defense. That meant backing the controversial antiballistic missile system, not only to provide assurances against the Russian bear but also to keep the wolf from the door. In addition, although Agnew was not mentioned by name, Nixon reemphasized his pledge that the South would not be disappointed in his choice of a running mate. It was relatively simple: they would have to take his word but, more than that, recognize that he, unlike Reagan, had the national support to win. That was also enough reason to pull Thurmond away from Reagan.[42]

At that Atlanta meeting, in an act of trust, and ratification of the understanding, Thurmond handed Nixon a small piece of paper containing three lists. One, showing the acceptables among potential vice presidential nominees, included the names of Reagan, Tower, Bush, Baker, Griffin, and Morton. Notably Agnew was in the second category, the one to which there were "no objections." Unacceptables were in the third column: Hatfield, Lindsay, and Rockefeller. Not only can it not be said that Thurmond dictated the choice, but it also becomes obvious that Agnew had not yet wormed his way into the heart of the South's leading unreconstructed power broker. Nixon, who recalls that he and John Mitchell decided to go with him, also maintains that Agnew "was not a closet Wallaceite, no way." So the southern strategy for 1968 was secured, insuring Nixon's first-ballot victory and preventing Reagan support from forcing a knock-down battle and a badly divided party.[43]

What reservations conservatives had about Agnew were, ironically, dissolved when liberal Republicans turned on Nixon's choice. Their revolt was rather perfunctory but long enough to delay his acceptance speech. A band of liberals headed by Senator Charles Goodell of New York claimed the support of 450 delegates, a figure that was never borne out. The dissidents, moreover, were far from unified. The one man who could have brought them together was Mayor Lindsay. But New York's liberal Republican mayor had his eyes on the 1972 convention. He withdrew his own name and went to the platform to second the Agnew nomination. But if conservatives had any doubts about Nixon's choice, the liberal revolt put them at ease.[44]

The nomination of Agnew secured, Nixon spoke informally before a joint session of the RNC and the party's finance committee. He explained that Agnew had become his choice only after rejecting an imposing list of far more prominent Republicans. The future president told them that he "wanted a man who could be President of the United States, who had the brains, who had the guts, who had the poise under pressure, so that if he ever sat there in that oval office, and an awesome decision had to be made, I would feel that here is a man I had confidence in." And then: "He is not known, nobody knows Spiro Agnew across the country, but they will. . . . He has got quality, class, poise under pressure. . . . Here is a man who has all the capability, intelligence, the strength, that America [is looking for], in this critical period when people are worried, wondering, looking for a sense of stability, but where they are also concerned about progress."[45]

By building on the process that had gone before, stretching all the way from the Dixiecrat revolt against Truman in 1948, to the "Eisencrats" of the 1950s, and the powerful support given by the region to Goldwater in 1964, Nixon's campaign represented a coming of age. Thirty-six years after Roosevelt's first election, the elements of a watershed were in place. To call it merely a southern strategy, however, misses the point. The big difference between Nixon in 1968 and his predecessors was that his was a *national* agenda that seized on a great dividing point of postwar American politics.

Out of power, the Republican party had little choice but to settle for Nixon. No one put it more bitterly than Garry Wills, then writing for the conservative *National Review*: "The Party had not undergone any great internal convulsion. It had simply caved, sifted and crumbled in upon its center, and the name of the resulting sandpile was Nixon."[46]

Such was the lamentation about consensus politics, so out of fashion to the sixties activists, whether of the left or the right. Somehow, according to this view, the failure was less that of men than of the system. Americans were always passive, merely "settling" for some aberration, meaning, of course, the imposition upon the public will of the unpalatable: national arm-twisting by manipulative salesmen forcing them to accept politicians like so much soap promoted by Madison Avenue. So book-buyers welcomed having best-sellers confirm their suspicions. None was more sensational than Joe McGinniss's *Selling of the President 1968,* which quotes Len Hall as explaining, "You sell your candidate and your programs the way a business sells its products."[47]

McGinniss did have an important message. Political salesmanship had become a high commercial art. Given even more importance by the new technology, especially television, it led to a new breed of affluent professionals who specialized in everything from speechwriting to sophisticated surveys of voter opinion. They mastered the technique of free advertising, and calculated how best to display everything: voice, looks, and quality of personality. Where once Gallup, Roper, and Harris had sufficed to gauge progress, the expert political handlers had become an essential part of *creating* progress.

To suggest, however, as does McGinniss, that somehow the American people merely swallowed bright packaging simplifies what happened. If that were the case, the entire image of Nixon's persona would have been recast. Nixon would have been transformed into someone more likable than the public found him. Few voted for him out of love. In fact, he just barely managed to beat the combination of Hubert Humphrey and Edwin Muskie; he was almost destroyed by a last-gasp regrouping of confused, divided, embittered liberals and radicals. Moreover, the candidate himself fought against and resisted the massive McLuhanesque attempts to divert the campaign from the issues.[48]

Exactly who was better at manipulating was never clear. Nixon was outraged by McGinniss-type portrayals. Kevin Phillips argued that the most effective work of the image-makers was in shaping the reporters' view of what really happened. "The three-man Nixon advertising committee," he argued, "were much better at selling McGinniss on their skills than they were at selling Richard Nixon to the American people." Insofar as the candidate himself was concerned, the fact that he was endorsed by over 80 percent of the country's newspapers did not keep the press from working hard to sell Humphrey.[49]

At the end of the campaign, Nixon had no choice but to head off a preelection disaster. A dramatic last-minute move toward peace by the administration could have been decisive at the polls, which was precisely what President Johnson tried to do. It was Henry Kissinger who alerted the Nixon campaign. Dr. Kissinger, the Harvard defense analyst and Rockefeller consultant, had been working at the Majestic Hotel in Paris with Democratic negotiators Averell Harriman and Cyrus Vance in a search for a diplomatic solution to the war.

The Communist regime in Hanoi was reluctant to settle, and for the best of military and strategic reasons. They pulled the strings of the National Liberation Front, which, in turn, worked with the Vietcong to undermine the government of South Vietnam. Half a million American troops were tied down, and guerrilla fighters had eliminated just about any remaining sanctuary around Saigon. Their success had most notably stigmatized the U.S. involvement and provoked such divisiveness as to goad Johnson into apoplectic desperation over a war he could not win and dared not lose. Sufficient Communist pressure against the South Vietnamese and Americans might conceivably push them to the breaking point. Washington might decide that the cause was impossible and not worth further blood and money. Ho Chi Minh, foremost a Vietnamese nationalist but also schooled in Moscow and reliant upon Soviet help, could afford to wait. For the people of Indochina, unlike the French and the Americans, war had become a way of life.

Still, even Ho could not control events. ROLLING THUNDER's bombs were devastating. Hanoi itself was no longer spared. And, for all the embarrassment the Tet offensive caused Johnson, Ho's stroke was costly. There were, moreover, indications that his most important backers, the Soviets, might well prefer to cut loose from their commitment. Changes in Kremlin leadership, especially the removal of Khrushchev, brought new uncertainties about Moscow's reliability. The Russians were not especially delighted about giving their Chinese "comrades" a pretext for matching their own influence in the area. Moreover, for Moscow as well as for Washington, the entire mess was too costly, not worth the advantage of keeping the Americans trapped in their quagmire. Secretary of State Dean Rusk reminded Ambassador Anatoly Dobrynin of all this when he met with the Russian in Washington to get Moscow's help. Polling expert Lou Harris, a friend of the two most recent Democratic presidents, was told by a member of the Russian delegation that a Vietnam settlement was in their best interest. If that alone was not enough to get Hanoi to the peace table, they could ultimately be bought off by such sweeteners from Washington as calling off the bombing entirely, not merely the limited reduction announced by Johnson in March. And there was always the National Liberation Front, that Communist umbrella arm for the guerrillas. Getting Washington to agree to recognize their existence as an interested party, which would mean including them at the negotiating table, would be an important face-saving gesture. Nixon, while still hedging his criticism of the administration, offered to go to Saigon or Paris to "get the negotiations off dead center."[50]

That was where Kissinger showed his hand. Kissinger, whose family had fled from Nazi Germany in time to escape the Holocaust, was brilliant, and no one appreciated that more than he. His credits included a published dissertation on Metternich, Castlereagh, and nineteenth-century European diplomacy. Two provocative books on the role of nuclear weapons in the cold war made the best-seller lists. He was blatantly ambitious and political, often brutal in his dealings with subordinates, and had a reputation for "playing both sides of the street," as Jack Kennedy knew in 1960 when told that Dr. Kissinger was also pushing for Rockefeller. Now, while he was in Paris, working for Lyndon Johnson and watching the progress of the Nixon-Humphrey contest, the probability of a Nixon victory offered another temptation. He had the chance to score some points with that camp by alerting them that the prospect for a preelection announcement of a Paris summit session to resolve the war had finally improved. Success in getting a conference started would dramatically undercut Nixon's advantage as the candidate best able to end the war. Kissinger made certain the Republicans knew what was going on.[51]

Cyrus Vance used the same intelligence to telephone the State Department with the triumphant news that "we've got everything we asked for." Their patience was quickly tested when Hanoi came up with additional obstacles, but the important point was that the north was willing. President Thieu was in no hurry to deal, and certainly not while the Democrats were still in power. Nixon seemed a shoo-in; having him in the White House heading a Republican administration, with a harder-line commitment to the war, would only strengthen Thieu's hand against the Communists. But Johnson had powerful leverage. He could call off the bombing or, at the very least, implicitly recognize the National Liberation Front, or both. The American ambassador in Saigon, Ellsworth Bunker, did his share of the arm-twisting by reminding the South Vietnamese leader what the withdrawal of Americans would do to his war. If all this made Thieu despondent, his mood was understandable. The Americans, he complained, were playing politics with the war. Finally, he seemed to have little choice but to give in. Lyndon Johnson, eager to pounce, told the world on October 31 that both sides were ready to talk peace. The impact on the American election was immediate. Humphrey, a sixteen-point underdog in mid-August, moved within easy sight of Nixon and, in a Harris poll, actually went ahead by 3 percent.[52]

Johnson, of course, was going to get what he wanted one way or another and then worry about what would happen next. The veteran pol, next to Nixon himself perhaps the most seasoned professional of them all, could not have been surprised that the Republican campaign was making its own moves. Cables intercepted by the National Security Agency from the South Vietnamese ambassador in Washington revealed that "the Nixon entourage," working through Anna C. Chennault, was pressuring Thieu to resist the peace talks. Saigon, he was reminded, should hold out for a new administration, presumably one headed by Nixon.[53]

Lyndon Johnson was hardly a stranger to wiretaps and FBI surveillance. In 1964, he had sent agents to bug dissident black Democrats from Mississippi at his party's convention in Atlantic City. During that year's campaign, FBI information on Barry Goldwater flowed to the White House. After a Johnson aide, Walter Jenkins, was forced to resign as the result of a homosexual encounter in a bathroom, the Bureau's resources were strained to keep up the president's requests for all it could learn about prospective appointees. The director, J. Edgar Hoover, entertained the president by letting him in on the dalliances of the Reverend Martin Luther King, Jr. Altogether, an enormous pile of raw FBI data swamped the White House.[54]

Once alerted about efforts to kill the peace talks, Johnson ordered telephone taps at the South Vietnamese embassy and on Chennault's line, and surveillance of the Nixon campaign. Senior FBI agent and former Hoover assistant Cartha DeLoach, who was placed in charge of the assignment, later told Senate Watergate Committee investigators that the White House "felt the Republicans . . . were attempting to slow down the South Vietnamese from going to the Paris peace talks and . . . wanted to know who either Mr. Nixon or Mr. Agnew had been in touch with." An FBI memorandum of October 30 stated that "it is widely known that [Mrs. Chennault] was involved in Republican political circles and, if it became known that the FBI was surveilling her this would put us in a most untenable and embarrassing position." The Bureau's files contain no direct evidence that they were ever able to pinpoint the exact source. Chennault's contention was that she acted at the direction of Nixon's law associate John Mitchell, who had taken charge of the campaign.[55]

Nixon was fighting back. It may be argued that Thieu did not need Nixon to tell him to resist going to Paris, but how could Nixon be sure? He wanted to win, and the dynamics of the campaign overwhelmed any other consideration. He had long cultivated the glamorous, extremely well connected widow of General Claire Chennault. Born in China, she was close to the Soong family and had access to many Asian leaders. Now an American citizen, she first met Nixon at a banquet in Formosa given in his honor by President and Madame Chiang Kai-shek when he was vice president.[56]

Years later, she talked while seated on a sofa near the center of the opulent living room of her penthouse apartment atop Washington's Watergate complex, a residence that was a museum of Chinese art treasures. She recalled Nixon as always well informed and eager to learn more about Asia. It was typical of him, then as well as later, to be diligent about pursuing information. He took care to limit direct contacts by having calls made by one of his friends, Robert Hill of New Hampshire, who had been an ambassador to several Latin American countries.[57] Nixon met with Chennault at the Broad Street office shortly after he returned to New York to practice law. Kept insufficiently informed by the State Department during the 1960s, not even briefed before his overseas trips, "he had to rely on people like myself," Chennault has written, "well-informed, trustworthy, and with solid connections to the Vietnamese leaders, to supply him with reliable information." In the spring of 1967, he asked her to serve as an adviser on Southeast Asian affairs. Then there were many other meetings, including some at Nixon's Fifth Avenue apartment with his law partner John Mitchell, who remained Chennault's main contact with Nixon. Chennault was Nixon's entrée to Ambassador Bui Diem, who was also being courted by the Democrats. Chennault recalled the ambassador's bitter complaints that "they tap my phone, they intercept my mail, they monitor messages I exchange with Saigon." Several complaints to the State Department were in vain.[58]

On the eve of the election, Thieu suddenly backed off, announcing that he could not go to Paris while the Hanoi regime represented the Vietcong. "The confusion that followed was enormous," Chennault has written, "punctuated with despairing questions. How could that be? How could Saigon have agreed and then reneged? Or was it Thieu who had given his agreement without his cabinet's approval, and if so why? Had he blundered, then retracted his offer? Or had he given no assurance in the first place? Worse, was Johnson playing politics at Vietnam's expense?" Nixon chose that moment, the Sunday before the election, to offer to go to Saigon if he could help bring peace.[59]

No one was more distraught than Hubert Humphrey. "I wonder if I should have blown the whistle on Anna Chennault and Nixon," he wrote in his diary. "He must have known about her call to Thieu. I *wish* I could have been sure. Damn Thieu. Dragging his feet this past weekend hurt us. I wonder if that call did it. If Nixon knew. Maybe I should have blasted them anyway."[60]

When Johnson wrote later that he "had no reason to think that . . . Nixon was himself involved in this maneuvering," he was plainly dissembling. The intercepted messages did not leave much to his imagination, but he knew more than he would, or could, let on. He could not advertise that American intelligence was poking into the communications being received in Saigon, where "secret" cables even got into the hands of an American correspondent. Chennault, for a time code-named Little Flower, was overheard telling the South Vietnamese embassy it would be best not to accept any peace terms before the election. Asked whether Nixon knew what she was doing, she said, "No, but our friend in New Mexico does." Agnew, then campaigning in Albuquerque, New Mexico, became the personal target of an order from President Johnson. FBI inspectors were to check his outgoing calls to find out whether he had contacted Little Flower on that November 2. Johnson's request, described as "most unusual," yielded nothing, which did not allay his suspicion that behind-the-scenes activity was trying to scuttle the peace talks. Herb Klein, one of the few Nixon people in touch with what was happening, recalls that he was with Bob Finch and Nixon in the Los Angeles hotel suite of the Century-Plaza when the president phoned to ask what the hell was going on.[61] There was that other factor: Johnson, annoyed at Humphrey's increasingly weak support of the war during the campaign, had reached the point where he was not about to help him at the price of discrediting Nixon. That circumstance probably went far toward creating the rapport that developed between the president and his successor. Nevertheless, the fact remains that it was not entirely clear that going public with that kind of charge so late in the campaign would not backfire.

Chennault talked later to the FBI about her involvement. Her comments left no doubt about the Nixon campaign's interest in the Paris talks. She provided an additional account in her book, which was published in 1980. Still, in her interview with this author, she added the tantalizing suggestion that the full story was far from known, that more confidential messages went from Washington to Saigon through couriers and not through Ambassador Diem. Diem, who published and edited the *Saigon Post,* was from an influential Vietnamese family. He first served the government as chief of staff, in effect, for the prime minister, and that was Nguyen Cao Ky, before going to the United States as ambassador in 1967. Thieu and Ky did not trust each other, and Diem was therefore on the wrong side. The lack of confidentiality between the two did not make the ambassador the best means of communication with the presidential palace in Saigon. Asked to name the other couriers, however, Chennault refused.[62]

Madame Chennault's statement implicitly questions how much of the affair was due to her intrigue, her manipulation, her desire for prominence. She credited herself with promoting early use of the word "Vietnamization" in a three-page paper that she said was sent to Nixon in 1967. When told Nixon thought she claimed too much credit for herself, she replied, "To have a woman, particularly an Asian woman, at that time, to tell a presidential candidate a possible solution made all the men look bad. They would not want to give us that credit."[63]

Shortly after Nixon's inauguration, anticipating charges that he had used Chennault to sabotage the agreement, he directed Bob Haldeman to review the details of what had happened. Haldeman got access to the highly confidential information. There was nothing in the FBI files or in the messages intercepted in Saigon that showed that Nixon personally used his influence to kill the Paris talks. There is, however, sufficient information to demonstrate that he was far from uninvolved and was rightly convinced that his political future was the target of Johnson's late-campaign ploy. Looking back upon those events, Haldeman agreed that he certainly was indiscreet about his meetings with Chennault and Diem.[64] Thieu was right: he was caught in an American political squeeze, and so, too, were U.S. politicians mired in intrigue, on and off the killing fields.

It was not the press that made the difference in 1968, but the state of the union, and it was the skill and craft of Richard Nixon that understood both the momentum behind a Wallace and what was happening to "poor Hubert," the Democratic candidate.

More than twenty years after Nixon's first election to the Congress, the convergence of the forces most responsible for the shape of postwar American society created the conditions for his resurrection. On May 16, several weeks before the Republican convention, he noted the changes in a radio speech that hailed the coming of new political relationships. FDR's coalition was obsolete, the old alliance of organized labor, minority groups, and southern Bourbons, progressives, and populists no longer viable. Nixon foresaw a realignment that would tie the new generation, with its post–New Deal values, to traditional Republican doctrines; once they were expressions of the confidence that accompanied the rise of industrial America. Now, in Nixon's words, Washington's role would be "to provide incentives for the private enterprise system to accept some social responsibility. In that context, liberals and conservatives will find themselves coming closer together rather than splitting apart." He called this new constituency, as had Democratic senator Paul Douglas earlier, the "silent center," a term that later evolved into "silent majority." Two years into Nixon's presidency, Garment noted to John Ehrlichman the trend among constituent groups to become "increasingly self-interested and independent and likely to respond for/against on the basis of intangibles . . . and less likely than ever to vote on the basis of party."[65] By building his following and by taking over the Republican party, especially its center, Nixon hoped to lay the basis for such a reconstruction.

Nixon did not discover these forces. Neither did Kevin Phillips, but the twenty-eight-year-old graduate of Colgate and Harvard Law School, who was raised in a middle-class family in the Parkchester neighborhood of the Bronx, tracked their political coming of age. Phillips's early experience as an administrative assistant to Congressman Paul Fino stimulated his analytical mind to the broader implications. He found that the largely ethnic area in Fino's northeastern Bronx district was a microcosm of middle America. He drew detailed maps that traced neighborhood voting patterns, and, following similar earlier models established by Samuel Lubell, Phillips emphasized that political responses could be gauged by knowing what voters were most eager to *oppose*. He tried to sell himself and his findings to the Rockefeller camp but was turned down. They were still attached, Phillips believes, to "elite notions of how to reach voters." Through William Timmons, who succeeded Bryce Harlow as Nixon's chief legislative leader, Phillips landed a spot with John Mitchell.[66]

Phillips assumed that the ongoing demographic changes, from northeast to southwest, from cities to suburbs, would combine with the expansion of the middle class and constitute a newly conservative electorate. If they could pick up disaffected Democrats, best represented by those attracted to a George Wallace, Republicans could achieve a new majority. Or, as Buchanan gleefully put it to Nixon later, "We are the beneficiaries of the visceral patriotism of the lower middle class."[67]

Later frequently overlooked, buried under that year's tumultuous events, was the Wallace factor. Well into the fight for the presidency, liberals and conservatives alike pondered a possible scenario: neither major party's candidate might gain the needed electoral majority to keep the vote from going to the House of Representatives. Wallace himself has acknowledged that whatever the case, even if he had managed to achieve an electoral college deadlock, Nixon would have gotten his support and won "because we were violently opposed to Mr. Humphrey's philosophy and ideology."[68]

That kind of victory was far from what Nixon wanted. Nixon, like Humphrey, viewed the southerner's candidacy with alarm. No one could, at the time, be certain of exactly how his power might influence the outcome, so there was apprehension in both major parties. Agnew himself, Nixon's antidote to Wallace, then became a major embarrassment. Nixon was forced to rush to his defense against suggestions that conflict-of-interest improprieties, which were first raised and defended when Agnew ran for the governorship, rendered him, in the words of a *New York Times* editorial, "not fit to stand one step away" from the presidency. Then there were Agnew's comments. Made both on and off the record, they contrasted with the wholesome, Lincolnesque, statesmanlike, reasoned approach taken by Humphrey's vice presidential candidate, Senator Muskie, whose major function was also to limit the Wallace damage. But, unlike Muskie, Agnew became an issue on his own, and a negative one. Instead of merely presenting the case for backing the Republican ticket, he came under fire for ethnic slurs and crudities. One of the ways America had changed during those reform years was the surge toward more sensitivity and appreciation for the nation's ethnic heritage, a development traceable to the assertions of "black power" by civil rights militants. It was no longer permissible, as Agnew found out, for a candidate to talk about "Polacks" instead of Polish Americans; nor, even in a relaxed moment in the privacy of his railroad car, to joke about 'the fat Jap." Agnew did both, and it did not sit well, undoubtedly not helped by the general tone of his campaigning. His rhetoric was further associated with the comment that "if you've seen one slum you've seen them all." No criticism stung as much as when the *Washington Post* declared that he was "perhaps the most eccentric political appointment since the Roman emperor Caligula named his horse a consul." For a time, dismayed by the fallout from Agnew's references to Polacks and fat Japs, Nixon began to separate himself from his running mate, but that failed to hide the use of Agnew to stem the Wallace threat.[69] Nevertheless, his role possibly even reinforced because the press attacked him for his indiscretions, Agnew became indispensable for blocking Wallace. Speechwriters Steve Hess and Pat Buchanan hurried to his campaign to guide his rhetoric.

Through the second half of September and into mid-October, surveys showed the Alabama governor attracting as much as one-fifth of the three-way vote. One of the most respected newspaper editors of the South, Virginius Dabney of Richmond, notified Senator A. Willis Robertson that *"Wallace is the real question mark, and I am constantly astonished at the size of his growing following."* Stephen Mitchell, until recently Democratic National Committee chairman, heard that laborers behind Wallace at a large Alcoa plant in Iowa consisted of ex-Klansmen, "anti-Catholics, a considerable number of Catholics and what I would call the backlash white vote. The latter people read the Chicago papers and feel that the negroes gave gotten too much already and do not appreciate what they have received." Leaders of New York's Central Labor Council acknowledged that only a last-minute union campaign kept an astonishingly large number of their members from voting for Wallace. As Nixon later noted to Bob Haldeman, "Our polls showed that Wallace was drawing approximately two votes from Nixon for every one that he drew from Humphrey." In Agnew, at least, the Nixon campaign gave Wallace some tough competition. Sometimes they were virtually indistinguishable, as when Agnew denounced "phony intellectuals . . . who don't understand what we mean by patriotism and hard work."[70]

Not since the Progressives of 1924 was there anything like it. Even the Henry Wallace Progressive Citizens of America had fizzled badly in 1948 after their Communist support was recognized. Geographically, the leftists had a narrow base. Half of their votes came from New York State. George Wallace appeared on the ballot in every state, most often as the candidate of the American Independent party, argued that there was not "a dime's worth of difference" between the two major political parties, and did remarkably well. "Wallace's candidacy was depriving me of a substantial number of votes, and anything I did to elevate Wallace would be self-destructive," Nixon later wrote.[71]

George Wallace cut deeply into Nixon's vote, especially from a wide variety of nonsouthern, eastern European ethnic groups, largely urban, Catholic, and middle-class. Considering the narrowness of his final victory over Humphrey, Nixon was fortunate to corral some three-fifths of those who defected from Wallace during the campaign. An analysis by the Survey Research Center of the University of Michigan agreed. "If Wallace had not run, we can have little confidence that they would have faithfully supported Humphrey and Muskie," reported the scholars. The majority of Wallace's votes were from "Democrats who otherwise preferred Nixon rather than from Republicans who might have given their favors to Humphrey," and it could not be demonstrated that Wallace affected the outcome. Nixon would have won anyway, but his popular vote margin might have been tripled.[72]

Had Wallace done better, of course, Nixon could have been in trouble. Humphrey closed the gap during those final days and finished with a deficit of some half-million popular votes. Some of the Wallace decline was predictable, the natural process in American politics of reluctance to "waste" votes on a third-party candidate. But he also hurt himself by making the unfortunate choice of "the bomber," General Curtis E. LeMay, as his running mate. The general, at one notable press conference, almost sounded euphoric about the atomic age, complaining that "we seem to have a phobia about nuclear weapons." As a mortified Wallace looked on and tried to intervene, LeMay stubbornly went on to make the statement that "I don't believe the world would end if we exploded a nuclear weapon." After the twenty tests at Bikini Atoll, LeMay reasoned, "the fish are all back in the lagoons; the coconut trees are growing coconuts; the guava bushes have fruit on them; the birds are back."[73]

Certain labor leaders were very nervous, for their own reasons. At a time of declining unionization, along with reduction in industrial employment, independent observers and pollsters were finding alarming numbers of workers leaning toward Wallace, possibly as many as 35 to 40 percent, especially among UAW members in Michigan. After scouting around the Homestead, Pennsylvania, area, the site of historic militant unionism in the steel mills, a *New York Times* reporter wrote, "This is wild Wallace country." "The experts had been assuming," wrote the three English journalists who have left the most thorough account of that election, "— it had become an axiom in Washington — that the white American worker was so affluent that he could no longer be reached by appeals to his pocket and that he no longer felt he needed a union to protect his interests." At the same time, big labor's leadership was divided, caught in the AFL-CIO rivalry between George Meany and Walter Reuther.[74]

The needs of internal union politics, the fear that leadership was losing control, and the reality that Wallace was exploiting racial tensions all worked to prompt a counterattack by labor's hierarchy. "We've got to stir these local union leaders to get a confrontation with their members," said the executive vice president of the Pennsylvania AFL-CIO. Meany himself, at odds with Reuther and wanting to beat both Nixon and Wallace, decided to throw the union's resources into an especially vigorous battle to "educate" the rank and file. In a campaign led by the AFL-CIO's Committee on Political Education, the men who worked the assembly lines were barraged by thousands of handbills that spelled out Wallace's antilabor record as governor and the realities of living conditions in Alabama. Indeed, for many workers the journey from Wallace to Humphrey, especially when shown the way by union leadership, was not as great as from Wallace to Nixon. Those blue-collar voters attracted to the southerner for shared resentments had little in common with traditional Nixon Republicans on economic issues. Nevertheless, Kevin Phillips argued, the Wallace movement was the inevitable way station for the white majority as they broke ranks with the old New Deal coalition.[75] Richard Scammon and Ben Wattenberg agreed: the "real America" was less dependent upon bread and butter and freer to return to pride in country.

The differences between a Richard Nixon and a George Wallace were profound. Wallace was a primitive populist, closely associated with violence and appealing to the visceral reactions of poor hardworking whites whose sweat seemed to be getting them nowhere except deeper in debt. He was, in the words of one incisive critic, the "greatest disturber of the political peace in this generation, a neurotic, raving egoist," and "a man whom violence follows."[76] Nixon, on the other hand, was always reflective, an intellectual in spite of himself; in his own way, urbane and sophisticated, and conscious that if the people did not have him, they would get Wallace or one of his clones.

That one was able to be elected twice while the other remained an outsider, his ultimate future made even more doubtful by an attempted assassination, gave the distinctive character to those next few years. Never loved as president, no Kennedy when it came to affection or inspiration, Nixon was, as during his student days, the guy who could get the job done.

Nixon and Wallace both gained at Humphrey's expense. Regardless of how close the final popular vote turned out, the vice president never had a chance. Either Wallace would get more votes and force the election to the House, where Wallace would wield great influence, or Nixon would defeat both Wallace and Humphrey. Of course, the latter occurred, and it was as clear a case as the nation is likely to see of the man matching the times. The New Deal presidents through LBJ labored under the shadow of FDR. Nixon, in the post–New Deal, post-Roosevelt period, never did avoid the specter that if he did not rule, George Wallace might. Even after Wallace was shot and wounded so seriously during the 1972 primary campaign, Nixon has pointed out, the ideas that drove him so far could not be assumed to have collapsed with the man.[77] America was ready for that, not for something better.

Insufficiently recognized at the time, almost lost in the attention given to Hubert Humphrey's ability to close in on Nixon during the final days of the 1968 campaign, was that a majority of Americans voted for either George Wallace or the Republican candidate. That figure, 57 percent, more properly indicated the sharp turn. The contrast with just four years earlier, when some 61 percent supported Lyndon Johnson, constituted one of the more remarkable turnabouts in American politics. Humphrey's share of the popular vote was almost 20 percent below Johnson's, a far more important indicator of what was happening than the simple fact that his loss was, at the end, by just about half a million out of the more than 73 million that were cast for all candidates combined. The change becomes even more emphatic in the absence of economic disaster. Seen from the distance of two decades, the revolutionary ingredients become sharper. The shift had been brewing for many years, long before people knew about the existence of Vietnam, and when rioting in the streets, burning cities, and fear of crime were still in the future. Finally, in 1968 the Republican National Committee's Research Division was able to report that, until Humphrey's recovery late in the campaign, "the Democratic coalition, forged in New Deal days of the big city vote, manual workers, Catholics, labor union members and Negroes, fell into brief disarray," and what had been the "Solid South" gave Nixon a 550,000 popular vote margin over Humphrey.[78]

The ultimate importance of Nixon's victory involved leadership for, as *Newsweek*'s survey of the "Troubled American" put it, "America's vast white middle-class majority."[79] The battle over who would inherit the next great movement in American political culture — the social force that would replace the New Deal — was the one that they fought and won. The "forgotten majority," the great petite bourgeoisie created by the social and economic changes of the past century, was on the verge of being discovered. Kevin Phillips had diagnosed the mood, but the accuracy of his prophecy had yet to be demonstrated. As Phillips himself acknowledged, and as Richard Nixon agreed, much hinged on the future course of George Wallace and his followers.

18

"I'm Not a Mushy Moderate"

WHEN RICHARD NIXON campaigned through Deshler, Ohio, in October 1968, the daughter of a Methodist minister held aloft a sign with a message that Nixon adopted as his theme. The young girl's actual words were "Bring Us Together Again," which Nixon recalled as "Bring Us Together." On the morning after the election, Nixon said that that would "be the great objective of this administration at the outset, to bring the American people together. This will be an open administration, open to new ideas, open to men and women of both parties, open to the critics as well as those who support us. . . . We want to bring America together."[1]

The message was portentous but not inappropriate, certainly given the crises Nixon inherited. Not since Lincoln's time was the nation so divided. When FDR took over in 1932, despair, even resignation, was more serious than disunity. Eleanor Roosevelt noted how "terrifying" it was that Americans were ready to give her husband whatever he wanted to enable him to cope with the crisis.[2]

Roosevelt told the American people that they had nothing to fear but "fear itself" and immediately began to tackle the national economic emergency. After Hoover's impotence, the new president had only to act, even comparing himself to a football coach trying play after play until he found one that worked. Anything was better than complacency, platitudes, and hollow promises.

Nixon faced a different sort of crisis; in many ways, it was more violent and divisive, and, in the long run, as potentially calamitous. As Daniel Patrick Moynihan reminded the president-elect that winter, "The sense of institutions being legitimate — especially the institutions of government — is the glue that holds society together." The challenge of the incoming administration, advised the Democrat who was about to become Nixon's assistant for urban affairs, was "to restore the authority of American institutions." Just before leaving office, President Johnson told the director of the Office of Emergency Preparations, General George A. Lincoln, that he had given too little thought to contingency plans. He hoped that the new administration, about to inherit a situation bound to worsen, would give the matter more attention. Things were not, however, completely left to chance. As they took over, Nixon's people received a batch of blank executive orders that needed only filling in for martial law to be declared in any affected city.[3]

Once again, the nation's leadership was under fire. However much Johnson had lost credibility and sacrificed respect, he had been masterful at getting what he wanted, signing more significant legislation than had any president since the 1930s. In each case, in his domestic programs as well as foreign policy, there remained powerful support for the pursuit of his reforms. Always, as he added his signature to still another measure, the comparisons with Kennedy remained; the martyrdom lived on to haunt his successors. Nothing was as burdensome as the myth that Jack Kennedy would have worked miracles.

Richard Nixon found it hard to reconcile himself to suggestions that he was indifferent about society's disadvantaged. As economic adviser Herbert Stein has suggested, he did not "bleed for the poor," but, Stein adds, in an obvious reference to the then current Reagan presidency, he was not about to "send them into the streets." "We were not zealots; we were not trying to return to a Calvin Coolidge era." Nixon recognized, as did the great theorist of liberal capitalism Adam Smith, that the free market created its own victims. He had always prided himself on not playing the racist game. He had hoped to remain in office long enough to do something about matters that government in America had scanted. His projected realignment would give him the strong political base for programs that extended leverage to those who did not belong to any dominant elite establishment. He had the resolve, the toughness to carry them out. "I'm not a mushy moderate," he maintained afterward. "I can't stand these people who put their finger in the air. Many of these positions I take are not popular." At the same time, he recalled, "I was not on the far right on social issues. You never heard me talk about abortion. As a matter of fact, I opposed federal subsidies for abortions, but I also sent the first population control measure to Congress, and I feel very strongly that it's a terrible mistake to try to export our views on abortion."[4]

Nixon understood the life-giving quality of successful programs. His populist instincts were strong enough to appreciate the injustice of programs that shifted responsibility to those already resentful of being ignored by government. The potential for revolt was that much greater when experimenting with social programs that were open to a thousand abuses. Favoritism to those in need, justifiable for humanitarian reasons, could only be tolerated if the recipients were judged by the majority as doing the utmost to find help through such benefits, without, of course, becoming threats to the social order. If they abused the charity and rejected middle-class standards, patience would soon run out, especially among those convinced that they were paying the bills for their own displacement. Neither they nor their grandparents, who had left the Old Country to begin new dreams in America, had been given such consideration. They had worked to make it on their own. The new, post-depression, postwar middle class, their memories blank about New Deal programs and the variety of wartime benefits for veterans, had become "rugged individualists" in the grand American tradition. It hardly mattered — they didn't give a damn — that, as Moynihan pointed out in 1967, the black poor and black working classes were *not* the beneficiaries of "legislation that would have meant for them what the New Deal measures meant for the population at large. Such programs were not even introduced."[5]

Nixon never doubted that men were instinctively selfish. Leadership, to be effective, had to guide man away from his own self-destructive tendencies. That was what society was all about. But all too often, and Nixon had seen it over and over again, the "leadership class" got its privileges for no better reason than the accident of birth and the advantages of wealth. That was Nixon the Calvinist, reserving for the chosen the responsibility for keeping man from self-destruction.[6]

He also fully appreciated how he had to battle the odds. By the time he reached the presidency, for example, he had long assumed foreign policy as his primary interest.[7] He had seen much of the world and, more than most American politicians, he read books. Nothing he had seen changed his mind about the inherent threats of the Marxist impulse. If the nonsocialist world relaxed, the appeal of the materialistic analysis, promoted by force and the self-interest of the Communist leadership class, would simply spread, choking the lifelines of free commerce.

Take the poor. That issue was a part of America's standing in the world. Governmental actions to ameliorate such social problems were potential admissions of weakness. Two days after the administration was sworn in, Agriculture Secretary Clifford Hardin asked about hunger and what should be done about it. Nixon, instead of dismissing the problem as one to be handled by the free market, expressed concern that admitting that it existed would be exploited by the Russians. Then, judiciously, he pigeonholed the matter by saying, "Let's get the facts" about the reality of the problem before plunging ahead.[8]

"If the United States withdraws into a new isolation," he warned long after his White House years were over, "there is no other power that shares our values and possesses the resources and the will to take our place. At the same time, we can be sure that another power hostile to our values and interests, the Soviet Union, will do so."[9] Nations, in their predatory instincts, were as aggressive as individuals, no more warranting trust because of special virtues. Those having systems without similar spiritual and cultural ethics, especially belief in individual progress, were the ones that most needed watching. Any changes would be illusory, evocative of great hope, but, alas, tactical and temporary; power and the preservation of socialism would continue as the long-term self-interest.

The concept of a "foreign policy" president had long been a cliché of American political leadership, the product of a federal system in which those in the Oval Office had the broadest constitutional responsibility and options. For a variety of reasons other than law, resistance to presidential leadership was also weakest when chief executives dealt with the rest of the world. The early Federalists had certainly made their moves, especially John Adams in his "quasi war" with France. James Monroe promulgated his doctrine. However, more activist internationalism intensified after Lincoln's day. Ulysses S. Grant had to be restrained by his secretary of state from undertaking a Caribbean adventure. From that point on, through America's second century, there was little holding back. William McKinley had his "splendid little war" over Cuba, then pushed over the Philippines. TR flexed the nascent military muscle in a dozen ways, with Congress given no choice but to foot the bills. William Howard Taft and Woodrow Wilson continued to press Yankee supremacy on the Latinos. When Wilson wanted neutrality in "thought as well as deed," so it was; when he wanted war, Congress fulminated, debated, and made sure everybody got behind the patriotic fight to "make the world safe for democracy." Even Warren Harding's administration, thanks to Charles Evans Hughes, led the way toward international naval agreements. Hoover held the line, keeping his "warrior" secretary of state from getting too excited about the Japanese in Manchuria. FDR, responding to a nation eager to thwart a new generation of "merchants of death," held back, even withdrawing after sounding the alarm about the Japanese invasion of China; in the end, however, he surreptitiously made confidential commitments to help a besieged British Empire and moved with stealth to prepare for the American involvement.

As a rising young politician, Nixon watched and applauded Truman's decisive steps to contain Soviet ambitions. He later supported and helped plan Eisenhower's covert operations. As vice president, he was closer to John Foster Dulles than to any other member of the cabinet.[10] By the time he reached the presidency, the country seemed exhausted by the hyperactive internationalism of Kennedy and Johnson. Leadership in foreign affairs came with the oath of office.

He had also seen checks on the commander in chief. The contrary forces were more likely to originate on the popular level and then sway

Congress. More than on domestic legislative matters — emphatically when it came to major bills — the national temper toward the world was felt on Capitol Hill, especially in the Senate. That the Foreign Relations Committee was Democratic-controlled did not help Johnson and, by 1968, the national frustration over Vietnam pushed the president from power. Nixon emerged as the "peace candidate." But, as he well knew, those major responsibilities, foreign and domestic, were inseparable.

Only two months after Nixon was sworn in, John Gardner, the Republican who had served Johnson as secretary of Health, Education, and Welfare, went to Harvard to deliver a series of three Godkin Lectures. Gardner began with the declaration that "these are dark days for the nation, days of controversy, days of violence and hostility." Gardner, who was a moderate man not known as an alarmist, added, "Every knowing person sees — first of all in himself — the anguish of the American people: the shattering of confidence, the anger, the bewilderment."[11]

Nixon read on, pen in hand, underlining as he went along, seizing on key words and paragraphs that confirmed his own analysis of the American condition. Gardner had his faith in the efficacy of private institutions over government, in the importance of restoring the "vitality of local leadership" over centralized planning. "We are just beginning to see how disorder and fragmentation can drain life of meaning, coherence and continuity," he went on; "in the name of freedom — he compulsively dissolves the limits on behavior and then finds himself unhappy in a world without limits. He sweeps aside rules, manners, formalities and standards of taste — anything that even slightly inhibits the free play of emotion and impulse." The Edmund Burke who recoiled at the sweep of the French Revolution would have cheered such words; so did Nixon.

The president's interest mounted as he read on. Gardner, it became clear, shared his view of man's character. Those so vehement about overturning society's foundations were innocents who, without any historical or anthropological evidence, persisted in believing "that man is naturally good, humane, decent, just and honorable, but that corrupt and wicked institutions have transformed the noble savage into a civilized monster." Nixon's pen went to the bottom of the page and wrote the word "Rousseau." Rousseau's children of nature had come into society and been corrupted. One stroke of Nixon's pen was not enough to applaud the next lines, and so he underscored them twice: "The collision between dissenters and lower middle class opponents is exceedingly dangerous. As long as the dissenters are confronting the top layers of the power structure, they are dealing with people who are reasonably secure, often willing to compromise, able to yield ground without anxiety. But when the dissenters collide with the lower middle class, they confront an insecure opponent, quick to anger and not prepared to yield an inch."

At the top of the first page, the president wrote a message to his "Cabinet & Top Staff." "I found John Gardner's Godkin Lectures expressed better than anything I have read — what I hope would be the philosophy of this Administration. I commend them for your weekend reading."[12]

The next day, Wednesday, March 26, 1969, the thirty-seventh president went to Walter Reed Army Hospital to visit the thirty-fourth. The general's system was giving out; repeated heart attacks had shortened his stay at Palm Desert; from his hospital bed, he had endorsed Nixon's nomination the summer before. Without him, and had he chosen differently during the secret fund crisis of that first national campaign, much of history would have been different; how, it would be impossible to say, but equally difficult to tell the story of America from midcentury on by ignoring both men. The general, seventy-nine that winter, heavily sedated, kept alive with oxygen and intravenous tubes, barely opened his eyes when the president walked in.

That last meeting was fresh in his mind when Nixon met with a delegation from the National Association of Manufacturers. He told them how Ike was pleased when he recognized his visitor, how he had the awareness to ask, "How's the Administration going?" When Nixon said, "We're going to do all right," the old man snapped, "You bet!" and his head dropped back, unconscious.[13]

Within forty-eight hours, Eisenhower was dead, another giant gone from a past era. "We think of the qualities of greatness and what his were that made him unique among us all," said President Nixon in his eulogy in the Rotunda of the Capitol early that Sunday evening. He "led the most powerful armies that the world has ever seen," and he was "a strong man. He was shrewd. He was decisive. . . . He restored calm to a divided nation. He gave Americans a new measure of self-respect. He invested his office with dignity and respect and trust. He made Americans proud of their President, proud of their country, proud of themselves." He led the greatest of armies and the greatest of nations, and "exercised a moral authority without parallel in America and the world."[14]

Had Eisenhower lived on, he would have seen the differences between himself and the man who can be called his protégé. The contrast was in part self-conscious and in part the product of Nixon's confrontation with the powers that he and other presidents fail to fully comprehend until faced with the complexities. For one who was labeled an "imperial president," it would later seem ironic to hear him talk about limitations, as did Kennedy before him and Jimmy Carter afterward. Carter admitted that he had "underestimated the inertia or the momentum of the federal bureaucracy." After Nixon's first two years on the job, as he confessed to four reporters who questioned him on national television right after New Year's Day in 1971, he, too, had discovered that it would be hard for his "actual performance" to fulfill his original expectations, so that "we must not become impatient." But Nixon *was* impatient. Finding himself stymied was worse than death itself. He was forever possessed, as Theodore White put it, with "How Things Work," how to get things done.[15]

Eisenhower could look good presiding as chairman of the board and pulling the strings from behind the scene. That was not Nixon's style. He was congenitally unable to abandon responsibility to others. Everything of consequence that came from his office, including the outpourings of his wordsmiths, had to carry his imprint. He *was* the president. As he told John Ehrlichman, he was the only one in the executive branch who had gotten there by being elected. Only he had faced the voters, and only he would have to do so again. "If he had to pay the political price for his Cabinet Secretaries' mistakes, then he, by God, had the right and obligation to correct these mistakes."[16] If the impossible needed to be done, he would give them impossible deadlines, and, by God, they had no choice but to meet them.

Comparisons with Eisenhower, the last Republican president before Nixon, are misleading on another level. By 1969, the "Ike age" was long gone; the eight years were eight decades. The country, as Nixon said in his inaugural, had "endured a long night of the American spirit." Instead of a "greening," the ultimate vision of such New Utopian theorists as Charles Reich, there was regression. A fractured society faced with bitterness the realities of how little could actually get done. It could have neither peace nor war, nor could it have prosperity without inflation, social justice without agitation, a Garden of Eden without weeds, politics without soul-wrenching.

In a time of recriminations, he later remembered, he thought of Churchill's advice about excluding the difficult but talented in favor of the pliable but mediocre. During the campaign, he told the nation that he did not "want a Cabinet of 'yes' men." His people would "be drawn from the broadest possible base — an Administration made up of Republicans, Democrats and independents, from politics, from career government service, from universities, from business, from the professions — one including not only executives and administrators, but scholars and thinkers."[17]

He took the office with the normal level of inflated expectations and was eager to establish his own imprimatur. He wanted recognition for his special achievements. He meant it about fulfilling his notions about executive management. "For one thing," he said before his nomination in 1968, "I would disperse power, spread it among able people. Men

operate best only if they are given the chance to operate at full capacity."
Domestic affairs would be within the realm of the cabinet. International
relations invariably ran head-on to frustrations, and he soon had to
conduct himself and organize the office in a manner that was designed
to give him better working control over the swollen apparatus of government. In Theodore Lowi's words, Nixon "built a bureaucracy to control the bureaucracy."[18]

Peter Flanigan, working under John Mitchell, led the talent search.
Altogether, 2,000 jobs needed to be filled, from chauffeurs and maids
to heading up the State Department. Only a relatively small number,
about 500, represented key posts on the White House staff. Flanigan
and his staff were primarily concerned with about 300 top positions. Of
that total, 35 were named by the time of Nixon's swearing-in, with another 64 assigned to the departments and agencies. All the rhetoric about
a reduced bureaucracy notwithstanding, the size of the White House
staff and Executive Office had grown enormously. Democrats or Republicans, liberals or conservatives, it made little difference. Growth went
on, nearly doubling between Truman's time and Eisenhower's, with the
number of full-timers reaching a new high under Nixon. However much
he tried, repeatedly altering organizational schemes, decentralizing and
centralizing and then decentralizing, the monster that was the federal
bureaucracy kept on growing. At Camp David, right after his reelection
in 1972, the president told his chief aides, "Cut the staff. Too many
people just stand around."[19]

He had a point. By that year, the White House staff had 550 full-
timers and the Executive Office staff was well over 5,000. Nixon's spontaneous comment fell into the category of just another futile presidential
desire. One measure showing the growth of the establishment was the
increase in Executive Office operating costs from $31 million when
Nixon took over to $71 million by the end of his first four years. The
size of the White House staff would remain much more vulnerable to a
variety of conditions beyond the control of any single president. Any
attempt to relate such growth to presidential influence, or to an executive
"grab for power," blatantly ignores that it was the world that was changing more than the voracity of the man in the White House.[20]

Nixon had also become convinced that his administration needed to
be open, without a protective palace guard. At one point after the nomination, his transition team even sent out form letters to those listed in
Who's Who in America inviting them to apply for a place in the new
government. The result was a lot of unanswered mail.[21]

Notably, Nixon's preparations for governing minimized partisanship
and he reached out as he later said, to "the other side of the aisle." His
"first choice for Secretary of Defense, a runaway choice, was Scoop Jackson." Henry Jackson, the hawkish Democrat from the state of Washing-

ton, also fought the good fight for military appropriations. "Look," said Jackson, as Nixon remembers it, "I want you to know that I think I can do more good for you in the Senate because the antiballistic missile thing is coming up and I'm the only one that can bring along Democrats." Another Democrat, Nixon's just-defeated rival, Hubert Humphrey, was asked to become ambassador to the United Nations (he even invited Eugene McCarthy to become a UN delegate). Nixon and Humphrey discussed the offer in Key Biscayne. But it was obvious that Humphrey, who had had to give up his seat to be vice president, wanted to get back into the Senate. Nixon also talked about filling a Supreme Court vacancy with Robert C. Byrd of West Virginia. Byrd was "a conservative, a lawyer, and respected," says Nixon, "and I knew we could get him through the Senate. What drove us off Bob was two things: One, like Justice Black, he had been a member of the Ku Klux Klan. For a liberal to have been a member of the Klan was no problem; for a conservative, I knew it was a problem. The second point was that he had gone to night law school. I thought that the American Bar Association would take a very dim view of almost anybody that hadn't come in first in his class at Harvard, that they would turn him down." Another Byrd, Harry, Jr., of Virginia, the son of the departed "boss" of the Old Commonwealth, a Democrat who made his own "halfway covenant" in 1970 by running as an independent, was also prepared to join with Nixon in forming a "new coalition" composed of the "new majority." Nixon expected it ultimately to be taken over by a Texas Democrat, John Connally, the one "best qualified" to become his successor.[22]

The Eisenhower experience was not entirely out of his system, and so he assumed the importance of a strong cabinet. By December 11, his choices made and with the television networks cooperating, the nation was treated to a video extravaganza. Never before had an incoming chief executive placed his team on stage with such fanfare, introducing each of the twelve "new men with new ideas" as they sat on a stage in Washington's Shoreham Hotel. They were seated in two rows facing the camera as Nixon stood at a microphone. "These are strong men, they're compassionate men, they're good men," he said, and went on with a reminder of how he did not want a cabinet of "yes-men." They were, instead, about to bring the country that "extra dimension," that "potential for great leadership." They were neither all politicians nor all businessmen.[23] As theater, it worked; the novelty was not lost on the American people. Neither was the image of mutuality in a cooperative effort, all laid out in the open for all to see. The new president and his working dozen started out as a model of an open administration.

With the exceptions of Bill Rogers, Bob Finch, and John Newton Mitchell — a relative newcomer to Nixon's close circle — who were placed at the head, respectively, of the State Department, Health, Education, and Welfare, and the Department of Justice — there were no intimate friends. One Republican he had come to know, Bill Scranton, turned down a chance to take over the State Department, and another, Edward Brooke of Massachusetts, bypassed becoming the first black ambassador to the United Nations. Nixon got a flat rejection when he wanted David Rockefeller as his secretary of the treasury. Nixon himself had never met George Shultz, but he took the forty-eight-year-old labor economist away from the University of Chicago's Graduate School of Business and made him secretary of labor, which was the start of the labor economist's long affair with government. A Goldwater supporter from Wisconsin, Melvin Laird, chairman of the Republican Conference and, in the words of a *National Journal* reporter, a "conservative congressional poker player," took over the Defense Department, the first elected politician to be put in charge of the Pentagon. Over the protests of environmentalists, he made Alaska governor Walter J. Hickel, one of Nixon's campaign leaders in the West, secretary of the interior. His former competitor, the governor of Michigan, George Romney, who thought of himself as a "realistic idealist," became secretary of housing and urban development. For transportation, Nixon chose a first-generation New England Italian, John Volpe, the governor of Massachusetts. Eisenhower's old director of the Bureau of the Budget, and one of the most effective fund-raisers to ever fuel the engines of American politicians, Maurice H. Stans, became director of the Commerce Department, while a Chicago banker, David M. Kennedy, was the new secretary of the treasury. One of Eisenhower's farm economists, Clifford N. Hardin, took over the Department of Agriculture. Notably, Nixon, "went South" for only one man, and that was for the bottom cabinet job, postmaster general. Winton M. Blount, a wealthy Alabama contractor, was a conservative and opponent of George Wallace.[24]

At least four, Romney, Hickel, Volpe, and Blount, can be described as self-made. Almost uniformly wealthy and belonging to the business and political establishment, they were described by the *New York Times* as "a team of moderates well-suited to the middle of the American political road without in fact being very 'balanced' in the conventional sense."[25]

The next day, the floodlights and cameras gone, Nixon met with his selected dozen at the Shoreham and got down to the facts of life. He warned that they were about to encounter adversarial relationships with the press. They and their families were bound to be upset to find themselves depicted as "ogres" by editorial writers, cartoonists, and columnists. They had to learn to let such criticism "roll off their backs," something Nixon had never mastered. The problem, of course, which had plagued his relationships with the press in the past, was in failing to distinguish between legitimate reportage and biased interpretations. As James Deakin has pointed out, he treated negative comments about himself as inherently "biased, slanted, distorted or erroneous." Ironically, on that particular occasion, he was indulging more in anticipation than reality. During those honeymoon days, the press was not eager to aggravate the already parlous state of the union. Even Nixon's principal nemesis, the cartoonist whose caricatures became engraved in the minds of a generation of liberals, was unusually gentle. Nixon, in Herblock's view, was off to a fresh start by going to a barbershop for a clean shave.[26]

Yet, for all Nixon's early faith in administration by cabinet, their influence was nil. During the first year, they met with the president just a dozen times. Rogers would ultimately leave the administration with bitterness, angered that his old friend let him be pushed aside and humiliated by Henry Kissinger and vowing to tell all someday in his own way. Shultz was a survivor, moving along with the administration's reorganization and playing the good soldier, but regarded by his boss as rather soft and trusting of the bureaucracy. Laird, the politician, remained a politician, arousing constant suspicions that his loyalty to potential constituents undermined his support for the administration's war effort. Hickel surprised the environmentalists by championing their cause, and then left the administration in frustration at being isolated as a pariah for defending student antiwar dissidents. He later complained that Nixon repeatedly called him an "adversary." Finch was overwhelmed and undermined by John Mitchell, and gave it all up to return to California and a political future that failed to materialize after being blamed for the inadequacy of his presentation of the administration's welfare reform bill before the Senate Finance Committee. Romney failed to get along and was notably ineffective. "If Richard Nixon, Wally Hickel and George Romney had back-packed together for four days in the Pecos wilderness," John Ehrlichman later wrote, "the first Nixon Cabinet would not have included either of these two former governors, I'd bet. They just didn't get along." David Kennedy was merely inadequate and lethargic. By the start of Nixon's second term, not one of the appointees remained at his original job.[27] Not until the final days, when Watergate tales fell like bombshells on the Nixon White House, did the cabinet gain power over the bunker.

Meanwhile, and most tellingly, much influence was in the hands of the White House staff. That, of course, placed them within Nixon's close control, an inner circle consisting of Kissinger and the fifty professionals on his National Security Council staff, Ehrlichman and his Domestic Affairs Council, and chief of staff Haldeman. Then, largely through the force of his convictions, personality, and grievances shared with Nixon, there was Daniel Patrick Moynihan.

*   *   *

"While a crisis in the international arena is likely to elicit approval, a crisis on the *domestic* scene is more likely to reflect discredit on the President," wrote analyst Burns Roper during the transition.[28] And, as the United States moved toward the inaugural, there was no shortage of domestic crises, overseas as well as at home. The most powerful protest had exploded with a coalition of French students and workers the previous spring. At the moment of Nixon's swearing-in, revolts of the young were continuing throughout the world. Spanish dictator Francisco Franco cracked down with limited martial law for the first time since the 1930s. Other outbreaks were reported from Czechoslovakia and Pakistan. There was more trouble in Paris, and the most violent demonstration was in Tokyo. Washington was not entirely spared.

There was no more raucous presidential inaugural than on that January 20. The day, wrote *New York Times* columnist Russell Baker, was "out of Edgar Allan Poe, dun and drear, with a chilling northeast wind that cut to the marrow, and a gray ugly overcast that turned the city the color of wet cement."[29] As though to ambush the incoming president, clusters of "crazies"— so labeled by the National Mobilization Committee to End the War in Vietnam — were scattered all along the Pennsylvania Avenue inaugural parade route. "Four more years of death! Four more years of death!" they shouted, and filled the streets with obscenities, smoke bombs, rocks, and bottles. Massed policemen, reinforced by paratroopers and shielding themselves from the barrage, tried to drive the demonstrators from the parade route. Intermittent scuffles between police and crazies went on for nearly two hours in front of the National Theater. The security forces were further provoked by chants of "Ho, Ho, Ho Chi Minh, the NLF is going to win." One poster said, "Nixon's the One — The No. 1 War Criminal." As the Marine band neared Pennsylvania and Thirteenth, a firecracker exploded on the street, then a smoke bomb landed at the feet of the armed forces color guard. The arrival of the presidential and cabinet limousines drew a new volley of missiles. One, a sphere of tinfoil the size of a softball, floated upward and sailed down toward the presidential limousine, which then suddenly sped ahead, the Secret Service men running ahead trying to deflect the objects; images of the nightmarish past, the Kennedy motorcade suddenly accelerating toward Parkland Hospital.

This time, unlike at the centennial in 1876, the man from the *Times* looked "across the street"— in reality, a few blocks from the Capitol steps where the new president took his oath of office — to where some of the city's many blacks lived. That neighborhood was another world, touched only by the overflow of the parked cars of surburbanites trying to get near the parade route. Entering the ghetto to report for his paper, Max Frankel talked to "a small group of sullen Negroes who said they shared with their neighbors the fear that they would now be forgotten in the seats of American power."[30]

Out of their sight, beyond the wall of people along the parade route and at Capitol plaza, were the two most admired women of the occasion. The most relaxed was Lady Bird Johnson; the most animated, Pat Nixon. The new first lady, colorfully dressed in a double-breasted coat of pink wool that flared from a belted waist, wore a beret of two-skin Russian sable. She told the press she wished Frank and Hannah were still alive to witness the ceremony. "Although my family entered the White House with great hopes that my father could help with the healing process," Julie wrote later, "we never underestimated the divisions caused by the war and by decades of racial injustice, nor forgot that the President who had lived in the White House before us had been broken by the bitterness and the unrest."[31]

Her father's inaugural address focused on that crisis. It sounded more like the words of an activist liberal than a mushy moderate. It reached out to both the young and the disaffected, and deplored the "raucous discord on earth." Nixon pointed out that "we are caught in war, wanting peace. We are torn by division, wanting unity. We see around us empty lives, wanting fulfillment. We see tasks that need doing, waiting for hands to do them. To a crisis of the spirit, we need an answer of the spirit. And to find that answer, we need only look within ourselves. . . . To lower our voices would be a simple thing." Then he pledged that "those who have been left out, we will try to bring in. Those left behind, we will try to catch up. For all of our people, we will set as our goal the decent order that makes progress possible and our lives secure." The goals of the new administration, spelled out in terms of domestic needs — in striking contrast to the cold warrior phrases that monopolized John F. Kennedy's address eight years earlier — included full employment, better housing, excellence in education. "In rebuilding our cities and improving our rural areas; in protecting our environment and enhancing the quality of life — in all these and more, we will and must press urgently forward. We shall now plan for the day when our wealth can be transferred from the destruction of war abroad to the urgent needs of our people at home," he added. "The American dream does not come to those who fall asleep." Then, Richard Nixon, the bane of America's liberals, added, "No man can be fully free while his neighbor is not. To go forward at all is to go forward together. This means black and white together, as one nation, not two. The laws have caught up with our conscience. What remains is to give life to what is the law: to insure at last that as all are born equal in dignity before God, all are born equal in dignity before man."

As the world watched and listened, he continued: "We seek an open world — open to ideas, open to the exchange of goods and people — a world in which no people, great or small, will live in angry isolation. We cannot expect to make everyone our friend, but we can try to make no one our enemy. Those who would be our adversaries, we invite to a peaceful competition — not in conquering territory or extending dominion, but in enriching the life of man. . . . We have endured a long night of the American spirit. But as our eyes catch the dimness of the first rays of dawn, let us not curse the remaining dark. Let us gather the light. . . . Let us go forward, firm in our faith, steadfast in our purpose, cautious of the dangers, but sustained by our confidence in the will of God and the promise of man."[32]

The next morning President Richard Nixon awoke to congratulatory messages from around the world. The *Times* of London, hailing the speech, noted that "though many people greet the advent of the Nixon era with misgivings, the omens are surprisingly favorable." Soviet Premier Aleksey N. Kosygin sent his best wishes and urged better American-Soviet relations "in the interests of peace." The president also found out that the violence encountered along the parade route after the speech went on unabated through the night, led by some three hundred to four hundred marauding youths. Police car windshields were a favorite target, and some downtown store and office windows were broken, including the large plate glass at the National Geographic Society and the windows of at least three banks. The site of the preinaugural concert attended by the Nixons the night before was painted with the letters: "Viva NLF." The Communist Chinese press agency, Hsinhau, noting the events, predicted the going would be more ominous for Mr. Nixon than for his predecessors, and reported that "some 10,000 youth and other people held a massive demonstration . . . to protest against the coming into office of this new chieftain of the reactionary United States ruling circles." To Peking, that meant that "the American people are rapidly awakening and portends a further upsurge of the American mass movement" described as "the raging flames of the American people's struggle."[33]

His first White House news summary also gave details of a District of Columbia that was a "city of fear and crime," in which the number of armed robberies was rising steadily. "In one 30-hour period a week ago," it reported, "six men died in the Washington area in three double killings involving holdups or the pursuit of holdup suspects. Two of the dead men were agents of the Federal Bureau of Investigation." On that page, the thirty-seventh president wrote, "We are going to make a major effort to reduce crime in nation — starting with D.C." To John Ehrlichman, he wrote, "It is of highest priority to do something meaningful on D.C. crime *now*. Talk to Mitchell — give me a timetable for action."[34]

To Bob Haldeman, his chief of staff, he gave instructions on sending thank-you notes to those who participated in the inaugural in one way or another, from those in charge of the arrangements to various aides and players in the bands and marching units.[35] As always, little escaped his attention.

On his way, he took along Pat Moynihan. Moynihan was not only a Democrat but a colorful controversialist with a tough, independent mind; closely associated with the Kennedy administration, Harvard, and the eastern intellectual community, he was something of an aberration in the new administration. He stirred the intelligence of Nixon's own dichotomies. As Stephen Hess has written, "The appointment of Moynihan was to carry the President down unfamiliar paths, often against the grain of his stated convictions." The professor also, as Hess further suggests, may have appealed to Nixon's "big play" instincts through his dramatic proposals.[36] Nixon clearly not only accepted the arguments of such people as Mel Laird and Len Garment in taking on Moynihan as his adviser on urban affairs but was excited by the Kennedyite's iconoclastic ideas on welfare reform. Pat Moynihan, the Harvard professor and former assistant in the Kennedy and Johnson labor departments, was an indulgence for Richard Nixon.

He was stimulating and exciting to have around; without him, the White House could be pretty lonely and grim. Pat was fascinating, his memos sparkling with wit and insight, his thinking provocative. His office in the West Wing was just off the president's, and Moynihan was close at hand, filling him with ideas and a purpose.

Moynihan was good for Nixon, and the president knew it. He took him on over unhappy noises from such conservatives as his congressional liaison chief, Bryce Harlow, and Arthur Burns, economist and counselor to the president. He kept him, and listened to his ideas, even when it meant resistance at the outset. James Jackson Kilpatrick, that strong-minded Virginia political writer, looked at what the president was doing and began to question the administration's dedication to conservatism. In a televised editorial on Nixon's first three weeks in office, Kilpatrick said, "We have had precious little to smile about." He and his conservative compatriots had relied on Nixon but there was "only one full blown conservative in the Cabinet," and he was in its least significant office.[37] Conservatives, for example, considered Milton Friedman the greatest economist in the country, but, lamented the journalist from the *Richmond News-Leader,* he is "still in Chicago." They wanted a conservative in the urban affairs post but got Moynihan; and for education commissioner got James Allen, "Mr. Busing." "It's been only three weeks," he concluded, "but conservatives are already asking, 'What's he done for us lately?' "[38]

Nixon's conversation told of the big things that could be done, a hundred ways to make that big play and so make a mark. Things that were right, that made sense because the time had come when he, as president of the United States, could achieve the positive. Moynihan, the liberal thinker, welcomed the prospect of being able to advance the kind of ideas on social policy that had been thwarted during infighting under the Democrats. In a strong sense, the Moynihan-Nixon marriage, dubious at the outset, got at the heart of the essential Nixon. Moynihan "wanted to succeed with the establishment," suggested Kevin Phillips, "but was also an outsider." Nixon appreciated the reality of the "whole failure of sociology" of the Great Society but allowed that side of him to be "buried by the Garments, Moynihans, and Finches."[39]

Phillips understood Moynihan's appeal to Nixon. He was the Irish kid from Hell's Kitchen whose mother ran a saloon on Forty-second Street, but he had made good and had played in the big leagues with the intellectuals. ("In the 1930's when I was growing up in New York City the Ivy League campuses were teeming with radical youth intent on redeeming the working man through the C.I.O. or whatever. We could not have cared less. From America Firsters to Young Communists they were all the same to us: 'rich college f---s.' I do not know, but strongly suspect, that especially to working class America, the misbehavior of students is seen as a form of class privilege. Which it is," Moynihan once reminisced to Nixon.[40] His liberalism was pure enough for vintage conservatism.

Moynihan had been to the world of Ivy Leaguers but had come from Nixon's America. At Cambridge, as director of the Joint Center for Urban Studies for Harvard and the Massachusetts Institute of Technology, he was the scholarship kid hacking his way socially in an upper-crust fraternity, wondering how he got there. When he called a student a "sociological phenomenon" for making Harvard just ten years after getting off a boat from the Chinese mainland, he was talking about himself. "I grew up in Hell's Kitchen," he said in 1965. "My father was a drunk. I know what life is like."[41] His father, a journalist and copy-writer, had another career as a gambler, alcoholic, and womanizer. When Pat was twelve, John Moynihan abandoned his family, leaving his wife and children to survive in a series of run-down West Side Manhattan apartments. She found wartime work in a defense plant, and enabled her family to upgrade itself from living with holes in the walls and paint flaking from the ceiling. Pat set up shop shining shoes in Times Square, establishing his sidewalk business on Forty-third Street near the old Paramount Theater. Taking advantage of the wartime work opportunities, he found a job as a stock boy in Gimbels and worked the West Side docks as a day laborer during the summer.

He read Karl Marx and Erskine Caldwell; for a while, but only briefly, he flirted with socialism. Mainly, he was devoted to Roosevelt and the Democratic party. Still, as with many Irish Catholics who were loyal to

FDR, Pat was impatient with theorists who wanted to make over the world. As a student in Manhattan's Benjamin Franklin High School, he was the only Irish kid among Puerto Ricans, blacks, and Italians. That, and working as a stevedore, gave him a good view of the working class. He got a firsthand view with the navy's wartime V-12 training program at little Middlebury College in Vermont. One fellow trainee, described as a "preppy friend," said afterward that "Moynihan was definitely an oddity. You really didn't know what to make of him." To them, he was radical, but when Truman ran into opposition from Henry Wallace and his Progressives, Moynihan was perceptive enough to understand that the president was being attacked by American Communists as a tactic to empower reactionaries and prove that capitalists were enemies of the people. For a time, he took up membership in a reform Democratic club and found how different those politicians were from their British counterparts, whom he had experienced while studying at the London School of Economics on a Fulbright scholarship. The Americans were interested in little but getting power and dispensing patronage. They knew little, and cared less, about laborers, and that was especially true of wealthy Manhattan reformers. As his biographer has written, he "believed he understood how working class people lived in a way that the upper middle class never could, and ultimately he came to resent them for presuming to speak for that stratum of society." When Richard Nixon wrote his memoirs, he quoted from a Moynihan memorandum about how America's "cultural elite" had "pretty generally rejected the values and activities of the larger society" since about 1840.[42]

One can, therefore, understand why Nixon found him so appealing, and why, for Moynihan, joining Nixon was a form of redemption. The new president was conservative, but that meant little. He was less dense than the liberals Moynihan had had to buck in the Labor Department and in the civil rights movement. Under the Democrats, Moynihan's ideas had drawn blanks. He tried to convince his liberal colleagues that civil rights legislation alone was not going to fill the stomachs of the poor. The underclass needed jobs, and no one else around Johnson believed more strongly that the most effective thing that could be done to save blacks from welfare and their own plight was to put them to work; Nixon really liked that about Moynihan.[43]

Still, it was the liberals around LBJ who gave Moynihan the most heartache. The best example was his report on the destruction of the black family. Moynihan was shocked to find himself denounced as a racist, even by civil rights leaders who should have known better; it was a "preposterous and fruitless controversy," he later wrote. They jumped all over him by interpreting the report as implying that since family structures were weak, any other remedies could only be futile. As Moynihan put it in a 1967 article, "You do not wipe away the scars of centuries by saying: Now you are free to go where you want, do as you desire; choose the leaders you please. You do not take a person who for years has been hobbled by chains and liberate him, bring him up to the starting line of a race and then say, 'You are free to compete with all the others,' and still justly believe that you have been completely fair." That sounded too much like Anatole France's point that the laws were fair to both the rich and the poor because they both had the right to sleep under bridges. No, argued Moynihan, black families had been hooked on welfare, and this country "simply cannot afford the luxury of having a large lower class that is at once deviant and dependent. . . . The time when white men, whatever their motives, could tell Negroes what was or was not good for them, is now definitely and decidedly over."[44]

Richard Nixon had also long agreed that employment was the first priority. Without money, all else would fail. That theme ran consistently through his political career, and through his administration's creation of the Philadelphia Plan and a program for minority enterprise that kept being known as "black capitalism." He still thinks along such lines when he maintains, in all earnestness, that his record on civil rights was "impeccable." "I want to see a program whereby we can cut substantially the subsidies for higher education," he informed his Domestic Affairs Council at the end of 1972, adding that "we might put a little more money into some of the black colleges. Certainly upgrading them a bit is infinitely more important and more needed than seeing that an assistant professor in an Ivy League college gets a higher income teaching than he could earn on the outside."[45] If one could be subsidized, so could the other. Moynihan's arguments about the evil of the welfare culture resembled the theories of conservative economist Milton Friedman, who had been advocating a negative income tax to subsidize families with very low incomes. Create a formula for putting money into people's hands, somehow, whether tied to income or jobs.

Attacking the "welfare chiselers" had grown through the sixties as a productive issue for all the ambitious in search of political paydirt. In Newburgh, New York, an enterprising city manager created a storm that went well beyond that Hudson Valley town by mandating forty hours of work each week with the city's building maintenance department for able-bodied men on relief. He also ordered the end to further support payments to mothers having additional children out of wedlock. Newburgh was immediately hailed for having seceded from the "Welfare State." The scheme aimed at sparing the town from further influxes of southern blacks by cutting off such payments.[46] The manager, Joseph McDowell Mitchell, finally got one able-bodied man to pick up papers from the city hall lawn. His plans ran into further difficulties in the courts, and he himself later left his job under a cloud to become an organizer for the John Birch Society. But the point had been made, and picked up all over the country.

The more sensational media led the way, and hair-raising stories about abuses of the nation's welfare system competed with accounts of crime in the streets. Everyone, it began to seem, either knew or had heard about some welfare cheat. Welfare queens were especially numerous, the stories telling all about how some black woman on the dole was using her Aid to Families with Dependent Children (AFDC) allowances for such "essentials" as color television sets; welfare kings were reportedly driving Caddies with funds from the public till. Then there were the welfare checks reported stolen or lost after having been cashed. More infuriating were accounts of how demonstrators demanding greater allowances had forced payments of additional millions. Nor was larceny confined to the poor, or the allegedly poor. Just as doctors and hospitals were profiteering from Medicaid, so were professionals dipping into the welfare till. A special study commissioned by the Massachusetts legislature found that all too often the intended recipients were being ripped off by unscrupulous vendors. In the Massachusetts case, the blame went to poor management by the state's welfare department. One antipoverty trainee in Boston was charged with stealing 352 welfare checks that gave him over $100,000. The Local Assistance Board of Elizabeth, New Jersey, discovered that 30 percent of those granted aid were not official residents of the city or state.[47]

Such stories were repeated with delight and there was little doubt, as the *New York Times* suggested editorially, that welfare was associated with "Negroes and sin." The anger behind the "white backlash" was all too ready to ignore the root of the problem and punish the "victims of society."[48]

In truth, however, there was little good to be said for the system, other than it kept some people alive. The problems were real. Even if one were to grant the total absence of cheating, something had to be done. Allowances varied egregiously from state to state. Requirements that eligible households had to be fatherless discouraged family cohesiveness. Even more serious to many, of greater concern than the abuses or the total cost to society, was that the culture of poverty was becoming a culture of welfare. A New York City University Center for Social Research Survey found that 15 percent of the mothers who were on welfare were the daughters of recipients. Making the point even more emphatic was that 46 percent of the mothers receiving such aid had been on welfare since before 1960.[49]

By 1968, hardly anyone had anything good to say about the system. The only defense was that a civilized society had to take some steps to counter starvation, especially when the victims were innocent children.

But the cost to society was becoming startling. New York City, and the Lindsay administration in particular, came under special fire because welfare costs had gotten out of control. For the first time in history, the city's payments had become the largest single item in its budget, going to fourteen thousand additional recipients each month. But costs were zooming on the West Coast, too, where Governor Reagan predicted that California's share of such expenditures for the 1968–1969 fiscal year would near $410 million. That the problem was national was underscored by President Johnson's appointment of a special study commission under industrialist Ben Heineman.[50]

The consensus seemed clear: the present system shortchanged both society and its dependents. Heineman's group urged that a floor be placed under income, an idea that was also expressed by schemes for income maintenance. Friedman's negative income tax, about the most prominent of such notions, was endorsed, in one way or another, by a commission appointed by Nelson Rockefeller, Moynihan's Joint Center for Urban Studies, the Arden House Committee for Public Welfare, the *New York Times*, and the Brookings Institution. Various schemes for providing bedrock subsistence had been around for over three decades, from FDR's 1935 urging that "health and decency" required a minimum welfare payment, through Truman's proposals for the protection of the working poor and the income maintenance suggestions of the Heineman Commission. As historian James Patterson has written, "Many supporters of a floor were conservatives who, like Friedman, hoped that some such plan could at once cut costs, enhance work incentives, and abolish the welfare bureaucracy." For them, Patterson adds, it promised "a quick, cheap solution to the 'crisis' of welfare."[51]

Both political parties called for a complete overhaul of the system in their national platforms, and Nixon seconded their point in his acceptance speech at Miami Beach. Tying income to work requirements, by creating jobs at the local level, was especially popular. Bobby Kennedy appeared headed in that direction. George Wallace certainly was already there. In a television interview in Providence, Rhode Island, that summer, the governor called for a reappraisal of the entire welfare program. Those who refused to work for reasonable wages should be excluded; the welfare rolls should be purged of persons "that ought not to be on them."[52] To some, the federal government had to do more than formulate new rules. It had to take on, as the Heineman Commission urged, a greater assumption of the costs, but it also had to do something about the differences that states were willing to pay out.

The greatest gap was between North and South. Southern states, it was suspected, kept relief payments low as a means of encouraging the departure of unneeded black labor. Indeed, as City Manager Mitchell assumed in Newburgh, the poor were wandering in search of higher welfare payments, a suspicion that was never adequately tested. Nevertheless, it was true that strains on the AFDC program were attributable to the massive movement of excess labor from southern farms to urban areas of the North.[53] That, together with the changing market for menial labor that characterized a modern technological society, was helping to create a permanent ghetto underclass.

The point became perhaps the sharpest preelection difference between Richard Nixon and his running mate. Spiro Agnew, accepting the premise that disparities from state to state motivated migrations, pulled no punches. He spoke out and wrote about the need for equalization of payments. In an interview that followed a speech in San Francisco, Agnew even said he would work to convince Nixon to support federalizing the program. Within little over a month, Nixon seemed to be moving toward that view, and he finally said so. At first, he called for a "national standard," then he followed that up with the clarification that he was talking about "equivalent but not necessarily equal" amounts.[54]

Nixon knew he had to act. There were several unavoidable truths about welfare: only crime was more closely linked with racial resentment and working middle-class anxiety; welfare dependency as a way of life was creating an underclass increasingly closed off from traditional routes of economic mobility; the expanding bureaucracy was equally dependent on the system; real destruction was being done to family units; and finally, hovering overhead as the incarnation of a gathering, and potentially ugly, protest force, there was the increasing Wallace threat. Somewhat less earthy when he pitched his message northward, Wallace used welfare to epitomize the evils of the federal bureaucracy. Moynihan, defensive before his liberal academic friends about his new Republican colleagues, explained that he found that they were "very nice people with a perfectly dreadful constituency." They had to cater to the Nixon and Wallace voters of 1968.[55]

If, as journalist Pete Hamill wrote, not all of Wallace's votes were "from red-necked racists," they nevertheless reflected growing conflict over how threatened the working class felt by aid to America's blacks.[56] Nobody so effectively stirred the anger of those who toiled for a wage, especially those who had not one job but two, and more likely than not, whose wives and children were also out trying to bring in more money. Wallace did not even have to say much about welfare directly. His message needed no interpreters.

Moynihan gave Nixon the spark for doing something specific. The Irishman from New York knew his hardworking laborers. He knew something about group interaction. He had joined with sociologist Nathan Glazer to write *Beyond the Melting Pot,* an important book about New York City's ethnic groups. The two authors (Glazer the major contributor) found not a loss of group identity, nor the realization of Israel

Zangwill's early twentieth-century dreamy prose ("Yes, East and West, and North and South, the palm and the pine, the pole and the equator, the crescent and the cross — how the great Alchemist melts and fuses them with his purging flame! Here shall they all unite to build the Republic of Man and the Kingdom of God"), but divisions and consciousness along clearly defined ethnic lines. Moynihan convinced Nixon that welfare had to be replaced with an income policy, one that avoided playing into and feeding mutual group jealousies and hostilities. As a conservative, the president had a chance to emulate British Tories and reach down to do something for the lower classes. Moynihan had not read Robert Blake's massive biography of Benjamin Disraeli, but he understood how Disraeli had taken hold of the social agenda. He understood Nixon, too. As Moynihan has since pointed out, "Nixon had a very thin life as a child, and his instinct was always to identify and sympathize with poor people"; he was even "prepared to use government where appropriate" to make life more equitable.[57]

Nixon would do well to read about Disraeli's life, Moynihan suggested. The president, who always did his homework, was impressed. Twice, in March of 1970, he quoted the English statesman in public statements about educational reform. At the very end of the year, Nixon told Moynihan and George Shultz that he had spent some of the past weekend with Blake's book. It was notable, he thought, that Disraeli, "born a Jew" and "in trouble during youth," became the "ablest practical politician of the late 1800's in Britain." He was even a novelist and a poet. That's what we need, said Nixon, "a little more poetry." He talked about Tolstoy and Churchill and their broader views of the cosmos, so unlike what one saw in Washington and much of the federal bureaucracy. The Disraeli device — and it was a device — was a fine way to convince Nixon that commitment to social concerns did not mean one had to abandon conservatism. It might even, as had such regimes as Bismarck's in Germany, promote the stability that conservatives were supposed to care about. Buying the idea, of course, did not make Nixon comfortable in his new clothes. Calling it "Family Security" would offend too many conservatives, but as Nixon reflected to one of Bob Finch's aides, he was hardly more at ease with the new name. "Family Assistance is, as you know," he said, "blah." Out of earshot of the HEW aide, and certainly not in Finch's presence, he later made the observation that for that department to handle welfare was like placing an alcoholic in charge of the bar.[58]

Reservations and all, Nixon had already made his play. Over a month before the inauguration, he announced that Moynihan would head a new Urban Affairs Council. The managerial model would be the National Security Council. Nixon immediately went to work, welfare becoming his chief domestic priority right from the start. Five days before January 20, setting the kind of draconian deadline that became his characteristic when he really wanted things done, he ordered Moynihan, Bob Finch, John Mitchell, and Bryce Harlow, to come up with a "thorough investigation" of the "New York welfare mess" by January 31. "The American people are outraged and, in my opinion, they should be," Nixon wrote.[59]

Over the objections of most of his cabinet, welfare reform became the centerpiece of what he called a New Federalism, which he announced on August 8, 1969. It called for a massive reordering of the way government went about doing things, a pullback from the concentration of power that had been going on ever since New Deal days. It was not designed to do for the disadvantaged what the Great Society had failed to accomplish. That kind of objective had little support from the administration, the Republican party, or the American people. George Will, the conservative journalist, put the matter very bluntly when he wrote that "most Americans are not much interested in poverty, and not at all interested in poverty programs."[60] They were not exactly interested, either, in having Washington destroy entitlements. They *were* most interested in who got what was spent and, if it was more controllable by having greater access on the local level, so much the better. Nixon did not set out to destroy the American welfare state; he tried to reconcile what remained to prevailing political realities; and, along the way, he had to be convinced that it was consistent with his own sense of social justice.

Calling it New Federalism, however, also did not seem very precise. Pat Buchanan, who suggested the term to speechwriter James Keogh, thought it might be a way of satisfying all hands, but that hardly made it adequate for signaling that the problem was being met. Safire thought the term landed "with a thud." Nixon himself feared that it might be understood that they were scheming to give "new powers to the Supreme Court." Arthur Burns, who took a dim view of the Moynihan-plotted direction, worried that New Federalism was "fine for the intellectuals, but the average man can't grasp it."[61]

Nixon, also unhappy about the name and desperately in search of something else to call his legislative package, was more concerned about the implications — and how it could be implemented. How, for example, could one truly sort out the appropriate level of government at which problems could best be handled? The Great Society's community action program, the target of Moynihan's most incisive critique, was a good example of what was considered "conservative": local people coping with local problems; local people knowing better than faraway bureaucrats what was best for them. But the reality was too often something different. Power at the grass-roots level still looked upward to state and federal agencies to preserve that very same power. The federal system itself, perhaps through the "genius" of the Founding Fathers, or maybe through their naïveté, set into motion competition for control. Roosevelt's original Social Security Act illustrated the dilemma. Inequities were built in through the idea of letting each state decide its own level of contribution. Now Nixon was calling for his New Federalism by floating the implication that Washington's role would be reduced while actually planning the opposite, a national standard for income maintenance — liberal ideas in conservative wrappings. "In essence," Safire has acknowledged, their "New Federalism" could be called "the Old Stinginess." Nixon's credentials as a conservative could not be justified without some scheme for decentralization; "*but*," writes Safire, "*not always*. In the understanding of that 'but,' the reason for major exceptions, is the idea of the New Federalism."[62]

But exactly where did that leave Nixon? True, he wanted stability; so would any true conservative; so did the American people when they elected him. Some of those who watched the new president were not sure whether he understood his own priorities or where he wanted to aim the country. Hardly any critic, either such conservatives as George Will or liberals like Daniel Schorr, went unnoticed by the White House. No administration, of course, can ignore public relations, and none experiences power without yeoman efforts at its manipulation. When CBS commentator Eric Sevareid followed Nixon's New Federalism proposals by raising speculation about the president's somewhat contradictory philosophy, a little group within the White House that was concerned with such problems — Safire was one, and Herb Klein, Len Garment, Pat Buchanan, Ray Price, and Jim Keogh were among the others — considered how to respond. As speechwriters and idea men, they were the ones primarily responsible for feeding the American people, directly or through the media, the character and ideas of Richard Nixon.[63]

Safire played around with such ideas on his typewriter. Any administration, he realized, was more likely to respond to events as of the moment rather than along the lines of a well-thought-out plan of action. So Safire's was more a contribution to the dialogue than a demarche. Reminiscent of the letters of Hamilton, Madison, and Jay in support of ratifying the Constitution of 1787, Safire's paper was called "New Federalist Paper #1" and, following the Hamilton-Madison-Jay precedent, was signed "Publius."

He recalled the patriotic celebration that greeted President Grant's opening of the Centennial Exposition in Philadelphia's Fairmount Park. When Nixon, due to play that role in 1976, opened the bicentennial, "there will be the customary excitement about space probes and scientific advance, but a patriotic fervor, with varying degrees of self-consciousness, will color the nation's emotions. It will be a time for a reaching for common purpose and a re-dedication to great ideals." In 1976, unlike 1876, the celebration "will be more localized than centralized, more soul-searching than breast-beating," and, paradoxically, we would be decentralizing the commemoration of how we established a nation by moving the disparate colonies toward centralization. True, he added, Americans relished the offerings of a strong central government, "a clear direction toward social goals, a willingness to counteract economic freezings and overheatings, a single voice in world affairs. But we are repelled by centralization's side effects: ineffective administration, inflexible bureaucracy and the resultant alienation and resentment." What was being called "the new Federalism," the modern-day Publius suggested, would be more accurately described as "national localism." Ultimately, after dismissal as another "middle of the road" concept, it might come to be appreciated as "a useful new development in American politics — and what has been represented as simple pragmatism may reveal some ideological subtlety."[64] Of course, that is what it turned out to be, a shifting from where government had gone under Roosevelt and the Democrats, toward a new set of shared responsibilities.

While the intellectuals around Nixon debated what they were doing, the reception from the nation's press was overwhelmingly favorable. Almost everyone applauded the merging of a work requirement with the Family Assistance Plan (FAP). Negative comments came from but a small minority. Not "more than 30" were essentially critical, reported Hess, and they reflected annoyance that he was, in effect, trying to continue the welfare state under a different guise. He was letting off mothers with dependent children too easily, not insisting on work requirements for them as well. Over four hundred newspapers were surveyed at the White House and, of that total, just five objected to FAP as an "insignificant attack on the root problems of poverty."[65] The press was with him, at least the preponderance of papers from all over America.

Moynihan's push for income equalization aimed at boosting the bottom so that it approximated the center of the income distribution scale. A plan to provide for family allowances would minimize resentments through a formula based on earnings, without pitting one group against another, or one class against another. The outcome would be a more stable society instead of the kind of divisions that could result in right-wing repression.[66]

If not through a negative income tax, the new plan might be accomplished through direct payments, perhaps tied to work. It would simultaneously make for efficiency by bypassing the bloated bureaucracy without depriving the needy, thereby increasing the efficiency of each dollar spent. Moreover, the present system rested on a bureaucracy that had grown for almost thirty-five years to include large staffs at the Department of Health, Education, and Welfare in Washington and at state and local governments. Altogether, the country's welfare process was in the hands of 1,152 separate units.[67]

Finally, after endless reconciliations of divergent views, the New Federalism program marked that great retreat from New Deal–era concentration of power in Washington. Introducing what was liberal as conservative, and what was conservative as liberal, Nixon announced the advent of revenue-sharing, which was Arthur Burns's pet plan. Federal money, at last, would be returned to the states to be controlled locally. Liberals distrustful of grass-roots priorities lamented that decisions would be made by regional power interests rather than by federal planners. On that same televised announcement, the president presented what Moynihan had been fighting for, with but minor alterations. Now known as the Family Assistance Plan, it envisioned a radical overhaul of the discredited welfare system. Instead of continuing the AFDC program, the federal government would set a national minimum income standard that would neither penalize those who worked nor encourage the breakup of families. "What I am proposing," explained the president, "is that the Federal Government build a foundation under the income of every American family with dependent children that cannot care for itself — and wherever in America that family may live." A minimum level would support all such families, with additional income possible through contributions by the states and outside earnings. Each dollar earned would reduce benefits by only fifty cents, so that "those who work would no longer be discriminated against." Finally, the government would recognize its obligation to the working poor as well as to the nonworking poor. Those accepting benefits would also have to accept work or suitable training, with the mothers of preschool children the only exceptions. "A guaranteed income establishes a right without any responsibilities," Nixon added; "family assistance recognizes a need and establishes a responsibility."[68]

Conservatives were clearly unhappy. Agnew, the vice president, wasn't at all shy about stating his objections when the cabinet met at Camp David just before the Senate was due to vote on acceptance of the antiballistic missile system. The problem with FAP, he stated at the open meeting while the president looked on, was that it "adds 13 million people to the welfare rolls." And then he asked, "Isn't it possible to fix the deficiencies of the present system — with regard to work incentives and day care — without adding these 13 million people to the rolls? Can't we repair and improve the present system?" At that point, George Romney chimed in with the thought about middle-class opposition. To all this, Nixon said nothing, which was not unusual when such views were expressed by the cabinet. Others, especially Agnew, however, were not about to drop the point. When the vice president was alerted that it was time to catch the helicopter so he could get back to the Hill for a possible Senate vote on the ABM system, he grinned at Nixon and said, "If it's a tie, Mr. President, I'll call and see if you have changed your mind about the welfare program."[69]

With Agnew gone, Nixon returned to the subject, acknowledging that welfare reform had less support than revenue-sharing and his manpower proposals. Cost, he explained, was principally behind the opposition, but then he concluded the meeting with a strong sales pitch. "I know the welfare road we have been on is the wrong road," he said. "It is a total disaster. I don't want to just patch it up; we must move in a new direction. We don't know that the program we have decided upon will solve the problem, but I like the balance between work and security. And now that the decision has been made, I ask that everyone join in the process of selling this as a very exciting new domestic program. As it was with the moon program, the word here should be 'Go.' "[70]

The pep talk was fine, but Nixon was a man of few illusions. He never underestimated the intransigence of those at the political extremes, and nothing that he heard and read came as a surprise. Nixon may have "couched" his proposal in the "rhetoric of conservatism," concluded the American Conservative Union, but the reality was that the Family Assistance Plan was guaranteed support for permanent indolence. Both the welfare proposal and the president's request for the creation of a National Institute of Education within the Department of Health, Education, and Welfare, which Nixon introduced to the Congress on September 11, 1970, were precisely opposed to where conservatives should be going. Revenue-sharing at least aimed at a historic decentralization, providing for a shift of power away from Washington. Keep that, John Ehrlichman told the president at San Clemente in January 1971; increase its funding, but cut FAP and health. Arthur Burns, who became Federal Reserve chairman in the fall of 1969, and his staff, including the brilliant young economist Martin Anderson, were also against the concept. James Kilpatrick was especially influential in spreading the alarm. Kilpatrick warned that Nixon was serving up "a pack of pretty rhetoric and tied with a bow of conservative blue. Sad to say, some of us who should have known better were fairly swept off our feet."[71] There was little love among the right wing for the concept of welfare in the first place, but to find a Republican president *guaranteeing* income — and with *federal* dollars — was a heresy not to be overlooked.

Nixon backed that up in his State of the Union message for 1971 with his call for a "New American Revolution" to implement such objectives as full employment, health care, environmental protection, reform of the federal bureaucracy, and revenue-sharing, as well as welfare reform, all, as he stated, through the framework of a governmental restructuring that might become "fully responsive to the needs and wishes of the American people." Of the six goals enumerated that day, he gave welfare reform the highest priority.[72]

Columnist Carl Rowan had it just about right when he noted at the outset of the administration that Nixon "is clearly not what he said he was, not what Democrats feared he was, nor even what Republicans hoped he was during the presidential campaign." More often, liberals remained skeptical about the president's motives. Programs that depended on more local powers, they suspected, were merely subterfuges for funneling federal money away from the urban poor and toward more traditional grass-roots Republicans. They were not far off. The ideology of self-help and individual initiative, as opposed to having the poor wedded to government largesse, remained a strong part of Nixon's makeup. When, for example, he wanted to boost the family assistance program in a statement at a conference on children, he suggested to Ray Price that "you might point out the fact that in the depression years I remember when my brother had tuberculosis for five years and we had to keep him in a hospital, my mother didn't buy a new dress for five years. We were really quite desperately poor, but as Eisenhower said it much more eloquently at Abilene in his opening campaign statement in 1952, the glory of it was that we didn't know it."[73]

But the mechanism of the American legislative system was incapable of achieving what sociologist Nathan Glazer called "the most enlightened and thoughtful legislation to have been introduced in the field of welfare in some decades."[74] At least it was true of that moment, during the Nixon era, during common acknowledgment that the current system had failed; and, though the administration retreated at the end, there had been genuine presidential urgings for adoption of FAP as a crucial part of his New Federalism.

What happened to FAP is an instructive case study, neither completely positive nor completely negative. It illustrated the barriers that doomed progress even in the presence of relatively substantial bipartisan consensus. American society, as Nixon and other presidents ultimately appreciated, had become so complex that movement, even if generally assumed to be desirable and necessary, became virtually impossible. That was less the case for the torrent of programs enacted by Johnson as part of his Great Society; but, it may be argued, they were specifically targeted, carried by the momentum of Kennedy's martyrdom and LBJ's talents for exploiting that mood, and, alas, poorly conceived and inadequately implemented in the rush to action.

With FAP, Nixon and his supporters faced something entirely different. Implications ranged from making decisions about what were the responsibilities of society and what were the best interests of the nation to gauging the impact upon constituent interest groups. The United

States Chamber of Commerce, for example, was vehemently opposed to supplementing the incomes of the working poor. It would only bloat the welfare rolls and costs, and, while redistributing wealth, would reduce self-reliance "from an ideal to an option." The attack by the major business organization, which represented some thirty-five thousand firms, was effective, pointing out that incomes would still flow to families with heads who rejected the work or training provisions. That slothful bodies would not actually be forced to enter the job market fed a skepticism about the nature of man that was shared by Nixon. "It's not the natural tendency of people to want to work," he said to a few of his speechwriters in the summer of 1972. By implication, at least, the president and the Chamber of Commerce shared an outlook that was not a sticking point with the National Association of Manufacturers, which supported the plan.[75]

However much assurances about the efficacy of "workfare" provisions were accepted or rejected, the fact remains that the Chamber of Commerce was the sole major business opponent of FAP. Far more were in support, including the more conservative, more upper-crust Committee for Economic Development. As Moynihan has pointed out, "There was business-conservative opposition to FAP, but it was never massive, and it was never unanimous."[76] The opposition tended to be less organized, ranging from Governor Reagan's objections to minimum standards and fear about the absence of a genuine work requirement, to those who claimed that the floor payments were too low or disliked anything sounding like a guaranteed annual income supported by the federal government.

Those in favor of reform, however, wanted just that — reform; the precise form was another matter. A Gallup survey that tried to determine popular reactions to guaranteeing all families of four an income of at least $3,200 a year by having the government supplement earnings that fell below that level, showed that 62 percent of the American people were opposed. When, however, Gallup asked whether they favored the guarantee not of income but of *work* that would yield the same income level, that kind of plan was welcomed by 79 percent.[77] There could be no suspicion that any new policy would constitute a government handout to the poor, a perception that would rise with any increase in the level of basic supports even with the workfare provision. Variations of the desired income suggested by advocacy groups went as high as $6,500 annually, which was urged by the more radical National Welfare Rights Organization. Organized labor had its own requirements, pegged to an hourly wage rate that would keep the unemployed from taking jobs away from existing union members. All in all, with the National Association of Counties taking the lead, meetings were held among some twenty participant groups, including religious, charity, civic, employee, and business groups. Meanwhile, John Gardner's self-proclaimed "citizen's lobby," Common Cause, kept the public informed of what was going on in an effort to mobilize support. Throughout the entire period, hearings were held on Capitol Hill by the House Ways and Means and the Senate Finance committees of the Ninety-first and Ninety-second Congresses.

Those hearings, which began in April 1970, illustrated the problem. The Senate Finance Committee was heavily rural and southern and, despite the disproportionate assistance such areas would receive through income equalization, those legislators were most resistant. Abe Ribicoff of Connecticut, a former HEW head under Kennedy, wanted a higher base rate. One of Ribicoff's colleagues on the Finance Committee, John Williams, just about undercut any movement toward the plan by pulling the bill apart brilliantly. When testifying at the hearings, Secretary Finch was no match for the able conservative from Delaware. Williams's detailed dissection of the proposed financing, when he considered it with other entitlement programs, portrayed FAP as something that would more than double the number of people on welfare. Moynihan, noting all this, has written that most of the committee had all but decided beforehand "that FAP would provide disincentives to work, *and that this could be shown.*"[78]

Moreover, in attempting to prod Wilbur Mills's House Ways and Means Committee, Finch hurt his own cause by his sharp criticism of the chairman in a speech before the National Press Club.[79] Nor did the administration, meanwhile, help itself with liberals by trying to placate the conservatives by adding more stringent workfare provisions.

When Nixon announced in February of 1973 that, after having resubmitted FAP three times before, he would not do so in the ninety-third Congress, he was only marking the official end of the effort. In late December, 1972, with just ten days left in the old session, a congressional conference committee stopped trying to reconcile irreconcilable differences. Welfare reform was dead, not to be achieved until late in the Reagan era fifteen years later with passage of the first federally mandated work requirement for welfare recipients. That bill, which required single parents on welfare whose children were over the age of three to find regular work and thereby get off the dole or to take job-training courses, had the chief sponsorship of Senator Daniel Patrick Moynihan of New York.[80]

Why the delay? Why Nixon's failure? "Everyone engaged in the battle has his own perceptions of what went wrong," wrote Senator Ribicoff. Ribicoff was the most active among the Democrats on the Finance Committee in holding out for higher levels of support; he faulted the White House's leadership after Moynihan left the administration at the end of 1970 to return to Harvard. Ribicoff was equally certain that Nixon himself had withdrawn from the battle.[81]

After the bill died in the Finance Committee in late 1970, the administration sent up a revised version to the next Congress with a $2,400 income floor but without a food stamp program and other protections for the poor. It got through Ways and Means, then passed the House handily, but again it was stalled in the Senate committee. When the administration announced a new economic policy on August 15, 1971, Nixon asked that welfare reform be delayed by a year.

That proved crucial. If all the inherent problems were not enough, the death blow came from a liberal Democrat, George McGovern of South Dakota. Senator McGovern's primary campaign en route to his party's nomination in 1972 advanced a proposal for a "demogrant" that would provide a thousand-dollar annual payment to every man, woman, and child in America. McGovern, who first announced his plan on January 13, 1972, thereby doomed whatever chance FAP had. His version of income subsistence became a laughingstock. Even Manolo Sanchez, Nixon's manservant, said that if it went into effect, "I quit — go on welfare." In a series of three debates with McGovern before the June 6 California primary, Hubert Humphrey exposed the political vulnerability of the idea, which suffered greatly from its sponsor's inadequate notion of the potential cost. Herb Stein, giving the McGovern proposal lengthy exposure before a bankers' meeting at Hot Springs, Virginia, concluded that "the plan amounts to shuffling around about $210-billion for the sake of giving something like $5-billion or $10-billion to the poor people." The real beneficiaries, he pointed out, would be those with $5,000 to $10,000 annual incomes rather than the poor.[82] He had, it seems, done McGovern's analysis for him; had it been done by the Democratic candidate, a lot of political grief would have been avoided. With neither liberals nor conservatives pleased, and with the idea of a guaranteed income apparently discredited, the administration had little reason to continue the fight.

When the president met with the cabinet at Camp David on April 21, 1972, some three months after McGovern unveiled his plan and eight months before the final congressional deadlock, Nixon suggested what to do about FAP. "Flush it," he said. "Blame it on the budget." He had already gotten an earful from Arthur Burns and Martin Anderson, and now he was ready to accept their advice. Charles Colson, special counsel to the president, agreed that as long as the Democrats were on the left, it made little sense for the administration to move toward the center. Nevertheless, at year's end, Nixon was surprised to find his Domestic Affairs Council still clinging to FAP among the programs for 1973. "I don't think I could have made it more clear over the past few months that I am convinced that the family assistance program is no longer viable," he responded sharply, "and that we must move in other directions in attacking the welfare mess. Yet the tired old reference to subsidizing the 'working poor' somehow found its way in the paper which was submitted to me."[83]

Nixon later recalled that "it wasn't because I gave up on the idea; I didn't. I thought it was still a good idea. It was because my operatives on the Hill, Bryce Harlow, Timmons, and the rest said we just can't hack it. Jerry Ford said it's not going to work." He was also "up against an unholy alliance. The right wing didn't want it, and I was bringing them along kicking and screaming. But you know the people that were against it — the people who had a vested interest, the damn social workers.

"Oh, I know it [abandoning FAP] was necessary, in order to keep the country together and to keep the coalition together. Politically, I wasn't going to pick up by reason of my support of FAP, by reason of my support of the Philadelphia Plan, by reason of my impeccable civil rights record, by reason of my minority business things, all of which were progressive ideas. I knew that I wasn't going to pick up a substantial number of the liberal Democrats, the black Democrats, et cetera. I knew that wasn't going to happen. . . . I had to at least take positions that the liberals didn't like. The liberals have a litmus test: you've got to be all for us or you're against us." He could have added that southern legislators remained unenthusiastic throughout the fight, even though their states would have been prime fiscal beneficiaries.[84] Equalization was evidently troublesome.

At Camp David after his first year in office, wondering what his presidency would look like by the time the nation celebrated its bicentennial in 1976, Nixon's mind reached for something distinctive. "Need for a name," he wrote on his yellow pad. "Square Deal. Fair Deal, New Deal, New Frontier, Great Society." It was Safire who pointed out the importance of having an idealistic theme in time for the bicentennial. Nixon, like the two Roosevelts, Truman, Kennedy, and Johnson, needed something positive, something consistent with the "national purpose and goals." Four days later, continuing to brood, he toted up his score so far and decided that he had reestablished dignity in the White House but was falling into the danger of looking like he was being "*managed* by planners." He wasn't sure where he stood, or where he ought to go — or, for that matter, what would be the force that *he* could lead. If he formed a new party, would it be conservative or would it be liberal? By late October 1970, he had decided that his "major role is moral leadership. I cannot exercise this adequately unless I speak out more often & more eloquently." Then he berated himself for allowing his time to be taken up by Haldeman and Kissinger "in purely instant discussion which could be left to others." What he really needed, he decided, was "for more stimulating people to talk to."[85] Just then, Moynihan was about to leave the White House staff.

The president had received just what he would expect from the Urban Affairs Council chairman, another long memo, a long good-bye, telling him, as though he did not already know, that, if anything, rejection of "the authority of American society has continued on the increase in the past two years. We have," Moynihan went on, "seen the beginning of organized terrorism, of a more or less classic Nihilist pattern of upper class youth blowing up the symbols of their parents' authority, and on occasion themselves as well." Then he added, calling it possibly "the most important point" he ever made to him:

> I do not know which has surprised me most: the sudden emergence of a revolutionary neo-Marxist critique of American society, or the almost total incapacity of the moderate-to-conservative forces of the society to argue back. The silent majority is silent because it has nothing to say. . . . Like Orwell's working class, it lives in a world not far removed from Victorian virtues. I for one find those virtues — confidence in the nation, love of the nation, a willingness to sacrifice for it — priceless. But the symbols of those beliefs are tattered, even at times tawdry. It is not fair. But it is true.[86]

Nixon would miss Moynihan. "Every time we get a little down, every time we need a little inspiration," he told the cabinet just before Christmas, "we're going to want to call him back to give it to us."[87]

19

"Tell It to Hanoi"

IF EVER A PRESIDENT could understand the ordeal of his predecessor, Richard Nixon understood Lyndon Johnson's. Rebels emanating from the campuses, the voices of America's privileged, had fired hatred, refusing to accept any explanation that tried to rationalize the war in Southeast Asia — whether in terms of morality, internationalism, or the predicament of a great power trapped, ridiculed, and searching for an honorable solution. Instead, they denounced, marched, carried candles, and threw whatever they could, even bombs. Weirdos, peaceniks, flower children, and just plain pot-smoking, free-love types threatened to paralyze the political system.[1] The televised "battle of Chicago" seen by millions at the time of the 1968 Democratic convention had few rivals in America as an instance of destructive class warfare. Certainly none had a larger audience. One onlooker, George Wallace, warned that increased militancy from "Marxist-Communist" protest groups would bring repression from the right, and that repression, he added, could even interfere with the freedoms of ordinary working people.[2]

As Richard Scammon, a precise pulse-taker of American politics, told an interviewer, Nixon and Johnson faced problems that were not really that different. He would not be surprised, added Scammon, to find Nixon "a successor to Lyndon Johnson and consensus, rather than a departure from them." What about the New Politics movement that worked so hard to dump LBJ? he was asked. "I think," said Scammon, "if there is to be a New Politics in America, it's going to be the New Politics of the gray flannel suit, of Nixon's pragmatic center. I don't think it'll be the New Politics of the beard and the sandal and the shades." Perhaps, said Scammon, recollecting the lessons learned by Len Hall, politicians were more likely to be prisoners than shapers of events.[3]

Johnson, in retirement at his Texas ranch, would have had to be Jesus himself not to feel vindicated. Interviewed in mid-1970, he couldn't help but gloat that Nixon was getting bogged down in Cambodia. Nor were the Nixon people so generous that a year later they failed to consider whether challenging the publication of classified Pentagon documents — the so-called Pentagon Papers — might be seen as helping to cover up Johnson's ill-advised policies.[4]

Beyond that, there were other similarities, not only in circumstances but in personalities. Each hated critics and could understand the other's discomfort. If Nixon was supersensitive about the press, Johnson was apoplectic, if only because he was less accustomed to their ways. Even their enemies were similar: the doves on the Hill; the boys who went to Harvard, Yale, and those other Ivy League schools, so different from the Whittiers and Southwest Texas State Teachers Colleges of Middle America. They bugged those who would do them in, both their enemies and their leakers. They, unlike the superintellectuals, *cared* about the Communist conspiracy and never minimized dangers to national security. Nixon went to Austin for the dedication of the Johnson Library and kept inviting the ex-president to visit him at the White House, but LBJ's heart problems got in the way. Now Nixon, as Johnson before him, faced the war on the streets. But, he wrote to Henry Kissinger, unlike LBJ, "I have the *will* in spades."[5]

And he seemed ready to stand up to it all. The summer of 1969 had not been all that bad. A scientific marvel had been accomplished for the ages. The spaceship *Apollo II*, with astronauts Neil A. Armstrong and Edwin "Buzz" Aldrin, Jr., landed at Tranquility Base on the moon. "Hello Neil and Buzz," said the president in a conversation that traveled through the universe, "I am talking to you by telephone from the Oval Room in the White House, and this certainly has to be the most historic telephone call ever made from the White House." The accidental drowning death of Mary Jo Kopechne, Senator Edward Kennedy's female companion, had just about eliminated Kennedy as a rival for 1972. Gallup polls were consistently showing Nixon's popularity in the mid-sixties, Eisenhower-style levels, despite all the noise. Nixon's economists were talking more about the value of compiling a budgetary surplus for full employment than about inflation. He even got his approval for the ABM system. Agnew, for all his bluster about making the president cry uncle about welfare reform, assured success for the weapons by casting the tie-breaking vote.[6]

The antiwar kids, souped up on anti-Nixon and antiestablishment passions, got together and let off some real steam by doing their thing. At least 300,000 — some estimates approached the half-million mark — made their way by car, foot, and even helicopter to the six-hundred-acre farm of Max Yasgur in the tiny Catskill town of Bethel, some seventy miles northwest of New York City. A rock festival for the ages, billed as

"Three Days of Peace and Music," brought together thirty of the top music groups and entertainment heroes of the counterculture. They were all there, it seemed — The Band, Sly and the Family Stone, Creedence Clearwater Revival, Jimi Hendrix, Sha-Na-Na, Joan Baez, The Who, Jefferson Airplane, Janis Joplin, and they were a magnet for the unmanageable numbers ready to join other New Utopians. Many paid eighteen dollars for the three days and nights of participation in the spiritual "greening" of their nonmaterialistic, love-filled, nonviolent "Woodstock Nation," which was nothing less than a "Festival of Life." They had created a great event in the development of American youth culture, said the young promoters. And, in many ways, it was true. One young man was unfortunately run over by a tractor as he lay tucked in his sleeping bag, and two others were victims of other accidents. But even the local police and townspeople, who were apprehensive about holding the event in the first place, said they had never met kids who were so polite. Things were also smooth for the beefed-up security that was imported from as far away as the Fillmore East rock club in Manhattan and a commune in New Mexico, which cost the promoters sixteen thousand dollars for a chartered airliner.[7]

The kids could feel like Christian martyrs, without enough toilet facilities and food, access to the site tied up by traffic jams that stretched along country roads for twenty miles, threatening to cancel the horse races at the Monticello track. Performers had to be air-dropped by helicopter. The hillside, facing the stage and the gigantic speakers that hovered overhead, was matted with the stripped-down torsos of men and women trying to find a spot on the grass. The August heat encouraged the removal of clothes, and some waded bare when cooling off in a nearby lake. Then came rainstorms that turned the well-churned ground into mud, which seemed but a minor inconvenience for freedom and virtue. Some made love on impulse, and there was pot-smoking, the sweet scent of marijuana everywhere. A handful were arrested for violating the drug laws, but mostly the problem was treating the nearly five thousand who had smoked too much or suffered from other distresses. Two apparently drug-related deaths were later reported. (Performers Jimi Hendrix and Janis Joplin had their young lives shortened by drugs not long afterward.) If it was, as some called it, a "Children's Crusade," it was also reminiscent of the Bacchanalian revelries.[8]

The president remained publicly silent but deplored the whole thing. Privately, he was offended at the rock culture, the double entendres of the music; it was a subtle, insidious underside of American life. Something ought to be done, perhaps by the Federal Communications Commission, which should monitor broadcasting such events to the public. "The most influential news media in the United States," complained Nixon speechwriter Jim Keogh, "told the youth of the country and the world that what had happened at Woodstock was beautiful."[9] Middle Americans shook their heads over the whole thing, especially the drug scene, and praised the Lord that their own children were not there.

Nixon, who later established the Drug Enforcement Agency, wanted to act right away. One thought was decriminalization of marijuana, which might ease drug enforcement. But he had his doubts that Middle America would go for it. How could they be sold that kind of notion? Such apprehensions were amply confirmed, including a report carried by the *Dallas Morning News* that showed a lopsided 85 percent opposing liberalization; 62 percent even favored cracking down harder. That, Nixon commented when he saw the item, was just about what he expected.[10]

Woodstock, the summit meeting of the Age of Aquarius, would never be matched. From there, it was all downhill for the counterculture. The SDS itself became more radicalized, perverted by the fanatics of the Maoist Progressive Labor Movement and the even more extreme Weathermen faction. On the West Coast that same month, another "way-out" group, cultists led by a bearded, charismatic, psychotic product of a tortured childhood, Charles Manson, invaded a Los Angeles mansion and killed five young people, including the actress Sharon Tate, who was eight months pregnant. "Dig it," said Weatherman Bernadine Dohrn. "First they killed those pigs, then they ate dinner in the same room with them, then they even shoved a fork into a victim's stomach. Wild!"[11]

Rivalry between the Weathermen and the Black Panthers led to the so-called Days of Rage in Chicago. Disappointed at not finding an army of white working-class kids ready to be led so the war could be "brought home," about eighty Weathermen wearing black helmets rampaged through the streets near Lincoln Park, smashing cars and throwing bricks before being beaten back and arrested by the police.[12]

The wild ones were destroying themselves. Nixon, alone with his thoughts that Labor Day weekend, reflected on the impotence of his office. It was supposed to be the most powerful in the world. "Each day [is] a chance," he wrote on his pad, "to do something memorable for some one," and then he added the thought about the "need to be good to do good." The presidency was as much personal as administrative. He had to be the one to set the example, to inspire and instill pride; public confidence would respond to displays of strength, compassion, and competence, and the image of a chief executive who had some "joy" in what he was doing. Those words kept being repeated on his paper: joy, serenity, confidence, inspirational. The leadership he contemplated was in his hands.[13] Big tests lay ahead that fall, especially with activists planning demonstrations to convince Americans about the immorality and futility of the entire Vietnamese enterprise. He would not end up like Johnson.

*   *   *

The basic tragedy was that Nixon was overconfident about ending the war early. He believed he could do what Johnson had not done. Criticizing from the outside was easy. In opposition, he had done the same thing to Johnson, and he meant it, but most sobering is the dissipation of presidential power when one is sworn into office. Even more relevant, in Nixon's case, was his fetish over being able to control events. He had the ideas and the means of putting them into effect, but managing an impatient people was another matter. "If for one month everybody would 'shut up' about the war," he told the cabinet at Camp David in September 1969, "we would be a long way toward getting it over." But that would not stop him. He did not intend to be the "first American President to lose a war"; he had three years and three months left in office, plenty of time to turn around "the Vietnam thing" as far as the world was concerned. If we lost the war in Vietnam or pulled an elegant bug-out, the United States would "retreat from the world," and the "*first defeat in history would destroy the confidence of the American people in themselves.*" It would all be over by the 1970 elections; "*we are going to be able by then to 'see the light at the end of the tunnel.'* " He kept saying that because he believed it. To a small group of senators who came in to see him a few days later, he emphasized that the United States was being misjudged by the enemy and acknowledged that there were still too many casualties. "One is too many," he said; but "it's moving," and the critics "won't look good in '70." With some bravado, he added, "Polls and editorials don't affect us much."[14]

Of course that was hyperbolic. He was convinced that was *exactly* why Hanoi doubted that the country could hold out. That was *exactly* why the effort was being undermined by the media, which were feeding the enemy an exaggerated view of American war-weariness. He kept pressing his staff, almost obsessively, for confirmation that the Communists were encouraged by the demonstrations and by critics' attacks on the administration. The irresponsible part of the press, a small and atypical but influential group, along with the television networks (now collectively more commonly called "the media"), was, in effect, giving aid and comfort to the enemy. Just the appearance of heeding the doves was enough to signal weakness.[15]

That was the problem, suggested Senator Hugh Scott. They were losing three battles, "the six o'clock, seven o'clock and 11 o'clock news." Almost from the moment he entered office, the president began not only the manipulation of the press but the process of generating "some non obvious ltrs [*sic*] to editors," supposedly from ordinary Americans, either to praise or condemn, as appropriate, the kind of coverage the administration was getting.[16]

Nixon thought he could cut down the bitterness before anybody got hurt. He spoke to the country in May of 1969 and made wide-ranging proposals for peace in the Far East, including a mutual withdrawal of all outside forces within one year and a cease-fire carried out under international supervision. Everything was negotiable, he said, but the United States would reserve the rights of the South Vietnamese to determine their own future. All sides would have to renounce force so the people of South Vietnam could "determine their own political future without outside interference." It was not very different, he added, from what the United States was trying to achieve in the continuing peace talks in Paris. Secretary of State Rogers, who was then in Saigon, swiftly arranged for Nixon to meet with President Thieu in Guam in mid-July. At a Pacific press conference on the twenty-fifth, he laid down the Nixon Doctrine, which became the guideline for Vietnamization. His plan did involve a retreat from overextended American military commitments, but that was not the same, he made clear, as writing off the world to chance. The United States would continue to provide the shield, including the potential of a nuclear response if national security were threatened. As long as the indigenous forces did their share on the ground, America would keep faith with its commitment by supplying money and military assistance. Then, in apparent contradiction, former defense secretary Clark M. Clifford led off a *Foreign Affairs* article with the declaration that "Viet Nam remains unquestionably the transcendent problem that confronts our nation."[17]

The policy of Vietnamization had been decided upon some time before its first formal enunciation. The direction was sealed after an earlier report from Defense Secretary Laird, who had returned from a trip to Southeast Asia in March. Laird's visit was followed by increased American equipment and a greater role in the training of Republic of Vietnam forces. Nixon, after his brief stay in Guam, flew from the mid-Pacific for a much broader inspection of the southeastern region, and, before leaving Saigon in late July, brought into line with his doctrine the scaling-down of American operations. "How this war is ended," he told troops of the First Infantry Division in Vietnam, "may well determine what happens to peace and freedom in all of Asia."[18]

In an increasingly divided America, the message was perhaps too subtle, or perhaps merely unconvincing given the remoteness of Vietnam and the doubts about saving that particular batch of mud and jungle from itself. Antiwar groups understood that however doubtful the enterprise, the war would go on until an "honorable" completion of American objectives. Nixon had come into office with some idea, even if he never said he had a secret plan, of how to end the war; instead, he seemed to be broadening the American military responsibility. After the Nixon-Thieu meeting, for example, and the announcement of the planned first withdrawal of twenty-five thousand troops, newsman John Chancellor said on NBC that the two leaders were only going through "all the traditional motions."[19]

In May 1969, the press had reported leaked information about the "secret" bombing of Cambodia, which meant, of course, that it was no longer a secret. The episode poisoned how the activists viewed Nixon, and at the same time Nixon became obsessed about betrayals within his own staff. With the approval of his advisor for National Security Affairs, Dr. Kissinger, wiretaps were placed on the telephones of key aides. The climate of mutual distrust was permeating the nation, from the streets to the national capital, and within the White House itself. To have, at that point, taken the administration's word that it was seeking an "honorable end" to the war would have required the sort of detachment from events that had become impossible, especially given the existing distrust of Mr. Nixon, his objectives, and *his* honor. Even those who granted that the president's intentions were good suggested that might not be enough to bring Thieu and his government into line.

Though questions existed about Washington's credibility, the doubts were far more serious when it came to the government in Saigon. A small number of American correspondents, David Halberstam, Peter Arnett, and Neil Sheehan, for example, had for some time seen the underside of the war and reported back that all was far from well.[20] Since the Kennedy assassination, confidence in South Vietnam was even lower than when Diem was alive. The press became more blunt about the failures of the strategic hamlet concept, and reported the Thieu regime's use of "tiger cage" cells for political prisoners. Hopeless corruption and cynicism among the South Vietnamese themselves began to limit enthusiasm for fighting the war. Qualms about continued American involvement had, of course, long since been voiced in the Congress, but they were no longer confined to the Senate Foreign Relations Committee, or to social justice activists for whom the war meant diverting funds that were needed for the disadvantaged at home.

Conditions had so deteriorated that the Nixon White House became more and more concerned with generating its own prowar press coverage for strategic placement. Larry Higby, Bob Haldeman's assistant, suggested that they might be able to place proadministration articles in such magazines as *Harper's* and the *New Republic*. When such senators as Harold Hughes of Iowa and Thomas Eagleton of Missouri tried to tie continued U.S. aid to Vietnam to the Saigon government's willingness to put a prompt end to repressive policies, Nixon directed Kissinger to get some Republican member of the House to counter with a speech demanding that Hanoi end *its* repressive policies in the north. When, that October, the president read in his daily news summary that fear of confrontation with student activists had led the University of Pennsylvania to retire its American flags for their own safety, he wrote in the margin, "My god!" David Broder wrote in the *Washington Post* that it was "becoming more obvious with every passing day that the men and the movement that broke Lyndon Johnson's authority in 1968 are out to break Richard Nixon in 1969."[21]

His people were with him; the president knew that. The FBI sent him an article that appeared in Hanoi telling all about the shock felt by ordinary Americans, their sense of a country out of control; the working classes, especially, were feeling cheated, and their rage was toward liberal intellectuals and liberal politicians, hippies, and militant blacks. A construction foreman from Baltimore was quoted as declaring that "the middle-class family is just forgotten." Some 85 percent of the public, according to the FBI report, were angered by the lack of resistance to black militants and college demonstrators.[22]

That, of course, was what the president was seeing. But the view from the White House was one thing; what the country saw was another. The administration's frequent observation that there was more to America than the supersophistication within the District of Columbia beltway was true enough, but it involved a certain amount of self-delusion, the belief that the antiwar movement was totally disconnected from nonactivists, or even that nonactivism meant complacency. In survey after survey, Nixon's level of approval held up, with the figure usually rising when the survey was confined to whites; the lowest wage-earners were his weakest supporters, the highest his strongest, but there was significant overlapping at the point where earnings and awareness coincided.

Findings by Gallup and others showed the dichotomy. The working classes were with him on national honor and "God and country" issues but suspected Republican policies toward wage-earners. A point not adequately grasped by the Johnson White House was also too upsetting for Nixon to acknowledge. Fully four-fifths of Americans, reported Lou Harris, had doubts about both the antiwar demonstrators *and* the war itself. The unease was reflected also in *Newsweek*'s special report "The Troubled American," which appeared in October 1969. Resentments against blacks and college students were especially strong because they were raising demands that, it was feared, threatened the patriotic, hard-working citizens' rightful place in the affluent society. There were too many explosive stories about uncontrolled students, with the so-called Battle of Berkeley erupting on that California campus in mid-May when a rally led to a clash of six thousand students and police over use of a "people's park." One died, many others were wounded, and Governor Reagan dispatched the National Guard, which finally brought peace by spraying tear gas from a helicopter. Dissidents of all kinds, reported *Newsweek,* were not bothered that "middle Americans" were seeing themselves as the "ultimate victims."[23]

What really mattered, the protesters believed, was getting attention and driving home their point. Anybody enlightened would inevitably agree. America was warring against poor, nonwhite Asians. America was even guilty of genocide, killing masses to save the country. Those in innocent ignorance had to be awakened to the truth; then they would care. The presence of a mad warrior in the White House would become all too obvious.

For the White House, the new war for the soul of America was the war that should have been fought all along. The loyal and patriotic would stand strong, inspired to even greater support in the face of such obvious denigration of their own country, thought Nixon. But, at the same time, arrangements were being made by two different antiwar groups, the Vietnam Moratorium Committee and the more radical National Mobilization Committee to End the War in Vietnam. Their rallies were planned for October 15 and November 15, respectively.

There was no doubt that, if the planners had their way, the demonstrators would do everything in their power to impugn the administration's conduct of the war. A series of monthly Moratoriums — the one on October 15 would be the first — had already been announced. They were going to go on, with or without White House approval; such was democracy. About the only say the executive office had in the matter was getting together with the leaders over routes to be used and where the crowds would gather. Security was, after all, important, not only for personnel but for government property. What should be done beyond that, though, that was the problem — how to react to the drumbeat of criticism that was sure to come, not only from way-outs waving Vietcong flags but from the older, more conservative folk, the highly regarded entertainers, the "father" of the baby boomers Dr. Benjamin Spock, and their supporters from the Hill, all ready to use microphones and bullhorns and fire the crowd about the "immoral war" being fought twelve thousand miles away. How to respond? What, if anything, could be done about it?

As Nixon learned, his own staff was not unified. One aide, Tom Whitehead, suggested facing the facts that there were a lot of well-educated young people out there; moreover, they "think for themselves; that they tend to be overly idealistic and unrealistic does not alter the fact." The worst thing the administration could do, thought Whitehead, was to appear to be "unresponsive, uncaring, and, perhaps worst, unhearing." Their good intentions should be recognized. Maybe staging a "Day of Prayer" would make a point, as well as "appeal to part of middle America." But it might be even better to accept it as any other activity by an interest group. Have the president welcome the "informational aspects" and even put together a paper to outline what America was doing in Vietnam in a way that would appear to show sensitivity about what was troubling the students. In either event, the risks were not great. "With luck, we might even get the initiative and follow-up to keep November 15 and December 15 under control." The worst that could happen would be to have the administration coming "out of the whole encounter neutral, and a fair chance that we could look pretty good." Lyn Nofziger agreed that ridiculing the demonstrations would backfire, and to "attempt to laugh off or sneer at any effort — however misguided — to stop it would be disastrous."[24]

Precisely, thought Nixon. That would be wrong. Responding to the Moratorium, suggested Buchanan, would honor the demonstration and be a sign of weak resolve. The president's own analysis of media coverage during the week of October 6 showed the danger of even appearing to react "with our decisions and actions," and that, he added, should "'serve as a lesson for the future." There could be no concession whatever. They discussed the possibility of getting some independent patriotic groups to organize countermarches — the Jaycees, the Veterans of Foreign Wars, and the American Legion. Best of all, Nixon said, would be to anticipate a turnout of twenty-five thousand for the demonstration, adding, "That's a good figure to shoot at, and when they don't get it, we'll call the thing a failure." Everybody laughed. It was vital, of course, to avoid appearing defensive. Better to ignore the entire thing, not respond to the provocations. He made that clear. He also told the press on September 26 that while he expected such demonstrations, "under no circumstances" would he be affected by them. He had another thought, however. To Bob Haldeman, he offered the idea that "perhaps we can turn the trick on them," while Dwight Chapin suggested that the more radical elements of the Moratorium group should be isolated and lumped together with the Mobilization people so that "their true purpose" could be exposed. When Nixon heard that the spiritual leaders of American reform Judaism had urged support for the October 15 demonstration, he suggested to Garment and Kissinger that "someone should tell them the consequences for Israel of an American bug-out in Viet Nam."[25]

When, increasingly on the defensive, he read that Olof Palme of the Swedish Democratic party, the same Olof Palme who had walked side by side with a North Vietnamese envoy in an antiwar parade, was about to become his country's next premier, Nixon directed the State Department to cut anything "we can with Sweden." Nixon, who watched little television except for the news and sports, heard about an NBC report that spent three minutes on a popular song that told about an American soldier paralyzed in Vietnam whose girlfriend walked out on him. The whole presentation was dreary, with pictures of a cemetery, wounded GIs, blood transfusions, a bleak deserted room, and wounded men on the battlefield. Noted Nixon in the margin of his news summary: "What has been done to complain? Give me a report!"[26]

Immediate groundwork must be laid with the press, Nixon suggested. Within a matter of weeks, on November 1, to be exact, Dean Burch, the conservative who managed Goldwater's 1964 campaign, was due to take over as head of the Federal Communications Commission. That would bolster the administration's efforts to employ the FCC as well as the Internal Revenue Service as a weapon against critics. Meanwhile, Nixon told the cabinet in late September, "you will have to use your 'Big Wheels' in the battle for network time." He wanted five monitoring committees set up to watch local television in five major markets — New York, Chicago, LA, Houston, Cleveland, for example — to monitor the television coverage the administration was getting in these areas, not on the national networks but on the local stations. At the same time, Walter Annenberg's *TV Guide* reported that the networks would be shifting their emphasis, from concentrating on what the left was doing to "exploring middle and lower-middle-class Americans."[27]

More than even at the start of the administration, Nixon scoured each presidential news summary that reached his desk and carefully made marginal notes about the pluses and minuses, the friends and the foes. There were those whose low blows must not be forgotten. Journalist Ted Lewis had advised, as Nixon wrote to Ehrlichman, "that if we appear soft and compromising in handling some of the domestic disputes that a foreign enemy may interpret this as meaning that we will have soft leadership generally in all areas." Crack down, soft-pedal "the open Administration line for the next two or three months"; that "theme has won us few friends among the public and despite the squealing of the press during the Johnson era has made us few friends with the press." A "hard list" of friends in the press must be drawn up, then given to Klein, Buchanan, and Ziegler, so they could have "their marching orders." How else could the public appreciate the administration's efforts? They should know that the president faced the press at conferences without any planted questions, with "no memorized answers; that the staff prepared material on 150 to 200 subjects and that RN develops the replies himself, deliberately on a non-fixed or memorized basis so as to maintain the extemporaneous character of the conference." The staff should put out word, too, about the "number of people RN sees, calls, etc., the length of work days, etc." Ron Ziegler "just can't get across what we do day to day," he complained to Haldeman; "because he cannot sell . . . he can only report. Somebody constantly has to be telling the press until it runs out of their ears that the President is working hard, even though he may be at Camp David, Florida or in California. Johnson was away from the White House almost more than any other President and yet his staff got across the fact that he was the hardest working

President in our history. . . . I am really quite disappointed that, since I have mentioned this on at least a dozen occasions over the past four months, we apparently have not followed up." As though that were not bad enough, too many on the Hill thought the controversy over nominating Clement Haynsworth to the Supreme Court would be damaging for Republican hopes in the midterm elections. Nixon suggested that Justice turn to Agnew for help.[28]

He could not show the pain, but it hurt just as much. His stoicism was always strained, a buffer against crises. After he said the same thing publicly, that "under no circumstances" would he be swayed by antiwar protests, a Georgetown student wrote to tell him that it was "ill-considered" to ignore the will of the people. The president answered back. The NBC evening news, which carried the response from the president, noted that the reply itself showed sensitivity to the needs of public relations. Nixon's answer to Randy J. Dicks was read only in part on the air, but the full text rejected compatibility between the democratic process and policy made "in the streets" and declared that abandoning policies based on "our best judgment" would "be an act of gross irresponsibility on my part."[29]

"From one end of the country to the other," wrote James Kilpatrick, "drums are rolling for the head of Richard Nixon and for the surrender to Hanoi"; and, continuing in the vein that characterized the many opposed to the war; "They are insatiable. Nothing that Nixon might do, short of absolute and precipitate withdrawal, would cool their fevers. . . . What do his critics want? They want his head; no more than that." Columnist Nick Thimmesch, also siding with the administration, scoffed that it was "easy for Dr. Spock's children to demonstrate," but "if we are ever to get on with the big job of fixing up America's poor, its cities, pollution, transportation and the rest, we'd better stick with Nixon's determined effort to end the war." Spiro Agnew met with the president and told reporters that support for the protest had come from the North Vietnamese themselves. The vice president next appeared on Walter Cronkite's television show to ask the Moratorium leaders to repudiate backing from the enemy, but Roger Mudd then slapped the administration for "trying to discredit the patriotism of millions of Americans who sincerely desire peace." That Monday evening, two nights before the October 15 protests, Howard K. Smith's commentary noted that the critics were on the offensive and the president was on the skids.[30]

And keeping him there, for the antiwar people, meant escalation on the streets to match what was happening on the battlefield. Continuing antiwar action carried inherent risks; anything less than an impressive show of strength was no longer enough. The whole country had to take notice. Newspapers, television, no source of public information could ignore the cries if they were loud enough. That was the essential reality

governing the organizers. When the Moratorium demonstrations followed on Wednesday, October 15, 1969, they made their point in cities
all over the country, not only in Washington, but in New York, San
Francisco, and Boston, which had the largest crowd, an estimated
100,000. Moreover, the demonstrators were not only the love-beaded
and long-haired, but, as telecaster Smith reported, they "looked like a
cross-section picked by the census bureau," cutting across age and class
groups. Nixon, satisfied that the media's coverage had not damaged the
administration, at the same time worried that weakness was showing.
Any other interpretation was self-deceptive: the peace movement had a
broad base, not resting on some way-out hippies and kooks. Middle-class
Americans were well represented and, misled or not, they could not be
ignored. No one was naive enough to think that they represented the
real America, but, as Nixon well knew, self-deception was another danger. A Harris poll showed that while 81 percent of the general public
took a dim view of the demonstrations, there was general agreement
that "they are raising real questions which ought to be discussed and
answered." The danger to the administration's position was further emphasized when Hugh Scott's call for a unilateral cease-fire between the
White House and its enemies was interpreted as a trial balloon. Even
the secretary of state, Bill Rogers, thought the protest showed a "dignified" concern for peace and advised that "we listen to these voices with
respect."[31]

For the moment, Nixon was on the defensive. One *National Review*
writer, who later joined Agnew's staff, estimated that the demonstrations
had garnered some $10 million to $15 million worth of free television
time for their cause, counting, of course, all production and promotion
costs. Moreover, Americans saw nothing that resembled the behavior of
the crazies at Chicago. But now the president had to turn his attention
to the more radical demonstration scheduled for the Lincoln Memorial
in mid-November, which certainly had to be violent. Nixon met with
Carl Albert and John McCormack on the morning of the twenty-fourth
and told the Congressional leaders, both House Democrats, that America
must not be brought down by street mobs. This democracy, unlike others,
must be defended from within as well as without. Both visitors agreed.
They were members of the opposition but, naturally, of the loyal opposition, and just as patriotically involved as Nixon himself. The elected
leaders were with him, except for the usual and by then well known
dissidents, but he was even more confident about the public. Never
comfortable on the defensive, congenitally restless on the bench, Richard
Nixon was ready to counterattack.

He had not been able to break through, and it wasn't for lack of trying.
In the last month alone, aide Jeb Magruder told Bob Haldeman, the

president had sent about twenty memos to Haldeman aide Ken Cole "requesting specific action relating to ... unfair news coverage." Between forty and sixty memos also went off to others in the White House urging a crackdown. All in all, he issued some sixty to eighty complaints against the news media during that one month alone. Letters also went out from the White House to newspapers and television stations, often under fictitious names, to set the record straight about unfair treatment, and it all worked in close conjunction with a detailed monitoring of what was being written and said almost anywhere in the nation. That's what Magruder had suggested, to riddle the media with bullets and not be subtle about who controlled the Federal Communications Commission.[32]

Another useful weapon was Spiro Agnew. He was second to none in his loathing of the press. He had already taken them to task when speaking in Hawaii that May, and on the nineteenth of October he was due in New Orleans. The occasion was innocuous enough, a Citizens Testimonial Dinner. Nixon talked to him about it the day before the Moratorium. He didn't have to tell the vice president what to say, just "to take off his gloves." Agnew was pretty competent; he could usually handle himself, and he did. He noted Nixon's comments, then wrote them out longhand before having them typed.[33]

The speech raked over the antiwar movement and the intellectual establishment. It also lifted Spiro Agnew from the Alexander Throttlebottom level of vice presidents. Not since Joe McCarthy's time had critics been so repudiated. They were not really critics. They were "gross." They were self-appointed spokesmen for the young. There was nothing subtle about their reasoning. We were seeing, Agnew went on, a time when "education is being redefined at the demand of the uneducated to suit the idea of the uneducated." They were the ones who were setting the climate. And, unfortunately, "a spirit of national masochism prevails, encouraged by an effete corps of impudent snobs who characterize themselves as intellectuals."[34]

The impact was dramatic. "Spiro Who?" finally became a household word. "Say It Again, Spiro," demanded bumper stickers. Dwight Chapin was right. He had foreseen it. The administration's offensive, to really carry the message, had to go over the heads of the media. They could not be trusted to do more than report their liberal analyses. The pundits had to be lobbied to make sure they got out the word that there really was a light at the end of the tunnel and that the president was strong, confident, undeterred, argued Chapin's "game plan." American flags should be worn in lapels, even the president's. Generate letters to Congressmen, and suggest to the networks that, if they really wanted peace, they should "tell it to Hanoi."[35] *Reader's Digest* cooperated and circulated thousands of little American flag decals. They soon appeared on the windows of Chevys, Fords, Buicks, Oldsmobiles, and every pickup truck imaginable all over the country as evidence that Americans were voting for the red, white, and blue.

And Agnew, he came through like a charm. The media had a fit but told all about him on page one. Nixon was amused, regarding the gathering storm as something of a vindication. The press was only doing what came naturally, he pointed out; it was traditional for them to drive wedges between the president and vice president. The same old game. For eight years, they had tried to divide him and Ike, but without much success. A few days later, after Agnew really opened up at Des Moines by delivering what one critic has called "the harshest and most insulting attack on the television networks that had ever been made by anyone in the top ranks of an Administration in power," an amused Nixon suggested that assassins now had a dilemma. "If they kill Nixon, they get Agnew." George Wallace, less impressed, doubted that Agnew's attacks would have "any real effect" unless they were "accompanied by policies as tough as the words."[36]

The next test was the "Mobe" march on Washington planned for November 15. Meanwhile, however, Nixon was on an escalator that led almost inexorably a year later to his memorandum of November 30, 1970, directing Bob Haldeman to develop a "list of those who are and will continue to be our major opponents between now and 1972. I refer not simply to press and TV, but the University community, religious organizations, finance, Eastern Establishment, the major Senate/House/Gubernatorial/Party leaders and minorities. . . . The purpose of this is to know who our opponents are and do nothing to build them up and to see that an intelligent program is developed to take them on where it is in our interest to do so."[37]

When *Newsweek*'s report "The Troubled American" reached the Oval Office, Nixon wanted to know what was being done about it. The administration had to sharpen its appeal to the "forgotten American." "We are going into this in detail," reported back Harry Dent, "using the information contained in the Newsweek article to good advantage," and a committee was being set up that would be operational within one week.[38]

Following through on the *Newsweek* story merely showed awareness of a widely noticed phenomenon. The backlash was not going unnoticed. Others were trying to arrive at an understanding of just who that "forgotten" person was. "The Forgotten Man is [Andrew] Jackson's man," wrote Peter Schrag in *Harper's*. "He is the vestigial American Democrat of 1840." A Teamsters research director in New York called them "underground people — *Untermenschen*." During the Johnson administration, urbanologist Robert Wood tried his hand and came up with a profile of low-income, low-career-prospect, large-family, and debt-burdened men who headed some 23 million households. Richard Harwood reported in the *Washington Post* that, "like specimens in a laboratory, they are being classified and labeled: 'The Forgotten American,' 'The Other American,' 'The Ethnic American' or, more simply, 'The Working American.'" But "the so-called forgotten Americans didn't forget," added Richard Scammon and Ben Wattenberg in *The Real Majority,* a book that rivaled Kevin Phillips's *Emerging Republican Majority* for influence; "they knew they were there all along."[39]

Richard P. Nathan of the Bureau of the Budget responded to the president's request and reported that the "group is not so simply defined. To single out such people statistically, it is necessary to use several population characteristics in combination." Agreeing with the basic Scammon-Wattenberg thesis that most voters were "unyoung, unpoor, unblack, *and* unpolitical," he hedged about a precise definition. More information was needed "before the forgotten American can become a serious subject for governmental programming."[40]

Of course, specialists such as Nathan, an economist, could not agree; nor could the sociologists, just as they argued about the validity of Moynihan and his black family or Oscar Lewis and the "culture of poverty." Nor could they measure the poor with the precision of a Michael Harrington, or agree that the only solution was to turn capitalism over to the masses or that raising the level from the top would help all boats to rise. If Nixon wanted that kind of agreement, he would have waited forever. The best thing was to shove the Nathan document into the "Middle American" file and go ahead and tell the forgotten exactly who they were and, whether they were silent, or whether they were a majority, get them behind him as a cohesive force by stimulating their apprehensions about the way America was going. "His years of political experience," wrote two scholars, " . . . had taught him that men who cannot unite on the basis of issues can nevertheless unite on the basis of a common enemy, a shared foe."[41] If the concept of forgotten Americans was inchoate, undefinable, create a definition, assert a mandate that indeed would bring them together.

It was Nixon's political genius that he put together hostility toward the counterculture, the antiwar movement, and the press, incorporating them all in that alliance of antipathies to create what Agnew called "positive polarization." Inseparable from the rest of the new majority was the maturation of a new ethnic consciousness, which had its roots not only with calls for racial equality but in the more threatening demands for black power. Historian Arthur Mann has noted that "it fed into, and was fed by, the divisiveness issuing from war, prejudice, poverty, welfare, violence, crime, pornography, pollution, the counter culture, the breakdown of authority, inflation, and everything else that called into question the legitimacy of American society."[42]

Nixon put it together and ran with it, finally organizing the constituency that had been dormant for so long. Only the illiterate could have missed what was happening that fall of 1969. Even as the demonstrators calculated how to increase their decibels, journalists were noting that *other* story. The pages of such magazines as *Commentary, Harper's,* and the *New Yorker* vied with each other for articles about white racism and the forgotten American.[43]

That was the social story preoccupying America. Father Andrew M. Greeley of Chicago, who came out of this ferment as a leading authority on ethnicity, later minimized what it all had to do with George Wallace. Polish Americans, he contended, were far less attracted to the southerner than everybody assumed; but, he also conceded, "the myth of the massive Polish vote for Wallace is so powerful that it is practically impossible to debunk." But, even if Greeley was right, his analysis came as an afterthought, some seven years later. One writer, for example, told in 1969 of visiting a blighted section of Pittsburgh known as Polish Hill, a place occupied by "Forgotten Americans." They were "deeply envious of black gains, deeply resentful of the Johnson years for 'giving the niggers everything,' " and, in their anger, were forming vigilante groups to protect themselves and their families. They were also planning to bolt from the Democratic party and vote for Wallace. Polish Hill, wrote Monroe W. Karmin, "which is 90 per cent white and undeniably poor, suggests that federal program administrators give the impression of being insensitive to the needs of the white poor." Marshall Frady's examination of Gary, Indiana, revealed workers among whom Wallace was "a kind of surly class assertion." They could identify with him as a class "as they couldn't with Goldwater — he talked like them, he angered like them, he even dressed like them." Wallace, wrote Frady, "represented an exasperated longing for the old village simplicities about life, and a retrenchment against sociologists, intellectuals, the entire national intelligentsia who have sought to impose on the nation a conscience which the harried common man has difficulty comprehending." When Governor Wallace arrived for a lunch with the editors of the liberal *Boston Globe,* he was pleased with the applause given to him by the printers as he entered the lobby. "I only hope I get as good a reception upstairs," said Wallace. "Don't count on it, George," replied one of the workers.[44]

Moreover, it was not only Wallace but Wallaceites who were in vogue that year. Up in Minneapolis, a city with an infinitesimal black population, where racial animosities were thought to have been bypassed, voters elected to city hall Charles Stenvig. A former detective and president of the Police Federation, he campaigned with the promise to "take the handcuffs off the police." After taking the primary, Stenvig won the general election with 61.8 percent of the vote, with the heaviest from the city's working-class districts. His areas of strength also coincided with

Goldwater's of 1964, and his supporters were antiestablishment and antimilitant. Sam Yorty became mayor of Los Angeles by exploiting division, especially Jews against blacks. (John P. Roche noted a description of Yorty as a man whose "idea of morality is to sell his grandmother, but deliver somebody else's.") In New York City, Mayor Lindsay, the Republican liberal and mainstay of the declining WASPs, had serious opposition from Mario Procaccino's success in appealing to the insecurities of white ethnics. When questioned by an interviewer, Wallace made the point that they were "making Alabama speeches with a Los Angeles, Minneapolis, and New York accent. The only thing they omitted was the drawl."[45]

Nixon began to keep his eye on another big-city ethnic politician, Frank Rizzo of Philadelphia. Rizzo, then a Democrat and the city's police commissioner, was ambitious. He was also the protégé of Walter Annenberg. Even more than that, he was a strong law-and-order man, and an Italian of great appeal to the city's ethnic whites. As Nixon reminded Chuck Colson just before the 1972 election, "We cannot assume that because we have moved up among Catholics and blue collar workers that that will hold. We must remember what happened in 1968. That is the use of Rizzo. The Italian labor leaders who have moved with us, the Italian political leaders who have moved with us, [Cardinal] Krol and the Polish group, etc., all these are of the very first priority at this time." Then he added, "In other words, the blue collar issues, and the Catholic issues, where McGovern simply cannot be appealing to them as we are."[46]

Annenberg, fond of the law-and-order police commissioner, got behind Rizzo's campaign for mayor. In that state, especially, it was good to have the powerful publisher on your side. Even after his sale of the *Inquirer,* his influence was enormous, and, of course, there was his bottomless pocketbook. For Rizzo, Annenberg's help meant being able to take over Philadelphia. For Nixon, the scenario was not hard to imagine. Having an ally in the city hall of that largely Democratic city could well make a difference in deciding Pennsylvania's large bloc of electoral votes. Their relationship, undoubtedly arranged by Annenberg, began well in advance of Rizzo's actual declaration of candidacy; they first met in January 1970, when the president and his wife visited the city. The commissioner, in charge of security for Nixon and his wife, escorted them to the train and wished them Godspeed. Within days, Rizzo announced that he was beefing up the city's narcotics squad and aiming to jail more pushers. All the time, while the city's incumbent mayor was being viewed as incompetent, Rizzo maintained his disinterest in politics. The local chapter of the Americans for Democratic Action hoped he meant it. But the same forces that were everywhere else were also present in Philadelphia. Racial polarization, ethnic pride, and social dislocation marked by ever-growing fear of rising urban crime inevitably led the

Annenberg-backed police commissioner toward city hall, which he won in 1971. Nixon had an ally in Pennsylvania's largest city.[47]

Suddenly, it seemed, everyone was aware of what Moynihan and Glazer had discovered years earlier: the newcomers had not "melted." Ethnics were coming forward, raising their hands with pride, wearing "Irish Power" and "Italian Power" buttons, proclaiming their national origins on bumper strips, and organizing their own civil rights congresses. Black power was being met by ethnic self-assertion. Conflicts among such groups, one writer recalled, had been "as American as cherry pie."[48] Each had a history of struggle to gain his place and was not about to yield. Studies about ethnicity as a political norm were multiplying. The "new ethnicity" virtually became a new field of investigation, with a growing body of literature.

Richard Nixon was never especially fond of calling them the silent majority. A "new majority," he later suggested to Haldeman, might be a better slogan. Either way, the point was clear. On November 3, 1969, he addressed the nation, and by appealing for their support, as one study later noted, he "consolidated this potential power base" of forgotten Americans. A Republican National Committee poll taken immediately afterward showed that nearly three-quarters of the voters thought they belonged to that classification. Moreover, Lou Harris found that, by 65 percent to 25 percent, the public was in agreement with his point that the "protesters against the war are giving aid and comfort to the Communists," which had little to do with their own desire for a speedy end to the war and their faith that the president shared that objective. Two political scientists have pointed out that using the phrase "silent majority" was effective because it "generated the illusory consciousness of a common identity among many traditionally hostile groups."[49]

It was Nixon's most effective speech, not eloquent but commanding, "a political masterpiece," commented Richard Strout, writing as TRB in the *New Republic*. "This remarkable speech was one of the most successful technical feats of political leadership in many, many years," wrote Joseph Alsop. It was successful, Nixon thought, "because we fought — dominated the dialogue." He could also have added that it worked because it so well represented his own concept of leadership. He knew exactly what he meant to say and went to work on the text during the evening after the October 15 Moratorium. Apprehensive about the damage done to American credibility by that demonstration, he was determined to spell out his administration's objectives, and, most essentially, to do so by going "over the heads of the press to the people and do this by TV." He also believed afterward, and with considerable justification, that it was one of the few speeches that have influenced the course of history.

Albeit he later had doubts that "silent majority" was the most appropriate term, he was to use "every possible device to keep this very real asset from wasting away."⁵⁰

The speech, written principally by Nixon with the help of Pat Buchanan, went through twelve drafts during long hours of labor at Camp David. It preoccupied him as little else. He had, of course, a substantial and talented speechwriting crew. All of them could be called upon from time to time. But this one was too important to be left to his staff. Nobody but Richard Nixon, with his gift for adversarial language honed since college days, could do the job. If Buchanan took it over, fire would come out, heated confrontational stuff that would only further divide, certainly not be presidential. Ray Price, on the other hand, would be too bland, *too* presidential, not right for this one. Safire was smart and sharp — almost too smart-alecky — and "too cute." "I think it probably could be said," the president observed to Bob Haldeman, "that with the exception of Theodore Roosevelt, Woodrow Wilson and Herbert Hoover, RN is the only President in this century who still sits down from time to time and completely writes a major speech." And that was one of the occasions when the enterprise was well worth the effort. At four o'clock one morning, after getting some advice from Mike Mansfield, he added a paragraph that called for support from "the great silent majority of Americans." Unable to sleep after that, he continued to write; at eight, he called Haldeman to say "The baby's just been born."⁵¹

The speech was effective for another reason. To a nation that had become jaundiced and war-weary, it was the most explicit elaboration yet heard. It acknowledged, for example, that "many Americans have lost confidence in what their Government has told them about our policy," and proceeded with a detailed recitation of how the war came about and how it had to end. The process of Vietnamization was being pursued "from strength and not from weakness," he explained, and added that "as South Vietnamese forces become stronger, the rate of American withdrawal can become greater." Nevertheless, he warned that Hanoi would find no profit in increased violence. There would be no precipitate withdrawal but perseverance until a "just peace through a negotiated settlement" became possible. "I know it may not be fashionable to speak of patriotism, or national destiny these days," he said near the end. "But I feel it is appropriate to do so on this occasion. . . . And so tonight — to you, the great silent majority of my fellow Americans — I ask for your support. . . . Let us understand: North Vietnam cannot defeat or humiliate the United States. Only Americans can do that."⁵²

"The White House Press Corps is dying because of the effect of that television speech," he said on November 5, "I'm not saying all the press is bad — some are responsible — but when you get on television, you can get across your point without having what you say strained through the press. And that," he added, "drives the press right up the wall."[53]

For the moment, it was the administration that was driven against the wall. One week before going on the air, Nixon advised Haldeman of the need to set up an "especially effective group" for the purpose "of monitoring the three television networks and hitting them hard on the positive side of the speech and taking them on if they take a negative view. I want this handled in more than a routine fashion and a strike force is to be set up for each network." He wanted another "special strike force" to track the *New York Times, Washington Post,* and two major news magazines, "strongly supporting and taking them on for whatever critical comment they may indulge in." A follow-up might include organizing three hundred or so letters from congressmen and senators backing the speech.[54]

What the administration was doing, of course, was policing the networks, ready to bring them into compliance for the future. Standing behind these actions was the implicit threat, later made explicit, of the licensing powers controlled by the FCC. Such powers were later strengthened with the creation within the White House of an Office of Telecommunications Policy under Clay T. Whitehead. Whitehead, backed by such staffers as Magruder and Colson, used the implicit regulatory powers to intimidate the networks. Their local television affiliates, which were overwhelmingly conservative and sympathetic to the administration, were pressured to help bring the nationals into line. "You didn't play ball during the campaign," Colson warned Frank Stanton of CBS. "We'll bring you to your knees in Wall Street and on Madison Avenue." Another way, of course, to break up the power of the three big networks and to control their liberal bias, as Colson later suggested to Haldeman, would be to "cable the country." "Just as Eisenhower's highway program permitted increased mobility for citizens and really fueled the whole era of economic expansion, so too can cable revolutionize communications with a profound impact on the future. It will have the important side benefit of destroying the present liberally controlled network news monopoly." The threat of a wired system was almost as ominous for the entire industry as the matter of license renewals. On September 15, 1972, after information about the Watergate break-in began appearing, Nixon predicted that the *Post* would "have damnable, damnable problems" with its two television stations, which were affiliated with the CBS network. "Well," he added, "the game has to be played awfully rough." Both stations, WJXT in Jacksonville and WPLG in Miami, became the only two of Florida's television outlets due for renewal that were challenged by groups friendly to the president. The stations weathered the crisis, but, as *New Yorker* writer Thomas Whiteside has written, "this development struck a very sensitive nerve in the entire broadcasting industry." Nixon later denied funding for public broadcasting, vetoing the bill with the complaint that the Corporation for Public Broadcasting was "becoming the center of power" in public broadcasting to the disadvantage of local noncommercial stations. At the end of that year, 1972, Clay Whitehead warned the networks that the "fairness doctrine" would be enforced with diligence when licenses came up for renewal.[55]

No presidency keeps its hands off public information. The care and feeding of the White House press corps is an old story, and that involves deciding what to withhold, what to leak, and, most of all, how and when a particular item should be sprung. In the years before Nixon took over, the game had shifted from beating the deadline before the morning papers went to bed to getting onto the evening news via the tube. Now, the major difference was the bold use of executive power to employ whatever means were at hand to keep recalcitrants in line. The decision to take on the network news organizations, Nixon has pointed out, was one result of the November 3 speech. The choice was the road to "positive polarization."[56]

All this underscores less Nixon's zest for dictatorial powers than his frustration at not being able to break through. The "instant analyses" carried by the networks after the November 3 speech expressed, "in one way or another," as Agnew later complained, "their hostility to what he had to say." Actually, few of their comments consisted of harsh condemnation. Most confined themselves to routine remarks that the president was speaking to the "silent majority" and that there was a national majority behind him in the country. One network used Averell Harriman to impugn the president's motives and handling of the war, and newscaster Tom Jarriel suggested that the president "has polarized attitudes in the country more than it ever has been into groups that are either for him or against him." When Agnew took the offensive at Des Moines ten days later, he argued that "seventy million Americans" were told what to think "by a small band of network commentators and self-appointed analysts," who showed hostility by their expressions, words, and inflections. That was the kind of power that "can create national issues overnight," that "can elevate men from local obscurity to national prominence within a week." Moreover, the "experts" who delivered these analyses lived and worked in the District of Columbia or New York City. "The views of this fraternity," he declared, "do *not* represent the views of America. That is why such a great gulf existed between how the nation received the President's address — and how the networks reviewed it." The time had come, he advised, for Americans to register their protest against public opinion being placed in the "hands of a small and unelected elite."[57]

Then there was the unspoken vexation. Television was functioning as had powerful elements of the press in earlier years, doing electronically what Herblock had accomplished by his cartoons, spelling out to the public the political motives behind the president's speech, confirming his old image as a crafty politician instead of a statesman. No matter what he did, Richard Nixon could not seem to escape that.

Two days after the Agnew speech, the National Mobilization Committee to End the War in Vietnam swamped Washington with at least a quarter of a million protesters, the largest antiwar demonstration in American history. They paraded down Pennsylvania Avenue, chanted their peace slogans, and carried their signs; then, in the frost of a rugged November day, they gathered at the foot of the Washington Monument. As at Woodstock, the crowd was orderly; and, again as at Woodstock, it was almost lily-white. To the dismay of many moderates present, especially older people who had traveled from afar by buses and automobiles, the assemblage listening to the speakers was dotted with flags of the National Liberation Front. A young group led by an old radical, David Dellinger, split away from the larger body and marched downtown, gathering in protest before the Justice Department. The volleys of tear gas fired from police canisters forced Saturday afternoon shoppers on K Street to cover their mouths with handkerchiefs. Later, the Justice Department said that seventeen windows were broken.[58]

The destructive radicals, "a minority of a minority," in the words of Todd Gitlin, were given commanding prominence in CBS's coverage, despite the objections of the anchorman, because it yielded "terrific pictures." John Mitchell's wife, Martha, taking it all in, said that the demonstration reminded her of the Bolshevik Revolution. The president, who had let it be known that he would sit it out by watching the Ohio State football game on television, then asked his attorney general for a "white paper" on the protest movement that, while pointing out the good, should "put more emphasis on the bad since the good has gotten more play than it should. The subversive backgrounds, of course, should be included since this will tend to drive some future participants away from the present leadership. The purpose of getting out this kind of report is to cool off the people who might lend their support to future marches and demonstrations if they were under the impression that it was 'just good clean fun.' "[59]

Agnew went to Montgomery, Alabama, on the twentieth and fired his next round, this time at the "irresponsible" press. His speech was powerful, effective, and targeted right at the *Washington Post, New York Times,* and *Newsweek.* He did not mind, he said, that he had been called by one magazine the "great polarizer" in American politics. But in fact it was those who marched up Pennsylvania and Constitution avenues who "sought to polarize the American people against the President's policy in Vietnam." And events and policies were being interpreted by an ever greater "concentration of more and more power in fewer and fewer hands." The public should discard any naive beliefs in the neutrality of American newspapers. The vice president, Nixon then reaffirmed, "always has the White House staff available to him for research and assistance on speeches subject to their first responsibility to prepare items for the President." "We have to remember," Nixon said in 1988, "that whatever Agnew was engaged in, apart from the fact that he fought with the press, was with my approval." There was little question that he had become, as at least one critic commented, "Nixon's Nixon."[60]

Agnew's speaking style, helped by such talents as his own aide Cynthia Rosenthal and presidential writers Pat Buchanan, Jim Keogh, and Vic Gold, cleverly employed alliterations that were also invaluable for gaining attention. The phrases simply made for good copy, and in the very media he was denouncing. The political dialogue suddenly filled with such "Agnewisms" as "radiclibs," who, he said when campaigning in Illinois against Adlai Stevenson III, had taken over the Democratic party. Then there were the "nattering nabobs of negativism," the "hopeless, hysterical hypochondriacs of history," and the charge that a "paralyzing permissive philosophy pervades every policy they espouse."[61]

His attacks naturally drew rebuttals from media stars, from Walter Cronkite on down. Especially common were such words as his "chilling effect" on a free press, along with complaints that Agnew was simply singling out the administration's opponents. Others, such as the *Louisville Courier-Journal*'s Norman Isaacs, then president of the American Society of Newspaper Publishers, noted with some alarm that the vice president's tone and message were somehow triggering a flow of anti-Semitic hate mail to his office.[62]

In the White House, the media monitoring apparatus found similar concerns being voiced by others. An increasing number of articles suggested that Agnew's rhetoric was responsible for bringing out anti-Semitism, not because of anything specific that he said but, presumably, because of the association that many made with Jews, the press, and power — and, especially, liberal power. The report for the period from December 15 to January 10 was shown to the president. It was typical of the left, he said, to call all opponents fascists. As far as he was concerned, he had no qualms. The vice president must not stop using his "rough, tough rhetoric."[63]

In the Oval Office on Christmas Eve 1970, the president told John Ehrlichman and press secretary Ron Ziegler that "seventy-five per cent of those guys hate my guts. They don't like to be beaten." He went on to tick off a litany of incidents that constituted encounters with media people who distorted every aspect of his career, especially such high points as the Hiss case, his vice presidential trips to Caracas and Moscow, the 1968 election (especially the inadequate coverage), and their analysis of his "silent majority" speech. He claimed that a drunken reporter had admitted how the president was hated by journalists.[64]

Reinforcing the administration's charges about a hostile media was the appearance in 1971 of a little book put out by an obscure publisher detailing the findings of a forty-nine-year-old staff writer for Walter Annenberg's *TV Guide*. Edith Efron's journalistic credits were impressive. They included the *New York Times Magazine, Time, Life, Look,* and writing for Mike Wallace's television show. Efron, who described herself as a "radical Libertarian" with about as many sympathies as differences with conservatives, detailed her findings about how the media handled the 1968 campaign.

Put most simply, the networks disliked Nixon. Their bias fell hard on the Democratic-liberal-left of opinion. Efron judged that they presented the issues in ways that often resembled the slant of "violent radicals." Her monitoring of CBS, NBC, and ABC led to the conclusion that all were partisan, and all actively behind Humphrey and the Democrats.[65]

Efron's charges appeared devastating, the most severe indictment ever made about biased reportage of a national election by the media. Her readers were presented with a mass of quantitative and anecdotal findings. How could one begin to contend with such data? She calculated, for example, that the three networks used 1,620 words to praise Nixon compared with 17,027 for critical reportage, while 8,458 positive words were spoken for Humphrey and only 8,307 on the negative side. Moreover, the Republican candidate was caricatured rather than described. ABC, according to Efron, presented him as an unkind automaton who was cold-bloodedly intent on marketing himself; he lacked qualities of mind and spirit, principles, clear vision, and compassion; he expressed the prejudices of whites against the young, the poor, and the black, and was a morally unprincipled racist; he was a mechanical, robotic man trying to set Americans against each other in mutual fear and suspicion; "a man who is in extreme conflict from holding in the desire to go for his enemy's jugular; a man whose nature is to go after an enemy with a club or a meat axe, a man with the psychology of a murderer." Viewers getting their impression from the CBS network saw someone who lacked ability, character, or principles, and was a "danger to the country," a cynical and irresponsible racist who was also an anti-Semite and a hypocrite; a programmed inhuman computing machine; "a square who believes in heroes." On NBC, he was portrayed as "a man unable to understand the epic forces that govern the world" and was "a cruelly mocking man"; a liar, a hypocrite, a name-caller; a man who failed to talk seriously to the public; a racist WASP who wanted to hold Negroes down economically; a hater of Negroes; a man whose audiences didn't like him and who were only responding to theatrical gimmicks; an opponent of racial and economic justice; a venal militarist. "If Richard Nixon is President of the United States today," she declared, "it is in spite of ABC-TV, CBS-TV, and NBC-TV. Together they broadcast the quantitative equivalent of a New York *Times* lead editorial against him every day — for five days a week for the seven weeks of his campaign period."[66]

Thus Efron reported her surveillance. How she counted, how she decided the pros and cons, her selective criteria, all were subjective, even her lists showing what she said was disproportionately pro-Humphrey newspaper reportage. Her methods were open to criticism that she was quantifying the unquantifiable, that in the case of electronic journalism especially, her "evidence" was beyond reasonable efforts of confirmation. Her descriptions were as unprovable as the CBS charge that "in story after story, there is just no resemblance between the story as broadcast and Miss Efron's description of that story. She sees sinister meanings where none were intended and none exist. Her conclusions are based, in large part, on nonexistent facts." The most apt comment came from the *Columbia Journalism Review*, which decided that the book "makes more sense as the history of an obsession."[67]

So inherently controversial a study was given more heat when Efron charged CBS with attempting to "suppress" the book, an act that turned out to be little more than the network's rejection of the validity of Efron's findings. Nevertheless, despite the obscurity of the publishing house and problems with distribution, sales were strong; by December it had climbed to the *New York Times* best-seller list and was in a third printing. Reviewers also fell into line, and with the inevitable results: the credibility of her data corresponded to the political bias of the critic.[68] Safire's own account of the Nixon presidency, despite his extended discussion of relations with the press, completely ignores Efron and her book, a civilized courtesy.

To Richard Nixon, Efron's findings were not only credible but a vindication. He reported in his memoirs that she found anti-Nixon word ratios of 11 to 1, 67 to 1, and 65 to 1. He was undoubtedly influenced by that book when he complained to John Dean about 8-to-1 media opposition in 1968.[69]

The Nixon White House did not sit by idly. At first, Pat Buchanan warned about getting the administration too closely involved with the book's fortunes lest it look like a "put up" job. By September, however, he changed his mind. The book, he agreed, "probably stretches for effect. But who cares about that. The networks with their painting of issues and people in stark black and white have no special claim to be treated with scrupulous fairness by their adversaries." But he cautioned against enabling the media to portray the controversy "as a White House versus networks battle."[70]

The administration then tried to have the *New York Times* promote the book through its best-seller list. A White House assistant, Henry C. Cashen II, got contacts in various parts of the country to make strategic purchases of the book in stores that would be included when numbers for the list were tabulated. He left Washington for that purpose, making arrangements to buy 650 copies of the book in New York during the week of November 8, while 350 were bought in the District of Columbia. The "Continuing Edith Efron Project," as one internal memorandum was called, followed sales and the author's appearances.[71]

Such was the administration's follow-through. However, there is no doubt that the study was funded to do exactly what it did, contribute to the hostility against the media. Efron's inspiration may or may not have been her own, but the backing for the book came from a highly interested group. The National Historical Foundation, which had been established by Alfred Kohlberg (the old China Lobby man), gave her an eight-thousand-dollar grant for the project.

Efron's thesis was consistent with Nixon's outlook. Old suspicions that the media's objective was to take dead aim at him in the manner of Herblock's cartoons rather than offer legitimate criticism were reinforced. "You see the way they hate to get up and look at the size of the crowds?" the campaigner said to some aides in Peoria, Illinois. "Remember — the press is the enemy." At about the same time, Safire reports, he sent a "Dear Ted" note to Agnew that said, "When news is concerned, nobody in the press is a friend — they are all enemies."[72]

The upshot of Nixon's war against the press includes not only the creation of counterhostility but also inadequate appreciation for the way he used them. He and his people envied JFK's ability to manipulate the media and to play the game without many scruples, but the emphasis on the antagonism he generated hides his development as an adequate practitioner. Packaging for a visual age was one matter, as Joe McGinniss points out, but the art clearly transcends the public relations specialist. Nixon, as a politician, became pretty good at the game.

Warring against the media was one thing, as Nixon well knew, even though it was becoming increasingly popular in an age of disillusionment; but continuing to wage unremitting battle against the nation's youth was quite another matter. More and more, despite his tough, uncompromising stance, he was on the defensive, illustrated most vividly, perhaps, by the lack of freedom of the president of the United States to visit major campuses for even routine addresses. For example, in September 1970 at Kansas State University, right there in mid-America and a triumphant stopover for Bobby Kennedy in 1968, his warnings about violence and unrest and his condemnation of youthful obsession with obscenities met with protests.[73] Earlier that year, after the Cambodian invasion and the killings at Kent State and Jackson State, he was not only a "murderer" but had called students "bums."

Later, in anticipation of a particularly threatening May Day demonstration around the White House in 1971, he descended to something even more offensive than admonishing or ignoring students. The situation was fraught with the elements of further polarization. Tens of thousands were in the city, disrupting all normal functions and services. They had to be countered by the district's 5,100-man police force just to minimize the damage, which was largely the result of pell-mell rampaging. The White House itself seemed besieged. Mrs. Nixon's aide, Connie Stuart, remembered that "it was like war." The air was filled with smoke and the sound of cherry bombs was audible from inside, where the usual security was reinforced. A tear gas canister, accidentally dropped by a guard while the president was working in the Executive Office Building, sent everybody out momentarily rubbing their eyes. All around the White House, just as during the massive outpouring one year earlier, a wall of buses was in place to provide additional protection. In Georgetown, near the university, troops lined M Street and Wisconsin Avenue. Police ordered protesters out of Potomac Park and arrested those who resisted, herding them by the hundreds to RFK Stadium, which was then likened to a "concentration camp." Ehrlichman, concerned about what was happening at the stadium, kept in touch with Attorney General Mitchell, who seemed unable to explain why so many were being arbitrarily rounded up. Ehrlichman's notes for that Sunday evening indicate that the arrest number had reached six thousand. At about eight o'clock, the domestic affairs adviser saw the president.

Nixon was fuming. Frustrated, he wanted to lash back. However, his political instincts were intact. He envisioned an outraged nation seeing pictures of their national capital being stormed by countless numbers of wild militants. Angrily, his thoughts on how the accounts would be received, he turned to Ehrlichman and said, "Be sure police are hurt tomorrow.... Be sure McGovern can't avoid [the responsibility for] these demonstrations." If Nixon continued in that vein, he might end up like Lyndon Johnson.[74]

He did not, of course, simply defy and deplore. He called in Dr. Alexander Heard of Vanderbilt University as an adviser on campus disruptions. But another presidential solution had been to appoint a commission, just as LBJ had one on civil unrest. His was headed by former Pennsylvania governor William Scranton, a genteel aristocrat who had had a crack at the State Department portfolio. Scranton, much milder than Nixon, much more concerned about Agnew as an incendiary element, was far more conciliatory. When the report of the President's Commission on Campus Unrest was delivered on September 26, 1970, it cited the president as the one person with "the platform and prestige to urge all Americans at once to step back from the battle line into which they are forming." In short, it called for a cease-fire; at a meeting with reporters right after its delivery, Scranton complained that "there has not been the kind of leadership to bring about the kind of reconciliation we're talking about."[75]

The report was received about as enthusiastically as Johnson received Otto Kerner's. Despite the interest shown by the press, Nixon kept mum for about as long as he could. Finally, one month after the report came out, Ehrlichman warned the president that continued silence might well be impossible. He should at least "finesse" the matter of blame. "Joke about everyone advising the President these days. Reaffirm your position on violent dissent and move on to other subjects. Then never comment on the report again and don't see Scranton again." Agnew, who was especially scathing, said it called for "neutrality between the fireman and the arsonist" and thought it was "pabulum for permissiveness." Over two months after its release, his delay stretched to its limits, Nixon responded at a press conference. Stepping back from Agnew's position, he commented that it was "certainly not pabulum," and then referred to a careful, noncommittal letter he had just sent to Scranton. The next day, he told his cabinet that he thought the report was "crap," although he conceded that it had made "one, two or three good recommendations." Bob Haldeman was just as incensed. Scranton's conclusions were "ridiculous," he said. Then, in a reference to the Kent State killings, he said, "If the time comes that any American President cannot be concerned and express concern about the deaths of people, then that man just isn't fit to be President."[76]

From all this, it followed quite naturally to Nixon that he go to "war" against the continued publication by the *New York Times* of the Pentagon's still-classified internal history of the war. The Pentagon Papers, as they came to be known, constituted a massive documentation of the American involvement in Vietnam from its start through the Johnson years. The exposure was made possible by a little rebellion by Daniel Ellsberg. Ellsberg, who had turned forty by the time he suddenly became a controversial figure, was a brilliant member of the Rand Corporation, a West Coast think tank. As a Defense Department consultant and supporter of the war, he participated in writing a classified detailed history of the war at the direction of Robert S. McNamara. After the death of President Kennedy, McNamara had continued to head the Defense Department and, in 1967, commissioned the history project.

Ellsberg's work on the study kindled his opposition. The war, he decided, was a wrongheaded and, in some ways, fraudulent undertaking. The American people had been continually deceived about its true nature and presidential leadership had avoided responsibility. The Harvard-educated Ellsberg began his rebellion, eventually joining a

Rand colleague, Anthony J. Russo, Jr., by duplicating the papers for reporter Neil Sheehan of the *Times;* the newspaper defied their classified status and began to make them public in mid-June 1971. The account was melancholy, a catalogue of mistakes and deceptions.[77]

Every event described predated the Nixon presidency. Nevertheless, although he could have remained detached and enjoyed what was essentially internecine warfare among Democrats, Nixon debated whether to act to prevent their publication. In the opinion of some of his aides, Nixon would be better off standing aside. The heartland of America wasn't interested in the matter, anyway, and it would soon be forgotten. Robert Dole, the Republican senator from Kansas and then the party's national chairman, was among those who thought they should let the opposition stew in its own embarrassment. Let the Democrats fight among themselves over the Kennedy versus Johnson responsibility for the war. Internal White House memoranda show that others warned that provoking a further fight might only stimulate deeper research into the conflict; the information might well demonstrate that Nixon was involved in what was going on by his hawkish support of the war instead of acting more wisely to check Johnson's escalation. A possible argument, as Charles Colson pointed out to Bob Haldeman, might be that Nixon should have known how bad it was and should have told the American people. He could even be shown as more responsible for the war's continuation than Senator Ed Muskie, the Maine Democrat who loomed as his most likely — and effective — opponent in 1972.[78]

They were the gut arguments that continued to float during the weeks after the papers were published. Some made sense, and the president himself seemed inclined not to let the Democrats off the hook, a point he made at the regular Tuesday session with congressional leaders on June 15. Additional reinforcement came at an Oval Office meeting on June 22 that included Henry Kissinger, along with his assistant General Al Haig. Bob Haldeman, who drafted an "action paper" afterward, noted that the group concluded that "the key now is to poison the Democratic well." The opportunities were plentiful, especially with calls coming from the press urging declassification of other potential embarrassments, everything from World War II and Korea to the Bay of Pigs and the Cuban Missile crisis. "All of this must be handled in a way that does not hit LBJ too directly or too hard," reported Haldeman. "Our whole concern now must be the public aspects of this. The morality issue is moot because the papers are already out. We must, however, get off the wicket of appearing to cover up for Johnson."[79]

Through all such sessions, however, Kissinger was clearly unhappy about not moving against Ellsberg, whom he considered, according to Colson's recollection, "a sexual pervert" and "the most dangerous man in America today," one who "must be stopped at all costs." As the administration's chief diplomatic troubleshooter, of course, Kissinger had abundant reasons for concern. He was, even at that moment, in secret negotiations with the North Vietnamese in Paris. Everything he was trying to do could collapse with a loss of confidence that the Americans could keep secrets. Similar considerations applied to efforts to deal with other Communist powers, especially in eastern Europe.[80]

Nixon, finally won over by Kissinger's arguments, took the case to the Supreme Court, arguing that the First Amendment did not give newspapers the right to publish stolen classified government documents that had a bearing on the national interest. "If we did not move against the *Times*," he has since written, "it would be a signal to every disgruntled bureaucrat in the government that he could leak anything he pleased while the government simply stood by." Forty-five thousand Americans had already died in Vietnam. Sensitive negotiations about ending the war were going on, and the *Times*, disregarding the national interest, acted through its own antiwar bias. Coming as it did, just weeks after the May Day demonstration, the publication of the papers risked even further aggravation of the situation. The decision to enter the fight against the Pentagon Papers also enabled Nixon to take on both the press and the antiwar movement, scoring points with the public even if he lost in the Supreme Court, which he did, by a 6–3 split.[81]

About all that could be done with the press was to put them on guard, get them to overcompensate. But, insofar as the student antiwar movement was concerned, there was a true solution, and Nixon had few reservations that it would work. He doubted that true idealism, real abhorrence of war, was behind the anger of most young militants. They were simply trying to save their own skins. They would shut up if Vietnam was not threatening their futures. During the 1968 campaign, he had vowed to end the draft, and he followed through. Finally, after receiving the report from a Commission on an All-Volunteer Armed Force that was headed by former defense secretary Thomas S. Gates, he endorsed its recommendations that there would be gains all around. Gradually, he phased out draft deferments, first on the basis of employment and then for undergraduates entering college in the fall of 1971. At the end of June 1972, he ruled out Vietnam duty for new draftees, and on August 28, after agreeing with Haldeman on the wisdom of acting before the presidential election, he announced the end of conscription after July of 1973. Nixon, despite himself, gave the students what they really wanted; he knew, more than they would admit, just what that was.[82]

Ironically, the man who was charged by his critics with widening the war simultaneously moved ahead with the troop-withdrawal aspect of Vietnamization. Ground combat forces were steadily reduced after the summer of 1969. By July 1972, 45,600 American soldiers remained, less than 9 percent of the total in the country when Nixon took over the presidency. That August, the last combat troops were removed. All in all, barring Vietnam duty for new draftees and taking out U.S. ground forces went far to undercut continued agitation at home, a point that became abundantly clear at the time of the intense carpet-bombing of North Vietnam at Christmastime in 1972.[83]

20

The Zigs and the Zags

WHEN NIXON WAS TOLD in May 1970 about the clubbing of dissenters by hard-hat laborers in New York's financial district, he reacted to the affair in his own way. He invited Peter Brennan, the head of the construction union, for a little ceremony in the Oval Office, and the president posed for cameras wearing one of their helmets, the new symbol for blue-collar hostility toward bourgeois radicals. Once again, the administration came under fire, not only from the far left, but from liberals who were outraged that the chief executive had sanctioned violence. It was a time when discord had reached a new high, when, having made his "big play" in Cambodia and touched off the reaction at home, he was accused of insensitivity by using the word "bums" to denounce young radicals. As though that were not enough, his sunrise encounter at the Lincoln Memorial was depicted as an unforgivable indulgence in banality. Instead of conveying the Christian humanity of a Lincoln, the thirty-seventh president came across as vindictive and contemptuous toward those who dared to engage in a national dialogue. However, like Lincoln, and unlike Truman and Johnson, Nixon refused to be undone by a war, not if he could help it.

The outlook for the congressional elections was grim. They would undoubtedly compound the bad news from Alabama, where George Wallace had forced incumbent governor Albert Brewer into a runoff primary, confirming what had already been evident at the original vote on May 5. Nixon and his people had done their best to cut him off at the pass, intervening in a statewide election in a way unmatched by any presidency, but without success. Despite the "laundering" of $400,000 to help Brewer, despite having the IRS investigate the tax irregularities of Wallace's brother, Gerald, which Jack Anderson made public three weeks before the first primary, George was still there.[1] And, one might add, stronger than ever, leaving no doubt about what he intended to do in 1972. He would run, even on a third-party ticket if necessary, and he could do much more this time than come away with 46 electoral votes from the South.

Nixon wondered, then, whether the trade-off had been worthwhile. He had worked hard to hold back the Wallace impulse. No doubt it was also a patriotic service, placing himself between the interests of the nation and the primitive populist. But he had paid the price. He had so temporized on civil rights that the old southern strategy had blossomed into a Wallace strategy.

A Wallace strategy was somewhat more national. It kept him competitive in the South while reaching out for the disaffected lower middle classes of the North. It could be done through "positive polarization." The cost, however, made Nixon despondent. He assumed that blacks should have understood his sympathy for racial equality. His ties with the civil rights movement went deep into the fifties, and included rapport with Martin Luther King, Jr., and other integrationists. His Senate votes as vice president had eased the way for overcoming anti–civil rights filibusters. He had never been a racist, even speaking out for desegregation in the deep South; most of his liberal opponents had never done that. But, unlike the Kennedys, he did not have the liberty to follow through in 1960.

His candidacy would have been hopeless without at least trying to reinforce Republican inroads in the South, a process that involved subduing suspicions about his own racial liberalism. In 1968, he kept southern Republicans, certainly largely racist, as he well knew, at bay and away from either Wallace or Reagan, by paying the price. That included selecting Agnew and going after the border state vote, and then campaigning with the theme that the South was, in effect, the whipping boy of the North, as Georgia's Charlie Bloch had warned the 1948 Democratic convention. Once in office, and encouraged by his attorney general, he moved to consolidate his gains, to cut the ground out from under Wallace.[2] Mitchell went to the Hill to try to oppose extending the Voting Rights Act of 1965. The Justice Department's guidelines sanctioned further delays of school desegregation, setting off a revolt of young lawyers under Attorney General Mitchell. At HEW, Bob Finch was caught in a crossfire between his own political ambitions and the administration's immediate needs. Pressed from one side by Mitchell, for whom Nixon's political requirements were paramount, and on the other by liberals, such as Leon Panetta, HEW's civil rights director, Finch tried hard to make everybody happy.[3]

Nixon flatly objected to busing schoolchildren as a device to correct racial imbalances. The experts themselves disagreed about the relative gains and losses. Yale law professor Alexander Bickel's warning that busing was an often fruitless and frequently subverted attempt for a principle of uncertain value and inequitable effects and was "fueling the politics of George Wallace" became must reading at the White House. Then, in April 1971, came the Supreme Court decision in the case of *Swann v. Charlotte-Mecklenburg Board of Education,* which upheld busing as an acceptable way of trying to undo institutionalized segregation, even if it meant sending children across district lines. Nixon thereupon repeated his misgivings about busing, especially of the cross-district type, which a court had also ordered for Richmond. For the moment, however, he asked that it be obeyed as the "law of the land"; but by August he declared his adamant opposition.[4]

Whether he was prepared to call for an antibusing constitutional amendment was another matter. That route was slow, and besides, argued some members of his staff, it would only tend to resegregate districts that had already complied with court orders. Nixon himself pointed out that the courts could always reinterpret amendments. Turning to his new HEW chief, Elliot Richardson, he said, "Elliot, let's get away from the hypocrisy that we get better education as a result of busing." Besides, what about the rural areas, where poor whites could not simply pack their children off to another, sometimes expensive, school? He was convinced that the entire idea was disastrous and inflammatory. *Newsweek* had reported that busing was favored by just 2 percent of the population. Other national surveys pretty much agreed. His opposition to busing, along with his approach to the crime issue, the calls for law and order, the crafting of a District of Columbia crime bill, with no-knock provisions that irked civil libertarians — all were attempts to diffuse the powerful thrust that was so forcefully represented by Wallace. On March 16, 1972, two days after Wallace won the Florida presidential primary following a campaign in which he vowed to stop busing, Nixon went on television to call for a "moratorium" on court-ordered busing until July 1, 1973, and an "equal educational opportunity" bill to provide compensatory funding for districts with mainly poor children and also to place more stringent controls on busing.[5]

Getting blacks and whites together under a single roof had long been the fighting faith of liberalism. Therefore, nothing else, with the possible exception of the war, subjected Nixon to as much criticism. When the Civil Rights Commission issued its thirteenth annual report, in October 1970, Father Theodore Hesburgh, its chairman, said that the new appraisal was among "the most important" of them all. The words were prudent but the message was clear: achieving "civil rights goals depends on the quality of leadership exercised by the President in moving the nation toward racial justice," and their findings of inadequacy raised "grave implications" capable of weakening "the fabric of the nation." The executive director of the NAACP, Roy Wilkins, bemoaned the fact that Nixon wanted to "turn the clock back on everything" and said he sided with "the enemies of little black children."[6]

"They're Whistlin' for Nixon in Dixie" headlined the *Miami Herald*. There was only praise for "treating the South as an equal partner with the rest of the nation." Republican state chairmen in several parts of the deep South were so exultant they even said he was "the most popular president in their states since FDR's early days." While Hubert Humphrey had already declared himself against busing, Senator Henry Jackson of Washington became the first prominent nonsouthern Democrat to sponsor an amendment. Wallace had, of course, already favored the constitutional route. The issue seemed designed to be exploited by those with an eye on the White House.[7]

Whatever else happened, Nixon knew he had to put southern conflicts behind him before 1972. As president, as commander-in-chief, as the man sworn to uphold the Constitution, he could hardly do less than back the courts in upholding long-overdue implementation of the 1954 *Brown* decision. Legal subterfuge upon legal subterfuge, many of dubious validity, combined with intimidation and such local realities as culture, custom, and financial limitations to inhibit compliance. One increasingly popular escape was the opening of "segregation academies," private schools beyond the reach of the courts.[8]

For Nixon, desegregating the South was certainly a political dead end, one of those issues that only people in Washington would applaud. He was realistic, he said; the left would never give him his due. "The NAACP would say the rhetoric was poor if I gave the Sermon on the Mount," he told several aides. But, he explained, "it is in our interest politically to get the issue behind us. I would prefer confrontations this year rather than in '72," and the way to go about it was by "low profile." Then, after some additional thought, he added, "Demagogues can force confrontations," but the real need for blacks was jobs.[9] The administration's two highly publicized approaches to the problem involved the bread-and-butter side of civil rights.

From the start, the administration gave its attention to an agency known as the Minority Business Enterprise program. On March 27, 1969, the president reminded representatives of the National Association of Manufacturers of the high failure rate of small businessmen, which was even higher for minority entrepreneurs.[10] Nixon had always favored jobs as the best route to racial equality. Therefore, nothing was more natural to him than assisting blacks to become capitalists and get a piece of the action for themselves. It was touted as the centerpiece of the administration's civil rights approach, a far better form of help than the Democratic idea of throwing money directly to the poor, money that

never became capital that could generate jobs. Giving blacks a chance
to go into business for themselves, whether through fast food franchises,
automobile dealerships, or local shops, was another matter.

The driving force was Commerce Secretary Maurice Stans. Stans and
the National Council on Minority Enterprises he set up were conscious
that loans could not legally be granted on race alone. But, as Stans said,
"one can seek to help businessmen," and why not operate under the
assumption that black businessmen would be given careful consideration? Nixon, in agreement, pointed out that the long-range objective
was to provide opportunities "for all to achieve to the limits of their
capabilities and ambitions, not the creation of a specified number of
minority owned businesses." For the first time, the subcommittee was
pleased to hear, the federal government was about to become accessible
to the unsophisticated and those in greatest need of help. The president's
executive order, issued on March 5, 1969, provided for creating an Office
of Minority Business Enterprise within the Department of Commerce,
to be coordinated with the Small Business Administration and administered by a newly appointed assistant to the secretary. When, a few days
later, he read that the financial plight of a manufacturing company was
jeopardizing the jobs of its two hundred ghetto employees, he wrote to
Stans: "This shows the enormous problems in our minority enterprise
program. 1) Any small business has a 75% chance of failing. 2) Minority
small business has a 90% chance of failing. Good luck!" The applause
was general. The *Wall Street Journal* liked the idea that the president's
executive order had "laid to rest the term 'black capitalism.' "[11]

By 1971, with $100 million appropriated, funds began to move
toward minority employers. All seemed well. There was, in fact, no
further need for the national council orginally set up by Stans. So,
when the group entered the Oval Office at noon on February 22, they
recommended that their functions be abolished. Nixon refused. This
was, he said, an exception; most of the time, he was delighted to see the
work of such groups come to an end. But his interest in what they were
doing was too great to let it go out of existence. Their request was
denied.[12]

The administration's "operation bootstrap" for blacks seemingly had
a companion piece, this one suggested by Labor Secretary Shultz. The
president's desegregation statement of 1970, while denying that the
administration was undermining the *Brown* decision, pointed with pride
to the cracking of the long-standing color barriers in construction unions.
The idea, Nixon explained, was to have builders "set specific goals of
minority manpower utilization" that complemented the existing requirements of the Office of Federal Contract Compliance.[13] Here, as in the
matter of minority enterprise, the apparatus was not really new; in this
case, even more than the former, it was fully consistent with the old

concern over discrimination being practiced by businessmen while fulfilling government contracts. What was new, and made as explicit as in
the minority enterprise program, was the need to hire a segment of
workers who were specifically determined by the government.

Implicit in the entire action was the assumption that the construction
industry's history of exclusion simply allowed no confidence in its own
recruitment methods and voluntary efforts to reform itself. The program
went into effect in September 1969, survived congressional attempts to
kill it, and expanded to include about fifty-five plans in various cities by
late 1972. Nevertheless, it continued to be known as the Philadelphia
Plan because that was where the first agreement was made.[14]

Each program was controversial in its own way. Liberals often argued
that they represented Nixon administration evasions of social justice
requirements. The point seemed validated by the president's obvious
sensitivity to the South and the revised guidelines for desegregation.
Neither program contradicted Nixon's faith in jobs and free enterprise
as the most effective means of uplifting disadvantaged minorities. At
the same time, the approach seemed well within what was acceptable to
both economic and social conservatives.

Labor and civil rights people were immediately skeptical. George
Meany doubted it would do anything to expand black employment.
Contractors, he explained, would simply shuttle their black workers
around, reassigning them from private to government projects and
thereby achieving compliance. Workers themselves assumed that it
would be effective, which was exactly why they worried. They feared
for their jobs and complained that their needs were being subordinated
to desires for social change. "We are 100 per cent opposed to a quota
system, whether it be called the Philadelphia Plan or whatever," said
G. C. Haggerty, president of the construction and building trades department of the AFL-CIO. The blacks who spoke out agreed that the design was divisive, "a calculated attempt coming right from the President's
desk to break up the coalition between Negroes and labor unions," complained Clarence Mitchell of the NAACP, adding that "most of the social
progress in this country has resulted from the alliance."[15]

That was not how either Shultz or the president saw it. Richard Nathan, who had done much to help the administration prepare its program
for welfare reform, insists that the Philadelphia Plan was "a quite liberal
civil rights plan" for the notoriously segregated industry. Assistant Attorney General Jerris Leonard called it "a major breakthrough in the
fight for equality of opportunity in employment" when he defended it
before the Senate Judiciary Committee. The usually perceptive conservative writer Kevin Phillips saw it as a wrongheaded assault against
the "emerging Republican majority" of "Northern blue-collar workers
and Catholics."[16] The fact remains, however, that the skeptics could not

be blamed for fearing that the plan was not so much an affirmative action program as a politically motivated wedge.

From the administration's often-stated ideological position, certainly its concern for the forgotten Americans or silent majority, it was a complete contradiction. It was a plan to engineer social change, and it gave every appearance of forcing those at the bottom to pay the price. From there it was easy to understand the fear that it was designed to split the prewar New Deal urban-labor-black coalition. The doubters were reinforced by its legislative history. A fine example was the crucial vote in the House on December 22, 1969, on an amendment that would have killed the Philadelphia Plan. The final count was 208 to 156, thus killing the amendment and saving the plan. That Republicans sided with the administration by about three to one is not surprising. More revealing is the Democratic vote. Of the sixty-seven southerners who voted, only six would have allowed Nixon's civil rights approach to die, while in the North there was much more of a split. Those Democrats favored it by just seventy-eight to fifty-four. Even more revealing were the varying patterns among northern Democrats. The New York City delegation, for example, went on record behind the plan almost en masse, with just two recorded in opposition, Mario Biaggi and Joseph Addabo, both from blue-collar districts. Those from Pennsylvania, however, where the plan originated, including from the major cities of Philadelphia and Pittsburgh, were against it by seven to one. An examination of the voting would reveal the influences, pro and con, of civil rights, labor, and industrial interests. Nixon, in explaining why the plan never fulfilled the expectations that it would become the administration's civil rights centerpiece, blames the national black leadership.[17]

One of the President's men, Ehrlichman, seemed to have a "better" idea of what the plan was all about. In a long memorandum to Nixon, he explained that "some non-conservative initiatives [have been] deliberately designed to furnish some zigs to go with our conservative zags in the same way we have included Moynihans with our Dents (rather than trying to recruit only those non-existent middle-of-the-roaders)." The welfare "reform effort has been a good zig, without damage to the Social issue, with promise of strong blue-collar appeal."

Some conservatives, unlike organized labor, failed to appreciate one striking purpose of the Philadelphia Plan. "Labor," Ehrlichman pointed out, "understands it and hates it," adding, for the president's information, that as it was both "anti-labor and pro-black" it succeeded in driving "a wedge between the Democrats and labor which has stretched the membrane. The Plan itself is not widely understood in non-labor circles. . . . In due time, if we administer it without undue zeal it can become a 'slow and reasonable' approach to civil rights."[18]

The other part of black capitalism, the minority enterprise program, also offered some additional value. Many businesses that were largely white but had some minority backers succeeded in getting the loans. The problem was sufficiently common for the Small Business Administration to finally clamp down on the practice. And there were not many investments in areas of high risk to enable substantial stimulation of employment.

Robert J. Brown, the black North Carolina businessman who became Stans's special assistant for the program, worked along with Paul Jones to raise funds from other blacks for the president's reelection. The objective was to get blacks to either support Nixon or to at least remain neutral. The Reverend Jesse Jackson, then just beginning his Operation Push program in Chicago, was one of those needing financial help. As a Jones memo noted about Jackson, "His support and or 'neutrality' could go far in favorably swinging black votes to R.N." Whether the transaction was made is not known. But Jackson did not take sides when McGovern opposed Nixon, explaining that he did not back the Democrat because of his differences with Mayor Daley.[19]

Derek Hansen, who worked in the minority business office, resigned and sent a memo to White House aide Ken Cole, charging that "its main purpose was political." Applicants were routinely expected to declare their allegiance to the president. Then, overwhelmingly, they found themselves under pressure, frequently via a direct call from Brown's office, for political contributions. Few minorities got their contracts without being solicited, a clear violation of federal law. The chairman of the Watts Labor Community Action Committee complained that the pressure on him "was almost unbearable," and that his failure to support Nixon's reelection effort in 1972 after warnings that he would not get any money unless he got "in line" cost him a $1.5 million contract. "We black people didn't create the system," said one cooperative businessman from Hollis, New York, "but we are going to work through the system just like the white folks do."[20]

At the head of it all was Commerce Secretary Maurice Stans. Evidence taken by the Senate Watergate Committee later showed that the pattern was little different from the politicization that contaminated other agencies. Stans, who became the finance chairman of the Committee for the Reelection of the President, helped to raise the staggering sum of $60 million for the 1972 campaign. His effective role, along with that of Nixon's West Coast attorney Herbert Kalmbach, involved some powerful dunning of companies with government contracts. Rich businessmen were, of course, prime targets. "Stans, Kalmbach and the rest marched through the corporate world like Sherman marched through Georgia," said Common Cause attorney Fred Wertheimer. At Bethlehem Steel, the company's chairman urged the creation of "truth squads" to fight the "antibusiness bias of Democratic candidates." Not neglected in the fund-raising were the businesses that were awaiting rulings from agencies or boards controlled by the administration. While contributions also went to Democrats in the usual manner, and several donated to both parties (Stewart R. Mott, for example, while giving $822,592 to liberal candidates and causes, was also generous to the other side), the Nixon campaign was particularly blessed by the "radical-liberal" reputation of its chief opponent. As Theodore White put it, Stans got money from the "terrified rich" by waving the specter of George McGovern's thousand-dollar-a-year "demogrants" and his ideas about raising inheritance and income taxes. One person, W. Clement Stone of Chicago, gave $2,141,655.94, a transaction made before disclosures of such contributions became mandatory. As Adlai Stevenson III declared on the floor of the Senate on September 21, 1972, "Mr. Stans' office safe emerges as the most fabulous piggy bank since the sheriff of Tammany Hall and his little tin box."[21]

As vital, perhaps, as raising money was Nixon's need to get the southern racial dilemma out of the way before 1972. Nobody could so effectively make political hay out of the issue as Mr. Wallace. The GOP state chairman from Texas warned Harry Dent that "in 1970 and 1972 it is entirely possible that Wallace and the American Independent Party candidates will be a factor in many U.S. Senate and congressional races. I certainly hope the Nixon administration is fully aware of what the consequences of this might be. It has more than just 'Southern' implications."[22]

On July 19, 1970, the president wrote on his pad, "Need to handle Wallace." The governor's success was undermining his own gains in the South. The only feasible counterattack, to avoid losing out on those crucial electoral votes, would be by pursuing the Wallace strategy vigorously against the Democrats. Deprive them of their northern working-class support by hanging the "race-liberal-student tag" on them. "Put in question," he wrote on his pad. "Demos stand for (?) principles. Do you support party which stands for those principles." Moreover, he was more convinced than ever that it was a mistake to assume that "R.N. picked up [support] as he became more liberal on Race, Welfare, environment, troop withdrawal."[23]

A strong Democratic candidate in 1972, such as Ed Muskie, who had been so impressive when running alongside Humphrey, could compete with Nixon so effectively in the North that those southern electors would be absolutely essential. School desegregation as a live issue, however, could easily undermine Nixon's position there. With Nixon needing to keep an eye on the North as well, he would be at a real disadvantage if he tried to tackle the South's most defiant voice. It was not hard to believe that Wallace might achieve in 1972 the electoral deadlock he had failed to create in 1968.

It therefore seems remarkable that, without serious confrontation and ugly headlines, the Nixon administration achieved the "impossible," the effective desegregation of the old dual system of schools. As recently as 1968, 68 percent of black children in the region were going to segregated schools. When the doors opened for classes in the fall of 1970, that number had dropped to 8 percent. "This miracle has happened almost unnoticed in the South," Shultz said before the cabinet that December.[24]

Nixon, after consulting with Garment, Dent, and Ehrlichman, had formed a working group, which was placed under the chairmanship of Vice President Agnew, an assignment that was most unwelcome. As Dent has written, Agnew did not relish becoming known as the "Number One Integrator of the South." Informally, his work was assumed by Secretary Shultz, the "president's economic superstar," who took on a wide range of tasks.[25]

Shultz began with the assumption that the South would eventually have to accept unitary (integrated) systems. The only way to do it was not by establishing an adversarial relationship between federal and local authorities, but by working with local leaders and offering enough federal funds to help certain districts expedite the task. Through the use of advisory committees, set up in the deep South where the strongest resistance was anticipated, Shultz placed local people in leadership positions. Influential blacks and whites were included; meanwhile, John Mitchell helped by communicating with and winning over local politicians. When such unhappy southerners as Strom Thurmond expressed their dismay at what was happening, it was Nixon who used his legal talents to explain why there were no other options. "Essentially," Ray Price has reported, "what the committees did was to shift the debate throughout the affected area from *whether* desegregation would finally take place to *how* it would take place — peacefully or violently, with the schools saved or destroyed." A bonus for each committee was having its members brought to the White House to meet the president. The whole process, as A. James Reichley has observed, was "an example of the invaluable contribution that a social establishment motivated by strong political leadership can bring to reform." Their operation resembled Jack Kennedy's enrollment of Birmingham's business establishment to help knock down the barriers there after the spring outrages of 1963. That accomplishment, when later followed by his position against school busing, effectively spared him further grief over civil rights. Meanwhile, ironically, northern big cities were actually resegregating, and places such as Boston became battlegrounds over court-ordered busing.[26]

"That was a helluva good job by Shultz," remarked Nixon many years later. Unmentioned was his own leadership in moving the program to the degree of success it ultimately achieved. In February and March of 1970, he engaged just about everybody on his staff who had to face up to the continuing civil rights problem. "You're not going to solve this race problem for a hundred years," he told them while they were assembled in the Oval Office. "Intermarriage and all that, assimilation, it will happen, but not in our time. Desegregation, though, that has to happen now." They all submitted ideas and drafts for a major statement by the president, but Nixon went through it line by line and became its chief author.[27]

On March 24, he delivered a ten-thousand-word statement that called for desegregating southern schools. It even called for additional appropriations from Congress to help make it possible. One and a half billion dollars was proposed for emergency aid to disadvantaged schools. The message also obliterated the distinction between de jure and de facto segregation and contained a strong call for finally doing away with all dual systems. Of the *Brown* decision, it said, "We are not backing away. The constitutional mandate will be enforced." All in all, while presenting a detailed examination of the problems involving the schools, the courts, and community complications, the president's statement made the clear point that "the focus is on race — and on the dismantling of all racial bars to equality of opportunity in the schools," and concluded by saying that "a system that leaves any segment of its people poorly educated serves the Nation badly; a system that educates all of its people well serves the Nation well."[28]

Newspaper reactions, studied carefully at the White House, were less skeptical than usual. Many applauded the grant proposal, although the *Baltimore Sun* thought it was a "sweetener" that said to "blacks still imprisoned in the ghetto, here's a few truckloads of cash to make you feel better." Even harsher, the *Milwaukee Journal* called it a "gilding of the ghetto schoolhouse," while the Long Island paper, *Newsday*, thought it was a "reward for the acceptance of apartheid." Those were the harshest. For the most part, the attitude was one of hope, of waiting to be convinced that the administration truly was not turning its back on desegregation. One black columnist, William Raspberry, wrote in the *Washington Post* that if Nixon "manages to find a way to improve the quality of education for black children, not only do his motives become insignificant, but real integration may become possible." Economic analyst Jude Wanniski concluded that the reactions showed that the president "accomplished what he set out to do — nullify suspicions that he had embarked on a major civil rights retreat and, at the same time, lay out an unequivocal Administration policy on school desegregation." The White House was pleased; the effort had been worthwhile. The statement, it was generally agreed, was far from inspirational but, as the *National Observer* pointed out, while it lacked the slogans and promised utopias that had been heard from LBJ and JFK, Nixon's message was "sensible, dispassionate, eloquent, sincere, timely, comprehensive and uncommonly wise."[29]

From there, the Cabinet Committee on Education took over. Even as they worked that spring and summer, administration conservatives were becoming somewhat hysterical. Haunted by the specter of a return of massive resistance, they feared a backfiring of the entire plan. "From the Wallace Victory and his ambitions," warned Buchanan, and the ardent integration plans of Georgia's black leader, Julian Bond, politically damaging explosions were inevitable in the fall. "We are already going to be between Wallace and Bond's friends — and my view is that we should be about equidistant." Then, concerned that the "silent majority" was slipping away from the administration, Buchanan added with emphasis, "*The working class is now the prize sought by both the Administration and the wiser heads on the left — as essential to their political majority; and we have not moved as effectively as we might have.*" Rather than take too seriously the promise to "bring us together," we must "*keep a wedge between the liberal elite and [their] former working class allies.*" Even in New York, Buchanan was finding, the liberal intellectual community was awakening to betrayal of the working people by the New Left and "the beautiful people." Right now, Buchanan advised, the president should stay above the fray; let Agnew, despite his talent for provoking strong counterpartisanship, go into the battle for the working-class vote. "The time will come soon enough for the so-called New Agnew."[30]

Buchanan was not in an unfamiliar role, but others, such as Harry Dent, seemed to confirm his anxieties. Images of massive resistance were popping up in the South; no violence as yet, but worry that the administration might be moving to the left, impressions that were being fanned with the help of Wallaceites. All kinds of rumors were floating around Dixie, including the imminent return to cutting off funds from segregated schools, an IRS policy to kill the "segregation academies" — all not helped by such people as Garment popping off about integrating every classroom. There could even be a retreat on the antibusing stance. The administration might send "Mixing Marshals" to force integration because it did not trust the southerners. The allegations, worried Dent, were widely believed, and they were undercutting the white moderates.[31]

Simultaneous changes affecting the Supreme Court became inseparable from Nixon's handling of North-South and liberal-conservative views on race. Had Hugo Black retired two years before he did, Nixon might have been spared the atmosphere that poisoned his fight over the Court. For thirty-four years, Black held the "southern seat," evolving from a youthful, small-town Alabama association with the KKK into one of the Court's foremost civil libertarians. In one of those accidents of history, however, it was not the Black seat that needed filling in late 1969, but the one that belonged to a Johnson man, Abe Fortas.

Fortas, who was both Jewish and a legal whiz, had come under sharp attack. His position was indefensible. *Life* came out with the revelation that, as he sat on the highest bench, he accepted annual fees of twenty thousand dollars from the foundation of Louis Wolfson, a wealthy industrialist. What really damned Fortas, however, was Wolfson's conviction for violating federal securities laws. Conservatives, who had no love for the liberal Fortas to begin with, and certainly no hesitation about condemning a "sleazy" Johnson choice, demanded his head. And they got it. For the first time in history, an associate justice resigned after being charged with misconduct.

Fortas's religion compounded the sensitivity of the whole matter. Ever since Louis Brandeis, there had been a "Jewish seat." Felix Frankfurter, and then Arthur Goldberg and Fortas, kept it going. Most Jews were also in tune with Fortas's liberalism. They were confident that the line of succession would not be breached. That was not how Nixon saw it, at least, not at that moment.

Had it been a matter of replacing Fortas at the start of the administration, the whole episode might have been very different. Then Nixon could have acted as he did when Chief Justice Earl Warren stepped down. Without much fuss at the time, he named a moderate conservative, Warren Burger of Minnesota, an old acquaintance from his early closeness to Harold Stassen. They had even worked together to get California's delegates to hold for Eisenhower in the 1952 convention, and Burger was rewarded with an assistant attorney generalship and then upped to the court of appeals.[32] Burger's nomination by Nixon came just a week after Fortas quit, but it was clear that, as the new chief justice, he was Earl Warren's replacement.

The Fortas vacancy was different. Arthur Goldberg, who acknowledged that Kennedy had appointed him because he was Jewish, said publicly that it should not be assumed that the Court must have a Jew, and Nixon agreed. "There is not a Jewish seat or a Catholic seat or a Negro seat on the Court," he said when Buchanan told him in October about pressures to name a "liberal" Jew. The nation's judicial branch must be "above politics." His only concern was whether, like Frankfurter, the potential nominee believed in a strict interpretation of the Constitution. Overwhelmingly in private, and sometimes openly, many who claimed to express the views of American Jews thought "they" should have the seat. After all, fair is fair, and that was the way of ethnic politics in America. But the rules of encounter had changed: Nixon's needs had to supercede such notions. And it was easy to see why he did not want to defer his own political considerations for what he increasingly understood to be doubtful benefits. He had gotten just about no credit from such groups as the American Jewish community for his decision to sell Phantom jets to Israel. "Because of this," went the explanation to Len Garment, who was in constant touch with minority needs, "he will be less inclined in the future to do things for the 'Jewish Community' because we might 'win' them." Garment and Kissinger, Nixon then explained, were the only friends Israel had in the administration. Kissinger, in order to get those planes to Tel Aviv, had to overrule both Mel Laird and Bill Rogers, whose "even-handed" approach hoped to mollify Arabs who were vulnerable to Russian romancing. Besides, complained Nixon, he only got 8 percent of the Jewish vote last time. Safire, much more optimistic about winning Jews from their Democratic ways, thought the figure was closer to 15 percent. But, conceded Nixon, still pondering the question, he would take a "good Jew"; they worked hard and were smart. Senate leader Hugh Scott, listening to all this, pointed out that it was "not pressing" to name a Jew, and Nixon rested the case by saying that a suitable one would be hard to find, anyway.[33]

He did find what he was looking for. From Johnson's experience, he told a group of reporters in his office that spring, he learned the risks of going with a personal friend. By summer, the attractions of turning to Dixie were more compelling. The desegregation cases were hotter. Nixon, pursuing his Wallace strategy, was trying to mollify recalcitrant southern districts, especially in Mississippi. In mid-August 1969, from a list of more than 170 names compiled by Attorney General Mitchell, Nixon chose a fifty-seven-year-old South Carolinian, the chief judge of the Fourth Circuit Court of Appeals and a man of considerable means, Clement F. Haynsworth, Jr.

His credentials seemed impeccable, and Nixon continues to believe the choice was appropriate. Haynsworth had graduated from Harvard Law School and, along with many old-line southern Democrats, left the party of Dixie and became a Republican after Eisenhower had placed him on the appeals court. If, from Nixon's point of view, the time called for a distinguished southern jurist, one who would signal confidence in the administration's friendship, it was also an unfortunate moment for a choice with enough blemishes to incite revenge-seeking liberals.[34]

A southern judge with any history of softness on civil rights would play right into their hands, which is what happened. The whole liberal establishment, or so it seemed, lined up in opposition. Haynsworth had sinned twice. He had voted against court-ordered desegregation efforts in Prince Edward County, Virginia. More important, and drawing the wrath of the AFL-CIO, was his promanagement adjudication over labor-management disputes. And, in one instance, he had ruled on a case even though he was a member of the board of the company involved. George Meany charged that he was not only antilabor but also a Thurmond segregationist.[35] The fact that Haynsworth had later resigned from the company's board and had, in fact, been cleared by Judge Simon E. Sobeloff of having had any involvement in its financial affairs, made no difference.

The ADA's vice chairman, Joseph L. Rauh, Jr., argued that Haynsworth's misdeed was "far worse than that of Justice Fortas" because his involved an actual conflict of interest while he sat on the bench. In the Senate, Birch Bayh of Indiana and Ted Kennedy led the attack, although Kennedy predicted eventual confirmation. The White House was outraged. "It really blew Haldeman and Ehrlichman up against the wall," said a member of Harlow's staff. There were those who suspected that the Democrats were more interested in scoring their political points, demonstrating how thoroughly Nixon was in bed with segregationists, and rich ones at that, than in defeating him. In fact, suggested Garment to Nixon, Kennedy really wanted him confirmed. Then, recalling that he had argued against sending up Haynsworth's name in the first place, the president should now demonstrate his "absence of rigidity, his openness to evidence and opinion," by withdrawing the nomination in the national interest. The idea of dropping Haynsworth was also suggested by some Republican liberals, especially those worried about the large number of blacks and unionists in their districts. Hugh Scott was among them.[36]

That really infuriated Nixon. He was a fighter; no softness about his backbone. "If we cave in on this one," he told legislative leaders on October 14, "they will think if you kick Nixon, you can get somewhere." He went all the way with Haynsworth, as far as his rejection in November on a roll-call vote of 45–55. Seventeen Republicans joined the majority, including both Scott and the assistant minority leader, Robert Griffin. "The liberals' opposition to Clement Haynsworth rankled and itched," Ehrlichman later wrote. "It was inevitable that the President would try to scratch the itch."[37]

He did "scratch," once, retaliating by asking the House minority leader to "get" Associate Justice William O. Douglas, who had become a symbol and hero of American liberalism. That effort, which appealed to those put off by Douglas's politics and life-style, went nowhere. But, at the same time, the mood was such that it was obvious that the president was going to really "shaft" the liberals. *Human Events,* a bible for the ultra-right, reported in April 1970 — and correctly, too — that Robert Byrd was a possible candidate, because it already appeared that Nixon's next choice, G. Harrold Carswell, a judge on Florida's court of appeals, would also fail.[38]

Eighteen years later, Nixon was still angry about Haynsworth. The conflict-of-interest charge was a "bad rap," but Carswell was different. He was a bad egg. Warren Burger had vouched for him, assuring Mitchell that he was "well qualified for promotion." He also had to be rejected, in spite of the Senate's reluctance to thwart the president for a second time. Carswell was indefensible. He had spoken out for white supremacy while an unsuccessful candidate for Georgia's legislature in 1948. Nothing about his judicial record since had shown any evidence of change. A substantial segment of the country's legal profession also joined in protests against Carswell as mediocre and undistinguished. Joseph Rauh testified that "Judge Carswell is Judge Haynsworth with a cutting edge, with a bitterness and a meanness that Judge Haynsworth never had." On April 8, the nomination was killed, the first time since 1894 that two consecutive Supreme Court nominations were rejected outright. Nixon issued a statement that accused the Senate of bias against men who were "born in the South."[39]

He also said that he would probably go elsewhere for his next choice. First, however, he talked to Ev Dirksen's son-in-law, Senator Howard Baker of Tennessee. "After Haynsworth and Carswell," explains Nixon, "we were looking for someone who could get approved."[40] When Baker turned it down, he did go elsewhere, to Minnesota for Harry Blackmun. Blackmun, a longtime friend of Burger's, was well respected and a circuit court judge. Getting him approved was easy. When two more appointment opportunities opened up in mid-September 1971 with the resignations of Justices Black and John M. Harlan, both of whom died shortly after, Nixon filled them without much trouble.

Lewis F. Powell, Jr., a sixty-four-year-old Virginian and a former president of the American Bar Association, was also recommended by Burger. Powell was a respected conservative with a good judicial mind, and his nomination was never in trouble. That cannot be said for the other man whose name was sent up that same day, William Rehnquist, a forty-seven-year Goldwaterite who had moved to Arizona to practice law. Rehnquist came under close grilling about his strict constructionist views, especially his opposition to the public accommodations section of the 1964 civil rights law, but both men were confirmed little over a month after having been nominated. Powell and Rehnquist became distinguished members, the latter finally becoming chief justice after Burger's retirement.

Despite the frustrations, Nixon had turned the Court around, although, in practice, not as sharply as conservatives had hoped. He had, however, begun the process, continued later by Ronald Reagan, of reversing the judicial activism that had lasted since the so-called Roosevelt Court. Conservatives who complained that Nixon had let them down on other matters had little cause for complaint about the judiciary.

Points were scored even in defeat. Viewing the president as cognizant of the importance of the South was helpful for a region then undergoing rapid school desegregation at the direction of HEW and the Justice Department. Suspicions, however, that Nixon sent up Haynsworth as a sacrificial lamb only to ingratiate himself with the South cannot be verified. He did expect confirmation, and failure fed his paranoia about northern liberals. (He would have agreed with Delmore Schwartz's observation that "just because you are paranoid doesn't mean they're not after you.") If anything, the reverse was true. Garment was probably right: the Bayhs and Kennedys assumed the political value in having Haynsworth and Carswell to kick Nixon around with. Even Carswell's nomination was not done with some perverse design. By rejecting Haynsworth, the Senate had done something it had not done in nearly forty years. That it would duplicate the action so soon afterward seemed far less likely in 1970 than it would much later in the cases of Robert Bork and Douglas Ginsberg.

As Nixon went on, he seemed to retreat further into the solitude of his office. Such members of the administration as Wally Hickel complained out loud about his inaccessibility. Near the close of 1970, twenty-eight White House journalists held an informal meeting at the Washington Hotel to decide how to get him to communicate more openly at press conferences, none of which had been held for the past nineteen weeks. His closest contacts were with Bob Haldeman, the administration's stage manager, and John Ehrlichman. Both were targets of complaints that, along with Henry Kissinger and Ron Ziegler, they constituted a "German wall" that isolated the president from the rest of the world. Yet, even those around him had some obvious difficulties. In October of 1970, for example, when Ehrlichman communicated via a long memorandum to the Oval Office, he made a point of saying, "I have been told that you believe this is a correct view. . . ." Kissinger, who found his own relationship one of mutual wariness, has noted how Nixon was filled "with an undefined dread" when meeting with anyone new.[41] Accounts of Nixon as a loner became commonplace.

And they were true. Nixon received strangers with courtesy, even kindness, but with apprehension that came from self-consciousness, or wondering what the other person really wanted. This self-consciousness or insecurity explains why he could be comfortable just sitting there with Bebe Rebozo for hours without responding — or even contemplating that he would have to respond — to any demands. In the presidency, overwhelmed with the realities of the frustrations of power, he more and more followed his natural proclivity to contemplate or even brood about the world around him: how well he was being served by his staff or understood by the people beyond Pennsylvania Avenue; how well he was providing that quality of leadership that he expected from himself; and whether all the things he wanted to bring together would ever fall into place. Gloomy Gus was not dead; he was alive and well and living in Washington, and with a lot to be gloomy about.

The war was a perfect example. It was winding down but kicking up storms. Vietnamization was working because the body count was reduced, but there was the Cambodian invasion and the continued heavy bombing, with more bombs being dropped over South Vietnam than above the seventeenth parallel. The crazies, who did not need much of an excuse to begin with, were wilder than ever. The violence was not in the South, as Buchanan, Dent, and Thurmond had feared, and was not aimed at desegregation, but at Nixon's widening use of the military.

Bombs exploded from coast to coast, seemingly at random but targeted at corporations, military facilities, universities, and at anything that could be tied in some way to the war culture. Since the start of the year, *Time* estimated in early November 1970, there had been three thousand explosions and more than fifty thousand threats of planted bombs. Unprovoked attacks had killed at least sixteen policemen. A police station in Cairo, Illinois, where racial tensions were high, was attacked by twenty blacks in army uniforms carrying rifles. The chief of police said they were seeing a "mild" form of revolution. At the University of Wisconsin, a so-called New Year's gang took credit for a bombing at an army-supported research center that killed a mathematics graduate student. If their demands were not met, they vowed "open warfare and kidnapping of prominent officials." In New York City's Greenwich Village earlier in the year, an expensive town house was accidentally demolished by a group of Weathermen who had turned the place into a bomb factory.[42]

As long as the war was going on, the country was being divided and not, as Nixon had promised at the outset, brought together. Johnson had considered Vietnam as something to get over with so he could get on with his Great Society. Nixon and Kissinger, although desiring to end the American role, were more concerned about not weakening the nation's international authority. It was all interrelated. At home, the end of the war meant a chance to put together what the Nixon people began to call the "new American majority."

As James Reston reminded the president in October 1970, "His main problem is not to win elections but to govern the country, and even if he wins in November, he may discover, like President Johnson, that he has missed the main point."[43]

Yet, to Nixon, Reston was fuzzy-minded; one could not govern the country without winning elections. That was typical of writers of his ilk, expressing themselves with platitudes totally removed from reality. When it came time to shore up his political supports, Nixon abandoned his solitude. He returned from a state trip to Europe that fall of 1970 and, fearing that Republican prospects were bleak and that at least two Senate seats could be lost, he outdid any previous president in campaigning across the country.[44] Away from the White House, out of his isolation, he slugged hard, suggesting less a "new" Nixon than the old campaigner whose language struck hard. He liked to get out on the stump and fight. Everybody who knew Nixon knew that.

Nixon was at his most partisan. At Phoenix, he was tough on law and order. Speaking in an airport hangar, he denounced the "violent thugs" and vowed to fight for "freedom from fear in America." Parents, college administrators, and faculties must stop coddling the radical few. Then, at San Jose, well-organized war protesters pelted his car with a variety of objects. Nixon himself was blamed for taunting them by standing up and waving a V sign. Unfortunately, film footage showing Nixon in an unseemly confrontation, looking more like a local sheriff running for office than the president of the United States, was selected for an election-eve campaign commercial over national television. The contrast with Senator Muskie was striking. Muskie spoke reasonably and dispassionately, and in full color, from his country home in Maine.

The *Times* called 1970 the year of the "non-emerging Republican majority." Democratic candidates did better than in 1968 by an average of 3 percent. Even in the South, there were more losses than gains. With George Wallace preparing for 1972, the *Times* suggested that Nixon might have to reconsider his strategy. Democrats had their biggest victory by taking away eleven governorships, always an important factor for an upcoming presidential election. The congressional picture appeared less gloomy, certainly less dim than such headlines that suggested Nixon had to change in order to "survive."[45] The Republicans gained two Senate seats while losing a dozen in the House. Such numerical changes in Congress were relatively minor, hardly what one might expect given the situation. Nixon quickly disputed reports that he was disappointed at the outcome. On the contrary, he said, there were reasons for optimism.

He and Agnew had campaigned hard in an effort that was unprecedented for an administration in an off-year election. Nixon's stridency was outdone by Agnew, who continued to hit hard at law and order. In fact, wrote Ray Price afterward, his speeches were "mixed with such bile that I think they lost much of their potential effectiveness, and in many cases became counter-productive." But Agnew had helped make a difference in New York, especially in the dumping of Senator Charles Goodell, whose dovishness developed when his constituency became statewide. The Goodell dumping was a case of purging an antiwar Republican, with the acquiescence of Governor Rockefeller, so the seat could be taken by the Conservative party candidate, James Buckley, brother of the *National Review* editor. From San Clemente right after the voting, Nixon expressed satisfaction that what had been achieved was more significant than could be measured by partisan numbers alone, "a working majority" ready to support his conduct of foreign policy and "the cause of peace generally." The important thing, he then told the press, was to "strengthen the Senate ideologically." The favored new-comers, both Democrats and Republicans, included Lloyd Bentsen in Texas, who defeated progressive Ralph W. Yarborough; William Brock, who edged out incumbent Albert Gore in a tough fight in Tennessee; Glenn Beall, Jr., over Joseph Tydings in Maryland; Robert Taft, Jr., beating out Howard Metzenbaum for the Ohio seat vacated by maverick Democrat Stephen Young; and Lowell Weicker, a Connecticut Repub-lican who knocked out the liberal Democratic candidate, Joseph Duffey. All in all, Nixon said, citing with satisfaction Buckley's White House–manufactured "upset" victory in New York, it was pretty good for an off year. Back in Washington a few days later, he and Mitchell had breakfast with Nelson Rockefeller. The Governor explained that his own success came from his "new constituency," those from ethnic groups that used to vote Democratic.[46]

Len Garment agreed with the assessment that the election had strengthened the president's hand. But, he cautioned, "it is well to rec-ognize that there are likely to be rough edges around the peace and prosperity issues as we move through 1971 and into 1972."[47]

Nixon's tough campaigning in 1970 was reminiscent of how hard he fought in 1966. That was also two years before a presidential campaign, another time of importance for shoring up the supports for the race to come. But there were two significant differences this time. For one, he was the incumbent, which actually strengthened his hand for picking up IOUs. The other was that never again would partisanship be as impor-tant. One more race for the presidency with the full party behind him, but also, he liked to think, with more defectors from the other camp. At least that was a way to build a new majority.

He noted with satisfaction that he continued to stand so high in the polls. Gallup found that people thought he was "doing his best in a hard job," that he was ending the war, and that he was "prudent and cautious." All fine for building for the future. Right now, though, however he analyzed what happened, and as optimistic as he appeared in public about the election results, he could not shake the general consensus that the administration had not succeeded, that the politics of polarization had actually backfired against Republican candidates. Even if surveys showed public approval holding above 60 percent, he could not escape the sense that he and Agnew were offering negative leadership.[48]

Four days after the election, before the meeting with Rockefeller, he sat down with some of his staff to "go over the game films" of the campaign, as one of Nixon's assistants said. What he saw confirmed that he had to change his style to have any chance in 1972. Afterward, in a meeting with his inner circle, headed by Mitchell, it was agreed that he had come on too strongly as a strident partisan. He had to become more presidential.[49]

He had, he felt, only himself to blame. It was *his* responsibility, he noted, to use his power "up to the hilt in areas where no one else could be effective." If his speechwriters were inadequate and his "idea" people such as Ray Price, the "house intellectual," were failing him, it had at least something to do with his own aloofness. The problems were overwhelming; and it certainly didn't help, as he scribbled on his pad, that "The Press, The Intellectual establishment, and the partisan Dems are hopelessly against — ." It was up to him to respond. He needed to do more reading and have more contacts with small groups. Except "purely for exercise," recreation had to stop. Too much time had been spent in matters that could be left to others, including letting Harlow "drag" him into too many congressional problems. He reached the conclusion that "the primary contribution a President can make is a Spiritual uplift," not material solutions; and he should make a point of finding such inspiration each Sunday. Some more optimism would help his psyche.[50]

Two weeks after reaching that conclusion, on November 30, he asked Haldeman for the compilation of names showing potential opponents and supporters that could be expected "between now and 1972." He thereby put into motion the rosters that became known as the "enemies list" after the Watergate scandal broke.[51]

It was all very depressing. How difficult to bottle all that up within himself while the world looked to him for leadership. Such thoughts were still with him when, on December 6, 1970, he sat up in the Lincoln Room and organized his thoughts in the form of a long list of dos and don'ts.

At the very time that some of the boys of the press were organizing to get together with Stuart Loory and John Osborne at the Washington Hotel to see how they could smoke him out, he was drawing up his own list of ways he could improve his communications. They were all there; he wrote them down one after another — press conferences; TV specials; radio messages; telephone calls; letters; meetings with his staff, cabinet, and congressional leaders; discussion groups; maybe even some surprise stops. "Fill the Canvas," he wrote; "lead 'up to the hilt.' Every day is the last. Make it count. . . . Is there anything I failed to do today. I will wish I could do when I no longer have powers to do it. . . . Everybody must feel he is participating & contributing."

At the top of a parallel column, he noted the need for "Visible Presidential Leader," and, right after that, parenthetically, added, "Don't let others dominate the dialogue." Below, he added a list of other needs: "Compassionate — humane — fatherly — warmth. . . . Noble slogans — 'This is a noble country.' . . . Hope, Confidence in future, optimistic — 'up beat.' . . . Courage — willingness to stand alone for what is right. . . . Candor — Honesty — openness — trustworthy. . . . ; Boldness — new leadership. . . . Fight for what he believes . . . " and so on, until he exhausted his list and space on the page, whereupon he added at the very bottom: "Some believe a President achieves every ambition when elected. But this is only the beginning — his ambition is not the election but what he can do after the election."[52]

The next few weeks brought a different atmosphere around the White House. It was noticed by the press corps. There was a "new mood there," noted Robert Semple in the *Times*, "which presumably reflects the president's own. His oratory has become more conciliatory, his approaches to the press and the Congress more open." He even began the new year by granting an interview to four correspondents. He told them that he would now "wear my hat as President of the United States."[53]

He was considering the future. Ten days after meeting with the reporters, he finally acted on an old source of irritation, Howard Hughes. Practically everybody who was anybody was on the "take" from Hughes, including Lawrence O'Brien, the chairman of the Democratic National Committee. Party chairmanships were then very much on the president's mind. He had just chosen Senator Robert Dole of Kansas to head the Republicans. But now, to expose the hypocrisy of the other side, he sent a memo to Haldeman. "It would seem that the time is approaching," wrote Nixon, "when Larry O'Brien is held accountable for his retainer with Hughes. Bebe has some information on this although it is, of course, not solid but there is no question that one of Hughes' people did have O'Brien on a very heavy retainer for 'services rendered' in the past. Perhaps Colson should make a check."[54]

Then, having in one way or another dealt with the chairmen of both parties, he upheld his nonpartisan vows in another way. With a small group of his friends, he set up what would become, in effect, his own campaign operation. There was nothing unprecedented about it. Kennedy's "Irish Mafia" operated almost independently of the Democratic party, and Johnson had control of his own funding, presided over by two of his loyal moneymen. Nixon had Stans and Kalmbach, and there were others ready to be helpful. His interests would be protected. By the time March came, they were in business in an office of the First National Bank Building at 1701 Pennsylvania Avenue. The outfit was called the Citizens Committee for the Reelection of the President, or, ultimately, CREEP by its critics and CREP or CRP by its friends.[55]

It was also time to do something about Agnew. He was effective, all right, and sharp; and he was saying everything he was supposed to say. But Nixon was hearing a lot, not only from Ray Price but from others, about the "bull in the china shop." He was "hard to work with," Ehrlichman has explained. "He had an enormous ego." Once, when in Africa, he openly criticized Nixon's China initiative. Bright but awkward and insensitive; came up with the damnedest things at the damnedest times. "A lot of people were down on him," remembers John Connally. Nixon thought often about getting rid of him. He never forgot how Agnew brought up the Supreme Court that first time they met in early 1968, before the Baltimore riots. He later recalled that he considered pushing him out of the vice presidency and giving the job to Connally.[56]

On November 1, 1970, they were in the Oval Office, along with Buchanan, Ziegler, and Richard Moore, a Nixon political aide. The president was ready to feed some speechmaking stuff to Agnew for Buchanan to write down. Suddenly, the vice president suggested he was hearing a lot of questions around the country about what the ticket would be like in 1972. Nixon, obviously not ready for that one, said that right now he was thinking about next Tuesday. Then, eager to change the subject and yet conscious of the other man's feelings, he directed Ziegler to put out some good word about the president's confidence in his vice president.[57] But no commitment.

Once the election was over, the vice president's role had to be recast. Agnew had a solid following out there. Conservatives, in particular, were lining up for him, even talking about him as the next president. The South loved him. But that base had no chance of expanding if he kept the same tune. He had to get out, make some positive noises, be seen as an advocate for the administration and its programs. Contacts with labor unions should be stepped up, but there was nothing in the advice about bridges to civil rights groups. Whatever, it would be wrong for him to be seen, Haldeman told the president, as "our only hatchet man." He should make certain he kept a good level of exposure to avoid the impression that he was being "trotted out to do a job and then shelved." All that until 1972, at least.[58]

Unlike Eisenhower, however, Nixon was not about to wait until the eleventh hour to make up his mind. He wanted Agnew not to delay even as long as 1972, to be persuaded to resign early. Then, using the Twenty-fifth Amendment, he could nominate Connally and put him in line as his successor to the presidency. Getting rid of Agnew and replacing him with Connally belonged to Nixon's party realignment scheme, an idea that seemed especially attractive with the Democrats destroying themselves by becoming the "new politics" party, a sure turnoff for the American heartland. Nixon, according to Herb Kalmbach, saw taking on Connally as part of "a populist, new Republican position." Connally was admired also because he was tough, self-confident, "a case of the attraction of the weak for the strong." He was, thought a later secretary of the treasury, William Simon, "a consummate politician. Brilliant, brilliant tactician." In July 1971, five months after Connally had joined the administration as Treasury Secretary, the president put all this to the Texas Democrat.[59]

Connally was not very interested. "I never gave that any serious thought," he recalls. "No man facing the victory that he was facing was about to remove his vice presidential nominee, for heaven's sake. I said, 'Mr. President, don't give any serious attention to all this talk. You're going to win this thing hands down.'" Nixon, however, held out hope that Connally could be persuaded and asked Ehrlichman to try to woo him. But, Ehrlichman believes, Mitchell objected. The attorney general and political tactician saw Connally as a "turncoat Democrat who probably couldn't be confirmed by the Democrat-controlled Senate."[60]

Given Agnew's following and the Wallace threat, dumping him did not make much sense, and that soon became apparent. Conservatives were restless. Nixon's requests that spring to his staff for clarifications of his programs showed his concern about moving toward the right. The administration was pushing what was still widely being called "guaranteed annual income" and continuing to fund such Great Society holdovers as the Office of Economic Opportunity. In January 1971, Nixon's State of the Union message, proclaiming his "New American Revolution," had called for "revolutionary" programs in the areas of health, the environment, and means of achieving a full employment economy. In July, after a secret preliminary diplomatic mission by Dr. Kissinger, the president announced acceptance of an invitation to visit the People's Republic of China sometime in the first half of 1972. That summer, "draft Reagan" drives became general, and Bill Buckley declared that he had gone about as far as he could with the administration. Lou Harris later noted that while 52 percent of Americans favored replacing the vice president, Republicans wanted him to remain. Of special interest was a North Carolina survey that showed voters favoring Agnew over Connally by 57 to 18 percent. The collective political sense of Richard Nixon and John Mitchell could hardly have escaped the conclusion that, as Kevin Phillips wrote in October, Agnew had to stay in order "to satisfy the right."[61]

That ended that. Agnew remained on the ticket in 1972, savoring the big victory against McGovern until, in the fall of the next year, he entered a plea of nolo contendere and became the second vice president to resign from office. Those charges that were first looked into by the press during the 1968 campaign had some truth. While in the governor's office, he had taken bribes from Maryland road contractors doing business with the state. So, deciding not to contest the charges, he resigned on October 15, 1973. With the administration then trying to ward off the mounting Watergate crisis and nobody wanting to complicate things any more than they had to, Nixon got assurances from Speaker Carl Albert that House minority leader Jerry Ford would be a shoo-in and nominated him as Agnew's successor. The only good thing that happened from that action was a quick confirmation.

Connally's role, meanwhile, was far from over. He became a prime force, if not *the* major force, in steering Nixon and his team toward acceptance of wage and price controls. The problem was twofold: continued rising inflation and a drain on gold through the international markets. Connally suggested a high-level meeting at Camp David in mid-August of 1971, and it was Connally who used the phase "closing the gold window" to describe their actions on convertibility. The United States no longer would, because it no longer could, keep open the "window" to allow the dollar to be exchanged for gold at the fixed price of thirty-five dollars an ounce in international trade. Out of that three-day session at Camp David, in the Catoctin Mountains of Maryland, also came the astonishing news that conservative Republicans, of all people, had imposed a system of controls on prices and wages. And so, as economics writer Leonard Silk has put it, "the two-and-half-year experiment in economic gradualism and laissez faire came to an abrupt end."[62]

That was the great Nixon turnabout in fiscal matters. Safire notes how "in every economic speech I had ever worked on with him, there was a boilerplate paragraph on the horrors of wage and price controls." In reality, his flexibility had been signaled earlier. After the 1970 elections, he remarked that "I am now a Keynesian," which meant that the economics of full employment was to get priority over budget-balancing. Nevertheless, the men around him who were, in effect, locked away from the rest of the world as they met in the living room of the Aspen Cottage, were, if not monetarists, traditional conservatives in the free market sense — Herb Stein, treasury under secretary Paul Volcker, George Shultz, Federal Reserve chairman Arthur Burns, and Paul McCracken, who headed the Council of Economic Advisers. Faced with the reality of the international monetary situation, combined with the president's need to do something to demonstrate both at home and abroad that action was being taken, they capitulated. "We need action," Nixon told them; "inflation robs the working man. He's on a treadmill."[63]

The gold window and convertibility problem was one thing, but whether that required the phased imposition of controls was another question. Connally contends that "we all knew the weakness of the wage and price controls. President Nixon hated them, had since World War II. We knew they were easy to get into, hell to get out of. But, again, we were taking some drastic steps. We were closing the gold window for the first time," and the controls were seen as insurance — included for psychological reasons — against a chaotic disruption of the world markets. Burns himself, in arguing against convertibility, had feared pandemonium and chaos on Wall Street.[64]

True conservatives never forgave Nixon. To them, it symbolized an abandonment of any convictions, a catering to political expediency. They liked to point out that lifting the phased system of controls removed the lid from the upward pressures and, during the last two years of his administration, prices shot upward.[65] It was almost as bad as going to China.

21

The Age of Nixon

IN FEBRUARY OF 1972, the world saw something that would have been unthinkable a few years earlier. Dick and Pat, the targets of South American leftists, were walking on top of the Great Wall of China. The president had just spent four hours with Premier Zhou Enlai. Merely seeing the two men together was a significant breakthrough, and no one was more appreciative of its importance than Nixon. He remembered the damage done by John Foster Dulles's snub of 1954. At that time, during the diplomatic conference at Geneva, the American secretary of state was so fearful of being seen in a harmonious pose with the Chinese leader that he turned his back as soon as he spotted news photographers. "When our hands met," wrote Nixon, "one era ended and another began." In the cold of that winter day, wearing a fur-collared coat, the president said, "As we look at this wall, what is most important is that we have an open world."[1]

The symbolic highlight — and symbolism was dominant — came when Nixon visited with Chairman Mao Zedong, the ideological and political leader of some one billion Chinese. Nixon soon found what the outside world did not know, that the chairman was beset with bronchitis and barely able to talk, which, Zhou had warned in advance, would limit their session to about ten minutes. But they went on for nearly a full hour.

The chairman reached out his hand to shake Nixon's, which the president later described as "probably the most moving moment." Mao also said that he had "voted" for Nixon in the last election. Undoubtedly, the president responded jocularly, that must have been because he was "the lesser of the two evils."

"I like rightists," answered Mao. Nixon, not losing the moment, replied in a more serious manner by saying, "I think the most important thing to note is that in America, at least at this time, those on the right can do what those on the left can only talk about."[2]

"The Chinese Army band played 'America the Beautiful' and 'Home on the Range,' " noted the euphoric *New York Times*. "President Nixon quoted Chairman Mao Zedong approvingly, used his chopsticks skillfully and clinked glasses with every Chinese official in sight. Premier Chou Enlai urged his guests to drink up, sent his greetings to the American people, and chatted amiably on camera in English with the Nixons." It looked more like a "reunion of old friends rather than the first social meeting of the leaders of two nations that have been bitterly hostile for more than two decades."[3]

After eight days of meetings, sightseeing, and drinking, and after sitting through a three-hour ballet, the American president parted exchanging pledges for the gradual increase in American-Chinese contacts. The United States also promised to begin to withdraw American forces from Formosa, Peking's chief irritant.[4]

Nixon was at his peak during that historic week, which began the normalization of relations between the two countries. It became trite to point out that his own past history had enabled him not only to get away with the move, but, except for the shock to the far right, to find himself applauded by the American public. The "China opening" remained the most widely approved single act of his presidency.

He was anxious to receive the primary credit for the initiative. When he first met Henry Kissinger, he was pleased to find that they were on "parallel tracks on China," Nixon told C. L. Sulzberger.[5] Charles de Gaulle and Conrad Adenauer had urged, in the mid-sixties, that the Americans had to act on Red China. U.S. politics had tied Washington's hands for years. So had the counterinsistence on the two-China concept and the question of replacing the government of Formosa in the Security Council of the United Nations with the Peking regime. Certainly, in the fifties, after Republicans had made so much about the "loss" of China and in the aftermath of the Korean War, such diplomacy was out of the question. Nixon himself, in his vice presidential trip through Southeast Asia in 1953, found dependence upon Washington and general fear of Peking-supported "wars of liberation."

To react by ignoring the People's Republic was another matter. For the Americans to maintain that kind of international posture was inherently unproductive. Unofficially, talks between representatives of the two nations took place in Warsaw for several years, but they had no real impact upon the climate in Asia. Neither Kennedy nor Johnson was sympathetic to the notion of ending the nonrecognition policy. Kennedy, as the first Democrat since Truman, felt it was a political impossibility, and Johnson, as he admitted in writing after leaving the White House, was still conscious of the "Who lost China?" syndrome. Moreover, there was the additional complication of seeing the Vietnamese war as necessary to counter expansionist ambitions of the People's Republic of China, an argument that was made with particular force by Dean Rusk as secretary of state under both JFK and LBJ. The Chinese, who boasted of their Marxist purity in contrast to the Soviets, were also major suppliers of Ho Chi Minh's forces. Their involvement was essential if any solutions were to be found to what Kissinger has described as the "agony of Vietnam." "For twenty years," he wrote, "U.S. policymakers considered China as a brooding, chaotic, fanatical, and alien realm difficult to comprehend and impossible to sway."[6]

The irony, of course, is that Nixon, as a certified hard-liner, had far more latitude to act. His reconsideration of American policy was encouraged by the French and West German leaders, who argued that Communist China was too big to be ignored, too vital for the United States to play a role in Asia without them; the Chinese were also sensitive to the history of abuse at the hands of western colonial powers.[7] Nixon began to understand that without relating to Peking, Washington's efforts to achieve a settlement in Vietnam would continue to be frustrated. He also began to appreciate the depth of the schism between Peking and Moscow. His talks with Pakistani and Filipino leaders indicated that the Chinese were turning around and that a different relationship should be sought. His 1967 article in *Foreign Affairs* was an important initial expression of that kind of thinking. When he was charged with boasting about a secret plan during the 1968 campaign, he really did have in mind a regional solution; not only what came to be known as Vietnamization but also the China initiative.

There were, in addition, too many other complicating factors in the region: commercial relations, nationalism, concerns about Japan all the way to the Asian subcontinent. Any influence in the area inevitably involved the People's Republic, so Nixon insisted that the war "was not the only reason I undertook the rapprochement with China. Had there been no Vietnam War, we would have had to seek new relations with China. We had to move in that direction. Nobody in a responsible position could fail to seek such a new relationship."[8]

At the same time, it was a flirtation of convenience. The Chinese had their "American card" to play. They were worried about any future revival of militarism in their old nemesis Japan and fearful of the threat from their ideological competitor, the Soviet Union. Moscow was in uncomfortable rapport with Washington, a consequence of the Kennedy initiatives on atmospheric nuclear testing and Johnson's opening of a dialogue about limiting strategic weapons.[9]

The highly publicized visit, the pictures of him on the Great Wall, visiting the Forbidden City, drinking champagne with Zhou, were invaluable for casting Nixon in the light he had always wanted to be seen, as a statesman. When the trip was first announced, reported Robert Pierpoint on CBS, the president's top aides were scarcely able to conceal their glee about what it would do to the Democrats. When he returned to Washington at the end of February, he told the large welcoming crowd that the visit had established "the basis of a structure for peace" without sacrificing the interests of America's allies.[10]

The nation was delighted. What it really meant for the long run was, of course, unknown; but a start had been made. It was also, in a real sense, a step toward the restoration of the historic "special relationship" between the two countries. The years since 1949 had been an aberration. The old conditioning, which included longstanding solicitude toward the Chinese people, especially when they were seen as victims of Japanese aggression, was permitting a dilution of the "China syndrome." Nixon used that relationship to make it possible.

Coming so soon after his wage-price freeze, however, it also cast him in the role of a centrist or opportunist instead of a legitimate conservative. "We've agreed that we will not negotiate the fate of other nations behind their backs," he said, while Senator James Buckley and other critics worried that he had indeed done just that, that he had signaled to our Pacific allies, especially Japan, that the Nixon Doctrine really meant a reduction in overall military support for the region. Jim's brother Bill deplored the loss of "any remaining sense of moral mission in the world." Nevertheless, decided Nixon when he studied the results of the New Hampshire primary less than two weeks after his return, there was no evidence that it had done much to sway Republican voters. Even more keenly disappointed, if for other reasons, was Secretary Rogers, who complained to the president soon afterward that the China trip upgraded Dr. Kissinger over the State Department.[11]

But Rogers was not in the cabinet for the purpose of designing foreign policy. He was the president's loyal friend and a good negotiator. Kissinger was the idea man. As Nixon said at Camp David later that year, Kissinger was a "ragmerchant" who started by bargaining at 50 percent to get to 25 percent. "That's why he's so good with the Russians."[12] Kissinger made headlines for his "shuttle diplomacy" in the Middle East, working between the Arabs and the Israelis toward a policy far less evenhanded than Rogers and the State Department desired, and became the administration's all-star glamour boy. It was inevitable, given Rogers's growing chagrin at all this, that he would soon drop out of the team and that the German-Jewish refugee with an accent as thick as his glasses would take over the State Department.

And their diplomacy was paying off. Three months after Peking came Moscow, where Nixon scored again, becoming the first American president to visit the Russian capital. There, in the company of both Rogers and Kissinger, he was received by Communist party secretary general Leonid I. Brezhnev and Premier Aleksey N. Kosygin. The greeting was subdued, unlike the Peking reception, under a cloud less because of the U.S. China opening than as a consequence of the recent bombing of the North Vietnamese capital of Hanoi and the port at Haiphong. Moscow claimed that four of its ships were hit.[13]

The Russians, however, were determined not to let such embarrassments intrude. They needed a nuclear agreement. The sessions then got down to a continuation of the strategic arms limitation talks (SALT) begun in Helsinki in 1969, and ended with Nixon and Brezhnev signing a series of historic documents in the Great Hall of the Kremlin. Most important was the antiballistic missile treaty. Never before had limits been placed on the growth of American and Soviet strategic missile arsenals. Seen at the time as a mere beginning, it was, nevertheless, a major gain in the long history of nuclear arms control legislation, freezing in place the recent Soviet buildup. Most significant perhaps, and not threatened to be undone until Ronald Reagan introduced his Strategic Defense Initiative, was the assumption that deterrence would remain most effective so long as superior offensive weapons made each superpower vulnerable to massive retaliation.[14]

More important than the accomplishments was keeping the dialogue alive, and the ability to go on despite what was happening in Vietnam. Or, to put it another way, the relationships with both Peking and Moscow had to be instrumental in affecting the course of the war in Vietnam.[15]

Yet, even what happened in Moscow was the culmination of a process begun during the Johnson presidency. The road to SALT I, as the Moscow agreements eventually became known, began with LBJ's warning to Soviet Premier Kosygin that the deployment of an antiballistic missile defense system around Moscow had created pressures within the United States "to increase greatly our capabilities to penetrate any defensive systems which you might establish."[16] Both countries proceeded to a treaty banning the spread of nuclear weapons to countries that did not have any and were ready to go on to talks about limiting offensive and defensive strategic weapons. Then came the Soviet invasion of Czechoslovakia in August 1968 and, with it, an end to any further progress, until the Nixon administration resumed negotiations at Helsinki.

The United States-Soviet dialogue naturally made Peking nervous and helped to move them toward playing their "American card." As the Chinese declared, "The United States-Soviet talks on so-called 'strategic arms limitation' are aimed at further developing their nuclear military alliance. They mainly hope to maintain a nuclear monopoly and carry out nuclear blackmail by nuclear threats against the Chinese people and the people of the world."[17]

*   *   *

In Vietnam, the intensification of the war was, in part, a response to new enemy offensives and in preparation for a further withdrawal of American troops. But the fighting had been going on for a long time, throughout nearly the full length of Nixon's term despite his election as the man who could end it. Such critics as Tom Wicker were arguing that "American soldiers are in jeopardy primarily because Mr. Nixon's own policies have kept them in Vietnam." Campus unrest also resumed in the spring of 1972, although on a noticeably smaller scale, and there was more heated debate on Capitol Hill. A number of college presidents joined in denouncing the escalation, and, in June, Nixon declared the end of Vietnam duty for draftees. Finally, after months of delicate secret negotiations, Kissinger stated that peace was "at hand." "Just how close at hand was a most beguiling question," suggested *Newsweek*, in an appropriate bit of speculation.[18]

Kissinger's statement came on October 26, 1972, less than two weeks before election day. But it was Kissinger who miscalculated. President Thieu was driving a harder bargain and, what Kissinger did not anticipate, Nixon was continuing to stand behind the South Vietnamese leader while Hanoi reneged on some vital concessions that appeared to have been made earlier. Thieu's gambit was to keep the war going by disrupting any possible Hanoi-Washington agreement, whereas Nixon was concerned that the peace, when it came, would be "with honor." American forces not only had to pull out, but their reason for having fought in the first place had to be secured.[19]

Both presidents were driving a hard bargain. Nixon's diplomacy, however, was more complicated. He had to achieve his goal not only by forcing the enemy to agree to terms but, as historian George Herring has put it, by bludgeoning "Thieu into submission."[20] But not even an additional $1 billion worth of military hardware was enough to move the South Vietnamese leader.

So there was no peace by that first Tuesday in November. After Nixon and Agnew were reelected, the president went all out by engaging in, as Kissinger put it, "jugular diplomacy." "I don't want any more of this crap about the fact that we couldn't hit this target or that one," he told Admiral Thomas Moorer, chairman of the Joint Chiefs of Staff. "This is your chance to use military power to win this war, and if you don't, I'll consider you responsible." The tonnage dropped over North Vietnam during a twelve-day period in December was greater than the power that had been used over the last two years. It was, said Senator George Aiken of Vermont, a "sorry Christmas present" for the American people, but it created the political and military opportunity for the U.S. agreement in January to end its role in the fighting.[21]

President Thieu nevertheless continued to resist a diplomatic solution. His confidence in ultimate victory was shared in retrospect at a gathering of some fifty U.S. scholars at the Smithsonian Institution on January 7–8, 1983. In what was, at the time, a remarkable consensus, they stressed that the war could have been won militarily and that it had, in fact, really been "won" in 1972. Some did, however, acknowledge that maintaining security in the area could have required a residual military presence for perhaps as long as thirty years, an undertaking that would never have been tolerated by the Congress or the American people.[22]

Nixon himself could not resist that kind of pressure. He compelled Thieu's acquiescence by giving him written assurances of renewed military support if the Hanoi regime violated the truce terms and attempted to undermine the country. The pledge was later reaffirmed when President Ford took over.[23]

On January 23, 1973, Nixon announced the conclusion of "an agreement to end the war and bring peace with honor in Vietnam and Southeast Asia." But later that same year, Congress asserted its own power with two strokes that coincided with the crippling of Nixon's presidency. First, in June, they voted to cut off the bombing of North Vietnam, thereby denying the administration's ability to retaliate. In November, overriding a presidential veto by Nixon, both houses passed the War Powers Resolution, which, as the *Wall Street Journal* pointed out, converted "the commander-in-chief into a committee-in-chief." In Vietnam itself, the war went on for another two years until, finally, that corner of Southeast Asia was taken over by the Communists.[24]

By the bicentennial year, Nixon later wrote, he had hoped to have "given America the beginning of a new leadership class whose values and aspirations were more truly reflective of the rest of the country."[25] That was, in effect, what the election of 1972 was all about.

Nixon's victory was never in doubt. The Democrats had doomed themselves, not only by the ineptitude of their candidate but by becoming regarded as disaffected from the mainstream of mid-America. *Christian Science Monitor* columnist Godfrey Sperling, Jr., in his coast-to-coast travels during the campaign, found "an overwhelming feeling of unhappiness . . . that can be described in no other terms than anti-youth and anti-black." Complaints about "permissiveness" singled out "the 'excesses' of blacks and against 'violence,' which, in the minds of many whites, is shorthand for 'black violence.' "[26] Nixon, meanwhile, although admonished by critics as an "imperial president," won the confidence of the majority as the one best able to promote stability at home and safeguard America's global role. He was still holding out in Vietnam, where the fighting had escalated in the spring, but, considering how long the war had been going on and the deepening frustration, conditions in the United States were remarkably calm. Even the instances of campus disturbances were more isolated. Finally, just weeks before the election,

Nixon was able to sign into law a key part of his New Federalism program. He went to Independence Hall in Philadelphia to put his signature on the revenue-sharing bill. It was not all that he wanted, but the change in direction was clear. Most emphatically, things were moving his way.

"I had no concern about McGovern," he has acknowledged. "My concern was about Wallace." Wallace was to bring the fruition of "my southern strategy," he added.[27] If the governor was not on the ballot, Nixon stood a fine chance of picking up the bulk of his votes.

The president always worried about Wallace, who, Johnny Apple later wrote in the *New York Times,* "has come to symbolize the frustrations of Southerners, ethnic Northerners and other traditional Democrats who think the party has moved too far left." When Wallace was asked in March of 1972 why he was entering the presidential primaries as a Democrat, he replied, "Once the Democratic party reflected true expressions of the rank-and-file citizens. They were its heart, the bulk of its strength and vitality." Along the way, by becoming the "party of the so-called intelligentsia," it moved away from "the working man and the businessman. It has been transformed into a party controlled by intellectual snobs, who ignore true expressions of rank-and-file citizens across America." He hoped, he added, to start a "grass-roots movement to take the Democratic party back unto themselves. It is a challenge to have again a real people's party."[28]

When competing outside the South for a national following, Wallace toned down his cruder racist appeals, which made him less offensive but no less effective. No poll ever showed him even remotely competitive with Nixon on a head-to-head basis, but as Nixon studied the surveys he saw the differences the Alabaman could make. Throughout 1971, for example, Ed Muskie, who had polled even higher than Nixon right after the congressional elections, generally remained only from four to eight points behind. The margin was usually approximated by Hubert Humphrey and Ted Kennedy. What became clear was that Wallace had his people. A large number were potential Nixonians, and their strength remained consistent with his third-party candidacy in 1968.[29] Still, Wallace had not even a remote chance of winning the nomination in a Democratic party substantially reshaped by reforms inspired by the New Left.

Nevertheless, Wallace posed potential trouble. He wavered throughout the early part of the year, first by declaring himself a Democratic party candidate, and then by temporarily indicating that he could return to his American Independent party line. By March, he was reported to have given up the third-party idea, but there was little trust in his intentions. In July, John Mitchell pointed out that it was still possible for Wallace to run as a third-party candidate in seventeen states.[30] That he was then in the early stages of recovery from the crippling gunshot wounds inflicted by a crazed would-be assassin at a Maryland shopping center on May 15 apparently made little difference. Nixon obviously did not dismiss the possibility that his candidacy could remain alive; after the shooting, he might even attract an additional sympathy vote, almost all at Nixon's expense. Nixon then dispatched John Connally to talk to the governor.

The Texan visited with Wallace on May 25 and told him he was Nixon's "closest political adviser," which was not much of an exaggeration. Connally reported back to Nixon that he had warned Wallace that he could not help himself by becoming "involved with a third party, and that the only way to get the Democratic Party back on its feet for the future was to 'beat the hell' out of McGovern in November." He did receive the reassurance he needed. Wallace would not flirt with the third-party idea, an important breakthrough. It negated the threat of a Wallace candidacy that could pick up the elements of the conservative, antigovernment, populist mood that was seizing Americans in reaction to the turbulence of recent years. As one political analyst put it, when Wallace voters were confronted by the idea that Nixon liked the rich and McGovern the poor, "they would rather identify with successful executives or money men than with what they consider the shiftless poor." Public confirmation that Wallace was out as a third-party threat came when he told the rightist American party convention in August that "I regret that my physical condition is such that I cannot answer the people's wish to draft me." Right after McGovern's defeat, Wallace announced that he fully intended to help reshape the Democratic party.[31]

Although he had been out of the administration since May, John Connally was very much a part of the Nixon campaign. He became head of Democrats for Nixon, which was the next best thing to having him replace Agnew on the ticket; in fact, a better idea. Nixon could then have both. Connally and Nixon, recalled Ehrlichman, had many conversations before the 1972 conventions about getting more Democrats on board, the left-wing "theft" of the party presumably simplifying the process. Now he was engaged in building a coalition that would occupy, said Ehrlichman, the "broadest part of the middle — all of the South and most of the North, leaving to the liberals what was left." Had Watergate not interfered, Connally calculated, the odds for the success of realignment would have been about fifty-fifty.[32]

Their projected realignment would have reshaped the Republican party. A key target was the southern leadership, which would have enabled the GOP to get into the region at the lower levels, where the Democrats were still in power. Connally assumed that successful realignment would have kept the Republican party from shifting to the far right by attracting a vast pool of conservative Democrats who were not, "in any sense," said Connally, "philosophical radicals." The planned re-grouping within the GOP would, hopefully, be biracial and attractive to middle-class whites and blacks from all regions of the country.[33]

Connally was a very persuasive fellow. Liberals thought of him as a high-flying robber-baron type of Texas gambler who rolled in millions. He was tarnished for a time by an alleged involvement in milk price-fixing but was finally acquitted, all of which had litttle to do with Big John's clout. He started out poor and made a lot of money through close involvement with the oil and gas industry. That self-made image was, of course, irresistible to Nixon. Someone once described Connally as an "LBJ with couth."

Associates within the administration could respect all that. But some saw him as a "funny money" populist. "You know, Texans are funny birds," said William Simon, who worked under him before eventually taking over at Treasury. "We call them southerners. We call them con-servatives. But when you take a look at their definitive recommendations, they say the way to bring interest rates down is for the Fed to print more money. Well, boy, that ain't the way to bring interest rates down. As a matter of fact, it's a way of doing just the opposite, and Shultz and I used to argue with John Connally until we were blue in the face. But forget it."[34]

If Simon, the man of high finance, regarded Connally as a populist, that was how Connally viewed Nixon. Connally recalls Nixon's assump-tions that the country was steadily moving away from liberalism, "away from the Roosevelt and Truman era, into a more moderate and more conservative area of political thought." He was, in fact, "very much more than a pragmatist. He was a populist."[35]

Nixon versus McGovern divided the country along not only the so-called social issues, but also ethnic, class, and cultural lines. The president had the support of local law-and-order people. Some, such as Frank Rizzo, who was elected Philadelphia's mayor in 1971, ultimately moved into the Republican party. Along the way to his 60 percent popular vote victory over McGovern, winning all electors outside the District of Co-lumbia and Massachusetts, Nixon made significant inroads among the middle and working classes who felt themselves alienated from the Dem-ocratic party. Analyses of urban voting patterns showed that that in-cluded a substantial portion of the Wallace vote.[36]

Liberalism had come to be associated, as Kevin Phillips has written, with "middle-class reformism and permissivism of avaricious economic, diplomatic, sociological and sexual hues" instead of, as under FDR, blue-collar politics. Of growing significance was the elite corps of neoconser-vatives, who were dedicated to the preservation of the "pre-1960s liberal ideals and interests." They had little trouble voting for the centrist, Richard Nixon, who got the votes of 90 perecent of moderate Republicans while McGovern managed to attract only half of the Democratic middle-of-the-roaders.[37]

He also succeeded, as had no other Republican, with the white ethnic vote, a descriptive term that virtually became a euphemism for Roman Catholics. For the first time ever, a majority of Catholics defected from their traditional affiliation with the Democratic party and backed a Republican for the presidency. The Republican Research Division afterward estimated that 59 percent of the ethnics voted Democratic when Humphrey was the candidate but, in a remarkable shift, they went for Nixon four years later by 56 percent.[38]

Nixon, of course, did everything to cultivate that vote. He stood with them on their traditional concern about aid to parochial schools and rejected federal funding of abortions. He even came out in favor of tax credits for private schools. As one complaining Democrat was quoted, "He does it by signs and symbols. He turns up in Philadelphia with Cardinal Krol to support Federal aid to Catholic schools; he writes a letter to Cardinal Cooke of New York opposing abortion; he rejects quota hiring and downplays the Philadelphia Plan of minority hiring on federally financed projects." That key component of his "new majority" had been moving his way since 1960. By 1968, Roman Catholic–dominated assembly districts were already firmly on his side.[39]

The black vote was another matter. Nixon himself, even while being defeated by Kennedy and in the face of the latter's efforts to get Martin Luther King, Jr., out of prison, had made a respectable showing in 1960. The Goldwater disaster of 1964, however, guaranteed a debacle, and black Republicans remained rare. In relative terms, blacks went to Nixon in greater numbers in 1972 than to any other Republican candidate since 1960, including George Bush's 1988 defeat of Michael Dukakis.[40] Even then, Nixon's gain was hardly more than a statistical blip, one that probably owed much to the growing black middle class which, as with most Americans, had little confidence in McGovern.

The administration had made no serious attempt to woo that component of Nixon's anticipated realignment. The efforts were largely confined to the limited network established by the minority enterprise program and sympathetic noises generated by the Philadelphia Plan. Southern school desegregation may have contributed to his improved standing among blacks in that area over 1968, giving him about 15 percent of their vote. For one who lauded his own civil rights program, and who genuinely believed that American blacks regarded him as a friend, the facts were quite another matter. The administration made no attempt to offer much hope to the urban black underclass. Its anti-busing vehemence, which led to the ouster of Father Hesburgh as chairman of the Civil Rights Commission, sent the opposite signal.[41] Nixon simply could not appeal to white middle-income workers, with their susceptibility to George Wallace, while trying to mitigate the damage done by racial inequities.

The reality became difficult for Nixon himself to contemplate. He wanted to believe that his civil rights record was impeccable. Still, there was probably no other single subject about which Nixon so thoroughly compromised his own convictions in order to be, as Herbert Stein has put it, "a very good synthesizer and effective articulator of opinion." His positions on both school busing and "forced" racial balancing were strongly with the dominant public view, and just as sharply opposed to a series of court decisions. In the case of school desegregation, where compliance with another verdict, *Brown v. Board of Education*, was cited as the reason for going ahead, the administration's activity was inspired more by a desire to remove that issue from Wallace by 1972. Of all significant ethnic groups, blacks were most resistant to his "new American majority," giving him 14 percent of their votes, an improvement of only 1 percent over 1968.[42]

In other ways, too, the outcome showed that, for all his realignment ideas, those who voted for Nixon marked not a change from the postwar pattern but a continuation of the process by which Republicanism was advancing as the faith of the more comfortable middle and upper classes. Only among southerners were there gains among lower status whites. Moreover, while fewer than half of Democrats at the conservative end of the political spectrum went for Eisenhower in 1956, over three-quarters of them voted for Nixon in 1972.[43] Not surprisingly, Nixon was unable to make a simultaneous appeal to both right-wing Democrats and blacks who had been with the party of FDR since 1936.

Nixon did better with Jewish voters in 1972 than any Republican since Eisenhower in 1956, but, of all white ethnic groups, that one continued to be the most elusive. Throughout his political career, even after he left office, he found himself forced to battle charges of anti-Semitism. The result was a continuing frustration over failure to understand why he never could make more headway among Jews, who, while relatively few in number, had a high turnout rate at the polls. Moreover, they included many heavy financial contributors. Detroit industrialist Max Fisher, for example, was a key Nixon fund-raiser as well as an activist in Jewish affairs.

Jews were, to be sure, overwhelmingly Democratic, having been brought solidly into the party of FDR. They gave him 90 percent of their vote in 1940. They also tended to be more liberal than most ethnic groups and more resistant to attractions on the right, a position that survived to a surprising degree even as they succeeded so well in advancing along with the nation's postwar prosperity.

Some Jewish intellectuals — notably Irving Kristol and Norman Podhoretz — were already on the right. The reasons for their shift usually differed from the motivations of much of the post–New Deal middle class. They were more likely to respond to ideological or group interests than economic. Just as did Podhoretz, Nixon emphasized that American isolationism born from opposition to Vietnam had important implications for what the United States might be expected to do in the Middle East. He often cited his own pro-Israel policy, one that included issuing a worldwide alert during the Yom Kippur War of 1973, when his airlift of urgent supplies to that Middle Eastern country risked the danger of Soviet intervention.[44]

Nixon undoubtedly had more high-level Jewish aides and advisers than any president, from Henry Kissinger on down. Their names constitute an imposing list: Arthur Burns, Herb Stein, Bill Safire, Leonard Garment, Steve Hess, among others. Then there were such friends as Walter Annenberg and Murray Chotiner, one of his earliest and most durable political advisers. A large number of the early sympathetic books about Nixon were written by such authors as Earl Mazo, Ralph de Toledano, and Victor Lasky. Writer Benjamin Stein, who joined the staff during the Watergate period and is the son of the economist, thought that Nixon was comfortable with Jews because he identified with them as an "outsider."[45]

Still, the matter had haunted him since his old congressional days, and, in his later years, certain things kept such suspicions alive. One was his failure to honor the "tradition" of a Jewish seat on the Supreme Court. Then there was the incident of Nixon's having instructed an aide, Frederic V. Malek, to do some checking into the backgrounds of Bureau of Labor Statistics employees because he suspected that Jews within the department were undermining the administration by skewing economic statistics. That first came to the public's attention in the 1976 book by Bob Woodward and Carl Bernstein, *The Final Days*. Later, in 1988, it gained new, and wider, publicity when another *Washington Post* reporter, Walter Pincus, uncovered a July 27, 1971, memo that showed Malek reporting to Haldeman that thirteen high officials of that department were Jewish. Malek then confirmed that the list had been prepared because the president had complained of a "Jewish cabal" in the bureau. Woodward and Bernstein also reported that Kissinger was convinced that Nixon was anti-Semitic.[46]

Safire has told about first hearing Nixon on the Watergate tape of June 23, 1972, where he complained that the arts were heavily influenced by leftist Jews. "Garment, Stein, and I all felt that sinking sensation in an especially personal way," he wrote. "It simply did not fit in all we knew about Nixon's attitude toward Jews, and it fit perfectly with most Jews' suspicions of latent anti-Semitism in Nixon, which all of us had worked so hard to allay."[47]

Woodward and Bernstein and Safire came to their conclusions without having seen another item, one from Ehrlichman's notes of meetings with the president. It reveals that the Bureau of Labor Statistics was not alone among the president's complaints. In conversations that took place on December 30, 1970, and March 28, 1972, he pointed out that the Internal Revenue Service and Commerce Department were both "overtopped" with Jews, and they were more concerned with the clock than with their responsibilities. Jews especially, Nixon said to Shultz and Moynihan, were "out by 4:50 P.M.," getting a jump on quitting time and heading for the parking lots.[48]

Such instances should not be surprising. They are not very different from the frequent complaints about the establishment or the intellectual elite and the media, or, for that matter, from other comments that showed his consciousness about ethnicity. These attitudes were not peculiar to Nixon but rather reflect those of his times and culture, including the reformers among American populists who resented Jews as leaders of the powerful, privileged, and rapacious "eastern money" interests, the Shylocks of the world. Still, there is no evidence that anyone felt that he was being treated differently by Nixon because he was Jewish. One might also point out that, given the history of suspicions by Jews toward Nixon, it would be surprising not to find him resentful.[49]

One Jew who became firmly identified with the president toward the end of his political career was a sixty-year-old rabbi from Rhode Island, Baruch Korff. Korff, who called himself "Nixon's most ardent defender," was upset that Jewish liberals seemed to be in the vanguard of the Nixon-haters. That made little sense to the Ukrainian-born rabbi. Nixon had worked for détente with Russia and freedom for Soviet Jews. In Rabbi Korff's view, American liberals were ready to sacrifice their own heritage for the fulfillment of utopian ideas about universal justice. With considerable flair for energy and self-promotion, the rabbi then went to work to organize the National Citizens Committee for Fairness to the Presidency. Years later, when asked about Nixon's anti-Semitism, he shrugged his shoulders and said, "Why should one expect anything else?" The rabbi defended Nixon until the end, and, one might say, beyond that.[50]

The thought of sitting in the White House when the nation celebrated the completion of its second century pleased Richard Nixon. If first terms are preoccupied with winning another four years, "lame duck" chief executives worry about what historians will write. Nixon was fatalistic about the matter. "There is no such thing as history," he said to his visitor; "there are historians, and eighty-five percent of them are on the left."[51]

The choice of Philadelphia as the official site of the two hundredth anniversary celebration was the most logical one for 1976, which seemed perfectly clear to the members of the Bicentennial Commission. On July 4, 1970, acting with the president's approval, Republican Senate leader Hugh Scott announced that the enterprise would be coordinated with federal, state, and city funds.

Nixon, as conscious of the broader implications of his role as any man who ever sat in the White House, opened the "Bicentennial Era" with a nationally televised broadcast. "To look at America with clear eyes today," he said in 1971, "is to see every reason for pride and little for shame, great cause for gratitude and little for regret, strong grounds for hope and none at all for despair. The crucial challenge now is to hold the high ground of confidence, courage, and faith that is rightly ours and to avoid the quicksand of fear and doubt." There seemed little reason for not celebrating the bicentennial with the theme that the "basic goal is to restore America's historic role as an *example* to the world."[52]

Then, as with so many other things, the grand plans came apart, realities shattering dreams. Environmentalists blocked the idea of holding the celebration in Fairmount Park. Another plan, one conceived as recognition of the urban black community in twentieth-century America, had the support of local leadership but collapsed when a majority of the residents feared that their neighborhood would be obliterated.

And so it went. Predominantly Polish, Irish, and Jewish districts voiced similar objections. Each feared being overrun by someone else. Philadelphia, noted a reporter, "still could not escape the deep divisions in America today." And, he asked, "what, in fact, *is* there to celebrate in a nation torn by a divisive war that cannot seem to be brought to a conclusion; by racial antagonisms that show little sign of abating; by vast gulfs separating young and old, rich and poor, city and suburb; by gigantic public and private bureaucracies that appear to be unresponsive to human needs; and by a political system that virtually thrives on ambiguity and meaningless hyperbole and is at the mercy of the guns of mad assassins?"[53]

Philadelphia's ambitions collapsed, the city's plans finally rejected by the Nixon-appointed commission. Frank Rizzo, then mayor-elect, lamented that "we may just have the police band at Independence Hall play the Star Spangled Banner and that would be it." The commission itself came under fire as being dominated by an elite bunch of fat cats who "undoubtedly would have been Tories had they been alive 200 years ago." Weren't those commissions political payoffs? Antiwar dissidents challenged their claim as representatives of the national spirit, and a countergroup was organized, the People's American Revolutionary Bicentennial Commission. In Washington, D.C., two black leaders tried their hand at creating an Afro-American Bicentennial Corporation.[54]

Others, mostly on the political right, thought that was the correct moment for a Bicentennial constitutional convention. Supporters urged the convening of an assembly that, as was being suggested, might completely "update" the work of the Founding Fathers so that "traditional values" would be safeguarded. At the same time, a new, reformist version of the Constitution was being urged by the liberal Center for Democratic Institutions at Santa Barbara, California. As early as 1969, applications to the Congress to call a Constitutional Convention had been approved by thirty-three of the required thirty-four states. Senator Sam Ervin of North Carolina, who loved to think of himself as a "Constitutional purist," tried to block any attempt to discard the document altogether. He introduced legislation to establish limitations and procedural safeguards, which were supported by the Nixon administration. These passed the Senate in 1971 but got stuck in the House. For a time, the specter of revisionists staging a "quiet revolution" with a new blueprint for the entire nation seemed almost plausible.[55]

Ervin's wariness was shared by Nixon's people even as the administration hoped to use the bicentennial to further its own political objectives. Its responsibility was to be upbeat, to inspire, to leave the public at the anniversary with a strong pride in the nation, to be sure, but also in the presidency.[56] Len Garment worried that there was something wrong about the American people feeling "considerably better about their own personal prospects than about the nation's." The administration's reputation was at stake, he wrote to H. R. Haldeman, and that would be affected by public perceptions as conditioned by information circulated during the next few years.

The bicentennial year, the period between September 1, 1975, and September 1, 1976, would be a crucial period for influencing that mood, Garment went on.

> In shorthand terms, a "successful" Bicentennial year would be evidence of the "success" of RN's policies. Such an event, participated in by millions from the U.S. and abroad and transmitted by telecommunications to still more millions, would also represent a publicly perceived vote of confidence in the President. There would then be less chance that the next Administration could reverse the President's work and swing the policy pendulum rapidly back in the old direction. A relationship of mutual respect with the media — particularly the networks — is an important part of planning for the Bicentennial year, for what should be the culminating educational event of RN's Presidency.[57]

Finally, with decentralized festivities gaining emphasis, the Nixon administration revamped the Bicentennial Commission. The plan, Garment advised the president, should be "to concentrate the Federal Bicentennial programs and expenditures in areas and institutions relating to history, culture, recreation, individual excellence, matters more or less concerned with the American 'spirit.' "[58]

As the *New York Times* later noted, "A wide variety of enduring public improvements had been proposed to mark our Revolution and 200 years; but none came to fruition." As for *Time* magazine's lament that the celebration would come and go with "no tangible symbol . . . left behind, for the betterment of the national life, the well being of its citizens," the bicentennial seemed destined to ultimately be as forgotten as the centennial.[59]

Then there was Watergate.

In the White House on March 29, 1974, Father John McLaughlin, the Jesuit priest who had joined the staff as a special aide and speechwriter — and a controversial figure in his own right — welcomed a visiting group from the Harvard Law School Republican Club. The cleric, a vigorous and articulate defender of the president, advised that those worrying about impeachment were overreacting from "a sense of doom. The United States is facing a measure of adversity as it moves toward its Bicentennial, but it faced a considerably larger measure of adversity when it moved toward the Civil War." Nixon, in fact, a "fellow sufferer," was reading a great deal about Lincoln, and he also identified himself with Andrew Johnson. The thirty-seventh president, like the seventeenth, Father McLaughlin told his audience, was brought up as "white trash."[60]

Father McLaughlin was articulate and outspoken, and that particular analogy was especially harsh. Later, he left the clergy, married, and became the successful host of a television news discussion program. During his brief stay at the White House, where he put his tongue and pen to use, he sometimes outraged both political opponents and those who hated having a clergyman on the president's personal staff. People tending to be cynical about Richard Nixon anyway assumed that Father McLaughlin was there as just another bid for the Roman Catholic vote.

And those who suspected the worst about Richard Nixon thought they found it when the cumulative scandals known simply as Watergate were exposed by journalists Woodward and Bernstein, who as a result became so familiar as a team that they came to be called by the collective name "Woodstein." They, "Deep Throat," "deep six," "stonewalling," "hush money," "dirty tricks," "laundering," tapes, eighteen and a half minutes, and "expletive deleted" became even more familiar than Agnew and Checkers. Not unnaturally, trying to contain the scandal consumed the administration's energies and the president's last two years as everything else became subordinated to "hanging tough." Before it shortened that second term, Watergate also led to the dismissal of both Ehrlichman and Haldeman, and caused the latter's replacement by General Al Haig as chief of staff. That, in a bit of administrative reorganizing that had not been anticipated, included rejuvenating a virtually dormant cabinet. As the investigation went on, it also mesmerized most Americans, many of whom hardly left their television sets so they could follow the hearings of the Senate Watergate Committee and, later, the impeachment proceedings of the House Judiciary Committee. Foreigners, for the most part, were puzzled by the whole thing, with Russians especially distressed. They had not expected the architect of détente to become the victim of a "coup."[61]

The two-year route to Nixon's downfall began during the night of June 17, 1972, when five men — first called "burglars" by the press — were caught breaking into Larry O'Brien's offices at the Democratic National Committee located in the Watergate complex of luxury condominiums and businesses on Washington's Virginia Avenue. From the back pages, the story advanced to major headlines when the men turned out to have connections with the FBI, CIA, and the Nixon White House. One of them, Gordon Liddy, was a former FBI agent and also a counsel to CREP. However, as hard as they tried, the McGovern Democrats failed to make the incident a major campaign issue.

The spring of 1973 brought a windfall for Nixon-haters. Almost daily headlines revealed campaign operations involving break-ins, sabotage, dirty tricks — especially one that helped to knock out Muskie as Nixon's potential rival — wiretaps, and financing by CREP, including payments of cover-up money. More startling news came that summer before the special Senate committee headed by Senator Sam Ervin, highlighted by the almost casual revelation by Alexander Butterfield of the president's staff that Nixon had routinely taped telephone calls to the Oval Office and, indeed, voices in the office itself. With Archibald Cox of Harvard Law called in as a special prosecutor, a battle followed over surrendering the tapes. The president, out to protect his staff along with his reputation, held back. In October, in a battle over subpoenas and pleas of executive privilege, Cox was fired, initiating the so-called Saturday night massacre, which included the resignations of Attorney General Elliot Richardson and his deputy William Ruckelshaus. The crisis deepened. When Nixon finally responded to court orders to release the tapes, he did so in segments. Much of the public that had been inattentive until then was upset when the frequent appearance of the phrase "expletive deleted" in the transcripts suggested heavy use of profanity in the White House. Equally dramatic was the revelation that eighteen and a half minutes of a key tape were mysteriously erased. Also under inspection, and all lumped together as "Watergate," were the president's tax returns and questions about excessive use of government funds to improve his homes at San Clemente and Key Biscayne.

Presidential pleas that "one year of Watergate is enough" were not sufficient. The battle continued to be waged in the courts, the Congress, and the press. During the summer of 1974, the House Judiciary Committee agreed to three resolutions of impeachment, for obstruction of justice, abuse of presidential powers, and violation by the president of his oath of office. With the White House already besieged came release of three transcripts of Oval Office conversations that dated back to June 23, 1972, just one week after the break-in. That was the "smoking gun" everybody had been looking for: conclusive proof that the president tried to cover up the break-in by telling Haldeman to get the FBI to stop its investigation.

On August 8, 1974, with his support in the Senate reduced to about a dozen and his popularity polls below 30 percent, Nixon announced on television that he would resign at noon the next day. On August 9, Gerald Ford was sworn in as the thirty-eighth president. One month later, President Ford dropped a Sunday morning bombshell by announcing that he had pardoned Mr. Nixon. The stroke of his pen raised enough of a storm finally to destroy Ford's chance to be elected on his own.

Ford, and Nixon's supporters generally, argued that a trial would have put both the ex-president and the nation through an extended trauma. He had already paid a "sufficient" price for the misdeeds. Still, in retrospect, the pardon was unfortunate in several ways. By accepting it, Nixon in effect acknowledged his guilt. Historically, it also deprived both the accused and the nation of an opportunity for the kind of examination that may have done much to sweep aside the more excessive allegations and suspicions. Nixon's argument that he was guilty of little that had not been done by his predecessors would have received a badly needed hearing. He would, at the same time, have been able to allay widely held suspicions of a power grab, which even included such fantastic rumors as a plot to cancel the presidential election of 1972. A joint survey conducted by *Newsweek* and ABC News on the tenth anniversary of the break-in tapped continuing confusion about what had really happened. More Americans, 10 percent more than on the day of Nixon's resignation, were convinced that he should have resigned while, by 56 to 35 percent, there was regret that he had not been made to stand trial. A full cross-examination, which would have been possible only by placing Mr. Nixon himself on the witness stand, could have done much to shed light on notions that he was merely the victim of what Paul Johnson has called "the first media Putsch in history."[62] Admittedly, the cost of such intelligence would have been great, but a free society has the right to consider the administration's malfeasance in its proper perspective.

President Ford apparently hoped a pardon, especially if given early in his administration, would cease to be an issue by 1976. He was also concerned that trying the case would cripple his administration's ability to engage the attention and direction of the country. For such reasons, or if only because he felt that he owed it to Nixon or, as some suspected, due to a prior understanding that had been worked out with Al Haig, Ford had acted.

Nixon, while raising the possibility that he was caught in a CIA plot, has admitted that he was trying to protect his people. It was, however, the president himself who called for evidence of the O'Brien-Hughes connection, and it was the president who had approved a plan by White House aide Tom Huston, which J. Edgar Hoover turned down, for gathering intelligence against his opponents.[63] All that took place well before the break-in at the Watergate.

Nixon did much to create the hostile climate within the White House, and his men were almost uniformly eager, ambitious, and in awe of their responsibility to protect the president and further his interests. They were bright but, alas, young and lacking in wisdom. The atmosphere of hitting back at the opposition by whatever means possible had been well established. Ideas were planted and their execution left to the aggressive and adventurous. John Ehrlichman, one of those who ended up with a jail term, has maintained, for example, that he wanted information from Daniel Ellsberg's psychiatrist but never thought that it would mean breaking into the doctor's office — exactly the point. Henry II didn't need to be more explicit about wanting to get rid of Thomas à Becket. Nixon himself later admitted, on a national television interview conducted by David Frost on May 4, 1977, that he had "let the American people down" by aiding the cover-up.[64]

Other circumstances may well have played a role in forcing the president out; certainly in destroying his level of popular approval. The worsening inflation of 1973 and 1974 did not help. The Arab oil cartel's forcing upward of prices combined with other factors in the economy traceable to the Johnson administration and the war made the increases a major concern. Kept relatively level by the wage-price freeze, the cost-of-living index shot upward after the lid was removed in January of 1973. Going against overwhelming contrary advice, including that from Herb Stein, the president chose to impose a second freeze, or stage of controls, in 1973, but it was not enough to contain inflation and the public's distress. As Nixon himself has pointed out, the American people do not necessarily punish corruption, as in the Iran-contra scandals or even Teapot Dome, but they do react to pocketbook issues.[65]

Had the national circumstances been different, there could have been a rebellion against the press. The president's men had hoped for exactly that, picturing themselves as the victims of journalistic persecution. When Rabbi Baruch Korff proclaimed himself a friend of Nixon's and set up his National Citizens Committee for Fairness to the Presidency, the response was revealing.

The Korff campaign, begun before the resignation, was, in effect, an uprising against the media, which were charged with playing the hangman's role. Letters that accompanied the $300,000 raised to help pay Nixon's legal fees almost unfailingly made that point. A cartoonist showed the presidential seal, the eagle replaced by a meek dove holding an olive branch in one claw and a piece of paper in another, being eaten up by three animated faces: a microphone, a newspaper, and a television set.[66]

If, as Theodore White has noted, Americans "voted for the end of the postwar world" by returning Richard Nixon to the White House in 1972, they also closed out the New Deal era.[67] Had Nixon made a clean breast of the Watergate break-in at the beginning and promised to take action against the intruders (an act that would have contradicted the hubris of the modern presidency), the scandal might have been contained; but, with the energy crisis distorting the economy, inflation alone would have been crippling. Nevertheless, during his term in office, Nixon achieved an important breakthrough in east-west relations (especially with the start of the SALT process), the end of America's involvement in Vietnam, and steps toward relaxation of the cumulative centralization of federal power. The influence of the New Deal could never be undone, but Nixon began the modifications that continued through the Ford, Carter, and Reagan years.

In foreign affairs, notably in its efforts to keep the regime of Salvador Allende from taking power in Chile and to thwart others regarded as hostile to U.S. interests, the administration's policies continued the long-standing assumptions behind American diplomacy. Other than the openings to China and the Soviets, however, the Nixon Doctrine began to alter the emphasis of American responsibility. With U.S. assistance, those nations faced with threats from leftist subversion were compelled to assume more of their own share of the burden.[68]

Interpretations of the part of the Nixon presidency that never happened tend to see Watergate as delaying the fruition of the subsequent conservative climate, or, in the rhetoric of his rightist opponents, as the sellout of a centrist. Podhoretz, in *The Present Danger*, wrote that Watergate "nullified" the conservative movement, while those more extreme accuse Nixon of sabotaging the cause. Republican stalwarts of the establishment variety, such as Hugh Scott, have had their view of realignment jaundiced by fruitless precedents.[69]

The conventional sequence of events would have Watergate as but an interruption of the inevitable conservative revolt against the world of New Deal economics and priorities. And there is enough evidence to show that, as the administration moved toward the right even while going to economic controls and to the China Wall, it was accommodating itself to traditional sources of Republican support. The executive officers of leading corporations established the Business Roundtable in 1972 to enhance their input into public policy. The American Enterprise Institute, growing up from modest beginnings, and with encouragement from within the Nixon White House, moved forward as a credible rival to the liberal Brookings Institution. Beer magnate Joseph Coors plunked down a quarter of a million dollars as seed money to enable Paul Weyrich to create the right-wing Heritage Foundation. Milton Friedman, speaking to a generation of conservatives who had earlier followed Hayek, was as upset at wage-price controls as was Buckley at seeing Nixon in Peking.[70]

The temptation to view Nixon as preparing the way for Reagan is great, and a number of political analysts have succumbed, but a clear line of post-Watergate continuity is almost inconceivable. There is too much that interferes with any attempt at delineating a logical progression. The consequences of the scandals themselves, including the pardon, altered both the politics and the climate. Other events, which had little to do with Nixon or Watergate, also got in the way: the energy crisis and double-digit inflation, which in most ways was more international than peculiarly American; the overthrow of the shah in Iran and the events at the embassy in Teheran, where fifty-two men were held hostage until Reagan took over from Carter. Beginning with New York City in 1975, American government at all levels began to contend with urban fiscal crises, which reinforced conservative arguments about continued heavy government spending. California, once again showing its propensity for the avant-garde, launched Proposition Thirteen, the revolt of taxpayers that bred copycats.

Making it all shakier was the nonelected, caretaker presidency of Gerald Ford and the quizzical, well-meaning, and often contradictory term of a southern Democrat, Jimmy Carter, whose Georgia origins made his election possible in the first place, and then, inevitably, assured his estrangement from traditional, northern sources of party support. Nor did the Russians help Carter, or the life of Nixon's détente, by continued insinuations of power in the Third World, especially the move into Afghanistan in 1979. All combined with fear of declining American authority and 20-plus percent interest rates to convince a wary electorate to take a chance with Ronald Reagan.

How a two-term Nixon presidency would have turned out is hard to say. Most observers have been perplexed by attempts to find consistency in Nixon. Safire has made the analogy of Nixon as a multilayer cake, with the progressive, the conservative, and the liberal each a part of the man. Still, his domestic legacy, ambiguous at best but most effective at encouraging the silent majority in their conservative populism, was too weak and, in the end, too flawed to sustain him in his prime area of strength, directing America's foreign policy.

Nixon's counterestablishment bias contained more of the essence of populism than of the pristine ideological right. In its last stage, even while the administration was contending with defending itself against the scandals, it was trying to adjust the welfare state to a new age. Welfare policies, for example, were sharply tightened when Caspar Weinberger became head of HEW in 1973. Under "Cap the Knife," the goal became less one of helping the poor than rooting out cheats and reducing services. Nixon fought hard to dismantle that holdover from Johnson's Great Society, the Office of Economic Opportunity, especially the controversial Community Action Program. In the face of congressional resistance, he brought in Howard Phillips to do the job. Phillips, who made Weinberger look like a left-liberal, was stopped by a federal district judge. But Nixon, determined to complete the work, appointed a successor by circumventing legislation and transferring programs to other agencies. By the end of 1973, OEO was left with three functions, legal services, economic development, and community action, all of which were dependent upon Congress for final action. Congress appropriated funds and the president impounded them, and the acrimony became sharper even as the Watergate revelations became more sensational. Still, the administration did manage to win approval for the National Environmental Policy Act and took the initiative in the matter of pollution control; and its efforts to aid education and design a national health insurance program all belonged to a time of greater, not less, cooperation between government and private enterprise. "Our economic policy actions and our trade actions and all the rest went on and on" through the trauma of Watergate, said William Simon. "And Nixon participated in them, right up until two weeks before he resigned. Incredible! Absolutely bizarre. He could pull the curtain down and deal for hours on these ethereal subjects."[71]

Abroad, as well as at home, there was a common denominator in Nixon's policies. He used not ideology but the carrot and the stick. The Nixon Doctrine did not inhibit his use of American power, especially in the air, to bring the enemy to the peace table by military pulverization. His way to end the war in Southeast Asia was by first extending it to interdict all supply routes, whether from North Vietnam into South Vietnam or into Cambodia, or from China and the USSR into Indochina. Nothing made the point more emphatic than his heavy "Christmas bombing" in 1972 or his demonstrations of military power to show the Soviets that he was ready for full-scale war if they attempted to counter supplies for Israel. Three of his postpresidential books, *The Real War, The Real Peace,* and *1999,* assume both continued east-west competition and avoidance of a nuclear holocaust by "managing conflict." The conservative who went to wage-price controls was the same anticommunist fighter who drank with Zhou and Mao. As he sat in his New Jersey exile in 1988 and pondered the *glasnost* and *perestroika* of Mikhail Gorbachev, he warned that the causes of the cold war had not disappeared and urged the west to keep up its guard "until he makes an irrevocable break with the Kremlin's past policies." We must, he warned, "make Gorbachev choose between a less confrontational relationship with the West and the retention of his imperial control over Eastern Europe." It was vintage Nixon to argue that we must be friends because "we cannot afford to be enemies." No woolly-headed reasoning there.[72]

On July 4, 1976, the nation celebrated its bicentennial. The outward mood was one of defiance against perceptions of a weakening America. As Vice President Rockefeller reminded a large crowd at the Washington Monument that evening, "Like every generation we face today what seems like insurmountable problems. . . . Every such challenge is an opportunity; it has been the creative response to such challenges of these 200 years that has brought America to greatness."[73]

The reality was something else. Opinion surveys confirmed the pervasiveness of drift and alienation, with a loss of confidence in key institutions. A Harris poll found that fully three-fifths of those queried also expressed dissatisfaction with their lives. Barbara Tuchman's bicentennial contribution to *Newsweek* typified expressions of anxiety. "Our sins in the twentieth century — greed, violence, inhumanity — have been profound, with the result that the pride and self-confidence of the nineteenth century have turned to disunity and self-distrust," she wrote. Then she added, even more portentously, about the First Amendment, "The U.S. has slid a long way from the original idea." Boston University president John Silber called his Independence Day oration at Faneuil Hall "Counterfeits of Democracy." "Increasingly," he warned, "we confuse the pursuit of happiness, guaranteed by the Declaration of Independence, with the pursuit of pleasure." Jon Nordheimer observed in the *New York Times*, "For many Americans, it is the age of anomie, when events, technology, communications, and social movement have contributed to confuse the national sense of purpose and values."[74]

"Indeed," as Christopher Lasch wrote, "Americans seem to wish to forget not only the sixties, the riots, the new left, the disruptions on college campuses, Vietnam, Watergate, and the Nixon presidency, but their entire collective past, even in the antiseptic form in which it was celebrated during the Bicentennial." The festivities were salutary, an antidote to the disillusionment of a decade, a reaffirmation of sacred values. "This country listened to Jerry Rubin too long," declared political statistician Richard Scammon. "We heard from the mass of America on July 4. They have always been this way." A Connecticut woman was

quoted as voicing what was undoubtedly the most representative sentiment. "It's nice that we're promoting our country for a change rather
than putting it down."[75]

"Oh, What a Lovely Party!" was *Time*'s heading for the magazine's
report of the national celebration. Thirty-three and a half tons of fireworks, the largest such display in the nation, were set off in the capital.
Communities throughout America featured their own pyrotechnics, pa-
rades, and mammoth birthday cakes. Races involved every conceivable
type of competition — balloons, greased poles, pie-eating. Reenactments
of Revolutionary War tableaux came into vogue, along with red, white,
and blue fire hydrants. In all fifty states and overseas American communities, bells marked the occasion. The National Anthem sounded
across Baltimore Harbor from its birthplace at Fort McHenry. At the
Charles River, nearly a half million crowded together along the Back
Bay waterfront to hear Arthur Fiedler's Boston Pops play the *1812
Overture*. Philadelphia police estimated that at least one million people
surged around Independence Square, where the signing of the Declaration of Independence was reenacted. At exactly 2:00 P.M., a soft mallet
struck the Liberty Bell. An enormous block party of twenty thousand
people turned out in Miami's Little Havana. Concern about protesters
had not disappeared, but the only significant negative expression took
place among dissidents in the national capital. At the Jefferson Memorial,
they blew a ram's horn to greet the sunrise, and then, five thousand
strong, marched to the Capitol carrying a banner that read, "Independence From Big Business."[76] But most Americans hardly noticed. Protest,
handwringing, and running the country down were distinctly out of
style. It was, instead, a time for jubilation, for reassertion of what Americans liked to consider their traditional values.

Exuberant throngs jammed Lower Manhattan. Sunshine, low humid-
ity, and a chance to view the glories of old naval days sparked old-
fashioned patriotic nostalgia. An armada of some 225 tall-masted ships
that comprised Operation Sail '76, having already journeyed from Bermuda to Newport, Rhode Island, floated into New York Harbor and up
the Hudson River. Hundreds of thousands filled the narrow downtown
streets along the waterfront, pushing their way to better vantage points.
Flags, vendors, and balloons were everywhere.

The sense of jubilation and national pride provided a sharp contrast
with the antiwar demonstrators who had only recently been so much a
part of the scene. All that now seemed eagerly forgotten; the light at
the end of the tunnel had been reached, if not as anticipated in Southeast
Asia, at least on the streets of America's cities. "By evening," reported
the *New York Times*, "hundreds of thousands jammed the shore along
lower Manhattan, some dangling from trees like Christmas decorations
to watch the dazzling fireworks explode over the harbor and the Statue

of Liberty." Lights of red, white, and blue crowned the Empire State Building. "New York City is what America is supposed to be," declared the local chairman of the Committee for July Fourth. "Did you get the same feeling as I got this weekend?" President Gerald Ford asked his companions as they flew in a helicopter over Mount Vernon. "It was just the feeling of people together."[77]

In Southern California, an exiled Richard Nixon was with his family at La Casa Pacifica estate near San Clemente. Their holiday celebration was limited to attendance at a bicentennial party at nearby Newport Beach that had been organized by a group of old friends. Other than that, they marked the two-hundredth birthday in a way that never could have been anticipated a little over two years earlier.

His earliest retirement days were made even more dismal by a severe return of the thrombophlebitis that had bothered him on and off since 1964. This time, however, the inflammation became a near-killer. An embolism formed from a blood clot in his left leg, threatening a blockage in a main artery and finally requiring surgery at Long Beach Memorial Hospital when his blood circulation was almost entirely shut down. After seven hours on the operating table in late October 1974, his system went into shock. Richard Nixon, disgraced and exiled, still waging legal battles over demands that he testify, was near death and his obituaries were being prepared.[78] Finally, on November 3, he was removed from the critical list and was back in San Clemente before Christmas.

At the moment of the bicentennial, Nixon's holiday was marred by additional setbacks. He had resigned from the California bar, but word came that New York had acted on its own to keep him from practicing there. Pat, now the "lonely lady of San Clemente," was rushed up the Pacific coast to a hospital in Long Beach, the victim of a stroke that partially paralyzed her left side. She had been reading Bob Woodward and Carl Bernstein's sensational account of their final days in the White House.[79]

Such developments failed to get much public attention that holiday weekend. Apart from local events, interest centered on the ceremonial activities of Gerald R. Ford. The thirty-eighth president, the first to reach the White House without the endorsement of any national election, projected a largely soothing, noncontroversial personality, his ebullient patriotism and obvious wholesomeness perfectly suiting the national mood.

Ford's day began at Valley Forge, Pennsylvania, where he delivered the opening comments at a ceremony that featured the arrival of twenty teams of horse-drawn covered wagons. He delivered a tribute to the national character, and then reminded his listeners that "though prosperity is a good thing, though compassionate charity is a good thing, though institutional reform is a good thing, a nation survives only so long as the spirit of sacrifice and self-discipline is strong within its people." Then he went on to Philadelphia. At Independence Hall, in what was the day's keynote address, the president asked, "Are 'the institutions under which we live' working the way they should? Are the foundations laid in 1776 and 1789 still strong enough and sound enough to resist the tremors of our times? Are the God-given rights secure, are our hard-won liberties protected?"[80]

By early afternoon, Ford joined the New York City celebration aboard the seventy-nine-thousand-ton aircraft carrier *Forrestal*. Before his brief remarks, at precisely 2:00 P.M., he rang the ship's bell thirteen times, one for each of the original thirteen colonies, and provided the cue for simultaneous ringing throughout America.

In Washington, he opened a time capsule that had been stored in a safe since the celebration of 1876. The cache contained photographs, autographs, inkstands, a book on temperance, and a list of the fewer than 100,000 who were then on the federal payroll. For the 2076 tricentennial, some Americans were already storing such items as credit cards and picket signs. Other suggestions included a Frisbee, a Beatles' record, birth control pills, a Big Mac hamburger, a chunk of moon rock, and a piece of the Watergate tapes.[81]

Epilogue

EIGHT YEARS after his resignation, an ABC–Washington Post poll showed that three-quarters of the American people held Richard Nixon responsible for the Watergate scandals. By a two-to-one margin, they also thought he should be excluded from future responsibility in national affairs. When Hofstra University, on Long Island, planned its Sixth Annual Presidential Conference, doubts were expressed about whether it would be appropriate to "honor" Nixon.[1]

Far more prolonged differences involved the creation of a Richard Nixon presidential library. That question joined the conflict between the National Archives and the former president for control of his papers, and was not resolved until the fall of 1987 with the decision to have the Nixon Presidential Archives Foundation build a Richard Nixon Library and Birthplace on a nine-acre tract in Yorba Linda. The solution ended a round of controversies about establishing a center at such possible places as Duke University, the University of Southern California, and San Clemente.

The problem began with a Supreme Court decision in 1977 that denied Nixon control over the papers of his administration, a ruling that rested on the argument that the circumstances of his resignation had placed him "in a different class from all other Presidents." Moreover, a 1974 congressional act had remanded control of the Nixon White House records to the National Archives. Any Nixon library, therefore, would have to exist without the presidential papers and recordings, thereby leaving its operation in the hands of the private funders, the "friends" of the ex-president. Scholars jaundiced about Nixon to begin with immediately feared that a foundation-run Nixon library would exist primarily to glorify his career rather than serve history.[2]

The battle to acquire a site for the library under the Nixon Foundation left little doubt that the issue was as much Nixon the individual as legalities. In San Clemente, for example, the proposal to establish a library there became involved with other local problems, but there were strong suspicions that it was stalled to death by an anti-Nixon minority within the city council. At Duke, careful attention was given to the academic considerations pertaining to control. Nevertheless, the report of the faculty committee concluded that "the academic community in this country was generally scandalized by Richard Nixon's political career, from Checkers to Watergate. Some of its members might shy away from any university that seemed to identify itself with the former president."[3]

The *Journal of American History* later published the results of a survey showing that specialists ranked his presidency below all of his predecessors except for the inept administrations of Ulysses S. Grant and Warren G. Harding. In only one area did Nixon place first: he was the most controversial, which at least implied that his overall ranking was subject to substantial change.[4]

Interestingly, Nixon's runner-up in the "controversiality" stakes was Lyndon B. Johnson. Johnson had had to contend with Vietnam and the turmoil at home; Nixon had both, and Watergate. But they also shared temperaments that were incapable of an Eisenhower-like detachment from the thunder and lightning. And Nixon, more than Johnson, was an ultranationalist.

His career was fought against enemies at home and abroad. An anticommunist battler from California days, he secured his national reputation during the effort to demonstrate Alger Hiss's guilt. For Nixon, communism in America was not the xenophobic crusade that it became for Joe McCarthy. There was overlapping, to be sure. Both exploited populism that lashed out at the "boys" in the "striped-pants" suits. To Nixon, it was a faith both dangerous and symptomatic of those for whom the American dream was more myth than the product of cultural exceptionalism. In denying that ideal, they were implicitly clinging to the advantages of a privileged elite. When, during the 1960s, internal subversion was no longer perceived as rooted in a Washington infiltrated by New Deal intellectuals, populism took on another form, one that denied the right and necessity of the United States to act as an international custodian of popular democracy. Nixon's exploitation of political opportunities was hardly more than an expression of the popular will.

In his unhappy retirement from public life, Nixon remained, in the words of his assistant John Taylor, an "extraordinarily practical intellectual" who continued to "live and breathe practical foreign policy." Finally freed from domestic political considerations, and having spent much of his retirement concentrating on the post-Nixon, post-Kissinger world, he found his expertise more valued with the multiplication of misfortunes under Ford, Carter, and Reagan. Although his own foreign policy record was far from unblemished, he built on the respect he had earned. He made several trips back to the scene of his greatest diplomatic triumph, China, and met with Deng Xiaoping. In a series of speeches, all personally written, and delivered before several key groups of opinion-makers, he emphasized a "new realism." In San Francisco, on April 21, 1986, he strongly supported the Reagan administration's military aid program toward the contra rebels in Nicaragua. As William Safire wrote that year about his ex-boss, in a self-confessed oxymoron, "He caws of 'hard-headed detente.'" After Nixon went to Moscow in the summer of 1986 and met Mikhail Gorbachev, he said he found the new Soviet leader to be "either the greatest actor the political world has produced or . . . a man totally in charge with the power and ability to chart his own course." The difference between the new Kremlin boss and the administration in Washington, he wrote, was that "he's playing chess while we're playing checkers."[5]

As Watergate became more distant, Nixon's standing improved. Increased requests for his campaign help began to come from various Republicans. A poll published in *Newsweek* in 1986 showed that 54 percent of Americans approved of the pardon.[6] His statements on foreign policy reappeared in such establishment journals as *Foreign Affairs* and the *Times* of London. Nixon's steady output of books, half a dozen in the last fifteen years, found large audiences and contributed to the debate about how best to reconcile the need for national security and American global interests with avoidance of a major war. The Reagan administration quietly consulted him about policy and strategy, both foreign and domestic. He urged Reagan, and later George Bush, not to ignore the power of the "new majority." After the 1989 massacre of protestors in the youth-led prodemocracy movement in Beijing, Nixon counseled the new administration in Washington to "stay the prudent course" and not overreact. "If we force them back into their isolation from the West," he wrote, "we risk prompting a potentially disastrous entente between the two great Communist powers that would be in nobody's interest but Gorbachev's."[7]

Into his mid-seventies, Nixon continued to work full days at 26 Federal Plaza in New York City, where, in 1985, he relieved the government of the $3 million annual cost for providing Secret Service protection by hiring his own people at his own expense. After he moved his office to a new complex in New Jersey, he maintained his customary routine, writing, keeping in touch with his friends, both American and foreign, and, above all, seeking respectability as an elder statesman, one who deserved to be taken seriously for his intimate and sophisticated view of the world. If he were twenty years younger, cynics would have been quick to conclude that he was merely planning another resurrection. Richard Nixon, whether leading the Orthogonians, the Republican party, or the nation, wondered what he had to do to be taken seriously. Such determined absorption in vital issues is rare among American politicians. However one views his public career, and the damage to the presidency caused by Watergate, Richard Nixon never was "just another politician." The nation, one suspects, will never be at peace with him, nor he with himself.

Notes

ABBREVIATIONS USED IN THE NOTES

CSU-F	California State University at Fullerton, Oral History Collection
GRFL	Gerald R. Ford Library
DDEL	Dwight D. Eisenhower Library
DNC	Democratic National Committee
HSTL	Harry S. Truman Library
JFKL	John F. Kennedy Library
LBJL	Lyndon B. Johnson Library
LAT	*Los Angeles Times*
NARA-LA	National Archives, Los Angeles Branch, at Laguna Niguel
NARA-Wash.	National Archives, Washington, D.C.
NPMP	Nixon Presidential Materials Project, Alexandria, Virginia
NYHT	*New York Herald Tribune*
NYT	*New York Times*
RNC	Republican National Committee
WP	*Washington Post*
WPNWE	*Washington Post National Weekly Edition*
WSJ	*Wall Street Journal*

Chapter 1. SUNRISE WITH LINCOLN

1. Interview with Egil Krogh, December 3, 1985.
2. Ibid.
3. Witcover, *White Knight*, p. 335; O'Neill, *Coming Apart*, p. 297.
4. Nixon notes, February 6, 1969, and January 16, 1970, PPF, Box 185, NPMP.
5. President's notes of analysis of first year, January 18, 1970, PPF, Box 185, NPMP.
6. Nixon notes, April 26, 1970, PPF, Box 185, NPMP.
7. Gitlin, *The Sixties*, p. 410; Herbert Klein to Nixon, May 6, 1970, Haldeman Papers, Box 152, NPMP; Nixon, *RN*, p. 458.
8. *NYT*, May 9, 1970.
9. Nixon, *RN*, p. 458.
10. John Ehrlichman, Notes of Meetings with the President, May 9, 1970, Ehrlichman Papers, Fenn Gallery, Santa Fe, New Mexico.
11. Interview with John Ehrlichman, June 17, 1985.

12. *NYT*, May 7, 1970.
13. Ibid.
14. *Public Papers: Nixon, 1970,* pp. 413–423.
15. *NYT*, May 9, 1970.
16. Nixon, *RN*, p. 459; Safire, *Before the Fall*, pp. 204–205.
17. Safire, *Before the Fall*, p. 205; Nixon, *RN*, p. 460.
18. Interview with Egil Krogh, December 3, 1985.
19. *NYT*, May 10, 1970; Safire, *Before the Fall*, pp. 202, 212.
20. Interview with Egil Krogh, December 3, 1985; Safire, *Before the Fall*, p. 205.
21. Nixon, *RN*, p. 461; interview with Egil Krogh, December 3, 1985.
22. Safire, *Before the Fall*, p. 212;

interview with Egil Krogh, December 3, 1985.
23. Safire, *Before the Fall*, p. 207; Nixon, *RN*, pp. 462–463; *Public Papers: Nixon, 1970,* pp. 424–425.
24. Nixon, *RN*, pp. 461, 464; Safire, *Before the Fall*, p. 207.
25. Safire, *Before the Fall*, pp. 205–206, 208.
26. Safire, *Before the Fall*, p. 211; *NYT*, May 9, 1970.
27. Price, *With Nixon*, pp. 169–170.
28. Safire, *Before the Fall*, pp. 209–210. Hannah Nixon died in September 1967.
29. Interview with Egil Krogh, December 3, 1985.
30. Ibid.

Chapter 2. THE THIRTY-SEVENTH PRESIDENT

1. McDermott, *Writings of William James*, p. 684; interview with Julie Nixon Eisenhower, January 21, 1986.
2. William Allen White, *Autobiography*, p. 619.
3. Barber, *Presidential Character*, p. 421.
4. Pious, "Richard M. Nixon," p. 637.
5. Hartz, *Liberal Tradition in America*, Brace & World, Inc., 1955, pp. 276, 291.
6. For a comprehensive sampling, see the following: Abrahamsen, *Nixon vs. Nixon;* Barber, *Presidential Character;* Brodie, *Richard Nixon;* Mazlish, *In Search of Nixon;* Woodstone, *Nixon's Head.*
7. Woodstone, *Nixon's Head*, p. 248.
8. Kopkind and Ridgeway, *Decade of Crisis*, p. 2.
9. Wills, *Nixon Agonistes*, p. 79; *NYT*, August 10, 1974.
10. Alsop, "Nixon and the Square Majority," p. 42.
11. Interview with Hugh Scott, June 10, 1986.
12. Nixon, *Leaders*, pp. 5, 320, 323, 333; Nixon, *RN*, p. 125.
13. Nixon, *Leaders*, p. 218; *The Sunday Times* (London), October 2, 1988.
14. Nixon, *Real War*, p. 238; Nixon, *RN*, p. 864.
15. John Ehrlichman Papers, seen at the Fenn Gallery, Santa Fe, New Mexico, now part of the NPMP, NARA-Alexandria; Solberg, *Hubert Humphrey*, p. 313; interview with H. R. Haldeman, January 25, 1985.
16. Wills, *Nixon Agonistes*, p. 184.
17. *NYT*, June 4, 1984.
18. Nixon soon afterward did away with government-paid Secret Service protection.
19. Safire, *Before the Fall*, p. 606.
20. Interview with Richard M. Nixon, June 4, 1984.
21. Ibid.
22. Interview with Richard M. Nixon, June 8, 1984.
23. Statement by Alger Hiss, October 20, 1983, news release issued by the National Emergency Civil Liberties Foundation.
24. Interview with Alger Hiss, April 5, 1984.
25. Ibid. "People have marveled, or been surprised, that I am not more bitter at Nixon," Hiss later told David Remnick of the *Washington Post*. "He didn't seem worth it." *Washington Post National Weekly Edition*, January 5, 1987, p. 10.
26. O'Neill, *A Better World*, p. 316.
27. Cf. *Commentary*, "Symposium: How Has the United States Met Its Major Challenges Since 1945?" pp. 25–107.
28. Nixon, *Six Crises*, p. 1.
29. Nixon handwritten notes for Lincoln Day speech, 1946, Nixon Non-Deeded Papers, Series 2, Box 1, NARA-LA; Nixon to Herman Perry, October 6, 1945, Nixon Non-Deeded Papers, Series 2, Box 1, NARA-LA; Garment, "Hill Case," p. 94.

Chapter 3. Two Centuries, One Nation

1. Sumner, *Forgotten Man*, p. 333.
2. Hofstadter, *Social Darwinism*, p. 32.
3. Garraty, *New American Commonwealth*, p. 332.
4. Spencer, *Social Status*, pp. 323–326, 353; Fleming, "Social Darwinism," p. 127.
5. Hofstadter, *Social Darwinism*, p. 66.
6. Sumner, *Forgotten Man*, p. 325.
7. *Guide to the Centennial Exposition*, p. 18.
8. Howells, "Sennight of the Centennial," p. 96.
9. *Guide to the Centennial Exposition*, p. 11; Page Smith, *Trial by Fire*, p. 934.
10. Howells, "Sennight of the Centennial," p. 95; Dee Brown, *Year of the Century*, p. 135; Page Smith, *Trial by Fire*, p. 940.
11. *Guide to the Centennial Exposition*, p. 12; Page Smith, *Trial by Fire*, p. 936; Dee Brown, *Year of the Century*, p. 139; Nevins, *Emergence of Modern America*, p. 309.
12. Rydell, *All the World's a Fair*, p. 22.
13. *Guide to the Centennial Exposition*, p. 16.
14. Jackson, *American Space*, p. 236; Dee Brown, *Year of the Century*, p. 21.
15. *NYT*, July 5, 1876; Rydell, *All the World's a Fair*, pp. 33–35.
16. Trachtenberg, *Incorporation of America*, p. 156.
17. Ibid., p. 47; Lynn, *William Dean Howells*, pp. 27, 273; Hough, *Quiet Rebel*, p. 23; Cady, *Road to Realism*, pp. 120, 232.
18. *NYT*, July 3, 1876.
19. Dee Brown, *Year of the Century*, p. 277; Bryce, *American Commonwealth*, v. 2, p. 241.
20. Cf. Edmund S. Morgan, *American Slavery, American Freedom*.
21. Cf. Dee Brown, *Bury My Heart at Wounded Knee*.
22. Rydell, *All the World's a Fair*, p. 27.
23. Trefousse, *Carl Schurz*, p. 222; Foner, *Reconstruction*, pp. 570–572; Page Smith, *Trial by Fire*, p. 900.
24. Bailyn, et al., *Great Republic*, v. 2, p. 545; Bryce, *American Commonwealth*, v. 2, p. 516.
25. Gabriel, *Course of American Democratic Thought*, pp. 137–138; H. Wayne Morgan, *Unity and Culture*, p. 64;

Bryce, *American Commonwealth*, v. 2, pp. 549–550; Fred A. Shannon, *Centennial Years*, p. 19.
26. Bryce, *American Commonwealth*, v. 2, p. 524.
27. Nevins, *Emergence of Modern America*, p. 310.
28. Jackson, *American Space*, p. 31; Trachtenberg, *Incorporation of America*, p. 48.
29. Parrington, *Main Currents*, v. 3, p. 23; Bryce, *American Commonwealth*, v. 1, pp. 637–638, v. 2, p. 156; Steffens, *Shame*, p. 138; Callow, *Tweed Ring*, p. 82.
30. Gillette, "Election of 1872," pp. 1304, 1305; Dobson, *Politics in the Gilded Age*, p. 62; Hoogenboom, "Spoilsmen and Reformers," p. 90.
31. McFeely, *Grant*, pp. 405–435.
32. Henry Adams, *Education*, p. 963.
33. Gillette, "Election of 1872," p. 1311.
34. Perlman, *Theory of the Labor Movement*, p. 177; Gillette, "Election of 1872," pp. 1308, 1312–1315.
35. Cady, *Road to Realism*, p. 179; Gillette, "Election of 1872," p. 1317.
36. Gillette, "Election of 1872," p. 1329.
37. Trefousse, *Carl Schurz*, p. 226; Kelley, *Transatlantic Persuasion*, p. 6; *NYT*, July 3, 1876; Sproat, *"The Best Men,"* p. 101.
38. Sumner, *Forgotten Man*, pp. 468–469, 491, 493.
39. Fleming, "Social Darwinism," p. 129; Wiebe, *Search for Order*, p. 139.
40. Matthew Arnold, "Dover Beach," in W. H. Auden and Norman Holmes Pearson, eds., *Poets of the English Language* (New York: The Viking Press, 1950), v. 5, p. 210.
41. Rosenman, *Public Papers . . . Franklin D. Roosevelt*, v. 1, p. 625; Freidel, *Franklin D. Roosevelt*, p. 268.
42. Aronowitz, *False Promises*, p. 300.
43. Moley, "Forgotten Majority," p. 23; Scammon and Wattenberg, *Real Majority*, p. 21; *NYT*, March 26, 1987, and July 19, 1988.
44. A Times Mirror Study of the American Electorate Conducted by the Gallup Organization, September 1987, *The People Press & Politics*, p. 17, and 1988 supplement, "Meet the God and Country Democrats."
45. Sumner, *Forgotten Man*, p. 323.

Chapter 4. IN THE LAND OF THE GOLDEN BEAR

1. Page Smith, *Trial by Fire*, p. 943; Starr, *Inventing the Dream*, p. 41.

2. Frederick Jackson Turner, "Significance of the Frontier in American History," p. 17.

3. Smalley, *Domestic Manners*, pp. 52, 58.

4. Gunther, *Inside U.S.A.*, pp. 43, 51; Thompson, *At the Edge of History*, pp. 4–5, 14–15; Wills, *Nixon Agonistes*, p. 77; Peirce, *Pacific States of America*, p. 24.

5. Starr, *Inventing the Dream*, pp. 76–91; Pomeroy, *Pacific Slope*, p. 168.

6. Bestor, *Backwards Utopias*, p. 1; Pomeroy, *Pacific Slope*, p. 44.

7. Kevin Starr lists the following examples: Riverside, Long Beach, Westminster, San Fernando, Alhambra, San Bernardino, Anaheim, Pomona, Ontario, Lompoc, and Pasadena. *Inventing the Dream*, p. 46.

8. For a recent view of this as a continuing process, see Wills, *Nixon Agonistes*, p. 75.

9. Cf. Muller, "Josiah Strong and American Nationalism."

10. Arthur M. Schlesinger, Jr., *Paths to the Present*, p. 75; Strong, *Our Country*, p. 42.

11. Bryce, *American Commonwealth*, v. 2, p. 482; Altschuler, *Race, Ethnicity, and Class*, p. 87.

12. Handlin, *Race and Nationality*, p. 85.

13. Bryce, *American Commonwealth*, v. 2, p. 482.

14. Gutman, "Work, Culture, and Society," p. 561; Holt, "Trade Unionism," p. 22.

15. Bryce, *American Commonwealth*, v. 2, pp. 482, 484.

16. Kornitzer, *Real Nixon*, p. 25.

17. Nixon, *RN*, pp. 11–13; Hoyt, *The Nixons*, pp. 111, 181–183; Schulte, *Young Nixon*, p. 12; CSU-F interviews by Mitch Haddad with Charlotte Otis Craig, April 28, 1970, OH-839, and Sheldon Beeson, April 23, 1970, OH-809.

18. Schulte, *Young Nixon*, p. 60; Washington Post, *Fall of a President*, p. xix.

19. James D. Hughes to Arthur W. Brothers, May 21, 1958, Nixon Pre-Presidential Files, Series 390, Box 2, NARA-LA.

20. Washington Post, *Fall of a President*, pp. xix–xx.

21. Schulte, *Young Nixon*, pp. 149--150; interview with John Ehrlichman, June 17, 1985.

22. Interview with Benjamin Stein, July 10, 1985; Nixon, *RN*, pp. 14, 19.

23. Hoyt, *The Nixons*, pp. 295–296; Schulte, *Young Nixon*, p. 164; Costello, *Facts About Nixon*, p. 179.

24. Interview with Richard M. Nixon, June 4, 1984; Safire, *Before the Fall*, p. 135; Buchanan, *Right from the Beginning*, p. 321.

25. Newspaper clipping, dated August 22, 1956, Whiteman File, Administrative Series, Box 28, DDEL.

26. Interview with Pat Brown, January 22, 1985.

27. Interviews with Herbert Kalmbach, July 1, 1985; Kevin Phillips, May 22, 1985; and Norman Podhoretz, October 23, 1984; Buckley, *Inveighing We Will Go*, p. 260; Buckley, *Up from Liberalism*, p. 102.

28. Interview with William F. Buckley, Jr., October 18, 1984.

29. Ibid.

30. Interview with William Rusher, October 2, 1984.

31. Interview with Roy Wilkins, August 11, 1970.

32. Statement by Ralph de Toledano, December 3, 1959, Nixon Pre-Presidential Papers, General Correspondence Series 320, Box 213, NARA-LA; *National Geographic*, December 1959, reprinted in Nixon, *Challenges We Face*, p. 215; interview with William Rusher, October 2, 1984.

33. Interview with Julie Nixon Eisenhower and David Eisenhower, January 21, 1986.

34. Interviews with Robert Finch, January 22, 1985, Herbert Klein, January 24, 1985, and H. R. Haldeman, January 25, 1985.

35. Interview with Richard M. Nixon, June 4, 1984; Mazo, *Richard Nixon*, p. 26.

36. Nixon, *RN*, pp. 16–17, 25, 35; Dean Triggs, interviewed by Steven Guttman, June 29, 1970, OH-971, CSU-F.

37. Kornitzer, *Real Nixon*, p. 102;

Jackson, "Young Nixon," p. 60; Osmyn Stout, interviewed by Terri Burton, February 5, 1972, OH-998, CSU-F.

38. Interview with Ola Florence Welch Jobe, August 28, 1986. CSU-F interviews: Hubert Perry, interviewed by Robert Davis, n.d., OH-929; Bruce Burchell, interviewed by Mitch Haddad, February 4, 1970, OH-824; Setsuko Tani, interviewed by Gregory Brolin, January 1, 1971, OH-964; Edwin Wunder, interviewed by Gregory Brolin, May 6, 1970, OH-990. Abrahamsen, *Nixon vs. Nixon*, pp. 84–87, 89, 90; Brodie, *Richard Nixon*, pp. 57, 122.

39. Mazo, *Richard Nixon*, p. 26; interview with Julie Nixon Eisenhower, January 21, 1986; Nixon, *RN*, p. 18.

40. *NYT*, February 13, 1986.

41. *NYT*, February 13, 1986.

42. Interview with William F. Buckley, Jr., October 18, 1984.

43. Interview with Julie Nixon Eisenhower, January 21, 1986.

44. Nixon, *RN*, pp. 14, 18–19.

45. Ibid., p. 19; Jewel Triggs, interviewed by Steven Guttman, June 13 and 29, 1970, OH-971, CSU-F.

46. CSU-F interviews: Ed Sowers, interviewed by Richard Gibbs, June 5, 1970, OH-954; Herman Fink, interviewed by John Donnelly, June 29, 1970, OH-854; and Emmett Ingrum, interviewed by Mitch Haddad, May 28, 1970, OH-883.

47. Gerald Shaw, interviewed by Jeff Jones, June 3, 1970, OH-946, CSU-F; Schulte, *Young Nixon*, p. 100.

48. Keogh, *This Is Nixon*, p. 27. CSU-F interviews: Hubert Perry, interviewed by Robert Davis, n.d., OH-929; Joseph E. Guadio, interviewed by Gregory Brolin, April 22, 1970, OH-860; G. Hoyt Corbit, interviewed by Milan Pavolovich, May 15, 1970, OH-838.

49. Schulte, *Young Nixon*, p. 211.

50. Ibid., pp. 34–35, 217; Hubert Perry, interviewed by Robert Davis, n.d. and 1977, OH-929, CSU-F; Kornitzer, *Real Nixon*, p. 56.

51. Schulte, *Young Nixon*, pp. 78, 187; Kornitzer, *Real Nixon*, p. 45; Mazo, *Richard Nixon*, p. 25.

52. Mazo, *Richard Nixon*, p. 26.

53. Nixon to Dean Claude Horack, April 23, 1942, Nixon Papers, Duke University Archives; Viorst, "Nixon of the O.P.A.," p. 72; Kornitzer, *Real Nixon*, p. 143.

54. Mazlish, *In Search of Nixon*, pp. 59–60; interview with Richard M. Nixon, June 4, 1984; Patrick J. Buchanan to Nixon, March 24, 1970, in Hoff-Wilson, *Papers*.

55. Karl, *Uneasy State*, p. 220.

56. Mazo, *Richard Nixon*, p. 14.

57. Schulte, *Young Nixon*, p. 187.

58. Mazo, *Richard Nixon*, pp. 15, 21; Jackson, "Young Nixon," p. 54B.

59. Osmyn Stout, interviewed by Terri Burton, February 5, 1972, OH-998, CSU-F.

60. Keogh, *This Is Nixon*, p. 27.

61. Kornitzer, *Real Nixon*, p. 106.

62. Hoyt, *The Nixons*, p. 210.

63. Brodie, *Richard Nixon*, p. 108; Nixon, *RN*, pp. 19–20.

64. Merton G. Wray, interviewed by Steve Prantalos, January 18, 1970, OH-987, CSU-F.

65. Hoyt, *The Nixons*, p. 192.

66. Keogh, *This Is Nixon*, p. 27.

67. George Jenkins, interviewed by Mitch Haddad, March 4, 1971, OH-886, CSU-F.

68. George Chisler, interviewed by Richard Gibbs, June 8, 1970, OH-833, CSU-F; Hoyt, *The Nixons*, pp. 198–199. CSU-F interviews: George Jenkins, interviewed by Mitch Haddad, March 4, 1971, OH-886; Rev. Charles Ball, interviewed by Mitch Haddad, December 22, 1969, OH-803; Oscar Marshburn, interviewed by John Donnelly, January 22, 1970, OH-902; Schulte, *Young Nixon*, p. 165.

69. Rev. Charles Ball, interviewed by Mitch Haddad, December 22, 1969, OH-803, CSU-F; Schulte, *Young Nixon*, p. 165.

70. CSU-F interviews: Louis T. Jones, interviewed by Glenn Barnett, December 11, 1969, OH-889; George Jenkins, interviewed by Mitch Haddad, March 4, 1971, OH-886.

71. Dr. Sheldon G. Jackson, interviewed by Mitch Haddad, April 9, 1970, OH-885, CSU-F.

72. Judge Gerald Kepple, interviewed by Greg Brolin, January 7, 1971,

OH-992, CSU-F; Trueblood, *People Called Quakers,* pp. 119, 122–123.

73. CSU-F interviews: C. Richard Harris, interviewed by Glenn Barnett, March 5, 1970, OH-874; Edwin Wunder, interviewed by Gregory Brolin, May 6, 1970, OH-990; Alsop, *Nixon and Rockefeller,* p. 227; Mazo, *Richard Nixon,* p. 37; Kornitzer, *Real Nixon,* pp. 147–149; Jackson, "Young Nixon," p. 66; Nixon, *RN,* p. 29.

74. Kornitzer, *Real Nixon,* p. 52; Jackson, "Young Nixon," p. 57.

75. Abrahamsen, *Nixon vs. Nixon,* p. 92; Brodie, *Richard Nixon,* pp. 106–108; Alsop, "Nixon on Nixon," p. 59.

76. Brodie, *Richard Nixon,* p. 108; Kenneth Ball, interviewed by John Donnelly, January 16, 1970, OH-804, CSU-F.

77. CSU-F interviews: Floyd Wildermuth, interviewed by Glenn Barnett, May 6, 1970, OH-983; Olive Marshburn, interviewed by John Donnelly, January 22, 1970, OH-902; Hubert Perry, interviewed by Robert Davis, n.d., OH-929; Osmyn Stout, interviewed by Terri Burton, February 5, 1972, OH-998.

78. de Toledano, *One Man Alone,* p. 24.

79. CSU-F interviews: Joseph E. Gaudio, interviewed by Gregory Brolin, April 22, 1970, OH-860; Newt Robinson, interviewed by John Donnelly, June 18, 1970, OH-939; Herman Fink, interviewed by John Donnelly, June 29, 1970, OH-854.

80. Alsop, "Nixon on Nixon," p. 58. Interviewed somewhat closer to the 1960 Republican convention, Nixon denied that he "instigated a social revolution by helping to organize the society." Kornitzer, *Real Nixon,* p. 101.

81. Merton G. Wray, interviewed by Steve Prantalos, January 18, 1970, OH-987, CSU-F.

82. CSU-F interviews: Dean Triggs, interviewed by Steven Guttman, June 13 and 29, 1970, OH-971; Herman Fink, interviewed by John Donnelly, June 29, 1970, OH-854.

83. Bruce Burchell, interviewed by Mitch Haddad, February 4, 1970, OH-824, CSU-F; Alsop, "Nixon On Nixon," p. 59.

84. Ambrose, *Nixon,* p. 60.

85. Interview with Ola Florence Welch

Jobe, August 28, 1986; Brodie, *Richard Nixon,* p. 108.

86. Alsop, *Nixon and Rockefeller,* p. 172.

87. Hubert Perry, interviewed by Robert Davis, n.d., OH-929, CSU-F.

88. C. Richard Harris, interviewed by Glenn Barnett, March 5, 1970, OH-874, CSU-F.

89. Osmyn Stout, interviewed by Terri Burton, February 5, 1972, OH-998, CSU-F. Nixon apparently made this point to many people, including in an interview with Stewart Alsop.

90. CSU-F interviews: C. Richard Harris, interviewed by Glenn Barnett, March 5, 1970, OH-874; Osmyn Stout, interviewed by Terri Burton, February 5, 1972, OH-998, CSU-F.

91. L. Wallace Black, interviewed by Steven Guttman, July 6, 1970, OH-812, CSU-F.

92. Nash, *Conservative Intellectual Movement,* pp. 5–13; Cf. Hayek, *Road to Serfdom,* and von Mises, *Omnipotent Government.*

93. Hamby, *Liberalism and Its Challengers,* p. 61.

94. Jackson, "Young Nixon," p. 61; Alsop, *Nixon and Rockefeller,* pp. 232, 236, 238.

95. Clarence E. Whitefield, "Not Many at Duke Knew Richard Nixon Well, but his Record in Law School is Enviable," mimeograph copy in Nixon Papers, Duke University Archives; Paul Fogleman, "Dick Nixon Remembered at Duke as Sober, Competitive Student," released by the Office of Information Services, Duke University, August 11, 1968, Nixon Papers, Duke University Archives.

96. Brodie, *Richard Nixon,* p. 128; Jewell Triggs, interviewed by Steven Guttman, June 13 and 29, 1970, OH-971, CSU-F.

97. Brodie, *Richard Nixon,* p. 124; interview with Ola Florence Welch Jobe, August 28, 1986.

98. Alsop, *Nixon and Rockefeller,* pp. 232, 237–238.

99. Jackson, "Young Nixon," p. 61. He was also admitted into the Order of the Coif, the national scholastic fraternity for honor law students.

100. Richard Gardner, "Fighting Quaker," p. 83, unpublished typescript in the Duke University

Archives; Hoyt, *The Nixons,* pp. 215–216.

101. Hoyt, *The Nixons,* p. 210.
102. Jackson, "Young Nixon," p. 61.
103. Nixon to Dean Horack, May 31, 1938, Nixon Papers, Duke University Archives.
104. Jackson, "Young Nixon," pp. 61–62.
105. Dean Horack to J. Edgar Hoover, October 6, 1937. Nixon Papers, Duke University Archives; Brodie, *Richard Nixon,* p. 132.
106. Dean Horack to Nixon, August 10, 1937, and Nixon to Horack, October 6, 1937, Nixon Papers, Duke University Archives.
107. Nixon to Dean Horack, November 3, 1937, Nixon Papers, Duke University Archives.
108. Costello, *Facts About Nixon,* p. 40.
109. Nixon to Dean Horack, October 6, 1937, Nixon Non-Deeded Papers, Series 2, Box 1, NARA-LA; Nixon to Horack, September 4, 1943, Nixon Papers, Duke University Archives.
110. Richard Gardner, "Fighting Quaker," p. 83, unpublished manuscript, Nixon Papers, Duke University Archives.
111. On December 8, 1972, in the presence of John Ehrlichman and a Texan about to be nominated for a federal judgeship [Sneed], Richard Nixon's comments turned to reflections of his old days at Duke. The Nixon who was then president of the United States thereupon made two points about the law school that seem to have been designed for his immediate audience. Duke, he said, had "many left-wing deans." The institution was also "elite," he added, which was an odd observation about a law school that was still trying to establish itself in the 1930s. Had Horack heard those remarks on a White House tape, they would have sounded as incongruous as the celebrated profanities. John Ehrlichman, memorandum, December 8, 1972, Ehrlichman Papers, Fenn Gallery, Santa Fe, New Mexico.
112. Jackson, "Young Nixon," p. 64.

113. Mazo, *Richard Nixon,* p. 41.
114. Julie Nixon Eisenhower, *Pat Nixon,* p. 19. CSU-F interviews: Marietta Malcolmson Baron, interviewed by Nancy Hunsaker, June 5, 1970, OH-805; C. Robert McCormick, interviewed by Mary Suzanne Simon, May 23, 1970, OH-908.
115. Jackson, "Young Nixon," p. 57; Lester David, *Lonely Lady of San Clemente,* p. 50; Brodie, *Richard Nixon,* p. 124.
116. Joyce F. Ernstberger, interviewed by Mary Suzanne Simon, April 17, 1970, OH-849, CSU-F.
117. CSU-F interviews: Morton Morehouse, interviewed by Nancy Hunsaker, May 28, 1970, OH-914; Marian Wilson Hodge, interviewed by Mary Suzanne Simon, May 15, 1970, OH-877. Julie Nixon Eisenhower, *Pat Nixon,* p. 23.
118. Marian Wilson Hodge, interviewed by Mary Suzanne Simon, May 15, 1970, OH-877, CSU-F.
119. CSU-F interviews: Marietta Malcolmson Baron, interviewed by Nancy Hunsaker, June 5, 1970, OH-805; Mable O. Myers, interviewed by Mitch Haddad, May 12, 1971, OH-910; Sheldon Beeson, interviewed by Mitch Haddad, April 23, 1970, OH-809.
120. CSU-F interviews: Dorothy Beeson, interviewed by Mitch Haddad, November 21, 1970, OH-810; Marian Wilson Hodge, interviewed by Mary Suzanne Simon, May 15, 1970, OH-877.
121. Paul Smith in Schulte, *Young Nixon,* p. 172.
122. CSU-F interviews: L. Wallace Black, interviewed by Steven Guttman, July 6, 1970, OH-812; Grant M. Garman, interviewed by Mary Suzanne Simon, June 1, 1970, OH-859.
123. Julie Nixon Eisenhower, *Pat Nixon,* p. 55; Judith Wingert Loubert, interviewed by Harry P. Jeffrey, June 1, 1970, OH-900, CSU-F.
124. Nixon, *RN,* p. 557; Abrahamsen, *Nixon vs. Nixon,* p. 115; Mazlish, *Nixon,* p. 69.

Chapter 5. A New Day for the Twelfth

1. Costello, *Facts About Nixon,* p. 39; Bowers and Blair, "How to Pick a Congressman," p. 132; Bullock, " 'Rabbits and Radicals,' " p. 322.

2. Harry A. Schuyler, interviewed by Terri Burton, January 31, 1972, OH-997, CSU-F.

3. Professionals, in the more precise meaning of that word, were more prominent in the campaign after Nixon won the primary. Frank Jorgensen to Rose Mary Woods, January 12, 1972, Nixon Non-Deeded Papers, Series 1, Box 1, NARA-LA.

4. Bowers and Blair, "How to Pick a Congressman," p. 31. Day later became the owner of the Day Printing Corporation of Pomona.

5. Bullock, " 'Rabbits and Radicals,' " p. 322; Day to Herman Perry, October 12, 1945, Nixon Non-Deeded Papers, Series 2, Box 1, NARA-LA; Frank E. Jorgensen, interviewed by Amelia R. Fry, April 1 and April 22, 1975, Bancroft Library.

6. Interview with Julie Nixon Eisenhower, January 21, 1986; interview with Patrick J. Hillings, July 10, 1985.

7. Gerald Kepple, interviewed by Greg Brolin, January 7, 1971, OH-992, CSU-F; Frank E. Jorgensen, interviewed by Amelia R. Fry, April 1 and 22, 1975, Bancroft Library; List of Members, Fact Finding Committee (1945), Nixon Non-Deeded Papers, Series 2, Box 1, NARA-LA; Costello, *Facts About Nixon*, p. 38; Mazo, *Richard Nixon*, p. 43.

8. Costello, *Facts About Nixon*, p. 39; Frank E. Jorgensen, interviewed by Amelia R. Fry, April 1 and April 22, 1975, Bancroft Library; L. Wallace Black, interviewed by Steven Guttman, July 6, 1970, OH-812, CSU-F.

9. Perry to G. Revelle Harrison, April 20, 1945, Nixon Non-Deeded Papers, Series 2, Box 1, NARA-LA.

10. Roy P. McLaughlin to Herman Perry, April 22, 1945, Nixon Non-Deeded Papers, Series 2, Box 1, NARA-LA.

11. Safire, *Before the Fall*, p. 183; Brodie, *Richard Nixon*, p. 271.

12. Day to Perry, October 12, 1945, Nixon Non-Deeded Papers, Series 2, Box 1, NARA-LA.

13. de Toledano, *Nixon*, pp. 39–40; Lance D. Smith to Herman Perry,

October 1, 1945, Nixon Non-Deeded Papers, Series 2, Box 1, NARA-LA; Robert L. King to Margaret J. Wiggs, February 1, 1957, Nixon Papers, Box 206, and Rose Mary Woods to Paul Harvey, March 7, 1960, Nixon Papers, Box 324, NARA-LA.

14. Bowers and Blair, "How to Pick a Congressman," p. 132; Bullock, " 'Rabbits and Radicals,' " p. 338; interview with Richard M. Nixon, June 4, 1984; Mazo, *Richard Nixon*, p. 44; Frank E. Jorgensen, interviewed by Amelia R. Fry, April 1 and April 22, 1975, Bancroft Library; Perry to Nixon, September 29, 1945, Nixon Non-Deeded Papers, Series 2, Box 1, NARA-LA.

15. Nixon to Perry, October 6, 1945, Nixon Non-Deeded Papers, Series 2, Box 1, NARA-LA.

16. Ibid.; Harry A. Schuyler, interviewed by Terri Burton, January 31, 1972, OH-997, CSU-F.

17. Nixon to Perry, October 6, 1945, Nixon Non-Deeded Papers, Series 2, Box 1, NARA-LA.

18. Gerald Kepple, interviewed by Gregory Brolin, January 7, 1971, OH-992, CSU-F; Frank E. Jorgensen, interviewed by Amelia R. Fry, April 1 and April 22, 1975, Bancroft Library.

19. Telegram from Herman Perry to Nixon, October 25, 1945, Nixon Non-Deeded Papers, Series 2, Box 1, NARA-LA; Kornitzer, *Real Nixon*, pp. 154–155; interview with Richard M. Nixon, June 4, 1986; Nixon, *RN*, p. 35; de Toledano, *Nixon*, p. 41.

20. Nixon to Perry, November 15, 1946, Nixon Non-Deeded Papers, Series 2, Box 1, NARA-LA.

21. Nixon, *RN*, p. 35; *LAT*, November 29, 1945; Perry to Nixon, November 30, 1945, Nixon Non-Deeded Papers, Series 2, Box 1, NARA-LA.

22. Nixon to Perry, December 17, 1945, Nixon Non-Deeded Papers, Series 2, Box 1, NARA-LA; *LAT*, February 6, 1946.

23. Nixon handwritten notes, Lincoln Day Speech, 1946, Nixon Non-Deeded Papers, Series 2, Box 1, NARA-LA.

24. Brochure used during Nixon's primary campaign, Nixon Papers, Duke University Archives.

25. Mazo, *Richard Nixon,* p. 45; de Toledano, *Nixon,* p. 42.
26. Gunther, *Inside U.S.A.,* p. 2.
27. Mazlish, *In Search of Nixon,* p. 42.
28. Sinclair, *The Brass Check,* p. 202; Adamic, *Dynamite,* p. 204.
29. Mowry, *California Progressives,* p. 48; Starr, *Inventing the Dream,* p. 74.
30. Starr, *Inventing the Dream,* pp. 208, 210–211; Pomeroy, *Pacific Slope,* p. 176.
31. Dubofsky, *Industrialism and the American Worker,* p. 107.
32. Preston, *Aliens and Dissenters,* pp. 227–229.
33. Adamic, *Dynamite,* pp. 200–201.
34. Mowry, *California Progressives,* pp. 9, 11; Starr, *Inventing the Dream,* pp. 199–201, 253–254; Bryce, *American Commonwealth,* v. 2, pp. 428, 442; Peirce, *Pacific States of America,* p. 27; Gunther, *Inside U.S.A.,* p. 13.
35. Pomeroy, *Pacific Slope,* p. 213.
36. Kornitzer, *Real Nixon,* p. 159; *LAT,* August 10, 1946.
37. Berges, *Life and Times of Los Angeles,* p. 74; Halberstam, *Powers That Be,* pp. 256–259.
38. *LAT,* September 22 and October 6, 1946.
39. Indeed, his columns were very long but, seemingly, could not find room even to mention Nixon's name. Cf. *LAT,* October 6 and 27, 1946.
40. Schneider, "Richard Nixon in 1946," unpublished article; *LAT,* March 25, 27, June 30, August 18, 23, October 12, 18, 27, 1946.
41. Costello, *Facts About Nixon,* p. 50; Nixon to Perry, August 16, 1946, Nixon Non-Deeded Papers, Series 2, Box 1, NARA-LA; de Toledano, *Nixon,* p. 42.
42. Costello, *Facts About Nixon,* p. 44.
43. Merton G. Wray, interviewed by Steve Prantalos, January 18, 1970, OH-987, CSU-F.
44. Roy Day, interviewed by Amelia R. Fry, February 21, 1975, Bancroft Library.
45. Goulden, *Best Years,* p. 47.
46. Bullock, " 'Rabbits and Radicals,' " p. 320; Nixon to Herman Perry, December 17, 1945, Nixon Pre-Presidential Papers, Non-Deeded Papers, Series 2, 1946 Campaign. NARA-LA.
47. Voorhis, *Confessions of a Congressman,* pp. 13–14; Bullock, " 'Rabbits and Radicals,' " p. 320; interview with Richard M. Nixon, June 4, 1984.
48. Mankiewicz, *Perfectly Clear,* p. 38; Bullock, " 'Rabbits and Radicals,' " pp. 320, 327.
49. Minutes of Meeting, UDA Conference, January 4, 1947, ADA Papers, Series 2, Box 71, Historical Society of Wisconsin; interview with Richard M. Nixon, June 4, 1984.
50. Roy P. McLaughlin to unknown, October 21, 1945, Nixon Non-Deeded Papers, Series 2, Box 1, NARA-LA; Bullock, " 'Rabbits and Radicals,' " p. 319; Nixon to Herman Perry, November 26, 1945, Nixon Non-Deeded Papers, Series 2, Box 1, NARA-LA.
51. Nixon to Herman Perry, December 2 and 17, 1945, Nixon Non-Deeded Papers, Series 2, Box 1, NARA-LA.
52. Interview with Herbert G. Klein, San Diego, California, January 24, 1985.
53. Costello, *Facts About Nixon,* p. 44; Halberstam, *Powers That Be,* p. 256.
54. Halberstam, *Powers That Be,* p. 257.
55. Alsop, *Nixon and Rockefeller,* p. 145.
56. Goldman, *Crucial Decade,* p. 25; Taft, *Organized Labor in American History,* pp. 567, 589.
57. Gallup, *Gallup Poll,* v. 1, p. 601.
58. Ibid., v. 1, pp. 285, 587.
59. Boylan, "Reconversion in Politics," unpublished Ph.D. dissertation. Brodie, *Richard Nixon,* p. 175; Costello, *The Facts About Nixon,* p. 54; Navasky, *Naming Names,* p. 24; *America,* November 2, 1946, p. 117.
60. Transcript of South Pasadena speech, September 13, 1946, Nixon Non-Deeded Papers, Series 2, Box 1, NARA-LA.
61. Blum, *Price of Vision,* pp. 664–666.
62. Markowitz, *Rise and Fall of the People's Century,* p. 181; Blum, *Price of Vision,* p. 665; Gilbert A. Harrison to Henry A. Wallace, September 13, 1946, and Josephus Daniels to Wallace, September 13, 1946, Henry A. Wallace Papers, Box 42; *New York Daily News,* September 13, 1946.
63. Hamby, *Beyond the New Deal,* p. 131.
64. *LAT,* October 24, 1946; Bullock, " 'Rabbits and Radicals,' " p. 359n.
65. Keogh, *This Is Nixon,* pp. 36–37.
66. Ibid., p. 80; L. Wallace Black, interviewed by Steven Guttman, July 6, 1970, OH-812, CSU-F.

67. *LAT*, October 12 and 17, 1946; Mazo, *Richard Nixon*, p. 48; Keogh, *This Is Nixon*, p. 34.
68. Keogh, *This Is Nixon*, pp. 92, 102.
69. Nixon, *RN*, p. 41; Parmet, *Democrats*, p. 62.
70. Bullock, " 'Rabbits and Radicals,' " pp. 328, 337.
71. Ibid., p. 328.
72. Ibid., pp. 329, 330.
73. Ibid., pp. 329, 331; Costello, *Facts About Nixon*, p. 53.
74. Bullock, " 'Rabbits and Radicals,' " pp. 331–332.
75. Voorhis, *Confessions of a Congressman*, p. 338.
76. Bullock, " 'Rabbits and Radicals,' " pp. 335–338; Gerald Kepple, interviewed by Greg Brolin, January 7, 1971, OH-992, CSU-F.
77. Bullock, " 'Rabbits and Radicals,' " p. 337.
78. Consolidation of Smear Charges and Refutations, Nixon Papers, Series 320, Box 701, Vice-President General Correspondence, NARA-LA; *LAT*, October 12, 1946; Voorhis, *Confessions of a Congressman*, p. 338.
79. *LAT*, May 20, 1946; Bullock, " 'Rabbits and Radicals,' " p. 341; Roy Day, interviewed by Amelia R. Fry, February 21, 1975, Bancroft Library.
80. Caute, *Great Fear*, p. 27; Bullock, " 'Rabbits and Radicals,' " p. 349.
81. *LAT*, November 7, 1946.
82. Reinhard, *Republican Right Since 1945*, p. 16; *LAT*, September 27, 1946.
83. Boykin to Walter George and Harry Byrd, November 11, 1946, Byrd Papers, Box 185, University of Virginia.
84. Laski, "American Political Scene," p. 583; Fuller, "Democrats After the Deluge," p. 715; Cochran, *Labor and Communism*, p. 260; Freeland, *Truman Doctrine*, p. 123; McCoy, *Presidency of Harry S. Truman*, p. 84.

Chapter 6. THE GAME OF GRUB

1. CSU-F interviews: C. Richard Harris, interviewed by Glenn Barnett, March 5, 1970, OH-874; Judith Wingert Loubert, interviewed by Harry P. Jeffrey, June 1, 1970, OH-900; Schulte, *Young Nixon*, pp. 149, 165.
2. Keogh, *This Is Nixon*, p. 80.
3. de Toledano, *Nixon*, p. 62; Costello, *Facts About Nixon*, p. 28. For Nixon as a reactionary, see Caute, *Great Fear*, p. 91, and especially the two-part series by Ernest Brashear called "Who Is Richard Nixon?" which appeared in the *New Republic* on September 1 and 8, 1952.
4. de Toledano, *Nixon*, p. 62.
5. Keogh, *This Is Nixon*, p. 79.
6. Lester David, *Lonely Lady of San Clemente*, p. 71; interview with Clare Boothe Luce, April 30, 1985.
7. Stephen Hess has made the point that Nixon's preoccupation with Kennedy should not be minimized. Interview with Hess, November 29, 1984.
8. *LAT*, November 6, 1946; Wright, "Nixon," p. B-2.
9. Parmet, *Jack*, pp. 164–170.
10. Ibid., p. 143.
11. Interview with Patrick J. Hillings, July 10, 1985.
12. Interview with William F. Price, July 11, 1985.
13. Schoenebaum, *Profiles of an Era*, p. 261.
14. Personal Resume, attached to Haldeman to Ray Arbuthnot, August 2, 1956, Nixon Pre-Presidential Papers, Series 320, Box 311, NARA-LA.
15. Rather and Gates, *Palace Guard*, pp. 217ff.; Evans and Novak, *Nixon in the White House*, p. 45.
16. *LAT*, November 28, 1960.
17. Cf. Lukacs, *Outgrowing Democracy*, p. 281; interview with H. R. Haldeman, January 25, 1985.
18. *Boston Herald*, March 3, 1950.
19. Mazo, *Nixon*, pp. 102–103; Costello, *Facts About Nixon*, p. 221; interviews with Frank E. Jorgensen, April 22, 1975, and Roy Crocker, February 20, 1975, by Amelia R. Fry, Bancroft Library; Brashear, "Who Is Richard Nixon?" p. 9.
20. Interview with John D. Ehrlichman, June 17, 1985.
21. Domhoff, *Bohemian Grove*, p. 53.
22. Reinhardt, "The Bohemian Club," v. 31, p. 82.
23. Domhoff, *Bohemian Grove*, pp. 11, 21; Reinhardt, "Bohemian Club," v. 31, p. 90.

24. Domhoff, *Bohemian Grove,* p. 57; Nixon, *RN,* p. 284.
25. Leonard Hall to Nixon, August 8, 1961, Nixon Papers, Box 313, NARA-LA.
26. Nixon to Albert C. Mattei, January 11, 1950, Nixon Non-Deeded Papers, Series 206, Box 5, NARA-LA; Nixon, *Leaders,* p. 128. Other than Nixon, those listed as present at that Cave Man encampment include the following: Members— Dr. L. R. Chandler; Fred G. Clark; Peter Grimm; Herbert Hoover, Sr.; Herbert Hoover, Jr.; Allan Hoover; Dr. George S. Johnson; Clarence Budington Kelland; Jeremiah Milbank; A. W. Peake; Edgar Rickard; Lowell Thomas; Dr. J. E. Wallace Sterling. Guests — Julius Ochs Adler, Joseph Binns, Guy George Gabrielson; H. V. Kaltenborn; James Kerney, Jr.; Raymond Moley; Robert C. Swain; Lt. Gen. Albert C. Wedemeyer; Richard Wilson. Eisenhower's name does not appear on the official list. Nixon Pre-Presidential Papers, Appearances File, Box 1, NARA-LA.
27. Interview with Richard M. Nixon, June 4, 1984. A comparison of names of those present at Bohemian Grove encampments in 1950 and 1962 shows that exactly the same number, seven out of twenty-three, came from California.
28. Interview with John D. Ehrlichman, June 17, 1985.
29. Minutes of UDA Conference, January 4, 1947. ADA Papers, Series 2, Box 71, Historical Society of Wisconsin.
30. Kornitzer, *Nixon,* p. 163; Martin, *My First Fifty Years in Politics,* p. 3; Julie Nixon Eisenhower, *Pat Nixon,* p. 96.
31. Nixon, *RN,* p. 44.
32. *LAT,* March 15, 1947; Hamby, *Beyond the New Deal,* p. 174; Theoharis, *Yalta Myths,* p. 58; Patterson, *Mr. Republican,* p. 335.
33. *Azusa* (California) *Herald,* January 20, 1949; Commager, *Documents of American History,* v. 2, pp. 539–540; Gallup, *Gallup Poll,* v. 1, pp. 537, 617.
34. *NYT,* January 1, 1947.
35. *NYT,* December 27, 1946.
36. *NYT,* January 4, 1947.
37. Gallup, *Gallup Poll,* v. 1, pp. 618,

621, 623; Lee, *Truman and Taft-Hartley,* pp. 11, 51; Goulden, *Best Years,* p. 123.
38. Lee, *Truman and Taft-Hartley,* pp. 35–36; Truman Longhand Notes File, n.d., 1946, President's Secretary's File, Harry S. Truman Library, Independence, Missouri; quoted in McCoy, *Truman,* p. 58.
39. Taft, *Organized Labor in American History,* p. 579; Hartmann, *Truman and the 80th Congress,* p. 29; Gallup, *Gallup Poll,* v. 1, p. 636.
40. Lee, *Truman and Taft-Hartley,* pp. 30, 50, 52.
41. Ibid., p. 55; Parmet, *Jack,* p. 175.
42. Lee, *Truman and Taft-Hartley,* pp. 61–67, 74–75.
43. McCoy, *Presidency of Harry S. Truman,* p. 99.
44. *Public Papers: Nixon, 1970,* p. 223; Costello, *Facts About Nixon,* p. 186.
45. House of Representatives, 80th Congress, 1st Session, *Hearings . . . on Un-American Activities,* v. 2, p. 482.
46. *Asusa* (California) *Herald,* January 20, 1949.
47. Keogh, *This Is Nixon,* p. 119; House of Representatives, 80th Congress, 1st Session, *Hearings . . . on Un-American Activities,* v. 2, p. 665; Nixon News Release, February 1947, Nixon Papers, NARA-LA; Reuben, *Honorable Mr. Nixon,* p. 9.
48. *Newsweek,* May 30, 1960, p. 96.
49. House of Representatives, 80th Congress, 1st Session, *Hearings . . . on Un-American Activities,* v. 2, p. 2071; Nixon to Carl Greenberg, May 11, 1959, Nixon Pre-Presidential Papers, Series 320, Box 643, NARA-LA.
50. House of Representatives, 80th Congress, 1st Session, *Hearings . . . on Un-American Activities,* v. 2, p. 665; *NYT,* February 23, 1947; Costello, *Facts About Nixon,* p. 179.
51. Interview with Blair Clark, March 18, 1977; *Boston Post,* April 15, 1947; *New York World-Telegram,* April 15, 1947; T. J. Reardon to Francis Morrissey, April 16, 1947, Pre-Presidential Papers, Box 98, John F. Kennedy Library; Parmet, *Jack,* p. 185.
52. Nixon, *RN,* p. 43; *McKeesport Daily News,* April 22, 1947.
53. McCoy, *Presidency of Harry S. Truman,* p. 99.
54. David Shannon, *Decline of American*

Communism, p. 48; *NYT*, November 10, 1952.

55. Brody, "Philip Murray," pp. 799–800; *NYT*, November 10, 1952.

56. Brody, *Workers in Industrial America*, pp. 216, 221; Radosh, *American Labor and United States Foreign Policy*, p. 357; Greenstone, *Labor in American Politics*, p. 54.

57. Brody, *Workers in Industrial America*, p. 225.

58. Gosnell, *Grass Roots Politics*, p. 4; Moscow, *Politics in the Empire State*, p. 40; Parmet and Hecht, *Never Again*, pp. 218–219; Marcus, *Father Coughlin*, p. 229; Lubell, *Future of American Politics*, pp. 212–213; Kane, *Catholic-Protestant Conflict in America*, pp. 214–215; Crosby, "The Angry Catholics," Ph.D. dissertation, pp. 7, 10–12; Gaddis, *United States and the Origins of the Cold War*, pp. 60–61, 142–143; Neal, *Dark Horse*, pp. 297–298, 302; Parmet, *Democrats*, p. 46.

59. MacDougall, *Gideon's Army*, v. 1, pp. 106–108; Taft, *Organized Labor in American History*, pp. 624–625.

60. *Boston Post*, March 14, 1947; Cochran, *Labor and Communism*, pp. 165–167; Parmet, *Jack*, pp. 181–182; Brody, *Workers in Industrial America*, pp. 223–226.

61. Brock, *Americans for Democratic Action*, p. 58; Cormier and Eaton, *Reuther*, pp. 279, 316; *America*, March 15, 1947, p. 648; David Shannon, *Decline of American Communism*, pp. 155, 217.

62. Cochran, *Labor and Communism*, p. 259.

63. Lubell, *Future of American Politics*, p. 45.

64. Gorer, *American People*, p. 26; Lerner, *America as a Civilization*, p. 89.

65. Pelling, *American Labor*, p. 221; Howe, *Socialism in America*, pp. 117–125; Lemons, *Troubled American*, p. 188; Aronowitz, *False Promises*, pp. 300–301; Brody, *Workers in Industrial America*, p. 17.

66. Perlman, *Theory of the Labor Movement*, p. 215.

67. *NYT*, November 10, 1952.

68. Aronowitz, *False Promises*, p. 332.

69. *NYT*, November 10, 1952.

70. Martin, *My First Fifty Years in Politics*, p. 194.

71. Nixon, *RN*, pp. 44–45; Nixon, *Six*

Crises, p. 13; Chambers, *Witness*, p. 536.

72. Costello, *Facts About Nixon*, pp. 182–183; Keogh, *This Is Nixon*, p. 39; Ambrose, *Nixon*, p. 143; Ambrose, *Eisenhower*, p. 55.

73. Interview with Richard M. Nixon, November 16, 1988; Cf. *Naming Names*, by Victor S. Navasky, who brackets Nixon as follows: "Men like Dies, Thomas, [Harold] Velde, Nixon, and McCarthy had in common political opportunism and a demagogic capacity to exploit nativism and know-nothing passions" (p. 311).

74. Stripling, *Red Plot Against America*, p. 57.

75. Ibid., pp. 15, 23, 36, 157–158.

76. Caute, *Great Fear*, pp. 90–92.

77. Carlson, *Under Cover*, pp. 233, 234; Gunther, *Inside U.S.A.*, p. 789; Sayre, *Running Time*, p. 17; Caute, *Great Fear*, p. 90; *NYT*, November 28, 1946. Actually, Rankin had a point. Joseph Scottoriggio, a Republican district captain and poll-watcher who had refused to overlook fraudulent voting, was beaten to death by two thugs. q.v. Warren Moscow, *Last of the Big-Time Bosses*, p. 68.

78. George Smathers interviewed by Don Wilson, July 10, 1964, JFKL-OH.

79. *Life Magazine*, November 14, 1947, quoted in Latham, *Communist Controversy in Washington*, p. 157.

80. Caute, *Great Fear*, p. 91.

81. J. Parnell Thomas to Richard Nixon, November 21, 1956, Nixon General Correspondence 320, NARA-LA.

82. Transcript, CBS "Open Hearing Forum," March 25, 1947, Nixon Non-Deeded Papers, Series 206, Box 6, NARA-LA. Historian Richard Freeland is undoubtedly on the right track when he observes that loyalty screening "reinforced the idea . . . that the global communist movement was at work and did constitute a present menace to American security." *Truman Doctrine*, p. 115.

83. Brodie, *Nixon*, p. 194; Goodman, *Committee*, p. 271.

84. This also applies to his conduct as a member of the Labor and Education Committee.

85. Carr, *House Committee on Un-American Activities,* pp. 48, 226, 229.
86. John W. Heselton to Nixon, May 19, 1948, Nixon Non-Deeded Papers, Congressional Files, Box 2, NARA-LA.
87. Carr, *House Committee on Un-American Activities,* p. 56; Goodman, *Committee,* p. 207.
88. Carr, *House Committee on Un-American Activities,* pp. 61–62, 229; Goodman, *Committee,* p. 208.
89. *NYT,* April 8, 1948.
90. Carr, *House Committee on Un-American Activities,* pp. 132, 138.
91. Carr, *House Committee on Un-American Activities,* pp. 131–132; Goodman, *Committee,* pp. 233, 238.
92. Carr, *House Committee on Un-American Activities,* pp. 141, 153; Chief investigator Stripling's book, *Red Plot Against America,* published before the complete letter became known, describes Hoover as "suggesting that Condon was a poor security risk." (p. 159); Andrews, *Washington Witch Hunt,* p. 146.
93. Goodman, *Committee,* p. 237; *NYT,* December 28, 1948.
94. Nixon news release, May 10, 1947, Nixon Non-Deeded Papers, Series 206, Box 6, NARA-LA; *LAT,* May 29, 1947; Hoyt, *The Nixons,* p. 253; Nixon to Hillings, July 20, 1949, Nixon Papers, Box 342, NARA-LA; Reeves, *Life and Times of Joe McCarthy,* p. 393; Nixon to Otis Chandler, March 16, 1961, Nixon Papers, Series 320, Box 142, NARA-LA.

Chapter 7. THE GREAT AWAKENING

1. Carr, *House Committee on Un-American Activities,* pp. 50–51.
2. Ibid., pp. 53–54.
3. Gallup, *Gallup Poll,* v. 1, pp. 639–640; Andrews, *Washington Witch Hunt,* p. 47.
4. Nixon, *RN,* p. 46; Goodman, *Committee,* p. 196.
5. House of Representatives, 80th Congress, 2d Session, *Hearings on . . . the Communist Party,* p. 493.
6. Nixon to Dulles, January 17, 1948, Nixon Papers, Non-Deeded Material, Congressional Files, Box 2, NARA-LA.
7. House of Representatives, 80th Congress, 2d Session, *Hearings on . . . the Communist Party,* p. 276.
8. Arnold, *Back When It All Began,* p. 7.
9. House of Representatives, 80th Congress, 2d Session, *Hearings on . . . the Communist Party,* pp. 252, 255, 258–259, 265, 267, 275.
10. Ibid., p. 265.
11. Ibid., p. 264.
12. Ibid., pp. 209, 214, 224, 225.
13. Ibid., pp. 225–226; Bentley, *Thirty Years of Treason,* pp. 264–265.
14. House of Representatives, 80th Congress, 2d Session, *Hearings on . . . the Communist Party,* p. 232.
15. Max M. Kampelman to Frank McCulloch, September 8, 1950, Harley Kilgore Papers, Box 2, Franklin D. Roosevelt Library; Bentley, *Thirty Years of Treason,* p. 271.
16. Burnham, *Struggle for the World,* pp. 9, 17, 161.
17. Ibid., p. 381.
18. Carr, *House Committee on Un-American Activities,* p. 81; Goodman, *Committee,* p. 227.
19. Bentley, *Thirty Years of Treason,* p. 287.
20. de Toledano, *One Man Alone,* pp. 67–68.
21. *NYT,* May 19, 1948; *Congress and the Nation,* v. 1, p. 1653.
22. *NYT,* May 7, 1948; Typescript of Remarks, Nixon Non-Deeded Papers, Series 206, Box 3, NARA-LA.
23. Goodman, *Committee,* pp. 229–230.
24. *NYT,* May 20, 1948.
25. Costello, *Facts About Nixon,* p. 189.
26. Caute, *Great Fear,* p. 39.
27. de Toledano, *Nixon,* p. 75; Jowitt, *Strange Case of Alger Hiss,* p. 147.
28. House of Representatives, 81st Congress, 2d Session, *Congressional Record,* pp. 1006–1007; Jowitt, *Strange Case of Alger Hiss,* p. 147; Koen, *China Lobby,* p. 80.
29. Henle, "This Man Nixon."
30. Stripling, *Red Plot Against America,* pp. 14, 160.
31. Nixon, *RN,* p. 47.
32. Weinstein, *Perjury,* p. 515.
33. Latham, *Communist Controversy in Washington,* pp. 149–150; David Shannon, *Decline of American Communism,* p. 190.
34. O'Neill, *Better World,* p. 279.

35. Latham, *Communist Controversy in Washington*, p. 152; Klehr, *Heyday of American Communism*, pp. 7, 11.
36. Nash, *Conservative Intellectual Movement*, p. 128.
37. Weinstein, *Perjury*, pp. 3–5; interview with Richard M. Nixon, June 4, 1984.
38. Nixon, "Lessons of the Hiss Case."
39. Nixon later noted that fact and regretted "that it was not the last" ("Lessons of the Hiss Case").
40. O'Neill, *Better World*, p. 368.
41. In addition to the present author, Father Cronin talked to Allen Weinstein, John Chabot Smith, and Garry Wills.
42. Richard Gid Powers, *Secrecy and Power*, p. 297; Wills, *Nixon Agonistes*, p. 26; *NYT*, March 24, 1947.
43. Interview with Father John Cronin, September 6, 1978; Nixon to the author, December 10, 1986; Wills, *Nixon Agonistes*, pp. 26–27; Kornitzer, *Real Nixon*, p. 172; Mazo, *Nixon*, p. 51; de Toledano, *One Man Alone*, p. 76; Ambrose, *Nixon*, pp. 137–138; interview with Richard M. Nixon, November 16, 1988; Weinstein, *Perjury*, pp. 8, 16.
44. Nixon, *Six Crises*, p. 10.
45. Ibid., p. 2; Nixon to the author, December 10, 1986; Kornitzer, *Real Nixon*, p. 175.
46. House of Representatives, 80th Congress, 2d Session, *Hearings Regarding Communist Espionage*, pp. 511–515; Weinstein, *Perjury*, p. 5; Stripling, *Red Plot Against America*, p. 96.
47. de Toledano and Lasky, *Seeds of Treason*, pp. 155–163; Weinstein, *Perjury*, pp. 19–21; Chambers, *Witness*, pp. 558–574; Hiss, *In the Court of Public Opinion*, pp. 68–69.
48. Cf. Andrews, *Washington Witch-Hunt;* interview with Richard M. Nixon, November 16, 1988; Weinstein, *Perjury*, p. 26; Berding, *Dulles on Diplomacy*, pp. 26–27; Nixon, *Six Crises*, pp. 20–21.
49. Nixon, *Six Crises*, p. 67.
50. Ibid., pp. 2, 11, 22.
51. John Ehrlichman, notes of conversation, December 24, 1969, Ehrlichman Papers, Fenn Gallery, Santa Fe, New Mexico.
52. Bendiner and Ascoli, "Case of Alger Hiss," p. 5.
53. Weinstein, *Perjury*, p. 447.
54. Cooke, *Generation on Trial*, p. 54; Weinstein, *Perjury*, p. 516; Fiedler, *End to Innocence*, p. 21; Navasky, *Naming Names*, p. 21; Brodie, *Richard Nixon*, p. 199; Chambers, *Witness*, p. 616.
55. Kempton, *Part of Our Time*, p. 17.
56. Ibid.; Brodie, *Richard Nixon*, pp. 213–214. It is noteworthy that Holmes lived long enough to have personal contacts with John Quincy Adams and Alger Hiss.
57. Kempton, *Part of Our Time*, pp. 26–27; Nixon, "Lessons of the Hiss Case."
58. Chambers, *Witness*, pp. 792n–793n.
59. Nixon, *Six Crises*, p. 16; Nixon, "Lessons of the Hiss Case."
60. Interview with Richard M. Nixon, November 16, 1988.
61. Nixon, *RN*, p. 176.
62. Nixon to the author, December 10, 1986.
63. Richard Gid Powers, *Secrecy and Power*, pp. 297–298.
64. Ibid., p. 299.
65. Interview with Richard M. Nixon, November 16, 1988.
66. Ibid.; House of Representatives, 81st Congress, 2d Session, *Congressional Record*, p. 1005.
67. Interview with Richard M. Nixon, November 16, 1988; Nixon to the author, November 17, 1988; Nixon, *Six Crises*, p. 58; Theoharis, *Beyond the Hiss Case*, p. 58.
68. Nixon, *RN*, p. 47; Nixon, *Six Crises*, pp. 61–62.
69. Nixon, *Six Crises*, pp. 65–66.
70. Gallup, *Gallup Poll*, v. 1, pp. 639, 664.
71. John Chabot Smith, *Alger Hiss*, p. 440; Nixon, *Six Crises*, pp. 69, 70; Weinstein, *Perjury*, p. xvii; John S. Burd, Jr., to Harvey Hancock, April 4, 1950, Nixon Non-Deeded Papers, Series 206, Box 5, NARA-LA.
72. Julius C. C. Edelstein to Herbert W. Beaser, September 17, 1956, Lehman Papers, School of International Relations Library, Columbia University.
73. Herbert W. Beaser to Julius C. C. Edelstein, September 19, 1956; Edelstein to Philip B. Perlman, September 22, 1956, Lehman Papers, School of International

Relations Library, Columbia
University.

74. Cooney, *Annenbergs*, pp. 279–280;
Philadelphia Inquirer, February 19,
1963.

75. Griffith, *Politics of Fear*, p. 48.

76. Donovan, "Birth of a Salesman,"
pp. 29–30; Nixon to Moley, August 12, 1949, Nixon Non-Deeded
Papers, "Congressional Files,
1950 Campaign," Box 5, NARA-
LA; Speech Transcript, Nixon
Non-Deeded Papers, Congressional Files 1950 Campaign, Box 5,
NARA-LA.

77. Chambers, *Witness*, p. 455.

78. Buckley, *Odyssey of a Friend*, pp. 59,
219.

79. Ibid., pp. 284–285.

80. Chambers to Nixon, February 2,
1961, Nixon Papers, Box 141,
NARA-LA.

81. Judis, "Two Faces of Whittaker
Chambers," pp. 25–32; Burnham,
Web of Subversion, pp. 15, 18.

82. *WPNWE*, January 5, 1987, p. 9; *New
Republic*, April 16, 1984, p. 32.

83. Buckley made the point on a Public
Broadcasting System documentary
called "The Conservatives" on
January 20, 1987; *NYT*, January 20,
1987.

Chapter 8. BREAKING THROUGH

1. Ranelagh, *Agency*, p. 116.

2. Nixon, *RN*, p. 72.

3. Father John Cronin to Nixon,
September 5, 1952, Nixon Pre-
Presidential Papers, Series 320, Box
191, NARA-LA.

4. Sanford, "Public Orientation to
Roosevelt," p. 213; Hamby, *Beyond
the New Deal*, p. 321.

5. Scott, *Come to the Party*, pp. 49–52;
interview with William F. Price, July
11, 1985.

6. Hillings to Nixon, July 2, 1949,
Nixon Non-Deeded Papers,
Congressional Files 1950 Campaign,
Box 4, NARA-LA.

7. Root, "Do We Need a Political
Realignment?," pp. 6–8.

8. Reinhard, *Republican Right*, p. 60;
NYT, August 29, 1950.

9. Costello, *Facts About Nixon*, p. 43.

10. *Alhambra Legionnaire*, June 1949.

11. Douglas to Nixon, June 4, 1949,
Nixon Non-Deeded Papers, Series
206, Box 5, NARA-LA.

12. Helen Gahagan Douglas, *Full Life*, p.
314.

13. Hamby, *Beyond the New Deal*, pp.
103, 171, 176, 207; de Toledano,
One Man Alone, p. 109; Brodie,
Richard Nixon, p. 239; Costello, *Facts
About Nixon*, p. 69.

14. Hamby, *Beyond the New Deal*, pp.
188, 359; Brodie, *Richard Nixon*, p.
238; Costello, *Facts About Nixon*, p.
73.

15. Hamby, *Beyond the New Deal*, p. 165;
Charles M. LaFollette to J. Howard
McGrath, November 1, 1949, Series
2, Box 59, ADA Papers, Historical
Society of Wisconsin; Douglas and

Arthur, *Autobiography of Melvyn
Douglas*, p. 8.

16. *Newsweek*, October 30, 1950, p. 21;
Roy Crocker, interviewed by Amelia
R. Fry, February 20, 1975, Bancroft
Library.

17. John S. Burd, Jr., to Harvey
Hancock, April 4, 1950, Nixon Non-
Deeded Papers, Series 206, Box 5,
NARA-LA; Roy Crocker,
interviewed by Amelia R. Fry,
February 20, 1975, Bancroft
Library; Mankiewicz, *Perfectly Clear*,
p. 49.

18. Keogh, *This Is Nixon*, pp. 193–194;
Roy Crocker, interviewed by Amelia
R. Fry, February 20, 1975, Bancroft
Library.

19. Nixon handwritten notes, 1950,
Nixon Non-Deeded Papers, Series
206, Box 5, NARA-LA.

20. John Walton Dinkelspiel,
interviewed by Amelia R. Fry,
January 31 and March 24, 1975,
Bancroft Library.

21. Brashear, "Who Is Richard Nixon?"
p. 12; Frank E. Jorgensen,
interviewed by Amelia R. Fry, April
1 and April 22, 1975, Bancroft
Library.

22. Brashear, "Who Is Richard Nixon?"
p. 11; Costello, *Facts About Nixon*, p.
69.

23. CSU-F interviews: Judith Wingert
Loubet, interviewed by Harry P.
Jeffrey, June 1, 1970, OH-900;
Guy N. Dixon, interviewed by
Steve Prantalos, June 12, 1970,
OH-845; Keogh, *This Is Nixon*, p.
86.

24. Mankiewicz, *Perfectly Clear*, p. 47;

Helen Gahagan Douglas, *Full Life,* p. 300; Nixon, *RN,* pp. 72, 74.

25. Frank E. Jorgensen, interviewed by Amelia R. Fry, April 1 and April 22, 1975, Bancroft Library; Kornitzer, *Real Nixon,* pp. 180, 182; *Newsweek,* June 5, 1950, p. 26; Mazo, *Richard Nixon,* p. 72; Nixon, *RN,* pp. 72–73.

26. Costello, *Facts About Nixon,* p. 64.

27. Wills, *Nixon Agonistes,* p. 46; Evans and Novak, *Nixon in the White House,* p. 71; de Toledano, *One Man Alone,* p. 104; Kornitzer, *Real Nixon,* p. 184.

28. Frank E. Jorgensen, interviewed by Amelia R. Fry, April 1 and 22, 1975, Bancroft Library.

29. Perry to Rose Mary Woods, September 3, 1953, Nixon Pre-Presidential Papers, Series 320, Vice-President's General Correspondence, Box 589, NARA-LA.

30. *Newsweek,* June 5, 1950, p. 25. Revealed only after the campaign was Boddy's $2 million indebtedness to various private oil interests. Boddy was also Downey's successor as their lobbyist. Mankiewicz, *Perfectly Clear,* p. 50; Helen Gahagan Douglas, *Full Life,* p. 298.

31. *Democratic News,* May 18, 1950, in Francis Keesling Papers, Box 27, Folder 239: California State Campaign, University of California Library, Berkeley; Mazo, *Richard Nixon,* pp. 75, 76; Helen Gahagan Douglas, *Full Life,* pp. 300, 301; *Los Angeles News,* June 5, 1950.

32. Wills, *Nixon Agonistes,* pp. 86–87.

33. Link and Catton, *American Epoch,* v. 2, p. 707; Reinhard, *Republican Right,* p. 67; Hyman, *Lives of William Benton,* p. 478.

34. DNC Papers, Newsclippings by Subject File, Box 16, John F. Kennedy Library; Lehman to Carmine DeSapio, May 2, 1950, Lehman Papers, School of International Relations Library, Columbia University.

35. Mazo, *Richard Nixon,* p. 80; Nixon Non-Deeded Papers, Congressional Files, 1950 Campaign, Box 5, NARA-LA; transcript of Douglas speech, October 4, 1950, Nixon Non-Deeded Papers, Series 206, Box 5, NARA-LA; Transcript of Douglas radio talk, October 30, 1950, Nixon Non-Deeded Papers, Series 206, Box 5, NARA-LA.

36. de Toledano, *One Man Alone,* p. 110.

37. Ronald Reagan, president of the Screen Actors Guild, supported Mrs. Douglas. Helen Gahagan Douglas, *Full Life,* p. 323.

38. Lash, *Eleanor,* p. 158; Parmet, *Democrats,* pp. 56, 97; Bundy, "Test of Yalta," p. 629; *Newsweek,* October 30, 1952, p. 21.

39. Hillings to Nixon, July 2, 1949, and August 25, 1949, Nixon Non-Deeded Material, Congressional Files 1950 Campaign, Box 4, NARA-LA.

40. Helen Gahagan Douglas, *Full Life,* ¡. 323; Costello, *Facts About Nixon,* p. 62.

41. Interview with Pat Brown, January 22, 1985; Mazo, *Richard Nixon,* p. 78.

42. Costello, *Facts About Nixon,* p. 61; Mazo, *Richard Nixon,* pp. 75, 79; Brodie, *Richard Nixon,* p. 243.

43. Costello, *Facts About Nixon,* p. 70; Brodie, *Richard Nixon,* p. 240.

44. Frank E. Jorgensen, interviewed by Amelia R. Fry, April 1 and 22, 1975, Bancroft Library; Lester David, *Lonely Lady of San Clemente,* p. 80; Brodie, *Richard Nixon,* p. 242; *ADL Bulletin,* September 1952, p. 7; Murray Chotiner to Nixon, January 24, 1956, Nixon Pre-Presidential Papers, Box 148, NARA-LA; interview with Pat Hillings, July 10, 1985; de Toledano, *One Man Alone,* p. 110.

45. de Toledano, *One Man Alone,* p. 110; interview with Pat Hillings, July 10, 1985; Sheed, *Clare Booth Luce,* p. 112.

46. Arnold Forster to ADL Regional Directors, August 19, 1952, Nixon Pre-Presidential Papers, Series 320, Box 45, NARA-LA.

47. Kahin, *Intervention,* p. 508n.

48. Elson, *World of Time Inc.,* p. 122.

49. Ibid.

50. Tuchman, *Stilwell,* p. 147; Seagrave, *Soong Dynasty,* p. 256. See especially Chapter 11, "All in the Family."

51. Seagrave, *Soong Dynasty,* p. 363.

52. Luce, *Mystery.*

53. Sheed, *Clare Boothe Luce,* p. 115; Steel, *Walter Lippmann,* p. 469; Seagrave, *Soong Dynasty,* pp. 434–435.

54. *The Reporter,* April 15, 1952, pp. 4–

24; Seagrave, *Soong Dynasty*, p. 367; Nash, *Conservative Intellectual Movement*, p. 89; Reeves, *Life and Times of Joe McCarthy*, p. 220; Keeley, *China Lobby Man*, p. 87.

55. Swanberg, *Luce*, p. 351; Steel, *Walter Lippmann*, p. 466; John Foster Dulles, "Memo of Telephone Conversation with the Vice President," October 17, 1955. Dulles Papers, Telephone Calls Series, DDEL.

56. Foster Rhea Dulles, *American Policy Toward Communist China*, p. 86.

57. Hamby, *Beyond the New Deal*, p. 433.

58. The situation was even more complex than that. The British, who had extended recognition almost right away, had some misgivings. Winston Churchill and Anthony Eden told Eisenhower at Bermuda in 1953 that it had proven to be a great mistake. Recognition had brought no gains for the British through any kind of access to the country or the people. It was not something they would do again if they had to do it over. (Interview with John W. Hanes, Jr., Dulles Oral History Collection, Princeton University.)

59. Hoopes, *Devil and John Foster Dulles*, p. 146; Swanberg, *Luce*, p. 352; telephone conversation between Dulles and Walter Judd, July 21, 1953, Dulles Papers, Telephone Calls, Box 1, DDEL; interviews with Judd and Roderic O'Connor in the Dulles Oral History Collection at Princeton; *NYT*, February 29, 1972.

60. Foster Rhea Dulles, *American Policy Toward Communist China*, p. 85; Swanberg, *Luce*, p. 351; Lerner, *America as a Civilization*, p. 771.

61. Theodore H. White, *In Search of History*, pp. 207, 211; Elson, *World of Time Inc.*, p. 146; Lerner, *America as a Civilization*, p. 771.

62. Sheed, *Clare Boothe Luce*, p. 85; Seagrave, *Soong Dynasty*, p. 312.

63. Elson, *World of Time Inc.*, p. 312.

64. *Life*, February 17, 1941; Elson, *World of Time Inc.*, pp. 223–224, 227, 312–313.

65. Kahn, *China Hands*, p. 50.

66. Keeley, *China Lobby Man*, pp. 14–19.

67. Reeves, *Life and Times of Joe McCarthy*, p. 221; Oshinsky,

Conspiracy So Immense, p. 123; *The Reporter*, April 15, 1952, p. 3.

68. Kahn, *China Hands*, p. 50; *The Reporter*, April 15, 1952, p. 14.

69. Westerfield, *Foreign Policy and Party Politics*, p. 246, n. 7, quoted in Koen, *China Lobby*, p. 153.

70. Koen, *China Lobby*, pp. 135–136; Keeley, *China Lobby Man*, pp. 81–85; Foster Rhea Dulles, *American Policy Toward Communist China*, pp. 87–88; *The Reporter*, April 15, 1952, p. 11; Reeves, *Life and Times of Joe McCarthy*, pp. 220–221, 262.

71. Koen, *China Lobby*, pp. 133–156.

72. Known as Peiping under the Kuomintang, then restored to Peking, and now called Beijing.

73. Charles Edison, et al., to Ralph Flanders, January 12, 1954, Flanders Papers, Syracuse University Library, Box 103; and to Sherman Adams, March 4, 1955, White House Central Files, Box 332, DDEL.

74. Adams to the Committee for One Million, March 11, 1955, White House Central Files, Box 332, DDEL.

75. Koen, *China Lobby*, p. 55; Costello, *Facts About Nixon*, p. 72; interview with Richard M. Nixon, November 16, 1988.

76. Reeves, *Life and Times of Joe McCarthy*, p. 387; Nixon to Editor, *Sacramento Bee*, November 1, 1950, Nixon Non-Deeded Papers, Congressional Files 1950 Campaign, Box 5, NARA-LA.

77. Kohlberg to Peter Frelinghuysen, May 5, 1958, Nixon Pre-Presidential Papers, Series 320, Box 423, NARA-LA.

78. de Toledano, *One Man Alone*, p. 108; Costello, *Facts About Nixon*, pp. 71–72; *The Reporter*, April 15, 1952, pp. 20–21.

79. Keeley, *China Lobby Man*, pp. 115, 134.

80. Theodore H. White, *In Search of History*, p. 375.

81. Swanberg, *Luce*, p. 299.

82. Ibid., pp. 298, 299, 327–329; Elson, *World of Time Inc.*, pp. 398, 461, 468.

83. Interview with Clare Boothe Luce, April 30, 1985.

84. Swanberg, *Luce*, p. 327.

85. *LAT*, January 10, 1960; Robert Gibbs, interviewed by Steven

Guttman, June 29, 1970, OH-971,
CSU-F; *NYT*, February 20, 1987.
86. Moscow, *Last of the Big-Time Bosses*,
pp. 58, 63; Klehr, *Heyday of American
Communism*, pp. 293, 294.
87. Nixon to George Creel, April 29,
1952, Nixon Pre-Presidential Papers,
Box 189, NARA-LA; anonymous
staff secretary to Ben Mandel, May
12, 1950, Nixon Non-Deeded
Papers, Series 206, Box 5, NARA-
LA; interview with Pat Hillings, July
10, 1985; Mazo, *Richard Nixon*, p.
78; telephone interview with Earl
Mazo, August 11, 1986; Nixon, *RN*,
p. 74; Costello, *Facts About Nixon*, p.
65.
88. Bernard Brennan, one of Nixon's
managers, had earlier issued a

statement that charged that they
coincided "353 times." Costello, *Facts
About Nixon*, p. 64.
89. Costello, *Facts About Nixon*, p. 66.
90. Francis Keesling Papers, Box 27,
Folder 239, University of California,
Berkeley; Roy Crocker, interviewed
by Amelia R. Fry, February 20,
1975, Bancroft Library.
91. Helen Gahagan Douglas, *Full Life*, p.
323; Brodie, *Richard Nixon*, p. 243;
Costello, *Facts About Nixon*, p. 73;
Donald F. Crosby, S.J., "Politics of
Religion," p. 37.
92. Kornitzer, *Real Nixon*, p. 182; Cort,
"Who Won the Election?" pp. 228–
229; Hamby, *Beyond the New Deal*, p.
421; Berman, *Politics of Civil Rights*,
p. 179.

Chapter 9. THE IDEAL RUNNING MATE

1. Unsigned, "Last Stand in
Mississippi," p. 36; Carter, "Two-
Party System in Dixie?" p. 9.
2. Patterson, "The Failure of Party
Realignment in the South," p. 602;
John U. Barr to Harry F. Byrd,
June 17, 1947, Byrd Papers, Box
184, University of Virginia; *NYT*,
November 16, 1952.
3. T. Coleman Andrews to Harry F.
Byrd, October 10, 1950, Byrd
Papers, Box 196, University of
Virginia; G. Fred Switzer to Wright
Morrow, November 26, 1951, Byrd
Papers, Box 227, University of
Virginia; A. Willis Robertson to Fred
M. Vinson, March 11, 1952, Vinson
Papers, Box 354, University of
Kentucky.
4. Cope, "Frustration of Harry Byrd,"
p. 23; A. Willis Robertson to
Howard W. Smith, February 3,
1945, Robertson Papers, College of
William and Mary.
5. Woodward, *Origins of the New South*,
p. 145; Gaston, *New South Creed*,
p. 189; Freidel, *F.D.R. and the South*,
p. 99; Parmet, *Democrats*, pp. 20–
21.
6. Open letter, Southern States
Industrial Council to "the
Industrialists of the South,"
February 8, 1947, Byrd Papers, Box
184, University of Virginia.
7. Rubin, *I'll Take My Stand*, pp. 199,
372.
8. Ravitch, *Troubled Crusade*, p. 116;
Key, *Southern Politics*, p. 519.

9. Harry Byrd to Watkins M. Abbitt,
March 27, 1946, Byrd Papers,
University of Virginia; Virginius
Dabney to Fred M. Davis, July 2,
1945, and J. K. M. Newton, August
2, 1945, Dabney Papers, Box 3,
University of Virginia.
10. Mrs. Jack Daniels Ames to Virginius
Dabney, July 10, 1945, Dabney
Papers, Box 9, University of
Virginia.
11. Harry Byrd to Watkins M. Abbitt,
March 27, 1946, Byrd Papers,
University of Virginia; Key, *Southern
Politics*, p. 518; Key, "New Voters in
the Making," p. 7.
12. Key, *Southern Politics*, p. 240.
13. Clark, *South Since Reconstruction*, p.
536; Woodward, *Origins of the New
South*, p. 396.
14. Clark, *South Since Reconstruction*, pp.
538–541.
15. Frederickson, *Black Image in the
White Mind*, pp. 198–200.
16. Cash, *Mind of the South*, p. 79.
17. Woodward, *Strange Career of Jim
Crow*, pp. 78, 80 (also see
Woodward, "Strange Career
Critics"); Frederickson, *Black Image
in the White Mind*, p. 200; U.S.
Bureau of the Census, *Historical
Statistics*, p. 218; Cash, *Mind of the
South*, p. 117.
18. Frederickson, *Black Image in the
White Mind*, p. 203; Woodward,
Strange Career of Jim Crow, p. 73;
Dollard, *Caste and Class in a Southern
Town*, p. 315.

19. Dollard, *Caste and Class in a Southern Town*, p. 321.
20. *The Reporter*, May 10, 1949, p. 24; Frank D. Bisbee to Harry Byrd, March 21, 1950, Byrd Papers, Box 203, University of Virginia.
21. Frady, *Wallace*, pp. 100–102.
22. Key, *Southern Politics*, pp. 239, 243–244; Chester M. Morgan, *Redneck Liberal*, p. 232; Percy, *Lanterns on the Levee*, p. 148. In addition to the collections listed on pages 255–256 of Charles Morgan's biography, Bilbo correspondence may be found with the Harry Byrd Papers at the University of Virginia.
23. Chester M. Morgan, *Redneck Liberal*, pp. 187, 205, 206, 208.
24. Bass and DeVries, *Transformation of Southern Politics*, pp. 38–39.
25. John Stennis to Lyndon B. Johnson, Senate Congressional File, Box 5, LBJL; Parmet, *Democrats*, p. 100.
26. Lewis Preston Collins, "The Memoirs and Analysis of Virginia's Participation in the Chicago National Democratic Convention," August 6, 1952, Byrd Papers, Box 198, University of Virginia; Statement of Senator Blair Moody, July 28, 1952, Neil Staebler Papers, Michigan Historical Collections, University of Michigan, Bentley Historical Library, Ann Arbor, Michigan; Hays, *Southern Moderate Speaks*, p. 81; Wilkinson, *Harry F. Byrd*, pp. 81–83, 84; Parmet, *Democrats*, p. 101; A. Willis Robertson to Kate H. Steele, October 22, 1952, Byrd Papers, Box 204, University of Virginia; Howard Smith to Robertson, October 14, 1952, Byrd Papers, Box 204, University of Virginia; Robertson to Harry Byrd, August 10, 1956, Robertson Papers, College of William and Mary.
27. Interview with Roy Wilkins, August 11, 1970; *NYT*, October 18, 1952.
28. *U.S. News & World Report*, August 29, 1952, p. 40.
29. *NYT*, October 14, 24, 1952; Ambrose, *Nixon*, p. 297.
30. Tindall, *Disruption of the Solid South*, p. 56; Paul T. David, *Presidential Nominating Politics in 1952*, v. 3, p. 349.
31. Bartley, *Rise of Massive Resistance*, pp. 48–50; Lubell, *Revolt of the Moderates*, pp. 178, 179–180; as

quoted in Chester Morgan, *Redneck Liberal*, p. 232.
32. Nixon, *RN*, pp. 81, 84.
33. *NYT*, July 13, 1952.
34. Schapsmeier and Schapsmeier, *Dirksen of Illinois*, p. 79; Richard Norton Smith, *Thomas E. Dewey and His Times*, p. 593; Patterson, *Mr. Republican*, p. 556.
35. Richard Norton Smith, *Thomas E. Dewey and His Times*, pp. 34, 320, 334.
36. Reinhard, *Republican Right*, p. 40; Ross, *Loneliest Campaign*, p. 32.
37. *NYT*, July 11, 1952.
38. Schapsmeier and Schapsmeier, *Dirksen of Illinois*, p. 79.
39. Reinhard, *Republican Right*, p. 89; Wills, *Reagan's America*, p. 286.
40. Statement by Joseph Polowsky attached to Julius Klein to Robert H. Finch, June 25, 1959, Nixon Pre-Presidential Papers, Series 320, Box 417, NARA-LA.
41. Ambrose, *Eisenhower*, p. 542.
42. Weeks to Sherman Adams, January 16, 1959, Adams Papers, Baker Library, Dartmouth.
43. Nixon, handwritten note, 1947, Nixon Non-Deeded Papers, Series 206, Box 7, NARA-LA; Nixon, *RN*, pp. 81–82.
44. Nixon to George Creel, August 30, 1951, Nixon Pre-Presidential Papers, Box 189, NARA-LA; Smith, *Dewey*, p. 595; Parmet, *Eisenhower*, p. 93; Nixon, *RN*, p. 83; interviews with Richard M. Nixon, June 4, 1984, and Sinclair Weeks, April 15, 1969.
45. *NYT*, July 3 and 10, 1952.
46. Ambrose, *Nixon*, p. 250.
47. Richard Norton Smith, *Thomas E. Dewey and His Times*, pp. 584, 595; interview with Richard M. Nixon, June 4, 1984.
48. Interviews with Henry Cabot Lodge, May 14, 1970, and Frank Carlson, June 20, 1984.
49. David Eisenhower, *Eisenhower at War*, p. 316.
50. Nixon's notes of his 1947 trip to Europe with the Herter Committee, attached to Rose Mary Woods to Stewart Alsop, March 10, 1958, Nixon Non-Deeded Papers, Congressional Files, Herter Committee, Box 7, NARA-LA.
51. Interview with Lucius Clay, April 8, 1969; David Eisenhower, *Eisenhower*

at War, p. 501; Dwight D. Eisenhower, *White House Years,* p. 20.

52. Interview with Henry Cabot Lodge, May 14, 1970.

53. Ibid.; Leverett Saltonstall, Eisenhower Oral History Project, Columbia University; Julie Nixon Eisenhower, *Pat Nixon,* p. 115.

54. Rovere, *Affairs of State,* pp. 26–27; *NYT,* July 8, 10, and 11, 1952.

55. Ibid., July 13, 1952.

56. Reinhard, *Republican Right,* pp. 90–91; Scott, *Come to the Party,* p. 68.

57. Interview with David Eisenhower, January 21, 1986.

58. Typescript, "Making a President," Robert Humphreys Papers, Box 4, n.d., DDEL.

59. *NYT,* September 19, 1952; *NYHT,* September 19, 1952; Dwight D. Eisenhower, *White House Years,* p. 65.

60. Nixon, *Six Crises,* p. 93; Ambrose, *Nixon,* p. 293.

61. Begeman, "Nixon: How the Press Suppressed the News," p. 11; Robert Humphreys to Sherman Adams, February 7, 1959, Adams Papers, Baker Library, Dartmouth.

62. Interview with Milton Eisenhower, June 19, 1969.

63. Parmet, *Eisenhower,* p. 136.

64. Ambrose, *Nixon,* pp. 256, 258; Costello, *Facts About Nixon,* p. 112.

65. Interviews with Milton Eisenhower, June 19, 1969, and Lucius Clay, April 8, 1969.

66. Sherman Adams, *Firsthand Report,* p. 37; interview with James C. Hagerty, April 11, 1969; Citizens for Eisenhower reports, September 22, 1962, Adams Papers, Baker Library, Dartmouth.

67. *NYT,* September 20, 1952.

68. Stassen to Nixon, September 21, 1952, Nixon Pre-Presidential Papers, General Correspondence 320, Box 724, NARA-LA.

69. Humphreys to Sherman Adams, February 7, 1959, Adams Papers, Baker Library, Dartmouth.

70. Memorandum of conversation between McCrary and Baruch, September 21, 1952, Sherman Adams Papers, Baker Library, Dartmouth; *NYT,* September 21, 1952.

71. Humphreys to Adams, February 7, 1959, Adams Papers, Baker Library,

Dartmouth; Dwight D. Eisenhower, *White House Years,* pp. 66–67.

72. Ambrose, *Nixon,* p. 295.

73. Ibid., pp. 277, 286; Humphreys to Adams, February 7, 1959, Adams Papers, Baker Library, Dartmouth; *NYT,* September 20, 1952; Parmet, *Eisenhower,* p. 136.

74. Mazo, *Richard Nixon,* p. 114; Richard Norton Smith, *An Uncommon Man,* p. 400; Ambrose, *Eisenhower,* p. 555; Sherman Adams, *Firsthand Report,* p. 38.

75. Nixon, *RN,* p. 99.

76. Nixon, *RN,* p. 97.

77. Sherman Adams, *Firthand Report,* p. 38; Nixon, *RN,* pp. 97–98; Parmet, *Eisenhower,* p. 136; *NYT,* September 22, 1952.

78. Nixon, *Six Crises,* p. 101; *NYT,* September 23, 1952.

79. Nixon, *Six Crises,* p. 110.

80. Kornitzer, *Real Nixon,* p. 107; Lester David, *Lonely Lady of San Clemente,* p. 85; Nixon, *Six Crises,* p. 87.

81. Interview with Milton Eisenhower, June 19, 1969.

82. Ambrose, *Nixon,* p. 289; Steel, *Walter Lippmann,* p. 483; Redlich, "Handbook for Demagogues," p. 290.

83. Parmet, *Eisenhower,* p. 138; Robert Humphreys to Sherman Adams, February 17, 1959, Adams Papers, Baker Library, Dartmouth; Cutler, *No Time for Rest,* pp. 285–286; Ambrose, *Nixon,* p. 289; Sherman Adams, *Firsthand Report,* pp. 40–41.

84. Hoyt, *The Nixons,* p. 276; CSU-F interviews: Newt Robinson, interviewed by John Donnelly, June 18, 1970, OH-939; Gerald Kepple, interviewed by Greg Brolin, January 7, 1971, OH-992; Cathcart and Schwartz, "New Nixon or Poor Richard," p. 12.

85. Gerald Kepple, interviewed by Greg Brolin, January 7, 1971, OH-992, CSU-F; Ambrose, *Nixon,* p. 290.

86. Humphreys to Adams, February 17, 1959, Adams Papers, Baker Library, Dartmouth; Swanberg, *Luce,* p. 329.

87. Parmet, *Eisenhower,* pp. 139–140; Ambrose, *Nixon,* p. 291.

88. Parmet, *Eisenhower,* p. 140; Julie Nixon Eisenhower, *Pat Nixon,* p. 124.

89. Humphreys to Adams, February 17,

1959, Adams Papers, Baker Library, Dartmouth.

90. Ibid.

Chapter 10. DICK AND IKE

1. Nixon, *Six Crises*, p. 133.
2. Nixon to Elliott V. Bell, October 10, 1955, Nixon Pre-Presidential Papers, Box 73, NARA-LA.
3. *NYT*, September 27, 1955.
4. Nixon, *Six Crises*, pp. 139, 140, 141, 149; interview with Richard M. Nixon, November 16, 1988; *NYT*, September 26, 1955.
5. Rovere, *Affairs of State*, p. 325; Ambrose, *Eisenhower*, p. 273; Parmet, *Eisenhower*, p. 417; interview with Richard Nixon in the John Foster Dulles Oral History Collection, Firestone Library, Princeton University.
6. Ambrose, *Eisenhower*, p. 273.
7. *NYT*, September 25, 1955; Julie Nixon Eisenhower, *Pat Nixon*, p. 154; *LAT*, December 2, 1957; memorandum of telephone call to Nixon by Dulles, September 26, 1955, Dulles Papers, Telephone Conversation Series, Box 4, DDEL.
8. Interview with Richard M. Nixon, June 8, 1984; I. F. Stone, *Haunted Fifties*, p. 67.
9. Memorandum of Telephone Conversation with Vice President Nixon, Dulles Papers, Telephone Conversations Series, Box 4, DDEL.
10. Parmet, *Eisenhower*, p. 422; *NYT*, October 18, 1955.
11. Karl Mundt to George Creel, August 11, 1951, Nixon Pre-Presidential Papers, Box 189, NARA-LA.
12. Larson, *Republican Looks at His Party*, pp. 10, 19.
13. Larson, *Eisenhower*, pp. 44–46; Ambrose, *Nixon*, p. 387.
14. Interview with Harold E. Stassen, August 23, 1971.
15. Parmet, *Eisenhower*, p. 450; Ambrose, *Nixon*, pp. 402, 406.
16. Larson, *Eisenhower*, p. 37; *U.S. News & World Report*, August 3, 1956, p. 34; Ambrose, *Eisenhower*, p. 285.
17. Nixon, *No More Vietnams*, p. 31; interview with Richard M. Nixon, June 5, 1984.
18. Ewald, *Who Killed Joe McCarthy?*, pp. 270–271.
19. Interviews with Sherman Adams, August 3, 1969, and David Eisenhower, January 21, 1986, *Washington Evening Star*, December 19, 1955.
20. *Washington Evening Star*, December 19, 1955; RNC, News Release, February 5, 1956, Nixon Pre-Presidential Papers, Series 296, Box 6, NARA-LA.
21. Ambrose, *Nixon*, p. 297. Far overshadowing the Texarkana speech that day was Joe McCarthy's nationally televised address that accused Stevenson of sympathizing and assisting the Communist cause.
22. Costello, *Facts About Nixon*, pp. 95, 117; Ambrose, *Nixon*, p. 336; Alsop, *Nixon and Rockefeller*, p. 147.
23. *Newsweek*, November 15, 1954.
24. Alsop, *Nixon and Rockefeller*, p. 147; Ambrose, *Nixon*, p. 354; Costello, *Facts About Nixon*, p. 128; Gillon, *Politics and Vision*, p. 110; Walter Johnson, *Papers of Adlai E. Stevenson*, v. 4, p. 409.
25. Nixon to Victor Lasky, November 18, 1954, Nixon General Correspondence, Series 320, Box 439, NARA-LA.
26. Notes of Cabinet Meeting, November 5, 1954, Whitman File, Cabinet Series, Box 4, DDEl.
27. Costello, *Facts About Nixon*, p. 130; Ambrose, *Nixon*, pp. 349, 406.
28. Ambrose, *Eisenhower*, p. 289; Ferrell, *Diary of James C. Hagerty*, pp. 243–245; Griffith, *Ike's Letters to a Friend*, pp. 153–154.
29. Griffith, *Ike's Letters to a Friend*, p. 159; Nixon, *RN*, p. 169–170; *Public Papers: Eisenhower, 1956*, p. 287.
30. For a clear indication of the promotion of Nixon's diplomatic prominence, see a Memorandum of Conversation between the President, Nixon, Dulles, and Jerry Persons, September 3, 1957, Dulles Papers, DDEL.
31. Interview with George Humphrey, July 2, 1969.
32. Memorandum of Conversation with

90. Ibid.
91. Nixon, *Six Crises*, p. 123.
92. Cf. Wright, *In the New World*, p. 230.

the President, February 27, 1956,
Dulles Papers, DDEL.

33. Ewald, *Eisenhower*, p. 185; Ambrose,
Eisenhower, p. 294; interview with
Leonard Hall, May 5, 1969.

34. Ewald, *Eisenhower*, p. 187; interview
with Leonard Hall, May 9, 1969;
Reinhard, *Republican Right*, p. 131;
Ambrose, *Eisenhower*, pp. 293–295;
Parmet, *Eisenhower*, p. 418.

35. *Newsweek*, March 19, 1956, pp. 31–
32; Mazo, *Richard Nixon*, p. 165;
Ambrose, *Nixon*, pp. 389, 390–391;
Ambrose, *Eisenhower*, p. 321; Nixon,
RN, p. 170.

36. Interview with Roy Wilkins, August
11, 1970; Schwartz, *Super Chief*, pp.
112–113; Warren, *Memoirs*, p. 291;
Larson, *Eisenhower*, p. 124; interview
with James C. Hagerty, April 9,
1969; interview with Steven
Benedict, April 9, 1969; Ambrose,
Eisenhower, p. 221.

37. Chafe, *Unfinished Journey*, p. 157;
Gallup, *Gallup Poll*, v. 2, p. 1337. On
election day, Eisenhower did even
better in the South than in 1952,
and even his support from blacks
improved.

38. Gallup, *Gallup Poll*, v. 2, p. 1352;
Parmet, *Eisenhower*, p. 441; E.
Frederick Morrow to Maxwell Rabb,
November 29, 1955. Morrow Papers,
Box 10, DDEL; interview with
Steven Benedict, April 9, 1969.

39. Ambrose, *Nixon*, pp. 395–396.

40. The sisters recall one black
girl as a schoolmate. Interview with
Julie Nixon Eisenhower, May 22,
1987.

41. See correspondence in Nixon
General Correspondence 320 File,
Box 617, containing responses to
public inquiries about the education
of the two girls, at NARA-LA;
interview with Julie Nixon
Eisenhower, May 22, 1987.

42. Interview with Roy Wilkins, August
11, 1970; Harris Wofford to Nixon,
December 30, 1957, Nixon General
Correspondence, Series 320, Box
828, NARA-LA; Garrow, *Bearing the
Cross*, p. 119.

43. Charles McWhorter to Nixon,
December 14, 1957, Nixon Pre-
Presidential Papers, Series 320, Box
153, NARA-LA; interview with Roy
Wilkins, August 11, 1970;
Eisenhower to Col. Percy W.

Thompson, August 17, 1960,
Whitman File, DDE Diary Series,
Box 52, DDEL.

44. Minutes of Cabinet Meeting,
December 18, 1959, Whitman File,
Cabinet Series, Box 15, DDEL.

45. Nixon, *Challenges We Face*, pp. 183,
184, 186; *NYT*, October 1, 1954;
NYHT, October 1, 1954; Nixon to
J. B. Rhine, October 2, 1957; Nixon
Pre-Presidential Papers, Box 228,
NARA-LA.

46. Keogh, *This Is Nixon*, pp. 104–105;
transcript of Lincoln Day Dinner
remarks, February 13, 1956, Nixon
Pre-Presidential Papers, Series 207,
NARA-LA.

47. Costello, *Facts About Nixon*, pp. 239–
240; Mazo and Hess, *Richard Nixon*,
p. 213.

48. A. Willis Robertson to Walter H.
Carter, October 2, 1964, Robertson
Papers, College of William and
Mary; Ambrose, *Eisenhower*, p. 222.

49. Chotiner to Nixon, January 24,
1956, Nixon Pre-Presidential Papers,
Box 148, NARA-LA.

50. ACLU News Release, June 7, 1956,
Nixon Pre-Presidential Papers, Box
148, NARA-LA; statement by
Murray M. Chotiner, June 4, 1956,
Nixon Pre-Presidential Papers,
Series 320, Box 148, NARA-LA.

51. Ambrose, *Eisenhower*, p. 293.

52. Ibid., p. 298.

53. Reinhard, *Republican Right*, pp. 131,
135–136; interview with Robert B.
Anderson, June 14, 1971; Ambrose,
Eisenhower, p. 294.

54. Reinhard, *Republican Right*, p. 131;
Parmet, *Eisenhower*, p. 424; Caspar
Weinberger, interview by Gabrielle
Morris, March 6, 1979, Bancroft
Library; Richard Berlin to Nixon,
February 24, 1956, Non-Deeded
Material, Nixon Pre-Presidential
Papers, Box 78, NARA-LA; Earl
Mazo to Thomas E. Dewey,
November 21, 1958, Nixon Pre-
Presidential Papers, NARA-LA; as
quoted in *The Reporter*, August 9,
1956, p. 4.

55. Nixon, *RN*, p. 171; Costello, *Facts
About Nixon*, p. 146; Brodie, *Richard
Nixon*, pp. 353–354; *Public Papers:
Eisenhower, 1956*, p. 302.

56. Pre-Press Briefing, February 29,
1956, Whitman File, Eisenhower
Diary Series, Box 13, DDEL.

57. Nixon, *RN,* p. 172; Memorandum, "Vice President Nixon's Appointment with the President," April 26, 1956, Whitman File, Administration Series, Box 28, DDEL.

58. "Vice President Nixon's Appointment with the President," Whitman File, Administration Series, Box 28, DDEL.

59. Nixon, *RN,* p. 173.

60. Transcript of Press Conference, April 26, 1956, Nixon General Correspondence, Series 320, Box 610, NARA-LA.

61. White House News Release, June 8, 1956, Weeks Papers, Box 10, Weeks Personal Collection; *NYT,* June 10 and 11, 1956; Parmet, *Eisenhower,* p. 449.

62. Gallup, *Gallup Poll,* v. 2, p. 1423.

63. Ibid. When the same question was asked of "independents," Dewey and Stassen were again runners-up and Herter near the bottom, one point ahead of Milton Eisenhower.

64. Parmet, *Eisenhower,* pp. 451–452; Ambrose, *Nixon,* p. 402; *NYHT,* July 24, 1956; Harold Stassen, Letter to Republican Delegates, and White House News Release, July 23, 1956, Weeks Papers, Box 19, Weeks Personal Collection.

65. Loie G. Gaunt, memo for the files, September 1958, Nixon General Correspondence 320, Box 724, NARA-LA; Harold E. Stassen to author, December 4, 1985.

66. *U.S. News & World Report,* August 3, 1956, p. 43.

67. *Washington Sunday Star,* February 19, 1956; Ann C. Whitman to Rose Mary Woods, February 22, 1956. Whitman File, Eisenhower Diary Series, Box 13, DDEL.

68. Stassen to Eisenhower, July 19, 1956, Whitman File, Administration Series, Box 34, DDEL; Stassen Memorandum, August 16, 1956; Whitman File, Administration Series, Box 34, DDEL; Ambrose, *Nixon,* p. 402; *U.S. News & World Report,* August 3, 1956, p. 44.

69. Stassen to Nixon, July 23, 1956, Nixon General Correspondence, Series 320, Box 724, NARA-LA.

70. *The Reporter,* August 9, 1956, pp. 3–4; interviews with David Eisenhower, January 21, 1986, and William F.

Buckley, Jr., October 18, 1984; *NYHT,* July 23 and 25, 1956; interview with Thomas E. Stephens, March 11, 1988.

71. Richard Norton Smith, *Thomas E. Dewey and His Times,* p. 623; Harold Stassen to Dwight Eisenhower, August 20, 1956, Whitman File, Administration Series, Box 34, DDEL; Mazo, *Richard Nixon,* p. 162; Javits, *Javits,* p. 212; Sigurd S. Larmon to Lucius Clay, Oveta Culp Hobby, et al., July 1956, Citizens for Eisenhower Papers, Box 1, DDEL; *NYHT,* August 8, 1956.

72. *Baltimore Evening Sun,* July 24, 1956; *NYHT,* July 23, 24, and 25, 1956.

73. *NYT,* July 24, 1956; John D. M. Hamilton to Sinclair Weeks, July 27, 1956, Weeks Papers, Box 19, Weeks Personal Collection; unsigned and undated note in Nixon General Correspondence, Series 320, Box 724, NARA-LA; Dwight D. Eisenhower, *Waging Peace,* p. 10; *NYHT,* July 26, 1956; Knebel, "Did Ike Really Want Nixon?," p. 26.

74. Morrow, *Black Man in the White House,* p. 85.

75. Interview with Richard M. Nixon, November 16, 1988; Ewald, *Eisenhower,* p. 179; telephone interview with William Bragg Ewald, Jr., June 5, 1987.

76. Ewald, *Eisenhower,* p. 256; In a telephone interview with the author on March 11, 1988, Stephens still refused to admit that he was doing anything other than practicing law in New York.

77. Sherman Adams, *Firsthand Report,* p. 430; telephone interview with William Bragg Ewald, Jr., June 5, 1987; interview with David Eisenhower, May 22, 1987.

78. Interview with Sherman Adams, August 3, 1969; interview with David Eisenhower, January 21, 1986; *Public Papers: Eisenhower, 1956,* p. 633; interview with William F. Price, July 11, 1985.

79. Interview with Patrick J. Hillings, July 10, 1985; Walter J. Minton to Robert L. King, May 21, 1956, Nixon Pre-Presidential Papers, Box 406, NARA-LA; Pat Hillings to Rose Mary Woods, July 18, 1956, Nixon

Pre-Presidential Papers, Box 342, NARA-LA; *Newsweek,* August 6, 1956, p. 20; Knebel, "Did Ike Really Want Nixon?," p. 26; interview with Richard M. Nixon, November 16, 1988; Goodman, "Fatal Passion of Harold Stassen," pp. 7–8; Republican Research Division, "Political Polls," RNC Papers, NARA-Wash., in Leuchtenburg and Kesaris, *Papers,* Part II, reel 2.
80. Ambrose, *Eisenhower,* p. 405.
81. Interview with Meade Alcorn, April 18, 1984.
82. Sherman Adams, *Firsthand Report,* p. 240.
83. D.D. to Nixon, July 12, 1956, Nixon Pre-Presidential Papers, Box 342, NARA-LA; William Randolph Hearst, Jr., to Nixon, September 12, 1956, Nixon Pre-Presidential Papers, Box 329, NARA-LA.
84. Interview with Meade Alcorn, April 18, 1984.
85. Interview with Clare Boothe Luce, April 30, 1985; interview with Richard M. Nixon, June 5, 1984; Hatch, *Ambassador Extraordinary,* p. 244; as quoted in Swanberg, *Luce,* p. 375.
86. Costello, *Facts About Nixon,* p. 152; Harold E. Stassen to Eisenhower, August 20, 1956, Whitman File, Administration Series, Box 34, DDEL; Earl Mazo to Thomas E. Dewey, November 21, 1958, Nixon Pre-Presidential Papers, Box 486, NARA-LA.
87. Telephone interview with Herbert Brownell, March 14, 1988.
88. William Randolph Hearst, Jr., to Nixon, September 12, 1956, Nixon Pre-Presidential Papers, Box 329, NARA-LA; Harold E. Stassen to Eisenhower, August 20, 1956, Whitman File, Administration Series, Box 34, DDEL.
89. Knebel, "Did Ike Really Want Nixon?," pp. 25–27.
90. Scott, *Come to the Party,* p. 148; Knebel, "Did Ike Really Want Nixon?," p. 27; *NYHT,* August 23, 1956; Parmet, *Eisenhower,* p. 457; interview with Richard M. Nixon, November 16, 1988.
91. Ambrose, *Nixon,* p. 406; Harold Boeschenstein to Eisenhower, August 24, 1956, White House Central Files, Box 17, DDEL.
92. Julie Nixon Eisenhower, *Pat Nixon,* p. 126; Nixon, *Six Crises,* p. 128; Caroli, *First Ladies,* p. 247.
93. Mazo, *Richard Nixon,* p. 139; Julie Nixon Eisenhower, *Pat Nixon,* p. 158.
94. Mazlish, *In Search of Nixon,* p. 69; Abrahamsen, *Nixon vs. Nixon,* p. 113; Julie Nixon Eisenhower, *Pat Nixon,* p. 158.
95. Julie Nixon Eisenhower, *Pat Nixon,* p. 158.
96. Ambrose, *Nixon,* pp. 392–394.
97. Julie Nixon Eisenhower, *Pat Nixon,* p. 145; Ambrose, *Nixon,* p. 350.
98. Judith Viorst, "Pat Nixon Is the Ultimate Good Sport," p. 26.
99. Nixon, *RN,* p. 537; Safire, *Before the Fall,* p. 607.
100. Caroli, *First Ladies,* pp. 252–253.
101. *NYT,* August 18, 1956.
102. *Boston Herald,* August 14, 1956; Chester Bowles to Hubert H. Humphrey, August 24, 1956, Bowles Papers, Yale.
103. Ewald, *Eisenhower,* p. 200.
104. Interview with William F. Buckley, Jr., October 18, 1984.
105. Interview with Meade Alcorn, April 18, 1984.
106. Ambrose, *Nixon,* p. 368.
107. Collier and Horowitz, *Rockefellers,* pp. 271, 275.
108. Interview with Hugh Scott, June 10, 1986.
109. *NYT,* August 27 and September 3, 1956; Kempton, *Part of Our Time,* p. 126.
110. Interview with David Eisenhower, May 22, 1987; *NYT,* August 23, 1956.
111. Sherman Adams, *Firsthand Report,* p. 241.
112. *NYHT,* August 23, 1956.
113. *NYT,* October 5, 1956.
114. Ambrose, *Nixon,* p. 420.
115. Gallup, *Gallup Poll,* v. 2, p. 1454.
116. Walter Johnson, *Papers of Adlai E. Stevenson,* v. 6, pp. 218, 306–307; *NYT,* October 28, 1956.
117. Walter Johnson, *Papers of Adlai E. Stevenson,* v. 6, p. 324.
118. Lash, *Eleanor,* p. 285; *NYT,* September 23, October 18, and October 24, 1956; I. F. Stone, *Haunted Fifties,* p. 163; Walter Johnson, *Papers of Adlai E. Stevenson,* v. 6, p. 306.
119. *Public Papers: Eisenhower, 1956,* p.

759; Parmet, *Eisenhower*, p. 492; Rischin, *"Our Own Kind,"* p. 34.

120. Rischin, *"Our Own Kind,"* p. 16; Garrow, "Black Civil Rights During the Eisenhower Years," p. 368; Parmet, *Eisenhower*, p. 492.

121. Rischin, *"Our Own Kind,"* pp. 15–16; *NYT*, November 2 and 4, 1956.

122. Palmer Hoyt to Nixon, September 26, 1956, Nixon Pre-Presidential Papers, Box 358, NARA-LA; *U.S. News & World Report*, March 29, 1957, pp. 62–67; Eulau, *Class and Party in the Eisenhower Years*, p. 2.

123. *WP*, November 12, 1956.

124. Claude Robinson Survey of 1956 Election, n. d., Nixon General Correspondence, Series 320, Box 647, NARA-LA; Republican Research Division, "Major Findings in Political Polls, October 11–30, 1956," RNC Papers, NARA-Wash., in Leuchtenburg and Kesaris, *Papers*, Part II, reel 2.

125. Republican Research Division, "Political Polls," RNC Papers, NARA-Wash., in Leuchtenburg and Kesaris, *Papers*, Part II, reel 2.

Chapter 11. THE GLOBAL VICE PRESIDENT

1. Nixon to John Ehrlichman and Ken Cole, December 28, 1972, President's Personal File, Box 4, NPMP.

2. MacLeish, "Conquest of America," pp. 17–22.

3. Rusher, *Rise of the Right*, p. 328; Nixon, *Challenges We Face*, p. 35.

4. Nixon to Raymond Moley, August 12, 1949, Nixon Non-Deeded Papers, Congressional Files, 1950 Campaign, Box 5, NARA-LA; Herbert Klein to Nixon, August 28, 1956, Nixon Pre-Presidential Papers, Box 416, NARA-LA.

5. Nixon, *RN*, pp. 48, 51; Martin, *My First Fifty Years in Politics*, p. 194; Nixon to Rose Mary Woods, March 12, 1958, Nixon Non-Deeded Papers, Series 206, Box 7, NARA-LA; Ambrose, *Nixon*, pp. 156–157.

6. Dictated notes of Nixon's Herter Committee trip, attached to Rose Mary Woods to Stewart Alsop, March 10, 1958, Nixon Non-Deeded Papers, Congressional Files, Herter Committee, Box 7, NARA-LA.

7. Ibid.

8. Ibid.

9. Ibid.

10. Ibid.; Nixon, *RN*, pp. 49–50, 52.

11. Nixon, *RN*, p. 51; dictated notes of Nixon's Herter Committee trip, attached to Rose Mary Woods to Stewart Alsop, March 10, 1958, Nixon Non-Deeded Papers, Congressional Files, Herter Committee, Box 7, NARA-LA.

12. Dictated notes of Nixon's Herter Committee trip, attached to Rose Mary Woods to Stewart Alsop, March 10, 1958, Nixon Non-Deeded

Papers, Congressional Files, Herter Committee, Box 7, NARA-LA.

13. Ibid.

14. Nixon, *RN*, pp. 50, 52. The "leadership" theme became the subject of a book he published after he left the presidency.

15. de Toledano, *Nixon*, p. 60.

16. *NYT*, September 18, 1947.

17. Nixon, *RN*, pp. 49, 52; Nixon handwritten notes, 1947, Nixon Non-Deeded Papers, Series 206, Box 7, NARA-LA.

18. Nixon News Release, March 14, 1947, Nixon Non-Deeded Papers, Series 206, Box 6, NARA-LA.

19. Ibid.

20. Ibid.

21. Goulden, *Korea*, p. 86.

22. Kaufman, *Korean War*, p. 36.

23. Ibid., pp. 1, 36–38; Truman, *Memoirs*, v. 2, p. 333; Patterson, *Mr. Republican*, p. 453; *NYT*, June 26, 1950; Goulden, *Korea*, p. 63; Goulden has argued that Truman's avoidance of a direct accusation was the basic flaw of the Truman-Acheson policy in Korea because that "in essence proved the Soviet point — that is, that the USSR could use satellites to nip at America's flanks without fear of provoking direct retaliation" (p. xviii).

24. Kaufman, *Korean War*, p. 32; Link and Catton, *American Epoch*, p. 707; Gallup, *Gallup Poll*, v. 2, p. 929.

25. Hastings, *Korean War*, pp. 42–45.

26. Kaufman, *Korean War*, p. 24.

27. Ibid., p. 37.

28. Goulden, *Korea*, p. 31.

29. Nixon made that point during his debates with Kennedy in 1960 when they had an exchange over the

offshore islands of Quemoy and Matsu.

30. Ambrose, *Nixon,* pp. 242, 323; Brodie, *Richard Nixon,* p. 249; transcript, "America's Town Meeting of the Air," May 1, 1951, Nixon Papers, Series 207, Appearances, NARA-LA; transcript of radio and television report by Vice President Nixon, December 23, 1953, Nixon Pre-Presidential Papers, Speaking Appearances, Box 15, NARA-LA.

31. *NYT,* February 29, 1972; Nixon, *Leaders,* p. 102.

32. Interview with Dwight D. Eisenhower by Dr. Philip Crowell for the John Foster Dulles Oral History Project, Firestone Library, Princeton.

33. Kahin, *Intervention,* pp. 34–36, 37; Parmet, "Making and Unmaking of Ngo Dinh Diem," pp. 38, 45.

34. Kahin, *Intervention,* p. 38.

35. Cf. Kahin, *Intervention,* p. 31.

36. The Senator Gravel Edition, *Pentagon Papers,* v. 1, pp. 385–386; Immerman, "Between the Unattainable and the Unacceptable," p. 121.

37. Vice President's Briefing Book, Far Eastern Trip File, Box 1, NARA-LA.

38. *Public Papers: Eisenhower, 1954,* p. 383; Hagerty Papers, Diary Entries, Box 1, DDEL; Dulles remarks before Los Angeles World Affairs Council, June 11, 1954, Dulles Papers, Subject Series, Box 8, DDEL; Notes of Cabinet Meeting, August 6, 1954, Hagerty Papers, Diary Entries, Box 1, DDEL.

39. Vice President's Briefing Book, Far Eastern Trip File, Box 1, NARA-LA; transcript of Nixon speech, December 23, 1953, Nixon Pre-Presidential Papers, Speaking Appearances, Box 15, NARA-LA; "Memorandum in Connection with the Trip," Nixon Pre-Presidential Papers, Far Eastern Trip File, Box 1, NARA-LA; Nixon, "Lessons of the Hiss Case."

40. Nixon, *RN,* pp. 121, 129.

41. Ibid., p. 152; Nixon Remarks, November 4, 1953, Nixon Far Eastern Trip Speech File, Box 1, NARA-LA; Nixon to Robert McClintock, November 9, 1953,

Nixon Pre-Presidential Papers, Far Eastern Trip File, Box 3, NARA-LA; Julie Nixon Eisenhower, *Pat Nixon,* p. 139.

42. Transcript of radio and television report by the vice president, December 23, 1953, Nixon Pre-Presidential Papers, Speaking Appearances, Box 15, NARA-LA.

43. de Toledano, *Nixon,* pp. 163, 164.

44. "Memorandum in Connection with the Trip," Nixon Pre-Presidential Papers, Far Eastern Trip File, Box 1, NARA-LA.

45. Ibid.

46. Alsop, *Nixon and Rockefeller,* p. 47; interview with Meade Alcorn, April 18, 1984.

47. *NYT,* April 18, 1954; Immerman, "Between the Unattainable and the Unacceptable," pp. 123, 132, 137; Hoopes, *Devil and John Foster Dulles,* p. 214.

48. Nixon also discounted Dulles's faith in the ability to achieve a united and independent Korea at Geneva. *NYT,* April 20, 1954; Nixon, *RN,* p. 151.

49. Hoopes, *Devil and John Foster Dulles,* pp. 208, 211; Nixon, *RN,* p. 150.

50. Quoted in Keogh, *This Is Nixon,* pp. 140–141; *NYT,* April 17, 1954.

51. Spector, *Advice and Support,* pp. 208–210; *NYT,* April 17, 18, and 20, 1954; House of Representatives, 83d Congress, 2d session, *Congressional Record,* v. 100, part 4, pp. 5289–5293; Gallup, *Gallup Poll,* v. 2, p. 1236.

52. Randle, *Geneva 1954,* pp. 93–94; Chamberlain, "Mr. Nixon's Position," p. 18.

53. *NYT,* April 18, 1954; telephone conversation with Vice President Nixon, April 19, 1954, Dulles Papers, Telephone Series, Box 2, DDEL; interview with Richard Nixon for the Dulles Oral History Project, Princeton.

54. Telephone conversation, Dulles and H. Alexander Smith, April 19, 1954, Dulles Papers, Telephone Calls Series, Box 2, DDEL; interview with Eleanor Lansing Dulles, January 9, 1970; Hoopes, *Devil and John Foster Dulles,* p. 307.

55. Randle, *Geneva 1954,* p. 118; Drummond, "Facts About Mr. Nixon's Speech"; Nixon, *RN,* p. 155;

Mazo, *Richard Nixon*, p. 256; Nixon, *No More Vietnams*, p. 31.

56. Kahin, *Intervention*, pp. 93–94, 98.

57. Ibid., p. 95.

58. Quoted in ibid., p. 97; Sulzberger, *World of Richard Nixon*, p. 158.

Chapter 12. HEIR APPARENT

1. Nixon, *RN*, p. 205.
2. Interview with Emmet J. Hughes, Dulles Oral History Project, Princeton; Mosley, *Dulles*, p. 336.
3. John Foster Dulles, Address to the Princeton National Alumni Luncheon, Princeton, New Jersey, February 22, 1952, Dulles Additional Papers, Folder AM 18643, Princeton; John Foster Dulles, "Memorandom of Conversation with the Vice President," February 8, 1953, Dulles Papers, DDEL.
4. Interview with Roscoe Drummond by John Luter, June 21, 1967, for the Eisenhower Oral History Project, Columbia.
5. Parmet, *Democrats*, pp. 97–98; Porter and Johnson, *National Party Platforms*, p. 499.
6. Mosley, *Dulles*, pp. 336, 344; Richard Harkness, Memorandum, Dulles Additional Papers, Folder AM 18874, Princeton.
7. Nixon, *RN*, p. 53; Weinstein, *Perjury*, pp. 448–449.
8. Neff, *Warriors at Suez*, p. 157.
9. Ferrell, *Eisenhower Diary*, p. 319; Stivers, "Eisenhower and the Middle East," p. 198; Sherman Adams, *Firsthand Report*, p. 249.
10. Neff, *Warriors at Suez*, pp. 107–108, 115, 126; Love, *Suez*, p. 302; Sherman Adams, *Firsthand Report*, p. 246.
11. Neff, *Warriors at Suez*, pp. 116, 123–136; Love, *Suez*, p. 204.
12. Interviews with Gen. Andrew Goodpaster, Eisenhower Oral History Project, Columbia; Herman Phleger, Dulles Oral History Project, Princeton; Childs, *Eisenhower, Captive Hero*, pp. 230–231; Hagerty *Eisenhower Diary*, p. 323; Neff, *Warriors at Suez*, p. 157.
13. Love, *Suez*, pp. 315, 327; interview with Dillon Anderson, Dulles Oral History Project, Princeton.
14. Interview with Dwight D. Eisenhower, Dulles Oral History Project, Princeton.
15. Memorandum of Conversation, October 21, 1955, Dulles Papers, Subject Files, DDEL; Notes of Telephone Conversation Between Dulles and Henry Luce, February 11, 1957, Dulles Papers, Telephone Calls Series, Box 6, DDEL; Telephone Call from Congressman Vorys, February 13, 1957, Dulles Papers, Telephone Calls Series, Box 6, DDEL.
16. John W. Hanes memorandum for John Foster Dulles, November 22, 1955, Dulles Papers, Subject Series, DDEL; Memorandum of Conversation, October 18, 1955, Dulles Papers, Subject Files, DDEL; Neff, *Warriors at Suez*, pp. 343, 348, 358, 360; Ambrose, *Eisenhower*, p. 365.
17. Interview with Richard Bissell, Dulles Oral History Project, Princeton; Parmet, *Eisenhower*, pp. 484–485.
18. Miller, *Henry Cabot Lodge*, p. 275; *NYT*, October 31, 1956; White House News Release, October 30, 1956, White House Central Files, Box 594, DDEL; Eden, *Full Circle*, p. 275.
19. Nixon telephone call to John Foster Dulles, October 31, 1956, Dulles Papers, Telephone Calls Series, Box 6, DDEL.
20. *NYT*, November 6 and 7, 1956; Rose Mary Woods to Ralph de Toledano, February 29, 1960, Nixon Pre-Presidential Papers, Series 320, Box 213, NARA-LA.
21. *NYT*, November 3, 1956; interview with Richard Nixon, Dulles Oral History Project, Princeton; de Toledano, *Nixon*, p. 196.
22. *Public Papers: Eisenhower, 1956*, p. 1072; Finer, *Dulles over Suez*, p. 458.
23. Interview with Julie Nixon Eisenhower, January 21, 1986.
24. Nixon, *RN*, p. 179; Nixon, *Real Peace*, p. 79; interview with Richard M. Nixon, November 16, 1988.
25. Rischin, "Our Own Kind," pp. 11, 23.
26. Sachar, *History of Israel*, pp. 512–513.
27. Nixon, *RN*, pp. 204–205; Ambrose, *Nixon*, p. 441; memoranda of

conversations, September 2 and 3,
1957, Dulles Papers, Subject Series,
Box 6, DDEL; Eisenhower to Nixon,
September 3, 1957, DDEL.
28. Interview with Richard Nixon,
Dulles Oral History Project,
Princeton; Phillips, "Nixon in '58,"
p. 69; Ambrose, *Nixon,* pp. 498–
499.
29. *NYT,* October 14, 1958.
30. Nixon to Chotiner, September 22,
1958, Nixon Pre-Presidential Papers,
Box 147, NARA-LA.
31. Telephone call, Rose Mary Woods to
Meade Alcorn, n.d., Whitman File,
Administration Series, Box 1,
DDEL; Robert Wood to Orville J.
Evans, June 7, 1957, and Nixon to
Robert Finch, June 28, 1957, Nixon
Pre-Presidential Papers, Series 320,
Box 259, NARA-LA.
32. Dictated message from Nixon to
Loie Gaunt, October 20, 1958,
Nixon General Correspondence,
Series 320, Box 622, NARA-LA.
33. Phillips, "Nixon in '58," pp. 68–69;
Congress and the Nation, 1945–1964,
p. 29; *NYT,* October 7 and
November 27, 1958.
34. *NYT,* October 21 and 23, 1958. In
his news conference right after the
election, Eisenhower refused to
retract his use of the word *radical,*
claimed he did not know who
devised the campaign strategy, and
vowed to carry out the fight against
their excessive spending proposals.
Public Papers: Eisenhower, 1958, pp.
827–828, 832.
35. *NYT,* October 15 and 24, 1958; Vice
President's Basic Speech, September
29, 1958, Nixon Pre-Presidential
Papers, DDEL.
36. *Life,* October 27, 1958, p. 38.
37. *NYT,* October 14, 1958; *Newsweek,*
October 6, 1958, p. 22.
38. Shannon, "Eisenhower as President,"
p. 390; Childs, *Eisenhower,* p. 292.
39. Gallup, *Gallup Poll,* v. 2, pp. 1570,
1571; *NYT,* October 12 and 14, 1958;
Newsweek, October 6, 1958, p. 22.
40. Gallup, *Gallup Poll,* v. 2, p. 1569.
41. Telephone Call from the Vice
President, September 25, 1958,
Dulles Papers, Telephone Calls
Series, DDEL; Telephone Call for
Arthur Dean, September 25, 1958;
Telephone Calls Series, DDEL.
42. Interview with Richard Nixon,

Dulles Oral History Project,
Princeton.
43. Chang, "To the Nuclear Brink," pp.
96–112; John J. McCloy to John
Foster Dulles, September 27, 1958,
Dulles Papers, Subject File, Box 6,
DDEL.
44. Dwight D. Eisenhower, *Waging
Peace,* p. 293; Divine, *Eisenhower and
the Cold War,* p. 66; Memorandum of
Telephone Conversation, August 18,
1955, Dulles Papers, Telephone
Calls Series, Box 4, DDEL.
45. Hoopes, *Devil and John Foster Dulles,*
p. 450; Divine, *Eisenhower and the
Cold War,* p. 56; Gerson, *Dulles,* p.
205; Goold-Adams, *Time of Power,* p.
287; Notes of Cabinet Meeting,
February 18, 1955, Ann Whitman
File, Cabinet Series, Box 4, DDEL.
46. Dwight D. Eisenhower, *Waging
Peace,* p. 304.
47. Hoopes, *Devil and John Foster Dulles,*
pp. 446, 451–452; Divine, *Eisenhower
and the Cold War,* p. 68; Phillips,
"Nixon in '58," pp. 69, 72.
48. Memorandum of Conversation,
September 23, 1958, Dulles Papers,
Telephone Calls Series, Box 9,
DDEL; Dulles Papers, Telephone
Calls Series, October 7, 1958,
DDEL.
49. *Kansas City Star,* September 15,
1958; Eisenhower to Dulles,
September 30, 1958, DDEL; Rod
O'Connor to Livingston Merchant,
April 9, 1955, Dulles Papers, Special
Assistants' Chronological Series, Box
7, DDEL; Gerson, *Dulles,* p. 202.
50. Dwight D. Eisenhower, *Waging
Peace,* p. 295.
51. *Fairbanks Daily News–Miner,*
November 3, 1958.
52. Charles McWhorter to Nixon,
November 20, 1957, Nixon Pre-
Presidential Papers, Series 320, Box
259, NARA-LA.
53. Meade Alcorn to Eisenhower,
December 15, 1958, and Charles
McWhorter to Nixon, November 23,
1958, Nixon Pre-Presidential Papers,
Series 320, Box 25, NARA-LA;
Dulles call to Nixon, November 5,
1958, Dulles Papers, Telephone
Calls Series, Box 9, DDEL; Nixon to
Barry Goldwater, December 30,
1958, Nixon Pre-Presidential Papers,
Series 320, Box 293, NARA-LA;
Goldwater to Nixon, December 16,

1958, Nixon Pre-Presidential Papers, Box 293, NARA-LA.

54. Nixon to Sheldon Glueck, December 16, 1958, Nixon Pre-Presidential Papers, Box 52, NARA-LA; *LAT,* April 11, 1988.

55. *NYT,* November 10, 1958.

56. John Bricker to Nixon, November 20, 1958, Nixon Pre-Presidential Papers, Series 320, Box 102, NARA-LA; Clarence B. Kelland to Meade Alcorn, November 15, 1958, Nixon Pre-Presidential Papers, Series 320, Box 402, NARA-LA.

57. Nixon to Fred Clark, January 2, 1959, Nixon Pre-Presidential Papers, Series 320, Box 643, NARA-LA.

58. Rockefeller Panel Reports, *Prospect for America,* pp. xxiv–xxvi; cf. Jessup, *National Purpose.*

59. Republican Committee on Programs and Progress, *Decisions for a Better America,* pp. 13–14, 190.

60. Jeffries, " 'Quest for National Purpose,' " pp. 457, 459.

61. Rockefeller Panel Reports, *Prospect for America,* pp. 401, 405, 409; American Assembly of Columbia University, *Goals for Americans,* p. 4.

62. Jessup, *National Purpose,* pp. 38, 127.

63. The entire essay has been reprinted in Jessup, *Ideas of Henry Luce,* pp. 106–120.

64. Gallup, *Gallup Poll,* v. 3, p. 1600.

65. Kennedy, "We Must Climb to the Hilltop," pp. 70B, 72, 75, 76.

66. Nixon, "Our Resolve Is Running Strong," pp. 87, 88, 93, 94.

67. Kennedy, *Strategy of Peace,* pp. 200–202.

68. Nixon to Henry Luce, September 23, 1958, Nixon Pre-Presidential Papers, Series 320, Box 464, NARA-LA.

69. Jeffries, " 'Quest for National Purpose,' " p. 460.

70. *NYT,* November 10, 1960; Nixon has indicated that a shift of one-half vote per precinct would have changed the result. Nixon, *RN,* p. 224; Bradlee, *Conversations with Kennedy,* p. 33; Nixon, *Six Crises,* pp.

412–413; Earl Mazo, interviewed by Ed Edwin, 1971, Columbia University, Oral History Research Office; Peirce, *People's President,* pp. 103–104.

71. Matusow, *Unraveling of America,* p. 26.

72. Memorandum, "Operation Security," Seaton Papers, Box 10, DDEL; Theodore H. White, *Breach of Faith,* p. 71; Kallina, "Was the 1960 Presidential Election Stolen?," pp. 113–118.

73. Lasky, *It Didn't Start with Watergate,* p. 51; Nixon, *Six Crises,* p. 413; Ambrose, *Eisenhower,* p. 604; Earl Mazo, interviewed by Ed Edwin, 1971, Columbia University, Oral History Research Office; Nixon, *RN,* p. 224.

74. Mazo and Hess, *Richard Nixon,* pp. 245–248; Lasky, *It Didn't Start With Watergate,* p. 49; Kevin McCann to Walter Williams, January 23, 1964, Nixon Pre-Presidential Papers, Series 238, Box 25, NARA-LA.

75. Colby, *Honorable Men,* p. 323; Lukas, *Nightmare,* pp. 38–39; Thomas Powers, *Man Who Kept the Secrets,* p. 330.

76. Memorandum, "Operation Integrity," Seaton Papers, Post-Presidency Series, Box 10, DDEL; Lukas, *Nightmare,* p. 107.

77. Ellis, *Short History of New York State,* p. 365; *NYT,* April 19, 1961.

78. Ann Whitman notes, November 9, 1960, Whitman File, DDE Diary Series, Box 54, DDEL; RNC Papers, NARA-Wash., in Leuchtenburg and Kesaris, *Papers,* Part II, reel 2; Nixon, *RN,* p. 214.

79. Nixon, *Six Crises,* pp. 418–419.

80. *WSJ,* July 22, 1964.

81. Paul T. David, *Presidential Election and Transition,* p. 166; Sundquist, *Politics and Policy,* p. 34.

82. Claude Robinson to Nixon, Leonard Hall, and Robert Finch, November 15, 1960, Nixon Pre-Presidential Papers, Series 320, Box 646, NARA-LA.

Chapter 13. Does It Make a Difference?

1. Sevareid, *Candidates 1960,* p. 10.

2. Ibid., pp. 3, 10, 11.

3. Quoted in Arthur Schlesinger, Jr., *Thousand Days,* pp. 64–65.

4. Arthur Schlesinger, Jr., *Kennedy or Nixon,* pp. 2, 3, 4, 5, 8, 18.

5. Agnes Meyer to Adlai Stevenson, August 10, 1960, Stevenson Papers, Box 795, Princeton; Arthur Schlesinger, Jr., to John F. Kennedy, August 30, 1960, Stevenson Papers, Box 798, Princeton; Arthur M.

Schlesinger, Jr., *Shape of National Politics to Come,* p. 17.

6. Alsop, *Nixon and Rockefeller,* pp. 34, 36.

7. Strong, *Our Country,* p. 42.

8. Meade Alcorn to Nixon, February 20, 1959, Nixon Pre-Presidential Papers, Series 320, Box 25, NARA-LA.

9. Ibid.; Connery and Benjamin, *Rockefeller of New York,* pp. 61–62; Sevareid, *Candidates 1960,* p. 51.

10. Kramer and Roberts, "*I Never Wanted to Be Vice-President of Anything!,*" p. 213.

11. William Loeb to Robert Finch, October 22, 1959, Nixon General Correspondence, Series 320, Box 458, NARA-LA.

12. Scott, *Come to the Party,* p. 162; Alsop, *Nixon and Rockefeller,* pp. 9, 37.

13. Wills, *Nixon Agonistes,* p. 241.

14. Collier and Horowitz, *Rockefellers,* p. 462; *Newsweek,* November 14, 1960, p. EE-10; Alsop, *Nixon and Rockefeller,* pp. 170, 178.

15. Nixon and Rockefeller Comparison on Issues, n.d., Nixon Pre-Presidential Papers, Series 320, Box 650, NARA-LA.

16. Parmet, *JFK,* p. 198; Wills, *Nixon Agonistes,* p. 214; Epstein, *Agency of Fear,* pp. 38, 270–271; Connery and Benjamin, *Rockefeller of New York,* pp. 267–269.

17. Persico, *Imperial Rockefeller,* pp. 142, 145.

18. Ibid., pp. 34–36.

19. Kramer and Roberts, "*I Never Wanted . . .,*" p. 14.

20. Persico, *Imperial Rockefeller,* pp. 16, 140–141; Sevareid, *Candidates 1960,* p. 49.

21. Robert Finch to Nixon, March 23, 1959, Nixon General Correspondence, Box 509, NARA-LA; Alsop, *Nixon and Rockefeller,* p. 167.

22. Charles McWhorter to Nixon, February 2, 1959, Nixon Pre-Presidential Papers, Series 320, Box 464, NARA-LA; Alsop, *Nixon and Rockefeller,* pp. 43, 109; Gallup, *Gallup Poll,* v. 3, p. 1588; Louis J. Taber to Fred J. Clark, February 13, 1959, Nixon Pre-Presidential Papers, Series 320, Box 155, NARA-LA; *Washington Star,* February 15, 1959.

23. Reinhard, *Republican Right,* pp. 150–151; *NYT,* January 24, 1959; Evans and Novak, *Lyndon B. Johnson,* p. 204.

24. Interview with Meade Alcorn, April 18, 1984; *NYT,* March 12, April 17 and 18, 1959.

25. Gallup, *Gallup Poll,* v. 3, p. 1588.

26. Nixon to Leonard Hall, November 2, 1959, and Nixon to Herbert Klein, November 2, 1959, Nixon General Correspondence, Series 320, Box 509, NARA-LA; Charles McWhorter to Robert Finch, March 24, 1959, Nixon Pre-Presidential Papers, Series 320, Box 400, NARA-LA.

27. Charles McWhorter to Nixon, March 28, 1959, Nixon Pre-Presidential Papers, Series 320, Box 320, NARA-LA; *NYT,* April 11, 1959; Pat Hillings to Robert Finch, June 11, 1959, Nixon Pre-Presidential Papers, Series 320, Box 341, NARA-LA; William Loeb to Herbert Klein, June 24, 1959, Nixon General Correspondence, Series 320, Box 458, NARA-LA.

28. Memorandum of Conversation, Nixon and John Foster Dulles, May 2, 1959, DDEL; Leonard Hall to Nixon, September 3, 1959, Nixon Pre-Presidential Papers, Series 238, Box 4, NARA-LA; Alsop, *Nixon and Rockefeller,* p. 87.

29. Memo dictated after conversation with Elmer Bobst, August 19, 1959, Nixon Pre-Inaugural Papers, Series 238, Box 4, NARA-LA; Walter Annenberg to Nixon, November 16, 1959, Nixon Non-Deeded Papers, NARA-LA; Charles McWhorter to Nixon, August 27, 1959, Nixon General Correspondence, Box 636, NARA-LA; William Loeb to Herb Klein, October 14, 1959, Nixon General Correspondence, Series 320, Box 458, NARA-LA.

30. National Review Forum, New York City, December 3, 1959. Remarks placed in the *Congressional Record* of February 25, 1960, by Robert Michel and contained with the Nixon collection of magazine and newspaper articles, Box 16, NARA-LA.

31. Clarence Budington Kelland to Nixon, April 1, 1960, and Rose Mary Woods to Robert Finch, May

6, 1960, Nixon Pre-Presidential Papers, Series 320, Box 402, NARA-LA; *Dallas Morning News,* April 7, 1960.

32. *WSJ,* January 4, 1960; *WP,* January 13, 1960; Arthur Krock, notes on conversation with Vice President Nixon, May 3, 1960, Krock Papers, Box 1, Folder 336, Princeton.

33. Transcript, "Open End," May 15, 1960; *NYT,* April 24, 1960; Nixon to Clarence Budington Kelland, May 10, 1960, Nixon Pre-Presidential Papers, Box 402, NARA-LA; *Newsweek,* May 16, 1960, p. 120; Moley to Nixon, July 4, 1960, Nixon General Correspondence, Series 320, Box 524, NARA-LA.

34. Richard Nixon, "Summary of Conversation Between the Vice President and Fidel Castro," April 19, 1959, enclosed with letter from John Taylor to the author, September 24, 1987.

35. Ibid.

36. O'Neill, *Coming Apart,* pp. 276n-277n; Miller and Nowak, *Fifties,* p. 396; Matusow, *Unraveling of America,* p. 310.

37. Excerpt of responses by Nixon to questions from newsmen, Station KQED, San Francisco, February 19, 1960, Nixon Pre-Presidential Papers, Box 144, NARA-LA; Brodie, *Richard Nixon,* p. 453.

38. Interview with Pat Brown, January 22, 1985; Klein, *Making It Perfectly Clear,* p. 64.

39. Nixon, *Six Crises,* p. 303; *Commonweal,* August 14, 1959, pp. 411–412.

40. Nixon to Henry Cabot Lodge, December 15, 1959, Nixon General Correspondence, Series 320, Box 457, NARA-LA; Nixon to Richard E. Berlin, September 10, 1959, Nixon Pre-Presidential Papers, Series 238, Box 78, NARA-LA.

41. Rusher, *Rise of the Right,* p. 77; John McCone to Nixon, August 31, 1959, Nixon General Correspondence, Series 320, Box 493, NARA-LA; Nixon to Richard E. Berlin, September 10, 1959, Nixon Pre-Presidential Papers, Series 238, Box 78, NARA-LA.

42. Gallup, *Gallup Poll,* v. 3, pp. 1629, 1631, 1645; Margaret Chase Smith to Nixon and Rockefeller, December

18, 1959, Nixon General Correspondence, Series 320, Box 707, NARA-LA.

43. Allan Oakley Hunter to Nixon, December 21, 1959, Nixon Pre-Presidential Papers, Series 320, Box 702, NARA-LA.

44. Theodore H. White, *Making of the President 1960,* p. 76; Alsop, *Nixon and Rockefeller,* pp. 161–162.

45. Gallup, *Gallup Poll,* v. 3, pp. 1647–1648; Claude Robinson to Nixon, December 31, 1959, Nixon Pre-Presidential Papers, Series 320, Box 646, NARA-LA; Nixon to Walter Annenberg, December 30, 1959, Nixon Non-Deeded Papers, NARA-LA.

46. Charles McWhorter to Nixon, April 13, 1960, Nixon Pre-Presidential Papers, Box 418, NARA-LA.

47. RNC Papers, NARA-Wash., in Leuchtenburg and Kesaris, *Papers,* Part I, reel 1.

48. *NYT,* April 17, 1959; Wright, *In the New World,* pp. 18, 26; *Dallas Morning News,* April 7, 1960; John Bricker to Nixon, May 24, 1960, Nixon Pre-Presidential Papers, Box 102, NARA-LA; Buckley, *Up from Liberalism,* p. ix.

49. Gallup, *Gallup Poll,* v. 3, p. 1651; *Newsweek,* November 14, 1960, p. EE-9; Nash, *Conservative Intellectual Movement,* pp. 207, 291.

50. Correspondence included in letter from John McCone to Nixon, August 31, 1959, Nixon General Correspondence, Series 320, Box 493, NARA-LA; Memorandum, "Political Behavior Report: Public Opinion, Richard Nixon, and U-2," n.d., Robert F. Kennedy Papers, Box 2, JFKL.

51. *NYT,* February 19, 1960.

52. *Syracuse Herald-Journal,* June 29, 1960.

53. Garrow, *Bearing the Cross,* p. 118; Tygiel, *Baseball's Great Experiment,* p. 340.

54. Charles McWhorter to Nixon, March 28, 1959, Nixon Vice-Presidential Papers, Series 320, Box 320, NARA-LA; transcript, "Face the Nation," April 19, 1959.

55. Eisenhower to Nixon, August 18, 1959, Whitman File, Administration Series, Box 28, DDEL; *NYT,* July 7, 1960; Ambrose, *Eisenhower,* p.

598; Goldwater, *With No Apologies,*
pp. 102–103; Eisenhower to
Tex McCrary, March 25, 1960,
DDEL; Gallup, *Gallup Poll,* v. 3,
p. 1672.

56. *NYT,* March 7, April 17, 1960;
Gallup, *Gallup Poll,* v. 3, p. 1657;
Raymond Moley, *Newsweek,* May 2,
1960, p. 95; Nixon to Moley, April
9, 1960, Nixon Pre-Presidential
Papers, Series 320, Box 524, NARA-
LA.

57. Nixon to Maurice Stans, April 25,
1960, Nixon Non-Deeded Papers,
Country File, Series 320, Box 1,
NARA-LA.

58. *NYT,* January 27 and 28, 1960.

59. Eisenhower to Tex McCrary, March
25, 1960, DDEL.

60. Ambrose, *Nixon,* p. 547; Arthur
Burns to Nixon, July 20, 1960,
Nixon Pre-Presidential Papers,
Series 238, Box 5, NARA-LA;
Theodore H. White, *Making of the
President 1960,* p. 181.

61. Theodore H. White, *Making of the
President 1960,* pp. 183–184; Kramer
and Roberts, "*I Never Wanted . . .,*"
pp. 228–229.

62. Nixon, *Challenges We Face,* passim;
NYT, June 10, 1960.

63. Theodore H. White, *Making of the
President 1960,* p. 192.

64. Reinhard, *Republican Right,* pp. 153–
154; Goldwater, *With No Apologies,* p.
112; Rusher, *Rise of the Right,* p. 88;
Persico, *Imperial Rockefeller,* p. 41.

65. Mazo and Hess, *Richard Nixon,* p.
227.

66. Nixon, *Six Crises,* p. 314; Nixon, *RN,*
p. 215.

67. Kramer and Roberts, "*I Never
Wanted . . .,*" pp. 232–233; Nixon,
Six Crises, p. 315.

68. Mazo and Hess, *Richard Nixon,* p.
227; Theodore H. White, *Making of
the President 1960,* p. 202; Nixon, *Six
Crises,* p. 315; Ambrose, *Nixon,* p.
552.

69. *NYT,* July 22, 1960.

70. First Draft of Civil Rights Plank,
William P. Rogers Papers, DDEL.

71. *NYT,* July 25, 1960.

72. Ibid., July 25 and 26, 1960.

73. Ibid., July 31, 1960.

74. Theodore H. White, *Making of the
President 1960,* p. 204.

75. Parmet, *JFK,* p. 177.

76. Sagan, "SIOP-62," v. 12, pp. 22–40.

77. *Newsweek,* November 14, 1960, p.
EE-9.

78. Interview with Julie Nixon
Eisenhower, January 21, 1986.

79. Judith Wingert Loubet, interviewed
by Harry P. Jeffrey, June 1, 1970,
OH-900, CSU-F; interview with
John D. Ehrlichman, June 17, 1985.
There are numerous examples of
individuals who have gone to
extraordinary lengths to exploit such
influences. The case of Ronald
Reagan's long-term friend and aide,
Michael Deaver, is only the most
recent.

80. Abrahamsen, *Nixon vs. Nixon,* p. 180.

81. Interview with Charles G. Rebozo,
June 4, 1985; Abrahamsen, *Nixon vs.
Nixon,* p. 180.

82. Lukas, *Nightmare,* p. 363.

83. Witcover, *Resurrection of Nixon,* p. 38;
Drosnin, *Citizen Hughes,* p. 301.

84. Lukas, *Nightmare,* p. 366; interview
with Charles G. Rebozo, June 4,
1985.

85. Nixon, *RN,* p. 964; Drosnin, *Citizen
Hughes,* p. 284.

86. Ehrlichman, *Witness to Power,* p. 61;
Cooney, *Annenbergs,* pp. 18–22.

87. Cooney, *Annenbergs,* pp. 14, 319.

88. Ibid., p. 14; interview with Walter
Annenberg, June 9, 1986.

89. Garment, "*Hill Case,*" p. 95;
interview with Charles G. Rebozo,
June 4, 1985; Elmer Bobst to Nixon,
May 25, 1954, Nixon Pre-
Presidential Papers, Box 90, NARA-
LA; interview with Robert H.
Abplanalp, March 21, 1985;
Mankiewicz, *Perfectly Clear,* p. 19.

90. Alexander, *Financing Politics,* p. 62.

91. Heiman, "How Don Kendall Put
New Pep in Pepsi," pp. 65–71.

92. Nixon to H. R. Haldeman, May 18,
1972, President's Personal File, Box
4, NPMP; interview with Donald
Kendall, October 24, 1985.

93. Stans, *Terrors of Justice,* pp. 135–136.

94. Heiman, "How Don Kendall Put
New Pep in Pepsi," p. 66; Donald M.
Kendall to Lyndon B. Johnson, May
4, 1965, Nixon Pre-Presidential
Papers, Series 238, Box 20, NARA-
LA.

95. Interview with Donald Kendall,
October 24, 1985.

96. Ibid.

97. Ibid., Donald M. Kendall to Charles
F. Willis, April 29, 1959, Nixon Pre-

Presidential Papers, Series 320, Box 404, NARA-LA.
98. *NYT*, January 17, 1970.
99. Interview with Donald Kendall, October 24, 1985; George Champion to Nixon, June 21, 1972, President's Personal File, Box 188, NPMP.
100. Donald Kendall to Nixon, April 26, 1961, Nixon Pre-Presidential Papers, Series 238, Box 20, NARA-LA; Ambrose, *Nixon*, p. 626.
101. Interview with Donald Kendall, October 24, 1985.

102. Interview with Robert Abplanalp, March 21, 1985; interview with John Connally, May 19, 1986; interview with Richard M. Nixon, November 16, 1988.
103. Interview with Robert Abplanalp, March 21, 1985.
104. Ibid.
105. Ibid., Lukas, *Nightmare*, p. 348.
106. Interview with Robert Abplanalp, March 21, 1985; Nixon, *RN*, p. 625.
107. Nixon, *RN*, p. 625.
108. Interview with Robert Abplanalp, March 21, 1985.

Chapter 14. A TWO-TIME LOSER

1. Phelan, *Howard Hughes*, p. xii.
2. Phelan, "Nixon Family and the Hughes Loan," p. 22.
3. *NYT*, April 6, 1976; Drosnin, *Citizen Hughes*, pp. 39, 53. Except for one Roman Catholic, his aides were also Mormons. Hughes had learned to appreciate their rejection of tobacco and alcohol.
4. *NYT*, April 7, 1976.
5. Phelan, *Howard Hughes*, p. x.
6. Lukas, *Nightmare*, p. 113; Drosnin, *Citizen Hughes*, pp. 48, 103–129; *NYT*, April 6 and May 12, 1976.
7. Price, *With Nixon*, p. 362; Drosnin, *Citizen Hughes*, p. 21.
8. Drosnin, *Citizen Hughes*, p. 42; Dietrich, *Howard*, pp. 10–11.
9. Alfred M. Landon to Nixon, March 12, 1964, and Nixon to Landon, April 20, 1964, Landon folder, Nixon Pre-Presidential Papers, NARA-LA.
10. CSU-F interviews: Sheldon Beeson, interviewed by Mitch Haddad, April 23, 1970, OH-809; William A. Milhous, interviewed by Mitch Haddad, June 25, 1970, OH-912; Herman Brannon, interviewed by Mitch Haddad, April 15, 1970, OH-818; William H. Barton, interviewed by Richard D. Curtiss, February 10, 1970, OH-807; Mr. and Mrs. Herman Brannon, interviewed by Mitch Haddad, April 15, 1970, OH-818; Theodore F. Marshburn interviewed by John Donnelly, December 31, 1969, OH-903; Harold A. McCabe, interviewed by Steve Prantalos, April 10, 1970, OH-962; Floyd Wildermuth, interviewed by Glenn Barnett, May 6, 1970, OH-983; Ehrlichman, *Witness to Power*, p.

171; interview with Richard M. Nixon, November 16, 1988; Lukas, *Nightmare*, p. 178.
11. Personal Statement of Donald Nixon, October 1960, DDEL.
12. Interview with Richard M. Nixon, November 16, 1988.
13. Dietrich, *Hughes*, p. 282.
14. Interview with Richard M. Nixon, November 16, 1988.
15. Anderson with Boyd, *Confessions of a Muckraker*, pp. 329, 331–332; Phelan, "Nixon Family and the Hughes Loan," p. 22; interview with Richard M. Nixon, November 16, 1988; Nixon, *Six Crises*, p. 398; Drosnin, *Citizen Hughes*, pp. 298–299.
16. Drosnin, *Citizen Hughes*, pp. 359–360; interview with Richard M. Nixon, November 16, 1988.
17. Interview with Richard M. Nixon, November 16, 1988.
18. *NYT*, November 13, 1960.
19. Anderson, *Confessions of a Muckraker*, pp. 330–332; Phelan, "Nixon Family and the Hughes Loan," p. 26.
20. Phelan, "Nixon Family and the Hughes Loan," p. 26; Personal Statement of Donald Nixon, October 1960, DDEL.
21. *NYT*, January 24, 1972.
22. Interview with Charles G. Rebozo, June 4, 1985; Nixon, *RN*, p. 243.
23. Nixon, *Six Crises*, p. 398.
24. Ambrose, *Nixon*, pp. 663–664; *NYT*, November 6, 1962.
25. Morgan, "Nixon's New Frontier," p. 91; notes by Arthur Krock on conversation with John F. Kennedy, December 31, 1962, Papers of Arthur Krock, Black Notebook III, Box 1, Princeton.

26. Caspar Weinberger, interviewed by Gabrielle Morris, March 29, 1979, Bancroft Library; Witcover, *Resurrection of Richard Nixon*, p. 32; interview with Julie Nixon Eisenhower, January 21, 1986.

27. Bryce Harlow telephone call to Rose Mary Woods, January 2, 1963, Nixon Pre-Presidential Papers, Series 320, Box 320, NARA-LA.

28. Raymond Moley to Nixon, December 14 and 15, 1960, Nixon Pre-Presidential Papers, Series 320, Box 524, NARA-LA.

29. Nixon to Raymond Moley, January 18, 1961, Nixon Pre-Presidential Papers, Series 320, Box 524, NARA-LA.

30. Robert D. Novak, *Agony of the GOP*, pp. 24, 49.

31. Interview with Stephen Hess, March 30, 1988.

32. Bryce Harlow to Nixon, March 6, 1961, Nixon Pre-Presidential Papers, Series 238, Box 15, NARA-LA; interviews with Stephen Hess, November 29, 1984, and March 30, 1988.

33. Klein, *Making It Perfectly Clear*, p. 47.

34. Mazo and Hess, *Richard Nixon*, p. 261; Caspar Weinberger, interviewed by Gabrielle Morris, March 29, 1979, Bancroft Library.

35. Nixon, "Lessons of the Hiss Case."

36. Whittaker Chambers to Nixon, February 2, 1961, Nixon Non-Deeded Materials, Box 141, NARA-LA.

37. Raymond Moley to Nixon, August 3, 1961, Nixon Pre-Presidential Papers, Series 238, Box 26, NARA-LA.

38. Raymond Moley to Nixon, August 16, 1961, Nixon Pre-Presidential Papers, Series 238, Box 26, NARA-LA; Moley to Nixon, September 19, 1961, Nixon Pre-Presidential Papers, Series 238, Box 26, NARA-LA.

39. *NYT*, October 7, 1962.

40. Herbert Klein to Nixon, June 28, 1961, Nixon Pre-Presidential Papers, Series 238, Box 416, NARA-LA.

41. Interview with H. R. Haldeman, January 25, 1985; Caspar Weinberger, interviewed by Gabrielle Morris, March 29, 1979, Bancroft Library; Claude Robinson to Nixon, July 24, 1961, Nixon Pre-Presidential Papers, Series 320, Box 646, NARA-LA; Klein, *Making It*

Perfectly Clear, p. 47; Berges, *Life and Times of Los Angeles*, p. 113; interview with Hugh Scott, June 10, 1986.

42. Transcript of Nixon Press Conference, September 27, 1961, Nixon General Correspondence, Series 320, Box 643, NARA-LA.

43. RNC Papers, NARA-Wash., in Leuchtenburg and Kesaris, *Papers*, Part I, reel 3.

44. *NYT*, June 6 and 7, 1962.

45. Ibid., March 5, June 8, and September 2, 1962.

46. Arthur Langlie to Nixon, June 13, 1961, Nixon General Correspondence, Series 320, Box 439, NARA-LA; *NYHT*, October 5, 1965; *NYT*, April 28, 1988.

47. Transcript of Nixon Press Conference, September 27, 1961, Nixon General Correspondence, Series 320, Box 643, NARA-LA.

48. Sheridan, *Fall and Rise of Jimmy Hoffa*, pp. 14, 31.

49. Ibid., pp. 31, 32; Moldea, *Hoffa Wars*, p. 58.

50. Brill, *Teamsters*, pp. 33, 364.

51. Sheridan, *Fall and Rise of Jimmy Hoffa*, p. 156; Brill, *Teamsters*, pp. 44, 210; Hougan, *Secret Agenda*, p. 89n; Allan Oakley Hunter to Nixon, December 21, 1959, Nixon Pre-Presidential Papers, Series 320, Box 702, NARA-LA.

52. Brill, *Teamsters*, p. 336; interview with Michael DiSalle, March 11, 1981; Michael DiSalle, interviewed by Ken Mack, November 24, 1964, JFKL-OH; Parmet, *Jack*, p. 505; Allan Oakley Hunter to Nixon, December 21, 1959, Nixon Pre-Presidential Papers, Series 320, Box 702, NARA-LA.

53. Allan Oakley Hunter to Nixon, December 21, 1959, Nixon Pre-Presidential Papers, Series 320, Box 702, NARA-LA; Hunter to Nixon, January 5, 1960, Nixon General Correspondence, Series 320, Box 701, NARA-LA.

54. Sheridan, *Fall and Rise of Jimmy Hoffa*, p. 157; Michael DiSalle, interviewed by Ken Mack, November 24, 1964, JFKL-OH; Drew Pearson column, *Los Angeles Mirror*, October 4, 1961.

55. *Los Angeles Mirror*, October 4, 1961. I am indebted to Alonzo Hamby for

the information on the voting in
Ohio.

56. Sheridan, *Fall and Rise of Jimmy Hoffa*, pp. 158, 165; Moldea, *Hoffa Wars*, pp. 108, 109; Arthur M. Schlesinger, Jr., *Robert Kennedy and His Times*, pp. 279–280.
57. Morgan, "Nixon's New Frontier," p. 132.
58. Ehrlichman, *Witness to Power*, p. 31; Lester David, *Lonely Lady of San Clemente*, p. 122; Witcover, *Resurrection of Nixon*, pp. 42–43; J. Edgar Hoover to Nixon, November 7, 1962, Nixon Non-Deeded Papers, Box 15, Country Files, Series 320, NARA-LA; Paul Trousdale to Nixon, November 10, 1964, Nixon Non-Deeded Papers, Series 238, Lawyer/Public Figure Correspondence, NARA-LA.
59. Transcript of Nixon Press Conference at the Statler-Hilton, Los Angeles, September 27, 1961, Nixon General Correspondence, Series 320, Box 643, NARA-LA.
60. Ibid.; Morgan, "Nixon's New Frontier," p. 131.
61. *NYT*, June 6 and November 11, 1962.
62. Epstein and Forster, *Radical Right*, pp. 143–152; Westin, "John Birch Society," pp. 261, 264, 267; Lipset and Raab, *Politics of Unreason*, p. 270; *NYT*, November 11, 1962; *Congress and the Nation, 1945–1964*, p. 80.
63. Interview with Stephen Hess, November 29, 1984; T. George Harris, "Rampant Right Invades the GOP," pp. 19–24; Robert D. Novak, *Agony of the GOP*, p. 391.
64. Transcript of remarks during question-and-answer period after Nixon's talk before the San Fernando Valley Chapter of the Los Angeles County Medical Association, February 22, 1962, Nixon General Correspondence, Series 320, Box 660, NARA-LA.
65. Interview with Pat Brown, January 22, 1985; *NYT*, June 20, 1962.
66. Nixon to Nelson Rockefeller, March 5, 1962, Nixon General Correspondence, Series 320, Box 650, NARA-LA.
67. Interview with Pat Brown, January 22, 1985.
68. Interview with Stephen Hess,

November 29, 1984; Caspar Weinberger, interviewed by Gabrielle Morris, March 29, 1979, Bancroft Library.
69. Interview with Richard M. Nixon, June 4, 1964; Robert D. Novak, *Agony of the GOP*, p. 87; RNC Papers, NARA-Wash., in Leuchtenburg and Kesaris, *Papers*, Part I, reel 3; *NYT*, November 11, and August 26, 1962; interview with Pat Brown, January 22, 1985.
70. Pat Hillings to Nixon, March 5, 1962, Nixon General Correspondence, Series 320, Box 341, NARA-LA.
71. State Senate of California, *Eleventh Report of the Senate Fact-Finding Subcommittee on Un-American Activities*, pp. 93, 99, and passim; transcript of press conference, September 18, 1962, in author's possession.
72. *NYT*, September 13 and 16, 1962.
73. Ibid., August 12, 1962; interview with H. R. Haldeman, January 25, 1985.
74. McWilliams, "Government by Whitaker and Baxter," pp. 346–348, 366–369, 418–421; Robert D. Novak, *Agony of the GOP*, p. 388.
75. Harris, *Sacred Trust*, p. 31; McWilliams, "Government by Whitaker and Baxter," p. 346.
76. Theodore H. White, *Breach of Faith*, p. 54; *NYT*, October 28, 1972; *LAT*, November 2, 1962; Klein, *Making It Perfectly Clear*, p. 63.
77. *LAT*, November 2, 1962; *NYT*, November 10, 1962, and October 28, 1972; interview with H. R. Haldeman, January 25, 1985; Klein, *Perfectly Clear*, p. 63.
78. Interview with Julie Nixon Eisenhower, January 21, 1986.
79. Transcript of press conference, September 18, 1962, in author's possession; *LAT*, October 23, 1962; transcript of Nixon Television Talk, October 27, 1962, Nixon Appearance Files, Series 207, NARA-LA; transcript of television speech by Ronald Reagan, November 4, 1962, Nixon General Correspondence, Series 320, Box 621, NARA-LA; *NYT*, November 6, 1962.
80. Ambrose, *Nixon*, p. 668; Nixon, *RN*, p. 226; Weinstein, *Perjury*, p. 531; Klein, *Making it Perfectly Clear*, p. 47.

81. Interview with Herbert Klein, January 24, 1985.

82. Klein, *Making It Perfectly Clear,* pp. 55-57; Ehrlichman, *Witness to Power,* pp. 33–34; interview with Herbert Klein, January 24, 1985; interview with Pat Hillings, July 10, 1985; Ambrose, *Nixon,* p. 671.

83. *LAT,* November 4, 1962; Klein, *Making It Perfectly Clear,* p. 58.

84. H. R. Haldeman to James J. Dunn, March 11, 1963, Nixon Pre-Presidential Papers, Series 320, Box 311, NARA-LA; Nixon to William Paley, August 20, 1962, Nixon General Correspondence, Series 320, Box 577, NARA-LA; Elmo Rober to Robert H. Finch, September 18, 1962, Nixon General Correspondence, Series 320, Box 577, NARA-LA.

85. Cf. Klein and Maccoby, "Newspaper Objectivity in the 1952 Campaign," pp. 285–296; Blumberg, *One Party Press?*; Efron, *News Twisters;* Edward Jay Epstein, *News From Nowhere;* Gitlin, *Whole World Is Watching;* Hallin, " 'Uncensored War' "; James Keogh, *President Nixon and the Press;* Klein, *Making It Perfectly Clear.*

86. Nixon, *Six Crises,* p. 397; Nixon to Richard E. Berlin, January 3, 1961, Nixon Pre-Presidential Papers, Box 78, NARA-LA; William H. G. FitzGerald to Hugh Scott, October 21, 1960, Robert Merriam Papers, DDEL.

87. *New Rochelle* (New York) *Standard-Star,* November 7, 1960; Baughman, *Henry R. Luce,* p. 183; interview with Richard M. Nixon, June 8, 1984; Cf. Efron, *News Twisters;* Henry C. Cashen III to Bruce Kehrli, November 5, 1971, Haldeman Papers, Box 123, NPMP.

88. Blumberg, *One Party Press?,* pp. 31, 45; cited in Deakin, *Straight Stuff,* p. 83.

89. Nixon to Richard E. Berlin, January 3, 1961, Nixon General Correspondence, Series 320, Box 78, NARA-LA.

90. Theodore H. White, *Making of the President 1960,* p. 336; Nixon, *Six Crises,* p. 397.

91. *NYT,* July 28, 1960; de Toledano, *One Man Alone,* pp. 221–223.

92. Theodore H. White, *Making of the President 1960,* pp. 336–337.

93. Peter Lisagor, interviewed by Ronald J. Grele, April 22, 1966, JFKL-OH; Robert D. Novak, *Agony of the GOP,* p. 8; John Ehrlichman to Nixon, April 6, 1961, Nixon Pre-Presidential Papers, Box 236, NARA-LA; Theodore H. White, *Making of the President 1960,* p. 337; Parmet, *JFK,* pp. 302–303.

94. *NYT,* July 28, 1960; Nixon to Fred Seaton, October 25, 1960, Seaton Papers, 1960 Campaign Series, Box 2, DDEL; Nixon, *Six Crises,* p. 397; Safire, *Before the Fall,* p. 345.

95. Matusow, *Unraveling of America,* pp. 3–4; Vigeurie, *New Right,* pp. 46, 91; Buchanan, *Conservative Votes,* p. 21.

96. Nixon to J. B. Rhine, October 31, 1957, and Nixon to Fred G. Clark, April 21, 1958, Nixon Pre-Presidential Papers, Box 228, NARA-LA; John Cowles to Nixon, May 5, 1960, Nixon Pre-Presidential Papers, Box 186, NARA-LA; Jennie M. Sessions to Robert H. Finch, April 19, 1960, Nixon Pre-Presidential Papers, Box 258, NARA-LA; *National Review,* January 31, 1959, pp. 486–488; Text of Address before the Economic Conference, Washington, November 2, 1959, Nixon Pre-Presidential Papers, Box 121, NARA-LA; Elmer H. Bobst to Nixon, January 2, 1958, Nixon Pre-Presidential Papers, Series 320, Box 90, NARA-LA.

97. Nixon to Henry Luce, September 23, 1958, Nixon Pre-Presidential Papers, Series 320, Box 464, NARA-LA; Tebbel and Watts, *Press and the Presidency,* p. 501.

98. Lichter, et al., *Media Elite,* p. 11.

99. Mills, *Power Elite,* p. 315.

100. Galbraith, *Affluent Society,* pp. 340–345; Bazelon, *Power in America,* pp. 308, 313, 318.

101. Broder, cited in Lichter, et al., *Media Elite,* p. 25.

102. Lichter, et al., *Media Elite,* chapter 2; interview with Richard M. Nixon, June 8, 1984; Safire, *Before the Fall,* pp. 353–354.

103. Wright, *In the New World,* pp. 44, 89, 124; Bazelon, *Power in America,* p. 320.

104. Mary McGrory comments in Press

Panel, interviewed by Fred Holborn, August 4, 1964, JFKL-OH.

105. Interview with Patrick J. Hillings,

July 10, 1985; interview with Julie and David Eisenhower, January 21, 1986.

Chapter 15. REVOLT OF THE RED-DIAPER BABIES

1. Interview with Julie Nixon Eisenhower, January 21, 1986.
2. Lowi, *End of Liberalism,* p. xiv.
3. Gallup, *Gallup Poll,* v. 1, p. 555.
4. Paul Johnson, *Modern Times,* p. 443; Lowi, *End of Liberalism,* p. xiii.
5. Hoffer, *True Believer,* p. 10.
6. Gitlin, *Sixties,* pp. 101–122.
7. Hayden, *Reunion,* p. 45.
8. John F. Kennedy to Ted Sorensen, February 8, 1961, Evelyn Lincoln's dictation file, Box 62, JFKL.
9. *Committee of Correspondence,* May 12, 1961, Warburg Papers, Box 42, JFKL; *NYT,* February 26, 1961, section 4, p. 5; Arthur M. Schlesinger, Jr., *Robert Kennedy and His Times,* pp. 330–335.
10. Rainwater and Yancey, *Moynihan Report,* p. 47.
11. Raymond Moley to Nixon, February 14, 1964, Nixon Pre-Presidential Papers, Non-Deeded Papers, Series 238, Lawyer/Public Figure Correspondence, NARA-LA.
12. Bernstein, "Profiles," p. 62.
13. Moynihan, "Employment, Income, and the Ordeal of the Negro Family," p. 755.
14. Ibid., p. 746; Kearns, *Lyndon Johnson,* p. 340.
15. Goldman, *Tragedy of Lyndon Johnson,* p. 257; Theodore H. White, *Making of the President 1964,* p. 257.
16. Degler, *At Odds,* p. 446.
17. *Harper's,* October 1962, pp. 117–118.
18. Chafe, *American Woman,* pp. 226, 238–39.
19. Bryce, *American Commonwealth,* v. 2, pp. 802–804.
20. Jacqueline Jones, *Labor of Love,* pp. 110–151; Fawcett and Thomas, *American Condition,* p. 87.
21. Chafe, *American Woman,* p. 217; Fawcett and Thomas, *American Condition,* p. 96; Degler, *At Odds,* pp. 499–500; Banner, *Women in Modern America,* p. 231.
22. Chafe, *American Woman,* p. 206; Degler, *At Odds,* p. 440; Fawcett and Thomas, *American Condition,* p. 86.
23. Degler, *At Odds,* p. 446; Fawcett and Thomas, *American Condition,* p. 83.

24. Chafe, *American Woman,* p. 218.
25. Degler, *At Odds,* p. 442.
26. Ibid., p. 444; Gitlin, *Sixties,* p. 367.
27. Degler, *At Odds,* p. 444.
28. Jacobs and Landau, *New Radicals,* p. 22.
29. Chang, "To the Nuclear Brink," pp. 97–98; Nixon, *RN,* pp. 234–235; *NYT,* May 10, 1961.
30. Nixon, "The Choice in Vietnam," March 15, 1965, mimeographed copy in the Vice President's File, DDEL; Nixon to Joseph Alsop, December 23, 1964, Nixon Pre-Presidential Papers, Non-Deeded Papers, NARA-LA, and *NYT,* February 17, 1985; interview with Richard M. Nixon, November 16, 1988.
31. Nixon to H. R. Haldeman, November 30, 1970, President's Personal File, Box 2, NPMP.
32. *NYT,* September 12, 14, and October 17, 1965.
33. Nixon to Joseph Alsop, December 23, 1964, Nixon Pre-Presidential Papers, Non-Deeded Papers, NARA-LA.
34. Donald Kendall to Lyndon B. Johnson, May 4, 1965, Nixon Pre-Presidential Papers, Series 238, Box 20, NARA-LA.
35. Nixon, "The Choice in Vietnam," March 15, 1965, mimeographed copy in the Vice President's File, DDEL.
36. Witcover, *Resurrection,* p. 109; Nixon to Barry Goldwater, February 10, 1965, Nixon Non-Deeded Papers, Series 238, NARA-LA; Berman, *William Fulbright,* p. 18; Julie Nixon Eisenhower, *Pat Nixon,* p. 229; Herring, *America's Longest War,* p. 141; Nixon to Robert T. Stevens, August 5, 1965, Nixon Non-Deeded Papers, Series 238, NARA-LA; Mazo and Hess, *Richard Nixon,* p. 255.
37. Ulam, *Dangerous Relations,* pp. 31–32; Cohen, *Dean Rusk,* p. 281; Parmet, *JFK,* p. 328; Chang, "JFK, China, and the Bomb," pp. 1287–1310.
38. Nixon, North American Newspaper Alliance Column, June 4, 1966, Pre-Presidential Papers, Special Name

File, 1961–1968, Box 8, DDEL; Berman, *William Fulbright,* p. 66.

39. Transcript of NBC-TV network speech from Cincinnati, Ohio, October 28, 1964, Nixon Pre-Presidential Papers, NARA-LA; Nixon to Albert Wedemeyer, March 16, 1966, Nixon Non-Deeded Papers, Series 230, Lawyer/Public Figure Correspondence, NARA-LA; Fred Panzer to Lyndon B. Johnson, September 19, 1967, White House Central File, PL, Box 2, LBJL.

40. Divine, *Exploring the Johnson Years,* p. 40.

41. Nixon to William Knowland, October 23, 1967, Nixon Non-Deeded Papers, Series 320, Lawyer/Public Figure Correspondence, NARA-LA.

42. Summers, *On Strategy,* p. 5.

43. Thomas Powers, *Vietnam,* p. 56; Matusow, *Unraveling of America,* pp. 318–319.

44. Beichman, "Study in Academic Freedom," p. 14.

45. Gitlin, *Whole World Is Watching,* pp. 89, 93, 98; Peirce, *Pacific States,* p. 69.

46. *NYT,* October 17, 26, and 27, 1965; Safire, *Before the Fall,* p. 22; Witcover, *Resurrection,* p. 118.

47. *NYT,* October 25, 27, and 29, 1965.

48. Nixon to Eisenhower, November 1, 1965, Eisenhower Post-Presidential Special Name File, 1961–1968, Box 8, DDEL; transcript, University of Rochester Commencement Address, June 5, 1966, Pre-Presidential Papers, Special Name File 1961–1968, Box 8, DDEL; Nixon to Julie Nixon, May 25, 1970, President's Personal File, Box 2, NPMP, NARA-Alexandria.

49. Statement of Richard Nixon on the Genovese Case, Morristown, New Jersey, October 24, 1965, attached to Nixon to Eisenhower, November 1, 1965, Eisenhower Post-Presidential Special Name File, 1961-1968, Box 8, DDEL.

50. Debs was later pardoned by the next Republican president, Warren Harding.

51. A convenient source for the text of Holmes's decision is Kutler, *Supreme Court and the Constitution,* pp. 328–

329; Cf. Swindler, *Court and Constitution in the 20th Century,* pp. 202–204, and Friedman, *History of American Law,* p. 578.

52. Cf. Link and Catton, *American Epoch,* v. 1, pp. 203, 321, and Preston, *Aliens and Dissenters,* passim.

53. Kelly and Harbison, *American Constitution,* pp. 906–914; Commager, *Documents of American History,* v. 2, p. 433.

54. See Chapter 4.

55. Beichman, "Study in Academic Freedom," p. 14.

56. Bruce Allen Murphy, *Fortas,* p. 230.

57. Garment, "Hill Case," pp. 94, 97.

58. Ibid.

59. Ibid., p. 98; Bruce Allen Murphy, *Fortas,* p. 230; Witcover, *Resurrection,* pp. 127–129.

60. Bruce Allen Murphy, *Fortas,* p. 232; Safire, *Before the Fall,* p. 26; Garment, "Hill Case," p. 109.

61. Unger, *Movement,* pp. 32–33; Jacobs and Landau, *New Radicals,* p. 22.

62. Unger, *Movement,* p. 34; Podhoretz, *Breaking Ranks,* p. 253; Daniel Patrick Moynihan to Richard Nixon, November 13, 1970, Box 163, Haldeman Papers, NPMP; Flacks, "Who Protests," pp. 135–143; Obear, "Student Activism in the Sixties," pp. 13, 17; Matusow, *Unraveling of America,* p. 309; Unger, *Movement,* pp. 31–32.

63. Ways, "Faculty Is the Heart of the Trouble," pp. 146–153.

64. Nixon to William Knowland, October 23, 1967, Nixon Non-Deeded Papers, Series 320, Lawyer/Public Figure Correspondence, NARA-LA; Witcover, *Resurrection,* p. 297.

65. Lou Harris, *Anguish of Change,* pp. 66–67, 70, 140–141; Robert G. Spivack, "Roving Reporter, Trip to New Hampshire," Marvin Watson file, Box 11, LBJL; Fred Panzer to Marvin Watson, Marvin Watson file, Box 11, LBJL; Converse, et al., "Continuity and Change in American Politics," pp. 1083–1105.

66. Interview with Norman Podhoretz, October 23, 1984.

67. Rusher, *Rise of the Right,* p. 328.

Chapter 16. MEN ON HORSEBACK

1. Thomas H. Kuchel to Nixon, December 12, 1962, Nixon General Correspondence, Series 320, Box 430, NARA-LA; H. L. Hunt to Nixon, January 24, 1963, Nixon Pre-Presidential Papers, Box 362, NARA-LA; Julie Nixon Eisenhower, *Pat Nixon,* p. 221; Nixon to Victor Lasky, December 22, 1964, Nixon Pre-Presidential Papers, Non-Deeded Papers, Series 238, Lawyer/Public Figure Correspondence, NARA-LA; interview with Richard M. Nixon, June 4, 1984.

2. Interview with Julie Nixon Eisenhower, January 21, 1986.

3. Kevin McCann to Walter Williams, January 23, 1964, Nixon Pre-Presidential Papers, Series 238, Box 25, NARA-LA.

4. Rose Mary Woods to Len Hall, November 13, 1963, and Hall to Woods, November 15, 1963, Nixon Non-Deeded Papers, Series 238, Lawyer/Public Figure Correspondence, NARA-LA.

5. Herbert Klein to Nixon, June 28, 1961, Nixon Pre-Presidential Papers, Box 416, NARA-LA; Len Hall to Nixon, September 29, 1961, Nixon Pre-Presidential Papers, Box 313, NARA-LA.

6. Nixon to John Bricker, March 11, 1963, Nixon Pre-Presidential Papers, Non-Deeded Papers, March 11, 1963, NARA-LA; Nixon to H. R. Haldeman, November 30, 1970, President's Personal File, Box 2, NPMP.

7. Nixon to Bryce Harlow, April 8, 1963, Nixon Pre-Presidential Papers, Box 320, NARA-LA.

8. Witcover, *Resurrection,* p. 48; *NYT,* April 21, 1963.

9. *NYT,* April 21, 1963.

10. Ibid.

11. Nixon to William R. Kintner, May 6, 1963, Nixon Papers, Box 320, NARA-LA; Nixon to William Knowland, October 16, 1963, Nixon Pre-Presidential Papers, Non-Deeded Papers, Series 230, Lawyer/Public Figure Correspondence, NARA-LA; Witcover, *Resurrection,* p. 57; Nixon to Karl Mundt, November 4, 1963, Nixon Pre-Presidential Papers, Non-Deeded Papers, Series 238, Lawyer/Public Figure Correspondence, NARA-LA; Nixon to Robert Humphreys, November 7, 1963, Nixon Pre-Presidential Papers, Non-Deeded Papers, NARA-LA.

12. Gallup, *Gallup Poll,* v. 3, pp. 1848, 1852; Parmet, *JFK,* p. 272.

13. Hess and Broder, Republican Establishment, p. 167; Gallup, *Gallup Poll,* v. 3, p. 1864; Witcover, *Resurrection,* p. 70; Fred A. Seaton to Nixon, January 31, 1964, Seaton Papers, Post-Presidency Series, Box 8, DDEL.

14. H. L. Hunt advised Nixon that he had weakened himself by supporting Eisenhower "tolerance of Communism." H. L. Hunt to Nixon, January 24, 1963, Nixon Pre-Presidential Papers, Box 362, NARA-LA.

15. Nash, *Conservative Intellectual Movement,* p. 69.

16. Reinhard, *Republican Right,* pp. 172–173.

17. Rusher, *Rise of the Right,* pp. 97–101, 137; Nash, *Conservative Intellectual Movement,* p. 292; Richard G. Kleindienst to Nixon, May 12, 1961, Nixon Pre-Presidential Papers, Series 320, Box 418, NARA-LA; *National Review,* February 12, 1963, p. 109.

18. Phillips, *Post-Conservative America,* p. 190; Crawford, *Thunder on the Right,* p. 6; Buchanan, *Conservative Votes,* p. 17.

19. Interview with William Rusher, October 2, 1984.

20. The *National Review,* for example, repudiated the John Birch Society as a disservice to the anticommunist cause and later backed the Panama Canal treaty during the Carter administration.

21. *National Review,* May 28, 1976, p. 566; Rusher, *Rise of the Right,* p. 101.

22. Nixon to Walter Annenberg, September 16, 1963, Nixon Pre-Presidential Papers, Non-Deeded Papers, NARA-LA.

23. Nixon to Victor Lasky, September 25, 1963, Nixon Pre-Presidential Papers, Series 238, Box 22, NARA-LA.

24. Kevin McCann to Walter Williams, January 23, 1964, Nixon Pre-

Presidential Papers, Series 238, Box 25, NARA-LA; Jim Hagerty to Rose Mary Woods, June 6, 1964, Nixon Pre-Presidential Papers, Series 238, Box 15, NARA-LA.

25. Witcover, *Resurrection*, p. 83; Reinhard, *Republican Right*, p. 188; Robert D. Novak, *Agony of the GOP*, p. 404.

26. Leonard Hall to Nixon, May 13, 1963, Nixon Pre-Presidential Papers, Box 313, NARA-LA; Reinhard, *Republican Right*, p. 177; Robert D. Novak, *Agony of the GOP*, p. 189.

27. Robert D. Novak, *Agony of the GOP*, pp. 326, 358n, 368, 369, 372; Hess and Broder, *Republican Establishment*, p. 167; Nixon Memorandum, March 12, 1964, Seaton Papers, Eisenhower Post Presidency Series, Box 8, DDEL; *NYT*, March 13, 1964. Seaton telephone call to Nixon, April 20, 1964, Seaton Papers, 1960 Campaign Series, Box 8, DDEL.

28. Robert D. Novak, *Agony of the GOP*, p. 379; Statement by Richard Nixon, May 27, 1964, Nixon Pre-Presidential Papers, Non-Deeded Papers, NARA-LA; Reinhard, *Republican Right*, p. 188.

29. Jim Hagerty telephone call to Rose Mary Woods, June 5, 1964, Nixon Pre-Presidential Papers, Series 238, Box 15.

30. Raymond Moley telephone call to Rose Mary Woods, June 8, 1964, Nixon Pre-Presidential Papers, Series 238, Box 26, NARA-LA; Robert D. Novak, *Agony of the GOP*, pp. 424–425; Reinhard, *Republican Right*, p. 190.

31. Jim Hagerty telephone call to Rose Mary Woods, June 10, 1964, Nixon Pre-Presidential Papers, Series 238, Lawyer/Public Figure Correspondence, Box 15, NARA-LA.

32. *Wisconsin State-Journal*, June 14, 1964.

33. Undated memorandum, Leonard Garment Papers, Box 1, Library of Congress.

34. Witcover, *Resurrection*, pp. 83–93; Robert D. Novak, *Agony of the GOP*, p. 433.

35. Theodore H. White, *Making of the President 1964*, p. 150; Gallup, *Gallup Poll*, pp. 1887–1888; *St. Louis Post-Dispatch*, December 6, 1962; *Detroit News*, March 10, 1963.

36. Undated memorandum, Leonard Garment Papers, Box 1, Library of Congress.

37. Jim Hagerty telephone call to Rose Mary Woods, June 10, 1964, Nixon Pre-Presidential Papers, Series 238, Box 15, NARA-LA.

38. Witcover, *Resurrection*, p. 96.

39. Theodore H. White, *Making of the President*, pp. 152–154.

40. Rusher, *Rise of the Right*, p. 168; Bernstein, "Profiles," p. 63.

41. Earle B. Mayfield, Jr., to Lyndon B. Johnson, July 21, 1966, PL, Box 1, White House Central File, LBJL; Nixon, *RN*, p. 674; Lyndon B. Johnson, *Vantage Point*, p. 555; Bornet, *Johnson*, p. 323; Ehrlichman, Notes of Meetings with the President, October 31, 1972, Ehrlichman Papers, Fenn Gallery, Santa Fe, New Mexico.

42. Theodore H. White, *Making of the President 1964*, pp. 214–215.

43. Bernstein, "Profiles," p. 62; Republican Research Division, "The 1964 Elections: A Summary Report with Supporting Tables," November 10, 1964, RNC Papers, NARA-Wash.

44. Nixon to H. R. Haldeman, November 30, 1970, President's Personal File, Box 2, NPMP, NARA-Alexandria.

45. Interview with Richard M. Nixon, June 4, 1984; interview with H. R. Haldeman, January 25, 1985.

46. Cannon, *Reagan*, pp. 13, 98. The speech had been carefully previewed by his wealthy California fund-raisers.

47. Tindall, *Disruption of the Solid South*, p. 64; Matthews and Protho, *Negroes and the New Southern Politics*, p. 374; Grantham, "South . . . and American Politics," p. 242.

48. Wicker, *JFK and LBJ*, p. 213; interview with Richard M. Nixon, June 4, 1984.

49. *NYT*, April 5, 1965; Kearns, *Lyndon Johnson*, p. 305.

50. Matusow, *Unraveling of America*, p. 214.

51. Evans and Novak, *Nixon*, p. 133n; *NYT*, February 13, 1964; Lyndon B. Johnson, *Vantage Point*, p. 451;

Kearns, *Lyndon Johnson,* p. 4; Nixon to Eisenhower, March 6, 1968, Eisenhower Post-Presidential Papers, Principal File 1968, Box 34, DDEL.

52. Parmet, *Democrats,* p. 243; Witcover, *Resurrection,* p. 170; Reinhard, *Republican Right,* pp. 216–217; Gallup, *Gallup Poll,* v. 3, p. 2034.

53. Greenfield, "LBJ and the Democrats," p. 11.

54. Gallup, *Gallup Poll,* v. 3, p. 1971; Erskine, "The Polls," pp. 656, 664, 667, 671; William Connell to Marvin Watson, September 13, 1967, PL, White House Central File, Box 2, LBJL; Ben Wattenberg to Lyndon B. Johnson, November 21, 1967, PL, White House Central File, Box 26, LBJL; Lippman, *Spiro Agnew's America,* p. 238; James Rowe to Lyndon B. Johnson, January 6, 1967, Marvin Watson papers, Box 30, LBJL; Matusow, *Unraveling of America,* p. 214; Kearns, *Lyndon Johnson,* p. 308.

55. *The Reporter,* October 19, 1967, p. 22; Joseph Napolitan, "Survey of Political Attitudes, Boston, Massachusetts, July 1967," Marvin Watson Papers, Box 8, LBJL; *NYT,* June 25, 1966; Witcover, *Shining Knight,* pp. 141–145, 149; Woodward, *Strange Career of Jim Crow,* p. 209.

56. Ted Van Dyk to Hubert H. Humphrey, November 14, 1966, White House Central File, Box 1, LBJL; Duscha, "Will California Stand Pat?" p. 42; Witcover, *White Knight,* p. 128.

57. Rieder, *Canarsie,* p. 77; *NYT,* August 18, 1969; Lemons, *Troubled American,* p. 81; unsigned memorandum to Lyndon B. Johnson, December 2, 1966, PL, Box 1, White House Central File, LBJL.

58. John Criswell to Marvin Watson, October 14, 1967, White House Central File, Box 2, LBJL.

59. Everett Dirksen to Victor Smith, December 8, 1964, Nixon Non-Deeded Materials, Series 238, Lawyer/Public Figure Correspondence File, NARA-LA.

60. McDonald, "Russell Kirk"; Nash, *Conservative Intellectual Movement,* p. 144; Auerbach, *Conservative Illusion,* pp. 145–150.

61. Nixon to Russell Kirk, December 5, 1968, Kirk Papers, Clarke Historical Library, Central Michigan University.

62. Reinhard, *Republican Right,* p. 218; Wallace and Gates, *Close Encounters,* p. 102; Witcover, *Resurrection,* p. 123; Califano, *Presidential Nation,* p. 112.

63. Witcover, *Resurrection,* pp. 130–131.

64. Ibid., p. 156; Statement by Richard M. Nixon, September 28, 1966, mimeographed copy in author's possession.

65. Statement by Richard M. Nixon, September 28, 1966, mimeographed copy in author's possession; Witcover, *Resurrection,* p. 156; Nixon to Eisenhower, October 13, 1966, Post-Presidential Papers, Special Name File, 1961–1968, Box 8, DDEL.

66. Witcover, *Resurrection,* p. 161; Safire, *Before the Fall,* p. 36.

67. Witcover, *Resurrection,* pp. 165–166; Safire, *Before the Fall,* pp. 38–39.

68. Richard M. Nixon, Summary of Remarks, Republican Coordinating Committee Meeting, October 3, 1966, DDEL; Witcover, *Resurrection,* pp. 154–155, 170; Hess and Broder, *Republican Establishment,* p. 174.

69. Kearns, *Lyndon Johnson,* p. 305; Republican Research Report No. 18, RNC Papers, NARA-Wash.

70. Boskin, "The Revolt of the Urban Ghettos," pp. 1–14; Ben Wattenberg to Lyndon B. Johnson, November 21, 1967, White House Central File, PL, Box 26, LBJL; *The Reporter,* November 2, 1967, p. 12; Louis Martin to John Criswell, August 29, 1967, White House Central File, Box 2, LBJL.

71. Interview with Norman Podhoretz, October 23, 1984; Mailer, *Armies of the Night,* pp. 101–102, 158.

72. Mailer, *Armies of the Night,* p. 158; Matusow, *Unraveling of America,* pp. 328, 387; Fred Panzer to Lyndon B. Johnson, September 19, 1967, White House Central File, PL, Box 2, LBJL.

73. Transcript of Nixon speech to the National Industrial Conference Board, September 12, 1967, Post-Presidential Papers, Special Name File, 1961–68, Box 12, DDEL;

Eisenhower to George Humphrey, February 14, 1967, DDEL; Republican Research Report No. 18, RNC Papers, NARA-Wash.

74. Nixon to John Volpe, June 7, 1965, Nixon Non-Deeded Papers, Series 238, Lawyer/Public Figure Correspondence, NARA-LA; Price, *With Nixon*, pp. 21, 24; Nixon, *RN*, p. 282.

75. Buchanan, *Right From the Beginning*, p. 325; Garment, "Hill Case," p. 95; Price, *With Nixon*, p. 29.

76. Nixon, *RN*, pp. 284–285.

77. Nixon, "Asia After Viet Nam," pp. 111–125.

78. James Rowe to Lyndon B. Johnson, May 31, 1967, Marvin Watson File, Box 30, LBJL; Albert Mark to Sherwin Markham, June 5, 1967, White House Central File, PL, Box 2, LBJL; Political Surveys and Analyses, "A National Survey of Attitudes Toward the Johnson Administration," August 3, 1967, White House Central File, PL, Box 2, LBJL; William Connell to Marvin Watson, September 13, 1967, White House Central File, PL, Box 2, LBJL; Ben Wattenberg to Lyndon B. Johnson, November 21, 1967, White House Central File, PL, Box 26, LBJL; Bornet, *Presidency of Lyndon B. Johnson*, p. 299; Moynihan, "President and the Negro," p. 31; Lekachman, "Death of a Slogan," p. 60; Lewis F. Powell to Preston M. Yancy, November 9, 1967, Dabney Papers, University of Virginia.

79. Schrag, "Forgotten Americans," p. 34; Frady, *Wallace*, p. 142; Peirce and Hagstrom, *Book of America*, p. 444; Parmet, *JFK*, pp. 266–267.

80. Lemons, *Troubled American*, p. 137; Frady, *Wallace*, p. 137; Sherrill, *Gothic Politics*, p. 270; Wicker, "George Wallace," p. 46.

81. Frady, *Wallace*, pp. 8, 14.

82. Marty Underwood to W. Marvin

Watson, n.d., Watson file, LBJL; Sherrill, *Gothic Politics*, p. 256; Fred Siegel, *Troubled Journey*, p. 160; Woodward, *Strange Career of Jim Crow*, p. 211.

83. Lemons, *Troubled American*, pp. 66–69, 79.

84. Converse, et al., "Continuity and Change in American Politics," p. 1086.

85. Marty Underwood to W. Marvin Watson, n.d., Watson File, LBJL; Richard Garbett to Leonard Garment, May 15, 1967, Garment Papers, Box 3, Library of Congress; W. Marvin Watson to Lyndon B. Johnson, January 12, 1968, Watson File, Box 5, LBJL; Gallup, *Gallup Poll*, v. 3, p. 2101.

86. Frady, *Wallace*, p. 137; Sherrill, *Gothic Politics*, p. 291.

87. Commager, *Documents of American History*, v. 2, p. 594.

88. Williams, "He's No Huey Long."

89. Peirce and Hagstrom, *Book of America*, p. 446.

90. *NYT*, May 5, 1975; Wooten, "Wallace's Last Hurrah?," p. 50; Whatley and Woods, *Alabama Message*, pp. 9, 20; Lipset and Raab, *Politics of Unreason*, p. 387; Black and Black, "Wallace Vote in Alabama," p. 732; Peirce and Hagstrom, *Book of America*, p. 447; Murphy and Gulliver, *Southern Strategy*, p. 56.

91. Sherrill, *Gothic Politics*, p. 259; *NYT*, November 30, 1973; *LAT*, September 17, 1968; Charles R. Baker to Frank Mankiewicz, March 15, 1972, Mankiewicz Papers, Box 21, JFKL; Chester, et al., *American Melodrama*, pp. 703–704; Bradford, "George Wallace and American Conservatives," p. 444.

92. Lemons, *Troubled American*, p. 67; *Newsweek*, October 6, 1969, pp. 29, 30.

Chapter 17. RESURRECTION

1. Nixon to Jerris Leonard, December 28, 1964, Nixon Pre-Presidential Papers, Non-Deeded Papers, NARA-LA.

2. Interview with John Ehrlichman, June 17, 1985; Jones, "Behind LBJ's Decision Not to Run in '68"; *NYT*, January 14, 1988; Bill Moyers to

George Christian, n.d., Watson File, Box 27, LBJL.

3. Clark, "How Eugene McCarthy Sank the Peace Effort — and Himself"; Interview with Allard Lowenstein, June 16, 1975.

4. Humphrey never did get those President's Club funds.

Solberg, *Hubert Humphrey*, p. 375.

5. Cf. Farber, *Chicago '68*, pp. 125, 128–130, 136.

6. Converse, et al., "Continuity and Change in American Politics," p. 1087; Farber, *Chicago '68*, pp. 205–206; Wills, *Nixon Agonistes*, p. 269.

7. Witcover, *Resurrection*, pp. 190–191.

8. Democratic State Chairmen reports, December 14, 1967, W. Marvin Watson File, Box 22, LBJL; Fred Panzer to Lyndon B. Johnson, March 4, 1968, W. Marvin Watson Papers, Box 11, LBJL.

9. Roberts, *First Rough Draft*, p. 252; James Rowe to Lyndon B. Johnson, March 19, 1968, W. Marvin Watson Papers, Box 30, LBJL.

10. Witcover, *Resurrection*, p. 229.

11. Nixon to Eisenhower, March 17, 1968, Post-Presidential Papers, Principal File 1968, Box 34, DDEL.

12. Safire, *You Could Look It Up*, p. 221; Republican Research Division, "Youth Issues Office Special Report," July 20, 1972, RNC Papers, NARA-Wash., in Leuchtenburg and Kesaris, *Papers*, Part II, reel 12.

13. Interview with Richard M. Nixon, November 16, 1988.

14. *NYT*, March 6, 1968.

15. Ibid.

16. Interview with Richard M. Nixon, November 16, 1988.

17. *NYT*, March 6, 1968.

18. Ibid., March 11 and 21, 1968; interview with Robert Semple, Jr., November 14, 1988; Safire, *You Could Look It Up*, pp. 220–221; interview with Richard M. Nixon, November 16, 1988.

19. Nixon, *RN*, p. 298; W. Marvin Watson, Memorandum for the Record, March 20, 1968, Watson File, Box 27, LBJL.

20. Interview with Richard M. Nixon, November 16, 1988; Safire, *Before the Fall*, p. 48; Witcover, *Resurrection*, p. 281.

21. Eisenhower to Nixon, October 24, 1968, Post-Presidential Papers, Principal File 1968, Box 34, DDEL.

22. Marvin Watson's notes of a telephone conversation between Governor Rockefeller and Saul Linowitz, January 22, 1968, Box 27, Marvin Watson Papers, LBJL; Dent, *Prodigal South*, pp. 93–94; Chester,

et al., *American Melodrama*, pp. 455–459.

23. Matusow, *Unraveling of America*, p. 403–404; Chester, et al., *American Melodrama*, p. 497.

24. Chester, et al., *American Melodrama*, p. 493; Dent, *Prodigal South*, p. 94.

25. Lippman, *Spiro Agnew's America*, p. 244.

26. Chester, et al., *American Melodrama*, p. 488; interview with Leonard Garment, February 27, 1985; Nixon to John Volpe, June 7, 1965, Nixon Non-Deeded Papers, Series 238, Lawyer/Public Figure Correspondence, NARA-LA.

27. Dent, *Prodigal South*, p. 103.

28. Interview with William Scranton, June 13, 1986; interview with Walter Annenberg, June 9, 1986.

29. Interview with Hugh Scott, June 10, 1986.

30. Interview with Robert Finch, January 22, 1985; Theodore H. White, *Making of the President 1968*, pp. 252–253; Chester, et al., *American Melodrama*, p. 489.

31. Interview with H. R. Haldeman, January 25, 1985.

32. Interviews with Richard M. Nixon, June 8, 1984, John Ehrlichman, June 17, 1985, Robert Finch, January 22, 1985.

33. Witcover, *White Knight*, p. 22; Chester, et al., *American Melodrama*, pp. 491–492.

34. Interview with Richard M. Nixon, November 16, 1988.

35. Witcover, *White Knight*, p. 5; Javits, *Autobiography*, p. 370.

36. Witcover, *White Knight*, pp. 27–28, 201; interview with Richard M. Nixon, November 14, 1988.

37. Witcover, *White Knight*, pp. 207, 220.

38. Chester, et al., *American Melodrama*, p. 489; Rusher, *Rise of the Right*, pp. 209, 216; interview with William Rusher, October 2, 1984; Buchanan, *Conservative Votes*, p. 3.

39. Buchanan, *Conservative Votes*, p. 3; Persico, *Imperial Rockefeller*, p. 80; *NYT*, January 27, 1974.

40. Goldwater, *With No Apologies*, p. 255; Rusher, *Rise of the Right*, p. 207; Wills, *Nixon Agonistes*, p. 256; Richard W. Garbett to Leonard Garment, Garment Papers, Box 3, Library of Congress.

41. Dent, *Prodigal South*, p. 101;

interview with Richard M. Nixon,
November 16, 1988.

42. Witcover, *Resurrection,* p. 312;
interview with Richard M. Nixon,
November 16, 1988.

43. Dent, *Prodigal South,* p. 103;
Interview with Richard M. Nixon,
November 16, 1988; Nixon, *RN,* p.
305; Persico, *Imperial Rockefeller,* p.
80; Dent, *Prodigal South,* pp. 96–97;
Chester, et al., *American Melodrama,*
pp. 486–487; Wills, *Nixon Agonistes,*
p. 271.

44. Dent, *Prodigal South,* p. 103; Chester
et al., *American Melodrama,* p. 493.

45. Mimeographed typescript of Nixon's
remarks, August 9, 1968, Miami
Beach, Florida, RNC Papers, NARA-
Wash., UPA, part 1, reel 7.

46. Wills, "Nixon Convention," p. 873.

47. McGinniss, *Selling of the President
1968,* p. 27.

48. Kevin Phillips, "Future of American
Politics."

49. Ibid.; Deakin, *Straight Stuff,* p. 275;
Keogh, *Nixon and the Press,* p. 3. An
Editor & Publisher survey showed
endorsements by about 84 percent
of the newspapers, a figure that can
be misleading without considering
actual circulation and other more
intangible matters of influence.

50. *Newsweek,* November 4, 1968, p. 44;
Lou Harris, *Anguish of Change,* p. 82;
Time, November 15, 1968, p. 24.

51. Parmet, *Jack,* p. 461; Hersh, *Price of
Power,* pp. 16–19; interview with
H. R. Haldeman, January 25, 1985.

52. Solberg, *Hubert Humphrey,* p. 393;
interview with Anna C. Chennault,
February 27, 1985; *Time,* November
15, 1968, p. 23.

53. Solberg, *Hubert Humphrey,* pp. 394–
395.

54. Garrow, *Bearing the Cross,* p. 347;
NYT, February 3, 1975.

55. Solberg, *Hubert Humphrey,* pp. 394–
395; Bui Diem with David Chanoff,
In the Jaws of History, pp. 244–245;
Thomas Powers, *Man Who Kept the
Secrets,* p. 252; *NYT,* February 3,
1975; Bruce Kehrli to Charles
Colson, June 29, 1972, News POF,
News Summaries, Box 41, NPMP;
cf. Nixon, *Submission of Recorded
Presidential Conversations,* p. 97, for
comments by John Dean; Lasky, *It
Didn't Start with Watergate,* pp. 216–
220; Theoharis, *Beyond the Hiss Case,*

pp. 30–31; Richard Gid Powers,
Secrecy and Power, p. 399; Hersh,
Price of Power, pp. 21–22; Sullivan,
Bureau, p. 78; Chennault, *Education
of Anna,* pp. 173–174.

56. Chennault, *Education of Anna,* p.
163.

57. President Nixon appointed Hill as
ambassador to Spain in 1969.

58. Chennault, *Education of Anna,* pp.
170, 175; Hung and Schecter, *Palace
File,* p. 23; interviews with Anna C.
Chennault, February 27, 1985, and
Bui Diem, November 30, 1984.

59. Chennault, *Education of Anna,* p.
189; Bornet, *Presidency of Lyndon B.
Johnson,* p. 320.

60. Humphrey, *Education of a Public
Man,* pp. 8–9.

61. Lyndon B. Johnson, *Vantage Point,*
p. 518; interview with Bui Diem,
November 30, 1984; Bui Diem, *Jaws
of History,* p. 243; *NYT,* June 27,
1973; interview with Herbert Klein,
January 24, 1985.

62. Interview with Anna C. Chennault,
February 27, 1985.

63. Interviews with Bui Diem,
November 30, 1984, and Anna C.
Chennault, February 27, 1985.

64. Interview with H. R. Haldeman,
January 25, 1985.

65. *NYT,* May 17, 1968; Safire, *Before the
Fall,* pp. 49–50; Nixon to H. R.
Haldeman, November 30, 1970,
President's Personal File, Box 2,
NPMP; Leonard Garment to John
Ehrlichman, April 1, 1971, Garment
Papers, Library of Congress, Box 1.

66. Interview with Kevin Phillips, May
22, 1985.

67. Ibid.; Wills, *Nixon Agonistes,* p. 268;
Patrick J. Buchanan to Richard
Nixon, June 17, 1970, Haldeman
Papers, Box 139, NPMP.

68. Peirce and Hagstrom, *Book of
America,* p. 445.

69. *NYT,* October 26, 1968; Lippman,
Spiro Agnew's America, pp. 155, 159–
160, 162.

70. Scammon and Wattenberg, *Real
Majority,* p. 191; Virginius Dabney to
A. Willis Robertson, September 12,
1968, Byrd Papers, Box 23,
University of Virginia; Eugene T.
Burke to Stephen Mitchell, October
10, 1968, Mitchell Papers, HSTL;
Schrag, "Forgotten Americans," p.
32; Richard Nixon to H. R.

Haldeman, November 30, 1970, PPF, Box 2, NPMP; Lippman, *Spiro Agnew's America,* pp. 154–167.

71. Black and Black, *Politics and Society in the South,* p. 262; Nixon, *RN,* p. 319.

72. Phillips, *Emerging Republican Majority,* p. 471; Price, *With Nixon,* p. 75; Lipset and Raab, *Politics of Unreason,* p. 396; Converse, et al., "Continuity and Change in American Politics," pp. 1091–1092; Broder, *Party's Over,* p. 82.

73. Chester, et al., *American Melodrama,* p. 699.

74. Ibid., pp. 706, 707–709.

75. Ibid., p. 706; Goulden, *Meany,* pp. 367–369; Levitan, *Blue-Collar Workers,* p. 123; Phillips, *Emerging Republican Majority,* pp. 462–463.

76. Sherrill, *Gothic Politics,* pp. 254, 266.

77. Interview with Richard M. Nixon, November 16, 1988.

78. Republican Research Division, "The 1968 Elections: A Summary with Supporting Tables," April 1969, RNC Papers, NARA-Wash., in Leuchtenburg and Kesaris, *Papers,* reel 8.

79. *Newsweek,* October 6, 1969, p. 29.

Chapter 18. "I'M NOT A MUSHY MODERATE"

1. Evans and Novak, *Nixon in the White House,* pp. 33–34.

2. Arthur M. Schlesinger, Jr., *Coming of the New Deal,* p. 1.

3. Robinson, *"To the Best of My Ability,"* p. 5; memorandum from Jim Keogh, July 10, 1969, in Hoff-Wilson, *Papers;* Lemann, "Unfinished War," p. 63.

4. Interview with Herbert Stein, December 14, 1984; interview with Richard M. Nixon, November 16, 1988.

5. Moynihan, "President and the Negro," p. 32.

6. Interview with Richard M. Nixon, June 8, 1984.

7. Interview with Richard M. Nixon, November 16, 1988.

8. Memorandum from John R. Price, April 14, 1969, in Hoff-Wilson, *Papers.*

9. Nixon, *1999,* p. 309.

10. Interview with Richard M. Nixon, November 16, 1988.

11. John Gardner, Transcript of Godkin Lectures, Harvard University, March 1969, PPF, Box 8, NPMP.

12. Ibid.

13. Alexander Butterfield memorandum for the president's file, March 27, 1969, in Hoff-Wilson, *Papers.*

14. *Public Papers: Nixon, 1969,* pp. 262–265.

15. *NYT,* October 23, 1977; *Public Papers: Nixon, 1971,* p. 6; *NYT,* October 23, 1977; Theodore H. White, *Breach of Faith,* p. 65.

16. Ehrlichman, *Witness to Power,* p. 88.

17. Interview with Richard M. Nixon, November 16, 1988; *NYT,* September 20, 1968.

18. Hess, *Organizing the Presidency,* p. 112; Lowi, *Personal President,* p. 144.

19. Ehrlichman Papers, November 14, 1972, Fenn Gallery, Santa Fe, New Mexico.

20. Lowi, *Personal President,* p. 5; Arthur Schlesinger, Jr., *Imperial Presidency,* p. 221; Bonafede, "Nixon's First-Year Appointments," pp. 182–192; Kernell and Popkin, *Chief of Staff,* pp. 2–3.

21. Hess, *Organizing the Presidency,* p. 116.

22. Interview with Richard M. Nixon, November 16, 1988.

23. Schell, *Time of Illusion,* pp. 23–24; Bonafede, "Nixon's Troubles," p. 1472.

24. Hess, *Organizing the Presidency,* pp. 114, 116; Theodore H. White, *Breach of Faith,* p. 103; Ehrlichman, *Witness to Power,* p. 94; Bonafede, "Nixon's First-Year Appointments," pp. 182–192.

25. *NYT,* December 12, 1968.

26. Keogh, *Nixon and the Press,* p. 2; Deakin, *Straight Stuff,* p. 275.

27. Bonafede, "Nixon's First-Year Appointments," p. 192; interview with William P. Rogers, November 15, 1983; Ehrlichman Papers, November 28, 1972, Fenn Gallery, Santa Fe, New Mexico; Broder, *Party's Over,* p. 103; Bonafede, "Nixon's Troubles," p. 1472; Evans and Novak, *Nixon in the White House,* p. 52; Ehrlichman, *Witness to Power,* p. 97; Safire, *Before the Fall,* p. 498.

28. Roper Research Associates, *The Public Pulse,* January 1969, Box 185, NPMP.

29. *NYT,* January 21, 1969.

30. Ibid.
31. Julie Nixon Eisenhower, *Pat Nixon,* p. 252.
32. *Public Papers: Nixon, 1969,* pp. 1–4.
33. *NYT,* January 21, 1969.
34. News Summaries, POF, Box 30, NPMP.
35. Nixon to H. R. Haldeman, January 21, 1969, POF, Box 1, NPMP.
36. Hess, *Organizing the Presidency,* pp. 120–121.
37. Kilpatrick meant Postmaster General Winton Malcolm Blount, who was certainly not an extremist.
38. White House News Summaries, February 1960, POF, Box 30, NPMP.
39. Schoen, *Pat,* pp. 145–146; Lemann, "Unfinished War," p. 59; interview with Kevin Phillips, May 22, 1985.
40. Daniel Patrick Moynihan to Nixon, November 13, 1970, Box 163, Haldeman Papers, NPMP.
41. Schoen, *Pat,* pp. 1, 121, 125.
42. Ibid.; Nixon, *RN,* p. 762.
43. Lemann, "Unfinished War," p. 59.
44. Moynihan, "President and the Negro," pp. 33–34.
45. Interview with Richard M. Nixon, November 16, 1988; Nixon to John Ehrlichman and Ken Cole, December 28, 1972, PPF, Box 4, NPMP.
46. *White Plains Reporter Dispatch,* June 27 and July 11, 1961.
47. *NYT,* January 17, February 4, July 4, September 18, November 24, and December 27, 1968.
48. *NYT,* May 17, 1968.
49. Ibid., March 24, 1968.
50. Ibid., January 6 and February 6, 1968; Patterson, *America's Struggle Against Poverty,* pp. 189–190.
51. Patterson, *America's Struggle Against Poverty,* p. 192. Governor Reagan was one exception; he disagreed that the federal government should impose any minimum standard.
52. Nathan, *Plot That Failed,* p. 15; *NYT,* July 25, 1968.
53. *NYT,* November 12, 1968.
54. Ibid., October 26 and 29, 1968.
55. Evans and Novak, *Nixon in the White House,* p. 56.
56. Nathan, *Plot That Failed,* p. 14; Moynihan, *Politics of Guaranteed Income,* p. 106.
57. Reichley, *Conservatives in an Age of Change,* p. 143.
58. *Public Papers: Nixon, 1970,* pp. 237, 276; Ehrlichman, Notes of Meetings with the President, December 30, 1970, March 23, 1971, and November 28, 1972, Ehrlichman Papers, Fenn Gallery, Santa Fe, New Mexico; Hoff-Wilson, *Papers,* October 24, 1969.
59. Moynihan, *Politics of Guaranteed Income,* p. 80.
60. Hess, *Organizing the Presidency,* p. 122; *Commentary,* May 1973, p. 58.
61. Patrick Buchanan memorandum to the president, August 13, 1969, in Hoff-Wilson, *Papers;* Safire, *Before the Fall,* p. 216; Ray Price memorandum to the president, August 25, 1969, in Hoff-Wilson, *Papers.*
62. Safire, *Before the Fall,* p. 220; Patrick Buchanan memorandum for the President's File, September 29, 1969, in Hoff-Wilson, *Papers.*
63. Safire, *Before the Fall,* p. 220.
64. William Safire to H. R. Haldeman, October 10, 1969, Haldeman Papers, Box 132, NPMP.
65. Stephen Hess to Nixon, September 11, 1969, Ehrlichman Papers, Box 40, NPMP.
66. Schoen, *Pat,* p. 131.
67. Ribicoff, "He Left at Half Time," p. 23.
68. *Public Papers: Nixon, 1969,* pp. 640–641.
69. Memorandum by James Keogh, August 6, 1969, in Hoff-Wilson, *Papers.* Agnew's "threat" was, of course, rhetorical; he went to the Senate and did cast the tie-breaking vote to save the ABM system.
70. Ibid.
71. *National Review,* February 24, 1970, p. 205; *Public Papers: Nixon, 1970,* p. 731; John Ehrlichman, Notes of Meetings with the President, January 6, 1971, Ehrlichman Papers, Fenn Gallery, Santa Fe, New Mexico; Evans and Novak, *Nixon in the White House,* p. 232.
72. *Public Papers: Nixon, 1971,* p. 51.
73. News Summaries, POF, Box 30, NPMP; Nixon to Ray Price, December 11, 1970, Haldeman Papers, Box 138, NPMP.
74. Glazer, "Limits of Social Policy," p. 57.
75. Moynihan, *Politics of a Guaranteed Income,* pp. 286–292, 294; Hoff-

Wilson, *Papers,* July 24, 1972; *Congress and the Nation,* v. 3, p. 625.

76. Moynihan, *Politics of a Guaranteed Income,* p. 294.

77. Gallup, *Gallup Poll,* v. 3, p. 2177.

78. Ribicoff, "He Left at Half Time," p. 23; Moynihan, *Politics of a Guaranteed Income,* p. 469.

79. Evans and Novak, *Nixon in the White House,* pp. 231–232.

80. *NYT,* October 1 and 2, 1988.

81. Ribicoff, "He Left at Half Time," p. 22; interview with Abraham Ribicoff, February 5, 1973.

82. Lemann, "Unfinished War," p. 66; Theodore H. White, *Making of the President 1972,* pp. 128–129; Ribicoff, "He Left at Half Time," p. 26; *NYT,* June 18, 1972.

83. John Ehrlichman, Notes of Meetings with the President, April 21, 1972, Ehrlichman Papers, Fenn Gallery, Santa Fe, New Mexico; Nixon to John Ehrlichman and Ken Cole, December 28, 1972, PPF, Box 4, NPMP.

84. Interview with Richard M. Nixon, November 16, 1988; *Congress and the Nation,* v. 3, p. 622; Moynihan, *Politics of a Guaranteed Income,* p. 545.

85. Nixon, handwritten notes, January 14, January 18, July 19, October 23, and November 15, 1970, PPF, Box 185, NPMP.

86. Daniel Patrick Moynihan to Nixon, November 13, 1970, Box 163, Haldeman papers, NPMP.

87. Schoen, *Pat,* p.175.

Chapter 19. "Tell It to Hanoi"

1. Peter Schrag was probably right when he wrote that "What upset the police at the Chicago convention most was not so much the politics of the demonstrators as their manners and their hair." "Forgotten Americans," p. 32.

2. *NYT,* January 2, 1970.

3. Whitworth, "One-Man Think Tank," pp. 54, 58, 65.

4. Interview with Lyndon B. Johnson, June 30, 1970, Johnson City, Texas; Haldeman Action Paper, June 22, 1971, Haldeman Subject File, Box 112, NPMP.

5. Small, *Johnson, Nixon, and the Doves,* pp. 17, 18, 37, 53, 105, 126; Tebbel and Watts, *Press and the Presidency,* pp. 489–500; Conkin, *Big Daddy from the Pedernales,* pp. 293–294; Gaddis, *Strategies of Containment,* p. 300.

6. *Public Papers: Nixon, 1969,* p. 530; Gallup, *Gallup Poll,* v. 3, pp. 2198, 2204, 2209; *NYT,* August 7 and September 3, 1969.

7. *NYT,* August 18, 1969; Reeves, "Mike Lang (groovy kid from Brooklyn) plus John Roberts (unlimited capital) Equals Woodstock," pp. 34, 122, 124, 126, 128, 130.

8. *NYT,* August 19 and 23, 1969; O'Neill, *Coming Apart,* p. 260; Douglas T. Miller, *Visions of America,* pp. 253–254.

9. John Ehrlichman, Notes of Meetings with the President, October 23, 1969, Ehrlichman Papers, Fenn Gallery, Santa Fe, New Mexico; Keogh, *Nixon and the Press,* p. 105.

10. John R. Brown III to John Ehrlichman, December 17, 1969, Ehrlichman Papers, Box 18, NPMP.

11. Unger, *Movement,* p. 181; O'Neill, *Coming Apart,* p. 263.

12. Matusow, *Unraveling of America,* p. 341.

13. Richard Nixon handwritten notes, September 7, 1969, PPF, Box 186, NPMP.

14. Patrick Buchanan memorandum for the President's File, September 27, 1969, in Hoff-Wilson, *Papers;* John Ehrlichman, Notes of Meetings with the President, October 2, 1969, Ehrlichman Papers, Fenn Gallery, Santa Fe, New Mexico.

15. Keogh, *Nixon and the Press,* p. 171; Kenneth Cole to John Ehrlichman, October 15, 1969, Ehrlichman Papers, Box 18, NPMP; Memorandum from Jim Keogh, November 5, 1969, in Hoff-Wilson, *Papers;* Nixon to Henry Kissinger, October 27, 1969, PPF, Box 1, NPMP.

16. Patrick Buchanan memorandum for the President, September 29, 1969, in Hoff-Wilson, *Papers;* News Summaries, February 7, 1969, POF, Box 30, NPMP.

17. *Public Papers: Nixon, 1969,* pp. 371,

544–556; Clifford, "Viet Nam Reappraisal," p. 601.

18. *Public Papers: Nixon, 1969,* p. 587; *NYT,* November 4, 1969.

19. Keogh, *Nixon and the Press,* p. 92.

20. Cf. Sheehan, *Bright Shining Lie,* pp. 277–278, 346.

21. Larry Higby to H. R. Haldeman, July 21, 1969, Box 195, Haldeman Papers, NPMP; News Summaries, POF, Box 31, NPMP; Julie Nixon Eisenhower, *Pat Nixon,* p. 274.

22. News Summaries, POF, Box 31, October 1, 1969.

23. Gallup, *Gallup Poll,* v. 3, pp. 2212, 2216; Lou Harris, *Anguish of Change,* p. 173; O'Neill, *Coming Apart,* p. 260; *Newsweek,* October 6, 1969, pp. 30–31.

24. Tom Whitehead to Peter Flanigan, and Lyn Nofziger to Bryce Harlow, September 29, 1969, Haldeman Subject File, Box 121, NPMP.

25. Kenneth Cole to John Ehrlichman, et al., October 15, 1969, Ehrlichman Papers, Box 18, NPMP; John Ehrlichman, Notes of Meetings with the President, October 1, 1969, Ehrlichman Papers, Fenn Gallery, Santa Fe, New Mexico; *Public Papers: Nixon, 1969,* p. 749; Magruder, *American Life,* pp. 75, 81; News Summaries, October 2, 1969, POF, Box 31, NPMP.

26. News Summaries, October 2 and October 7, 1969, POF, Box 31, NPMP.

27. Whiteside, "Annals of Television," pp. 41–42; Patrick Buchanan memorandum for the president, September 29, 1969, in Hoff-Wilson, *Papers;* Gitlin, *Whole World Is Watching,* p. 279.

28. Memoranda in PPF, Box 1, Nixon to John Ehrlichman and two to H. R. Haldeman, October 1, 1969; Nixon to H. R. Haldeman, October 10, 1969, Haldeman Subject File, Box 138, NPMP; Whiteside, "Annals of Television," pp. 42–43.

29. *Public Papers: Nixon, 1969,* p. 799; Gitlin, *Whole World Is Watching,* p. 220; Price, *With Nixon,* p. 159.

30. Syndicated column by James J. Kilpatrick, October 14, 1969, NPMP; News Summaries, POF, Box 31, NPMP; Lippman, *Agnew,* p. 186; Gitlin, *Whole World Is Watching,* p. 220; Ken Cole to John Ehrlichman,

et al., October 15, 1969, Ehrlichman Papers, Box 18, NPMP.

31. Lippman, *Agnew,* pp. 187, 189; Gitlin, *Whole World Is Watching,* p. 221; Ken Cole to John Ehrlichman, et al., October 15, 1969, Ehrlichman Papers, Box 18, NPMP; Lou Harris, *Anguish of Change,* p. 173; Nixon, *RN,* p. 404; Lippman, *Agnew,* p. 189.

32. Deakin, *Straight Stuff,* p. 290; Magruder, *American Life,* pp. 72–77; Tebbel and Watts, *Press and the Presidency,* pp. 507–508; John R. Brown III to John Ehrlichman, December 17, 1969, Ehrlichman Papers, Box 18, NPMP.

33. Coyne, *Impudent Snobs,* p. 36; Lippman, *Agnew,* p. 189.

34. Coyne, *Impudent Snobs,* pp. 36–37.

35. Magruder, *One Man's Life,* pp. 81–83.

36. John Ehrlichman, Notes of Meetings with the President, October 29, 1969, Ehrlichman Papers, Fenn Gallery, Santa Fe, New Mexico; Schell, *Time of Illusion,* p. 67; Coyne, *Impudent Snobs,* pp. 265–270; John Ehrlichman Notes of Meetings with the President, November 14, 1969, Fenn Gallery, Santa Fe, New Mexico; *NYT,* January 2, 1970.

37. Nixon to H. R. Haldeman, November 30, 1970, Haldeman Papers, Box 138, NPMP.

38. Harry Dent to Ken Cole, October 9, 1969, Dent Papers, Box 8, NPMP.

39. Schrag, "Forgotten Americans," pp. 27–28, 29; Scammon and Wattenberg, *Real Majority,* pp. 223–224.

40. Scammon and Wattenberg, *Real Majority,* p. 225; Richard P. Nathan to Harry Dent, November 4, 1969, Dent Papers, Box 8, NPMP.

41. King and Anderson, "Nixon, Agnew, and the 'Silent Majority,'" pp. 243–244.

42. Mann, *One and the Many,* p. 18

43. Cf. Frady, "Gary, Indiana," pp. 34–45; Schrag, "Forgotten Americans," pp. 27–34; Friedman, "Is White Racism the Problem?," pp. 61–65; Glazer, "Blacks, Jews and the Intellectuals," pp. 33–39; Goldbloom, "Is There a Backlash Vote?," pp. 17–26; Whitworth, "One-Man Think Tank," pp. 50–89; Karmin, "Polish Hill," pp. 35–39.

44. Greeley, "Ethnic Miracle," p. 33;

Karmin, "Polish Hill," pp. 35, 38; Frady, "Gary, Indiana," p. 37; Lukas, *Common Ground*, p. 495.

45. Goldbloom, "Is There a Backlash Vote?" p. 18; Lemons, *Troubled American*, p. 137.

46. Nixon to Charles Colson and H. R. Haldeman, August 9, 1972, Haldeman Papers, Box 162, NPMP.

47. *Philadelphia Inquirer*, January 25, 28, and February 6, 1970; Cooney, *Annenbergs*, p. 345. Rizzo became a Republican. Later, after the end of his administration, Walter Annenberg told this writer confidentially that he would reemerge the next year as the GOP's mayoral candidate, which he did, and lost.

48. Friedman, "Is White Racism the Problem?," p. 61.

49. Nixon to Bob Haldeman, March 2, 1970, Haldeman Papers, Box 138, NPMP; King and Anderson, "Nixon, Agnew, and the 'Silent Majority,'" pp. 243, 247; Harry Dent to John Brown III, February 25, 1970, Dent Papers, Box 8, NPMP; Lou Harris, *Anguish of Change*, p. 67.

50. *New Republic*, April 4 and 11, 1970, p. 6; *WP*, December 29, 1969; Nixon, handwritten notes, March 16, 1971, PPF, Box 186, NPMP; Julie Nixon Eisenhower, *Pat Nixon*, p. 275; memorandum from Jim Keogh, November 5, 1969, in Hoff-Wilson, *Papers*; Nixon, *RN*, p. 409; Nixon to H. R. Haldeman, December 30, 1969, PPF, Box 1, NPMP.

51. John Ehrlichman, Notes of Meetings with the President, December 2, 1969, Ehrlichman Papers, Fenn Gallery, Santa Fe, New Mexico; Nixon to H. R. Haldeman, PPF, Box 1, November 24, 1969, NPMP; Nixon, *RN*, pp. 408–409; Buchanan, *Right from the Beginning*, p. 325.

52. *Public Papers: Nixon, 1969*, pp. 901–909.

53. Memorandum from Jim Keogh, November 5, 1969, in Hoff-Wilson, *Papers*.

54. Nixon to H. R. Haldeman, October 26, 1969, President's General File, Box 1, NPMP.

55. Whiteside, "Annals of Television," pp. 62, 69–70; Charles Colson to H. R. Haldeman, February 14, 1973, Haldeman Papers, Box 181, NPMP;

House of Representatives, 93d Congress, 2d Session, *Hearings Before the Committee on the Judiciary*, p. 15; *Public Papers: Nixon, 1972*, pp. 718–719.

56. Nixon, *RN*, p. 411; Schell, *Time of Illusion*, p. 184; Safire, *Before the Fall*, p. 313.

57. Keogh, *Nixon and the Press*, p. 172; Coyne, *Impudent Snobs*, pp. 265–270.

58. *NYT*, November 16, 1969.

59. Gitlin, *Whole World Is Watching*, pp. 224, 227; Nixon to H. R. Haldeman, November 24, 1969, PPF, Box 1, NPMP; Magruder, *One Man's Life*, p. 83.

60. Coyne, *Impudent Snobs*, pp. 270–274; Nixon to H. R. Haldeman, November 24, 1969, PPF, Box 1, NPMP; Whiteside, "Annals of Television," p. 43; interview with Richard M. Nixon, November 16, 1988.

61. Lippman, *Spiro Agnew's America*, p. 213.

62. *NYT*, November 20, 1969.

63. John R. Brown III memo to John Ehrlichman, January 14, 1970, Ehrlichman Papers, Box 18, NPMP.

64. John Ehrlichman, Notes of Meetings with the President, December 24, 1969, Ehrlichman Papers, Fenn Gallery, Santa Fe, New Mexico.

65. Efron, *News Twisters*, p. 47.

66. Ibid., pp. 32–33, 52–55; Nixon, *RN*, p. 330.

67. CBS News Release, October 1, 1971, Haldeman Papers, Box 123, NPMP; *Columbia Journalism Review* 10 (November–December 1971), p. 60.

68. Memorandum by W. Richard Howard, December 13, 1971, Haldeman Papers, Box 123, NPMP; Cf. Box 123 of the Haldeman Papers, NPMP, especially with reviews by Charles Winick and Irving Kristol.

69. Nixon, *RN*, p. 330; *Recorded Presidential Conversations*, February 28, 1973, p. 9.

70. Bruce Kehrli to H. R. Haldeman, August 9, 1971, Box 123, NPMP; Patrick J. Buchanan to H. R. Haldeman, September 24, 1971, Haldeman Papers, Box 123, NPMP.

71. Memorandum by W. Richard Howard, December 13, 1971, Haldeman Papers, Box 123, NPMP.

72. Safire, *Before the Fall*, pp. 70, 75.

73. *Public Papers: Nixon, 1970*, pp. 758–763; Schell, *Time of Illusion*, p. 120; *NYT*, September 17, 1970.

74. Julie Nixon Eisenhower, *Pat Nixon*, p. 317; John Ehrlichman office diary, May 2 and 3, 1971, Ehrlichman Papers, Fenn Gallery, Santa Fe, New Mexico.

75. *NYT*, September 27, 1970.

76. John Ehrlichman to Nixon, October 21, 1970, Ehrlichman Papers, Fenn Gallery, Santa Fe, New Mexico; Lippman, *Spiro Agnew's America*, pp. 209–210; Kenneth Cole memorandum for the President's file, December 11, 1970, in Hoff-Wilson, *Papers;* H. R. Haldeman to Patrick Buchanan, January 21, 1971, Haldeman Papers, Box 195, NPMP; *NYT*, December 13, 1970; *Public Papers: Nixon, 1970*, pp. 1103, 1109.

77. Unger, *Papers and the Papers*, pp. 12, 66.

78. Ibid., p. 110; Charles Colson to H. R. Haldeman, June 25, 1971, and Doug Hallett to Colson, July 9, 1971, Haldeman Papers, Box 130, NPMP.

79. Ibid.; H. R. Haldeman Action Paper, June 22, 1971, Haldeman Papers, Box 112, NPMP.

80. Hersh, *Price of Power*, pp. 384–385.

81. Nixon, *Leaders*, p. 28, and *RN*, pp. 508–511.

82. *NYT*, June 29, 1972; Nixon to H. R. Haldeman, August 14, 1962, Haldeman Papers, Box 162, NPMP; Howard A. Cohen to the president, September 18, 1972, Haldeman Papers, Box 103, NPMP; Lubell, *Hidden Crisis in American Politics*, pp. 199–205, 208–209.

83. Olson, *Directory*, p. 490.

Chapter 20. THE ZIGS AND THE ZAGS

1. Interview with Richard M. Nixon, November 16, 1988; Lukas, *Nightmare*, pp. 148–149.

2. Dent, *Prodigal South*, p. 123.

3. Evans and Novak, *Nixon in the White House*, pp. 59–60.

4. Bickel, "Where Do We Go From Here?," pp. 20–22; *NYT*, February 22, 1970, and April 21, 1971; Reichley, *Conservatives in an Age of Change*, p. 192; Orfield, *Must We Bus?*, pp. 14, 332.

5. *NYT*, February 11, 1972; Edward L. Morgan for the President's File, February 14, 1972, in Hoff-Wilson, *Papers; Newsweek*, October 6, 1969, p. 45; Schell, *Time of Illusion*, pp. 41–42, 47; *Public Papers: Nixon, 1972*, pp. 425–429.

6. *NYT*, October 13, 1970, and May 26, 1972.

7. News Summaries, October 12, 1969, POF, Box 31, NPMP; *NYT*, February 12, 1972; *Christian Science Monitor*, February 16, 1972.

8. Orfield, *Must We Bus?*, p. 59.

9. John Ehrlichman, Notes of Meetings with the President, August 4, 1970, Ehrlichman Papers, Fenn Gallery, Santa Fe, New Mexico.

10. Alexander Butterfield memorandum for the President's File, March 27, 1969, in Hoff-Wilson, *Papers*.

11. Memorandum from John R. Price, February 12, 1969, in Hoff-Wilson, *Papers; Public Papers: Nixon, 1969*, pp. 197–198; *NYT*, November 18, 1973; Robert J. Brown to the President, March 5, 1969, in Hoff-Wilson, *Papers;* News Summaries, March 10, 1969, POF, Box 30, NPMP.

12. Donald Rumsfeld for the President's File, February 22, 1971, PPF, Box 23, NPMP.

13. *Public Papers: Nixon, 1970*, p. 319.

14. Nathan, *Plot That Failed*, p. 16; Ray Marshall, "Blacks and Blue-Collar Workers and Unions," in Levitan, *Blue-Collar Workers*, p. 188; *Congress and the Nation, 1969–1972*, p. 498.

15. *Congress and the Nation, 1969–1972*, p. 711; *Philadelphia Inquirer*, January 13, 1970.

16. Nathan, *Plot That Failed*, p. 16; *Congress and the Nation, 1969–1972*, p. 498; *WP*, September 25, 1970.

17. *Congress and the Nation, 1969–1972*, pp. 12a–13a; Nixon, *RN*, p. 438.

18. John Erlichman to Nixon, October 21, 1970, Ehrlichman Papers, Fenn Gallery, Santa Fe, New Mexico.

19. Lukas, *Nightmare*, p. 21; John Ehrlichman memo for the President's File, January 28, 1971, in Hoff-Wilson, *Papers; NYT*, June 12, 1974.

20. *NYT*, November 18, 1973; *The New Republic*, October 7, 1972, p. 8.

21. *WSJ*, December 13, 1973; *NYT*, July

13 and 17, 1973; Theodore H. White, *Making of the President 1972,* p. 120; Lukas, *Nightmare,* pp. 109–110; Alexander, *Financing Politics,* pp. 61, 86–87; Staff of the New York Times, *Watergate Hearings,* pp. 229–246; House of Representatives, 92d Congress, 2d Session, *Congressional Record,* September 21, 1972, pp. S 15532–15533.

22. Peter O'Donnell, Jr., to Harry Dent, March 25, 1969, Dent Papers, Box 8, NPMP.

23. Nixon, handwritten notes, July 19, 1970, PPF, Box 185, NPMP.

24. Reichley, *Conservatives in an Age of Change,* p. 189; Price, *With Nixon,* p. 205; Ray Price memo for the files, December 21, 1970, in Hoff-Wilson, *Papers.*

25. Dent, *Prodigal South,* p. 136.

26. *Public Papers: Nixon, 1970,* pp. 304–320; Safire, *Before the Fall,* p. 242; Price, *With Nixon,* pp. 206–210; Reichley, *Conservatives in an Age of Change,* pp. 188–189; *NYT,* May 13, 1973; Cf. Lukas, *Common Ground,* passim; Orfield, *Must We Bus?,* p. 57.

27. Interview with Richard M. Nixon, November 16, 1988; Safire, *Before the Fall,* p. 237.

28. Statement on Civil Rights, March 24, 1970, in Republican Research Division, "1970 Campaign Factbook," RNC Papers, NARA-Wash., in Leuchtenburg and Kesaris, *Papers,* reel 9.

29. Editorial and Column Reaction to the President's Message on School Desegregation, April 3, 1970, POF Box 31, NPMP.

30. Patrick Buchanan memorandum for the president, June 23, 1970, Haldeman Subject File, June 23, 1970, Box 139, NPMP.

31. Harry Dent to the president, July 21, 1970, Haldeman Papers, Box 122, NPMP.

32. Interview with Richard M. Nixon, November 16, 1988.

33. Glass, "Nixon Gives Israel Massive Aid," p. 57; *NYT,* May 23, 1967; interview with Arthur J. Goldberg, March 10, 1981; Ken Cole to Len Garment, September 29, 1969, Garment Papers, Box 1, Library of Congress; John Ehrlichman, Notes of Meetings with the President, October 2, 1969, Ehrlichman Papers,

Fenn Gallery, Santa Fe, New Mexico; Safire, *Before the Fall,* p. 572.

34. Interview with Richard M. Nixon, November 16, 1988; Evans and Novak, *Nixon in the White House,* pp. 159–161.

35. Goulden, *Meany,* p. 411.

36. Evans and Novak, *Nixon in the White House,* p. 163; Reichley, *Conservatives in an Age of Change,* pp. 95, 96; Len Garment to H. R. Haldeman, October 1, 1969, Garment Papers, Box 1, Library of Congress; Bryce Harlow memo for the Staff Secretary, October 29, 1969, in Hoff-Wilson, *Papers;* Nixon to Bryce Harlow, November 12, 1969, PPF, Box 1, NPMP.

37. Pat Buchanan memo for the president, October 15, 1969, in Hoff-Wilson, *Papers; NYT,* November 22, 1969; Evans and Novak, *Nixon in the White House,* p. 163; *Congress and the Nation, 1969–1972,* pp. 292–294; Ehrlichman, *Witness,* p. 122.

38. Ehrlichman, *Witness,* p. 122; Ford, *Time to Heal,* p. 93.

39. Interview with Richard M. Nixon, November 16, 1988; Warren Burger to John Mitchell, April 4, 1969, attached to John Ehrlichman, Notes of Meetings with the President, October 13, 1971, Ehrlichman Papers, Fenn Gallery, Santa Fe, New Mexico; *Congress and the Nation, 1969–1972,* p. 296; *Public Papers: Nixon, 1970,* p. 346.

40. Interview with Richard M. Nixon, November 16, 1988.

41. Crouse, *Boys on the Bus,* pp. 232–233; John Ehrlichman to the president, October 21, 1970, attached to Ehrlichman, Notes of Meetings with the President, September 25, 1970, Ehrlichman Papers, Fenn Gallery, Santa Fe, New Mexico; Kissinger, *White House Years,* p. 78.

42. Unger, *Movement,* pp. 182–183.

43. *NYT,* October 25, 1970.

44. Herbert Klein memo for the President's File, March 5, 1970, in Hoff-Wilson, *Papers.*

45. *NYT,* November 8, 1970, section 4, p. 1, and December 7, 1970.

46. Ray Price memo to Nixon, November 13, 1970, PPF, Box 185,

NPMP; John Mitchell memo for the
President's File, November 27, 1970,
and Herbert Klein memo for the
President's File, November 5, 1970,
in Hoff-Wilson, *Papers.*

47. Len Garment to H. R. Haldeman,
November 11, 1970, Garment
Papers, Box 9, Library of Congress.

48. Nixon to H. R. Haldeman,
December 1, 1970, PPF, Box 2,
NPMP; Lukas, *Nightmare,* p. 5.

49. Lukas, *Nightmare,* pp. 5–6.

50. Nixon, handwritten notes,
November 15, 1970, PPF, Box 185,
NPMP.

51. Nixon to H. R. Haldeman,
November 30, 1970, Haldeman
Papers, Box 138, NPMP.

52. Nixon, handwritten notes, December
6, 1970, PPF, 186, NPMP.

53. *NYT,* January 5 and 21, 1971.

54. Nixon to H. R. Haldeman, January
14, 1971, PPF, Box 3, NPMP.

55. Lukas, *Nightmare,* p. 6.

56. Interview with John Ehrlichman,
June 17, 1985; interview with John
Connally, May 19, 1986;
Ehrlichman, *Witness,* p. 136n.

57. Ehrlichman, *Witness,* p. 153; John
Ehrlichman, Notes of Meetings with
the President, November 1, 1970,
Ehrlichman Papers, Fenn Gallery,
Santa Fe, New Mexico.

58. H. R. Haldeman to the president,
December 1, 1970, in Hoff-Wilson,
Papers.

59. Ehrlichman, *Witness,* p. 261;
interviews with John Ehrlichman,
June 25, 1985, Herbert Kalmbach,
July 1, 1985, Benjamin Stein, July
10, 1985, William Simon, October 9,
1984, and John Connally, May 19,
1986.

60. Interview with John Connally, May
19, 1986; Ehrlichman, *Witness,* p.
261.

61. H. R. Haldeman to Ray Price, April
23, 1971, and to John Ehrlichman,
May 26, 1971, Box 196, NPMP;
Public Papers: Nixon, 1971, pp. 50–
58, 819–820; Lippman, *Spiro
Agnew's America,* p. 244; *The American
Political Report,* October 11 and 25,
1971.

62. Silk, *Nixonomics,* p. 16.

63. Safire, *Before the Fall,* pp. 509, 517;
Silk, *Nixonomics,* p. 14.

64. Interview with John Connally, May
19, 1986.

65. Interviews with Herbert Stein,
December 14, 1984, William Rusher,
October 2, 1984, William F. Buckley,
Jr., October 18, 1984, and William
Simon, October 9, 1984.

Chapter 21. THE AGE OF NIXON

1. Nixon, *RN,* p. 559; *NYT,* February
24, 1972.

2. Nixon, *RN,* p. 562.

3. *NYT,* February 22, 1972.

4. Ibid.

5. Sulzberger, *World and Richard Nixon,*
p. 181.

6. Kissinger, *White House Years,* p. 685.

7. Interview with Richard M. Nixon,
June 8, 1984.

8. Ibid.

9. Kissinger, *White House Years,* p. 689.

10. *NYT,* February 29, 1972.

11. News Summaries, July 19, 1971,
POF, Box 33, NPMP; *NYT,*
February 29, 1972; Buckley,
Inveighing We Will Go, p. 95; H. R.
Haldeman memo for the President's
File, March 8, 1972, Haldeman
Papers, Box 163, NPMP; Nixon to
H. R. Haldeman, March 11, 1972,
PPF, Box 3, NPMP.

12. John Erlichman, Notes of Meetings with the President, November

14, 1972, Ehrlichman Papers,
Fenn Gallery, Santa Fe, New
Mexico.

13. Interview with Vladimir Pechatnov, April 12, 1985; *NYT,* April 18,
1972.

14. Reichley, *Conservatives in an Age of
Change,* p. 121; *NYT,* May 27,
1972.

15. *Congress and the Nation, 1969–1972,*
pp. 894–895; Nixon, *RN,* p. 346.

16. Lyndon B. Johnson, *Vantage Point,*
p. 480.

17. Ulam, *Dangerous Relations,* p. 52.

18. *NYT,* April 20, May 9, June 28, and
October 27, 1972; *Newsweek,*
November 6, 1972, p. 33.

19. Herring, *America's Longest War,* pp.
251–252; Lewy, *America in Vietnam,*
p. 412.

20. Herring, *America's Longest War,* p.
253.

21. Ibid., pp. 253–255; Lewy, *America in
Vietnam,* pp. 412, 416–417; *NYT,*

January 24, 1973; Nixon, *RN,* pp. 747–751.

22. Peter Braestrup, *Vietnam as History,* passim.

23. Hung and Schecter, *Palace File,* pp. 2–3, 144, and 353.

24. *NYT,* January 24, 1973; *WSJ,* May 2, 1988; Nixon, *RN,* pp. 747–751; Herring, *America's Longest War,* pp. 253–255; Lewy, *America in Vietnam,* pp. 412, 416–417.

25. Nixon, *RN,* p. 762.

26. *Christian Science Monitor,* November 11, 1972.

27. Interview with Richard M. Nixon, November 16, 1988.

28. *NYT,* March 1, 1972, and July 5, 1973.

29. Gallup, *Gallup Poll,* v. 3, pp. 2296, 2323, 2330.

30. *Christian Science Monitor,* March 15, 1972; John Ehrlichman, Notes of Meetings with the President, July 6, 1972, Ehrlichman Papers, Fenn Gallery, Santa Fe, New Mexico.

31. Nixon, *RN,* pp. 657–658; *NYT,* August 5, October 16, and November 8, 1972.

32. Interview with John Connally, May 19, 1986.

33. Ibid.

34. Interview with William Simon, October 9, 1984.

35. Interview with John Connally, May 19, 1986.

36. Republican Research Division, "1972 Election Report," November 27, 1972, RNC Papers, NARA-Wash., in Leuchtenburg and Kesaris, *Papers,* Part II, reel 12.

37. Phillips, *Post-Conservative America,* pp. 32, 43; *Milwaukee Journal,* November 8, 1972.

38. Republican Research Division, "1972 Election Report," November 22, 1972, RNC Papers, NARA-Wash.

39. *NYT,* September 24, 1972; *Christian Science Monitor,* October 30, 1972; Phillips, *Emerging Republican Majority,* pp. 172–175.

40. *NYT,* November 9 and 10, 1988.

41. Ibid., November 18, 1972; Black and Black, *Politics and Society in the South,* p. 270.

42. Interview with Herbert Stein, December 14, 1984; Theodore H. White, *Making of the President 1972,* p. 347.

43. Nie, et al., *Changing American Voter,* pp. 239, 334.

44. Nixon, *RN,* pp. 939–943.

45. Interview with Benjamin Stein, July 10, 1985.

46. Woodward and Bernstein, *Final Days,* p. 169; *NYT,* September 12, 1988.

47. Safire, *Before the Fall,* p. 577.

48. Ehrlichman Papers, December 30, 1970, and November 28, 1972, Fenn Gallery, Santa Fe, New Mexico.

49. See discussion of populism and anti-Semitism in Handlin, *Truth in History,* pp. 339–343.

50. *NYT,* May 25, 1980; interview with Rabbi Baruch Korff, October 10, 1984.

51. Cf. Mayer and Shafer, "Reagan's Aides Prepare for Their Final Battle." Note Ronald Reagan's designation of Edmund Morris as his official presidential biographer. Interview with Richard M. Nixon, November 16, 1988.

52. Duscha, "American Tragicomedy," p. 33; Leonard Garment to H. R. Haldeman, January 20, 1970, Garment Papers, Box 2, Library of Congress.

53. Duscha, "American Tragicomedy," p. 30.

54. *Boston Globe,* December 9, 1971; Duscha, "American Tragicomedy," pp. 28–32.

55. Leonard Garment to John Ehrlichman, January 15, 1973, Garment Papers, Box 2, Library of Congress; Duscha, "American Tragicomedy," pp. 32–33.

56. Nixon, handwritten notes, November 24, 1971, PPF, Box 185, NPMP.

57. Garment to H. R. Haldeman, January 19, 1973, Garment Papers, Box 1, Library of Congress.

58. Leonard Garment to Nixon, December 8, 1972, Garment Papers, Box 2, Library of Congress.

59. *NYT,* July 5, 1976; *Time,* July 12, 1976, p. 8.

60. Briefing of Harvard Law School Republican Club at the White House, March 29, 1974, by Father John McLaughlin. Tape recording at the NPMP.

61. Interview with Vladimir Pechatnov, April 12, 1985.

62. Anson, *Exile,* p. 275n; Paul Johnson,

"In Praise of Richard Nixon," p. 52.

63. Lukas, *Nightmare*, p. 33; Richard Gid Powers, *Secrecy and Power*, p. 456; interview with Richard M. Nixon, November 16, 1988.

64. Interview with John Ehrlichman, June 17, 1985; *NYT*, May 5, 1977.

65. *WSJ*, January 11, 1973; *NYT*, January 12, 1973, and October 26, 1974; interviews with Herbert Stein, December 14, 1984, and Richard M. Nixon, November 16, 1988.

66. Rabbi Baruch Korff Papers, Hay Library, Brown University.

67. Theodore H. White, *Making of the President 1972*, p. 349.

68. Margulies, "U.S. Policies in Chile," unpublished paper; Szulc, *Illusion of Peace*, pp. 353–369, 720–725; Hersh, *Price of Power*, pp. 258–261.

69. Blumenthal, *Rise of the Counter-Establishment*, p. 144; Podhoretz, *Present Danger*, p. 14; interview with Hugh Scott, June 10, 1986.

70. Blumenthal, *Rise of the Counter-Establishment*, pp. 55, 60, 111.

71. Randall, "Presidential Power versus Bureaucratic Intransigence," pp. 796–799; *Congress and the Nation, 1973–1976*, p. 410; interview with William Simon, October 9, 1984.

72. Nixon, "American Foreign Policy," pp. 199, 219.

73. *NYT*, July 5, 1976.

74. Ibid.; Tuchman, "On Our Birthday," p. 9.

75. Lasch, *Culture of Narcissism*, p. 5; Sidey, "A Feeling of People Together," p. 27; *Newsweek*, July 12, 1976, p. 13.

76. *Time*, July 19, 1976, p. 27; *Newsweek*, July 12, 1976, p. 13.

77. *Newsweek*, July 12, 1976, p. 13; *Time*, July 19, 1976, p. 27.

78. Anson, *Exile*, p. 79.

79. *Time*, July 19, 1976, p. 27; Julie Nixon Eisenhower, *Pat Nixon*, pp. 447, 452.

80. *Public Papers: Ford, 1976–77*, v. 2, p. 644; *NYT*, July 5, 1976.

81. *Newsweek*, July 12, 1976, p. 12; *Time*, July 12, 1976, p. 8.

Epilogue

1. *LAT*, March 8, 1984; *NYT*, November 23, 1987.

2. John Ehrlichman, "Should Richard Nixon's Papers Be Public?," *Parade Magazine*, November 30, 1986, p. 5; *Orange County* (California) *Register*, November 15, 1987; *LAT*, November 29, 1987.

3. *Orange County Register*, November 15, 1987; *LAT*, November 6 and 7, 1987; *San Clemente Sun Post*, November 1, 1987; "Report to the Academic Council of the

Subcommittee on Library Relations" (1981), Duke University Archives, Durham, North Carolina.

4. Murray and Blessing, "Presidential Performance Study," p. 540.

5. *NYT*, January 12, 1986; *Time*, April 4, 1987, p. 23, and November 30, 1987, p. 18.

6. *Newsweek*, May 19, 1986, p. 29.

7. Michael Balzano to Nixon, April 25, 1989, letter in Mr. Nixon's possession; *Newsday*, June 25, 1989.

Bibliography

INTERVIEWS CITED

Robert Abplanalp, 3/21/85; Sherman Adams, 8/3/69; Meade Alcorn, 4/18/84; Robert B. Anderson, 6/14/71; Walter Annenberg, 6/9/86; Steven Benedict, 4/9/69; Pat Brown, 1/22/85; Herbert Brownell, 3/14/88; William F. Buckley, Jr., 10/14/84; Frank Carlson, 6/20/84; Anna C. Chennault, 2/27/85; Blair Clark, 3/18/77; Lucius Clay, 4/8/69; John Connally, 5/19/86; Father John Cronin, 9/6/68; Bui Diem, 11/30/84; Michael DiSalle, 3/11/71; Eleanor Lansing Dulles, 1/9/70; John D. Ehrlichman, 6/17/85; David Eisenhower, 1/21/86 and 5/22/87; Julie Nixon Eisenhower, 1/21/86; William Bragg Ewald, Jr., 6/5/87; Robert Finch, 1/22/85; Leonard Garment, 2/27/85; Arthur J. Goldberg, 3/10/81; Martha Griffiths, 1/17/73; James C. Hagerty, 4/11/69; H. R. Haldeman, 1/25/85; Leonard Hall, 5/9/69; Stephen Hess, 11/29/84; Patrick J. Hillings, 7/10/85; Alger Hiss, 4/5/84; George Humphrey, 7/2/69; Ola Florence Welch Jobe, 8/28/86; Lyndon B. Johnson, 6/30/70; Herbert Kalmbach, 7/1/85; Donald Kendall, 10/24/85; Herbert Klein, 1/24/85; Rabbi Baruch M. Korff, 10/10/84; Egil Krogh, 12/3/85; Henry Cabot Lodge, 5/14/70; Clare Booth Luce, 4/30/85; Richard M. Nixon, 6/4, 6/5, 6/8/84 and 11/16/88; Kevin Phillips, 5/22/85; Norman Podhoretz, 10/23/84; Raymond Price, 4/12/84; William F. Price, 7/11/85; Charles G. "Bebe" Rebozo, 6/4/85; Abraham Ribicoff, 2/5/73; William P. Rogers, 11/15/83; William Rusher, 10/2/84; James St. Clair, 11/11/84; Hugh Scott, 6/10/86; William Scranton, 6/13/86; Robert Semple, Jr., 11/14/88; William Simon, 10/9/84; Harold E. Stassen, 8/23/71; Benjamin Stein, 7/10/85; Herbert Stein, 12/14/84; Thomas C. Stephens, 3/11/88; John Taylor, 3/10/86; Sinclair Weeks, 4/15/69; Roy Wilkins, 8/11/70; Ronald Ziegler, 12/14/84.

ARCHIVAL SOURCES

The principal primary sources for this work came from five different repositories. The Dwight D. Eisenhower Library at Abilene, Kansas, was used for the White House Central Files, the Whitman File, the Nixon Vice-Presidential Papers, the Citizens for Eisenhower Papers, the Post-Presidential Special Name File, and the papers of Fred Seaton, James Hagerty, Robert Humphreys, John Foster Dulles, William P. Rogers, and Robert Merriam, in addition to transcripts of interviews from the Bancroft Library Oral History Project of the University of California at Berkeley. The Los Angeles branch of the National Archives located at Laguna Niguel, California, was used for the Nixon Pre-Presidential Papers, Nixon Non-Deeded Papers, and the files under the following subtopics: General Correspondence, Appearances, Trips, Lawyer/Public Figure Correspondence, Congressional Files, and Country Files. The essential material for examining the Nixon presidency is available through the Nixon Presidential Materials Project at the Alexandria, Virginia, branch of the National Archives, where the following collections were used: the President's Personal Files, the President's Office Files, and the papers of H. R. Haldeman, John

Ehrlichman, Ray Price, Charles Colson, John Dean, Harry Dent, and Patrick J. Buchanan. The Library of Congress was useful for the papers of Leonard Garment, and the Richard M. Nixon Project of California State University at Fullerton houses a valuable collection of interviews with contemporaries who recollect Nixon's early years.

Ancillary background material came from the Lyndon B. Johnson Oral History Project, the White House Central File, the Senate Congressional File, and the papers of Marvin Watson, Barefoot Sanders, Bill Moyers, and James Rowe at the Johnson Library in Austin, Texas; also, from various collections, especially the Kennedy Oral History Project, of the John F. Kennedy Library, Boston, Massachusetts, and from the Gerald R. Ford Library at Ann Arbor, Michigan.

Additional archival sources were the Baruch Korff Papers at the Hay Library, Brown University, Providence, Rhode Island; Francis Keesling Papers, University of California, Berkeley; Russel Kirk Papers, Clarke Historical Library, Central Michigan University, Mount Pleasant, Michigan; Herbert Lehman Papers at the School of International Relations Library and the files of the Oral History Research Office, both at Columbia University, New York City; the papers of Sherman Adams and Sinclair Weeks at the Special Collections of the Dartmouth College Library, Hanover, New Hampshire; the Richard Nixon Papers at Duke University, Durham, North Carolina; the Henry Wallace Papers at the University of Iowa, Iowa City; the Fred M. Vinson Papers at the University of Kentucky in Lexington; the Sam Ervin Papers at the University of North Carolina in Chapel Hill; from Princeton University, the Dulles Additional Papers and the Dulles Oral History Collection at the Firestone Library and the papers of Arthur Krock and Adlai E. Stevenson at the Seeley G. Mudd Library; the Stephen Mitchell Papers at the Harry S. Truman Library, Independence, Missouri; the papers of Harry Byrd and Virginius Dabney at the University of Virginia, Charlottesville; the A. Willis Robertson Papers at the College of William and Mary, Williamsburg, Virginia; the files of the Americans for Democratic Action at the Historical Society of Wisconsin, Madison; and the Chester Bowles Papers at the Sterling Library, Yale University.

The following collections were made available via microfilm and microfiche copies from University Publications of America, Frederick, Maryland: William E. Leuchtenburg and Paul L. Kesaris, eds., *Papers of the Republican Party,* and Joan Hoff-Wilson, ed., *Papers of the Nixon White House,* Part 2, "The President's Meeting Files, 1969–1974."

GOVERNMENT DOCUMENTS

House of Representatives, Committee on the Judiciary, *Submission of Recorded Presidential Conversations to the Committee on the Judiciary of the House of Representatives by President Richard Nixon, April 30, 1974.* Washington, D.C.: U.S. Government Printing Office, 1974.

House of Representatives, 80th Congress, 1st Session, *Hearings Before the Subcommittee of the Committee on Un-American Activities.* Washington, D.C.: U.S. Government Printing Office, 1947.

House of Representatives, 80th Congress, 2d Session, *Hearings Before the Subcommittee of the Committee on Un-American Activities.* Washington, D.C.: U.S. Government Printing Office, 1948.

House of Representatives, 80th Congress, 2d Session, *Hearings Regarding Communist Espionage in the United States Government.* Washington, D.C.: U.S. Government Printing Office, 1948.

House of Representatives, 80th Congress, 2d Session, *Hearings on Proposed Legislation to Curb or Control the Communist Party of the United States,* February 5, 6, 9–11, 19, 20, 1948. Washington, D.C.: U.S. Government Printing Office, 1948.

House of Representatives, 81st Congress, 2d Session, *Congressional Record.* Washington, D.C.: U.S. Government Printing Office, 1950.

House of Representatives, 93rd Congress, 2d Session, *Hearings Before the Committee on the Judiciary.* Washington, D.C.: U.S. Government Printing Office, 1974.

Public Papers of the Presidents: Dwight D. Eisenhower, 1956. Washington, D.C.: U.S. Government Printing Office, 1958.

Public Papers of the Presidents: Richard Nixon, 1969–1974, 5 vols. Washington, D.C.: U.S. Government Printing Office, 1971–1975.

Public Papers of the Presidents: Gerald R. Ford, 1976–1977, vol. 2. Washington, D.C.: U.S. Government Printing Office, 1979.

The Senator Gravel Edition, *The Pentagon Papers*, 5 vols. Boston: Beacon Press, 1972.

Nixon, Richard. *Submission of Recorded Presidential Conversations to the Committee on the Judiciary of the House of Representatives, April 30, 1974*. Washington: U.S. Government Printing Office, 1974.

State Senate of California. *Eleventh Report of the Senate Fact-Finding Subcommittee on Un-American Activities*. Sacramento: Senate of the State of California, 1961.

U.S. Bureau of the Census. *Historical Statistics of the United States, Colonial Times to 1957*. Washington, D.C.: U.S. Government Printing Office, 1960.

UNPUBLISHED PAPERS AND DISSERTATIONS

Boylan, James Richard. "Reconversion in Politics: The New Deal Coalition and the Election of the Eightieth Congress." Ph.D. dissertation, Columbia University, 1971.

Crosby, Donald F. "The Angry Catholics: American Catholics and Senator Joseph R. McCarthy, 1950–1957." Ph.D. dissertation, Brandeis University, 1973.

Gardner, Richard. "Fighting Quaker." Manuscript in Duke University Archives.

Guerra, David M. "Network Television News Policy and the Nixon Administration: A Comparison." Ph.D. dissertation, New York University, 1974.

Kisteneff, Alexis P. "The New Federalism of Richard Nixon as Counter-Revolution to the American Liberal State: A Study in Political Theory and Public Policy." Ph.D. dissertation, Brown University, 1977.

Margulies, Mario. "U.S. Policies in Chile and the Fall of Salvador Allende." Unpublished paper, The Graduate Center of the City University of New York, 1988.

Nixon, Richard. "The Choice in Vietnam." Typescript in the Vice President's File, DDEL.

———. "Lessons of the Hiss Case." Address prepared for delivery at the Annual Meeting of the Pumpkin Papers Irregulars, October 31, 1985. Mimeographed typescript in author's possession.

Sandler, Samuel. "Reconciling Domestic and International Politics: The Eisenhower and Nixon Presidencies." Ph.D. dissertation, Johns Hopkins University, 1977.

Schneider, Jeff. "Richard Nixon in 1946: The Liberal as Existentialist." Unpublished paper, The Graduate Center of the City University of New York, 1987.

Whitefield, Clarence E. "Not Many at Duke Knew Richard Nixon Well, but his Record in Law School is Enviable." Manuscript in Nixon Papers, Duke University Archives.

ARTICLES

Alsop, Stewart. "Nixon on Nixon." *Saturday Evening Post*, July 12, 1958.

———. "Nixon and the Square Majority." *The Atlantic*, February 1972.

Alter, Robert. "A Fever of Ethnicity." *Commentary*, July 1972.

Anderson, Totton J., and Eugene C. Lee. "The 1962 Election in California." *Western Political Quarterly* XVI (June 1963)

Auerbach, Joel D., and Bert A. Rockman. "Clashing Beliefs within the Executive Branch: The Nixon Administration Bureaucracy." *American Political Science Review* 70 (June 1976).

Banfield, Edward C., Nathan Glazer, Michael Harrington, Tom Kahn, Christopher Lasch, Robert Lekachman, Bayard Rustin, Gus Tyler, and George F. Will. "Nixon, the Great Society, and the Future of Social Policy: A Symposium." *Commentary* 55 (May 1973).

Begeman, Jean. "Nixon: How the Press Suppressed the News." *New Republic*, October 6, 1952.

Beichman, Arnold. "Study in Academic Freedom." *New York Times Magazine*, December 19, 1965.

Bendiner, Robert K., and Max Ascoli. "The Case of Alger Hiss." *The Reporter*, August 30, 1949.

Berger, Peter and Brigitte. "The Blueing of America." *New York Times*, February 15, 1971.

Berlin, Ira, and Herbert G. Gutman. "Natives and Immigrants, Free Men and Slaves: Urban Workingmen in the Antebellum South." *American Historical Review* 88 (December 1983).

Bernstein, Burton. "Profiles: Barry Goldwater." *The New Yorker*, April 25, 1988.

Bickel, Alexander M. "Where Do We Go from Here?" *The New Republic*, February 7, 1970.

Black, Earl, and Merle Black. "The Wallace Vote in Alabama: A Multiple Analysis." *Journal of Politics* 35 (August 1973).

Blumin, Stuart M. "The Hypothesis of Middle-Class Formation in Nineteenth-Century America: A Critique and Some Proposals." *The American Historical Review* 90 (April 1985).

Bonafede, Dom. "Agencies Resist Nixon Directive to Cut Back Spending on Public Relations." *National Journal* 3 (July 24, 1971).

———. "Nixon Personnel Staff Works to Restructure Federal Policies." *National Journal* 3 (December 11, 1971).

———. "Nixon's First-Year Appointments Reveal Pattern of His Administration." *National Journal* 2 (January 24, 1970).

———. "Nixon's Troubles Bring Enhanced Role for Cabinet, Better Working Relationships." *National Journal* 5 (October 6, 1973).

———. "Speechwriters Play Strategic Role in Conveying, Shaping Nixon's Policies." *National Journal* 4 (February 19, 1972).

———, and Jonathan Cottin. "Nixon, in Reorganization Plan, Seeks Tighter Rein on Bureaucracy." *National Journal* 2 (March 21, 1970).

Boskin, Joseph. "The Revolt of the Urban Ghettos, 1964–1967." *The Annals* (March 1969).

Bowers, Lynn, and Dorothy Blair. "How to Pick a Congressman." *Saturday Evening Post,* March 19, 1949.

Bradford, M. E. "George Wallace and American Conservatives." *National Review,* April 25, 1975.

Brashear, Ernest. "Who Is Richard Nixon?" *New Republic,* September 1, 1952.

Brody, David. "Philip Murray," in John A. Garraty and Jerome L. Sternstein, eds., *Encyclopedia of American Biography.* New York: Harper and Row, 1974.

Brogan, Dennis W. "The Illusion of American Omnipotence." *Harper's Magazine,* December 1952.

Bullock, Paul. " 'Rabbits and Radicals': Richard Nixon's 1946 Campaign Against Jerry Voorhis." *Southern California Quarterly,* Fall 1973.

Bundy, McGeorge. "The Test of Yalta." *Foreign Affairs* (July 1949).

Carter, Hodding. "A Two-Party System in Dixie?" *The Reporter,* March 28, 1950.

Cathcart, Robert S., and Edward A. Schwartz. "The New Nixon or Poor Richard?" *North American Review* 253 (September/October 1968).

Chace, James, "Five-Power World of Richard Nixon." *New York Times Magazine,* February 20, 1972.

Chamberlain, John. "Mr. Nixon's Position." *Barron's,* May 10, 1954.

Chang, Gordon H. "JFK, China, and the Bomb." *Journal of American History* 74 (March 1988).

———. "To the Nuclear Brink: Eisenhower, Dulles, and the Quemoy-Matsu Crisis." *International Security* 12 (Spring 1988).

Clark, Blair, "How Eugene McCarthy Sank the Peace Effort — and Himself." *Berkshire Eagle,* August 7, 1988.

Clifford, Clark. "A Viet Nam Reappraisal." *Foreign Affairs,* July 1969.

Commentary. "Symposium: How Has the United States Met Its Major Challenges Since 1945?" November 1945.

Converse, Philip E., Warren E. Miller, et al. "Continuity and Change in American Politics: Parties and Issues in the 1968 Election." *American Political Science Review* 63 (December 1969).

Cope, Richard. "The Frustration of Harry Byrd." *The Reporter,* November 21, 1950.

Cort, John E. "Who Won the Election?" *Commonweal,* December 8, 1950.

Crosby, Donald F., S.J. "The Politics of Religion," in Robert Griffith and Athan Theoharis, eds., *The Specter,* New York: New Viewpoints, 1974.

Donovan, Richard. "Birth of a Salesman." *The Reporter,* October 14, 1952.

Drew, Elizabeth. "Washington: The Nixon Court." *Atlantic Monthly* 230 (November 1972).

Drummond, Roscoe. "The Facts About Mr. Nixon's Speech." *New York Herald Tribune,* April 22, 1954.

Duscha, Julius. "An American Tragicomedy." *Saturday Review,* July 1, 1972.

Erskine, Hazel G. "The Polls: Demonstrations and Race Riots." *Public Opinion Quarterly* 31 (Winter 1967–68).

Fiedler, Leslie. "Hiss, Chambers, and the Age of Innocence." *Commentary,* December 1950.

Flacks, Richard. "Who Protests: The Social Bases of the Student Movement," in Julian and Durward Long, eds., *Protest! Student Activism in America*. New York: William Morrow and Company.

Flannery, Harry W. "Red Smear in California." *The Commonweal*, December 8, 1950.

Fleming, Donald. "Social Darwinism," in Arthur M. Schlesinger, Jr., and Morton White, eds., *Paths of American Thought*. Boston: Houghton Mifflin, 1963.

Frady, Marshall. "Gary, Indiana." *Harper's*, August 1969.

Friedman, Murray. "Is White Racism the Problem?" *Commentary*, January 1969.

Fuller, Helen. "Democrats After the Deluge." *The New Republic*, December 2, 1946.

Furlow, Barbara. "Portrait of Two Presidents: Nixon and Johnson." *U.S. News & World Report*, July 28, 1969.

Garment, Leonard. "The Hill Case," *The New Yorker*, April 17, 1989.

Garrow, David J. "Black Civil Rights During the Eisenhower Years." *Constitutional Commentary* 3 (Summer 1986).

Gillette, William. "Election of 1872," in Arthur M. Schlesinger, Jr., and Fred L. Israel, eds., *History of American Presidential Elections, 1789–1978*, 4 vols. New York: Chelsea House, 1971.

Glass, Andrew J. "Nixon Gives Israel Massive Aid but Reaps No Jewish Political Harvest." *National Journal* 4 (January 8, 1972).

Glazer, Nathan. "Blacks, Jews, and Intellectuals." *Commentary*, April 1969.

———. "The Limits of Social Policy." *Commentary*, September 1971.

Goldbloom, Maurice J. "Is There a Backlash Vote?" *Commentary*, August 1969.

Goodman, William. "Fatal Passion of Harold Stassen." *The New Republic*, August 6, 1956.

Grantham, Dewey W., Jr. "The South and Reconstruction of American Politics." *Journal of American History* 53 (September 1966).

Greeley, Andrew M., "The Ethnic Miracle." *The Public Interest* 45 (Fall 1976).

Greenfield, Meg. "LBJ and the Democrats." *The Reporter*, June 2, 1966.

Gutman, Herbert. "Work, Culture, and Society in Industrializing America, 1815–1919." *American Historical Review* 78 (June 1973).

Hacker, Andrew. "Is There a New Republican Majority?" *Commentary*, November 1969.

Haight, Timothy R., and Richard A. Brody. "Mass Media and Presidential Popularity: Presidential Broadcasting and News in the Nixon Administration." *Communication Research* 4 (January 1977).

Hamill, Pete. "The Revolt of the White Lower-Middle Class," in Louise Kapp Howe, ed., *The White Majority*. New York: Random House, 1970.

Harris, T. George. "The Rampant Right Invades the GOP." *Look*, July 16, 1963.

Heale, M. J., "Red Scare Politics: California's Campaign against Un-American Activities, 1940–1970." *Journal of American Studies* 20 (April 1986).

Heiman, Grover. "How Don Kendall Put New Pep in Pepsi." *Nation's Business*, May 1981.

Henle, Ray. "This Man Nixon." *Town Journal*, May 1956.

Herring, George C. "The War In Vietnam," in Robert A. Divine, ed., *Exploring the Johnson Years*. Austin: University of Texas Press, 1981.

Holt, James. "Trade Unionism in the British and U.S. Steel Industries, 1880–1914: A Comparative Study." *Labor History* 18 (1977).

Homan, William H. "The Men Behind Nixon's Speeches." *New York Times Magazine*, January 19, 1969.

Hoogenboom, Ari. "Spoilsmen and Reformers: Civil Service Reform and Public Morality," in H. Wayne Morgan, ed., *The Gilded Age: A Reappraisal*. Syracuse, New York: Syracuse University Press, 1963.

Horton, Philip. "The China Lobby, Part II." *The Reporter*, April 29, 1952.

Howells, William Dean. "A Sennight of the Centennial." *Atlantic Monthly* 30 (July 1876).

Hoxie, R. Gordon. "The Nixon Resignation and the Watergate Era Reforms Viewed Ten Years Later." *Presidential Studies Quarterly* 14 (Fall 1984).

Immerman, Richard H. "Between the Unattainable and the Unacceptable: Eisenhower and Dienbienphu," in Richard Melanson and David Mayers, eds., *Reevaluating Eisenhower*. Urbana: University of Illinois Press, 1987.

Jackson, Donald. "The Young Nixon." *Life*, November 6, 1970.

Jeffries, John W. "The 'Quest for National Purpose' of 1960." *American Quarterly* 30 (Fall 1978).

Johnson, Paul. "In Praise of Richard Nixon." *Commentary,* October 1988.

Jones, James R. "Behind LBJ's Decision Not to Run in '68." *New York Times,* April 16, 1988.

Judis, John B. "Apocalypse Now and Then." *The New Republican,* August 31, 1987.

———. "The Two Faces of Whittaker Chambers." *The New Republic,* April 16, 1984.

Kallina, Edmund F. "Was the 1960 Presidential Election Stolen? The Case of Illinois." *Presidential Studies Quarterly* 15 (Winter 1985).

Karmin, Monroe W. "Polish Hill: The White Ethnics Complain." *The Washington Monthly,* April 1969.

Kelley, Robert. "Ideology and Political Culture from Jefferson to Nixon." *American Historical Review* 82 (June 1977).

Kennedy, John F. "We Must Climb to the Hilltop." *Life,* August 22, 1960.

Key, V. O., Jr. "New Voters in the Making." *The Reporter,* December 6, 1949.

Kilpatrick, Carroll. "Leonard Garment Is Bright, Musical, a Known New York Liberal, and a Man Close to Richard Nixon." *Washington Post,* June 7, 1970.

King, Andrew A., and Floyd D. Anderson. "Nixon, Agnew, and the 'Silent Majority': A Case Study in the Rhetoric of Polarization." *Western Speech* 35 (Fall 1971).

Klein, Malcolm W., and Nathan Maccoby. "Newspaper Objectivity in the 1952 Campaign." *Journalism Quarterly* 31 (Summer 1954).

Knebel, Fletcher. "Did Ike Really Want Nixon?" *Look,* October 30, 1956.

Koenig, Louis. "Reassessing the 'Imperial Presidency,' " in Richard M. Pious, ed., *The Power to Govern.* New York: The Academy of Political Science, 1981.

Laing, Robert B., and Robert L. Stevenson. "Public Opinion Trends in the Last Days of the Nixon Administration." *Journalism Quarterly* 53 (Summer 1976).

Laski, Harold J. "The American Political Scene." *The Nation,* November 23, 1946.

"Last Stand in Mississippi." *The Reporter,* June 7, 1949.

Lekachman, Robert. "Death of a Slogan — The Great Society 1967." *Commentary,* January 1967.

Lemann, Nicholas. "The Unfinished War." *The Atlantic,* January 1989.

Lewis, Flora. "The Nixon Doctrine." *Atlantic Monthly* 226 (November 1970).

MacLeish, Archibald. "The Conquest of America." *The Atlantic,* August 1949.

Mayer, Jane, and Ronald G. Shafer. "Reagan's Aides Prepare for Their Final Battle." *Wall Street Journal,* October 18, 1955.

McDonald, Wesley W. "Russell Kirk: Conservatism's Seasoned Sage." *Wall Street Journal,* November 19, 1984.

McWilliams, Carey. "Government by Whitaker and Baxter." *The Nation,* April 14, April 21, and May 5, 1951.

Moley, Raymond. "The Forgotten Majority." *Newsweek,* August 4, 1952.

———. "Nixon vs. Douglas." *Newsweek,* August 28, 1950.

Morgan, Neil. "Nixon's New Frontier." *Esquire,* February 1962.

Moynihan, Daniel Patrick. "Employment, Income, and the Ordeal of the Negro Family." *Daedalus,* Fall 1965.

———. "The President and the Negro: The Moment Lost." *Commentary,* February 1967.

Muller, Dorothea R. "Josiah Strong and the American Nationalism: A Reevaluation." *Journal of American History* 53 (December 1966).

Murray, Robert K., and Tim H. Blessing. "The Presidential Performance Study: A Progress Report." *Journal of American History* 70 (December 1983).

Nixon, Richard. "Our Resolve Is Running Strong." *Life,* August 29, 1960.

———. "American Foreign Policy: The Bush Agenda." *Foreign Affairs, America and the World, 1988/89* 68.

———. "Asia After Viet Nam." *Foreign Affairs* 46 (October 1967).

———. "Lessons of the Alger Hiss Case." *New York Times,* January 8, 1986.

Obear, Frederick W. "Student Activism in the Sixties," in Julian Foster and Durward Long, eds., *Protest! Student Activism in America.* New York: William Morrow and Co., 1970.

Osborne, John. "Summing Up of a Nixon-Watcher." *New Republic* 159 (October 26, 1968).

Parmet, Herbert S. "The Making and Unmaking of Ngo Dinh Diem," in John Schlight, ed., *The Second Indochina War.* Washington, D.C.: Center of Military History, U.S. Army, 1986.

Patterson, James T. "The Failure of Party Realignment in the South, 1937–1939." *Journal of Politics*, August 1965.

Phelan, James R. "The Nixon Family and the Hughes Loan." *The Reporter*, August 16, 1962.

Phillips, Cabell. "Nixon in '58 — and Nixon in '60." *New York Times Magazine*, October 26, 1958.

———. "One-Man Task Force of the G.O.P." *New York Times Magazine*, October 24, 1954.

Phillips, Kevin. "The Future of American Politics." *National Review*, December 22, 1972.

———. "The Selling of the President 1968." King Features syndicated column, January 31, 1972.

Pious, Richard Matthew. "Richard M. Nixon," in Henry F. Graff, ed., *The Presidents: A Reference History*. New York: Charles Scribner's Sons, 1984.

Podhoretz, Norman. "Between Nixon and the New Politics." *Commentary*, September 1972.

Poirier, Richard. "Horatio Alger in the White House." *Harper's*, September 1972.

Randall, Ronald. "Presidential Power versus Bureaucratic Intransigence: The Influence of the Nixon Administration on Welfare Policy." *American Political Science Review* 73 (September 1979).

Real, Michael R. "Popular Culture, Media Propaganda, and the 1972 'CREEP Campaign.' " *Journal of Popular Culture* 8 (Winter 1974).

Redlich, Norman. "A Handbook for Demagogues." *The Nation*, October 4, 1952.

Reeves, Richard. "Mike Lang (groovy kid from Brooklyn) plus John Roberts (unlimited capital) Equals Woodstock." *New York Times Magazine*, September 7, 1969.

Reinhardt, Richard. "The Bohemian Club." *American Heritage*, June–July 1980.

Rezneck, Samuel. "Distress, Relief, and Discontent in the United States during the Depression of 1873–78." *Journal of Political Economy* 58 (1950).

Ribicoff, Abraham. "He Left at Half Time." *The New Republic*, February 17, 1973.

Root, Oren. "Do We Need a Political Realignment?" *The Commonweal*, April 15, 1949.

Rovere, Richard H. "Nixon: Most Likely to Succeed." *Harper's*, September 1955.

———. "A Reporter at Large: The Campaign: Nixon." *The New Yorker*, October 13, 1956.

Safford, Jeffrey J. "The Nixon-Castro Meeting of 19 April 1959." *Diplomatic History* 4 (Fall 1980).

Sagan, Scott D. "SIOP-62: The Nuclear War Plan Briefing to President Kennedy." *International Security* 12 (Summer 1987).

Sanford, Fillmore H. "Public Orientation to Roosevelt." *Public Opinion Quarterly*, Summer 1951.

Schrag, Peter. "The Forgotten Americans." *Harper's Magazine*, August 1969.

Scobie, Ingrid W. "Helen Gahagan Douglas and Her 1950 Senate Race with Richard M. Nixon." *Southern California Quarterly* 58 (Spring 1976).

Semple, Robert B., Jr. "The Nixon Phenomenon." *New York Times Magazine*, January 21, 1968.

———. "Nixon's Presidency Is a Very Private Affair." *New York Times Magazine*, November 2, 1969.

———. "The Middle American Who Edits Ideas for Nixon." *New York Times Magazine*, April 12, 1970.

———. "The Three Strategies of a Master Politician." *New York Times Magazine*, November 1, 1970.

Shannon, William V. "Eisenhower as President." *Commentary*, November 1958.

Sidey, Hugh. "A Feeling of People Together." *Time*, July 19, 1976.

Simmons, Robert R. "The Communist Side: an Exploratory Sketch," in Francis H. Heller, ed., *The Korean War*. Lawrence: The Regents Press of Kansas, 1977.

Stivers, William. "Eisenhower and the Middle East," in Richard A. Melanson and David Mayer, eds., *Reevaluating Eisenhower: American Foreign Policy in the 1950s*. Urbana: University of Illinois Press, 1986.

Tuchman, Barbara. "On Our Birthday — America as Idea." *Newsweek*, July 12, 1976.

Turner, Frederick Jackson. "The Significance of the Frontier in Amercian History," in George Rogers Taylor, ed., *The Turner Thesis*. Boston: D. C. Heath and Company, 1956.

Viorst, Judith. "Pat Nixon Is the Ultimate Good Sport." *New York Times Magazine*, September 13, 1970.

Viorst, Milton. "Nixon of the O.P.A." *New York Times Magazine*, October 3, 1971.

Warner, Sam Bass, Jr. "If All the World Were Philadelphia." *American Historical Review* 74 (1968).

Ways, Max. "The Faculty Is the Heart of the Trouble," in *Youth and Turmoil*, New York: Time-Life Books, 1969

Wells, Samuel F., Jr. "The Lessons of War." *Wilson Quarterly* 2 (Summer 1978).

Wertenbaker, Charles. "China Lobby." *The Reporter*, April 15, 1952.

Westin, Alan F. "The John Birch Society: 'Radical Right' and 'Extreme Left' in the Political Context of Post World War II." First published in 1962, reprinted in Daniel Bell, ed., *The Radical Right*, rev. ed. Garden City, New York: Anchor, 1964.

Whiteside, Thomas. "Annals of Television: Shaking the Tree." *The New Yorker*, March 17, 1975.

Whitworth, William. "One-Man Think Tank." *The New Yorker*, September 20, 1969.

Wicker, Tom. "George Wallace: A Gross and Simple Heart." *Harper's*, April 1967.

Williams, T. Harry. "He's No Huey Long." *New York Times*, April 6, 1972.

Wills, Garry. "The Nixon Convention." *National Review* 20 (August 17, 1968).

Woodward, C. Vann. "Strange Career Critics: Long May They Persevere." *Journal of American History* 75 (December 1988).

Wooten, James T. "Wallace's Last Hurrah?" *New York Times Magazine*, January 11, 1976.

Wright, Lawrence. "Nixon — Then, Now, Forever." *Albany Sunday Times Union*, December 7, 1986.

Books

Abrahamsen, David. *Nixon vs. Nixon: an Emotional Tragedy*. New York: Signet Books, 1978.

Adamic, Louis. *Dynamite: The Story of Class Violence in America*, rev. ed. Gloucester, Massachusetts: Peter Smith, 1963.

Adams, Henry. *The Education of Henry Adams*. New York: Library of America, 1983.

Adams, Sherman. *Firsthand Report*. New York: Harper and Bros., 1961.

Alexander, Herbert E. *Financing the 1968 Election*. Lexington, Massachusetts: Lexington Books, 1971.

————. *Financing Politics*, 3d. ed. Washington, D.C.: Congressional Quarterly Press, 1984.

Alsop, Stewart. *Nixon and Rockefeller: A Double Portrait*. Garden City, New York: Doubleday and Co., 1960.

Altschuler, Glenn C. *Race, Ethnicity, and Class in American Social Thought*. Arlington Heights, Illinois: Harlan Davidson, 1982.

Ambrose, Stephen E. *Eisenhower, the President*. New York: Simon and Schuster, 1984.

————. *Nixon: The Education of a Politician, 1913–1962*. New York: Simon and Schuster, 1987.

The American Assembly of Columbia University. *Goals for Americans*. Englewood Cliffs, New Jersey: Prentice-Hall, 1960.

Anderson, Jack, with James Boyd. *Confessions of a Muckraker: The Inside Story of Life in Washington During the Truman, Eisenhower, Kennedy and Johnson Years*. New York: Random House, 1979.

Andrews, Bert. *Washington Witch-Hunt*. New York: Random House, 1948.

Anson, Robert Sam. *Exile: The Unquiet Oblivion of Richard M. Nixon*. New York: Simon and Schuster, 1984.

Apple, R. W., Jr., et al. *The Watergate Hearings, Break-in and Cover-Up: Proceedings of the Senate Select Committee on Presidential Campaign Activities as edited by the staff of The New York Times*. New York: Viking Press, 1973.

Arnold, William A. *Back When It All Began: The Early Years*. New York: Vantage Press, 1975.

Aronowitz, Stanley. *False Promises: The Shaping of American Working Class Consciousness*. New York: McGraw-Hill, 1973.

Auerbach, Morton. *The Conservative Illusion*. New York: Columbia University Press, 1959.

Bachrak, Stanley. *The Committee of One Million: China Politics, 1953–1971 Lobby*. New York: Columbia University Press, 1976.

Bagdikian, Ben. *The Effete Conspiracy and Other Crimes by the Press*. New York: Harper and Row, 1972.

Bailyn, Bernard, David Brion Davis, et al., *The Great Republic*. Lexington, Massachusetts: D.C. Heath, 1981.

Banner, Lois W. *Women in Modern America: A Brief History*. New York: Harcourt Brace and Jovanovich, 1974.

Barber, James David. *The Presidential Character*. Englewood Cliffs, New Jersey: Prentice-Hall, 1972.

Baritz, Loren. *Backfire: A History of How American Culture Led Us into Vietnam and Made Us Fight the Way We Did*. New York: William Morrow, 1985.

Barnour, Eric. *Tube of Plenty*. New York: Oxford University Press, 1977.

Bartley, Numan V. *The Rise of Massive Resistance*. Baton Rouge: Louisiana University Press, 1969.

Bass, Jack, and Walter DeVries. *The Transformation of Southern Politics: Social Change and Political Consequences Since 1945*. New York: Basic Books, 1976.

Baughman, James L. *Henry Luce and the Rise of the American News Media*. Boston: Twayne Publishers, 1987.

Bazelon, David T. *Power in America: The Politics of the New Class*. New York: New American Library, 1967.

Bell, Daniel. *The Coming of the Post-Industrial Society: A Venture in Social Forecasting*. New York: Basic Books, 1974.

———. *The End of Ideology*, rev. ed. New York: Free Press, 1962.

———. ed. *The Radical Right*. Garden City, New York: Anchor Books, 1964.

Bentley, Eric, ed. *Thirty Years of Treason*. New York: Viking Press, 1971.

Berding, Andrew H. *Dulles on Diplomacy*. Princeton, New Jersey: D. Van Nostrand Company, 1965.

Berges, Marshall. *The Life and Times of Los Angeles: A Newspaper, a Family and a City*. New York: Atheneum, 1984.

Berman, Larry. *Planning a Tragedy: The Americanization of the War in Vietnam*. New York: W. W. Norton, 1982.

Berman, Ronald. *America in the Sixties: An Intellectual History*. New York: Free Press, 1968.

Berman, William C. *The Politics of Civil Rights*. Columbus: Ohio State University Press, 1970.

———. *William Fulbright and the Vietnam War*. Kent, Ohio: Kent State University Press, 1988.

Bernstein, Carl, and Bob Woodward. *All the President's Men*. New York: Simon and Schuster, 1974.

Berthoff, Rowland. *An Unsettled People: Social Order and Disorder in American History*. New York: Harper and Row, 1971.

Bestor, Arthur Eugene, Jr. *Backwards Utopias*. Philadelphia: University of Philadelphia Press, 1950.

Black, Earl, and Merle Black. *Politics and Society in the South*. Cambridge, Massachusetts: Harvard University Press, 1987.

Blum, John Morton, ed. *The Price of Vision: The Diary of Henry A. Wallace, 1942–1946*. Boston: Houghton Mifflin, 1973.

Blumberg, Nathan B. *One-Party Press? Coverage of the 1952 Presidential Campaign in 35 Daily Newspapers*. Lincoln: University of Nebraska Press, 1952.

Blumenthal, Sidney. *The Rise of the Counter-Establishment*. New York: Times Books, 1986.

Bolner, James, and Robert Stanley. *Busing: The Political and Judicial Process*. New York: Praeger, 1974.

Bornet, Vaughan. *The Presidency of Lyndon B. Johnson*. Lawrence: University of Kansas Press, 1983.

Boorstin, Daniel J. *The Decline of Radicalism: Reflections on America Today*. New York: Vintage Books, 1970.

Bowler, Marion K. *The Nixon Guaranteed Income Proposal: Substance and Process in Policy Change*. Cambridge, Massachusetts: Ballinger, 1974.

Bradlee, Ben. *Conversations with Kennedy*. New York: W. W. Norton, 1975.

Braestrup, Peter. *The Big Story: How the American Press and Television Reported and Interpreted the Crisis of Tet 1968 in Vietnam and Washington*, rev. ed. New Haven, Connecticut: Yale University Press, 1983.

———, ed. *Vietnam as History: Ten Years After the Paris Peace Accords*. Washington, D.C.: University Press of America, 1984.

Braley, Russell. *Bad News: The Foreign Policy of the New York Times*. Chicago: Regnery Gateway, 1984.

Brill, Steve. *The Teamsters*. New York: Simon and Schuster, 1978.

Brock, Clifton. *Americans for Democratic Action*. Washington, D.C.: Public Affairs Press, 1962.

Broder, David. *The Party's Over*. New York: Harper and Row, 1972.

Brodie, Fawn. *Richard Nixon: The Shaping of His Character*. New York: W. W. Norton, 1981.

Brody, David. *Workers in Industrial America: Essays on the 20th Century Struggle*. New York: Oxford University Press, 1980.

Brown, Dee. *Bury My Heart at Wounded Knee*. New York: Holt, Rinehart and Winston, 1970.

———. *The Year of the Century: 1876*. New York: Charles Scribner's Sons, 1966.

Brown, Seyom. *The Faces of Power*. New York: Columbia University Press, 1983.

Bruce, Robert V. *1877: Year of Violence*. Indianapolis: Bobbs-Merrill, 1959.

Bryce, James. *The American Commonwealth*, 2 vols. New York: Macmillan, 1901.

Buchanan, Patrick. *Conservative Votes, Liberal Victories*. New York: Quadrangle/The New York Times Book Company, 1975.

———. *The New Majority*. Philadelphia: 1973.

———. *Right from the Beginning*. Boston: Little, Brown, 1988.

Buckley, William F., Jr. *Inveighing We Will Go*. New York: G. P. Putnam's, 1970.

———, ed. *Odyssey of a Friend*. New York: G. P. Putnam's, 1969.

———. *Up from Liberalism*. New Rochelle, New York: Arlington House, 1968.

Burke, Robert E. *Olson's New Deal for California*. Berkeley and Los Angeles: University of California Press, 1953.

Burnham, James. *The Coming Defeat of Communism*. New York: John Day, 1950.

———. *The Current Crisis in American Politics*. New York: Oxford University Press, 1982.

———. *The Struggle for the World*. New York: John Day, 1947.

———. *The Web of Subversion*. New York: John Day, 1954.

Burns, James MacGregor. *The Power to Lead: The Crisis of the Modern Presidency*. New York: Simon and Schuster, 1984.

———. *The Workshop of Democracy*. New York: Alfred A. Knopf, 1985.

Cady, Edwin. *The Road to Realism*. Syracuse, New York: Syracuse University Press, 1956.

———. *The Realist at War*. Syracuse, New York: Syracuse University Press, 1958.

Califano, Joseph. *A Presidential Nation*. New York: W. W. Norton, 1975.

Calleo, David P. *The Imperious Economy*. Cambridge, Massachusetts: Harvard University Press, 1982.

Callow, Alexander B. *The Tweed Ring*. New York: Oxford University Press, 1966.

Cannon, Lou. *Reagan*. New York: G. P. Putnam's, 1982.

Caridi, Ronald J. *The Korean War and American Politics: The Republican Party as a Case Study*. Philadelphia: University of Pennsylvania Press, 1968.

Carlson, John Roy. *Under Cover*. Philadelphia: The Blakiston Company, 1943.

Caroli, Betty Boyd. *First Ladies*. New York: Oxford University Press, 1987.

Carr, Robert K. *The House Committee on Un-American Activities, 1945–1950*. Ithaca, New York: Cornell University Press, 1952.

Cash, W. J. *The Mind of the South*. Garden City, New York: Doubleday Anchor Books, 1956.

Caute, David. *The Great Fear*. New York: Simon and Schuster, 1978.

———. *The Year of the Barricades: A Journey Through 1968*. New York: Harper and Row, 1988.

Chafe, William H. *The American Woman*. New York: Oxford University Press, 1972.

———. *The Unfinished Journey: America Since World War II*. New York: Oxford University Press, 1985.

Chambers, Whittaker. *Witness*. New York: Random House, 1952.

Chennault, Anna C. *The Education of Anna*. New York: Times Books, 1980.

Chester, Lewis, Godfrey Hodgson, and Bruce Page. *An American Melodrama*. New York: Viking Press, 1969.

Childs, Marquis. *Eisenhower: Captive Hero*. New York: Harcourt Brace and Company, 1958.

Clark, Thomas D., ed. *The South Since Reconstruction*. Indianapolis and New York: Bobbs-Merrill, 1973.

Cochran, Bert. *Labor and Communism: The Conflict That Shaped American Unions*. Princeton: Princeton University Press, 1977.

Cohen, Warren I. *Dean Rusk*. Totawa, New Jersey: Cooper Square Publishers, 1980.

Colby, William. *Honorable Men: My Life in the CIA*. New York: Simon and Schuster, 1978.

Collier, Peter, and David Horowitz. *The Rockefellers*. New York: Holt, Rinehart and Winston, 1976.

Colson, Charles. *Born Again*. Old Tappan, New Jersey: Chosen Books, 1976.

Commager, Henry Steele. *Documents of American History*, 9th ed. Englewood Cliffs, New Jersey: Prentice-Hall, 1973.

Congress and the Nation, 1945–1964. Washington, D.C.: Congressional Quarterly Service, 1965.

Congress and the Nation, 1969–1972. Washington, D.C.: Congressional Quarterly Service, 1973.

Congress and the Nation, 1973–1976. Washington, D.C.: Congressional Quarterly Service, 1977.

Conkin, Paul K. *Big Daddy from the Pedernales*. Boston: Twayne Publishers, 1986.

Connery, Robert H., and Gerald Benjamin. *Rockefeller of New York*. Ithaca, New York: Cornell University Press, 1979.

Cooke, Alistair. *A Generation on Trial*. New York: Knopf, 1950.

Cooney, John. *The Annenbergs: The Salvaging of a Tainted Dynasty*. New York: Simon and Schuster, 1982.

Cormier, Frank, and William J. Eaton. *Reuther*. Englewood Cliffs, New Jersey: Prentice-Hall, 1970.

Costello, William. *The Facts About Nixon: An Unauthorized Biography*. New York: Viking Press, 1960.

Coyne, John R. *The Impudent Snobs: Agnew vs. the Intellectual Establishment*. New Rochelle, New York: Arlington House, 1972.

Cox, Archibald. *The Court and the Constitution*. Boston: Houghton Mifflin, 1987.

Crawford, Alan. *Thunder on the Right: The 'New Right' and the Politics of Resentment*. New York: Pantheon Books, 1980.

Crosby, Donald F. *God, Church, and Flag: Senator Joseph R. McCarthy and the Catholic Church, 1950–1957*. Chapel Hill: University of North Carolina Press, 1978.

Crouse, Timothy. *The Boys on the Bus*. New York: Random House, 1973.

Cutler, Robert. *No Time for Rest*. Boston: Little, Brown, 1965.

David, Lester. *The Lonely Lady of San Clemente: The Story of Pat Nixon*. New York: Crowell, 1978.

David, Paul T., ed. *Presidential Nominating Politics in 1952*, 5 vols. Baltimore: Johns Hopkins Press, 1954.

———, ed. *The Presidential Election and Transition, 1960–1961*. Washington, D.C.: The Brookings Institution, 1961.

Deakin, James. *Straight Stuff: The Reporters, the White House and the Truth*. New York: Morrow, 1984.

Dean, John. *Blind Ambition: The White House Years*. New York: Simon and Schuster, 1976.

———. *Lost Honor: The Rest of the Story*. Los Angeles: Stratford Press, 1982.

Degler, Carl N. *At Odds: Women and the Family in America from the Revolution to the Present*. New York: Oxford University Press, 1980.

———. *Out of Our Past: The Forces That Shaped Modern America*. New York: Harper Colophon Books, 1962.

Dent, Harry S. *The Prodigal South Returns to Power*. New York: John Wiley and Sons, 1978.

de Toledano, Ralph. *Nixon*. New York: Holt, 1956.

———. *One Man Alone*. New York: Funk and Wagnalls, 1969.

———, and Victor Lasky. *The Seeds of Treason*. New York: Funk and Wagnalls, 1959.

Diem, Bui, with David Chanoff. *In the Jaws of History*. Boston: Houghton Mifflin, 1987.

Dietrich, Noah. *Howard: The Amazing Mr. Hughes*. Greenwich, Connecticut: Fawcett Books, 1972.

Diggins, John P. *The Lost Soul of American Politics: Virtue, Self-Interest, and the Foundations of Liberalism*. New York: Basic Books, 1984.

———. *The Proud Decades: America in War and in Peace, 1941–1960*. New York: W. W. Norton and Company, 1988.

Divine, Robert A. *Eisenhower and the Cold War*. New York: Oxford University Press, 1981.

————, ed. *Exploring the Johnson Years*. Austin: University of Texas Press, 1981.

Dobson, John M. *Politics in the Gilded Age: A New Perspective on Reform*. New York: Praeger, 1972.

Dollard, John. *Caste and Class in a Southern Town*. Garden City, New York: Doubleday Anchor Books, 1957.

Domhoff, G. William. *The Bohemian Grove and Other Retreats*. New York: Harper and Row, 1974.

Donovan, Robert J. *Conflict and Crisis: The Presidency of Harry S Truman, 1945–1948*. New York: W. W. Norton, 1977.

————. *The Future of the Republican Party*. New York: Signet Books, 1964.

————. *Tumultuous Years: The Presidency of Harry S. Truman, 1949–1953*. New York: W. W. Norton, 1982.

Douglas, Helen Gahagan. *A Full Life*. New York: Doubleday and Company, 1982.

Douglas, Melvyn, and Tom Arthur. *See You at the Movies: The Autobiography of Melvyn Douglas*. Lanham, Maryland: University Press of America, 1987.

Drew, Elizabeth. *Washington Journal: The Events of 1973–1974*. New York: Random House, 1975.

Drosnin, Michael. *Citizen Hughes: In His Own Words — How Howard Hughes Tried to Buy America*. New York: Holt, Rinehart and Winston, 1985.

Dubofsky, Melvin. *Industrialism and the American Worker, 1865–1920*. New York: Thomas Y. Crowell Company, 1975.

————. *We Shall Be All*. Chicago: Quadrangle Books, 1969.

Dulles, Foster Rhea. *American Policy Toward Communist China*. New York: Thomas Y. Crowell, 1972.

Eden, Anthony. *Full Circle*. London: Cassell and Co., 1960.

Efron, Edith. *The News Twisters*. Los Angeles: Nash, 1971.

Ehrlichman, John. *Witness to Power: The Nixon Years*. New York: Simon and Schuster, 1982.

Eisenhower, David. *Eisenhower at War, 1943–1945*. New York: Random House, 1986.

Eisenhower, Dwight D. *The White House Years: Mandate for Change, 1953–1956*. Garden City, New York: Doubleday and Co., 1963.

————. *Waging Peace, 1956–1961*. Garden City, New York: Doubleday and Co., 1965.

Eisenhower, Julie Nixon. *Pat Nixon: The Untold Story*. New York: Simon and Schuster, 1986.

Ekirch, Arthur A., Jr. *Ideologies and Utopias: The Impact of the New Deal on American Thought*. Chicago: Quadrangle Books, 1969.

Ellis, David M., James A. Frost, et al. *A Short History of New York State*. Ithaca, New York: Cornell University Press, 1957.

Elson, Robert T. *The World of Time Inc*. New York: Atheneum, 1973.

Epstein, Benjamin, R., and Arnold Forster. *The Radical Right: Report on the John Birch Society and Its Allies*. New York: Random House, 1966.

Epstein, Edward Jay. *Agency of Fear*. New York: Putnam's, 1977.

————. *News from Nowhere: Television and the News*. New York: Random House, 1973.

Eulau, Heinz. *Class and Party in the Eisenhower Years*. New York: Free Press, 1962.

Evans, Rowland, Jr., and Robert D. Novak. *Lyndon B. Johnson: The Exercise of Power*. New York: New American Library, 1966.

————. *Nixon in the White House: The Frustration of Power*. New York: Random House, 1971.

Ewald, William Bragg, Jr. *Eisenhower the President*. Englewood Cliffs, New Jersey: Prentice-Hall, 1981.

————. *Who Killed Joe McCarthy?* New York: Simon and Schuster, 1984.

Farber, David. *Chicago '68*. Chicago: University of Chicago Press, 1987.

Fawcett, Edward and Tony Thomas. *The American Condition*. New York: Harper and Row, 1982.

Ferrell, Robert H., ed. *The Eisenhower Diaries*. New York: W. W. Norton and Co., 1981.

————. *The Diary of James C. Hagerty*. Bloomington: Indiana University Press, 1983.

Fiedler, Leslie. *An End to Innocence: Essays on Culture and Politics*. Boston: Beacon Press, 1952.

Finer, Herman. *Dulles over Suez*. Chicago: Quadrangle Books, 1964.

Foner, Eric. *Reconstruction*. New York: Harper and Row, 1958.

Ford, Gerald R. *A Time to Heal: The Autobiography of Gerald R. Ford*. New York: Harper and Row, 1979.

Foster, Julian, and Durward Long, eds. *Protest! Student Activism in America*. New York: William Morrow and Co., 1970.

Frady, Marshall. *Billy Graham: A Parable of American Righteousness*. Boston: Little, Brown, 1979.

———. *Wallace*. New York and Cleveland: World Publishing Company, 1968.

Frederickson, George M. *The Black Image in the White Mind*. New York: Harper and Row, 1971.

Freeland, Richard M. *The Truman Doctrine and the Origins of McCarthyism*. New York: Alfred A. Knopf, 1972.

Freidel, Frank. *F.D.R. and the South*. Baton Rouge: Louisiana State University Press, 1967.

———. *Franklin D. Roosevelt: The Triumph*. Boston: Little, Brown, 1956.

Friedman, Lawrence M. *A History of American Law*. New York: Simon and Schuster, 1973.

Frost, David. *The Presidential Debate, 1968*. New York: Stein and Day, 1968.

Fuchs, Lawrence, ed. *American Ethnic Politics*. New York: Harper and Row, 1968.

———. *The Political Behavior of American Jews*. Glencoe, Illinois: Free Press, 1956.

Gabriel, Ralph. *The Course of American Democratic Thought*, 2d. ed. New York: Ronald Press, 1956.

Gaddis, John Lewis. *Strategies of Containment*. New York: Oxford University Press, 1982.

———. *The United States and the Origins of the Cold War, 1941–1947*. New York: Columbia University Press, 1972.

Galbraith, John Kenneth. *The Affluent Society*. Boston: Houghton Mifflin, 1958.

Gallup, George H., ed. *The Gallup Poll: Public Opinion, 1935–1971*, 3 vols. New York: Random House, 1972.

Garraty, John. *The New American Commonwealth*. New York: Harper Torchbooks, 1968.

Garrow, David J. *Bearing the Cross: Martin Luther King, Jr., and the Southern Christian Leadership Conference*. New York: William Morrow and Co., 1986.

Garthoff, Raymond L. *Detente and Confrontation: American-Soviet Relations from Nixon to Reagan*. Washington: The Brookings Institution, 1985.

Gaston, Paul M. *The New South Creed: A Study in Southern Mythmaking*. New York: Vintage Books, 1973.

Gerson, Louis L. *John Foster Dulles*. New York: Cooper Square Publishers, 1968.

Gillon, Steven M. *Politics and Vision: The ADA and American Liberalism, 1947–1985*. New York: Oxford University Press, 1987.

Gitlin, Todd. *The Sixties: Years of Hope, Days of Rage*. New York: Random House, 1987.

———. *The Whole World Is Watching*. Berkeley and Los Angeles: University of California Press, 1980.

Goldman, Eric F. *The Crucial Decade — and After*. New York: Vintage Books, 1961.

———. *The Tragedy of Lyndon Johnson*. New York: Alfred A. Knopf, 1969.

Goldwater, Barry. *The Conscience of a Conservative*. Shepherdsville, Kentucky: Victor Publishing Company, 1960.

———. *Goldwater*. New York: Doubleday, 1988.

———. *With No Apologies*. New York: William Morrow and Co., 1979.

Goodman, Walter. *The Committee*. New York: Farrar, Straus and Giroux, 1968.

Goodwyn, Lawrence. *Democratic Promise: The Populist Movement in America*. New York: Oxford University Press, 1976.

Goold-Adams, Richard. *The Time of Power*. London: Weidenfeld and Nicolson, 1962.

Gorer, Geoffrey. *The American People: A Study in National Character*, rev. ed. New York: Norton, 1963.

Gosnell, Harold F., *Grass Roots Politics: National Voting Behavior of Typical States*. New York: Russell and Russell, 1970.

Gottlieb, Robert, and Irene Wolt. *Empires in the Sun: The Story of the Los Angeles Times*. New York: G. P. Putnam's, 1977.

———, and Peter Wiley. *Empires in the Sun: The Rise of the New American West*. New York: G. P. Putnam's, 1982.

Goulden, Joseph C. *The Best Years, 1945–1950*. New York: Atheneum, 1976.

———. *Korea: The Untold Story of the War*. New York: Times Books, 1983.

———. *Meany*. New York: Atheneum, 1972.

Greenstone, J. David. *Labor in American Politics*. New York: Vintage Books, 1969.

Griffith, Robert W., ed. *Ike's Letters to a Friend, 1941–1958.* Lawrence: University Press of Kansas, 1984.

———. *The Politics of Fear: Joseph R. McCarthy and the Senate.* Lexington: University of Kentucky Press, 1970.

Griffith, Robert, and Athan Theoharis, eds. *The Specter: Original Essays on the Cold War and the Origins of McCarthyism.* New York: New Viewpoints, 1974.

Guhin, Michael A. *John Foster Dulles: A Statesman and His Times.* New York and London: Columbia University Press, 1972.

Guide to the Centennial Exposition and Fairmount Park. Philadelphia: J. Henry Smythe, 1876.

Gunther, John. *Inside U.S.A.* New York: Harper and Brothers, 1947.

Halberstam, David. *The Powers That Be.* New York: Knopf, 1979.

Haldeman, H. R. *The Ends of Power.* New York: New York Times Books, 1978.

Hallin, Daniel C. *The "Uncensored War": The Media and Vietnam.* New York: Oxford University Press, 1986.

Hamby, Alonzo L. *Beyond the New Deal: Harry S. Truman and American Liberalism.* New York: Columbia University Press, 1973.

———. *Liberalism and Its Challengers: F.D.R. to Reagan.* New York: Oxford University Press, 1985.

———. *The Imperial Years: The U.S. Since 1939.* New York: Weybright and Talley, 1976.

Handlin, Oscar. *Race and Nationality in American Life.* Garden City, New York: Doubleday Anchor Books, 1957.

———. *Truth in History.* Cambridge, Massachusetts: Harvard University Press, 1979.

Harris, Lou. *The Anguish of Change.* New York: W. W. Norton and Co., 1973.

Harris, Richard. *A Sacred Trust.* New York: New American Library, 1966.

Hartmann, Susan M. *Truman and the 80th Congress.* Columbia: University of Missouri Press, 1971.

Hartz, Louis. *The Liberal Tradition in America.* New York: Harcourt, Brace and World, 1955.

Hastings, Max. *The Korean War.* New York: Simon and Schuster, 1987.

Hatch, Alden. *Ambassador Extraordinary: Clare Booth Luce.* New York: Henry Holt and Company, 1956.

Hayden, Tom. *Reunion: A Memoir.* New York: Random House, 1988.

———. *Trial.* New York: Rinehart and Winston, 1970.

Hayek, Friedrich von. *The Road to Serfdom.* Chicago: University of Chicago Press, 1944.

Hays, Brooks. *A Southern Moderate Speaks.* Chapel Hill: University of North Carolina Press, 1959.

Heller, Francis H., ed. *The Korean War: A 25–Year Perspective.* Lawrence: Regents Press of Kansas, 1977.

Herring, George C. *America's Longest War,* 2d ed. New York: John Wiley and Sons, 1986.

Hersh, Seymour M. *The Price of Power: Kissinger in the Nixon White House.* New York: Summit Books, 1983.

Hess, Stephen. *Organizing the Presidency.* Washington, D.C.: The Brookings Institution, 1976.

———, and David S. Broder. *The Republican Establishment.* New York: Harper and Row, 1967.

Hill, Gladwyn. *The Dancing Bear: An Inside Look at California Politics.* New York: World Publishing Company, 1968.

Hiss, Alger. *In the Court of Public Opinion.* New York: Alfred A. Knopf, 1957.

Hodgson, Godfrey. *America in Our Time.* Garden City, New York: Doubleday, 1976.

Hoffer, Eric. *The True Believer.* New York: Perennial Library, 1951.

———. *The Temper of Our Time.* New York: Harper and Row, 1964.

Hoffman, Paul. *The New Nixon.* New York: Tower Publications, 1970.

Hoff-Wilson, Joan, ed. *Papers of the Nixon White House,* Part 2, "The President's Meeting Files, 1969–1974." Frederick, Maryland: University Publications of America, 1988. Microfilm.

Hofstadter, Richard. *Anti-Intellectualism in American Life.* New York: Alfred A. Knopf, 1963.

———. *The Paranoid Style in American Politics.* New York: Alfred A. Knopf, 1965.

———. *Social Darwinism in American Thought,* rev. ed. New York: George Braziller, 1959.

Hoopes, Townsend. *The Devil and John Foster Dulles.* Boston: Little, Brown, 1973.

Hougan, Jim. *Secret Agenda: Watergate, Deep Throat and the CIA.* New York: Random House, 1984.

Hough, Robert L. *The Quiet Rebel: William Dean Howells as Social Commentator.* Hamden, Connecticut: Archon Books, 1968.

Howe, Irving. *Socialism in America.* San Diego: Harcourt Brace Jovanovich, 1985.

————, ed. *The World of the Blue-Collar Worker.* New York: Quadrangle Books, 1972.

Hoyt, Edwin Palmer. *The Nixons: An American Family.* New York: Random House, 1972.

Humphrey, Hubert H. *The Education of a Public Man: My Life and Politics.* Garden City, New York: Doubleday, 1976.

Hung, Nguyen Tien, and Jerrold L. Schecter. *The Palace File.* New York: Harper and Row, 1986.

Huntington, Samuel P. *American Politics: The Promise of Disharmony.* Cambridge, Massachusetts: Harvard University Press, 1981.

Hyman, Sidney. *The Lives of William Benton.* Chicago: University of Chicago Press, 1969.

Isaacson, Walter, and Evan Thomas. *The Wise Men.* New York: Simon and Schuster, 1986.

Jackson, John B. *American Space: The Centennial Years, 1865–1876.* New York: W. W. Norton, 1972.

Jacobs, Paul, and Saul Landau. *The New Radicals.* Baltimore: Pelican Books, 1967.

James, D. Clayton. *The Years of MacArthur,* 3 vols. Boston: Houghton Mifflin, 1985.

Javits, Jacob K. *Javits: The Autobiography of a Public Man.* Boston: Houghton Mifflin, 1981.

Jessup, John K., ed. *The Ideas of Henry Luce.* New York: Atheneum, 1969.

Jessup, John K., Adlai Stevenson, et al. *The National Purpose.* New York: Holt, Rinehart and Winston, 1960.

Johnson, Lyndon B. *The Vantage Point.* New York: Holt, Rinehart and Winston, 1971.

Johnson, Paul. *Modern Times: The World from the Twenties to the Eighties.* New York: Harper and Row, 1983.

Johnson, Walter, ed. *The Papers of Adlai E. Stevenson,* 8 vols. Boston: Little, Brown, 1972–1979.

Jones, Howard Mumford. *The Age of Energy: Varieties of American Experience, 1865–1915.* New York: Viking Press, 1970.

Jones, Jacqueline. *Labor of Love, Labor of Sorrow: Black Women, Work, and the Family from Slavery to the Present.* New York: Basic Books, 1985.

Jowitt, Earl. *The Strange Case of Alger Hiss.* Garden City, New York: Doubleday, 1953.

Kahin, George M. *Intervention: How America Became Involved in Vietnam.* New York: Alfred A. Knopf, 1986.

Kahn, E. J., Jr. *The China Hands.* New York: Viking Press, 1975.

Kane, John J. *Catholic-Protestant Conflict in America.* Chicago: Regnery, 1955.

Karl, Barry D. *The Uneasy State: The United States from 1915 to 1945.* Chicago: University of Chicago Press, 1983.

Karnow, Stanley. *Vietnam: A History.* New York: Viking Press, 1983.

Kaufman, Burton. *The Korean War.* New York: Alfred A. Knopf, 1986.

Kearns, Doris. *Lyndon Johnson and the American Dream.* New York: Harper and Row, 1976.

Keeley, Joseph. *The China Lobby Man: The Story of Alfred Kohlberg.* New York: Funk and Wagnalls, 1968.

Kelley, Robert. *The Transatlantic Persuasion: The Liberal-Democratic Mind in the Age of Gladstone.* New York: Alfred A. Knopf, 1969.

Kelly, Alfred H., and Winfred A. Harbison. *The American Constitution,* 5th ed. New York: W. W. Norton and Co., 1976.

Kempton, Murray. *Part of Our Time: Some Monuments and Ruins of the Thirties.* New York: Dell, 1967.

Kennedy, John F. *The Strategy of Peace.* New York: Harper and Brothers, 1960.

Keogh, James. *President Nixon and the Press.* New York: Funk and Wagnalls, 1972.

————. *This Is Nixon.* New York: Putnam, 1956.

Kernell, Samuel, and Samuel L. Popkin, eds. *Chief of Staff: Twenty-Five Years of Managing the Presidency.* Berkeley and Los Angeles: University of California Press, 1986.

Key, V. O., Jr. *Southern Politics.* New York: Vintage Books, 1949.

Kissinger, Henry. *White House Years.* Boston: Little, Brown, 1979.

————. *Years of Upheaval.* Boston: Little, Brown, 1982.

Klehr, Harvey. *The Heyday of American Communism: The Depression Decade*. New York: Basic Books, 1984.

Klein, Herbert G. *Making It Perfectly Clear*. Garden City, New York: Doubleday, 1980.

Koen, Ross Y. *The China Lobby in American Politics*. New York: Octagon Books, 1974.

Kopkind, Andrew, and James Ridgeway, eds. *Decade of Crisis: America in the '60s*. New York: World Publishing Company, 1969.

Kornitzer, Bela. *The Real Nixon: A Political and Personal Portrait*. New York: Harper and Row, 1969.

Kramer, Michael, and Sam Roberts. *"I Never Wanted to Be Vice President of Anything!"* New York: Basic Books, 1976.

Kutler, Stanley I., ed. *The Supreme Court and the Constitution: Readings in American Constitutional History*. New York: W. W. Norton, 1977.

Larson, Arthur. *A Republican Looks at His Party*. New York: Harper and Brothers, 1956.

———. *Eisenhower: The President Nobody Knew*. New York: Charles Scribner's Sons, 1968.

Lasch, Christopher. *The Culture of Narcissism: American Life in an Age of Diminishing Expectations*. New York: W. W. Norton, 1978.

Lash, Joseph P. *Eleanor: The Years Alone*. New York: W. W. Norton, 1972.

Lasky, Victor. *It Didn't Start with Watergate*. New York: Dial Press, 1977.

Latham, Earl. *The Communist Controversy in Washington*. New York: Atheneum, 1969.

Lee, R. Alton. *Truman and Taft-Hartley*. Lexington: University of Kentucky Press, 1966.

Lemons, Richard. *The Troubled American*. New York: Simon and Schuster Clarion Paperback, 1971.

Lerner, Max. *America as a Civilization*. New York: Simon and Schuster, 1957.

———. *The Unfinished Country*. New York: Simon and Schuster, 1959.

Leuchtenburg, William, and Paul L. Kesaris, eds. *Papers of the Republican Party*. Frederick, Maryland: University Publications of America, 1986. Microfilm, two parts.

Levitan, Sar A., ed. *Blue-Collar Workers: A Symposium on Middle America*. New York: McGraw-Hill, 1971.

Lewy, Guenter. *America in Vietnam*. New York: Oxford University Press, 1978.

Lichter, S. Robert, Standley Rothman, and Linda S. Lichter. *The Media Elite: America's New Powerbrokers*. Bethesda, Maryland: Adler and Adler, 1986.

Link, Arthur S., and William B. Catton. *American Epoch: A History of the United States Since 1900*, 5th ed., 2 vols. New York: Alfred A. Knopf, 1980.

Lippman, Theo, Jr. *Spiro Agnew's America*. New York: W. W. Norton, 1972.

Lipset, Seymour Martin, and Earl Raab. *The Politics of Unreason: Right-Wing Extremism in America, 1790–1970*. New York: Harper and Row, 1970.

———, and Gerald M. Schaflander. *Passion and Politics: Student Activism in America*. Boston: Little, Brown, 1971.

Litwak, Robert. *Detente and the Nixon Doctrine: American Foreign Policy and the Pursuit of Stability, 1969–1976*. Cambridge: Cambridge University Press, 1984.

Love, Kenneth. *Suez: The Twice-Fought War*. New York: McGraw-Hill, 1969.

Lowi, Theodore J. *The End of Liberalism*. New York: W. W. Norton, 1969.

———. *The Personal President: Power Invested, Promise Unfulfilled*. Ithaca, New York: Cornell University Press, 1985.

———. *The Politics of Disorder*. New York: Basic Books, 1971.

Lubell, Samuel. *The Future of American Politics*, 3rd ed. New York: Harper Colophon Books, 1965.

———. *The Future While It Happened*. New York: Norton, 1973.

———. *The Hidden Crisis in American Politics*. New York: W. W. Norton, 1970.

———. *The Revolt of the Moderates*. New York: Harper and Brothers, 1956.

Luce, Clare Booth. *The Mystery of American Policy in China*. New York: Plain Talk, 1949.

Lukacs, John. *Outgrowing Democracy: A History of the United States in the Twentieth Century*. Garden City, New York: Doubleday, 1984.

Lukas, J. Anthony. *Common Ground: A Turbulent Decade in the Lives of Three American Families*. New York: Knopf, 1985.

———. *Nightmare: The Underside of the Nixon Years*. New York: Viking Press, 1976.

Lynn, Kenneth S. *William Dean Howells: An American Life*. New York: Harcourt Brace Jovanovich, 1971.

MacDonald, Callum A. *Korea: The War Before Vietnam.* New York: Free Press, 1987.

MacDougall, Curtis D. *Gideon's Army,* 3 vols. New York: Marzani and Munsell, 1965.

Magruder, Jeb Stuart. *An American Life: One Man's Road to Watergate.* New York: Atheneum, 1974.

Mailer, Norman. *Armies of the Night.* New York: Signet Books, 1968.

———. *Cannibals and Christians.* New York: Dial Press, 1966.

———. *Some Honorable Men: Political Conventions, 1960–1972.* Boston: Little, Brown, 1976.

Mankiewicz, Frank. *Perfectly Clear: Nixon from Whittier to Watergate.* New York: Quadrangle Books, 1973.

Mann, Arthur. *The One and the Many.* Chicago: University of Chicago Press, 1979.

Marcus, Sheldon. *Father Coughlin: The Tumultuous Life of the Priest of the Little Flower.* Boston: Little, Brown, 1973.

Markovitz, Norman D. *The Rise and Fall of the People's Century: Henry Wallace and American Liberalism, 1941–1948.* New York: Free Press, 1973.

Martin, Joe. *My First Fifty Years in Politics.* New York: McGraw-Hill, 1960.

Matthews, Donald R., and James W. Protho. *Negroes and the New Southern Politics.* New York: Harcourt, Brace and World, 1966.

Matusow, Allen J. *The Unraveling of America: A History of Liberalism in the 1960s.* New York: Harper and Row, 1984.

May, Ernest. *The Truman Administration and China.* Philadelphia: J. B. Lippincott, 1975.

Mayer, George. *The Republican Party, 1854–1966,* 2nd ed. New York: Oxford University Press, 1967.

Mazlish, Bruce. *In Search of Nixon.* Baltimore: Penguin Books, 1972.

Mazo, Earl. *Richard Nixon: A Political and Personal Portrait.* New York: Harper and Row, 1968.

———, and Stephen Hess. *Richard Nixon: A Political Portrait.* New York: Harper and Row, 1968.

McCoy, Donald R. *The Presidency of Harry S. Truman.* Lawrence: University of Kansas Press, 1984.

McDermott, John J., ed. *The Writings of William James.* New York: Random House, 1967.

McFeely, William S. *Grant: A Biography.* New York: W. W. Norton, 1981.

McGinniss, Joe. *The Selling of the President 1968.* New York: Trident Press, 1968.

McWilliams, Carey. *Ill Fares the Wind.* New York: Arno Press, 1976.

———. *Southern California Country: An Island on the Land.* New York: Duell, Sloan, and Pearce, 1946.

Melanson, Richard A., and David Mayers, eds. *Reevaluating Eisenhower: American Foreign Policy in the Fifties.* Urbana and Chicago: University of Illinois Press, 1987.

Miller, Douglas T. *Visions of America.* New York and Los Angeles: West Publishing Company, 1988.

———, and Marion Nowak. *The Fifties: The Way We Really Were.* Garden City, New York: Doubleday, 1977.

Miller, James. *"Democracy Is In the Streets": From Port Huron to the Siege of Chicago.* New York: Simon and Schuster, 1987.

Miller, William J. *Henry Cabot Lodge.* New York: James H. Heineman, 1967.

Mills, C. Wright. *The Power Elite.* New York: Oxford University Press, 1956.

Moldea, Dan E. *The Hoffa Wars: Teamsters, Rebels, Politicians, and the Mob.* New York and London: Paddington Press, 1978.

Morgan, Chester M. *Redneck Liberal: Theodore G. Bilbo and the New Deal.* Baton Rouge: Louisiana State University Press, 1985.

Morgan, Edmund S. *American Slavery, American Freedom.* New York: W. W. Norton, 1975.

Morgan, H. Wayne, ed. *The Gilded Age,* rev. ed. Syracuse, New York: Syracuse University Press, 1970.

———. *Unity and Culture: The United States, 1877–1900.* London: Penguin Press, 1971.

Morrow, E. Frederic. *Black Man in the White House.* New York: Coward-McCann, 1963.

Moscow, Warren. *The Last of the Big-Time Bosses.* New York: Stein and Day, 1971.

———. *Politics in the Empire State.* New York: Alfred Knopf, 1948.

Mosley, Leonard. *Dulles: A Biography of Eleanor, Allen and John Foster Dulles and Their Family Network.* New York: Dial Press/James Wade, 1978.

Mowry, George. *The California Progressives*. Chicago: Quadrangle Paperbacks, 1963.

Moynihan, Daniel P. *Coping: On the Practice of Government*. New York: Random House, 1973.

————. *Maximum Feasible Misunderstanding*. New York: Free Press, 1969.

————. *The Politics of a Guaranteed Income: The Nixon Administration and the Family Assistance Plan*. New York: Random House, 1973.

Mumford, Lewis. *The Story of Utopias*. New York: Viking Press Compass Books, 1962.

Murphy, Bruce Allen. *Fortas: The Rise and Ruin of a Supreme Court Justice*. New York: William Morrow, 1988.

Murphy, Reg, and Hal Gulliver. *The Southern Strategy*. New York: Charles Scribner's, 1971.

Myrdal, Gunnar. *An American Dilemma: The Negro Problem and Modern Democracy*, Twentieth Anniversary Edition. New York: Harper and Row, 1962.

Nash, George H. *The Conservative Intellectual Movement in America Since 1945*. New York: Harper Colophon Books, 1979.

Nathan, Richard P. *The Plot That Failed: Nixon and the Administrative Presidency*. New York: Wiley, 1975.

Navasky, Victor S. *Naming Names*. New York: Viking Press, 1980.

Neal, Steve. *Dark Horse: A Biography of Wendell Willkie*. Garden City, New York: Doubleday, 1984.

Neff, Donald. *Warriors at Suez*. New York: Linden Press/Simon and Schuster, 1981.

Negley, Glenn, and M. Max Patrick. *The Quest for Utopia*. Garden City, New York: Doubleday Anchor Books, 1962.

Nevins, Allan. *The Emergence of Modern America, 1865–1878*. New York: Macmillan, 1927.

New York Times. *The End of a Presidency*. New York: Bantam, 1974.

Nie, Norman H., Sidney Verba, and John R. Petrocik. *The Changing American Voter*. Cambridge, Massachusetts: Harvard University Press, 1976.

Nixon, Richard. *The Challenges We Face*. New York: McGraw-Hill, 1960.

————. *Leaders*. New York: Warner Books, 1982.

————. *1999: Victory Without War*. New York: Simon and Schuster, 1988.

————. *No More Vietnams*. New Rochelle, New York: Arbor House, 1985.

————. *The Real War*. New York: Warner Books, 1980.

————. *RN: The Memoirs of Richard Nixon*. New York: Grosset and Dunlap, 1978.

————. *Setting the Course: The First Year*. New York: Funk and Wagnalls, 1970.

————. *Six Crises*. Garden City, New York: Doubleday and Co., 1962.

Noble, David. *The End of American History*. Minneapolis: University of Minnesota Press, 1985.

Novak, Michael. *Choosing Our King*. New York: Macmillan, 1974.

————. *The Rise of the Unmeltable Ethnics*. New York: Macmillan, 1972.

Novak, Robert D. *The Agony of the G.O.P.: 1964*. New York: Macmillan, 1965.

Olson, James S., ed. *Directory of the Vietnam War*. Westport, Connecticut: Greenwood Press, 1988.

O'Neill, William L. *A Better World*. New York: Simon and Schuster Touchstone Books, 1982.

————. *Coming Apart: An Informal History of America in the 1960's*. Chicago: Quadrangle Books, 1971.

Orfield, Gary. *Must We Bus? Segregated Schools and National Policy*. Washington: Brookings Institution, 1978.

Oshinksy, David M. *A Conspiracy So Immense*. New York: Free Press, 1983.

Paley, William S. *As It Happened*. Boston: Houghton Mifflin, 1977.

Panetta, Leon E., and Peter Gall. *Bring Us Together: The Nixon Team and the Civil Rights Retreat*. Philadelphia: Lippincott, 1971.

Parmet, Herbert S. *The Democrats: The Years After FDR*. New York: Macmillan, 1976.

————. *Eisenhower and the American Crusades*. New York: Macmillan, 1972.

————. *Jack: The Struggles of John F. Kennedy*. New York: Dial Press, 1980.

————. *JFK: The Presidency of John F. Kennedy*. New York: Dial Press, 1983.

————, and Marie B. Hecht. *Never Again: A President Runs for a Third Term*. New York: Macmillan, 1968.

Parrington, Vernon L. *Main Currents in American Thought*. New York: Harcourt, Brace and Co., 1927.

Patterson, James T. *America's Struggle Against Poverty, 1900–1980*. Cambridge, Massachusetts: Harvard University Press, 1981.

———. *Mr. Republican: A Biography of Robert A. Taft*. Boston: Houghton Mifflin, 1972.

Peirce, Neal R. *The Pacific States of America*. New York: W. W. Norton, 1972.

———. *The People's President*. New York: Simon and Schuster, 1968.

———, and Jerry Hagstrom. *The Book of America: Inside 50 States Today*. New York: W. W. Norton and Co., 1983.

Pelling, Henry. *American Labor*. Chicago: University of Chicago Press, 1960.

Pells, Richard H. *The Liberal Mind in a Conservative Age: American Intellectuals in the 1940s and 1950s*. New York: Harper and Row, 1985.

Percy, William Alexander. *Lanterns on the Levee: Recollections of a Planter's Son*. Baton Rouge: Louisiana State University Press, 1973.

Perlman, Selig. *A Theory of the Labor Movement*, reprint ed. New York: Augustus M. Kelley, 1968.

Perrett, Geoffrey. *A Dream of Greatness: The American People, 1945–1963*. New York: Coward-McCann, 1979.

Persico, Joseph. *The Imperial Rockefeller*. New York: Simon and Schuster, 1982.

Phelan, James R. *Howard Hughes: The Hidden Years*. New York: Random House, 1976.

Phillips, Kevin P. *The Emerging Republican Majority*. New Rochelle, New York: Arlington House, 1969.

———. *Mediacracy: American Parties and Politics in the Communications Age*. Garden City, New York: Doubleday and Co., 1975.

———. *Post-Conservative America*. New York: Random House, 1982.

Pious, Richard M. *The American Presidency*. New York: Basic Books, 1979.

Podhoretz, Norman. *Breaking Ranks*. New York: Harper and Row, 1979.

———. *The Present Danger*. New York: Simon and Schuster, 1982.

Pomeroy, Earl. *The Pacific Slope: A History of California, Oregon, Washington, Idaho, Utah and Nevada*. New York: Knopf, 1965.

Porter, Kirk H., and Donald Bruce Johnson, eds. *National Party Platforms*. Urbana: The University of Illinois Press, 1961.

Powers, Richard Gid. *Secrecy and Power: The Life of J. Edgar Hoover*. New York: Free Press, 1987.

Powers, Thomas. *The Man Who Kept the Secrets: Richard Helms and the CIA*. New York: Pocket Books, 1981.

———. *Vietnam: The War at Home*. Boston: G. K. Hall and Co., 1984.

Preston, William, Jr. *Aliens and Dissenters: Federal Suppression of Radicals, 1903–1933*. New York: Harper Torchbooks, 1966.

Price, Raymond. *With Nixon*. New York: Viking, 1977.

Radosh, Ronald. *American Labor and United States Foreign Policy*. New York: Random House, 1969.

———, and Joyce Milton. *The Rosenberg File*. New York: Holt, Rinehart and Winston, 1983.

Rainwater, Lee, and William L. Yancey. *The Moynihan Report and the Politics of Controversy*. Cambridge, Massachusetts: The MIT Press, 1967.

Randle, Robert F. *Geneva 1954: The Settlement of the Indochinese War*. Princeton, New Jersey: Princeton University Press, 1969.

Ranelagh, John. *The Agency: The Rise and Decline of the CIA*. New York: Simon and Schuster, 1986.

Rather, Dan, and Gary Paul Gates. *The Palace Guard*. New York: Harper and Row, 1974.

Ravitch, Diane. *The Troubled Crusade: American Education, 1945–1980*. New York: Basic Books, 1983.

Reeves, Thomas C. *The Life and Times of Joe McCarthy*. New York: Stein and Day, 1982.

Reichley, A. James. *Conservatives in an Age of Change: The Nixon and Ford Administrations*. Washington: Brookings Institution, 1981.

Reinhard, David W. *The Republican Right Since 1945*. Lexington: University Press of Kentucky, 1983.

Republican Committee on Programs and Progress. *Decisions for a Better America*. Garden City, New York: Doubleday, 1960.

Rieder, Jonathan. *Canarsie: The Jews and Italians of Brooklyn Against Liberalism*. Cambridge, Massachusetts: Harvard University Press, 1985.

Rischin, Moses. *"Our Own Kind": Voting by Race, Creed, or National Origin*. Santa Barbara, California: Center for the Study of Democratic Institutions, 1960.

Roberts, Chalmers. *First Rough Draft*. New York: Praeger, 1973.

Robinson, Donald L. *"To the Best of My Ability": The Presidency and the Constitution*. New York: W. W. Norton, 1987.

Rockefeller Panel Reports. *Prospect for America*. Garden City, New York: Doubleday, 1961.

Roland, Charles P. *The Improbable Era: The South Since World War II*. Lexington: University Press of Kentucky, 1975.

Rolling Stone, eds. *The Age of Paranoia*. New York: Pocket Books, 1972.

Rosenman, Samuel I., ed. *The Public Papers and Addresses of Franklin D. Roosevelt*, 13 vols. New York: Russell and Russell, 1969.

Ross, Irving. *The Loneliest Campaign: The Truman Victory of 1948*. New York: New American Library, 1968.

Rossiter, Clinton. *The American Presidency*, rev. ed. New York: Mentor Books, 1960.

———. *Conservatism in America*. New York: Vintage Books, 1962.

Roth, Philip. *Our Gang*. New York: Random House, 1971.

Rovere, Richard. *Affairs of State: The Eisenhower Years*. New York: Farrar, Straus and Cudahy, 1956.

———. *Final Reports: Personal Reflections on Politics and History in Our Time*. Garden City, New York: Doubleday, 1984.

Rubin, Louis D., Jr., et al. *I'll Take My Stand*. New York: Harper Torchbooks, 1962.

Rusher, William. *The Rise of the Right*. New York: William Morrow, 1984.

Rydell, Robert W. *All the World's a Fair: Visions of Empire at American International Expositions, 1876–1916*. Chicago: University of Chicago Press, 1985.

Sachar, Howard M. *A History of Israel*. New York: Alfred A. Knopf, 1976.

Safire, William. *Before the Fall*. Garden City, New York: Doubleday, 1975.

———. *You Could Look It Up*. New York: Times Books, 1988.

Sale, Kirkpatrick. *SDS*. New York: Random House, 1973.

Sayre, Norma. *Running Time: Films of the Cold War*. New York: Dial Press, 1982.

Scammon, Richard M., and Ben J. Wattenberg. *The Real Majority*. New York: Coward-McCann, 1970.

Schandler, Herbert Y. *The Unmaking of a President: Lyndon Johnson and Vietnam*. Princeton, New Jersey: Princeton University Press, 1977.

Schapsmeier, Edward L., and Frederick H. Schapsmeier. *Dirksen of Illinois: Senatorial Statesman*. Chicago: University of Illinois Press, 1985.

Schell, Jonathan. *The Time of Illusion*. New York: Knopf, 1976.

Schlesinger, Arthur M., Jr. *The Coming of the New Deal*. Boston: Houghton Mifflin, 1958.

———. *The Crisis of Confidence*. Boston: Houghton Mifflin, 1969.

———. *The Cycles of American History*. Boston: Houghton Mifflin, 1986.

———. *The Imperial Presidency*. Boston: Houghton Mifflin, 1973.

———. *Kennedy or Nixon: Does It Make Any Difference?* New York: Macmillan, 1960.

———. *Paths to the Present*. Boston: Houghton Mifflin, 1964.

———. *Robert Kennedy and His Times*. Boston: Houghton Mifflin, 1978.

———. *The Shape of National Politics to Come*. Private publication, 1959.

———. *A Thousand Days*. Boston: Houghton Mifflin, 1965.

———. *The Vital Center*. Boston: Houghton Mifflin, 1949.

Schlesinger, Arthur M., Sr. *The Rise of Modern America, 1865–1951*. New York: Macmillan, 1951.

Schlicht, John, ed. *Second Indochina War Symposium*. Washington, D.C.: Center of Military History, U.S. Army, 1986.

Schoen, Douglas. *Pat: A Biography of Daniel Patrick Moynihan*. New York: Harper and Row, 1979.

Schoenebaum, Eleanora W., ed. *Profiles of an Era: The Nixon/Ford Years*. New York: Harcourt Brace Jovanovich, 1979.

Schulte, Renee K., ed. *The Young Nixon*. Fullerton: California State University Press, 1978.

Schwartz, Bernard. *Super Chief: Earl Warren and His Supreme Court — A Judicial Biography*. New York: New York University Press, 1983.

Scott, Hugh. *Come to the Party*. Englewood Cliffs, New Jersey: Prentice-Hall, 1968.

Seagrave, Sterling. *The Soong Dynasty*. New York: Harper and Row, 1985.

Sennett, Richard, and Jonathan Cobb. *The Hidden Injuries of Class*. New York: Alfred A. Knopf, 1972.

Sevareid, Eric, ed. *Candidates 1960*. New York: Basic Books, 1959.

Sexton, Patricia, and Brendan Sexton. *Blue Collars and Hard Hats*. New York: Random House, 1971.

Shannon, David. *The Decline of American Communism*. New York: Harcourt, Brace, 1959.

Shannon, Fred. *Centennial Years: America from the Late 1870's to the Early 1890's*. Garden City, New York: Doubleday, 1967.

Shawcross, William. *Sideshow: Kissinger, Nixon and the Destruction of Cambodia*. New York: Simon and Schuster, 1979.

Sheed, Wilfrid. *Clare Booth Luce*. New York: E. P. Dutton, 1982.

Sheehan, Neil. *A Bright Shining Lie: John Paul Vann and America in Vietnam*. New York: Random House, 1988.

Sheridan, Walter. *The Fall and Rise of Jimmy Hoffa*. New York: Saturday Review Press, 1972.

Sherrill, Robert. *Gothic Politics in the Deep South*. New York: Grossman Publishers, 1968.

Siegel, Frederick F. *Troubled Journey: From Pearl Harbor to Ronald Reagan*. New York: Hill and Wang, 1984.

Silk, Leonard. *Nixonomics*. New York: Praeger, 1973.

Simmons, Robert H. *The Strained Alliance: Peking, Pyongyang, Moscow and the Politics of the Korean Civil War*. New York: Free Press, 1975.

Sinclair, Upton. *The Brass Check: A Study of American Journalism*. Pasadena, California: private publication, 1919.

Small, Melvin. *Johnson, Nixon, and the Doves*. New Brunswick, New Jersey: Rutgers University Press, 1988.

Smalley, Donald, ed. *Domestic Manners of the Americans by Mrs. Frances Trollope*. New York: Vintage Books, 1960.

Smith, John Chabot. *Alger Hiss: The True Story*. New York: Penguin Books, 1977.

Smith, Page. *Trial by Fire: Volume Five of a People's History of the United States*. New York: McGraw Hill, 1982.

Smith, Richard Norton. *An Uncommon Man: The Triumph of Herbert Hoover*. New York: Simon and Schuster, 1984.

————. *Thomas E. Dewey and His Times*. New York: Simon and Schuster, 1982.

Solberg, Carl. *Hubert Humphrey: A Political Biography*. New York: Norton, 1984.

Spector, Ronald H. *Advice and Support: The Early Years of the U.S. Army in Vietnam, 1941–1960*. New York: Free Press, 1985.

Spencer, Herbert. *Social Status*. London, 1850.

Sperber, A. M. *Murrow: His Life and Times*. New York: Freundlich Books, 1986.

Sproat, John G. *"The Best Men": Liberal Reformers in the Gilded Age*. New York: Oxford University Press, 1968.

Stans, Maurice. *The Terrors of Justice*. New York: Everest House, 1978.

Starr, Kevin. *Americans and the California Dream, 1850–1915*. New York: Oxford University Press, 1973.

————. *Inventing the Dream: California Through the Progressive Era*. New York: Oxford University Press, 1985.

Steel, Ronald. *Walter Lippmann and the American Century*. Boston: Atlantic–Little, Brown, 1980.

Steffens, Lincoln. *The Shame of the Cities*. New York: Hill and Wang, 1957.

Stein, Herbert. *Presidential Economics: The Making of Economic Policy From Roosevelt to Reagan and Beyond*. New York: Simon and Schuster, 1984.

Stone, David M. *Nixon and the Politics of Public Television*. New York: Garland Publishing, 1985.

Stone, I. F. *The Haunted Fifties*. New York: Viking Books, 1969; reiss. Boston: Little, Brown, 1988.

Stripling, Robert E. *The Red Plot Against America*. Drexel Hill, Pennsylvania: Bell Publishing Co., 1949.

Strong, Josiah. *Our Country*, edited by Jurgen Herbst. Cambridge, Massachusetts: Harvard University Press, 1963.

Sullivan, William C. *The Bureau: My Thirty Years in Hoover's FBI*. New York: W. W. Norton, 1979.

Sulzberger, Cyrus L. *The World of Richard Nixon*. Englewood Cliffs, New Jersey: Prentice Hall, 1987.

Summers, Harry G., Jr. *On Strategy: A Critical Analysis of the Vietnam War*. Novato, California: Presidio Press, 1982.

Sumner, William Graham. *The Forgotten Man and Other Essays*. Freeport, New York: Books for Libraries Press, 1969.

Sundquist, James L. *Politics and Policy: The Eisenhower, Kennedy, and Johnson Years*. Washington, D.C.: Brookings Institution, 1968.

Swanberg, W. A. *Luce and His Empire*. New York: Charles Scribner's, 1972.

Swindler, William F. *Court and Constitution in the 20th Century*. Indianapolis and New York: Bobbs Merrill Company, 1969.

Szulc, Tad. *The Illusion of Peace: Foreign Policy in the Nixon-Kissinger Years*. New York: Viking, 1978.

Taft, Philip. *Organized Labor in American History*. New York: Harper and Row, 1964.

Tebbel, John, and Sarah Miles Watts. *The Press and the Presidency: From George Washington to Ronald Reagan*. New York: Oxford University Press, 1985.

Theoharis, Athan. *Beyond the Hiss Case: The FBI, Congress, and the Cold War*. Philadelphia: Temple University Press, 1982.

———. *The Yalta Myths*. Columbia: University of Missouri Press, 1970.

Thompson, William Irwin. *At the Edge of History*. New York: Harper and Row, 1971.

Tindall, George Brown. *The Disruption of the Solid South*. Athens: University of Georgia Press, 1972.

Trachtenberg, Alan. *The Incorporation of America: Culture and Society in the Gilded Age*. New York: Hill and Wang, 1982.

Trefousse, Hans L. *Carl Schurz: A Biography*. Knoxville: University of Tennessee Press, 1982.

Trueblood, E. Elton. *The People Called Quakers*. New York: Harper and Row, 1966.

Truman, Harry S. *Memoirs*, 2 vols. Garden City, New York: Doubleday, 1955–1956.

Tuchman, Barbara. *Stillwell and the American Experience in China, 1911–45*. New York: Macmillan, 1971.

Tucker, Nancy Bernkopf. *Patterns in the Dust: Chinese-American Relations and the Recognition Controversy*. New York: Columbia University Press, 1983.

Turner, Kathleen J. *Lyndon Johnson's Dual War: Vietnam and the Press*. Chicago: University of Chicago Press, 1985.

Tygiel, Jules. *Baseball's Great Experiment: Jackie Robinson and His Legacy*. New York: Vintage Books, 1984.

Ulam, Adam B. *Dangerous Relations: The Soviet Union in World Politics, 1970–1982*. New York: Oxford University Press, 1983.

Unger, Irwin. *The Movement: A History of the American New Left, 1959–1972*. New York: Dodd, Mead and Company, 1974.

Unger, Sanford J. *The Papers and the Papers*. New York: E. P. Dutton, 1972.

Veroff, Joseph, Elizabeth Douvan, and Richard A. Kulka. *The Inner American: A Self-Portrait from 1957 to 1976*. New York: Basic Books, 1981.

Viguerie, Richard A. *The New Right: We're Ready to Lead*. Falls Church, Virginia: Viguerie Company, 1981.

Viorst, Milton. *Fall From Grace: The Republican Party and the Puritan Ethic*. New York: New American Library, 1968.

———. *Fire in the Streets: America in the 1960s*. New York: Simon and Schuster, 1979.

Vogelsgang, Sandy. *The Long Dark Night of the Soul: The American Intellectual Left and the Vietnam War*. New York: Harper, 1972.

von Mises, Ludwig. *Omnipotent Government*. New Haven, Connecticut: Yale University Press, 1944.

Voorhis, Horace Jeremiah. *Confessions of a Congressman*. Garden City, New Jersey: Doubleday, 1947.

———. *The Strange Case of Richard Milhous Nixon*. New York: Paul S. Eriksson, 1972.

Wallace, Mike, and Gary Paul Gates. *Close Encounters*. New York: William Morrow, 1984.

Warren, Earl. *The Memoirs of Chief Justice Earl Warren.* Garden City, New York: Doubleday, 1977.

Washington Post. *The Fall of a President.* New York: Dell, 1974.

Weinstein, Allen. *Perjury: The Hiss-Chambers Case.* New York: Alfred A. Knopf, 1978.

Westerfield, H. Bradford. *Foreign Policy and Party Politics: Pearl Harbor to Korea.* New Haven: Yale University Press, 1955.

Whalen, Richard J. *Catch the Falling Flat: A Republican Challenger to His Party.* Boston: Houghton Mifflin, 1972.

Whatley, Joe, Jr., and Richard P. Woods. *The Alabama Message: A View from Within.* Tuscaloosa, Alabama: Alabama Political Research Group, 1976.

White, Theodore H. *America in Search of Itself.* New York: Harper and Row, 1982.

———. *Breach of Faith: The Fall of Richard Nixon.* New York: Atheneum, 1975.

———. *The Making of the President 1960.* New York: Atheneum, 1961.

———. *The Making of the President 1964.* New York: Atheneum, 1965.

———. *The Making of the President 1968.* New York: Atheneum, 1969.

———. *The Making of the President 1972.* New York: Atheneum, 1973.

———. *In Search of History — A Personal Expedition.* New York: Harper and Row, 1978.

White, William Allen. *The Autobiography of William Allen White.* New York: Macmillan, 1946.

Wicker, Tom. *JFK and LBJ.* New York: William Morrow, 1968.

Wiebe, Robert H. *The Search for Order, 1877–1920.* New York: Hill and Wang, 1967.

Wilkinson, J. Harvie, III. *Harry F. Byrd and the Changing Face of Virginia Politics, 1945–1966.* Charlottesville: University Press of Virginia, 1968.

Wills, Garry, *Nixon Agonistes.* New York: Mentor Books, 1971.

———. *Reagan's America: Innocents at Home.* Garden City, New York: Doubleday, 1987.

Witcover, Jules. *The Resurrection of Richard Nixon.* New York: Putnam's, 1970.

———. *White Knight: The Rise of Spiro Agnew.* New York: Random House, 1972.

Wolfe, Tom. *Radical Chic and Mau-Mauing the Flak Catchers.* New York: Farrar, Straus and Giroux, 1970.

Woodstone, Arthur, *Nixon's Head.* New York: St. Martin's Press, 1972.

Woodward, Bob, and Carl Bernstein. *The Final Days.* New York: Simon and Schuster, 1976.

Woodward, C. Vann. *Origins of the New South, 1877–1913.* Baton Rouge: Louisiana State University Press, 1951.

———. *The Strange Career of Jim Crow,* 3rd rev. ed. New York: Oxford University Press, 1974.

Wright, Lawrence. *In The New World: Growing Up with America, 1960–1984.* New York: Alfred Knopf, 1987.

Zaroulis, Nancy, and Gerald Sullivan. *Who Spoke Up? American Protest Against the War in Vietnam 1963–1975.* Garden City, New York: Doubleday, 1984.

Index

People's World, 112
Pepper, Claude, 214, 224–225
PepsiCo, 396, 397–399
Percy, Charles, 348, 372, 385, 487
    party platform and, 386–387
perestroika, 643
Perlman, Selig, 43, 139
Perón, Juan, 367
Perry, Herman, 83, 89–94, 96, 101–
    102, 104–105, 125, 141, 191, 193,
    299
Perry, Hubert, 75
Persico, Joseph, 367–368
Petee, Harold F. "Jack," 103
Peters, Jean, 405
Peterson, Esther, 449
Peterson, J. Hardin, 143
Philadelphia Inquirer, 177, 445, 579
Philadelphia Plan, 546, 560, 599–600, 630
Phillips, Howard, 642
Phillips, Kevin, 58–59, 517, 577, 617
    background of, 523–524
    on Nixon-Moynihan relationship, 544
    Nixon's black capitalism programs and,
    599
    Nixon's presidential candidacy and,
    524, 527–528, 629–630
Pierpoint, Robert, 623
Plain Talk, 207
Plessy v. Ferguson, 223
PM, 108
Podhoretz, Norman, 59, 464, 466, 493,
    631–632, 640
Point Four Program, 368
Poland, uprising against Soviet Union of,
    292–294, 327
"Political Obituary of Richard M. Nixon,
    The," 428–429
Pomeroy, Earl, 100
Pomona Progress-Bulletin, 109
Porter, Paul, 149
Port Huron Statement, 473
Potter, Philip, 7–8
Powell, Adam Clayton, Jr., 294
Powell, Lewis F., Jr., 463, 609
Powell, Wesley, 477
Powers, Dave, 118–119
Powers, Richard Gid, 175
Precision Valve Corporation, 400
Present Danger, The (Podhoretz), 640
President's Commission on Campus Un-
    rest, 589–590
President's Commission on National
    Goals, 348–349, 354
Price, Ray, 12, 494–495, 603, 612, 614–
    615
    Nixon's welfare program and, 552, 556
    Vietnam War and, 581
Price, William, 119–120

"Problem of American Communism, The"
    (Cronin), 167
Procaccino, Mario, 488, 579
Progressive Citizens of America, 124, 138,
    303
Pueblo affair, 505
Push, Operation, 601

Quaker Campus, 78
Quantico group, 290
Quayle, Oliver, 446, 505
Quemoy and Matsu, China's shelling of,
    337, 339–344, 451

racial strife, 484–485, 487, 492–493
    as campaign issue, 527–528
    King's assassination and, 503, 512
Radford, Arthur, 260, 317–318, 323, 341
Rankin, John E., 142–144, 151, 178, 180,
    200
    in hearings on anticommunist legisla-
    tion, 151–155, 157
Raspberry, William, 604
Rauh, Joseph L., Jr., 290, 608–609
Rayburn, Sam, 113
Reader's Digest, 76, 575
Reagan, Ronald, 18, 23–25, 59–61, 63,
    180, 252, 299, 346–347, 367, 624
    Battle of Berkeley and, 569
    conservatism of, 474
    contra aid program of, 649
    Cuban missile crisis and, 428
    domestic programs of, 530
    Goldwater's presidential candidacy and,
    482–483
    gubernatorial campaign of, 486–487
    Nixon's gubernatorial campaign and,
    417
    Nixon's legacy and, 641
    Nixon's presidential candidacy and,
    508–509, 512–516, 595
    presidential candidacy of, 475, 508–
    509, 514–516, 595, 617
    Supreme Court appointees of, 609
    welfare system and, 548, 557–558
Real Majority, The (Scammon and Watten-
    berg), 577
Real Peace, The (Nixon), 642
Real War, The (Nixon), 22, 642
Reardon, L. F., 382
Rebozo, Charles G. "Bebe," 4–5, 286, 401
    background of, 392–393
    Hughes and, 393–394, 405, 408, 410,
    615
    Nixon's relationship with, 288–289,
    392–396, 399–400, 610
Reece, Carroll, 113–114
Reed, Stanley, 170
Rehnquist, William, 609

Smith Act, 459
Smylie, Robert E., 281
Sobeloff, Simon E., 608
Social Darwinism, 31–32, 47
Social Security, 552
Social Statistics (Spencer), 31
Sokolsky, George, 431
Somervell, Brehon, 235
Soong Dynasty, 201–203
South:
　blacks in, 219–226, 229
　civil rights issue in, 266–269
　counterrevolution among whites in,
　　297–298
　Dixiecrat movement in, 216–218, 229
　in Eisenhower's reelection, 295
　Goldwater's strength in, 480, 483
　in 1952 campaign and election, 225–
　　229
　Nixon's approach to, 491, 627–628
　Nixon's black capitalism programs and,
　　599
　Nixon's popularity in, 270, 383–384,
　　510, 515–516, 595, 597, 602–603,
　　605, 630–631
　Nixon's school desegregation plan for,
　　603–605, 630
　Nixon's Supreme Court appointees and,
　　609–610
　poor whites in, 220–224
　Reagan's popularity in, 512–514
Southern Christian Leadership Confer-
　ence, 298
Southern Pacific Railway Company (SP),
　99–100
Southern Regional Council (SRC), 220,
　500
Southern States Industrial Council, 218
Soviet-Nazi alliance, 164
Soviet Union, 7, 25, 28, 60, 396
　ballistic capability of, 383
　Chinese relations with, 343–344, 622,
　　624
　Czechoslovakia invaded by, 624
　Dulles on, 325
　expansionism of, 182–183
　Jewish emigration from, 397–398, 633
　Korean War and, 306–309
　Nixon's domestic programs and, 531
　Nixon's opening to, 623–624
　Polish and Hungarian uprisings against,
　　292–294, 327, 333
　Suez crisis and, 329–331, 333, 335
　technological advances of, 340, 352,
　　375, 433–434
　U.S. détente with, 398
　Vietnam War and, 319, 454, 518, 624
　Watergate scandal and, 637
Sparkman, John J., 227, 247

Spellman, Francis Cardinal, 197–198
Spencer, Herbert, 30–32, 354
Spencer-Roberts, 426
Sperling, Godfrey, Jr., 626
Spivack, Robert G., 465
Spock, Benjamin, 570, 573
Sprague, J. Russel, 234–235, 282
Spruce Goose, 404
Sputnik, 340, 375, 433–434
Stalin, Joseph, 164, 183, 254, 263, 300
Standard Oil, 420
Stans, Maurice H., 385, 397, 489, 538,
　615
　minority enterprise program of, 598,
　　601–602
Stanton, Elizabeth Cady, 34
Stanton, Frank, 582
Starr, Kevin, 51–52, 98
Stassen, Harold, 160, 177, 184, 237, 241,
　244, 256, 258–259, 290, 407
　Herter's vice presidential candidacy
　　promoted by, 276–285
　Nixon's vice presidential nomination
　　supported by, 291–292
State Department, U.S., 26, 140, 174, 398,
　536, 538, 623
　China Lobby and, 202, 205, 210
　under Dulles, 253–254, 324–325, 336–
　　337
　Hiss case and, 163, 166–167, 175
　Korean War and, 306
　Nixon on political attacks on, 315–316
　Suez crisis and, 330, 334
　Vietnam War and, 310, 320, 519, 521,
　　571
Steele, Walter S., 151–152
Steel Workers Organizing Committee, 135
Steffens, Lincoln, 42
Stein, Benjamin, 632
Stein, Herbert, 530, 559, 618, 631, 639
Stennis, John, 226, 457
Stenvig, Charles, 578–579
Stephens, Thomas E., 278–280
Stevens, Robert T., 453–454
Stevenson, Adlai, III, 79, 262, 297, 348,
　353, 448, 585, 602,
　Kennedy-Nixon campaign and, 361
　Nixon attacked by, 293–294
　presidential campaigns of, 227–229,
　　247, 251–252, 261, 264, 289, 292–
　　295, 333, 335, 358
Stone, I. F., 293
Stone, W. Clement, 395, 602
Stout, Osmyn, 75, 78–79
Strachey, John, 301
strategic arms limitation talks (SALT I),
　624
Strategic Defense Initiative, 624
Stripling, Robert, 27, 142–143, 146